W9-BIC-158

HOLT McDOUGAL

LARSON ALGEBRA 1

Ron Larson

Laurie Boswell

Timothy D. Kanold

Lee Stiff

HOLT McDOUGAL

 HOUGHTON MIFFLIN HARCOURT

Printed in the U.S.A.

ISBN 978-0-547-64713-5

2 3 4 5 6 7 8 9 10 0914 20 19 18 17 16 15 14 13 12 11
4500309084 ^ B C D E F G

About *Larson Algebra 1*

The content of *Algebra 1* is organized around families of functions, with special emphasis on linear and quadratic functions. As you study each family of functions, you will learn to represent them in multiple ways—as verbal descriptions, equations, tables, and graphs. You will also learn to model real-world situations using functions in order to solve problems arising from those situations.

In addition to its algebra content, *Algebra 1* includes lessons on probability and data analysis as well as numerous examples and exercises involving geometry. These math topics often appear on standardized tests, so maintaining your familiarity with them is important. To help you prepare for standardized tests, *Algebra 1* provides instruction and practice on standardized test questions in a variety of formats—multiple choice, short response, extended response, and so on. Technology support for both learning algebra and preparing for standardized tests is available at my.hrw.com.

About the Authors

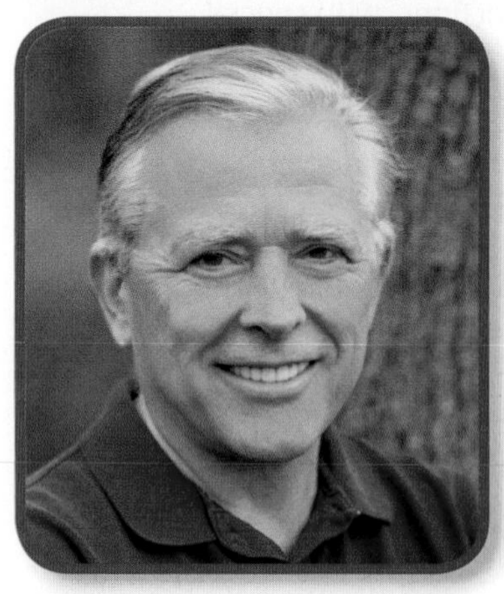

Ron Larson

"My goal is to write books that are mathematically correct, instructionally sound, and student friendly."

I think of myself as a facilitator of teaching and learning—writing instructional materials that teachers have told me they need. Over the years, my greatest input has come from the thousands of teachers that have used our books in real classes with real students. Based on this input, we have written books that meet a variety of teaching and learning needs.

Ron Larson is a professor of mathematics at Penn State University at Erie, where he has taught since receiving his Ph.D. in mathematics from the University of Colorado. Dr. Larson is well known as the author of a comprehensive program for mathematics that spans middle school, high school, and college courses. Dr. Larson's numerous professional activities keep him in constant touch with the needs of teachers and supervisors. He closely follows developments in mathematics standards and assessment.

Laurie Boswell

"To reach all students, you need to address different learning styles."

As a mathematics teacher, I quickly learned that to engage all students, I needed to provide for different learning styles. I also learned the importance of designing lessons that would challenge and motivate students. Using a balance of direct instruction, student-engaged activities, and meaningful communication has enabled me to help all students learn.

Laurie Boswell is a mathematics teacher at The Riverside School in Lyndonville, Vermont, as well as a Regional Director of the National Council of Supervisors of Mathematics. She has taught mathematics at all levels, elementary through college. She is the recipient of the Presidential Award for Excellence in Mathematics and Science Teaching, and a past president of the Council for Presidential Awardees in Mathematics. She served on the NCTM Board of Directors (2002–2005), and she speaks frequently at regional and national conferences.

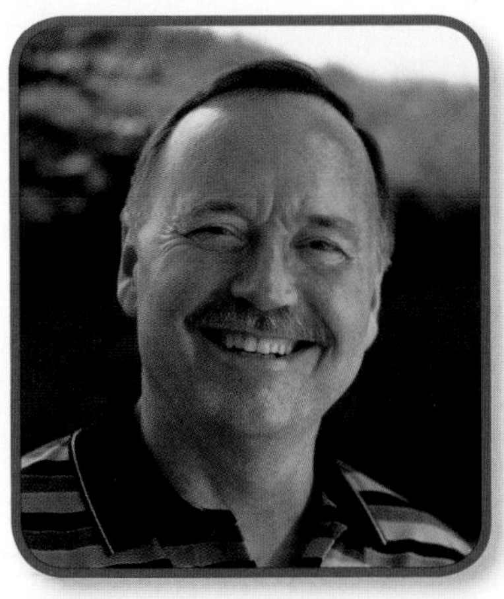

Timothy D. Kanold

"Relevance and meaning are key to successful learning."

Key to creating a mathematics program that will help students be successful are relevance and meaningfulness. Student access to relevant and meaningful mathematics is a critical equity issue in this decade. Our authorship team has worked hard to ensure that we present a balanced curriculum that builds mathematical skills and conceptual understanding simultaneously. We believe students should experience lessons considered to be important, engaging, and meaningful to the context and culture of the student.

Timothy D. Kanold is a past president of the NCSM and a former superintendent of Adlai E. Stevenson High School District 125 in Lincolnshire, Illinois, where he also taught and directed mathematics and science for 22 years. He received a Presidential Award for Excellence in Mathematics and Science Teaching. He also received the prestigious 2010 Damen Award from Loyola University Chicago, for outstanding contributions to education, including work with professional learning communities and the common core state standards recommendations.

Lee Stiff

"All students must have opportunities to take rigorous, high-quality mathematics."

I am proud to be a part of an author team that shares my goals and commitment to setting high mathematics standards for all students. Our focus in writing this program has been to help all students acquire the knowledge, skills, and problem-solving abilities they need in order to become successful adults.

Lee Stiff is a professor of mathematics education in the College of Education of North Carolina State University at Raleigh and has taught mathematics at the high school and middle school levels. He served on the NCTM Board of Directors and was elected President of NCTM for the years 2000–2002. He was a Fulbright Scholar to the University of Ghana and a recipient of the W. W. Rankin Award for Excellence in Mathematics Education presented by the North Carolina Council of Teachers of Mathematics.

Advisers and Reviewers

Curriculum Advisers and Reviewers

Cindy Branson
Mathematics Teacher
Creekview High School
Carrollton, TX

Rhonda Foote
Secondary Math Resource Specialist
North Kansas City School District
Kansas City, MO

Michael J. Klein
Educational Consultant
Macomb ISD
Clinton Township, MI

Fizza Munaim
Mathematics Teacher
Riverside Middle School
El Paso, TX

Dr. Anne Papakonstantinou
Director, School Mathematics Project
Rice University
Houston, TX

Richard Parr
Director, School Mathematics Project and Instructional Programs, School Mathematics Project
Rice University
Houston, TX

Rebecca S. Poe
Mathematics Teacher
Winnsboro High School
Winnsboro, TX

Teacher Panels

Leticia Alvarado
Mathematics Department Chair
Hornedo Middle School
El Paso, TX

Arlene Banks
Mathematics Teacher
Westridge Middle School
Overland Park, KS

Monette Bartel
Associate Adjunct Professor
College of the Canyons
Valencia, CA

Janice Beauchamp
Mathematics Teacher
Buchanan High School
Clovis, CA

Jan Berghaus
Mathematics Teacher
Shawnee Mission West High School
Overland Park, KS

Dennis Dickson
Mathematics Teacher
Leavenworth High School
Leavenworth, KS

Teacher Panels *(continued)*

Pauline Embree
Mathematics Department Chair
Rancho San Joaquin Middle School
Irvine, CA

Coleen Floberg
Mathematics Teacher
Highland Park High School
Topeka, KS

Alberto Hernandez Galindo
Mathematics Department Chair
San Jose High Academy
San Jose, CA

Phillip Gegen
Mathematics Teacher
Oak Park High School
Kansas City, MO

Jason Godfrey
Mathematics Teacher
Grandview High School
Grandview, MO

Leticia Gonzales-Reynolds
Mathematics Teacher
Crockett High School
Austin, TX

Maria Gossett
Mathematics Department Chair
E.M. Daggett Middle School
Fort Worth, TX

Tom Griffith
Mathematics Department Chair
Scripps Ranch High School
San Diego, CA

Debra Konvalin
Mathematics Teacher
Hiram W. Johnson High School
Sacramento, CA

William Lee Littles
Mathematics Teacher
Central High School
Beaumont, TX

Maria Magdalena Lucio
Lead Teacher for Algebra 1
Homer Hanna High School
Brownsville, TX

Deborah Reilly
Mathematics Teacher
West Middle School
Leavenworth, KS

Jon Simon
National Board Certified
Mathematics Teacher
Casa Grande High School
Petaluma, CA

Karen S. Skinner
Mathematics Teacher
New Mark Middle School
Kansas City, MO

Steve Snider
Mathematics Teacher
Benton High School
St. Joseph, MO

Bertha Stimac
Instructional Specialist
Elsik High School
Houston, TX

Karen Stohlmann
Mathematics Teacher
Blue Valley Northwest High School
Overland Park, KS

Deborah Sylvester
Mathematics Teacher
Wamego High School
Wamego, KS

Tommie L. Walsh
Mathematics Teacher (retired)
Smylie Wilson Junior High School
Lubbock, TX

Mary Warner
Mathematics Teacher
Richard King High School
Corpus Christi, TX

Maureen Williams
Mathematics Department Chair
Southwest Junior High School
Lawrence, KS

CHAPTER 1

Problem Solving, p. 29
$0.1s + 0.6 = 2$

Expressions, Equations, and Functions

COMMON CORE

CHAPTER 2

Solving Equations, p. 93
$8517 = 2117 + 64d$

Solving Linear Equations

COMMON CORE

CHAPTER

3

Graphing Linear Equations, p. 169
$2x + y = 128$

Graphing Linear Equations and Functions

COMMON CORE

Rick Havner/AP/Wide World Photos

CHAPTER

4

Slopes of Lines, p. 260
$12y = -7x + 42$

Writing Linear Equations

COMMON CORE

CHAPTER 5

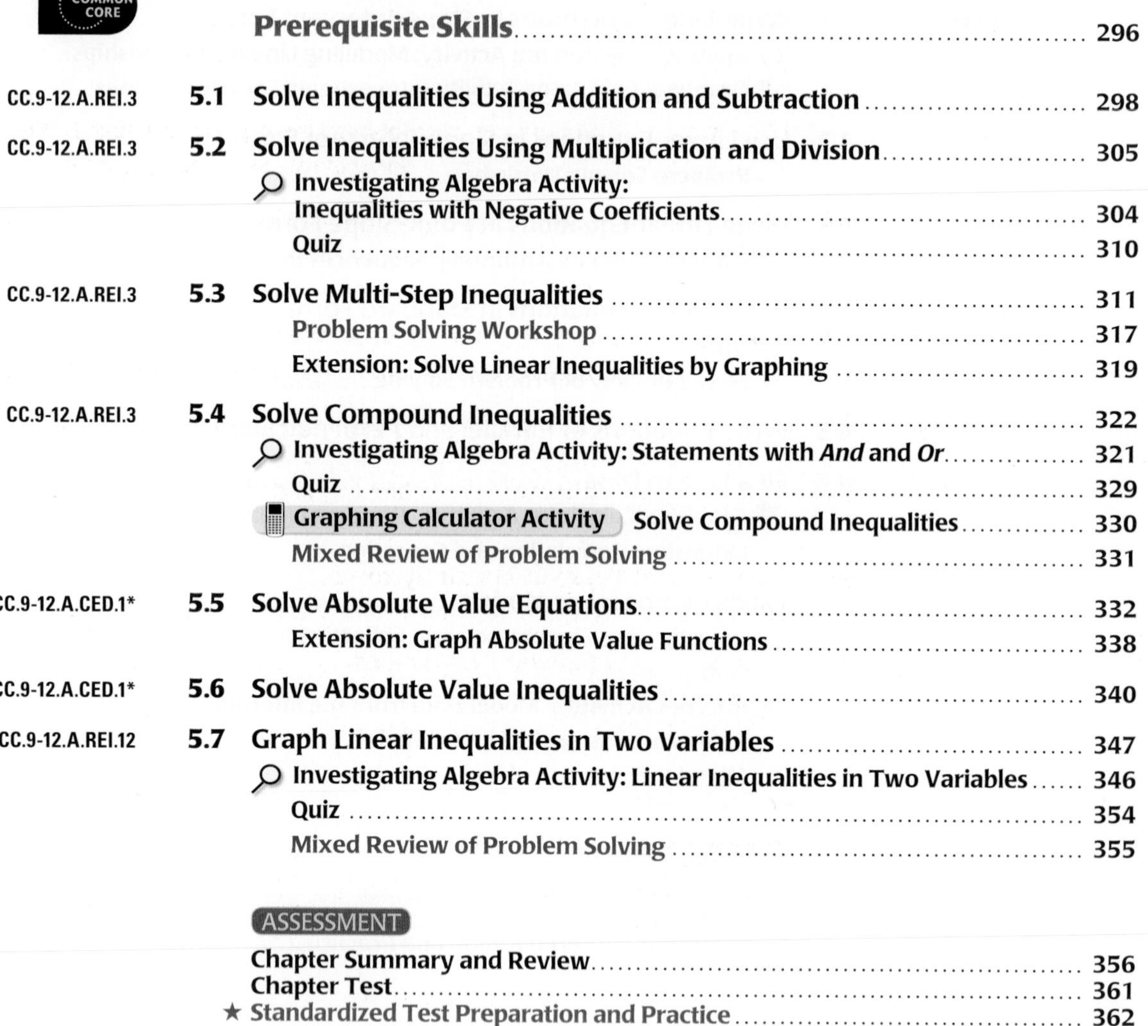

Graphing Inequalities, p. 298
$T \leq 134$

Solving and Graphing Linear Inequalities

COMMON CORE

Morey Milbradt/Brand X Pictures/Jupiterimages/Getty Images

CHAPTER

6

Solving Linear Systems, p. 388
$x - y = 4, x + y = 6$

Systems of Equations and Inequalities

COMMON CORE

CHAPTER 7

Order of Magnitude, p. 439
Solar system radius: 10^{13} m

Exponents and Exponential Functions

COMMON CORE

CHAPTER

8

Subtracting Polynomials, p. 500

$B = -0.0262t^3 + 0.376t^2 - 0.574t + 9.67$

Polynomials and Factoring

COMMON CORE

John Burcham/Getty Images

CHAPTER 9

Solving Quadratic Equations, p. 590
$y = -0.04x^2 + 1.2x$

Quadratic Equations and Functions

COMMON CORE

Donald Miralle/Getty Images

CHAPTER

10

Constructing Data Displays, p. 685
Min. = 173, Med. = 239, Max. = 295

Data Analysis

COMMON CORE

CHAPTER 11

Using Permutations, p. 719
$\text{Probability} = \frac{{}_5P_5}{{}_7P_7}$

Probability

COMMON CORE

Contents of Student Resources

Additional Lesson

Interpreting Linear Models

GOAL Interpret the slope and the y-intercept of a linear model.

Recall that you can interpret the slope of a nonvertical line as a rate of change. You have also seen that the y-intercept of a nonvertical line is the y-coordinate of the point where the line crosses the y-axis. In many linear models, the y-intercept represents an initial value or starting point.

CC.9-12.S.ID.7 Interpret the slope (rate of change) and the intercept (constant term) of a linear model in the context of the data.*

EXAMPLE 1 Interpret the slope and y-intercept

BIOLOGY A lion cub is born at a zoo. At birth, the cub weighs 5 pounds. After six months, the cub's weight has increased to 95 pounds. A linear model is used to represent the weight of the cub over this time period. What does the slope represent? What does the y-intercept represent?

Solution

STEP 1 **Interpret** the slope. The slope is the average rate of change in the cub's weight over the given time.

$$\text{Slope} = \frac{\text{change in weight (pounds)}}{\text{change in time (months)}} = \frac{90\text{ lb}}{6\text{ mo}} = 15\text{ lb/mo}$$

The slope tells you that the average rate at which the cub's weight is changing over the time period is 15 pounds per month.

STEP 2 **Interpret** the y-intercept. The y-intercept corresponds to an x-value of 0. For this example, $x = 0$ represents the time of the cub's birth. So, the y-intercept represents the weight of the cub when it was born, 5 pounds.

▸ The slope, 15, represents the cub's average growth rate in pounds per month. The y-intercept, 5, represents the cub's weight at birth.

EXAMPLE 2 Interpret a negative slope

RECREATION A linear model represents the height of a hot air balloon as a function of time for a given period. What does a negative slope represent in this context?

Solution

$$\text{Slope} = \text{rate of change} = \frac{\text{change in height}}{\text{change in time}}$$

Since the rate of change is negative, the height of the hot air balloon must be decreasing during the time period.

▸ A negative slope represents a hot air balloon that is descending.

PRACTICE

EXAMPLE 1
for Exs. 1–4

For each linear model, interpret what the slope and y-intercept represent.

1. **HOBBIES** When you begin to add water to an aquarium, it contains 10 gallons of water. Eight minutes later, the aquarium contains 34 gallons. A linear model represents the amount of water in the aquarium over time.

2. **HIKING** Beginning at the seashore, you hike on a trail up a mountain canyon. After 2 hours, your elevation is 1600 feet above sea level. A linear model represents your elevation as a function of time.

3. **TRANSPORTATION** A taxi service charges \$3 plus an amount based on distance. A 3-mile ride costs a total of \$10.50. A 5-mile ride costs a total of \$15.50. A linear model represents the cost of a taxi ride as a function of distance.

4. **PATTERNS** The figure shows three stages of a pattern made from square tiles. A linear model represents the number of tiles needed to build the pattern as a function of the stage number.

Stage 0

Stage 1

Stage 2

EXAMPLE 2
for Exs. 5–8

In Exercises 5–8, each model has a negative slope. Explain what the negative slope represents in the context of the linear model.

5. **POOLS** A linear model represents the amount of water in a swimming pool as a function of time.

6. **TECHNOLOGY** A linear model represents the price of a computer over time.

7. **EXERCISE** A linear model gives the maximum heart rate during exercise as a function of a person's age.

8. **BUSINESS** A linear model gives the number of cups of hot apple cider sold each day at a cafe as a function of the daily high temperature.

9. **FREEZERS** A scientist notes the temperature (in degrees Celsius) inside a laboratory freezer. She decides to adjust the temperature and writes a linear model to represent the temperature inside the freezer over time.

   a. What does a positive slope represent in this context?

   b. What does a negative y-intercept represent in this context?

10. **ELEVATORS** A linear model represents the height of an elevator over time.

    a. Explain what the slope represents (height in feet, time in seconds).

    b. For one elevator, the slope is 10. For another it is 16. What does this tell you?

    c. Suppose the slope for a time period is 0. What does this tell you?

11. **REASONING** In Exercise 2, how does the slope change on the return trip if you hike back to your starting point in the same amount of time? Explain.

12. **REASONING** A linear model represents the amount of time it takes to download an MP3 file as a function of the file's size. What do you expect the y-intercept to be? Explain why this makes sense.

Additional Lesson

Modeling with Combined Functions

GOAL Use arithmetic operations to combine functions.

You can perform arithmetic operations on functions in much the same way that you add, subtract, multiply, and divide algebraic expressions.

CC.9-12.F.BF.1b Combine standard function types using arithmetic operations.

EXAMPLE 1 Combine linear functions

HIGH SCHOOL SPORTS During the period 2000–2009, participation in high school sports (in millions) by male students M and female students F can be modeled by

$M = 0.06t + 3.8$ and

$F = 0.04t + 2.7$

where t is the number of years since 2000.

a. About how many students participated in high school sports in 2007?

b. About how many more male students than female students participated in high school sports in 2009?

Solution

a. Add the models for the participation by male and female students to find a model for the total participation P (in millions) by all students.

$P = (0.06t + 3.8) + (0.04t + 2.7)$ **Add the models.**

$= (0.06t + 0.04t) + (3.8 + 2.7)$ **Combine like terms.**

$= 0.1t + 6.5$ **Simplify.**

Substitute 7 for t in the model because 2007 is 7 years after 2000.

$P = 0.1(7) + 6.5 = 7.2$

▶ About 7.2 million students participated in high school sports in 2007.

b. Subtract the model for the participation by female students from the model for participation by male students to find a model for the difference in participation D (in millions).

$D = (0.06t + 3.8) - (0.04t + 2.7)$ **Find the difference of the models.**

$= (0.06t - 0.04t) + (3.8 - 2.7)$ **Combine like terms.**

$= 0.02t + 1.1$ **Simplify.**

Substitute 9 for t in the model because 2009 is 9 years after 2000.

$D = 0.02(9) + 1.1 = 1.28$

▶ About 1.28 million more male students than female students participated in high school sports in 2009.

EXAMPLE 2 Combine linear and exponential functions

POPULATION During the period 2000–2010, the populations (in thousands) of Boone County, Illinois, and Kendall County, Illinois, can be modeled by

Boone County: $B = 1.2t + 42.1$ and

Kendall County: $K = 55.2(1.076)^t$

where t is the number of years since 2000. What was the approximate total population P of the two counties in 2010?

Solution

STEP 1 **Add** the models for the populations to find a model for the total population P (in thousands) of the two counties.

$$P = (1.2t + 42.1) + 55.2(1.076)^t$$

STEP 2 **Substitute** 10 for t in the model because 2010 is 10 years after 2000.

$$P = 1.2(10) + 42.1 + 55.2(1.076)^{10} = 54.1 + 55.2(1.076)^{10} \approx 169$$

▶ The total population of the two counties in 2010 was about 169,000.

PRACTICE

EXAMPLE 1
for Ex. 1

1. **AGRICULTURE** During the period 2005 to 2009, the number of acres (in millions) of oats O and rye R planted in the United States can be modeled by

   $O = -0.26t + 4.3$ and $R = -0.05t + 1.4$

   where t is the number of years since 2005.

   a. Write a function for the total acres A (in millions) of oats and rye. About how many total acres of these crops were planted in 2009?

   b. Write a function for the difference in acres D (in millions) of oats and rye. About how many more acres of oats than rye were planted in 2009?

EXAMPLE 2
for Ex. 2

2. **STOCK MARKET** The dollar value of each share of the stock for Company A and for Company B for the period from 2005 to 2012 can be modeled by

   $A = 40(1.06)^t$ and $B = 2.6t + 60$

   where t is the number of years since 2005.

   a. Mia owns 100 shares of stock in each company. Write a model for the total value V of her stocks.

   b. What was the approximate total value of Mia's stock in Company A and Company B in 2012?

3. **A COOLING LIQUID** You pour boiling water into a cup to make tea. The temperature of the tea (in degrees Fahrenheit) as it cools to room temperature is modeled by the function $T = 140(0.97)^m + 72$ where m is the number of minutes after you pour the water. Explain how T is a combination of two functions, and explain what each function represents.

Additional Lesson

Use Inverse Functions

GOAL Find and apply inverse functions.

Key Vocabulary
- **inverse relation**
- **inverse function**

CC.9-12.F.BF.4 Find inverse functions.
a. Solve an equation of the form $f(x) = c$ for a simple function f that has an inverse, and write an expression for the inverse.

Recall that you learned that a relation is a pairing of input values with output values. An **inverse relation** interchanges the input and output values of the original relation. This means that the domain and range are also interchanged.

Original relation

x	0	1	2	3	4
y	6	4	2	0	−2

Inverse relation

x	6	4	2	0	−2
y	0	1	2	3	4

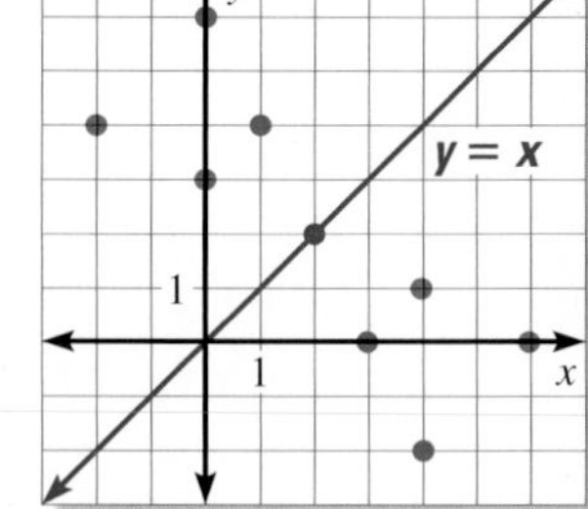

The graph of an inverse relation is a *reflection* of the graph of the original relation. The line of reflection is $y = x$. To find the inverse of a relation given by an equation in x and y, switch the roles of x and y and solve for y.

EXAMPLE 1 Find an inverse relation

Find an equation for the inverse of the relation $y = 3x - 5$.

$y = 3x - 5$	**Write original relation.**
$x = 3y - 5$	**Switch x and y.**
$x + 5 = 3y$	**Add 5 to each side.**
$\frac{1}{3}x + \frac{5}{3} = y$	**Solve for y. This is the inverse relation.**

In Example 1, both the original relation and the inverse relation happen to be functions. In such cases, the two functions are called **inverse functions**.

READING
The symbol −1 in f^{-1} is not to be interpreted as an exponent. In other words, $f^{-1}(x) \neq \frac{1}{f(x)}$.

KEY CONCEPT *For Your Notebook*

Inverse Functions

Functions f and g are inverses of each other provided:

$$f(g(x)) = x \qquad \text{and} \qquad g(f(x)) = x$$

The function g is denoted by f^{-1}, read as "f inverse."

As you have seen, to evaluate $f(2)$ for a function $f(x)$, you substitute 2 for x in the function. In the same way, you can evaluate $f(3x - 5)$ by substituting the expression $3x - 5$ for x in the function. So, to evaluate $f(g(x))$, you substitute the expression that represents the function $g(x)$ for x in the function $f(x)$.

EXAMPLE 2 Verify that functions are inverses

Verify that $f(x) = 3x - 5$ and $f^{-1}(x) = \frac{1}{3}x + \frac{5}{3}$ are inverse functions.

Solution

STEP 1 **Show** that $f(f^{-1}(x)) = x$.

$$f(f^{-1}(x)) = f\left(\frac{1}{3}x + \frac{5}{3}\right)$$
$$= 3\left(\frac{1}{3}x + \frac{5}{3}\right) - 5$$
$$= x + 5 - 5$$
$$= x \checkmark$$

STEP 2 **Show** that $f^{-1}(f(x)) = x$.

$$f^{-1}(f(x)) = f^{-1}(3x - 5)$$
$$= \frac{1}{3}(3x - 5) + \frac{5}{3}$$
$$= x - \frac{5}{3} + \frac{5}{3}$$
$$= x \checkmark$$

EXAMPLE 3 Solve a multi-step problem

FITNESS Elastic bands can be used in exercising to provide a range of resistance. A band's resistance R (in pounds) can be modeled by $R = \frac{3}{8}L - 5$ where L is the total length of the stretched band (in inches).

- Find the inverse of the model.
- Use the inverse function to find the length at which the band provides 19 pounds of resistance.

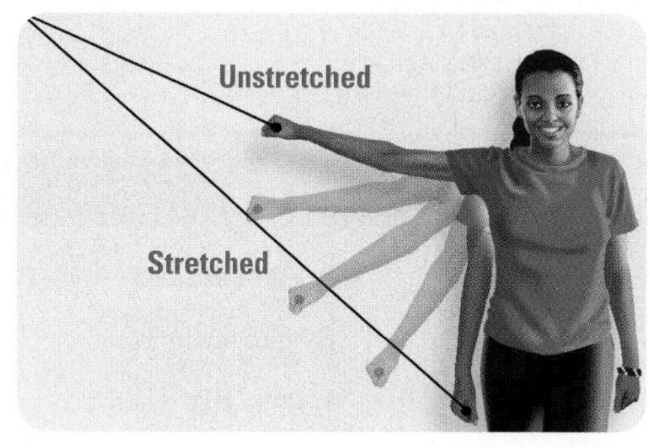

Solution

FIND INVERSES
Notice that you do not switch the variables when you are finding inverses of models. This would be confusing because the letters are chosen to remind you of the real-life quantities they represent.

STEP 1 **Find** the inverse function.

$R = \frac{3}{8}L - 5$ **Write original model.**

$R + 5 = \frac{3}{8}L$ **Add 5 to each side.**

$\frac{8}{3}R + \frac{40}{3} = L$ **Multiply each side by $\frac{8}{3}$.**

STEP 2 **Evaluate** the inverse function when $R = 19$.

$$L = \frac{8}{3}R + \frac{40}{3} = \frac{8}{3}(19) + \frac{40}{3} = \frac{152}{3} + \frac{40}{3} = \frac{192}{3} = 64$$

▸ The band provides 19 pounds of resistance when it is stretched to 64 inches.

✓ GUIDED PRACTICE for Examples 1, 2, and 3

Find the inverse of the given function. Then verify that your result and the original function are inverses.

1. $f(x) = x + 4$ **2.** $f(x) = 2x - 1$ **3.** $f(x) = -3x + 1$

4. FITNESS Use the inverse function in Example 3 to find the length at which the band provides 13 pounds of resistance.

EXAMPLE 4 Find the inverse of a function

Find the inverse of $f(x) = x^2, x \geq 0$. Then graph f and f^{-1}.

Solution

$f(x) = x^2$ **Write original function.**

$y = x^2$ **Replace $f(x)$ with y.**

$x = y^2$ **Switch x and y.**

$\pm\sqrt{x} = y$ **Take square roots of each side.**

The domain of f is restricted to nonnegative values of x. So, the range of f^{-1} must also be restricted to nonnegative values, and therefore the inverse is $f^{-1}(x) = \sqrt{x}$. (If the domain were restricted to $x \leq 0$, you would choose $f^{-1}(x) = -\sqrt{x}$.)

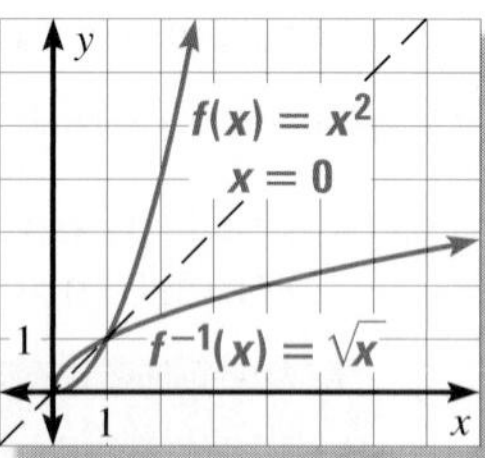

CHECK SOLUTION

You can check the solution of Example 4 by noting that the graph of

$f^{-1}(x) = \sqrt{x}$

is the reflection of the graph of $f(x) = x^2, x \geq 0$, in the line $y = x$.

PRACTICE

EXAMPLE 1
for Exs. 1–11

INVERSE RELATIONS Find an equation for the inverse relation.

1. $y = 4x - 1$
2. $y = -2x + 5$
3. $y = 7x - 6$
4. $y = 10x - 28$
5. $y = 12x + 7$
6. $y = -18x - 5$
7. $y = 5x + \frac{1}{3}$
8. $y = -\frac{2}{3}x + 2$
9. $y = -\frac{3}{5}x + \frac{7}{5}$

ERROR ANALYSIS *Describe* and correct the error in finding the inverse of the relation.

10.

$y = 6x - 11$

$x = 6y - 11$

$x + 11 = 6y$

$\frac{x}{6} + 11 = y$

11.

$y = -x + 3$

$-x = y + 3$

$-x - 3 = y$

12. ★ **OPEN-ENDED MATH** Write a function f such that the graph of f^{-1} is a line with a slope of 3.

EXAMPLE 2
for Exs. 13–18

VERIFYING INVERSE FUNCTIONS Verify that f and g are inverse functions.

13. $f(x) = x + 4, g(x) = x - 4$
14. $f(x) = 2x + 3, g(x) = \frac{1}{2}x - \frac{3}{2}$
15. $f(x) = \frac{1}{4}x^3, g(x) = (4x)^{1/3}$
16. $f(x) = \frac{1}{5}x - 1, g(x) = 5x + 5$
17. $f(x) = 4x + 9, g(x) = \frac{1}{4}x - \frac{9}{4}$
18. $f(x) = 5x^2 - 2, x \geq 0; g(x) = \left(\frac{x + 2}{5}\right)^{1/2}$

EXAMPLE 3
for Exs. 19–20

19. **EXCHANGE RATES** The *euro* is the unit of currency for the European Union. On a certain day, the number E of euros that could be obtained for D dollars was given by this function:

$$E = 0.81419D$$

Find the inverse of the function. Then use the inverse to find the number of dollars that could be obtained for 250 euros on that day.

20. ★ **EXTENDED RESPONSE** At the start of a dog sled race in Anchorage, Alaska, the temperature was 5°C. By the end of the race, the temperature was −10°C. The formula for converting temperatures from degrees Fahrenheit F to degrees Celsius C is $C = \frac{5}{9}(F - 32)$.

    a. Find the inverse of the given model. *Describe* what information you can obtain from the inverse.

    b. Find the Fahrenheit temperatures at the start and end of the race.

    c. Use a graphing calculator to graph the original function and its inverse. Find the temperature that is the same on both temperature scales.

EXAMPLE 4
for Exs. 21–23

INVERSES OF NONLINEAR FUNCTIONS Find the inverse of the function.

21. $f(x) = \frac{1}{3}x^2, x \geq 0$

22. $f(x) = \frac{1}{2}x^3$

23. $f(x) = \frac{1}{4}x^2 - 1, x \geq 0$

24. **BOAT SPEED** The maximum hull speed v (in knots) of a boat with a displacement hull can be approximated by

$$v = 1.34\sqrt{\ell}$$

where ℓ is the length (in feet) of the boat's waterline. Find the inverse of the model. Then find the waterline length needed to achieve a maximum speed of 7.5 knots.

25. **CHALLENGE** Consider the function $g(x) = -x$.

    a. Graph $g(x) = -x$ and explain why it is its own inverse. Also verify that $g(x) = g^{-1}(x)$ algebraically.

    b. Graph other linear functions that are their own inverses. Write equations of the lines you graphed.

    c. Use your results from part (b) to write a general equation describing the family of linear functions that are their own inverses.

26. Find the inverse of the function $f(x) = \frac{x+1}{x-1}, x \neq 1$.

    Verify that your answer is the inverse of $f(x)$.

27. **CHALLENGE** Show that the inverse of any linear function $f(x) = mx + b$, where $m \neq 0$, is also a linear function. Give the slope and y-intercept of the graph of f^{-1} in terms of m and b.

Rod Taylor/AP/Wide World Photos

Additional Lesson

Investigate Polynomials and Closure

GOAL Determine whether a set is closed under an operation.

COMMON CORE

CC.9-12.A-APR-1. Understand that polynomials form a system analogous to the integers, namely, they are closed under the operations of addition, subtraction, and multiplication; add, subtract, and multiply polynomials.

If an operation is performed on members of a set and the result is always a member of that set, the set is *closed* under that operation. For example, the set {0, 1} is closed under multiplication since every possible product of the set members ($0 \bullet 0 = 0$, $0 \bullet 1 = 0$, and $1 \bullet 1 = 1$) is a member of the set. On the other hand, the set is not closed under addition since the sum $1 + 1 = 2$ is not a member of the set.

The table below lists several subsets of the set of real numbers and indicates whether they are closed under the four basic operations.

CLOSURE AND DIVISION
Exclude the undefined case of division by 0 when determining whether a set is closed under division.

Set of numbers	Closed under addition?	Closed under subtraction?	Closed under multiplication?	Closed under division?
Whole numbers	Yes	No	Yes	No
Integers	Yes	Yes	Yes	No
Rational numbers	Yes	Yes	Yes	Yes
Real numbers	Yes	Yes	Yes	Yes

Sets of algebraic expressions, like sets of numbers, can either be closed or not closed under an operation.

EXAMPLE 1 Polynomials and addition

Tell whether the set of polynomials in a single variable with real number coefficients is closed under addition.

Recall that a polynomial is a monomial or a sum of monomials.

Let $p_1(x)$ and $p_2(x)$ be two polynomials with real number coefficients as shown below. (Some terms in one or both polynomials may be 0.)

$$p_1(x) = a_0x^0 + a_1x^1 + \cdots + a_kx^k$$

$$p_2(x) = b_0x^0 + b_1x^1 + \cdots + b_kx^k$$

So, the coefficients $a_0, a_1, \ldots, a_k$ and $b_0, b_1, \ldots, b_k$ are real numbers, and the exponents $0, 1, \ldots, k$ are whole numbers. To add polynomials, add like terms:

$$p_1(x) + p_2(x) = (a_0 + b_0)x^0 + (a_1 + b_1)x^1 + \cdots + (a_k + b_k)x^k$$

Since the original coefficients are real numbers and the set of real numbers is closed under addition, each new coefficient, $(a_0 + b_0)$, $(a_1 + b_1)$, and so on, is a real number. The exponents do not change. So, the sum $p_1(x) + p_2(x)$ is itself a polynomial, and the set of polynomials is closed under addition.

EXAMPLE 2 Polynomials under multiplication and division

Tell whether the set of polynomials in a single variable with real coefficients is closed under (a) multiplication and (b) division.

a. Let $p_1(x)$ and $p_2(x)$ be two polynomials with real number coefficients $a_0, a_1, \ldots, a_j$ and $b_0, b_1, \ldots, b_k$, as shown below ($j \le k$).

$$p_1(x) = a_0x^0 + \cdots + a_jx^j$$

$$p_2(x) = b_0x^0 + \cdots + b_jx^j + \cdots + b_kx^k$$

To multiply two polynomials, use the distributive property to multiply each term of one polynomial with each term of the other:

$$p_1(x) \bullet p_2(x) = (a_0 \bullet b_0)x^{0+0} + \cdots + (a_0 \bullet b_k)x^{0+k} + \cdots + (a_j \bullet b_0)x^{j+0} + \ldots + (a_j \bullet b_k)x^{j+k}$$

Because each term of the product has a coefficient (from $a_0 \bullet b_0$ to $a_j \bullet b_k$) that is a product of real numbers, and the set of real numbers is closed under multiplication, the new coefficients are real numbers. Because the exponent of each term (from $0 + 0$ to $j + k$) is a sum of whole numbers, and the set of whole numbers is closed under addition, each exponent is a whole number.

So, the product $p_1(x) \bullet p_2(x)$ is itself a polynomial, and the set of polynomials is closed under multiplication.

b. To prove that a set is *not* closed under an operation, you need to provide only a single example where the result is not a member of the original set. The quotient of the polynomials $x + 1$ and $x - 1$ is $\frac{x+1}{x-1}$. This rational expression cannot be simplified and is not a polynomial, so the set of polynomials is not closed under division.

PRACTICE

1. Give an example showing that the set of integers is not closed under division.

2. Give an example showing that the set of whole numbers is not closed under subtraction.

3. Determine whether the set of polynomials in one variable with real coefficients is closed under subtraction.

4. Based on the operations under which the given set is closed, tell whether the set of polynomials in one variable with real coefficients is most like *the set of whole numbers, the set of integers,* or *the set of rational numbers.*

5. Consider the set of quadratic expressions in one variable with real coefficients: $q_1(x) = a_1x^2 + b_1x + c_1$, $a_1 \neq 0$. This set is not closed under addition because the coefficient of the x^2 term in the sum can be zero.

   a. Give an example of the situation described above.

   b. Based on the information above, determine whether this set is closed under any of the operations subtraction, multiplication, or division.

Additional Lesson

Translate Between Recursive and Explicit Rules for Sequences

GOAL Translate between recursive and explicit rules for arithmetic and geometric sequences.

CC.9-12.F.BF.2 Write arithmetic and geometric sequences both recursively and with an explicit formula, use them to model situations, and translate between the two forms.*

The box below summarizes the recursive and explicit rules for arithmetic sequences with common difference d, and for geometric sequences with common ratio r.

KEY CONCEPT *For Your Notebook*

Sequence Formulas

	Arithmetic Sequence	Geometric Sequence
Recursive Formula	$a_n = a_{n-1} + d$	$a_n = r \cdot a_{n-1}$
Explicit Formula	$a_n = a_1 + (n - 1)d$	$a_n = a_1 r^{n-1}$

To translate from an explicit rule to a recursive rule for an arithmetic sequence, find the first term a_1 and the common difference d. To translate from an explicit rule to a recursive rule for a geometric sequence, find a_1 and the common ratio r.

EXAMPLE 1 Translate from an explicit rule to a recursive rule

Write a recursive rule for the sequence.

a. $a_n = -6 + 8n$

b. $a_n = -3\left(\frac{1}{2}\right)^{n-1}$

Solution

a. $a_n = -6 + 8n$ — **Write explicit rule.**

$a_1 = -6 + 8(1) = 2$ — **Substitute 1 for *n*.**

$d = 8$ — **The coefficient of *n* is *d*.**

$a_1 = 2,\ a_n = a_{n-1} + 8$ — **Write recursive rule.**

b. $a_n = -3\left(\frac{1}{2}\right)^{n-1}$ — **Write explicit rule.**

$a_1 = -3\left(\frac{1}{2}\right)^0 = -3$ — **Substitute 1 for *n*.**

$r = \frac{1}{2}$ — **The common ratio is $\frac{1}{2}$.**

$a_1 = -3,\ a_n = \frac{1}{2}a_{n-1}$ — **Write recursive rule.**

To translate from a recursive rule to an explicit rule for an arithmetic sequence, find the common difference d. To translate from a recursive rule to an explicit rule for a geometric sequence, find the common ratio r.

EXAMPLE 2 Translate from a recursive rule to an explicit rule

Write an explicit rule for the sequence.

a. $a_1 = -5, a_n = a_{n-1} - 2$

b. $a_1 = 10, a_n = 2a_{n-1}$

Solution

a. $a_1 = -5, a_n = a_{n-1} - 2$ — Write recursive rule.

$d = -2$ — The number added or subtracted is d.

$a_n = -5 + (n - 1)(-2)$ — Substitute -5 for a_1 and -2 for d.

$a_n = -3 - 2n$ — Simplify to write explicit rule.

b. $a_1 = 10, a_n = 2a_{n-1}$ — Write recursive rule.

$r = 2$ — The coefficient of a_{n-1} is r.

$a_n = 10(2)^{n-1}$ — Substitute 10 for a_1 and 2 for r to write explicit rule.

PRACTICE

EXAMPLE 1 for Exs. 1–4

Write a recursive rule for the sequence.

1. $a_n = 17 - 4n$

2. $a_n = 126 + 12.5n$

3. $a_n = 16(3)^{n-1}$

4. $a_n = 100{,}000(1.02)^{n-1}$

EXAMPLE 2 for Exs. 5–8

Write an explicit rule for the sequence.

5. $a_1 = -12, a_n = a_{n-1} + 16$

6. $a_1 = 158, a_n = a_{n-1} - 7$

7. $a_1 = 2, a_n = -6a_{n-1}$

8. $a_1 = -\frac{1}{2}, a_n = 100a_{n-1}$

9. SAVINGS Juliana has saved \$82 so far to buy a bicycle. She saves an additional \$30 each month. The explicit rule $a_n = 30n + 82$ gives the amount saved after n months. Write a recursive rule for the amount Juliana has saved n months from now.

10. SOUP CANS A grocery store arranges cans in a pyramid-shaped display with 20 cans in the bottom row and 2 fewer cans in each subsequent row going up. The number of cans in each row is represented by the recursive rule $a_1 = 20, a_n = a_{n-1} - 2$. Write an explicit rule for the number of cans in row n.

11. SALARY Linda's salary is given by the explicit rule $a_n = 35{,}000(1.04)^{n-1}$, where n is the number of years she has worked. Write a recursive rule for her salary.

12. DEPRECIATION The value of Tim's car is given by the recursive rule $a_1 = 25{,}600$, $a_n = 0.86a_{n-1}$, where n is the number of years since Tim bought the car. Write an explicit rule for the value of Tim's car after n years.

Additional Lesson

Write Quadratic Equations

GOAL Write a quadratic equation given its roots or its graph.

COMMON CORE

CC.9-12.A.SSE.3 Choose and produce an equivalent form of an expression to reveal and explain properties of the quantity represented by the expression.

You are already familiar with the property of zero: For any real number a, $a \bullet 0 = 0$. This is equivalent to the following statement:

For real numbers a and b, if $a = 0$ or $b = 0$, then $ab = 0$.

If you are given the roots of a quadratic equation, you can use the property of zero to write the equation.

EXAMPLE 1 Write a quadratic equation given its roots

Write a quadratic equation in standard form with the roots −2 and 1.

Solution

$x = -2$ or $x = 1$	**Write the roots as solutions to two equations.**
$x + 2 = 0$ or $x - 1 = 0$	**Rewrite each equation with 0 on one side.**
$(x + 2)(x - 1) = 0$	**Property of zero**
$x^2 + x - 2 = 0$	**Multiply.**

▶ A quadratic equation with the roots −2 and 1 is $x^2 + x - 2 = 0$.

CHECK Check the equation by substituting the roots into the equation.

$$(-2)^2 + (-2) - 2 \stackrel{?}{=} 0 \qquad 1^2 + 1 - 2 \stackrel{?}{=} 0$$

$$4 - 2 - 2 \stackrel{?}{=} 0 \qquad 1 + 1 - 2 \stackrel{?}{=} 0$$

$$0 = 0 \checkmark \qquad 0 = 0 \checkmark$$

EQUATIONS AND GRAPHS You can also show that the equation $x^2 + x - 2 = 0$ has the roots −2 and 1 by graphing the related quadratic function $y = x^2 + x - 2$. The graph shows that $y = x^2 + x - 2$ has x-intercepts −2 and 1. This means that $x = -2$ and $x = 1$ are zeros of the function $y = x^2 + x - 2$ and roots of the equation $x^2 + x - 2 = 0$.

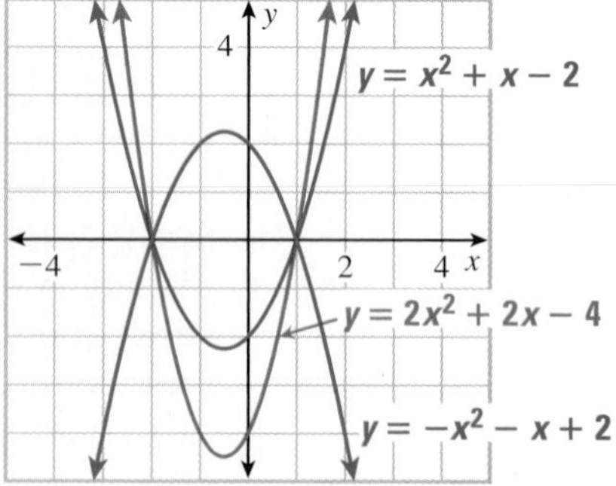

The graph also shows that there are other quadratic functions with the same zeros, including the functions $y = 2x^2 + 2x - 4$ and $y = -x^2 - x + 2$. In order to determine a unique quadratic function, you need to know the two zeros and another piece of information, such as another point on the graph.

EXAMPLE 2 Write a quadratic function given its graph

Write a quadratic function in standard form for the parabola shown.

Solution

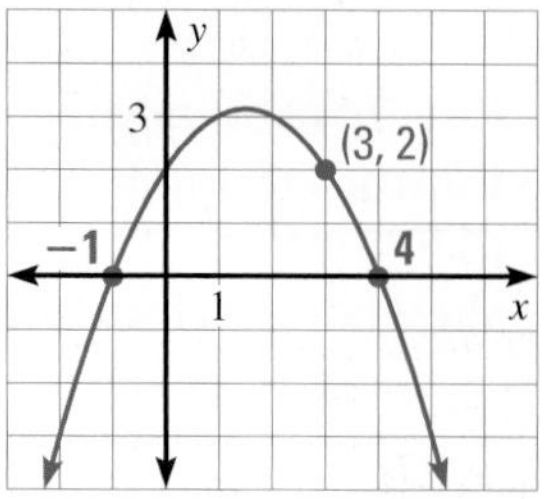

Because the x-intercepts are given, use the intercept form of a quadratic function.

$y = a(x - p)(x - q)$ **Intercept form**

$y = a(x + 1)(x - 4)$ **Substitute −1 for p and 4 for q.**

Use the other given point, (3, 2) to find a.

$2 = a(3 + 1)(3 - 4)$ **Substitute.**

$2 = -4a$ **Multiply.**

$-\frac{1}{2} = a$ **Solve for a.**

Write the function $y = -\frac{1}{2}(x + 1)(x - 4)$ in standard form.

$y = -\frac{1}{2}(x^2 - 3x - 4)$ **Multiply the binomials.**

$y = -\frac{1}{2}x^2 + \frac{3}{2}x + 2$ **Distributive property**

▶ A quadratic function for the parabola is $y = -\frac{1}{2}x^2 + \frac{3}{2}x + 2$.

AVOID ERRORS
Be sure to substitute the x-intercepts and the coordinates of the given point for the correct letters in $y = a(x - p)(x - q)$.

PRACTICE

EXAMPLE 1 for Exs. 1–6

Write a quadratic equation in standard form with the given roots.

1. 2 and 5 **2.** −3 and 4 **3.** 1 and −5

4. −2 and −3 **5.** 7 and −5 **6.** −4 and 0

EXAMPLE 2 for Exs. 7–9

Write a quadratic function in standard form for the parabola shown.

7. (0, 6); −2; 3

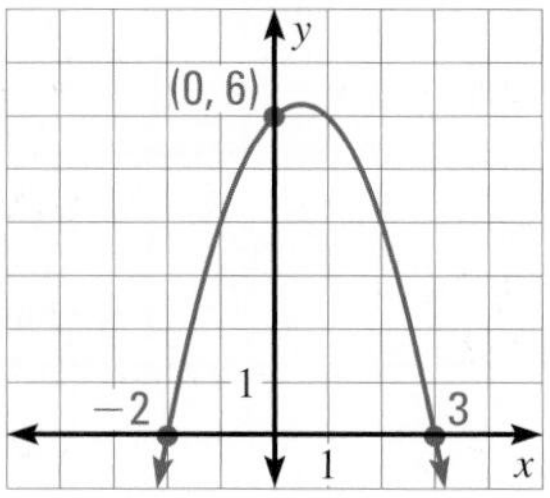

8. (−3, 3); −6; −4

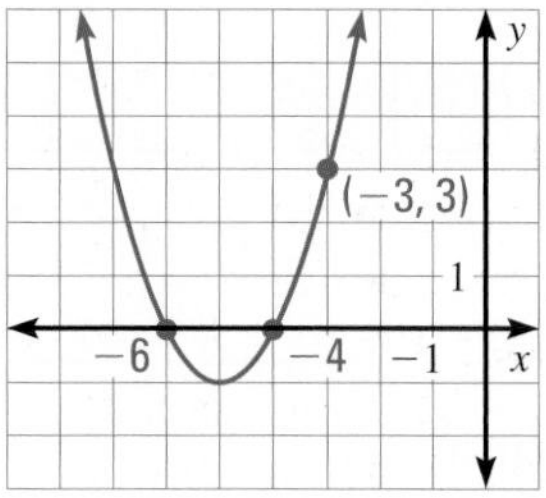

9. −3; 3; (1, −4)

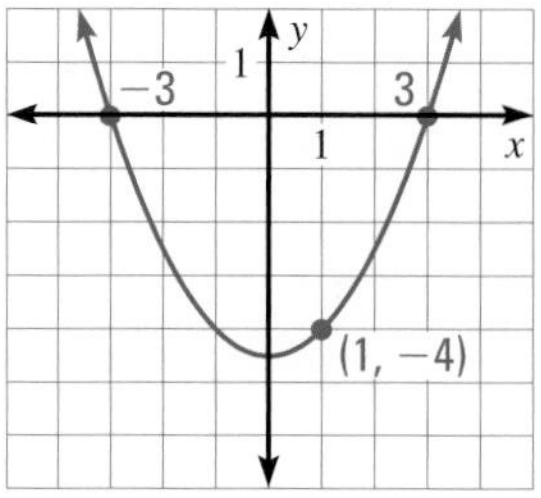

10. REASONING Once you write a quadratic equation that has given roots, explain how you can find additional quadratic equations with those roots.

11. CHALLENGE Write a quadratic equation in standard form with −2 as a repeated root.

Additional Lesson

Data Distributions

GOAL Compare and interpret the shape, center, and spread of data sets.

Key Vocabulary
- **mound-shaped distribution**
- **skewed distribution**

CC.9-12.S.ID.3 Interpret differences in shape, center, and spread in the context of the data sets, accounting for possible effects of extreme data points (outliers).*

Histograms can help you compare the shapes of data distributions. A **mound-shaped distribution** is approximately symmetrical, with the data frequency in each interval generally increasing toward the center of the distribution. In a **skewed distribution**, the intervals with the greatest data frequency occur toward one end of the histogram.

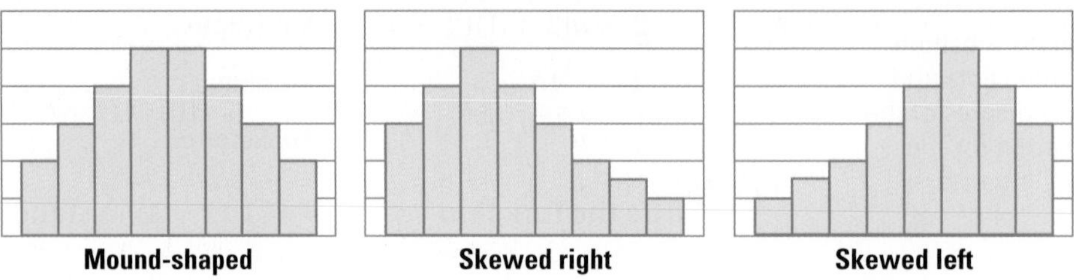

Notice that in the skewed right distribution, the longer "tail" of the distribution extends to the right, and in the skewed left distribution the tail extends to the left.

EXAMPLE 1 Compare the shapes of data sets

MEDIA The histograms below display the ages of 50 randomly-chosen subscribers to two magazines. Compare the shapes of the data distributions, and interpret the differences in shape.

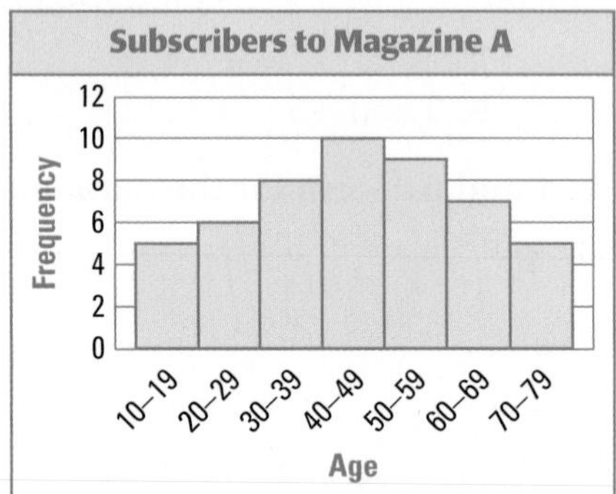

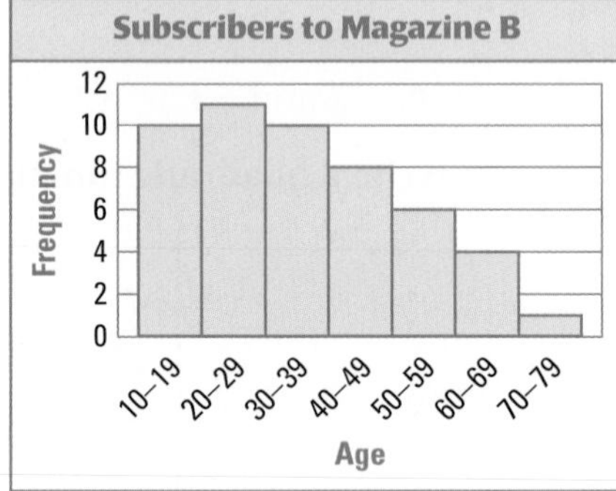

Solution

STEP 1 **Compare** the shapes of the histograms.

The distribution in the histogram for Magazine A is mound-shaped. The distribution in the histogram for Magazine B is skewed right.

STEP 2 **Interpret** the differences in the shapes.

Magazine A is most popular with middle-aged readers. The number of subscribers decreases symmetrically with decreasing and increasing age. Magazine B appeals especially to teenagers and young adults, with fewer and fewer subscribers as age increases.

COMPARING CENTER AND SPREAD In order to compare the center and spread of data sets it is often best to use box-and-whisker plots, which make it easy to compare the medians, ranges, and interquartile ranges. You can also use box-and-whisker plots to identify *outliers,* data values that fall far outside the main distribution.

EXAMPLE 2 Compare the centers and spreads of data sets

ELECTORAL VOTES The table shows the number of electoral votes of states in the West and Midwest according to the U.S. Census Bureau. Compare and interpret differences in the centers and spreads of the data sets.

Electoral Votes of States in the 2012 Presidential Election													
West	3	3	3	4	4	5	6	6	7	9	11	12	55
Midwest	3	3	5	6	6	10	10	10	11	16	18	20	

Solution

STEP 1 **Draw** a double box-and-whisker plot to compare the data.

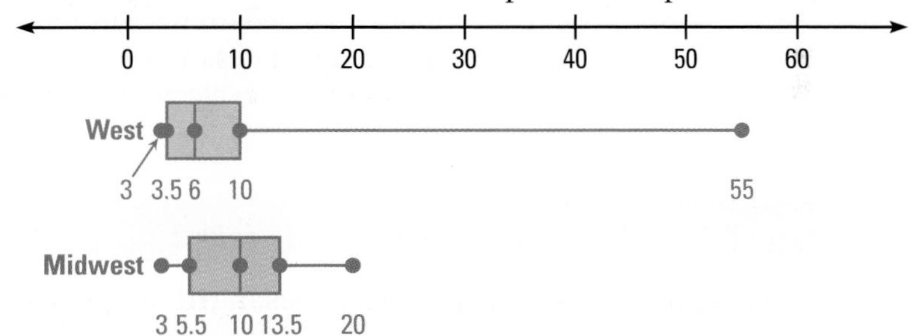

STEP 2 **Compare** the centers and spreads of the data.

Find the median, range, and interquartile range for each region.

Region	Median	Range	Interquartile Range
West	6	52	6.5
Midwest	10	17	8

STEP 3 **Interpret** the differences in the centers and spreads.

Each box represents the center half of its data set. The differences in the medians and positions of the boxes show that in general, states in the Midwest tend to have more electoral votes than states in the West.

The interquartile ranges show that the center half of the Midwest data is a little more spread out than in the West. The West's much greater range, however, means that the West's total spread is much greater. The data value 55 appears to be an outlier.

OUTLIERS A data value is an outlier if it is more than 1.5 times the interquartile range below the first quartile or above the third quartile, that is, if it lies more than 1.5 "box widths" to the left or right of the box on a box-and-whisker plot. Because outliers affect measures of the center and spread, it is useful to compare data sets with and without outliers.

EXAMPLE 3 Describe the effect of outliers

Describe the effect of outliers in comparing the data sets from Example 2.

STEP 1 **Identify** any data values that are outliers.

For the West, 1.5 times the interquartile range is $1.5(6.5) = 9.75$. The upper quartile is 10. Any data value greater than $10 + 9.75 = 19.75$ is an outlier. So, the data value 55 is an outlier.

STEP 2 **Determine** the measures of center and spread without the outlier.

Region	Median	Range	Interquartile Range
West	5.5	9	4.5
Midwest	10	17	8

STEP 3 **Interpret** the changes in the measures of center and spread.

The median for the West changed only from 6 to 5.5, but the interquartile range changed from 6.5 to 4.5, and the range from 52 to only 9. Without the outlier, states in the West show significantly fewer and significantly less variation in electoral votes than those in the Midwest.

PRACTICE

EXAMPLE 1
for Exs. 1–2

Compare and interpret differences in the shapes of the data sets.

1. **PLANTS** The histograms display data about the heights (to the nearest centimeter) of two sets of bean plants.

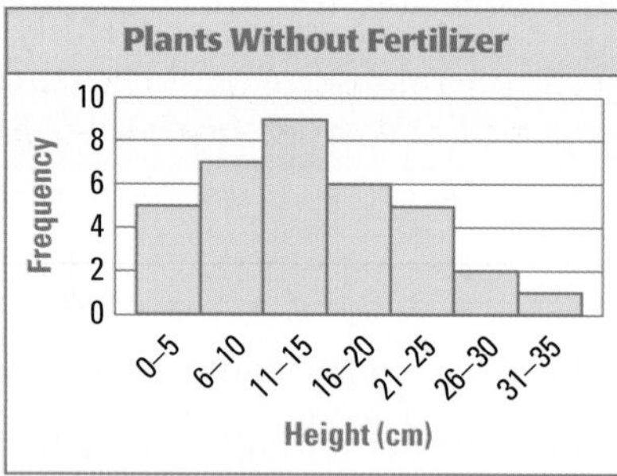

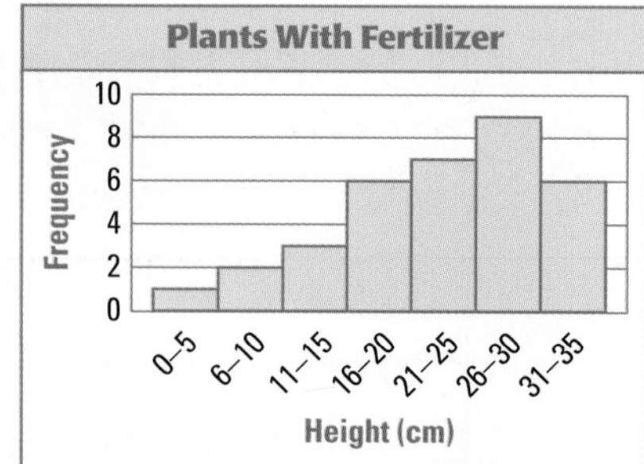

2. **SHOPPING** The histograms display data about the total amount spent (to the nearest dollar) by 40 customers at each of two grocery stores.

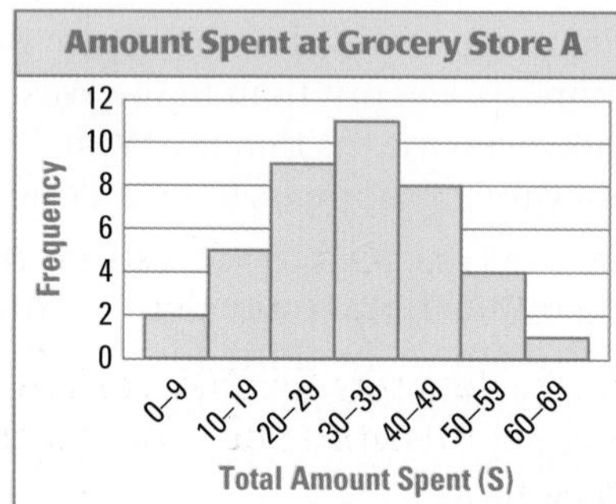

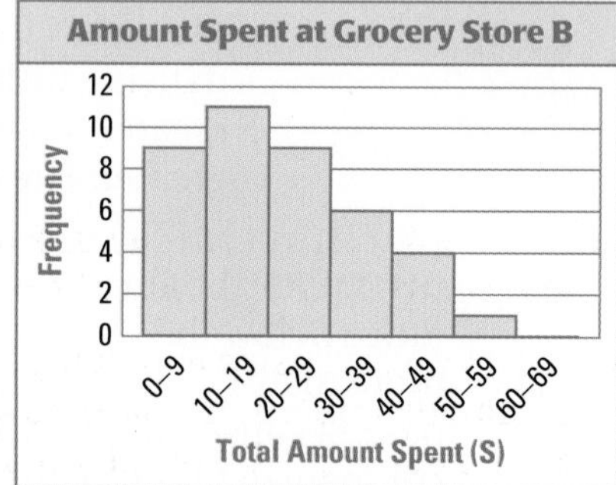

EXAMPLE 2
for Exs. 3–4

Compare and interpret differences in the centers and spreads of the data sets.

3. **GOVERNMENT** The table shows the age at inauguration of 20th century presidents and vice-presidents.

Age at Inauguration	
Presidents	42 43 46 51 51 51 52 54 55 55 56 56 60 61 62 64 69
Vice-Presidents	40 41 42 44 48 49 50 52 52 52 53 53 56 58 59 60 60 64 66 69 71

4. **TOURNAMENTS** The table shows the time (in minutes) for competitors to complete a crossword puzzle at a tournament.

Time to Complete a Crossword Puzzle															
Experts	3	7	7	8	8	9	9	9	10	10	10	10	11	12	14
Rookies	12	12	12	13	13	13	14	16	16	16	16	16	19	19	20

EXAMPLE 3
for Exs. 5–6

5. **OUTLIERS** Identify and describe the effect of outliers in comparing the data sets from Exercise 4.

6. **BASEBALL** The table shows the number of home runs hit by two baseball players over 13 seasons. Describe the effect of any outliers in comparing the centers and spreads of the data sets.

Home Runs Per Season													
Player A	10	11	11	12	14	15	16	17	19	20	20	20	34
Player B	17	17	17	18	20	21	22	24	24	25	26	27	27

7. **CLIMATE** The box-and-whisker plot shows the average monthly high temperature (in degrees Fahrenheit) each month in Honolulu, San Francisco, and New York. Use what you know about these cities to match the box-and-whisker plots to the cities. Explain your choices.

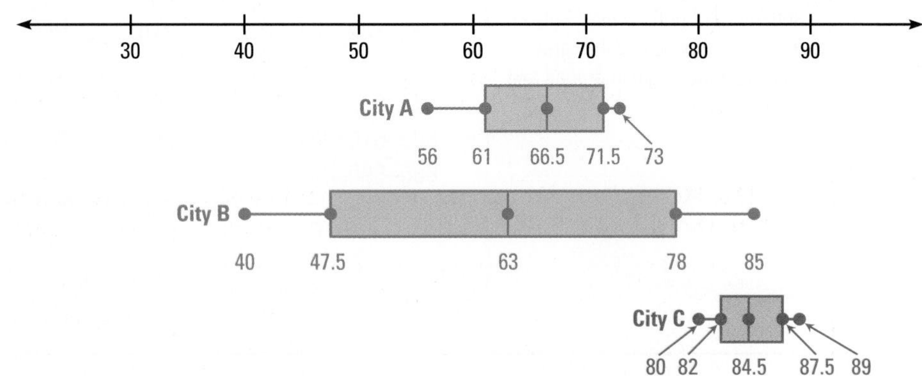

8. **REASONING** Every value in a data set is doubled to form a new data set. Compare the centers and spreads of the original and new data sets.

9. **OPEN-ENDED** Give an example of two data sets that have different centers but identical spreads. Explain how these similarities and differences would be reflected in the data sets' box-and-whisker plots.

Standards for Mathematical Content

Correlation for Holt McDougal Larson Algebra 1, Geometry, Algebra 2

Standards	Descriptor	Algebra 1	Geometry	Algebra 2
Standards for Mathematical Content				
(+ = advanced; * = also a Modeling Standard)				
Number and Quantity				
CC.9-12.N.RN.1	Explain how the definition of the meaning of rational exponents follows from extending the properties of integer exponents to those values, allowing for a notation for radicals in terms of rational exponents.	SE: 455–456		SE: 166–171, 211, 218, 221, 473, EP4
CC.9-12.N.RN.2	Rewrite expressions involving radicals and rational exponents using the properties of exponents.	SE: 455–456	SE: 131, 419, 445, 451–453	SE: 172–179, 219, 221, 257, EP4
CC.9-12.N.RN.3	Explain why the sum or product of two rational numbers is rational; that the sum of a rational number and an irrational number is irrational; and that the product of a nonzero rational number and an irrational number is irrational.	SE: 80–81		
CC.9-12.N.Q.1	Use units as a way to understand problems and to guide the solution of multi-step problems; choose and interpret units consistently in formulas; choose and interpret the scale and the origin in graphs and data displays.*	SE: 17–18, 19–20, 27, 43, 48, 50–51, 53, 54, 87, 90–91, 165–166, 168–170, 371, 374–375, 551, 554–555, 556, 607, 609–610, 684, 685–690, 691, 694	SE: 55, 60, 66, 70, 89, 152, 189, 319, 523, 695, 711–716, 719–725, 727, 731–732, 739, 749, 750, 752–757, 759, 763–770, 775–781, 786–790, 795, 798, 800, 801–802, 803, 810–811, SR10, SR20–SR21, EP3, EP23–EP24	SE: 5, 8–9, 30, 103, 114, 116, 374, 492, 494–495, 500–501, 507, SR13, SR17–SR19, SR21

SE = Student Edition

Standards	Descriptor	Algebra 1	Geometry	Algebra 2
Standards for Mathematical Content				
(+ = advanced; * = also a Modeling Standard)				
Number and Quantity				
CC.9-12.N.Q.2	Define appropriate quantities for the purpose of descriptive modeling.*	SE: 168, 277, 282, 686, 689, 691		SE: 5, 20, 27, 28, 114, 131, 147, 312, 469
CC.9-12.N.Q.3	Choose a level of accuracy appropriate to limitations on measurement when reporting quantities.*	SE: 35–40	SE: 476, 727, 729–732	
CC.9-12.N.CN.1	Know there is a complex number i such that $i^2 = -1$, and every complex number has the form $a + bi$ with a and b real.			SE: 41–42
CC.9-12.N.CN.2	Use the relation $i^2 = -1$ and the commutative, associative, and distributive properties to add, subtract, and multiply complex numbers.			SE: AL2–AL3, 42–44, 45–47, 57, 78–79, 81, 93, EP2
CC.9-12.N.CN.3	(+) Find the conjugate of a complex number; use conjugates to find moduli and quotients of complex numbers.			SE: 44–46, 57, 79, 81, EP2
CC.9-12.N.CN.4	(+) Represent complex numbers on the complex plane in rectangular and polar form (including real and imaginary numbers), and explain why the rectangular and polar forms of a given complex number represent the same number.			SE: 44–46
CC.9-12.N.CN.5	(+) Represent addition, subtraction, multiplication, and conjugation of complex numbers geometrically on the complex plane; use properties of this representation for computation.			SE: 47, 48

SE = Student Edition

Standards	Descriptor	Algebra 1	Geometry	Algebra 2
Standards for Mathematical Content				
(+ = advanced; * = also a Modeling Standard)				
Number and Quantity				
CC.9-12.N.CN.6	(+) Calculate the distance between numbers in the complex plane as the modulus of the difference, and the midpoint of a segment as the average of the numbers at its endpoints.			SE: 47, 48
CC.9-12.N.CN.7	Solve quadratic equations with real coefficients that have complex solutions.			SE: 41, 45, 57, 81, 85, EP2
CC.9-12.N.CN.8	(+) Extend polynomial identities to the complex numbers.			SE: 138–140, 142, 159
CC.9-12.N.CN.9	(+) Know the Fundamental Theorem of Algebra; show that it is true for quadratic polynomials.			SE: AL6, 137–143, 157, 159
CC.9-12.N.VM.1	(+) Recognize vector quantities as having both magnitude and direction. Represent vector quantities by directed line segments, and use appropriate symbols for vectors and their magnitudes (e.g., ***v***, |***v***|, ||***v***||, *v*).	*This standard is outside the Common Core college and career ready standards.*		
CC.9-12.N.VM.2	(+) Find the components of a vector by subtracting the coordinates of an initial point from the coordinates of a terminal point.	*This standard is outside the Common Core college and career ready standards.*		
CC.9-12.N.VM.3	(+) Solve problems involving velocity and other quantities that can be represented by vectors.	*This standard is outside the Common Core college and career ready standards.*		

SE = Student Edition

Standards	Descriptor	Algebra 1	Geometry	Algebra 2
Standards for Mathematical Content				
(+ = advanced; * = also a Modeling Standard)				
Number and Quantity				
CC.9-12.N.VM.4	(+) Add and subtract vectors. a. Add vectors end-to-end, component-wise, and by the parallelogram rule. Understand that the magnitude of a sum of two vectors is typically not the sum of the magnitudes. b. Given two vectors in magnitude and direction form, determine the magnitude and direction of their sum. c. Understand vector subtraction $\mathbf{v} - \mathbf{w}$ as $\mathbf{v} + (-\mathbf{w})$, where $-\mathbf{w}$ is the additive inverse of $\mathbf{w}$, with the same magnitude as $\mathbf{w}$ and pointing in the opposite direction. Represent vector subtraction graphically by connecting the tips in the appropriate order, and perform vector subtraction component-wise.	*This standard is outside the Common Core college and career ready standards.*		
CC.9-12.N.VM.5	(+) Multiply a vector by a scalar. a. Represent scalar multiplication graphically by scaling vectors and possibly reversing their direction; perform scalar multiplication component-wise, e.g., as $c(v_x, v_y) = (cv_x, cv_y)$. b. Compute the magnitude of a scalar multiple $c\mathbf{v}$ using $\|\|c\mathbf{v}\|\| = \|c\|\mathbf{v}$. Compute the direction of $c\mathbf{v}$ knowing that when $\|c\|\mathbf{v} \neq 0$, the direction of $c\mathbf{v}$ is either along $\mathbf{v}$ (for $c > 0$) or against $\mathbf{v}$ (for $c < 0$).	*This standard is outside the Common Core college and career ready standards.*		
CC.9-12.N.VM.6	(+) Use matrices to represent and manipulate data, e.g., to represent payoffs or incidence relationships in a network.		SE: 575, 578–579	

SE = Student Edition

Standards	Descriptor	Algebra 1	Geometry	Algebra 2
Standards for Mathematical Content				
(+ = advanced; * = also a Modeling Standard)				
Number and Quantity				
CC.9-12.N.VM.7	(+) Multiply matrices by scalars to produce new matrices, e.g., as when all of the payoffs in a game are doubled.		SE: 619–623, 631, EP20	
CC.9-12.N.VM.8	(+) Add, subtract, and multiply matrices of appropriate dimensions.		SE: 573, 576–577, 579, EP19	
CC.9-12.N.VM.9	(+) Understand that, unlike multiplication of numbers, matrix multiplication for square matrices is not a commutative operation, but still satisfies the associative and distributive properties.		SE: 574–575, 578, 579, EP19	
CC.9-12.N.VM.10	(+) Understand that the zero and identity matrices play a role in matrix addition and multiplication similar to the role of 0 and 1 in the real numbers. The determinant of a square matrix is nonzero if and only if the matrix has a multiplicative inverse.	*This standard is outside the Common Core college and career ready standards.*		
CC.9-12.N.VM.11	(+) Multiply a vector (regarded as a matrix with one column) by a matrix of suitable dimensions to produce another vector. Work with matrices as transformations of vectors.		SE: 574, 584–586, 592, 595	
CC.9-12.N.VM.12	(+) Work with 2 × 2 matrices as a transformations of the plane, and interpret the absolute value of the determinant in terms of area.		SE: 584–586, 592, 595	

SE = Student Edition

Standards	Descriptor	Algebra 1	Geometry	Algebra 2
Standards for Mathematical Content				
(+ = advanced; * = also a Modeling Standard)				
Algebra				
CC.9-12.A.SSE.1	Interpret expressions that represent a quantity in terms of its context.* a. Interpret parts of an expression, such as terms, factors, and coefficients. b. Interpret complicated expressions by viewing one or more of their parts as a single entity.	SE: 78, 182–183, 185–187, 191, 193, 194	SE: 427–429, 431, 433, 649–650, 689–690, 711, 713, 719–721, 727, 752–754, 797	SE: 5, 20, 27, 28, 95, 105, 114, 131, 147, 183, 469
CC.9-12.A.SSE.2	Use the structure of an expression to identify ways to rewrite it.	SE: 497–498, 503, 504–505, 511–512, 524, 525–526, 528–530, 534, 535–536, 538–539, 542–543, 545–546, 548–550, 552	SE: 98, 703, 751–754, 763–765, SR4, SR5	SE: 18–19, 21–22, 25–26, 29–30, 31, 77–78, 81, 104–105, 111–113, 114–115
CC.9-12.A.SSE.3	Choose and produce an equivalent form of an expression to reveal and explain properties of the quantity represented by the expression. a. Factor a quadratic expression to reveal the zeros of the function it defines. b. Complete the square in a quadratic expression to reveal the maximum or minimum value of the function it defines. c. Use the properties of exponents to transform expressions for exponential functions.	SE: AL6–AL7, AL14–AL15, 462, 474, 535, 536, 537, 539, 540, 543, 544, 545, 546, 549, 551, 554, 583–584, 589, 611–612		SE: 11–12, 14, 15, 21–22, 27–28, 53, 55–56, 240–241, 242–243, 248
CC.9-12.A.SSE.4	Derive the formula for the sum of a finite geometric series (when the common ratio is not 1), and use the formula to solve problems.			SE: 452–453, 455–457, 458, 460, 479, 481, 483, 487, 576, EP8

SE = Student Edition

Standards	Descriptor	Algebra 1	Geometry	Algebra 2
Standards for Mathematical Content				
(+ = advanced; * = also a Modeling Standard)				
Algebra				
CC.9-12.A.APR.1	Understand that polynomials form a system analogous to the integers, namely, they are closed under the operations of addition, subtraction, and multiplication; add, subtract, and multiply polynomials.	SE: AL10–AL11, 496–498, 499–501, 503, 504–507, 508–510, 511–513, 514–516, 522, 523, 531, 547, 557, 558–559, 563, 566		SE: 104–106, 107–110, 126, 127, 155, 159, 179, 343–344
CC.9-12.A.APR.2	Know and apply the Remainder Theorem: For a polynomial $p(x)$ and a number a, the remainder on division by $x - a$ is $p(a)$, so $p(a) = 0$ if and only if $(x - a)$ is a factor of $p(x)$.			SE: 121–123, 124–125, 129–131, 132–133, 156, 159, 163, 203, EP3
CC.9-12.A.APR.3	Identify zeros of polynomials when suitable factorizations are available, and use the zeros to construct a rough graph of the function defined by the polynomial.	SE: 549, 583–584		SE: 111–114, 115–117, 120–123, 124–126, 127, 128–131, 132–135, 138, 140, 142, 145, 148–149, 153, 156–157, 159, 171, 203
CC.9-12.A.APR.4	Prove polynomial identities and use them to describe numerical relationships.	SE: 511–513, 514–516, 542–544, 545–547		SE: AL4–AL5, 105–106, 107–108, 111–113, 114–117
CC.9-12.A.APR.5	(+) Know and apply the Binomial Theorem for the expansion of $(x + y)^n$ in powers of x and y for a positive integer n, where x and y are any numbers, with coefficients determined for example by Pascal's Triangle. (The Binomial Theorem can be proved by mathematical induction or by a combinatorial argument.)			SE: AL8, 381–382, 383, 385, EP7

SE = Student Edition

Standards	Descriptor	Algebra 1	Geometry	Algebra 2
Standards for Mathematical Content				
(+ = advanced; * = also a Modeling Standard)				
Algebra				
CC.9-12.A.APR.6	Rewrite simple rational expressions in different forms; write $a(x)/b(x)$ in the form $q(x) + r(x)/b(x)$, where $a(x)$, $b(x)$, $q(x)$, and $r(x)$ are polynomials with the degree of $r(x)$ less than the degree of $b(x)$, using inspection, long division, or, for the more complicated examples, a computer algebra system.			SE: 120–122, 124, 135, 156, 159, 317–318, EP3
CC.9-12.A.APR.7	(+) Understand that rational expressions form a system analogous to the rational numbers, closed under addition, subtraction, multiplication, and division by a nonzero rational expression; add, subtract, multiply, and divide rational expressions.	SE: 756		SE: 327–331, 332–334, 335, 336–339, 340–342, 343–344, 351, 366, 369, 371, 501, EP6
CC.9-12.A.CED.1	Create equations and inequalities in one variable and use them to solve problems. Include equations arising from linear and quadratic functions, and simple rational and exponential functions.*	SE: 87, 88–90, 93, 95–96, 100, 102–103, 105, 108–109, 300, 302–303, 307, 309–310, 313, 314–316, 322–323, 325, 327–328	SE: 13, 16, 19, 26, 30, 36, 39, 41, 45, 56, 57, 61, 311, 313, 315, 327, 332, 334, 341, 347, 350, 681–683, 684–685	SE: 35, 36–37, 56, 61, 72, 114, 131, 134, 268, 350–351, 356, 641
CC.9-12.A.CED.2	Create equations in two or more variables to represent relationships between quantities; graph equations on coordinate axes with labels and scales.*	SE: 43, 45–46, 156, 157–159, 164–166, 167–170, 183, 185–187, 192–193, 195–197, 201, 203, 205–206, 223–225, 226–229, 232–235, 236–239, 243–245, 246–248, 253, 255–256	SE: 165–166, 167–169, 172–175, 176–179	SE: 3–9, 11–17, 95–102, 103, 145–150, 198–203, 228–235, 236–241, 251–257, 281–288, 496–501, 502–508, 510–515, 518–524

SE = Student Edition

Standards	Descriptor	Algebra 1	Geometry	Algebra 2
Standards for Mathematical Content				
(+ = advanced; * = also a Modeling Standard)				
Algebra				
CC.9-12.A.CED.3	Represent constraints by equations or inequalities, and by systems of equations and/or inequalities, and interpret solutions as viable or nonviable options in a modeling context.*	SE: 29, 32–33, 43, 45–46, 100, 102–103, 225, 228–229, 350, 352–353, 379, 380, 382–383, 395, 398–399, 416, 419–420, 421		SE: 3–9, 11–17, 95–102, 103, 145–150, 198–203, 228–235, 236–241, 251–257, 281–288, 496–501, 502–508, 510–515, 518–524
CC.9-12.A.CED.4	Rearrange formulas to highlight a quantity of interest, using the same reasoning as in solving equations.*	SE: 126–128, 129–131, 132, 133, 138, 139, 141, 152, EP3	SE: 477, 480–481, 779, SR9	
CC.9-12.A.REI.1	Explain each step in solving a simple equation as following from the equality of numbers asserted at the previous step, starting from the assumption that the original equation has a solution. Construct a viable argument to justify a solution method.	SE: 84–86, 87–88, 91–93, 94, 98–99, 100, 104–106, 111–112, 120–121, 126–128, 133, 134–138	SE: 96, 97–98, 100–101, 103, 111, 128, 130, 170, SR21	
CC.9-12.A.REI.2	Solve simple rational and radical equations in one variable, and give examples showing how extraneous solutions may arise.	SE: 756		SE: 204–207, 208–211, 212–213, 214–215, 216, 217, 220, 221, 225, 250, 265, 309, 345–348, 349–351, 352–353, 354–355, 356, 365, 366, 370, 371, 495

SE = Student Edition

Standards	Descriptor	Algebra 1	Geometry	Algebra 2
Standards for Mathematical Content				
(+ = advanced; * = also a Modeling Standard)				
Algebra				
CC.9-12.A.REI.3	Solve linear equations and inequalities in one variable, including equations with coefficients represented by letters.	SE: 82–83, 84–87, 88–90, 91–93, 94–96, 98–100, 101–103, 104–106, 107–109, 110, 113, 115–116, 117–119, 125, 126–128, 129–131, 132, 133, 134–136, 138, 139, 296, 298–300, 301–303, 304, 305–307, 308–310, 311–313, 314–316, 319–320, 322–325, 326–329, 330, 332–334, 335–337	SE: 16, 26, 29, 37, 44, 76, 81, 83, 147, 150, 153, 178, 219, 266, 268, 305, 313, 325, 332, 341, 379	
CC.9-12.A.REI.4	Solve quadratic equations in one variable. a. Use the method of completing the square to transform any quadratic equation in x into an equation of the form $(x - p)^2 = q$ that has the same solutions. Derive the quadratic formula from this form. b. Solve quadratic equations by inspection (e.g., for $x^2 = 49$), taking square roots, completing the square, the quadratic formula and factoring, as appropriate to the initial form of the equation. Recognize when the quadratic formula gives complex solutions and write them as $a \pm bi$ for real numbers a and b.	SE: 527, 528, 531, 537–538, 539, 541, 544, 545, 547, 555, 560–561, 563, 564–565, 594–596, 597–600, 601, 603, 606–607, 608–610, 613–615, 616–618, 619, 647, 650–651, 653, 654–655	SE: 493, SR14–SR15	SE: 18–21, 22–24, 25–28, 29–31, 32–35, 36–37, 38–39, 40, 48, 50–52, 54–57, 58–61, 62–65, 77–79, 81
CC.9-12.A.REI.5	Prove that, given a system of two equations in two variables, replacing one equation by the sum of that equation and a multiple of the other produces a system with the same solutions.	SE: 400–401		

SE = Student Edition

Standards	Descriptor	Algebra 1	Geometry	Algebra 2
Standards for Mathematical Content				
(+ = advanced; * = also a Modeling Standard)				
Algebra				
CC.9-12.A.REI.6	Solve systems of linear equations exactly and approximately (e.g., with graphs), focusing on pairs of linear equations in two variables.	SE: 368, 369–372, 373–375, 376, 377–380, 381–383, 384, 385, 386–388, 389–392, 393–396, 397–399, 402, 403–405, 406–409, 420, 421, 422, 423–426, 427, 428–429, 430–431, 454	SE: 175, 178, SR12	
CC.9-12.A.REI.7	Solve a simple system consisting of a linear equation and a quadratic equation in two variables algebraically and graphically.	SE: 621–627		SE: 534–537, 538–540, 543, 548, 549, 550–551, 553, EP9
CC.9-12.A.REI.8	(+) Represent a system of linear equations as a single matrix equation in a vector variable.	*This standard is outside the Common Core college and career ready standards.*		
CC.9-12.A.REI.9	(+) Find the inverse of a matrix if it exists and use it to solve systems of linear equations (using technology for matrices of dimension 3×3 or greater).	*This standard is outside the Common Core college and career ready standards.*		
CC.9-12.A.REI.10	Understand that the graph of an equation in two variables is the set of all its solutions plotted in the coordinate plane, often forming a curve (which could be a line).	SE: 153		

SE = Student Edition

Standards	Descriptor	Algebra 1	Geometry	Algebra 2
Standards for Mathematical Content				
(+ = advanced; * = also a Modeling Standard)				
Algebra				
CC.9-12.A.REI.11	Explain why the *x*-coordinates of the points where the graphs of the equations $y = f(x)$ and $y = g(x)$ intersect are the solutions of the equation $f(x) = g(x)$; find the solutions approximately, e.g., using technology to graph the functions, make tables of values, or find successive approximations. Include cases where $f(x)$ and/or $g(x)$ are linear, polynomial, rational, absolute value, exponential, and logarithmic functions.*	SE: 189–190, 207–208, 585–588, 589–591, 593, 596		SE: 38–39, 118–119, 130, 132–133, 140–141, 145, 207, 212–213, 270, 275–277, 278–309, 635, 638, 642–643
CC.9-12.A.REI.12	Graph the solutions to a linear inequality in two variables as a half-plane (excluding the boundary in the case of a strict inequality), and graph the solution set to a system of linear inequalities in two variables as the intersection of the corresponding half-planes.	SE: 346, 347–350, 351–354, 355, 360, 361, 364–365, 409, 414–416, 417–420, 421, 422, 426, 427, 440, 501, 510, 522	SE: 199, SR13	SE: 57, 65
Functions				
CC.9-12.F.IF.1	Understand that a function from one set (called the domain) to another set (called the range) assigns to each element of the domain exactly one element of the range. If *f* is a function and *x* is an element of its domain, then $f(x)$ denotes the output of *f* corresponding to the input *x*. The graph of *f* is the graph of the equation $y = f(x)$.	SE: 41–42, 44, 49–51, 54, 55–56, 58, 62, 65, 119, 201, 202, 204–206		
CC.9-12.F.IF.2	Use function notation, evaluate functions for inputs in their domains, and interpret statements that use function notation in terms of a context.	SE: 200–203, 204–206, 209, 214, 215, 219, 270, 338–339, EP4		SE: 24, 31, 57, 73, 137–141, 142–143, 146–147, 148–149, 171, 180–183, 184–186, 187, 189, 191–193, 195, 197

SE = Student Edition

Standards	Descriptor	Algebra 1	Geometry	Algebra 2
Standards for Mathematical Content				
(+ = advanced; * = also a Modeling Standard)				
Functions				
CC.9-12.F.IF.3	Recognize that sequences are functions, sometimes defined recursively, whose domain is a subset of the integers.	SE: 249–250, 477–478, 479–481	SE: 70	SE: 434, 466, 467–470, 471–473, 475, 478, 479, 482, 483, 484, 486–487, EP8
CC.9-12.F.IF.4	For a function that models a relationship between two quantities, interpret key features of graphs and tables in terms of the quantities, and sketch graphs showing key features given a verbal description of the relationship. Key features include: intercepts; intervals where the function is increasing, decreasing, positive, or negative; relative maximums and minimums; symmetries; end behavior; and periodicity.*	SE: 165–166, 168–170, 171, 176, 179–180, 205, 253, 255, 275–277, 279–281, 573, 575–576, 579, 581–582, 588, 590–591, 638–644		SE: 5, 7–9, 12–13, 16–17, 94, 97, 145–147, 148–150, 242–243, 357–364, 612–615, 616–618
CC.9-12.F.IF.5	Relate the domain of a function to its graph and, where applicable, to the quantitative relationship it describes.*	SE: 50–51, 52, 57, 62, 65, 155–156, 157–159, 166, 170, 171, 201, 205, 253, 255, 464, 573, 575		SE: 17, 102, 149, 198–201, 202–203, 229, 232, 234, 237–238, 239, 241, 245–246, 248, 250, 255, 256, 311–313, 314–315, 319, 615
CC.9-12.F.IF.6	Calculate and interpret the average rate of change of a function (presented symbolically or as a table) over a specified interval. Estimate the rate of change from a graph.*	SE: 175–176, 178–180, 209, 234–235, 239, 241, 244–245, 247, 266, 267–270, 645		SE: 357–364

SE = Student Edition

Standards	Descriptor	Algebra 1	Geometry	Algebra 2
Standards for Mathematical Content				
(+ = advanced; * = also a Modeling Standard)				
Functions				
CC.9-12.F.IF.7	Graph functions expressed symbolically and show key features of the graph, by hand in simple cases and using technology for more complicated cases.* a. Graph linear and quadratic functions and show intercepts, maxima, and minima. b. Graph square root, cube root, and piecewise-defined functions, including step functions and absolute value functions. c. Graph polynomial functions, identifying zeros when suitable factorizations are available, and showing end behavior. d. (+) Graph rational functions, identifying zeros and asymptotes when suitable factorizations are available, and showing end behavior. e. Graph exponential and logarithmic functions, showing intercepts and end behavior, and trigonometric functions, showing period, midline, and amplitude.	SE: 154–156, 157–158, 160, 163–166, 167–169, 182–184, 185–188, 189–190, 192, 195, 197, 200–203, 204–206, 209, 212–214, 215, 243, 246, 253, 255, 338–339, 411–412, 459, 462–463, 470–471, 473–474, 502, 570–573, 574–576, 577–578, 580, 583–584, 585–588, 589, 592–593, 611–612, 636–637	SE: 174, 177–178, 493, SR14–SR15	SE: 2–5, 6–9, 11–14, 15–17, 94, 97–99, 100–102, 103, 145–147, 148–150, 198–201, 202–203, 228–230, 232–234, 236–238, 239–241, 245–246, 248–249, 254–255, 256–257, 310–313, 314–315, 316, 319–321, 322–325, 612–616, 617–618, 619–623, 624–626
CC.9–12.F.IF.8	Write a function defined by an expression in different but equivalent forms to reveal and explain different properties of the function. a. Use the process of factoring and completing the square in a quadratic function to show zeros, extreme values, and symmetry of the graph, and interpret these in terms of a context. b. Use the properties of exponents to interpret expressions for exponential functions.	SE: 163–166, 167–168, 182–184, 185–188, 223–225, 226–229, 232–235, 236–239, 242–244, 245–248, 251–253, 254–256, 286, 460, 461, 472, 473, 577–578, 580–582, 583–584, 611–612		SE: 2–5, 6–9, 10, 11–14, 15–17, 31, 228–231, 232–233, 236, 239, 242–243

SE = Student Edition

Standards	Descriptor	Algebra 1	Geometry	Algebra 2
Standards for Mathematical Content				
(+ = advanced; * = also a Modeling Standard)				
Functions				
CC.9-12.F.IF.9	Compare properties of two functions each represented in a different way (algebraically, graphically, numerically in tables, or by verbal descriptions).	SE: 338–339, 459, 470, 570–572, 638–644		SE: 357–364
CC.9-12.F.BF.1	Write a function that describes a relationship between two quantities.* a. Determine an explicit expression, a recursive process, or steps for calculation from a context. b. Combine standard function types using arithmetic operations. c. (+) Compose functions.	SE: AL4–AL5, 225, 228–229, 234–235, 238–239, 244–245, 247–248, 253, 255–256, 266–267, 268–270, 271–272, 274, 275–278, 279–281, 282, 285, 290, 291, 294, 295, 458, 460–461, 462–463, 468, 469, 471, 473, 475, 630–631, 653		SE: 74, 80, 81, 85, 152, 158, 159, 162–163, 180–183, 184–186, 187, 280, 281–285, 286–288, 294, 295, 299, 422, 426, 427, 431, 466, 467–470, 471–473, 645–647, 648–651
CC.9-12.F.BF.2	Write arithmetic and geometric sequences both recursively and with an explicit formula, use them to model situations, and translate between the two forms.*	SE: AL12–AL13, 249–250, 477–478, 479–481		SE: 438, 442–444, 446–448, 450–452, 454–456, 466, 467–470, 471–473, 476–477, 478, 479, 481–482, 483, 484–485, 486
CC.9-12.F.BF.3	Identify the effect on the graph of replacing $f(x)$ by $f(x) + k$, $kf(x)$, $f(kx)$, and $f(x + k)$ for specific values of k (both positive and negative); find the value of k given the graphs. Experiment with cases and illustrate an explanation of the effects on the graph using technology. Include recognizing even and odd functions from their graphs and algebraic expressions for them.	SE: 201–203, 204–206, 209, 214, 230–231, 338–339, 459, 462, 470, 473–474, 611–612		SE: 2–3, 6, 11, 15, 198–200, 201–202, 229, 232, 237, 239, 242–243, 245, 248, 255, 256, 310–311, 313–314, 357–365, 613–616, 617, 619–623, 624–626, 645–647, 648–651

SE = Student Edition

Standards	Descriptor	Algebra 1	Geometry	Algebra 2
Standards for Mathematical Content				
(+ = advanced; * = also a Modeling Standard)				
Functions				
CC.9-12.F.BF.4	Find inverse functions. a. Solve an equation of the form $f(x) = c$ for a simple function f that has an inverse and write an expression for the inverse. b. (+) Verify by composition that one function is the inverse of another. c. (+) Read values of an inverse function from a graph or a table, given that the function has an inverse. d. (+) Produce an invertible function from a non-invertible function by restricting the domain.	SE: AL6–AL9	SE: 477, 479, 480–482	SE: 189, 190–194, 195–197, 205, 210, 251, 253–254, 258, 268, 271, 274, 578, 579–581, 582–584, 635–638, 639–641
CC.9-12.F.BF.5	(+) Understand the inverse relationship between exponents and logarithms and use this relationship to solve problems involving logarithms and exponents.			SE: 251–254, 255–257, 258, 263, 265, 268–271, 272–274, 282–284, 290, 293–294, 295, 297, 298, EP5
CC.9-12.F.LE.1	Distinguish between situations that can be modeled with linear functions and with exponential functions.* a. Prove that linear functions grow by equal differences over equal intervals, and that exponential functions grow by equal factors over equal intervals. b. Recognize situations in which one quantity changes at a constant rate per unit interval relative to another. c. Recognize situations in which a quantity grows or decays by a constant percent rate per unit interval relative to another.	SE: 458–461, 462–465, 469, 473, 477–478, 628–631, 632–635, 636–637, 638–644		SE: 449

SE = Student Edition

Standards	Descriptor	Algebra 1	Geometry	Algebra 2
Standards for Mathematical Content				
(+ = advanced; * = also a Modeling Standard)				
Functions				
CC.9-12.F.LE.2	Construct linear and exponential functions, including arithmetic and geometric sequences, given a graph, a description of a relationship, or two input-output pairs (include reading these from a table).*	SE: 50–51, 52–53, 223–225, 226–229, 232–235, 236–239, 242–245, 246–248, 249–250, 251–253, 254–256, 257, 258, 260, 261–262, 266, 267–270, 275–278, 279–281, 282, 458–461, 462–465, 468, 469–472, 473–476, 477–478		SE: 230–231, 233–235, 238, 239–241, 247, 248–249, 280, 281–282, 285–287, 438, 442–444, 446–448, 450–452, 454–456, 466, 467–470, 471–473, 478, 479, 481–482, 483, 484–485, 486
CC.9-12.F.LE.3	Observe using graphs and tables that a quantity increasing exponentially eventually exceeds a quantity increasing linearly, quadratically, or (more generally) as a polynomial function.*	SE: 638–644		SE: 299, 357–364
CC.9-12.F.LE.4	For exponential models, express as *a* logarithm the solution to $ab^{ct} = d$ where *a*, *c*, and *d* are numbers and the base *b* is 2, 10, or *e*; evaluate the logarithm using technology.*			SE: 268, 272–274, 283, 288, 289, 290, 294, 295
CC.9-12.F.LE.5	Interpret the parameters in a linear or exponential function in terms of a context.*	SE: 225, 234–235, 239, 244, 267, 269–270, 460–461, 465, 471–472, 475		SE: 230–231, 232, 236, 239, 246
CC.9-12.F.TF.1	Understand radian measure of an angle as the length of the arc on the unit circle subtended by the angle.			SE: 564–566, 567–569

SE = Student Edition

Standards	Descriptor	Algebra 1	Geometry	Algebra 2
Standards for Mathematical Content				
(+ = advanced; * = also a Modeling Standard)				
Functions				
CC.9-12.F.TF.2	Explain how the unit circle in the coordinate plane enables the extension of trigonometric functions to all real numbers, interpreted as radian measures of angles traversed counterclockwise around the unit circle.			SE: 563–565, 570–574, 575–576, 603
CC.9-12.F.TF.3	(+) Use special triangles to determine geometrically the values of sine, cosine, tangent for $\pi/3$, $\pi/4$ and $\pi/6$, and use the unit circle to express the values of sine, cosines, and tangent for x, $\pi + x$, and $2\pi - x$ in terms of their values for x, where x is any real number.			SE: 557–558, 572, 578
CC.9-12.F.TF.4	(+) Use the unit circle to explain symmetry (odd and even) and periodicity of trigonometric functions.			SE: 570–574, 612–616, 628
CC.9-12.F.TF.5	Choose trigonometric functions to model periodic phenomena with specified amplitude, frequency, and midline.*			SE: 614–615, 617–618, 620, 625–626, 644, 645–647, 648–651, 652, 667, 671, 673, 676
CC.9-12.F.TF.6	(+) Understand that restricting a trigonometric function to a domain on which it is always increasing or always decreasing allows its inverse to be constructed.			SE: 579, 601, 603
CC.9-12.F.TF.7	(+) Use inverse functions to solve trigonometric equations that arise in modeling contexts; evaluate the solutions using technology, and interpret them in terms of the context.*			SE: 635–638, 639–641, 642–643, 644, 651, 658, 668, 671, 673, 677, EP11

SE = Student Edition

Standards	Descriptor	Algebra 1	Geometry	Algebra 2
Standards for Mathematical Content				
(+ = advanced; * = also a Modeling Standard)				
Functions				
CC.9-12.F.TF.8	Prove the Pythagorean identity $\sin^2(\theta) + \cos^2(\theta) = 1$ and use it to calculate trigonometric ratios.		SE: 472	SE: 628–631, 632–633, 638, 651, 658, 662, 670, 673, 677, EP11
CC.9-12.F.TF.9	(+) Prove the addition and subtraction formulas for sine, cosine, and tangent and use them to solve problems.			SE: 653–655, 656–658, 666, 668, 672, 673, 677, EP11
Geometry				
CC.9-12.G.CO.1	Know precise definitions of angle, circle, perpendicular line, parallel line, and line segment, based on the undefined notions of point, line, distance along a line, and distance around a circular arc.	SE: 184, 185, 258–259, 261	SE: 2–3, 24–25, 73, 74, 139, 641, 710–711, 713	SE: 563, 565
CC.9-12.G.CO.2	Represent transformations in the plane using, e.g., transparencies and geometry software; describe transformations as functions that take points in the plane as inputs and give other points as outputs. Compare transformations that preserve distance and angle to those that do not (e.g., translation versus horizontal stretch).		SE: 223–224, 225–230, 271, 273–275, 276–279, 285, 288, 291, 293, 402, 403–405, 406–409, 412, 417, 418, 423, 564–566, 568–571, 573, 577, 580, 581–582, 584, 585–586, 588, 589, 591–592, 594–595, 597, 598, 599, 600–601, 604–605, 607, 620, 622–623, 625	SE: SR14–SR15
CC.9-12.G.CO.3	Given a rectangle, parallelogram, trapezoid, or regular polygon, describe the rotations and reflections that carry it onto itself.		SE: 611–613, 615–616, 631, 632, 792–793	

SE = Student Edition

Standards	Descriptor	Algebra 1	Geometry	Algebra 2
Standards for Mathematical Content				
(+ = advanced; * = also a Modeling Standard)				
Geometry				
CC.9-12.G.CO.4	Develop definitions of rotations, reflections, and translations in terms of angles, circles, perpendicular lines, parallel lines, and line segments.		SE: 564–566, 568–571, 580, 581–584, 585–588, 590–593, 594–597, 599, 600–603, 604–607	
CC.9-12.G.CO.5	Given a geometric figure and a rotation, reflection, or translation, draw the transformed figure using, e.g., graph paper, tracing paper, or geometry software. Specify a sequence of transformations that will carry a given figure onto another.	SE: SR13	SE: 271, 273–275, 276, 278, 279, 280, 285, 288, 293, 564, 566, 568–570, 579, 580, 581–582, 585–586, 589, 590–591, 594–595, 598, 599, 600–603, 604–606, 608–610	
CC.9-12.G.CO.6	Use geometric descriptions of rigid motions to transform figures and to predict the effect of a given rigid motion on a given figure; given two figures, use the definition of congruence in terms of rigid motions to decide if they are congruent.		SE: 223–224, 225–230, 272–275, 276–279, 280, 285, 288, 291, 292–293, 564–567, 568–571, 573, 576–577, 579, 580, 581–584, 585–588, 589, 590–593, 594–597, 598, 599, 600–603, 604–607, 608–610, 626, 627, 628–630, 632	
CC.9-12.G.CO.7	Use the definition of congruence in terms of rigid motions to show that two triangles are congruent if and only if corresponding pairs of sides and corresponding pairs of angles are congruent.		SE: 223–224, 225–230	
CC.9-12.G.CO.8	Explain how the criteria for triangle congruence (ASA, SAS, and SSS) follow from the definition of congruence in terms of rigid motions.		SE: 254–255	

SE = Student Edition

Standards	Descriptor	Algebra 1	Geometry	Algebra 2
Standards for Mathematical Content				
(+ = advanced; * = also a Modeling Standard)				
Geometry				
CC.9-12.G.CO.9	Prove geometric theorems about lines and angles. Theorems include: vertical angles are congruent; when a transversal crosses parallel lines, alternate interior angles are congruent and corresponding angles are congruent; points on a perpendicular bisector of a line segment are exactly those equidistant from the segment's endpoints.		SE: 105–106, 110, 116–118, 121–122, 129, 145, 147–148, 151–152, 154–155, 160, 169, 182–184, 188, 305, 310	
CC.9-12.G.CO.10	Prove theorems about triangles. Theorems include: measures of interior angles of a triangle sum to 180°; base angles of isosceles triangles are congruent; the segment joining midpoints of two sides of a triangle is parallel to the third side and half the length; the medians of a triangle meet at a point.		SE: 206, 208–209, 214, 264–265, 269, 296, 297, 299, 302–303, 305–307, 310, 312, 314, 317–318, 320, 321–323, 325–326, 328–329, 330–331, 332, 336, 337, 340, 342–343	
CC.9-12.G.CO.11	Prove theorems about parallelograms. Theorems include: opposite sides are congruent, the diagonals of a parallelogram bisect each other, and conversely, rectangles are parallelograms with congruent diagonals.		SE: 508, 509–511, 512–515, 516–519, 520–523, 524–525, 527–530, 531–534, 544–545, 546–549, 551, 553–555, 556	
CC.9-12.G.CO.12	Make formal geometric constructions with a variety of tools and methods (compass and straightedge, string, reflective devices, paper folding, dynamic geometry software, etc.). Copying a segment; copying an angle; bisecting a segment; bisecting an angle; constructing perpendicular lines, including the perpendicular bisector of a line segment; and constructing a line parallel to a given line through a point not on the line.		SE: 33–34, 161, 190–191, 233, 258, 261–262, 307, 309, 314, 316, 325, 395, 402, 521, 617, 621, 655, 661, 731	

SE = Student Edition

Standards	Descriptor	Algebra 1	Geometry	Algebra 2
Standards for Mathematical Content				
(+ = advanced; * = also a Modeling Standard)				
Geometry				
CC.9-12.G.CO.13	Construct an equilateral triangle, a square, and a regular hexagon inscribed in a circle.		SE: 670–671, 731	
CC.9-12.G.SRT.1	Verify experimentally the properties of dilations given by a center and a scale factor: a. A dilation takes a line not passing through the center of the dilation to a parallel line, and leaves a line passing through the center unchanged. b. The dilation of a line segment is longer or shorter in the ratio given by the scale factor.		SE: 366, 367–373, 402, 408, 617, 623, 625	
CC.9-12.G.SRT.2	Given two figures, use the definition of similarity in terms of similarity transformations to decide if they are similar; explain using similarity transformations the meaning of similarity for triangles as the equality of all corresponding angles and the proportionality of all corresponding pairs of sides.		SE: 367–374	
CC.9-12.G.SRT.3	Use the properties of similarity transformations to establish the AA criterion for two triangles to be similar.		SE: 374	
CC.9-12.G.SRT.4	Prove theorems about triangles. Theorems include: a line parallel to one side of a triangle divides the other two proportionally, and conversely; the Pythagorean Theorem proved using triangle similarity.		SE: 382–384, 388–389, 391–392, 396–397, 442, 443, 446, 449–450, 451, 453, 457	

SE = Student Edition

Standards	Descriptor	Algebra 1	Geometry	Algebra 2
Standards for Mathematical Content				
(+ = advanced; * = also a Modeling Standard)				
Geometry				
CC.9-12.G.SRT.5	Use congruence and similarity criteria for triangles to solve problems and prove relationships in geometric figures.		SE: 215–218, 219–221, 232–234, 235–237, 238–240, 241–244, 246, 247–250, 251–253, 256–258, 259–263, 283–284, 288, 292–293, 302, 358–361, 362–365, 375–377, 378–381, 382–385, 386–389, 391–393, 394–397, 399, 412, 416–417, 418, 420, 422, 443–446, 447–450, 451–454, 455–458	
CC.9-12.G.SRT.6	Understand that by similarity, side ratios in right triangles are properties of the angles in the triangle, leading to definitions of trigonometric ratios for acute angles.		SE: 460–461, 463, 467, 471	SE: 556–557
CC.9-12.G.SRT.7	Explain and use the relationship between the sine and cosine of complementary angles.		SE: AL2–AL3, 474	SE: 628, 631–632, 670
CC.9-12.G.SRT.8	Use trigonometric ratios and the Pythagorean Theorem to solve right triangles in applied problems.		SE: 428, 431–433, 437, 439–440, 459, 462, 465–466, 468–470, 473–474, 476, 478–479, 481–482, 486, 490, 492, 494, 497	SE: 559, 561–562, 569, 581, 583–584, 600, 603, 605, 606–607, 618
CC.9-12.G.SRT.9	(+) Derive the formula $A = \frac{1}{2} ab \sin(C)$ for the area of a triangle by drawing an auxiliary line from a vertex perpendicular to the opposite side.		SE: 473	SE: 589, 591

SE = Student Edition

Standards	Descriptor	Algebra 1	Geometry	Algebra 2
Standards for Mathematical Content				
(+ = advanced; * = also a Modeling Standard)				
Geometry				
CC.9-12.G.SRT.10	(+) Prove the Laws of Sines and Cosines and use them to solve problems.		SE: 484–485	SE: 585, 586–588, 590–592, 593–595, 596–598, 600, 601, 604, 605, EP10
CC.9-12.G.SRT.11	(+) Understand and apply the Law of Sines and the Law of Cosines to find unknown measurements in right and non-right triangles (e.g., surveying problems, resultant forces).		SE: AL4–AL9, AL10–AL13, 484–485	SE: 585, 586–588, 590–592, 593–595, 596–598, 600, 601, 604, 605, EP10
CC.9-12.G.C.1	Prove that all circles are similar.		SE: 367–373	
CC.9-12.G.C.2	Identify and describe relationships among inscribed angles, radii, and chords. Include the relationship between central, inscribed, and circumscribed angles; inscribed angles on a diameter are right angles; the radius of a circle is perpendicular to the tangent where the radius intersects the circle.		SE: 640, 643–644, 646–648, 649–651, 652–653, 654–656, 657–660, 661, 662–665, 666–669, 695, 699–700, 702	
CC.9-12.G.C.3	Construct the inscribed and circumscribed circles of a triangle, and prove properties of angles for a quadrilateral inscribed in a circle.		SE: 308, 309, 314, 316, 665, 668	
CC.9-12.G.C.4	(+) Construct a tangent line from a point outside a given circle to the circle.		SE: 670–671	
CC.9-12.G.C.5	Derive using similarity the fact that the length of the arc intercepted by an angle is proportional to the radius, and define the radian measure of the angle as the constant of proportionality; derive the formula for the area of a sector.		SE: 711, 713, 717–718, 720, 722	SE: 564–565

SE = Student Edition

Standards	Descriptor	Algebra 1	Geometry	Algebra 2
Standards for Mathematical Content				
(+ = advanced; * = also a Modeling Standard)				
Geometry				
CC.9-12.G.GPE.1	Derive the equation of a circle of given center and radius using the Pythagorean Theorem; complete the square to find the center and radius of a circle given by an equation.		SE: 689, 693	SE: 502, 532, 540, 548, 549, EP9
CC.9-12.G.GPE.2	Derive the equation of a parabola given a focus and directrix.		SE: AL14–AL17	SE: 496–498
CC.9–12.G.GPE.3	(+) Derive the equations of ellipses and hyperbolas given foci and directrices.			SE: 514, 522
CC.9-12.G.GPE.4	Use coordinates to prove simple geometric theorems algebraically.		SE: 296, 298–299, 300–303, 304, 311, 318, 322–323, 324, 346, 352–353, 511, 512–513, 519, 520–521, 525, 526, 532, 536, 540–541, 543, 547	SE: 490, 493, 495
CC.9-12.G.GPE.5	Prove the slope criteria for parallel and perpendicular lines and use them to solve geometric problems (e.g., find the equation of line parallel or perpendicular to a given line that passes through a given point).	SE: 258–260, 261–263, 270, 285, 289, 291, 295	SE: 164–165, 167–168, 171, 172–173, 177–178, 185, 187, 189, 193, 196–197, 198, 201, 202–203	
CC.9-12.G.GPE.6	Find the point on a directed line segment between two given points that partitions the segment in a given ratio.		SE: 410–411	

SE = Student Edition

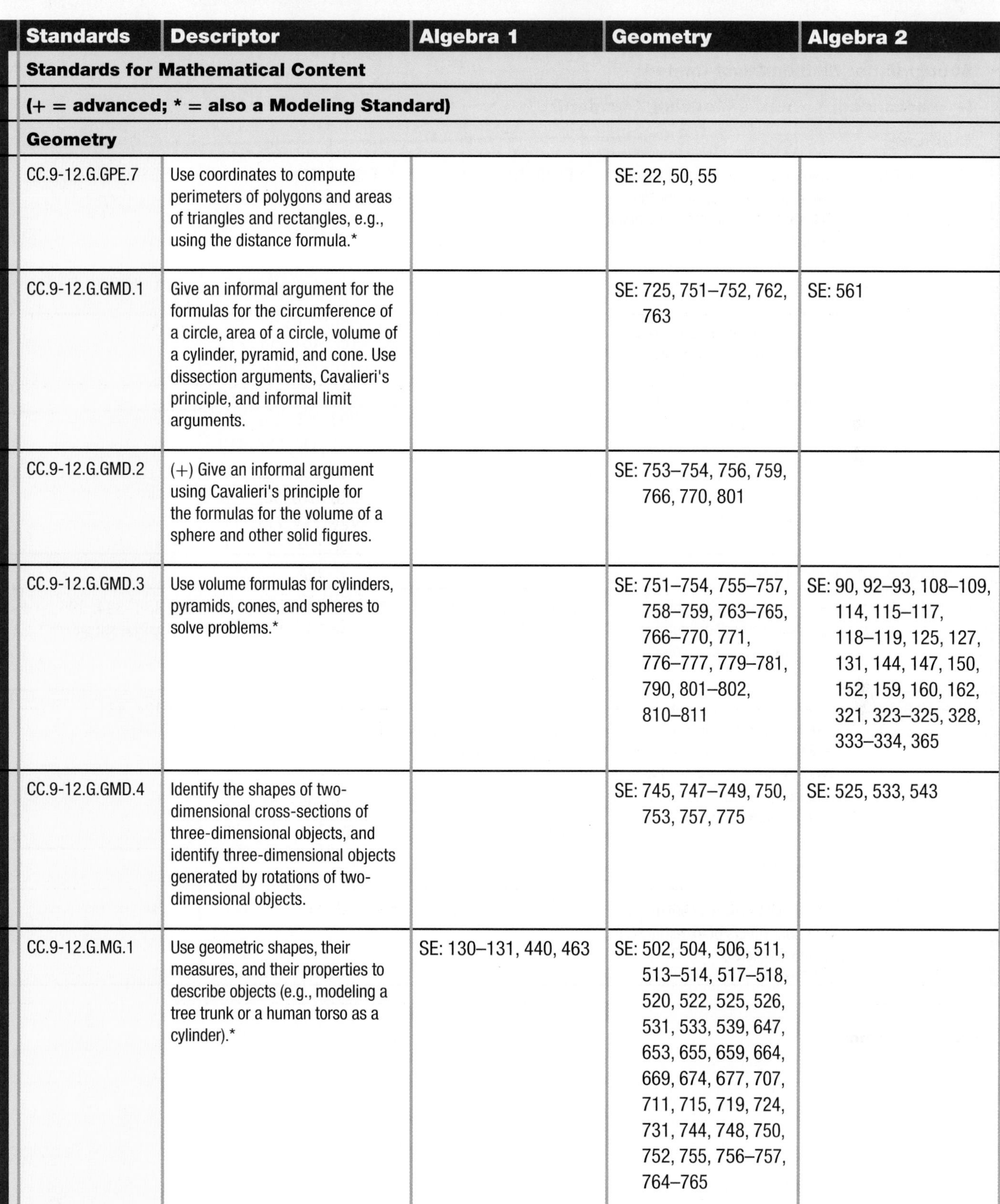

Standards	Descriptor	Algebra 1	Geometry	Algebra 2
Standards for Mathematical Content				
(+ = advanced; * = also a Modeling Standard)				
Geometry				
CC.9-12.G.GPE.7	Use coordinates to compute perimeters of polygons and areas of triangles and rectangles, e.g., using the distance formula.*		SE: 22, 50, 55	
CC.9-12.G.GMD.1	Give an informal argument for the formulas for the circumference of a circle, area of a circle, volume of a cylinder, pyramid, and cone. Use dissection arguments, Cavalieri's principle, and informal limit arguments.		SE: 725, 751–752, 762, 763	SE: 561
CC.9-12.G.GMD.2	(+) Give an informal argument using Cavalieri's principle for the formulas for the volume of a sphere and other solid figures.		SE: 753–754, 756, 759, 766, 770, 801	
CC.9-12.G.GMD.3	Use volume formulas for cylinders, pyramids, cones, and spheres to solve problems.*		SE: 751–754, 755–757, 758–759, 763–765, 766–770, 771, 776–777, 779–781, 790, 801–802, 810–811	SE: 90, 92–93, 108–109, 114, 115–117, 118–119, 125, 127, 131, 144, 147, 150, 152, 159, 160, 162, 321, 323–325, 328, 333–334, 365
CC.9-12.G.GMD.4	Identify the shapes of two-dimensional cross-sections of three-dimensional objects, and identify three-dimensional objects generated by rotations of two-dimensional objects.		SE: 745, 747–749, 750, 753, 757, 775	SE: 525, 533, 543
CC.9-12.G.MG.1	Use geometric shapes, their measures, and their properties to describe objects (e.g., modeling a tree trunk or a human torso as a cylinder).*	SE: 130–131, 440, 463	SE: 502, 504, 506, 511, 513–514, 517–518, 520, 522, 525, 526, 531, 533, 539, 647, 653, 655, 659, 664, 669, 674, 677, 707, 711, 715, 719, 724, 731, 744, 748, 750, 752, 755, 756–757, 764–765	

SE = Student Edition

Standards	Descriptor	Algebra 1	Geometry	Algebra 2
Standards for Mathematical Content				
(+ = advanced; * = also a Modeling Standard)				
Geometry				
CC.9-12.G.MG.2	Apply concepts of density based on area and volume in modeling situations (e.g., persons per square mile, BTUs per cubic foot).*	SE: 30, 103, 354, 668	SE: 760–761	
CC.9-12.G.MG.3	Apply geometric methods to solve design problems (e.g., designing an object or structure to satisfy physical constraints or minimize cost; working with typographic grid systems based on ratios).*		SE: 7, 23, 31, 50, 60, 99, 124, 143, 151, 162, 181, 207, 213, 216, 220, 234, 236, 240, 269, 274, 278, 293, 297, 302, 319, 331, 344, 384, 412, 449, 482, 530, 533, 608–610, 667, 669, 721, 744, 771	
Statistics and Probability				
CC.9-12.S.ID.1	Represent data with plots on the real number line (dot plots, histograms, and box plots).*	SE: 678, 680–683, 684, 685–690, 691, 694, 751, 754–755, EP11	SE: SR20–SR21	SE: 388–394, 395, SR34–SR35
CC.9-12.S.ID.2	Use statistics appropriate to the shape of the data distribution to compare center (median, mean) and spread (interquartile range, standard deviation) of two or more different data sets.*	SE: 664, 665–668, 669–670, 681, 683, 685, 689–690, 691, 692–693, 751, SR10	SE: SR19	SE: 427, 431
CC.9-12.S.ID.3	Interpret differences in shape, center, and spread in the context of the data sets, accounting for possible effects of extreme data points (outliers).*	SE: AL16–AL19, 668, 670, 683, 686, 689, 690, 691, 694, 751		

SE = Student Edition

Standards	Descriptor	Algebra 1	Geometry	Algebra 2
Standards for Mathematical Content				
(+ = advanced; * = also a Modeling Standard)				
Statistics and Probability				
CC.9-12.S.ID.4	Use the mean and standard deviation of a data set to fit it to a normal distribution and to estimate population percentages. Recognize that there are data sets for which such a procedure is not appropriate. Use calculators, spreadsheets, and tables to estimate areas under the normal curve.*			SE: 397–398, 400–404, 425, 427, EP7
CC.9-12.S.ID.5	Summarize categorical data for two categories in two-way frequency tables. Interpret relative frequencies in the context of the data (including joint, marginal, and conditional relative frequencies). Recognize possible associations and trends in the data.*	SE: 673–677, 708, 711, 712, 725		SE: SR34
CC.9-12.S.ID.6	Represent data on two quantitative variables on a scatter plot, and describe how the variables are related.* a. Fit a function to the data; use functions fitted to data to solve problems in the context of the data. Use given functions or choose a function suggested by the context. Emphasize linear and exponential models. b. Informally assess the fit of a function by plotting and analyzing residuals. c. Fit a linear function for a scatter plot that suggests a linear association.	SE: 266–270, 271–272, 275–281, 282, 283–284, 285, 290, 291, 294–295, EP5		SE: 37, 81, 85, 152, 282, 284–287, 289, 295, 299, 426, 427, 431, 647, 650, 651, 673, EP3, EP7

SE = Student Edition

Standards	Descriptor	Algebra 1	Geometry	Algebra 2
Standards for Mathematical Content				
(+ = advanced; * = also a Modeling Standard)				
Statistics and Probability				
CC.9-12.S.ID.7	Interpret the slope (rate of change) and the intercept (constant term) of a linear model in the context of the data.*	SE: AL2–AL3, 175–176, 178–179, 183, 186–187, 244–245, 278, 280, 281	SE: 165, 169–170, 174, 178	
CC.9-12.S.ID.8	Compute (using technology) and interpret the correlation coefficient of a linear fit.*	SE: 272, 273		
CC.9-12.S.ID.9	Distinguish between correlation and causation.*	SE: 273		
CC.9-12.S.IC.1	Understand statistics as a process for making inferences about population parameters based on a random sample from that population.*	SE: 660–661, 664	SE: 817–818	SE: 410–411, 412–413
CC.9-12.S.IC.2	Decide if a specified model is consistent with results from a given data-generating process, e.g., using simulation.*	SE: 713–714	SE: 817–818, 838	SE: 386–387
CC.9-12.S.IC.3	Recognize the purposes of and differences among sample surveys, experiments, and observational studies; explain how randomization relates to each.*	SE: 661, 663–664		SE: 406–407, 409, 414–419, 422, EP7
CC.9-12.S.IC.4	Use data from a sample survey to estimate a population mean or proportion; develop a margin of error through the use of simulation models for random sampling.*	SE: 660		SE: 408–411, 412–413, 422, 427, EP7
CC.9-12.S.IC.5	Use data from a randomized experiment to compare two treatments; use simulations to decide if differences between parameters are significant.*	SE: 664, 673–677, 714		SE: 420–421
CC.9-12.S.IC.6	Evaluate reports based on data.*	SE: 664		SE: 411, 414–419

SE = Student Edition

Standards	Descriptor	Algebra 1	Geometry	Algebra 2
Standards for Mathematical Content				
(+ = advanced; * = also a Modeling Standard)				
Statistics and Probability				
CC.9-12.S.CP.1	Describe events as subsets of a sample space (the set of outcomes) using characteristics (or categories) of the outcomes, or as unions, intersections, or complements of other events ("or," "and," "not").*	SE: 707–710, 727–729, 735–738, EP12	SE: 811–816, 831–833, 839–842, EP24	SE: 396, EP7
CC.9-12.S.CP.2	Understand that two events *A* and *B* are independent if the probability of *A* and *B* occurring together is the product of their probabilities, and use this characterization to determine if they are independent.*	SE: 735–738, EP12	SE: 839–846, EP24	
CC.9-12.S.CP.3	Understand the conditional probability of *A* given *B* as *P*(*A* and *B*)/*P*(*B*), and interpret independence of *A* and *B* as saying that the conditional probability of *A* given *B* is the same as the probability of *A*, and the conditional probability of *B* given *A* is the same as the probability of *B*.*	SE: 735–742, 752–753	SE: 839–846, 856–857	
CC.9-12.S.CP.4	Construct and interpret two-way frequency tables of data when two categories are associated with each object being classified. Use the two-way table as a sample space to decide if events are independent and to approximate conditional probabilities.*	SE: 708, 711–712, 725, 737, 740–741, 743–744	SE: 812, 815–816, 829, 841, 844–845, 847–848	SE: AL10–AL11
CC.9-12.S.CP.5	Recognize and explain the concepts of conditional probability and independence in everyday language and everyday situations.*	SE: 735–742	SE: 839–846	
CC.9-12.S.CP.6	Find the conditional probability of *A* given *B* as the fraction of *B*'s outcomes that also belong to *A*, and interpret the answer in terms of the model.*	SE: 735–742	SE: 839–846	

SE = Student Edition

Standards	Descriptor	Algebra 1	Geometry	Algebra 2
Standards for Mathematical Content				
(+ = advanced; * = also a Modeling Standard)				
Statistics and Probability				
CC.9-12.S.CP.7	Apply the Addition Rule, $P(A \text{ or } B) = P(A) + P(B) - P(A \text{ and } B)$, and interpret the answer in terms of the model.*	SE: 727–733	SE: 831–837	
CC.9-12.S.CP.8	(+) Apply the general Multiplication Rule in a uniform probability model, $P(A \text{ and } B) = P(A)P(B \mid A) = P(B)P(A \mid B)$, and interpret the answer in terms of the model.*	SE: 735–742	SE: 839–846	
CC.9-12.S.CP.9	(+) Use permutations and combinations to compute probabilities of compound events and solve problems.*	SE: 715–719, 720–723, 727–733	SE: 819–823, 824–827, 831–837	
CC.9-12.S.MD.1	(+) Define a random variable for a quantity of interest by assigning a numerical value to each event in a sample space; graph the corresponding probability distribution using the same graphical displays as for data distributions.*			SE: 388–389, 391–392
CC.9-12.S.MD.2	(+) Calculate the expected value of a random variable; interpret it as the mean of the probability distribution.*	*This standard is outside the scope of the Holt McDougal Larson AGA series*		
CC.9-12.S.MD.3	(+) Develop a probability distribution for a random variable defined for a sample space in which theoretical probabilities can be calculated; find the expected value. *			SE: 388–390, 391–394, 395, 396

SE = Student Edition

Standards	Descriptor	Algebra 1	Geometry	Algebra 2
Standards for Mathematical Content				
(+ = advanced; * = also a Modeling Standard)				
Statistics and Probability				
CC.9-12.S.MD.4	(+) Develop a probability distribution for a random variable defined for a sample space in which probabilities are assigned empirically; find the expected value.*			SE: 390–393
CC.9-12.S.MD.5	(+) Weigh the possible outcomes of a decision by assigning probabilities to payoff values and finding expected values.* a. Find the expected payoff for a game of chance. b. Evaluate and compare strategies on the basis of expected values.	*This standard is outside the scope of the Holt McDougal Larson AGA series*		
CC.9-12.S.MD.6	(+) Use probabilities to make fair decisions (e.g., drawing by lots, using a random number generator).*	SE: 743–744	SE: 847–848	SE: AL10–AL11, 406–407
CC.9-12.S.MD.7	(+) Analyze decisions and strategies using probability concepts (e.g., product testing, medical testing, pulling a hockey goalie at the end of a game).*	SE: 711, 743–744	SE: 815, 847–848	SE: AL10–AL11, 414–418

SE = Student Edition

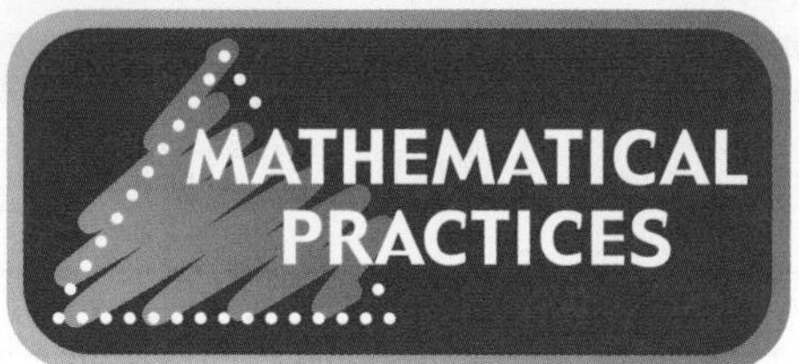

Mastering the Standards

for Mathematical Practice

The topics described in the Standards for Mathematical Content will vary from year to year. However, the *way* in which you learn, study, and think about mathematics will not. The Standards for Mathematical Practice describe skills that you will use in all of your math courses. These pages show some features of your book that will help you gain these skills and use them to master this year's topics.

1 Make sense of problems and persevere in solving them.

Mathematically proficient students start by explaining to themselves the meaning of a problem... They analyze givens, constraints, relationships, and goals. They make conjectures about the form... of the solution and plan a solution pathway...

In your book

Verbal Models and the **Problem Solving Plan** help you translate the information in a problem into a model and then analyze your solution.

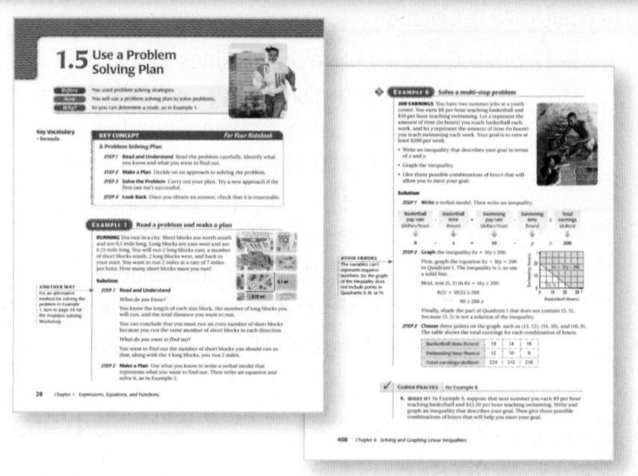

2 Reason abstractly and quantitatively.
3 Construct viable arguments and critique the reasoning of others.

Mathematically proficient students... justify their conclusions, [and]... distinguish correct... reasoning from that which is flawed.

In your book

What if?, Error Analysis, and **Reasoning** exercises ask you to evaluate statements, explain relationships, apply mathematical principles, and justify your reasoning.

WHAT IF? In Exercise 2, suppose the price of the 60 inch bookshelf was $99.30. Can you still solve the problem? *Explain.*

ERROR ANALYSIS *Describe* and correct the error in writing an equation of the line shown.

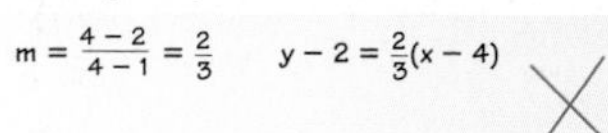

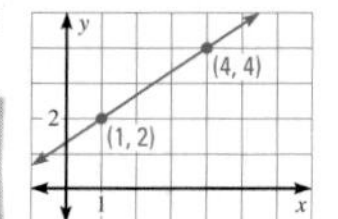

REASONING Give a counterexample for the following statement: If the graphs of the equations of a linear system have the same slope, then the linear system has no solution.

④ Model with mathematics.

Mathematically proficient students can apply... mathematics... to... problems... in everyday life, society, and the workplace...

In your book

Application exercises and **Mixed Reviews of Problem Solving** apply mathematics to other disciplines and in real-world scenarios.

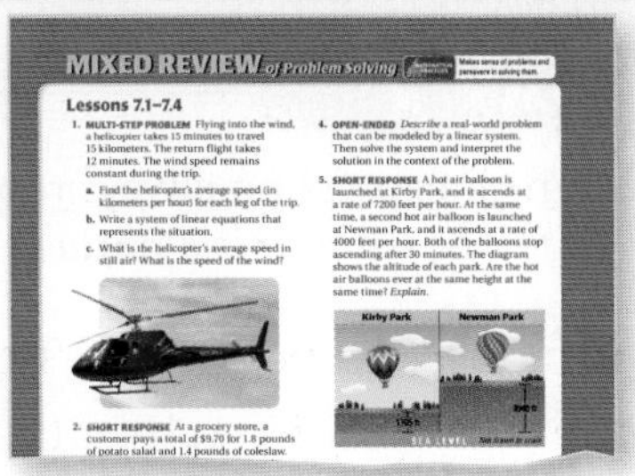

MIXED REVIEW of Problem Solving

Lessons 7.1–7.4

1. MULTI-STEP PROBLEM Flying into the wind, a helicopter takes 15 minutes to travel 15 kilometers. The return flight takes 12 minutes. The wind speed remains constant during the trip.
   a. Find the helicopter's average speed (in kilometers per hour) for each leg of the trip.
   b. Write a system of linear equations that represents the situation.
   c. What is the helicopter's average speed in still air? What is the speed of the wind?

2. SHORT RESPONSE At a grocery store, a customer pays a total of $9.70 for 1.8 pounds of potato salad and 1.4 pounds of coleslaw.

4. OPEN-ENDED *Describe* a real-world problem that can be modeled by a linear system. Then solve the system and interpret the solution in the context of the problem.

5. SHORT RESPONSE A hot air balloon is launched at Kirby Park, and it ascends at a rate of 7200 feet per hour. At the same time, a second hot air balloon is launched at Newman Park, and it ascends at a rate of 4000 feet per hour. Both of the balloons stop ascending after 30 minutes. The diagram shows the altitude of each park. Are the hot air balloons ever at the same height at the same time? *Explain.*

⑤ Use appropriate tools strategically.

Mathematically proficient students consider the available tools when solving a... problem... [and] are... able to use technological tools to explore and deepen their understanding...

In your book

Problem Solving Workshops explore alternative methods as tools for problem solving. A variety of **Activities** use concrete and technological tools to explore mathematical concepts.

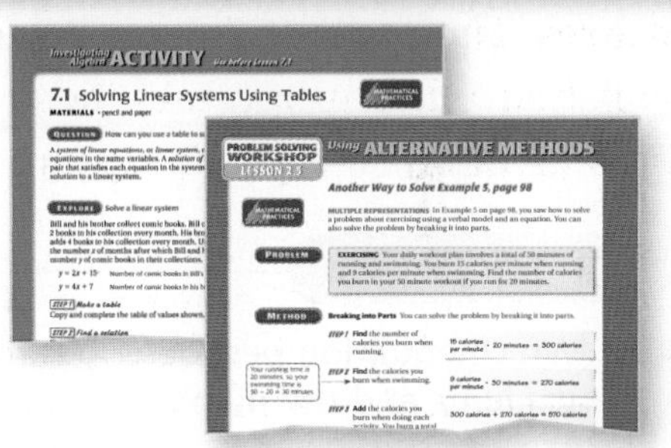

Investigating Algebra ACTIVITY

7.1 Solving Linear Systems Using Tables

MATERIALS • pencil and paper

QUESTION How can you use a table to s

EXPLORE Solve a linear system

STEP 1 Make a table

Copy and complete the table of values shown.

STEP 2 Find a solution

PROBLEM SOLVING WORKSHOP Using ALTERNATIVE METHODS

Another Way to Solve Example 5, page 98

MULTIPLE REPRESENTATIONS In Example 5 on page 98, you saw how to solve a problem about exercising using a verbal model and an equation. You can also solve the problem by breaking it into parts.

PROBLEM EXERCISING Your daily workout plan involves a total of 50 minutes of running and swimming. You burn 15 calories per minute when running and 9 calories per minute when swimming. Find the number of calories you burn in your 50 minute workout if you run for 20 minutes.

METHOD Breaking into Parts You can solve the problem by breaking it into parts.

STEP 1 Find the number of calories you burn when running. 15 calories per minute · 20 minutes = 300 calories

STEP 2 Find the calories you burn when swimming. 9 calories per minute · 30 minutes = 270 calories

STEP 3 Add the calories you burn when doing each activity. 300 calories + 270 calories = 570 calories

⑥ Attend to precision.

Mathematically proficient students... communicate precisely... with others and in their own reasoning... [They] give carefully formulated explanations...

In your book

Multiple Representations and **Extended Response exercises** ask you to explain your reasoning to help you learn to communicate mathematics precisely.

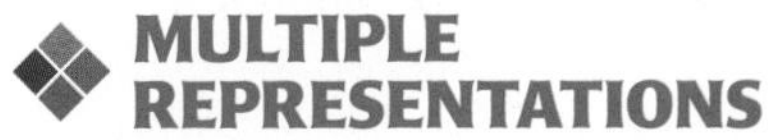

⑦ Look for and express regularity in repeated reasoning.
⑧ Look for and make use of structure.

Mathematically proficient students... look both for general methods and for shortcuts...

In your book

Lesson examples group similar types of problems together, and the solutions are carefully stepped out. This allows you to make generalizations about—and notice variations in—the underlying structures.

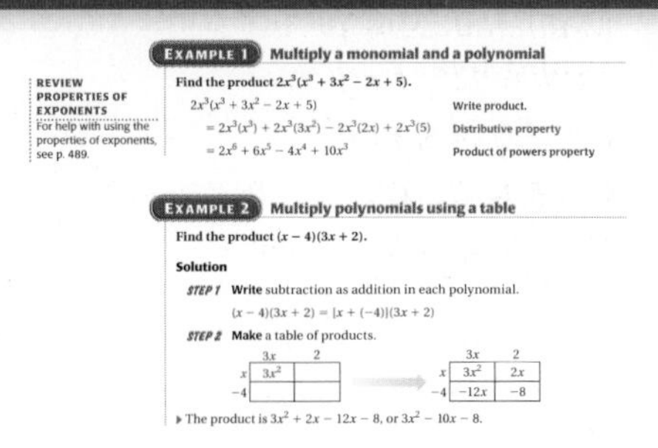

EXAMPLE 1 Multiply a monomial and a polynomial

REVIEW PROPERTIES OF EXPONENTS
For help with using the properties of exponents, see p. 489.

Find the product $2x^3(x^3 + 3x^2 - 2x + 5)$.

$2x^3(x^3 + 3x^2 - 2x + 5)$ — Write product.

$= 2x^3(x^3) + 2x^3(3x^2) - 2x^3(2x) + 2x^3(5)$ — Distributive property

$= 2x^6 + 6x^5 - 4x^4 + 10x^3$ — Product of powers property

EXAMPLE 2 Multiply polynomials using a table

Find the product $(x - 4)(3x + 2)$.

Solution

STEP 1 Write subtraction as addition in each polynomial.

$(x - 4)(3x + 2) = [x + (-4)](3x + 2)$

STEP 2 Make a table of products.

	$3x$	2
x	$3x^2$	
-4		

	$3x$	2
x	$3x^2$	$2x$
-4	$-12x$	-8

▸ The product is $3x^2 + 2x - 12x - 8$, or $3x^2 - 10x - 8$.

WEEK 1

DAY 1

Which expression always represents an odd number when n is a natural number?

(A) $n^2 + 1$

(B) $2n + 1$

(C) n^2

(D) $n + 1$

DAY 2

Cell phone bills are based on a flat monthly fee and the number of minutes used. In the equation $c = 0.07m + 29.99$, what does the variable m represent?

(F) The number of months billed

(G) The total amount of the bill

(H) The number of minutes used

(J) The phone number

DAY 3

Which equation best describes the relationship between the number of students and the number of tables in the cafeteria?

Students (n)	Tables (t)
720	18
600	15
960	24

(A) $n = 40t$

(B) $n = 35t + 90$

(C) $t = 40n$

(D) $n = 45t - 90$

DAY 4

Which expression represents the verbal phrase "the sum of three times a number and five"?

(F) $3(n + 5)$

(G) $3 + n \cdot 5$

(H) $3n + 5$

(J) $3 + (n + 5)$

DAY 5

What is the next term in the pattern?

$$-3, 6, -12, 24, \_\_\_, \ldots$$

(A) 36

(B) 30

(C) −32

(D) −48

Countdown to Mastery

WEEK 2

DAY 1

What is the next term in the pattern?

$$-1, \frac{1}{2}, -\frac{1}{4}, \frac{1}{8}, \_\_\_\_, \ldots$$

Ⓐ $-\frac{1}{10}$

Ⓑ $-\frac{1}{16}$

Ⓒ $\frac{1}{16}$

Ⓓ $\frac{1}{10}$

DAY 2

Which expression is equivalent to $2(3x - 4) - 8x + 3$?

Ⓕ $2x + 11$

Ⓖ $-2x - 5$

Ⓗ $2x - 5$

Ⓙ $-2x - 11$

DAY 3

Based on the table, which inequality correctly shows the relationship between x and y?

x	2	3	5	6
y	−3	−8	−10	−9

Ⓐ $x > -y$

Ⓑ $2x < -y$

Ⓒ $x < -y$

Ⓓ $2x > -y$

DAY 4

The sum of three consecutive even numbers is 42. The sum can be represented by the equation $n + (n + 2) + (n + 4) = 42$. What does n represent?

Ⓕ The greatest number

Ⓖ The average of the numbers

Ⓗ The middle number

Ⓙ The least number

DAY 5

A job advertisement states that the position pays \$12 an hour. Which equation represents the relationship between the salary s and the number of hours h worked?

Ⓐ $s = 12 + h$

Ⓑ $s = 12h$

Ⓒ $h = 12s$

Ⓓ $h = 12 + s$

DAY 1

Which expression is equivalent to 2^3?

(A) $2 \cdot 3$

(B) $3 + 3$

(C) $2 + 2 + 2$

(D) $2 \cdot 2 \cdot 2$

DAY 2

Which number is not a solution of $-7y + 19 < 75$?

(F) 13

(G) 0

(H) −2

(J) −8

DAY 3

Lydia received a gift card for $25.00 worth of smoothies from the Smoothie Spot. If the cost of each smoothie is $3.25, which table best describes *b*, the balance remaining on the gift card after she buys *n* smoothies?

(A)

n	*b*
1	$21.75
3	$15.25
4	$12.00
7	$2.25

(C)

n	*b*
1	$21.75
2	$18.50
5	$15.25
7	$12.00

(B)

n	*b*
2	$18.50
4	$12.00
6	$6.50
8	$0

(D)

n	*b*
2	$18.50
3	$15.25
5	$7.75
6	$4.50

DAY 4

The band is trying to raise money to take a field trip to the Rock and Roll Hall of Fame. They decide to sell sweatshirts. The equation for the amount of money *a* that they will make for selling *t* sweatshirts is $a = 22t - 350$. In order to make at least $2100, how many sweatshirts do the band members need to sell?

(F) 112

(G) 111

(H) 80

(J) 79

DAY 5

What is the solution to the equation $8x - 10 = 54$?

(A) 5.5

(B) 6.75

(C) 8

(D) 12

Countdown to Mastery

WEEK 4

DAY 1

Which expression is equivalent to $2x(3x + 5) - x^2 + 8$?

Ⓐ $-x^2 + 6x + 18$

Ⓑ $5x^2 + 10x + 8$

Ⓒ $10x + 14$

Ⓓ $-x^2 + 16x + 8$

DAY 2

What is the value of $3x^2 - 5x + 2$ when $x = -4$?

Ⓕ -66

Ⓖ -26

Ⓗ 30

Ⓙ 70

DAY 3

Which graph matches the values from the table?

x	-3	-1	2	4
y	6	2	-4	-8

Ⓐ
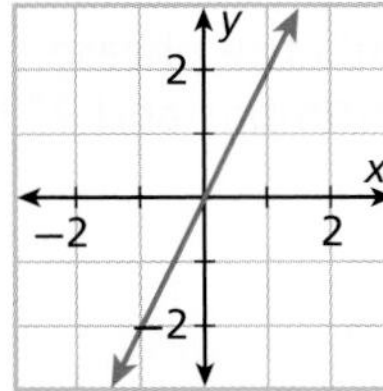

Ⓒ
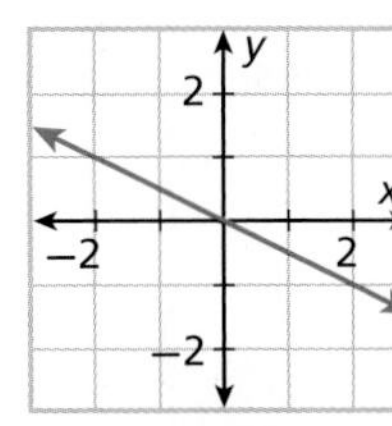

Ⓑ
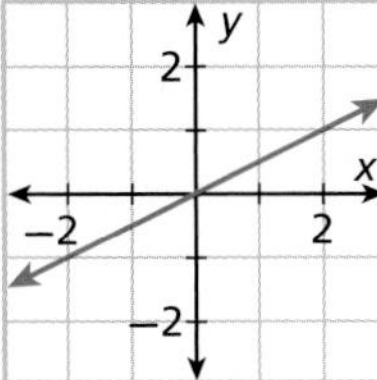

Ⓓ
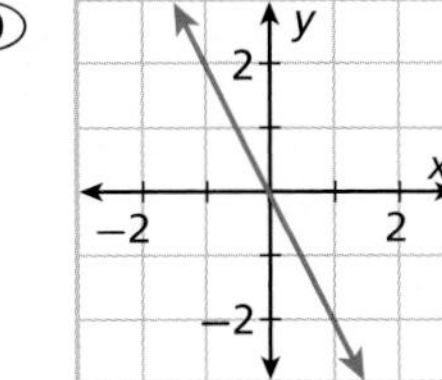

DAY 4

A rectangle has a length of 8 m and a width of 3 m. If a similar rectangle has a length of 22 m, what is its width?

Ⓕ 58.67 m

Ⓖ 17 m

Ⓗ 8.25 m

Ⓙ 9 m

DAY 5

Simplify the algebraic expression $4(x + 5) - 2(x + 5)$.

Ⓐ $2x + 10$

Ⓑ $2x + 30$

Ⓒ $6x + 30$

Ⓓ $-8x^2 - 200$

Countdown to Mastery

WEEK 5

DAY 1

Which description of the relationship between x and y best represents the table below?

x	9	0	−6	1
y	3	0	−2	$\frac{1}{3}$

Ⓐ The value of y is three times the value of x.

Ⓑ The value of x is three more than the value of y.

Ⓒ The value of x is three less than the value of y.

Ⓓ The value of x is three times the value of y.

DAY 2

Claire's father is 6 years more than 3 times her age. If her father is 39 years old, how old is Claire?

Ⓕ 15 years old

Ⓖ 11 years old

Ⓗ 7 years old

Ⓙ 6 years old

DAY 3

Which expression represents the phrase "four times the sum of a number and 2"?

Ⓐ $4n + 2$

Ⓑ $4(2n)$

Ⓒ $4(n + 2)$

Ⓓ $4 \cdot n + 2$

DAY 4

What is the solution to $-8x - 3 = -4x + 5$?

Ⓕ −4

Ⓖ −2

Ⓗ 2

Ⓙ 4

DAY 5

The cheerleaders are selling tickets to a pasta dinner to raise money for new competition outfits. They plan to charge \$6 per person, and their total expenses for dinner are \$135. Which value for the number of tickets sold would result in the cheerleaders not making a profit?

Ⓐ 46

Ⓑ 45

Ⓒ 23

Ⓓ 22

DAY 1

Which equation matches the data in the table?

x	3	1	−2	6
y	2	4	7	−1

Ⓐ $y = -x + 5$

Ⓑ $y = 2x - 1$

Ⓒ $y = x + 3$

Ⓓ $y = -3x + 11$

DAY 2

The drama club charges $3 admission to the one-act play festival. Their expenses are $115. In order for the club to make exactly $110 after expenses, how many people must attend the festival?

Ⓕ 39

Ⓖ 75

Ⓗ 114

Ⓙ 152

DAY 3

Melissa's brother is 6 years less than twice her age. The sum of her age and her brother's age is 27. Which equation best shows this information?

Ⓐ $x + (6 - 2x) = 27$

Ⓑ $x + (2x - 6) = 27$

Ⓒ $2x - 6 = 27$

Ⓓ $x = 2x - 6$

DAY 4

A rectangle has a length of 5 inches and a width of 3 inches. If a similar rectangle has a width of 15 inches, what is its length?

Ⓕ 5 inches

Ⓖ 9 inches

Ⓗ 15 inches

Ⓙ 25 inches

DAY 5

A bus company sells an annual bus pass for $8.50, and then charges a rider $0.25 per ride. Use the equation $c = 0.25b + 8.5$ to answer the following question: How much will it cost for someone to ride the bus 38 times?

Ⓐ $118.00

Ⓑ $20.00

Ⓒ $18.00

Ⓓ $9.50

Countdown to Mastery

WEEK 7

DAY 1

Daniel's recipe for 24 cookies calls for $2\frac{1}{2}$ cups of flour. How much flour will Daniel need to make 60 cookies?

Ⓐ 1 cup

Ⓑ $6\frac{1}{4}$ cups

Ⓒ $6\frac{1}{2}$ cups

Ⓓ $7\frac{1}{2}$ cups

DAY 2

What is the value of $2x^2 + 3x - 5$ when $x = -2$?

Ⓕ -7

Ⓖ -3

Ⓗ 5

Ⓙ 9

DAY 3

Which graph shows a line where each value of y is three more than half of x?

Ⓐ

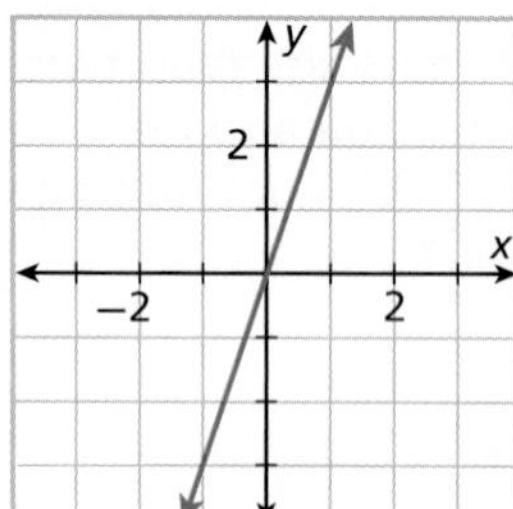

Ⓒ

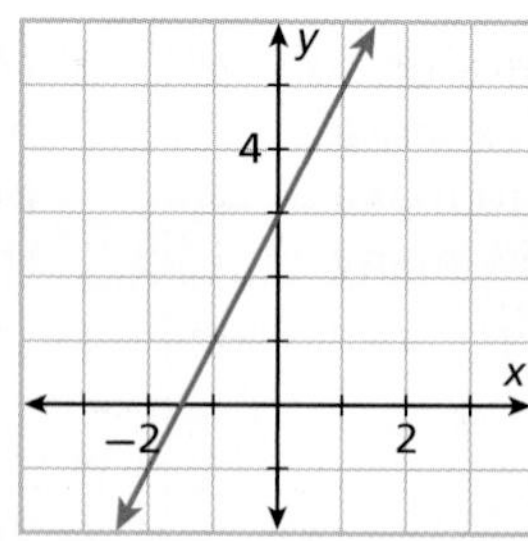

Ⓑ

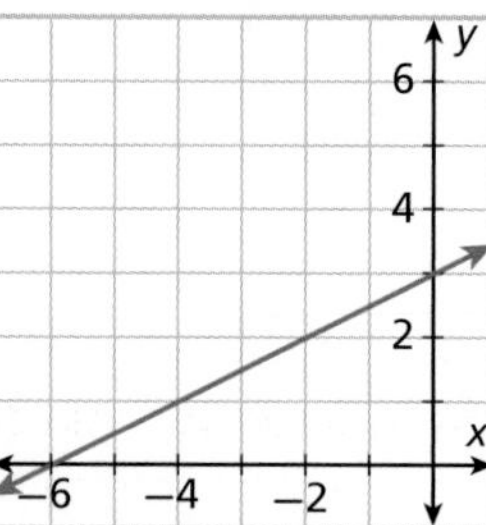

Ⓓ

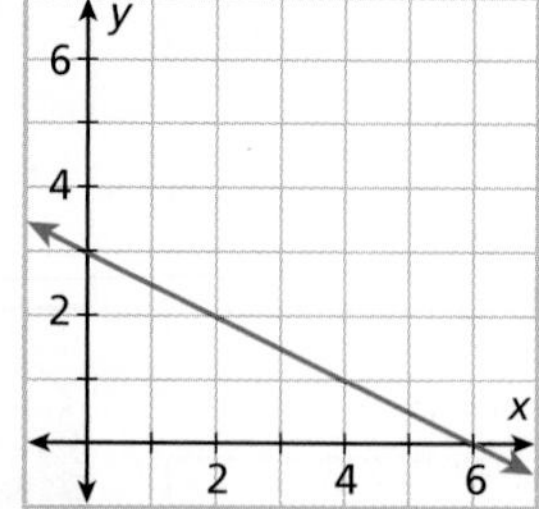

DAY 4

What is the solution to $2x + 8 < 3x - 4$?

Ⓕ $x < 12$

Ⓖ $x > \frac{12}{5}$

Ⓗ $x > 12$

Ⓙ $x < \frac{12}{5}$

DAY 5

Simplify the expression $3(5x - 8) + 2(4x - 1)$.

Ⓐ $23x + 26$

Ⓑ $23x + 22$

Ⓒ $23x - 22$

Ⓓ $23x - 26$

Countdown to Mastery — WEEK 8

DAY 1

A swimming pool charges an annual $75 membership fee, and it costs $1.50 each time a member brings a guest. Which equation shows the yearly cost y in terms of the number of guests g?

(A) $y = 75g + 1.5$

(B) $y = -1.5g + 75$

(C) $y = 1.5g + 75$

(D) $y = 1.5g + 75g$

DAY 2

On a certain standardized test, the equation $s = 9q + 218$ is used to determine a student's score. In this equation, s is the score and q is the number of questions answered correctly. If the maximum score on the test is 650, how many questions are on the test?

(F) 96 questions

(G) 72 questions

(H) 48 questions

(J) 24 questions

DAY 3

If you belong to Lowell's Gym and plan to work out 82 times in a year, what is your total cost for the year?

Lowell's Gym	
Membership fee	$75
Workout fee (per visit)	$2

(A) $89 (B) $157 (C) $164 (D) $239

DAY 4

A publishing company must ship boxes of a particular book to bookstores around the country. The boxes used for shipping can hold a maximum of 35 pounds. If the company wants to ship at least 10 books per box, what is the maximum weight of a book that can be put in the box?

(F) 3 pounds

(G) $3\frac{1}{2}$ pounds

(H) 4 pounds

(J) 25 pounds

DAY 5

Which verbal description does not match the function $f(x) = -\frac{1}{3}x - 5$?

(A) The function value is the difference between x times $-\frac{1}{3}$ and 5.

(B) The function value is 5 less than the product of x and $-\frac{1}{3}$.

(C) The function value is $-\frac{1}{3}$ of x subtracted from 5.

(D) The function value is $-\frac{1}{3}$ of x decreased by 5.

Countdown to Mastery

WEEK 9

DAY 1

Brian calculates the charge for each lawn he mows by using the function $f(t) = 10t + 5.5$, where t is the number of hours spent mowing the lawn. He always works for at least one full hour. Which statement cannot be inferred from this information?

Ⓐ Brian's hourly rate is $10.

Ⓑ Brian includes a charge of $5.50 for all lawns.

Ⓒ Brian uses $5.50 worth of gas for each job.

Ⓓ The minimum that Brian will make for each lawn is $15.50.

DAY 2

Which of the following relationships has a negative correlation?

Ⓕ A person's height and weight

Ⓖ The number of minutes spent studying and a test grade

Ⓗ The outside temperature and the number of layers of clothes a person wears

Ⓙ The number of years a person spent in school and the person's salary

DAY 3

The graph shows the value of a car over a period of years. Which of the following statements cannot be concluded from the graph?

Ⓐ The car started at a value of approximately $8400.

Ⓑ The car's value depreciates more quickly at the beginning, and then less quickly as time goes on.

Ⓒ The car is worth approximately $3000 when it is 5 years old.

Ⓓ The car should be sold before its worth drops below $2000.

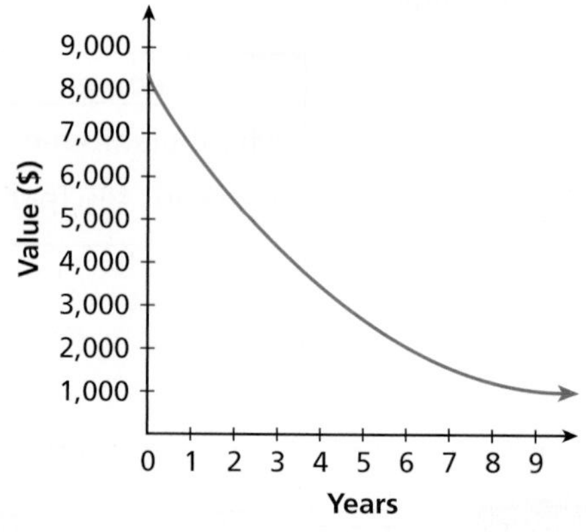

DAY 4

Which function best matches the table?

x	−3	0	3	6
y	2	4	6	8

Ⓕ $y = -\frac{2}{3}x$

Ⓖ $y = 2x + 4$

Ⓗ $y = \frac{2}{3}x + 4$

Ⓙ $y = \frac{1}{3}x + 3$

DAY 5

To change from degrees Celsius to degrees Fahrenheit, you can use the equation $f = \frac{9}{5}c + 32$. If the temperature is at least 55 degrees Fahrenheit, what inequality can you use to find the temperature in Celsius?

Ⓐ $55 \geq \frac{9}{5}c + 32$

Ⓑ $f \geq \frac{9}{5} \cdot 55 + 32$

Ⓒ $55 \leq \frac{9}{5}c + 32$

Ⓓ $f \leq \frac{9}{5} \cdot 55 + 32$

Countdown to Mastery

WEEK 10

DAY 1

A function relating two quantities is $f(x) = \frac{1}{5}x + 6$. What will always be true based on this function?

(A) $f(x)$ will be less than x.

(B) If x is positive, then $f(x)$ will be positive.

(C) If x is negative, then $f(x)$ will be negative.

(D) $f(x)$ will be greater than x.

DAY 2

In the equation $p = -40q + 163$, which relationship between p and q is true?

(F) You cannot determine the relationship based on this information.

(G) q is dependent on p.

(H) p and q are independent of each other.

(J) p is dependent on q.

DAY 3

What is the equation of the line shown?

(A) $y = 2x$

(B) $y = -2x$

(C) $y = \frac{1}{2}x$

(D) $y = -\frac{1}{2}x$

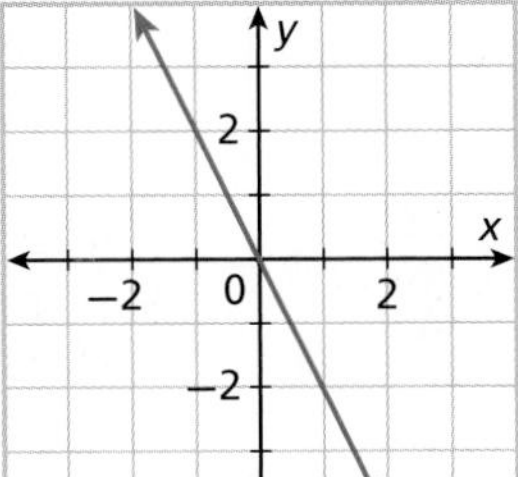

DAY 4

What is the solution to $-8x - 3 \geq -4x + 5$?

(F) $x \leq -2$

(G) $x \geq 2$

(H) $x \leq 2$

(J) $x \geq -2$

DAY 5

The sum of three consecutive integers is 54. What is the greatest of the three integers?

(A) 17

(B) 18

(C) 19

(D) 20

Countdown to Mastery

WEEK 11

DAY 1

Darian has a picture that is 4 inches wide and 6 inches long. He wants to enlarge the picture so that it has a width of 18 inches. What is the length of the enlarged picture?

Ⓐ 27 inches

Ⓑ 24 inches

Ⓒ 20 inches

Ⓓ 12 inches

DAY 2

At a computer repair shop, the function $f(t) = 40t + 35$ is used to calculate fees, where t is the number of hours technicians spend working on the computer. If you pay \$315 to get your computer repaired, how long did the technician work on repairing your computer?

Ⓕ 8.75 hours

Ⓖ 7.875 hours

Ⓗ 7.5 hours

Ⓙ 7 hours

DAY 3

The scatter plot shows the relationship between the size of a diamond in Carats and its retail price. What is the approximate retail price of a 0.30 Carat diamond?

Ⓐ \$400

Ⓑ \$600

Ⓒ \$800

Ⓓ \$1000

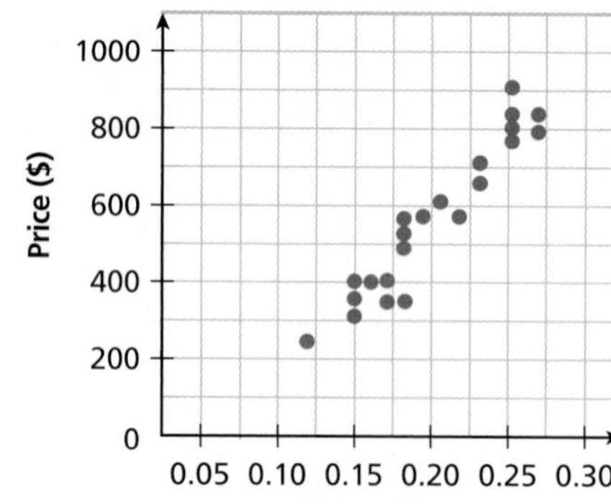

DAY 4

What is the next term in the pattern?

50, 10, 2, $\frac{2}{5}$, ___, ...

Ⓕ $\frac{1}{25}$

Ⓖ $\frac{2}{25}$

Ⓗ $\frac{2}{10}$

Ⓙ $\frac{1}{5}$

DAY 5

Which expression is equivalent to $5x - 35$?

Ⓐ $5(x - 35)$

Ⓑ $5(x - 7)$

Ⓒ $5(x + 35)$

Ⓓ $5(x + 7)$

Countdown to Mastery

WEEK 12

DAY 1

Based on the information in the table, what is the relationship between the weight of the object and its volume?

Weight (lb)	2	5	8	12
Volume (in^3)	0.5	1.25	2	3

Ⓐ The weight is 1.5 more than the volume.

Ⓑ The volume is 4 times the weight.

Ⓒ The weight is 4 times the volume.

Ⓓ The volume is 6 less than the weight.

DAY 2

What is the range of the function shown in the table?

x	1	3	5	8
$f(x)$	2	−2	0	2

Ⓕ {1, 3, 5, 8}

Ⓖ {4}

Ⓗ {−2, 0, 2}

Ⓙ {7}

DAY 3

Which graph shows a linear function?

Ⓐ

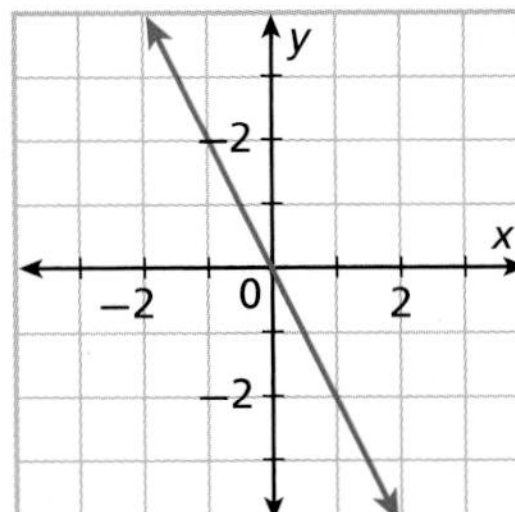

Ⓒ

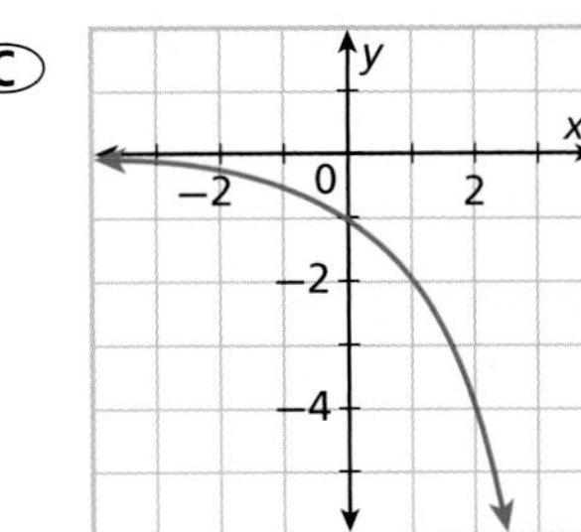

Ⓑ

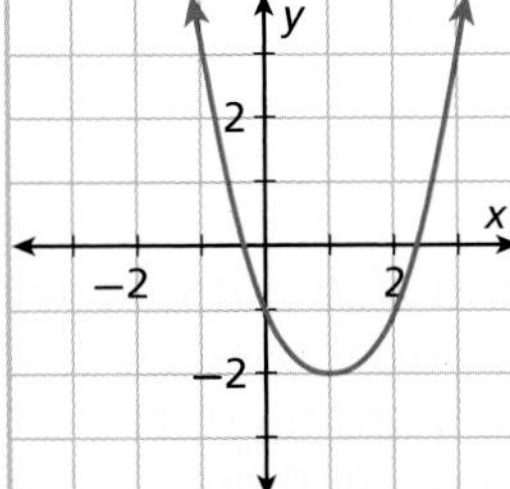

Ⓓ

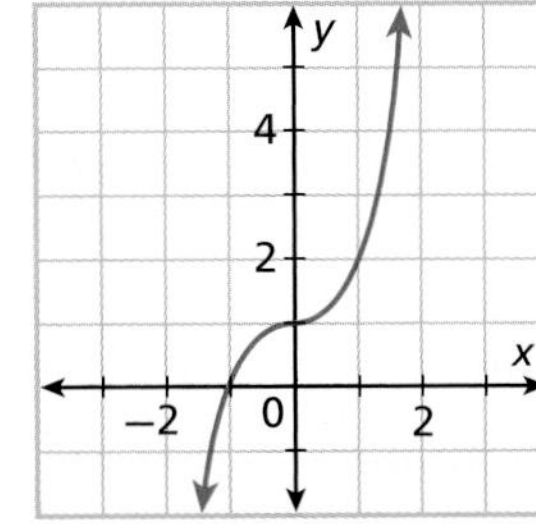

DAY 4

What is the solution to the equation $6(x - 9) = -12x + 36$?

Ⓕ $x = 5$

Ⓖ $x = 2.5$

Ⓗ $x = -1$

Ⓙ $x = -5$

DAY 5

Simplify the algebraic expression $5x - 2(4x - 3) + 7$.

Ⓐ $-3x + 1$

Ⓑ $13x + 13$

Ⓒ $-3x + 13$

Ⓓ $3x + 1$

DAY 1

The slope of a line is $-\frac{1}{4}$, and the y-intercept is –3. What is the equation of the line?

(A) $x + y = -3$

(B) $y = -\frac{1}{4}x + 1$

(C) $y = -\frac{1}{4}x - 3$

(D) $x - 4y = -3$

DAY 2

A taxi company charges a $2.50 fee per ride plus an additional $2.10 per mile traveled. If the taxi fee increases to $2.75, which characteristic of this function would change?

(F) The slope

(G) The x-intercept

(H) The y-intercept

(J) There would be no changes

DAY 3

Which description of the relationship between x and y best matches the graph below?

(A) The value of y is 3 times the value of x.

(B) The value of x is 2 more than the value of y.

(C) The value of x is 2 less than the value of y.

(D) The value of x is 3 times the value of y.

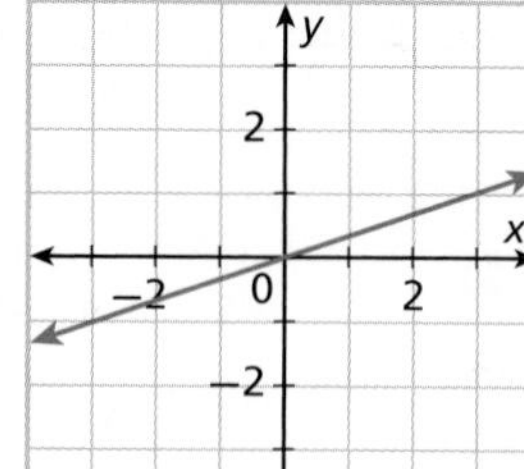

DAY 4

In which relationship are the two quantities independent of one another?

(F) The amount of tax paid for an item and the price of the item

(G) The number of snacks bought from a snack machine and the amount of money in the machine

(H) The number of hours worked at $6.50 per hour and the amount of money earned

(J) The age of a person and the number of televisions in his or her home

DAY 5

The linear function $f(x) = 3x + 15$ models the cost of renting x movies over the course of a year from a certain store. What range restrictions will there be if you graph this function?

(A) $f(x) \geq 0$

(B) $f(x) \geq 15$

(C) $f(x) > 0$

(D) $0 \leq f(x) \leq 15$

Countdown to Mastery

WEEK 14

DAY 1

Which function matches the data in the table?

x	-3	2	5
$f(x)$	15	0	15

Ⓐ $f(x) = -3x + 6$

Ⓑ $f(x) = -5x$

Ⓒ $f(x) = x^2 - 2x$

Ⓓ $f(x) = 3x^2 - 12$

DAY 2

A consultant charges her clients for her services based on an equation relating the total bill $f(h)$ to the number of hours worked h. The best interpretation of this function $f(h) = 125h + 150$ is:

Ⓕ She charges \$150 per hour plus a \$125 flat fee.

Ⓖ She charges \$125 per hour plus a \$150 flat fee.

Ⓗ She charges \$275 per hour.

Ⓙ Her hourly charges vary from \$125 to \$150 depending on the job.

DAY 3

A rectangle has the dimensions shown. Which value for the area has the correct number of significant digits?

Ⓐ 55.728 square centimeters

Ⓑ 55.73 square centimeters

Ⓒ 55.7 square centimeters

Ⓓ 56 square centimeters

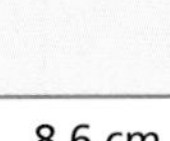

6.48 cm

8.6 cm

DAY 4

What is the range of the function $f(x) = 2x + 3$?

Ⓕ All real numbers

Ⓖ $f(x) \geq 3$

Ⓗ $f(x) \geq 0$

Ⓙ $f(x) \geq -3$

DAY 5

At Terry's TVs, profit is calculated using the equation $p = 0.4c - 125$, where p is the profit and c is the wholesale cost. If the company makes a profit of \$375 on one TV, what is the wholesale cost of the TV?

Ⓐ \$25

Ⓑ \$937.50

Ⓒ \$1250

Ⓓ \$1062.50

DAY 1

Which graph shows a linear function?

Ⓐ
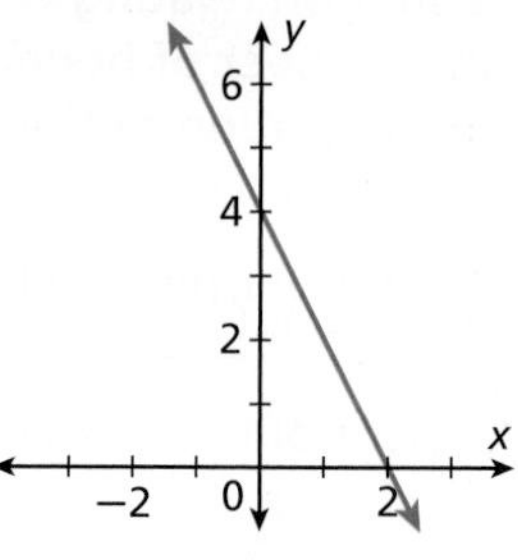

Ⓒ
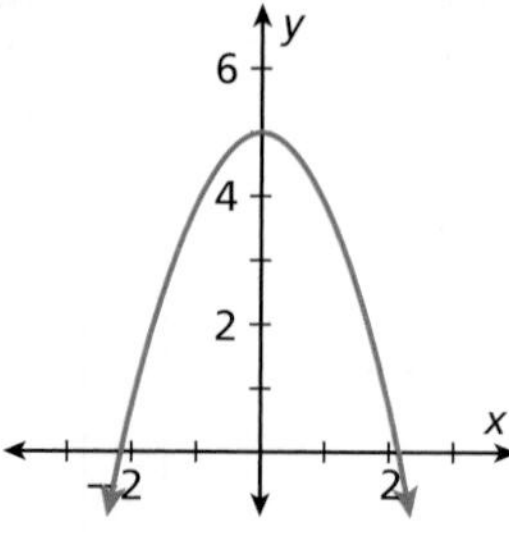

Ⓑ
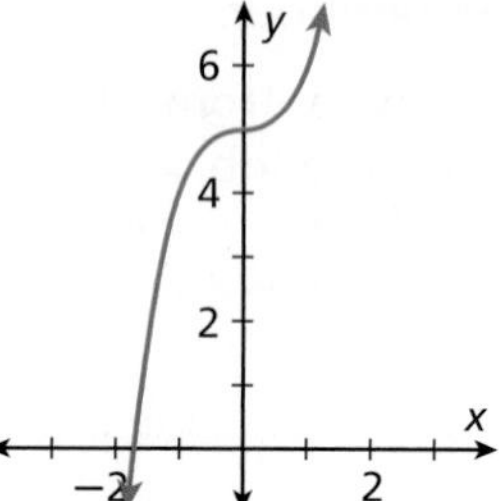

Ⓓ
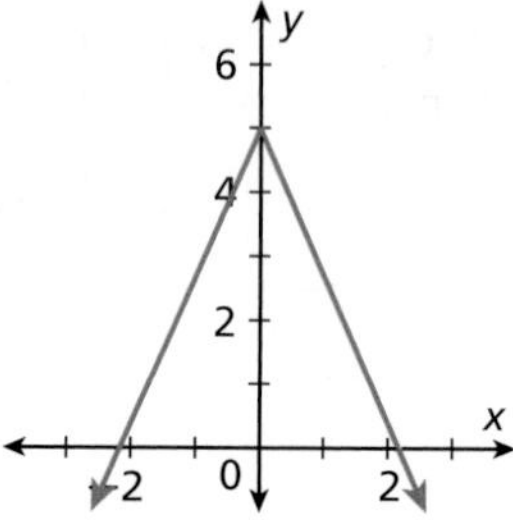

DAY 2

The relationship between which two quantities can be represented by a linear function?

Ⓕ The volume of a cube and its side length

Ⓖ The perimeter of a rectangle and its area

Ⓗ The perimeter of an equilateral triangle and its side length

Ⓙ The area of a square and its side length

DAY 3

Which equation represents a linear function with a slope of $\frac{2}{3}$?

Ⓐ $y = \frac{3}{2}x$

Ⓑ $y = \frac{2}{3}x + 4$

Ⓒ $y = x + \frac{2}{3}$

Ⓓ $y = \frac{2}{3}$

DAY 4

What are the x- and y-intercepts of $y = \frac{2}{5}x - 2$?

Ⓕ x-intercept: –2; y-intercept: 5

Ⓖ x-intercept: $\frac{2}{5}$; y-intercept: –2

Ⓗ x-intercept: 0; y-intercept: –2

Ⓙ x-intercept: 5; y-intercept: –2

DAY 5

A system of equations is set up to determine how many pounds of hazelnut coffee and how many pounds of Colombian coffee were mixed together to make a blend. The total mixture was 20 pounds of coffee. Which of the following is not a possible solution to the system?

Ⓐ (7, 13)

Ⓑ (32, –12)

Ⓒ (11, 9)

Ⓓ (1, 19)

Countdown to Mastery

WEEK 16

DAY 1

If a graph shows the relationship between the amount of sand in the top of an hourglass y over time x, what quantity does the x-intercept represent?

Ⓐ The amount of sand that is in the top of the hourglass originally

Ⓑ The speed at which the sand passes to the bottom of the hourglass

Ⓒ The height of the hourglass

Ⓓ The amount of time it takes for all of the sand to pass to the bottom of the hourglass

DAY 2

Which equation represents a line parallel to the one shown?

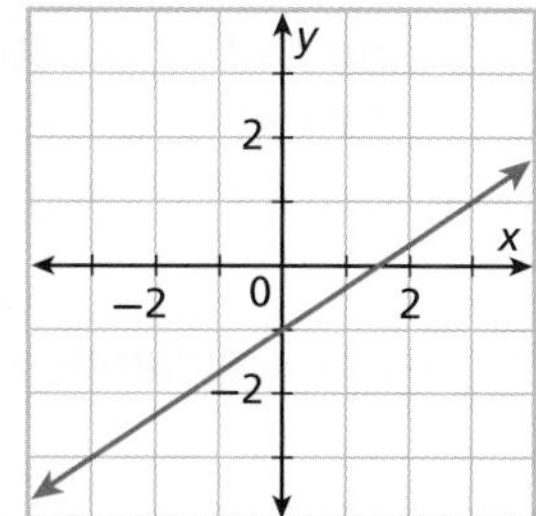

Ⓕ $y = \frac{3}{2}x + 1$

Ⓗ $y = \frac{2}{3}x + 1$

Ⓖ $y = -\frac{3}{2}x - 1$

Ⓙ $y = -\frac{2}{3}x$

DAY 3

The Whartons are planting a rectangular vegetable garden. Suppose the width of the garden is x feet and the length of the garden is $5 - x$ feet. Which type of function can you use to model the area y of the garden in terms of its width?

Ⓐ linear

Ⓑ quadratic

Ⓒ exponential decay

Ⓓ exponential growth

DAY 4

Your school is selling candles to raise money. If profit y is related to the number of items sold x, what are reasonable restrictions on the domain?

Ⓕ $y \geq 0$

Ⓖ No restrictions

Ⓗ $x \geq 0$

Ⓙ $0 \leq y \leq 2000$

DAY 5

What is the solution to the system of equations graphed below?

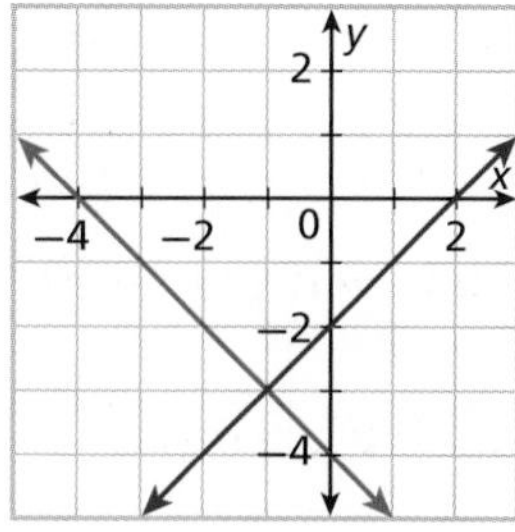

Ⓐ $(-1, 3)$

Ⓒ $(-3, -1)$

Ⓑ $(-1, -3)$

Ⓓ $(3, -1)$

Countdown to Mastery

WEEK 17

DAY 1

A store manager increases the wholesale cost of an item by 35%. Which statement best represents the functional relationship between the wholesale cost of the item and the markup on the item?

Ⓐ The markup is dependent on the wholesale cost.

Ⓑ The wholesale cost is dependent on the markup.

Ⓒ The markup and the wholesale cost are independent of each other.

Ⓓ The relationship cannot be determined.

DAY 2

Which situation can best be represented by a linear function?

Ⓕ The distance that an airplane is away from the airport as it comes in for a landing and time

Ⓖ The distance traveled by a car moving at a constant speed and time

Ⓗ The number of apples on a tree and the number of trees in the orchard

Ⓙ The height from the ground of a person riding a roller coaster and time

DAY 3

The scatter plot shows the percent of households that own a car versus the household income. What is a reasonable estimate for the percent of households that own a car if the household income is $50,000?

Ⓐ 50%

Ⓑ 65%

Ⓒ 77%

Ⓓ 85%

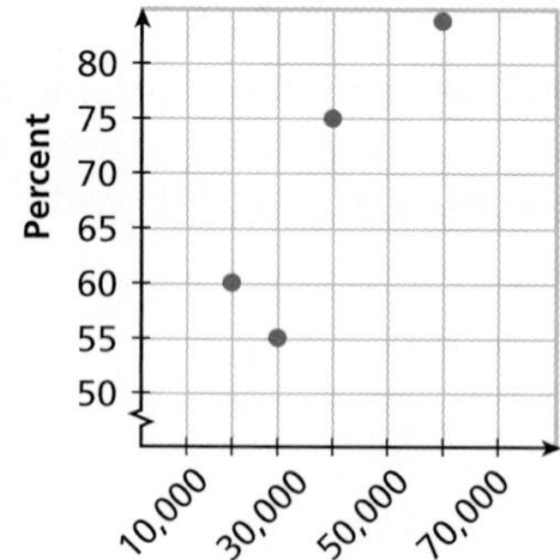

DAY 4

What is the slope of the line with equation $3x - 5y = 12$?

Ⓕ -3

Ⓖ $-\frac{3}{5}$

Ⓗ $\frac{3}{5}$

Ⓙ 3

DAY 5

Joy and a friend start a business. What linear function relates the total income and each partner's share of the profit based on the data in the table?

Total Income (t)	Profit Share (p)
$350.00	$50.00
$425.00	$87.50
$500.00	$125.00

Ⓐ $p = \frac{1}{2}t - 125$

Ⓑ $p = \frac{1}{4}t - 37.5$

Ⓒ $p = t - 300$

Ⓓ $p = \frac{1}{7}t$

Countdown to Mastery

WEEK 18

DAY 1

What is the range of the function $f(x) = 2x^2 + 1$ if the domain is $\{-2, 0, 3\}$?

Ⓐ $\{1, 9, 19\}$

Ⓑ $\{0, 8, 18\}$

Ⓒ $\{-9, 1, 19\}$

Ⓓ $\{-2, 0, 3\}$

DAY 2

Which function has a *y*-intercept of -2 and a graph whose slope is $\frac{5}{4}$?

Ⓕ $5x + 4y = 2$

Ⓖ $y = \frac{5}{4}x + 2$

Ⓗ $y = -\frac{5}{4}x + 2$

Ⓙ $y = \frac{5}{4}x - 2$

DAY 3

The graph represents a residual plot for a data set and a linear model. Based on the residual plot, which statement best describes the goodness of fit of the linear model?

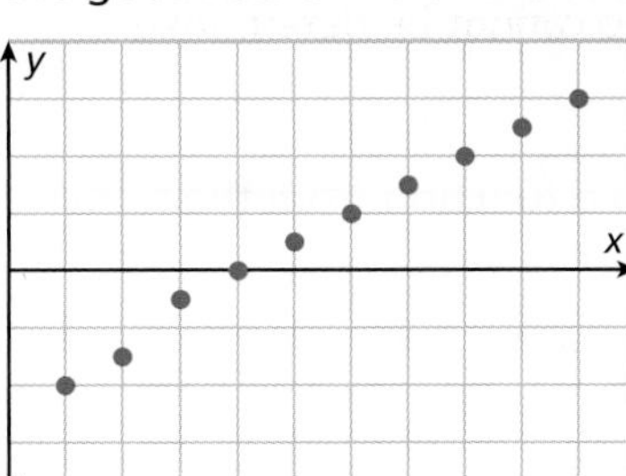

Ⓐ The line is a good fit for the data.

Ⓑ The line is in the wrong place.

Ⓒ The data are not linear.

Ⓓ The data may have relatively no correlation.

DAY 4

Which of the following cannot be represented by a linear function?

Ⓕ The amount of water *w* coming out of a dripping faucet over *m* minutes

Ⓖ The height *h* of a person over *t* years

Ⓗ The gross sales *s* made from the sale of *c* CDs priced at $14 each

Ⓙ The amount of sales tax on a purchase of *d* dollars if the rate is 6%

DAY 5

The graph shows the distance that a person is from home while driving at a constant speed. What quantity is represented by the *y*-intercept?

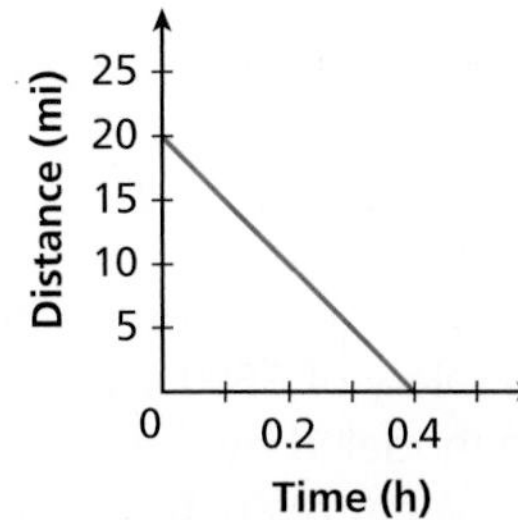

Ⓐ The speed at which the person is driving

Ⓑ The distance from home at the start

Ⓒ The amount of time it takes to get home

Ⓓ The distance from home at the end

DAY 1

Assuming that the graph below has the same x- and y-scale, which is the best estimate for the solution to the system?

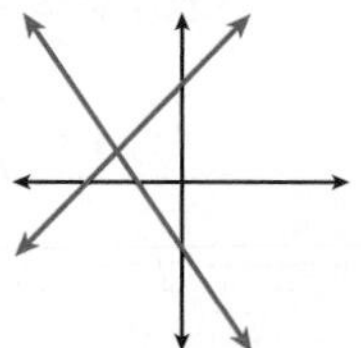

(A) $(-5, 10)$
(B) $(-4, 2)$
(C) $(3, -6)$
(D) $(8, -4)$

DAY 2

What is the y-intercept of the function whose graph has a slope of $-\frac{1}{3}$ and passes through the point $(-6, 4)$?

(F) 6

(G) 2

(H) −2

(J) −6

DAY 3

Which graph shows a function from the family $f(x) = x^2$?

(A)

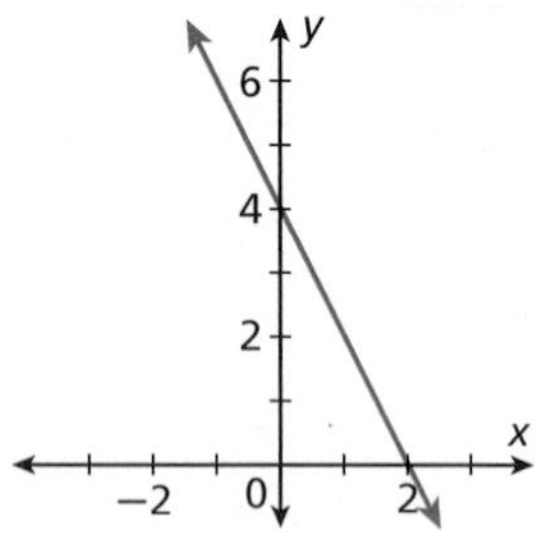

(C)

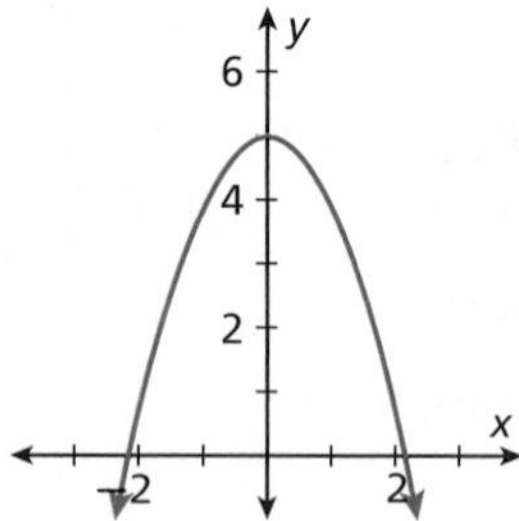

(B)

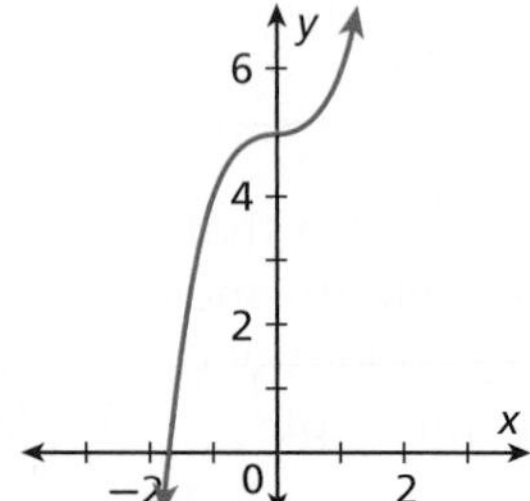

(D)

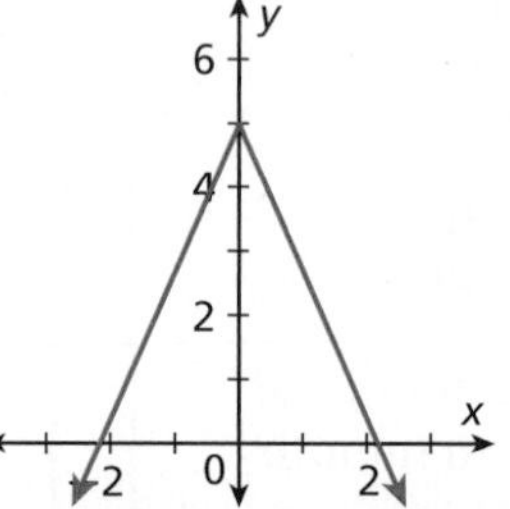

DAY 4

Miguel earns a 15% commission on his sales in addition to a salary of \$500 a week. His earnings can be modeled by the equation $p = 0.15s + 500$. What restrictions on the values of p and s best fit this situation?

(F) $p \geq 0$, s can be any value.

(G) $s \geq 0$, p can be any value.

(H) $s \geq 500$, $p \geq 0$

(J) $s \geq 0$, $p \geq 500$

DAY 5

If $f(x) = \frac{1}{2}x$, what best describes the relationship between x and $f(x)$?

(A) As the value of x increases by 1, the value of $f(x)$ will increase by 2.

(B) As the value of x increases by 1, the value of $f(x)$ will remain the same.

(C) As the value of x increases by 1, the value of $f(x)$ will increase by $\frac{1}{2}$.

(D) The value of x will not affect the value of $f(x)$.

Countdown to Mastery

WEEK 20

DAY 1

On Saturday, Suzie's Pretzel Stand sells a total of 12 items. Suzie charges \$3 for a pretzel and \$2 for a milkshake. If she took in \$32 on Saturday, which system of equations can be used to determine how many pretzels and how many milkshakes were sold?

Ⓐ $\begin{cases} 3x + 2y = 12 \\ x + y = 32 \end{cases}$

Ⓑ $\begin{cases} 3x - 2y = 32 \\ x + y = 12 \end{cases}$

Ⓒ $\begin{cases} 3x - 2y = 12 \\ x + y = 32 \end{cases}$

Ⓓ $\begin{cases} x + y = 12 \\ 3x + 2y = 32 \end{cases}$

DAY 2

What is the slope of the line shown?

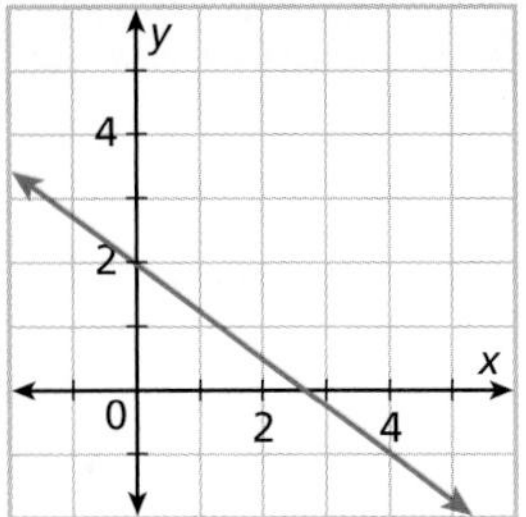

Ⓕ $-\frac{4}{3}$

Ⓖ $-\frac{3}{4}$

Ⓗ $\frac{3}{4}$

Ⓙ $\frac{4}{3}$

DAY 3

If the x-intercept of the function graphed below were to stay the same and the slope of the line decreased, what impact would that have on the y-intercept?

Ⓐ The y-intercept will decrease.

Ⓑ The y-intercept will remain the same.

Ⓒ The y-intercept will increase.

Ⓓ The y-intercept will double.

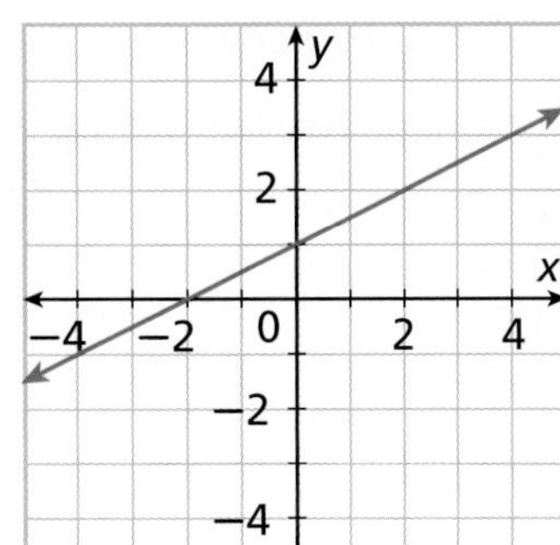

DAY 4

A system of equations is set up to determine the number of nickels and the number of quarters that Elissa has. Which ordered pair does not represent a valid solution to this system?

Ⓕ (0, 15)

Ⓖ (12, −5)

Ⓗ (31, 4)

Ⓙ (7, 0)

DAY 5

A gym membership costs \$25 a month plus \$3 per visit. This is modeled by the function $c = 3v + 25$, where c is the cost per month and v is the number of visits. If the slope of this function's graph were to increase, what would that mean about the prices that the gym charges?

Ⓐ The gym raised its monthly fee.

Ⓑ The gym lowered the cost per visit.

Ⓒ The gym raised the cost per visit.

Ⓓ The gym lowered its monthly fee.

DAY 1

Which of the functions, when graphed, will result in the most narrow parabola?

Ⓐ $y = 5x^2$

Ⓑ $y = \frac{1}{5}x^2$

Ⓒ $y = x^2$

Ⓓ $y = \frac{1}{2}x^2$

DAY 2

How do the graphs of the functions $f(x) = x^2 - 5$ and $g(x) = x^2 + 4$ relate to each other?

Ⓕ The graph of $f(x)$ is 9 units to the left of the graph of $g(x)$.

Ⓖ The graph of $f(x)$ is 1 unit below the graph of $g(x)$.

Ⓗ The graph of $f(x)$ is 9 units below the graph of $g(x)$.

Ⓙ The graph of $f(x)$ is 1 unit to the left of the graph of $g(x)$.

DAY 3

The graph shows the proposed balance in Jake's bank account if Jake saves an average of $15 a week. Which statement would not be true if the slope of the line were to increase?

Ⓐ Jake is saving more money per week.

Ⓑ Jake started with more money in his bank account.

Ⓒ It will take less time for Jake's bank balance to reach $120.

Ⓓ After 6 weeks Jake will have more than $90 in his bank account.

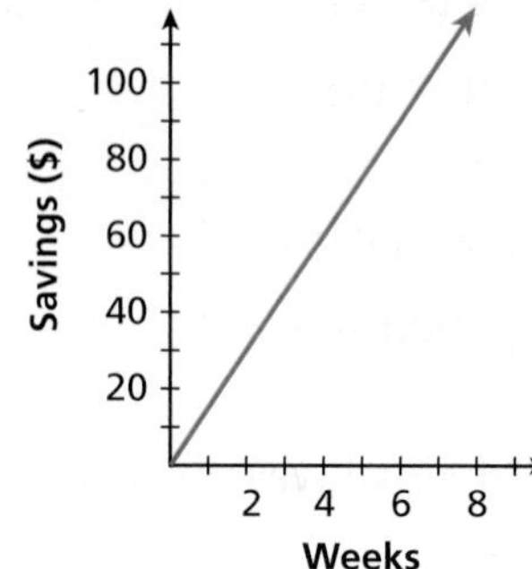

DAY 4

What are the roots of the function $f(x) = (2x - 1)(x + 5)$?

Ⓕ $\frac{1}{2}$ and -5

Ⓖ -1 and 5

Ⓗ 1 and -5

Ⓙ $-\frac{1}{2}$ and 5

DAY 5

For a typical shot in basketball, the ball's height in feet will be a function of time in seconds, modeled by an equation such as $h = -16t^2 + 25t + 6$. Which inequality shows the restrictions that should be put on the domain of this function?

Ⓐ $t \leq 0$

Ⓑ $h \leq 0$

Ⓒ $h \geq 0$

Ⓓ $t \geq 0$

Countdown to Mastery

WEEK 22

DAY 1

What are the roots of the graphed function?

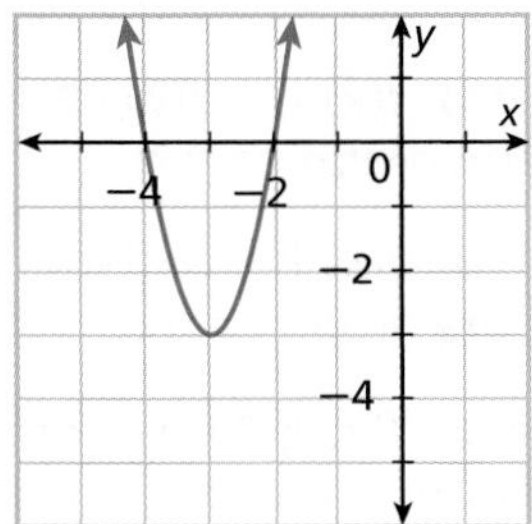

Ⓐ 2 and 4

Ⓑ −2 and −4

Ⓒ −2 and 4

Ⓓ 2 and −4

DAY 2

What is the range of the function shown?

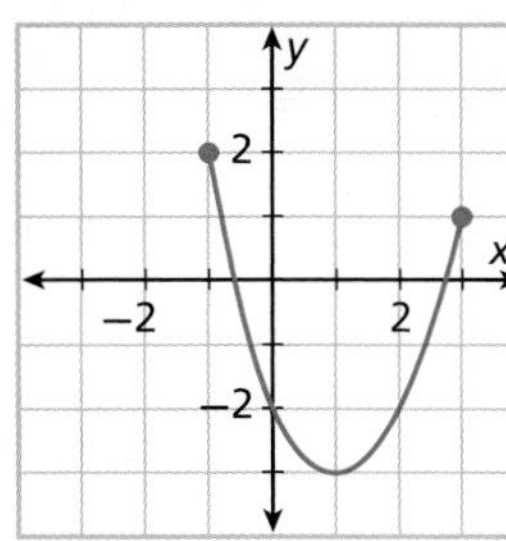

Ⓕ $-2 < y < 3$

Ⓖ $-3 < y \leq 2$

Ⓗ $-3 \leq y \leq 2$

Ⓙ $-2 \leq y \leq 3$

DAY 3

The graph shows the height of a baseball from the time it is thrown until the time it hits the ground. What value is not shown on the graph?

Ⓐ The amount of time that the ball was in the air

Ⓑ The height at which the ball started

Ⓒ The maximum height that the ball reached

Ⓓ The speed at which the ball was thrown

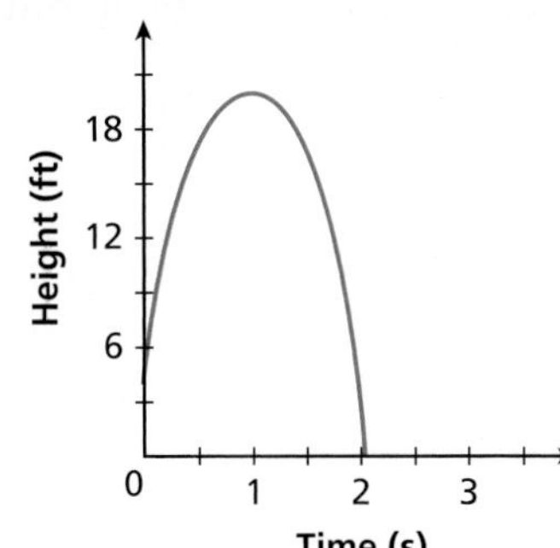

DAY 4

What are the solution(s) of the equation $x^2 - 10x - 24 = 0$?

Ⓕ $x = -4, 6$

Ⓖ $x = 2, -12$

Ⓗ $x = -2, 12$

Ⓙ $x = 4, -6$

DAY 5

What is the solution to the system of equations?

$$\begin{cases} 3x - 4y = 19 \\ y = 2x - 11 \end{cases}$$

Ⓐ (5, −1)

Ⓑ (−5, −21)

Ⓒ (5, 1)

Ⓓ (−5, −8.5)

Countdown to Mastery

WEEK 23

DAY 1

Which graph shows a function $y = ax^2$ when $a > 1$?

Ⓐ 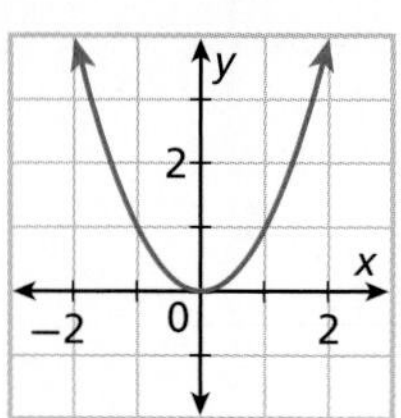

Ⓒ 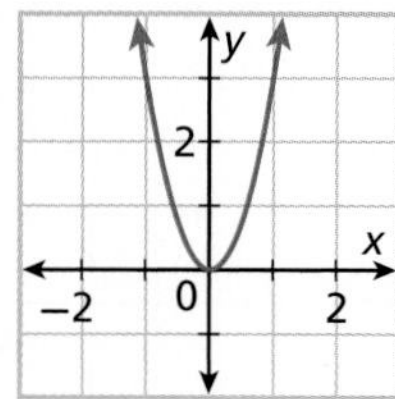

Ⓑ 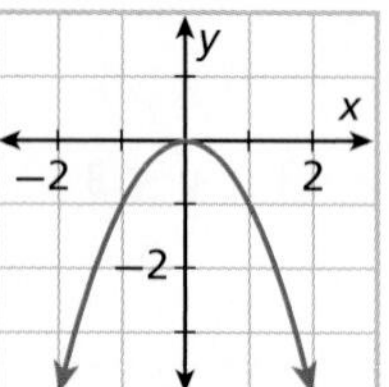

Ⓓ 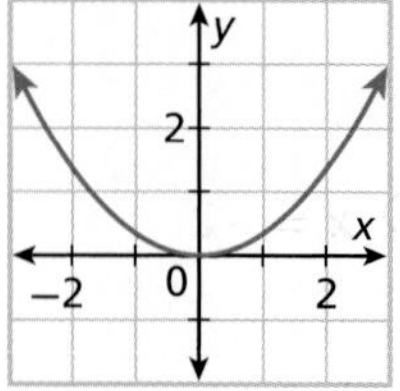

DAY 2

Which best describes the difference between the graphs of $f(x) = x^2$ and $g(x) = x^2 - 3$?

Ⓕ The graph of $g(x)$ is translated 3 units up from the graph of $f(x)$.

Ⓖ The graph of $g(x)$ is translated 3 units left from the graph of $f(x)$.

Ⓗ The graph of $g(x)$ is translated 3 units right from the graph of $f(x)$.

Ⓙ The graph of $g(x)$ is translated 3 units down from the graph of $f(x)$.

DAY 3

The graph shows the height of water coming out of a fountain over time. How many seconds pass before the water reaches the ground?

Ⓐ 0

Ⓑ 2

Ⓒ 4

Ⓓ 18

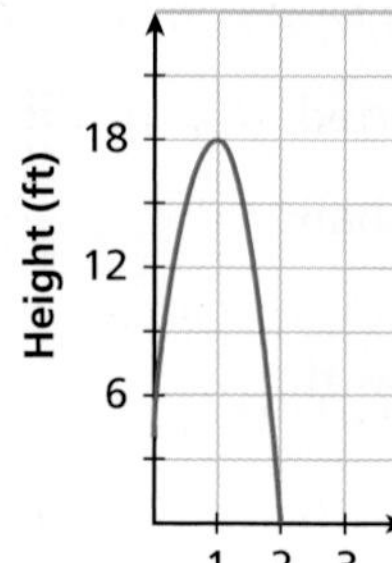

DAY 4

What is one solution to the equation $2x^2 + 7x + 3 = 0$?

Ⓕ $x = 3$

Ⓖ $x = \frac{1}{2}$

Ⓗ $x = -\frac{1}{2}$

Ⓙ $x = -1$

DAY 5

What is the solution to the system of equations $4x + 2y = -8$ and $x - 2y = 13$?

Ⓐ (25, 6)

Ⓑ (1, 6)

Ⓒ (−1, −6)

Ⓓ (1, −6)

Countdown to Mastery

WEEK 24

DAY 1

Which is the parent function of the graph shown?

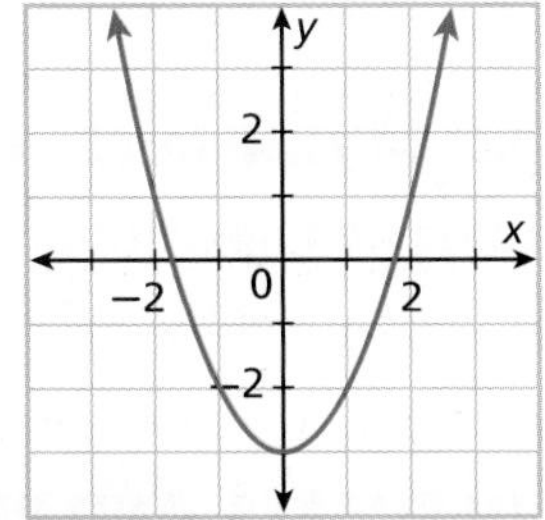

Ⓐ $y = x$

Ⓑ $y = |x|$

Ⓒ $y = x^2$

Ⓓ $y = x^3$

DAY 2

What is the x-intercept of the function shown?

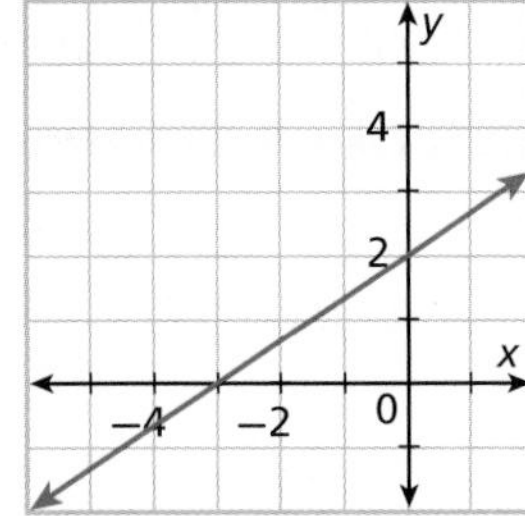

Ⓕ $x = -3$

Ⓖ $x = -2$

Ⓗ $x = 2$

Ⓙ $x = 3$

DAY 3

Which situation cannot be described by a linear function?

Ⓐ The amount of commission earned on a sale if the commission rate is 12%

Ⓑ The area of a square given its side length

Ⓒ The cost of renting a car if the charge is \$25 plus \$0.15 per mile

Ⓓ The amount paid for babysitting *h* hours if you charge \$8.25 per hour

DAY 4

What is the equation of the line that passes through the points $(-4, 2)$ and $(-8, 8)$?

Ⓕ $y = -\frac{3}{2}x - 4$

Ⓖ $y = -\frac{3}{2}x - 20$

Ⓗ $y = -\frac{3}{2}x - 8$

Ⓙ $y = -\frac{3}{2}x + 4$

DAY 5

What is the slope of the line given the equation $3x - 4y = -8$?

Ⓐ $m = 3$

Ⓑ $m = 2$

Ⓒ $m = \frac{3}{4}$

Ⓓ $m = -3$

Skills Readiness

Pre-Course Test

WHOLE NUMBER OPERATIONS

Solve.

1. $548 - 485$ **2.** 29×17

3. $774 \div 18$

ADD AND SUBTRACT DECIMALS

Add or subtract.

4. $34.26 + 25.7$ **5.** $24.8 - 6.23$

MULTIPLY DECIMALS

Multiply.

6. 3.4×0.7 **7.** 5.3×2.4

DIVIDE DECIMALS

Divide.

8. $18.9 \div 7$ **9.** $0.85 \div 0.5$

MULTIPLY AND DIVIDE FRACTIONS

Multiply or divide. Give your answer in simplest form.

10. $\frac{3}{8} \times \frac{4}{6}$ **11.** $\frac{7}{10} \div 7$

ADD AND SUBTRACT FRACTIONS

Add or subtract. Give your answer in simplest form.

12. $\frac{4}{5} + \frac{7}{10}$ **13.** $1\frac{3}{7} - \frac{5}{7}$

ADD AND SUBTRACT INTEGERS

Perform each indicated operation.

14. $-63 + 47$ **15.** $-21 - (-33)$

MULTIPLY AND DIVIDE INTEGERS

Perform each indicated operation.

16. $16(-3)$ **17.** $-42 \div (-7)$

FRACTIONS, DECIMALS, AND PERCENTS

For each problem, write an equivalent decimal and percent.

18. $\frac{3}{20}$ **19.** $\frac{11}{8}$

ORDER OF OPERATIONS

Evaluate each expression.

20. $16 + 4 \div 4$ **21.** $5 + 4 \times 3^2$

DISTRIBUTIVE PROPERTY

Simplify each expression.

22. $6(14 + t)$ **23.** $(h - 7)8$

RATES AND UNIT RATES

Find each unit rate.

24. $33 for 6 sandwiches

25. 98 photos in 7 days

CONNECT WORDS AND ALGEBRA

26. Eloise has collected $195 for charity. Each week she will collect an additional $15. Write an equation representing the total amount t (in dollars) that Eloise will have collected after w weeks.

GRAPH NUMBERS ON A NUMBER LINE

Identify each number on the number line.

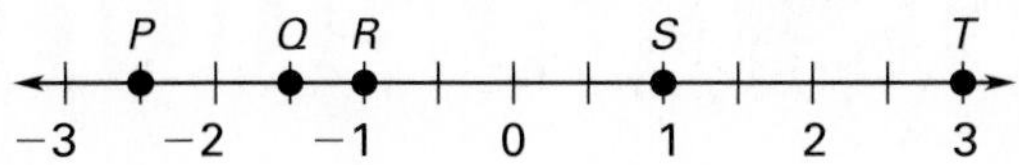

27. 3

28. −1.5

29. −2.5

COMPARE AND ORDER REAL NUMBERS

Compare. Use <, >, or =.

30. $\frac{8}{15}$ ____ $\frac{3}{5}$

31. 30% ____ 0.030

32. $\frac{8}{20}$ ____ 40%

EVALUATE EXPRESSIONS

Evaluate each expression for the given value of the variable.

33. $6g - 15$ for $g = 7$

34. $13 + \frac{3}{4}d$ for $d = -8$

SOLVE ONE-STEP EQUATIONS

Solve.

35. $6t = 144$ **36.** $18 + u = -8$

COMBINE LIKE TERMS

Combine like terms to simplify each expression.

37. $4c^2 - 23 + 5c^2$

38. $-4h + 5j - 4j + 7h$

SOLVE MULTI-STEP EQUATIONS

Solve.

39. $3y + 13 = 40$ **40.** $4(w - 3) - 6 = 42$

SOLVE PROPORTIONS

Solve each proportion.

41. $\frac{3}{5} = \frac{r}{15}$ **42.** $\frac{9}{18} = \frac{6}{q}$

FUNCTION TABLES

Generate ordered pairs for each function for $x = -2, -1, 0, 1, 2$.

43. $y = 3x + 7$

44. $y = (x - 3)^2$

ORDERED PAIRS

Identify each point on the coordinate grid.

45. $D(-1, 3)$ **46.** $E(4, 0)$

GRAPH LINEAR FUNCTIONS

Graph each function.

47. $y = x + 4$ **48.** $y = -\frac{1}{2}x + \frac{1}{2}$

SOLVE AND GRAPH INEQUALITIES

Solve and graph each inequality.

49. $q - 5 \leq -2$ **50.** $-3g < 12$

1 Expressions, Equations, and Functions

Lesson	
1.1	CC.9-12.N.Q.1*
1.2	CC.9-12.A.SSE.1*
1.3	CC.9-12.A.SSE.1*
1.4	CC.9-12.A.CED.1*
1.5	CC.9-12.A.CED.1*
1.6	CC.9-12.N.Q.3*
1.7	CC.9-12.A.CED.2*
1.8	CC.9-12.F.IF.4*

Before

Previously, you learned the following skills, which you'll use in this chapter: using fractions and percents, and finding area.

Prerequisite Skills

VOCABULARY CHECK

Copy and complete the statement.

1. In the fraction $\frac{2}{3}$, _?_ is the numerator and _?_ is the denominator.
2. Two fractions that represent the same number are called _?_ fractions.
3. The word *percent* (%) means "divided by _?_."

SKILLS CHECK

Perform the indicated operation.

4. $\frac{3}{5} \times \frac{2}{3}$
5. $1\frac{1}{4} \times \frac{3}{5}$
6. $\frac{1}{2} \div \frac{5}{8}$
7. $6 \div \frac{3}{4}$

Write the percent as a decimal.

8. 4%
9. 23%
10. 1.5%
11. 2.5%
12. Find the area of the rectangle.

$4\frac{1}{2}$ in.

11 in.

Now

In this chapter, you will apply the big ideas listed below and reviewed in the Chapter Summary. You will also use the key vocabulary listed below.

Big Ideas

1. **Writing and evaluating algebraic expressions**
2. **Using expressions to write equations and inequalities**
3. **Representing functions as verbal rules, equations, tables, and graphs**

KEY VOCABULARY

- variable
- algebraic expression
- power, exponent, base
- order of operations
- verbal model
- rate, unit rate
- open sentence
- equation, inequality
- solution of an equation or inequality
- formula
- precision
- significant digits
- function, domain, range
- independent variable
- dependent variable

Why?

You can use multiple representations to describe a real-world situation. For example, you can solve an equation, make a table, or draw a diagram to determine a running route.

Animated Algebra

The animation illustrated below helps you answer a question from this chapter: How does the number of blocks you run affect the total distance?

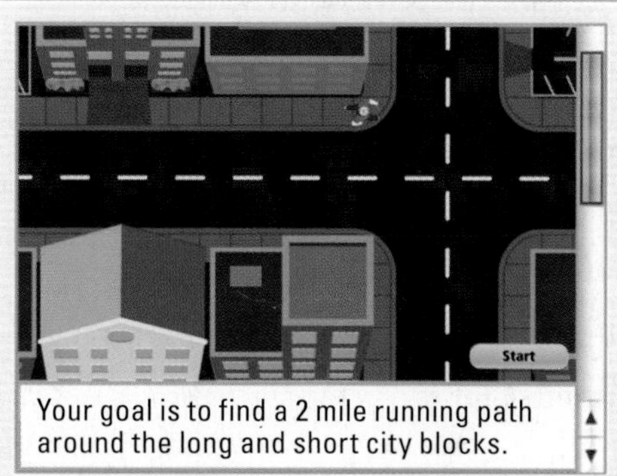

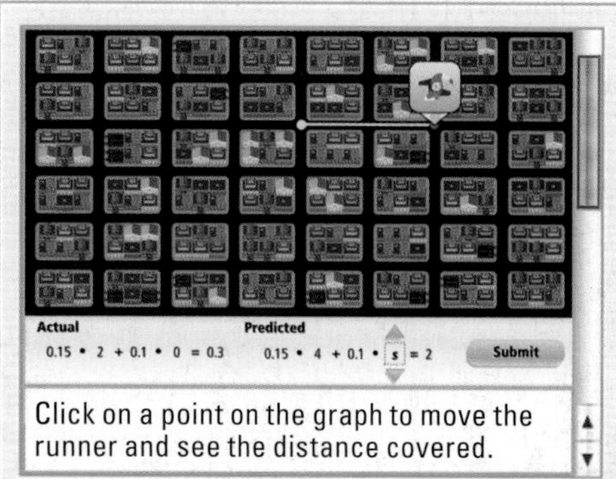

1.1 Evaluate Expressions

Before	You used whole numbers, fractions, and decimals.
Now	You will evaluate algebraic expressions and use exponents.
Why	So you can calculate sports statistics, as in Ex. 50.

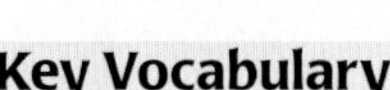

Key Vocabulary
- **variable**
- **algebraic expression**
- **power**
- **base**
- **exponent**

CC.9-12.N.Q.1 Use units as a way to understand problems and to guide the solution of multi-step problems; choose and interpret units consistently in formulas; choose and interpret the scale and the origin in graphs and data displays.*

A **variable** is a letter used to represent one or more numbers. The numbers are the values of the variable. *Expressions* consist of numbers, variables, and operations. An **algebraic expression**, or *variable expression*, is an expression that includes at least one variable.

Algebraic expression	Meaning	Operation
$5(n)$ $\quad 5 \cdot n$ $\quad 5n$	5 times n	Multiplication
$\frac{14}{y}$ $\quad 14 \div y$	14 divided by y	Division
$6 + c$	6 plus c	Addition
$8 - x$	8 minus x	Subtraction

To **evaluate an algebraic expression**, substitute a number for each variable, perform the operation(s), and simplify the result, if necessary.

EXAMPLE 1 Evaluate algebraic expressions

Evaluate the expression when $n = 3$.

USE A PROPERTY
Part (a) of Example 1 illustrates the transitive property of equality: If $a = b$ and $b = c$, then $a = c$. Because $13 \cdot n = 13 \cdot 3$ and $13 \cdot 3 = 39$, $13 \cdot n = 39$. Two other properties of equality are the reflexive property ($a = a$) and the symmetric property (if $a = b$, then $b = a$).

a. $13 \cdot n = 13 \cdot 3$ **Substitute 3 for *n*.**

$= 39$ **Multiply.**

b. $\frac{9}{n} = \frac{9}{3}$ **Substitute 3 for *n*.**

$= 3$ **Divide.**

c. $n - 1 = 3 - 1$ **Substitute 3 for *n*.**

$= 2$ **Subtract.**

d. $n + 8 = 3 + 8$ **Substitute 3 for *n*.**

$= 11$ **Add.**

GUIDED PRACTICE for Example 1

Evaluate the expression when $y = 2$.

1. $6y$ **2.** $\frac{8}{y}$ **3.** $y + 4$ **4.** $11 - y$

EXAMPLE 2 Evaluate an expression

MOVIES The total cost of seeing a movie at a theater can be represented by the expression $a + r$ where a is the cost (in dollars) of admission and r is the cost (in dollars) of refreshments. Suppose you pay \$7.50 for admission and \$7.25 for refreshments. Find the total cost.

Solution

Total cost $= a + r$	**Write expression.**
$= 7.50 + 7.25$	**Substitute 7.50 for *a* and 7.25 for *r*.**
$= 14.75$	**Add.**

▶ The total cost is \$14.75.

EXPRESSIONS USING EXPONENTS A **power** is an expression that represents repeated multiplication of the same factor. For example, 81 is a power of 3 because $81 = 3 \cdot 3 \cdot 3 \cdot 3$. A power can be written in a form using two numbers, a **base** and an **exponent**. The exponent represents the number of times the base is used as a factor, so 81 can be written as 3^4.

base ↓ exponent ↙

$$\underbrace{3^4}_{\text{power}} = \underbrace{3 \cdot 3 \cdot 3 \cdot 3}_{\text{4 factors of 3}}$$

EXAMPLE 3 Read and write powers

Write the power in words and as a product.

WRITE EXPONENTS
For a number raised to the first power, you usually do not write the exponent 1. For instance, you write 7^1 simply as 7.

Power	Words	Product
a. 7^1	seven to the first power	7
b. 5^2	five to the second power, or five *squared*	$5 \cdot 5$
c. $\left(\frac{1}{2}\right)^3$	one half to the third power, or one half *cubed*	$\frac{1}{2} \cdot \frac{1}{2} \cdot \frac{1}{2}$
d. z^5	z to the fifth power	$z \cdot z \cdot z \cdot z \cdot z$

GUIDED PRACTICE for Examples 2 and 3

5. WHAT IF? In Example 2, suppose you go back to the theater with a friend to see an afternoon movie. You pay for both admissions. Your total cost (in dollars) can be represented by the expression $2a$. If each admission costs \$4.75, what is your total cost?

Write the power in words and as a product.

6. 9^5 **7.** 2^8 **8.** n^4

EXAMPLE 4 Evaluate powers

USE A PROPERTY

Example 4 illustrates the substitution property of equality: If $a = b$, then a can be substituted for b in any expression or equation. Because $x = 2$, $x^4 = 2^4$.

Evaluate the expression.

a. x^4 when $x = 2$

b. n^3 when $n = 1.5$

Solution

a. $x^4 = 2^4$

$= 2 \cdot 2 \cdot 2 \cdot 2$

$= 16$

b. $n^3 = 1.5^3$

$= (1.5)(1.5)(1.5)$

$= 3.375$

GUIDED PRACTICE for Example 4

Evaluate the expression.

9. x^3 when $x = 8$

10. k^2 when $k = 2.5$

11. d^4 when $d = \frac{1}{3}$

REVIEW AREA AND VOLUME

For help with area and volume, see pp. SR14 and SR17.

AREA AND VOLUME Exponents are used in the formulas for the area of a square and the volume of a cube. In fact, the words *squared* and *cubed* come from the formula for the area of a square and the formula for the volume of a cube.

$A = s^2$ s s

$V = s^3$ s s s

EXAMPLE 5 Evaluate a power

STORAGE CUBES Each edge of the medium-sized pop-up storage cube shown is 14 inches long. The storage cube is made so that it can be folded flat when not in use. Find the volume of the storage cube.

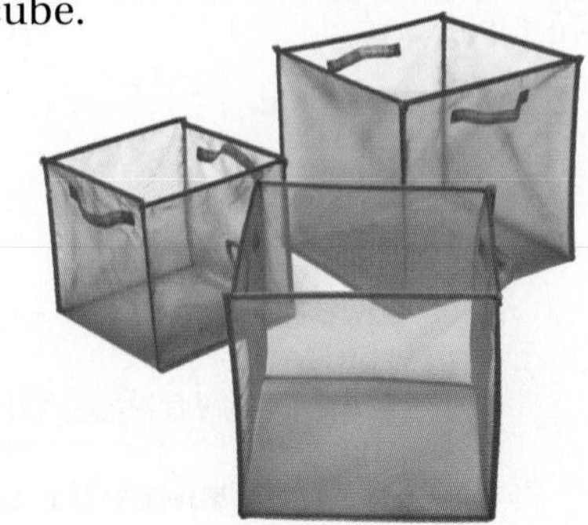

Solution

$V = s^3$ **Write formula for volume.**

$= 14^3$ **Substitute 14 for *s*.**

$= 2744$ **Evaluate power.**

▶ The volume of the storage cube is 2744 cubic inches.

GUIDED PRACTICE for Example 5

12. WHAT IF? In Example 5, suppose the storage cube is folded flat to form a square. Find the area of the square.

1.1 EXERCISES

HOMEWORK KEY

○ = See WORKED-OUT SOLUTIONS Exs. 19, 35, and 51

★ = STANDARDIZED TEST PRACTICE Exs. 2, 15, 44, 45, 52, and 54

SKILL PRACTICE

1. **VOCABULARY** Identify the exponent and the base in the expression 6^{12}.

2. ★ **WRITING** *Describe* the steps you would take to evaluate the expression n^5 when $n = 3$. Then evaluate the expression.

EXAMPLE 1 for Exs. 3–15

EVALUATING EXPRESSIONS Evaluate the expression.

3. $15x$ when $x = 4$
4. $0.4r$ when $r = 6$
5. $w - 8$ when $w = 20$
6. $1.6 - g$ when $g = 1.2$
7. $5 + m$ when $m = 7$
8. $0.8 + h$ when $h = 3.7$
9. $\frac{24}{f}$ when $f = 8$
10. $\frac{t}{5}$ when $t = 4.5$
11. $2.5m$ when $m = 4$
12. $\frac{1}{2}k$ when $k = \frac{2}{3}$
13. $y - \frac{1}{2}$ when $y = \frac{5}{6}$
14. $h + \frac{1}{3}$ when $h = 1\frac{1}{3}$

15. ★ **MULTIPLE CHOICE** What is the value of $2.5m$ when $m = 10$?

Ⓐ 0.25 Ⓑ 2.5 Ⓒ 12.5 Ⓓ 25

EXAMPLE 3 for Exs. 16–25

WRITING POWERS Write the power in words and as a product.

16. 12^5
17. 7^3
18. $(3.2)^2$
19. $(0.3)^4$
20. $\left(\frac{1}{2}\right)^8$
21. n^7
22. y^6
23. t^4

ERROR ANALYSIS ***Describe*** **and correct the error in evaluating the power.**

24. $(0.4)^2 = 2(0.4) = 0.8$ 

25. $5^4 = 4 \cdot 4 \cdot 4 \cdot 4 \cdot 4 = 1024$ 

EXAMPLE 4 for Exs. 26–37

EVALUATING POWERS Evaluate the power.

26. 3^2
27. 10^2
28. 1^5
29. 11^3
30. 5^3
31. 3^5
32. 2^6
33. 6^4
34. $\left(\frac{1}{4}\right)^2$
35. $\left(\frac{3}{5}\right)^3$
36. $\left(\frac{2}{3}\right)^4$
37. $\left(\frac{1}{6}\right)^3$

EVALUATING EXPRESSIONS Evaluate the expression.

38. x^2 when $x = \frac{3}{4}$
39. p^2 when $p = 1.1$
40. $x + y$ when $x = 11$ and $y = 6.4$
41. kn when $k = 9$ and $n = 4.5$
42. $w - z$ when $w = 9.5$ and $z = 2.8$
43. $\frac{b}{c}$ when $b = 24$ and $c = 2.5$

44. ★ **MULTIPLE CHOICE** Which expression has the greatest value when $x = 10$ and $y = 0.5$?

Ⓐ xy Ⓑ $x - y$ Ⓒ $\frac{x}{y}$ Ⓓ $\frac{y}{x}$

45. ★ **MULTIPLE CHOICE** Let b be the number of tokens you bought at an arcade, and let u be the number you have used. Which expression represents the number of tokens remaining?

Ⓐ $b + u$ Ⓑ $b - u$ Ⓒ bu Ⓓ $\frac{b}{u}$

46. **COMPARING POWERS** Let x and y be whole numbers greater than 0 with $y > x$. Which has the greater value, 3^x or 3^y? *Explain.*

47. **CHALLENGE** For which whole number value(s) of x greater than 0 is the value of x^2 greater than the value of 2^x? *Explain.*

PROBLEM SOLVING

EXAMPLE 2 for Exs. 48–50

48. **GEOMETRY** The perimeter of a square with a side length of s is given by the expression $4s$. What is the perimeter of the square shown?

7.5 m

49. **LEOPARD FROG** You can estimate the distance (in centimeters) that a leopard frog can jump using the expression 13ℓ where ℓ is the frog's length (in centimeters). What distance can a leopard frog that is 12.5 centimeters long jump?

50. **MULTI-STEP PROBLEM** Jen was the leading scorer on her soccer team. She scored 120 goals and had 20 assists in her high school career.

a. The number n of points awarded for goals is given by $2g$ where g is the number of goals scored. How many points did Jen earn for goals?

b. The point total is given by $n + a$ where a is the number of assists. Use your answer from part (a) to find Jen's point total.

EXAMPLE 3 for Exs. 51–52

51. **MULTI-STEP PROBLEM** You are buying a tank for three fish. You have a flame angel that is 3.5 inches long, a yellow sailfin tang that is 5.5 inches long, and a coral beauty that is 3 inches long. The area (in square inches) of water surface the fish need is given by the expression $12f$ where f is the sum of the lengths (in inches) of all the fish in the tank.

a. What is the total length of the three fish?

b. How many square inches of water surface do the fish need?

52. ★ **MULTIPLE CHOICE** For a snow sculpture contest, snow is packed into a cube-shaped box with an edge length of 8 feet. The box is frozen and removed, leaving a cube of snow. One cubic foot of the snow weighs about 30 pounds. You can estimate the weight (in pounds) of the cube using the expression $30V$ where V is the volume (in cubic feet) of the snow. About how much does the uncarved cube weigh?

Ⓐ 240 pounds Ⓑ 1920 pounds

Ⓒ 15,360 pounds Ⓓ 216,000 pounds

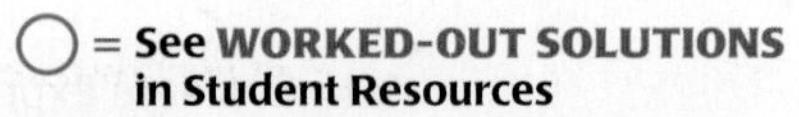
= See **WORKED-OUT SOLUTIONS** in Student Resources

★ = **STANDARDIZED TEST PRACTICE**

53. **FOOTBALL** A football team's net score for the regular season is given by the expression $a - b$ where a is the total number of points the team scored and b is the total number of points scored against the team. The table shows the point totals for the 2003 National Football League Conference Champions. Which team's net score was greater?

Team	Points scored, a	Points scored against, b
New England Patriots	336	238
Carolina Panthers	325	304

54. ★ **EXTENDED RESPONSE** A manufacturer produces three different sizes of cube-shaped stacking bins with edge lengths as shown.

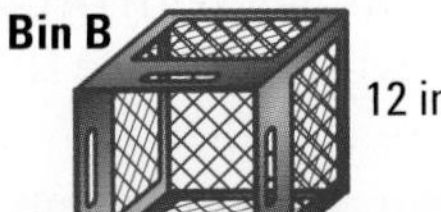

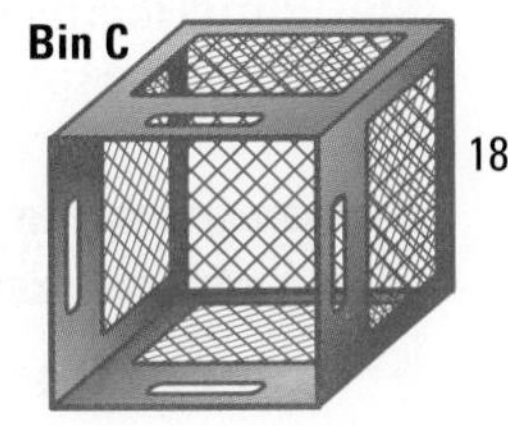

a. **Evaluate** Find the volume of each bin.

b. **Compare** How many times greater is the edge length of bin B than the edge length of bin A? How many times greater is the volume of bin B than the volume of bin A?

c. **Compare** Answer the questions in part (b) for bin A and bin C.

d. **CHALLENGE** *Explain* how multiplying the edge length of a cube by a number n affects the volume of the cube. *Justify* your explanation.

at my.hrw.com

55. **CHALLENGE** You purchase a set of 100 cube-shaped miniature magnets, each with an edge length of $\frac{1}{8}$ inch. You arrange the cubes to form larger cubes, each one with a different edge length. How many cubes can you form? What is their total volume?

1.2 Apply Order of Operations

Before You evaluated algebraic expressions and used exponents.

Now You will use the order of operations to evaluate expressions.

Why? So you can determine online music costs, as in Ex. 35.

Key Vocabulary
- **order of operations**

Mathematicians have established an **order of operations** to evaluate an expression involving more than one operation.

COMMON CORE

CC.9-12.A.SSE.1 Interpret expressions that represent a quantity in terms of its context.*

KEY CONCEPT *For Your Notebook*

Order of Operations

STEP 1 **Evaluate** expressions inside grouping symbols.

STEP 2 **Evaluate** powers.

STEP 3 **Multiply** and **divide** from left to right.

STEP 4 **Add** and **subtract** from left to right.

EXAMPLE 1 Evaluate expressions

Evaluate the expression $27 \div 3^2 \times 2 - 3$.

STEP 1 There are no grouping symbols, so go to Step 2.

STEP 2 **Evaluate** powers.

$27 \div 3^2 \times 2 - 3 = 27 \div 9 \times 2 - 3$ **Evaluate power.**

STEP 3 **Multiply** and **divide** from left to right.

$27 \div 9 \times 2 - 3 = 3 \times 2 - 3$ **Divide.**

$3 \times 2 - 3 = 6 - 3$ **Multiply.**

STEP 4 **Add** and **subtract** from left to right.

$6 - 3 = 3$ **Subtract.**

▶ The value of the expression $27 \div 3^2 \times 2 - 3$ is 3.

GUIDED PRACTICE for Example 1

Evaluate the expression.

1. $20 - 4^2$ **2.** $2 \cdot 3^2 + 4$ **3.** $32 \div 2^3 + 6$ **4.** $15 + 6^2 - 4$

GROUPING SYMBOLS Grouping symbols such as parentheses ( ) and brackets [ ] indicate that operations inside the grouping symbols should be performed first. For example, to evaluate $2 \cdot 4 + 6$, you multiply first, then add. To evaluate $2(4 + 6)$, you add first, then multiply.

EXAMPLE 2 Evaluate expressions with grouping symbols

Evaluate the expression.

a. $7(13 - 8) = 7(5)$ — Subtract within parentheses.

$= 35$ — Multiply.

b. $24 - (3^2 + 1) = 24 - (9 + 1)$ — Evaluate power.

$= 24 - 10$ — Add within parentheses.

$= 14$ — Subtract.

c. $2[30 - (8 + 13)] = 2[30 - 21]$ — Add within parentheses.

$= 2[9]$ — Subtract within brackets.

$= 18$ — Multiply.

AVOID ERRORS
When grouping symbols appear inside other grouping symbols, work from the innermost grouping symbols outward.

FRACTION BARS A fraction bar can act as a grouping symbol. Evaluate the numerator and denominator before you divide:

$$\frac{8 + 4}{5 - 2} = (8 + 4) \div (5 - 2) = 12 \div 3 = 4$$

EXAMPLE 3 Evaluate an algebraic expression

Evaluate the expression when $x = 4$.

$\frac{9x}{3(x + 2)} = \frac{9 \cdot 4}{3(4 + 2)}$ — Substitute 4 for x.

$= \frac{9 \cdot 4}{3 \cdot 6}$ — Add within parentheses.

$= \frac{36}{18}$ — Multiply.

$= 2$ — Divide.

Animated Algebra at my.hrw.com

✓ GUIDED PRACTICE for Examples 2 and 3

Evaluate the expression.

5. $4(3 + 9)$ **6.** $3(8 - 2^2)$ **7.** $2[(9 + 3) \div 4]$

Evaluate the expression when $y = 8$.

8. $y^2 - 3$ **9.** $12 - y - 1$ **10.** $\frac{10y + 1}{y + 1}$

★ **EXAMPLE 4** **Standardized Test Practice**

A group of 12 students volunteers to collect litter for one day. A sponsor provides 3 juice drinks and 2 sandwiches for each student and pays \$30 for trash bags. The sponsor's cost (in dollars) is given by the expression $12(3j + 2s) + 30$ where j is the cost of a juice drink and s is the cost of a sandwich. A juice drink costs \$1.25. A sandwich costs \$2. What is the sponsor's cost?

Ⓐ \$79 Ⓑ \$123 Ⓒ \$129 Ⓓ \$210

ELIMINATE CHOICES
You can eliminate choices A and D by estimating. When j is about 1 and s is 2, the value of the expression is about $12(3 + 4) + 30$, or \$114.

Solution

$12(3j + 2s) + 30 = 12(3 \cdot 1.25 + 2 \cdot 2) + 30$ **Substitute 1.25 for j and 2 for s.**

$= 12(3.75 + 4) + 30$ **Multiply within parentheses.**

$= 12(7.75) + 30$ **Add within parentheses.**

$= 93 + 30$ **Multiply.**

$= 123$ **Add.**

▶ The sponsor's cost is \$123. The correct answer is B. Ⓐ Ⓑ Ⓒ Ⓓ.

✓ **GUIDED PRACTICE** for Example 4

11. WHAT IF? In Example 4, suppose the number of volunteers doubles. Does the sponsor's cost double as well? *Explain.*

1.2 EXERCISES

HOMEWORK KEY

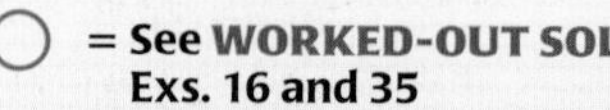

○ = **See WORKED-OUT SOLUTIONS Exs. 16 and 35**

★ = **STANDARDIZED TEST PRACTICE Exs. 2, 19, 31, 37, 39, and 40**

SKILL PRACTICE

1. VOCABULARY According to the order of operations, which operation would you perform first in simplifying $50 - 5 \times 4^2 \div 2$?

2. ★ WRITING *Describe* the steps you would use to evaluate the expression $2(3x + 1)^2$ when $x = 3$.

EXAMPLES 1 and 2 for Exs. 3–21

EVALUATING EXPRESSIONS **Evaluate the expression.**

3. $13 - 8 + 3$ **4.** $8 - 2^2$ **5.** $3 \cdot 6 - 4$ **6.** $5 \cdot 2^3 + 7$

7. $48 \div 4^2 + \frac{3}{5}$ **8.** $1 + 5^2 \div 50$ **9.** $2^4 \cdot 4 - 2 \div 8$ **10.** $4^3 \div 8 + 8$

11. $(12 + 72) \div 4$ **12.** $24 + 4(3 + 1)$ **13.** $12(6 - 3.5)^2 - 1.5$ **14.** $24 \div (8 + 4^2)$

15. $\frac{1}{2}(21 + 2^2)$ **(16.)** $\frac{1}{6}(6 + 18) - 2^2$ **17.** $\frac{3}{4}[13 - (2 + 3)]^2$ **18.** $8[20 - (9 - 5)^2]$

19. ★ **MULTIPLE CHOICE** What is the value of $3[20 - (7 - 5)^2]$?

(A) 48 (B) 56 (C) 192 (D) 972

ERROR ANALYSIS ***Describe*** **and correct the error in evaluating the expression.**

20. $(1 + 13) \div 7 + 7 = 14 \div 7 + 7$
$= 14 \div 14$
$= 1$ ✗

21. $20 - \frac{1}{2} \cdot 6^2 = 20 - 3^2$
$= 20 - 9$
$= 11$ ✗

EXAMPLE 3 for Exs. 22–31

EVALUATING EXPRESSIONS **Evaluate the expression.**

22. $4n - 12$ when $n = 7$
23. $2 + 3x^2$ when $x = 3$
24. $6t^2 - 13$ when $t = 2$
25. $11 + r^3 - 2r$ when $r = 5$
26. $5(w - 4)$ when $w = 7$
27. $3(m^2 - 2)$ when $m = 1.5$
28. $\frac{9x + 4}{3x + 1}$ when $x = 7$
29. $\frac{k^2 - 1}{k + 3}$ when $k = 5$
30. $\frac{b^3 - 21}{5b + 9}$ when $b = 3$

31. ★ **MULTIPLE CHOICE** What is the value of $\frac{x^2}{25} + 3x$ when $x = 10$?

(A) 26 (B) 34 (C) 43 (D) 105

CHALLENGE **Insert grouping symbols in the expression so that the value of the expression is 14.**

32. $9 + 39 + 22 \div 11 - 9 + 3$
33. $2 \times 2 + 3^2 - 4 + 3 \times 5$

PROBLEM SOLVING

EXAMPLE 4 for Exs. 34–37

34. **SALES** Your school's booster club sells school T-shirts. Half the T-shirts come from one supplier at a cost of \$5.95 each, and half from another supplier at a cost of \$6.15 each. The average cost (in dollars) of a T-shirt is given by the expression $\frac{5.95 + 6.15}{2}$. Find the average cost.

35. **MULTI-STEP PROBLEM** You join an online music service. The total cost (in dollars) of downloading 3 singles at \$.99 each and 2 albums at \$9.95 each is given by the expression $3 \cdot 0.99 + 2 \cdot 9.95$.

a. Find the total cost.

b. You have \$25 to spend. How much will you have left?

36. **PHYSIOLOGY** If you know how tall you were at the age of 2, you can estimate your adult height (in inches). Girls can use the expression $25 + 1.17h$ where h is the height (in inches) at the age of 2. Boys can use the expression $22.7 + 1.37h$. Estimate the adult height of each person to the nearest inch.

a. A girl who was 34 inches tall at age 2

b. A boy who was 33 inches tall at age 2

37. ★ **OPEN-ENDED** Write a numerical expression including parentheses that has the same value when you remove the parentheses.

38. **ONLINE SHOPPING** The regular shipping fee (in dollars) for an online computer store is given by the expression $0.5w + 4.49$ where w is the weight (in pounds) of the item. The fee (in dollars) for rush delivery is given by $0.99w + 6.49$. You purchase a 26.5 pound computer. How much do you save using regular shipping instead of rush delivery?

39. ★ **SHORT RESPONSE** You make and sell flags for $10 each. Each flag requires $4.50 worth of fabric. You pay $12.99 for a kit to punch holes to hang the flags. Your expenses (in dollars) are given by the expression $4.50m + 12.99$ where m is the number of flags you make. Your income is given by the expression $10s$ where s is the number of flags you sell. Your profit is equal to the difference of your income and your expenses.

   a. You make 50 flags and sell 38 of them. Find your income and your expenses. Then find your profit.

   b. *Explain* how you could use a single expression to determine your profit.

40. ★ **EXTENDED RESPONSE** Each year Heisman Trophy voters select the outstanding college football player. Each voter selects three players ranked first to third. A first place vote is worth 3 points, a second place vote is worth 2 points, and a third place vote is worth 1 point. Let f, s, and t be, respectively, the number of first place, second place, and third place votes a player gets. The table shows the votes for the winner and the runner-up in 2003.

Player	First place	Second place	Third place
Jason White	319	204	116
Larry Fitzgerald	253	233	128

   a. **Analyze** *Explain* why the expression $3f + 2s + t$ represents a player's point total.

   b. **Calculate** Use the expression in part (a) to determine how many more points Jason White got than Larry Fitzgerald got.

   c. **CHALLENGE** Can you rearrange the order of the votes for each player in such a way that Larry Fitzgerald would have won? *Explain*.

See **EXTRA PRACTICE** in Student Resources **ONLINE QUIZ** at my.hrw.com

Use Order of Operations

MATHEMATICAL PRACTICES

Use appropriate tools strategically.

QUESTION How can you use a graphing calculator to evaluate an expression?

You can use a graphing calculator to evaluate an expression. When you enter the expression, it is important to use grouping symbols so that the calculator performs operations in the correct order.

EXAMPLE Evaluate an expression

Use a graphing calculator to evaluate an expression.

Lean body mass is the mass of the skeleton, muscles, and organs. Physicians use lean body mass to determine dosages of medicine.

Scientists have developed separate formulas for the lean body masses of men and women based on their mass m (in kilograms) and height h (in meters). Lean body mass in measured in units called BMI (Body Mass Index) units.

Men: $1.10m - \frac{128m^2}{10{,}000h^2}$ **Women:** $1.07m - \frac{148m^2}{10{,}000h^2}$

Find the lean body mass (in BMI units) of a man who is 1.8 meters tall and has a mass of 80 kilograms.

Solution

Enter the expression for men in the calculator. Substitute 80 for m and 1.8 for h. Because the fraction bar is a grouping symbol, enter the denominator using parentheses.

Use the following keystrokes.

1.10 [×] 80 [−] 128 [×] 80 [x²] [÷] [(] 10000 [×] 1.8 [x²] [)]

▶ The lean body mass of a man who is 1.8 meters tall and has a mass of 80 kilograms is about 62.7 BMI units.

PRACTICE

Use a calculator to evaluate the expression for $n = 4$. Round to the nearest thousandth.

1. $3 + 5 \cdot n \div 10$
2. $2 + \frac{3n^2}{4}$
3. $\frac{83}{3n^2} - 1.3$
4. $\frac{14.2n}{8 + n^3}$
5. $\frac{7 - n}{n^2}$
6. $5n^2 + \frac{4n^3 + 1}{3}$
7. Find the lean body mass (to the nearest tenth of a BMI unit) of a woman who is 1.6 meters tall and has a mass of 54 kilograms.

Animated Algebra
my.hrw.com

Patterns and Expressions

Look for and make use of structure.

MATERIALS • graph paper

QUESTION **How can you use an algebraic expression to describe a pattern?**

EXPLORE **Create and describe a pattern**

STEP 1

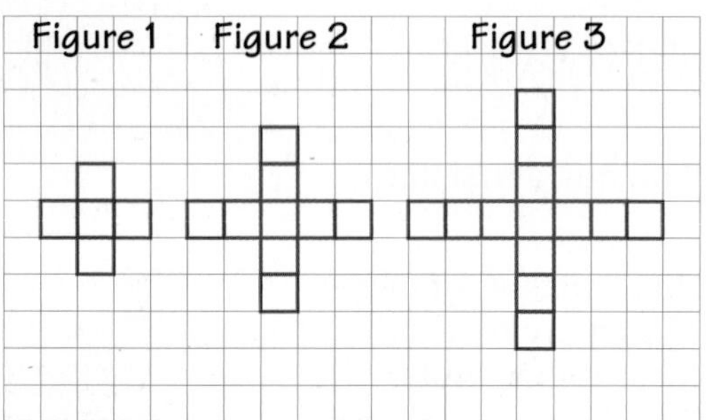

Draw a figure Draw a unit square on graph paper. Then draw a unit square against each side of the first square to form figure 1.

Copy figure 1 and draw a square on each "arm" to form figure 2. Use the same method to form figure 3.

STEP 2

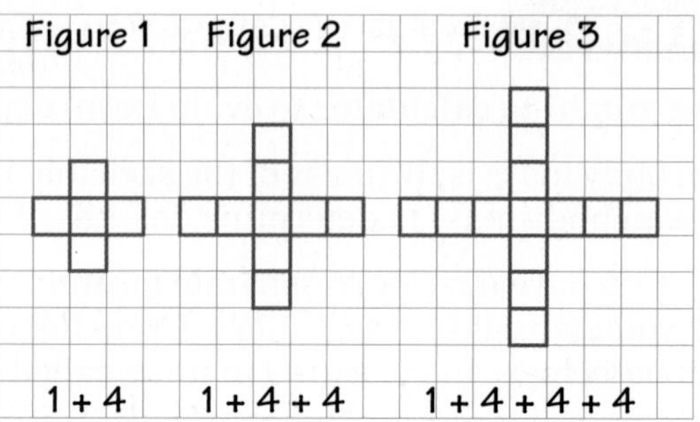

Write expressions For each figure, write a numerical expression that describes the number of squares in the figure.

DRAW CONCLUSIONS **Use your observations to complete these exercises**

In Exercises 1–3, use the pattern in Steps 1 and 2 above.

1. How is the figure number related to the number of times 4 is added in the numerical expression? Predict the number of squares in the fourth figure. Create figure 4 and check your prediction.
2. *Describe* how to calculate the number of squares in the nth figure.
3. Write an algebraic expression for the number of squares in the nth figure. (*Hint:* Remember that repeated addition can be written as multiplication.)
4. **a.** Write an algebraic expression for the number of squares in the nth figure of the pattern shown.

   b. *Explain* why the expression n^2 is not an appropriate answer to part (a). Create a pattern that can be described by the expression n^2.

Figure 1 **Figure 2** **Figure 3** **Figure 4**

1.3 Write Expressions

Before You evaluated expressions.

Now You will translate verbal phrases into expressions.

Why? So you can find a bicycling distance, as in Ex. 36.

Key Vocabulary
- **verbal model**
- **rate**
- **unit rate**

CC.9-12.A.SSE.1 Interpret expressions that represent a quantity in terms of its context.*

To translate verbal phrases into expressions, look for words that indicate mathematical operations.

KEY CONCEPT *For Your Notebook*

Translating Verbal Phrases

Operation	Verbal Phrase	Expression
Addition: sum, plus, total, more than, increased by	The sum of 2 and a number x	$2 + x$
	A number n plus 7	$n + 7$
Subtraction: difference, less than, minus, decreased by	The difference of a number n and 6	$n - 6$
	A number y minus 5	$y - 5$
Multiplication: times, product, multiplied by, of	12 times a number y	$12y$
	$\frac{1}{3}$ of a number x	$\frac{1}{3}x$
Division: quotient, divided by, divided into	The quotient of a number k and 2	$\frac{k}{2}$

Order is important when writing subtraction and division expressions. For instance, "the difference of a number n and 6" is written $n - 6$, *not* $6 - n$, and "the quotient of a number k and 2" is written $\frac{k}{2}$, *not* $\frac{2}{k}$.

EXAMPLE 1 Translate verbal phrases into expressions

AVOID ERRORS
When you translate verbal phrases, the words "the quantity" tell you what to group. In part (a), you write $6n - 4$, *not* $(6 - 4)n$.

	Verbal Phrase	Expression
a.	4 less than the quantity 6 times a number n	$6n - 4$
b.	3 times the sum of 7 and a number y	$3(7 + y)$
c.	The difference of 22 and the square of a number m	$22 - m^2$

GUIDED PRACTICE for Example 1

1. Translate the phrase "the quotient when the quantity 10 plus a number x is divided by 2" into an expression.

EXAMPLE 2 Write an expression

CHOOSE A VARIABLE
To write an expression for a real-world problem, choose a letter that reminds you of the quantity represented, such as ℓ for length.

CUTTING A RIBBON A piece of ribbon ℓ feet long is cut from a ribbon 8 feet long. Write an expression for the length (in feet) of the remaining piece.

Solution

Draw a diagram and use a specific case to help you write the expression.

Suppose the piece cut is 2 feet long.

8 ft

(8 − 2) ft | 2 ft

The remaining piece is (8 − 2) feet long.

Suppose the piece cut is ℓ feet long.

8 ft

$(8 - \ell)$ ft | ℓ ft

The remaining piece is $(8 - \ell)$ feet long.

▶ The expression $8 - \ell$ represents the length (in feet) of the remaining piece.

VERBAL MODEL A **verbal model** describes a real-world situation using words as labels and using math symbols to relate the words. You can replace the words with numbers and variables to create a *mathematical model*, such as an expression, for the real-world situation.

EXAMPLE 3 Use a verbal model to write an expression

TIPS You work with 5 other people at an ice cream stand. All the workers put their tips into a jar and share the amount in the jar equally at the end of the day. Write an expression for each person's share (in dollars) of the tips.

Solution

STEP 1 **Write** a verbal model.

STEP 2 **Translate** the verbal model into an algebraic expression. Let a represent the amount (in dollars) in the jar.

Amount in jar	÷	Number of people
a	÷	6

AVOID ERRORS
Read the statement of the problem carefully. The number of people sharing tips is 6.

▶ An expression that represents each person's share (in dollars) is $\frac{a}{6}$.

✓ GUIDED PRACTICE for Examples 2 and 3

2. **WHAT IF?** In Example 2, suppose that you cut the original ribbon into p pieces of equal length. Write an expression that represents the length (in feet) of each piece.

3. **WHAT IF?** In Example 3, suppose that each of the 6 workers contributes an equal amount for an after-work celebration. Write an expression that represents the total amount (in dollars) contributed.

RATES A **rate** is a fraction that compares two quantities measured in different units. If the denominator of the fraction is 1 unit, the rate is called a **unit rate**.

EXAMPLE 4 Find a unit rate

> **READING**
> *Per* means "for each" or "for every" and can also be represented using the symbol /, as in mi/h.

A car travels 120 miles in 2 hours. Find the unit rate in feet per second.

$$\frac{120 \text{ miles}}{2 \text{ hours}} = \frac{120 \cancel{\text{ miles}}}{2 \cancel{\text{ hours}}} \cdot \frac{5280 \text{ feet}}{1 \cancel{\text{ mile}}} \cdot \frac{1 \cancel{\text{ hour}}}{60 \cancel{\text{ minutes}}} \cdot \frac{1 \cancel{\text{ minute}}}{60 \text{ seconds}} = \frac{88 \text{ feet}}{1 \text{ second}}$$

▶ The unit rate is 88 feet per second.

EXAMPLE 5 Solve a multi-step problem

TRAINING For a training program, each day you run a given distance and then walk to cool down. One day you run 2 miles and then walk for 20 minutes at a rate of 0.1 mile per 100 seconds. What total distance do you cover?

Solution

STEP 1 **Convert** your walking rate to miles per minute.

$$\frac{0.1 \text{ mile}}{100 \cancel{\text{ seconds}}} \cdot \frac{60 \cancel{\text{ seconds}}}{1 \text{ minute}} = \frac{6 \text{ miles}}{100 \text{ minutes}} = \frac{0.06 \text{ mile}}{1 \text{ minute}}$$

STEP 2 **Write** a verbal model and then an expression. Let m be the number of minutes you walk.

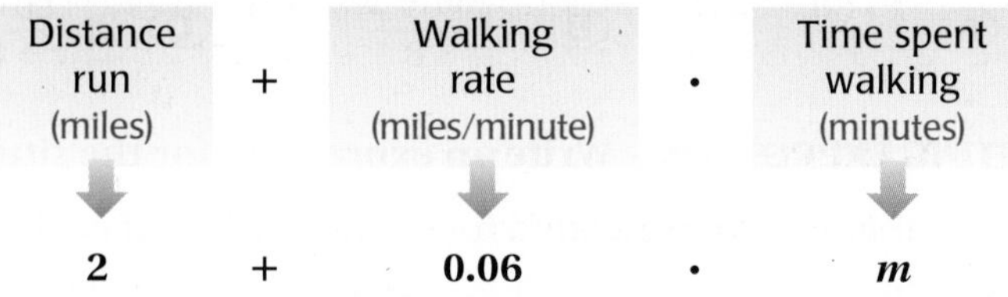

Use *unit analysis* to check that the expression $2 + 0.06m$ is reasonable.

$$\text{miles} + \frac{\text{miles}}{\cancel{\text{minute}}} \cdot \cancel{\text{minutes}} = \text{miles} + \text{miles} = \text{miles}$$

Because the units are miles, the expression is reasonable.

> **USE UNIT ANALYSIS**
> You expect the answer to be a distance in miles. You can use unit analysis, also called *dimensional analysis*, to check that the expression produces an answer in miles.

STEP 3 **Evaluate** the expression when $m = 20$.

$2 + 0.06(20) = 3.2$

▶ You cover a total distance of 3.2 miles.

✓ GUIDED PRACTICE for Examples 4 and 5

4. WHAT IF? In Example 5, suppose tomorrow you run 3 miles and then walk for 15 minutes at a rate of 0.1 mile per 90 seconds. What total distance will you cover?

1.3 EXERCISES

HOMEWORK KEY ○ = See **WORKED-OUT SOLUTIONS** Exs. 11, 21, and 33
★ = **STANDARDIZED TEST PRACTICE** Exs. 2, 13, 14, 34, and 37

SKILL PRACTICE

1. **VOCABULARY** Copy and complete: A(n) __?__ is a fraction that compares two quantities measured in different units.

2. ★ **WRITING** *Explain* how to write $\frac{20 \text{ miles}}{4 \text{ hours}}$ as a unit rate.

EXAMPLE 1 for Exs. 3–14

TRANSLATING PHRASES Translate the verbal phrase into an expression.

3. 8 more than a number x
4. The product of 6 and a number y
5. $\frac{1}{2}$ of a number m
6. 50 divided by a number h
7. The difference of 7 and a number n
8. The sum of 15 and a number x
9. The quotient of twice a number t and 12
10. 3 less than the square of a number p
11. 7 less than twice a number k
12. 5 more than 3 times a number w

13. ★ **MULTIPLE CHOICE** Which expression represents the phrase "the product of 15 and the quantity 12 more than a number x"?

Ⓐ $15 + 12 \cdot x$ Ⓑ $(15 + 12)x$ Ⓒ $15(x + 12)$ Ⓓ $15 \cdot 12 + x$

14. ★ **MULTIPLE CHOICE** Which expression represents the phrase "twice the quotient of 50 and the sum of a number y and 8"?

Ⓐ $\frac{2 \cdot 50}{y} + 8$ Ⓑ $2\left(\frac{50 + y}{8}\right)$ Ⓒ $2\left(\frac{50}{y + 8}\right)$ Ⓓ $\frac{2}{50} + (y + 8)$

EXAMPLES 2 and 3 for Exs. 15–21

WRITING EXPRESSIONS Write an expression for the situation.

15. Number of tokens needed for v video games if each game takes 4 tokens
16. Number of pages of a 5 page article left to read if you've read p pages
17. Each person's share if p people share 16 slices of pizza equally
18. Amount you spend if you buy a shirt for \$20 and jeans for j dollars
19. Number of days left in the week if d days have passed so far
20. Number of hours in m minutes
21. Number of months in y years

EXAMPLE 4 for Exs. 22–27

UNIT RATES Find the unit rate in feet per second.

22. $\frac{300 \text{ yards}}{1 \text{ minute}}$
23. $\frac{240 \text{ yards}}{1 \text{ hour}}$
24. $\frac{180 \text{ miles}}{2 \text{ hours}}$
25. $\frac{171 \text{ miles}}{3 \text{ hours}}$

ERROR ANALYSIS ***Describe*** **and correct the error in the units.**

26. $\frac{\$2}{\text{foot}} \cdot 24 \text{ feet} = \frac{\$48}{\text{ft}^2}$ 

27. $9 \text{ yards} \cdot \frac{3 \text{ feet}}{1 \text{ yard}} \cdot \frac{\$2}{\text{foot}} = \frac{\$54}{\text{ft}}$ 

COMPARING RATES In Exercises 28 and 29, tell which rate is greater.

28. $1\frac{1}{4}$ miles in 2 minutes and 4 seconds, or $1\frac{3}{16}$ miles in 1 minute and 55 seconds

29. $1.60 for 5 minutes, or $19.50 for 1 hour

30. CHALLENGE Look for a pattern in the expressions shown below. Use the pattern to write an expression for the sum of the whole numbers from 1 to n. Then find the sum of the whole numbers from 1 to 50.

$1 + 2 = \frac{2 \cdot 3}{2}$ $\quad$ $1 + 2 + 3 = \frac{3 \cdot 4}{2}$ $\quad$ $1 + 2 + 3 + 4 = \frac{4 \cdot 5}{2}$

PROBLEM SOLVING

EXAMPLE 5 for Exs. 31–34

31. TICKET PRICES Tickets to a science museum cost $19.95 each. There is a $3 charge for each order no matter how many tickets are ordered. Write an expression for the cost (in dollars) of ordering tickets. Then find the total cost if you order 5 tickets.

32. FOSSIL FUELS Fossil fuels are produced by the decay of organic material over millions of years. To make one gallon of gas, it takes about 98 tons of organic material, roughly the amount of wheat that could be harvested in a 40 acre field. Write an expression for the amount (in tons) of organic material it takes to make g gallons of gas. How many tons would it take to make enough gas to fill a car's 20 gallon gas tank?

33. MULTI-STEP PROBLEM A 48 ounce container of juice costs $2.64. A 64 ounce container of the same juice costs $3.84.

a. Find the cost per ounce of each container.

b. Which size container costs less per ounce?

c. You want to buy 192 ounces of juice. How much do you save using the container size from your answer to part (b)?

34. ★ OPEN-ENDED *Describe* a real-world situation that can be modeled by the rate $\frac{30}{x}$ where x is a period of time (in hours). Identify the units for 30. Choose a value for x and find the unit rate.

35. WILDLIFE EDUCATION A wildlife center presents a program about birds of prey. The center charges a basic fee of $325 and an additional fee for each bird exhibited. If 5 birds are exhibited, the additional fee is $125. What is the total cost if 7 birds are exhibited?

36. CYCLING To prepare for a bicycling event, you warm up each day at a moderate pace and then you ride hard for a number of miles. One day, you warm up for 15 minutes at a rate of 0.1 mile per 25 seconds and then you ride hard for 12 miles. What total distance do you cover?

37. ★ **EXTENDED RESPONSE** A national survey determines the champion tree in a species. The champion is the tree with the greatest score, based on the tree's girth, its height, and its crown spread as shown.

A tree's score is the sum of the girth in inches, the height in feet, and $\frac{1}{4}$ the crown spread in feet. The data for three champion trees are given. Note that the girth is given in feet.

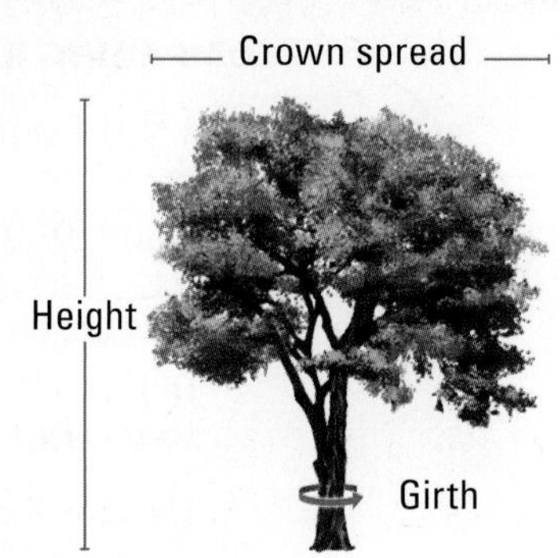

Species	Girth (ft)	Height (ft)	Crown spread (ft)
Narrowleaf cottonwood	12	97	24
Green ash	21.5	95	95
Green buttonwood	14.5	51	68

a. **Write** Write an expression for a tree's score.

b. **Evaluate** Find the score for each tree in the table.

c. **CHALLENGE** Let n be any number greater than 0. Which change would have the greatest effect on a tree's score, an increase of n feet in the girth, in the height, or in the crown spread? *Explain* your reasoning.

QUIZ

Evaluate the expression.

1. $y + 10$ when $y = 43$
2. $15 - b$ when $b = 9$
3. t^2 when $t = 20$
4. $3n - 5$ when $n = 8$
5. $2y^2 - 1$ when $y = 5$
6. $\frac{3x - 6}{8}$ when $x = 8$

Translate the verbal phrase into an expression.

7. 7 less than a number y
8. 5 more than a number t
9. Twice a number k
10. **CAMPING** The rental cost for a campsite is \$25 plus \$2 per person. Write an expression for the total cost. Then find the total cost for 5 people.

See **EXTRA PRACTICE** in Student Resources **ONLINE QUIZ** at my.hrw.com

1.4 Write Equations and Inequalities

Before You translated verbal phrases into expressions.

Now You will translate verbal sentences into equations or inequalities.

Why So you can calculate team competition statistics, as in Ex. 41.

Key Vocabulary
- equation
- inequality
- open sentence
- solution of an equation
- solution of an inequality

CC.9-12.A.CED.1 Create equations and inequalities in one variable and use them to solve problems.*

An **equation** is a mathematical sentence formed by placing the symbol = between two expressions. An **inequality** is a mathematical sentence formed by placing one of the symbols <, ≤, >, or ≥ between two expressions.

An **open sentence** is an equation or an inequality that contains an algebraic expression.

KEY CONCEPT *For Your Notebook*

Symbol	Meaning	Associated Words
$=$	is equal to	the same as
$<$	is less than	fewer than
$\le$	is less than or equal to	at most, no more than
$>$	is greater than	more than
$\ge$	is greater than or equal to	at least, no less than

COMBINING INEQUALITIES Sometimes two inequalities are combined. For example, the inequalities $x > 4$ and $x < 9$ can be combined to form the inequality $4 < x < 9$, which is read "x is greater than 4 and less than 9."

EXAMPLE 1 Write equations and inequalities

	Verbal Sentence	Equation or Inequality
a.	The difference of twice a number k and 8 is 12.	$2k - 8 = 12$
b.	The product of 6 and a number n is at least 24.	$6n \ge 24$
c.	A number y is no less than 5 and no more than 13.	$5 \le y \le 13$

 Animated Algebra at my.hrw.com

✓ **GUIDED PRACTICE** for Example 1

1. Write an equation or an inequality: The quotient of a number p and 12 is at least 30.

SOLUTIONS When you substitute a number for the variable in an open sentence like $x + 2 = 5$ or $2y > 6$, the resulting statement is either true or false. If the statement is true, the number is a **solution of the equation** or a **solution of the inequality**.

EXAMPLE 2 Check possible solutions

Check whether 3 is a solution of the equation or inequality.

Equation/Inequality	Substitute	Conclusion
a. $8 - 2x = 2$	$8 - 2(3) \stackrel{?}{=} 2$	$2 = 2$ ✓ 3 is a solution.
b. $4x - 5 = 6$	$4(3) - 5 \stackrel{?}{=} 6$	$7 = 6$ ✗ 3 is *not* a solution.
c. $2z + 5 > 12$	$2(3) + 5 \stackrel{?}{>} 12$	$11 > 12$ ✗ 3 is *not* a solution.
d. $5 + 3n \le 20$	$5 + 3(3) \stackrel{?}{\le} 20$	$14 \le 20$ ✓ 3 is a solution.

READING
A question mark above a symbol indicates a question. For instance, $8 - 2(3) \stackrel{?}{=} 2$ means "Is $8 - 2(3)$ equal to 2?"

USING MENTAL MATH Some equations are simple enough to solve using mental math. Think of the equation as a question. Once you answer the question, check the solution.

EXAMPLE 3 Use mental math to solve an equation

Equation	Think	Solution	Check
a. $x + 4 = 10$	What number plus 4 equals 10?	6	$6 + 4 = 10$ ✓
b. $20 - y = 8$	20 minus what number equals 8?	12	$20 - 12 = 8$ ✓
c. $6n = 42$	6 times what number equals 42?	7	$6(7) = 42$ ✓
d. $\frac{a}{5} = 9$	What number divided by 5 equals 9?	45	$\frac{45}{5} = 9$ ✓

✓ **GUIDED PRACTICE** for Examples 2 and 3

Check whether the given number is a solution of the equation or inequality.

2. $9 - x = 4$; 5 **3.** $b + 5 < 15$; 7 **4.** $2n + 3 \ge 21$; 9

Solve the equation using mental math.

5. $m + 6 = 11$ **6.** $5x = 40$ **7.** $\frac{r}{4} = 10$

EXAMPLE 4 Solve a multi-step problem

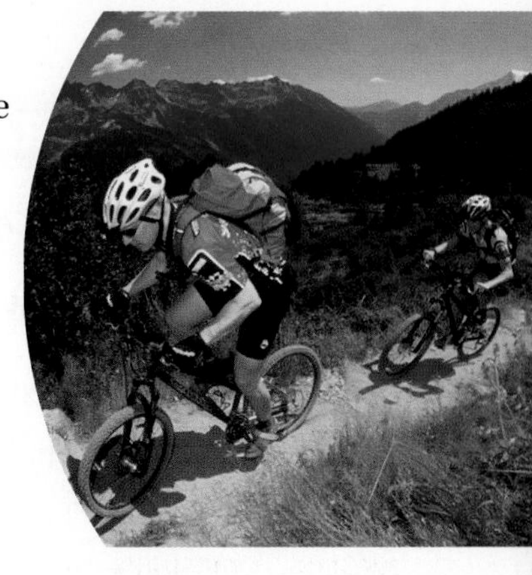

MOUNTAIN BIKING The last time you and 3 friends went to a mountain bike park, you had a coupon for \$10 off and paid \$17 for 4 tickets. What is the regular price of 4 tickets? If you pay the regular price this time and share it equally, how much does each person pay?

Solution

STEP 1 **Write** a verbal model. Let p be the regular price of 4 tickets. Write an equation.

Regular price	−	Amount of coupon	=	Amount paid
↓		↓		↓
p	−	10	=	17

STEP 2 **Use** mental math to solve the equation $p - 10 = 17$. Think: 10 less than what number is 17? Because $27 - 10 = 17$, the solution is 27.

▶ The regular price for 4 tickets is \$27.

STEP 3 **Find** the cost per person: $\frac{\$27}{4 \text{ people}} = \$6.75$ per person

▶ Each person pays \$6.75.

EXAMPLE 5 Write and check a solution of an inequality

BASKETBALL A basketball player scored 351 points last year. If the player plays 18 games this year, will an average of 20 points per game be enough to beat last year's total?

Solution

STEP 1 **Write** a verbal model. Let p be the average number of points per game. Write an inequality.

Number of games	•	Points per game	>	Total points last year
↓		↓		↓
18	•	p	>	351

USE UNIT ANALYSIS
Unit analysis shows that games $\cdot \frac{\text{points}}{\text{games}} =$ points, so the inequality is reasonable.

STEP 2 **Check** that 20 is a solution of the inequality $18p > 351$. Because $18(20) = 360$ and $360 > 351$, 20 is a solution. ✓

▶ An average of 20 points per game will be enough.

✓ GUIDED PRACTICE for Examples 4 and 5

8. **WHAT IF?** In Example 4, suppose that the price of 4 tickets with a half-off coupon is \$15. What is each person's share if you pay full price?

9. **WHAT IF?** In Example 5, suppose that the player plays 16 games. Would an average of 22 points per game be enough to beat last year's total?

1.4 EXERCISES

HOMEWORK KEY

○ = See **WORKED-OUT SOLUTIONS** Exs. 7 and 41

★ = **STANDARDIZED TEST PRACTICE** Exs. 2, 16, 37, 44, 45, and 46

SKILL PRACTICE

1. **VOCABULARY** Give an example of an open sentence.

2. ★ **WRITING** *Describe* the difference between an expression and an equation.

EXAMPLE 1 for Exs. 3–16

WRITING OPEN SENTENCES **Write an equation or an inequality.**

3. The sum of 42 and a number n is equal to 51.
4. The difference of a number z and 11 is equal to 35.
5. The difference of 9 and the quotient of a number t and 6 is 5.
6. The sum of 12 and the quantity 8 times a number k is equal to 48.
7. The product of 9 and the quantity 5 more than a number t is less than 6.
8. The product of 4 and a number w is at most 51.
9. The sum of a number b and 3 is greater than 8 and less than 12.
10. The product of 8 and a number k is greater than 4 and no more than 16.
11. The difference of a number t and 7 is greater than 10 and less than 20.

STORE SALES **Write an inequality for the price p (in dollars) described.**

12. 

13. 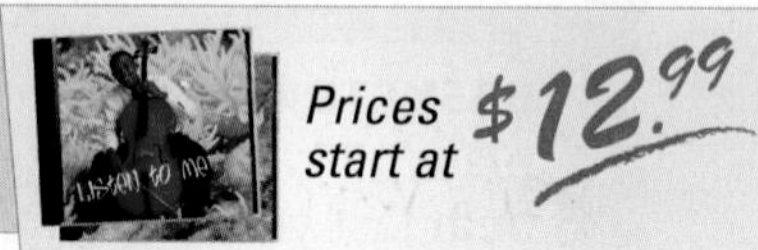

ERROR ANALYSIS ***Describe*** **and correct the error in writing the verbal sentence as an equation or an inequality.**

14. The sum of a number n and 4 is no more than 13.

$n + 4 < 13$ ✗

15. The quotient of a number t and 4.2 is at most 15.

$\frac{t}{4.2} > 15$ ✗

16. ★ **MULTIPLE CHOICE** Which inequality corresponds to the sentence "The product of a number b and 3 is no less than 12"?

Ⓐ $3b < 12$　Ⓑ $3b \le 12$　Ⓒ $3b > 12$　Ⓓ $3b \ge 12$

EXAMPLE 2 for Exs. 17–28

CHECK POSSIBLE SOLUTIONS **Check whether the given number is a solution of the equation or inequality.**

17. $x + 9 = 17; 8$
18. $9 + 4y = 17; 1$
19. $6f - 7 = 29; 5$
20. $\frac{k}{5} + 9 = 11; 10$
21. $\frac{r}{3} - 4 = 4; 12$
22. $\frac{x-5}{3} \ge 2.8; 11$
23. $15 - 4y > 6; 2$
24. $y - 3.5 < 6; 9$
25. $2 + 3x \le 8; 2$
26. $2p - 1 \ge 7; 3$
27. $4z - 5 < 3; 2$
28. $3z + 7 > 20; 4$

EXAMPLE 3
for Exs. 29–34

MENTAL MATH **Solve the equation using mental math.**

29. $x + 8 = 13$ **30.** $y + 16 = 25$ **31.** $z - 11 = 1$

32. $5w = 20$ **33.** $8b = 72$ **34.** $\frac{f}{6} = 4$

EQUATIONS AND INEQUALITIES **In Exercises 35 and 36, write an open sentence. Then check whether $3\frac{1}{2}$ is a solution of the open sentence.**

35. 2 less than the product of 3 and a number x is equal to the sum of x and 5.

36. 4 more than twice a number k is no greater than the sum of k and 11.

37. ★ **MULTIPLE CHOICE** Which equation has the same solution as $z - 9 = 3$?

Ⓐ $z - 4 = 16$ Ⓑ $\frac{1}{2}z = 7$ Ⓒ $z + 15 = 27$ Ⓓ $5z = 45$

38. **CHALLENGE** Use mental math to solve the equation $3x + 4 = 19$. *Explain* your thinking.

PROBLEM SOLVING

EXAMPLES 4 and 5
for Exs. 39–43

39. **CHARITY WALK** You are taking part in a charity walk, and you have walked 12.5 miles so far. Your goal is to walk 20 miles. How many more miles do you need to walk to meet your goal?

40. **COMPACT DISCS** You buy a storage rack that holds 40 CDs. You have 27 CDs. Write an inequality that describes how many more CDs you can buy and still have no more CDs than the rack can hold. You buy 15 CDs. Will they all still fit?

41. **ECO-CHALLENGE** Eco-Challenge Fiji was a competition that included jungle trekking, ocean swimming, mountain biking, and river kayaking. In 2002, the U.S. team finished second about 6 hours after the winning team from New Zealand. The U.S. team finished in about 173 hours. What was the winning team's time?

42. **BAKING MEASUREMENTS** You are baking batches of cookies for a bake sale. Each batch takes 2.5 cups of flour. You have 18 cups of flour. Can you bake 8 batches? *Explain.*

43. **EMPLOYMENT** Your friend takes a job cleaning up a neighbor's yard and mowing the grass, and asks you and two other friends to help. Your friend divides the amount the neighbor pays equally among all the members of the group. Each of you got \$25. How much did the neighbor pay?

44. ★ **OPEN-ENDED** Describe a real-world situation you could model using the equation $5x = 50$. Use mental math to solve the equation. *Explain* what the solution means in this situation.

45. ★ **SHORT RESPONSE** You have two part-time jobs. You earn $6 per hour running errands and $5 per hour walking dogs. You can work a total of 10 hours this weekend and hope to earn at least $55. Let r be the number of hours you spend running errands.

a. Write an inequality that describes the situation. Your inequality should involve only one variable, r.

b. If you spend the same amount of time at each job, will you meet your goal? *Explain.*

c. Can you meet your goal by working all 10 hours at only one job? *Explain.*

46. ★ **EXTENDED RESPONSE** Your school's service club is sponsoring a dance in the school gym to raise money for a local charity. The expenses will be $600. The club members will sell tickets for $10. They hope to raise enough money to cover the expenses and have enough left to donate $1000 to the charity.

a. How many tickets must they sell to cover their expenses?

b. How many tickets must they sell to cover their expenses and meet their goal?

c. The school allows no more than 200 students in the gymnasium for a dance. Can the club members sell enough tickets to exceed their goal? What is the greatest possible amount by which they can exceed their goal? *Explain* your reasoning.

47. CHALLENGE You and your friend are reading the same series of science fiction books. You tell your friend, "I've read 3 times as many books as you have." Your friend replies, "You've read only 4 more books than I have." How many books have each of you read?

48. CHALLENGE Each of the long sides of a rectangle has a length of x inches. Each of the other sides is 1 inch shorter than the long sides. The perimeter of the rectangle is 22 inches. Find the length and the width of the rectangle. *Justify* your answer.

MIXED REVIEW *of Problem Solving*

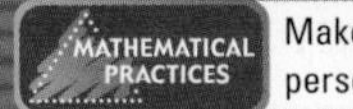

Make sense of problems and persevere in solving them.

1. **MULTI-STEP PROBLEM** You are making a photo quilt by transferring photos to squares of fabric. Each square should be big enough so that you can turn over an edge $\frac{5}{8}$ inch long on each side and have a finished square with a side length of $5\frac{3}{4}$ inches.
   a. What are the dimensions of each fabric square?
   b. How many square inches of fabric do you need if you want to include 48 squares?
   c. The fabric you buy is 36 inches wide. How long a piece of fabric do you need?
   d. You buy a piece of fabric that has the length you found in part (c). Once you've cut all the squares, how many square inches of fabric are left over?

2. **MULTI-STEP PROBLEM** A rule of thumb states that the ideal weight (in ounces) of a baseball bat for a high school baseball player is 5 ounces more than one third of the player's height (in inches).

   a. Write an expression that describes the ideal weight (in ounces) of a bat for a high school baseball player who is h inches tall.
   b. One player was 66 inches tall last year. This year the player is 69 inches tall. How much heavier should the player's new bat be than the bat used last year?

3. **SHORT RESPONSE** You collect miniature cars and display them on shelves that hold 20 cars each.
   a. Which expression would you evaluate to find the number of shelves you need for x cars: $20x$, $\frac{x}{20}$, or $\frac{20}{x}$? *Justify* your choice.
   b. Find the number of shelves you need to display 120 cars.

4. **OPEN-ENDED** *Describe* a real-world situation that you could model with the inequality $3x < 15$. *Explain* what a solution of the inequality means in this situation.

5. **SHORT RESPONSE** You pay \$7.50 for 3 quarts of strawberries. You realize that you need more strawberries for your recipe. You return to the store with \$4.50. Will you have enough money to buy 2 more quarts of strawberries? *Explain* your reasoning.

6. **EXTENDED RESPONSE** The number of calories in one serving of any food is the sum of the calories from fat, protein, and carbohydrate. The table shows the calories in 1 gram of each of the three food components.

Component	Calories in 1 gram
Fat	9
Protein	4
Carbohydrate	4

   a. Write an expression for the total number of calories in a serving of food that contains f grams of fat, p grams of protein, and c grams of carbohydrate.
   b. A serving of cheddar cheese contains 14 grams of fat, 11 grams of protein, and 1 gram of carbohydrate. How many calories are in a serving of cheddar cheese?
   c. A 100 pound teenager requires about 45 grams of protein per day. If the teenager tried to get all the required protein for one day from cheddar cheese, how many calories would the teenager consume? *Explain.*

7. **GRIDDED ANSWER** You are comparing two dorm-size refrigerators, both with cube-shaped interiors. One model has an interior edge length of 14 inches. Another model has an interior edge length of 16 inches. How many more cubic inches of storage space does the larger model have?

1.5 Use a Problem Solving Plan

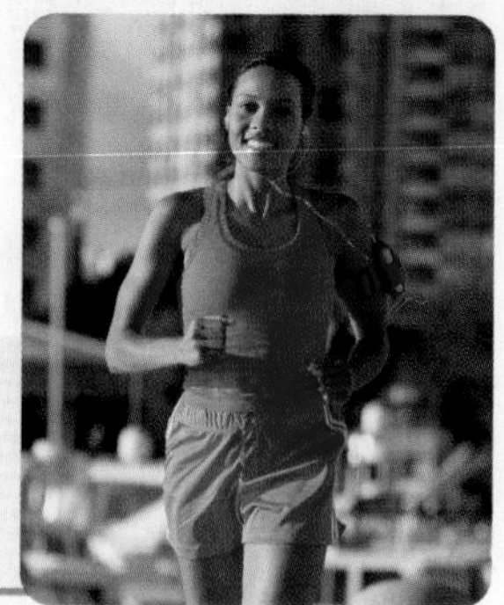

Before You used problem solving strategies.

Now You will use a problem solving plan to solve problems.

Why? So you can determine a route, as in Example 1.

Key Vocabulary
- formula

CC.9-12.A.CED.1 Create equations and inequalities in one variable and use them to solve problems.*

KEY CONCEPT *For Your Notebook*

A Problem Solving Plan

STEP 1 **Read and Understand** Read the problem carefully. Identify what you know and what you want to find out.

STEP 2 **Make a Plan** Decide on an approach to solving the problem.

STEP 3 **Solve the Problem** Carry out your plan. Try a new approach if the first one isn't successful.

STEP 4 **Look Back** Once you obtain an answer, check that it is reasonable.

EXAMPLE 1 Read a problem and make a plan

RUNNING You run in a city. Short blocks are north-south and are 0.1 mile long. Long blocks are east-west and are 0.15 mile long. You will run 2 long blocks east, a number of short blocks south, 2 long blocks west, and back to your start. You want to run 2 miles at a rate of 7 miles per hour. How many short blocks must you run?

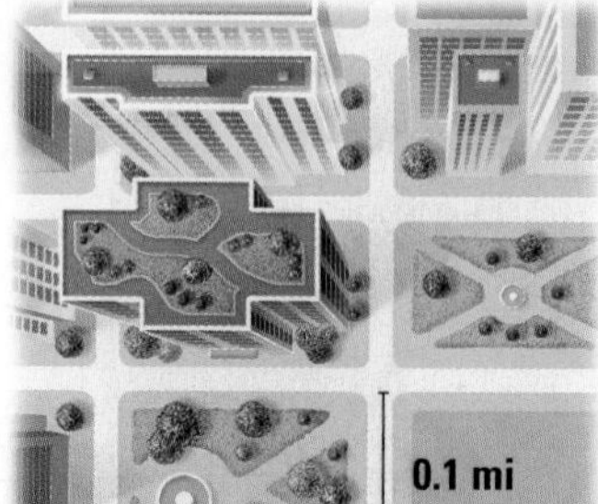

Solution

ANOTHER WAY For an alternative method for solving the problem in Example 1, see the **Problem Solving Workshop**.

STEP 1 **Read and Understand**

What do you know?

You know the length of each size block, the number of long blocks you will run, and the total distance you want to run.

You can conclude that you must run an even number of short blocks because you run the same number of short blocks in each direction.

What do you want to find out?

You want to find out the number of short blocks you should run so that, along with the 4 long blocks, you run 2 miles.

STEP 2 **Make a Plan** Use what you know to write a verbal model that represents what you want to find out. Then write an equation and solve it, as in Example 2.

EXAMPLE 2 Solve a problem and look back

Solve the problem in Example 1 by carrying out the plan. Then check your answer.

Solution

> **IDENTIFY IRRELEVANT INFORMATION**
> The rate at which you run is given, but it is not needed to solve the problem. That information is irrelevant. All other given information is relevant, and no information needed to solve the problem is missing.

STEP 3 **Solve the Problem** Write a verbal model. Then write an equation. Let s be the number of short blocks you run.

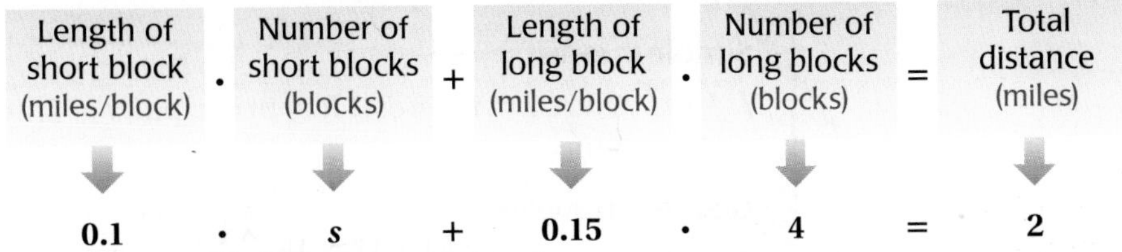

The equation is $0.1s + 0.6 = 2$. One way to solve the equation is to use the strategy *guess, check, and revise.*

Guess an even number that is easily multiplied by 0.1. Try 20.

Check whether 20 is a solution.

$0.1s + 0.6 = 2$ **Write equation.**

$0.1(20) + 0.6 \stackrel{?}{=} 2$ **Substitute 20 for *s*.**

$2.6 = 2$ ✗ **Simplify; 20 does not check.**

Revise. Because $2.6 > 2$, try an even number less than 20. Try 14.

Check whether 14 is a solution.

$0.1s + 0.6 = 2$ **Write equation.**

$0.1(14) + 0.6 \stackrel{?}{=} 2$ **Substitute 14 for *s*.**

$2 = 2$ ✓ **Simplify.**

▶ To run 2 miles, you should run 14 short blocks along with the 4 long blocks you run.

STEP 4 **Look Back** Check your answer by making a table. You run 0.6 mile on long blocks. Each two short blocks add 0.2 mile.

Short blocks	0	2	4	6	8	10	12	14
Total distance	0.6	0.8	1.0	1.2	1.4	1.6	1.8	2.0

The total distance is 2 miles when you run 4 long blocks and 14 short blocks. The answer in Step 3 is correct.

at my.hrw.com

✓ GUIDED PRACTICE for Examples 1 and 2

1. **WHAT IF?** In Example 1, suppose that you want to run a total distance of 3 miles. How many short blocks should you run?

FORMULAS A **formula** is an equation that relates two or more quantities. You may find it helpful to use formulas in problem solving.

REVIEW FORMULAS
For additional formulas, see pp. SR16–SR20 and the Table of Formulas on pp. T2–T3.

KEY CONCEPT — *For Your Notebook*

Formulas

Temperature

$C = \frac{5}{9}(F - 32)$ where F = degrees Fahrenheit and C = degrees Celsius

Simple interest

$I = Prt$ where I = interest, P = principal, r = interest rate (as a decimal), and t = time

Distance traveled

$d = rt$ where d = distance traveled, r = rate (constant or average speed), and t = time

Profit

$P = I - E$ where P = profit, I = income, and E = expenses

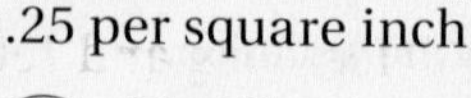

Standardized Test Practice

You are making a leather book cover. You need a rectangular piece of leather as shown. Find the cost of the piece if leather costs $.25 per square inch.

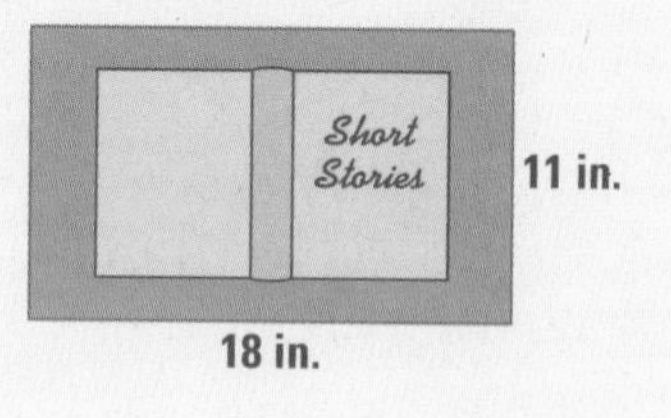

Ⓐ $14.50 Ⓑ $49.50

Ⓒ $58.00 Ⓓ $198.00

ELIMINATE CHOICES
You can eliminate choices A and D by estimating. The area of the piece of leather is about 200 square inches, and $.25(200) is about $50.

Solution

Use the formula for the area of a rectangle, $A = \ell w$, with $\ell = 18$ inches and $w = 11$ inches.

$A = \ell w$	**Write area formula.**
$= 18(11)$	**Substitute 18 for ℓ and 11 for w.**
$= 198$	**Simplify.**

The area is 198 square inches, so the total cost is $.25(198) = $49.50.

▶ The correct answer is B. Ⓐ Ⓑ Ⓒ Ⓓ

GUIDED PRACTICE for Example 3

2. **GARDENING** A gardener determines the cost of planting daffodil bulbs to be $2.40 per square foot. How much will it cost to plant daffodil bulbs in a rectangular garden that is 12 feet long and 5 feet wide?

Ⓐ $40.80 Ⓑ $60 Ⓒ $81.60 Ⓓ $144

1.5 EXERCISES

HOMEWORK KEY

○ = See **WORKED-OUT SOLUTIONS** Exs. 5 and 17

★ = **STANDARDIZED TEST PRACTICE** Exs. 2, 11, 12, 20, and 22

◆ = **MULTIPLE REPRESENTATIONS** Ex. 21

SKILL PRACTICE

1. **VOCABULARY** Give an example of a formula.

2. ★ **WRITING** *Describe* how you can use a formula to solve the following problem: The inner edges of a cube-shaped pot have a length of 1.5 feet. How much does it cost to fill the planter if soil costs $4 per cubic foot?

EXAMPLES 1 and 2 for Exs. 3–5

READING AND UNDERSTANDING In Exercises 3–5, identify what you know and what you need to find out. Identify any missing or irrelevant information. You do *not* need to solve the problem.

3. **CRAFT SHOW** You make dog collars and anticipate selling all of them at a craft fair. You spent $85 for materials and hope to make a profit of $90. How much should you charge for each collar?

4. **DISTANCE RUNNING** One day Paul ran at a rate of 0.15 mile per minute for 40 minutes. The next day Paul and Jen ran together at a rate of 0.16 mile per minute for 50 minutes. How far did Paul run altogether?

5. **TEMPERATURE** One day, the temperature in Rome, Italy, was 30°C. The temperature in Dallas, Texas, was 83°F. Which temperature was higher?

ERROR ANALYSIS *Describe* and correct the error in solving the problem.

A town is fencing a rectangular field that is 200 feet long and 150 feet wide. At $10 per foot, how much will it cost to fence the field?

6.
$P = 200 + 150 = 350$
$\$10(350) = \$3500$ ✗

7.
$A = (200)(150) = 30{,}000$
$\$10(30{,}000) = \$300{,}000$

EXAMPLE 3 for Exs. 8–12

CHOOSING A FORMULA In Exercises 8–10, state the formula that is needed to solve the problem. You do *not* need to solve the problem.

8. The temperature is 68°F. What is the temperature in degrees Celsius?

9. A store buys a baseball cap for $5 and sells it for $20. What is the profit?

10. Find the area of a triangle with a base of 25 feet and a height of 8 feet.

11. ★ **MULTIPLE CHOICE** What is the interest on $1200 invested for 2 years in an account that earns simple interest at a rate of 5% per year?

Ⓐ $12 Ⓑ $60 Ⓒ $120 Ⓓ $240

12. ★ **MULTIPLE CHOICE** A car travels at an average speed of 55 miles per hour. How many miles does the car travel in 2.5 hours?

Ⓐ 22 miles Ⓑ 57.5 miles Ⓒ 110 miles Ⓓ 137.5 miles

13. **CHALLENGE** Write a formula for the length ℓ of a rectangle given its perimeter P and its width w. *Justify* your thinking.

PROBLEM SOLVING

EXAMPLES 1, 2, and 3 for Exs. 14–18

14. **DVD STORAGE** A stackable storage rack holds 22 DVDs and costs $21. How much would it cost to buy enough racks to hold 127 DVDs?

15. **FRAMING** For an art project, you make a square print with a side length of 8 inches. You make a frame using strips of wood $1\frac{1}{4}$ inches wide. What is the area of the frame?

16. **MOUNTAIN BOARDS** You have saved $70 to buy a mountain board that costs $250. You plan to save $10 each week. How many weeks will it take to save for the mountain board?

17. **HIKING** You are hiking. The total weight of your backpack and its contents is $13\frac{3}{8}$ pounds. You want to carry no more than 15 pounds. How many extra water bottles can you add to your backpack if each bottle weighs $\frac{3}{4}$ pound?

18. **PIZZA** Thick crust pizza requires about 0.15 ounce of dough per square inch of surface area. You have two rectangular pans, one that is 16 inches long and 14 inches wide, and one that is 15.5 inches long and 10 inches wide. How much more dough do you need to make a thick crust pizza in the larger pan than in the smaller one?

19. **SONAR** A diver uses a sonar device to determine the distance to her diving partner. The device sends a sound wave and records the time it takes for the wave to reach the diving partner and return to the device. Suppose the wave travels at a rate of about 4800 feet per second.

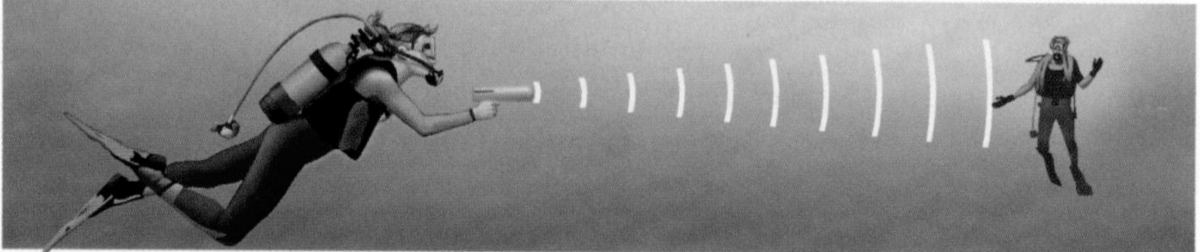

   a. The wave returns 0.2 second after it was sent. How far did the wave travel?

   b. How far away is the diving partner?

20. ★ **EXTENDED RESPONSE** A gardener is reseeding a city park that has the shape of a right triangle with a base of 150 feet and a height of 200 feet. The third side of the park is 250 feet long.

   a. One bag of grass seed covers 3750 square feet and costs $27.50. How many bags are needed? What is the total cost?

   b. Wire fencing costs $23.19 for each 50 foot roll. How much does it cost to buy fencing to enclose the area?

   c. Fence posts cost $3.19 each and should be placed every 5 feet. How many posts are needed, and how much will they cost altogether? *Explain.*

○ = See **WORKED-OUT SOLUTIONS** in Student Resources ★ = **STANDARDIZED TEST PRACTICE** ◆ = **MULTIPLE REPRESENTATIONS**

21. ◆ **MULTIPLE REPRESENTATIONS** Homeowners are building a square closet in a rectangular room that is 24 feet long and 18 feet wide. They want the remaining floor area to be at least 400 square feet. Because they don't want to cut any of the 1 foot by 1 foot square floor tiles, the side length of the closet floor should be a whole number of feet.

a. **Making a Table** Make a table showing possible side lengths of the closet floor and the remaining area for each side length.

b. **Writing an Inequality** Write an inequality to describe the situation. Use your table to find the greatest possible side length of the closet floor.

22. ★ **SHORT RESPONSE** A farmer plans to build a fence around a rectangular pen that is 16 feet long. The area of the pen is 80 square feet. Is 40 feet of fencing enough to fence in the pen? *Explain.*

23. **CHALLENGE** You and your friend live 12 miles apart. You leave home at the same time and travel toward each other. You walk at a rate of 4 miles per hour and your friend bicycles at a rate of 11 miles per hour.

a. How long after you leave home will you meet? How far from home will each of you be?

b. Suppose your friend bicycles at a rate of 12 miles per hour. How much sooner will you meet? How far from home will each of you be?

QUIZ

Write an equation or an inequality.

1. 4 more than twice a number n is equal to 25.
2. The quotient of a number x and 2 is no more than 9.

Check whether the given number is a solution of the equation or inequality.

3. $13 - 2x = 5$; 4
4. $5d - 4 \geq 16$; 4
5. $4y + 3 \geq 15$; 3
6. **CAR TRAVEL** One car travels about 28.5 miles on each gallon of gas. Suppose the average price of gas is $2 per gallon. About how much would the gas for a 978 mile trip cost?

PROBLEM SOLVING WORKSHOP
LESSON 1.5

Using ALTERNATIVE METHODS

Another Way to Solve Example 1

Make sense of problems and persevere in solving them.

MULTIPLE REPRESENTATIONS In Example 1, you saw how to solve a problem about running using an equation. You can also solve the problem by using the strategy *draw a diagram.*

PROBLEM

RUNNING You run in a city. Short blocks are north-south and are 0.1 mile long. Long blocks are east-west and are 0.15 mile long. You will run 2 long blocks east, a number of short blocks south, 2 long blocks west, and back to your start. You want to run 2 miles at a rate of 7 miles per hour. How many short blocks must you run?

METHOD

Drawing a Diagram You can draw a diagram to solve the problem.

STEP 1 **Read** the problem carefully. It tells you the lengths of a short block and a long block. You plan to run 4 long blocks and a distance of 2 miles.

STEP 2 **Draw** a pair of rectangles to represent running 1 short block in each direction. The total distance is $4(0.15) + 2(0.1) = 0.8$ mile. Continue adding pairs of rectangles until the total distance run is 2 miles.

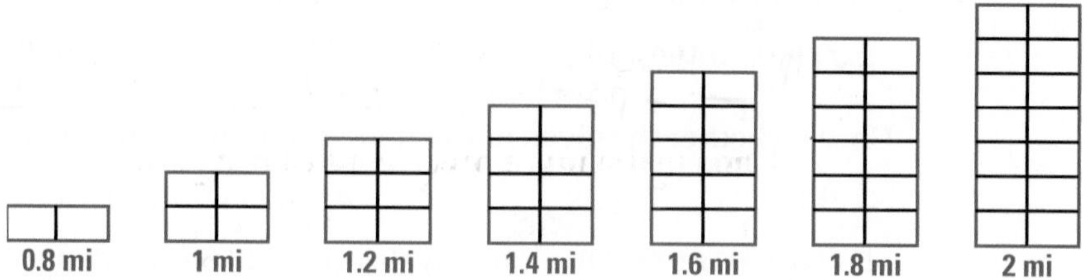

▸ You should run 14 short blocks.

Animated Algebra at my.hrw.com

PRACTICE

1. **BAKING** A cake pan is 9 inches wide and 11 inches long. How many 3 inch by 3 inch square pieces can you cut? Solve this problem using an equation. Then draw a diagram. *Explain* why a diagram is useful.

2. **SWIMMING** A 12 foot rope strung through 4 floats marks off the deep end of a pool. Each end of the rope is 3 feet from a float. The floats are equally spaced. How far apart are they? Solve this problem using two different methods.

3. **ERROR ANALYSIS** *Describe* and correct the error in solving Exercise 2.

$$4x + 6 = 12$$
$$4(1.5) + 6 = 12$$

The floats are 1.5 feet apart.

4. **GEOMETRY** The length of a rectangle is twice its width. The perimeter is 72 inches. What is its length? Solve this problem using two different methods.

1.6 Use Precision and Measurement

Before You measured using a ruler and protractor.

Now You will compare measurements for precision.

Why? So you can determine which measurement is more precise, as in Ex. 31.

Key Vocabulary
- **precision**
- **significant digits**

CC.9-12.N.Q.3 Choose a level of accuracy appropriate to limitations on measurement when reporting quantities.*

You ask two friends for the time. Noah says that it is about 2:30. Mia says it is 2:28 and 19 seconds. Mia gives a more *precise* measurement of the time.

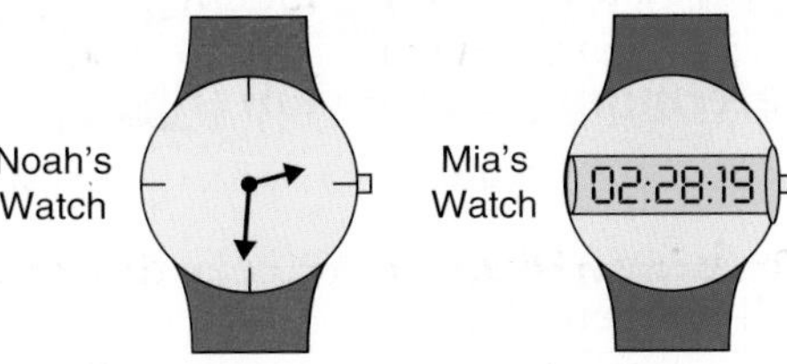

PRECISION **Precision** is the level of detail that an instrument can measure. Mia's watch is more precise than Noah's watch because it gives the time to the nearest second. In a similar way, a ruler marked in millimeters is more precise than a ruler marked only in centimeters, since a millimeter is a smaller unit than a centimeter.

EXAMPLE 1 Compare precision of measurements

Choose the more precise measurement.

a. 7 cm; 7.3 cm **b.** 5 yd; 16 ft **c.** 1 pint; 16 ounces

Solution

AVOID ERRORS
Remember that the smaller number is not always the more precise measurement. Always examine the units of measure.

a. The units are the same. Because tenths are smaller than ones, 7.3 centimeters is more precise than 7 centimeters.

b. The units are different. Because a foot is a smaller unit of measure than a yard, 16 feet is a more precise unit of measure.

c. The units are different. Because an ounce is a smaller unit of measure than a pint, 16 ounces is a more precise measurement even though 1 pint is equal to 16 ounces.

GUIDED PRACTICE for Example 1

Choose the more precise measurement.

1. 21.13 oz; 21.4 oz

2. $14\frac{1}{2}$ in.; $2\frac{5}{8}$ in.

3. 14 mm; 2 cm

4. 2.5 hr; 90 min

SIGNIFICANT DIGITS To the nearest centimeter, the diameter of a United States quarter is 2 centimeters. Measured to the nearest millimeter, the diameter of the quarter is 24 millimeters. The measurement 24 millimeters is more precise because it is given using a smaller unit of length.

In the two coin measurements, notice that the numerical value 24 has more digits than the value 2. You can use the number of significant digits to describe the precision of a measurement. **Significant digits** are the digits in a measurement that carry meaning contributing to the precision of the measurement.

KEY CONCEPT — For Your Notebook

Determining Significant Digits

Rule	Example	Significant digits	Number of significant digits
All nonzero digits	281.39	**281.39**	5
Zeros that are to the right of both the last nonzero digit and the decimal point	0.0070	0.00**70**	2
Zeros between significant digits	500.7	**500.7**	4

Zeros at the end of a whole number are usually assumed to be nonsignificant. For example, 220 centimeters has 2 significant digits, while 202 centimeters has 3 significant digits.

EXAMPLE 2 Identify significant digits

Determine the number of significant digits in each measurement.

a. 290.01 g **b.** 0.8500 km **c.** 4000 mi

Solution

a. The digits 2, 9, and 1 are nonzero digits, so they are significant digits. The zeros are between significant digits, so they are also significant digits.

There are 5 significant digits: **290.01**.

b. The digits 8 and 5 are nonzero digits, so they are significant digits. The two zeros to the right of the last nonzero digit are also to the right of the decimal point, so they are significant digits.

There are 4 significant digits: 0.**8500**.

c. The digit 4 is a nonzero digit, so it is a significant digit. The zeros at the end of a whole number are not significant.

There is 1 significant digit: **4**000.

AVOID ERRORS
Remember that not all zeros are significant. Be careful when deciding whether a zero in a number is significant or not.

SIGNIFICANT DIGITS IN CALCULATIONS When you perform calculations involving measurements, the number of significant digits that you write in your result depends on the number of significant digits in the given measurements.

KEY CONCEPT *For Your Notebook*

Determining Significant Digits in Calculations

Operations	Rule	Example
Addition and Subtraction	Round the sum or difference to the same place as the last significant digit of the least precise measurement.	3.24 ← hundredths + 7.3 ← tenths **10.54** ← tenths
Multiplication and Division	The product or quotient must have the same number of significant digits as the least precise measurement.	40 ← 1 sig digit × 31 ← 2 sig digits 1240 ← exact answer **1000** ← 1 sig digit

EXAMPLE 3 Calculating with significant digits

Perform the indicated operation. Write the answer with the correct number of significant digits.

a. 45.1 cm + 19.45 cm **b.** 6.4 ft × 2.15 ft

Solution

a. 45.1 cm + 19.45 cm = 64.55 cm

The least precise measurement is 45.1 centimeters. Its last significant digit is in the tenths place. Round the sum to the nearest tenth.

The correct sum is 64.6 centimeters.

b. 6.4 ft × 2.15 ft = 13.76 ft^2

The least precise measurement is 6.4 feet. It has two significant digits. Round the product to two significant digits.

The correct product is 14 square feet.

✓ **GUIDED PRACTICE** for Examples 2 and 3

Determine the number of significant digits in each measurement.

5. 800.20 ft **6.** 0.005 cm **7.** 36,900 mi

Perform the indicated operation. Write the answer with the correct number of significant digits.

8. 27.23 m − 12.7 m **9.** 45.16 yd^2 ÷ 4.25 yd

1.6 EXERCISES

HOMEWORK KEY

○ = See **WORKED-OUT SOLUTIONS** Exs. 3, 11, 21, and 33

★ = **STANDARDIZED TEST PRACTICE** Exs. 2, 20, 29, 30, and 37

SKILL PRACTICE

1. **VOCABULARY** Copy and complete: The level of detail that an instrument can measure is known as its __?__.

2. ★ **WRITING** Which number, 0.023 or 301, has the fewer significant digits? Explain.

EXAMPLE 1 for Exs. 3–10

COMPARING PRECISION **Choose the more precise measurement.**

3. 14.2 gal; 7 gal
4. 0.02 mm; 0.1 mm
5. 90 ft; 71 in.
6. 57.65 lb; 34.9 lb
7. 14.1 m; 29.3 cm
8. 36 yd; 17.2 yd

ERROR ANALYSIS **Describe and correct the error in the statement.**

9. Heidi told her friend Mike that 1.5 hours is a more precise measurement of time than 85 minutes.

10. Eric's new fishing rod was advertised as being 4 feet long. He measured it to be 47 inches long. Eric's friend says that 4 feet is the more precise measurement.

EXAMPLE 2 for Exs. 11–20

IDENTIFYING SIGNIFICANT DIGITS **Determine the number of significant digits in the measurement.**

11. 312.5 cm
12. 100 hr
13. 0.030 gal
14. 16.007 lb
15. 1020 mm
16. 0.0025 sec
17. 38.0 m
18. 8.375 ft
19. 205.7140 mi

20. ★ **MULTIPLE CHOICE** The measurement 0.007 grams contains how many significant digits?

Ⓐ 1 Ⓑ 2 Ⓒ 3 Ⓓ 4

EXAMPLE 3 for Exs. 21–30

CALCULATING WITH SIGNIFICANT DIGITS **Perform the indicated operation. Write the answer with the correct number of significant digits.**

21. 97.2 m − 16.04 m
22. 8 ft × 11.2 ft
23. 257.64 oz ÷ 2.4 oz
24. 0.043 yd + 0.22 yd
25. 6.42 mm × 7.51 mm
26. 2.8 mi + 3.56 mi
27. 245 kg − 18.32 kg
28. 9.05 cm^2 ÷ 18 cm

29. ★ **WRITING** Describe how to find the number of significant digits to give for the area of a rectangle with side lengths 8.2 meters and 20 meters.

30. ★ **MULTIPLE CHOICE** The quotient 97.3 hr ÷ 5.5 hr contains how many significant digits?

Ⓐ 4 Ⓑ 3 Ⓒ 2 Ⓓ 1

CHALLENGE **Perform the indicated operation. Write the answer with the correct number of significant digits.**

31. 0.40 ft × 2.25 ft
32. 23.175 km^2 ÷ 10.30 km

PROBLEM SOLVING

EXAMPLE 1 for Exs. 33–36

33. COINS According to the United States Mint, a one-dollar coin has a mass of 8.1 grams. Justine finds the mass of a one-dollar coin and reports a mass of 8.05 grams. Steven finds that the mass of his one-dollar coin is 8.2 grams. Whose measurement is more precise?

COMPARING MEASUREMENTS For Exercises 34–36, three students are asked to measure a piece of string that has a length of exactly 15.2 centimeters. Their measurements are shown in the table.

Student	Measurement
Alex	15.35 cm
Chandra	14.9 cm
Luis	154 mm

34. Which student made the most precise measurement?

35. Which student made the least precise measurement?

36. Which student's answer is closest to the actual length of the string?

EXAMPLES 2 and 3 for Exs. 37–49

37. ★ SHORT RESPONSE Brian drives 426 miles and uses 19.3 gallons of gas for the trip. Brian's calculator shows that $\frac{426}{19.3} \approx 22.07253886$, so he states that his car gets 22.07253886 miles per gallon. Do you agree with Brian's statement? *Explain* your answer.

38. REFLECTING POOL The Reflecting Pool is a rectangular body of water in front of the Lincoln Memorial in Washington, D.C. A surveyor determines that the length of the pool to the nearest foot is 2029 feet and the width of the pool to the nearest foot is 167 feet.

a. How should the surveyor report the perimeter of the pool using the correct number of significant digits?

b. How should the surveyor report the area of the pool using the correct number of significant digits?

39. HEALTH When Kyle went for his annual physical the nurse weighed him and told him he weighed 118.5 pounds. After seeing the doctor, Kyle was sent for some tests where he was weighed again. This time he was told he weighed 119 pounds. Which of the two measurements is more precise? *Explain* your answer.

40. GARDENING A student measures the length of a rectangular garden plot to the nearest tenth of a meter and finds that the length is 6.4 meters. Another student measures the width of the plot to the nearest meter and finds that the width is 2 meters. Using the correct number of significant digits, what are the perimeter and area of the plot?

41. **CHARITY RUN** Nicole and Renee are participating in a charity run to raise money for their school's library. Both girls have sponsors who will pay them $1 for each mile they collectively run. If Nicole ran 7.2 miles and Renee ran 6.03 miles, how should they report their cumulative miles to their sponsors using the correct number of significant digits?

★ OPEN-ENDED In Exercises 42–46, give an example of the described measurement.

42. A 5-digit distance in miles that has 3 significant digits

43. A measurement greater than 1000 centimeters that has 2 significant digits

44. A measurement less than 1 millimeter that has 4 significant digits

45. A 4-digit area that has 3 significant digits and 2 digits that are zeros

46. A weight less than 10 pounds that has 5 significant digits

47. **POSTERS** The area of a rectangular poster is 852 square inches. The length of the poster is 36 inches. Using the correct number of significant digits, what is the width of the poster?

48. **SCIENCE** Tanya and Edmond are lab partners in science class. They each measure the volume of a beaker of a solution. Tanya found the volume to be 2.25 liters, while Edmond reported the volume as 2300 milliliters. Who gave the more precise measurement? *Explain* your answer.

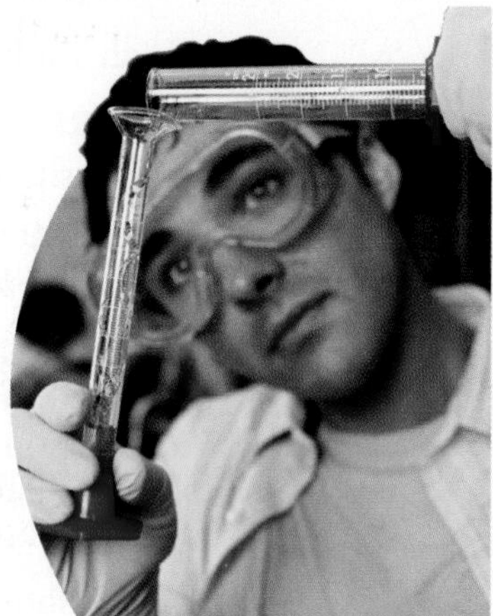

49. **REALTORS** When a realtor first lists a home for sale, it is very important to calculate the living area of the home. Carrie measured the length and width of a house she is about to list and found that it measured 52.5 feet long by 35 feet wide. Using the correct number of significant digits, how should Carrie report the area of the house?

50. **CHALLENGE** A student measures the length of a cube and records the length as 3.5 centimeters. Using the correct number of significant digits, how should the student report the volume of the cube?

51. **CHALLENGE** Suppose the average 12-ounce aluminum drink can weighs approximately 13.6 grams and the liquid inside weighs approximately 453.59 grams. Using the correct number of significant digits, how much do the 24 drink cans in a carton weigh?

1.7 Represent Functions as Rules and Tables

Before You wrote algebraic expressions and equations.
Now You will represent functions as rules and as tables.
Why? So you can describe consumer costs, as in Example 1.

Key Vocabulary
- **function**
- **domain**
- **range**
- **independent variable**
- **dependent variable**

When you pump gas, the total cost depends on the number of gallons pumped. The total cost is a *function* of the number of gallons pumped.

A **function** consists of:

- A set called the **domain** containing numbers called **inputs**, and a set called the **range** containing numbers called **outputs**.
- A pairing of inputs with outputs such that each input is paired with exactly one output.

CC.9-12.A.CED.2 Create equations in two or more variables to represent relationships between quantities; graph equations on coordinate axes with labels and scales.*

EXAMPLE 1 Identify the domain and range of a function

The input-output table shows the cost of various amounts of regular unleaded gas from the same pump. Identify the domain and range of the function.

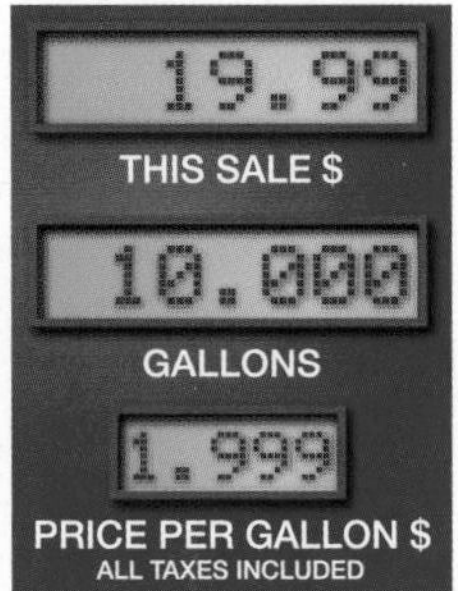

Input (gallons)	10	12	13	17
Output (dollars)	19.99	23.99	25.99	33.98

Solution

▶ The domain is the set of inputs: 10, 12, 13, and 17. The range is the set of outputs: 19.99, 23.99, 25.99, and 33.98.

GUIDED PRACTICE for Example 1

1. Identify the domain and range of the function.

Input	0	1	2	4
Output	5	2	2	1

MAPPING DIAGRAMS A function may be represented by a *mapping diagram.* Notice that an output may be paired with more than one input, but no input is paired with more than one output.

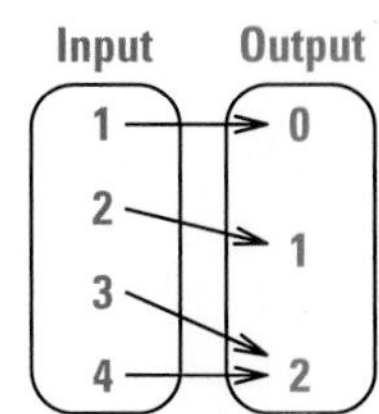

EXAMPLE 2 Identify a function

Tell whether the pairing is a function.

a.

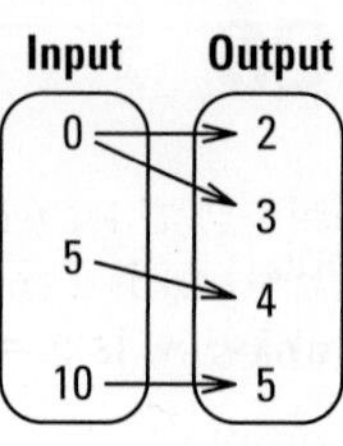

The pairing is *not* a function because the input 0 is paired with both 2 and 3.

b.

Input	Output
0	0
1	2
4	8
6	12

The pairing is a function because each input is paired with exactly one output.

✓ GUIDED PRACTICE for Example 2

Tell whether the pairing is a function.

2.

Input	3	6	9	12
Output	1	2	2	1

3.

Input	2	2	4	7
Output	0	1	2	3

FUNCTION RULES A function may be represented using a rule that relates one variable to another. The input variable is called the **independent variable.** The output variable is called the **dependent variable** because its value depends on the value of the input variable.

READING
Function rules typically give the dependent variable in terms of the independent variable. In an equation like $y = x + 3$, you know that y is the dependent variable.

KEY CONCEPT *For Your Notebook*

Functions

Verbal Rule
The output is 3 more than the input.

Equation
$y = x + 3$

Table

Input, x	0	1	2	3	4
Output, y	3	4	5	6	7

EXAMPLE 3 Make a table for a function

The domain of the function $y = 2x$ is 0, 2, 5, 7, and 8. Make a table for the function, then identify the range of the function.

Solution

x	0	2	5	7	8
$y = 2x$	$2(0) = 0$	$2(2) = 4$	$2(5) = 10$	$2(7) = 14$	$2(8) = 16$

The range of the function is 0, 4, 10, 14, and 16.

EXAMPLE 4 Write a function rule

Write a rule for the function.

Input	0	1	4	6	10
Output	2	3	6	8	12

Solution

Let x be the input, or independent variable, and let y be the output, or dependent variable. Notice that each output is 2 more than the corresponding input. So, a rule for the function is $y = x + 2$.

EXAMPLE 5 Write a function rule for a real-world situation

CONCERT TICKETS You are buying concert tickets that cost \$15 each. You can buy up to 6 tickets. Write the amount (in dollars) you spend as a function of the number of tickets you buy. Identify the independent and dependent variables. Then identify the domain and the range of the function.

Solution

CHOOSE A VARIABLE
To write a function rule for a real-world situation, choose letters for the variables that remind you of the quantities represented.

Write a verbal model. Then write a function rule. Let n represent the number of tickets purchased and A represent the amount spent (in dollars).

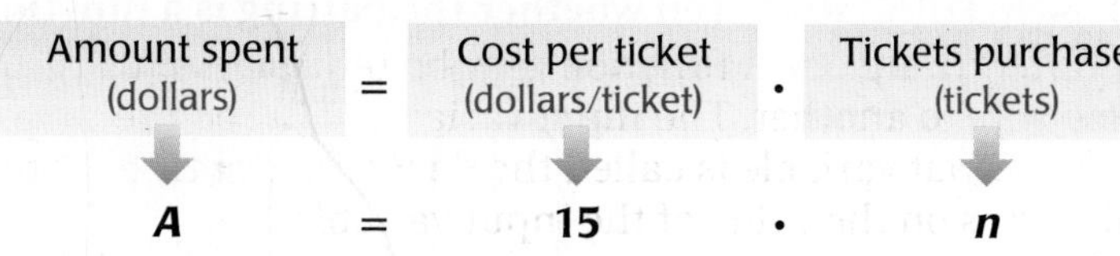

So, the function rule is $A = 15n$. The amount spent depends on the number of tickets bought, so n is the independent variable and A is the dependent variable.

Because you can buy up to 6 tickets, the domain of the function is 0, 1, 2, 3, 4, 5, and 6. Make a table to identify the range.

Number of tickets, n	0	1	2	3	4	5	6
Amount (dollars), A	0	15	30	45	60	75	90

The range of the function is 0, 15, 30, 45, 60, 75, and 90.

Animated Algebra at my.hrw.com

✓ GUIDED PRACTICE for Examples 3, 4, and 5

4. Make a table for the function $y = x - 5$ with domain 10, 12, 15, 18, and 29. Then identify the range of the function.

5. Write a rule for the function. Identify the domain and the range.

Time (hours)	1	2	3	4
Pay (dollars)	8	16	24	32

1.7 EXERCISES

HOMEWORK KEY

○ = See **WORKED-OUT SOLUTIONS** Exs. 7 and 23

★ = **STANDARDIZED TEST PRACTICE** Exs. 2, 11, 12, 13, 26, and 27

◆ = **MULTIPLE REPRESENTATIONS** Exs. 23 and 24

SKILL PRACTICE

1. **VOCABULARY** Copy and complete: A(n) _?_ is a number in the domain of a function. A(n) _?_ is a number in the range of a function.

2. ★ **WRITING** In the equation $b = a - 2$, which variable is the independent variable and which is the dependent variable? *Explain.*

EXAMPLES 1 and 2 for Exs. 3–11

DOMAIN AND RANGE **Identify the domain and range of the function.**

3.

Input	Output
0	5
1	7
2	15
3	44

4.

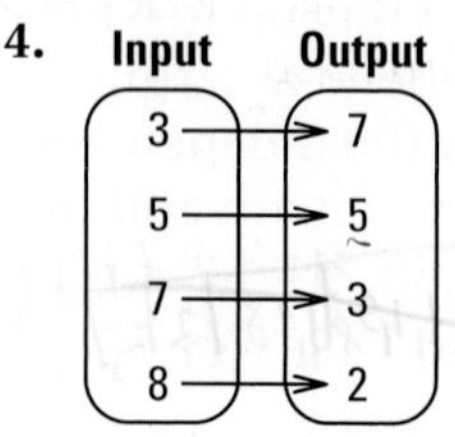

5.

Input	Output
6	5
12	7
21	10
42	17

IDENTIFYING FUNCTIONS **Tell whether the pairing is a function.**

6.

Input	Output
0	7.5
1	9.5
2	11.5
3	13.5

7.

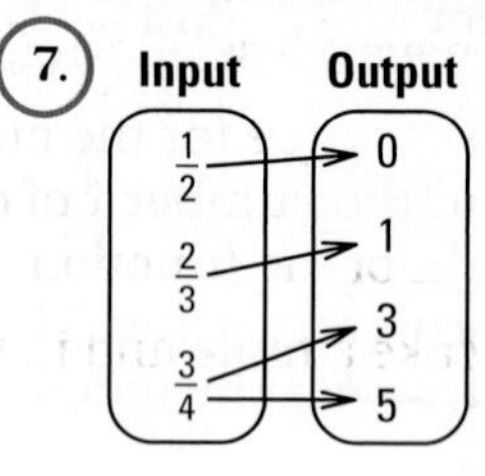

8.

Input	Output
7	13
11	8
21	13
35	20

ERROR ANALYSIS **In Exercises 9 and 10, describe and correct the error related to the function represented by the table.**

Input, *x*	1	2	3	4	5
Output, *y*	6	7	8	6	9

9. The pairing is not a function. One output is paired with two inputs. ✗

10. The pairing is a function. The range is 1, 2, 3, 4, and 5.

11. ★ **OPEN-ENDED** Draw a mapping diagram for a function with 6 inputs. Then make a table to represent the function.

EXAMPLES 3 and 4 for Exs. 12–21

12. ★ **MULTIPLE CHOICE** The domain of the function $y = 5x - 1$ is 1, 3, 4, 5, and 6. Which number is in the range of the function?

Ⓐ 0 Ⓑ 4 Ⓒ 9 Ⓓ 15

13. ★ **MULTIPLE CHOICE** Each output of a function is 0.5 less than the corresponding input. Which equation is a rule for the function?

Ⓐ $y = x - 0.5$ Ⓑ $y = x + 0.5$ Ⓒ $y = 0.5 - x$ Ⓓ $y = 0.5x$

TABLES **Make a table for the function. Identify the range of the function.**

14. $y = x - 3$
Domain: 12, 15, 22, 30

15. $y = x + 3.5$
Domain: 4, 5, 7, 8, 12

16. $y = 3x + 4$
Domain: 0, 5, 7, 10

17. $y = \frac{1}{2}x + 3$
Domain: 4, 6, 9, 11

18. $y = \frac{2}{3}x + \frac{1}{3}$
Domain: 4, 6, 8, 12

19. $y = \frac{0.5x + 1}{2}$
Domain: 0, 2, 4, 6

FUNCTION RULES **Write a rule for the function.**

20.

Input, x	0	1	2	3
Output, y	2.2	3.2	4.2	5.2

21.

Input, x	15	20	21	30	42
Output, y	7	12	13	22	34

22. CHALLENGE Fill in the table in such a way that when t is the independent variable, the pairing is a function, and when t is the dependent variable, the pairing is not a function.

t	?	?	?	?
v	?	?	?	?

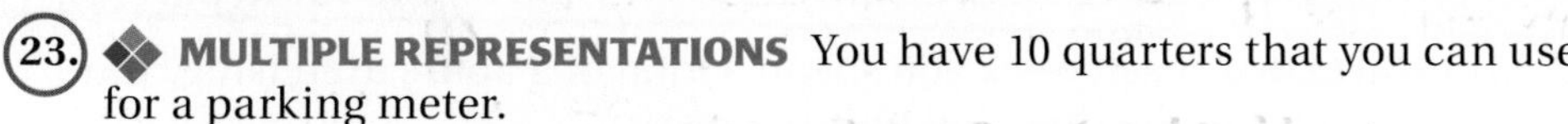

PROBLEM SOLVING

EXAMPLE 5 for Exs. 23–26

23. ◆ **MULTIPLE REPRESENTATIONS** You have 10 quarters that you can use for a parking meter.

a. **Describing in Words** Copy and complete: Each time you put 1 quarter in the meter, you have 1 less quarter, so _?_ is a function of _?_.

b. **Writing a Rule** Write a rule for the number y of quarters that you have left as a function of the number x of quarters you have used so far. Identify the domain of the function.

c. **Making a Table** Make a table and identify the range of the function.

24. ◆ **MULTIPLE REPRESENTATIONS** At a yard sale, you find 5 paperback books by your favorite author. Each book is priced at $.75.

a. **Describing in Words** Copy and complete: For each book you buy, you spend $.75, so _?_ is a function of _?_.

b. **Writing a Rule** Write a rule for the amount (in dollars) you spend as a function of the number of books you buy. Identify the domain of the function.

c. **Making a Table** Make a table and identify the range of the function.

25. SAVINGS You have $100 saved and plan to save $20 each month. Write a rule for the amount saved (in dollars) as a function of the number of months from now. Identify the independent and dependent variables, the domain, and the range. How much will you have saved altogether 12 months from now?

26. ★ **OPEN-ENDED** Write a function rule that models a real-world situation. Identify the independent variable and the dependent variable.

27. ★ **SHORT RESPONSE** Consider a pairing of the digits 2 through 9 on a telephone keypad with the associated letters.

a. Make a table showing the pairing with the digits as inputs and the letters as outputs. Is the pairing a function? *Explain.*

b. Make a table showing the pairing with the letters as inputs and the digits as outputs. Is the pairing a function? *Explain.*

28. **MULTI-STEP PROBLEM** The table shows the fuel efficiency of four compact cars from one manufacturer for model year 2004.

City fuel efficiency (mi/gal), c	24	26	27	28
Highway fuel efficiency (mi/gal), h	32	34	35	36

a. Write a Rule Use the table to write a rule for the cars' highway fuel efficiency as a function of their city fuel efficiency.

b. Predict Another of the manufacturer's compact cars has a city fuel efficiency of 30 miles per gallon. Predict the highway fuel efficiency.

c. Calculate A study found that if gas costs \$2 per gallon, you can use the expression $\frac{11,550}{c} + \frac{9450}{h}$ to estimate a car's annual fuel cost (in dollars) for a typical driver. Evaluate the expression for the car in part (b).

29. **CHALLENGE** Each week you spend a total of 5 hours exercising. You swim part of the time and bike the rest.

300 calories per hour   440 calories per hour

a. Write a rule for the total number of calories you burn for the whole 5 hours as a function of the time you spend swimming.

b. One week you spend half the time swimming. How many calories do you burn during the whole 5 hours?

See **EXTRA PRACTICE** in Student Resources   **ONLINE QUIZ** at my.hrw.com

Graphing Calculator ACTIVITY *Use after Represent Functions as Rules and Tables*

my.hrw.com
Keystrokes

Make a Table

Use appropriate tools strategically.

QUESTION **How can you use a graphing calculator to create a table for a function?**

You can use a graphing calculator to create a table for a function when you want to display many pairs of input values and output values or when you want to find the input value that corresponds to a given output value.

In the example below, you will make a table to compare temperatures in degrees Celsius and temperatures in degrees Fahrenheit for temperatures at or above the temperature at which water freezes, 32°F.

EXAMPLE **Use a graphing calculator to make a table**

The formula $C = \frac{5}{9}(F - 32)$ gives the temperature in degrees Celsius as a function of the temperature in degrees Fahrenheit. Make a table for the function.

STEP 1 ***Enter equation***

Rewrite the function using x for F and y for C. Press Y= and enter $\frac{5}{9}(x - 32)$.

STEP 2 ***Set up table***

Go to the TABLE SETUP screen. Use a starting value (TblStart) of 32 and an increment (ΔTbl) of 1.

STEP 3 ***View table***

Display the table. Scroll down to see pairs of inputs and outputs.

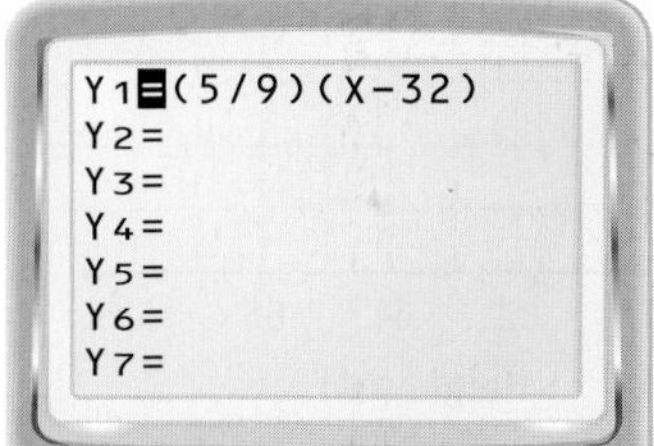

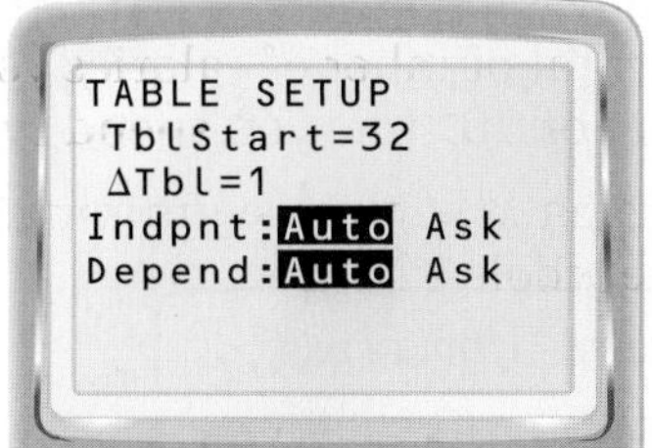

X	Y1	Y2
32	0	
33	.55556	
34	1.1111	
35	1.6667	
36	2.2222	
37	2.7778	

PRACTICE

1. You see a sign that indicates that the outdoor temperature is 10°C. Find the temperature in degrees Fahrenheit. *Explain* how you found your answer.
2. Water boils at 100°C. What is the temperature in degrees Fahrenheit?

Make a table for the function. Use the given starting value and increment.

3. $y = \frac{3}{4}x + 5$
   TblStart = 0, ΔTbl = 1
4. $y = 4x + 2$
   TblStart = 0, ΔTbl = 0.5
5. $y = 7.5x - 0.5$
   TblStart = 1, ΔTbl = 1
6. $y = 0.5x + 6$
   TblStart = 3, ΔTbl = 3

Scatter Plots and Functions

MATHEMATICAL PRACTICES

Model with mathematics.

MATERIALS • tape measure • graph paper

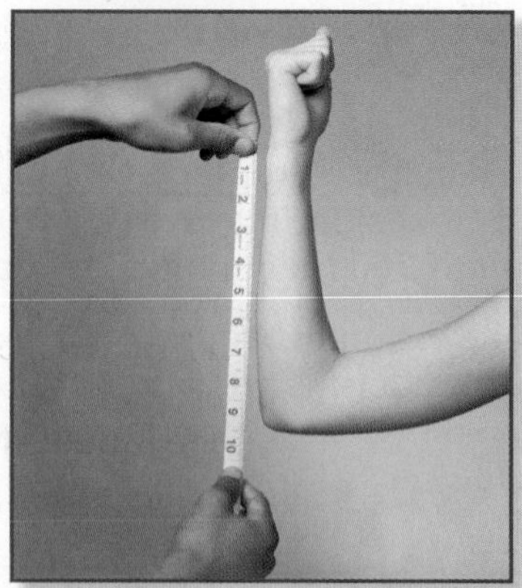

QUESTION **How can you tell whether a graph represents a function?**

A *scatter plot* is a type of display for paired data. Each data pair is plotted as a point. In this activity, you will work in a group to make a scatter plot. You will measure the height of each student in your group and the length of his or her forearm. The length of the forearm is the distance from the elbow to the wrist.

EXPLORE **Collect data and make a scatter plot**

STEP 1 ***Collect data*** Measure the height of each student in your group and the length of his or her forearm. Record the results for each student in one row of a table like the one shown.

Height (inches)	Forearm length (inches)
63	10
?	?

STEP 2 ***Make a scatter plot*** Use graph paper to draw axes labeled as shown. Then plot the data pairs (*height, forearm length*). For example, plot the point (63, 10) for a student with a height of 63 inches and a forearm length of 10 inches.

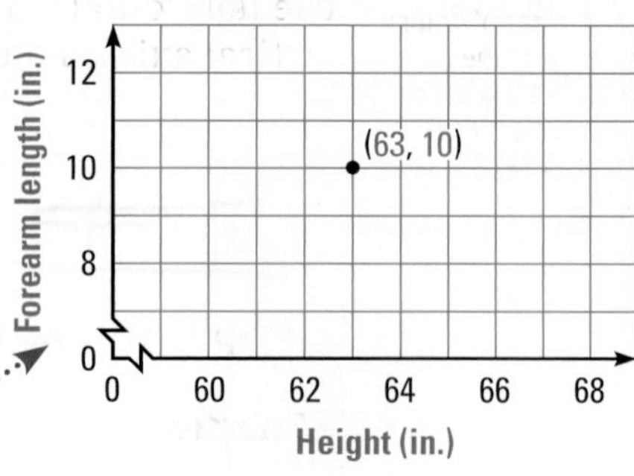

The symbol ⌇ on an axis represents a break in the axis.

DRAW CONCLUSIONS **Use your observations to complete these exercises**

1. Examine your scatter plot. What does it suggest about the relationship between a person's height and the person's forearm length?
2. Compare your table with those of the other groups in your class. Determine which of the tables represent functions and which do not.
3. Is it possible to determine whether a table represents a function by looking at the corresponding scatter plot? *Explain.*

1.8 Represent Functions as Graphs

Before	You represented functions as rules and tables.
Now	You will represent functions as graphs.
Why?	So you can describe sales trends, as in Example 4.

Key Vocabulary
- **function**
- **domain**
- **range**

REVIEW THE COORDINATE PLANE
For help with the coordinate plane, see p. SR11.

CC.9-12.F.IF.4 For a function that models a relationship between two quantities, interpret key features of graphs and tables in terms of the quantities, and sketch graphs showing key features given a verbal description of the relationship.*

You can use a graph to represent a function. Given a table that represents a function, each corresponding pair of input and output values forms an ordered pair of numbers that can be plotted as a point. The x-coordinate is the input. The y-coordinate is the output.

Table

Input, x	Output, y
1	2
2	3
4	5

Ordered Pairs

(input, output)
(1, 2)
(2, 3)
(4, 5)

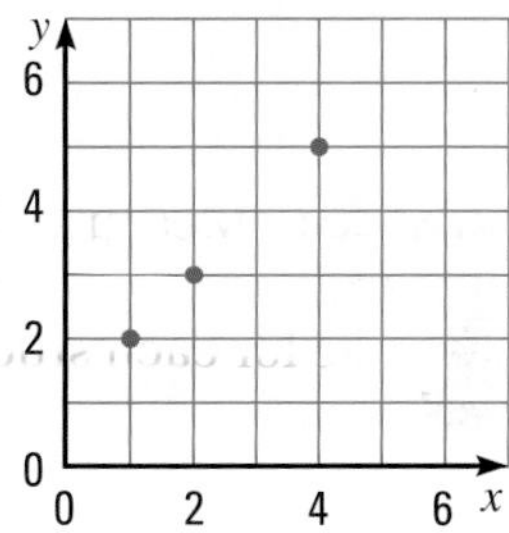

The horizontal axis of the graph is labeled with the input variable. The vertical axis is labeled with the output variable.

EXAMPLE 1 Graph a function

Graph the function $y = \frac{1}{2}x$ with domain 0, 2, 4, 6, and 8.

Solution

STEP 1 **Make** an input-output table.

x	0	2	4	6	8
y	0	1	2	3	4

STEP 2 **Plot** a point for each ordered pair (x, y).

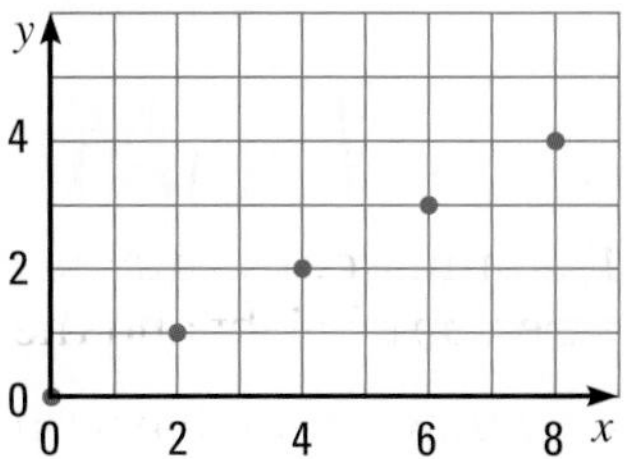

GUIDED PRACTICE for Example 1

1. Graph the function $y = 2x - 1$ with domain 1, 2, 3, 4, and 5.

EXAMPLE 2 Graph a function

SAT SCORES The table shows the average score s on the mathematics section of the Scholastic Aptitude Test (SAT) in the United States from 1997 to 2003 as a function of the time t in years since 1997. In the table, 0 corresponds to the year 1997, 1 corresponds to 1998, and so on. Graph the function.

Years since 1997, t	0	1	2	3	4	5	6
Average score, s	511	512	511	514	514	516	519

Solution

READING
The symbol ⦚ on the vertical number line represents a break in the axis.

STEP 1 **Choose** a scale. The scale should allow you to plot all the points on a graph that is a reasonable size.

- The t-values range from 0 to 6, so label the t-axis from 0 to 6 in increments of 1 unit.
- The s-values range from 511 to 519, so label the s-axis from 510 to 520 in increments of 2 units.

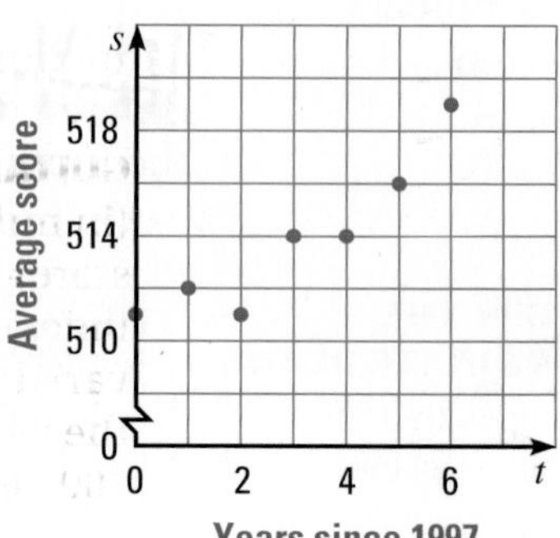

STEP 2 **Plot** the points.

✓ GUIDED PRACTICE for Example 2

2. **WHAT IF?** In Example 2, suppose that you use a scale on the s-axis from 0 to 520 in increments of 1 unit. *Describe* the appearance of the graph.

EXAMPLE 3 Write a function rule for a graph

Write a rule for the function represented by the graph. Identify the domain and the range of the function.

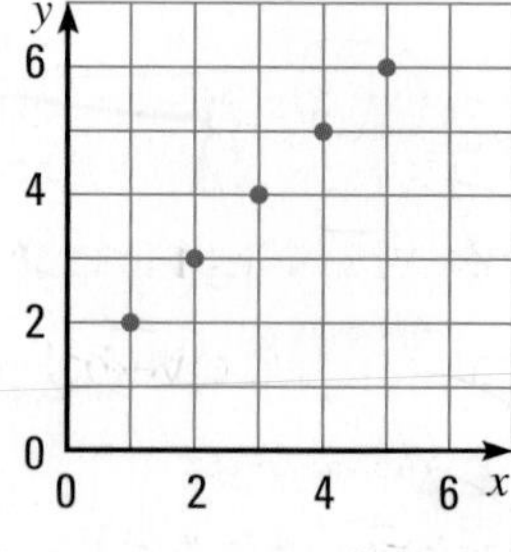

Solution

STEP 1 **Make** a table for the graph.

x	1	2	3	4	5
y	2	3	4	5	6

STEP 2 **Find** a relationship between the inputs and the outputs. Notice from the table that each output value is 1 more than the corresponding input value.

STEP 3 **Write** a function rule that describes the relationship: $y = x + 1$.

▶ A rule for the function is $y = x + 1$. The domain of the function is 1, 2, 3, 4, and 5. The range is 2, 3, 4, 5, and 6.

GUIDED PRACTICE for Example 3

Write a rule for the function represented by the graph. Identify the domain and the range of the function.

3.

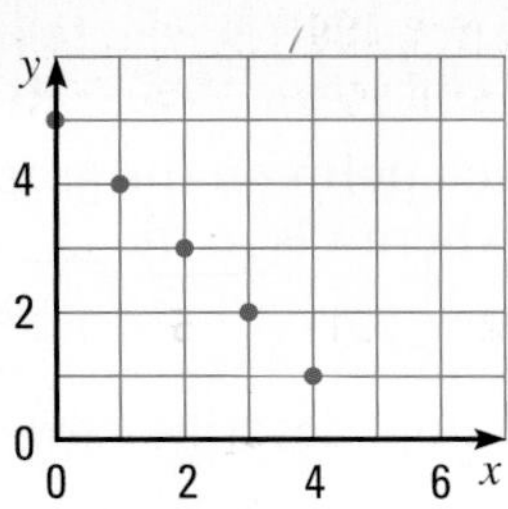

4.

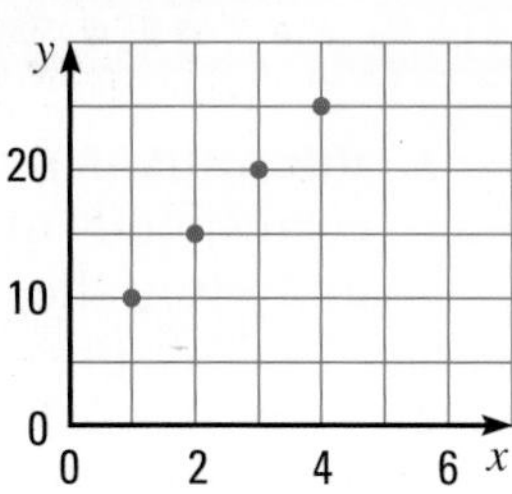

EXAMPLE 4 Analyze a graph

GUITAR SALES The graph shows guitar sales (in millions of dollars) for a chain of music stores for the period 1999–2005. Identify the independent variable and the dependent variable. Describe how sales changed over the period and how you would expect sales in 2006 to compare to sales in 2005.

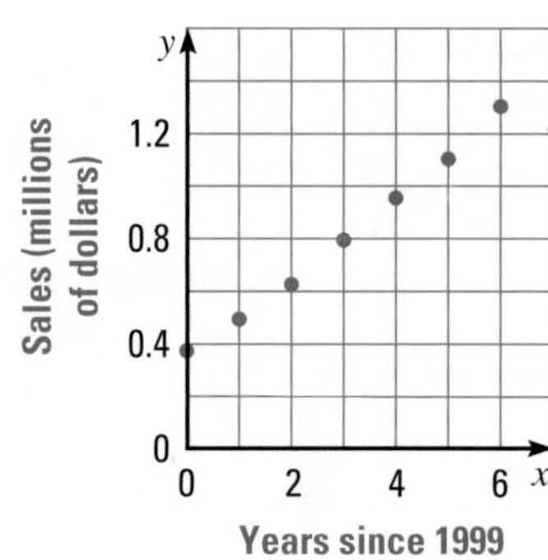

Solution

The independent variable is the number of years since 1999. The dependent variable is the sales (in millions of dollars). The graph shows that sales were increasing. If the trend continued, sales would be greater in 2006 than in 2005.

GUIDED PRACTICE for Example 4

5. REASONING Based on the graph in Example 4, is $1.4 million a reasonable prediction of the chain's sales for 2006? *Explain.*

CONCEPT SUMMARY *For Your Notebook*

Ways to Represent a Function

You can use a verbal rule, an equation, a table, or a graph to represent a function.

Verbal Rule

The output is 1 less than twice the input.

Equation

$y = 2x - 1$

Table

x	y
1	1
2	3
3	5
4	7

Graph

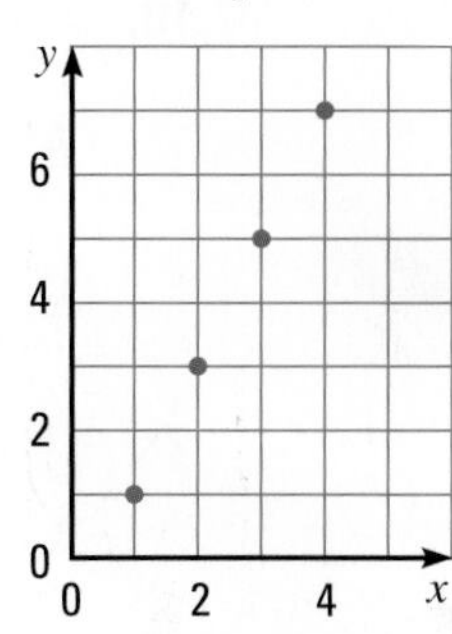

1.8 EXERCISES

HOMEWORK KEY

○ = See WORKED-OUT SOLUTIONS Exs. 3 and 17

★ = STANDARDIZED TEST PRACTICE Exs. 2, 13, 18, 19, and 20

SKILL PRACTICE

1. **VOCABULARY** Copy and complete: Each point on the graph of a function corresponds to an ordered pair (x, y) where x is in the _?_ of the function and y is in the _?_ of the function.

2. ★ **WRITING** Given the graph of a function, describe how to write a rule for the function.

EXAMPLE 1 for Exs. 3–9

GRAPHING FUNCTIONS Graph the function.

3. $y = x + 3$; domain: 0, 1, 2, 3, 4, and 5
4. $y = \frac{1}{2}x + 1$; domain: 0, 1, 2, 3, 4, and 5
5. $y = 2x + 2$; domain: 0, 2, 5, 7, and 10
6. $y = 3x - 1$; domain: 1, 2, 3, 4, and 5
7. $y = x + 5$; domain: 0, 2, 4, 6, 8, and 10
8. $y = 2.5x$; domain: 0, 1, 2, 3, and 4

9. **ERROR ANALYSIS** *Describe* and correct the error in graphing the function $y = x - 1$ with domain 1, 2, 3, 4, and 5.

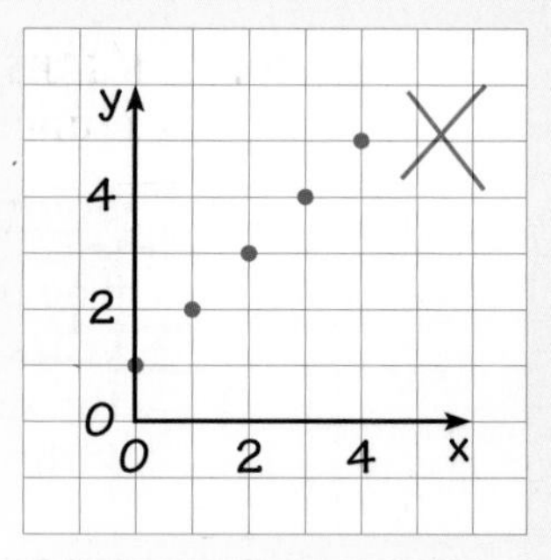

EXAMPLE 3 for Exs. 10–12

WRITING FUNCTION RULES Write a rule for the function represented by the graph. Identify the domain and the range of the function.

10.

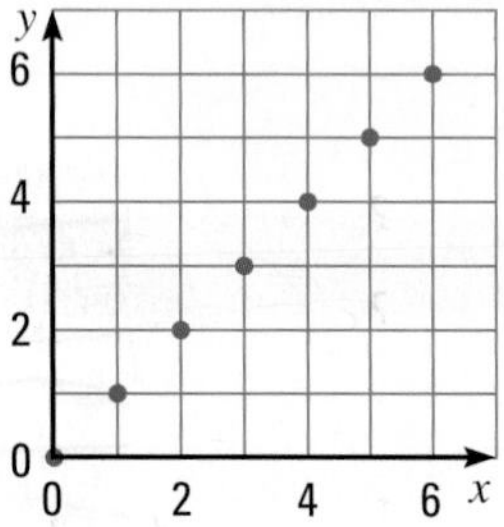

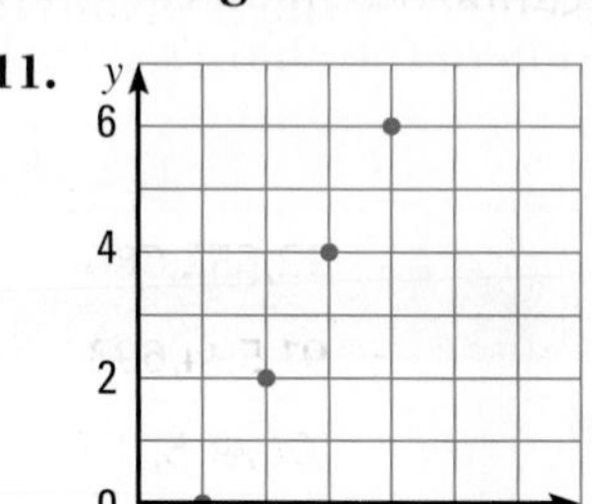

11.

12.

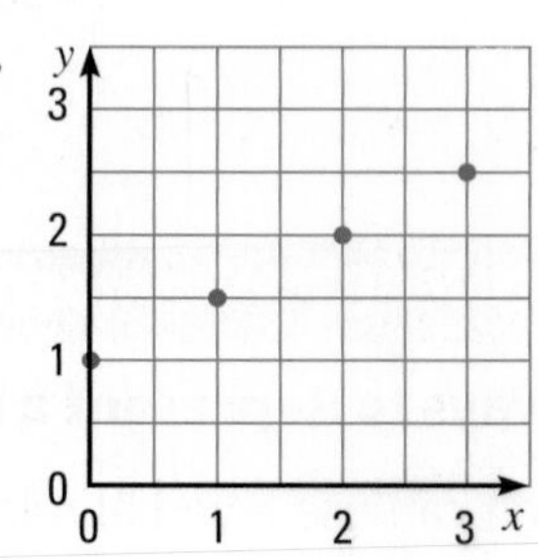

13. ★ **MULTIPLE CHOICE** The graph of which function is shown?

Ⓐ $y = \frac{1}{2}x + \frac{1}{2}$ Ⓑ $y = x + \frac{1}{2}$

Ⓒ $y = \frac{3}{2}x + \frac{1}{2}$ Ⓓ $y = 2x + \frac{1}{2}$

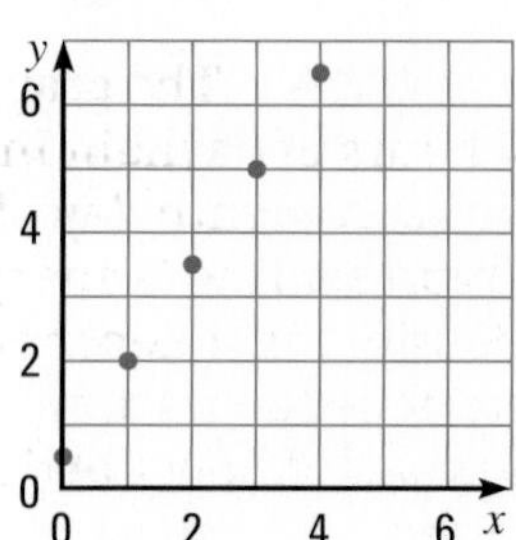

14. **CHALLENGE** The graph represents a function.

a. Write a rule for the function.

b. Find the value of y so that $(1.5, y)$ is on the graph of the function.

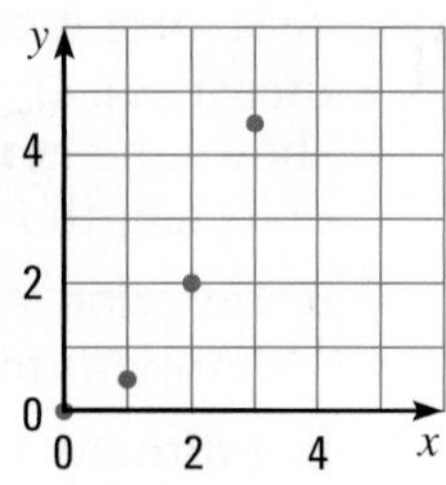

PROBLEM SOLVING

EXAMPLE 2 for Exs. 15–17

15. **ADVERTISING** The table shows the cost C (in millions of dollars) of a 30 second Super Bowl ad on TV as a function of the time t (in years) since 1997. Graph the function.

Years since 1997, t	0	1	2	3	4	5	6	7
Cost (millions of dollars), C	1.2	1.3	1.6	2.1	2.1	1.9	2.1	2.3

16. **CONGRESS** The table shows the number r of U.S. representatives for Texas as a function of the time t (in years) since 1930. Graph the function.

Years since 1930, t	0	10	20	30	40	50	60	70
Number of representatives, r	21	21	22	23	24	27	30	32

17. **ELECTIONS** The table shows the number v of voters in U.S. presidential elections as a function of the time t (in years) since 1984. First copy and complete the table. Round to the nearest million. Then graph the function represented by the first and third columns.

Years since 1984	Voters	Voters (millions)
0	92,652,680	?
4	91,594,693	?
8	104,405,155	?
12	96,456,345	?
16	105,586,274	?

EXAMPLE 4 for Exs. 18–19

18. ★ **WRITING** The graph shows the number of hours of daylight in Houston, Texas, on the fifteenth day of the month, with 1 representing January, and so on. Identify the independent variable and the dependent variable. *Describe* how the number of hours of daylight changes over a year.

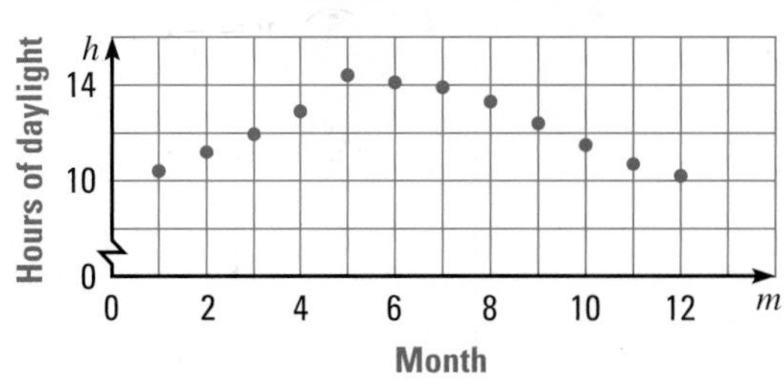

19. ★ **SHORT RESPONSE** A field biologist collected and measured alligator snapping turtle eggs. The graph shows the mass m (in grams) of an egg as a function of its length ℓ (in millimeters).

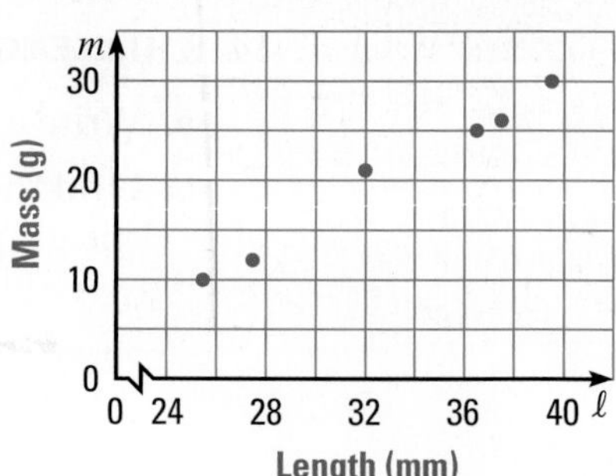

a. **Describe** As the lengths of the eggs increase, what happens to the masses of the eggs?

b. **Estimate** Is 27.5 g a reasonable estimate for the mass of an egg that is 38 mm long? *Explain.*

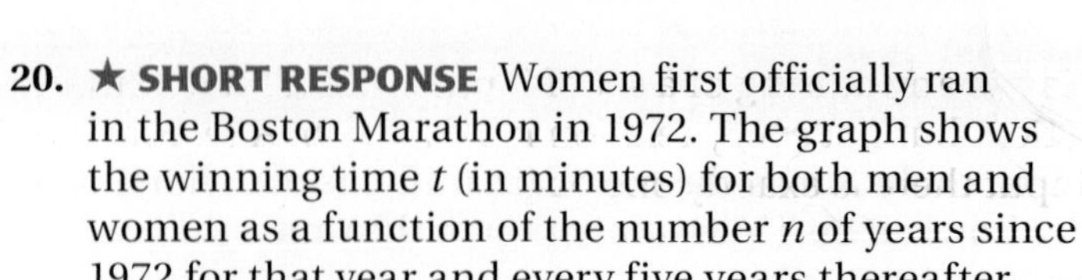

20. ★ **SHORT RESPONSE** Women first officially ran in the Boston Marathon in 1972. The graph shows the winning time t (in minutes) for both men and women as a function of the number n of years since 1972 for that year and every five years thereafter.

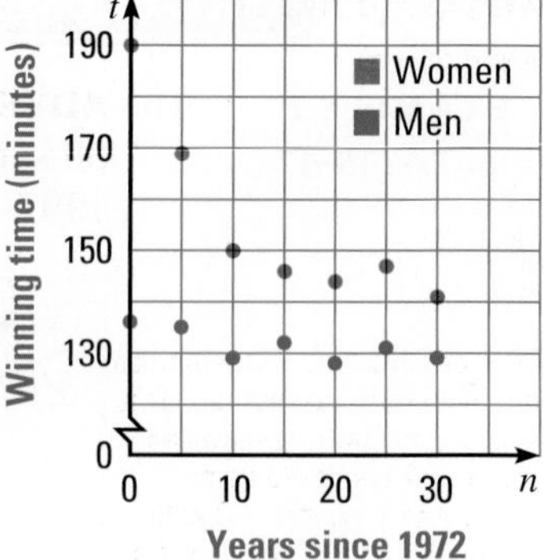

a. **CHALLENGE** *Explain* how you can estimate the difference in the men's and women's winning time for any year shown.

b. **CHALLENGE** *Compare* any trends you see in the graphs.

QUIZ

Choose the more precise measurement.

1. 1.5 ft; 18 in.
2. 25 mm or 1.2 m
3. 1.7 cm or 2.45 cm
4. **SIGNIFICANT DIGITS** Identify the number of significant digits in the measurement **(a)** 16.002 m and **(b)** 10.05.
5. The domain of the function $y = 12 - 2x$ is 0, 2, 3, 4, and 5. Make a table for the function, then identify the range of the function.

Tell whether the pairing is a function.

6.

x	5	6	7	11
y	1	2	3	7

7.

x	4	6	9	15
y	1	3	6	3

Graph the function.

8. $y = 2x - 5$; domain: 5, 6, 7, 8, and 9
9. $y = 7 - x$; domain: 1, 2, 3, 4, and 5

Extension Determine Whether a Relation Is a Function

GOAL Determine whether a relation is a function when the relation is represented by a table or a graph.

Key Vocabulary
- **relation**

CC.9-12.F.IF.1 Understand that a function from one set (called the domain) to another set (called the range) assigns to each element of the domain exactly one element of the range. If f is a function and x is an element of its domain, then $f(x)$ denotes the output of f corresponding to the input x. The graph of f is the graph of the equation $y = f(x)$.

A **relation** is any pairing of a set of inputs with a set of outputs. Every function is a relation, but not every relation is a function. A relation is a function if for every input there is exactly one output.

EXAMPLE 1 Determine whether a relation is a function

Determine whether the relation is a function.

a.

Input	4	4	5	6	7
Output	0	1	2	3	4

b.

Input	3	5	7	9
Output	1	2	3	2

Solution

a. The input 4 has two different outputs, 0 and 1. So, the relation is *not* a function.

b. Every input has exactly one output, so the relation is a function.

USING THE GRAPH OF A RELATION You can use the *vertical line test* to determine whether a relation represented by a graph is a function. When a relation is *not* a function, its graph contains at least two points with the same x-coordinate and different y-coordinates. Those points lie on a vertical line.

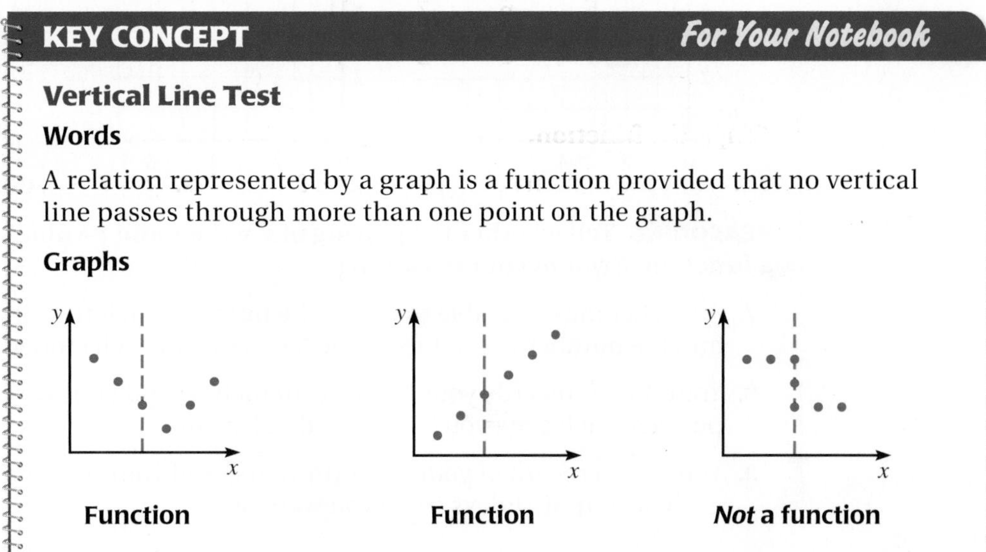

EXAMPLE 2 Use the vertical line test

Determine whether the graph represents a function.

a.

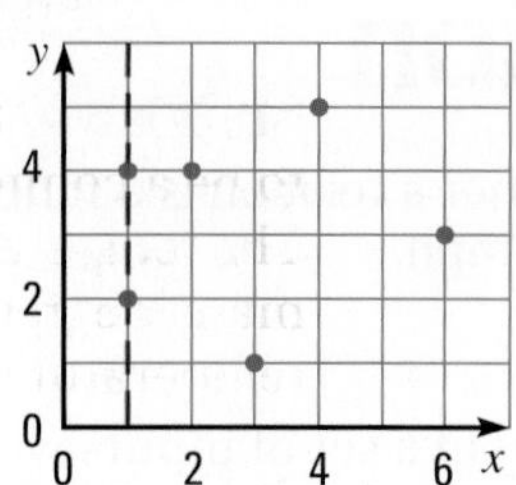

You can draw a vertical line through the points (1, 2) and (1, 4). The graph does *not* represent a function.

Animated Algebra at my.hrw.com

b.

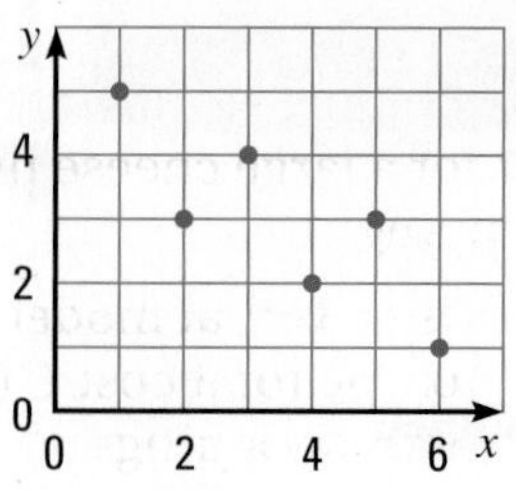

No vertical line can be drawn through more than one point. The graph represents a function.

PRACTICE

EXAMPLE 1 for Exs. 1–3

IDENTIFYING FUNCTIONS **Determine whether the relation is a function.**

1.

Input	Output
0	1
2	6
5	12
7	5
8	4

2.

Input	Output
3	7
4	8
4	9
5	10
6	11

3.

Input	Output
0.7	1.9
1.2	2.4
3.5	4.7
7.5	8.7
7.5	9.7

EXAMPLE 2 for Exs. 4–6

IDENTIFYING FUNCTIONS **Determine whether the graph represents a function.**

4.

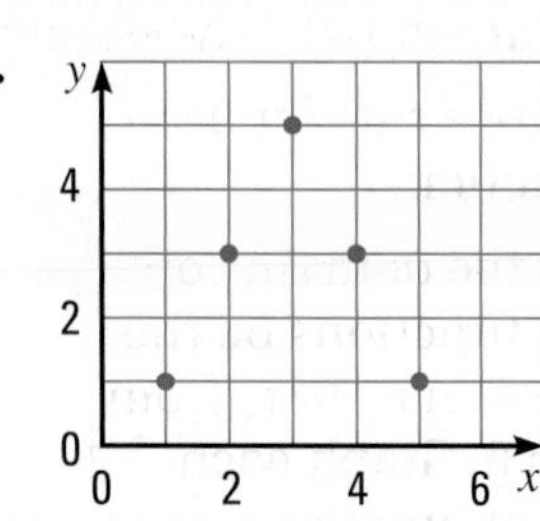

5.

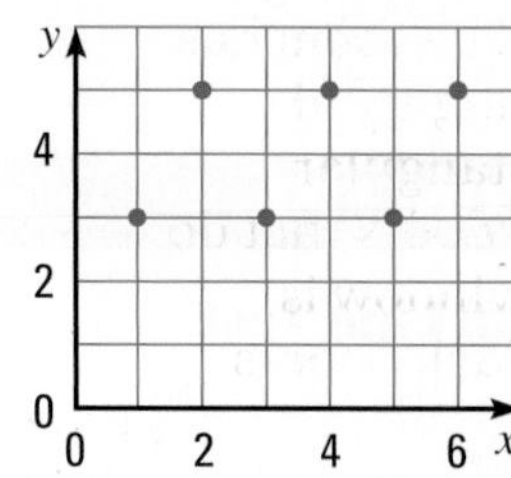

6.

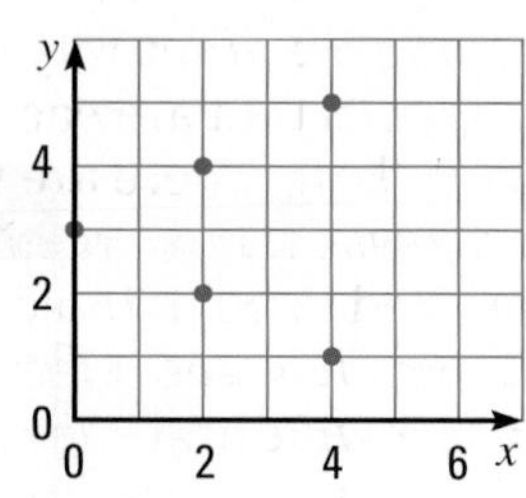

REASONING **Tell whether the pairing of x-values and y-values is necessarily a function. *Explain* your reasoning.**

7. A teacher makes a table that lists the number x of letters in the first name and the number y of letters in the last name of each student in the class.

8. Your doctor records your height x (in inches) and your weight y (in pounds) each time you have a medical exam.

9. You have a record of your age x (in years) and your height y (in inches) on each of your birthdays since you were born.

MIXED REVIEW *of Problem Solving*

Make sense of problems and persevere in solving them.

1. **MULTI-STEP PROBLEM** A pizza shop charges \$7 for a large cheese pizza plus \$.95 for each topping.

   a. Use a verbal model to write an equation for the total cost C (in dollars) of a pizza with n toppings.

   b. The pizza shop offers 10 toppings. Write an input-output table for the total cost (in dollars) of a pizza as a function of the number n of toppings. *Explain* why the table represents a function and describe the domain and range of the function.

   c. You have \$15 to spend on a large pizza. What is the greatest number of toppings you can afford?

2. **SHORT RESPONSE** Your class is planning a car wash. You need \$75 worth of materials.

   a. Use a verbal model to write an equation that relates your profit to the number of cars you wash. Find your profit if you wash 120 cars.

   b. Does doubling the number of cars you wash double your profit? *Explain.*

3. **MULTI-STEP PROBLEM** You are painting a room in a community center. The room has four walls that are each 9 feet high and 25 feet long. There are two rectangular windows and two rectangular doors that do not need to be painted. Each window is 3.5 feet wide and 4 feet high. Each door is 3.5 feet wide and 7 feet high.

   a. Find the combined area of the windows and doors.

   b. Find the combined area of all four walls, excluding the windows and the doors.

   c. A gallon of paint covers about 400 square feet. How many one-gallon cans of paint will you need in order to give the room one coat of paint?

   d. The paint costs \$24.95 per gallon. How much will it cost for one coat of paint?

4. **GRIDDED ANSWER** You consider 68°F to be a comfortable room temperature. The temperature in a room is 18°C. How many degrees Celsius should you raise the temperature so that it will be 68°F?

5. **SHORT RESPONSE** Your family is driving from Charleston, South Carolina, to Jacksonville, Florida, a total distance of about 250 miles. You leave Charleston at 1:00 P.M. You travel at an average speed of 55 miles per hour without stopping. Will you get to Jacksonville before the 5:00 P.M. rush hour? *Explain.*

6. **GRIDDED ANSWER** A person invests \$1200 in an account earning 3% simple annual interest. How much will be in the account after 2 years?

7. **OPEN-ENDED** Write a problem that involves a real-world situation and that can be solved using the formula for distance traveled. Solve the problem and explain what the solution means in the situation.

8. **EXTENDED RESPONSE** You pay \$40 per hour for windsurfing lessons and rent equipment for \$20 per hour. The cost (in dollars) of lessons and the cost (in dollars) of rentals are both functions of the time (in hours).

   a. Write a rule for each function.

   b. Let the domains of the functions be the whole numbers from 0 to 6. Graph each function.

   c. You rent equipment for every lesson you take. What function gives your total cost? How would the graph of this function compare with the graphs in part (b)?

1 CHAPTER SUMMARY

BIG IDEAS

For Your Notebook

Big Idea 1

Writing and Evaluating Algebraic Expressions

The cost of admission for one student at a planetarium is \$6. You can use a verbal model to write an expression for the total cost of admission for any number of students.

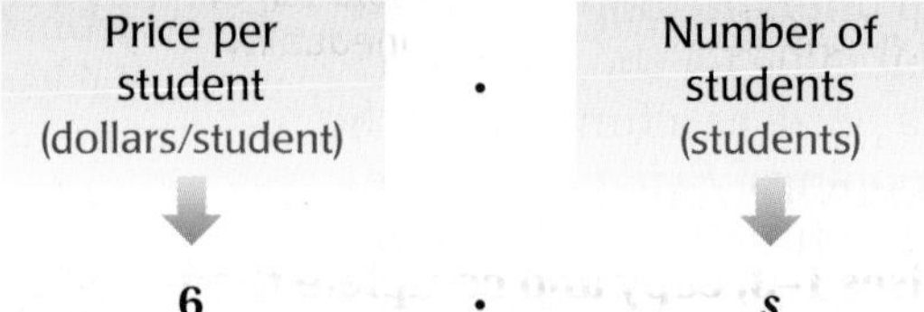

6 • *s*

An expression is $6s$. Because $\frac{\text{dollars}}{\cancel{\text{student}}} \cdot \cancel{\text{students}} = \text{dollars}$, the expression produces an answer in dollars. The expression is reasonable.

Big Idea 2

Using Expressions to Write Equations and Inequalities

You can use symbols to write an equation or inequality that compares the expression $6s$ to another expression.

The total cost of admission to the planetarium for *s* students at a rate of \$6 per student is \$150.

$6s = 150$ **Equation**

The total cost of admission to the planetarium for *s* students at a rate of \$6 per student is no more than \$150.

$6s \leq 150$ **Inequality**

Big Idea 3

Representing Functions as Verbal Rules, Equations, Tables, and Graphs

You can use a verbal description, an equation, a table, or a graph to represent a function.

Words The total cost (in dollars) of admission to the planetarium is 6 times the number of students.

Equation

$C = 6s$

Table

Input, *s*	Output, *C*
0	0
1	6
2	12
3	18

Graph

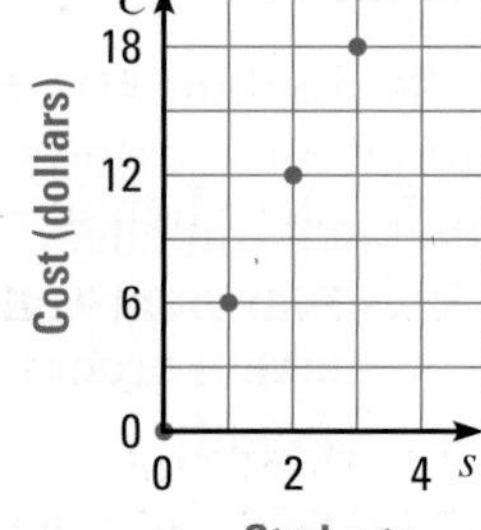

1 CHAPTER REVIEW

@HomeTutor
my.hrw.com
- Multi-Language Glossary
- Vocabulary practice

REVIEW KEY VOCABULARY

- variable
- algebraic expression
- evaluate an algebraic expression
- power, exponent, base
- order of operations
- verbal model
- rate, unit rate
- equation, inequality
- open sentence
- solution of an equation or inequality
- formula
- precision
- significant digits
- function, domain, range
- independent variable
- dependent variable

VOCABULARY EXERCISES

In Exercises 1–3, copy and complete the statement.

1. In the power 7^{12}, _?_ is the base and _?_ is the exponent.

2. A(n) _?_ is a statement that contains the symbol =.

3. A(n) _?_ is an expression that includes at least one variable.

4. **WRITING** *Describe* how you can tell by looking at the graph of a function which variable is the input variable and which is the output variable.

REVIEW EXAMPLES AND EXERCISES

Use the review examples and exercises below to check your understanding of the concepts you have learned in each lesson of this chapter.

1.1 Evaluate Expressions

EXAMPLE

Evaluate $6 - n$ when $n = 4$.

$6 - n = 6 - 4$ **Substitute 4 for *n*.**

$= 2$ **Simplify.**

EXERCISES

EXAMPLES 1, 4, and 5 for Exs. 5–12

Evaluate the expression.

5. $3 + x$ when $x = 13$

6. $y - 2$ when $y = 18$

7. $\frac{20}{k}$ when $k = 2$

8. $40w$ when $w = 0.5$

9. z^2 when $z = 20$

10. w^3 when $w = 0.1$

11. **DVD STORAGE** A DVD storage sleeve has the shape of a square with an edge length of 5 inches. What is the area of the front of the sleeve?

12. **NOTEPAPER** You store square notepaper in a cube-shaped box with an inside edge length of 3 inches. What is the volume of the box?

1 CHAPTER REVIEW

1.2 Apply Order of Operations

EXAMPLE

Evaluate $(5 + 3)^2 \div 2 \times 3$.

$(5 + 3)^2 \div 2 \times 3 = 8^2 \div 2 \times 3$ **Add within parentheses.**

$= 64 \div 2 \times 3$ **Evaluate power.**

$= 32 \times 3$ **Divide.**

$= 96$ **Multiply.**

EXERCISES

EXAMPLES 1, 2, and 3 for Exs. 13–21

Evaluate the expression.

13. $12 - 6 \div 2$

14. $1 + 2 \cdot 9^2$

15. $3 + 2^3 - 6 \div 2$

16. $15 - (4 + 3^2)$

17. $\dfrac{20 - 12}{5^2 - 1}$

18. $50 - [7 + (3^2 \div 2)]$

Evaluate the expression when $x = 4$.

19. $15x - 8$

20. $3x^2 + 4$

21. $2(x - 1)^2$

1.3 Write Expressions

EXAMPLE

Write an expression for the entry fee in a jazz band competition if there is a base fee of \$50 and a charge of \$1 per member.

Write a verbal model. Then translate the verbal model into an algebraic expression. Let n represent the number of band members.

Base fee (dollars) + Cost per member (dollars/member) • Number of members (members)

50 + **1** • ***n***

▸ An expression for the entry fee (in dollars) is $50 + n$.

EXERCISES

EXAMPLES 1, 2, and 3 for Exs. 22–27

Translate the verbal phrase into an expression.

22. The sum of a number k and 7

23. 5 less than a number z

24. The quotient of a number k and 12

25. 3 times the square of a number x

26. TOLL ROADS A toll road charges trucks a toll of \$3 per axle. Write an expression for the total toll for a truck.

27. SCHOOL SUPPLIES You purchase some notebooks for \$2.95 each and a package of pens for \$2.19. Write an expression for the total amount (in dollars) that you spend.

@HomeTutor
my.hrw.com
Chapter Review Practice

1.4 Write Equations and Inequalities

EXAMPLE

Write an inequality for the sentence "The sum of 3 and twice a number k is no more than 15". Then check whether 4 is a solution of the inequality.

An inequality is $3 + 2k \le 15$.

To check whether 4 is a solution of the inequality, substitute 4 for k.

$3 + 2(4) \overset{?}{\le} 15$ **Substitute 4 for *k*.**

$11 \le 15$ ✓ **The solution checks. So, 4 is a solution.**

EXERCISES

EXAMPLES 1 and 2 for Exs. 28–32

Write an equation or an inequality.

28. The product of a number z and 12 is 60.

29. The sum of 13 and a number t is at least 24.

Check whether the given number is a solution of the equation or inequality.

30. $3x - 4 = 10; 5$

31. $4y - 2 \ge 2; 3$

32. $2d + 4 < 9d - 7; 3$

1.5 Use a Problem Solving Plan

EXAMPLE

A rectangular banner is 12 feet long and has an area of 60 square feet. What is the perimeter of the banner?

STEP 1 **Read and Understand** You know the length of the rectangular banner and its area. You want to find the perimeter.

STEP 2 **Make a Plan** Use the area formula for a rectangle to find the width. Then use the perimeter formula for a rectangle.

STEP 3 **Solve the Problem** Substituting 12 for ℓ in the formula $A = \ell w$, $60 = 12w$. Because $12 \cdot 5 = 60$, $w = 5$. Then substituting 12 for ℓ and 5 for w in the formula $P = 2\ell + 2w$, $P = 2(12) + 2(5) = 34$ feet.

STEP 4 **Look Back** Use estimation. Since $\ell \approx 10$ and $A = 60$, $w \approx 6$. Then $P \approx 2(10) + 2(6) = 32$ feet, so your answer is reasonable.

EXERCISES

EXAMPLES 1, 2, and 3 for Exs. 33–34

33. U.S. HISTORY The flag that inspired the national anthem was a rectangle 30 feet wide and 42 feet long. Pieces of the flag have been lost. It is now 30 feet wide and 34 feet long. How many square feet have been lost?

34. PATTERNS A grocery clerk stacks three rows of cans of fruit for a display. Each of the top two rows has 2 fewer cans than the row beneath it. There are 30 cans altogether. How many cans are there in each row?

1.6 Use Precision and Measurement

EXAMPLE

Determine the number of significant digits in the measurement 7020 kilometers.

The digits 7 and 2 are nonzero digits, so they are significant digits. There is a zero between two significant digits, so that is a significant digit. Because 7020 is a whole number, the zero at the end is nonsignificant.

There are 3 significant digits.

EXERCISES

EXAMPLES 1 and 2 for Exs. 35–38

Determine the number of significant digits in the measurement.

35. 15.02 meters

36. 10.302 miles

37. 0.0020 centimeters

38. PRECISION In a woodworking class, students measure a board that has a length of exactly 30.25 centimeters. Lorraine reports the length to be 303 millimeters. Arnie reports the length to be 30 centimeters. Whose measurement is more precise?

1.7 Represent Functions as Rules and Tables

EXAMPLE

The domain of the function $y = 3x - 5$ is 2, 3, 4, and 5. Make a table for the function, then identify the range of the function.

x	2	3	4	5
$y = 3x - 5$	$3(2) - 5 = 1$	$3(3) - 5 = 4$	$3(4) - 5 = 7$	$3(5) - 5 = 10$

The range of the function is 1, 4, 7, and 10.

EXERCISES

EXAMPLES 1, 2, and 3 for Exs. 39–42

Make a table for the function. Identify the range of the function.

39. $y = x - 5$
Domain: 10, 12, 15, 20, 21

40. $y = 3x + 1$
Domain: 0, 2, 3, 5, 10

Write a rule for the function.

41.

Input, x	0	2	4	5
Output, y	4	6	8	9

42.

Input, x	0	3	4	6
Output, y	0	15	20	30

@HomeTutor
my.hrw.com
Chapter Review Practice

1.8 Represent Functions as Graphs

EXAMPLE

Write a rule for the function represented by the graph. Identify the domain and the range of the function.

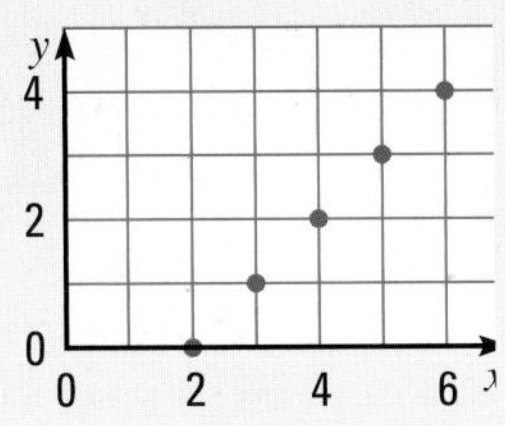

Make a table for the graph.

x	2	3	4	5	6
y	0	1	2	3	4

Each y-value is 2 less than the corresponding x-value. A rule for the function is $y = x - 2$. The domain is 2, 3, 4, 5, and 6. The range is 0, 1, 2, 3, and 4.

EXERCISES

EXAMPLES 1, 3, and 4 for Exs. 43–44

43. Graph the function $y = 4x - 3$ with domain 1, 2, 3, 4, and 5.

44. Write a rule for the function represented by the graph. Identify the domain and the range of the function.

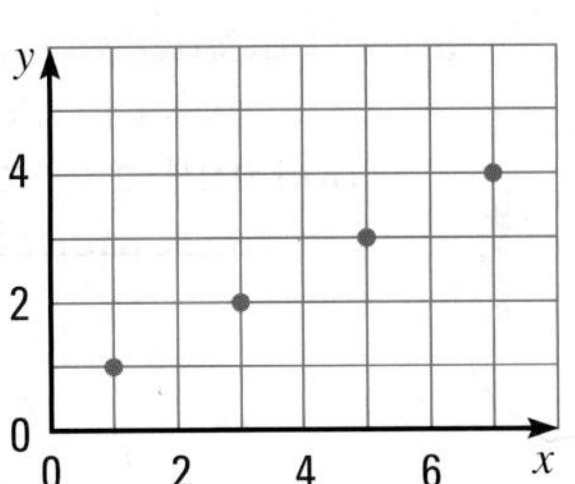

1 CHAPTER TEST

Evaluate the expression.

1. $7 + 3^2 \cdot 2$

2. $(5^2 + 17) \div 7$

3. $(24 - 11) - (3 + 2) \div 4$

4. $\frac{x}{5}$ when $x = 30$

5. n^3 when $n = 20$

6. $15 - t$ when $t = 11$

7. $12 + 4x$ when $x = 1\frac{1}{2}$

8. $3z^2 - 7$ when $z = 6$

9. $2(4n + 5)$ when $n = 2$

Write an expression, an equation, or an inequality.

10. The sum of 19 and the cube of a number x

11. The product of 3 and a number y is no more than 21.

12. Twice the difference of a number z and 12 is equal to 10.

Check whether the given number is a solution of the equation or inequality.

13. $2 + 3x = 10$; 2

14. $8 + 3b > 15$; 2

15. $11y - 5 \leq 30$; 3

16. Perform the operation 15.2 feet × 2.4 feet. Write the answer with the correct number of significant digits.

17. Refer to the graph.

a. *Explain* why the graph represents a function.

b. Identify the domain and the range.

c. Write a rule for the function.

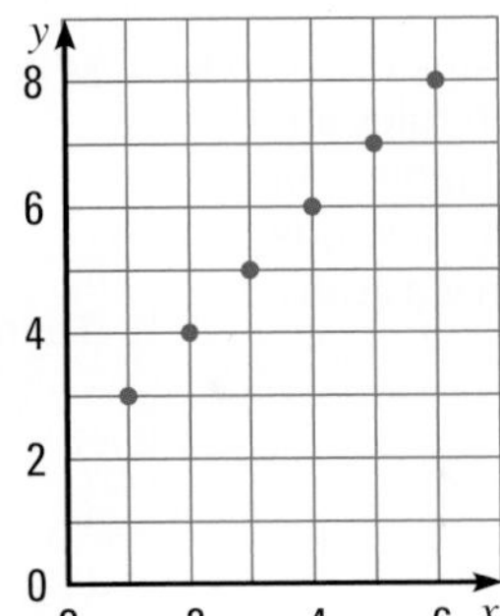

18. FOOD PREPARATION You buy tomatoes at \$1.29 per pound and peppers at \$3.99 per pound to make salsa. Write an expression for the total cost of the ingredients. Then find the total cost of 5 pounds of tomatoes and 2 pounds of peppers.

19. CAR EXPENSES A family determined the average cost of maintaining and operating the family car to be about \$.30 per mile. On one trip, the family drove at an average rate of 50 miles per hour for a total of 6.5 hours. On a second trip, they drove at an average rate of 55 miles per hour for a total of 6 hours. Which trip cost more? How much more?

20. SHOE SIZES A man's size 6 shoe is the same size as a woman's size $7\frac{1}{2}$. The table shows other corresponding sizes of men's and women's shoes.

Men's size, x	6	$6\frac{1}{2}$	7	$7\frac{1}{2}$	8	$8\frac{1}{2}$	9
Women's size, y	$7\frac{1}{2}$	8	$8\frac{1}{2}$	9	$9\frac{1}{2}$	10	$10\frac{1}{2}$

a. Using the data in the table, write a rule for women's shoe size as a function of men's shoe size. Identify the domain and the range.

b. Graph the function.

Scoring Rubric

Full Credit
- solution is complete and correct

Partial Credit
- solution is complete but has errors,
or
- solution is without error but incomplete

No Credit
- no solution is given,
or
- solution makes no sense

SHORT RESPONSE QUESTIONS

PROBLEM

Mike and Aaron are inflating helium balloons for a graduation party. Mike can inflate 3 balloons per minute, and Aaron can inflate 2 balloons per minute. If Mike and Aaron start inflating balloons at the same time, how many minutes will it take them to inflate a total of 30 balloons? *Explain* your answer.

Below are sample solutions to the problem. Read each solution and the comments on the left to see why the sample represents full credit, partial credit, or no credit.

SAMPLE 1: Full credit solution

For each person, the number of balloons inflated is a function of the number of minutes. Let t be the time (in minutes) that Mike and Aaron have been inflating balloons, and let b be the number of balloons inflated.

The function rules are correct. The tables and explanation show how the problem was solved.

Mike: $b = 3t$

t	1	2	3	4	5	6
b	3	6	9	12	15	18

Aaron: $b = 2t$

t	1	2	3	4	5	6
b	2	4	6	8	10	12

The tables show that in 6 minutes Mike will have inflated 18 balloons, and Aaron will have inflated 12 balloons.

The solution is correct.

Since $18 + 12 = 30$, it will take Mike and Aaron 6 minutes to inflate a total of 30 balloons.

SAMPLE 2: Partial credit solution

The reasoning and the function rule are correct.

Since Mike can inflate 3 balloons per minute and Aaron can inflate 2 balloons per minute, together they can inflate 5 balloons per minute.

Use the function $b = 5t$ where t is the time (in minutes) and b is the number of balloons inflated.

The solution is incorrect. The student substituted 30 for t instead of for b.

$$b = 5t$$
$$= 5(30)$$
$$= 150$$

So, it will take 150 minutes, or 2.5 hours, to inflate 30 balloons.

SAMPLE 3: Partial credit solution

The solution is without error but incomplete. There is no explanation of how the graph was used to find the answer.

Mike can inflate 3 balloons per minute, and Aaron can inflate 2 balloons per minute. Let t represent the time in minutes and b represent the total number of balloons the friends inflate. Graph the function $b = 5t$.

It will take 6 minutes to inflate 30 balloons.

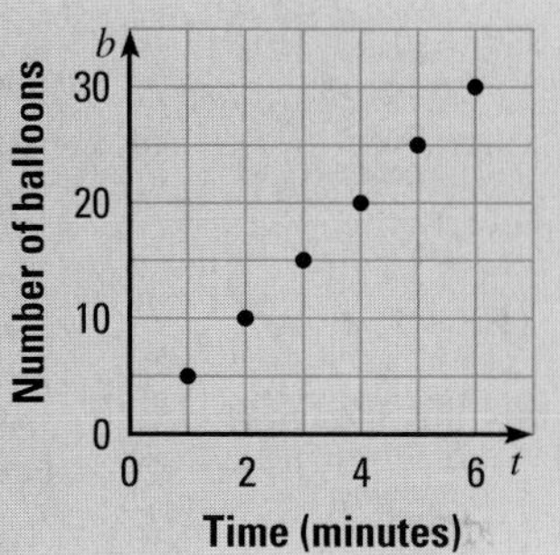

SAMPLE 4: No credit solution

The solution makes no sense. Each boy takes less time working alone.

Mike takes $30 \div 3 = 10$ minutes to inflate 30 balloons. Aaron takes $30 \div 2 = 15$ minutes to inflate 30 balloons. Because $10 + 15 = 25$, it will take Mike and Aaron 25 minutes to inflate 30 balloons.

PRACTICE Apply the Scoring Rubric

Score the solution to the problem below as *full credit, partial credit,* or *no credit. Explain* your reasoning.

PROBLEM Jessica and Graciela start exercising at the same time. Jessica jogs at a rate of 600 feet per minute. Graciela walks in the same direction at a rate of 400 feet per minute. If the girls start at the same time, in how many minutes will they be 4000 feet apart? *Explain.*

1. Because $4000 \div 200 = 20$, Jessica and Graciela will be 4000 feet apart after 20 minutes.

2. For every minute they exercise, the girls travel a total of 1000 feet. Let t be time (in minutes) and d be distance (in feet). Then $d = 1000t$, and when $t = 4$, $d = 4000$. The answer is 4 minutes.

3. Let t be the time (in minutes) and d be the distance (in feet). For Jessica, $d = 600t$. For Graciela, $d = 400t$.

t	5	10	15	20
d	3000	6000	9000	12,000

t	5	10	15	20
d	2000	4000	6000	8000

When $t = 20$, $600t = 12{,}000$ and $400t = 8000$, so the girls are 4000 feet apart. The answer is 20 minutes.

1 ★ Standardized TEST PRACTICE

SHORT RESPONSE

1. A punch recipe uses 2 parts pineapple juice to 3 parts apple juice. The table shows the number of calories in each type of juice.

Juice	Calories in one cup
pineapple	140
apple	120

Would you expect there to be fewer than 120 calories, between 120 and 140 calories, or more than 140 calories in 1 cup of the punch? Exactly how many calories are there in 1 cup of the punch? *Explain.*

2. Ming has saved $340 to spend on an MP3 player and music. Music for the MP3 player costs $.99 per song, and Ming wants to buy at least 100 songs. Which models of MP3 player should she consider purchasing? *Explain* your reasoning.

Model	Price (dollars)
A	230
B	241
C	275
D	299

3. An animal shelter has 200 calendars to sell at a fair as a fundraiser. Each of the calendars costs $3 to make. The shelter hopes to sell all the calendars and make a total profit of $1800.
   a. What should the selling price of each calendar be?
   b. If the shelter hopes to make a profit of $2000, what should the selling price of each calendar be? *Explain* your reasoning.

4. Mark works at a grocery store where employees make one and a half times their regular hourly wage when they work on a Saturday or a Sunday. Mark works an 8 hour shift 5 days per week, sometimes including weekends. His regular hourly wage is $8.50. What is the maximum amount that he could earn in one week? *Explain* your reasoning.

5. The Ruizes offer each of their children two different options for increasing the child's weekly allowance.

   Option 1: Increase the allowance by one half of the current allowance.

   Option 2: Increase the allowance by $3 per week.

   Describe under what conditions each option is preferable. *Justify* your answers.

6. A pizzeria charges $11 for a large cheese pizza. The pizzeria is offering a special deal. If you buy 3 large cheese pizzas, you can choose to get a fourth cheese pizza free.
   a. Make a table showing the cost (in dollars) of 1, 2, 3, or 4 pizzas.
   b. Is the cost of the pizzas a function of the number of pizzas purchased? *Explain.*
   c. Is the number of pizzas purchased a function of the cost (in dollars)? *Explain.*

7. You buy 5 feet of ribbon to decorate the edge of a rectangular placemat. You have 6 inches of ribbon left over after you decorate the placemat. What is the width of the placemat? *Explain* your method.

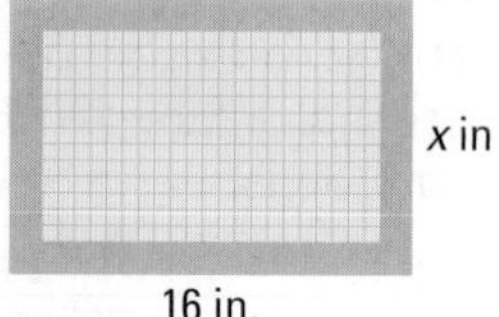

8. Two buses leave the same stop at the same time and travel the same route. One is an express bus and doesn't make any stops along the way. The other is a local bus and makes stops along the way.

   The express bus travels at an average speed of 40 miles per hour, and the local bus travels at an average speed of 30 miles per hour. The route is 10 miles long and the local bus makes 5 two-minute stops. How many minutes do you save by taking the express bus instead of the local bus? *Explain.*

MULTIPLE CHOICE

9. Which is a rule for the function given by the input-output table?

Input, x	8	10	12	14
Output, y	5	7	9	11

Ⓐ $y = x - 3$ Ⓑ $y = x - 2$

Ⓒ $y = x + 3$ Ⓓ $y = x + 2$

10. The number of adult tickets sold at a school talent show is 5 less than 3 times the number c of children's tickets sold. Which expression represents the number of adult tickets sold?

Ⓐ $3c + 5$ Ⓑ $5 - 3c$

Ⓒ $5c + 3$ Ⓓ $3c - 5$

11. The function $y = 2x + 4$ has a domain of 2, 3, 5, 7, and 8. Which number is *not* in the range of the function?

Ⓐ 8 Ⓑ 12

Ⓒ 18 Ⓓ 20

GRIDDED ANSWER

12. What is the value of the expression $202 - 2(2 + 3)^2$?

13. What is the value of $x^2 - 2x + 7$ when $x = 3$?

14. What is the solution of the equation $54 = 9x$?

15. What is the volume (in cubic inches) of the cube?

16. A rectangular field is twice as long as it is wide. A golf cart traveling at 12 miles per hour takes 7.5 minutes to travel the perimeter of the field. What is the length (in miles) of the field?

17. The table represents a function that can also be represented by a rule. What is the missing value in the table?

Input, x	7	8	11	12
Output, y	0	?	4	5

EXTENDED RESPONSE

18. Mario deposits \$140 in an account that earns simple interest at a rate of 5% per year. On the same day, Andy deposits \$150 in an account that earns simple interest at a rate of 3% per year. Mario and Andy plan to keep the accounts for at least 5 years, but make no additional deposits.

a. For each account, write a rule for the the amount I (in dollars) of interest as a function of the time t (in years) that the account has been open.

b. Let the domain of each function in part (a) be 1, 2, 3, 4, and 5. Make a table for each function.

c. After how many years will the total amount in each account be the same? How much will be in each account? *Justify* your answer.

19. A dance floor is made from square wooden tiles with a side length of 1 foot. The floor can be laid out as a square or as a rectangle. The width of the rectangular floor is 10 feet less than the width of the square floor, and its length is 15 feet greater than the length of the square floor.

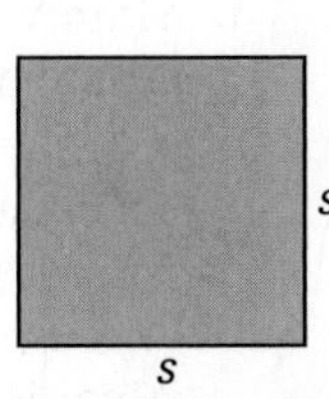

a. How much greater is the length of the rectangular dance floor than the width? *Justify* your answer.

b. The perimeter of the rectangular dance floor is 130 feet. What are the length and width of the dance floor? *Explain* your reasoning.

c. How many square tiles make up the dance floor?

2 Solving Linear Equations

COMMON CORE

Lesson	
2.1	CC.9-12.N.Q.1*
2.2	CC.9-12.A.REI.3
2.3	CC.9-12.A.REI.3
2.4	CC.9-12.A.REI.3
2.5	CC.9-12.A.REI.3
2.6	CC.9-12.A.CED.1*
2.7	CC.9-12.A.CED.1*
2.8	CC.9-12.A.CED.4*

Before

Previously, you learned the following skills, which you'll use in this chapter: simplifying expressions, writing percents as decimals, and using formulas.

Prerequisite Skills

VOCABULARY CHECK

Copy and complete the statement.

1. In the expression $3x + 7 + 7x$, __?__ and __?__ are like terms.
2. The reciprocal of $\frac{5}{8}$ is __?__.

SKILLS CHECK

Simplify the expression.

3. $5x - (6 - x)$ 4. $3(x - 9) - 16$ 5. $23 + 4(x + 2)$ 6. $x(7 + x) + 9x^2$

Write the percent as a decimal.

7. 54% 8. 99% 9. 12.5% **10.** 150%

Find the perimeter of the rectangle.

11. 16 ft by 7 ft **12.** 20 cm by 14 cm **13.** 11 in. by 4 in.

Now

In this chapter, you will apply the big ideas listed below and reviewed in the Chapter Summary. You will also use the key vocabulary listed below.

Big Ideas

1. **Solving equations in one variable**
2. **Solving proportions**
3. **Rewriting equations in two or more variables**

KEY VOCABULARY

- square root
- radicand
- perfect square
- irrational number
- real numbers
- inverse operations
- equivalent equations
- identity
- ratio
- proportion
- cross product
- scale drawing
- scale model
- scale
- literal equation

Why?

Knowing how to solve a linear equation can help you solve problems involving distance, rate, and time. For example, you can solve an equation to find the time it takes a jellyfish to travel a given distance at a given rate.

Animated Algebra

The animation illustrated below helps you answer a question from this chapter: How long does it take the jellyfish to travel 26 feet?

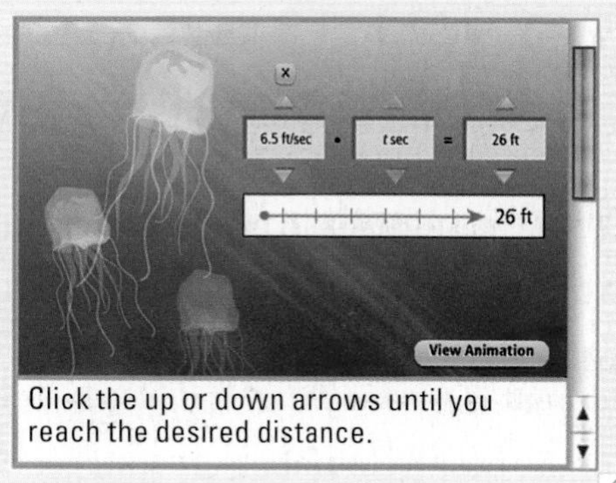

Animated Algebra at my.hrw.com

Writing Statements in If-Then Form

Look for and make use of structure.

MATERIALS • paper and pencil

QUESTION **How can you write an *all* or *none* statement in if-then form?**

EXPLORE **Tell whether certain statements are true about a group**

STEP 1 ***Answer questions*** Copy the questions below and write your answers beside them.

1. Do you play an instrument?

2. Do you participate in a school sport?

3. Are you taking an art class?

4. Do you walk to school?

STEP 2 ***Write if-then statements*** Each of the *all* or *none* statements below can be written in if-then form. Copy each statement and complete its equivalent if-then form. The first one is done for you as an example.

1. All of the students in our group play an instrument.
If a student is in our group, then the student plays an instrument.

2. None of the students in our group participates in a school sport.
If __?__, then __?__.

3. None of the students in our group is taking an art class.
If __?__, then __?__.

4. All of the students in our group walk to school.
If __?__, then __?__.

STEP 3 ***Analyze statements*** Form a group with 2 or 3 classmates. Tell whether each if-then statement in Step 2 is *true* or *false* for your group. If the statement is false, give a counterexample.

DRAW CONCLUSIONS **Use your observations to complete these exercises**

1. *Describe* the similarity and difference in the if-then forms of the following statements:

All of the students in our group listen to rock music.

None of the students in our group listens to rock music.

Rewrite the given conditional statement in if-then form. Then tell whether the statement is *true* or *false*. If it is false, give a counterexample.

2. All of the positive numbers are integers.

3. All of the rational numbers can be written as fractions.

4. None of the negative numbers is a whole number.

5. None of the rational numbers has an opposite equal to itself.

2.1 Find Square Roots and Compare Real Numbers

Before You found squares of numbers and compared rational numbers.

Now You will find square roots and compare real numbers.

Why? So you can find side lengths of geometric shapes, as in Ex. 52.

Key Vocabulary
- **square root**
- **radicand**
- **perfect square**
- **irrational number**
- **real numbers**

CC.9-12.N.Q.1 Use units as a way to understand problems and to guide the solution of multi-step problems; choose and interpret units consistently in formulas; choose and interpret the scale and the origin in graphs and data displays.*

Recall that the square of 4 is $4^2 = 16$ and the square of -4 is $(-4)^2 = 16$. The numbers 4 and -4 are called the *square roots* of 16. In this lesson, you will find the square roots of nonnegative numbers.

KEY CONCEPT *For Your Notebook*

Square Root of a Number

Words If $b^2 = a$, then b is a **square root** of a.

Example $3^2 = 9$ and $(-3)^2 = 9$, so 3 and -3 are square roots of 9.

All positive real numbers have two square roots, a positive square root (or *principal* square root) and a negative square root. A square root is written with the radical symbol $\sqrt{\ }$. The number or expression inside a radical symbol is the **radicand.**

radical symbol ⟶ $\sqrt{a}$ ⟵ **radicand**

Zero has only one square root, 0. Negative real numbers do not have real square roots because the square of every real number is either positive or 0.

EXAMPLE 1 Find square roots

Evaluate the expression.

READING The symbol $\pm$ is read as "plus or minus" and refers to both the positive square root and the negative square root.

a. $\pm\sqrt{36} = \pm 6$ **The positive and negative square roots of 36 are 6 and −6.**

b. $\sqrt{49} = 7$ **The positive square root of 49 is 7.**

c. $-\sqrt{4} = -2$ **The negative square root of 4 is −2.**

✓ **GUIDED PRACTICE** for Example 1

Evaluate the expression.

1. $-\sqrt{9}$ **2.** $\sqrt{25}$ **3.** $\pm\sqrt{64}$ **4.** $-\sqrt{81}$

PERFECT SQUARES The square of an integer is called a **perfect square**. As shown in Example 1, the square root of a perfect square is an integer. As you will see in Example 2, you need to approximate a square root if the radicand is a whole number that is *not* a perfect square.

EXAMPLE 2 Approximate a square root

FURNITURE The top of a folding table is a square whose area is 945 square inches. Approximate the side length of the tabletop to the nearest inch.

Solution

You need to find the side length s of the tabletop such that $s^2 = 945$. This means that s is the positive square root of 945. You can use a table to determine whether 945 is a perfect square.

Number	28	29	30	31	32
Square of number	784	841	900	961	1024

As shown in the table, 945 is *not* a perfect square. The greatest perfect square less than 945 is 900. The least perfect square greater than 945 is 961.

$900 < 945 < 961$ **Write a compound inequality that compares 945 with both 900 and 961.**

$\sqrt{900} < \sqrt{945} < \sqrt{961}$ **Take positive square root of each number.**

$30 < \sqrt{945} < 31$ **Find square root of each perfect square.**

The average of 30 and 31 is 30.5, and $(30.5)^2 = 930.25$. Because $945 > 930.25$, $\sqrt{945}$ is closer to 31 than to 30.

▶ The side length of the tabletop is about 31 inches.

USING A CALCULATOR In Example 2, you can use a calculator to obtain a better approximation of the side length of the tabletop.

The value shown can be rounded to the nearest hundredth, 30.74, or to the nearest tenth, 30.7. In either case, the length is closer to 31 than to 30.

GUIDED PRACTICE for Example 2

Approximate the square root to the nearest integer.

5. $\sqrt{32}$ **6.** $\sqrt{103}$ **7.** $-\sqrt{48}$ **8.** $-\sqrt{350}$

IRRATIONAL NUMBERS The square root of a whole number that is not a perfect square is an example of an *irrational number*. An **irrational number**, such as $\sqrt{945} = 30.74085\ldots$, is a number that cannot be written as a quotient of two integers. The decimal form of an irrational number neither terminates nor repeats.

REAL NUMBERS The set of **real numbers** is the set of all rational and irrational numbers, as illustrated in the Venn diagram below. Every point on the real number line represents a real number.

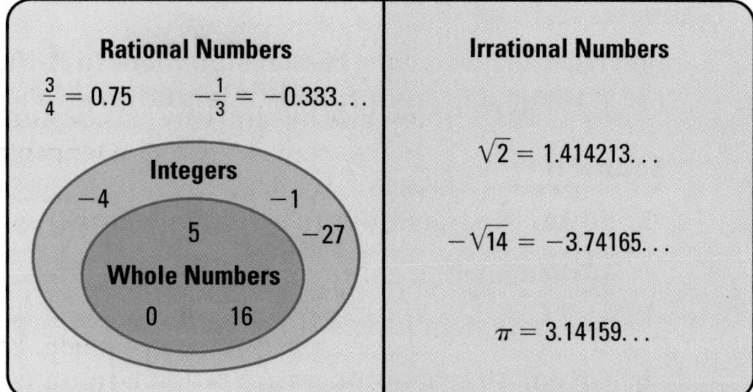

READING
If you exclude 0 from the whole numbers, the resulting set is called the *natural numbers.*

EXAMPLE 3 Classify numbers

Tell whether each of the following numbers is a real number, a rational number, an irrational number, an integer, or a whole number: $\sqrt{24}$, $\sqrt{100}$, $-\sqrt{81}$.

Number	Real number?	Rational number?	Irrational number?	Integer?	Whole number?
$\sqrt{24}$	Yes	No	Yes	No	No
$\sqrt{100}$	Yes	Yes	No	Yes	Yes
$-\sqrt{81}$	Yes	Yes	No	Yes	No

EXAMPLE 4 Graph and order real numbers

Order the numbers from least to greatest: $\frac{4}{3}$, $-\sqrt{5}$, $\sqrt{13}$, -2.5, $\sqrt{9}$.

Solution

Begin by graphing the numbers on a number line.

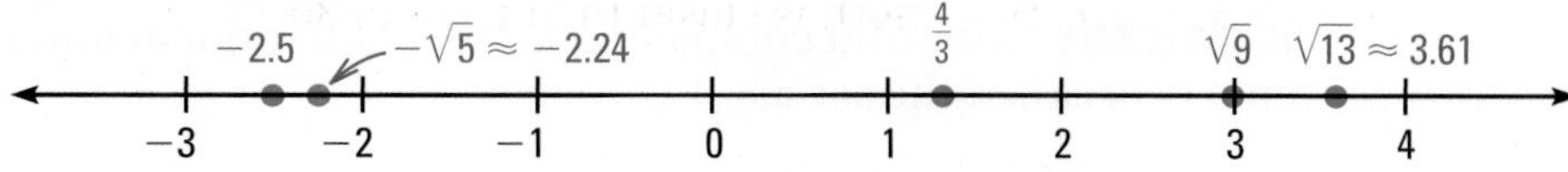

▶ Read the numbers from left to right: -2.5, $-\sqrt{5}$, $\frac{4}{3}$, $\sqrt{9}$, $\sqrt{13}$.

✓ GUIDED PRACTICE for Examples 3 and 4

9. Tell whether each of the following numbers is a real number, a rational number, an irrational number, an integer, or a whole number: $-\frac{9}{2}$, 5.2, 0, $\sqrt{7}$, 4.1, $-\sqrt{20}$. Then order the numbers from least to greatest.

CONDITIONAL STATEMENTS A conditional statement not in if-then form can be written in that form.

EXAMPLE 5 Rewrite a conditional statement in if-then form

Rewrite the given conditional statement in if-then form. Then tell whether the statement is *true* or *false*. If it is false, give a counterexample.

Solution

a. Given: No fractions are irrational numbers.

If-then form: If a number is a fraction, then it is not an irrational number.

The statement is true.

b. Given: All real numbers are rational numbers.

If-then form: If a number is a real number, then it is a rational number.

The statement is false. For example, $\sqrt{2}$ is a real number but *not* a rational number.

✓ GUIDED PRACTICE for Example 5

Rewrite the conditional statement in if-then form. Then tell whether the statement is *true* or *false*. If it is false, give a counterexample.

10. All square roots of perfect squares are rational numbers.

11. All repeating decimals are irrational numbers.

12. No integers are irrational numbers.

2.1 EXERCISES

HOMEWORK KEY

○ = See WORKED-OUT SOLUTIONS Exs. 9, 19, and 47

★ = STANDARDIZED TEST PRACTICE Exs. 2, 23, 41, 42, 48, and 51

◆ = MULTIPLE REPRESENTATIONS Ex. 52

SKILL PRACTICE

1. VOCABULARY Copy and complete: The set of all rational and irrational numbers is called the set of __?__.

2. ★ WRITING Without calculating, how can you tell whether the square root of a whole number is rational or irrational?

EXAMPLE 1 for Exs. 3–14

EVALUATING SQUARE ROOTS Evaluate the expression.

3. $\sqrt{4}$	**4.** $-\sqrt{49}$	**5.** $-\sqrt{9}$	**6.** $\pm\sqrt{1}$
7. $\sqrt{196}$	**8.** $\pm\sqrt{121}$	**9.** $\pm\sqrt{2500}$	**10.** $-\sqrt{256}$
11. $-\sqrt{225}$	**12.** $\sqrt{361}$	**13.** $\pm\sqrt{169}$	**14.** $-\sqrt{1600}$

EXAMPLE 2 for Exs. 15–22

APPROXIMATING SQUARE ROOTS Approximate the square root to the nearest integer.

15. $\sqrt{10}$ **16.** $-\sqrt{18}$ **17.** $-\sqrt{3}$ **18.** $\sqrt{150}$

19. $-\sqrt{86}$ **20.** $\sqrt{40}$ **21.** $\sqrt{200}$ **22.** $-\sqrt{65}$

23. ★ **MULTIPLE CHOICE** Which number is between −30 and −25?

Ⓐ $-\sqrt{1610}$ Ⓑ $-\sqrt{680}$ Ⓒ $-\sqrt{410}$ Ⓓ $-\sqrt{27}$

EXAMPLES 3 AND 4 for Exs. 24–29

CLASSIFYING AND ORDERING REAL NUMBERS Tell whether each number in the list is a real number, a rational number, an irrational number, an integer, or a whole number. Then order the numbers from least to greatest.

24. $\sqrt{49}$, 8, $-\sqrt{4}$, −3

25. $-\sqrt{12}$, −3.7, $\sqrt{9}$, 2.9

26. −11.5, $-\sqrt{121}$, −10, $\frac{25}{2}$, $\sqrt{144}$

27. $\sqrt{8}$, $-\frac{2}{5}$, −1, 0.6, $\sqrt{6}$

28. $-\frac{8}{3}$, $-\sqrt{5}$, 2.6, −1.5, $\sqrt{5}$

29. −8.3, $-\sqrt{80}$, $-\frac{17}{2}$, −8.25, $-\sqrt{100}$

EXAMPLE 5 for Exs. 30–33

ANALYZING CONDITIONAL STATEMENTS Rewrite the conditional statement in if-then form. Then tell whether the statement is *true* or *false*. If it is false, give a counterexample.

30. All whole numbers are real numbers.

31. All real numbers are irrational numbers.

32. No perfect squares are whole numbers.

33. No irrational numbers are whole numbers.

EVALUATING EXPRESSIONS Evaluate the expression for the given value of x.

34. $3 + \sqrt{x}$ when $x = 9$

35. $11 - \sqrt{x}$ when $x = 81$

36. $4 \cdot \sqrt{x}$ when $x = 49$

37. $-7 \cdot \sqrt{x}$ when $x = 36$

38. $-3 \cdot \sqrt{x} - 7$ when $x = 121$

39. $6 \cdot \sqrt{x} + 3$ when $x = 100$

40. REASONING Tell whether each of the following sets of numbers has an additive identity, additive inverses, a multiplicative identity, and multiplicative inverses: whole numbers, integers, rational numbers, real numbers. Use a table similar to the one in Example 3 to display your results.

41. ★ **MULTIPLE CHOICE** If $x = 36$, the value of which expression is a perfect square?

Ⓐ $\sqrt{x} + 17$ Ⓑ $87 - \sqrt{x}$ Ⓒ $5 \cdot \sqrt{x}$ Ⓓ $8 \cdot \sqrt{x} + 2$

42. ★ **WRITING** Let $x > 0$. Compare the values of x and $\sqrt{x}$ for $0 < x < 1$ and for $x > 1$. Give examples to justify your thinking.

43. CHALLENGE Find the first five perfect squares x such that $2 \cdot \sqrt{x}$ is also a perfect square. *Describe* your method.

44. CHALLENGE Let n be any whole number from 1 to 1000. For how many values of n is $\sqrt{n}$ a rational number? *Explain* your reasoning.

PROBLEM SOLVING

EXAMPLE 1 for Exs. 45, 47

45. ART The area of a square painting is 3600 square inches. Find the side length of the painting.

EXAMPLE 2 for Exs. 46, 48

46. SOCCER Some soccer drills are practiced in a square section of a field. If the section of a field for a soccer drill is 1620 square yards, find the side length of the section. Round your answer to the nearest yard.

47. MAZES The table shows the locations and areas of various life-size square mazes. Find the side lengths of the mazes. Then tell whether the side lengths are *rational* or *irrational* numbers.

Location of maze	Area (ft^2)
Dallas, Texas	1225
San Francisco, California	576
Corona, New York	2304
Waterville, Maine	900

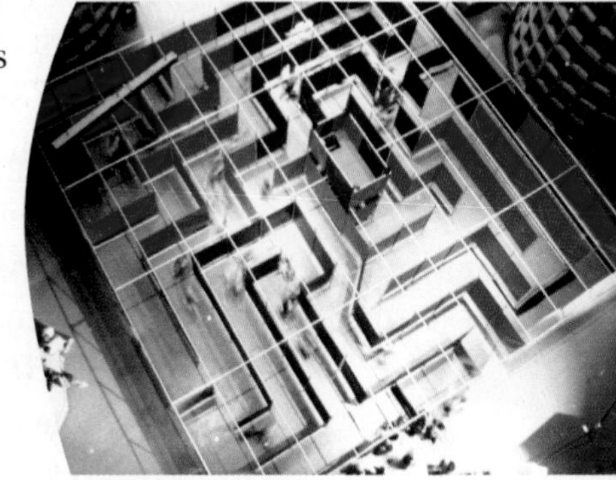

Maze at Corona, New York

48. ★ SHORT RESPONSE You plan to use a square section of a park for a small outdoor concert. The section should have an area of 1450 square feet. You have 150 feet of rope to use to surround the section. Do you have enough rope? *Explain* your reasoning.

49. STORAGE CUBES If $b^3 = a$, then b is called the *cube root* of a, written $\sqrt[3]{a}$. For instance, $14^3 = 2744$, so 14 is the cube root of 2744, or $14 = \sqrt[3]{2744}$. Suppose a storage cube is advertised as having a volume of 10 cubic feet. Use a calculator to approximate the edge length of the storage cube to the nearest tenth of a foot.

50. MULTI-STEP PROBLEM The Kelvin temperature scale was invented by Lord Kelvin in the 19th century and is often used for scientific measurements. To convert a temperature from degrees Celsius (°C) to kelvin (K), you add 273 to the temperature in degrees Celsius.

a. Convert 17°C to kelvin.

b. The speed s (in meters per second) of sound in air is given by the formula $s = 20.1 \cdot \sqrt{K}$ where K is the temperature in kelvin. Find the speed of sound in air at 17°C. Round your answer to the nearest meter per second.

51. ★ SHORT RESPONSE A homeowner is building a square patio and will cover the patio with square tiles. Each tile has an area of 256 square inches and costs \$3.45. The homeowner has \$500 to spend on tiles.

a. Calculate How many tiles can the homeowner buy?

b. Explain Find the side length (in feet) of the largest patio that the homeowner can build. *Explain* how you got your answer.

52. **MULTIPLE REPRESENTATIONS** The diagram shows the approximate areas (in square meters) of the square bases for the pyramids of Giza.

a. **Making a Table** Make a table that gives the following quotients (rounded to the nearest tenth) for each of the 3 pairs of pyramids:

- (area of larger base) ÷ (area of smaller base)
- (side length of larger base) ÷ (side length of smaller base)

For each pair of pyramids, how are the two quotients related?

b. **Writing an Equation** Write an equation that gives the quotient q of the side lengths as a function of the quotient r of the areas.

53. **CHALLENGE** Write an equation that gives the edge length ℓ of a cube as a function of the surface area A of the cube.

Extension Use Real and Rational Numbers

GOAL Identify whether sets of rational and irrational numbers are closed under operations.

Key Vocabulary
- **closure**

RATIONAL AND IRRATIONAL NUMBERS Recall that a *rational number* is a number $\frac{a}{b}$ where a and b are integers with $b \neq 0$. An *irrational number* is any number that cannot be written as a quotient of two integers.

CC.9-12.N.RN.3 Explain why the sum or product of two rational numbers is rational; that the sum of a rational number and an irrational number is irrational; and that the product of a nonzero rational number and an irrational number is irrational.

EXAMPLE 1 Sums of rational numbers

Prove that the sum of two rational numbers is rational.

Solution

Let x and y be two rational numbers.

By the definition of rational numbers, x can be written as $\frac{a}{b}$ and y can be written as $\frac{c}{d}$ where a, b, c, and d are integers with $b \neq 0$ and $d \neq 0$.

$x + y = \frac{a}{b} + \frac{c}{d}$ **Add x and y.**

$x + y = \frac{ad + bc}{bd}$ **Rewrite $\frac{a}{b} + \frac{c}{d}$ using a common denominator.**

Because the sum or product of two integers will always be integers, the expressions $ad + bc$ and bd are both integers.

Therefore, the sum $x + y$ is equal to the ratio of two integers. So by definition, this sum is a rational number.

CLOSURE As you saw in Example 1, the sum of two rational numbers is rational. The set of rational numbers has *closure* or is *closed* under multiplication.

KEY CONCEPT ***For Your Notebook***

Closure

A set has **closure** or is closed under a given operation if the number that results from performing the operation on any two numbers in the set is also in the set.

Example: The sum of any two rational numbers is a rational number. The set of rationals is closed under addition.

$\frac{1}{2} + \frac{1}{3} = \frac{5}{6}$ $\frac{1}{2} + \frac{3}{2} = 2$

Non-example: The quotient of two integers is not necessarily an integer. The set of integers is not closed under division.

$6 \div 2 = 3$ $-6 \div 5 = -\frac{6}{5}$

EXAMPLE 2 Sum of a rational and an irrational number

Solve the equation $x - 3 = \sqrt{2}$. Is the solution *rational* or *irrational*?

Solution

$x - 3 = \sqrt{2}$ **Write original equation.**

$x - 3 + 3 = \sqrt{2} + 3$ **Add 3 to both sides.**

$x = \sqrt{2} + 3$ **Simplify.**

▶ The solution is *irrational*.

SUMS OF IRRATIONAL NUMBERS Example 2 shows a single case where the sum of a rational number and an irrational number is irrational. To prove that this is always true, you must first assume that such a sum is rational. This results in a contradiction which proves that the assumption must be false.

Let a be rational and b be irrational. Let c be the sum of a and b, and assume that c is rational.

$a + b = c$ **Assume c is rational.**

$b = c - a$ **Subtract a from each side.**

By Example 1, you know that $c - a$ is rational. But a rational number cannot be equal to an irrational number, so this is a contradiction. Therefore the sum of a rational number and an irrational number must be irrational.

PRACTICE

1. Use Example 1 as a model to prove that the product of two rational numbers is rational.

2. Copy and complete: Prove that the product of a nonzero rational number and an irrational number is irrational.

> Let x be a nonzero rational number and y be an __?__ number. By definition, $x = \frac{a}{b}$, where a and b are __?__ with $b \neq 0$. Now assume that the product xy is a __?__ number. Therefore xy can be written as the quotient of integers c and d with $d \neq 0$.
>
> __?__ **The product xy can be written as $\frac{c}{d}$.**
>
> __?__ **Substitute $\frac{a}{b}$ for x.**
>
> __?__ **Multiply both sides by __?__.**
>
> __?__ **Simplify.**
>
> By definition, __?__ is a rational number which means that y must be rational. But y is an irrational number, meaning the assumption that __?__ is rational must be false. Therefore, __?__.

3. Use an indirect proof like the one following Example 2 to prove that the sum of a rational number and an irrational number is irrational.

Modeling One-Step Equations

Use appropriate tools strategically.

MATERIALS • algebra tiles

QUESTION How can you use algebra tiles to solve one-step equations?

You can model one-step equations using algebra tiles.

1-tile | ***x*-tile**

A 1-tile represents the number 1. An x-tile represents the variable x.

EXPLORE 1 Solve an equation using subtraction

Solve $x + 2 = 5$.

STEP 1 Model $x + 2 = 5$ using algebra tiles.

STEP 2 To find the value of x, isolate the x-tile on one side of the equation. You can do this by removing two 1-tiles from each side.

STEP 3 The x-tile is equal to three 1-tiles. So, the solution of $x + 2 = 5$ is 3.

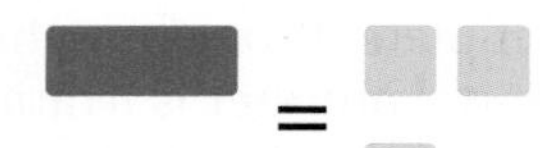

PRACTICE

Write the equation modeled by the algebra tiles.

1. 

2. 

Use algebra tiles to model and solve the equation.

3. $x + 3 = 9$
4. $x + 2 = 7$
5. $x + 8 = 8$
6. $x + 3 = 7$
7. $x + 2 = 12$
8. $x + 7 = 12$
9. $15 = x + 5$
10. $13 = x + 10$

EXPLORE 2 Solve an equation using division

Solve $2x = 12$.

STEP 1 Model $2x = 12$ using algebra tiles.

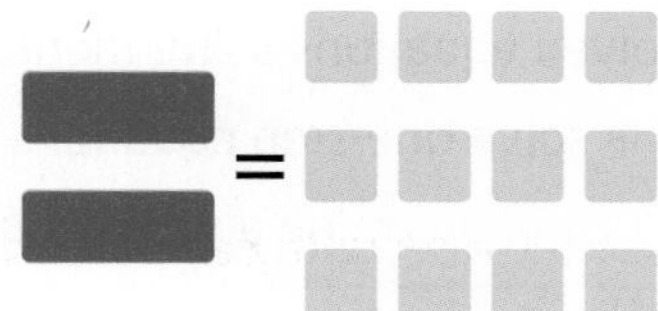

STEP 2 There are two x-tiles, so divide the x-tiles and 1-tiles into two equal groups.

STEP 3 An x-tile is equal to six 1-tiles. So, the solution of $2x = 12$ is 6.

PRACTICE

Write the equation modeled by the algebra tiles.

11.

12.

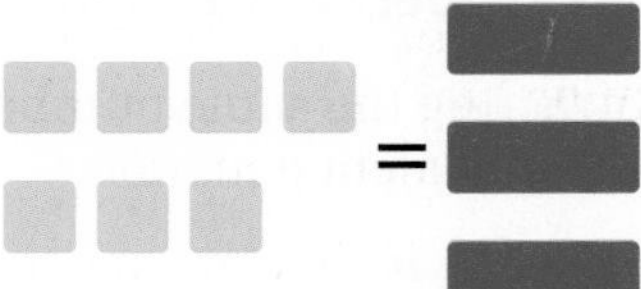

Use algebra tiles to model and solve the equation.

13. $2x = 10$ **14.** $3x = 12$ **15.** $3x = 18$ **16.** $4x = 16$

17. $6 = 2x$ **18.** $12 = 4x$ **19.** $20 = 5x$ **20.** $21 = 7x$

DRAW CONCLUSIONS Use your observations to complete these exercises

21. An equation and explanation that correspond to each step in Explore 1 are shown below. Copy and complete the equations and explanations.

$x + 2 = 5$	**Original equation**
$x + 2 - \underline{\ ?\ } = 5 - \underline{\ ?\ }$	**Subtract _?_ from each side.**
$x = \underline{\ ?\ }$	**Simplify. Solution is _?_.**

22. Write an equation that corresponds to the algebra tile equation in each step of Explore 2. Based on your results, describe an algebraic method that you can use to solve $12x = 180$. Then use your method to find the solution.

2.2 Solve One-Step Equations

Before You solved equations using mental math.

Now You will solve one-step equations using algebra.

Why? So you can determine a weight limit, as in Ex. 56.

Key Vocabulary
- **inverse operations**
- **equivalent equations**
- **reciprocal**

CC.9-12.A.REI.3 Solve linear equations and inequalities in one variable, including equations with coefficients represented by letters.

Inverse operations are two operations that undo each other, such as addition and subtraction. When you perform the same inverse operation on each side of an equation, you produce an *equivalent equation*. **Equivalent equations** are equations that have the same solution(s).

KEY CONCEPT — *For Your Notebook*

Addition Property of Equality

Words Adding the same number to each side of an equation produces an equivalent equation.

Algebra If $x - a = b$, then $x - a + a = b + a$, or $x = b + a$.

Subtraction Property of Equality

Words Subtracting the same number from each side of an equation produces an equivalent equation.

Algebra If $x + a = b$, then $x + a - a = b - a$, or $x = b - a$.

EXAMPLE 1 Solve an equation using subtraction

Solve $x + 7 = 4$.

$x + 7 = 4$ — **Write original equation.**

$x + 7 - 7 = 4 - 7$ — **Use subtraction property of equality: Subtract 7 from each side.**

$x = -3$ — **Simplify.**

▶ The solution is -3.

AVOID ERRORS
To obtain an equivalent equation, be sure to subtract the same number from each side.

CHECK Substitute -3 for x in the original equation.

$x + 7 = 4$ — **Write original equation.**

$-3 + 7 \stackrel{?}{=} 4$ — **Substitute −3 for *x*.**

$4 = 4$ ✓ — **Simplify. Solution checks.**

EXAMPLE 2 Solve an equation using addition

USE HORIZONTAL FORMAT

In Example 2, both horizontal and vertical formats are used. In the rest of the book, equations will be solved using the horizontal format.

Solve $x - 12 = 3$.

Horizontal format		Vertical format
$x - 12 = 3$	**Write original equation.**	$x - 12 = \quad 3$
$x - 12 + 12 = 3 + 12$	**Add 12 to each side.**	$+ 12 \quad + 12$
$x = 15$	**Simplify.**	$x \quad = \quad 15$

MULTIPLICATION AND DIVISION EQUATIONS Multiplication and division are inverse operations. So, the multiplication property of equality can be used to solve equations involving division, and the division property of equality can be used to solve equations involving multiplication.

KEY CONCEPT *For Your Notebook*

Multiplication Property of Equality

Words Multiplying each side of an equation by the same nonzero number produces an equivalent equation.

Algebra If $\frac{x}{a} = b$ and $a \neq 0$, then $a \cdot \frac{x}{a} = a \cdot b$, or $x = ab$.

Division Property of Equality

Words Dividing each side of an equation by the same nonzero number produces an equivalent equation.

Algebra If $ax = b$ and $a \neq 0$, then $\frac{ax}{a} = \frac{b}{a}$, or $x = \frac{b}{a}$.

EXAMPLE 3 Solve an equation using division

Solve $-6x = 48$.

$-6x = 48$ **Write original equation.**

$\frac{-6x}{-6} = \frac{48}{-6}$ **Divide each side by −6.**

$x = -8$ **Simplify.**

✓ GUIDED PRACTICE for Examples 1, 2, and 3

Solve the equation. Check your solution.

1. $y + 7 = 10$ **2.** $x - 5 = 3$ **3.** $q - 11 = -5$ **4.** $6 = t - 2$

5. $4x = 48$ **6.** $-65 = -5y$ **7.** $6w = -54$ **8.** $24 = -8n$

EXAMPLE 4 Solve an equation using multiplication

Solve $\frac{x}{4} = 5$.

Solution

$\frac{x}{4} = 5$ Write original equation.

$4 \cdot \frac{x}{4} = 4 \cdot 5$ Multiply each side by 4.

$x = 20$ Simplify.

✓ **GUIDED PRACTICE** for Example 4

Solve the equation. Check your solution.

9. $\frac{t}{-3} = 9$ **10.** $6 = \frac{c}{7}$ **11.** $13 = \frac{z}{-2}$ **12.** $\frac{a}{5} = -11$

USING RECIPROCALS Recall that the product of a number and its reciprocal is 1. You can isolate a variable with a fractional coefficient by multiplying each side of the equation by the reciprocal of the fraction.

EXAMPLE 5 Solve an equation by multiplying by a reciprocal

Solve $-\frac{2}{7}x = 4$.

REVIEW RECIPROCALS
For help with finding reciprocals, see p. SR7.

Solution

The coefficient of x is $-\frac{2}{7}$. The reciprocal of $-\frac{2}{7}$ is $-\frac{7}{2}$.

$-\frac{2}{7}x = 4$ Write original equation.

$-\frac{7}{2}\left(-\frac{2}{7}x\right) = -\frac{7}{2}(4)$ Multiply each side by the reciprocal, $-\frac{7}{2}$.

$x = -14$ Simplify.

▶ The solution is −14. Check by substituting −14 for x in the original equation.

CHECK $-\frac{2}{7}x = 4$ Write original equation.

$-\frac{2}{7}(-14) \stackrel{?}{=} 4$ Substitute −14 for x.

$4 = 4$ ✓ Simplify. Solution checks.

GUIDED PRACTICE for Example 5

Solve the equation. Check your solution.

13. $\frac{5}{6}w = 10$ **14.** $\frac{2}{3}p = 14$ **15.** $9 = -\frac{3}{4}m$ **16.** $-8 = -\frac{4}{5}v$

EXAMPLE 6 Write and solve an equation

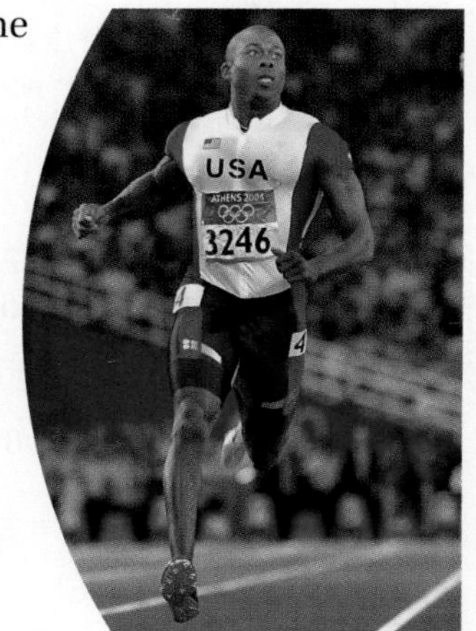

OLYMPICS In the 2004 Olympics, Shawn Crawford won the 200 meter dash. His winning time was 19.79 seconds. Find his average speed to the nearest tenth of a meter per second.

Solution

Let r represent Crawford's speed in meters per second. Write a verbal model. Then write and solve an equation.

Distance (meters)	=	Rate (meters/second)	·	Time (seconds)
↓		↓		↓
200	=	r	·	**19.79**

$$\frac{200}{19.79} = \frac{19.79r}{19.79}$$

$$10.1 \approx r$$

▶ Crawford's average speed was about 10.1 meters per second.

GUIDED PRACTICE for Example 6

17. **WHAT IF?** In Example 6, suppose Shawn Crawford ran 100 meters at the same average speed he ran the 200 meters. How long would it take him to run 100 meters? Round your answer to the nearest tenth of a second.

2.2 EXERCISES

HOMEWORK KEY

○ = See **WORKED-OUT SOLUTIONS** Exs. 13 and 55

★ = **STANDARDIZED TEST PRACTICE** Exs. 2, 15, 16, 57, 58, and 61

◆ = **MULTIPLE REPRESENTATIONS** Ex. 59

SKILL PRACTICE

1. **VOCABULARY** Copy and complete: Two operations that undo each other are called __?__.

2. ★ **WRITING** Which property of equality would you use to solve the equation $14x = 35$? *Explain.*

EXAMPLES 1 and 2 for Exs. 3–14

SOLVING ADDITION AND SUBTRACTION EQUATIONS **Solve the equation. Check your solution.**

3. $x + 5 = 8$
4. $m + 9 = 2$
5. $11 = f + 6$
6. $13 = 7 + z$
7. $6 = 9 + h$
8. $-3 = 5 + a$
9. $y - 4 = 3$
10. $t - 5 = 7$
11. $14 = k - 3$
12. $6 = w - 7$
13. $-2 = n - 6$
14. $-11 = b - 9$

EXAMPLES 1 and 2 for Exs. 15, 16

15. ★ **MULTIPLE CHOICE** What is the solution of $-8 = d - 13$?

Ⓐ -21 Ⓑ -5 Ⓒ 5 Ⓓ 21

16. ★ **MULTIPLE CHOICE** What is the solution of $22 + v = -65$?

Ⓐ -87 Ⓑ -43 Ⓒ 43 Ⓓ 87

EXAMPLES 3 and 4 for Exs. 17–30

SOLVING MULTIPLICATION AND DIVISION EQUATIONS Solve the equation. Check your solution.

17. $5g = 20$
18. $-4q = 52$
19. $48 = 8c$
20. $-108 = 9j$
21. $15 = -h$
22. $187 = -17r$
23. $\frac{y}{3} = 5$
24. $\frac{m}{2} = 14$
25. $8 = \frac{x}{6}$
26. $7 = \frac{t}{-7}$
27. $-11 = \frac{z}{-2}$
28. $-3 = \frac{d}{14}$

In Exercises 29 and 30, refer to the method shown, which a student used to write a repeating decimal as a fraction.

Let $x = 0.\overline{63}$. Then $100x = 63.\overline{63}$.

Subtract: $100x = 63.636363\ldots$

$-x = -0.636363\ldots$

$99x = 63$

$x = \frac{63}{99} = \frac{7}{11}$

29. *Explain* the student's method.

30. Write the repeating decimal as a fraction.

a. $0.\overline{7}$ **b.** $0.\overline{18}$

SOLVING EQUATIONS Solve the equation. Check your solution.

31. $b - 0.4 = 3.1$
32. $-3.2 + z = -7.4$
33. $-5.7 = w - 4.6$
34. $-6.1 = p + 2.2$
35. $8.2 = -4g$
36. $-3.3a = 19.8$
37. $\frac{3}{4} = \frac{1}{8} + v$
38. $\frac{n}{4.6} = -2.5$
39. $-0.12 = \frac{y}{-0.5}$

EXAMPLE 5 for Exs. 40–48

40. $\frac{1}{2}m = 21$
41. $\frac{1}{3}c = 32$
42. $-7 = \frac{1}{5}x$
43. $\frac{3}{2}k = 18$
44. $-21 = -\frac{3}{5}t$
45. $-\frac{2}{7}v = 16$
46. $\frac{8}{5}x = \frac{4}{15}$
47. $\frac{1}{3}y = \frac{1}{5}$
48. $-\frac{4}{3} = \frac{2}{3}z$

GEOMETRY The rectangle or triangle has area A. Write and solve an equation to find the value of x.

49. $A = 54 \text{ in.}^2$

x

12 in.

50. $A = 72 \text{ cm}^2$

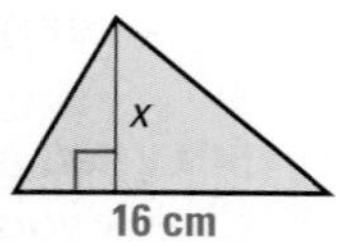

CHALLENGE Find the value of b using the given information.

51. $4a = 6$ and $b = a - 2$

52. $a - 6.7 = 3.1$ and $b = 5a$

○ = See WORKED-OUT SOLUTIONS in Student Resources ★ = STANDARDIZED TEST PRACTICE ◆ = MULTIPLE REPRESENTATIONS

PROBLEM SOLVING

EXAMPLE 6 for Exs. 53–57

53. **THE DEAD SEA** For the period 1999–2004, the maximum depth of the Dead Sea decreased by 9.9 feet. The maximum depth in 2004 was 1036.7 feet. What was the maximum depth in 1999?

54. **CRAFTS** You purchase a cane of polymer clay to make pendants for necklaces. The cane is 50 millimeters long. How thick should you make each pendant so that you will have 20 pendants of uniform thickness?

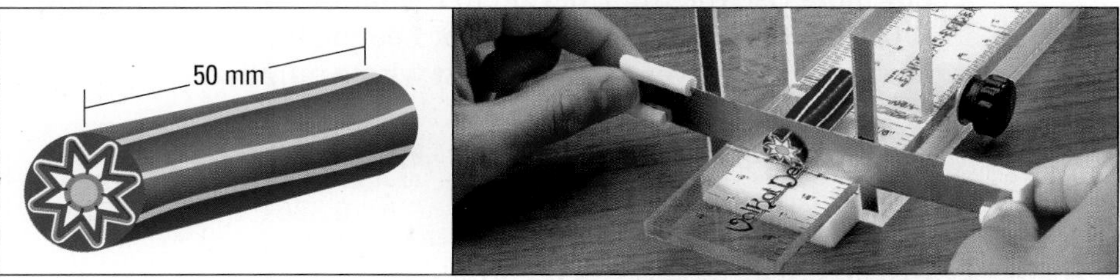

55. **TRAMPOLINES** A rectangular trampoline has an area of 187 square feet. The length of the trampoline is 17 feet. What is its width?

56. **WHEELCHAIRS** The van used to transport patients to and from a rehabilitation facility is equipped with a wheelchair lift. The maximum lifting capacity for the lift is 300 pounds. The wheelchairs used by the facility weigh 55 pounds each. What is the maximum weight of a wheelchair occupant who can use the lift?

57. ★ **SHORT RESPONSE** In Everglades National Park in Florida, there are 200 species of birds that migrate. This accounts for $\frac{4}{7}$ of all the species of birds sighted in the park.

    a. Write an equation to find the number of species of birds that have been sighted in Everglades National Park.

    b. There are 600 species of plants in Everglades National Park. Are there more species of birds or of plants in the park? *Explain.*

58. ★ **OPEN-ENDED** *Describe* a real-world situation that can be modeled by the equation $15x = 135$. Solve the equation and explain what the solution means in this situation.

59. **MULTIPLE REPRESENTATIONS** A box jellyfish can travel at a rate of 6.5 feet per second.

    a. **Making a Table** Make a table that shows the distance d the jellyfish can travel after 1, 2, 3, 4, and 5 seconds.

    b. **Drawing a Graph** Graph the ordered pairs from the table in a coordinate plane. How long does it take the jellyfish to travel 26 feet?

    c. **Writing an Equation** Write and solve an equation to find the time it takes the jellyfish to travel 26 feet.

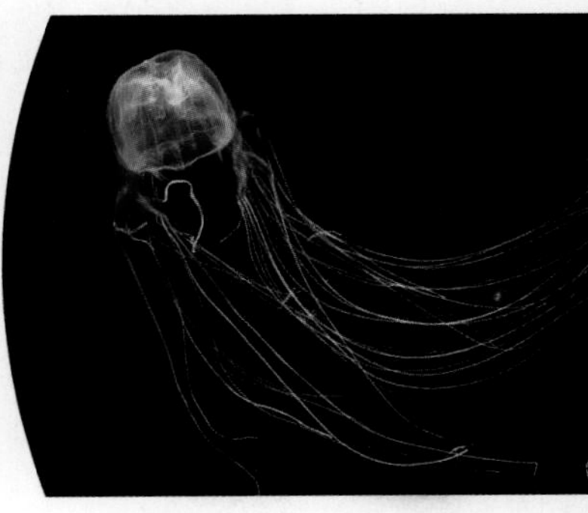

Animated Algebra at my.hrw.com

60. **MULTI-STEP PROBLEM** Tatami mats are a floor covering used in Japan. Tatami mats are equal in size, unless they are cut in half. The floor shown has an area of 81 square feet and is covered with 4.5 tatami mats.

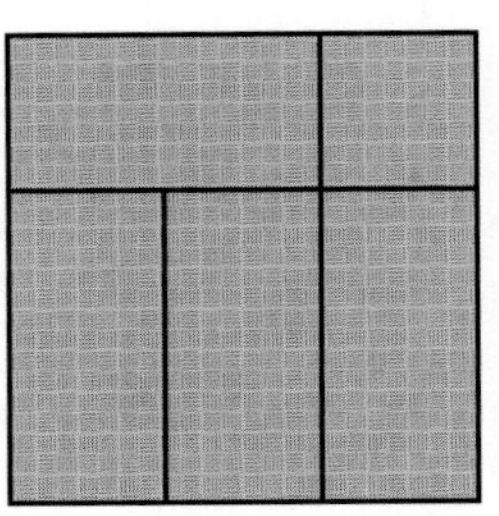

a. What is the area of one tatami mat?

b. What is the length of one tatami mat if it has a width of 3 feet?

61. ★ **EXTENDED RESPONSE** In baseball, a player's batting average is calculated by dividing the number of hits by the number of at bats.

a. **Calculate** Use the information in the table to find the number of hits Bill Mueller had in the 2003 Major League Baseball regular season. Round your answer to the nearest whole number.

Player	Team	Batting average	At bats
Bill Mueller	Boston Red Sox	0.326	524

b. **Calculate** The number of hits Bill Mueller had was 44 less than the number of hits Vernon Wells of the Toronto Blue Jays had in the 2003 regular season. How many hits did Vernon Wells have?

c. **Compare** In the 2003 regular season, Mueller had a higher batting average than Wells. Did Wells have fewer at bats than Mueller? *Explain* your reasoning.

62. **AMERICAN FLAGS** An American flag has a length that is 1.9 times its width. What is the area of a flag that has a length of 9.5 feet?

63. **CHALLENGE** At a farm where you can pick your own strawberries, the cost of picked strawberries is calculated using only the weight of the strawberries. The total weight of a container full of strawberries is 2.1 pounds. The cost of the strawberries is $4.68. The weight of the container is 0.3 pound. What is the cost per pound for strawberries?

See **EXTRA PRACTICE** in Student Resources **ONLINE QUIZ** at my.hrw.com

2.3 Solve Two-Step Equations

Before You solved one-step equations.

Now You will solve two-step equations.

Why? So you can find a scuba diver's depth, as in Example 4.

Key Vocabulary
- like terms
- input
- output

CC.9-12.A.REI.3 Solve linear equations and inequalities in one variable, including equations with coefficients represented by letters.

The equation $\frac{x}{2} + 5 = 11$ involves two operations performed on x: division by 2 and addition by 5. You typically solve such an equation by applying the inverse operations in the reverse order of the order of operations. This is shown in the table below.

Operations performed on x	Operations to isolate x
1. Divide by 2. 2. Add 5.	1. Subtract 5. 2. Multiply by 2.

EXAMPLE 1 Solve a two-step equation

Solve $\frac{x}{2} + 5 = 11$.

$\frac{x}{2} + 5 = 11$ Write original equation.

$\frac{x}{2} + 5 - 5 = 11 - 5$ Subtract 5 from each side.

$\frac{x}{2} = 6$ Simplify.

$2 \cdot \frac{x}{2} = 2 \cdot 6$ Multiply each side by 2.

$x = 12$ Simplify.

▶ The solution is 12. Check by substituting 12 for x in the original equation.

CHECK $\frac{x}{2} + 5 = 11$ Write original equation.

$\frac{12}{2} + 5 \stackrel{?}{=} 11$ Substitute 12 for x.

$11 = 11$ ✓ Simplify. Solution checks.

GUIDED PRACTICE for Example 1

Solve the equation. Check your solution.

1. $5x + 9 = 24$ **2.** $4y - 4 = 16$ **3.** $-1 = \frac{z}{3} - 7$

EXAMPLE 2 Solve a two-step equation by combining like terms

REVIEW LIKE TERMS
You may want to review combining like terms before solving two-step equations.

Solve $7x - 4x = 21$.

$7x - 4x = 21$ Write original equation.

$3x = 21$ Combine like terms.

$\frac{3x}{3} = \frac{21}{3}$ Divide each side by 3.

$x = 7$ Simplify.

EXAMPLE 3 Find an input of a function

The output of a function is 3 less than 5 times the input. Find the input when the output is 17.

Solution

STEP 1 **Write** an equation for the function. Let x be the input and y be the output.

$y = 5x - 3$ y is 3 less than 5 times x.

STEP 2 **Solve** the equation for x when $y = 17$.

$y = 5x - 3$ Write original function.

$17 = 5x - 3$ Substitute 17 for y.

$17 + 3 = 5x - 3 + 3$ Add 3 to each side.

$20 = 5x$ Simplify.

$\frac{20}{5} = \frac{5x}{5}$ Divide each side by 5.

$4 = x$ Simplify.

▶ An input of 4 produces an output of 17.

CHECK $y = 5x - 3$ Write original function.

$17 \stackrel{?}{=} 5(4) - 3$ Substitute 17 for y and 4 for x.

$17 \stackrel{?}{=} 20 - 3$ Multiply 5 and 4.

$17 = 17$ ✓ Simplify. Solution checks.

✓ GUIDED PRACTICE for Examples 2 and 3

Solve the equation. Check your solution.

4. $4w + 2w = 24$
5. $8t - 3t = 35$
6. $-16 = 5d - 9d$
7. The output of a function is 5 more than -2 times the input. Find the input when the output is 11.
8. The output of a function is 4 less than 4 times the input. Find the input when the output is 3.

EXAMPLE 4 Solve a multi-step problem

SCUBA DIVING As a scuba diver descends into deeper water, the pressure of the water on the diver's body steadily increases.

The pressure at the surface of the water is 2117 pounds per square foot (lb/ft^2). The pressure increases at a rate of 64 pounds per square foot for each foot the diver descends. Find the depth at which a diver experiences a pressure of 8517 pounds per square foot.

ANOTHER WAY
For an alternative method for solving Example 4, see the **Problem Solving Workshop**.

Solution

STEP 1 **Write** a verbal model. Then write an equation.

Pressure at given depth (lb/ft^2)	=	Pressure at surface (lb/ft^2)	+	Rate of change of pressure (lb/ft^2 per foot of depth)	•	Diver's depth (ft)
P	=	2117	+	64	•	d

STEP 2 **Find** the depth at which the pressure is 8517 pounds per square foot.

$P = 2117 + 64d$ **Write equation.**

$8517 = 2117 + 64d$ **Substitute 8517 for *P*.**

$8517 - 2117 = 2117 - 2117 + 64d$ **Subtract 2117 from each side.**

$6400 = 64d$ **Simplify.**

$\frac{6400}{64} = \frac{64d}{64}$ **Divide each side by 64.**

$100 = d$ **Simplify.**

▶ A diver experiences a pressure of 8517 pounds per square foot at a depth of 100 feet.

CHECK

$P = 2117 + 64d$ **Write original equation.**

$8517 \stackrel{?}{=} 2117 + 64(100)$ **Substitute 8517 for *P* and 100 for *d*.**

$8517 \stackrel{?}{=} 2117 + 6400$ **Multiply 64 and 100.**

$8517 = 8517$ ✓ **Simplify. Solution checks.**

✓ GUIDED PRACTICE for Example 4

9. **WHAT IF?** In Example 4, suppose the diver experiences a pressure of 5317 pounds per square foot. Find the diver's depth.

10. **JOBS** Kim has a job where she makes \$8 per hour plus tips. Yesterday, Kim made \$53 dollars, \$13 of which was from tips. How many hours did she work?

2.3 EXERCISES

HOMEWORK KEY

○ = See **WORKED-OUT SOLUTIONS** Exs. 13, 19, and 39

★ = **STANDARDIZED TEST PRACTICE** Exs. 2, 21, 40, 41, and 44

◆ = **MULTIPLE REPRESENTATIONS** Ex. 43

SKILL PRACTICE

1. **VOCABULARY** Copy and complete: To solve the equation $2x + 3x = 20$, you would begin by combining $2x$ and $3x$ because they are _?_.

2. ★ **WRITING** *Describe* the steps you would use to solve the equation $4x + 7 = 15$.

EXAMPLE 1 for Exs. 3–14

SOLVING TWO-STEP EQUATIONS **Solve the equation. Check your solution.**

3. $3x + 7 = 19$
4. $5h + 4 = 19$
5. $7d - 1 = 13$
6. $2g - 13 = 3$
7. $10 = 7 - m$
8. $11 = 12 - q$
9. $\frac{a}{3} + 4 = 6$
10. $17 = \frac{w}{5} + 13$
11. $\frac{b}{2} - 9 = 11$
12. $-6 = \frac{z}{4} - 3$
13. $7 = \frac{5}{6}c - 8$
14. $10 = \frac{2}{7}n + 4$

EXAMPLE 2 for Exs. 15–23

COMBINING LIKE TERMS **Solve the equation. Check your solution.**

15. $8y + 3y = 44$
16. $2p + 7p = 54$
17. $11x - 9x = 18$
18. $36 = 9x - 3x$
19. $-32 = -5k + 13k$
20. $6 = -7f + 4f$

21. ★ **MULTIPLE CHOICE** What is the first step you can take to solve the equation $6 + \frac{x}{3} = -2$?

Ⓐ Subtract 2 from each side.
Ⓑ Add 6 to each side.
Ⓒ Divide each side by 3.
Ⓓ Subtract 6 from each side.

ERROR ANALYSIS ***Describe*** **and correct the error in solving the equation.**

22.
$$7 - 3x = 12$$
$$4x = 12$$
$$x = 3$$

23.
$$-2x + x = 10$$
$$\frac{-2x + x}{-2} = \frac{10}{-2}$$
$$x = -5$$

EXAMPLE 3 for Exs. 24–26

FINDING AN INPUT OF A FUNCTION **Write an equation for the function described. Then find the input.**

24. The output of a function is 7 more than 3 times the input. Find the input when the output is -8.

25. The output of a function is 4 more than 2 times the input. Find the input when the output is -10.

26. The output of a function is 9 less than 10 times the input. Find the input when the output is 11.

SOLVING EQUATIONS **Solve the equation. Check your solution.**

27. $5.6 = 1.1p + 1.2$

28. $7.2y + 4.7 = 62.3$

29. $1.2j - 4.3 = 1.7$

30. $16 - 2.4d = -8$

31. $14.4m - 5.1 = 2.1$

32. $-5.3 = 2.2v - 8.6$

33. $\frac{c}{5.3} + 8.3 = 11.3$

34. $3.2 + \frac{x}{2.5} = 4.6$

35. $-1.2 = \frac{z}{4.6} - 2.7$

36. **CHALLENGE** Solve the equations $3x + 2 = 5$, $3x + 2 = 8$, and $3x + 2 = 11$. Predict the solution of the equation $3x + 2 = 14$. *Explain.*

PROBLEM SOLVING

EXAMPLE 4 for Exs. 37–40

37. **DANCE CLASSES** A dance academy charges \$24 per class and a one-time registration fee of \$15. A student paid a total of \$687 to the academy. Find the number of classes the student took.

38. **CAR REPAIR** Tyler paid \$124 to get his car repaired. The total cost for the repairs was the sum of the amount paid for parts and the amount paid for labor. Tyler was charged \$76 for parts and \$32 per hour for labor. Find the amount of time it took to repair his car.

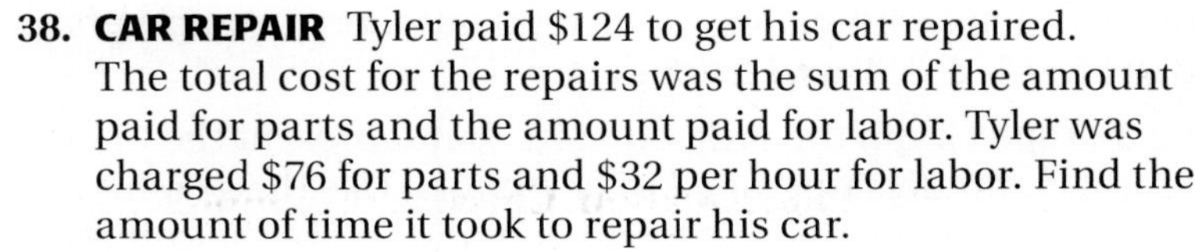

39. **ADVERTISING** A science museum wants to promote an upcoming exhibit by advertising on city buses for one month. The costs of the two types of advertisements being considered are shown. The museum has budgeted \$6000 for the advertisements. The museum decides to have 1 full bus wrap advertisement. How many half-side advertisements can the museum have?

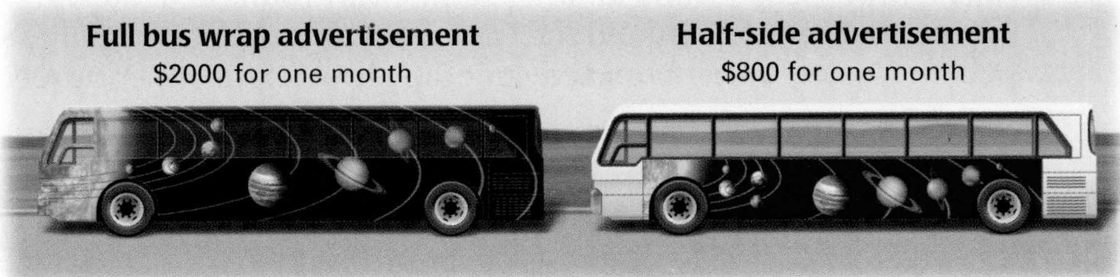

40. ★ **MULTIPLE CHOICE** A skateboarding park charges \$7 per session to skate and \$4 per session to rent safety equipment. Jared rents safety equipment every time he skates. During one year, he spends \$99 for skating charges and equipment rentals. Which equation can be used to find x, the number of sessions Jared attended?

(A) $99 = 7x$ (B) $99 = 7x + 4x$ (C) $99 = 7x + 4$ (D) $99 = 4x + 7$

41. ★ **SHORT RESPONSE** A guitar store offers a finance plan where you give a \$50 down payment on a guitar and pay the remaining balance in 6 equal monthly payments. You have \$50 and you can afford to pay up to \$90 per month for a guitar. Can you afford a guitar that costs \$542? *Explain.*

42. **MULTI-STEP PROBLEM** The capacity of a landfill is 4,756,505 tons. The landfill currently holds 2,896,112 tons. A cell is added to the landfill every day, and each cell averages 1600 tons.

a. Write an equation that gives the amount y (in tons) in the landfill as a function of the number x of days from now.

b. After how many days will the landfill reach capacity? Round your answer to the nearest day.

c. Use estimation to check your answer to part (b).

43. **MULTIPLE REPRESENTATIONS** Two computer technicians are upgrading the software on the 54 computers in a school. On average, Marissa upgrades 5 computers in 1 hour and Ryan upgrades 7 computers in 1 hour.

a. **Writing an Equation** Write an equation that gives the total number y of computers upgraded as a function of the number x of hours worked.

b. **Making a Table** Make a table that shows the number of computers upgraded by each technician and the total number of computers upgraded after 1, 2, 3, 4, and 5 hours.

c. **Drawing a Graph** Graph the ordered pairs that represent the total number y of computers upgraded after x hours. Use the graph to estimate the number of hours it took to upgrade all of the computers.

44. ★ **SHORT RESPONSE** At a restaurant, customers can dine inside the restaurant or pick up food at the take-out window. On an average day, 400 customers are served inside the restaurant, and 120 customers pick up food at the take-out window. After how many days will the restaurant have served 2600 customers? *Explain.*

45. **CHALLENGE** During a 1 mile race, one runner is running at a rate of 14.6 feet per second, and another runner is running at a rate of 11.3 feet per second. One lap around the track is 660 feet. After how many seconds will the faster runner be exactly one lap ahead of the other runner?

QUIZ

1. Tell whether each of the following numbers is a real number, a rational number, an irrational number, an integer, or a whole number: -3, $-\sqrt{5}$, -3.7, $\sqrt{3}$. Then order the numbers from least to greatest.

2. Rewrite the following conditional statement in if-then form: "No irrational numbers are negative numbers." Tell whether the statement is *true* or *false*. If it is false, give a counterexample.

Solve the equation. Check your solution.

3. $-7b = -56$

4. $\frac{z}{4} = 6$

5. $-\frac{4}{3}t = -12$

6. $9w - 4 = 14$

7. $23 = 1 - d$

8. $66 = 4m + 7m$

See **EXTRA PRACTICE** in Student Resources **ONLINE QUIZ** at my.hrw.com

PROBLEM SOLVING WORKSHOP
LESSON 2.3

Using ALTERNATIVE METHODS

Another Way to Solve Example 4

Make sense of problems and persevere in solving them.

MULTIPLE REPRESENTATIONS In Example 4, you saw how to solve a problem about scuba diving by using an equation. You can also solve the problem using a table.

PROBLEM

SCUBA DIVING As a scuba diver descends into deeper water, the pressure of the water on the diver's body steadily increases. The pressure at the surface of the water is 2117 pounds per square foot (lb/ft^2). The pressure increases at a rate of 64 pounds per square foot for each foot the diver descends. Find the depth at which a diver experiences a pressure of 8517 pounds per square foot.

METHOD

Making a Table An alternative approach is to make a table.

STEP 1 **Make** a table that shows the pressure as the depth increases. Because you are looking for a fairly high pressure, use larger increments in depth, such as 20 feet.

Depth (ft)	Pressure (lb/ft^2)
0	2117
1	2181
2	2245
20	3397
40	4677
60	5957
80	7237
100	8517

Every 1 ft of depth increases the pressure by 64 lb/ft^2.

Every 20 ft of depth increases the pressure by $64(20) = 1280\ lb/ft^2$.

STEP 2 **Look** for the depth at which the pressure reaches 8517 pounds per square foot. This happens at a depth of 100 feet.

PRACTICE

1. **BASKETBALL** A sports club offers an organized basketball league. A team pays $600 to join the league. In addition to paying their share of the $600, team members who are not members of the sports club must pay a $25 fee to play. A team pays a total of $775. How many team members who are not club members are on the team? Solve this problem using two different methods.

2. **WHAT IF?** In Exercise 1, suppose you are on a team, but not a club member. The $600 cost is divided equally among the team members. How many players must there be on your team for you to pay $100 to play? Make a table to find the answer.

3. **FURNITURE** You have $370 to spend on a dining table and chairs. A table costs $220, and each chair costs $35. How many chairs can you buy in addition to the table? Solve this problem using two different methods.

2.4 Solve Multi-Step Equations

Before You solved one-step and two-step equations.
Now You will solve multi-step equations.
Why? So you can solve a problem about lifeguarding, as in Ex. 40.

Key Vocabulary
- **like terms**
- **distributive property**
- **reciprocal**

CC.9-12.A.REI.3 Solve linear equations and inequalities in one variable, including equations with coefficients represented by letters.

Solving a linear equation may take more than two steps. Start by simplifying one or both sides of the equation, if possible. Then use inverse operations to isolate the variable.

EXAMPLE 1 Solve an equation by combining like terms

Solve $8x - 3x - 10 = 20$.

$8x - 3x - 10 = 20$	Write original equation.
$5x - 10 = 20$	Combine like terms.
$5x - 10 + 10 = 20 + 10$	Add 10 to each side.
$5x = 30$	Simplify.
$\frac{5x}{5} = \frac{30}{5}$	Divide each side by 5.
$x = 6$	Simplify.

EXAMPLE 2 Solve an equation using the distributive property

Solve $7x + 2(x + 6) = 39$.

Solution

When solving an equation, you may feel comfortable doing some steps mentally. Method 2 shows a solution where some steps are done mentally.

REVIEW PROPERTIES
You may want to review the distributive property before studying these methods.

METHOD 1 Show All Steps

$$7x + 2(x + 6) = 39$$
$$7x + 2x + 12 = 39$$
$$9x + 12 = 39$$
$$9x + 12 - 12 = 39 - 12$$
$$9x = 27$$
$$\frac{9x}{9} = \frac{27}{9}$$
$$x = 3$$

METHOD 2 Do Some Steps Mentally

$$7x + 2(x + 6) = 39$$
$$7x + 2x + 12 = 39$$
$$9x + 12 = 39$$
$$9x = 27$$
$$x = 3$$

EXAMPLE 3 Standardized Test Practice

Which equation represents Step 2 in the solution process?

Step 1 $5x - 4(x - 3) = 17$

Step 2 $\boxed{}$

Step 3 $x + 12 = 17$

Step 4 $x = 5$

Ⓐ $5x - 4x - 12 = 17$ Ⓑ $5x - 4x - 3 = 17$

Ⓒ $5x - 4x + 3 = 17$ Ⓓ $5x - 4x + 12 = 17$

ELIMINATE CHOICES
You can eliminate choices B and C because -4 has not been distributed to *both* terms in the parentheses.

Solution

In Step 2, the distributive property is used to simplify the left side of the equation. Because $-4(x - 3) = -4x + 12$, Step 2 should be $5x - 4x + 12 = 17$.

▶ The correct answer is D. Ⓐ Ⓑ Ⓒ Ⓓ

GUIDED PRACTICE for Examples 1, 2, and 3

Solve the equation. Check your solution.

1. $9d - 2d + 4 = 32$
2. $2w + 3(w + 4) = 27$
3. $6x - 2(x - 5) = 46$

USING RECIPROCALS Although you can use the distributive property to solve an equation such as $\frac{3}{2}(3x + 5) = -24$, it is easier to multiply each side of the equation by the reciprocal of the fraction.

EXAMPLE 4 Multiply by a reciprocal to solve an equation

Solve $\frac{3}{2}(3x + 5) = -24$.

$\frac{3}{2}(3x + 5) = -24$	Write original equation.
$\frac{2}{3} \cdot \frac{3}{2}(3x + 5) = \frac{2}{3}(-24)$	Multiply each side by $\frac{2}{3}$, the reciprocal of $\frac{3}{2}$.
$3x + 5 = -16$	Simplify.
$3x = -21$	Subtract 5 from each side.
$x = -7$	Divide each side by 3.

GUIDED PRACTICE for Example 4

Solve the equation. Check your solution.

4. $\frac{3}{4}(z - 6) = 12$
5. $\frac{2}{5}(3r + 4) = 10$
6. $-\frac{4}{5}(4a - 1) = 28$

EXAMPLE 5 Write and solve an equation

SUMMER CAMP You are planning a scavenger hunt for 21 campers. You plan to have 5 teams. One camper from each team will be the recorder and the rest will be searchers. How many searchers will each team have?

Solution

Let s be the number of searchers on each team. Then $1 + s$ is the total number of campers on each team.

Number of campers	=	Number of teams	·	Number of campers on each team
21	=	**5**	·	**$(1 + s)$**

$21 = 5(1 + s)$ **Write equation.**

$21 = 5 + 5s$ **Distributive property**

$16 = 5s$ **Subtract 5 from each side.**

$3.2 = s$ **Divide each side by 5.**

CHECK REASONABLENESS
The number of searchers must be a whole number.

▶ Because 4 searchers per team would require a total of $5(1 + 4) = 25$ campers, 4 teams will have 3 searchers and 1 team will have 4 searchers.

GUIDED PRACTICE for Example 5

7. **WHAT IF?** In Example 5, suppose you decide to use only 4 teams. How many searchers should there be on each team?

2.4 EXERCISES

HOMEWORK KEY
○ = **See WORKED-OUT SOLUTIONS** Exs. 17 and 39
★ = **STANDARDIZED TEST PRACTICE** Exs. 2, 18, 35, 36, and 41
◆ = **MULTIPLE REPRESENTATIONS** Ex. 42

SKILL PRACTICE

1. **VOCABULARY** What is the reciprocal of the fraction in the equation $\frac{3}{5}(2x + 8) = 18$?

2. ★ **WRITING** *Describe* the steps you would use to solve the equation $3(4y - 7) = 6$.

EXAMPLE 1 for Exs. 3–11

COMBINING LIKE TERMS **Solve the equation. Check your solution.**

3. $p + 2p - 3 = 6$
4. $12v + 14 + 10v = 80$
5. $11w - 9 - 7w = 15$
6. $5a + 3 - 3a = -7$
7. $6c - 8 - 2c = -16$
8. $9 = 7z - 13z - 21$
9. $-2 = 3y - 18 - 5y$
10. $23 = -4m + 2 + m$
11. $35 = -5 + 2x - 7x$

EXAMPLES 2 and 3
for Exs. 12–18, 25

USING THE DISTRIBUTIVE PROPERTY **Solve the equation. Check your solution.**

12. $3 + 4(z + 5) = 31$ **13.** $14 + 2(4g - 3) = 40$ **14.** $5m + 2(m + 1) = 23$

15. $5h + 2(11 - h) = -5$ **16.** $27 = 3c - 3(6 - 2c)$ **17.** $-3 = 12y - 5(2y - 7)$

18. ★ **MULTIPLE CHOICE** What is the solution of $7v - (6 - 2v) = 12$?

Ⓐ -3.6 Ⓑ -2 Ⓒ 2 Ⓓ 3.6

EXAMPLE 4
for Exs. 19–24, 26

MULTIPLYING BY A RECIPROCAL **Solve the equation. Check your solution.**

19. $\frac{1}{3}(d + 3) = 5$ **20.** $\frac{3}{2}(x - 5) = -6$ **21.** $\frac{4}{3}(7 - n) = 12$

22. $4 = \frac{2}{9}(4y - 2)$ **23.** $-32 = \frac{8}{7}(3w - 1)$ **24.** $-14 = \frac{2}{5}(9 - 2b)$

ERROR ANALYSIS ***Describe*** **and correct the error in solving the equation.**

25.

$5x - 3(x - 6) = 2$
$5x - 3x - 18 = 2$
$2x - 18 = 2$
$2x = 20$
$x = 10$

26.

$\frac{1}{2}(2x - 10) = 4$
$2x - 10 = 2$
$2x = 12$
$x = 6$

SOLVING EQUATIONS **Solve the equation. Check your solution.**

27. $8.9 + 1.2(3a - 1) = 14.9$ **28.** $-11.2 + 4(2.1 + q) = -0.8$

29. $1.3t + 3(t + 8.2) = 37.5$ **30.** $1.6 = 7.6 - 5(k + 1.1)$

31. $0.5 = 4.1x - 2(1.3x - 4)$ **32.** $8.7 = 3.5m - 2.5(5.4 - 6m)$

REVIEW CONVERTING UNITS
For help with converting units of measurement, see SR19.

GEOMETRY **Find the value of x for the triangle or rectangle. Be sure to use the same units for the side lengths and the perimeters.**

33. Perimeter = 288 inches

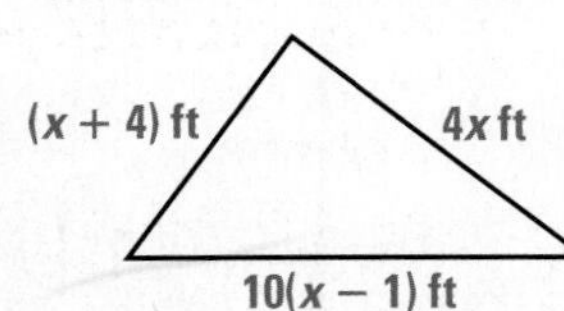

34. Perimeter = 2600 centimeters

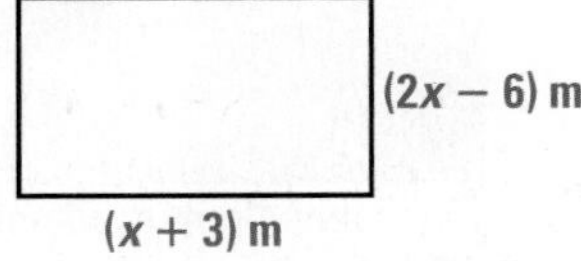

35. ★ **WRITING** The length of a rectangle is 3.5 inches more than its width. The perimeter of the rectangle is 31 inches. Find the length and the width of the rectangle. *Explain* your reasoning.

36. ★ **SHORT RESPONSE** Solve each equation by first dividing each side of the equation by the number outside the parentheses. When would you recommend using this method to solve an equation? *Explain.*

a. $9(x - 4) = 72$ **b.** $8(x + 5) = 60$

37. **CHALLENGE** An even integer can be represented by the expression $2n$. Find three consecutive even integers that have a sum of 54.

PROBLEM SOLVING

EXAMPLE 5 for Exs. 38–40

38. **BASKETBALL** A ticket agency sells tickets to a professional basketball game. The agency charges \$32.50 for each ticket, a convenience charge of \$3.30 for each ticket, and a processing fee of \$5.90 for the entire order. The total charge for an order is \$220.70. How many tickets were purchased?

39. **HANGING POSTERS** You want to hang 3 equally-sized travel posters on the wall in your room so that the posters on the ends are each 3 feet from the end of the wall. You want the spacing between posters to be equal. How much space should you leave between the posters?

40. **LIFEGUARD TRAINING** To qualify for a lifeguard training course, you have to swim continuously for 500 yards using either the front crawl or the breaststroke. You swim the front crawl at a rate of 45 yards per minute and the breaststroke at a rate of 35 yards per minute. You take 12 minutes to swim 500 yards. How much time did you spend swimming the front crawl? Use the verbal model below.

Distance = Rate for front crawl · Time for front crawl + Rate for breaststroke (Total time − Time for front crawl)

41. ★ **EXTENDED RESPONSE** The Busk-Ivanhoe Tunnel on the Colorado Midland Railway was built in the 1890s with separate work crews starting on opposite ends at different times. The crew working from Ivanhoe started 0.75 month later than the crew working from Busk.

Cutaway of Busk-Ivanhoe Tunnel

a. Starting at the time construction began on the Busk end, find the time it took to complete a total of 8473 feet of the tunnel. Round your answer to the nearest month.

b. After 8473 feet were completed, the work crews merged under the same supervision. The combined crew took 3 months to complete the remaining 921 feet of the tunnel. Find the rate at which the remainder of the tunnel was completed.

c. Was the tunnel being completed more rapidly before or after the work crews merged? *Explain* your reasoning.

○ = See **WORKED-OUT SOLUTIONS** in Student Resources ★ = **STANDARDIZED TEST PRACTICE** ◆ = **MULTIPLE REPRESENTATIONS**

42. **MULTIPLE REPRESENTATIONS** A roofing contractor gives estimates for shingling a roof in cost per square, where a square is a 10 foot by 10 foot section of roof. The contractor estimates \$27.50 per square for materials, \$17 per square for labor, \$30 per square for overhead and profit, and a total of \$750 for miscellaneous expenses.

   a. **Writing an Equation** Write an equation that gives the estimate y (in dollars) as a function of the number x of squares of a roof. The contractor gives an estimate of \$2314.50. About how many squares does the roof have?

   b. **Making a Table** Make a table that shows the estimates for shingling a roof that has 5, 10, 15, 20, or 25 squares. Use your table to check your answer to part (a).

43. **CHALLENGE** Jan says that she has quarters and dimes that total \$2.80, and that the number of dimes is 8 more than the number of quarters. Demonstrate algebraically that Jan must be mistaken.

2.5 Solve Equations with Variables on Both Sides

Before You solved equations with variables on one side.

Now You will solve equations with variables on both sides.

Why? So you can find the cost of a gym membership, as in Ex. 52.

Key Vocabulary
- **identity**

Some equations have variables on both sides. To solve such equations, you can collect the variable terms on one side of the equation and the constant terms on the other side of the equation.

EXAMPLE 1 Solve an equation with variables on both sides

Solve $7 - 8x = 4x - 17$.

$7 - 8x = 4x - 17$	Write original equation.
$7 - 8x + 8x = 4x - 17 + 8x$	Add $8x$ to each side.
$7 = 12x - 17$	Simplify each side.
$24 = 12x$	Add 17 to each side.
$2 = x$	Divide each side by 12.

▶ The solution is 2. Check by substituting 2 for x in the original equation.

CHECK

$7 - 8x = 4x - 17$	Write original equation.
$7 - 8(2) \stackrel{?}{=} 4(2) - 17$	Substitute 2 for x.
$-9 \stackrel{?}{=} 4(2) - 17$	Simplify left side.
$-9 = -9$ ✓	Simplify right side. Solution checks.

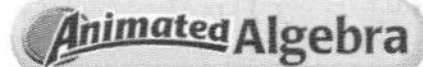 at my.hrw.com

ANOTHER WAY
You could also begin solving the equation by subtracting $4x$ from each side to obtain $7 - 12x = -17$. When you solve this equation for x, you get the same solution, 2.

COMMON CORE

CC.9-12.A.REI.3 Solve linear equations and inequalities in one variable, including equations with coefficients represented by letters.

EXAMPLE 2 Solve an equation with grouping symbols

Solve $9x - 5 = \frac{1}{4}(16x + 60)$.

$9x - 5 = \frac{1}{4}(16x + 60)$	Write original equation.
$9x - 5 = 4x + 15$	Distributive property
$5x - 5 = 15$	Subtract $4x$ from each side.
$5x = 20$	Add 5 to each side.
$x = 4$	Divide each side by 5.

GUIDED PRACTICE for Examples 1 and 2

Solve the equation. Check your solution.

1. $24 - 3m = 5m$ **2.** $20 + c = 4c - 7$ **3.** $9 - 3k = 17 - 2k$

4. $5z - 2 = 2(3z - 4)$ **5.** $3 - 4a = 5(a - 3)$ **6.** $8y - 6 = \frac{2}{3}(6y + 15)$

EXAMPLE 3 Solve a real-world problem

CAR SALES A car dealership sold 78 new cars and 67 used cars this year. The number of new cars sold by the dealership has been increasing by 6 cars each year. The number of used cars sold by the dealership has been decreasing by 4 cars each year. If these trends continue, in how many years will the number of new cars sold be twice the number of used cars sold?

Solution

Let x represent the number of years from now. So, $6x$ represents the increase in the number of new cars sold over x years and $-4x$ represents the decrease in the number of used cars sold over x years. Write a verbal model.

New cars sold this year + Increase in new cars sold over x years = 2 (Used cars sold this year + Decrease in used cars sold over x years)

$$78 + 6x = 2(67 + (-4x))$$

$78 + 6x = 2(67 - 4x)$ **Write equation.**

$78 + 6x = 134 - 8x$ **Distributive property**

$78 + 14x = 134$ **Add $8x$ to each side.**

$14x = 56$ **Subtract 78 from each side.**

$x = 4$ **Divide each side by 14.**

▶ The number of new cars sold will be twice the number of used cars sold in 4 years.

CHECK You can use a table to check your answer.

Year	0	1	2	3	4
Used cars sold	67	63	59	55	51
New cars sold	78	84	90	96	102

The number of new cars sold is twice the number of used cars sold in 4 years.

GUIDED PRACTICE for Example 3

7. WHAT IF? In Example 3, suppose the car dealership sold 50 new cars this year instead of 78. In how many years will the number of new cars sold be twice the number of used cars sold?

NUMBER OF SOLUTIONS Equations do not always have one solution. An equation that is true for all values of the variable is an **identity**. So, the solution of an identity is all real numbers. Some equations have no solution.

EXAMPLE 4 Identify the number of solutions of an equation

Solve the equation, if possible.

a. $3x = 3(x + 4)$

b. $2x + 10 = 2(x + 5)$

Solution

a. $3x = 3(x + 4)$ **Original equation**

$3x = 3x + 12$ **Distributive property**

The equation $3x = 3x + 12$ is not true because the number $3x$ cannot be equal to 12 more than itself. So, the equation has no solution. This can be demonstrated by continuing to solve the equation.

$3x - 3x = 3x + 12 - 3x$ **Subtract $3x$ from each side.**

$0 = 12$ ✗ **Simplify.**

▶ The statement $0 = 12$ is not true, so the equation has no solution.

b. $2x + 10 = 2(x + 5)$ **Original equation**

$2x + 10 = 2x + 10$ **Distributive property**

▶ Notice that the statement $2x + 10 = 2x + 10$ is true for all values of x. So, the equation is an identity, and the solution is all real numbers.

✓ **GUIDED PRACTICE** for Example 4

Solve the equation, if possible.

8. $9z + 12 = 9(z + 3)$

9. $7w + 1 = 8w + 1$

10. $3(2a + 2) = 2(3a + 3)$

SOLVING LINEAR EQUATIONS You have learned several ways to transform an equation to an equivalent equation. These methods are combined in the steps listed below.

CONCEPT SUMMARY *For Your Notebook*

Steps for Solving Linear Equations

STEP 1 **Use** the distributive property to remove any grouping symbols.

STEP 2 **Simplify** the expression on each side of the equation.

STEP 3 **Use** properties of equality to collect the variable terms on one side of the equation and the constant terms on the other side of the equation.

STEP 4 **Use** properties of equality to solve for the variable.

STEP 5 **Check** your solution in the original equation.

2.5 EXERCISES

HOMEWORK KEY

○ = See **WORKED-OUT SOLUTIONS** Exs. 13 and 51

★ = **STANDARDIZED TEST PRACTICE** Exs. 2, 15, 16, 17, 29, and 53

◆ = **MULTIPLE REPRESENTATIONS** Ex. 52

SKILL PRACTICE

1. **VOCABULARY** Copy and complete: An equation that is true for all values of the variable is called a(n) __?__.

2. ★ **WRITING** *Explain* why the equation $4x + 3 = 4x + 1$ has no solution.

EXAMPLES 1 and 2 for Exs. 3–17

SOLVING EQUATIONS **Solve the equation. Check your solution.**

3. $8t + 5 = 6t + 1$
4. $k + 1 = 3k - 1$
5. $8c + 5 = 4c - 11$
6. $8 + 4m = 9m - 7$
7. $10b + 18 = 8b + 4$
8. $19 - 13p = -17p - 5$
9. $9a = 6(a + 4)$
10. $5h - 7 = 2(h + 1)$
11. $3(d + 12) = 8 - 4d$
12. $7(r + 7) = 5r + 59$
13. $40 + 14j = 2(-4j - 13)$
14. $5(n + 2) = \frac{3}{5}(5 + 10n)$

15. ★ **MULTIPLE CHOICE** What is the solution of the equation $8x + 2x = 15x - 10$?

Ⓐ -2 Ⓑ 0.4 Ⓒ 2 Ⓓ 5

16. ★ **MULTIPLE CHOICE** What is the solution of the equation $4y + y + 1 = 7(y - 1)$?

Ⓐ -4 Ⓑ -3 Ⓒ 3 Ⓓ 4

17. ★ **WRITING** *Describe* the steps you would use to solve the equation $3(2z - 5) = 2z + 13$.

EXAMPLE 4 for Exs. 18–28

SOLVING EQUATIONS **Solve the equation, if possible.**

18. $w + 3 = w + 6$
19. $16d = 22 + 5d$
20. $8z = 4(2z + 1)$
21. $12 + 5v = 2v - 9$
22. $22x + 70 = 17x - 95$
23. $2 - 15n = 5(-3n + 2)$
24. $12y + 6 = 6(2y + 1)$
25. $5(1 + 4m) = 2(3 + 10m)$
26. $2(3g + 2) = \frac{1}{2}(12g + 8)$

ERROR ANALYSIS ***Describe*** **and correct the error in solving the equation.**

27.

$3(x + 5) = 3x + 15$
$3x + 5 = 3x + 15$
$5 = 15$
The equation has no solution.

28.

$6(2y + 6) = 4(9 + 3y)$
$12y + 36 = 36 + 12y$
$12y = 12y$
$0 = 0$
The solution is $y = 0$.

29. ★ **OPEN-ENDED** Give an example of an equation that has no solution. *Explain* why your equation does not have a solution.

SOLVING EQUATIONS **Solve the equation, if possible.**

30. $8w - 8 - 6w = 4w - 7$

31. $3x - 4 = 2x + 8 - 5x$

32. $-15c + 7c + 1 = 3 - 8c$

33. $\frac{3}{2} + \frac{3}{4}a = \frac{1}{4}a - \frac{1}{2}$

34. $\frac{5}{8}m - \frac{3}{8} = \frac{1}{2}m + \frac{7}{8}$

35. $n - 10 = \frac{5}{6}n - 7 - \frac{1}{3}n$

36. $3.7b + 7 = 8.1b - 19.4$

37. $6.2h + 5 - 1.4h = 4.8h + 5$

38. $0.7z + 1.9 + 0.1z = 5.5 - 0.4z$

39. $5.4t + 14.6 - 10.1t = 12.8 - 3.5t - 0.6$

40. $\frac{1}{8}(5y + 64) = \frac{1}{4}(20 + 2y)$

41. $14 - \frac{1}{5}(j - 10) = \frac{2}{5}(25 + j)$

42. $5(1.2k + 6) = 7.1k + 34.4$

43. $-0.25(4v - 8) = 0.5(4 - 2v)$

GEOMETRY **Find the perimeter of the square.**

44.

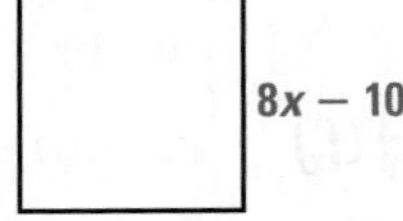

45.

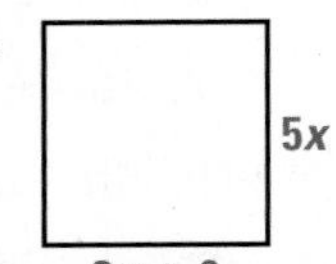

46.

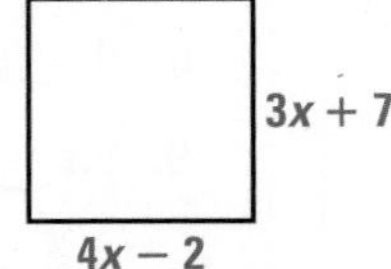

CHALLENGE **Find the value(s) of *a* for which the equation is an identity.**

47. $a(2x + 3) = 9x + 12 - x$

48. $10x - 35 + 3ax = 5ax - 7a$

PROBLEM SOLVING

EXAMPLE 3 for Exs. 49–51

49. CAMPING The membership fee for joining a camping association is \$45. A local campground charges members of the camping association \$35 per night for a campsite and nonmembers \$40 per night for a campsite. After how many nights of camping is the total cost for members, including the membership fee, the same as the total cost for nonmembers?

50. HIGH-SPEED INTERNET Dan and Sydney are getting high-speed Internet access at the same time. Dan's provider charges \$60 for installation and \$42.95 per month. Sydney's provider has free installation and charges \$57.95 per month. After how many months will Dan and Sydney have paid the same amount for high-speed Internet service?

51. LANGUAGES Information about students who take Spanish and students who take French at a high school is shown in the table. If the trends continue, in how many years will there be 3 times as many students taking Spanish as French?

Language	Students enrolled this year	Average rate of change
Spanish	555	33 more students each year
French	230	2 fewer students each year

○ = See WORKED-OUT SOLUTIONS in Student Resources ★ = STANDARDIZED TEST PRACTICE ◆ = MULTIPLE REPRESENTATIONS

52. **MULTIPLE REPRESENTATIONS** For \$360, a rock-climbing gym offers a yearly membership where members can climb as many days as they want and pay \$4 per day for equipment rental. Nonmembers pay \$10 per day to use the gym and \$6 per day for equipment rental.

   a. **Writing an Equation** Write an equation to find the number of visits after which the total cost for a member and the total cost for a nonmember are the same. Then solve the equation.

   b. **Making a Table** Make a table for the costs of members and nonmembers after 5, 10, 15, 20, 25, 30, and 35 visits. Use the table to check your answer to part (a).

53. ★ **EXTENDED RESPONSE** Flyball is a relay race for dogs. In each of the four legs of the relay, a dog jumps over hurdles, retrieves a ball from a flybox, and runs back over the hurdles. The last leg of a relay is shown below. The collie starts the course 0.3 second before the sheepdog.

   a. Let t represent the time (in seconds) it takes the collie to run the last leg. Write and solve an equation to find the number of seconds after which the sheepdog would catch up with the collie.

   b. How long does it take the collie to run the last leg?

   c. Use your answers from parts (a) and (b) to determine whether the sheepdog catches up and passes the collie during the last leg of the relay. *Explain* your reasoning.

CHALLENGE Find the length and the width of the rectangle described.

54. The length is 12 units more than the width. The perimeter is 7 times the width.

55. The length is 4 units less than 3 times the width. The perimeter is 22 units more than twice the width.

QUIZ

Solve the equation. Check your solution.

1. $x + 2x - 1 = 38$

2. $2v + 5v - 8 = 13$

3. $2a - 6(a - 4) = -4$

4. $\frac{6}{5}(5 - 4g) = -18$

Solve the equation, if possible.

5. $y - 2 = y + 2$

6. $2x - 14 = -3x + 6$

7. $10z - 4 = 2(5z - 2)$

8. $6m + 5 - 3m = 7(m - 1)$

9. $2(7 - g) = 9g + 14 - 11g$

10. $13k + 3(k + 11) = 8k - 7$

Spreadsheet ACTIVITY *Use after Solve Equations with Variables on Both Sides*

my.hrw.com Keystrokes

Solve Equations Using Tables

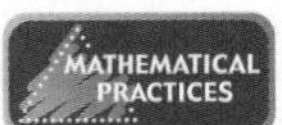

Use appropriate tools strategically.

QUESTION How can you use a spreadsheet to solve an equation with variables on both sides?

You can use a spreadsheet to solve an equation with variables on both sides by evaluating the left side of the equation and the right side of the equation using the same value of the variable. If the left side and right side are equal, then the value of the variable is a solution.

EXAMPLE Solve an equation using a spreadsheet

Solve $19(x - 1) - 72 = 6x$.

STEP 1 ***Enter data and formulas***

Label columns for possible solutions, left side, and right side in row 1. Enter the integers from 0 through 10 as possible solutions in column A. Then enter the formulas for the left side and the right side of the equation in columns B and C.

	A	B	C
1	Possible solutions	Left side	Right side
2	0	=19*(A2−1)−72	=6*A2
3	1	=19*(A3−1)−72	=6*A3
...	...	...	...
12	10	=19*(A12−1)−72	=6*A12

STEP 2 ***Compare columns***

Compare the values of the left side and the values of the right side. The left side and right side values are equal when $x = 7$. So, the solution is 7.

	A	B	C
1	Possible solutions	Left side	Right side
...	...	...	...
8	6	23	36
9	7	42	42
10	8	61	48

DRAW CONCLUSIONS Use your observations to complete these exercises

In Exercises 1–3, use a spreadsheet to solve the equation.

1. $15x + 6 = 6x + 24$ **2.** $8x - 17 = 5x + 70$ **3.** $18 - 2(x + 3) = x$

4. Not all equations have integer solutions. Consider the equation $4.9 + 4.8(7 - x) = 6.2x$.

a. Follow Step 1 above using $4.9 + 4.8(7 - x) = 6.2x$.

b. Add a fourth column that shows the difference of the value of the left side and the value of the right side. Find consecutive possible solutions between which the differences of the values of the left side and right side change sign.

c. Repeat Step 1. This time use the lesser of the two possible solutions from part (b) as the first possible solution, and increase each possible solution by 0.1. Can you identify a solution now? If so, what is it?

Apply Properties of Equality

GOAL Use algebraic properties to help solve equations.

Key Vocabulary
- **equation**
- **solve an equation**

CC.9-12.A.REI.1 Explain each step in solving a simple equation as following from the equality of numbers asserted at the previous step, starting from the assumption that the original equation has a solution. Construct a viable argument to justify a solution method.

When you *solve an equation,* you use properties of real numbers. In particular you use the *algebraic properties of equality* and the *distributive property.*

KEY CONCEPT *For Your Notebook*

Algebraic Properties of Equality

Let a, b, and c be real numbers.

Addition Property	If $a = b$, then $a + c = b + c$.
Subtraction Property	If $a = b$, then $a - c = b - c$.
Multiplication Property	If $a = b$, then $ac = bc$.
Division Property	If $a = b$ and $c \neq 0$, then $\frac{a}{c} = \frac{b}{c}$.
Substitution Property	If $a = b$, then a can be substituted for b in any equation or expression.

EXAMPLE 1 Write reasons for each step

Solve $4x + 7 = -2x - 5$. Write reasons for each step.

Solution

Equation	Explanation	Reason
$4x + 7 = -2x - 5$	Write original equation.	Given
$4x + 7 + \mathbf{2x} = -2x - 5 + \mathbf{2x}$	Add $2x$ to each side.	Addition Property of Equality
$6x + 7 = -5$	Combine like terms.	Simplify.
$6x + 7 - \mathbf{7} = -5 - \mathbf{7}$	Subtract 7 from each side.	Subtraction Property of Equality
$6x = -12$	Combine like terms.	Simplify.
$x = -2$	Divide each side by 6.	Division Property of Equality

▶ The value of x is -2.

GUIDED PRACTICE for Example 1

Solve the equation. Write a reason for each step.

1. $5x - 7 = 8$

2. $13 - 2x = x + 25$

KEY CONCEPT — *For Your Notebook*

Distributive Property

$a(b + c) = ab + ac$, where a, b, and c are real numbers.

EXAMPLE 2 Use the Distributive Property

Solve $7(5 - x) = 14$. Write reasons for each step.

Solution

Equation	Explanation	Reason
$7(5 - x) = 14$	Write original equation.	Given
$35 - 7x = 14$	Multiply.	Distributive Property
$-7x = -21$	Subtract 35 from each side.	Subtraction Property of Equality
$x = 3$	Divide each side by -7.	Division Property of Equality

▶ The value of x is 3.

PRACTICE

Copy the logical argument. Write a reason for each step.

1. $3x - 12 = 7x + 8$ Given
   $-4x - 12 = 8$?
   $-4x = 20$?
   $x = -5$?

2. $5(x - 1) = 4x + 3$ Given
   $5x - 5 = 4x + 3$?
   $x - 5 = 3$?
   $x = 8$?

For Exercises 3–14, solve the equation. Write a reason for each step.

3. $5x - 10 = -40$
4. $4x + 9 = 16 - 3x$
5. $5 - x = 17$
6. $2x - 3 = x - 5$
7. $19 - 2x = -17$
8. $-3x = -5x + 12$
9. $5(3x - 20) = -10$
10. $3(2x + 11) = 9$
11. $2(-x - 5) = 12$
12. $4(5x - 9) = -2(x + 7)$
13. $13 - x = -2(x + 3)$
14. $3(7x - 9) - 19x = -15$

15. **ERROR ANALYSIS** Describe and correct the error in solving for x.

$7x = x + 24$ Given
$8x = 24$ Addition Property of Equality
$x = 3$ Division Property of Equality

16. **DEBATE** Mrs. Sinclair divided her 30 history students into 6 debate teams, with each team consisting of a secretary to take notes during the debates and x debaters. The solution of the equation $6(x + 1) = 30$ represents the number of debaters on each team. Solve the equation and write a reason for each step.

MIXED REVIEW *of Problem Solving*

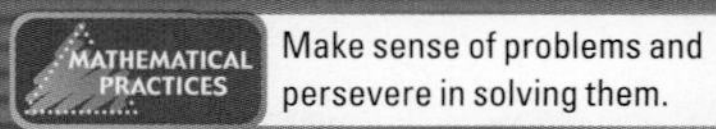

Make sense of problems and persevere in solving them.

1. **MULTI-STEP PROBLEM** A phone company charges \$.25 for the first minute of a long-distance call and \$.07 for each additional minute.

   a. Write an equation that gives the cost C of a long-distance call as a function of the length t (in minutes) of the call.

   b. Find the duration of a long-distance call that costs \$2.

2. **GRIDDED ANSWER** A veterinary assistant steps on a scale while holding a cat. The weight of the cat and assistant is 175 pounds. The assistant weighs 162 pounds. Find the weight (in pounds) of the cat.

3. **EXTENDED RESPONSE** A bowling alley charges \$1.50 for bowling shoes and \$3.75 for each game. Paul and Brandon each have \$15 to spend at the bowling alley.

   a. Paul brings his own bowling shoes. How many games can he bowl?

   b. Brandon needs to pay for bowling shoes. How many games can he bowl? Round your answer down to the nearest whole number.

   c. Both Paul and Brandon decide to bowl the number of games that Brandon can afford to bowl. Does Paul have enough money to buy a slice of pizza and a soda that cost a total of \$3.25? *Explain* your reasoning.

4. **GRIDDED ANSWER** The triangle has a perimeter of 82 inches. What is x?

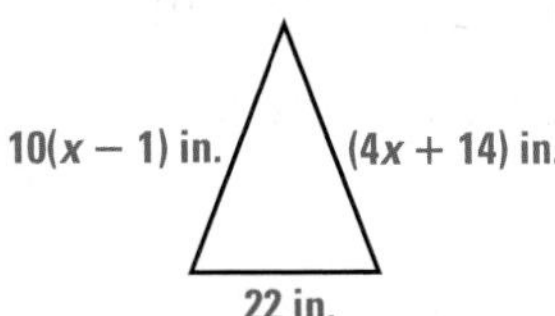

5. **SHORT RESPONSE** You are folding origami cranes that will be used as decorations at a wedding. If you make cranes for 1 hour without a break, you can make 40 cranes. During a 3 hour period, you make 100 cranes. How much time did you spend *not* making cranes? *Explain* your reasoning.

6. **SHORT RESPONSE** A ski resort offers a super-saver pass for \$90. The lift ticket rates with and without the super-saver pass are listed below.

Pass	Weekday lift ticket	Weekend/holiday lift ticket
With	\$22.50	\$36.00
Without	\$45.00	\$48.00

   Suppose a skier skis only on weekdays. After how many visits to the ski resort will the cost for the super-saver pass and the lift tickets be equal to the cost of the lift tickets without the pass? *Explain* your reasoning.

7. **SHORT RESPONSE** The eruption of Mount St. Helens in 1980 decreased its elevation by 1313 feet. The current elevation is 8364 feet. What was the elevation of the volcano before the eruption? *Explain* your reasoning.

8. **EXTENDED RESPONSE** A garden supply store sells daffodil bulbs for \$.60 per bulb.

   a. Jen spends \$24 on daffodil bulbs. How many daffodil bulbs did she purchase?

   b. Jen decides to plant the daffodil bulbs along one side of her house that is 30 feet long. How many inches apart should she plant the bulbs so that they are equally spaced?

   c. Jen thinks that the daffodils will look better if the bulbs are planted 6 inches apart. How many more bulbs does she need? *Explain* your reasoning.

9. **OPEN-ENDED** *Describe* a real-world situation that can be modeled by the equation $4x + 15 = 47$. Then solve the equation and explain what your solution means in this situation.

2.6 Write Ratios and Proportions

Before You solved equations involving division.

Now You will find ratios and write and solve proportions.

Why? So you can find a ratio involving a contest, as in Ex. 46.

Key Vocabulary
- ratio
- proportion
- simplest form

CC.9-12.A.CED.1 Create equations and inequalities in one variable and use them to solve problems.*

Throughout this book you have been using rates, such as 50 miles per hour. A rate is a special type of *ratio.*

KEY CONCEPT *For Your Notebook*

Ratios

A **ratio** uses division to compare two quantities. You can write the ratio of two quantities a and b, where b is not equal to 0, in three ways.

a to b $\qquad a : b \qquad \frac{a}{b}$

Each ratio is read "the ratio of a to b." Ratios should be written in simplest form.

EXAMPLE 1 Write a ratio

VOLLEYBALL A volleyball team plays 14 home matches and 10 away matches.

a. Find the ratio of home matches to away matches.

b. Find the ratio of home matches to all matches.

Solution

a. $\frac{\text{home matches}}{\text{away matches}} = \frac{14}{10} = \frac{7}{5}$

b. $\frac{\text{home matches}}{\text{all matches}} = \frac{14}{14 + 10} = \frac{14}{24} = \frac{7}{12}$

GUIDED PRACTICE for Example 1

Derek and his brother decide to combine their CD collections. Derek has 44 CDs, and his brother has 52 CDs. Find the specified ratio.

1. The number of Derek's CDs to the number of his brother's CDs
2. The number of Derek's CDs to the number of CDs in the entire collection

PROPORTIONS A **proportion** is an equation that states that two ratios are equivalent. The general form of a proportion is given below.

READING
This proportion is read *"a is to b as c is to d."*

$$\frac{a}{b} = \frac{c}{d} \text{ where } b \neq 0, d \neq 0$$

If one of the numbers in a proportion is unknown, you can solve the proportion to find the unknown number. To solve a proportion with a variable in the numerator, you can use the same methods you used to solve equations.

EXAMPLE 2 Solve a proportion

Solve the proportion $\frac{11}{6} = \frac{x}{30}$.

$\frac{11}{6} = \frac{x}{30}$	**Write original proportion.**
$30 \cdot \frac{11}{6} = 30 \cdot \frac{x}{30}$	**Multiply each side by 30.**
$\frac{330}{6} = x$	**Simplify.**
$55 = x$	**Divide.**

GUIDED PRACTICE for Example 2

Solve the proportion. Check your solution.

3. $\frac{w}{35} = \frac{4}{7}$ 4. $\frac{9}{2} = \frac{m}{12}$ 5. $\frac{z}{54} = \frac{5}{9}$

SETTING UP A PROPORTION There are different ways to set up a proportion. Consider the following problem.

A recipe for tomato salsa calls for 30 tomatoes to make 12 pints of salsa. How many tomatoes are needed to make 4 pints of salsa?

The tables below show two ways of arranging the information from the problem. In each table, x represents the number of tomatoes needed to make 4 pints of salsa. The proportions follow from the tables.

AVOID ERRORS
You cannot write a proportion that compares pints to tomatoes and tomatoes to pints.

$$\frac{\text{pints}}{\text{tomatoes}} \neq \frac{\text{tomatoes}}{\text{pints}}$$

	Tomatoes	Pints
Smaller recipe	x	4
Normal recipe	30	12

Proportion: $\frac{x}{30} = \frac{4}{12}$

	Smaller recipe	Normal recipe
Tomatoes	x	30
Pints	4	12

Proportion: $\frac{x}{4} = \frac{30}{12}$

EXAMPLE 3 Solve a multi-step problem

ELEVATORS The elevator that takes passengers from the lobby of the John Hancock Center in Chicago to the observation level travels 150 feet in 5 seconds. The observation level is located on the 94th floor, at 1029 feet above the ground. Find the time it takes the elevator to travel from the lobby to the observation level.

Solution

STEP 1 **Write** a proportion involving two ratios that compare the amount of time the elevator has ascended with the distance traveled.

$$\frac{5}{150} = \frac{x}{1029}$$ ← **seconds** / ← **feet**

STEP 2 **Solve** the proportion.

$\frac{5}{150} = \frac{x}{1029}$ **Write proportion.**

$1029 \cdot \frac{5}{150} = 1029 \cdot \frac{x}{1029}$ **Multiply each side by 1029.**

$\frac{5145}{150} = x$ **Simplify.**

$34.3 = x$ **Use a calculator.**

▶ The elevator travels from the lobby to the observation level in 34.3 seconds.

CHECK You can use a table to check the reasonableness of your answer.

GENERATE TABLE
As the amount of time increases by 5 seconds, the distance traveled increases by 150 feet.

Time (sec)	5	10	15	20	25	30	35
Distance traveled (ft)	150	300	450	600	750	900	1050

The solution, 34.3 seconds, is slightly less than 35 seconds, and 1029 feet is slightly less than 1050 feet. So, the solution is reasonable.

✓ GUIDED PRACTICE for Example 3

6. **WHAT IF?** In Example 3, suppose the elevator travels 125 feet in 5 seconds. Find the time it will take for the elevator to travel from the lobby to the observation level.

7. **ASTRONOMY** When two full moons appear in the same month, the second full moon is called a blue moon. On average, 2 blue moons occur every 5 years. Find the number of blue moons that are likely to occur in the next 25 years.

2.6 EXERCISES

HOMEWORK KEY

○ = See **WORKED-OUT SOLUTIONS** Exs. 17 and 49
★ = **STANDARDIZED TEST PRACTICE** Exs. 2, 19, 20, 43, and 54
◆ = **MULTIPLE REPRESENTATIONS** Ex. 52

SKILL PRACTICE

1. **VOCABULARY** Copy and complete: A proportion is an equation that states that two __?__ are equivalent.

2. ★ **WRITING** Write a ratio of two quantities in three different ways.

SIMPLIFYING RATIOS **Tell whether the ratio is in simplest form. If not, write it in simplest form.**

3. 14 to 18
4. 5 : 13
5. $\frac{24}{25}$
6. 28 to 32

EXAMPLE 2 for Exs. 7–22

SOLVING PROPORTIONS **Solve the proportion. Check your solution.**

7. $\frac{2}{5} = \frac{x}{3}$
8. $\frac{4}{1} = \frac{z}{16}$
9. $\frac{c}{8} = \frac{11}{4}$
10. $\frac{36}{12} = \frac{x}{2}$
11. $\frac{16}{7} = \frac{m}{21}$
12. $\frac{k}{9} = \frac{10}{18}$
13. $\frac{5}{8} = \frac{t}{24}$
14. $\frac{d}{5} = \frac{80}{100}$
15. $\frac{v}{20} = \frac{8}{4}$
16. $\frac{r}{60} = \frac{40}{50}$
17. $\frac{16}{48} = \frac{n}{36}$
18. $\frac{49}{98} = \frac{s}{112}$

19. ★ **MULTIPLE CHOICE** What is the value of x in the proportion $\frac{8}{5} = \frac{x}{20}$?

Ⓐ 2 Ⓑ 23 Ⓒ 32 Ⓓ 40

20. ★ **MULTIPLE CHOICE** What is the value of z in the proportion $\frac{z}{15} = \frac{28}{35}$?

Ⓐ 8 Ⓑ 12 Ⓒ 18.75 Ⓓ 425

ERROR ANALYSIS ***Describe*** **and correct the error in solving the proportion.**

21.
$$\frac{3}{4} = \frac{x}{6}$$
$$\frac{1}{6} \cdot \frac{3}{4} = \frac{1}{6} \cdot \frac{x}{6}$$
$$\frac{1}{8} = x$$

22.
$$\frac{m}{10} = \frac{50}{20}$$
$$10 \cdot \frac{m}{10} = 20 \cdot \frac{50}{20}$$
$$m = 50$$

WRITING AND SOLVING PROPORTIONS **Write the sentence as a proportion. Then solve the proportion.**

23. 3 is to 8 as x is to 32.
24. 5 is to 7 as a is to 49.
25. x is to 4 as 8 is to 16.
26. y is to 20 as 9 is to 5.
27. b is to 10 as 7 is to 2.
28. 4 is to 12 as n is to 3.
29. 12 is to 18 as d is to 27.
30. t is to 21 as 40 is to 28.

SOLVING PROPORTIONS **Solve the proportion. Check your solution.**

31. $\frac{b}{0.5} = \frac{9}{2.5}$

32. $\frac{1.1}{1.2} = \frac{n}{3.6}$

33. $\frac{2.1}{7.7} = \frac{v}{8.8}$

34. $\frac{36}{54} = \frac{2x}{6}$

35. $\frac{3a}{4} = \frac{36}{12}$

36. $\frac{10h}{108} = \frac{5}{9}$

37. $\frac{6r}{10} = \frac{36}{15}$

38. $\frac{12}{42} = \frac{4w}{56}$

39. $\frac{m+3}{8} = \frac{40}{64}$

40. $\frac{5}{13} = \frac{k-4}{39}$

41. $\frac{7}{112} = \frac{c-3}{8}$

42. $\frac{6+n}{60} = \frac{15}{90}$

43. ★ **SHORT RESPONSE** Is it possible to write a proportion using the numbers 3, 4, 6, and 8? *Explain* your reasoning.

44. **CHALLENGE** If $\frac{a}{b} = \frac{c}{d}$ for nonzero numbers *a, b, c,* and *d,* is it also true that $\frac{a}{c} = \frac{b}{d}$? *Explain.*

PROBLEM SOLVING

EXAMPLE 1 for Exs. 45–49

45. **GOVERNMENT** There are 435 representatives in the U.S. House of Representatives. Of the 435 representatives, 6 are from Kentucky. Find the ratio of the number of representatives from Kentucky to the total number of representatives.

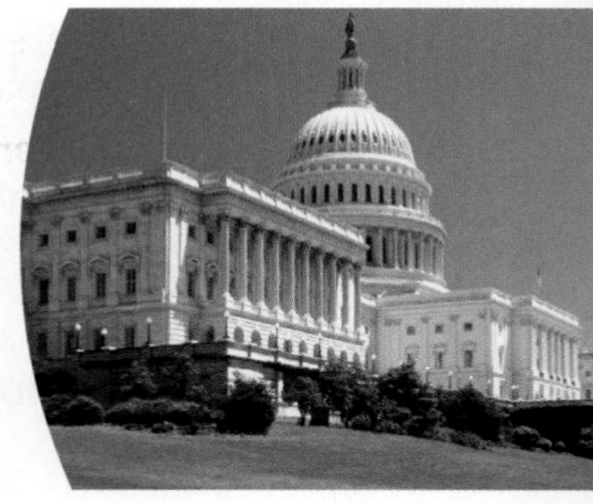

46. **CONTEST** Of the 30 champions of the National Spelling Bee from 1974 to 2003, 16 are boys. Find the ratio of the number of champions who are girls to the number who are boys.

PIZZA SALES **The table shows the number of pizzas sold at a pizzeria during a week. Use the information to find the specified ratio.**

47. Small pizzas to large pizzas

48. Medium pizzas to large pizzas

(49.) Large pizzas to all pizzas

Size	Small	Medium	Large
Pizzas	96	144	240

EXAMPLE 3 for Exs. 50–52

50. **READING** A student can read 7 pages of a book in 10 minutes. How many pages of the book can the student read in 30 minutes?

51. **SOCCER** In the first 4 games of the season, a soccer team scored a total of 10 goals. If this trend continues, how many goals will the team score in the 18 remaining games of the season?

52. ◆ **MULTIPLE REPRESENTATIONS** A movie is filmed so that the ratio of the length to the width of the image on the screen is 1.85 : 1.

   a. **Writing a Proportion** Write and solve a proportion to find the length of the image on the screen when the width of the image is 38 feet.

   b. **Making a Table** Make a table that shows the length of an image when the width of the image is 20, 25, 30, 35, and 40 feet. Use your table to check the reasonableness of your answer to part (a).

○ = See **WORKED-OUT SOLUTIONS** in Student Resources ★ = **STANDARDIZED TEST PRACTICE** ◆ = **MULTIPLE REPRESENTATIONS**

53. **MULTI-STEP PROBLEM** One day, the ratio of skiers to snowboarders on the mountain at a ski resort was 13 : 10. The resort sold a total of 253 lift tickets during the day.

a. Find the ratio of snowboarders on the mountain to all of the skiers and snowboarders on the mountain.

b. Use the ratio from part (a) to find the number of lift tickets sold to snowboarders during the day.

c. During the same day, the ratio of snowboarders who rented snowboards to snowboarders that have their own snowboards is 4 : 7. Find the number of snowboarders who rented a snowboard.

54. ★ **EXTENDED RESPONSE** You and a friend are waiting in separate lines to purchase concert tickets.

a. **Interpret** Every 10 minutes, the cashier at the head of your line helps 3 people. There are 11 people in line in front of you. Write a proportion that can be used to determine how long you will have to wait to purchase tickets.

b. **Interpret** Every 5 minutes, the cashier at the head of your friend's line helps 2 people. There are 14 people in line in front of your friend. Write a proportion that can be used to determine how long your friend will have to wait to purchase tickets.

c. **Compare** Will you or your friend be able to purchase concert tickets first? *Explain.*

55. **CHALLENGE** A car traveling 50 miles per hour goes 15 miles farther in the same amount of time as a car traveling 30 miles per hour. Find the distance that each car travels.

2.7 Solve Proportions Using Cross Products

Before You solved proportions using the multiplication property of equality.
Now You will solve proportions using cross products.
Why? So you can find the height of a scale model, as in Ex. 39.

Key Vocabulary
- **cross product**
- **scale drawing**
- **scale model**
- **scale**

CC.9-12.A.CED.1 Create equations and inequalities in one variable and use them to solve problems.*

In a proportion, a **cross product** is the product of the numerator of one ratio and the denominator of the other ratio. The following property involving cross products can be used to solve proportions.

KEY CONCEPT — *For Your Notebook*

Cross Products Property

Words The cross products of a proportion are equal.

Example $\frac{3}{4} = \frac{6}{8}$ $\quad 4 \cdot 6 = 24$, $\ 3 \cdot 8 = 24$

Algebra If $\frac{a}{b} = \frac{c}{d}$ where $b \neq 0$ and $d \neq 0$, then $ad = bc$.

The proportion $\frac{3}{4} = \frac{6}{8}$ can be written as $3:4 = 6:8$. In this form, 4 and 6 are called the *means* of the proportion, and 3 and 8 are called the *extremes* of the proportion. This is why the cross products property is also called the *means-extremes property.*

EXAMPLE 1 Use the cross products property

Solve the proportion $\frac{8}{x} = \frac{6}{15}$.

$\frac{8}{x} = \frac{6}{15}$	Write original proportion.
$8 \cdot 15 = x \cdot 6$	Cross products property
$120 = 6x$	Simplify.
$20 = x$	Divide each side by 6.

▶ The solution is 20. Check by substituting 20 for x in the original proportion.

CHECK $\frac{8}{20} \stackrel{?}{=} \frac{6}{15}$	Substitute 20 for x.
$8 \cdot 15 \stackrel{?}{=} 20 \cdot 6$	Cross products property
$120 = 120$ ✓	Simplify. Solution checks.

★ EXAMPLE 2 Standardized Test Practice

What is the value of x in the proportion $\frac{4}{x} = \frac{8}{x-3}$?

Ⓐ -6 Ⓑ -3 Ⓒ 3 Ⓓ 6

Solution

ANOTHER WAY
Because 8 is twice 4, you can reason that $x - 3$ must be twice x:
$x - 3 = 2x$
$-3 = x$

$\frac{4}{x} = \frac{8}{x-3}$ **Write original proportion.**

$4(x - 3) = x \cdot 8$ **Cross products property**

$4x - 12 = 8x$ **Simplify.**

$-12 = 4x$ **Subtract $4x$ from each side.**

$-3 = x$ **Divide each side by 4.**

▶ The value of x is -3. The correct answer is B. Ⓐ Ⓑ Ⓒ Ⓓ

EXAMPLE 3 Write and solve a proportion

SEALS Each day, the seals at an aquarium are each fed 8 pounds of food for every 100 pounds of their body weight. A seal at the aquarium weighs 280 pounds. How much food should the seal be fed per day?

Solution

STEP 1 **Write** a proportion involving two ratios that compare the amount of food with the weight of the seal.

$\frac{8}{100} = \frac{x}{280}$ ← **amount of food** / ← **weight of seal**

STEP 2 **Solve** the proportion.

ANOTHER WAY
You can also solve the proportion by multiplying each side of the equation by 280.

$\frac{8}{100} = \frac{x}{280}$ **Write proportion.**

$8 \cdot 280 = 100 \cdot x$ **Cross products property**

$2240 = 100x$ **Simplify.**

$22.4 = x$ **Divide each side by 100.**

▶ A 280 pound seal should be fed 22.4 pounds of food per day.

GUIDED PRACTICE for Examples 1, 2, and 3

Solve the proportion. Check your solution.

1. $\frac{4}{a} = \frac{24}{30}$

2. $\frac{3}{x} = \frac{2}{x-6}$

3. $\frac{m}{5} = \frac{m-6}{4}$

4. **WHAT IF?** In Example 3, suppose the seal weighs 260 pounds. How much food should the seal be fed per day?

SCALE DRAWINGS AND SCALE MODELS The floor plan below is an example of a *scale drawing.* A **scale drawing** is a two-dimensional drawing of an object in which the dimensions of the drawing are in proportion to the dimensions of the object. A **scale model** is a three-dimensional model of an object in which the dimensions of the model are in proportion to the dimensions of the object.

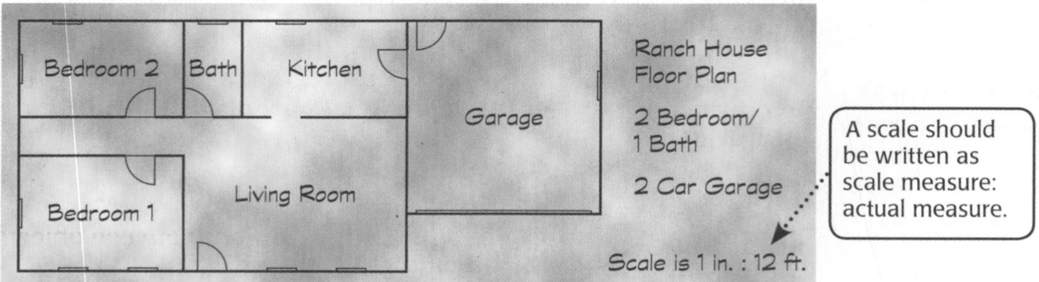

A scale should be written as scale measure: actual measure.

The **scale** of a scale drawing or scale model relates the drawing's or model's dimensions and the actual dimensions. For example, the scale 1 in. : 12 ft on the floor plan means that 1 inch in the floor plan represents an actual distance of 12 feet.

EXAMPLE 4 Use the scale on a map

MAPS Use a metric ruler and the map of Ohio to estimate the distance between Cleveland and Cincinnati.

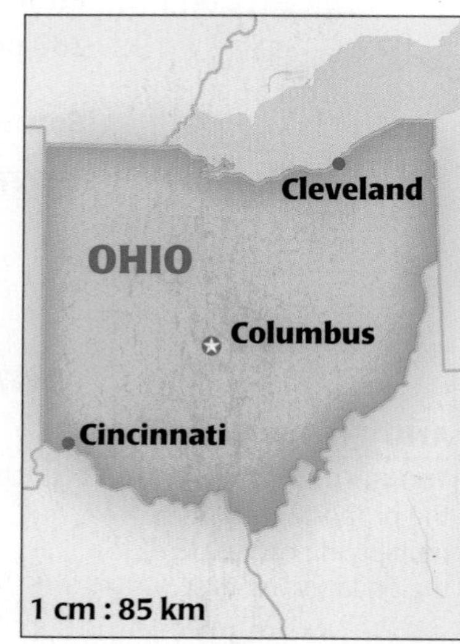

Solution

From the map's scale, 1 centimeter represents 85 kilometers. On the map, the distance between Cleveland and Cincinnati is about 4.2 centimeters.

Write and solve a proportion to find the distance d between the cities.

$$\frac{1}{85} = \frac{4.2}{d} \quad \begin{array}{l}\leftarrow \textbf{centimeters} \\ \leftarrow \textbf{kilometers}\end{array}$$

$1 \cdot d = 85 \cdot 4.2$ **Cross products property**

$d = 357$ **Simplify.**

▶ The actual distance between Cleveland and Cincinnati is about 357 kilometers.

✓ **GUIDED PRACTICE** for Example 4

5. Use a metric ruler and the map in Example 4 to estimate the distance (in kilometers) between Columbus and Cleveland.

6. **MODEL SHIPS** The ship model kits sold at a hobby store have a scale of 1 ft : 600 ft. A completed model of the *Queen Elizabeth II* is 1.6 feet long. Estimate the actual length of the *Queen Elizabeth II.*

2.7 EXERCISES

HOMEWORK KEY

○ = See WORKED-OUT SOLUTIONS Exs. 13 and 39

★ = STANDARDIZED TEST PRACTICE Exs. 2, 15, 16, 41, and 42

◆ = MULTIPLE REPRESENTATIONS Ex. 40

SKILL PRACTICE

1. **VOCABULARY** Copy and complete: In a proportion, a(n) __?__ is the product of the numerator of one ratio and the denominator of the other ratio.

2. ★ **WRITING** A scale drawing has a scale of 1 cm : 3 m. *Explain* how the scale can be used to find the actual distance between objects in the drawing.

EXAMPLES 1 and 2 for Exs. 3–18

SOLVING PROPORTIONS **Solve the proportion. Check your solution.**

3. $\frac{2}{3} = \frac{4}{x}$
4. $\frac{3}{y} = \frac{15}{35}$
5. $\frac{13}{6} = \frac{52}{z}$
6. $\frac{10}{45} = \frac{v}{27}$
7. $\frac{5m}{6} = \frac{10}{12}$
8. $\frac{3k}{27} = \frac{2}{3}$
9. $\frac{-49}{7} = \frac{a+7}{6}$
10. $\frac{6}{t+4} = \frac{42}{77}$
11. $\frac{8}{12} = \frac{r}{r+1}$
12. $\frac{n}{n-12} = \frac{9}{5}$
13. $\frac{11}{w} = \frac{33}{w+24}$
14. $\frac{18}{d+13} = \frac{6}{d-13}$

15. ★ **MULTIPLE CHOICE** What is the value of h in the proportion $\frac{15}{-2h} = \frac{5}{12}$?

(A) −36 (B) −18 (C) 18 (D) 36

16. ★ **MULTIPLE CHOICE** What is the value of s in the proportion $\frac{7}{s-14} = \frac{21}{s+18}$?

(A) −48 (B) −16 (C) 3 (D) 30

ERROR ANALYSIS ***Describe*** **and correct the error in solving the proportion.**

17.

$$\frac{4}{3} = \frac{16}{x}$$
$$4 \cdot 16 = 4 \cdot x$$
$$64 = 4x$$
$$16 = x$$

18.

$$\frac{18}{14} = \frac{b+2}{b}$$
$$18b = 14b + 2$$
$$4b = 2$$
$$b = 0.5$$

SOLVING PROPORTIONS **Solve the proportion. Check your solution.**

19. $\frac{7}{3} = \frac{2x+5}{x}$
20. $\frac{a}{9a-2} = \frac{1}{8}$
21. $\frac{24}{5z+4} = \frac{4}{z-1}$
22. $\frac{c-8}{-2} = \frac{11-4c}{11}$
23. $\frac{k-8}{7+k} = \frac{-1}{5}$
24. $\frac{2}{-3} = \frac{4v+4}{2v+14}$
25. $\frac{m+1}{4} = \frac{3m+6}{7}$
26. $\frac{6}{4+2w} = \frac{-2}{w-10}$
27. $\frac{n+0.3}{n-3.2} = \frac{9}{2}$
28. $\frac{-3}{11} = \frac{5-h}{h+1.4}$
29. $\frac{4}{b-3.9} = \frac{2}{b+1}$
30. $\frac{16.5+3t}{3} = \frac{0.9-t}{-5}$

31. **REASONING** The statements below justify the cross products property. Copy and complete the justification.

$\frac{a}{b} = \frac{c}{d}$	**Given**
$bd \cdot \frac{a}{b} = bd \cdot \frac{c}{d}$	**a.** ___?___
$\frac{bd \cdot a}{b} = \frac{bd \cdot c}{d}$	**b.** ___?___
$ad = cb$	**c.** ___?___

32. **CHALLENGE** In the proportion $\frac{5}{h} = \frac{k}{14}$, what happens to the value of h as the value of k increases? *Explain.*

PROBLEM SOLVING

EXAMPLE 3 for Exs. 33–34

33. **RECIPES** A recipe that yields 12 buttermilk biscuits calls for 2 cups of flour. How much flour is needed to make 30 biscuits?

34. **DIGITAL PHOTOGRAPHS** It took 7.2 minutes to upload 8 digital photographs from your computer to a website. At this rate, how long will it take to upload 20 photographs?

EXAMPLE 4 for Exs. 35–39

MAPS A map has a scale of 1 cm : 15 km. Use the given map distance to find the actual distance.

35. 6 cm
36. 3.2 cm
37. 0.5 cm
38. 4.7 cm

39. **SCALE MODEL** An exhibit at Tobu World Square in Japan includes a scale model of the Empire State Building. The model was built using a scale of 1 m : 25 m. The height of the actual Empire State Building is 443.2 meters. What is the height of the model?

40. ◆ **MULTIPLE REPRESENTATIONS** The diameter of the burst of a firework is proportional to the diameter of the shell of the firework.

    a. **Writing a Proportion** Use the information in the diagram to find the burst diameter for a 4.75 inch shell.

    b. **Making a Table** Make a table of burst diameters for 2, 3, 4, 5, and 6 inch shells. Use the table to check your answer to part (a).

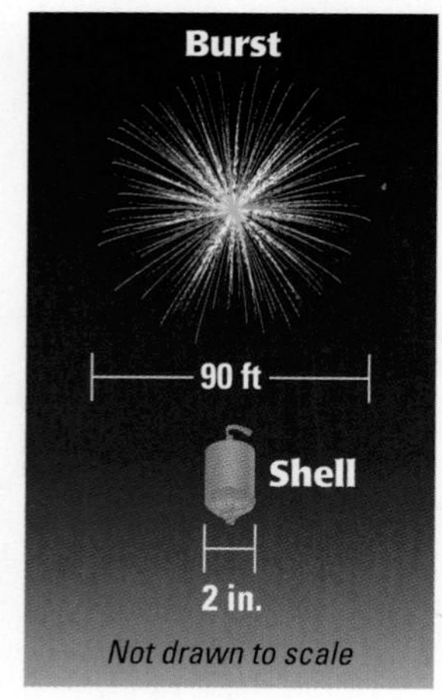

Not drawn to scale

41. ★ **SHORT RESPONSE** The ratio of the length of a soccer field to the width of the field is 3 : 2. A scale drawing of a soccer field has a scale of 1 in. : 20 yd. The length of the field in the drawing is 6 inches. What is the actual width of the field? *Explain* your reasoning.

○ = See WORKED-OUT SOLUTIONS in Student Resources

★ = STANDARDIZED TEST PRACTICE

◆ = MULTIPLE REPRESENTATIONS

42. ★ **EXTENDED RESPONSE** A mole is a unit of measurement used in chemistry. The masses of one mole of three elements are in the table.

Element	Mass of 1 mole
Hydrogen	1.008 grams
Carbon	12.011 grams
Oxygen	15.999 grams

a. A 100 gram sample of ascorbic acid contains 4.58 grams of hydrogen. To the nearest tenth, find the number of moles of hydrogen.

b. A 100 gram sample of ascorbic acid contains 54.5 grams of oxygen. To the nearest tenth, find the number of moles of oxygen in the sample.

c. The ratio of moles of hydrogen to moles of carbon in ascorbic acid is 4:3. How does this ratio compare with the ratio of moles of hydrogen to moles of oxygen in ascorbic acid? *Explain.*

43. **CHALLENGE** In one high school, there are 90 seniors, 142 juniors, 175 sophomores, and 218 freshmen. Ideally, in the apportionment of the 30 seats on the student council, the number of seats each class has is proportional to the number of class members. Assign a number of seats on the council to each class. *Explain* your reasoning.

2.8 Rewrite Equations and Formulas

Before You wrote functions and used formulas.
Now You will rewrite equations and formulas.
Why? So you can solve a problem about bowling, as in Ex. 33.

Key Vocabulary
- **literal equation**
- **formula**

The equations $2x + 5 = 11$ and $6x + 3 = 15$ have the general form $ax + b = c$. The equation $ax + b = c$ is called a **literal equation** because the coefficients and constants have been replaced by letters. When you solve a literal equation, you can use the result to solve any equation that has the same form as the literal equation.

COMMON CORE

CC.9-12.A.CED.4 Rearrange formulas to highlight a quantity of interest, using the same reasoning as in solving equations.*

EXAMPLE 1 Solve a literal equation

Solve $ax + b = c$ for x. Then use the solution to solve $2x + 5 = 11$.

Solution

STEP 1 **Solve** $ax + b = c$ for x.

$ax + b = c$ — **Write original equation.**

$ax = c - b$ — **Subtract b from each side.**

$x = \frac{c - b}{a}$ — **Assume $a \neq 0$. Divide each side by a.**

STEP 2 **Use** the solution to solve $2x + 5 = 11$.

$x = \frac{c - b}{a}$ — **Solution of literal equation**

$= \frac{11 - 5}{2}$ — **Substitute 2 for a, 5 for b, and 11 for c.**

$= 3$ — **Simplify.**

▶ The solution of $2x + 5 = 11$ is 3.

VARIABLES IN DENOMINATORS In Example 1, you must assume that $a \neq 0$ in order to divide by a. In general, if you have to divide by a variable when solving a literal equation, you should assume that the variable does not equal 0.

GUIDED PRACTICE for Example 1

Solve the literal equation for x. Then use the solution to solve the specific equation.

1. $a - bx = c$; $12 - 5x = -3$

2. $ax = bx + c$; $11x = 6x + 20$

TWO OR MORE VARIABLES An equation in two variables, such as $3x + 2y = 8$, or a formula in two or more variables, such as $A = \frac{1}{2}bh$, can be rewritten so that one variable is a function of the other variable(s).

EXAMPLE 2 Rewrite an equation

Write $3x + 2y = 8$ so that y is a function of x.

$3x + 2y = 8$ **Write original equation.**

$2y = 8 - 3x$ **Subtract $3x$ from each side.**

$y = 4 - \frac{3}{2}x$ **Divide each side by 2.**

EXAMPLE 3 Solve and use a geometric formula

The area A of a triangle is given by the formula $A = \frac{1}{2}bh$ where b is the base and h is the height.

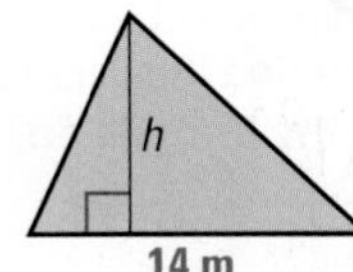

a. Solve the formula for the height h.

b. Use the rewritten formula to find the height of the triangle shown, which has an area of 64.4 square meters.

Solution

a. $A = \frac{1}{2}bh$ **Write original formula.**

$2A = bh$ **Multiply each side by 2.**

$\frac{2A}{b} = h$ **Divide each side by b.**

b. Substitute 64.4 for A and 14 for b in the rewritten formula.

$h = \frac{2A}{b}$ **Write rewritten formula.**

$= \frac{2(64.4)}{14}$ **Substitute 64.4 for A and 14 for b.**

$= 9.2$ **Simplify.**

▶ The height of the triangle is 9.2 meters.

USE UNIT ANALYSIS
When area is measured in square meters and the base is measured in meters, dividing twice the area by the base gives a result measured in meters.

Animated **Algebra** at my.hrw.com

✓ GUIDED PRACTICE for Examples 2 and 3

3. Write $5x + 4y = 20$ so that y is a function of x.

4. The perimeter P of a rectangle is given by the formula $P = 2\ell + 2w$ where ℓ is the length and w is the width.

a. Solve the formula for the width w.

b. Use the rewritten formula to find the width of the rectangle shown.

$P = 19.2$ ft
w
7.2 ft

EXAMPLE 4 Solve a multi-step problem

TEMPERATURE You are visiting Toronto, Canada, over the weekend. A website gives the forecast shown. Find the low temperatures for Saturday and Sunday in degrees Fahrenheit. Use the formula $C = \frac{5}{9}(F - 32)$ where C is the temperature in degrees Celsius and F is the temperature in degrees Fahrenheit.

3 Day Forecast for Toronto		
Friday	**Saturday**	**Sunday**
Sunny High 21°C Low 13°C	Sunny High 22°C Low 14°C	Partly Cloudy High 16°C Low 10°C

REWRITE FORMULAS

When using a formula for multiple calculations, you may find it easier to rewrite the formula first.

Solution

STEP 1 **Rewrite** the formula. In the problem, degrees Celsius are given and degrees Fahrenheit need to be calculated. The calculations will be easier if the formula is written so that F is a function of C.

$C = \frac{5}{9}(F - 32)$ **Write original formula.**

$\frac{9}{5} \cdot C = \frac{9}{5} \cdot \frac{5}{9}(F - 32)$ **Multiply each side by $\frac{9}{5}$, the reciprocal of $\frac{5}{9}$.**

$\frac{9}{5}C = F - 32$ **Simplify.**

$\frac{9}{5}C + 32 = F$ **Add 32 to each side.**

▶ The rewritten formula is $F = \frac{9}{5}C + 32$.

STEP 2 **Find** the low temperatures for Saturday and Sunday in degrees Fahrenheit.

Saturday (low of 14°C)

$$F = \frac{9}{5}C + 32$$
$$= \frac{9}{5}(14) + 32$$
$$= 25.2 + 32$$
$$= 57.2$$

▶ The low for Saturday is 57.2°F.

Sunday (low of 10°C)

$$F = \frac{9}{5}C + 32$$
$$= \frac{9}{5}(10) + 32$$
$$= 18 + 32$$
$$= 50$$

▶ The low for Sunday is 50°F.

GUIDED PRACTICE for Example 4

5. Use the information in Example 4 to find the high temperatures for Saturday and Sunday in degrees Fahrenheit.

2.8 EXERCISES

HOMEWORK KEY

○ = See WORKED-OUT SOLUTIONS Exs. 17 and 33

★ = STANDARDIZED TEST PRACTICE Exs. 2, 23, 29, 35, and 36

◆ = MULTIPLE REPRESENTATIONS Ex. 34

SKILL PRACTICE

1. **VOCABULARY** Copy and complete: When you write the equation $3x + 2 = 8$ as $ax + b = c$, the equation $ax + b = c$ is called a(n) __?__ because the coefficients and constants have been replaced by letters.

2. ★ **WRITING** *Describe* the steps you would take to solve $I = prt$ for t.

EXAMPLE 1 for Exs. 3–10

LITERAL EQUATIONS **Solve the literal equation for *x*. Then use the solution to solve the specific equation.**

3. $ax = bx - c$; $8x = 3x - 10$
4. $a(x + b) = c$; $2(x + 1) = 9$
5. $c = \frac{x + a}{b}$; $2 = \frac{x + 5}{7}$
6. $\frac{x}{a} = \frac{b}{c}$; $\frac{x}{8} = \frac{4.5}{12}$
7. $\frac{x}{a} + b = c$; $\frac{x}{4} + 6 = 13$
8. $ax + b = cx - d$; $2x + 9 = 7x - 1$

ERROR ANALYSIS ***Describe*** **and correct the error in solving the equation for *x*.**

9.
$ax + b = 0$
$ax = b$
$x = \frac{b}{a}$

10.
$c = ax - bx$
$c = (a - b)x$
$c(a - b) = x$

EXAMPLE 2 for Exs. 11–19

REWRITING EQUATIONS **Write the equation so that *y* is a function of *x*.**

11. $2x + y = 7$
12. $5x + 4y = 10$
13. $12 = 9x + 3y$
14. $18x - 2y = 26$
15. $14 = 7y - 6x$
16. $8x - 8y = 5$
17. $30 = 9x - 5y$
18. $3 + 6x = 11 - 4y$
19. $2 + 6y = 3x + 4$

EXAMPLE 3 for Exs. 20–23

REWRITING FORMULAS **Solve the formula for the indicated variable.**

20. Volume of a rectangular prism: $V = \ell wh$. Solve for w.
21. Surface area of a prism: $S = 2B + Ph$. Solve for h.
22. Length of movie projected at 24 frames per second: $\ell = 24f$. Solve for f.

Animated **Algebra** at my.hrw.com

23. ★ **MULTIPLE CHOICE** The formula for the area of a trapezoid is $A = \frac{1}{2}(b_1 + b_2)h$. Which equation is *not* equivalent to the formula?

(A) $h = \frac{2A}{b_1 + b_2}$ (B) $b_1 = \frac{2A}{h} - b_2$ (C) $b_2 = \frac{2A}{b_1} - h$ (D) $b_2 = \frac{2A}{h} - b_1$

REWRITING EQUATIONS **Write the equation so that *y* is a function of *x*.**

24. $4.2x - 2y = 16.8$
25. $9 - 0.5y = 2.5x$
26. $8x - 5x + 21 = 36 - 6y$

GEOMETRY **Solve the formula for the indicated variable. Then evaluate the rewritten formula for the given values. (Use 3.14 for π.)**

27. Surface area of a cone: $S = \pi r\ell + \pi r^2$. Solve for ℓ. Find ℓ when $S = 283\text{ cm}^2$ and $r = 5$ cm.

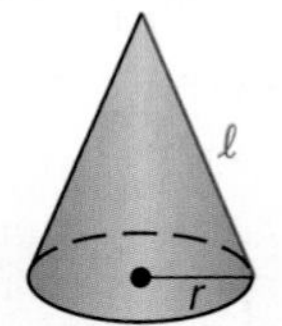

28. Area of a circular ring: $A = 4\pi pw$. Solve for p. Find p when $A = 905\text{ ft}^2$ and $w = 9$ ft.

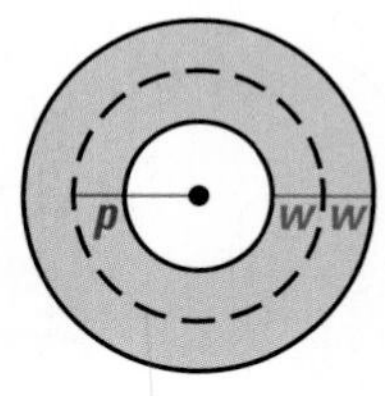

29. ★ **OPEN-ENDED** *Describe* a real-world situation where you would want to solve the distance traveled formula $d = rt$ for t.

CHALLENGE **Solve the literal equation for *a*.**

30. $x = \dfrac{a + b + c}{ab}$

31. $y = x\left(\dfrac{ab}{a - b}\right)$

PROBLEM SOLVING

EXAMPLE 4 for Exs. 32–34

32. CARPENTRY The penny size d of a nail is given by $d = 4n - 2$ where n is the length (in inches) of the nail.

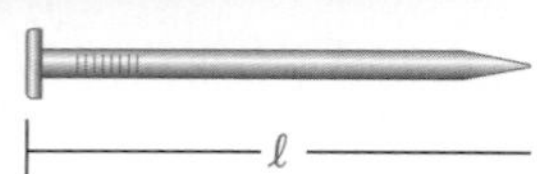

a. Solve the formula for n.

b. Use the new formula to find the lengths of nails with the following penny sizes: 5, 12, 16, and 20.

33. BOWLING To participate in a bowling league, you pay a \$25 sign-up fee and \$12 for each league night that you bowl. So, the total cost C (in dollars) is given by the equation $C = 12x + 25$ where x is the number of league nights you bowled.

a. Solve the equation for x.

b. How many league nights have you bowled if you spent a total of \$145? \$181? \$205?

34. ◆ **MULTIPLE REPRESENTATIONS** An athletic facility is building an indoor track like the one shown. The perimeter P (in feet) of the track is given by $P = 2\pi r + 2x$.

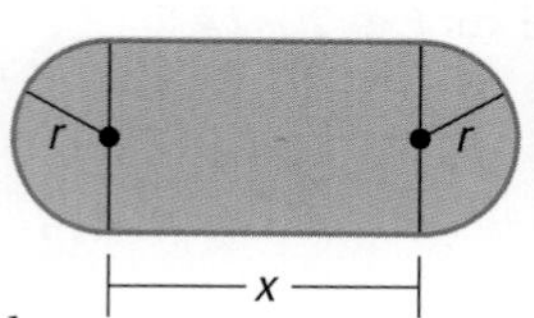

a. Writing an Equation Solve the formula for x.

b. Making a Table The perimeter of the track will be 660 feet. Use the rewritten formula to make a table that shows values of x to the nearest foot when r is 50 feet, 51 feet, 52 feet, and 53 feet. (Use 3.14 for π.)

c. Drawing a Graph Plot the ordered pairs from your table. Look for a pattern in the points. Use the pattern to find x when r is 54 feet.

35. ★ **WRITING** You work as a server at a restaurant. During your shift, you keep track of the bills that you give the tables you serve and the tips you receive from the tables. You want to calculate the tip received from each table as a percent of the bill. *Explain* how to rewrite the percent equation to make it easier to calculate the percent tip from each table.

36. ★ **EXTENDED RESPONSE** One type of stone formation found in Carlsbad Caverns in New Mexico is called a column. This cylindrical stone formation is connected to the ceiling and the floor of a cave.

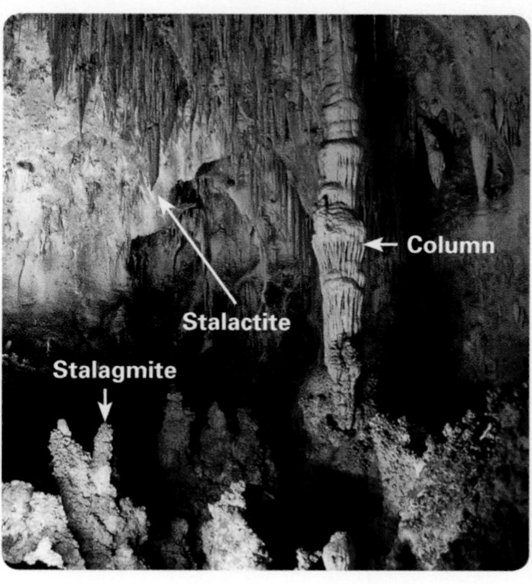

a. Rewrite the formula for the circumference of a circle, $C = 2\pi r$, so that you can easily calculate the radius of a column given its circumference.

b. What is the radius, to the nearest tenth of a foot, of a column that has a circumference of 7 feet? 8 feet? 9 feet? (Use 3.14 for π.)

c. *Explain* how you can find the *area* of a cross section of a column if you know its circumference.

37. **CHALLENGE** The distance d (in miles) traveled by a car is given by $d = 55t$ where t is the time (in hours) the car has traveled. The distance d (in miles) traveled is also given by $d = 20g$ where g is the number of gallons of gasoline used by the car. Write an equation that expresses g as a function of t.

QUIZ

Solve the proportion. Check your solution.

1. $\frac{24}{20} = \frac{x}{5}$
2. $\frac{6}{-7} = \frac{3z}{42}$
3. $\frac{14}{12} = \frac{w + 11}{18}$
4. $\frac{18}{5a} = \frac{3}{-5}$
5. $\frac{10}{17} = \frac{k}{2k - 3}$
6. $\frac{h - 1}{3} = \frac{2h + 1}{9}$

Write the equation so that y is a function of x.

7. $5x - 3y = 9$
8. $3x + 2y + 5x = 12$
9. $4(2x - y) = 6$

10. **GEOMETRY** The volume V of a cylinder is given by the formula $V = \pi r^2 h$ where r is the radius of the cylinder and h is the height of the cylinder. Solve the formula for h.

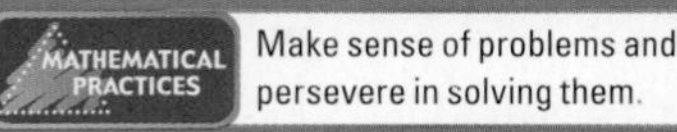

1. **MULTI-STEP PROBLEM** The table below shows the results of a survey in which students at a school were asked to name their favorite sport to watch on TV.

Sport	Students
Baseball	7
Basketball	6
Football	10
Other	8

   a. There are 1209 students at the school. Write a proportion that you can use to predict the number of students at the school who would name baseball as their favorite sport to watch on TV.

   b. Solve the proportion.

2. **MULTI-STEP PROBLEM** The ratio of male students to female students in the freshman class at a high school is 4 : 5. There are 216 students in the freshman class.

   a. Find the ratio of female students to all students.

   b. Use the ratio to find the number of female students in the freshman class.

3. **SHORT RESPONSE** During a vacation, your family's car used 7 gallons of gasoline to travel 154 miles. Your family is planning another vacation in which you will travel 770 miles by car. If gasoline costs about \$2 per gallon, how much money should your family budget for gasoline for this vacation? *Explain* your reasoning.

4. **SHORT RESPONSE** In biology, the surface-area-to-volume quotient Q of a single spherical cell is given by the formula $Q = \frac{3}{r}$ where r is the radius of the cell. Suppose you need to calculate the diameters of cells given the surface-area-to-volume quotients of the cells. Given that $d = 2r$, explain how to write a formula for the diameter d of a cell given its surface-area-to-volume quotient.

5. **GRIDDED ANSWER** A basketball player made 60% of his free-throws during a season. The player made 84 free-throws. How many free-throw attempts did he have?

6. **EXTENDED RESPONSE** When a real estate agent sells a house, the agent receives 6% of the sale price as a commission. The agent lists the sale price for a house as \$208,000.

   a. How much of a commission should the agent expect to receive for selling this house at full price?

   b. The house actually sells for \$205,000. How much of a commission does the agent receive?

   c. The real estate agent gives 10% of her commission to her assistant. What percent of the selling price does the agent's assistant receive? *Explain* your reasoning.

7. **SHORT RESPONSE** The area A of a rhombus is given by the formula $A = \frac{1}{2}d_1d_2$ where d_1 and d_2 are the lengths of the diagonals.

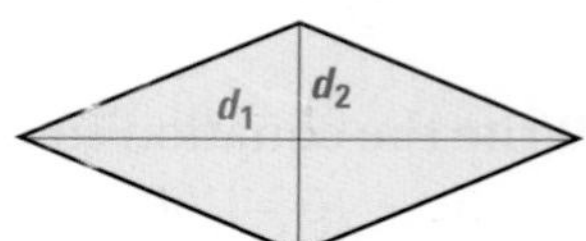

Suppose you need to find d_1 for different values of A and d_2. *Explain* how to rewrite the area formula to make it easier to find values for d_1.

8. **OPEN-ENDED** *Describe* how the dimensions of the rectangular garden below can be altered to increase the area of the garden by 25%.

2 CHAPTER SUMMARY

BIG IDEAS *For Your Notebook*

Big Idea 1

Solving Equations in One Variable

You can solve equations in one variable by adding, subtracting, multiplying by, or dividing by the same number on each side.

Property	Words	Algebra
Addition Property of Equality	Add the same number to each side.	If $x - a = b$, then $x - a + a = b + a$, or $x = b + a$.
Subtraction Property of Equality	Subtract the same number from each side.	If $x + a = b$, then $x + a - a = b - a$, or $x = b - a$.
Multiplication Property of Equality	Multiply each side by the same nonzero number.	If $\frac{x}{a} = b$ and $a \neq 0$, then $a \cdot \frac{x}{a} = a \cdot b$, or $x = ab$.
Division Property of Equality	Divide each side by the same nonzero number.	If $ax = b$ and $a \neq 0$, then $\frac{ax}{a} = \frac{b}{a}$, or $x = \frac{b}{a}$.

Big Idea 2

Solving Proportions

When solving a proportion, you can take the cross products, then use properties of equality.

$\frac{x - 3}{40} = \frac{4}{5}$ **Original proportion**

$5(x - 3) = 40 \cdot 4$ **Cross products property**

$5x - 15 = 160$ **Simplify.**

$5x = 175$ **Addition property of equality: Add 15 to each side.**

$x = 35$ **Division property of equality: Divide each side by 5.**

Big Idea 3

Rewriting Equations in Two or More Variables

If you have an equation in two or more variables, you can solve for one variable in terms of the others using properties of equality. For example, the formula for the perimeter P of a rectangle can be solved for the length ℓ.

$P = 2\ell + 2w$ (rectangle with width w and length ℓ)

$P = 2\ell + 2w$ **Original formula**

$P - 2w = 2\ell$ **Subtraction property of equality: Subtract 2*w* from each side.**

$\frac{P - 2w}{2} = \ell$ **Division property of equality: Divide each side by 2.**

2 CHAPTER REVIEW

@HomeTutor
my.hrw.com
- Multi-Language Glossary
- Vocabulary practice

REVIEW KEY VOCABULARY

- square root
- radicand
- perfect square
- irrational number
- real numbers
- inverse operations
- equivalent equations
- identity
- ratio
- proportion
- cross product
- scale drawing
- scale model
- scale
- literal equation

VOCABULARY EXERCISES

1. Copy and complete: A(n) __?__ is a two-dimensional drawing of an object in which the dimensions of the drawing are in proportion to the dimensions of the object.
2. Copy and complete: When you perform the same inverse operation on each side of an equation, you produce a(n) __?__ equation.
3. *Explain* why the equation $2x + 8x = 3x + 7x$ is an identity.
4. Copy and complete: In the proportion $\frac{7}{8} = \frac{28}{32}$, $7 \cdot 32$ and $8 \cdot 28$ are __?__.
5. *Describe* the steps you would take to write the equation $6x - 2y = 16$ in function form.

REVIEW EXAMPLES AND EXERCISES

Use the review examples and exercises below to check your understanding of the concepts you have learned in each lesson of this chapter.

2.1 Find Square Roots and Compare Real Numbers

EXAMPLE

Order the following numbers from least to greatest: $\sqrt{25}$, $-\sqrt{18}$, -4, 3.2.

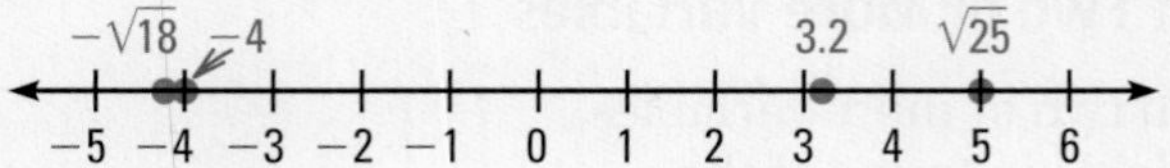

From least to greatest, the numbers are $-\sqrt{18}$, -4, 3.2, and $\sqrt{25}$.

EXERCISES

EXAMPLES 1, 2, and 4 for Exs. 6–15

Evaluate the expression.

6. $\sqrt{121}$
7. $-\sqrt{36}$
8. $\pm\sqrt{81}$
9. $\pm\sqrt{225}$

Approximate the square root to the nearest integer.

10. $\sqrt{97}$
11. $-\sqrt{48}$
12. $-\sqrt{142}$
13. $\sqrt{300}$

Order the numbers in the list from least to greatest.

14. $-\sqrt{49}$, -6.8, 2, $\sqrt{3}$, 1.58
15. 1.25, $\sqrt{11}$, -0.3, 0, $-\sqrt{4}$

@HomeTutor
my.hrw.com
Chapter Review Practice

2.2 Solve One-Step Equations

EXAMPLE

Solve $\frac{x}{5} = 14$.

$\frac{x}{5} = 14$	**Write original equation.**
$5 \cdot \frac{x}{5} = 5 \cdot 14$	**Multiply each side by 5.**
$x = 70$	**Simplify.**

EXERCISES

EXAMPLES 1, 2, 3, 4 and 5 for Exs. 16–22

Solve the equation. Check your solution.

16. $x - 4 = 3$

17. $-8 + a = 5$

18. $4m = -84$

19. $-5z = 75$

20. $11 = \frac{r}{6}$

21. $-27 = \frac{3}{4}w$

22. PARKS A rectangular city park has an area of 211,200 square feet. If the length of the park is 660 feet, what is the width of the park?

2.3 Solve Two-Step Equations

EXAMPLE

Solve $4x - 9 = 3$.

$4x - 9 = 3$	**Write original equation.**
$4x - 9 + 9 = 3 + 9$	**Add 9 to each side.**
$4x = 12$	**Simplify.**
$\frac{4x}{4} = \frac{12}{4}$	**Divide each side by 4.**
$x = 3$	**Simplify.**

EXERCISES

EXAMPLES 1 and 2 for Exs. 23–28

Solve the equation. Check your solution.

23. $9b + 5 = 23$

24. $11 = 5y - 4$

25. $\frac{n}{3} - 4 = 2$

26. $\frac{3}{2}v + 2 = 20$

27. $3t + 9t = 60$

28. $-110 = -4c - 6c$

2 CHAPTER REVIEW

2.4 Solve Multi-Step Equations

EXAMPLE

Solve $5x - 2(4x + 3) = 9$.

$5x - 2(4x + 3) = 9$	**Write original equation.**
$5x - 8x - 6 = 9$	**Distributive property**
$-3x - 6 = 9$	**Combine like terms.**
$-3x = 15$	**Add 6 to each side.**
$x = -5$	**Divide each side by −3.**

EXERCISES

EXAMPLES 1, 2, 3 and 4 for Exs. 29–37

Solve the equation. Check your solution.

29. $3w + 4w - 2 = 12$

30. $z + 5 - 4z = 8$

31. $c + 2c - 5 - 5c = 7$

32. $4y - (y - 4) = -20$

33. $8a - 3(2a + 5) = 13$

34. $16h - 4(5h - 7) = 4$

35. $\frac{3}{2}(b + 1) = 3$

36. $\frac{4}{3}(2x - 1) = -12$

37. $\frac{6}{5}(8k + 2) = -36$

2.5 Solve Equations with Variables on Both Sides

EXAMPLE

Solve the equation, if possible.

$-2(x - 5) = 7 - 2x$	**Original equation**
$-2x + 10 = 7 - 2x$	**Distributive property**
$-2x + 3 = -2x$	**Subtract 7 from each side.**

▶ The equation $-2x + 3 = -2x$ is not true because the number $-2x$ cannot be equal to 3 more than itself. So, the equation has no solution.

EXERCISES

Solve the equation, if possible.

38. $-3z - 1 = 8 - 3z$

39. $16 - 2m = 5m + 9$

40. $2.9w + 5 = 4.7w - 7.6$

41. $2y + 11.4 = 2.6 - 0.2y$

42. $4(x - 3) = -2(6 - 2x)$

43. $6(2a + 10) = 5(a + 5)$

EXAMPLES 1, 2, and 4 for Exs. 38–46

44. $\frac{1}{12}(48 + 24b) = 2(17 - 4b)$

45. $1.5(n + 20) = 0.5(n + 60)$

46. **GEOMETRY** Refer to the square shown.

a. Find the value of x.

b. Find the perimeter of the square.

6x + 5

8x − 3

@HomeTutor
my.hrw.com
Chapter Review Practice

2.6 Write Ratios and Proportions

EXAMPLE

You know that 5 pizzas will feed 20 people. How many pizzas do you need to order to feed 88 people?

$\frac{5}{20} = \frac{x}{88}$ ← **number of pizzas** / ← **number of people**

$88 \cdot \frac{5}{20} = 88 \cdot \frac{x}{88}$ **Multiply each side by 88.**

$22 = x$ **Simplify.**

▶ You need to order 22 pizzas.

EXERCISES

EXAMPLES 2 and 3 for Exs. 47–53

Solve the proportion. Check your solution.

47. $\frac{56}{16} = \frac{x}{2}$ **48.** $\frac{y}{9} = \frac{25}{15}$ **49.** $\frac{2}{7} = \frac{m}{91}$

50. $\frac{5z}{3} = \frac{105}{6}$ **51.** $\frac{9}{4} = \frac{3a}{20}$ **52.** $\frac{c+2}{45} = \frac{8}{5}$

53. PAINTING The label on a can of paint states that one gallon of the paint will cover 560 square feet. How many gallons of that paint are needed to cover 1400 square feet?

2.7 Solve Proportions Using Cross Products

EXAMPLE

Solve the proportion $\frac{3}{10} = \frac{12}{x}$.

$\frac{3}{10} = \frac{12}{x}$ **Write original proportion.**

$3 \cdot x = 10 \cdot 12$ **Cross products property**

$3x = 120$ **Simplify.**

$x = 40$ **Divide each side by 3.**

EXERCISES

EXAMPLES 1 and 4 for Exs. 54–60

Solve the proportion. Check your solution.

54. $\frac{5}{7} = \frac{20}{r}$ **55.** $\frac{6}{z} = \frac{12}{5}$ **56.** $\frac{126}{56} = \frac{9}{4b}$

57. $\frac{10}{3m} = \frac{-5}{6}$ **58.** $\frac{n+8}{5n-2} = \frac{3}{8}$ **59.** $\frac{5-c}{3} = \frac{2c+2}{-4}$

60. MAPS A map has a scale of 1 cm : 12 km. The distance between two cities on the map is 6.8 centimeters. Estimate the actual distance between the cities.

2 CHAPTER REVIEW

2.8 Rewrite Equations and Formulas

EXAMPLE

Write $5x + 4y - 7 = 5$ so that y is a function of x.

$5x + 4y - 7 = 5$	**Write original equation.**
$5x + 4y = 12$	**Add 7 to each side.**
$4y = 12 - 5x$	**Subtract $5x$ from each side.**
$y = 3 - \frac{5}{4}x$	**Divide each side by 4.**

EXERCISES

EXAMPLES 2 and 3 for Exs. 61–64

Write the equation so that y is a function of x.

61. $x + 7y = 0$

62. $3x = 2y - 18$

63. $4y - x = 20 - y$

64. AQUARIUMS A pet store sells aquariums that are rectangular prisms. The volume V of an aquarium is given by the formula $V = \ell wh$ where ℓ is the length, w is the width, and h is the height.

a. Solve the formula for h.

b. Use the rewritten formula to find the height of the aquarium shown, which has a volume of 5850 cubic inches.

2 CHAPTER TEST

Tell whether the number is a real number, a rational number, an irrational number, an integer, or a whole number.

1. $-\frac{1}{4}$ **2.** $\sqrt{90}$ **3.** $-\sqrt{144}$ **4.** 8.95

Order the numbers in the list from least to greatest.

5. $-\frac{5}{3}, -2, 3, \frac{1}{2}, -1.07$ **6.** $\sqrt{15}, -4.3, 4.2, 0, -\sqrt{25}$

Solve the equation. Check your solution.

7. $5 + r = -19$ **8.** $z - 8 = -12$ **9.** $-11x = -77$

10. $\frac{a}{9} = 6$ **11.** $15q - 17 = 13$ **12.** $3y + 2 = 26$

13. $\frac{b}{4} + 5 = 14$ **14.** $\frac{m}{10} - 6 = 20$ **15.** $6j + 5j = 33$

16. $4k - 9k = 10$ **17.** $14c - 8c + 7 = 37$ **18.** $4w - 21 + 5w = 51$

19. $-19.4 - 15d + 22d = 4.4$ **20.** $-12h + 39 = -4h - 17$ **21.** $-5.7v - 44.2 = -8.3v$

22. $-6.5t + 15 = -9.7t + 43.8$ **23.** $3(3n + 4) = 54 + 6n$ **24.** $\frac{1}{3}(24p - 66) = 3p + 43$

Solve the proportion. Check your solution.

25. $\frac{3}{4} = \frac{z}{16}$ **26.** $\frac{72}{45} = \frac{8}{w}$ **27.** $\frac{k}{9} = \frac{63}{81}$

28. $\frac{-5n}{4} = \frac{15}{2}$ **29.** $\frac{34}{6} = \frac{2x + 1}{3}$ **30.** $\frac{-4a - 1}{-10a} = \frac{3}{8}$

Write the equation so that *y* is a function of *x*.

31. $8x + y = 14$ **32.** $-9x + 3y = 18$ **33.** $4x = -2y + 26$

34. MOVIES The ticket prices at a movie theater are shown in the table. A family purchases tickets for 2 adults and 3 children, and the family purchases 3 boxes of popcorn of the same size. The family spent a total of $40.25. How much did each box of popcorn cost?

Ticket	Price
Adults	$8.50
Children	$5.50

35. ICE SKATING To become a member of an ice skating rink, you have to pay a $30 membership fee. The cost of admission to the rink is $5 for members and $7 for nonmembers. After how many visits to the rink is the total cost for members, including the membership fee, the same as the total cost for nonmembers?

36. SCALE DRAWING You are making a scale drawing of your classroom using the scale 1 inch : 3 feet. The floor of your classroom is a rectangle with a length of 21 feet and a width of 18 feet. What should the length and width of the floor in your drawing be?

2 ★ Standardized TEST PREPARATION

MULTIPLE CHOICE QUESTIONS

If you have difficulty solving a multiple choice problem directly, you may be able to use another approach to eliminate incorrect answer choices and obtain the correct answer.

PROBLEM 1

Sid's car gets 34 miles per gallon when driven on the highway and 26 miles per gallon when driven in the city. If Sid drove 414 miles on 13 gallons of gas, how many highway miles and how many city miles did Sid drive?

Ⓐ 91 highway miles, 323 city miles

Ⓑ 182 highway miles, 232 city miles

Ⓒ 232 highway miles, 182 city miles

Ⓓ 323 highway miles, 91 city miles

METHOD 1

SOLVE DIRECTLY Write and solve an equation for the situation.

STEP 1 **Write** an equation. Let x represent the amount of gas (in gallons) used for highway driving. Then $13 - x$ represents the amount of gas used for city driving.

$$414 = 34x + 26(13 - x)$$

STEP 2 **Solve** the equation.

$$414 = 34x + 338 - 26x$$

$$414 = 8x + 338$$

$$76 = 8x$$

$$9.5 = x$$

STEP 3 **Calculate** the number of highway miles driven.

$$34(9.5) = 323$$

STEP 4 **Calculate** the number of city miles driven.

$$26(13 - 9.5) = 91$$

Sid drove 323 highway miles and 91 city miles.

The correct answer is D. Ⓐ Ⓑ Ⓒ Ⓓ

METHOD 2

ELIMINATE CHOICES Another method is to consider the extremes to eliminate incorrect answer choices.

STEP 1 **Consider** driving all highway miles and all city miles.

All highway: $13 \text{ gal} \cdot \frac{34 \text{ mi}}{1 \text{ gal}} = 442 \text{ mi}$

All city: $13 \text{ gal} \cdot \frac{26 \text{ mi}}{1 \text{ gal}} = 338 \text{ mi}$

Because 414 is closer to 442 than to 338, you know that more highway miles were driven than city miles. So, you can eliminate choices A and B.

STEP 2 **Calculate** the gallons of gas that would be used for the remaining choices.

Choice C: $232 \text{ mi} \cdot \frac{1 \text{ gal}}{34 \text{ mi}} \approx 6.8 \text{ gal}$

$182 \text{ mi} \cdot \frac{1 \text{ gal}}{26 \text{ mi}} = 7 \text{ gal}$

Choice D: $323 \text{ mi} \cdot \frac{1 \text{ gal}}{34 \text{ mi}} = 9.5 \text{ gal}$

$91 \text{ mi} \cdot \frac{1 \text{ gal}}{26 \text{ mi}} = 3.5 \text{ gal}$

In choice D, the total number of gallons of gas is 13.

The correct answer is D. Ⓐ Ⓑ Ⓒ Ⓓ

PROBLEM 2

What is the value of x in the proportion $\frac{3}{2x - 10} = \frac{12}{x + 9}$?

(A) 4 (B) 6 (C) 7 (D) 8

METHOD 1

SOLVE DIRECTLY Find the value of x by using the cross products property to solve the proportion.

$$\frac{3}{2x - 10} = \frac{12}{x + 9}$$

$$3(x + 9) = (2x - 10) \cdot 12$$

$$3x + 27 = 24x - 120$$

$$147 = 21x$$

$$7 = x$$

The correct answer is C. (A) (B) (C) (D)

METHOD 2

ELIMINATE CHOICES Substitute each answer choice for x in the proportion and simplify.

Choice A: $\frac{3}{2(4) - 10} \stackrel{?}{=} \frac{12}{4 + 9}$

$\frac{3}{-2} = \frac{12}{13}$ ✗

Choice B: $\frac{3}{2(6) - 10} \stackrel{?}{=} \frac{12}{6 + 9}$

$\frac{3}{2} = \frac{4}{5}$ ✗

Choice C: $\frac{3}{2(7) - 10} \stackrel{?}{=} \frac{12}{7 + 9}$

$\frac{3}{4} = \frac{3}{4}$ ✓

The correct answer is C. (A) (B) (C) (D)

PRACTICE

Explain why you can eliminate the highlighted answer choice.

1. What is the solution of the equation $5(x + 13) = 8(4 + x)$?

   (A) −11 (B) −4 (C) ✗ 0 (D) 11

2. 45 is 80% of what number?

   (A) ✗ 36 (B) 56.25 (C) 60 (D) 64.5

3. A grocery store sells apples by the pound. A 3 pound bag of apples costs \$2.99. About how much does a 5 pound bag of apples cost?

   (A) \$3.24 (B) \$3.45 (C) \$4.98 (D) ✗ \$5.98

4. The surface area S of a cylinder is given by the formula $S = 2\pi rh + 2\pi r^2$ where r is the radius and h is the height of the cylinder. Which of the given formulas is *not* equivalent to the original formula?

   (A) $S = 2\pi r(h + r)$ (B) $h = 2\pi rS + 2\pi r^2$

   (C) ✗ $h = \frac{S - 2\pi r^2}{2\pi r}$ (D) $h = \frac{S}{2\pi r} - r$

2 ★ Standardized TEST PRACTICE

MULTIPLE CHOICE

1. How many solutions does the equation $3(x - 3) = 3x - 6$ have?

   Ⓐ None　Ⓑ 1
   Ⓒ 2　Ⓓ Infinitely many

2. A karate studio offers a 6 week session for \$175. How much would you expect to pay for a 9 week session?

   Ⓐ \$117　Ⓑ \$200
   Ⓒ \$229　Ⓓ \$262.50

3. Andrew decides to get cable TV for \$43 per month. Doug buys a satellite dish for \$104 and pays \$30 per month for satellite TV. After how many months will Andrew and Doug have paid the same amount for their TV services?

   Ⓐ 7　Ⓑ 8
   Ⓒ 9　Ⓓ 10

4. The rates for using a swimming facility are given below. After how many visits will a family of 4 save money by having a membership rather than paying for all 4 family members for each visit?

Admission Prices	
One-day visit	\$3 per person
Family membership (unlimited visits)	\$150

   Ⓐ 12　Ⓑ 13
   Ⓒ 38　Ⓓ 50

5. The record for the longest distance and longest time ever flown by a model airplane was set in 2003 by Maynard Hill. The airplane flew 1888 miles from Canada to Ireland in 38 hours and 53 minutes. What was the plane's average speed?

   Ⓐ About 36 mi/h　Ⓑ About 45 mi/h
   Ⓒ About 49 mi/h　Ⓓ About 71,744 mi/h

6. The perimeter of the triangle shown is 16.5 inches. What is the length of the shortest side?

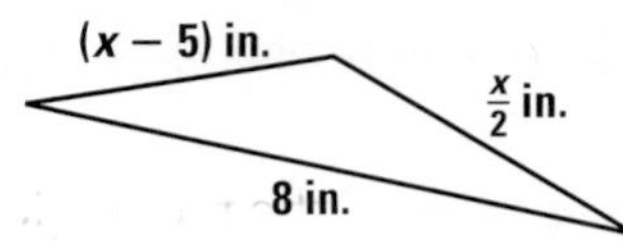

   Ⓐ 3.5 in.　Ⓑ 4 in.
   Ⓒ 4.5 in.　Ⓓ 9 in.

7. Jeanie completed a 27 mile duathlon (a race that is a combination of running and biking) in exactly 2 hours. She ran an average speed of 8.5 miles per hour and biked an average speed of 16 miles per hour. For how long did Jeanie bike during the race?

   Ⓐ 1 hour 20 minutes
   Ⓑ 1 hour 15 minutes
   Ⓒ 45 minutes
   Ⓓ 40 minutes

8. A model of the Gateway Arch in St. Louis, Missouri, was built using a scale of 1 ft : 500 ft. The model is 1.26 feet tall. What is the actual height of the Gateway Arch?

   Ⓐ 75.6 ft　Ⓑ 396.8 ft
   Ⓒ 630 ft　Ⓓ 7560 ft

9. A mountain biking park has a total of 48 trails, 37.5% of which are beginner trails. The rest are divided evenly between intermediate and expert trails. How many of each kind of trail is there?

   Ⓐ 12 beginner, 18 intermediate, 18 expert
   Ⓑ 18 beginner, 15 intermediate, 15 expert
   Ⓒ 18 beginner, 12 intermediate, 18 expert
   Ⓓ 30 beginner, 9 intermediate, 9 expert

10. What percent of 256 is 140.8?

   Ⓐ 45%　Ⓑ 50%
   Ⓒ 52.5%　Ⓓ 55%

GRIDDED ANSWER

11. The circumference of a circle is 12 feet. What is the radius (in feet) of the circle? Round your answer to the nearest tenth.

12. What is the value of x in the equation $75 = 15x - 6(x + 7)$?

13. The perimeter of the rectangle shown is 41 centimeters. What is the value of x?

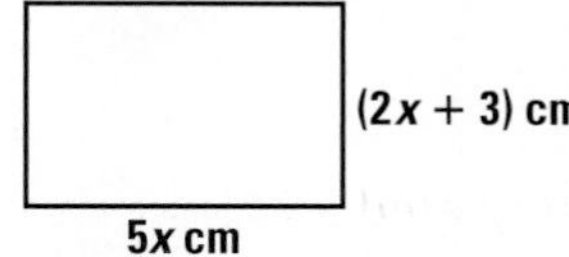

14. Chris pays \$.29 for each digital photo he has printed. Debbie buys a photo printer for \$180. It costs \$.14 per photo for ink and paper to print a photo using the printer. After how many prints will Chris and Debbie have paid the same amount?

SHORT RESPONSE

15. Kendra is painting her dining room white and her living room blue. She spends a total of \$132 on 5 cans of paint. The white paint costs \$24 per can, and the blue paint costs \$28 per can.

a. Write and solve an equation to find the number of cans of each color paint that Kendra bought.

b. How much would Kendra have saved by switching the colors of the dining room and living room? *Explain.*

16. Kim and Sandy are each knitting a scarf. Kim can knit 3 rows in 5 minutes. Sandy can knit 4 rows in 6 minutes. They start knitting at the same time and do not take any breaks. Kim wants her scarf to be 84 rows long. Sandy wants her scarf to be 88 rows long. Who will finish her scarf first? *Explain.*

EXTENDED RESPONSE

17. You are shopping for tools. You find two stores at which the regular prices of the tools are the same. Store A is currently offering \$30 off any purchase of \$100 or more. Store B is currently offering 12% off any purchase.

a. Compare the costs of buying \$200 worth of tools from each store.

b. Compare the costs of buying \$300 worth of tools from each store.

c. Let x be the regular price (in dollars) of your purchase, and assume that x is greater than 100. Write an equation you could use to find the value of x for which the costs of the tools after the discounts are the same. *Explain* how you wrote the equation.

d. Solve the equation from part (c). How can the solution help you to decide from which store you should buy the tools? *Explain.*

18. The circle graph shows the results of a survey that asked 225 randomly selected people how they get driving directions.

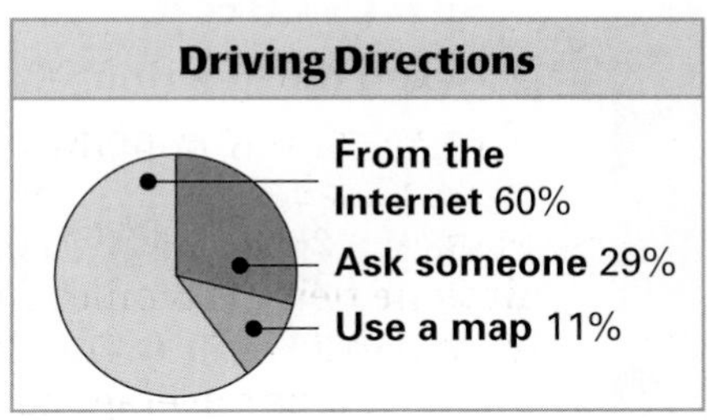

a. How many people said that they get directions from the Internet?

b. Suppose 15 more people were surveyed, and all 15 said that they get directions from the Internet. Calculate the new percent for the "From the Internet" category. *Explain* how you found your answer.

c. Instead of 15 more people, suppose x more people are surveyed and they all said that they get directions from the Internet. What value of x would make the percent for the "From the Internet" category be 70%? Your response should include a proportion and an explanation of how you used the proportion to find your answer.

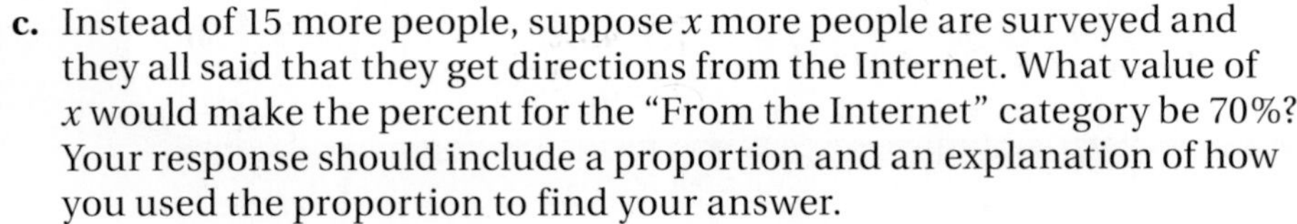

3 Graphing Linear Equations and Functions

COMMON CORE

Lesson	
3.1	CC.9-12.F.IF.7*
3.2	CC.9-12.F.IF.7a*
3.3	CC.9-12.F.IF.7a*
3.4	CC.9-12.F.IF.6*
3.5	CC.9-12.F.IF.7a*
3.6	CC.9-12.A.CED.2*
3.7	CC.9-12.F.IF.7a*

Before

Previously, you learned the following skills, which you'll use in this chapter: graphing functions and writing equations and functions.

Prerequisite Skills

VOCABULARY CHECK

Copy and complete the statement.

1. The set of inputs of a function is called the __?__ of the function. The set of outputs of a function is called the __?__ of the function.
2. A(n) __?__ uses division to compare two quantities.

SKILLS CHECK

Graph the function.

3. $y = x + 6$; domain: 0, 2, 4, 6, and 8
4. $y = 2x + 1$; domain: 0, 1, 2, 3, and 4
5. $y = \frac{2}{3}x$; domain: 0, 3, 6, 9, and 12
6. $y = x - \frac{1}{2}$; domain: 1, 2, 3, 4, and 5
7. $y = x - 4$; 5, 6, 7, and 9
8. $y = \frac{1}{2}x + 1$; 2, 4, 6, and 8

Write the equation so that *y* is a function of *x*.

9. $6x + 4y = 16$
10. $x + 2y = 5$
11. $-12x + 6y = -12$

Now

In this chapter, you will apply the big ideas listed below and reviewed in the Chapter Summary. You will also use the key vocabulary listed below.

Big Ideas

1. **Graphing linear equations and functions using a variety of methods**
2. **Recognizing how changes in linear equations and functions affect their graphs**
3. **Using graphs of linear equations and functions to solve real-world problems**

KEY VOCABULARY

- quadrant
- standard form of a linear equation
- linear function
- *x*-intercept
- *y*-intercept
- slope
- rate of change
- slope-intercept form
- parallel
- direct variation
- constant of variation
- function notation
- family of functions
- parent linear function

Why?

You can graph linear functions to solve problems involving distance. For example, you can graph a linear function to find the time it takes and in-line skater to travel a particular distance at a particular speed.

Animated Algebra

The animation illustrated below helps you answer a question from this chapter: How can you graph a function that models the distance an in-line skater travels over time?

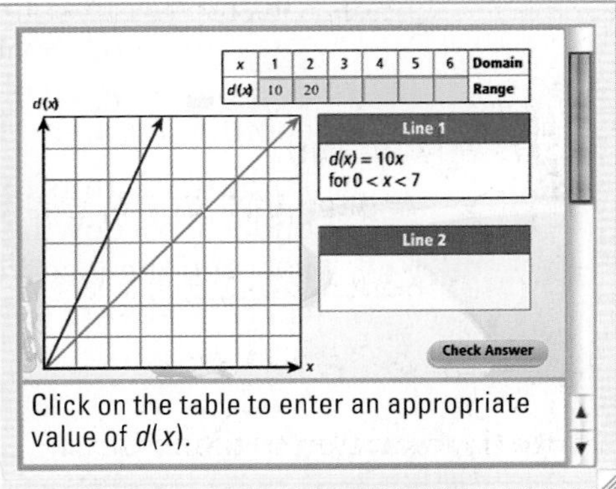

Animated Algebra at my.hrw.com

3.1 Plot Points in a Coordinate Plane

Before You graphed numbers on a number line.

Now You will identify and plot points in a coordinate plane.

Why? So you can interpret photos of Earth taken from space, as in Ex. 36.

Key Vocabulary
- **quadrants**
- **coordinate plane**
- **ordered pair**

You have used a coordinate plane to graph ordered pairs whose coordinates were nonnegative. If you extend the x-axis and y-axis to include negative values, you divide the coordinate plane into four regions called **quadrants**, labeled I, II, III, and IV as shown.

Points in Quadrant I have two positive coordinates. Points in the other three quadrants have at least one negative coordinate.

For example, point P is in Quadrant IV and has an x-coordinate of 3 and a y-coordinate of -2. A point on an axis, such as point Q, is not considered to be in any of the four quadrants.

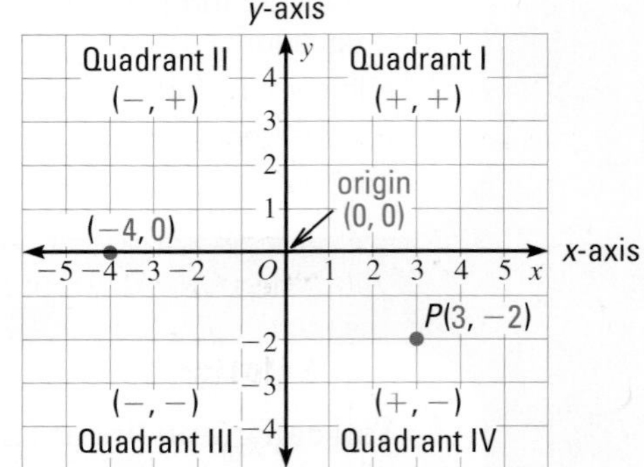

READING
The x-coordinate of a point is sometimes called the *abscissa*. The y-coordinate of a point is sometimes called the *ordinate*.

COMMON CORE

CC.9-12.F.IF.7 Graph functions expressed symbolically and show key features of the graph, by hand in simple cases and using technology for more complicated cases.*

EXAMPLE 1 Name points in a coordinate plane

Give the coordinates of the point.

a. A **b.** B

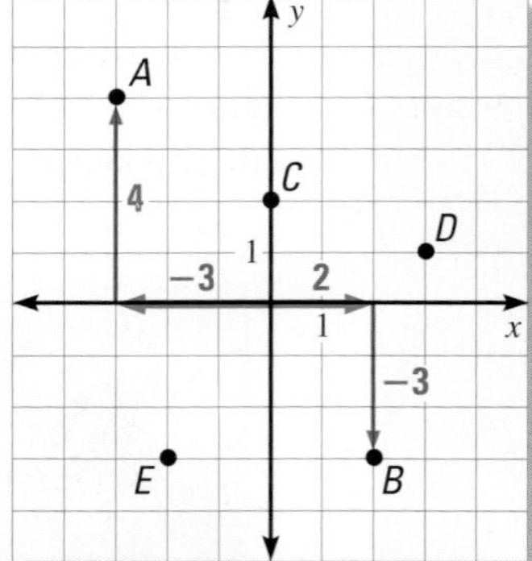

Solution

a. Point A is 3 units to the left of the origin and 4 units up. So, the x-coordinate is -3, and the y-coordinate is 4. The coordinates are $(-3, 4)$.

b. Point B is 2 units to the right of the origin and 3 units down. So, the x-coordinate is 2, and the y-coordinate is -3. The coordinates are $(2, -3)$.

✓ **GUIDED PRACTICE** for Example 1

1. Use the coordinate plane in Example 1 to give the coordinates of points C, D, and E.
2. What is the y-coordinate of any point on the x-axis?

EXAMPLE 2 Plot points in a coordinate plane

Plot the point in a coordinate plane. Describe the location of the point.

a. $A(-4, 4)$ **b.** $B(3, -2)$ **c.** $C(0, -4)$

Solution

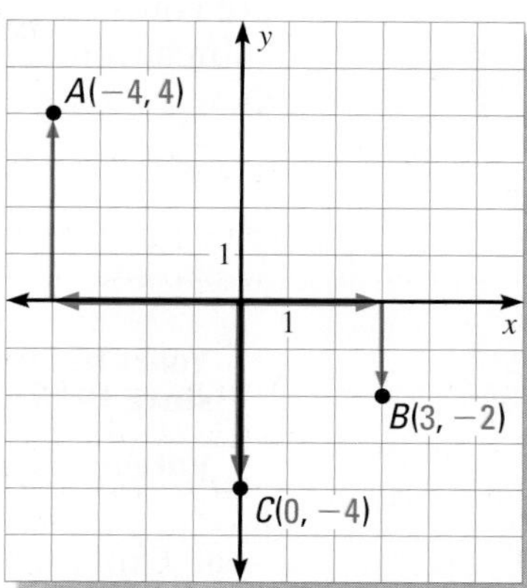

a. Begin at the origin. First move 4 units to the left, then 4 units up. Point A is in Quadrant II.

b. Begin at the origin. First move 3 units to the right, then 2 units down. Point B is in Quadrant IV.

c. Begin at the origin and move 4 units down. Point C is on the y-axis.

at my.hrw.com

EXAMPLE 3 Graph a function

Graph the function $y = 2x - 1$ with domain $-2, -1, 0, 1$, and 2. Then identify the range of the function.

Solution

STEP 1 **Make** a table by substituting the domain values into the function.

x	$y = 2x - 1$
−2	$y = 2(-2) - 1 = -5$
−1	$y = 2(-1) - 1 = -3$
0	$y = 2(0) - 1 = -1$
1	$y = 2(1) - 1 = 1$
2	$y = 2(2) - 1 = 3$

STEP 2 **List** the ordered pairs: $(-2, -5)$, $(-1, -3)$, $(0, -1)$, $(1, 1)$, $(2, 3)$. Then graph the function.

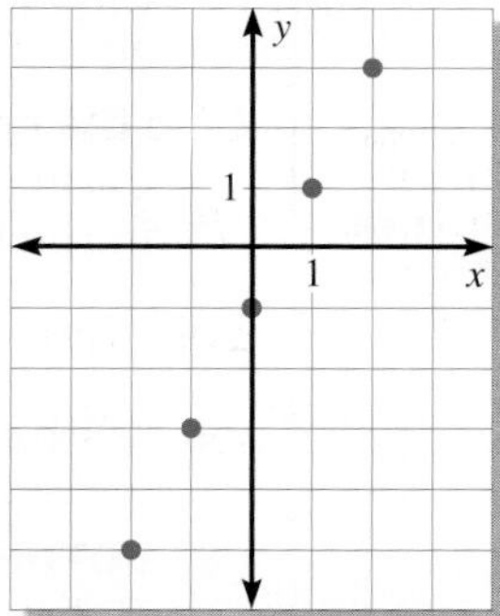

ANALYZE A FUNCTION

The function in Example 3 is called a *discrete* function. The graphs of discrete functions consist of isolated points.

STEP 3 **Identify** the range. The range consists of the y-values from the table: $-5, -3, -1, 1$, and 3.

✓ GUIDED PRACTICE for Examples 2 and 3

Plot the point in a coordinate plane. *Describe* the location of the point.

3. $A(2, 5)$ **4.** $B(-1, 0)$ **5.** $C(-2, -1)$ **6.** $D(-5, 3)$

7. Graph the function $y = -\frac{1}{3}x + 2$ with domain $-6, -3, 0, 3$, and 6. Then identify the range of the function.

EXAMPLE 4 Graph a function represented by a table

VOTING In 1920 the ratification of the 19th amendment to the United States Constitution gave women the right to vote. The table shows the number (to the nearest million) of votes cast in presidential elections both before and since women were able to vote.

Presidential campaign button

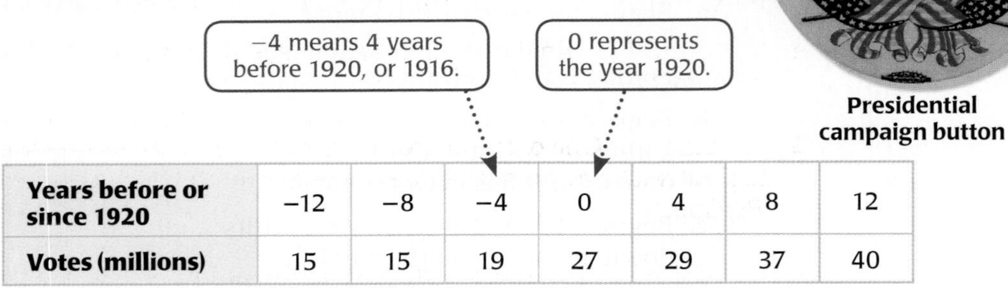

Years before or since 1920	−12	−8	−4	0	4	8	12
Votes (millions)	15	15	19	27	29	37	40

a. Explain how you know that the table represents a function.

b. Graph the function represented by the table.

c. Describe any trend in the number of votes cast.

Solution

a. The table represents a function because each input has exactly one output.

b. To graph the function, let x be the number of years before or since 1920. Let y be the number of votes cast (in millions).

The graph of the function is shown.

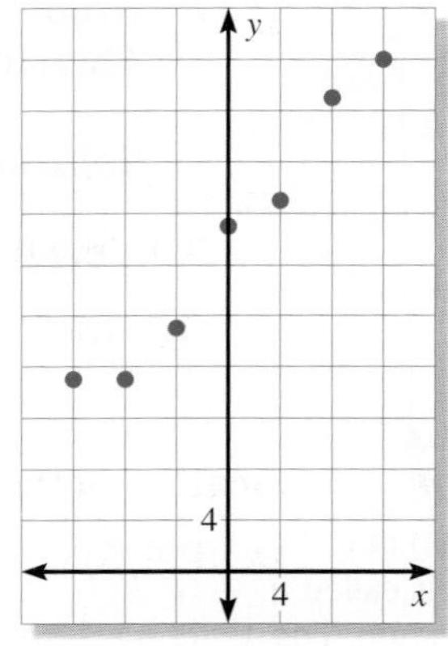

c. In the three election years before 1920, the number of votes cast was less than 20 million. In 1920, the number of votes cast was greater than 20 million. The number of votes cast continued to increase in the three election years since 1920.

✓ GUIDED PRACTICE for Example 4

8. VOTING The presidential election in 1972 was the first election in which 18-year-olds were allowed to vote. The table shows the number (to the nearest million) of votes cast in presidential elections both before and since 1972.

Years before or since 1972	−12	−8	−4	0	4	8	12
Votes (millions)	69	71	73	78	82	87	93

a. *Explain* how you know the graph represents a function.

b. Graph the function represented by the table.

c. *Describe* any trend in the number of votes cast.

3.1 EXERCISES

HOMEWORK KEY

○ = See WORKED-OUT SOLUTIONS Exs. 15, 25, and 37

★ = STANDARDIZED TEST PRACTICE Exs. 2, 13, 23, 33, and 41

◆ = MULTIPLE REPRESENTATIONS Ex. 40

SKILL PRACTICE

1. **VOCABULARY** What is the x-coordinate of the point $(5, -3)$? What is the y-coordinate?

2. ★ **WRITING** One of the coordinates of a point is negative while the other is positive. Can you determine the quadrant in which the point lies? *Explain.*

EXAMPLE 1 for Exs. 3–13

NAMING POINTS Give the coordinates of the point.

3. A 4. B
5. C 6. D
7. E 8. F
9. G 10. H
11. J 12. K

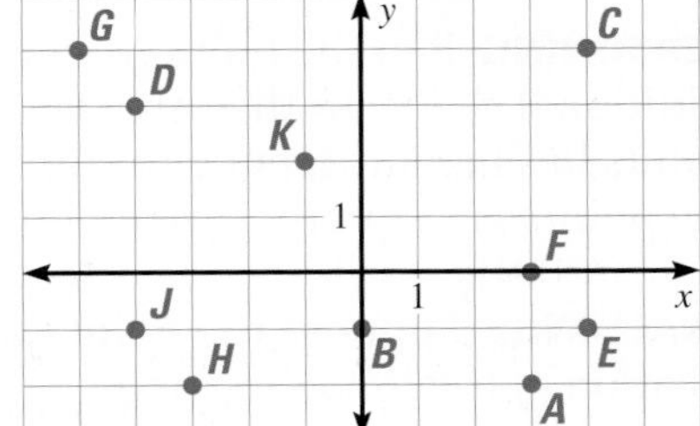

13. ★ **MULTIPLE CHOICE** A point is located 3 units to the left of the origin and 6 units up. What are the coordinates of the point?

Ⓐ $(3, 6)$ Ⓑ $(-3, 6)$ Ⓒ $(6, 3)$ Ⓓ $(6, -3)$

EXAMPLE 2 for Exs. 14–22

PLOTTING POINTS Plot the point in a coordinate plane. *Describe* the location of the point.

14. $P(5, 5)$ 15. $Q(-1, 5)$ 16. $R(-3, 0)$ 17. $S(0, 0)$
18. $T(-3, -4)$ 19. $U(0, 6)$ 20. $V(1.5, 4)$ 21. $W(3, -2.5)$

22. **ERROR ANALYSIS** *Describe* and correct the error in describing the location of the point $W(6, -6)$.

Point W(6, −6) is 6 units to the left of the origin and 6 units up.

EXAMPLE 3 for Exs. 23–27

23. ★ **MULTIPLE CHOICE** Which number is in the range of the function whose graph is shown?

Ⓐ -2 Ⓑ -1
Ⓒ 0 Ⓓ 2

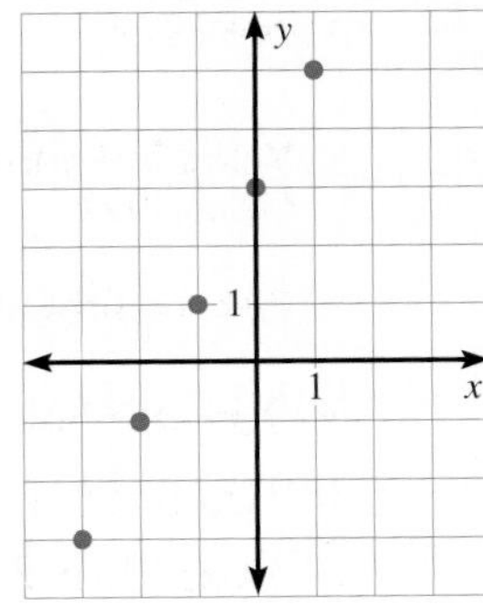

GRAPHING FUNCTIONS Graph the function with the given domain. Then identify the range of the function.

24. $y = -x + 1$; domain: −2, −1, 0, 1, 2

25. $y = 2x - 5$; domain: −2, −1, 0, 1, 2

26. $y = -\frac{2}{3}x - 1$; domain: −6, −3, 0, 3, 6

27. $y = \frac{1}{2}x + 1$; domain: −6, −4, −2, 0, 2

28. **GEOMETRY** Plot the points $W(-4, -2)$, $X(-4, 4)$, $Y(4, 4)$, and $Z(4, -2)$ in a coordinate plane. Connect the points in order. Connect point Z to point W. Identify the resulting figure. Find its perimeter and area.

REASONING Without plotting the point, tell whether it is in Quadrant I, II, III, or IV. *Explain* your reasoning.

29. (4, −11)

30. (40, −40)

31. (−18, 15)

32. (−32, −22)

33. ★ **WRITING** *Explain* how can you tell by looking at the coordinates of a point whether the point is on the x-axis or on the y-axis.

34. **REASONING** Plot the point $J(-4, 3)$ in a coordinate plane. Plot three additional points in the same coordinate plane so that each of the four points lies in a different quadrant and the figure formed by connecting the points is a square. *Explain* how you located the points.

35. **CHALLENGE** Suppose the point (a, b) lies in Quadrant IV. *Describe* the location of the following points: (b, a), $(2a, -2b)$, and $(-b, -a)$. *Explain* your reasoning.

PROBLEM SOLVING

36. **ASTRONAUT PHOTOGRAPHY** Astronauts use a coordinate system to describe the locations of objects they photograph from space. The x-axis is the equator, 0° latitude. The y-axis is the prime meridian, 0° longitude. The names and coordinates of some lakes photographed from space are given. Use the map to determine on which continent each lake is located.

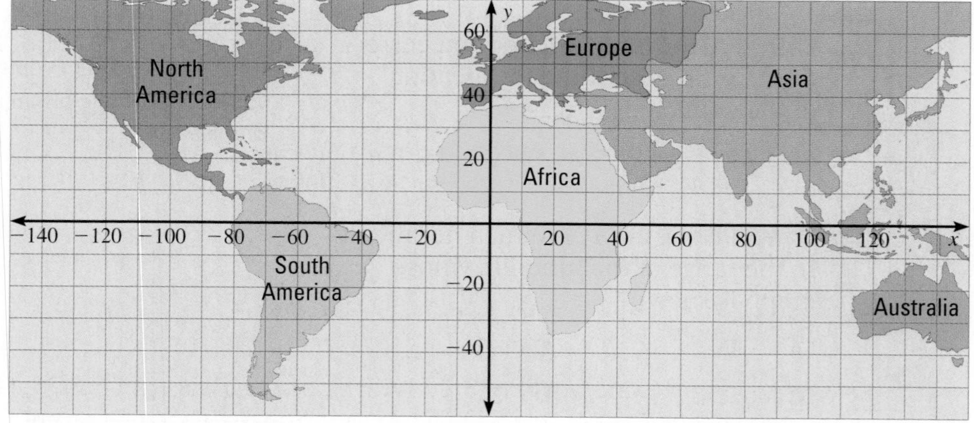

a. Lake Kulundinskoye: (80, 53)

b. Lake Champlain: (−73, 45)

c. Lake Van: (43, 39)

d. Lake Viedma: (−73, −50)

e. Lake Saint Clair: (−83, 43)

f. Starnberger Lake: (12, 48)

○ = See **WORKED-OUT SOLUTIONS** in Student Resources ★ = **STANDARDIZED TEST PRACTICE** ◆ = **MULTIPLE REPRESENTATIONS**

EXAMPLE 4
for Exs. 37–39

37. **RECORD TEMPERATURES** The table shows the record low temperatures (in degrees Fahrenheit) for Odessa, Texas, for each day in the first week of February. *Explain* how you know the table represents a function. Graph the data from the table.

Day in February	1	2	3	4	5	6	7
Record low (degrees Fahrenheit)	−8	−11	10	8	10	9	11

38. **STOCK VALUE** The table shows the change in value (in dollars) of a stock over five days.

Day	1	2	3	4	5
Change in value (dollars)	−0.30	0.10	0.15	0.35	0.11

a. *Explain* how you know the table represents a function. Graph the data from the table.

b. *Describe* any trend in the change in value of the stock.

39. **MULTI-STEP PROBLEM** The difference between what the federal government collects and what it spends during a fiscal year is called the federal surplus or deficit. The table shows the federal surplus or deficit (in billions of dollars) in the 1990s. (A negative number represents a deficit.)

Years since 1990	0	1	2	3	4	5	6	7	8	9
Surplus or deficit (billions)	−221	−269	−290	−255	−203	−164	−108	−22	69	126

a. Graph the function represented by the table.

b. What conclusions can you make from the graph?

40. **MULTIPLE REPRESENTATIONS** Low-density lipoproteins (LDL) transport cholesterol in the bloodstream throughout the body. A high LDL number is associated with an increased risk of cardiovascular disease. A patient's LDL number in 1999 was 189 milligrams per deciliter (mg/dL). To lower that number, the patient went on a diet. The annual LDL numbers for the patient in years after 1999 are 169, 154, 145, 139, and 136

Years since 1999	1	2	?	?	?
Annual changes in LDL (mg/dL)	−20	−15	?	?	?

a. **Making a Table** Use the given information to copy and complete the table that shows the annual change in the patient's LDL number since 1999.

b. **Drawing a Graph** Graph the ordered pairs from the table.

c. **Describing in Words** Based on the graph, what can you conclude about the diet's effectiveness in lowering the patient's LDL number?

41. ★ **EXTENDED RESPONSE** In a scientific study, researchers asked men to report their heights and weights. Then the researchers measured the actual heights and weights of the men. The data for six men are shown in the table. One row of the table represents the data for one man.

Height (inches)			Weight (pounds)		
Reported	**Measured**	**Difference**	**Reported**	**Measured**	**Difference**
70	68	$70 - 68 = 2$	154	146	$154 - 146 = 8$
70	67.5	?	141	143	?
78.5	77.5	?	165	168	?
68	69	?	146	143	?
71	72	?	220	223	?
70	70	?	176	176	?

a. **Calculate** Copy and complete the table.

b. **Graph** For each participant, write an ordered pair (x, y) where x is the difference of the reported and measured heights and y is the difference of the reported and measured weights. Then plot the ordered pairs in a coordinate plane.

c. **CHALLENGE** What does the origin represent in this situation?

d. **CHALLENGE** Which quadrant has the greatest number of points? *Explain* what it means for a point to be in that quadrant.

See **EXTRA PRACTICE** in Student Resources

ONLINE QUIZ at my.hrw.com

3.2 Graph Linear Equations

Before	You plotted points in a coordinate plane.
Now	You will graph linear equations in a coordinate plane.
Why?	So you can find how meteorologists collect data, as in Ex. 40.

Key Vocabulary
- **standard form of a linear equation**
- **linear function**

An example of an equation in two variables is $2x + 5y = 8$. A **solution of an equation in two variables**, x and y, is an ordered pair (x, y) that produces a true statement when the values of x and y are substituted into the equation.

EXAMPLE 1 Standardized Test Practice

CC.9-12.F.IF.7a Graph linear and quadratic functions and show intercepts, maxima, and minima.*

Which ordered pair is a solution of $3x - y = 7$?

Ⓐ (3, 4) Ⓑ (1, −4) Ⓒ (5, −3) Ⓓ (−1, −2)

Solution

Check whether each ordered pair is a solution of the equation.

Test (3, 4):	$3x - y = 7$	**Write original equation.**
	$3(3) - 4 \stackrel{?}{=} 7$	**Substitute 3 for *x* and 4 for *y*.**
	$5 = 7$ ✗	**Simplify.**
Test (1, −4):	$3x - y = 7$	**Write original equation.**
	$3(1) - (-4) \stackrel{?}{=} 7$	**Substitute 1 for *x* and −4 for *y*.**
	$7 = 7$ ✓	**Simplify.**

So, (3, 4) is *not* a solution, but (1, −4) is a solution of $3x - y = 7$.

▶ The correct answer is B. Ⓐ Ⓑ Ⓒ Ⓓ

✓ **GUIDED PRACTICE** for Example 1

1. Tell whether $\left(4, -\frac{1}{2}\right)$ is a solution of $x + 2y = 5$.

GRAPHS The **graph of an equation in two variables** is the set of points in a coordinate plane that represent all solutions of the equation. If the variables in an equation represent real numbers, one way to graph the equation is to make a table of values, plot enough points to recognize a pattern, and then connect the points. When making a table of values, choose convenient values of x that include negative values, zero, and positive values.

EXAMPLE 2 Graph an equation

Graph the equation $-2x + y = -3$.

Solution

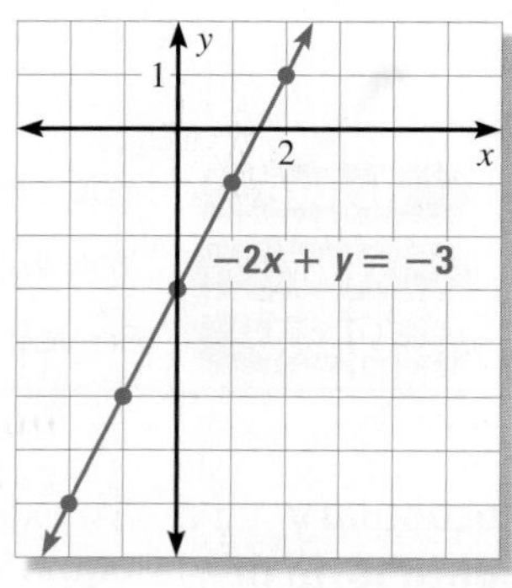

STEP 1 **Solve** the equation for y.

$$-2x + y = -3$$

$$y = 2x - 3$$

DRAW A GRAPH
If you continued to find solutions of the equation and plotted them, the line would fill in.

STEP 2 **Make** a table by choosing a few values for x and finding the values of y.

x	−2	−1	0	1	2
y	−7	−5	−3	−1	1

STEP 3 **Plot** the points. Notice that the points appear to lie on a line.

STEP 4 **Connect** the points by drawing a line through them. Use arrows to indicate that the graph goes on without end.

LINEAR EQUATIONS A **linear equation** is an equation whose graph is a line, such as the equation in Example 2. The **standard form** of a linear equation is

$$Ax + By = C$$

where A, B, and C are real numbers and A and B are not both zero.

Consider what happens when $A = 0$ or when $B = 0$. When $A = 0$, the equation becomes $By = C$, or $y = \frac{C}{B}$. Because $\frac{C}{B}$ is a constant, you can write $y = b$. Similarly, when $B = 0$, the equation becomes $Ax = C$, or $x = \frac{C}{A}$, and you can write $x = a$.

EXAMPLE 3 Graph $y = b$ and $x = a$

Graph (a) $y = 2$ and (b) $x = -1$.

Solution

FIND A SOLUTION
The equations $y = 2$ and $0x + 1y = 2$ are equivalent. For any value of x, the ordered pair $(x, 2)$ is a solution of $y = 2$.

a. For every value of x, the value of y is 2. The graph of the equation $y = 2$ is a horizontal line 2 units above the x-axis.

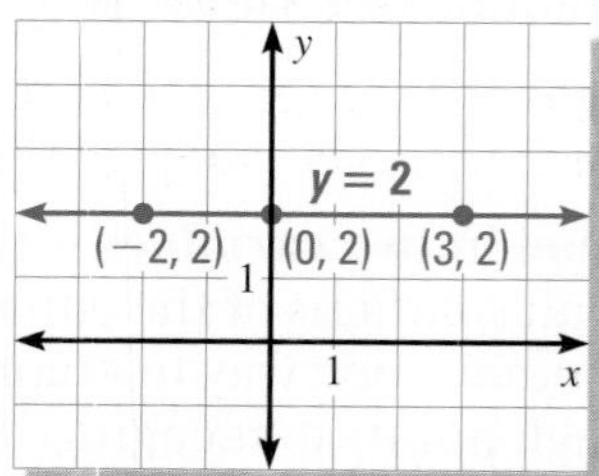

b. For every value of y, the value of x is −1. The graph of the equation $x = -1$ is a vertical line 1 unit to the left of the y-axis.

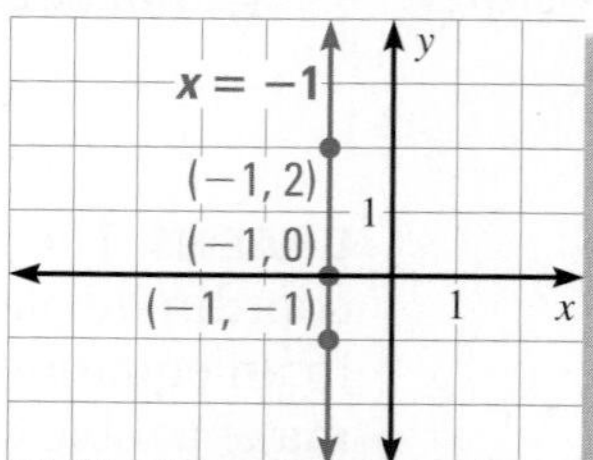

Animated Algebra at my.hrw.com

KEY CONCEPT — *For Your Notebook*

Equations of Horizontal and Vertical Lines

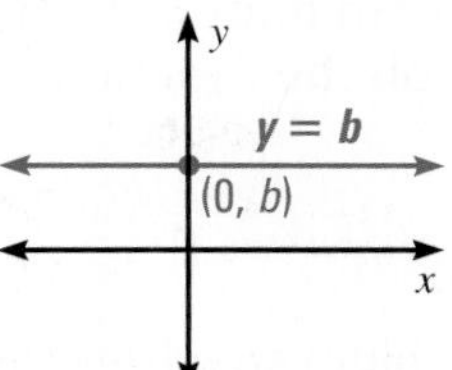

The graph of $y = b$ is a horizontal line. The line passes through the point $(0, b)$.

The graph of $x = a$ is a vertical line. The line passes through the point $(a, 0)$.

✓ GUIDED PRACTICE for Examples 2 and 3

Graph the equation.

2. $y + 3x = -2$ **3.** $y = 2.5$ **4.** $x = -4$

IDENTIFY A FUNCTION

The function $y = 2$ is a *constant function.* The graph of a constant function is a horizontal line.

LINEAR FUNCTIONS In Example 3, $y = 2$ is a function, while $x = -1$ is not a function. The equation $Ax + By = C$ represents a **linear function** provided $B \neq 0$ (that is, provided the graph of the equation is not a vertical line). If the domain of a linear function is not specified, it is understood to be all real numbers. The domain can be restricted, as shown in Example 4.

EXAMPLE 4 Graph a linear function

Graph the function $y = -\frac{1}{2}x + 4$ with domain $x \geq 0$. Then identify the range of the function.

Solution

STEP 1 **Make** a table.

x	0	2	4	6	8
y	4	3	2	1	0

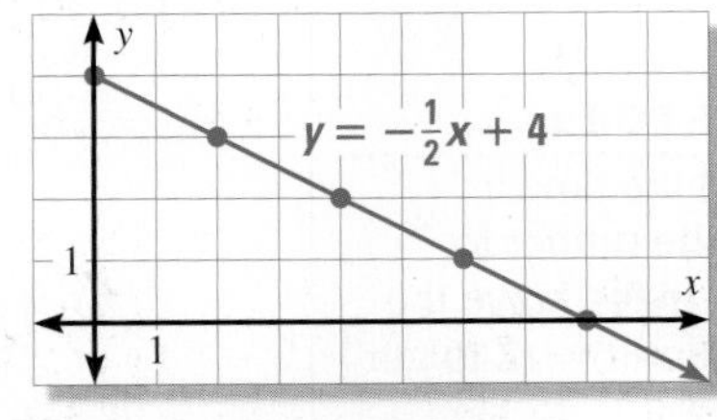

STEP 2 **Plot** the points.

STEP 3 **Connect** the points with a ray because the domain is restricted.

STEP 4 **Identify** the range. From the graph, you can see that all points have a y-coordinate of 4 or less, so the range of the function is $y \leq 4$.

ANALYZE A FUNCTION

The function in Example 4 is called a *continuous* function. The graphs of continuous functions are unbroken.

✓ GUIDED PRACTICE for Example 4

5. Graph the function $y = -3x + 1$ with domain $x \leq 0$. Then identify the range of the function.

EXAMPLE 5 Solve a multi-step problem

RUNNING The distance d (in miles) that a runner travels is given by the function $d = 6t$ where t is the time (in hours) spent running. The runner plans to go for a 1.5 hour run. Graph the function and identify its domain and range.

Solution

STEP 1 **Identify** whether the problem specifies the domain or the range. You know the amount of time the runner plans to spend running. Because time is the independent variable, the domain is specified in this problem. The domain of the function is $0 \le t \le 1.5$.

STEP 2 **Graph** the function. Make a table of values. Then plot and connect the points.

t (hours)	0	0.5	1	1.5
d (miles)	0	3	6	9

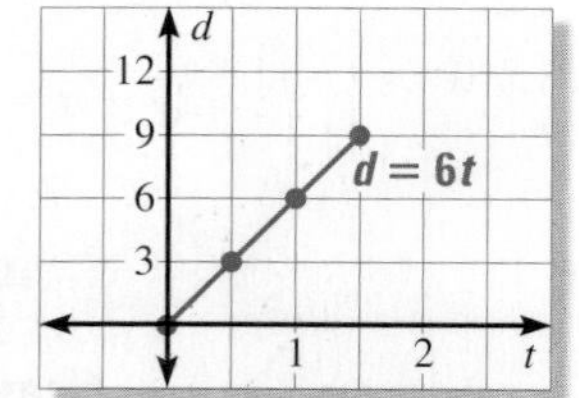

STEP 3 **Identify** the unspecified domain or range. From the table or graph, you can see that the range of the function is $0 \le d \le 9$.

ANALYZE GRAPHS
In Example 2, the domain is unrestricted, and the graph is a *line*. In Example 4, the domain is restricted to $x \ge 0$, and the graph is a *ray*. Here, the domain is restricted to $0 \le t \le 1.5$, and the graph is a *line segment*.

EXAMPLE 6 Solve a related problem

WHAT IF? Suppose the runner in Example 5 instead plans to run 12 miles. Graph the function and identify its domain and range.

Solution

STEP 1 **Identify** whether the problem specifies the domain or the range. You are given the distance that the runner plans to travel. Because distance is the dependent variable, the range is specified in this problem. The range of the function is $0 \le d \le 12$.

STEP 2 **Graph** the function. To make a table, you can substitute d-values (be sure to include 0 and 12) into the function $d = 6t$ and solve for t.

t (hours)	0	1	2
d (miles)	0	6	12

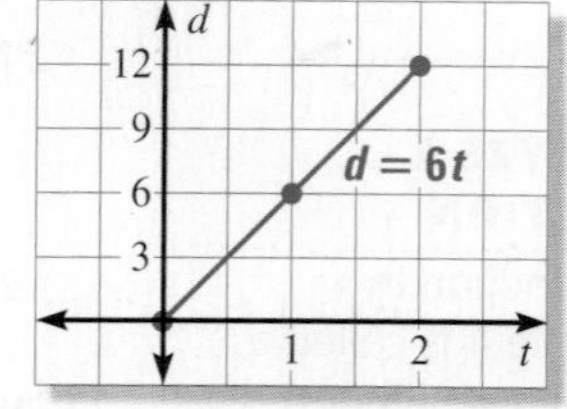

STEP 3 **Identify** the unspecified domain or range. From the table or graph, you can see that the domain of the function is $0 \le t \le 2$.

SOLVE FOR t
To find the time it takes the runner to run 12 miles, solve the equation $6t = 12$ to get $t = 2$.

✓ GUIDED PRACTICE for Examples 5 and 6

6. **GAS COSTS** For gas that costs \$2 per gallon, the equation $C = 2g$ gives the cost C (in dollars) of pumping g gallons of gas. You plan to pump \$10 worth of gas. Graph the function and identify its domain and range.

3.2 EXERCISES

HOMEWORK KEY

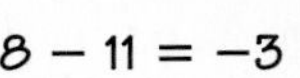
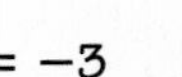

○ = See WORKED-OUT SOLUTIONS Exs. 3, 11, and 37

★ = STANDARDIZED TEST PRACTICE Exs. 2, 10, 32, 33, 39, and 41

◆ = MULTIPLE REPRESENTATIONS Ex. 40

SKILL PRACTICE

1. **VOCABULARY** The equation $Ax + By = C$ represents a(n) __?__ provided $B \neq 0$.

2. ★ **WRITING** Is the equation $y = 6x + 4$ in standard form? *Explain.*

EXAMPLE 1 for Exs. 3–10

CHECKING SOLUTIONS **Tell whether the ordered pair is a solution of the equation.**

3. $2y + x = 4$; $(-2, 3)$
4. $3x - 2y = -5$; $(-1, 1)$
5. $x = 9$; $(9, 6)$
6. $y = -7$; $(-7, 0)$
7. $-7x - 4y = 1$; $(-3, -5)$
8. $-5y - 6x = 0$; $(-6, 5)$

9. **ERROR ANALYSIS** *Describe* and correct the error in determining whether (8, 11) is a solution of $y - x = -3$.

$y - x = -3$
$8 - 11 = -3$
$-3 = -3$ (8, 11) is a solution.

10. ★ **MULTIPLE CHOICE** Which ordered pair is a solution of $6x + 3y = 18$?

Ⓐ $(-2, -10)$ Ⓑ $(-2, 10)$ Ⓒ $(2, 10)$ Ⓓ $(10, -2)$

EXAMPLES 2 and 3 for Exs. 11–25

GRAPHING EQUATIONS **Graph the equation.**

11. $y + x = 2$
12. $y - 2x = 5$
13. $y - 3x = 0$
14. $y + 4x = 1$
15. $2y - 6x = 10$
16. $3y + 4x = 12$
17. $x - 2y = 3$
18. $3x + 2y = 8$
19. $x = 0$
20. $y = 0$
21. $y = -4$
22. $x = 2$

MATCHING EQUATIONS WITH GRAPHS **Match the equation with its graph.**

23. $y - x = 0$
24. $x = -2$
25. $y = -1$

A.
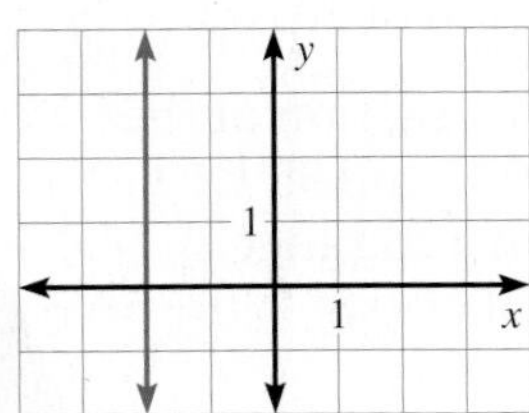

B.
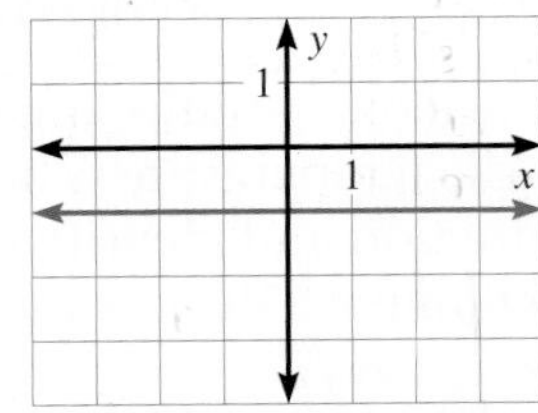

C.
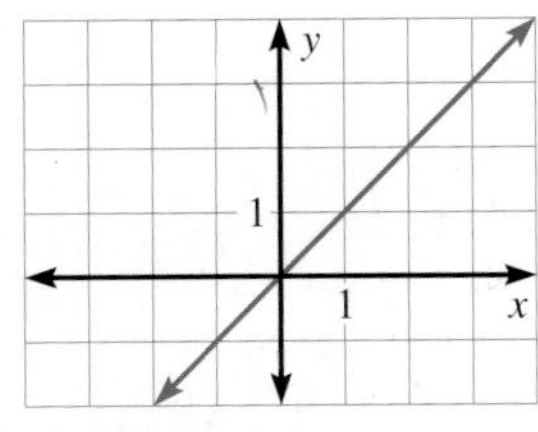

EXAMPLE 4 for Exs. 26–31

GRAPHING FUNCTIONS **Graph the function with the given domain. Then identify the range of the function.**

26. $y = 3x - 2$; domain: $x \geq 0$
27. $y = -5x + 3$; domain: $x \leq 0$
28. $y = 4$; domain: $x \leq 5$
29. $y = -6$; domain: $x \geq 5$
30. $y = 2x + 3$; domain: $-4 \leq x \leq 0$
31. $y = -x - 1$; domain: $-1 \leq x \leq 3$

32. ★ **OPEN-ENDED** Graph $x - y = 3$ and $2x - 2y = 6$. *Explain* why the equations look different but have the same graph. Find another equation that looks different from the two given equations but has the same graph.

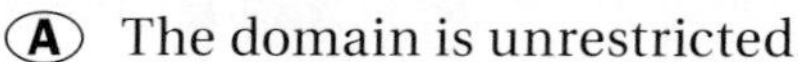

33. ★ **MULTIPLE CHOICE** Which statement is true for the function whose graph is shown?

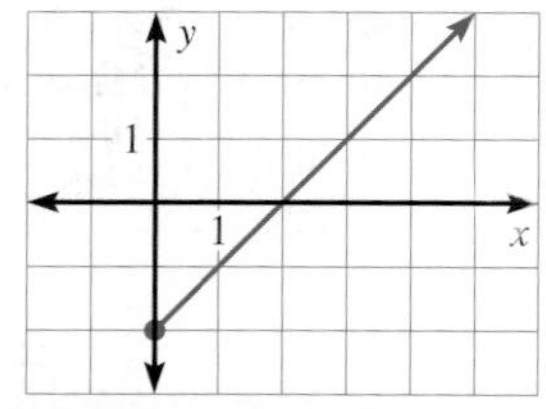

Ⓐ The domain is unrestricted.

Ⓑ The domain is $x \leq -2$.

Ⓒ The range is $y \leq -2$.

Ⓓ The range is $y \geq -2$.

34. **CHALLENGE** If $(3, n)$ is a solution of $Ax + 3y = 6$ and $(n, 5)$ is a solution of $5x + y = 20$, what is the value of A?

PROBLEM SOLVING

EXAMPLES 5 and 6 for Exs. 35–39

35. **BAKING** The weight w (in pounds) of a loaf of bread that a recipe yields is given by the function $w = \frac{1}{2}f$ where f is the number of cups of flour used. You have 4 cups of flour. Graph the function and identify its domain and range. What is the weight of the largest loaf of bread you can make?

36. **TRAVEL** After visiting relatives who live 200 miles away, your family drives home at an average speed of 50 miles per hour. Your distance d (in miles) from home is given by $d = 200 - 50t$ where t is the time (in hours) spent driving. Graph the function and identify its domain and range. What is your distance from home after driving for 1.5 hours?

37. **EARTH SCIENCE** The temperature T (in degrees Celsius) of Earth's crust can be modeled by the function $T = 20 + 25d$ where d is the distance (in kilometers) from the surface.

a. A scientist studies organisms in the first 4 kilometers of Earth's crust. Graph the function and identify its domain and range. What is the temperature at the deepest part of the section of crust?

b. Suppose the scientist studies organisms in a section of the crust where the temperature is between 20°C and 95°C. Graph the function and identify its domain and range. How many kilometers deep is the section of crust?

38. **MULTI-STEP PROBLEM** A fashion designer orders fabric that costs \$30 per yard. The designer wants the fabric to be dyed, which costs \$100. The total cost C (in dollars) of the fabric is given by the function

$$C = 30f + 100$$

where f is the number of yards of fabric.

a. The designer orders 3 yards of fabric. How much does the fabric cost? *Explain.*

b. Suppose the designer can spend \$500 on fabric. How many yards of fabric can the designer buy? *Explain.*

39. ★ **SHORT RESPONSE** An emergency cell phone charger requires you to turn a small crank in order to create the energy needed to recharge the phone's battery. If you turn the crank 120 times per minute, the total number r of revolutions that you turn the crank is given by

$$r = 120t$$

where t is the time (in minutes) spent turning the crank.

a. Graph the function and identify its domain and range.

b. Identify the domain and range if you stop turning the crank after 4 minutes. *Explain* how this affects the appearance of the graph.

40. **MULTIPLE REPRESENTATIONS** The National Weather Service releases weather balloons twice daily at over 90 locations in the United States in order to collect data for meteorologists. The height h (in feet) of a balloon is a function of the time t (in seconds) after the balloon is released, as shown.

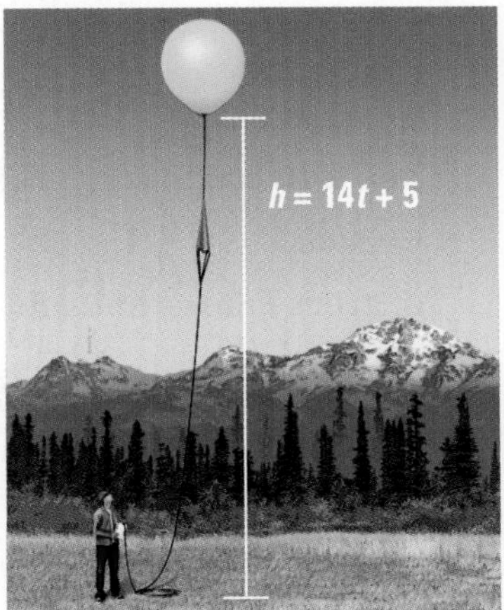

a. Making a Table Make a table showing the height of a balloon after t seconds for $t = 0$ through $t = 10$.

b. Drawing a Graph A balloon bursts after a flight of about 7200 seconds. Graph the function and identify the domain and range.

41. ★ **EXTENDED RESPONSE** Students can pay for lunch at a school in one of two ways. Students can either make a payment of \$30 per month or they can buy lunch daily for \$2.50 per lunch.

a. Graph Graph the function $y = 30$ to represent the monthly payment plan. Using the same coordinate plane, graph the function $y = 2.5x$ to represent the daily payment plan.

b. CHALLENGE What are the coordinates of the point that is a solution of both functions? What does that point mean in this situation?

c. CHALLENGE A student eats an average of 15 school lunches per month. How should the student pay, daily or monthly? *Explain.*

my.hrw.com
Keystrokes

Graphing Linear Equations

MATHEMATICAL PRACTICES
Use appropriate tools strategically.

QUESTION How do you graph an equation on a graphing calculator?

EXAMPLE Use a graph to solve a problem

The formula to convert temperature from degrees Fahrenheit to degrees Celsius is $C = \frac{5}{9}(F - 32)$. Graph the equation. At what temperature are degrees Fahrenheit and degrees Celsius equal?

STEP 1 ***Rewrite and enter equation***

Rewrite the equation using x for F and y for C. Enter the equation into the Y= screen. Put parentheses around the fraction $\frac{5}{9}$.

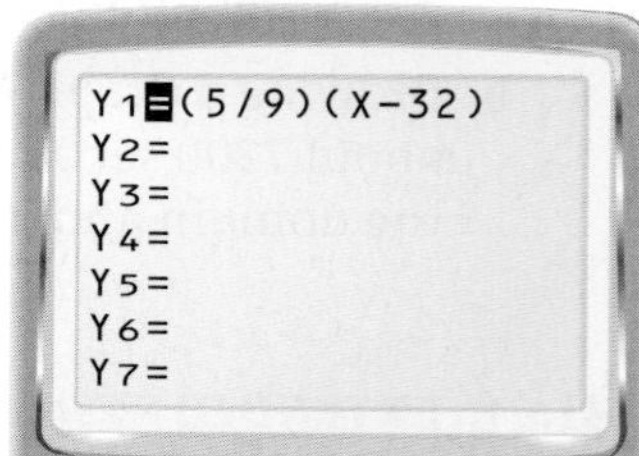

STEP 2 ***Set window***

The screen is a "window" that lets you look at part of a coordinate plane. Press WINDOW to set the borders of the graph. A friendly window for this equation is $-94 \le x \le 94$ and $-100 \le y \le 100$.

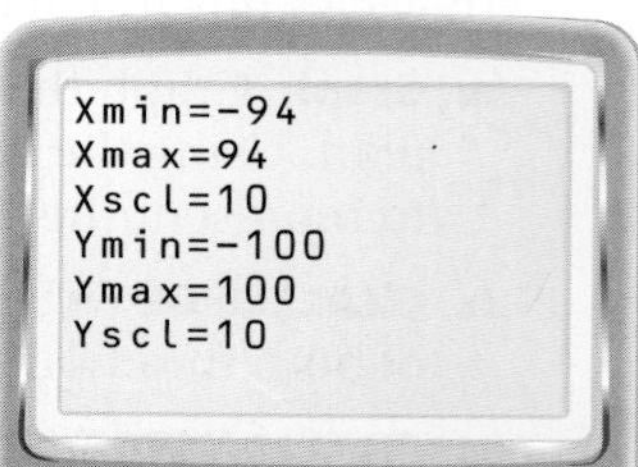

STEP 3 ***Graph and trace equation***

Press TRACE and use the left and right arrows to move the cursor along the graph until the x-coordinate and y-coordinate are equal. From the graph, you can see that degrees Fahrenheit and degrees Celsius are equal at -40.

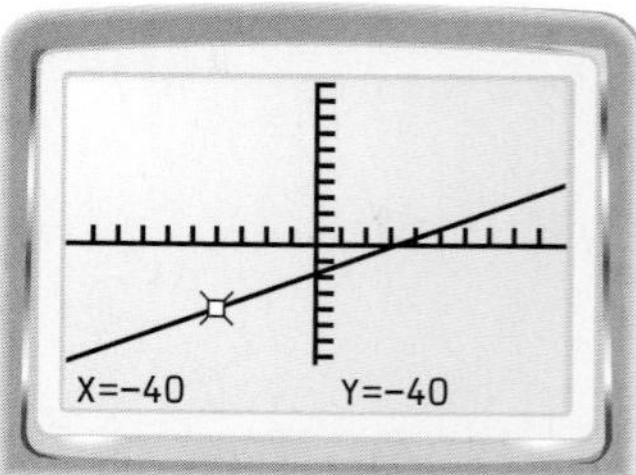

PRACTICE

Graph the equation. Find the unknown value in the ordered pair.

1. $y = 8 - x$; (2.4, ?) **2.** $y = 2x + 3$; (?, 0.8) **3.** $y = -4.5x + 1$; (1.4, ?)

4. SPEED OF SOUND The speed s (in meters per second) of sound in air can be modeled by $s = 331.1 + 0.61T$ where T is the air temperature in degrees Celsius. Graph the equation. Estimate the speed of sound when the temperature is 20°C.

Extension Identify Discrete and Continuous Functions

GOAL Graph and classify discrete and continuous functions.

Key Vocabulary
- **discrete function**
- **continuous function**

CC.9-12.F.IF.5 Relate the domain of a function to its graph and, where applicable, to the quantitative relationship it describes.*

The graph of a function can consist of individual points, as in the graph at the left below. The graph of a function can also be a line or a part of a line with no breaks, as in the graph at the right below.

KEY CONCEPT *For Your Notebook*

Identifying Discrete and Continuous Functions

A **discrete function** has a graph that consists of isolated points.

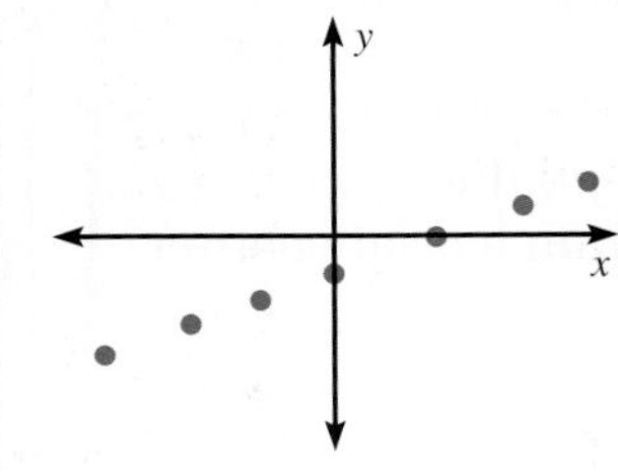

A **continuous function** has a graph that is unbroken.

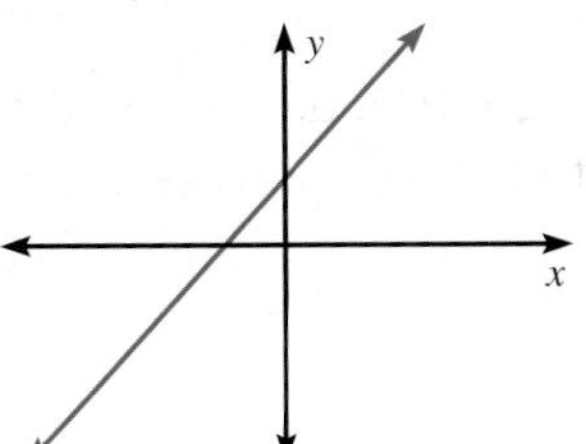

EXAMPLE 1 **Graph and classify a function**

Graph the function $y = 2x - 1$ with the given domain. Classify the function as discrete or continuous.

a. Domain: $x = 0, 1, 2, 3$

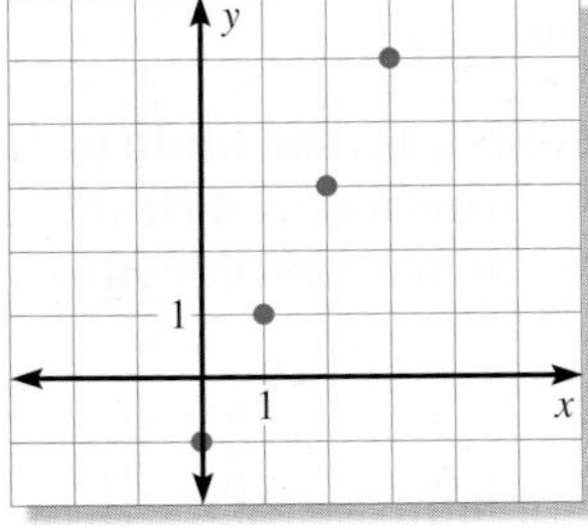

The graph consists of individual points, so the function is discrete.

b. Domain: $x \geq 0$

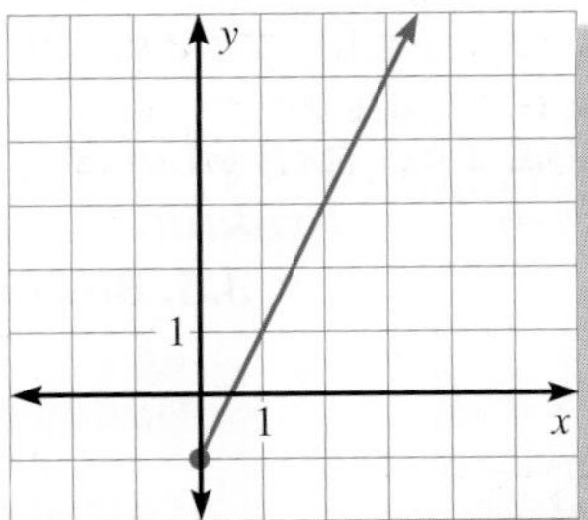

The graph is unbroken, so the function is continuous.

GRAPHS As a general rule, you can tell that a function is continuous if you do not have to lift your pencil from the paper to draw its graph, as in part (b) of Example 1.

EXAMPLE 2 Classify and graph a real-world function

Tell whether the function represented by the table is discrete or continuous. Explain. If continuous, graph the function and find the value of y when $x = 1.5$.

Duration of storm (hours), x	1	2	3
Amount of rain (inches), y	0.5	1	1.5

Solution

Although the table shows the amount of rain that has fallen after whole numbers of hours only, it makes sense to talk about the amount of rain after any amount of time during the storm. So, the table represents a continuous function.

The graph of the function is shown. To find the value of y when $x = 1.5$, start at 1.5 on the x-axis, move up to the graph, and move over to the y-axis. The y-value is about 0.75. So, about 0.75 inch of rain has fallen after 1.5 hours.

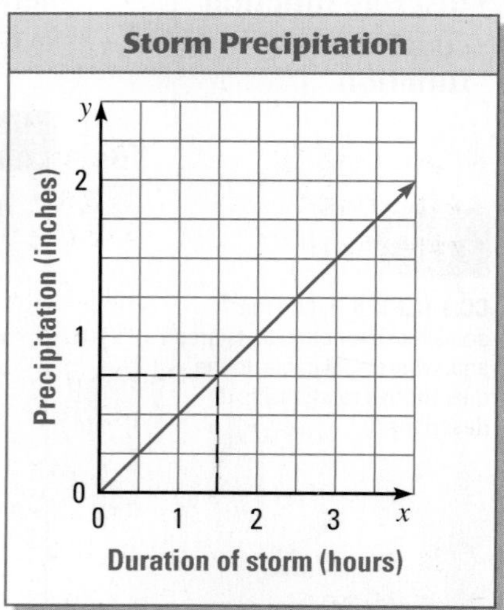

PRACTICE

EXAMPLE 1 for Exs. 1–6

Graph the function with the given domain. Classify the function as discrete or continuous.

1. $y = -2x + 3$; domain: $-2, -1, 0, 1, 2$
2. $y = x$; domain: all real numbers
3. $y = -\frac{1}{3}x + 1$; domain: $-12, -6, 0, 6, 12$
4. $y = 0.5x$; domain: $-2, -1, 0, 1, 2$
5. $y = 3x - 4$; domain: $x \leq 0$
6. $y = \frac{2}{3}x + \frac{1}{3}$; domain: $x \geq -2$

EXAMPLE 2 for Exs. 7–9

Tell whether the function represented by the table is discrete or continuous. *Explain.* If continuous, graph the function and find the value of y when $x = 3.5$. Round your answer to the nearest hundredth.

7.

Number of DVD rentals, x	1	2	3	4
Cost of rentals (dollars), y	4.50	9.00	13.50	18.00

8.

Hours since 12 P.M., x	2	4	6	8
Distance driven (miles), y	100	200	300	400

9.

Volume of water (cubic inches), x	3	6	9	12
Approximate weight of water (pounds), y	0.1	0.2	0.3	0.4

3.3 Graph Using Intercepts

Before You graphed a linear equation using a table of values.

Now You will graph a linear equation using intercepts.

Why So you can find a submersible's location, as in Example 5.

Key Vocabulary
- *x*-intercept
- *y*-intercept

You can use the fact that two points determine a line to graph a linear equation. Two convenient points are the points where the graph crosses the axes.

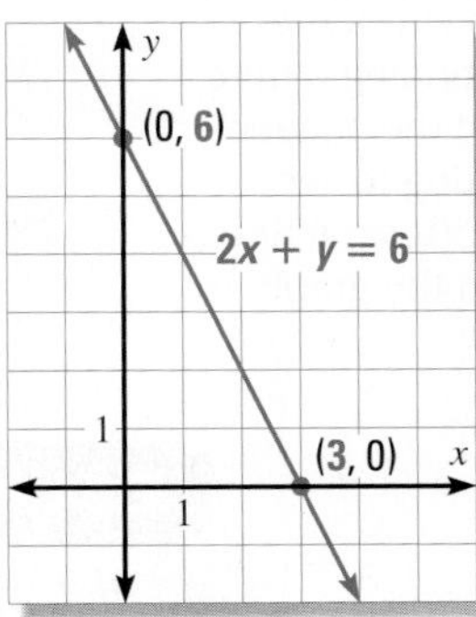

An ***x*-intercept** of a graph is the *x*-coordinate of a point where the graph crosses the *x*-axis. A ***y*-intercept** of a graph is the *y*-coordinate of a point where the graph crosses the *y*-axis.

To find the *x*-intercept of the graph of a linear equation, find the value of x when $y = 0$. To find the *y*-intercept of the graph, find the value of y when $x = 0$.

COMMON CORE

CC.9-12.F.IF.7a Graph linear and quadratic functions and show intercepts, maxima, and minima.*

EXAMPLE 1 Find the intercepts of the graph of an equation

Find the *x*-intercept and the *y*-intercept of the graph of $2x + 7y = 28$.

Solution

To find the *x*-intercept, substitute 0 for y and solve for x.

$2x + 7y = 28$ **Write original equation.**

$2x + 7(0) = 28$ **Substitute 0 for *y*.**

$x = \frac{28}{2} = 14$ **Solve for *x*.**

To find the *y*-intercept, substitute 0 for x and solve for y.

$2x + 7y = 28$ **Write original equation.**

$2(0) + 7y = 28$ **Substitute 0 for *x*.**

$y = \frac{28}{7} = 4$ **Solve for *y*.**

▶ The *x*-intercept is 14. The *y*-intercept is 4.

GUIDED PRACTICE for Example 1

Find the *x*-intercept and the *y*-intercept of the graph of the equation.

1. $3x + 2y = 6$
2. $4x - 2y = 10$
3. $-3x + 5y = -15$

EXAMPLE 2 Use intercepts to graph an equation

Graph the equation $x + 2y = 4$.

Solution

STEP 1 **Find** the intercepts.

$x + 2y = 4$	$x + 2y = 4$
$x + 2(0) = 4$	$0 + 2y = 4$
$x = 4 \leftarrow$ **x-intercept**	$y = 2 \leftarrow$ **y-intercept**

STEP 2 **Plot** points. The x-intercept is 4, so plot the point $(4, 0)$. The y-intercept is 2, so plot the point $(0, 2)$. Draw a line through the points.

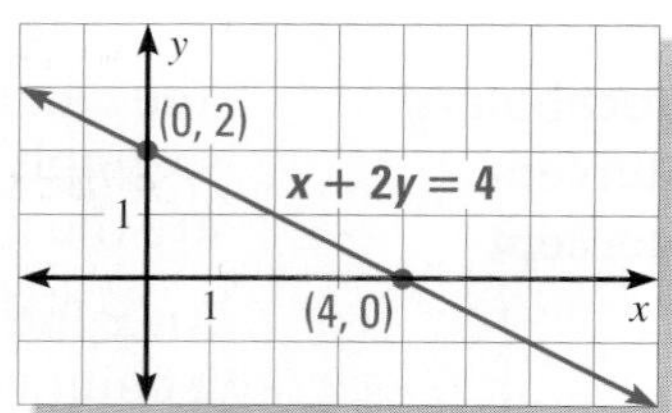

Animated Algebra at my.hrw.com

CHECK A GRAPH
Be sure to check the graph by finding a third solution of the equation and checking to see that the corresponding point is on the graph.

EXAMPLE 3 Use a graph to find intercepts

The graph crosses the x-axis at $(2, 0)$. The x-intercept is 2. The graph crosses the y-axis at $(0, -1)$. The y-intercept is -1.

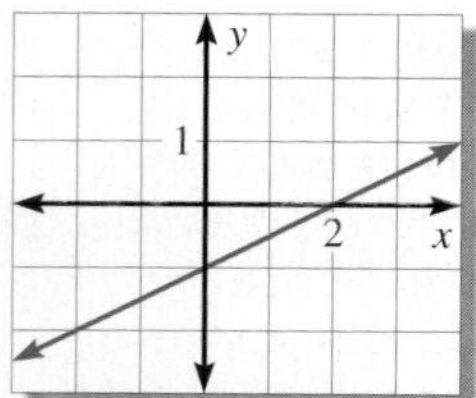

✓ GUIDED PRACTICE for Examples 2 and 3

4. Graph $6x + 7y = 42$. Label the points where the line crosses the axes.
5. Identify the x-intercept and the y-intercept of the graph shown at the right.

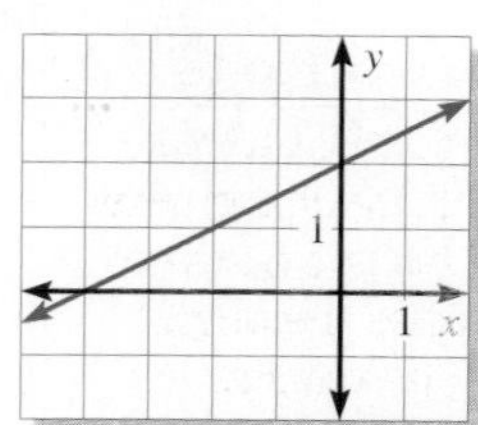

KEY CONCEPT *For Your Notebook*

Relating Intercepts, Points, and Graphs

Intercepts	Points
The x intercept of a graph is a.	The graph crosses the x-axis at $(a, 0)$.
The y-intercept of a graph is b.	The graph crosses the y-axis at $(0, b)$.

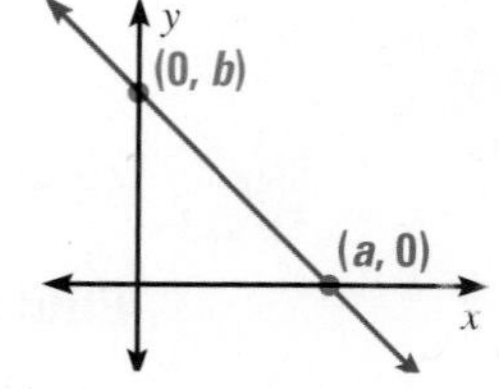

EXAMPLE 4 Solve a multi-step problem

EVENT PLANNING You are helping to plan an awards banquet for your school, and you need to rent tables to seat 180 people. Tables come in two sizes. Small tables seat 4 people, and large tables seat 6 people. This situation can be modeled by the equation

$$4x + 6y = 180$$

where x is the number of small tables and y is the number of large tables.

- Find the intercepts of the graph of the equation.
- Graph the equation.
- Give four possibilities for the number of each size table you could rent.

Solution

STEP 1 **Find** the intercepts.

$4x + 6y = 180$	$4x + 6y = 180$
$4x + 6(0) = 180$	$4(0) + 6y = 180$
$x = 45 \leftarrow$ **x-intercept**	$y = 30 \leftarrow$ **y-intercept**

DRAW A GRAPH
Although x and y represent whole numbers, it is convenient to draw an unbroken line segment that includes points whose coordinates are not whole numbers.

STEP 2 **Graph** the equation.

The x-intercept is 45, so plot the point (45, 0). The y-intercept is 30, so plot the point (0, 30).

Since x and y both represent numbers of tables, neither x nor y can be negative. So, instead of drawing a line, draw the part of the line that is in Quadrant I.

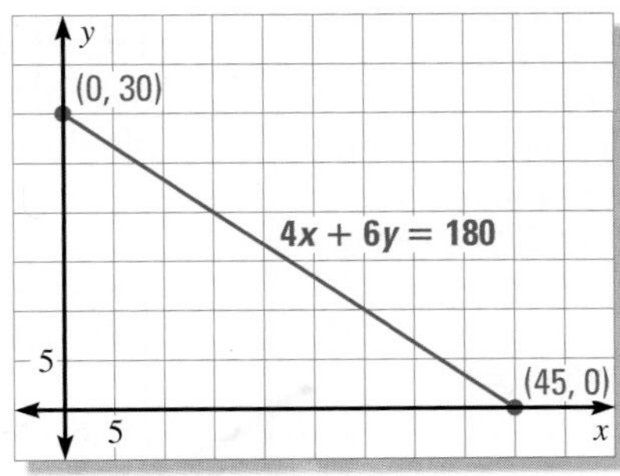

FIND SOLUTIONS
Other points, such as (12, 22), are also on the graph but are not as obvious as the points shown here because their coordinates are not multiples of 5.

STEP 3 **Find** the number of tables. For this problem, only whole-number values of x and y make sense. You can see that the line passes through the points **(0, 30)**, **(15, 20)**, **(30, 10)**, and **(45, 0)**.

So, four possible combinations of tables that will seat 180 people are: 0 small and 30 large, 15 small and 20 large, 30 small and 10 large, and 45 small and 0 large.

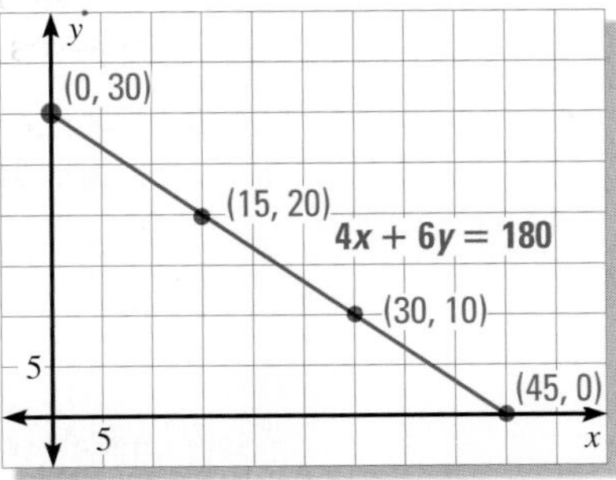

✓ GUIDED PRACTICE for Example 4

6. **WHAT IF?** In Example 4, suppose the small tables cost \$9 to rent and the large tables cost \$14. Of the four possible combinations of tables given in the example, which rental is the least expensive? *Explain.*

EXAMPLE 5 Use a linear model

SUBMERSIBLES A submersible designed to explore the ocean floor is at an elevation of −13,000 feet (13,000 feet below sea level). The submersible ascends to the surface at an average rate of 650 feet per minute. The elevation e (in feet) of the submersible is given by the function

$$e = 650t - 13{,}000$$

where t is the time (in minutes) since the submersible began to ascend.

- Find the intercepts of the graph of the function and state what the intercepts represent.
- Graph the function and identify its domain and range.

Solution

STEP 1 **Find** the intercepts.

$0 = 650t - 13{,}000$	$e = 650(0) - 13{,}000$
$13{,}000 = 650t$	$e = -13{,}000 \leftarrow$ **e-intercept**
$20 = t \leftarrow$ **t-intercept**	

NAME INTERCEPTS
Because t is the independent variable, the horizontal axis is the t-axis, and you refer to the "t-intercept" of the graph of the function. Similarly, the vertical axis is the e-axis, and you refer to the "e-intercept."

The t-intercept represents the number of minutes the submersible takes to reach an elevation of 0 feet (sea level). The e-intercept represents the elevation of the submersible after 0 minutes (the time the ascent begins).

STEP 2 **Graph** the function using the intercepts.

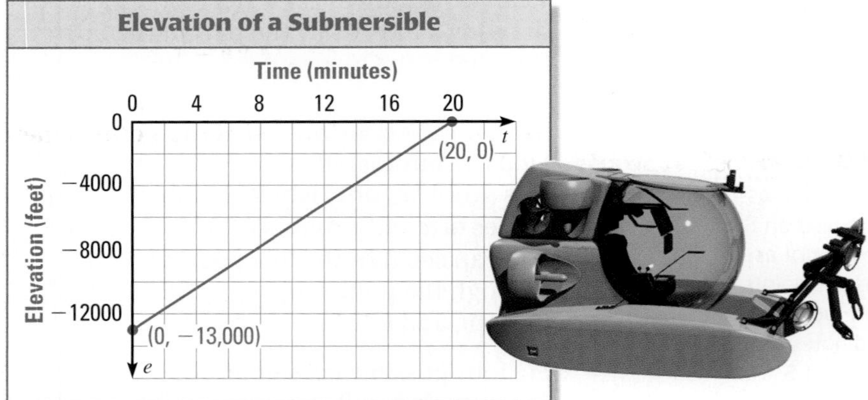

The submersible starts at an elevation of −13,000 feet and ascends to an elevation of 0 feet. So, the range of the function is $-13{,}000 \le e \le 0$. From the graph, you can see that the domain of the function is $0 \le t \le 20$.

GUIDED PRACTICE for Example 5

7. **WHAT IF?** In Example 5, suppose the elevation of a second submersible is given by $e = 500t - 10{,}000$. Graph the function and identify its domain and range.

3.3 EXERCISES

HOMEWORK KEY

○ = See **WORKED-OUT SOLUTIONS** Exs. 21 and 47

★ = **STANDARDIZED TEST PRACTICE** Exs. 2, 37, 41, 49, and 50

◆ = **MULTIPLE REPRESENTATIONS** Ex. 44

SKILL PRACTICE

1. **VOCABULARY** Copy and complete: The _?_ of the graph of an equation is the value of x when y is zero.

2. ★ **WRITING** What are the x-intercept and the y-intercept of the line passing through the points (0, 3) and (−4, 0)? *Explain.*

3. **ERROR ANALYSIS** *Describe* and correct the error in finding the intercepts of the line shown.

The x-intercept is 1, and the y-intercept is −2.

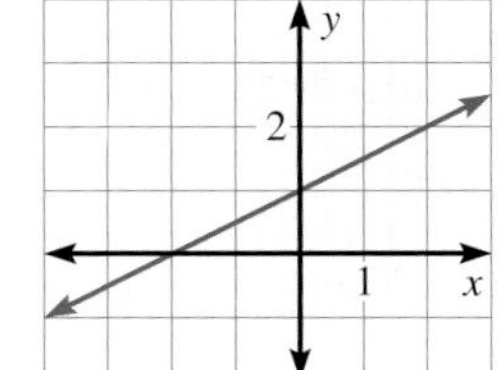

EXAMPLE 1 for Exs. 4–15

FINDING INTERCEPTS Find the x-intercept and the y-intercept of the graph of the equation.

4. $5x - y = 35$
5. $3x - 3y = 9$
6. $-3x + 9y = -18$
7. $4x + y = 4$
8. $2x + y = 10$
9. $2x - 8y = 24$
10. $3x + 0.5y = 6$
11. $0.2x + 3.2y = 12.8$
12. $y = 2x + 24$
13. $y = -14x + 7$
14. $y = -4.8x + 1.2$
15. $y = \frac{3}{5}x - 12$

EXAMPLE 2 for Exs. 16–27

GRAPHING LINES Graph the equation. Label the points where the line crosses the axes.

16. $y = x + 3$
17. $y = x - 2$
18. $y = 4x - 8$
19. $y = 5 + 10x$
20. $y = -2 + 8x$
21. $y = -4x + 3$
22. $3x + y = 15$
23. $x - 4y = 18$
24. $8x - 5y = 80$
25. $-2x + 5y = 15$
26. $0.5x + 3y = 9$
27. $y = \frac{1}{2}x + \frac{1}{4}$

EXAMPLE 3 for Exs. 28–30

USING GRAPHS TO FIND INTERCEPTS Identify the x-intercept and the y-intercept of the graph.

28.

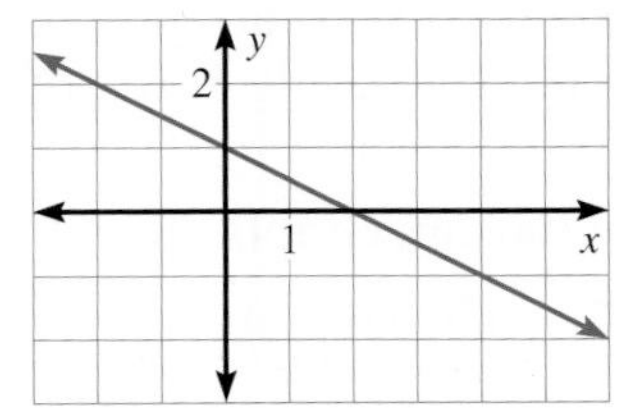

29.

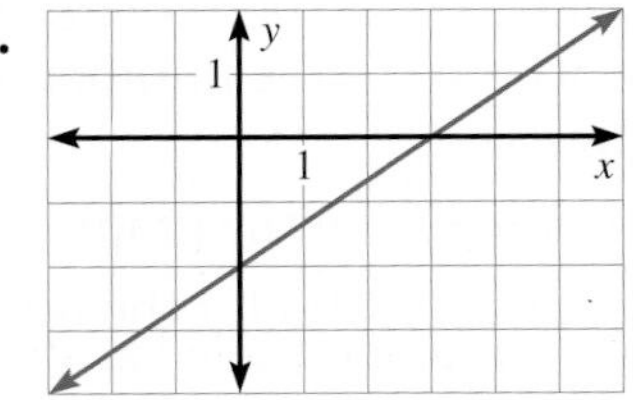

30.

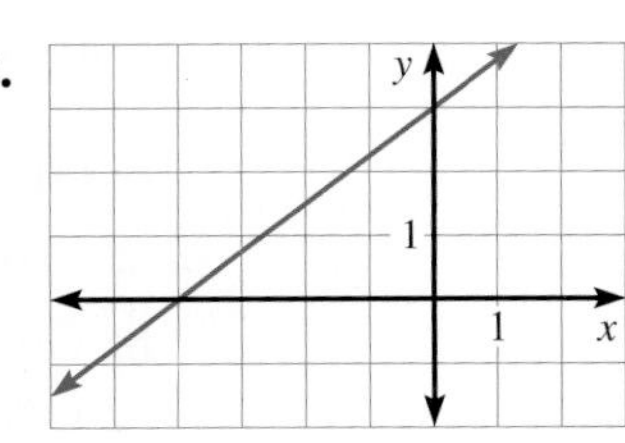

USING INTERCEPTS **Draw the line that has the given intercepts.**

31. x-intercept: 3
y-intercept: 5

32. x-intercept: -2
y-intercept: 4

33. x-intercept: -5
y-intercept: 6

34. x-intercept: 9
y-intercept: -1

35. x-intercept: -8
y-intercept: -11

36. x-intercept: -2
y-intercept: -6

37. ★ **MULTIPLE CHOICE** The x-intercept of the graph of $Ax + 5y = 20$ is 2. What is the value of A?

Ⓐ 2 Ⓑ 5 Ⓒ 7.5 Ⓓ 10

MATCHING EQUATIONS WITH GRAPHS **Match the equation with its graph.**

38. $2x - 6y = 6$

39. $2x - 6y = -6$

40. $2x - 6y = 12$

A.

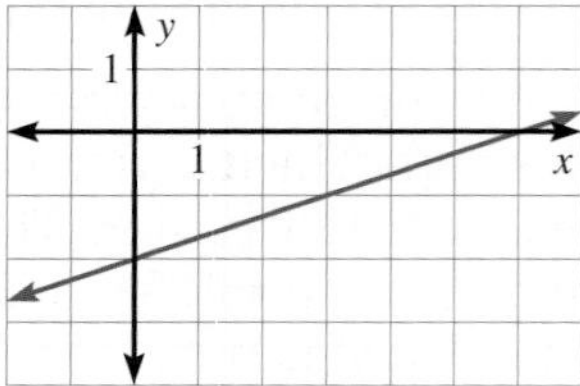

B.

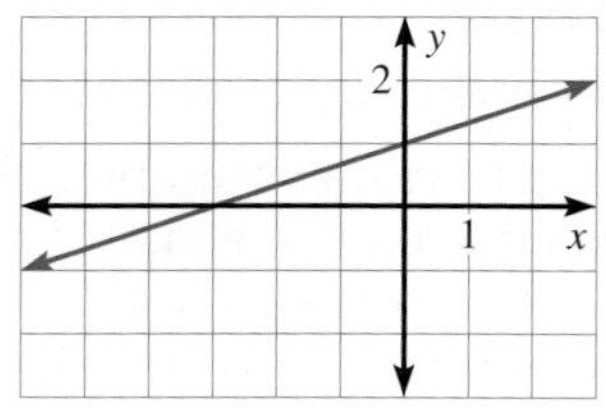

C.

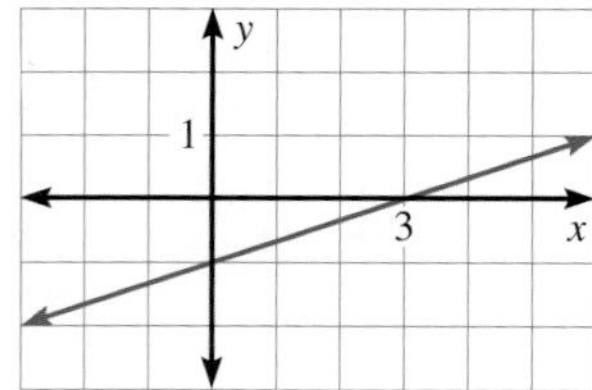

41. ★ **WRITING** Is it possible for a line *not* to have an x-intercept? Is it possible for a line *not* to have a y-intercept? *Explain.*

42. **REASONING** Consider the equation $3x + 5y = k$. What values could k have so that the x-intercept and the y-intercept of the equation's graph would both be integers? *Explain.*

43. **CHALLENGE** If $a \neq 0$, find the intercepts of the graph of $y = ax + b$ in terms of a and b.

PROBLEM SOLVING

EXAMPLES 4 and 5 for Exs. 44–47

44. ◆ **MULTIPLE REPRESENTATIONS** The perimeter of a rectangular park is 72 feet. Let x be the park's width (in feet) and let y be its length (in feet).

a. **Writing an Equation** Write an equation for the perimeter.

b. **Drawing a Graph** Find the intercepts of the graph of the equation you wrote. Then graph the equation.

45. **RECYCLING** In one state, small bottles have a refund value of \$.04 each, and large bottles have a refund value of \$.08 each. Your friend returns both small and large bottles and receives \$.56. This situation is given by $4x + 8y = 56$ where x is the number of small bottles and y is the number of large bottles.

a. Find the intercepts of the graph of the equation. Graph the equation.

b. Give three possibilities for the number of each size bottle your friend could have returned.

46. **MULTI-STEP PROBLEM** Before 1979, there was no 3-point shot in professional basketball; players could score only 2-point field goals and 1-point free throws. In a game before 1979, a team scored a total of 128 points. This situation is given by the equation $2x + y = 128$ where x is the possible number of field goals and y is the possible number of free throws.

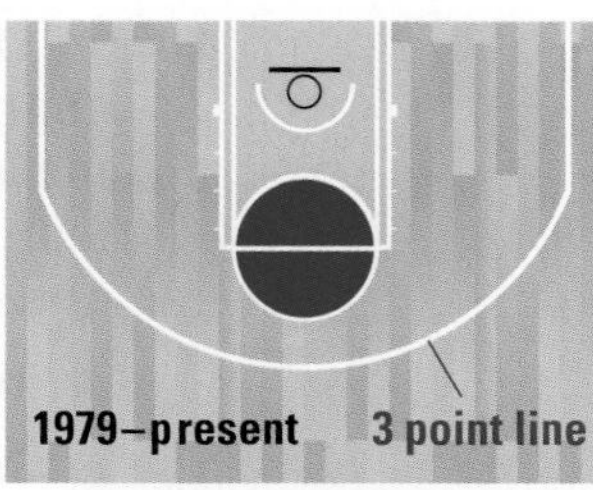

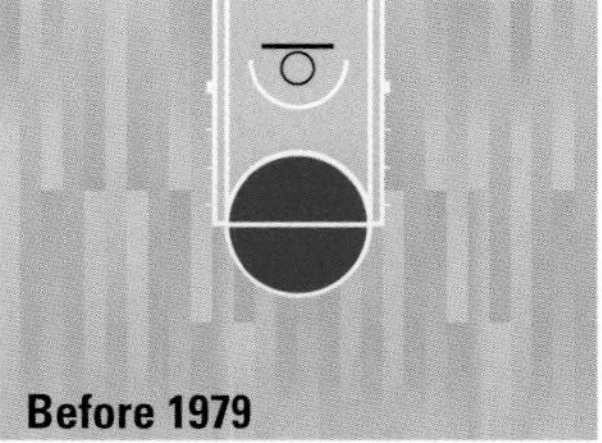

a. Find the intercepts of the graph of the equation. Graph the equation.

b. What do the intercepts mean in this situation?

c. What are three possible numbers of field goals and free throws the team could have scored?

d. If the team made 24 free throws, how many field goals were made?

47. **COMMUNITY GARDENS** A family has a plot in a community garden. The family is going to plant vegetables, flowers, or both. The diagram shows the area used by one vegetable plant and the area of the entire plot. The area f (in square feet) of the plot left for flowers is given by $f = 180 - 1.5v$ where v is the number of vegetable plants the family plants.

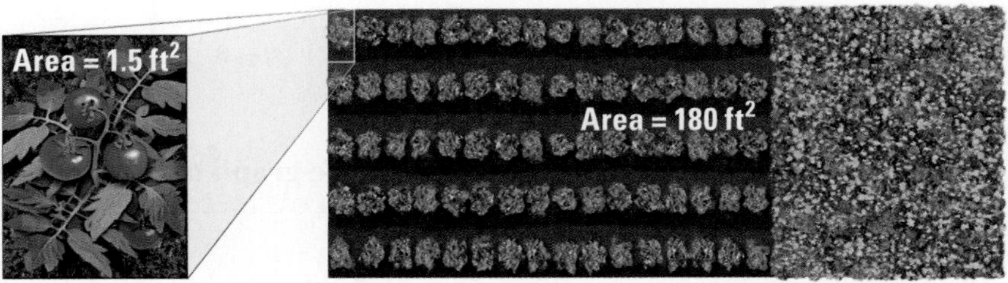

a. Find the intercepts of the graph of the function and state what the intercepts represent.

b. Graph the function and identify its domain and range.

c. The family decides to plant 80 vegetable plants. How many square feet are left to plant flowers?

48. **CAR SHARING** A member of a car-sharing program can use a car for \$6 per hour and \$.50 per mile. The member uses the car for one day and is charged \$44. This situation is given by

$$6t + 0.5d = 44$$

where t is the time (in hours) the car is used and d is the distance (in miles) the car is driven. Give three examples of the number of hours the member could have used the car and the number of miles the member could have driven the car.

49. ★ **SHORT RESPONSE** A humidifier is a device used to put moisture into the air by turning water to vapor. A humidifier has a tank that can hold 1.5 gallons of water. The humidifier can disperse the water at a rate of 0.12 gallon per hour. The amount of water w (in gallons) left in the humidifier after t hours of use is given by the function

$$w = 1.5 - 0.12t.$$

After how many hours of use will you have to refill the humidifier? *Explain* how you found your answer.

50. ★ **EXTENDED RESPONSE** You borrow \$180 from a friend who doesn't charge you interest. You work out a payment schedule in which you will make weekly payments to your friend. The balance B (in dollars) of the loan is given by the function $B = 180 - pn$ where p is the weekly payment and n is the number of weeks you make payments.

   a. **Interpret** Without finding the intercepts, state what they represent.

   b. **Graph** Graph the function if you make weekly payments of \$20.

   c. **Identify** Find the domain and range of the function in part (b). How long will it take to pay back your friend?

   d. **CHALLENGE** Suppose you make payments of \$20 for three weeks. Then you make payments of \$15 until you have paid your friend back. How does this affect the graph? How many payments do you make?

QUIZ

Plot the point in a coordinate plane. *Describe* the location of the point.

1. $(-7, 2)$
2. $(0, -5)$
3. $(2, -6)$

Graph the equation.

4. $-4x - 2y = 12$
5. $y = -5$
6. $x = 6$

Find the x-intercept and the y-intercept of the graph of the equation.

7. $y = x + 7$
8. $y = x - 3$
9. $y = -5x + 2$
10. $x + 3y = 15$
11. $3x - 6y = 36$
12. $-2x - 5y = 22$

13. **SWIMMING POOLS** A public swimming pool that holds 45,000 gallons of water is going to be drained for maintenance at a rate of 100 gallons per minute. The amount of water w (in gallons) in the pool after t minutes is given by the function $w = 45{,}000 - 100t$. Graph the function. Identify its domain and range. How much water is in the pool after 60 minutes? How many minutes will it take to empty the pool?

See **EXTRA PRACTICE** in Student Resources **ONLINE QUIZ** at my.hrw.com

MIXED REVIEW *of Problem Solving*

1. **MULTI-STEP PROBLEM** An amusement park charges \$20 for an all-day pass and \$10 for a pass after 5 P.M. On Wednesday the amusement park collected \$1000 in pass sales. This situation can be modeled by the equation $1000 = 20x + 10y$ where x is the number of all-day passes sold and y is the number of passes sold after 5 P.M.

   a. Find the x-intercept of the graph of the equation. What does it represent?

   b. Find the y-intercept of the graph of the equation. What does it represent?

   c. Graph the equation using a scale of 10 on the x- and y-axes.

2. **MULTI-STEP PROBLEM** A violin player who plays every day received a violin with new strings. Players who play every day should replace the strings on their violins every 6 months. A particular brand of strings costs \$24 per pack. The table shows the total spent a (in dollars) on replacement strings with respect to time t (in months).

t (months)	a (dollars)
6	24
12	48
18	72
24	96
30	120

   a. *Explain* how you know the table represents a function.

   b. Graph the function.

3. **OPEN-ENDED** Create a table that shows the number of minutes you think you will spend watching TV next week. Let Monday be day 1, Tuesday be day 2, and so on. Graph the data. Does the graph represent a function? *Explain.*

4. **SHORT RESPONSE** You can hike at an average rate of 3 miles per hour. Your total hiking distance d (in miles) can be modeled by the function $d = 3t$ where t is the time (in hours) you hike. You plan on hiking for 10 hours this weekend.

   a. Is the domain or range specified in the problem? *Explain.*

   b. Graph the function and identify its domain and range. Use the graph to find how long it takes to hike 6 miles.

5. **EXTENDED RESPONSE** The table shows the departure d (in degrees Fahrenheit) from the normal monthly temperature in New England for the first six months of 2004. For example, in month 1, $d = -3$. So, the average temperature was 3 degrees below the normal temperature for January.

M (month)	1	2	3	4	5	6
d (°F)	−3	−1	2	2	4	−1

   a. *Explain* how you know the table represents a function.

   b. Graph the function and identify its domain and range.

   c. What does a point in Quadrant IV mean in terms of this situation?

6. **GRIDDED ANSWER** The graph shows the possible combinations of T-shirts and tank tops that you can buy with the amount of money you have. If you buy only T-shirts, how many can you buy?

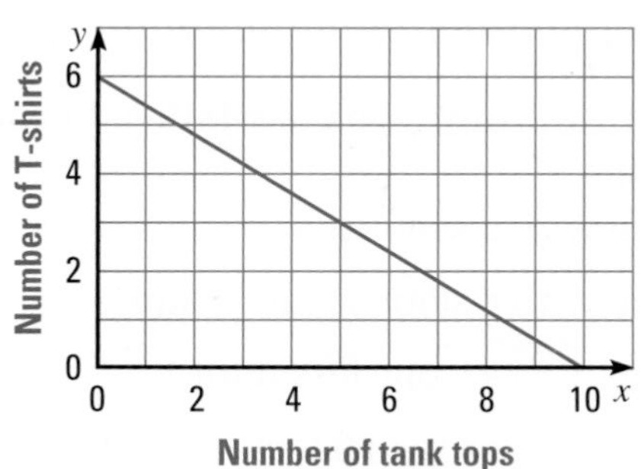

Slopes of Lines

Use appropriate tools strategically.

MATERIALS • several books • two rulers

QUESTION How can you use algebra to describe the slope of a ramp?

You can use the ratio of the vertical rise to the horizontal run to describe the *slope* of a ramp.

$$\text{slope} = \frac{\text{rise}}{\text{run}}$$

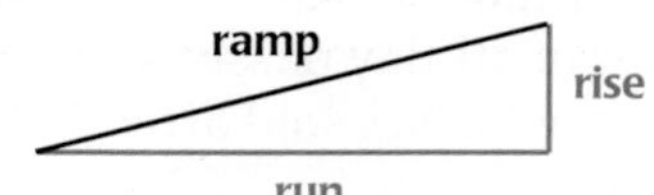

EXPLORE Calculate the slopes of ramps

STEP 1

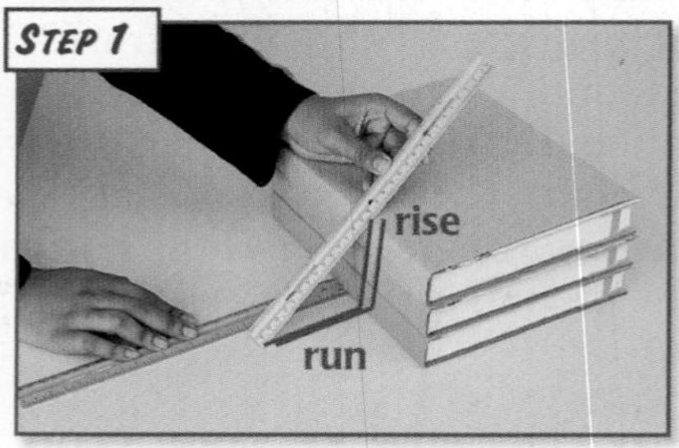

Make a ramp Make a stack of three books. Use a ruler as a ramp. Measure the rise and run of the ramp, and record them in a table. Calculate and record the slope of the ramp in your table.

STEP 2

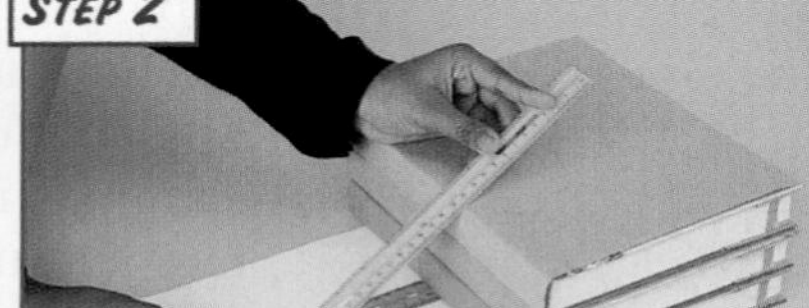

Change the run Without changing the rise, make three ramps with different runs by moving the lower end of the ruler. Measure and record the rise and run of each ramp. Calculate and record each slope.

STEP 3

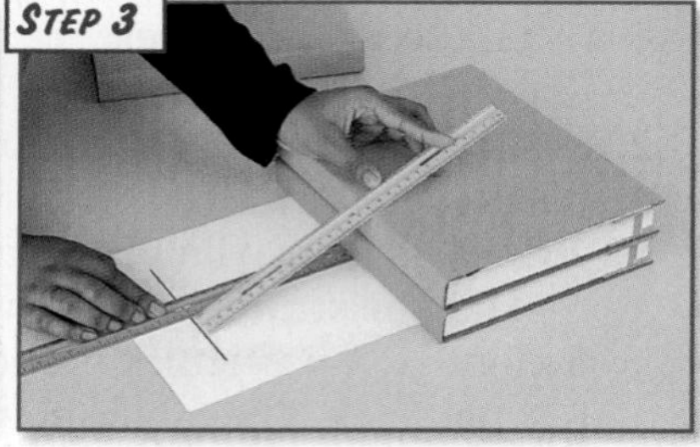

Change the rise Without changing the run, make three ramps with different rises by adding or removing books. Measure and record the rise and run of each ramp. Calculate and record each slope.

DRAW CONCLUSIONS Use your observations to complete these exercises

Describe **how the slope of the ramp changes given the following conditions. Give three examples that support your answer.**

1. The run of the ramp increases, and the rise stays the same.
2. The rise of the ramp increases, and the run stays the same.

In Exercises 3–5, describe the relationship between the rise and the run of the ramp.

3. A ramp with a slope of 1
4. A ramp with a slope greater than 1
5. A ramp with a slope less than 1
6. Ramp A has a rise of 6 feet and a run of 2 feet. Ramp B has a rise of 10 feet and a run of 4 feet. Which ramp is steeper? How do you know?

3.4 Find Slope and Rate of Change

Before You graphed linear equations.

Now You will find the slope of a line and interpret slope as a rate of change.

Why? So you can find the slope of a boat ramp, as in Ex. 23.

Key Vocabulary
- **slope**
- **rate of change**

CC.9-12.F.IF.6 Calculate and interpret the average rate of change of a function (presented symbolically or as a table) over a specified interval. Estimate the rate of change from a graph.*

READING
Read x_1 as "x sub one." Think "x-coordinate of the first point."
Read y_1 as "y sub one." Think "y-coordinate of the first point."

The **slope** of a nonvertical line is the ratio of the vertical change (the *rise*) to the horizontal change (the *run*) between any two points on the line. The slope of a line is represented by the letter m.

KEY CONCEPT — *For Your Notebook*

Finding the Slope of a Line

Words

The slope m of the nonvertical line passing through the two points (x_1, y_1) and (x_2, y_2) is the ratio of the rise (change in y) to the run (change in x).

$$\text{slope} = \frac{\text{rise}}{\text{run}} = \frac{\text{change in } y}{\text{change in } x}$$

Symbols

$$m = \frac{y_2 - y_1}{x_2 - x_1}$$

Graph

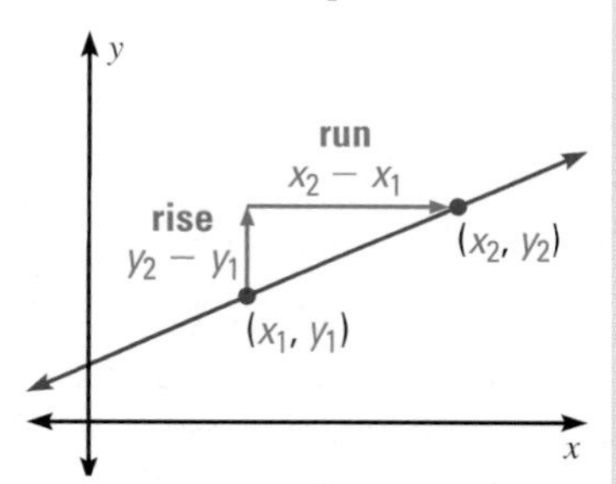

EXAMPLE 1 Find a positive slope

Find the slope of the line shown.

Let $(x_1, y_1) = (-4, 2)$ and $(x_2, y_2) = (2, 6)$.

$m = \frac{y_2 - y_1}{x_2 - x_1}$ **Write formula for slope.**

$= \frac{6 - 2}{2 - (-4)}$ **Substitute.**

$= \frac{4}{6} = \frac{2}{3}$ **Simplify.**

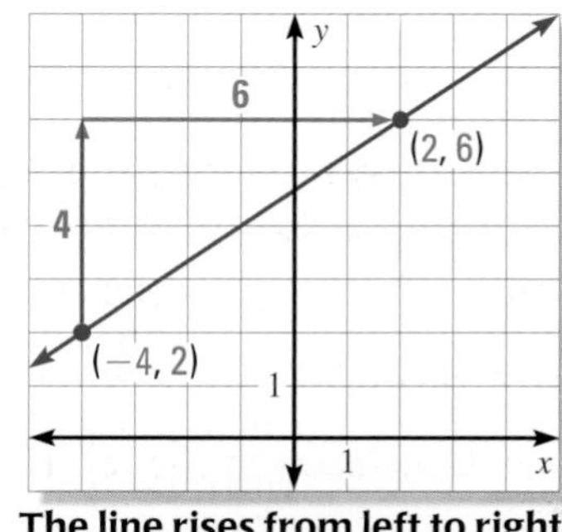

The line rises from left to right. The slope is positive.

AVOID ERRORS
Be sure to keep the x- and y-coordinates in the same order in both the numerator and denominator when calculating slope.

✓ GUIDED PRACTICE for Example 1

Find the slope of the line that passes through the points.

1. (5, 2) and (4, −1) **2.** (−2, 3) and (4, 6) **3.** $\left(\frac{9}{2}, 5\right)$ and $\left(\frac{1}{2}, -3\right)$

EXAMPLE 2 Find a negative slope

FIND SLOPE
In Example 2, if you used two other points on the line, such as (4, 3) and (5, 1), in the slope formula, the slope would still be −2.

Find the slope of the line shown.

Let $(x_1, y_1) = (3, 5)$ and $(x_2, y_2) = (6, -1)$.

$m = \frac{y_2 - y_1}{x_2 - x_1}$ **Write formula for slope.**

$= \frac{-1 - 5}{6 - 3}$ **Substitute.**

$= \frac{-6}{3} = -2$ **Simplify.**

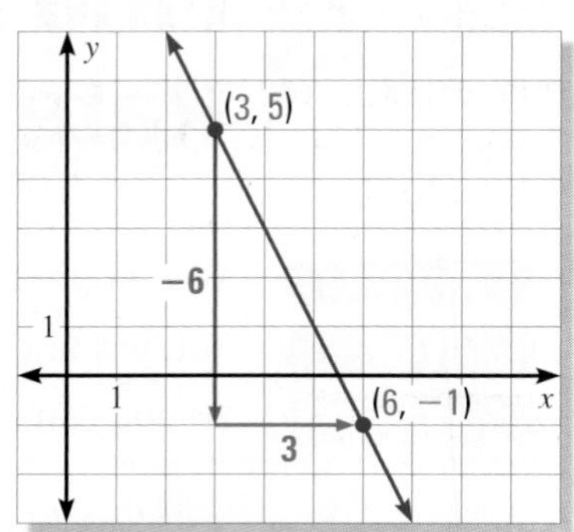

The line falls from left to right. The slope is negative.

EXAMPLE 3 Find the slope of a horizontal line

Find the slope of the line shown.

Let $(x_1, y_1) = (-2, 4)$ and $(x_2, y_2) = (4, 4)$.

$m = \frac{y_2 - y_1}{x_2 - x_1}$ **Write formula for slope.**

$= \frac{4 - 4}{4 - (-2)}$ **Substitute.**

$= \frac{0}{6} = 0$ **Simplify.**

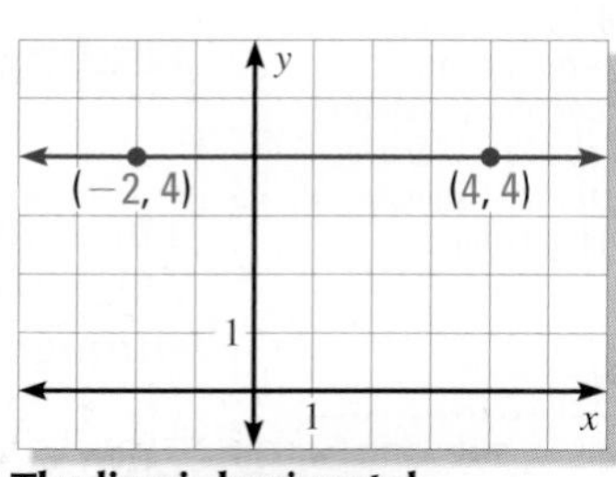

The line is horizontal. The slope is zero.

EXAMPLE 4 Find the slope of a vertical line

Find the slope of the line shown.

Let $(x_1, y_1) = (3, 5)$ and $(x_2, y_2) = (3, 1)$.

$m = \frac{y_2 - y_1}{x_2 - x_1}$ **Write formula for slope.**

$= \frac{1 - 5}{3 - 3}$ **Substitute.**

$= \frac{-4}{0}$ **Division by zero is undefined.**

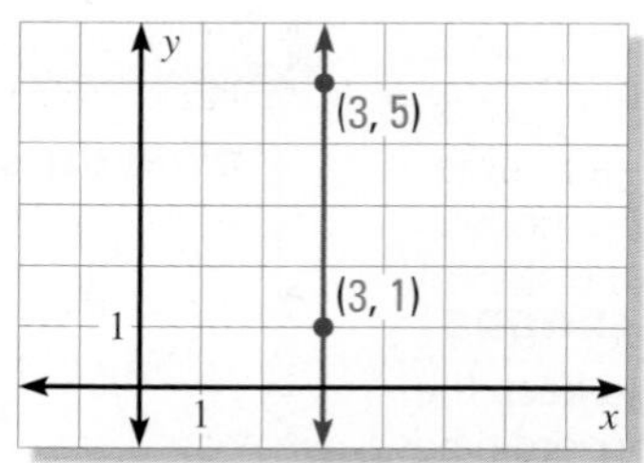

The line is vertical. The slope is undefined.

▶ Because division by zero is undefined, the slope of a vertical line is undefined.

✓ GUIDED PRACTICE for Examples 2, 3, and 4

Find the slope of the line that passes through the points.

4. (5, 2) and (5, −2)
5. (0, 4) and (−3, 4)
6. (0, 6) and (5, −4)

CONCEPT SUMMARY
For Your Notebook

Classification of Lines by Slope

A line with positive slope ($m > 0$) *rises* from left to right.

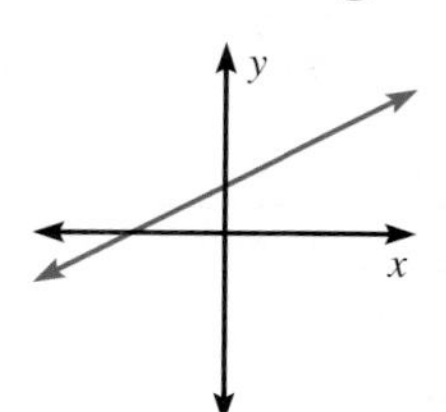

A line with negative slope ($m < 0$) *falls* from left to right.

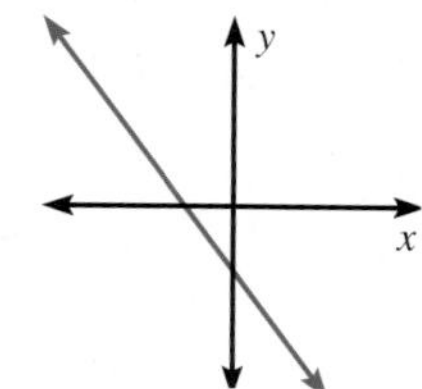

A line with zero slope ($m = 0$) is *horizontal.*

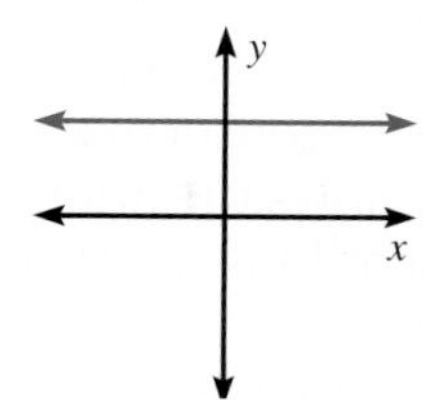

A line with undefined slope is *vertical.*

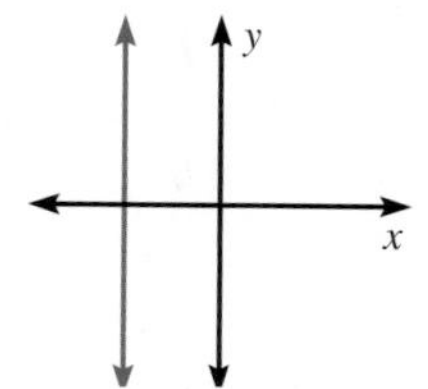

RATE OF CHANGE A **rate of change** compares a change in one quantity to a change in another quantity. For example, if you are paid $60 for working 5 hours, then your hourly wage is $12 per hour, a rate of change that describes how your pay increases with respect to time spent working.

EXAMPLE 5 Find a rate of change

INTERNET CAFE The table shows the cost of using a computer at an Internet cafe for a given amount of time. Find the rate of change in cost with respect to time.

Time (hours)	2	4	6
Cost (dollars)	7	14	21

Solution

ANALYZE UNITS
Because the cost is in dollars and time is in hours, the rate of change in cost with respect to time is expressed in dollars per hour.

$$\textbf{Rate of change} = \frac{\text{change in cost}}{\text{change in time}}$$

$$= \frac{14 - 7}{4 - 2} = \frac{7}{2} = 3.5$$

▶ The rate of change in cost is $3.50 per hour.

GUIDED PRACTICE for Example 5

7. **EXERCISE** The table shows the distance a person walks for exercise. Find the rate of change in distance with respect to time.

Time (minutes)	Distance (miles)
30	1.5
60	3
90	4.5

SLOPE AND RATE OF CHANGE You can interpret the slope of a line as a rate of change. When given graphs of real-world data, you can compare rates of change by comparing slopes of lines.

EXAMPLE 6 Use a graph to find and compare rates of change

COMMUNITY THEATER A community theater performed a play each Saturday evening for 10 consecutive weeks. The graph shows the attendance for the performances in weeks 1, 4, 6, and 10. Describe the rates of change in attendance with respect to time.

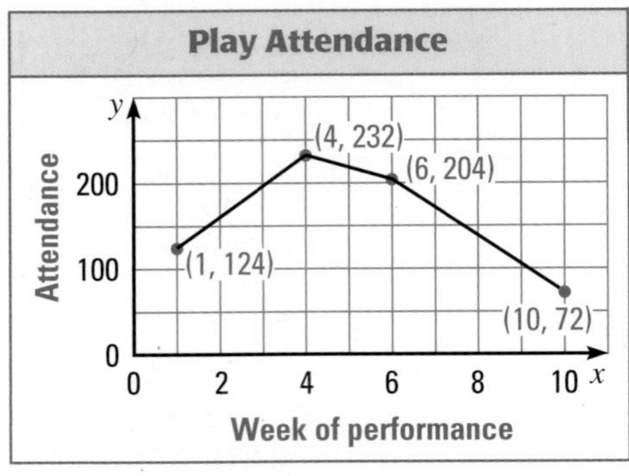

Solution

Find the rates of change using the slope formula.

Weeks 1–4: $\frac{232 - 124}{4 - 1} = \frac{108}{3} = 36$ people per week

INTERPRET RATE OF CHANGE
A negative rate of change indicates a decrease.

Weeks 4–6: $\frac{204 - 232}{6 - 4} = \frac{-28}{2} = -14$ people per week

Weeks 6–10: $\frac{72 - 204}{10 - 6} = \frac{-132}{4} = -33$ people per week

▶ Attendance increased during the early weeks of performing the play. Then attendance decreased, slowly at first, then more rapidly.

EXAMPLE 7 Interpret a graph

COMMUTING TO SCHOOL A student commutes from home to school by walking and by riding a bus. Describe the student's commute in words.

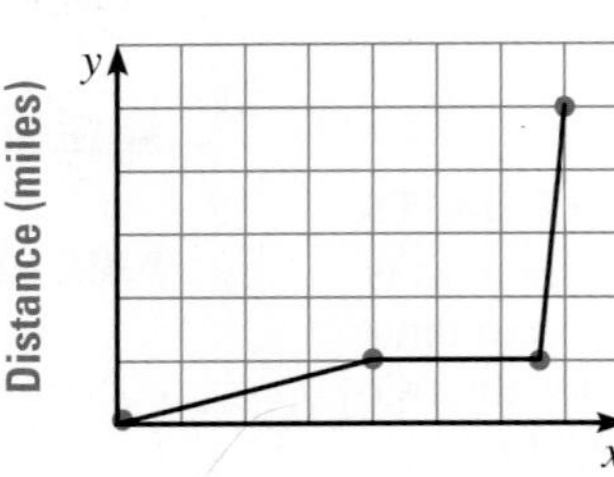

Solution

The first segment of the graph is not very steep, so the student is not traveling very far with respect to time. The student must be walking. The second segment has a zero slope, so the student must not be moving. He or she is waiting for the bus. The last segment is steep, so the student is traveling far with respect to time. The student must be riding the bus.

Animated Algebra at my.hrw.com

✓ GUIDED PRACTICE for Examples 6 and 7

8. **WHAT IF?** How would the answer to Example 6 change if you knew that attendance was 70 people in week 12?

9. **WHAT IF?** Using the graph in Example 7, draw a graph that represents the student's commute from school to home.

3.4 EXERCISES

HOMEWORK KEY

○ = See **WORKED-OUT SOLUTIONS** Exs. 11 and 37

★ = **STANDARDIZED TEST PRACTICE** Exs. 2, 17, 18, 34, and 40

SKILL PRACTICE

1. **VOCABULARY** Copy and complete: The __?__ of a nonvertical line is the ratio of the vertical change to the horizontal change between any two points on the line.

2. ★ **WRITING** Without calculating the slope, how can you tell that the slope of the line that passes through the points (−5, −3) and (2, 4) is positive?

3. **ERROR ANALYSIS** *Describe* and correct the error in calculating the slope of the line passing through the points (5, 3) and (2, 6).

$$m = \frac{6-3}{5-2} = \frac{3}{3} = 1$$ ✗

EXAMPLES 1,2,3, and 4 for Exs. 4–18

FINDING SLOPE Tell whether the slope of the line is *positive, negative, zero,* or *undefined*. Then find the slope if it exists.

4.
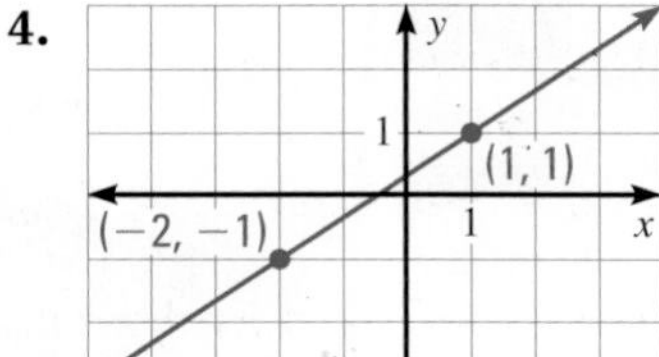

5.
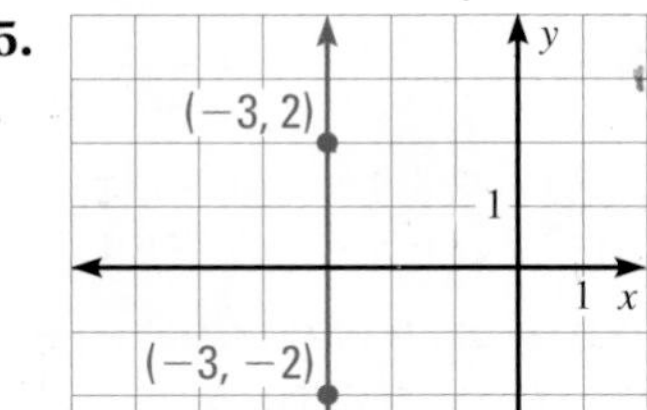

6.
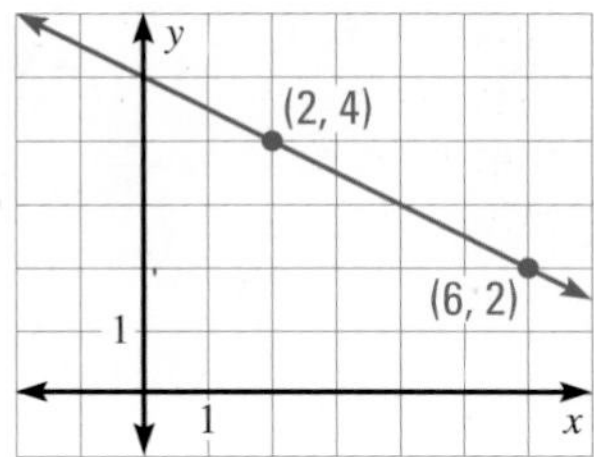

7. **ERROR ANALYSIS** *Describe* and correct the error in calculating the slope of the line shown.

$$m = \frac{12-6}{0-3} = \frac{6}{-3} = -2$$ ✗

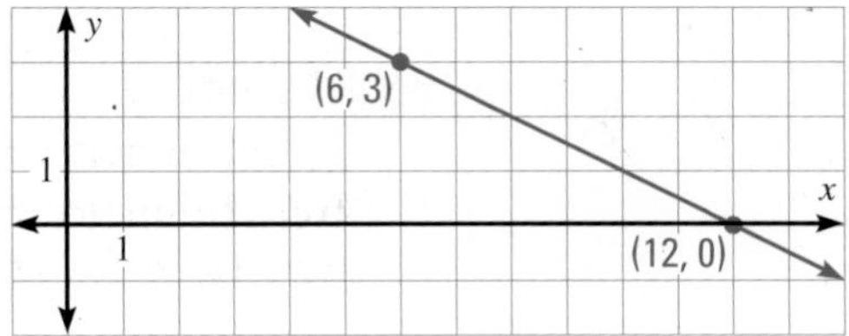

FINDING SLOPE Find the slope of the line that passes through the points.

8. (−2, −1) and (4, 5)
9. (−3, −2) and (−3, 6)
10. (5, −3) and (−5, −3)
11. (1, 3) and (3, −2)
12. (−3, 4) and (4, 1)
13. (1, −3) and (7, 3)
14. (0, 0) and (0, −6)
15. (−9, 1) and (1, 1)
16. (−10, −2) and (−8, 8)

17. ★ **MULTIPLE CHOICE** The slope of the line that passes through the points (−2, −3) and (8, −3) is __?__.

Ⓐ positive Ⓑ negative Ⓒ zero Ⓓ undefined

18. ★ **MULTIPLE CHOICE** What is the slope of the line that passes through the points (7, −9) and (−13, −6)?

Ⓐ $-\frac{3}{20}$ Ⓑ $\frac{3}{20}$ Ⓒ $\frac{3}{4}$ Ⓓ $\frac{5}{2}$

EXAMPLE 5
for Exs. 19–20

19. **MOVIE RENTALS** The table shows the number of days you keep a rented movie before returning it and the total cost of renting the movie. Find the rate of change in cost with respect to time and interpret its meaning.

Time (days)	4	5	6	7
Total cost (dollars)	6.00	8.25	10.50	12.75

20. **AMUSEMENT PARK** The table shows the amount of time spent at an amusement park and the admission fee the park charges. Find the rate of change in the fee with respect to time spent at the park and interpret its meaning.

Time (hours)	4	5	6
Admission fee (dollars)	34.99	34.99	34.99

FINDING SLOPE **Find the slope of the object. Round to the nearest tenth.**

21. Skateboard ramp

22. Pet ramp

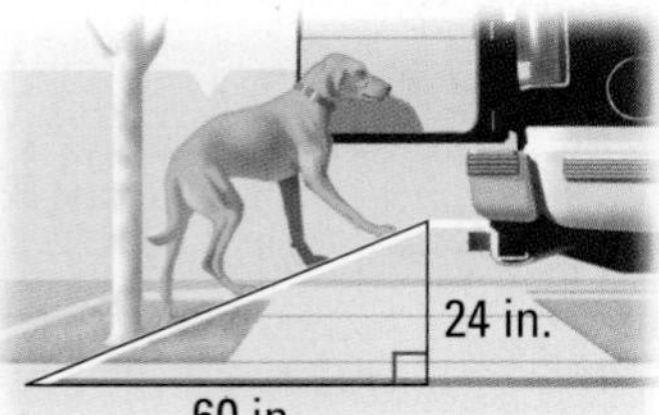

23. Boat ramp

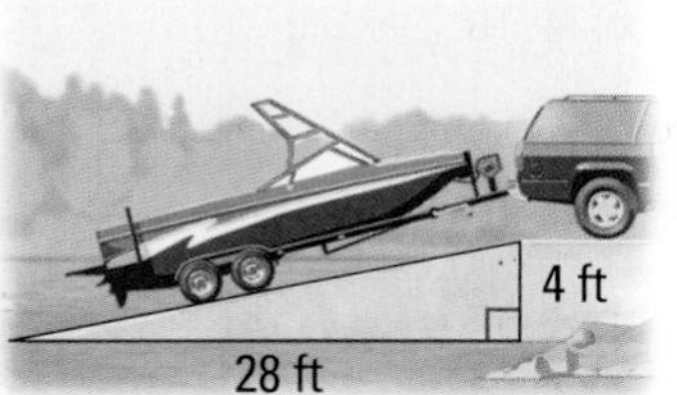

In Exercises 24–32, use the example below to find the value of x or y so that the line passing through the given points has the given slope.

EXAMPLE **Find a coordinate given the slope of a line**

Find the value of x so that the line that passes through the points $(2, 3)$ and $(x, 9)$ has a slope of $\frac{3}{2}$.

Solution

Let $(x_1, y_1) = (2, 3)$ and $(x_2, y_2) = (x, 9)$.

$m = \frac{y_2 - y_1}{x_2 - x_1}$ **Write formula for slope.**

$\frac{3}{2} = \frac{9 - 3}{x - 2}$ **Substitute values.**

$3(x - 2) = 2(9 - 3)$ **Cross products property**

$3x - 6 = 12$ **Simplify.**

$x = 6$ **Solve for *x*.**

24. $(x, 4), (6, -1); m = \frac{5}{6}$

25. $(0, y), (-2, 1); m = -8$

26. $(8, 1), (x, 7); m = -\frac{1}{2}$

27. $(5, 4), (-5, y); m = \frac{3}{5}$

28. $(-9, y), (0, -3); m = -\frac{7}{9}$

29. $(x, 9), (-1, 19); m = 5$

30. $(9, 3), (-6, 7y); m = 3$

31. $(-3, y + 1), (0, 4); m = 6$

32. $\left(\frac{x}{2}, 7\right), (-10, 15); m = 4$

○ = See **WORKED-OUT SOLUTIONS** in Student Resources

★ = **STANDARDIZED TEST PRACTICE**

33. REASONING The point $(-1, 8)$ is on a line that has a slope of -3. Is the point $(4, -7)$ on the same line? *Explain* your reasoning.

34. ★ WRITING Is a line with undefined slope the graph of a function? *Explain.*

35. CHALLENGE Given two points (x_1, y_1) and (x_2, y_2) such that $x_1 \neq x_2$, show that $\frac{y_2 - y_1}{x_2 - x_1} = \frac{y_1 - y_2}{x_1 - x_2}$. What does this result tell you about calculating the slope of a line?

PROBLEM SOLVING

EXAMPLE 6 for Exs. 36–37

36. OCEANOGRAPHY Ocean water levels are measured hourly at a monitoring station. The table shows the water level (in meters) on one particular morning. *Describe* the rates of change in water levels throughout the morning.

Hours since 12:00 A.M.	1	3	8	10	12
Water level (meters)	2	1.4	0.5	1	1.8

37. MULTI-STEP PROBLEM Firing a piece of pottery in a kiln takes place at different temperatures for different amounts of time. The graph shows the temperatures in a kiln while firing a piece of pottery (after the kiln is preheated to 250°F).

a. Determine the time interval during which the temperature in the kiln showed the greatest rate of change.

b. Determine the time interval during which the temperature in the kiln showed the least rate of change.

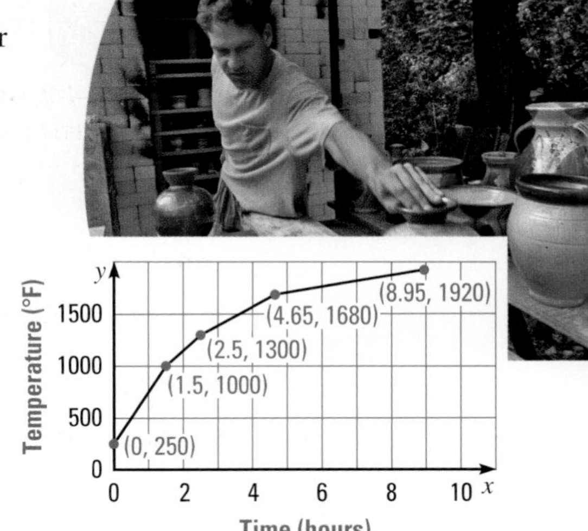

EXAMPLE 7 for Exs. 38–39

38. FLYING The graph shows the altitude of a plane during 4 hours of a flight. Give a verbal description of the flight.

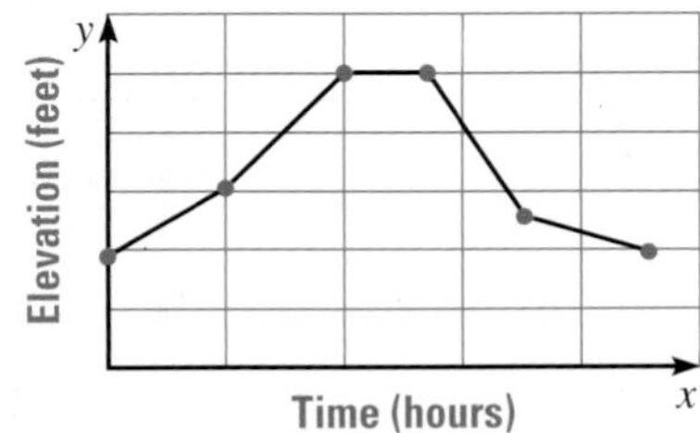

39. HIKING The graph shows the elevation of a hiker walking on a mountain trail. Give a verbal description of the hike.

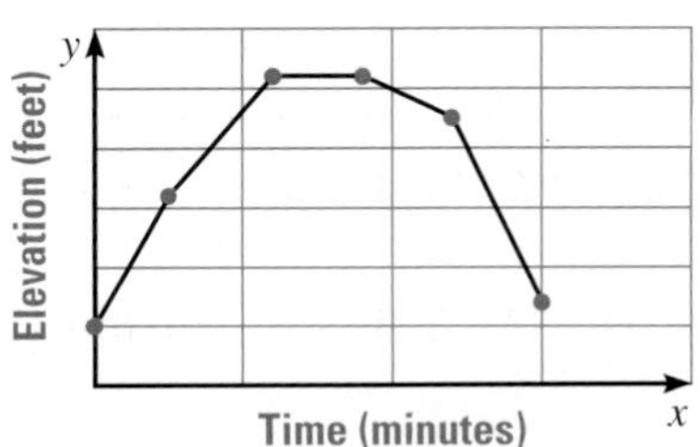

40. ★ **EXTENDED RESPONSE** The graph shows the number (in thousands) of undergraduate students who majored in biological science, engineering, or liberal arts in the United States from 1990 to 2000.

a. During which two-year period did the number of engineering students decrease the most? Estimate the rate of change for this time period.

b. During which two-year period did the number of liberal arts students increase the most? Estimate the rate of change for this time period.

c. How did the total number of students majoring in biological science, engineering, and liberal arts change in the 10 year period? *Explain* your thinking.

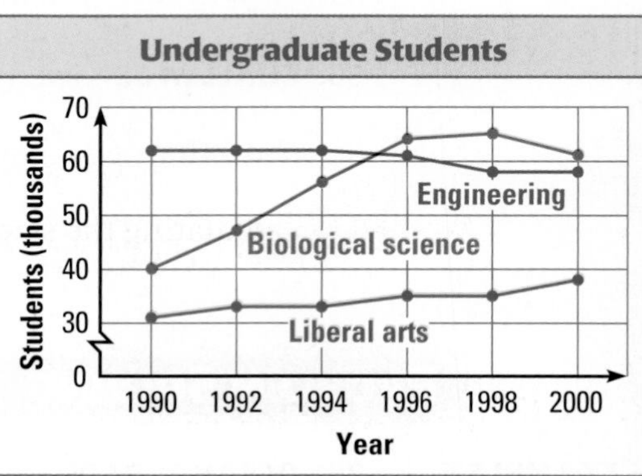

41. **CHALLENGE** Imagine the containers below being filled with water at a constant rate. Sketch a graph that shows the water level for each container during the time it takes to fill the container with water.

a. 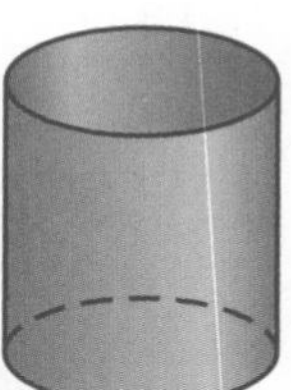

b. 

c. 

Slope and *y*-Intercept

Reason abstractly and quantitatively.

QUESTION **How can you use the equation of a line to find its slope and *y*-intercept?**

EXPLORE **Find the slopes and the *y*-intercepts of lines**

STEP 1 ***Find y when x = 0***
Copy the table below. Let $x_1 = 0$ and find y_1 for each equation. Use your answers to complete the second and fifth columns in the table.

STEP 2 ***Find y when x = 2***
Let $x_2 = 2$ and find y_2 for each equation. Use your answers to complete the third column in the table.

STEP 3 ***Compute the slope***
Use the slope formula and the ordered pairs you found in the second and third columns to complete the fourth column.

Line	$(0, y_1)$	$(2, y_2)$	Slope	*y*-intercept
$y = 4x + 3$	(0, 3)	(2, 11)	$\frac{11-3}{2-0} = 4$	3
$y = -2x + 3$	(0, ?)	(2, ?)	?	?
$y = \frac{1}{2}x + 4$	(0, ?)	(2, ?)	?	?
$y = -4x - 3$	(0, ?)	(2, ?)	?	?
$y = -\frac{1}{4}x - 3$	(0, ?)	(2, ?)	?	?

DRAW CONCLUSIONS **Use your observations to complete these exercises**

1. *Compare* the slope of each line with the equation of the line. What do you notice?
2. *Compare* the *y*-intercept of each line with the equation of the line. What do you notice?

Predict the slope and the *y*-intercept of the line with the given equation. Then check your predictions by finding the slope and *y*-intercept as you did in the table above.

3. $y = -5x + 1$
4. $y = \frac{3}{4}x + 2$
5. $y = -\frac{3}{2}x - 1$

6. **REASONING** Use the procedure you followed to complete the table above to show that the *y*-intercept of the graph of $y = mx + b$ is b and the slope of the graph is m.

3.5 Graph Using Slope-Intercept Form

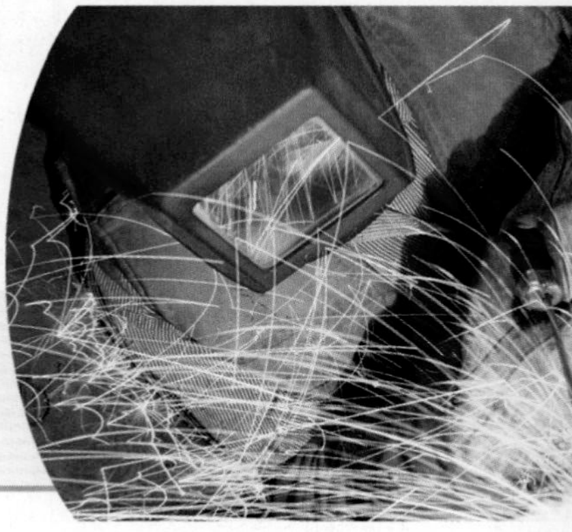

Before You found slopes and graphed equations using intercepts.

Now You will graph linear equations using slope-intercept form.

Why? So you can model a worker's earnings, as in Ex. 43.

Key Vocabulary
- **slope-intercept form**
- **parallel**

CC.9-12.F.IF.7a Graph linear and quadratic functions and show intercepts, maxima, and minima.*

In the activity, you saw how the slope and y-intercept of the graph of a linear equation in the form $y = mx + b$ are related to the equation.

KEY CONCEPT *For Your Notebook*

Finding the Slope and y-Intercept of a Line

Words

A linear equation of the form $y = mx + b$ is written in **slope-intercept form** where m is the slope and b is the y-intercept of the equation's graph.

Symbols

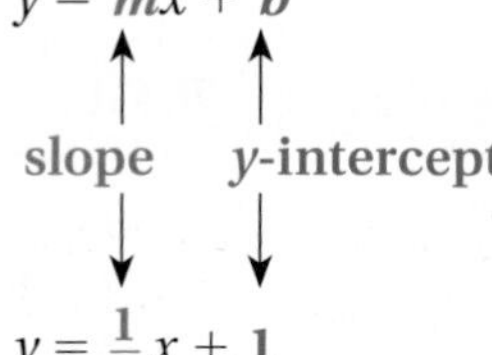

Graph

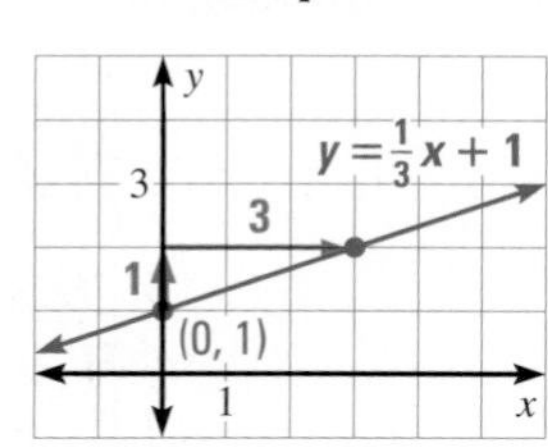

EXAMPLE 1 Identify slope and y-intercept

Identify the slope and y-intercept of the line with the given equation.

a. $y = 3x + 4$

b. $3x + y = 2$

Solution

a. The equation is in the form $y = mx + b$. So, the slope of the line is 3, and the y-intercept is 4.

b. Rewrite the equation in slope-intercept form by solving for y.

$3x + y = 2$ **Write original equation.**

$y = -3x + 2$ **Subtract $3x$ from each side.**

▶ The line has a slope of -3 and a y-intercept of 2.

REWRITE EQUATIONS
When you rewrite a linear equation in slope-intercept form, you are expressing y as a function of x.

GUIDED PRACTICE for Example 1

Identify the slope and y-intercept of the line with the given equation.

1. $y = 5x - 3$

2. $3x - 3y = 12$

3. $x + 4y = 6$

EXAMPLE 2 Graph an equation using slope-intercept form

Graph the equation $2x + y = 3$.

Solution

STEP 1 **Rewrite** the equation in slope-intercept form.

$y = -2x + 3$

STEP 2 **Identify** the slope and the y-intercept.

$m = -2$ and $b = 3$

STEP 3 **Plot** the point that corresponds to the y-intercept, $(0, 3)$.

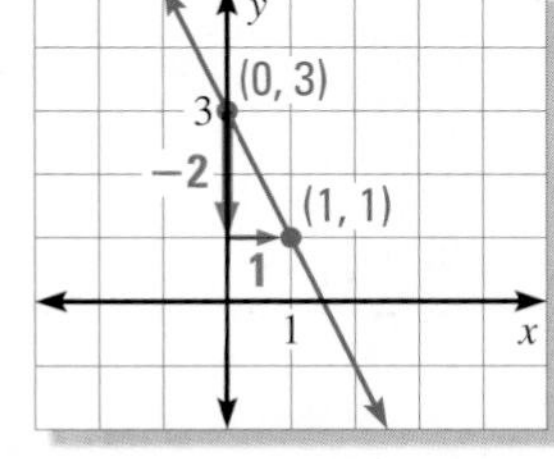

STEP 4 **Use** the slope to locate a second point on the line. Draw a line through the two points.

CHECK REASONABLENESS
To check the line drawn in Example 2, substitute the coordinates of the second point into the original equation. You should get a true statement.

Animated **Algebra** at my.hrw.com

MODELING In real-world problems that can be modeled by linear equations, the y-intercept is often an initial value, and the slope is a rate of change.

EXAMPLE 3 Change slopes of lines

ESCALATORS To get from one floor to another at a library, you can take either the stairs or the escalator. You can climb stairs at a rate of 1.75 feet per second, and the escalator rises at a rate of 2 feet per second. You have to travel a vertical distance of 28 feet. The equations model the vertical distance d (in feet) you have left to travel after t seconds.

Stairs: $d = -1.75t + 28$ **Escalator:** $d = -2t + 28$

a. Graph the equations in the same coordinate plane.

b. How much time do you save by taking the escalator?

Solution

a. Draw the graph of $d = -1.75t + 28$ using the fact that the d-intercept is 28 and the slope is -1.75. Similarly, draw the graph of $d = -2t + 28$. The graphs make sense only in the first quadrant.

b. The equation $d = -1.75t + 28$ has a t-intercept of 16. The equation $d = -2t + 28$ has a t-intercept of 14. So, you save $16 - 14 = 2$ seconds by taking the escalator.

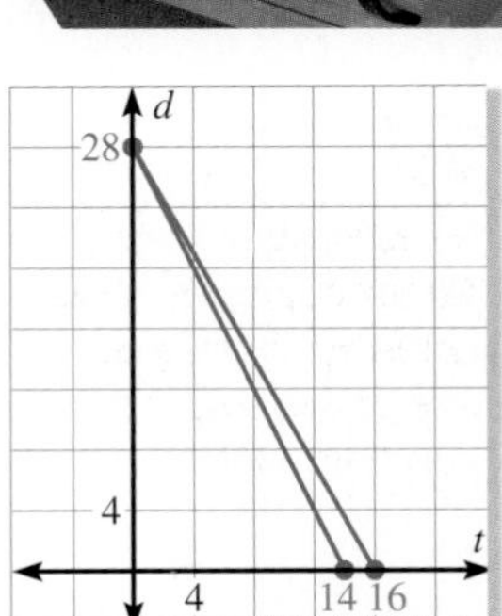

✓ **GUIDED PRACTICE** for Examples 2 and 3

4. Graph the equation $y = -2x + 5$.

5. **WHAT IF?** In Example 3, suppose a person can climb stairs at a rate of 1.4 feet per second. How much time does taking the escalator save?

EXAMPLE 4 Change intercepts of lines

TELEVISION A company produced two 30 second commercials, one for \$300,000 and the second for \$400,000. Each airing of either commercial on a particular station costs \$150,000. The cost C (in thousands of dollars) to produce the first commercial and air it n times is given by $C = 150n + 300$. The cost to produce the second and air it n times is given by $C = 150n + 400$.

a. Graph both equations in the same coordinate plane.

b. Based on the graphs, what is the difference of the costs to produce each commercial and air it 2 times? 4 times? What do you notice about the differences of the costs?

Solution

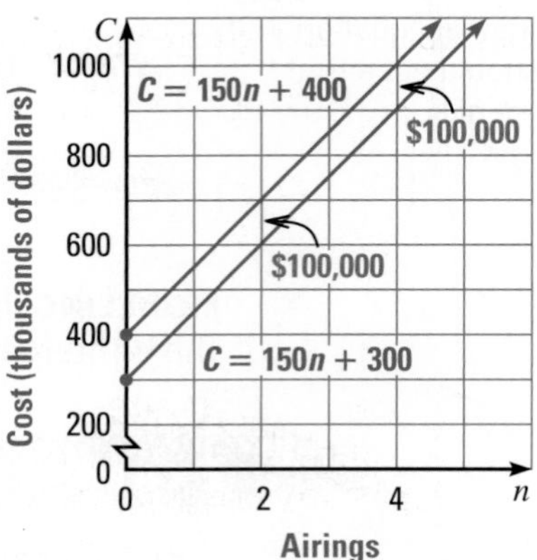

a. The graphs of the equations are shown.

b. You can see that the vertical distance between the lines is \$100,000 when $n = 2$ and $n = 4$.

The difference of the costs is \$100,000 no matter how many times the commercials are aired.

PARALLEL LINES Two lines in the same plane are **parallel** if they do not intersect. Because slope gives the rate at which a line rises or falls, two nonvertical lines with the same slope are parallel.

EXAMPLE 5 Identify parallel lines

Determine which of the lines are parallel.

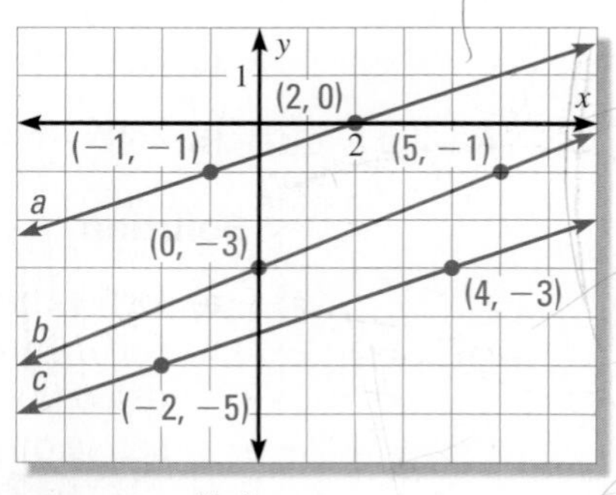

Find the slope of each line.

Line *a*: $m = \frac{-1 - 0}{-1 - 2} = \frac{-1}{-3} = \frac{1}{3}$

Line *b*: $m = \frac{-3 - (-1)}{0 - 5} = \frac{-2}{-5} = \frac{2}{5}$

Line *c*: $m = \frac{-5 - (-3)}{-2 - 4} = \frac{-2}{-6} = \frac{1}{3}$

▶ Line a and line c have the same slope, so they are parallel.

✓ GUIDED PRACTICE for Examples 4 and 5

6. **WHAT IF?** In Example 4, suppose that the cost of producing and airing a third commercial is given by $C = 150n + 200$. Graph the equation. Find the difference of the costs of the second commercial and the third.

7. Determine which lines are parallel: line a through $(-1, 2)$ and $(3, 4)$; line b through $(2, 2)$ and $(5, 8)$; line c through $(-9, -2)$ and $(-3, 1)$.

3.5 EXERCISES

HOMEWORK KEY

◯ = See **WORKED-OUT SOLUTIONS** Exs. 11, 21, and 41

★ = **STANDARDIZED TEST PRACTICE** Exs. 2, 9, 10, 36, 42, and 44

SKILL PRACTICE

1. **VOCABULARY** Copy and complete: Two lines in the same plane are _?_ if they do not intersect.

2. ★ **WRITING** What is the slope-intercept form of a linear equation? *Explain* why this form is called slope-intercept form.

EXAMPLE 1 for Exs. 3–16

SLOPE AND *y*-INTERCEPT Identify the slope and *y*-intercept of the line with the given equation.

3. $y = 2x + 1$
4. $y = -x$
5. $y = 6 - 3x$
6. $y = -7 + 5x$
7. $y = \frac{2}{3}x - 1$
8. $y = -\frac{1}{4}x + 8$

9. ★ **MULTIPLE CHOICE** What is the slope of the line with the equation $y = -18x - 9$?

Ⓐ -18 Ⓑ -9 Ⓒ 9 Ⓓ 18

10. ★ **MULTIPLE CHOICE** What is the *y*-intercept of the line with the equation $x - 3y = -12$?

Ⓐ -12 Ⓑ -4 Ⓒ 4 Ⓓ 12

REWRITING EQUATIONS Rewrite the equation in slope-intercept form. Then identify the slope and the *y*-intercept of the line.

11. $4x + y = 1$
12. $x - y = 6$
13. $6x - 3y = -9$
14. $-12x - 4y = 2$
15. $2x + 5y = -10$
16. $-x - 10y = 20$

EXAMPLE 2 for Exs. 17–29

MATCHING EQUATIONS WITH GRAPHS Match the equation with its graph.

17. $2x + 3y = 6$
18. $2x + 3y = -6$
19. $2x - 3y = 6$

A.
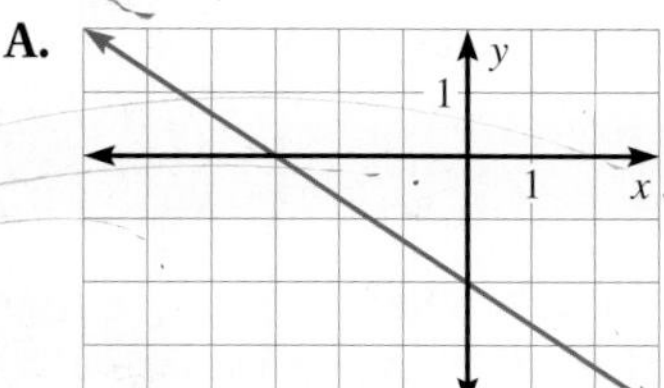

B.
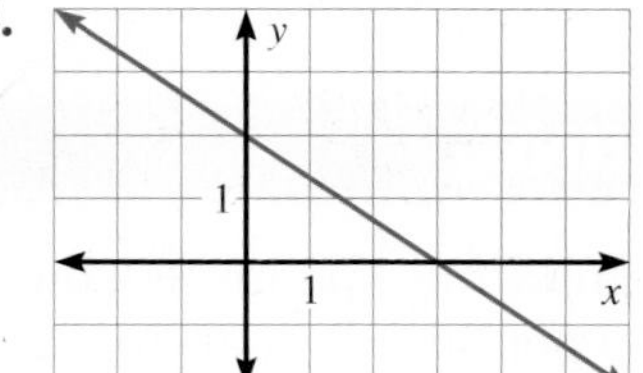

C.
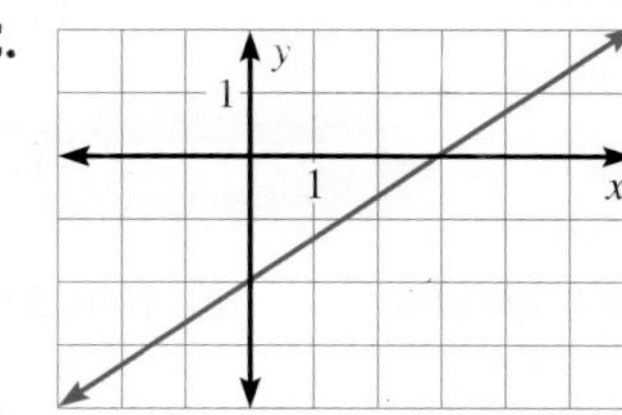

20. **ERROR ANALYSIS** *Describe* and correct the error in graphing the equation $y = 4x - 1$.

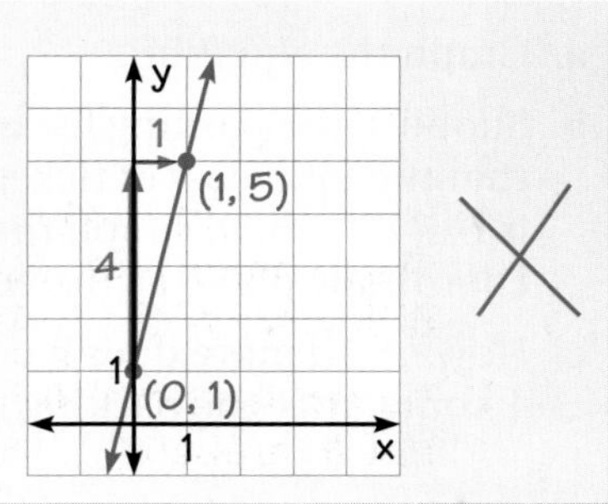

GRAPHING EQUATIONS **Graph the equation.**

(21.) $y = -6x + 1$ 22. $y = 3x + 2$ 23. $y = -x + 7$

24. $y = \frac{2}{3}x$ 25. $y = \frac{1}{4}x - 5$ 26. $y = -\frac{5}{2}x + 2$

27. $7x - 2y = -11$ 28. $-8x - 2y = 32$ 29. $-x - 0.5y = 2.5$

EXAMPLE 5
for Exs. 30–35

PARALLEL LINES **Determine which lines are parallel.**

30. 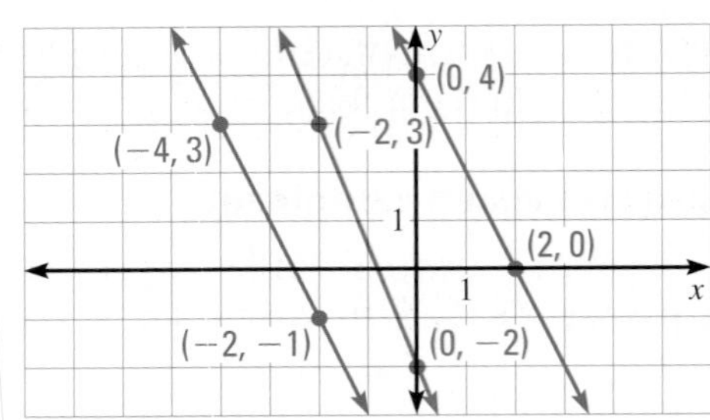

31. 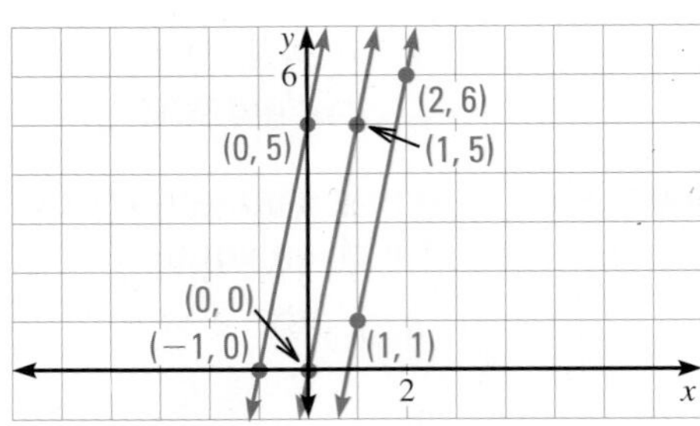

PARALLEL LINES **Tell whether the graphs of the two equations are parallel lines. *Explain* your reasoning.**

32. $y = 5x - 7$, $5x + y = 7$ 33. $y = 3x + 2$, $-7 + 3x = y$

34. $y = -0.5x$, $x + 2y = 18$ 35. $4x + y = 3$, $x + 4y = 3$

36. ★ **OPEN-ENDED** Write the equation of a line that is parallel to $6x + y = 24$. *Explain* your reasoning.

REASONING **Find the value of k so that the lines through the given points are parallel.**

37. Line 1: $(-4, -2)$ and $(0, 0)$
Line 2: $(2, 7)$ and $(k, 5)$

38. Line 1: $(-1, 9)$ and $(-6, -6)$
Line 2: $(-7, k)$ and $(0, -2)$

39. **CHALLENGE** To show that the slope of a line is constant, let (x_1, y_1) and (x_2, y_2) be any two points on the line $y = mx + b$. Use the equation of the line to express y_1 in terms of x_1 and y_2 in terms of x_2. Then show that the slope between the two points is m.

PROBLEM SOLVING

EXAMPLES 3 and 4
for Exs. 40–44

40. **HOCKEY** Your family spends \$60 on tickets to a hockey game and \$4 per hour for parking. The total cost C (in dollars) is given by $C = 60 + 4t$ where t is the time (in hours) your family's car is parked.

a. Graph the equation.

b. Suppose the parking fee is raised to \$5.50 per hour so that the total cost of tickets and parking for t hours is $C = 60 + 5.5t$. Graph the equation in the same coordinate plane as the equation in part (a).

c. How much more does it cost to go to a game for 4 hours after the parking fee is raised?

○ = See **WORKED-OUT SOLUTIONS** in Student Resources ★ = **STANDARDIZED TEST PRACTICE**

41. SPEED LIMITS In 1995 Pennsylvania changed its maximum speed limit on rural interstate highways, as shown below. The diagram also shows the distance d (in miles) a person could travel driving at the maximum speed limit for t hours both before and after 1995.

a. Graph both equations in the same coordinate plane.

b. Use the graphs to find the difference of the distances a person could drive in 3 hours before and after the speed limit was changed.

42. ★ SHORT RESPONSE A service station charges \$40 per hour for labor plus the cost of parts to repair a car. Parts can either be ordered from the car dealership for \$250 or from a warehouse for \$200. The equations below give the total repair cost C (in dollars) for a repair that takes t hours using parts from the dealership or from the warehouse.

Dealership: $C = 40t + 250$ **Warehouse:** $C = 40t + 200$

a. Graph both equations in the same coordinate plane.

b. Use the graphs to find the difference of the costs if the repair takes 3 hours. What if the repair takes 4 hours? What do you notice about the differences of the costs? *Explain.*

43. FACTORY SHIFTS Welders at a factory can work one of two shifts. Welders on the first shift earn \$12 per hour while workers on the second shift earn \$14 per hour. The total amount a (in dollars) a first-shift worker earns is given by $a = 12t$ where t is the time (in hours) worked. The total amount a second-shift worker earns is given by $a = 14t$.

a. Graph both equations in the same coordinate plane. What do the slopes and the a-intercepts of the graphs mean in this situation?

b. How much more money does a welder earn for a 40 hour week if he or she works the second shift rather than the first shift?

44. ★ EXTENDED RESPONSE An artist is renting a booth at an art show. A small booth costs \$350 to rent. The artist plans to sell framed pictures for \$50 each. The profit P (in dollars) the artist makes after selling p pictures is given by $P = 50p - 350$.

a. Graph the equation.

b. If the artist decides to rent a larger booth for \$500, the profit is given by $P = 50p - 500$. Graph this equation on the same coordinate plane you used in part (a).

c. The artist can display 80 pictures in the small booth and 120 in the larger booth. If the artist is able to sell all of the pictures, which booth should the artist rent? *Explain.*

45. **CHALLENGE** To use a rock climbing wall at a college, a person who does not attend the college has to pay a \$5 certification fee plus \$3 per visit. The total cost C (in dollars) for a person who does not attend the college is given by $C = 3v + 5$ where v is the number of visits to the rock climbing wall. A student at the college pays only an \$8 certification fee, so the total cost for a student is given by $C = 8$.

a. Graph both equations in the same coordinate plane. At what point do the lines intersect? What does the point of intersection represent?

b. When will a nonstudent pay more than a student? When will a student pay more than a nonstudent? *Explain.*

QUIZ

Find the slope of the line that passes through the points.

1. $(3, -11)$ and $(0, 4)$
2. $(2, 1)$ and $(8, 4)$
3. $(-4, -1)$ and $(-1, -1)$

Identify the slope and *y*-intercept of the line with the given equation.

4. $y = -x + 9$
5. $2x + 9y = -18$
6. $-x + 6y = 21$

Graph the equation.

7. $y = -2x + 11$
8. $y = \frac{5}{3}x - 8$
9. $-3x - 4y = -12$

10. **RED OAKS** Red oak trees grow at a rate of about 2 feet per year. You buy and plant two red oak trees, one that is 6 feet tall and one that is 8 feet tall. The height h (in feet) of the shorter tree can be modeled by $h = 2t + 6$ where t is the time (in years) since you planted the tree. The height of the taller tree can be modeled by $h = 2t + 8$.

a. Graph both equations in the same coordinate plane.

b. Use the graphs to find the difference of the heights of the trees 5 years after you plant them. What is the difference after 10 years? What do you notice about the difference of the heights of the two trees?

Extension

Solve Linear Equations by Graphing

GOAL Use graphs to solve linear equations.

You have learned how to solve linear equations in one variable algebraically. You can also solve linear equations graphically.

COMMON CORE

CC.9-12.A.REI.11 Explain why the x-coordinates of the points where the graphs of the equations $y = f(x)$ and $y = g(x)$ intersect are the solutions of the equation $f(x) = g(x)$; find the solutions approximately, e.g., using technology to graph the functions, make tables of values, or find successive approximations. Include cases where $f(x)$ and/or $g(x)$ are linear, polynomial, rational, absolute value, exponential, and logarithmic functions.*

KEY CONCEPT *For Your Notebook*

Steps for Solving Linear Equations Graphically

Use the following steps to solve a linear equation in one variable graphically.

STEP 1 **Write** the equation in the form $ax + b = 0$.

STEP 2 **Write** the related function $y = ax + b$.

STEP 3 **Graph** the equation $y = ax + b$.

The solution of $ax + b = 0$ is the x-intercept of the graph of $y = ax + b$.

EXAMPLE 1 Solve an equation graphically

Solve $\frac{5}{2}x + 2 = 3x$ graphically. Check your solution algebraically.

Solution

STEP 1 **Write** the equation in the form $ax + b = 0$.

$\frac{5}{2}x + 2 = 3x$ **Write original equation.**

$-\frac{1}{2}x + 2 = 0$ **Subtract 3x from each side.**

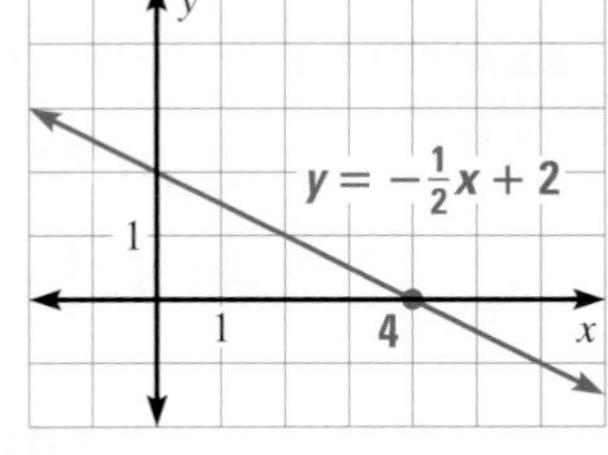

STEP 2 **Write** the related function $y = -\frac{1}{2}x + 2$.

STEP 3 **Graph** the equation $y = -\frac{1}{2}x + 2$. The x-intercept is 4.

▶ The solution of $\frac{5}{2}x + 2 = 3x$ is 4.

CHECK Use substitution.

$\frac{5}{2}x + 2 = 3x$ **Write original equation.**

$\frac{5}{2}(4) + 2 \stackrel{?}{=} 3(4)$ **Substitute 4 for x.**

$10 + 2 = 12$ **Simplify.**

$12 = 12$ ✓ **Solution checks.**

EXAMPLE 2 Approximate a real-world solution

POPULATION The United States population P (in millions) can be modeled by the function $P = 2.683t + 213.1$ where t is the number of years since 1975. In approximately what year will the population be 350 million?

Solution

Substitute 350 for P in the linear model. You can answer the question by solving the resulting linear equation $350 = 2.683t + 213.1$.

STEP 1 **Write** the equation in the form $ax + b = 0$.

$350 = 2.683t + 213.1$ **Write equation.**

$0 = 2.683t - 136.9$ **Subtract 350 from each side.**

$0 = 2.683x - 136.9$ **Substitute *x* for *t*.**

STEP 2 **Write** the related function: $y = 2.683x - 136.9$.

SET THE WINDOW
Use the following viewing window for Example 2.
Xmin=−5
Xmax=60
Xscl=5
Ymin=−150
Ymax=10
Yscl=10

STEP 3 **Graph** the related function on a graphing calculator. Use the *trace* feature to approximate the x-intercept. You will know that you've crossed the x-axis when the y-values change from negative to positive. The x-intercept is about 51.

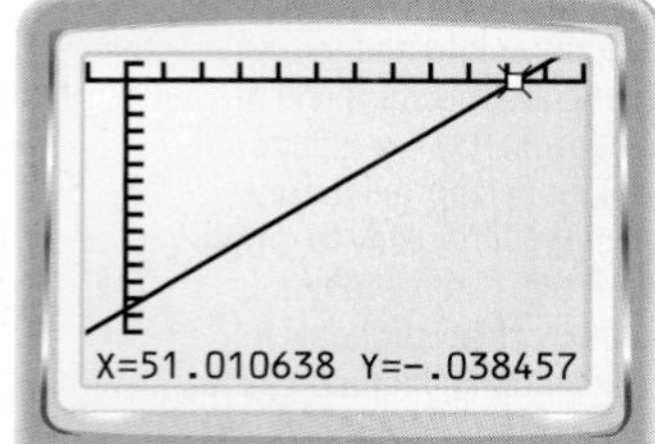

▶ Because x is the number of years since 1975, you can estimate that the population will be 350 million about 51 years after 1975, or in 2026.

PRACTICE

EXAMPLE 1 for Exs. 1–6

Solve the equation graphically. Then check your solution algebraically.

1. $6x + 5 = -7$
2. $-7x + 18 = -3$
3. $2x - 4 = 3x$
4. $\frac{1}{2}x - 3 = 2x$
5. $-4 + 9x = -3x + 2$
6. $10x - 18x = 4x - 6$

EXAMPLE 2 for Exs. 7–9

7. **CABLE TELEVISION** The number s (in millions) of cable television subscribers can be modeled by the function $s = 1.79t + 51.1$ where t is the number of years since 1990. Use a graphing calculator to approximate the year when the number of subscribers was 70 million.

8. **EDUCATION** The number b (in thousands) of bachelor's degrees in Spanish earned in the U.S. can be modeled by the function $b = 0.281t + 4.26$ where t is the number of years since 1990. Use a graphing calculator to approximate the year when the number of degrees will be 9000.

9. **TRAVEL** The number of miles m (in billions) traveled by vehicles in New York can be modeled by $m = 2.56t + 113$ where t is the number of years since 1994. Use a graphing calculator to approximate the year in which the number of vehicle miles of travel in New York was 130 billion.

3.6 Model Direct Variation

Before You wrote and graphed linear equations.

Now You will write and graph direct variation equations.

Why? So you can model distance traveled, as in Ex. 40.

Key Vocabulary
- **direct variation**
- **constant of variation**

Two variables x and y show **direct variation** provided $y = ax$ and $a \neq 0$. The nonzero number a is called the **constant of variation**, and y is said to *vary directly* with x.

The equation $y = 5x$ is an example of direct variation, and the constant of variation is 5. The equation $y = x + 5$ is *not* an example of direct variation.

COMMON CORE

CC.9-12.A.CED.2 Create equations in two or more variables to represent relationships between quantities; graph equations on coordinate axes with labels and scales.*

EXAMPLE 1 Identify direct variation equations

Tell whether the equation represents direct variation. If so, identify the constant of variation.

a. $2x - 3y = 0$ **b.** $-x + y = 4$

Solution

To tell whether an equation represents direct variation, try to rewrite the equation in the form $y = ax$.

a. $2x - 3y = 0$ **Write original equation.**

$-3y = -2x$ **Subtract 2*x* from each side.**

$y = \frac{2}{3}x$ **Simplify.**

▶ Because the equation $2x - 3y = 0$ can be rewritten in the form $y = ax$, it represents direct variation. The constant of variation is $\frac{2}{3}$.

b. $-x + y = 4$ **Write original equation.**

$y = x + 4$ **Add *x* to each side.**

▶ Because the equation $-x + y = 4$ cannot be rewritten in the form $y = ax$, it does not represent direct variation.

GUIDED PRACTICE for Example 1

Tell whether the equation represents direct variation. If so, identify the constant of variation.

1. $-x + y = 1$ **2.** $2x + y = 0$ **3.** $4x - 5y = 0$

DIRECT VARIATION GRAPHS Notice that a direct variation equation, $y = ax$, is a linear equation in slope-intercept form, $y = mx + b$, with $m = a$ and $b = 0$. The graph of a direct variation equation is a line with a slope of a and a y-intercept of 0. So, the line passes through the origin.

EXAMPLE 2 Graph direct variation equations

Graph the direct variation equation.

a. $y = \frac{2}{3}x$

b. $y = -3x$

Solution

a. Plot a point at the origin. The slope is equal to the constant of variation, or $\frac{2}{3}$. Find and plot a second point, then draw a line through the points.

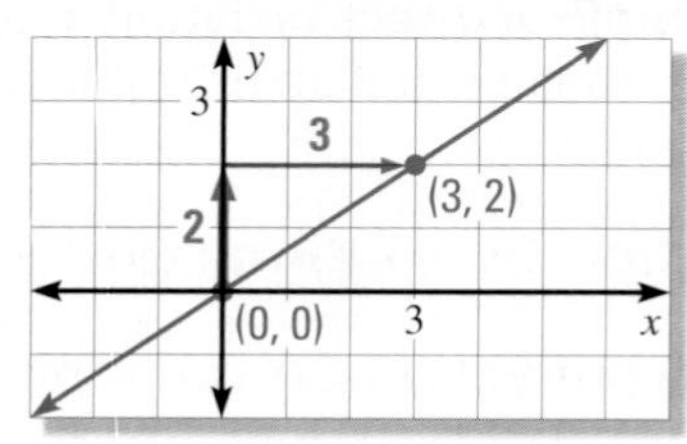

b. Plot a point at the origin. The slope is equal to the constant of variation, or -3. Find and plot a second point, then draw a line through the points.

DRAW A GRAPH
If the constant of variation is positive, the graph of $y = ax$ passes through Quadrants I and III. If the constant of variation is negative, the graph of $y = ax$ passes through Quadrants II and IV.

Animated Algebra at my.hrw.com

EXAMPLE 3 Write and use a direct variation equation

The graph of a direct variation equation is shown.

a. Write the direct variation equation.

b. Find the value of y when $x = 30$.

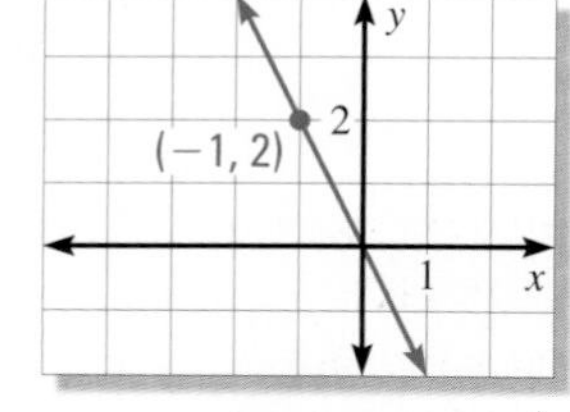

Solution

a. Because y varies directly with x, the equation has the form $y = ax$. Use the fact that $y = 2$ when $x = -1$ to find a.

$y = ax$	**Write direct variation equation.**
$2 = a(-1)$	**Substitute.**
$-2 = a$	**Solve for a.**

▸ A direct variation equation that relates x and y is $y = -2x$.

b. When $x = 30$, $y = -2(30) = -60$.

✓ GUIDED PRACTICE for Examples 2 and 3

4. Graph the direct variation equation $y = 2x$.

5. The graph of a direct variation equation passes through the point (4, 6). Write the direct variation equation and find the value of y when $x = 24$.

KEY CONCEPT — *For Your Notebook*

Properties of Graphs of Direct Variation Equations

- The graph of a direct variation equation is a line through the origin.
- The slope of the graph of $y = ax$ is a.

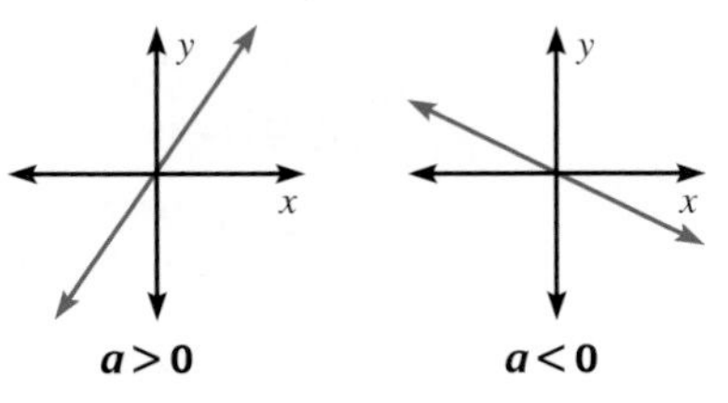

EXAMPLE 4 Solve a multi-step problem

ANOTHER WAY
For alternative methods for solving Example 4, see the **Problem Solving Workshop**.

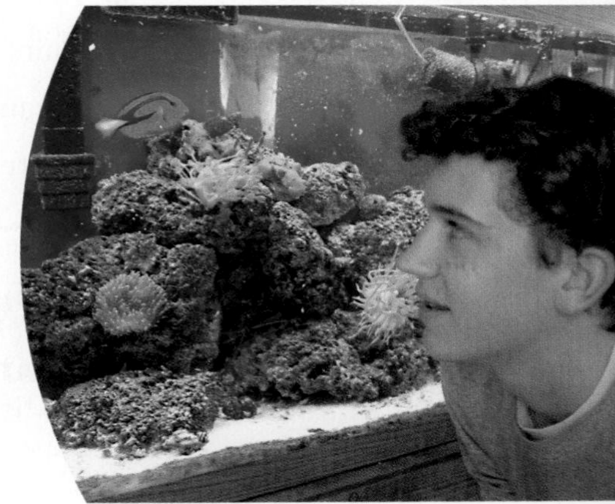

SALTWATER AQUARIUM The number s of tablespoons of sea salt needed in a saltwater fish tank varies directly with the number w of gallons of water in the tank. A pet shop owner recommends adding 100 tablespoons of sea salt to a 20 gallon tank.

- Write a direct variation equation that relates w and s.
- How many tablespoons of salt should be added to a 30 gallon saltwater fish tank?

Solution

STEP 1 **Write** a direct variation equation. Because s varies directly with w, you can use the equation $s = aw$. Also use the fact that $s = 100$ when $w = 20$.

$s = aw$ **Write direct variation equation.**

$100 = a(20)$ **Substitute.**

$5 = a$ **Solve for *a*.**

RECOGNIZE RATE OF CHANGE
The value of a in Example 4 is a rate of change: 5 tablespoons of sea salt per gallon of water.

▶ A direct variation equation that relates w and s is $s = 5w$.

STEP 2 **Find** the number of tablespoons of salt that should be added to a 30 gallon saltwater fish tank. Use your direct variation equation from Step 1.

$s = 5w$ **Write direct variation equation.**

$s = 5(30)$ **Substitute 30 for *w*.**

$s = 150$ **Simplify.**

▶ You should add 150 tablespoons of salt to a 30 gallon fish tank.

GUIDED PRACTICE for Example 4

6. **WHAT IF?** In Example 4, suppose the fish tank is a 25 gallon tank. How many tablespoons of salt should be added to the tank?

RATIOS The direct variation equation $y = ax$ can be rewritten as $\frac{y}{x} = a$ for $x \neq 0$. So, in a direct variation, the ratio of y to x is constant for all nonzero data pairs (x, y).

EXAMPLE 5 Use a direct variation model

ONLINE MUSIC The table shows the cost C of downloading s songs at an Internet music site.

a. Explain why C varies directly with s.

b. Write a direct variation equation that relates s and C.

Number of songs, s	Cost, C (dollars)
3	2.97
5	4.95
7	6.93

CHECK RATIOS
For real-world data, the ratios may not be exactly equal. You may still be able to use a direct variation model when the ratios are approximately equal.

Solution

a. To explain why C varies directly with s, compare the ratios $\frac{C}{s}$ for all data pairs (s, C): $\frac{2.97}{3} = \frac{4.95}{5} = \frac{6.93}{7} = 0.99$.

Because the ratios all equal 0.99, C varies directly with s.

b. A direct variation equation is $C = 0.99s$.

✓ GUIDED PRACTICE for Example 5

7. **WHAT IF?** In Example 5, suppose the website charges a total of \$1.99 for the first 5 songs you download and \$.99 for each song after the first 5. Is it reasonable to use a direct variation model for this situation? *Explain.*

3.6 EXERCISES

HOMEWORK KEY

○ = **See WORKED-OUT SOLUTIONS Exs. 7, 21, and 43**

★ = **STANDARDIZED TEST PRACTICE Exs. 2, 9, 28, 38, 43, 44, and 46**

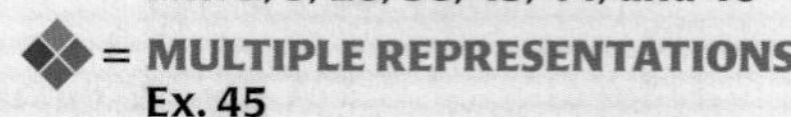

◆ = **MULTIPLE REPRESENTATIONS Ex. 45**

SKILL PRACTICE

1. **VOCABULARY** Copy and complete: Two variables x and y show __?__ provided $y = ax$ and $a \neq 0$.

2. ★ **WRITING** A line has a slope of -3 and a y-intercept of 4. Is the equation of the line a direct variation equation? *Explain.*

EXAMPLE 1
for Exs. 3–10

IDENTIFYING DIRECT VARIATION EQUATIONS **Tell whether the equation represents direct variation. If so, identify the constant of variation.**

3. $y = x$

4. $y = 5x - 1$

5. $2x + y = 3$

6. $x - 3y = 0$

7. $8x + 2y = 0$

8. $2.4x + 6 = 1.2y$

9. ★ **MULTIPLE CHOICE** Which equation is a direct variation equation?

Ⓐ $y = 7 - 3x$ Ⓑ $3x - 7y = 1$ Ⓒ $3x - 7y = 0$ Ⓓ $3y = 7x - 1$

10. **ERROR ANALYSIS** *Describe* and correct the error in identifying the constant of variation for the direct variation equation $-5x + 3y = 0$.

$-5x + 3y = 0$
$3y = 5x$
The constant of variation is 5.

EXAMPLE 2 for Exs. 11–22

GRAPHING EQUATIONS **Graph the direct variation equation.**

11. $y = x$ 12. $y = 3x$ 13. $y = -4x$ 14. $y = 5x$

15. $y = \frac{4}{3}x$ 16. $y = \frac{1}{2}x$ 17. $y = -\frac{1}{3}x$ 18. $y = -\frac{3}{2}x$

19. $12y = -24x$ 20. $10y = 25x$ 21. $4x + y = 0$ 22. $y - 1.25x = 0$

EXAMPLE 3 for Exs. 23–25

WRITING EQUATIONS **The graph of a direct variation equation is shown. Write the direct variation equation. Then find the value of y when $x = 8$.**

23. 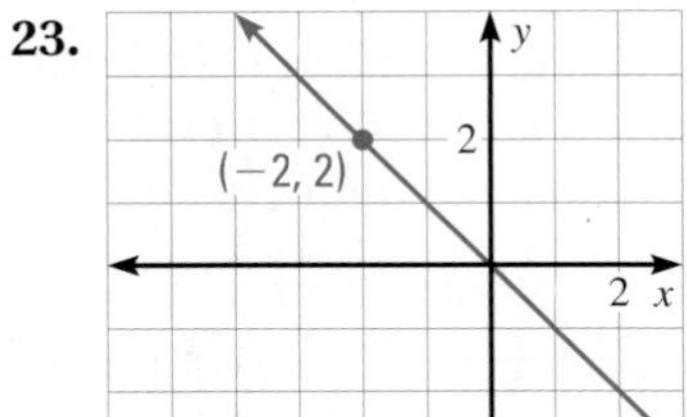

24. 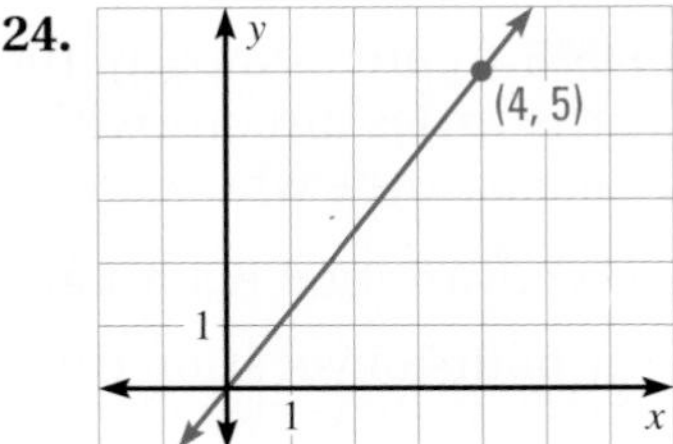

25. 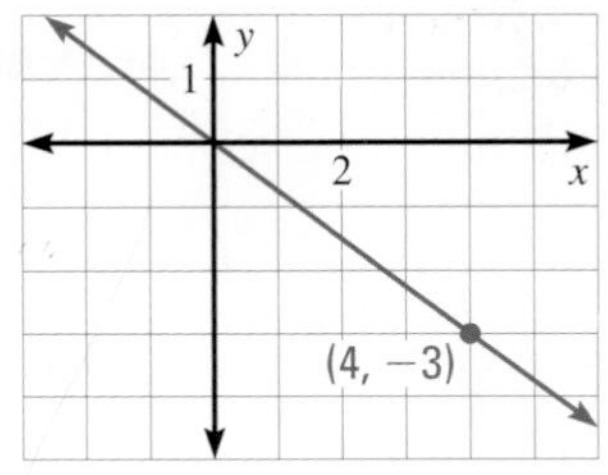

IDENTIFYING DIRECT VARIATION EQUATIONS **Tell whether the table represents direct variation. If so, write the direct variation equation.**

26.

x	1	2	3	4	6
y	5	10	15	20	30

27.

x	−3	−1	1	3	5
y	−2	0	2	4	6

28. ★ **WRITING** A student says that a direct variation equation can be used to model the data in the table. *Explain* why the student is mistaken.

x	2	4	8	16
y	1	2	4	6

WRITING EQUATIONS **Given that y varies directly with x, use the specified values to write a direct variation equation that relates x and y.**

29. $x = 3, y = 9$ 30. $x = 2, y = 26$ 31. $x = 14, y = 7$

32. $x = 15, y = -5$ 33. $x = -2, y = -2$ 34. $x = -18, y = -4$

35. $x = \frac{1}{4}, y = 1$ 36. $x = -6, y = 15$ 37. $x = -5.2, y = 1.4$

38. ★ **WRITING** If y varies directly with x, does x vary directly with y? If so, what is the relationship between the constants of variation? *Explain.*

39. **CHALLENGE** The slope of a line is $-\frac{1}{3}$, and the point $(-6, 2)$ lies on the line. Use the formula for the slope of a line to determine if the equation of the line is a direct variation equation.

PROBLEM SOLVING

EXAMPLE 4 for Exs. 40–42

40. **BICYCLES** The distance d (in meters) you travel on a bicycle varies directly with the number r of revolutions that the rear tire completes. You travel about 2 meters on a mountain bike for every revolution of the tire.

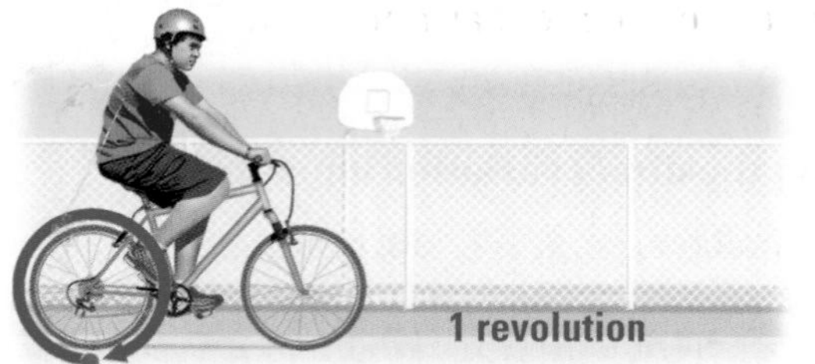

a. Write a direct variation equation that relates r and d.

b. How many meters do you travel in 1500 tire revolutions?

41. **VACATION TIME** At one company, the amount of vacation v (in hours) an employee earns varies directly with the amount of time t (in weeks) he or she works. An employee who works 2 weeks earns 3 hours of vacation.

a. Write a direct variation equation that relates t and v.

b. How many hours of vacation time does an employee earn in 8 weeks?

42. **LANDSCAPING** Landscapers plan to spread a layer of stone on a path. The number s of bags of stone needed depends on the depth d (in inches) of the layer. They need 10 bags to spread a layer of stone that is 2 inches deep. Write a direct variation equation that relates d and s. Then find the number of bags needed to spread a layer that is 3 inches deep.

EXAMPLE 5 for Exs. 43–44

43. ★ **SHORT RESPONSE** At a recycling center, computers and computer accessories can be recycled for a fee f based on weight w, as shown in the table.

Weight, w (pounds)	Fee, f (dollars)
10	2.50
15	3.75
30	7.50

a. *Explain* why f varies directly with w.

b. Write a direct variation equation that relates w and f, and identify the rate of change that the constant of variation represents. Find the total recycling fee for an 18 pound computer and a 10 pound printer.

44. ★ **SHORT RESPONSE** You can buy gold chain by the inch. The table shows the price of gold chain for various lengths.

Length, ℓ (inches)	7	9	16	18
Price, p (dollars)	8.75	11.25	20.00	22.50

a. *Explain* why p varies directly with ℓ.

b. Write a direct variation equation that relates ℓ and p, and identify the rate of change that the constant of variation represents. If you have \$30, what is the longest chain that you can buy?

○ = See WORKED-OUT SOLUTIONS in Student Resources ★ = STANDARDIZED TEST PRACTICE ◆ = MULTIPLE REPRESENTATIONS

45. ◆ **MULTIPLE REPRESENTATIONS** The total cost of riding the subway to and from school every day is $1.50.

a. Making a Table Make a table that shows the number d of school days and the total cost C (in dollars) for trips to and from school for some values of d. Assume you travel to school once each school day and home from school once each school day.

b. Drawing a Graph Graph the ordered pairs from the table and draw a ray through them.

c. Writing an Equation Write an equation of the graph from part (b). Is it a direct variation equation? *Explain.* If there are 22 school days in one month, what will it cost to ride the subway to and from school for that month?

46. ★ **EXTENDED RESPONSE** The table shows the average number of field goals attempted t and the average number of field goals made m per game for all NCAA Division I women's basketball teams for 9 consecutive seasons.

Attempted field goals, t	61.8	61.9	61.8	60.8	59.5	59.0	58.9	59.2	58.4
Field goals made, m	25.7	25.6	25.6	25.2	24.5	24.6	24.5	24.3	24.0

a. Write Why is it reasonable to use a direct variation model for this situation? Write a direct variation equation that relates t and m. Find the constant of variation to the nearest tenth.

b. Estimate The highest average number of attempted field goals in one season was 66.2. Estimate the number of field goals made that season.

c. Explain If the average number of field goals made was increasing rather than decreasing and the number of attempted field goals continued to decrease, would the data show direct variation? *Explain.*

47. CHALLENGE In Exercise 40, you found an equation showing that the distance traveled on a bike varies directly with the number of revolutions that the rear tire completes. The number r of tire revolutions varies directly with the number p of pedal revolutions. In a particular gear, you travel about 1.3 meters for every 5 revolutions of the pedals. Show that distance traveled varies directly with pedal revolutions.

PROBLEM SOLVING WORKSHOP
LESSON 3.6

Using ALTERNATIVE METHODS

Another Way to Solve Example 4

Make sense of problems and persevere in solving them.

MULTIPLE REPRESENTATIONS In Example 4, you saw how to solve the problem about how much salt to add to a saltwater fish tank by writing and using a direct variation equation. You can also solve the problem using a graph or a proportion.

PROBLEM

SALTWATER AQUARIUM The number s of tablespoons of sea salt needed in a saltwater fish tank varies directly with the number w of gallons of water in the tank. A pet shop owner recommends adding 100 tablespoons of sea salt to a 20 gallon tank. How many tablespoons of salt should be added to a 30 gallon saltwater fish tank?

METHOD 1

Using a Graph An alternative approach is to use a graph.

STEP 1 **Read** the problem. It tells you an amount of salt for a certain size fish tank. You can also assume that if a fishtank has no water, then no salt needs to be added. Write ordered pairs for this information.

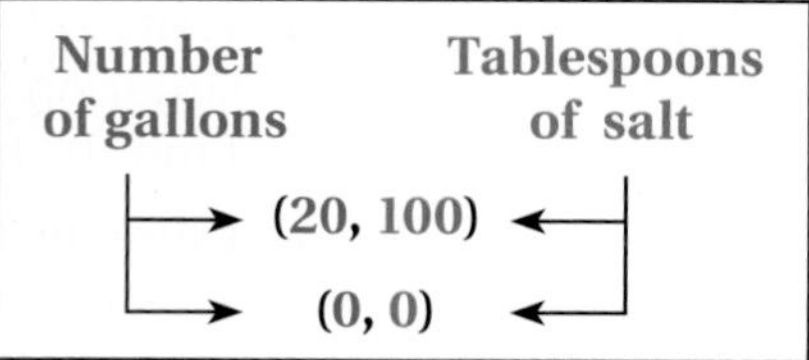

STEP 2 **Graph** the ordered pairs. Draw a line through the points.

The coordinates of points on the line give the amounts of salt that should be added to fish tanks of various sizes.

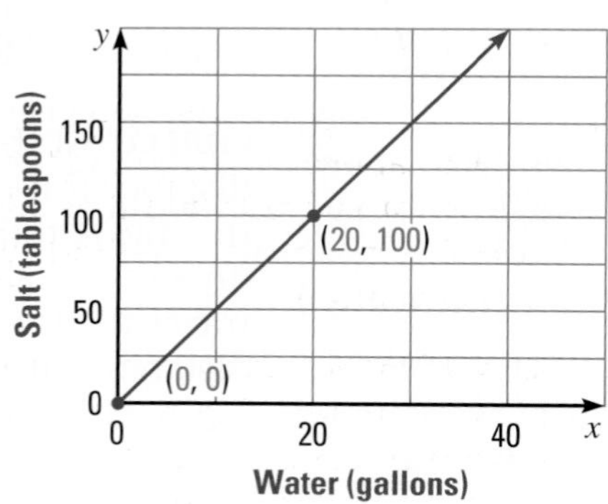

STEP 3 **Find** the point on the graph that has an x-coordinate of 30. The y-coordinate of this point is 150, so 150 tablespoons of salt should be added to a 30 gallon tank.

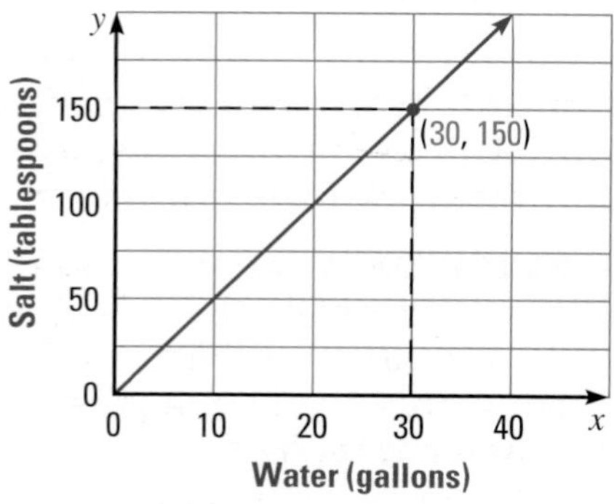

METHOD 2 **Writing a Proportion** Another alternative approach is to write and solve a proportion.

STEP 1 **Write** a proportion involving two ratios that each compare the amount of water (in gallons) to the amount of salt (in tablespoons).

$$\frac{20}{100} = \frac{30}{s}$$

30 ← amount of water (gallons)
s ← amount of salt (tablespoons)

STEP 2 **Solve** the proportion.

$\frac{20}{100} = \frac{30}{s}$ **Write proportion.**

$20s = 100 \cdot 30$ **Cross products property**

$20s = 3000$ **Simplify.**

$s = 150$ **Divide each side by 20.**

▶ You should add 150 tablespoons of salt to a 30 gallon tank.

CHECK Check your answer by writing each ratio in simplest form.

$\frac{20}{100} = \frac{1}{5}$ and $\frac{30}{150} = \frac{1}{5}$

Because each ratio simplifies to $\frac{1}{5}$, the answer is correct.

PRACTICE

1. **WHAT IF?** Suppose the fish tank in the problem above is a 22 gallon tank. How many tablespoons of salt should be added to the tank? *Describe* which method you used to solve this problem.

2. **ADVERTISING** A local newspaper charges by the word for printing classified ads. A 14 word ad costs $5.88. How much would a 21 word ad cost? Solve this problem using two different methods.

3. **REASONING** In Exercise 2, how can you quickly determine the cost of a 7 word ad? *Explain* how you could use the cost of a 7 word ad to solve the problem.

4. **NUTRITION** A company sells fruit smoothies in two sizes of bottles: 6 fluid ounces and 10 fluid ounces. You know that a 6 ounce bottle contains 96 milligrams of sodium. How many milligrams of sodium does a 10 ounce bottle contain?

5. **ERROR ANALYSIS** A student solved the problem in Exercise 4 as shown. *Describe* and correct the error made.

> Let x = the number of milligrams of sodium in a 10 ounce bottle.
>
> $\frac{6}{x} = \frac{10}{96}$
>
> $576 = 10x$
>
> $57.6 = x$
>
> ✗

6. **SLEEPING** You find an online calculator that calculates the number of calories you burn while sleeping. The results for various sleeping times are shown. About how many more calories would you burn by sleeping for 9.5 hours than for 8 hours? Choose any method for solving the problem.

Hours of sleep	6.5	7	8.5	9
Calories burned	390	420	510	540

3.7 Graph Linear Functions

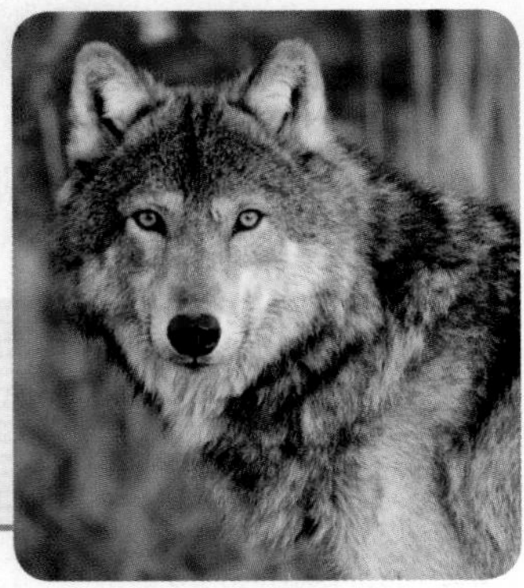

Before You graphed linear equations and functions.

Now You will use function notation.

Why? So you can model an animal population, as in Example 3.

Key Vocabulary
- function notation
- family of functions
- parent linear function

You have seen linear functions written in the form $y = mx + b$. By naming a function f, you can write it using **function notation**.

$$f(x) = mx + b \quad \textbf{Function notation}$$

The symbol $f(x)$ is another name for y and is read as "the value of f at x," or simply as "f of x." It does *not* mean f times x. You can use letters other than f, such as g or h, to name functions.

CC.9-12.F.IF.7a Graph linear and quadratic functions and show intercepts, maxima, and minima.*

EXAMPLE 1 Standardized Test Practice

What is the value of the function $f(x) = 3x - 15$ when $x = -3$?

Ⓐ −24 Ⓑ −6 Ⓒ −2 Ⓓ 8

Solution

$f(x) = 3x - 15$ **Write original function.**

$f(-3) = 3(-3) - 15$ **Substitute −3 for x.**

$= -24$ **Simplify.**

▶ The correct answer is A. Ⓐ Ⓑ Ⓒ Ⓓ

✓ GUIDED PRACTICE for Example 1

1. Evaluate the function $h(x) = -7x$ when $x = 7$.

EXAMPLE 2 Find an *x*-value

For the function $f(x) = 2x - 10$, find the value of x so that $f(x) = 6$.

$f(x) = 2x - 10$ **Write original function.**

$6 = 2x - 10$ **Substitute 6 for $f(x)$.**

$8 = x$ **Solve for x.**

▶ When $x = 8$, $f(x) = 6$.

DOMAIN AND RANGE The domain of a function consists of the values of x for which the function is defined. The range consists of the values of $f(x)$ where x is in the domain of f. The graph of a function f is the set of all points $(x, f(x))$.

EXAMPLE 3 Graph a function

INTERPRET MODELS
The rate of change in the wolf population actually varied over time. The model simplifies the situation by assuming a steady rate of change.

GRAY WOLF The gray wolf population in central Idaho was monitored over several years for a project aimed at boosting the number of wolves. The number of wolves can be modeled by the function $f(x) = 37x + 7$ where x is the number of years since 1995. Graph the function and identify its domain and range.

Solution

To graph the function, make a table.

x	$f(x)$
0	$37(0) + 7 = 7$
1	$37(1) + 7 = 44$
2	$37(2) + 7 = 81$

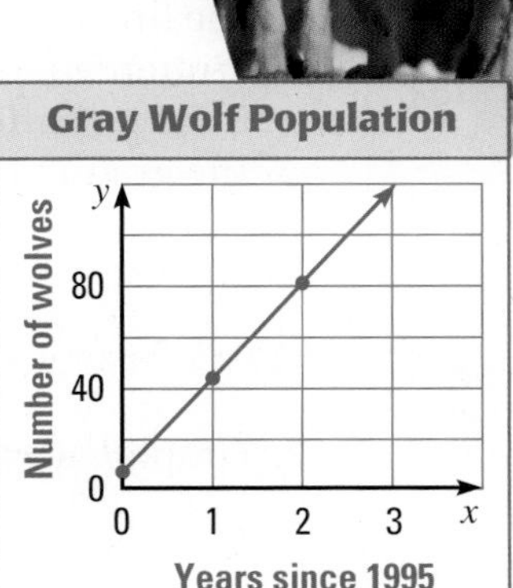

The domain of the function is $x \geq 0$. From the graph or table, you can see that the range of the function is $f(x) \geq 7$.

GUIDED PRACTICE for Examples 2 and 3

2. **WOLF POPULATION** Use the model from Example 3 to find the value of x so that $f(x) = 155$. *Explain* what the solution means in this situation.

IDENTIFY PARAMETERS
Particular members of the family of linear functions are determined by the values of m and b, called *parameters*, in the general form $y = mx + b$.

FAMILIES OF FUNCTIONS A **family of functions** is a group of functions with similar characteristics. For example, functions that have the form $f(x) = mx + b$ constitute the family of *linear* functions.

KEY CONCEPT *For Your Notebook*

Parent Function for Linear Functions

The most basic linear function in the family of all linear functions, called the **parent linear function**, is:

$$f(x) = x$$

The graph of the parent linear function is shown.

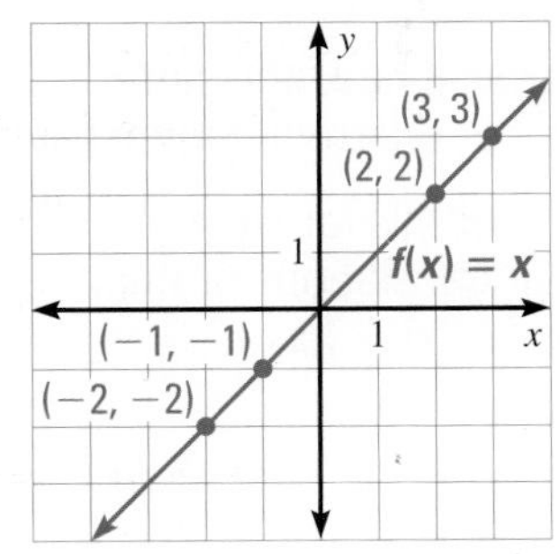

READING
The parent linear function is also called the *identity function*.

EXAMPLE 4 Compare graphs with the graph $f(x) = x$

Graph the function. Compare the graph with the graph of $f(x) = x$.

a. $g(x) = x + 3$ **b.** $h(x) = 2x$

Solution

a.

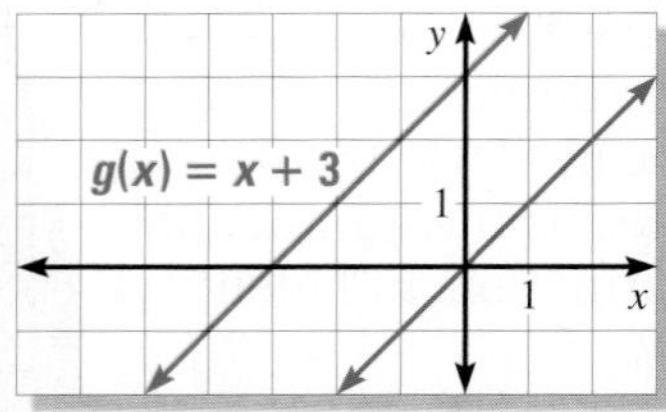

Because the graphs of g and f have the same slope, $m = 1$, the lines are parallel. Also, the y-intercept of the graph of g is 3 more than the y-intercept of the graph of f.

b.

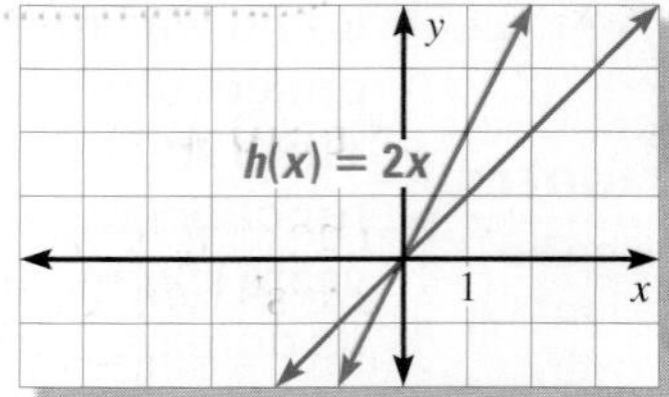

Because the slope of the graph of h is greater than the slope of the graph of f, the graph of h rises faster from left to right. The y-intercept for both graphs is 0, so both lines pass through the origin.

GUIDED PRACTICE for Example 4

3. Graph $h(x) = -3x$. Compare the graph with the graph of $f(x) = x$.

CONCEPT SUMMARY *For Your Notebook*

Comparing Graphs of Linear Functions with the Graph of $f(x) = x$

Changing m or b in the general linear function $g(x) = mx + b$ creates families of linear functions whose graphs are related to the graph of $f(x) = x$.

$g(x) = x + b$

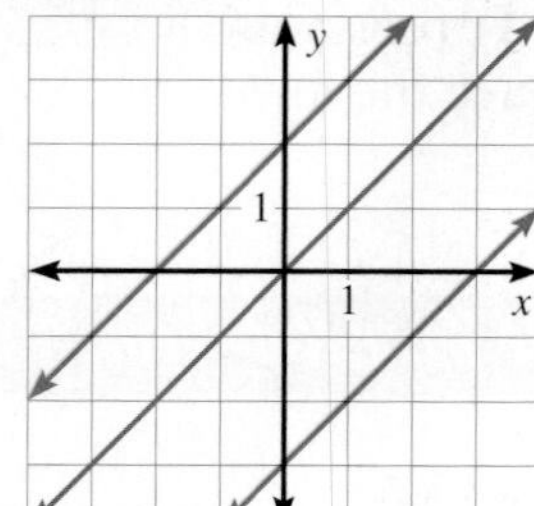

- The graphs have the same slope, but different y-intercepts.
- Graphs of this family are vertical translations of the graph of $f(x) = x$.

$g(x) = mx$ where $m > 0$

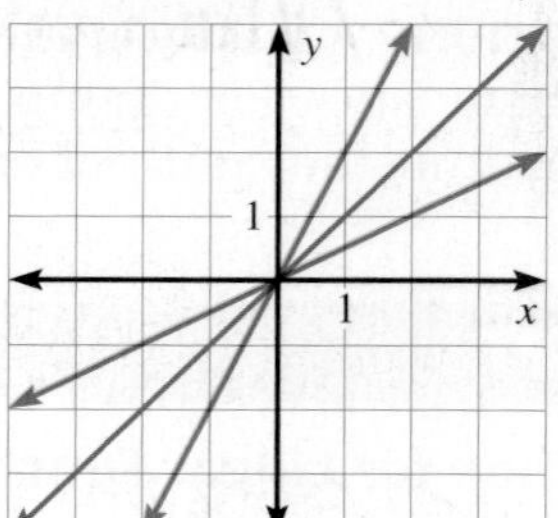

- The graphs have different (positive) slopes, but the same y-intercept.
- Graphs of this family are vertical stretches or shrinks of the graph of $f(x) = x$.

$g(x) = mx$ where $m < 0$

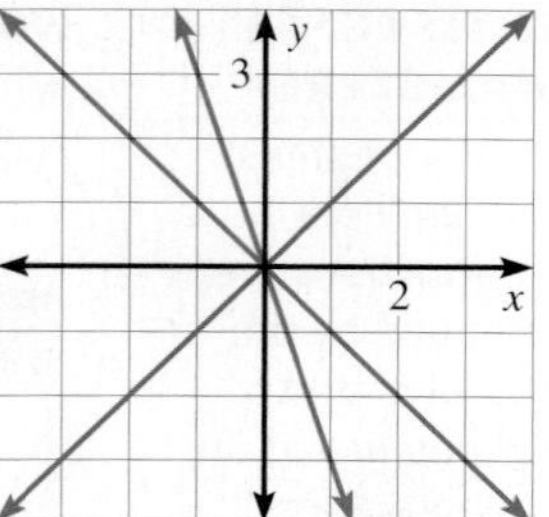

- The graphs have different (negative) slopes, but the same y-intercept.
- Graphs of this family are vertical stretches or shrinks with reflections in the x-axis of the graph of $f(x) = x$.

EXAMPLE 5 Graph real-world functions

CABLE A cable company charges new customers \$40 for installation and \$60 per month for its service. The cost to the customer is given by the function $f(x) = 60x + 40$ where x is the number of months of service. To attract new customers, the cable company reduces the installation fee to \$5. A function for the cost with the reduced installation fee is $g(x) = 60x + 5$. Graph both functions. How is the graph of g related to the graph of f?

Solution

The graphs of both functions are shown. Both functions have a slope of 60, so they are parallel. The y-intercept of the graph of g is 35 less than the graph of f. So, the graph of g is a vertical translation of the graph of f.

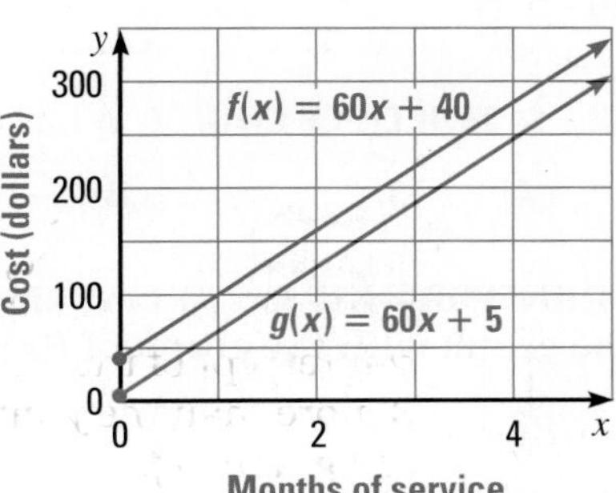

REVIEW TRANSFORMATIONS
For help with transformations, see pp. SR12–SR13.

GUIDED PRACTICE for Example 5

4. **WHAT IF?** In Example 5, suppose the monthly fee is \$70 so that the cost to the customer is given by $h(x) = 70x + 40$. Graph f and h in the same coordinate plane. How is the graph of h related to the graph of f?

3.7 EXERCISES

HOMEWORK KEY

○ = See **WORKED-OUT SOLUTIONS** Exs. 3, 17, and 39

★ = **STANDARDIZED TEST PRACTICE** Exs. 2, 13, 22, 35, 36, 44, and 45

SKILL PRACTICE

1. **VOCABULARY** When you write the function $y = 3x + 12$ as $f(x) = 3x + 12$, you are using __?__.

2. ★ **WRITING** Would the functions $f(x) = -9x + 12$, $g(x) = -9x - 2$, and $h(x) = -9x$ be considered a family of functions? *Explain.*

EXAMPLE 1 for Exs. 3–13

EVALUATING FUNCTIONS **Evaluate the function when $x = -2, 0,$ and 3.**

3. $f(x) = 12x + 1$
4. $g(x) = -3x + 5$
5. $p(x) = -8x - 2$
6. $h(x) = 2.25x$
7. $m(x) = -6.5x$
8. $f(x) = -0.75x - 1$
9. $s(x) = \frac{2}{5}x + 3$
10. $d(x) = -\frac{3}{2}x + 5$
11. $h(x) = \frac{3}{4}x - 6$

12. **ERROR ANALYSIS** *Describe* and correct the error in evaluating the function $g(x) = -5x + 3$ when $x = -3$.

$g(-3) = -5(-3) + 3$
$-3g = 18$
$g = -6$

13. ★ **MULTIPLE CHOICE** Given $f(x) = -6.8x + 5$, what is the value of $f(-2)$?

Ⓐ -18.6 Ⓑ -8.6 Ⓒ 8.6 Ⓓ 18.6

EXAMPLE 2 for Exs. 14–22

FINDING X-VALUES Find the value of *x* so that the function has the given value.

14. $f(x) = 6x + 9;\ 3$
15. $g(x) = -x + 5;\ 2$
16. $h(x) = -7x + 12;\ -9$
17. $j(x) = 4x + 11;\ -13$
18. $m(x) = 9x - 5;\ -2$
19. $n(x) = -2x - 21;\ -6$
20. $p(x) = -12x - 36;\ -3$
21. $q(x) = 8x - 32;\ -4$

22. ★ **MULTIPLE CHOICE** What value of x makes $f(x) = 5$ if $f(x) = -2x + 25$?

Ⓐ -15 Ⓑ -10 Ⓒ 10 Ⓓ 15

EXAMPLE 4 for Exs. 23–34

TRANSFORMATIONS OF LINEAR FUNCTIONS Graph the function. Compare the graph with the graph of $f(x) = x$.

23. $g(x) = x + 5$
24. $h(x) = 6 + x$
25. $q(x) = x - 1$
26. $m(x) = x - 6$
27. $d(x) = x + 7$
28. $t(x) = x - 3$
29. $r(x) = 4x$
30. $w(x) = 5x$
31. $h(x) = -3x$
32. $k(x) = -6x$
33. $g(x) = \frac{1}{3}x$
34. $m(x) = -\frac{7}{2}x$

35. ★ **MULTIPLE CHOICE** The graph of which function is shown?

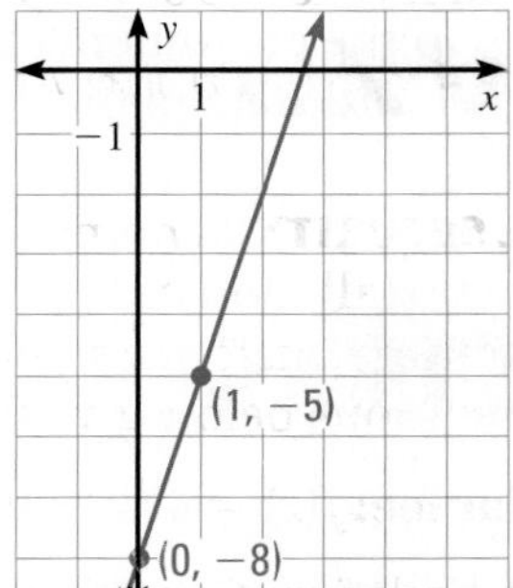

Ⓐ $f(x) = 3x + 8$

Ⓑ $f(x) = 3x - 8$

Ⓒ $f(x) = 8x + 3$

Ⓓ $f(x) = 8x - 3$

36. ★ **OPEN-ENDED** In this exercise you will compare the graphs of linear functions when their slopes and y-intercepts are changed.

   a. Choose a linear function of the form $f(x) = mx + b$ where $m \neq 0$. Then graph the function.

   b. Using the same m and b values as in part (a), graph the function $g(x) = 2mx + b$. How are the slope and y-intercept of the graph of g related to the slope and y-intercept of the graph of f?

   c. Using the same m and b values as in part (a), graph the function $h(x) = mx + (b - 3)$. How are the slope and y-intercept of the graph of h related to the slope and y-intercept of the graph of f?

37. **REASONING** How is the graph of $g(x) = 1$ related to the graph of $h(x) = -1$?

38. **CHALLENGE** Suppose that $f(x) = 4x + 7$ and $g(x) = 2x$. What is a rule for $g(f(x))$? What is a rule for $f(g(x))$?

PROBLEM SOLVING

EXAMPLE 3
for Exs. 39–41

39. **MOVIE TICKETS** The average price of a movie ticket in the United States from 1980 to 2000 can be modeled by the function $f(x) = 0.10x + 2.75$ where x is the number of years since 1980.

a. Graph the function and identify its domain and range.

b. Find the value of x so that $f(x) = 4.55$. *Explain* what the solution means in this situation.

40. **DVD PLAYERS** The number (in thousands) of DVD players sold in the United States from 1998 to 2003 can be modeled by $f(x) = 4250x + 330$ where x is the number of years since 1998.

a. Graph the function and identify its domain and range.

b. Find the value of x so that $f(x) = 13{,}080$. *Explain* what the solution means in this situation.

41. **IN-LINE SKATING** An in-line skater's average speed is 10 miles per hour. The distance traveled after skating for x hours is given by the function $d(x) = 10x$. Graph the function and identify its domain and range. How long did it take the skater to travel 15 miles? *Explain.*

Animated Algebra at my.hrw.com

EXAMPLE 5
for Exs. 42–43

42. **HOME SECURITY** A home security company charges new customers \$155 for the installation of security equipment and a monthly fee of \$40. To attract more customers, the company reduces its installation fee to \$75. The functions below give the total cost for x months of service:

Regular fee: $f(x) = 40x + 155$ **Reduced fee:** $g(x) = 40x + 75$

Graph both functions. How is the graph of g related to the graph of f?

43. **THEATERS** A ticket for a play at a theater costs \$16. The revenue (in dollars) generated from the sale of x tickets is given by $s(x) = 16x$. The theater managers raise the cost of tickets to \$20. The revenue generated from the sale of x tickets at that price is given by $r(x) = 20x$. Graph both functions. How is the graph of r related to the graph of s?

44. ★ **EXTENDED RESPONSE** The cost of supplies, such as mustard and napkins, a pretzel vendor needs for one day is \$75. Each pretzel costs the vendor \$.50 to make. The total daily cost to the vendor is given by $C(x) = 0.5x + 75$ where x is the number of pretzels the vendor makes.

a. **Graph** Graph the cost function.

b. **Graph** The vendor sells each pretzel for \$3. The revenue is given by $R(x) = 3x$ where x is the number of pretzels sold. Graph the function.

c. **Explain** The vendor's profit is the difference of the revenue and the cost. *Explain* how you could use the graphs to find the vendor's profit for any given number of pretzels made and sold.

45. ★ **EXTENDED RESPONSE** The number of hours of daylight in Austin, Texas, during the month of March can be modeled by the function $\ell(x) = 0.03x + 11.5$ where x is the day of the month.

a. **Graph** Graph the function and identify its domain and range.

b. **Graph** The number of hours of darkness can be modeled by the function $d(x) = 24 - \ell(x)$. Graph the function on the same coordinate plane as you used in part (a). Identify its domain and range.

c. **CHALLENGE** *Explain* how you could have obtained the graph of d from the graph of ℓ using translations and reflections.

d. **CHALLENGE** What does the point where the graphs intersect mean in terms of the number of hours of daylight and darkness?

QUIZ

Given that y varies directly with x, use the specified values to write a direct variation equation that relates x and y.

1. $x = 5, y = 10$
2. $x = 4, y = 6$
3. $x = 2, y = -16$

Evaluate the function.

4. $g(x) = 6x - 5$ when $x = 4$
5. $h(x) = 14x + 7$ when $x = 2$
6. $j(x) = 0.2x + 12.2$ when $x = 244$
7. $k(x) = \frac{5}{6}x + \frac{1}{3}$ when $x = 4$

Graph the function. Compare the graph to the graph of $f(x) = x$.

8. $g(x) = -4x$
9. $h(x) = x - 2$

10. **HOURLY WAGE** The table shows the number of hours that you worked for each of three weeks and the amount that you were paid. What is your hourly wage?

Hours	12	16	14
Pay (dollars)	84	112	98

See **EXTRA PRACTICE** in Student Resources **ONLINE QUIZ** at my.hrw.com

Solving Linear Equations by Graphing Each Side

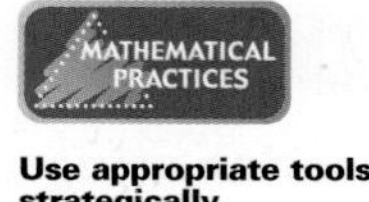

Use appropriate tools strategically.

QUESTION How can a graphing calculator be used to solve a linear equation?

You can solve a linear equation in one variable by graphing each side of the equation and finding the point of intersection. The x-value of the intersection is the solution of the equation.

EXAMPLE 1 Solve a linear equation

Solve the linear equation $\frac{4}{5}x + 8 = 20$ using a graphing calculator.

STEP 1 ***Create two equations***

Write two functions by setting each side of the equation equal to y.

$$\frac{4}{5}x + 8 = 20$$

$$y = \frac{4}{5}x + 8 \text{ and } y = 20$$

STEP 2 ***Enter equations***

Enter the equations from Step 1 as Y_1 and Y_2.

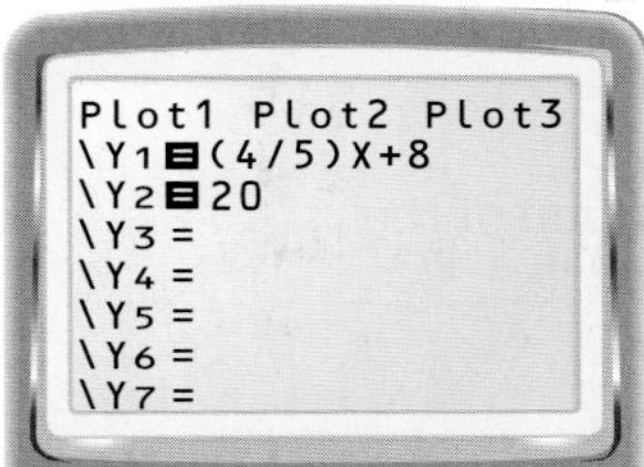

STEP 3 ***Graph the equations***

Choose a viewing window that allows you to see the intersection.

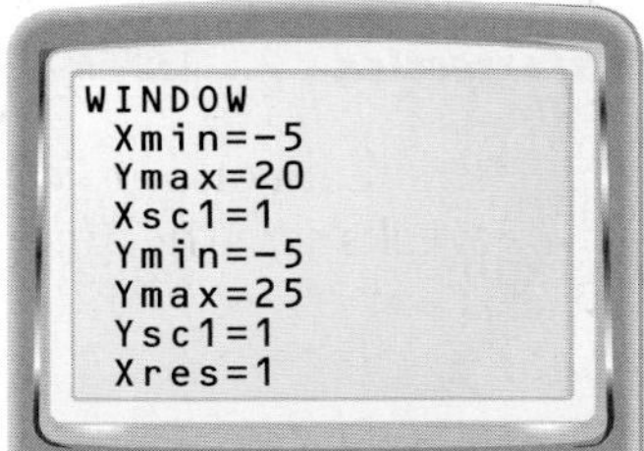

STEP 4 ***Find the point of intersection***

Use the *Intersect* feature on the graphing calculator to find the point of intersection. The graphs intersect at (15, 20).

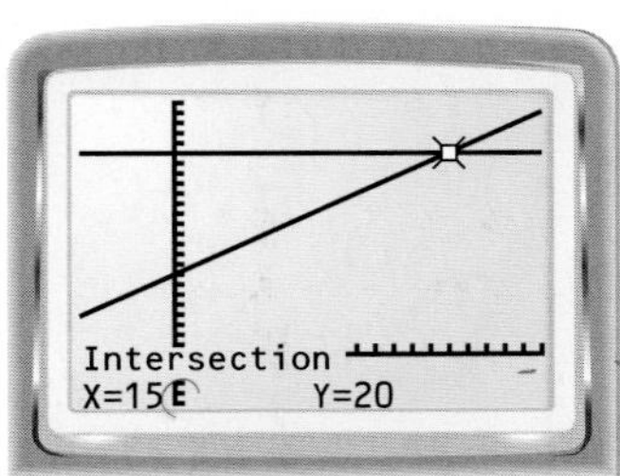

STEP 5 ***Check the solution***

The x-value of the point of intersection, 15, is the solution of the equation. Check by substituting 15 for x in the original equation.

Check:

$$\frac{4}{5}x + 8 \stackrel{?}{=} 20$$

$$\frac{4}{5}(15) + 8 \stackrel{?}{=} 20$$

$$12 + 8 \stackrel{?}{=} 20$$

$$20 = 20 \checkmark$$

You can use this method to find a solution for any type of equation in one variable. You can also use this method to check a solution that you found algebraically.

PRACTICE 1

Solve the equation using a graphing calculator.

1. $6x - 5 = 19$ **2.** $3 = 2x + 5$ **3.** $-3q + 4 = 13$

4. $3 + \frac{8}{7}x = -1$ **5.** $7 - \frac{5}{3}c = 17$ **6.** $\frac{1}{3}x + \frac{2}{5}x = 22$

EXAMPLE 2 Solve a linear equation

Solve the linear equation $2t - 1 = -3t + 9$ using a graphing calculator.

STEP 1 ***Create two equations***

Set each side of the equation equal to y and change t to x.

$$y = 2x - 1 \qquad y = -3x + 9$$

STEP 2 ***Enter equations***

```
Plot1 Plot2 Plot3
\Y1=2X-1
\Y2=-3X+9
\Y3=
\Y4=
\Y5=
\Y6=
\Y7=
```

STEP 3 ***Graph the equations***

```
WINDOW
 Xmin=-10
 Ymax=10
 Xscl=1
 Ymin=-10
 Ymax=10
 Yscl=1
 Xres=1
```

STEP 4 ***Find the point of intersection***

Use the *Intersect* feature on the graphing calculator to find the point of intersection. The graphs intersect at (2, 3).

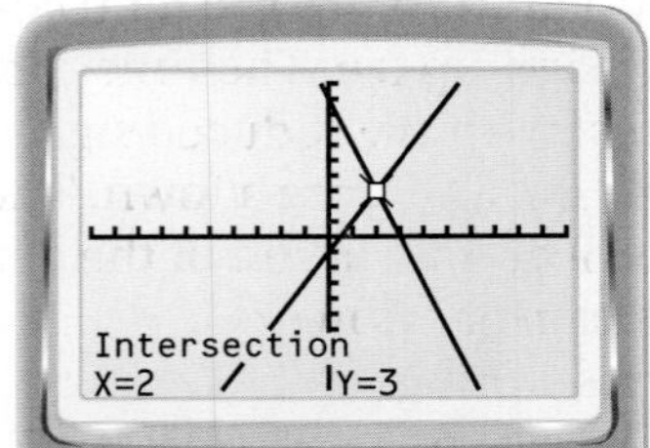

STEP 5 ***Check the solution***

The x-value of the point of intersection, 2, is the solution of the equation.

Check: $2t - 1 \stackrel{?}{=} -3t + 9$

$2(2) - 1 \stackrel{?}{=} -3(2) + 9$

$3 = 3$ ✓

PRACTICE 2

Solve the equation using a graphing calculator.

7. $-5x + 2 = 4x - 7$ **8.** $7x - 4 = 9x - 8$ **9.** $-3x + 1 = -7x - 11$

10. $8x = 12x - 20$ **11.** $2x - 7 = 3x + 11$ **12.** $-x + 4 = x - 2$

13. DRAW CONCLUSIONS Describe the graphs when you solve an equation with a variable on one side by graphing each side of the equation. What is different about the graphs when the original equation has a variable on each side?

MIXED REVIEW of Problem Solving

Make sense of problems and persevere in solving them.

1. **MULTI-STEP PROBLEM** The amount of drink mix d (in tablespoons) that you need to add to w fluid ounces of water is given by $d = \frac{1}{4}w$.
   a. Graph the equation.
   b. Use the graph to find the amount of drink mix you need if you want to make enough drinks to serve 4 people. Assume 1 serving is 8 fluid ounces.

2. **MULTI-STEP PROBLEM** A water park charges \$25 per ticket for adults. Let s be the amount of money the park receives from adult ticket sales, and let t be the number of adult tickets sold.

   a. Write a direct variation equation that relates t and s.
   b. How much money does the park earn when 90 adult tickets are sold?
   c. The park collected \$3325 in adult ticket sales in one day. How many tickets did the park sell?

3. **SHORT RESPONSE** You and your friend are each reading an essay that is 10 pages long. You read at a rate of 1 page per minute. Your friend reads at a rate of $\frac{2}{3}$ page per minute. The models below give the number p of pages you and your friend have left to read after reading for m minutes.

   You: $p = -m + 10$

   Your friend: $p = -\frac{2}{3}m + 10$

   Graph both equations in the same coordinate plane. *Explain* how you can use the graphs to find how many more minutes it took your friend to read the essay than it took you to read the essay.

4. **OPEN-ENDED** Draw a graph that represents going to a movie theater, watching a movie, and returning home from the theater. Let the x-axis represent time and the y-axis represent your distance from home.

5. **EXTENDED RESPONSE** A central observatory averages and then reports the number of sunspots recorded by various observatories. The table shows the average number of sunspots reported by the central observatory in years since 1995.

Years since 1995	Average number of sunspots
0	17.5
2	21.0
4	93.2
6	110.9

   a. Draw a line graph of the data.
   b. During which two-year period was the increase in sunspots the greatest? Find the rate of change for this time period.
   c. During which two-year period was the increase in sunspots the least? Find the rate of change for this time period.
   d. *Explain* how you could find the overall rate of change for the time period shown.

6. **GRIDDED ANSWER** To become a member at a gym, you have to pay a sign-up fee of \$125 and a monthly fee of \$40. To attract new customers, the gym lowers the sign-up fee to \$75. The function f gives the total cost with the regular sign-up fee. The function g gives the total cost with the reduced sign-up fee. The graphs of f and g are shown. The graph of g is a vertical translation of the graph of f by how many units down?

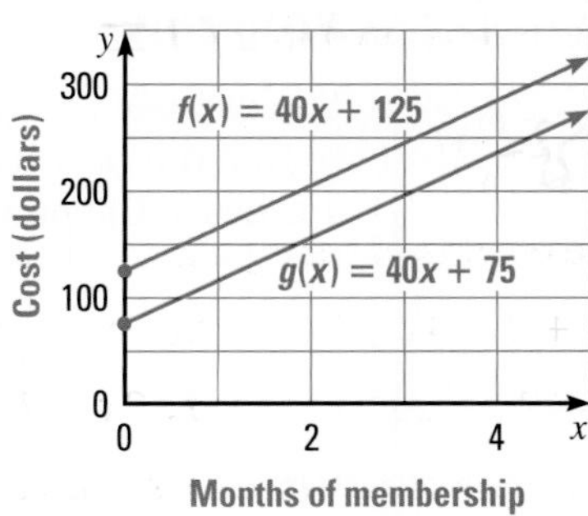

3 CHAPTER SUMMARY

Animated Algebra
my.hrw.com
Electronic Function Library

BIG IDEAS — For Your Notebook

Big Idea 1 Graphing Linear Equations and Functions Using a Variety of Methods

You can graph a linear equation or function by making a table, using intercepts, or using the slope and y-intercept.

A taxi company charges a $2 fee to pick up a customer plus $1 per mile to drive to the customer's destination. The total cost C (in dollars) that a customer pays to travel d miles is given by $C = d + 2$. Graph this function.

Method: Make a table.

d	C
0	2
1	3
2	4
3	5

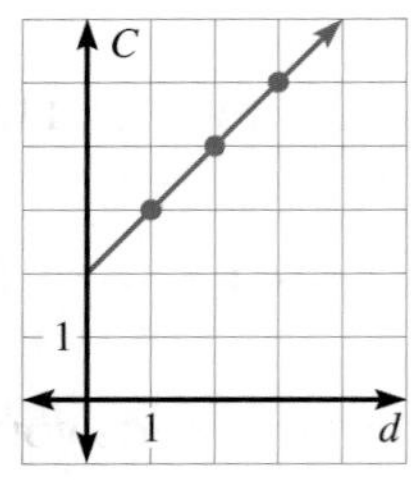

Method: Use slope and C-intercept.

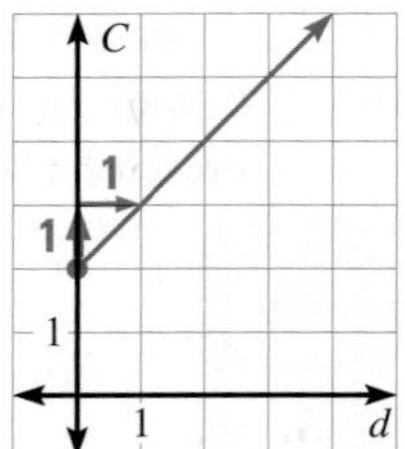

Big Idea 2 Recognizing How Changes in Linear Equations and Functions Affect Their Graphs

When you change the value of m or b in the equation $y = mx + b$, you produce an equation whose graph is related to the graph of the original equation.

Suppose the taxi company raises its rate to $1.50 per mile. The total amount that a customer pays is given by $C = 1.5d + 2$. Graph the function.

You can see that the graphs have the same C-intercept, but different slopes.

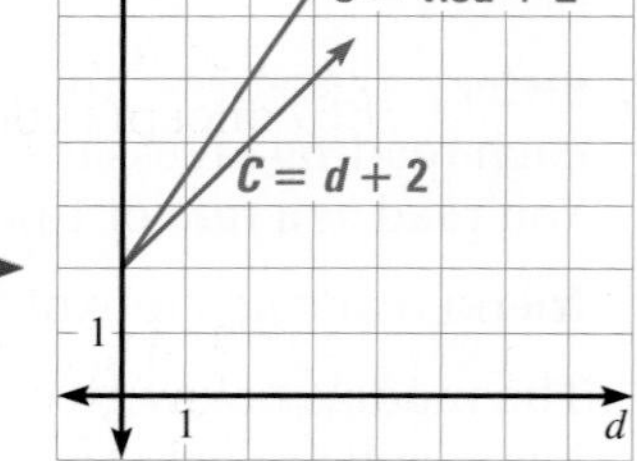

Big Idea 3 Using Graphs of Linear Equations and Functions to Solve Real-world Problems

You can use the graphs of $C = d + 2$ and $C = 1.5d + 2$ to find out how much more a customer pays to travel 4 miles at the new rate than at the old rate.

A customer pays $2 more to travel 4 miles at the new rate.

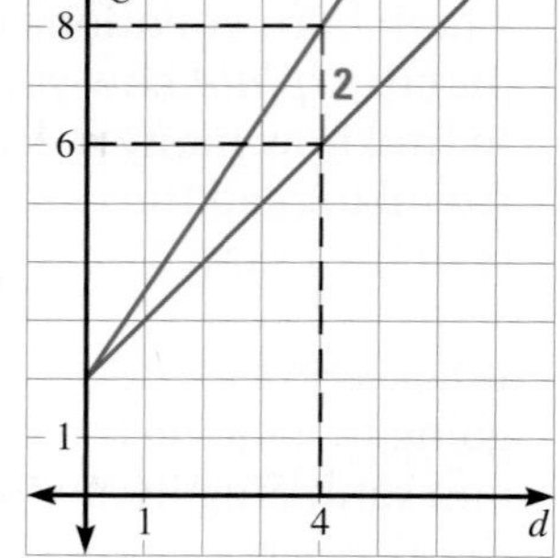

3 CHAPTER REVIEW

@HomeTutor
my.hrw.com
- Multi-Language Glossary
- Vocabulary practice

REVIEW KEY VOCABULARY

- quadrant
- solution of an equation in two variables
- graph of an equation in two variables
- linear equation
- standard form of a linear equation
- linear function
- *x*-intercept
- *y*-intercept
- slope
- rate of change
- slope-intercept form
- parallel
- direct variation
- constant of variation
- function notation
- family of functions
- parent linear function

VOCABULARY EXERCISES

1. Copy and complete: The __?__ of a nonvertical line is the ratio of vertical change to horizontal change.

2. Copy and complete: When you write $y = 2x + 3$ as $f(x) = 2x + 3$, you use __?__.

3. **WRITING** *Describe* three different methods you could use to graph the equation $5x + 3y = 12$.

4. Tell whether the equation is written in slope-intercept form. If the equation is not in slope-intercept form, write it in slope-intercept form.

   a. $3x + y = 6$ **b.** $y = 5x + 2$ **c.** $x = 4y - 1$ **d.** $y = -x + 6$

REVIEW EXAMPLES AND EXERCISES

Use the review examples and exercises below to check your understanding of the concepts you have learned in each lesson of this chapter.

3.1 Plot Points in a Coordinate Plane

EXAMPLE

Plot the points $A(-2, 3)$ and $B(0, -2)$ in a coordinate plane. Describe the location of the points.

Point $A(-2, 3)$: Begin at the origin and move 2 units to the left, then 3 units up. Point A is in Quadrant II.

Point $B(0, -2)$: Begin at the origin and move 2 units down. Point B is on the y-axis.

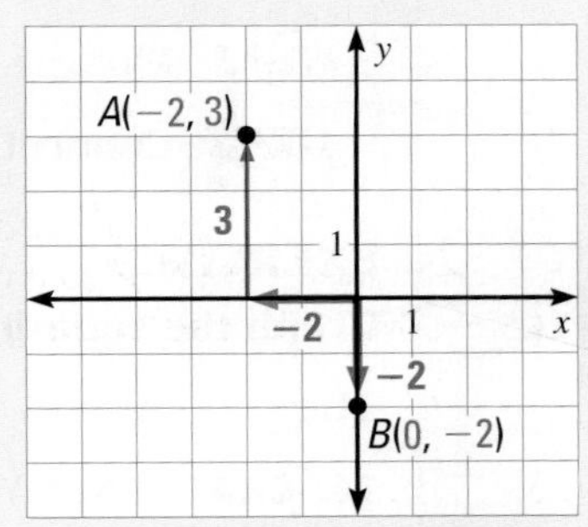

EXERCISES

EXAMPLE 2 for Exs. 5–7

Plot the point in a coordinate plane. *Describe* the location of the point.

5. $A(3, 4)$ 6. $B(-5, 0)$ 7. $C(-7, -2)$

3 CHAPTER REVIEW

3.2 Graph Linear Equations

EXAMPLE

Graph the equation $y + 3x = 1$.

STEP 1 **Solve** the equation for y.

$$y + 3x = 1$$
$$y = -3x + 1$$

STEP 2 **Make** a table by choosing a few values for x and finding the values for y.

x	−1	0	1
y	4	1	−2

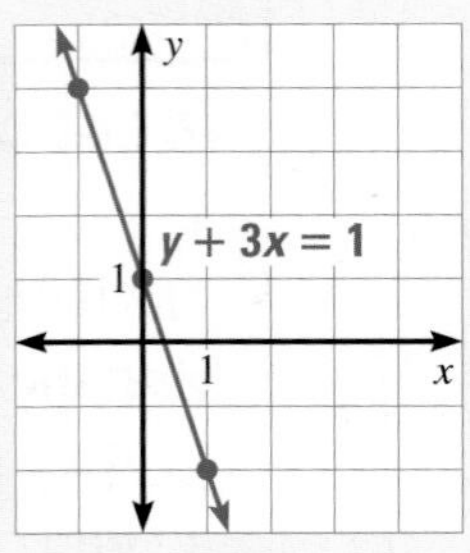

STEP 3 **Plot** the points.

STEP 4 **Connect** the points by drawing a line through them.

EXERCISES

EXAMPLE 2 for Exs. 8–10

Graph the equation.

8. $y + 5x = -5$ **9.** $2x + 3y = 9$ **10.** $2y - 14 = 4$

3.3 Graph Using Intercepts

EXAMPLE

Graph the equation $-0.5x + 2y = 4$.

STEP 1 **Find** the intercepts.

$$-0.5x + 2y = 4 \qquad -0.5x + 2y = 4$$
$$-0.5x + 2(0) = 4 \qquad -0.5(0) + 2y = 4$$
$$x = -8 \leftarrow \textbf{x-intercept} \qquad y = 2 \leftarrow \textbf{y-intercept}$$

STEP 2 **Plot** the points that correspond to the intercepts: (−8, 0) and (0, 2).

STEP 3 **Connect** the points by drawing a line through them.

EXERCISES

EXAMPLES 2 and 4 for Exs. 11–14

Graph the equation.

11. $-x + 5y = 15$ **12.** $4x + 4y = -16$ **13.** $2x - 6y = 18$

14. CRAFT FAIR You sell necklaces for \$10 and bracelets for \$5 at a craft fair. You want to earn \$50. This situation is modeled by the equation $10n + 5b = 50$ where n is the number of necklaces you sell and b is the number of bracelets you sell. Find the intercepts of the graph of the equation. Then graph the equation. Give three possibilities for the number of bracelets and necklaces that you could sell.

@HomeTutor
my.hrw.com
Chapter Review Practice

3.4 Find Slope and Rate of Change

EXAMPLE

Find the slope of the line shown.

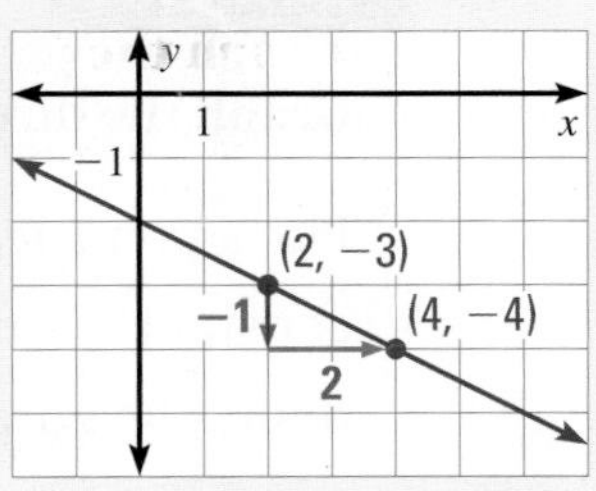

Let $(x_1, y_1) = (2, -3)$ and $(x_2, y_2) = (4, -4)$.

$m = \frac{y_2 - y_1}{x_2 - x_1}$ **Write formula for slope.**

$= \frac{-4 - (-3)}{4 - 2}$ **Substitute values.**

$= -\frac{1}{2}$ **Simplify.**

EXAMPLES 1,2,3, and 4 for Exs. 15–17

EXERCISES

Find the slope of the line that passes through the points.

15. (−1, 11) and (2, 10) **16.** (−2, 0) and (4, 9) **17.** (−5, 4) and (1, −8)

3.5 Graph Using Slope-Intercept Form

EXAMPLE

Graph the equation $2x + y = -1$.

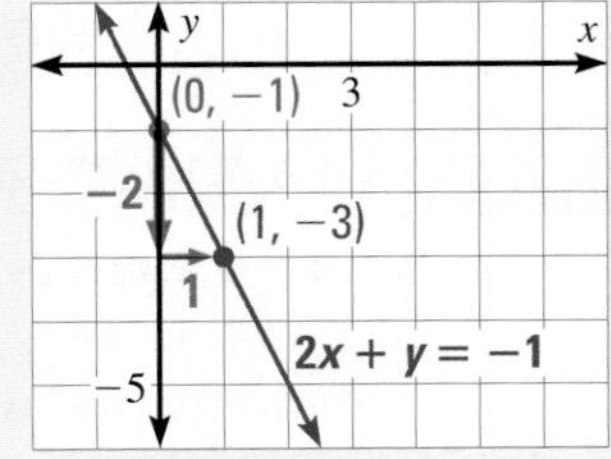

STEP 1 **Rewrite** the equation in slope-intercept form.

$2x + y = -1 \rightarrow y = -2x - 1$

STEP 2 **Identify** the slope and the *y*-intercept.

$m = -2$ and $b = -1$

STEP 3 **Plot** the point that corresponds to the *y*-intercept, (0, −1).

STEP 4 **Use** the slope to locate a second point on the line. Draw a line through the two points.

EXAMPLES 2 and 3 for Exs. 18–21

EXERCISES

Graph the equation.

18. $4x - y = 3$ **19.** $3x - 6y = 9$ **20.** $-3x + 4y - 12 = 0$

21. RUNNING One athlete can run a 60 meter race at an average rate of 7 meters per second. A second athlete can run the race at an average rate of 6 meters per second. The distance *d* (in meters) the athletes have left to run after *t* seconds is given by the following equations:

Athlete 1: $d = -7t + 60$ **Athlete 2**: $d = -6t + 60$

Graph both models in the same coordinate plane. About how many seconds faster does the first athlete finish the race than the second athlete?

3 CHAPTER REVIEW

3.6 Model Direct Variation

EXAMPLE

Graph the direct variation equation $y = -\frac{2}{3}x$.

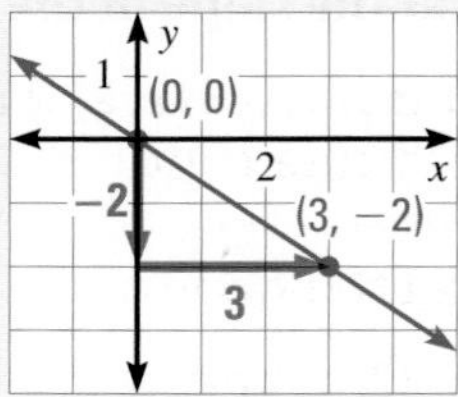

Plot a point at the origin. The slope is equal to the constant of variation, $-\frac{2}{3}$. Find and plot a second point, then draw a line through the points.

EXERCISES

EXAMPLES 1, 2, and 4 for Exs. 22–28

Tell whether the equation represents direct variation. If so, identify the constant of variation.

22. $x - y = 3$ **23.** $x + 2y = 0$ **24.** $8x - 2y = 0$

Graph the direct variation equation.

25. $y = 4x$ **26.** $-5y = 3x$ **27.** $4x + 3y = 0$

28. SNOWSTORMS The amount s (in inches) of snow that fell during a snowstorm varied directly with the duration d (in hours) of the storm. In the first 2 hours of the storm 5 inches of snow fell. Write a direct variation equation that relates d and s. How many inches of snow fell in 6 hours?

3.7 Graph Linear Functions

EXAMPLE

Evaluate the function $f(x) = -6x + 5$ when $x = 3$.

$f(x) = -6x + 5$ **Write function.**

$f(3) = -6(3) + 5$ **Substitute 3 for *x*.**

$= -13$ **Simplify.**

EXERCISES

EXAMPLES 1 and 3 for Exs. 29–34

Evaluate the function.

29. $g(x) = 2x - 3$ when $x = 7$ **30.** $h(x) = -\frac{1}{2}x - 7$ when $x = -6$

Graph the function. Compare the graph with the graph of $f(x) = x$.

31. $j(x) = x - 6$ **32.** $k(x) = -2.5x$ **33.** $t(x) = 2x + 1$

34. MOUNT EVEREST Mount Everest is rising at a rate of 2.4 inches per year. The number of inches that Mount Everest rises in x years is given by the function $f(x) = 2.4x$. Graph the function and identify its domain and range. Find the value of x so that $f(x) = 250$. *Explain* what the solution means in this situation.

3 CHAPTER TEST

Plot the point in a coordinate plane. *Describe* the location of the point.

1. $A(7, 1)$ **2.** $B(-4, 0)$ **3.** $C(3, -9)$

Draw the line that has the given intercepts.

4. x-intercept: 2
y-intercept: -6

5. x-intercept: -1
y-intercept: 8

6. x-intercept: -3
y-intercept: -5

Find the slope of the line that passes through the points.

7. (2, 1) and (8, 4) **8.** $(-2, 7)$ and $(0, -1)$ **9.** (3, 5) and (3, 14)

Identify the slope and y-intercept of the line with the given equation.

10. $y = -\frac{3}{2}x - 10$ **11.** $7x + 2y = -28$ **12.** $3x - 8y = 48$

Tell whether the equation represents direct variation. If so, identify the constant of variation.

13. $x + 4y = 4$ **14.** $-\frac{1}{3}x - y = 0$ **15.** $3x - 3y = 0$

Graph the equation.

16. $x = 3$ **17.** $y + x = 6$ **18.** $2x + 8y = -32$

Evaluate the function for the given value.

19. $f(x) = -4x$ when $x = 2.5$ **20.** $g(x) = \frac{5}{2}x - 6$ when $x = -2$

21. BUSINESS To start a dog washing business, you invest $300 in supplies. You charge $10 per hour for your services. Your profit P (in dollars) for working t hours is given by $P = 10t - 300$. Graph the equation. You will break even when your profit is $0. Use the graph to find the number of hours you must work in order to break even.

22. PEDIATRICS The dose d (in milligrams) of a particular medicine that a pediatrician prescribes for a patient varies directly with the patient's mass m (in kilograms). The pediatrician recommends a dose of 150 mg of medicine for a patient whose mass is 30 kg.

a. Write a direct variation equation that relates m and d.

b. What would the dose of medicine be for a patient whose mass is 50 kg?

23. SCISSOR LIFT The scissor lift is a device that can lower and raise a platform. The maximum and minimum heights of the platform of a particular scissor lift are shown. The scissor lift can raise the platform at a rate of 3.5 inches per second. The height of the platform after t seconds is given by $h(t) = 3.5t + 48$. Graph the function and identify its domain and range.

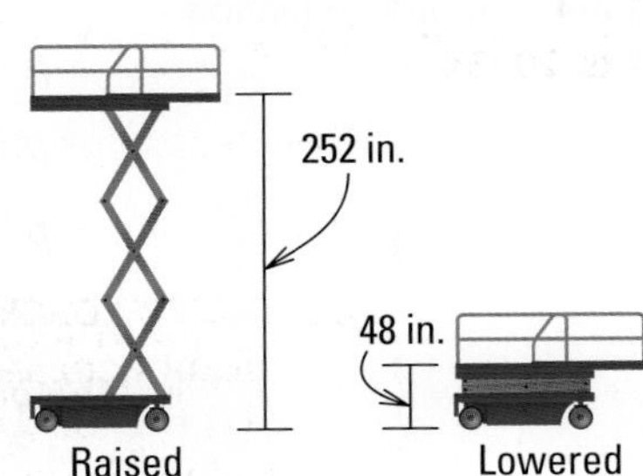

CONTEXT-BASED MULTIPLE CHOICE QUESTIONS

Some of the information you need to solve a context-based multiple choice question may appear in a table, a diagram, or a graph.

PROBLEM 1

A recipe from a box of pancake mix is shown. The number p of pancakes you can make varies directly with the number m of cups of mix you use. A full box of pancake mix contains 9 cups of mix. How many pancakes can you make when you use the full box?

Ⓐ 63 Ⓑ 65

Ⓒ 126 Ⓓ 131

2 cups pancake mix
1 cup milk
2 eggs
Combine ingredients. Pour batter on hot greased griddle. Flip when edges are dry. Makes 14 pancakes.

Plan

INTERPRET THE INFORMATION Use the number of pancakes and the number of cups of mix given in the recipe to write a direct variation equation. Then use the equation to find the number of pancakes that you can make when you use 9 cups of mix.

Solution

STEP 1
Use the values given in the recipe to find a direct variation equation.

Because the number p of pancakes you can make varies directly with the number m of cups of mix you use, you can write the equation $p = am$. From the recipe, you know that $p = 14$ when $m = 2$.

$p = am$ **Write direct variation equation.**

$\mathbf{14} = a(\mathbf{2})$ **Substitute.**

$7 = a$ **Solve for *a*.**

So, a direct variation equation that relates p and m is $p = 7m$.

STEP 2
Substitute 9 for m in the direct variation equation and solve for p.

Use the direct variation equation to find the number of pancakes you can make when you use a full box of mix.

$p = 7\mathbf{m}$ **Write direct variation equation.**

$p = 7(\mathbf{9})$ **Substitute 9 for *m*.**

$p = 63$ **Simplify.**

You can make 63 pancakes when you use a full box of mix.

The correct answer is A. Ⓐ Ⓑ Ⓒ Ⓓ

PROBLEM 2

At a yard sale, Jack made $54 selling cassettes for $1 each and CDs for $3 each. This situation is modeled by the equation $x + 3y = 54$ where x is the number of cassettes and y is the number of CDs that Jack sold. The graph of the equation is shown. Which is a possible combination of cassettes and CDs that Jack sold?

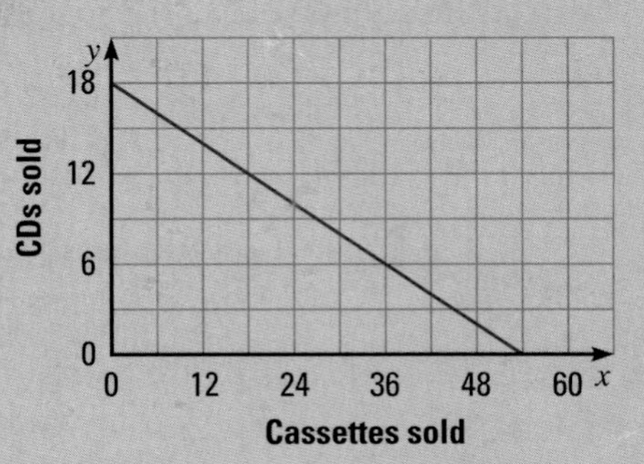

Ⓐ 12 cassettes, 4 CDs Ⓑ 4 cassettes, 12 CDs

Ⓒ 18 cassettes, 12 CDs Ⓓ 28.5 cassettes, 8.5 CDs

Plan

INTERPRET THE INFORMATION Each point on the line represents a solution of the equation. Identify the answer choice that describes a point on the graph shown and that makes sense in the context of the problem.

Solution

STEP 1 Write an ordered pair for each answer choice.

The answer choices correspond to the following ordered pairs.

Ⓐ (12, 4) Ⓑ (4, 12) Ⓒ (18, 12) Ⓓ (28.5, 8.5)

STEP 2 Eliminate points not on the line and points that don't make sense. Check ordered pairs not eliminated to find the solution.

You can eliminate answer choices A and B because the points do not lie on the graph shown. You can also eliminate answer choice D because only whole number solutions make sense in this situation. Check that (18, 12) is a solution of the equation.

$x + 3y = 54$ **Write original equation.**

$\mathbf{18} + 3(\mathbf{12}) = 54$ **Substitute.**

$54 = 54$ ✓ **Solution checks.**

The correct answer is C. Ⓐ Ⓑ Ⓒ Ⓓ

PRACTICE

1. In Problem 2, what is the greatest number of CDs Jack could have sold?

   Ⓐ 3 Ⓑ 18 Ⓒ 36 Ⓓ 54

2. The table shows the total cost for a certain number of people to ice skate at a particular rink. What is the cost per person?

   Ⓐ $.20 Ⓑ $1

   Ⓒ $5 Ⓓ $10

Number of people	Cost (dollars)
2	10
4	20
6	30

3 ★ Standardized TEST PRACTICE

MULTIPLE CHOICE

In Exercises 1 and 2, use the graph below.

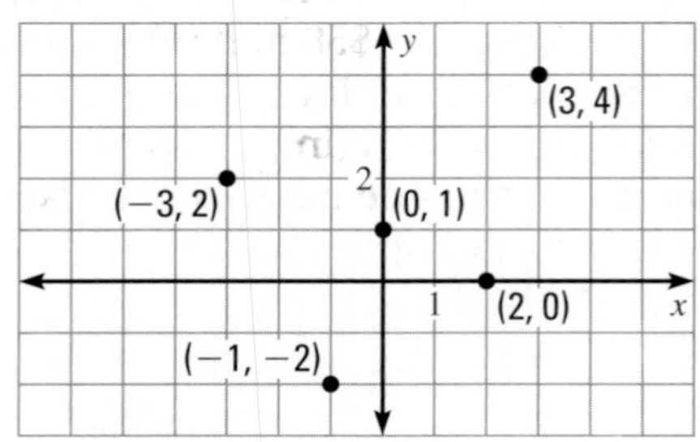

1. The graph represents a function. Which number is in the domain of the function?

   (A) −2 (B) −1

   (C) 1 (D) 4

2. The graph would no longer represent a function if which point were included?

   (A) (−4, −2) (B) (−2, 0)

   (C) (1, 3) (D) (3, −1)

In Exercises 3 and 4, use the graph below, which shows a traveler's movements through an airport to a terminal. The traveler has to walk and take a shuttle bus to get to the terminal.

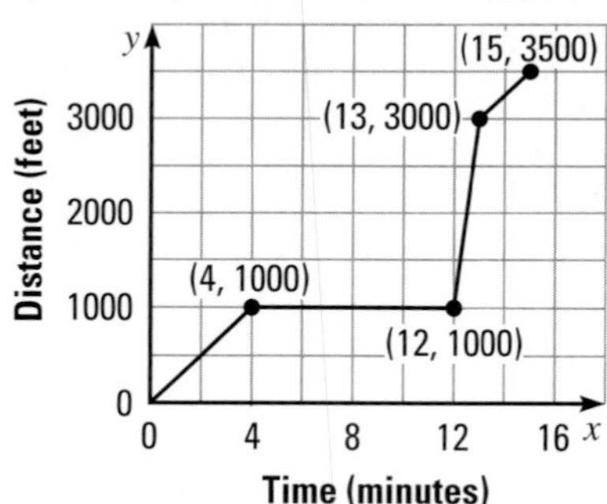

3. For how many minutes does the traveler wait for the shuttle bus?

   (A) 1 min (B) 2 min

   (C) 4 min (D) 8 min

4. For about what distance does the traveler ride on the shuttle bus?

   (A) 100 ft (B) 1000 ft

   (C) 2000 ft (D) 3000 ft

In Exercises 5–7, use the following information.

At a yoga studio, new members pay a sign-up fee of \$50 plus a monthly fee of \$25. The total cost C (in dollars) of a new membership is given by $C = 25m + 50$ where m is the number of months of membership. The owner of the studio is considering changing the cost of a new membership. A graph of four different options for changing the cost is shown.

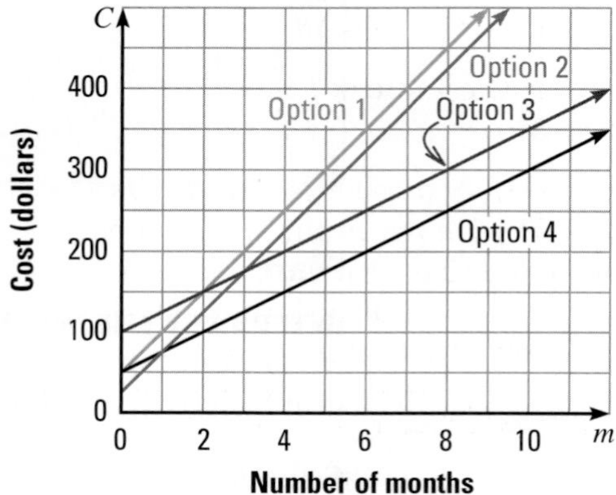

5. For which option are the sign-up fee and monthly fee kept the same?

   (A) Option 1 (B) Option 2

   (C) Option 3 (D) Option 4

6. For which option is the sign-up fee kept the same and the monthly fee raised?

   (A) Option 1 (B) Option 2

   (C) Option 3 (D) Option 4

7. For which option is the monthly fee kept the same and the sign-up fee raised?

   (A) Option 1 (B) Option 2

   (C) Option 3 (D) Option 4

8. The table shows the cost of a therapeutic massage for a given amount of time. What is the cost per minute?

Time (minutes)	30	45	60
Cost (dollars)	42.00	63.00	84.00

   (A) \$.71 (B) \$1.40

   (C) \$2.80 (D) \$14.00

GRIDDED ANSWER

9. What is the slope of the line shown?

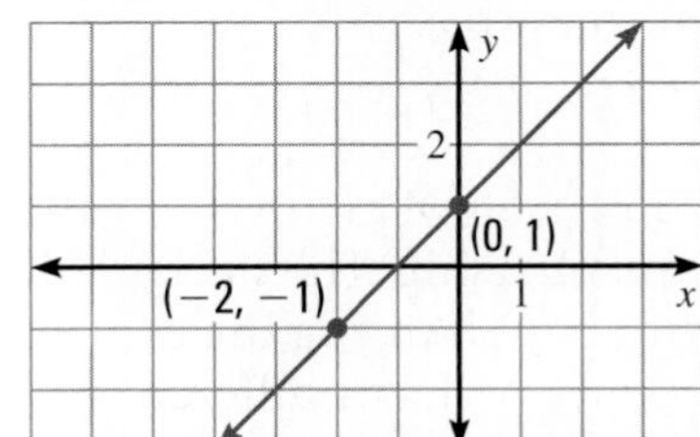

10. What is the y-intercept of the graph of the equation $4x + 8y = 16$?

11. What is the value of $f(x) = -1.8x - 9$ when $x = -5$?

12. The number w of cups of water varies directly with the number u of cups of uncooked rice. Use the table to find the value of the constant of variation a in the direct variation equation $w = au$.

Uncooked rice, *u* (cups)	$\frac{1}{2}$	1	$1\frac{1}{2}$
Water, *w* (cups)	$\frac{3}{4}$	$1\frac{1}{2}$	$2\frac{1}{4}$

SHORT RESPONSE

13. Patricia takes a bus to and from her job. She can either pay \$1.75 each way or get a monthly bus pass for \$58 and ride the bus an unlimited number of times. The functions below give the costs C (in dollars) of riding the bus n times in one month. The graphs of the functions are shown.

Monthly pass: $C = 58$

Pay per ride: $C = 1.75n$

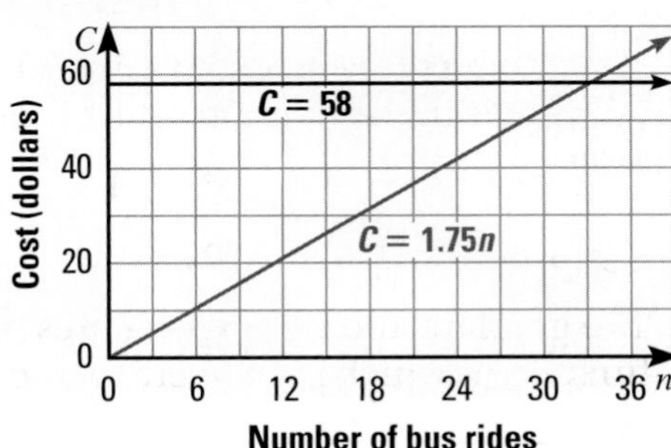

How many days in a month would Patricia need to take the bus to and from work to make buying a monthly pass worth the cost? *Explain.*

EXTENDED RESPONSE

14. A fog machine has a tank that holds 32 fluid ounces of fog fluid and has two settings: low and high. The low setting uses 0.2 fluid ounce of fluid per minute, and the high setting uses 0.25 fluid ounce per minute. The functions below give the amount f (in fluid ounces) of fluid left in the tank after t minutes when the machine starts with a full tank of fluid.

Low setting: $f = -0.2t + 32$ **High setting:** $f = -0.25t + 32$

a. Identify the slope and y-intercept of each function.

b. Graph each function in the same coordinate plane.

c. How much longer can the machine be run on the low setting than on the high setting? *Explain* how you found your answer.

15. At a pizzeria, a cheese pizza costs \$9. Toppings cost \$1.50 each.

a. The cost of a pizza is given by the function $f(x) = 1.5x + 9$ where x is the number of toppings. Graph the function.

b. You have \$14 and buy only a pizza. How many toppings can you get?

c. The pizzeria's owner decides to change the price of toppings to \$2 each. The new cost of a pizza is given by the function $g(x) = 2x + 9$. Graph the function in the same coordinate plane you used in part (a).

d. Can you get the same number of toppings at the new price as you did in part (b)? *Explain.*

4 Writing Linear Equations

Lesson
4.1 CC.9-12.A.CED.2*
4.2 CC.9-12.A.CED.2*
4.3 CC.9-12.A.CED.2*
4.4 CC.9-12.A.CED.2*
4.5 CC.9-12.F.LE.2*
4.6 CC.9-12.S.ID.6c*
4.7 CC.9-12.S.ID.6a*

Before

Previously, you learned the following skills, which you'll use in this chapter: evaluating functions and finding the slopes and *y*-intercepts of lines.

Prerequisite Skills

VOCABULARY CHECK

Copy and complete the statement.

1. For the graph of the equation $y = mx + b$, the value of m is the __?__ .
2. For the graph of the equation $y = mx + b$, the value of b is the __?__ .
3. Two lines are __?__ if their slopes are equal.

SKILLS CHECK

Identify the slope and the *y*-intercept of the line with the equation.

4. $y = x + 1$
5. $y = \frac{3}{4}x - 6$
6. $y = -\frac{2}{5}x - 2$

Tell whether the graphs of the two equations are parallel lines.

7. $y = 3x + 5$
   $y = 3x - 2$
8. $y = \frac{1}{4}x - 1$
   $y = 4x + 3$
9. $y = \frac{1}{2}x + 4$
   $y = \frac{1}{2}x - 4$

Evaluate the function when $x = -2, 0,$ and 4.

10. $f(x) = x - 10$
11. $f(x) = 2x + 4$
12. $f(x) = -5x - 7$

Now

In this chapter, you will apply the big ideas listed below and reviewed in the Chapter Summary. You will also use the key vocabulary listed below.

Big Ideas

1. **Writing linear equations in a variety of forms**
2. **Using linear models to solve problems**
3. **Modeling data with a line of fit**

KEY VOCABULARY

- point-slope form
- converse
- perpendicular
- scatter plot
- correlation
- line of fit
- best-fitting line
- linear regression
- interpolation
- extrapolation
- zero of a function

Why?

You can use linear equations to solve problems involving a constant rate of change. For example, you can write an equation that models how traffic delays affected excess fuel consumption over time.

Animated Algebra

The animation illustrated below helps you to answer a question from this chapter: In what year was a certain amount of excess fuel consumed?

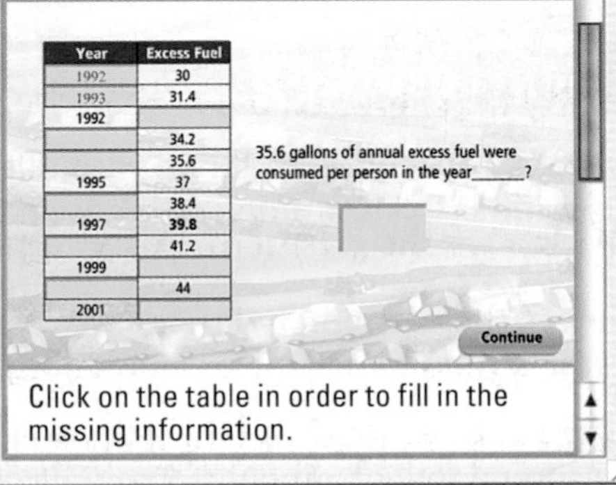

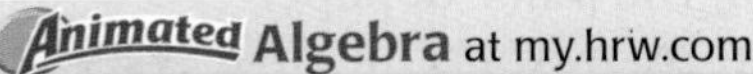

Modeling Linear Relationships

Reason abstractly and quantitatively.

MATERIALS • 8.5 inch by 11 inch piece of paper • inch ruler

QUESTION How can you model a linear relationship?

You know that the perimeter of a rectangle is given by the formula $P = 2\ell + 2w$. In this activity, you will find a linear relationship using that formula.

EXPLORE Find perimeters of rectangles

STEP 1 ***Find perimeter***

Find the perimeter of a piece of paper that is 8.5 inches wide and 11 inches long. Record the result in a table like the one shown.

Width of fold (inches)	Perimeter of rectangle (inches)
0	39
1	?
2	?
3	?
4	?

STEP 2 ***Change paper size***

Measure 1 inch from a short edge of the paper. Fold over 1 inch of the paper. You now have a rectangle with the same width and a different length than the original piece of paper. Find the perimeter of this new rectangle and record it in your table.

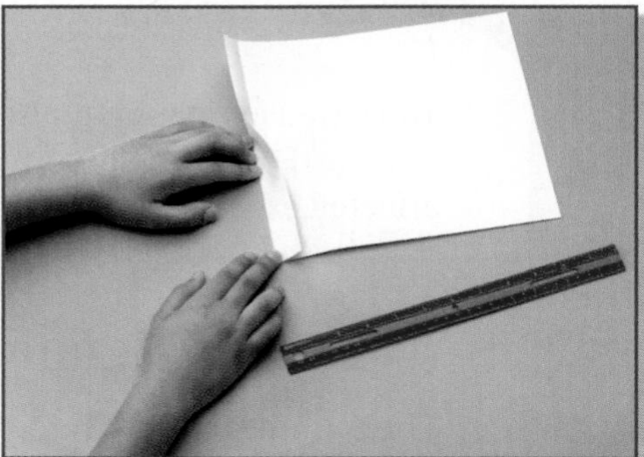

STEP 3 ***Find additional perimeters***

Unfold the paper and repeat Step 2, this time folding the paper 2 inches from a short edge. Find the perimeter of this rectangle and record the result in your table. Repeat with a fold of 3 inches and a fold of 4 inches.

DRAW CONCLUSIONS Use your observations to complete these exercises

1. What were the length and the width of the piece of paper before it was folded? By how much did these dimensions change with each fold?
2. What was the perimeter of the piece of paper before it was folded? By how much did the perimeter change with each fold?
3. Use the values from your table to predict the perimeter of the piece of paper after a fold of 5 inches. *Explain* your reasoning.
4. Write a rule you could use to find the perimeter of the piece of paper after a fold of n inches. Use the data in the table to show that this rule gives accurate results.

4.1 Write Linear Equations in Slope-Intercept Form

Before You graphed equations of lines.

Now You will write equations of lines.

Why? So you can model distances in sports, as in Ex. 52.

Key Vocabulary
- *y*-intercept
- slope
- slope-intercept form

Recall that the graph of an equation in slope-intercept form, $y = mx + b$, is a line with a slope of m and a y-intercept of b. You can use this form to write an equation of a line if you know its slope and y-intercept.

EXAMPLE 1 Use slope and *y*-intercept to write an equation

Write an equation of the line with a slope of −2 and a *y*-intercept of 5.

$y = mx + b$ **Write slope-intercept form.**

$y = -2x + 5$ **Substitute −2 for *m* and 5 for *b*.**

EXAMPLE 2 Standardized Test Practice

Which equation represents the line shown?

Ⓐ $y = -\frac{2}{5}x + 3$ Ⓑ $y = -\frac{5}{2}x + 3$

Ⓒ $y = -\frac{2}{5}x + 1$ Ⓓ $y = 3x + \frac{2}{5}$

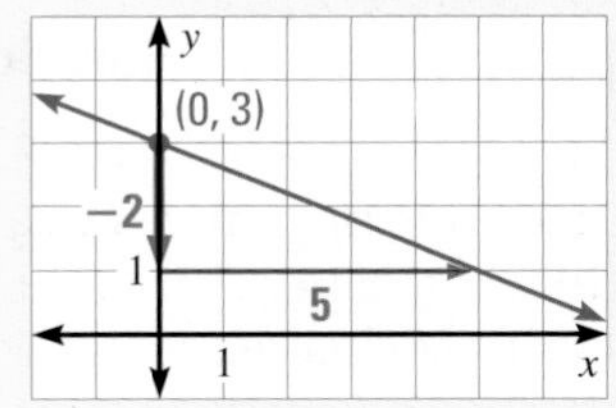

ELIMINATE CHOICES
In Example 2, you can eliminate choices C and D because the *y*-intercepts of the graphs of these equations are not 3.

The slope of the line is $\frac{\text{rise}}{\text{run}} = \frac{-2}{5} = -\frac{2}{5}$.

The line crosses the y-axis at (0, 3). So, the y-intercept is 3.

$y = mx + b$ **Write slope-intercept form.**

$y = -\frac{2}{5}x + 3$ **Substitute $-\frac{2}{5}$ for *m* and 3 for *b*.**

▶ The correct answer is A. Ⓐ Ⓑ Ⓒ Ⓓ

CC.9-12.A.CED.2 Create equations in two or more variables to represent relationships between quantities; graph equations on coordinate axes with labels and scales.*

Animated Algebra at my.hrw.com

GUIDED PRACTICE for Examples 1 and 2

Write an equation of the line with the given slope and *y*-intercept.

1. Slope is 8; y-intercept is −7.
2. Slope is $\frac{3}{4}$; y-intercept is −3.

USING TWO POINTS If you know the point where a line crosses the y-axis and any other point on the line, you can write an equation of the line.

EXAMPLE 3 Write an equation of a line given two points

Write an equation of the line shown.

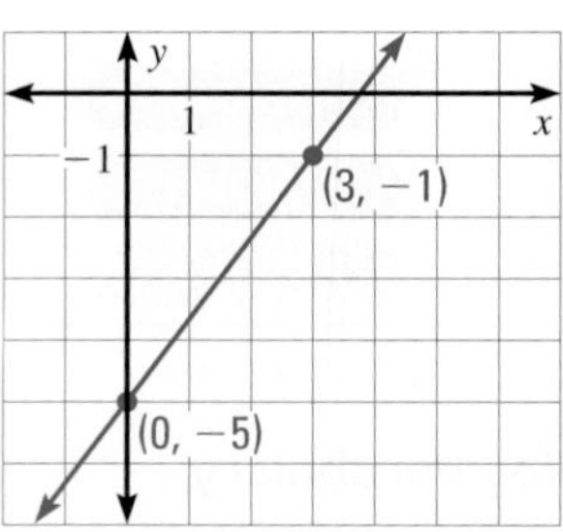

Solution

STEP 1 **Calculate** the slope.

$$m = \frac{y_2 - y_1}{x_2 - x_1} = \frac{-1 - (-5)}{3 - 0} = \frac{4}{3}$$

STEP 2 **Write** an equation of the line. The line crosses the y-axis at $(0, -5)$. So, the y-intercept is -5.

$y = mx + b$ **Write slope-intercept form.**

$y = \frac{4}{3}x - 5$ **Substitute $\frac{4}{3}$ for m and -5 for b.**

WRITING FUNCTIONS Recall that the graphs of linear functions are lines. You can use slope-intercept form to write a linear function.

EXAMPLE 4 Write a linear function

REVIEW FUNCTIONS
You may want to review function notation before writing an equation for a function.

Write an equation for the linear function f with the values $f(0) = 5$ and $f(4) = 17$.

Solution

STEP 1 **Write** $f(0) = 5$ as $(0, 5)$ and $f(4) = 17$ as $(4, 17)$.

STEP 2 **Calculate** the slope of the line that passes through $(0, 5)$ and $(4, 17)$.

$$m = \frac{y_2 - y_1}{x_2 - x_1} = \frac{17 - 5}{4 - 0} = \frac{12}{4} = 3$$

STEP 3 **Write** an equation of the line. The line crosses the y-axis at $(0, 5)$. So, the y-intercept is 5.

$y = mx + b$ **Write slope-intercept form.**

$y = 3x + 5$ **Substitute 3 for m and 5 for b.**

▶ The function is $f(x) = 3x + 5$.

✓ GUIDED PRACTICE for Examples 3 and 4

3. Write an equation of the line shown.

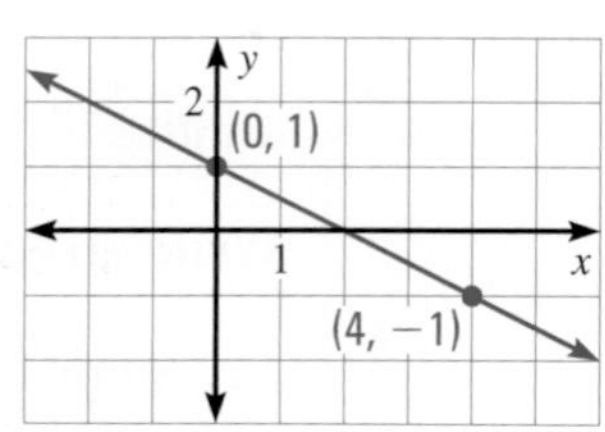

Write an equation for the linear function f with the given values.

4. $f(0) = -2, f(8) = 4$
5. $f(-3) = 6, f(0) = 5$

READING
The value b is a starting value in a real-world situation modeled by $y = mx + b$, because when $x = 0$, the value of y is b.

MODELING REAL-WORLD SITUATIONS When a quantity y changes at a constant rate with respect to a quantity x, you can use the equation $y = mx + b$ to model the relationship. The value of m is the constant rate of change, and the value of b is an initial, or starting, value for y.

EXAMPLE 5 Solve a multi-step problem

RECORDING STUDIO A recording studio charges musicians an initial fee of $50 to record an album. Studio time costs an additional $35 per hour.

a. Write an equation that gives the total cost of an album as a function of studio time (in hours).

b. Find the total cost of recording an album that takes 10 hours of studio time.

Solution

a. The cost changes at a constant rate, so you can write an equation in slope-intercept form to model the total cost.

STEP 1 **Identify** the rate of change and the starting value.

Rate of change, *m*: cost per hour
Starting value, *b*: initial fee

STEP 2 **Write** a verbal model. Then write the equation.

Total cost (dollars)	=	Cost per hour (dollars per hour)	•	Studio time (hours)	+	Initial fee (dollars)
C	=	35	•	t	+	50

CHECK Use unit analysis to check the equation.

$$\text{dollars} = \frac{\text{dollars}}{\cancel{\text{hour}}} \cdot \cancel{\text{hours}} + \text{dollars} \checkmark$$

▶ The total cost C is given by the function $C = 35t + 50$ where t is the studio time (in hours).

b. Evaluate the function for $t = 10$.

$C = 35(10) + 50 = 400$ **Substitute 10 for *t* and simplify.**

▶ The total cost for 10 hours of studio time is $400.

✓ GUIDED PRACTICE for Example 5

6. WHAT IF? In Example 5, suppose the recording studio raises its initial fee to $75 and charges $40 per hour for studio time.

a. Write an equation that gives the total cost of an album as a function of studio time (in hours).

b. Find the total cost of recording an album that takes 10 hours of studio time.

4.1 EXERCISES

HOMEWORK KEY

◯ = **See WORKED-OUT SOLUTIONS** Exs. 11, 19, and 47

★ = **STANDARDIZED TEST PRACTICE** Exs. 2, 9, 40, 43, 48, and 50

◆ = **MULTIPLE REPRESENTATIONS** Ex. 49

SKILL PRACTICE

1. **VOCABULARY** Copy and complete: The ratio of the rise to the run between any two points on a nonvertical line is called the _?_.

2. ★ **WRITING** *Explain* how you can use slope-intercept form to write an equation of a line given its slope and y-intercept.

EXAMPLE 1 for Exs. 3–9, 16

WRITING EQUATIONS **Write an equation of the line with the given slope and y-intercept.**

3. slope: 2, y-intercept: 9
4. slope: 1, y-intercept: 5
5. slope: -3, y-intercept: 0
6. slope: -7, y-intercept: 1
7. slope: $\frac{2}{3}$, y-intercept: -9
8. slope: $\frac{3}{4}$, y-intercept: -6

9. ★ **MULTIPLE CHOICE** Which equation represents the line with a slope of -1 and a y-intercept of 2?

Ⓐ $y = -x + 2$ Ⓑ $y = 2x - 1$ Ⓒ $y = x - 2$ Ⓓ $y = 2x + 1$

EXAMPLE 2 for Exs. 10–15

WRITING EQUATIONS **Write an equation of the line shown.**

10. 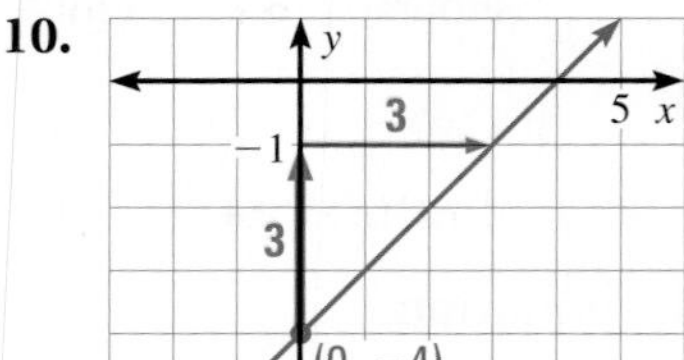

11. 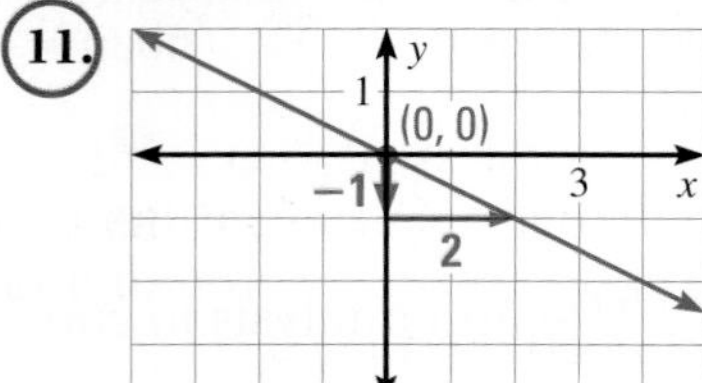

12. 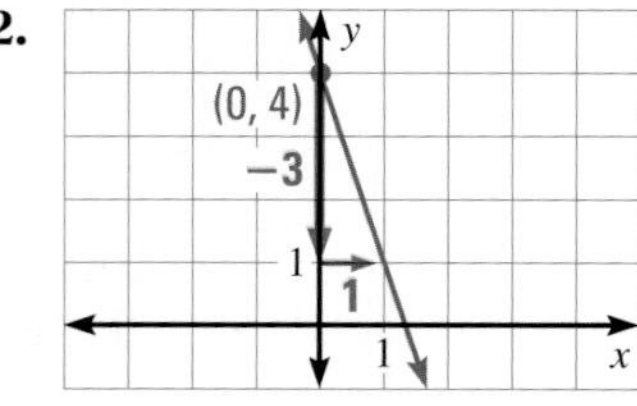

13. 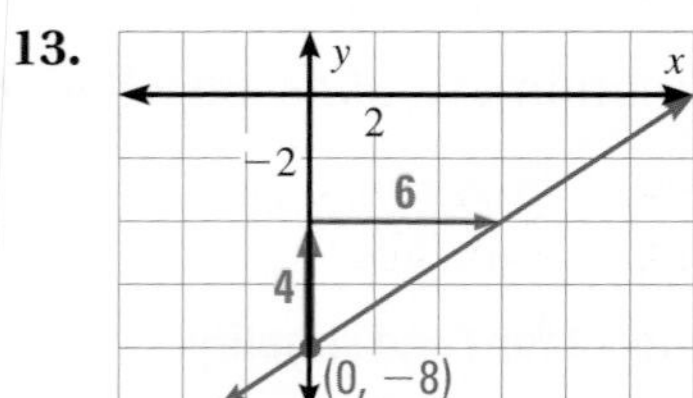

14. 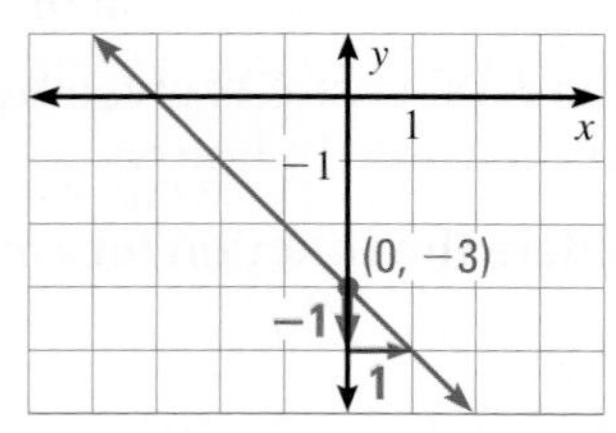

15. 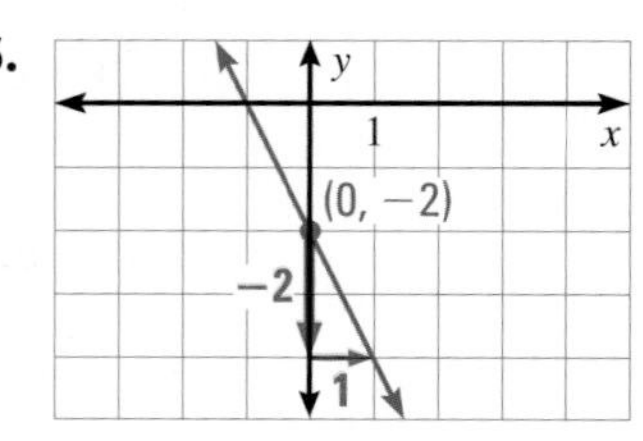

16. **ERROR ANALYSIS** *Describe* and correct the error in writing an equation of the line with a slope of 2 and a y-intercept of 7.

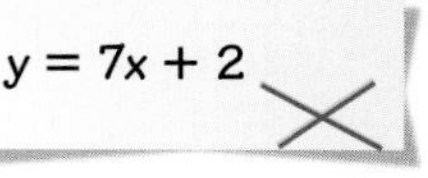

EXAMPLE 3 for Exs. 17–29

17. **ERROR ANALYSIS** *Describe* and correct the error in writing an equation of the line shown.

$$\text{slope} = \frac{0-4}{0-5} = \frac{-4}{-5} = \frac{4}{5}$$

$$y = \frac{4}{5}x + 4$$

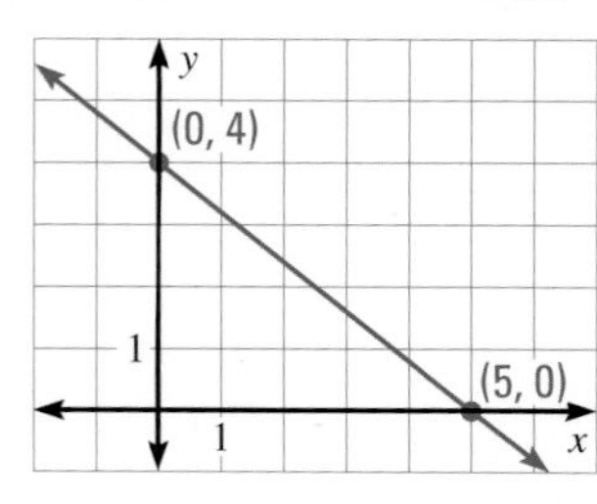

USING A GRAPH **Write an equation of the line shown.**

18.

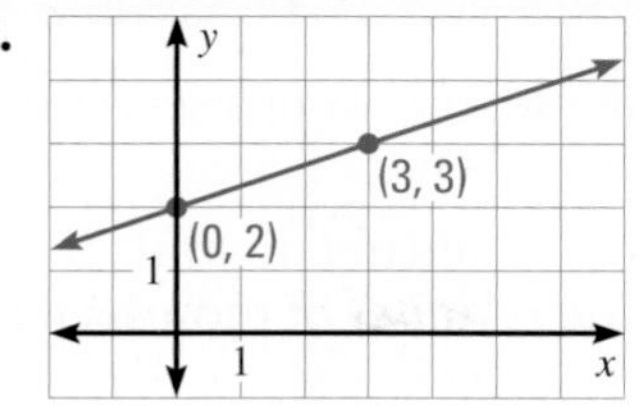

19.

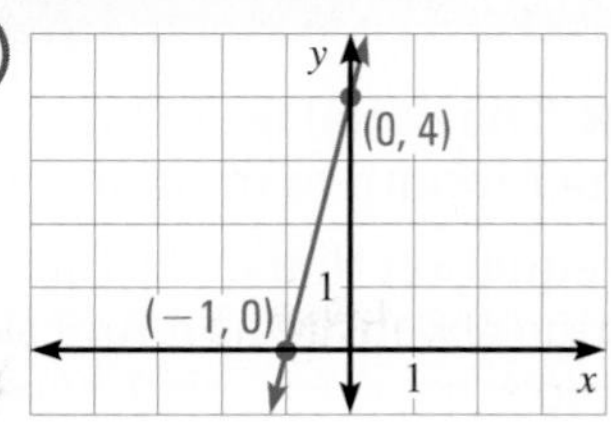

20.

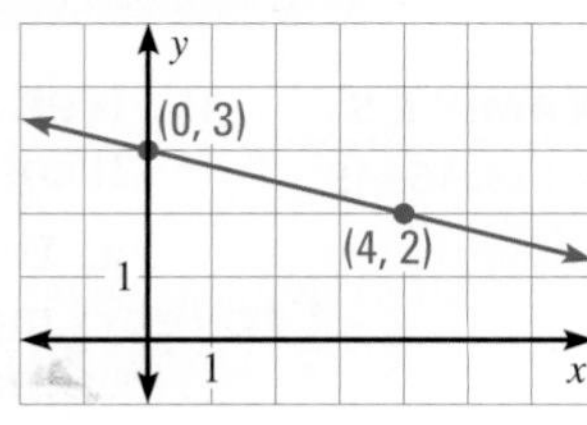

21.

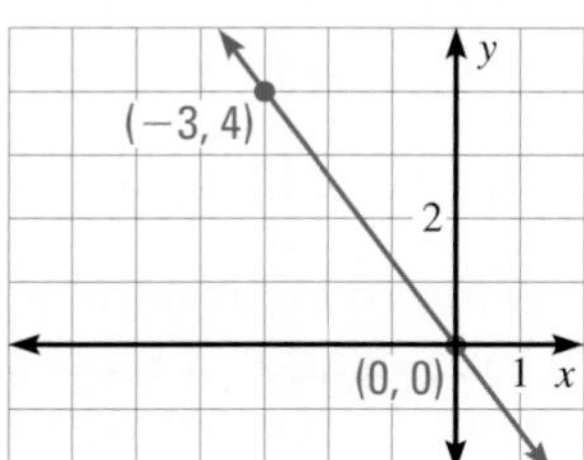

22.

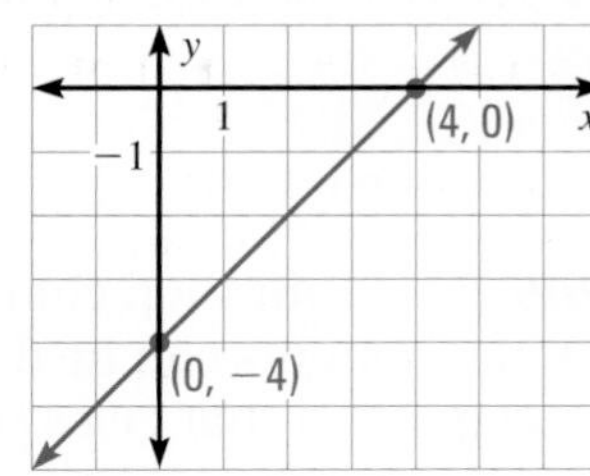

23.

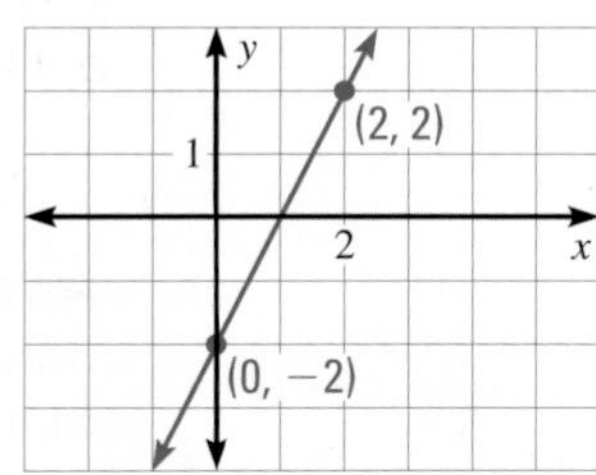

USING TWO POINTS **Write an equation of the line that passes through the given points.**

24. (−3, 1), (0, −8)
25. (2, −7), (0, −5)
26. (2, −4), (0, −4)
27. (0, 4), (8, 3.5)
28. (0, 5), (1.5, 1)
29. (−6, 0), (0, −24)

EXAMPLE 4
for Exs. 30–38

WRITING FUNCTIONS **Write an equation for the linear function *f* with the given values.**

30. $f(0) = 2, f(2) = 4$
31. $f(0) = 7, f(3) = 1$
32. $f(0) = -2, f(4) = -3$
33. $f(0) = -1, f(5) = -5$
34. $f(-2) = 6, f(0) = -4$
35. $f(-6) = -1, f(0) = 3$
36. $f(4) = 13, f(0) = 21$
37. $f(0) = 9, f(3) = 0$
38. $f(0.2) = 1, f(0) = 0.6$

39. **VISUAL THINKING** Line ℓ passes through the points (0, 1) and (3, 0). What change(s) in the parameters m and b in the slope-intercept equation of k occurred to produce the slope-intercept equation of ℓ?

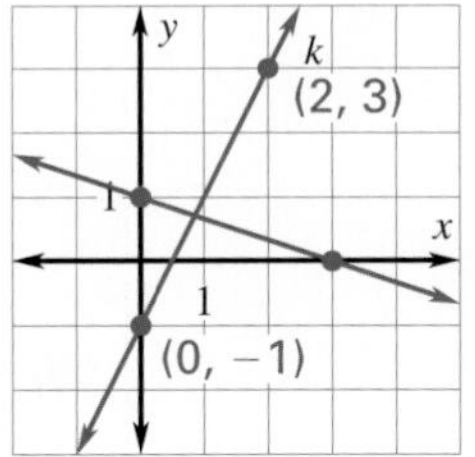

40. ★ **OPEN-ENDED** *Describe* a real-world situation that can be modeled by the function $y = 4x + 9$.

USING A DIAGRAM OR TABLE **Write an equation that represents the linear function shown in the mapping diagram or table.**

41.

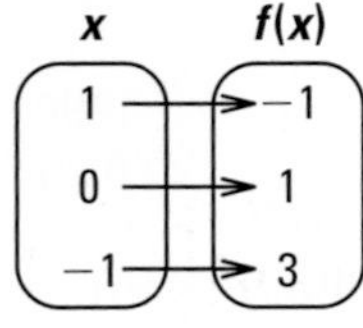

42.

x	$f(x)$
−4	−2
−2	−1
0	0

43. ★ **WRITING** A line passes through the points (3, 5) and (3, −7). Is it possible to write an equation of the line in slope-intercept form? *Justify* your answer.

44. **CHALLENGE** Show that the equation of the line that passes through the points $(0, b)$ and $(1, b + m)$ is $y = mx + b$. *Explain* how you can be sure that the point $(-1, b - m)$ also lies on the line.

PROBLEM SOLVING

EXAMPLE 5 for Exs. 45–49

45. **WEB SERVER** The initial fee to have a website set up using a server is \$48. It costs \$44 per month to maintain the website.
   a. Write an equation that gives the total cost of setting up and maintaining a website as a function of the number of months it is maintained.
   b. Find the total cost of setting up and maintaining the website for 6 months.

46. **PHOTOGRAPHS** A camera shop charges \$3.99 for an enlargement of a photograph. Enlargements can be delivered for a charge of \$1.49 per order. Write an equation that gives the total cost of an order with delivery as a function of the number of enlargements. Find the total cost of ordering 8 photograph enlargements with delivery.

47. **AQUARIUM** Your family spends \$30 for tickets to an aquarium and \$3 per hour for parking. Write an equation that gives the total cost of your family's visit to the aquarium as a function of the number of hours that you are there. Find the total cost of 4 hours at the aquarium.

48. ★ **SHORT RESPONSE** Scientists found that the number of ant species in Clark Canyon, Nevada, increases at a rate of 0.0037 species per meter of elevation. There are approximately 3 ant species at sea level.
   a. Write an equation that gives the number of ant species as a function of the elevation (in meters).
   b. Identify the dependent and independent variables in this situation.
   c. *Explain* how you can use the equation from part (a) to approximate the number of ant species at an elevation of 2 meters.

49. ◆ **MULTIPLE REPRESENTATIONS** The timeline shows the approximate total area of glaciers on Mount Kilimanjaro from 1970 to 2000.

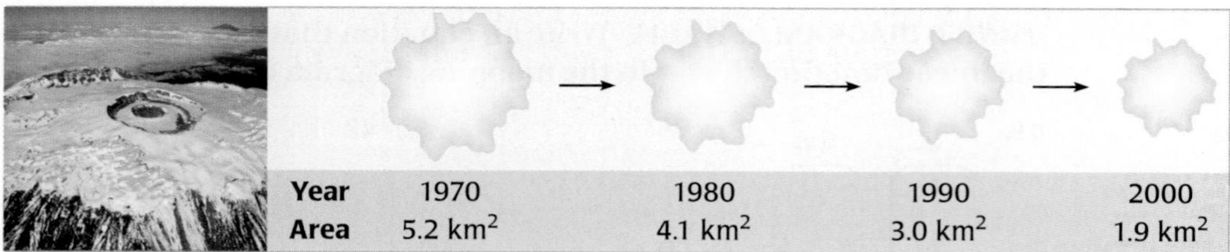

Year	1970	1980	1990	2000
Area	5.2 km^2	4.1 km^2	3.0 km^2	1.9 km^2

   a. **Making a Table** Make a table that shows the number of years x since 1970 and the area of the glaciers y (in square kilometers).
   b. **Drawing a Graph** Graph the data in the table. *Explain* how you know the area of glaciers changed at a constant rate.
   c. **Writing an Equation** Write an equation that models the area of glaciers as a function of the number of years since 1970. By how much did the area of the glaciers decrease each year from 1970 to 2000?

○ = See **WORKED-OUT SOLUTIONS** in Student Resources ★ = **STANDARDIZED TEST PRACTICE** ◆ = **MULTIPLE REPRESENTATIONS**

50. ★ **EXTENDED RESPONSE** The Harris Dam in Maine releases water into the Kennebec River. From 10:00 A.M. to 1:00 P.M. during each day of whitewater rafting season, water is released at a greater rate than usual.

Time interval	Release rate (gallons per hour)
12:00 A.M. to 10:00 A.M.	8.1 million
10:00 A.M. to 1:00 P.M.	130 million

a. On a day during rafting season, how much water is released by 10:00 A.M.?

b. Write an equation that gives, for a day during rafting season, the total amount of water (in gallons) released as a function of the number of hours since 10:00 A.M.

c. What is the domain of the function from part (b)? *Explain.*

51. **FIREFIGHTING** The diagram shows the time a firefighting aircraft takes to scoop water from a lake, fly to a fire, and drop the water on the fire.

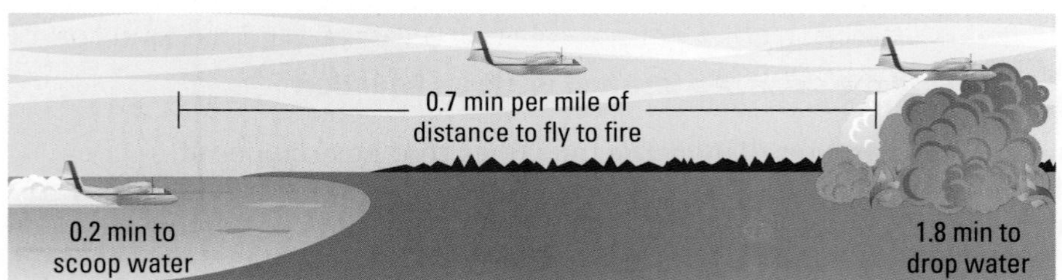

a. **Model** Write an equation that gives the total time (in minutes) that the aircraft takes to scoop, fly, and drop as a function of the distance (in miles) flown from the lake to the fire.

b. **Predict** Find the time the aircraft takes to scoop, fly, and drop if it travels 20 miles from the lake to the fire.

52. **CHALLENGE** The elevation at which a baseball game is played affects the distance a ball travels when hit. For every increase of 1000 feet in elevation, the ball travels about 7 feet farther. Suppose a baseball travels 400 feet when hit in a ball park at sea level.

a. **Model** Write an equation that gives the distance (in feet) the baseball travels as a function of the elevation of the ball park in which it is hit.

b. **Justify** *Justify* the equation from part (a) using unit analysis.

c. **Predict** If the ball were hit in exactly the same way at a park with an elevation of 3500 feet, how far would it travel?

Investigate Families of Lines

Use appropriate tools strategically.

QUESTION How can you use a graphing calculator to find equations of lines using slopes and y-intercepts?

Recall that you can create families of lines by varying the value of either m or b in $y = mx + b$. The constants m and b are called *parameters*. Given the value of one parameter, you can determine the value of the other parameter if you also have information that uniquely identifies one member of the family of lines.

EXAMPLE 1 Find the slope of a line and write an equation

In the same viewing window, display the four lines that have slopes of −1, −0.5, 0.5, and 1 and a y-intercept of 2. Then use the graphs to determine which line passes through the point (12, 8). Write an equation of the line.

STEP 1 *Enter equations*

Press Y= and enter the four equations. Because the lines all have the same y-intercept, they constitute a family of lines and can be entered as shown.

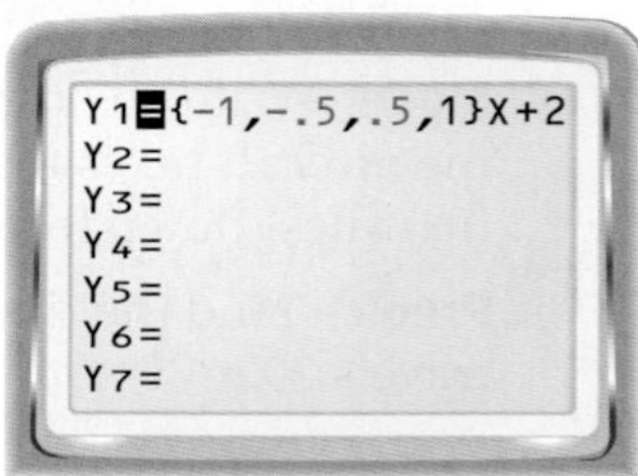

STEP 2 *Display graphs*

Graph the equations in an appropriate viewing window. Press TRACE and use the left and right arrow keys to move along one of the lines until $x = 12$. Use the up and down arrow keys to see which line passes through (12, 8).

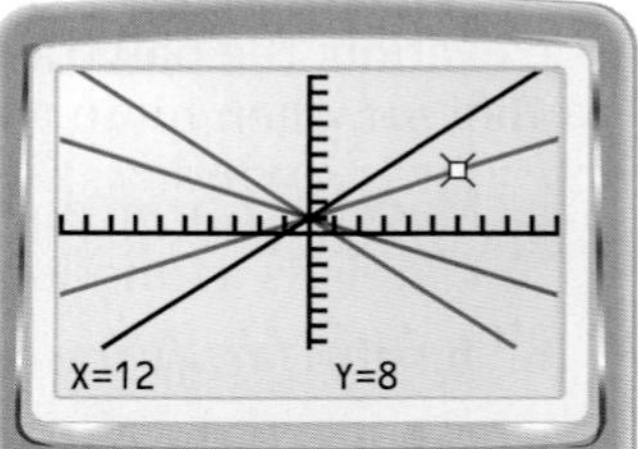

STEP 3 *Find the line*

The line that passes through (12, 8) is the line with a slope of 0.5. So, an equation of the line is $y = 0.5x + 2$.

PRACTICE

Display the lines that have the same y-intercept but different slopes, as given, in the same viewing window. Determine which line passes through the given point. Write an equation of the line.

1. Slopes: −3, −2, 2, 3; y-intercept: 5; point: (−3, 11)
2. Slopes: 4, −2.5, 2.5, 4; y-intercept: −1; point: (4, −11)
3. Slopes: −2, −1, 1, 2; y-intercept: 1.5; point: (1, 3.5)

my.hrw.com
Keystrokes

EXAMPLE 2 Find the y-intercept of a line and write an equation

In the same viewing window, display the five lines that have a slope of 0.5 and y-intercepts of −2, −1, 0, 1, and 2. Then use the graphs to determine which line passes through the point (−2, −2). Write an equation of the line.

STEP 1 ***Enter equations***

Press [Y=] and enter the five equations. Because the lines all have the same slope, they constitute a family of lines and can be entered as shown below.

STEP 2 ***Display graphs***

Graph the equations in an appropriate viewing window. Press [TRACE] and use the left and right arrow keys to move along one of the lines until $x = -2$. Use the up and down arrow keys to see which line passes through (−2, −2).

STEP 3 ***Find the line***

The line that passes through (−2, −2) is the line with a y-intercept of −1. So, an equation of the line is $y = 0.5x - 1$.

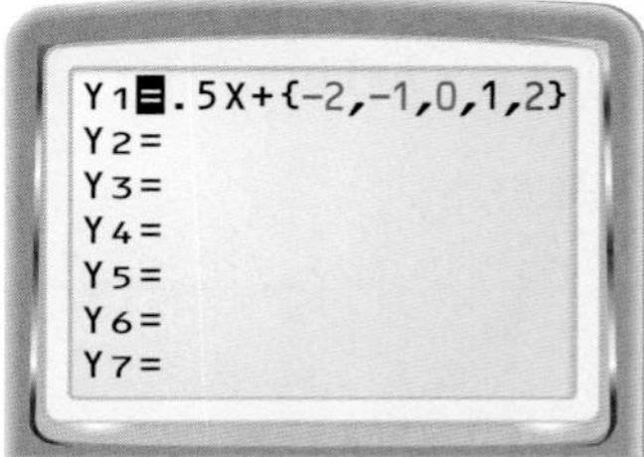

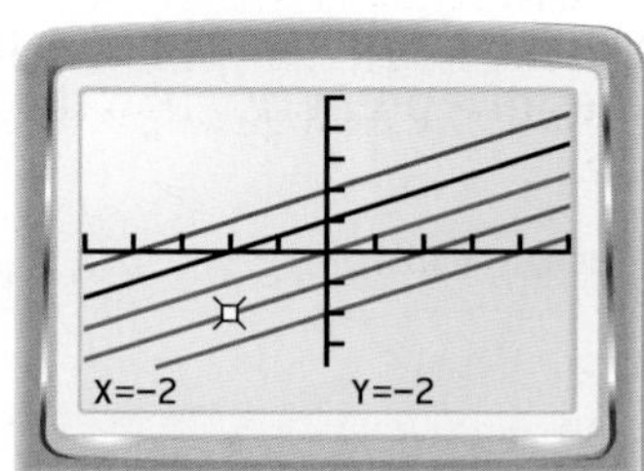

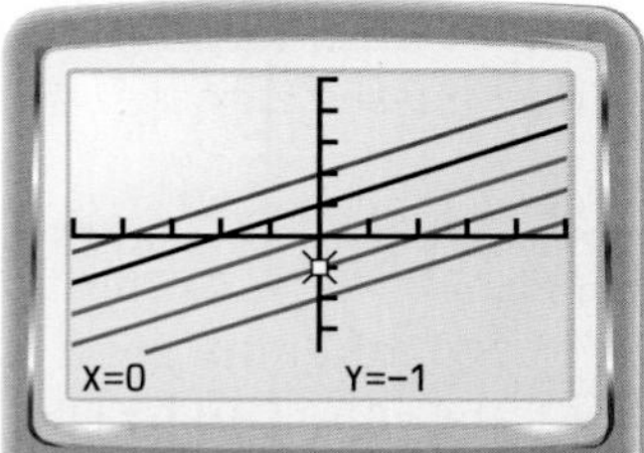

PRACTICE

Display the lines that have the same slope but different y-intercepts, as given, in the same viewing window. Determine which line passes through the given point. Write an equation of the line.

4. Slope: −3; y-intercepts: −2, −1, 0, 1, 2; point: (4, −13)
5. Slope: 1.5; y-intercepts: −2, −1, 0, 1, 2; point: (−2, −1)
6. Slope: −0.5; y-intercepts: −3, −1.5, 0, 1.5, 3; point: (−4, 3.5)
7. Slope: 4; y-intercepts: −3, −1, 0, 1, 3; point: (2, 5)
8. Slope: 2; y-intercepts: −6, −3, 0, 3, 6; point: (−2, −7)

DRAW CONCLUSIONS

9. Of all the lines having equations of the form $y = 0.5x + b$, which one passes through the point (2, 2)? *Explain* how you found your answer.
10. *Describe* a process you could use to find an equation of a line that has a slope of −0.25 and passes through the point (8, −2).

4.2 Use Linear Equations in Slope-Intercept Form

Before You wrote an equation of a line using its slope and y-intercept.

Now You will write an equation of a line using points on the line.

Why So you can write a model for total cost, as in Example 5.

Key Vocabulary
- y-intercept
- slope
- slope-intercept form

CC.9-12.A.CED.2 Create equations in two or more variables to represent relationships between quantities; graph equations on coordinate axes with labels and scales.*

KEY CONCEPT *For Your Notebook*

Writing an Equation of a Line in Slope-Intercept Form

STEP 1 **Identify** the slope m. You can use the slope formula to calculate the slope if you know two points on the line.

STEP 2 **Find** the y-intercept. You can substitute the slope and the coordinates of a point (x, y) on the line in $y = mx + b$. Then solve for b.

STEP 3 **Write** an equation using $y = mx + b$.

EXAMPLE 1 Write an equation given the slope and a point

Write an equation of the line that passes through the point $(-1, 3)$ and has a slope of -4.

Solution

STEP 1 **Identify** the slope. The slope is -4.

STEP 2 **Find** the y-intercept. Substitute the slope and the coordinates of the given point in $y = mx + b$. Solve for b.

$y = mx + b$ **Write slope-intercept form.**

$3 = -4(-1) + b$ **Substitute -4 for m, -1 for x, and 3 for y.**

$-1 = b$ **Solve for b.**

AVOID ERRORS
When you substitute, be careful not to mix up the x- and y-values.

STEP 3 **Write** an equation of the line.

$y = mx + b$ **Write slope-intercept form.**

$y = -4x - 1$ **Substitute -4 for m and -1 for b.**

GUIDED PRACTICE for Example 1

1. Write an equation of the line that passes through the point $(6, 3)$ and has a slope of 2.

EXAMPLE 2 Write an equation given two points

Write an equation of the line that passes through (−2, 5) and (2, −1).

Solution

STEP 1 **Calculate** the slope.

$$m = \frac{y_2 - y_1}{x_2 - x_1} = \frac{-1 - 5}{2 - (-2)} = \frac{-6}{4} = -\frac{3}{2}$$

ANOTHER WAY
You can also find the y-intercept using the coordinates of the other given point, (2, −1):
$y = mx + b$
$-1 = -\frac{3}{2}(2) + b$
$2 = b$

STEP 2 **Find** the y-intercept. Use the slope and the point (−2, 5).

$y = mx + b$ — **Write slope-intercept form.**

$5 = -\frac{3}{2}(-2) + b$ — **Substitute $-\frac{3}{2}$ for m, −2 for x, and 5 for y.**

$2 = b$ — **Solve for b.**

STEP 3 **Write** an equation of the line.

$y = mx + b$ — **Write slope-intercept form.**

$y = -\frac{3}{2}x + 2$ — **Substitute $-\frac{3}{2}$ for m and 2 for b.**

★ EXAMPLE 3 Standardized Test Practice

Which function has the values $f(4) = 9$ and $f(-4) = -7$?

Ⓐ $f(x) = 2x + 10$ Ⓑ $f(x) = 2x + 1$

Ⓒ $f(x) = 2x - 13$ Ⓓ $f(x) = 2x - 14$

ELIMINATE CHOICES
You can also evaluate each function when $x = 4$ and $x = -4$. Eliminate any choices for which $f(4) \neq 9$ or $f(-4) \neq -7$.

STEP 1 **Calculate** the slope. Write $f(4) = 9$ as (4, 9) and $f(-4) = -7$ as (−4, −7).

$$m = \frac{y_2 - y_1}{x_2 - x_1} = \frac{-7 - 9}{-4 - 4} = \frac{-16}{-8} = 2$$

STEP 2 **Find** the y-intercept. Use the slope and the point (4, 9).

$y = mx + b$ — **Write slope-intercept form.**

$9 = 2(4) + b$ — **Substitute 2 for m, 4 for x, and 9 for y.**

$1 = b$ — **Solve for b.**

STEP 3 **Write** an equation for the function. Use function notation.

$f(x) = 2x + 1$ — **Substitute 2 for m and 1 for b.**

▶ The answer is B. Ⓐ Ⓑ Ⓒ Ⓓ

✓ GUIDED PRACTICE for Examples 2 and 3

2. Write an equation of the line that passes through (1, −2) and (−5, 4).
3. Write an equation for the linear function with the values $f(-2) = 10$ and $f(4) = -2$.

CONCEPT SUMMARY — For Your Notebook

How to Write Equations in Slope-Intercept Form

Given slope m and y-intercept b

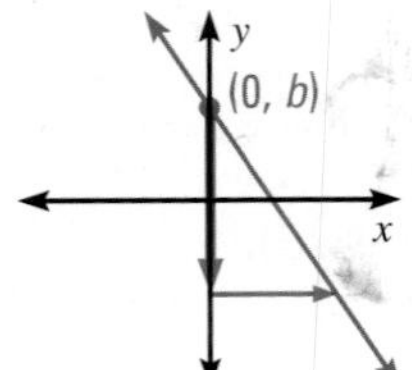

Substitute m and b in the equation $y = mx + b$.

Given slope m and one point

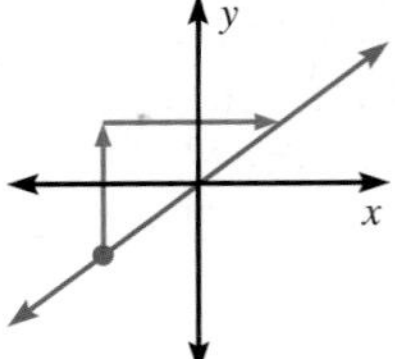

Substitute m and the coordinates of the point in $y = mx + b$. Solve for b. Write the equation.

Given two points

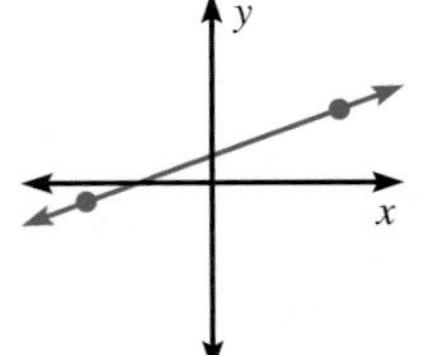

Use the points to find the slope m. Then follow the same steps described at the left.

MODELING REAL-WORLD SITUATIONS You can model a real-world situation that involves a constant rate of change with an equation in slope-intercept form.

EXAMPLE 4 Solve a multi-step problem

GYM MEMBERSHIP Your gym membership costs \$33 per month after an initial membership fee. You paid a total of \$228 after 6 months. Write an equation that gives the total cost as a function of the length of your gym membership (in months). Find the total cost after 9 months.

Solution

STEP 1 **Identify** the rate of change and starting value.

Rate of change, *m*: monthly cost, \$33 per month
Starting value, *b*: initial membership fee

STEP 2 **Write** a verbal model. Then write an equation.

Total cost	=	Monthly cost	•	Number of months	+	Membership fee
C	=	33	•	t	+	b

STEP 3 **Find** the starting value. Membership for 6 months costs \$228, so you can substitute 6 for t and 228 for C in the equation $C = 33t + b$.

$228 = 33(6) + b$ **Substitute 6 for *t* and 228 for *C*.**

$30 = b$ **Solve for *b*.**

STEP 4 **Write** an equation. Use the function from Step 2.

$C = 33t + 30$ **Substitute 30 for *b*.**

STEP 5 **Evaluate** the function when $t = 9$.

$C = 33(9) + 30 = 327$ **Substitute 9 for *t*. Simplify.**

▶ Your total cost after 9 months is \$327.

EXAMPLE 5 Solve a multi-step problem

BMX RACING In Bicycle Moto Cross (BMX) racing, racers purchase a one year membership to a track. They also pay an entry fee for each race at that track. One racer paid a total of $125 after 5 races. A second racer paid a total of $170 after 8 races. How much does the track membership cost? What is the entry fee per race?

ANOTHER WAY
For alternative methods for solving the problem in Example 5, see the **Problem Solving Workshop**.

Solution

STEP 1 **Identify** the rate of change and starting value.

Rate of change, *m*: entry fee per race
Starting value, *b*: track membership cost

STEP 2 **Write** a verbal model. Then write an equation.

Total cost	=	Entry fee per race	·	Races entered	+	Membership cost
C	=	m	·	r	+	b

STEP 3 **Calculate** the rate of change. This is the entry fee per race. Use the slope formula. Racer 1 is represented by (5, 125). Racer 2 is represented by (8, 170).

$$m = \frac{y_2 - y_1}{x_2 - x_1} = \frac{170 - 125}{8 - 5} = \frac{45}{3} = 15$$

STEP 4 **Find** the track membership cost b. Use the data pair (5, 125) for racer 1 and the entry fee per race from Step 3.

$C = mr + b$ **Write the equation from Step 2.**

$125 = 15(5) + b$ **Substitute 15 for *m*, 5 for *r*, and 125 for *C*.**

$50 = b$ **Solve for *b*.**

▶ The track membership cost is $50. The entry fee per race is $15.

✓ GUIDED PRACTICE for Examples 4 and 5

4. **GYM MEMBERSHIP** A gym charges $35 per month after an initial membership fee. A member has paid a total of $250 after 6 months. Write an equation that gives the total cost of a gym membership as a function of the length of membership (in months). Find the total cost of membership after 10 months.

5. **BMX RACING** A BMX race track charges a membership fee and an entry fee per race. One racer paid a total of $76 after 3 races. Another racer paid a total of $124 after 7 races.
   a. How much does the track membership cost?
   b. What is the entry fee per race?
   c. Write an equation that gives the total cost as a function of the number of races entered.

4.2 EXERCISES

HOMEWORK KEY

○ = **See WORKED-OUT SOLUTIONS** Exs. 5, 11, and 49

★ = **STANDARDIZED TEST PRACTICE** Exs. 2, 29, 34–37, 41, and 49

◆ = **MULTIPLE REPRESENTATIONS** Ex. 53

SKILL PRACTICE

1. **VOCABULARY** What is the y-coordinate of a point where a graph crosses the y-axis called?

2. ★ **WRITING** If the equation $y = mx + b$ is used to model a quantity y as a function of the quantity x, why is b considered to be the starting value?

EXAMPLE 1 for Exs. 3–9

WRITING EQUATIONS Write an equation of the line that passes through the given point and has the given slope m.

3. $(1, 1)$; $m = 3$
4. $(5, 1)$; $m = 2$
5. $(-4, 7)$; $m = -5$
6. $(5, -5)$; $m = -2$
7. $(8, -4)$; $m = -\frac{3}{4}$
8. $(-3, -11)$; $m = \frac{1}{2}$

9. **ERROR ANALYSIS** *Describe* and correct the error in finding the y-intercept of the line that passes through the point $(6, -3)$ and has a slope of -2.

$y = mx + b$
$6 = -2(-3) + b$
$6 = 6 + b$
$0 = b$ ✗

EXAMPLE 4 for Ex. 10

10. **ERROR ANALYSIS** An Internet service provider charges \$18 per month plus an initial set-up fee. One customer paid a total of \$81 after 2 months of service. *Describe* and correct the error in finding the set-up fee.

$C = mt + b$
$81 = m(2) + 18$
$63 = m(2)$
$31.50 = m$ ✗

EXAMPLE 2 for Exs. 11–22

USING TWO POINTS Write an equation of the line that passes through the given points.

11. $(1, 4), (2, 7)$
12. $(3, 2), (4, 9)$
13. $(10, -5), (-5, 1)$
14. $(-2, 8), (-6, 0)$
15. $\left(\frac{9}{2}, 1\right), \left(-\frac{7}{2}, 7\right)$
16. $\left(-5, \frac{3}{4}\right), \left(-2, -\frac{3}{4}\right)$

USING A GRAPH Write an equation of the line shown.

17.
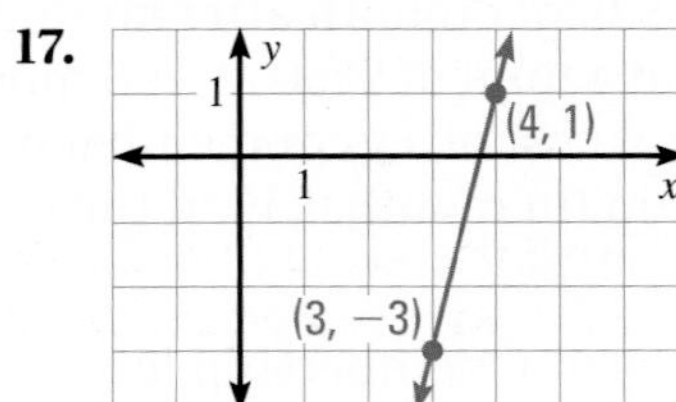

18.
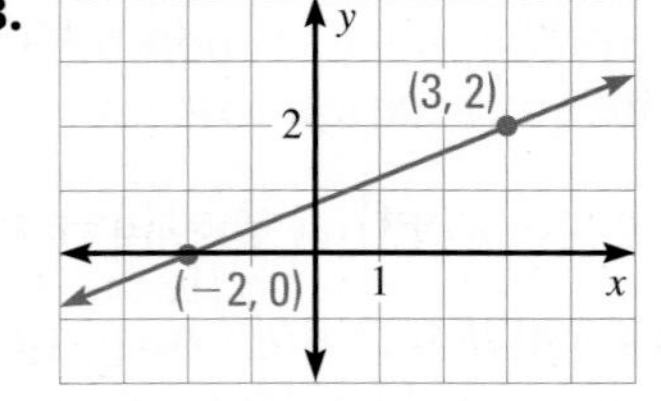

19.
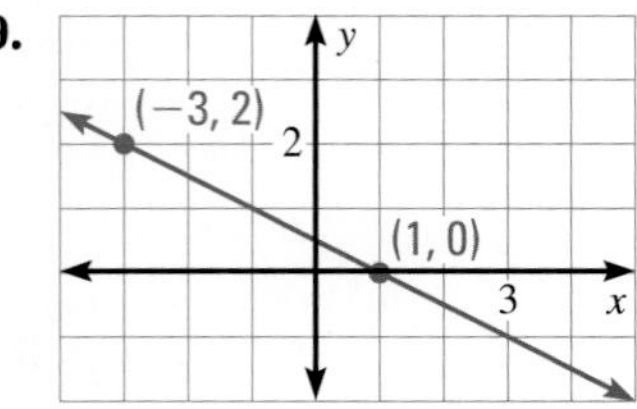

20.
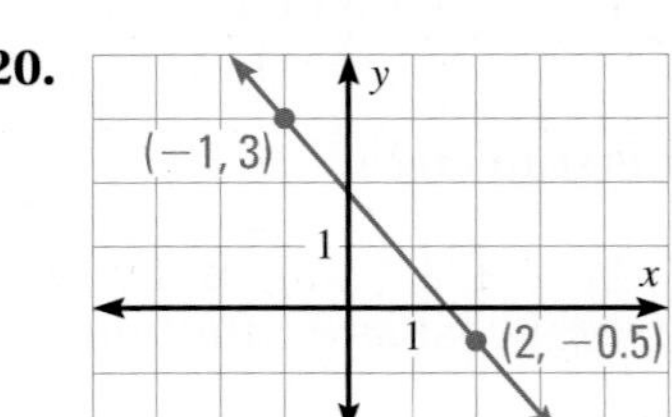

21.
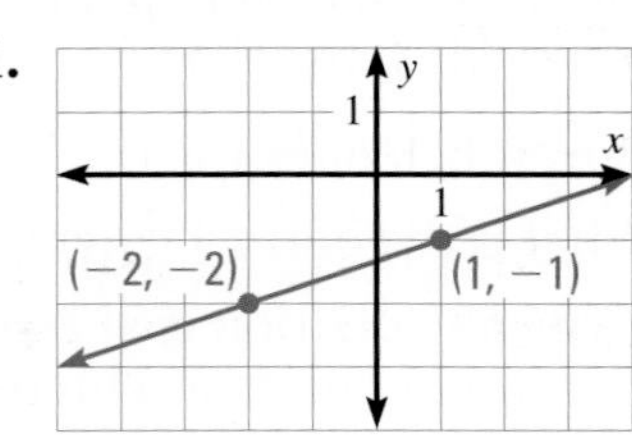

22.
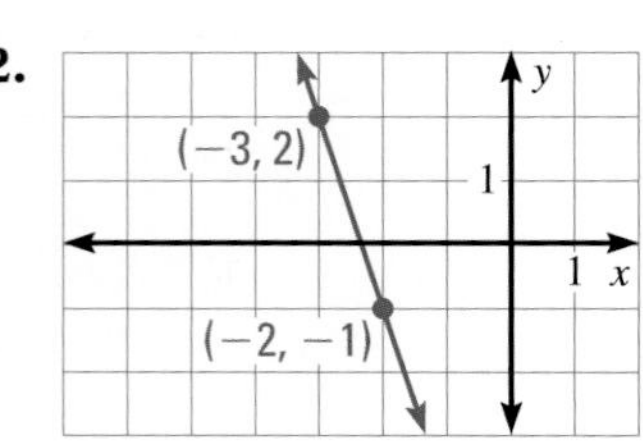

EXAMPLE 3
for Exs. 23–33

WRITING LINEAR FUNCTIONS Write an equation for a linear function f that has the given values.

23. $f(-2) = 15, f(1) = 9$

24. $f(-2) = -2, f(4) = -8$

25. $f(2) = 7, f(4) = 6$

26. $f(-4) = -8, f(-8) = -11$

27. $f(3) = 1, f(6) = 4$

28. $f(-5) = 9, f(11) = -39$

29. ★ **MULTIPLE CHOICE** Which function has the values $f(4) = -15$ and $f(7) = 57$?

Ⓐ $f(x) = 14x - 71$

Ⓑ $f(x) = 24x - 1361$

Ⓒ $f(x) = 24x + 360$

Ⓓ $f(x) = 24x - 111$

USING A TABLE OR DIAGRAM Write an equation that represents the linear function shown in the table or mapping diagram.

30.

x	$f(x)$
−4	6
4	4
8	3
12	2

31.

x	$f(x)$
−3	8
3	4
6	2
9	0

32.

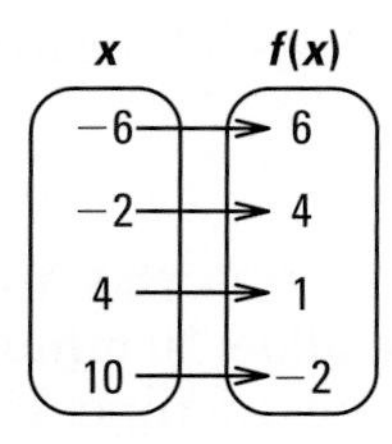

33.

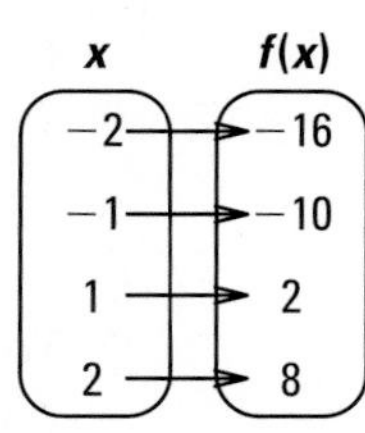

★ **SHORT RESPONSE Tell whether the given information is enough to write an equation of a line. *Justify* your answer.**

34. Two points on the line

35. The slope and a point on the line

36. The slope of the line

37. Both intercepts of the line

USING A GRAPH In Exercises 38–41, use the graph at the right.

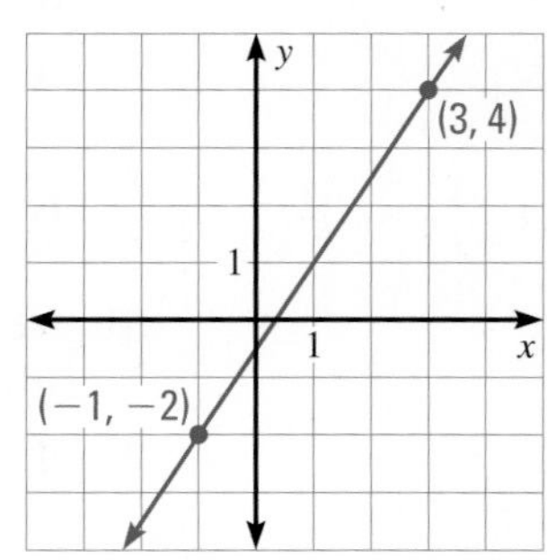

38. Write an equation of the line shown.

39. Write an equation of a line that has the same y-intercept as the line shown but has a slope that is 3 times the slope of the line shown.

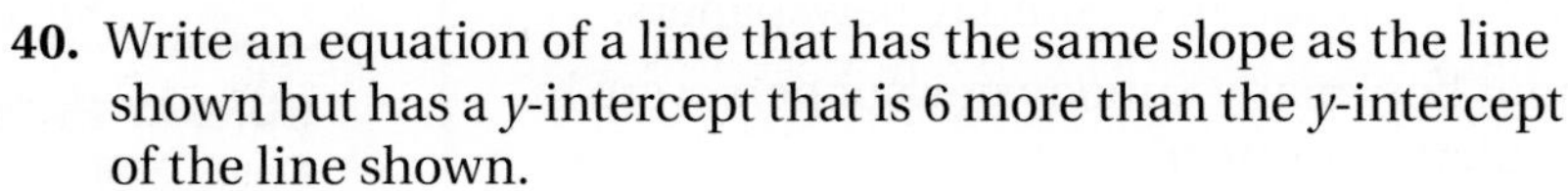

40. Write an equation of a line that has the same slope as the line shown but has a y-intercept that is 6 more than the y-intercept of the line shown.

41. ★ **WRITING** Which of the lines from Exercises 38–40 intersect? Which of the lines never intersect? *Justify* your answers.

REASONING Decide whether the three points lie on the same line. *Explain* how you know. If the points do lie on the same line, write an equation of the line that passes through all three points.

42. $(-4, -2), (2, 2.5), (8, 7)$

43. $(2, 2), (-4, 5), (6, 1)$

44. $(-10, 4), (-3, 2.8), (-17, 6.8)$

45. $(-5.5, 3), (-7.5, 4), (-4, 5)$

46. **CHALLENGE** A line passes through the points $(-2, 3)$, $(2, 5)$, and $(6, k)$. Find the value of k. *Explain* your steps.

PROBLEM SOLVING

EXAMPLES 4 and 5 for Exs. 47–50

47. **BIOLOGY** Four years after a hedge maple tree was planted, its height was 9 feet. Eight years after it was planted, the hedge maple tree's height was 12 feet. What is the growth rate of the hedge maple? What was its height when it was planted?

48. **TECHNOLOGY** You have a subscription to an online magazine that allows you to view 25 articles from the magazine's archives. You are charged an additional fee for each article after the first 25 articles viewed. After viewing 28 archived articles, you paid a total of $34.80. After viewing 30 archived articles, you paid a total of $40.70.

    a. What is the cost per archived article after the first 25 articles viewed?

    b. What is cost of the magazine subscription?

49. ★ **SHORT RESPONSE** You are cooking a roast beef until it is well-done. You must allow 30 minutes of cooking time for every pound of beef, plus some extra time. The last time you cooked a 2 pound roast, it was well-done after 1 hour and 25 minutes. How much time will it take to cook a 3 pound roast? *Explain* how you found your answer.

HINT In part (b), let *t* represent the number of years since 1981.

50. **TELEPHONE SERVICE** The annual household cost of telephone service in the United States increased at a relatively constant rate of $27.80 per year from 1981 to 2001. In 2001 the annual household cost of telephone service was $914.

    a. What was the annual household cost of telephone service in 1981?

    b. Write an equation that gives the annual household cost of telephone service as a function of the number of years since 1981.

    c. Find the household cost of telephone service in 2000.

51. **NEWSPAPERS** Use the information in the article about the circulation of Sunday newspapers.

    a. About how many Sunday newspapers were in circulation in 1970?

    b. Write an equation that gives the number of Sunday newspapers in circulation as a function of the number of years since 1970.

    c. About how many Sunday newspapers were in circulation in 2000?

Sunday Edition 

SUNDAY PAPERS INCREASE

From 1970 to 2000, the number of Sunday newspapers in circulation increased at a relatively constant rate of 11.8 newspapers per year. In 1997 there were 903 Sunday newspapers in circulation.

52. **AIRPORTS** From 1990 to 2001, the number of airports in the United States increased at a relatively constant rate of 175 airports per year. There were 19,306 airports in the United States in 2001.

    a. How many U.S. airports were there in 1990?

    b. Write an equation that gives the number of U.S. airports as a function of the number of years since 1990.

    c. Find the year in which the number of U.S. airports reached 19,200.

○ = See **WORKED-OUT SOLUTIONS** in Student Resources ★ = **STANDARDIZED TEST PRACTICE** 

53. **MULTIPLE REPRESENTATIONS** A hurricane is traveling at a constant speed on a straight path toward a coastal town, as shown below.

Hurricane position at 1:00 P.M.

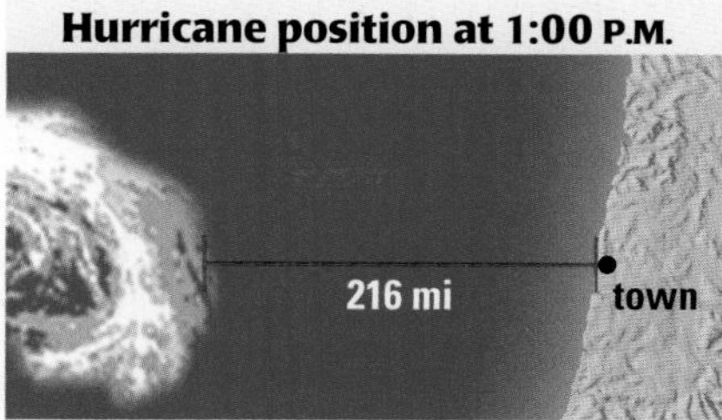

Hurricane position at 5:00 P.M.

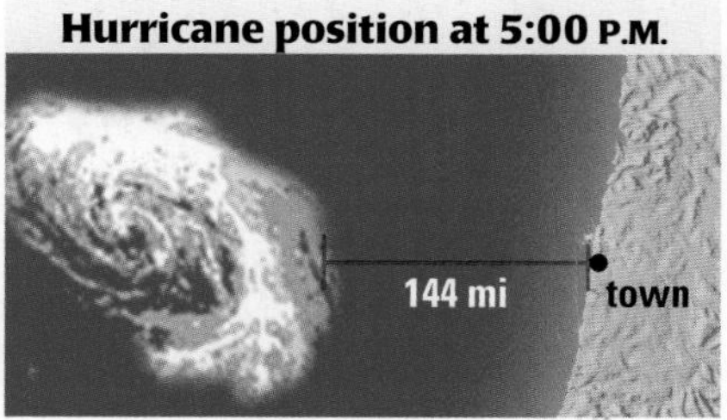

a. **Writing an Equation** Write an equation that gives the distance (in miles) of the hurricane from the town as a function of the number of hours since 12:00 P.M.

b. **Drawing a Graph** Graph the equation from part (a). *Explain* what the slope and the y-intercept of the graph mean in this situation.

c. **Describing in Words** Predict the time at which the hurricane will reach the town. Your answer should include the following information:

- an explanation of how you used your equation
- a description of the steps you followed to obtain your prediction

54. **CHALLENGE** An in-line skater practices at a race track. In two trials, the skater travels the same distance going from a standstill to his top racing speed. He then travels at his top racing speed for different distances.

Trial number	Time at top racing speed (seconds)	Total distance traveled (meters)
1	24	300
2	29	350

a. **Model** Write an equation that gives the total distance traveled (in meters) as a function of the time (in seconds) at top racing speed.

b. **Justify** What do the rate of change and initial value in your equation represent? *Explain* your answer using unit analysis.

c. **Predict** One lap around the race track is 200 meters. The skater starts at a standstill and completes 3 laps. Predict the number of seconds the skater travels at his top racing speed. *Explain* your method.

Using ALTERNATIVE METHODS

Another Way to Solve Example 5

Make sense of problems and persevere in solving them.

MULTIPLE REPRESENTATIONS In Example 5, you saw how to solve a problem about BMX racing using an equation. You can also solve this problem using a graph or a table.

PROBLEM

BMX RACING In Bicycle Moto Cross (BMX) racing, racers purchase a one year membership to a track. They also pay an entry fee for each race at that track. One racer paid a total of \$125 after 5 races. A second racer paid a total of \$170 after 8 races. How much does the track membership cost? What is the entry fee per race?

METHOD 1

Using a Graph One alternative approach is to use a graph.

STEP 1 **Read** the problem. It tells you the number of races and amount paid for each racer. Write this information as ordered pairs.

Racer 1: (5, 125)
Racer 2: (8, 170)

STEP 2 **Graph** the ordered pairs. Draw a line through the points.

The y-intercept is 50.
So, the track membership is \$50.

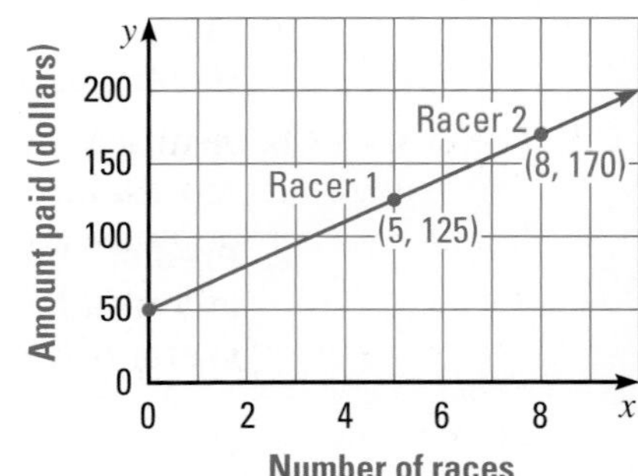

STEP 3 **Find** the slope of the line. This is the entry fee per race.

$$\text{Fee} = \frac{\textbf{45 dollars}}{\textbf{3 races}} = \$15 \text{ per race}$$

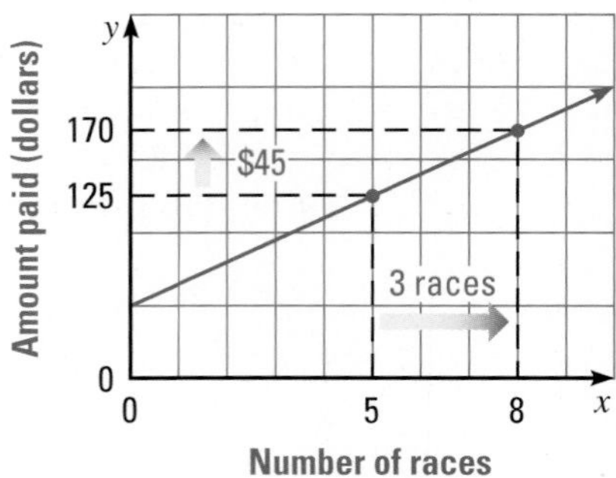

METHOD 2 **Using a Table** Another approach is to use a table showing the amount paid for various numbers of races.

STEP 1 **Calculate** the race entry fee.

Number of races	Amount paid
5	$125
6	?
7	?
8	$170

+ 3   + $45

The number of races increased by 3, and the amount paid increased by $45, so the race entry fee is $45 ÷ 3 = $15.

STEP 2 **Find** the membership cost.

Number of races	Amount paid
0	$50
1	$65
2	$80
3	$95
4	$110
5	$125

− $15 − $15 − $15 − $15 − $15

The membership cost is the cost with no races. Use the race entry fee and work backwards to fill in the table. The membership cost is $50.

PRACTICE

1. **CALENDARS** A company makes calendars from personal photos. You pay a delivery fee for each order plus a cost per calendar. The cost of 2 calendars plus delivery is $43. The cost of 4 calendars plus delivery is $81. What is the delivery fee? What is the cost per calendar? Solve this problem using two different methods.

2. **BOOKSHELVES** A furniture maker offers bookshelves that have the same width and depth but that differ in height and price, as shown in the table. Find the cost of a bookshelf that is 72 inches high. Solve this problem using two different methods.

Height (inches)	Price (dollars)
36	56.54
48	77.42
60	98.30

3. **WHAT IF?** In Exercise 2, suppose the price of the 60 inch bookshelf was $99.30. Can you still solve the problem? *Explain.*

4. **CONCERT TICKETS** All tickets for a concert are the same price. The ticket agency adds a fixed fee to every order. A person who orders 5 tickets pays $93. A person who orders 3 tickets pays $57. How much will 4 tickets cost? Solve this problem using two different methods.

5. **ERROR ANALYSIS** A student solved the problem in Exercise 4 as shown below. *Describe* and correct the error.

Let p = price paid for 4 tickets

$$\frac{57}{3} = \frac{p}{4}$$

$$228 = 3p$$

$$76 = p$$

4.3 Write Linear Equations in Point-Slope Form

Before You wrote linear equations in slope-intercept form.

Now You will write linear equations in point-slope form.

Why? So you can model sports statistics, as in Ex. 43.

Key Vocabulary
- **point-slope form**

CC.9-12.A.CED.2 Create equations in two or more variables to represent relationships between quantities; graph equations on coordinate axes with labels and scales.*

Consider the line that passes through the point (2, 3) with a slope of $\frac{1}{2}$.

Let (x, y) where $x \neq 2$ be another point on the line. You can write an equation relating x and y using the slope formula, with $(x_1, y_1) = (2, 3)$ and $(x_2, y_2) = (x, y)$.

$m = \frac{y_2 - y_1}{x_2 - x_1}$ **Write slope formula.**

$\frac{1}{2} = \frac{y - 3}{x - 2}$ **Substitute $\frac{1}{2}$ for m, 3 for y_1, and 2 for x_1.**

$\frac{1}{2}(x - 2) = y - 3$ **Multiply each side by $(x - 2)$.**

The equation in *point-slope form* is $y - 3 = \frac{1}{2}(x - 2)$.

USE POINT-SLOPE FORM
When an equation is in point-slope form, you can read the x- and y-coordinates of a point on the line and the slope of the line.

KEY CONCEPT — *For Your Notebook*

Point-Slope Form

The **point-slope form** of the equation of the nonvertical line through a given point (x_1, y_1) with a slope of m is $y - y_1 = m(x - x_1)$.

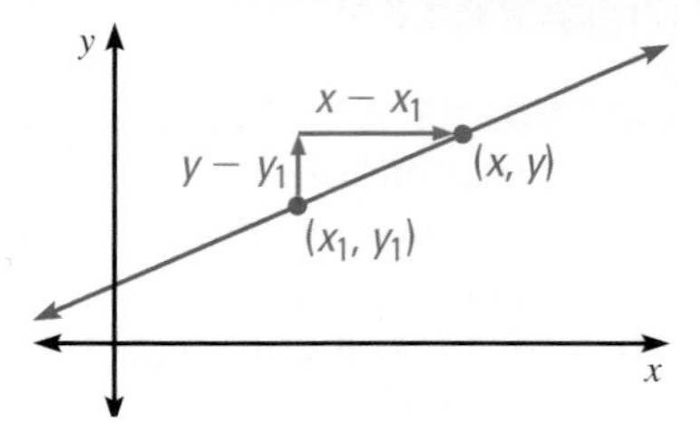

EXAMPLE 1 Write an equation in point-slope form

Write an equation in point-slope form of the line that passes through the point (4, −3) and has a slope of 2.

$y - y_1 = m(x - x_1)$ **Write point-slope form.**

$y + 3 = 2(x - 4)$ **Substitute 2 for m, 4 for x_1, and −3 for y_1.**

✓ GUIDED PRACTICE for Example 1

1. Write an equation in point-slope form of the line that passes through the point (−1, 4) and has a slope of −2.

EXAMPLE 2 Graph an equation in point-slope form

Graph the equation $y + 2 = \frac{2}{3}(x - 3)$.

Solution

Because the equation is in point-slope form, you know that the line has a slope of $\frac{2}{3}$ and passes through the point $(3, -2)$.

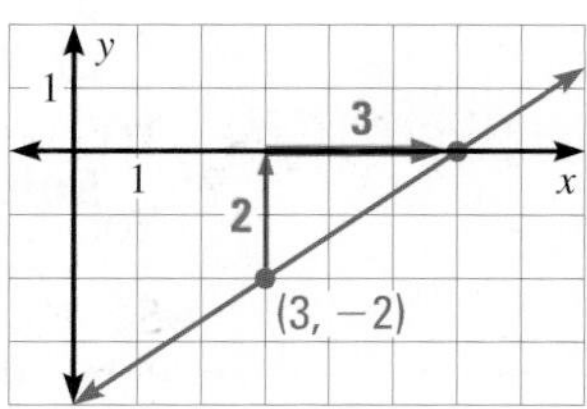

Plot the point $(3, -2)$. Find a second point on the line using the slope. Draw a line through both points.

✓ GUIDED PRACTICE for Example 2

2. Graph the equation $y - 1 = -(x - 2)$.

EXAMPLE 3 Use point-slope form to write an equation

Write an equation in point-slope form of the line shown.

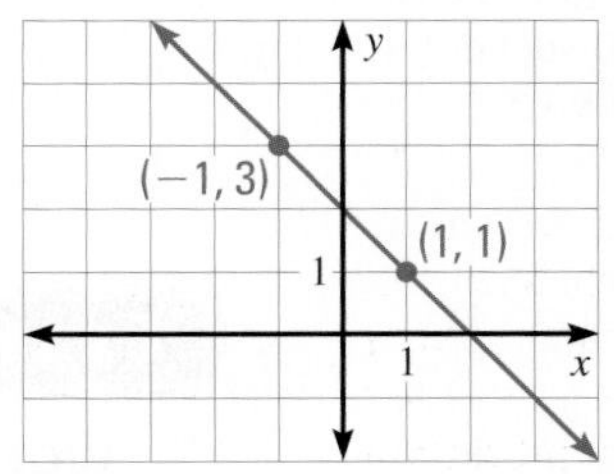

Solution

STEP 1 **Find** the slope of the line.

$$m = \frac{y_2 - y_1}{x_2 - x_1} = \frac{3 - 1}{-1 - 1} = \frac{2}{-2} = -1$$

STEP 2 **Write** the equation in point-slope form. You can use either given point.

Method 1 Use $(-1, 3)$.	**Method 2** Use $(1, 1)$.
$y - y_1 = m(x - x_1)$	$y - y_1 = m(x - x_1)$
$y - 3 = -(x + 1)$	$y - 1 = -(x - 1)$

CHECK Check that the equations are equivalent by writing them in slope-intercept form.

$y - 3 = -x - 1$	$y - 1 = -x + 1$
$y = -x + 2$	$y = -x + 2$

Animated Algebra activity at my.hrw.com

✓ GUIDED PRACTICE for Example 3

3. Write an equation in point-slope form of the line that passes through the points $(2, 3)$ and $(4, 4)$.

EXAMPLE 4 Solve a multi-step problem

STICKERS You are designing a sticker to advertise your band. A company charges \$225 for the first 1000 stickers and \$80 for each additional 1000 stickers. Write an equation that gives the total cost (in dollars) of stickers as a function of the number (in thousands) of stickers ordered. Find the cost of 9000 stickers.

Solution

STEP 1 **Identify** the rate of change and a data pair. Let C be the cost (in dollars) and s be the number of stickers (in thousands).

Rate of change, m: \$80 per 1 thousand stickers
Data pair (s_1, C_1): (1 thousand stickers, \$225)

STEP 2 **Write** an equation using point-slope form. Rewrite the equation in slope-intercept form so that cost is a function of the number of stickers.

$C - C_1 = m(s - s_1)$ **Write point-slope form.**

$C - 225 = 80(s - 1)$ **Substitute 80 for m, 1 for s_1, and 225 for C_1.**

$C = 80s + 145$ **Solve for C.**

STEP 3 **Find** the cost of 9000 stickers.

$C = 80(9) + 145 = 865$ **Substitute 9 for s. Simplify.**

▶ The cost of 9000 stickers is \$865.

AVOID ERRORS
Remember that s is given in thousands. To find the cost of 9000 stickers, substitute 9 for s.

EXAMPLE 5 Write a real-world linear model from a table

WORKING RANCH The table shows the cost of visiting a working ranch for one day and night for different numbers of people. Can the situation be modeled by a linear equation? *Explain.* If possible, write an equation that gives the cost as a function of the number of people in the group.

Number of people	4	6	8	10	12
Cost (dollars)	250	350	450	550	650

Solution

STEP 1 **Find** the rate of change for consecutive data pairs in the table.

$$\frac{350 - 250}{6 - 4} = 50, \quad \frac{450 - 350}{8 - 6} = 50, \quad \frac{550 - 450}{10 - 8} = 50, \quad \frac{650 - 550}{12 - 10} = 50$$

Because the cost increases at a constant rate of \$50 per person, the situation can be modeled by a linear equation.

STEP 2 **Use** point-slope form to write the equation. Let C be the cost (in dollars) and p be the number of people. Use the data pair (4, 250).

$C - C_1 = m(p - p_1)$ **Write point-slope form.**

$C - 250 = 50(p - 4)$ **Substitute 50 for m, 4 for p_1, and 250 for C_1.**

$C = 50p + 50$ **Solve for C.**

 **GUIDED PRACTICE** for Examples 4 and 5

4. **WHAT IF?** In Example 4, suppose a second company charges \$250 for the first 1000 stickers. The cost of each additional 1000 stickers is \$60.

   a. Write an equation that gives the total cost (in dollars)of the stickers as a function of the number (in thousands) of stickers ordered.

   b. Which company would charge you less for 9000 stickers?

5. **MAILING COSTS** The table shows the cost (in dollars) of sending a single piece of first class mail for different weights. Can the situation be modeled by a linear equation? *Explain.* If possible, write an equation that gives the cost of sending a piece of mail as a function of its weight (in ounces).

Weight (ounces)	1	4	5	10	12
Cost (dollars)	0.37	1.06	1.29	2.44	2.90

4.3 EXERCISES

HOMEWORK KEY
○ = See **WORKED-OUT SOLUTIONS** Exs. 3 and 39
★ = **STANDARDIZED TEST PRACTICE** Exs. 2, 12, 30–34, 38, and 41

SKILL PRACTICE

1. **VOCABULARY** Identify the slope of the line given by the equation $y - 5 = -2(x + 5)$. Then identify one point on the line.

2. ★ **WRITING** *Describe* the steps you would take to write an equation in point-slope form of the line that passes through the points $(3, -2)$ and $(4, 5)$.

EXAMPLE 1 for Exs. 3–13

WRITING EQUATIONS **Write an equation in point-slope form of the line that passes through the given point and has the given slope *m*.**

3. $(2, 1)$, $m = 2$
4. $(3, 5)$, $m = -1$
5. $(7, -1)$, $m = -6$
6. $(5, -1)$, $m = -2$
7. $(-8, 2)$, $m = 5$
8. $(-6, 6)$, $m = \frac{3}{2}$
9. $(-11, -3)$, $m = -9$
10. $(-3, -9)$, $m = \frac{7}{3}$
11. $(5, -12)$, $m = -\frac{2}{5}$

12. ★ **MULTIPLE CHOICE** Which equation represents the line that passes through the point $(-6, 2)$ and has a slope of -1?

    (A) $y + 2 = -(x + 6)$
    (B) $y + 2 = -(x - 6)$
    (C) $y - 2 = -(x + 6)$
    (D) $y + 1 = -2(x + 6)$

13. **ERROR ANALYSIS** *Describe* and correct the error in writing an equation of the line that passes through the point $(1, -5)$ and has a slope of -2.

$y - 5 = -2(x - 1)$ ✗

EXAMPLE 2
for Exs. 14–19

GRAPHING EQUATIONS **Graph the equation.**

14. $y - 5 = 3(x - 1)$ **15.** $y + 3 = -2(x - 2)$ **16.** $y - 1 = 3(x + 6)$

17. $y + 8 = -(x + 4)$ **18.** $y - 1 = \frac{3}{4}(x + 1)$ **19.** $y + 4 = -\frac{5}{2}(x - 3)$

EXAMPLE 3
for Exs. 20–30

USING A GRAPH **Write an equation in point-slope form of the line shown.**

20.

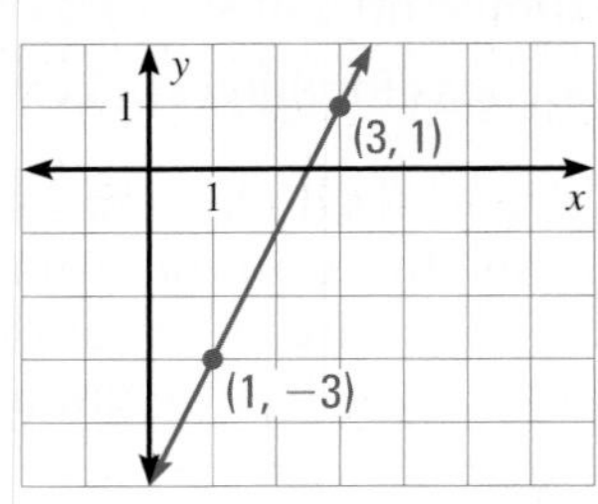

21.

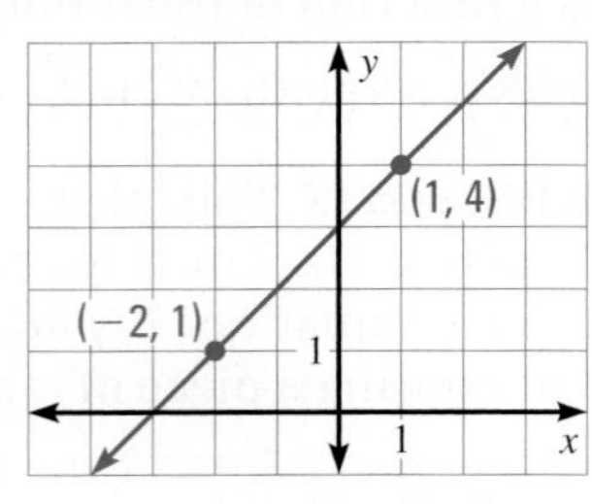

22.

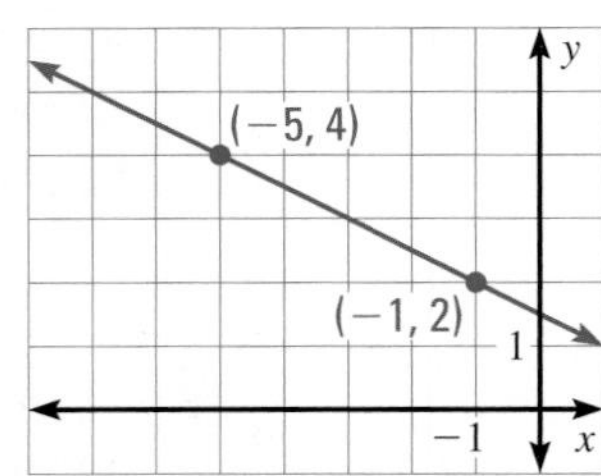

WRITING EQUATIONS **Write an equation in point-slope form of the line that passes through the given points.**

23. (7, 2), (2, 12) **24.** (6, −2), (12, 1) **25.** (−4, −1), (6, −7)

26. (4, 5), (−4, −5) **27.** (−3, −20), (4, 36) **28.** (−5, −19), (5, 13)

29. **ERROR ANALYSIS** *Describe* and correct the error in writing an equation of the line shown.

$m = \frac{4-2}{4-1} = \frac{2}{3}$ $y - 2 = \frac{2}{3}(x - 4)$ ✗

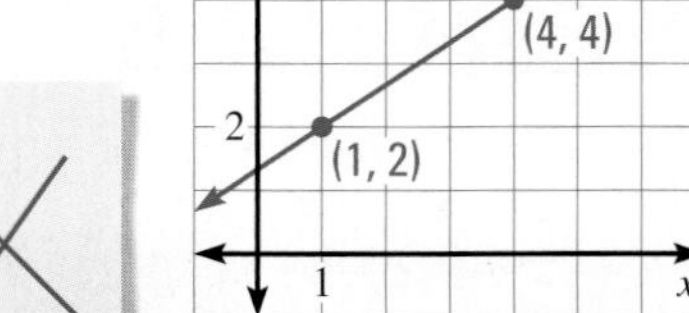

30. ★ **MULTIPLE CHOICE** The graph of which equation is shown?

Ⓐ $y + 4 = -3(x + 2)$ Ⓑ $y - 4 = -3(x - 2)$

Ⓒ $y - 4 = -3(x + 2)$ Ⓓ $y + 4 = -3(x - 2)$

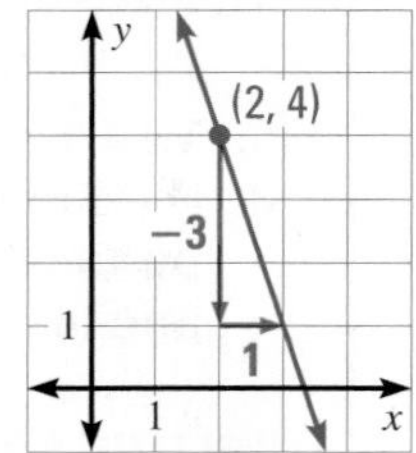

★ **SHORT RESPONSE** **Tell whether the data in the table can be modeled by a linear equation.** ***Explain.*** **If possible, write an equation in point-slope form that relates** ***y*** **and** ***x*****.**

31.

x	2	4	6	8	10
y	−1	5	15	29	47

32.

x	1	2	3	5	7
y	1.2	1.4	1.6	2	2.4

33.

x	1	2	3	4	5
y	2	−3	4	−5	6

34.

x	−3	−1	1	3	5
y	16	10	4	−2	−8

CHALLENGE **Find the value of** ***k*** **so that the line passing through the given points has slope** ***m*****. Write an equation of the line in point-slope form.**

35. $(k, 4k), (k + 2, 3k), m = -1$ **36.** $(-k + 1, 3), (3, k + 3), m = 3$

○ = See **WORKED-OUT SOLUTIONS** in Student Resources ★ = **STANDARDIZED TEST PRACTICE**

PROBLEM SOLVING

EXAMPLE 4 for Exs. 37, 39, 40

37. **TELEVISION** In order to use an excerpt from a movie in a new television show, the television producer must pay the director of the movie \$790 for the first 2 minutes of the excerpt and \$130 per minute after that.

    a. Write an equation that gives the total cost (in dollars) of using the excerpt as a function of the length (in minutes) of the excerpt.

    b. Find the total cost of using an excerpt that is 8 minutes long.

EXAMPLE 5 for Exs. 38, 41

38. ★ **SHORT RESPONSE** A school district pays an installation fee and a monthly fee for Internet service. The table shows the total cost of Internet service for the school district over different numbers of months. *Explain* why the situation can be modeled by a linear equation. What is the installation fee? What is the monthly service fee?

Months of service	2	4	6	8	10	12
Total cost (dollars)	9,378	12,806	16,234	19,662	23,090	26,518

39. **COMPANY SALES** During the period 1994–2004, the annual sales of a small company increased by \$10,000 per year. In 1997 the annual sales were \$97,000. Write an equation that gives the annual sales as a function of the number of years since 1994. Find the sales in 2000.

    Animated Algebra at my.hrw.com

40. **TRAFFIC DELAYS** From 1990 to 2001 in Boston, Massachusetts, the annual excess fuel (in gallons per person) consumed due to traffic delays increased by about 1.4 gallons per person each year. In 1995 each person consumed about 37 gallons of excess fuel.

    a. Write an equation that gives the annual excess fuel (in gallons per person) as a function of the number of years since 1990.

    b. How much excess fuel was consumed per person in 2001?

    Animated Algebra at my.hrw.com

41. ★ **EXTENDED RESPONSE** The table shows the cost of ordering sets of prints of digital photos from an online service. The cost per print is the same for the first 30 prints. There is also a shipping charge.

Number of prints	1	2	5	8
Total cost (dollars)	1.98	2.47	3.94	5.41

    a. *Explain* why the situation can be modeled by a linear equation.

    b. Write an equation in point-slope form that relates the total cost (in dollars) of a set of prints to the number of prints ordered.

    c. Find the shipping charge for up to 10 prints.

    d. The cost of 15 prints is \$9.14. The shipping charge increases after the first 10 prints. Find the shipping charge for 15 prints.

42. **AQUACULTURE** Aquaculture is the farming of fish and other aquatic animals. World aquaculture increased at a relatively constant rate from 1991 to 2002. In 1994 world aquaculture was about 20.8 million metric tons. In 2000 world aquaculture was about 35.5 million metric tons.

a. Write an equation that gives world aquaculture (in millions of metric tons) as a function of the number of years since 1991.

b. In 2001 China was responsible for 70.2% of world aquaculture. Approximate China's aquaculture in 2001.

43. **MARATHON** The diagram shows a marathon runner's speed at several outdoor temperatures.

a. Write an equation in point-slope form that relates running speed (in feet per second) to temperature (in degrees Fahrenheit).

b. Estimate the runner's speed when the temperature is 80°F.

44. **CHALLENGE** The number of cans recycled per pound of aluminum recycled in the U.S. increased at a relatively constant rate from 1972 to 2002. In 1977 about 23.5 cans per pound of aluminum were recycled. In 2000, about 33.1 cans per pound of aluminum were recycled.

a. Write an equation that gives the number of cans recycled per pound of aluminum recycled as a function of the number of years since 1972.

b. In 2002, there were 53.8 billion aluminum cans collected for recycling. Approximately how many pounds of aluminum were collected? *Explain* how you found your answer.

Extension

Relate Arithmetic Sequences to Linear Functions

GOAL Identify, graph, and write the general form of arithmetic sequences.

Key Vocabulary
- **sequence**
- **arithmetic sequence**
- **common difference**

CC.9-12.F.IF.3 Recognize that sequences are functions, sometimes defined recursively, whose domain is a subset of the integers.

A **sequence** is an ordered list of numbers. The numbers in a sequence are called *terms*. In an **arithmetic sequence**, the difference between consecutive terms is constant. The constant difference is called the **common difference**.

An arithmetic sequence has the form $a_1, a_1 + d, a_1 + 2d, \ldots$ where a_1 is the first term and d is the common difference. For instance, if $a_1 = 2$ and $d = 6$, then the sequence $2, 2 + 6, 2 + 2(6), \ldots$ or $2, 8, 14, \ldots$ is arithmetic.

EXAMPLE 1 Identify an arithmetic sequence

Tell whether the sequence is arithmetic. If it is, find the next two terms.

a. $-4, 1, 6, 11, 16, \ldots$

b. $3, 5, 9, 15, 23, \ldots$

Solution

a. The first term is $a_1 = -4$. Find the differences of consecutive terms.

$a_2 - a_1 = 1 - (-4) = 5$ $\quad$ $a_3 - a_2 = 6 - 1 = 5$

$a_4 - a_3 = 11 - 6 = 5$ $\quad$ $a_5 - a_4 = 16 - 11 = 5$

▶ Because the terms have a common difference ($d = 5$), the sequence is arithmetic. The next two terms are $a_6 = 21$ and $a_7 = 26$.

b. The first term is $a_1 = 3$. Find the differences of consecutive terms.

$a_2 - a_1 = 5 - 3 = 2$ $\quad$ $a_3 - a_2 = 9 - 5 = 4$

$a_4 - a_3 = 15 - 9 = 6$ $\quad$ $a_5 - a_4 = 23 - 15 = 8$

▶ There is no common difference, so the sequence is not arithmetic.

GRAPHING A SEQUENCE To graph a sequence, let a term's position number in the sequence be the x-value. The term is the corresponding y-value.

EXAMPLE 2 Graph a sequence

Graph the sequence $-4, 1, 6, 11, 16, \ldots$.

Make a table pairing each term with its position number.

Position, x	1	2	3	4	5
Term, y	−4	1	6	11	16

Plot the pairs in the table as points in a coordinate plane.

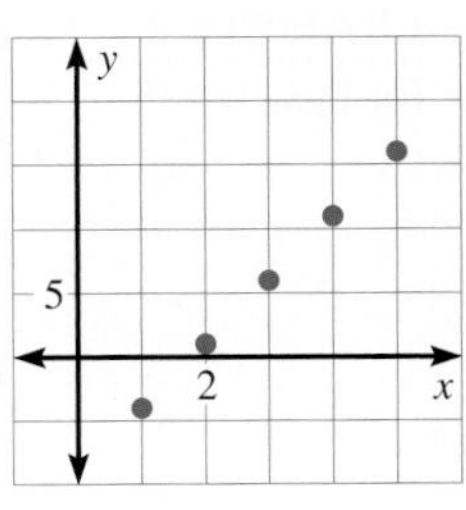

USE FUNCTION NOTATION

You can write the arithmetic sequence with first term a_1 and common difference d in function notation as $f(x) = a_1 + d(x - 1)$.

FUNCTIONS Notice that the points plotted in Example 2 appear to lie on a line. In fact, an arithmetic sequence is a linear function. You can think of the common difference d as the slope and $(1, a_1)$ as a point on the graph of the function. An equation in point-slope form for the function is $a_n - a_1 = d(n - 1)$. This equation can be rewritten as $a_n = a_1 + (n - 1)d$.

KEY CONCEPT *For Your Notebook*

Rule for an Arithmetic Sequence

The nth term of an arithmetic sequence with first term a_1 and common difference d is given by $a_n = a_1 + (n - 1)d$.

EXAMPLE 3 Write a rule for the *n*th term of a sequence

Write a rule for the *n*th term of the sequence −4, 1, 6, 11, 16, ... Find a_{100}.

Solution

The first term of the sequence is $a_1 = -4$, and the common difference is $d = 5$.

$a_n = a_1 + (n - 1)d$	**Write general rule for an arithmetic sequence.**
$a_n = -4 + (n - 1)5$	**Substitute −4 for a_1 and 5 for d.**

Find a_{100} by substituting 100 for n.

$a_n = -4 + (n - 1)5$	**Write the rule for the sequence.**
$a_{100} = -4 + (100 - 1)5$	**Substitute 100 for n.**
$a_{100} = 491$	**Evaluate.**

PRACTICE

EXAMPLE 1 for Exs. 1–3

Tell whether the sequence is arithmetic. If it is, find the next two terms. If it is not, explain why not.

1. 17, 14, 11, 8, 5, . . .
2. 1, 4, 16, 64, 256, . . .
3. −8, −15, −22, −29, −36, . . .

EXAMPLE 2 for Exs. 4–9

Graph the sequence.

4. 1, 4, 7, 11, 14, . . .
5. 4, −3, −10, −17, −24, . . .
6. 5, −1, −7, −13, −19, . . .
7. $2, 3\frac{1}{2}, 5, 6\frac{1}{2}, 8, \ldots$
8. 0, 2, 4, 6, 8, . . .
9. −3, −4, −5, −6, −7, . . .

EXAMPLE 3 for Exs. 10–15

Write a rule for the *n*th term of the sequence. Find a_{100}.

10. −12, −5, 2, 9, 16, . . .
11. 51, 72, 93, 114, 135, . . .
12. 0.25, −0.75, −1.75, −2.75, . . .
13. $\frac{1}{4}, \frac{3}{8}, \frac{1}{2}, \frac{5}{8}, \frac{3}{4}, \ldots$
14. 0, −5, −10, −15, −20, . . .
15. $1, 1\frac{1}{3}, 1\frac{2}{3}, 2, 2\frac{1}{3}, \ldots$
16. **REASONING** For an arithmetic sequence with a first term of a_1 and a common difference of d, show that $a_{n+1} - a_n = d$.

4.4 Write Linear Equations in Standard Form

Before You wrote equations in point-slope form.

Now You will write equations in standard form.

Why? So you can find possible combinations of objects, as in Ex. 41.

Key Vocabulary
- **standard form**

Recall that the linear equation $Ax + By = C$ is in standard form, where A, B, and C are real numbers and A and B are not both zero. All linear equations can be written in standard form.

COMMON CORE

CC.9-12.A.CED.2 Create equations in two or more variables to represent relationships between quantities; graph equations on coordinate axes with labels and scales.*

EXAMPLE 1 Write equivalent equations in standard form

Write two equations in standard form that are equivalent to $2x - 6y = 4$.

Solution

To write one equivalent equation, multiply each side by 2.

$$4x - 12y = 8$$

To write another equivalent equation, multiply each side by 0.5.

$$x - 3y = 2$$

EXAMPLE 2 Write an equation from a graph

Write an equation in standard form of the line shown.

(1, 1)

(2, −2)

Solution

STEP 1 **Calculate** the slope.

$$m = \frac{1 - (-2)}{1 - 2} = \frac{3}{-1} = -3$$

STEP 2 **Write** an equation in point-slope form. Use (1, 1).

$y - y_1 = m(x - x_1)$ **Write point-slope form.**

$y - 1 = -3(x - 1)$ **Substitute 1 for y_1, −3 for m, and 1 for x_1.**

STEP 3 **Rewrite** the equation in standard form.

$3x + y = 4$ **Simplify. Collect variable terms on one side, constants on the other.**

Animated Algebra at my.hrw.com

✓ GUIDED PRACTICE for Examples 1 and 2

1. Write two equations in standard form that are equivalent to $x - y = 3$.
2. Write an equation in standard form of the line through $(3, -1)$ and $(2, -3)$.

HORIZONTAL AND VERTICAL LINES Recall that equations of horizontal lines have the form $y = a$. Equations of vertical lines have the form $x = b$. You cannot write an equation for a vertical line in slope-intercept form or point-slope form, because a vertical line has no slope. However, you can write an equation for a vertical line in standard form.

EXAMPLE 3 Write an equation of a line

Write an equation of the specified line.

a. Blue line **b.** Red line

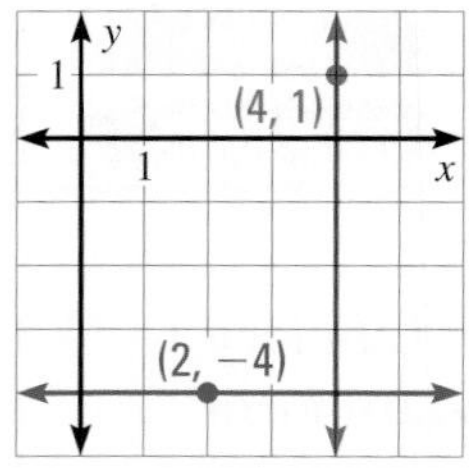

Solution

ANOTHER WAY
Using the slope-intercept form to find an equation of the horizontal line gives you $y = 0x - 4$, or $y = -4$.

a. The y-coordinate of the given point on the blue line is -4. This means that all points on the line have a y-coordinate of -4. An equation of the line is $y = -4$.

b. The x-coordinate of the given point on the red line is 4. This means that all points on the line have an x-coordinate of 4. An equation of the line is $x = 4$.

EXAMPLE 4 Complete an equation in standard form

Find the missing coefficient in the equation of the line shown. Write the completed equation.

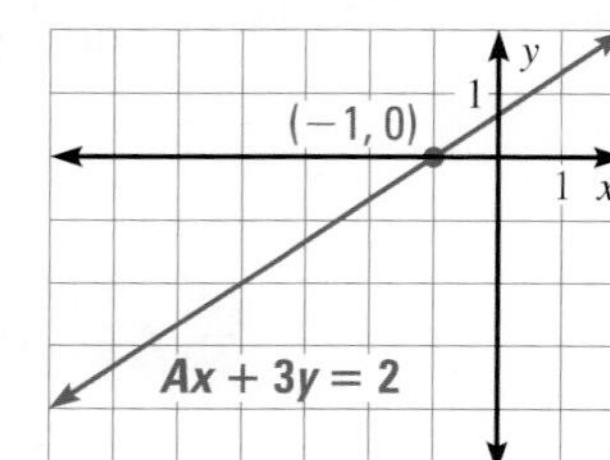

Solution

STEP 1 **Find** the value of A. Substitute the coordinates of the given point for x and y in the equation. Solve for A.

$$Ax + 3y = 2 \quad \text{Write equation.}$$

$$A(-1) + 3(0) = 2 \quad \text{Substitute } -1 \text{ for } x \text{ and } 0 \text{ for } y.$$

$$-A = 2 \quad \text{Simplify.}$$

$$A = -2 \quad \text{Divide by } -1.$$

STEP 2 **Complete** the equation.

$$-2x + 3y = 2 \quad \text{Substitute } -2 \text{ for } A.$$

✓ GUIDED PRACTICE for Examples 3 and 4

Write equations of the horizontal and vertical lines that pass through the given point.

3. $(-8, -9)$ **4.** $(13, -5)$

Find the missing coefficient in the equation of the line that passes through the given point. Write the completed equation.

5. $-4x + By = 7, (-1, 1)$ **6.** $Ax + y = -3, (2, 11)$

EXAMPLE 5 Solve a multi-step problem

LIBRARY Your class is taking a trip to the public library. You can travel in small and large vans. A small van holds 8 people and a large van holds 12 people. Your class could fill 15 small vans and 2 large vans.

a. **Write** an equation in standard form that models the possible combinations of small vans and large vans that your class could fill.

b. **Graph** the equation from part (a).

c. **List** several possible combinations.

Solution

a. Write a verbal model. Then write an equation.

Capacity of small van	·	Number of small vans	+	Capacity of large van	·	Number of large vans	=	People on trip
8	·	s	+	12	·	ℓ	=	p

Because your class could fill 15 small vans and 2 large vans, use (15, 2) as the s- and ℓ-values to substitute in the equation $8s + 12\ell = p$ to find the value of p.

$8(15) + 12(2) = p$ **Substitute 15 for s and 2 for ℓ.**

$144 = p$ **Simplify.**

Substitute 144 for p in the equation $8s + 12\ell = p$.

▶ The equation $8s + 12\ell = 144$ models the possible combinations.

b. Find the intercepts of the graph.

Substitute 0 for s. Substitute 0 for ℓ.

$8(0) + 12\ell = 144$ $8s + 12(0) = 144$

$\ell = 12$ $s = 18$

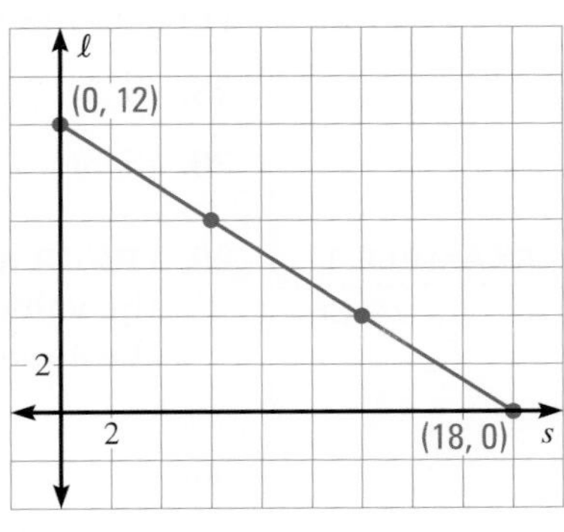

Plot the points (0, 12) and (18, 0). Connect them with a line segment. For this problem only nonnegative whole-number values of s and ℓ make sense.

c. The graph passes through (0, 12), (6, 8), (12, 4), and (18, 0). So, four possible combinations are 0 small and 12 large, 6 small and 8 large, 12 small and 4 large, 18 small and 0 large.

LISTING COMBINATIONS
Other combinations of small and large vans are possible. Another way to find possible combinations is by substituting values for s or ℓ in the equation.

GUIDED PRACTICE for Example 5

7. **WHAT IF?** In Example 5, suppose that 8 students decide not to go on the class trip. Write an equation that models the possible combinations of small and large vans that your class could fill. List several possible combinations.

4.4 EXERCISES

HOMEWORK KEY

○ = See **WORKED-OUT SOLUTIONS** Exs. 17 and 39

★ = **STANDARDIZED TEST PRACTICE** Exs. 4, 30, 40, and 42

◆ = **MULTIPLE REPRESENTATIONS** Ex. 41

SKILL PRACTICE

VOCABULARY Identify the form of the equation.

1. $2x + 8y = -3$ **2.** $y = -5x + 8$ **3.** $y + 4 = 2(x - 6)$

4. ★ **WRITING** *Explain* how to write an equation of a line in standard form when two points on the line are given.

EXAMPLE 1 for Exs. 5–10

EQUIVALENT EQUATIONS Write two equations in standard form that are equivalent to the given equation.

5. $x + y = -10$ **6.** $5x + 10y = 15$ **7.** $-x + 2y = 9$

8. $-9x - 12y = 6$ **9.** $9x - 3y = -12$ **10.** $-2x + 4y = -5$

EXAMPLE 2 for Exs. 11–22

WRITING EQUATIONS Write an equation in standard form of the line that passes through the given point and has the given slope *m* or that passes through the two given points.

11. $(-3, 2)$, $m = 1$ **12.** $(4, -1)$, $m = 3$ **13.** $(0, 5)$, $m = -2$

14. $(-8, 0)$, $m = -4$ **15.** $(-4, -4)$, $m = -\frac{3}{2}$ **16.** $(-6, -10)$, $m = \frac{1}{6}$

17. $(-8, 4)$, $(4, -4)$ **18.** $(-5, 2)$, $(-4, 3)$ **19.** $(0, -1)$, $(-6, -9)$

20. $(3, 9)$, $(1, 1)$ **21.** $(10, 6)$, $(-12, -5)$ **22.** $(-6, -2)$, $(-1, -2)$

EXAMPLE 3 for Exs. 23–28

HORIZONTAL AND VERTICAL LINES Write equations of the horizontal and vertical lines that pass through the given point.

23. $(3, 2)$ **24.** $(-5, -3)$ **25.** $(-1, 3)$

26. $(5, 3)$ **27.** $(-1, 4)$ **28.** $(-6, -2)$

EXAMPLE 4 for Exs. 29–36

29. **ERROR ANALYSIS** *Describe* and correct the error in finding the value of *A* for the equation $Ax - 3y = 5$, if the graph of the equation passes through the point $(1, -4)$.

$A(-4) - 3(1) = 5$
$A = -2$ ✗

30. ★ **WRITING** The *intercept form* of the equation of a line with an *x*-intercept of *a* and a *y*-intercept of *b* is $\frac{x}{a} + \frac{y}{b} = 1$. Write the equation $2x + 3y = 12$ in intercept form. *Describe* your method.

COMPLETING EQUATIONS Find the missing coefficient in the equation of the line that passes through the given point. Write the completed equation.

31. $Ax + 3y = 5$, $(2, -1)$ **32.** $Ax - 4y = -1$, $(6, 1)$ **33.** $-x + By = 10$, $(-2, -2)$

34. $8x + By = 4$, $(-5, 4)$ **35.** $Ax - 3y = -5$, $(1, 0)$ **36.** $2x + By = -4$, $(-3, 7)$

37. **CHALLENGE** Write an equation in standard form of the line that passes through $(0, a)$ and $(b, 0)$ where $a \neq 0$ and $b \neq 0$.

PROBLEM SOLVING

EXAMPLE 5 for Exs. 38–41

38. **GARDENING** The diagram shows the prices of two types of ground cover plants. Write an equation in standard form that models the possible combinations of vinca and phlox plants a gardener can buy for $300. List three of these possible combinations.

39. **NUTRITION** A snack mix requires a total of 120 ounces of some corn cereal and some wheat cereal. Corn cereal comes in 12 ounce boxes.
    a. The last time you made this mix, you used 5 boxes of corn cereal and 4 boxes of wheat cereal. How many ounces are in a box of wheat cereal?
    b. Write an equation in standard form that models the possible combinations of boxes of wheat and corn cereal you can use.
    c. List all possible combinations of whole boxes of wheat and corn cereal you can use to make the snack mix.

40. ★ **SHORT RESPONSE** A dog kennel charges $20 per night to board your dog. You can also have a doggie treat delivered to your dog for $5. Write an equation that models the possible combinations of nights at the kennel and doggie treats that you can buy for $100. Graph the equation. *Explain* what the intercepts of the graph mean in this situation.

41. **MULTIPLE REPRESENTATIONS** As the student council treasurer, you prepare the budget for your class rafting trip. Each large raft costs $100 to rent, and each small raft costs $40 to rent. You have $1600 to spend.
    a. **Writing an Equation** Write an equation in standard form that models the possible combinations of small rafts and large rafts that you can rent.
    b. **Drawing a Graph** Graph the equation from part (a).
    c. **Making a Table** Make a table that shows several combinations of small and large rafts that you can rent.

42. ★ **SHORT RESPONSE** One bus ride costs $.75. One subway ride costs $1.00. A monthly pass can be used for unlimited subway and bus rides and costs the same as 36 subway rides plus 36 bus rides.
    a. Write an equation in standard form that models the possible combinations of bus and subway rides with the same value as the pass.
    b. You ride the bus 60 times in one month. How many times must you ride the subway in order for the cost of the rides to equal the value of the pass? *Explain* your answer.

43. **GEOMETRY** Write an equation in standard form that models the possible lengths and widths (in feet) of a rectangle having the same perimeter as a rectangle that is 10 feet wide and 20 feet long. Make a table that shows five possible lengths and widths of the rectangle.

44. **CHALLENGE** You are working in a chemistry lab. You have 1000 milliliters of pure acid. A dilution of acid is created by adding pure acid to water. A 40% dilution contains 40% acid and 60% water. You have been asked to make a 40% dilution and a 60% dilution of pure acid.

    a. Write an equation in standard form that models the possible quantities of each dilution you can prepare using all 1000 milliliters of pure acid.

    b. You prepare 700 milliliters of the 40% dilution. How much of the 60% dilution can you prepare?

    c. How much water do you need to prepare 700 milliliters of the 40% dilution?

QUIZ

Write an equation in slope-intercept form of the line that passes through the given point and has the given slope *m*.

1. (2, 5), $m = 3$
2. (−1, 4), $m = -2$
3. (0, −7), $m = 5$

Write an equation in slope-intercept form of the line that passes through the given points.

4. (0, 2), (9, 5)
5. (5, 7), (19, 14)
6. (4, 24), (−11, 19)

Write an equation in (a) point-slope form and (b) standard form of the line that passes through the given points.

7. (−5, 2), (−4, 3)
8. (0, −1), (−6, −9)
9. (3, 9), (1, 1)

10. **DVDS** The table shows the price per DVD for different quantities of DVDs. Write an equation that models the price per DVD as a function of the number of DVDs purchased.

Number of DVDs purchased	1	2	3	4	5	6
Price per DVD (dollars)	20	18	16	14	12	10

See **EXTRA PRACTICE** in Student Resources **ONLINE QUIZ** at my.hrw.com

MIXED REVIEW of Problem Solving

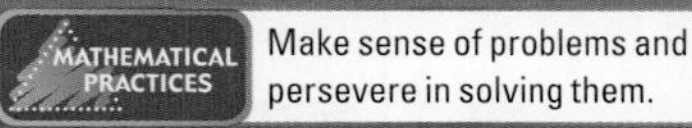

Make sense of problems and persevere in solving them.

1. **MULTI-STEP PROBLEM** A satellite radio company charges a monthly fee of \$13 for service. To use the service, you must first buy equipment that costs \$100.
   a. Identify the rate of change and starting value in this situation.
   b. Write an equation that gives the total cost of satellite radio as a function of the number of months of service.
   c. Find the total cost after 1 year of satellite radio service.

2. **MULTI-STEP PROBLEM** You hike 5 miles before taking a break. After your break, you continue to hike at an average speed of 3.5 miles per hour.

   a. Write an equation that gives the distance (in miles) that you hike as a function of the time (in hours) since your break.
   b. You hike for 4 hours after your break. Find the total distance you hike for the day.

3. **EXTENDED RESPONSE** The table shows the cost of a catered lunch buffet for different numbers of people.

Number of people	Cost (dollars)
12	192
18	288
24	384
30	480
36	576
42	672

   a. *Explain* why the situation can be modeled by a linear equation.
   b. Write an equation that gives the cost of the lunch buffet as a function of the number of people attending.
   c. What is the cost of a lunch buffet for 120 people?

4. **SHORT RESPONSE** You use a garden hose to fill a swimming pool at a constant rate. The pool is empty when you begin to fill it. The pool contains 15 gallons of water after 5 minutes. After 30 minutes, the pool contains 90 gallons of water. Write an equation that gives the volume (in gallons) of water in the pool as a function of the number of minutes since you began filling it. *Explain* how you can find the time it takes to put 150 gallons of water in the pool.

5. **EXTENDED RESPONSE** A city is paving a bike path. The same length of path is paved each day. After 4 days, there are 8 miles of path remaining to be paved. After 6 more days, there are 5 miles of path remaining to be paved.
   a. *Explain* how you know the situation can be modeled by a linear equation.
   b. Write an equation that gives the distance (in miles) remaining to be paved as a function of the number of days since the project began.
   c. In how many more days will the entire path be paved?

6. **OPEN-ENDED** Write an equation in standard form that models the possible combinations of nickels and dimes worth a certain amount of money (in dollars). List several of these possible combinations.

7. **GRIDDED ANSWER** You are saving money to buy a stereo system. You have saved \$50 so far. You plan to save \$20 each week for the next few months. How much money do you expect to have saved in 7 weeks?

8. **GRIDDED ANSWER** The cost of renting a moving van for a 26 mile trip is \$62.50. The cost of renting the same van for a 38 mile trip is \$65.50. The cost changes at a constant rate with respect to the length (in miles) of the trip. Find the total cost of renting the van for a 54 mile trip.

4.5 Write Equations of Parallel and Perpendicular Lines

Before You used slope to determine whether lines are parallel.
Now You will write equations of parallel and perpendicular lines.
Why? So you can analyze growth rates, as in Ex. 33.

Key Vocabulary
- converse
- perpendicular lines
- conditional statement

The **converse** of a conditional statement interchanges the hypothesis and conclusion. The converse of a true statement is not necessarily true.

You have learned that the statement "If two nonvertical lines have the same slope, then they are parallel" is true. Its converse is also true.

COMMON CORE

CC.9-12.F.LE.2 Construct linear and exponential functions, including arithmetic and geometric sequences, given a graph, a description of a relationship, or two input-output pairs (include reading these from a table).*

KEY CONCEPT *For Your Notebook*

Parallel Lines

- If two nonvertical lines in the same plane have the same slope, then they are parallel.
- If two nonvertical lines in the same plane are parallel, then they have the same slope.

EXAMPLE 1 Write an equation of a parallel line

Write an equation of the line that passes through $(-3, -5)$ and is parallel to the line $y = 3x - 1$.

Solution

STEP 1 **Identify** the slope. The graph of the given equation has a slope of 3. So, the parallel line through $(-3, -5)$ has a slope of 3.

STEP 2 **Find** the y-intercept. Use the slope and the given point.

$y = mx + b$	**Write slope-intercept form.**
$-5 = 3(-3) + b$	**Substitute 3 for *m*, −3 for *x*, and −5 for *y*.**
$4 = b$	**Solve for *b*.**

STEP 3 **Write** an equation. Use $y = mx + b$.

$y = 3x + 4$	**Substitute 3 for *m* and 4 for *b*.**

CHECK REASONABLENESS
You can check that your answer is reasonable by graphing both lines.

GUIDED PRACTICE for Example 1

1. Write an equation of the line that passes through $(-2, 11)$ and is parallel to the line $y = -x + 5$.

PERPENDICULAR LINES Two lines in the same plane are **perpendicular** if they intersect to form a right angle. Horizontal and vertical lines are perpendicular to each other.

Compare the slopes of the perpendicular lines shown below.

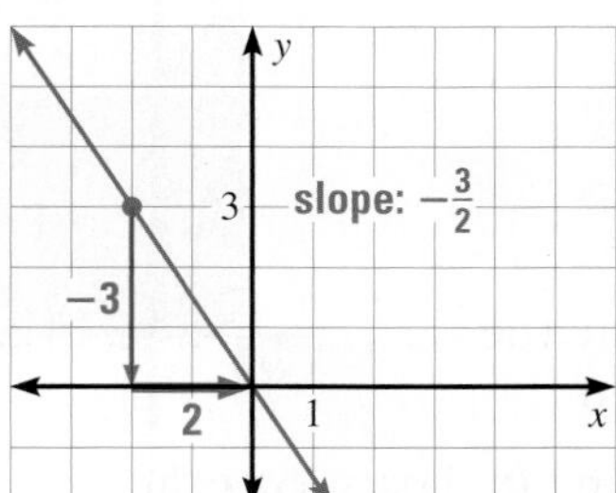

Rotate the line 90° in a clockwise direction about the origin to find a perpendicular line.

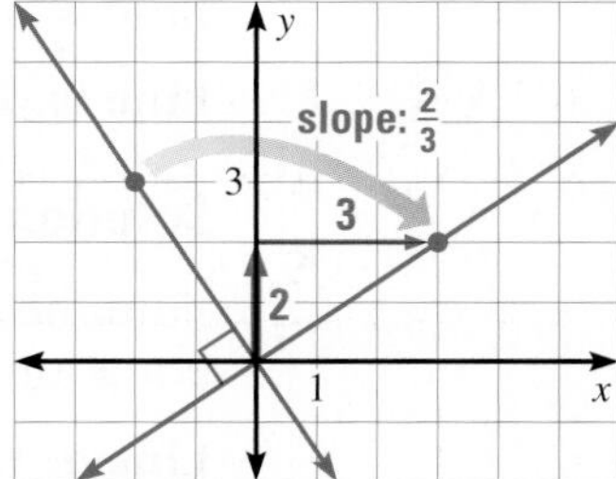

KEY CONCEPT — *For Your Notebook*

USE FRACTIONS
The product of a nonzero number m and its negative reciprocal is −1:
$m\left(-\frac{1}{m}\right) = -1$.

Perpendicular Lines

- If two nonvertical lines in the same plane have slopes that are negative reciprocals, then the lines are perpendicular.
- If two nonvertical lines in the same plane are perpendicular, then their slopes are negative reciprocals.

EXAMPLE 2 Determine whether lines are parallel or perpendicular

Determine which lines, if any, are parallel or perpendicular.

Line *a*: $y = 5x - 3$ **Line *b*:** $x + 5y = 2$ **Line *c*:** $-10y - 2x = 0$

Solution

Find the slopes of the lines.

Line *a*: The equation is in slope-intercept form. The slope is 5.

Write the equations for lines b and c in slope-intercept form.

Line *b*: $x + 5y = 2$

$5y = -x + 2$

$y = -\frac{1}{5}x + \frac{2}{5}$

Line *c*: $-10y - 2x = 0$

$-10y = 2x$

$y = -\frac{1}{5}x$

▶ Lines b and c have slopes of $-\frac{1}{5}$, so they are parallel. Line a has a slope of 5, the negative reciprocal of $-\frac{1}{5}$, so it is perpendicular to lines b and c.

✓ GUIDED PRACTICE for Example 2

2. Determine which lines, if any, are parallel or perpendicular.

Line *a*: $2x + 6y = -3$ **Line *b*:** $y = 3x - 8$ **Line *c*:** $-1.5y + 4.5x = 6$

EXAMPLE 3 Determine whether lines are perpendicular

STATE FLAG The Arizona state flag is shown in a coordinate plane. Lines a and b appear to be perpendicular. Are they?

Line a: $12y = -7x + 42$

Line b: $11y = 16x - 52$

Solution

Find the slopes of the lines. Write the equations in slope-intercept form.

Line a: $12y = -7x + 42$ **Line b:** $11y = 16x - 52$

$y = -\frac{7}{12}x + \frac{42}{12}$ $y = \frac{16}{11}x - \frac{52}{11}$

▸ The slope of line a is $-\frac{7}{12}$. The slope of line b is $\frac{16}{11}$. The two slopes are not negative reciprocals, so lines a and b are not perpendicular.

EXAMPLE 4 Write an equation of a perpendicular line

Write an equation of the line that passes through (4, −5) and is perpendicular to the line $y = 2x + 3$.

Solution

STEP 1 **Identify** the slope. The graph of the given equation has a slope of 2. Because the slopes of perpendicular lines are negative reciprocals, the slope of the perpendicular line through (4, −5) is $-\frac{1}{2}$.

STEP 2 **Find** the y-intercept. Use the slope and the given point.

$y = mx + b$ **Write slope-intercept form.**

$-5 = -\frac{1}{2}(4) + b$ **Substitute $-\frac{1}{2}$ for m, 4 for x, and −5 for y.**

$-3 = b$ **Solve for b.**

STEP 3 **Write** an equation.

$y = mx + b$ **Write slope-intercept form.**

$y = -\frac{1}{2}x - 3$ **Substitute $-\frac{1}{2}$ for m and −3 for b.**

GUIDED PRACTICE for Examples 3 and 4

3. Is line a perpendicular to line b? *Justify* your answer using slopes.

   Line a: $2y + x = -12$ **Line b:** $2y = 3x - 8$

4. Write an equation of the line that passes through (4, 3) and is perpendicular to the line $y = 4x - 7$.

4.5 EXERCISES

HOMEWORK KEY

○ = See WORKED-OUT SOLUTIONS Exs. 19 and 33

★ = STANDARDIZED TEST PRACTICE Exs. 2, 16, 17, 28, 30, 34, and 36

SKILL PRACTICE

1. **VOCABULARY** Copy and complete: Two lines in a plane are _?_ if they intersect to form a right angle.

2. ★ **WRITING** *Explain* how you can tell whether two lines are perpendicular, given the equations of the lines.

EXAMPLE 1 for Exs. 3–11

PARALLEL LINES Write an equation of the line that passes through the given point and is parallel to the given line.

3. $(-1, 3), y = 2x + 2$
4. $(6, 8), y = -\frac{5}{2}x + 10$
5. $(5, -1), y = -\frac{3}{5}x - 3$
6. $(-1, 2), y = 5x + 4$
7. $(1, 7), -6x + y = -1$
8. $(18, 2), 3y = x - 12$
9. $(-2, 5), 2y = 4x - 6$
10. $(9, 4), y - x = 3$
11. $(-10, 0), -y + 3x = 16$

EXAMPLE 2 for Exs. 12–16

PARALLEL OR PERPENDICULAR Determine which lines, if any, are parallel or perpendicular.

12. Line a: $y = 4x - 2$, Line b: $y = -\frac{1}{4}x$, Line c: $y = -4x + 1$
13. Line a: $y = \frac{3}{5}x + 1$, Line b: $5y = 3x - 2$, Line c: $10x - 6y = -4$
14. Line a: $y = 3x + 6$, Line b: $3x + y = 6$, Line c: $3y = 2x + 18$
15. Line a: $4x - 3y = 2$, Line b: $3x + 4y = -1$, Line c: $4y - 3x = 20$

16. ★ **MULTIPLE CHOICE** Which statement is true of the given lines?

Line a: $-2x + y = 4$ Line b: $2x + 5y = 2$ Line c: $x + 2y = 4$

Ⓐ Lines a and b are parallel. Ⓑ Lines a and c are parallel.

Ⓒ Lines a and b are perpendicular. Ⓓ Lines a and c are perpendicular.

17. ★ **SHORT RESPONSE** Determine which of the lines shown, if any, are parallel or perpendicular. *Justify* your answer using slopes.

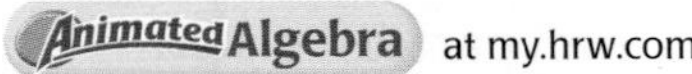

at my.hrw.com

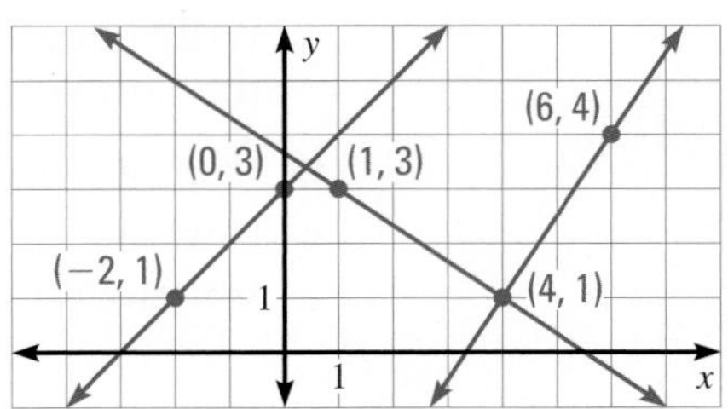

EXAMPLE 4 for Exs. 18–27

PERPENDICULAR LINES Write an equation of the line that passes through the given point and is perpendicular to the given line.

18. $(3, -3), y = x + 5$
19. $(-9, 2), y = 3x - 12$
20. $(5, 1), y = 5x - 2$
21. $(7, 10), y = 0.5x - 9$
22. $(-2, -4), y = -\frac{2}{7}x + 1$
23. $(-4, -1), y = \frac{4}{3}x + 6$
24. $(3, 3), 2y = 3x - 6$
25. $(-5, 2), y + 3 = 2x$
26. $(8, -1), 4y + 2x = 12$

27. **ERROR ANALYSIS** *Describe* and correct the error in finding the y-intercept of the line that passes through (2, 1) and is perpendicular to the line $y = -\frac{1}{2}x + 3$.

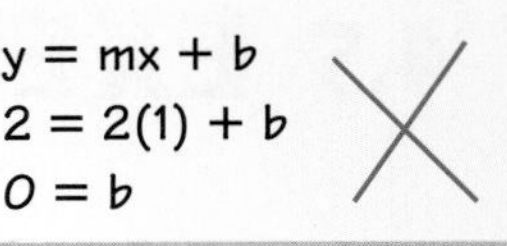

28. ★ **MULTIPLE CHOICE** Which equation represents the line that passes through (0, 0) and is parallel to the line passing through (2, 3) and (6, 1)?

Ⓐ $y = \frac{1}{2}x$ Ⓑ $y = -\frac{1}{2}x$ Ⓒ $y = -2x$ Ⓓ $y = 2x$

29. **REASONING** Is the line through (4, 3) and (3, −1) perpendicular to the line through (−3, 3) and (1, 2)? *Justify* your answer using slopes.

30. ★ **OPEN-ENDED** Write equations of two lines that are parallel. Then write an equation of a line that is perpendicular to those lines.

31. **CHALLENGE** Write a formula for the slope of a line that is perpendicular to the line through the points (x_1, y_1) and (x_2, y_2).

PROBLEM SOLVING

EXAMPLES 3 and 4 for Exs. 32, 34

32. **HOCKEY** A hockey puck leaves the blade of a hockey stick, bounces off a wall, and travels in a new direction, as shown.
 a. Write an equation that models the path of the puck from the blade of the hockey stick to the wall.
 b. Write an equation that models the path of the puck after it bounces off the wall.
 c. Does the path of the puck form a right angle? *Justify* your answer.

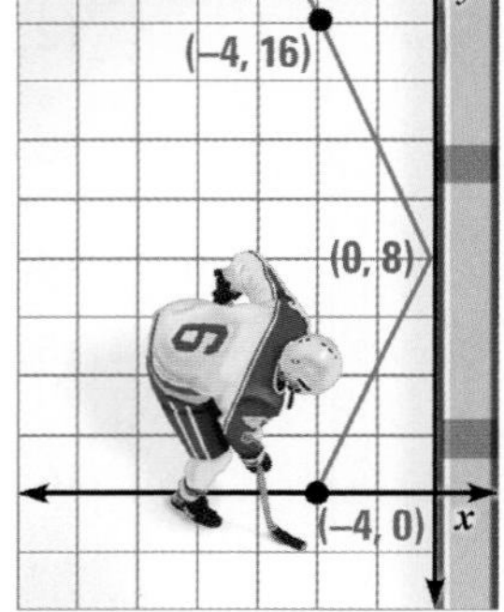

33. **BIOLOGY** While nursing, blue whale calves can gain weight at a rate of 200 pounds per day. Two particular calves weigh 6000 pounds and 6250 pounds at birth.
 a. Write equations that model the weight of each calf as a function of the number of days since birth.
 b. How much is each calf expected to weigh 30 days after birth?
 c. How are the graphs of the equations from part (a) related? *Justify* your answer.

34. ★ **SHORT RESPONSE** The map shows several streets in a city. Determine which of the streets, if any, are parallel or perpendicular. *Justify* your answer using slopes.

Park: $3y - 2x = 12$ Main: $y = -6x + 44$

2nd St.: $3y = 2x - 13$ Sea: $2y = -3x + 37$

35. **SOFTBALL** A softball training academy charges students a monthly fee plus an initial registration fee. The total amounts paid by two students are given by the functions $f(x)$ and $g(x)$ where x is the numbers of months the students have been members of the academy. The graphs of f and g are parallel lines. Did the students pay different monthly fees or different registration fees? How do you know?

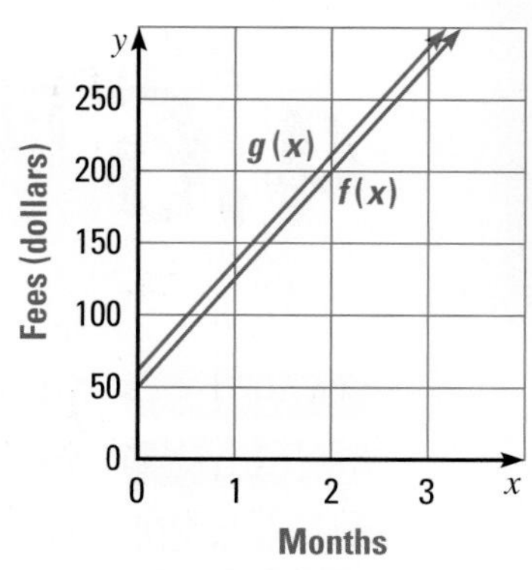

36. ★ **EXTENDED RESPONSE** If you are one of the first 100 people to join a new health club, you are charged a joining fee of \$49. Otherwise, you are charged a joining fee of \$149. The monthly membership cost is \$38.75.

   a. Write an equation that gives the total cost (in dollars) of membership as a function of the number of months of membership if you are one of the first 100 members to join.

   b. Write an equation that gives the total cost (in dollars) of membership as a function of the number of months of membership if you are *not* one of the first 100 members to join.

   c. How are the graphs of these functions related? How do you know?

   d. After 6 months, what is the difference in total cost for a person who paid \$149 to join and a person who paid \$49 to join? after 12 months?

37. **CHALLENGE** You and your friend have gift cards to a shopping mall. Your card has a value of \$50, and your friend's card has a value of \$30. If neither of you uses the cards, the value begins to decrease at a rate of \$2.50 per month after 6 months.

   a. Write two equations, one that gives the value of your card and another that gives the value of your friend's card as functions of the number of months after 6 months of nonuse.

   b. How are the graphs of these functions related? How do you know?

   c. What are the x-intercepts of the graphs of the functions, and what do they mean in this situation?

4.6 Fit a Line to Data

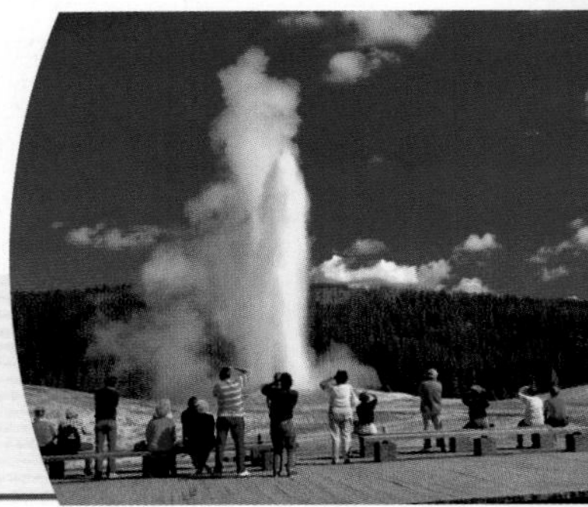

Before You modeled situations involving a constant rate of change.

Now You will make scatter plots and write equations to model data.

Why? So you can model scientific data, as in Ex. 19.

Key Vocabulary
- **scatter plot**
- **correlation**
- **line of fit**

CC.9-12.S.ID.6c Fit a linear function for a scatter plot that suggests a linear association.*

A **scatter plot** is a graph used to determine whether there is a relationship between paired data. Scatter plots can show trends in the data.

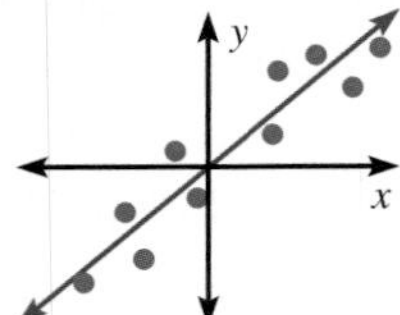

If y tends to increase as x increases, the paired data are said to have a **positive correlation**.

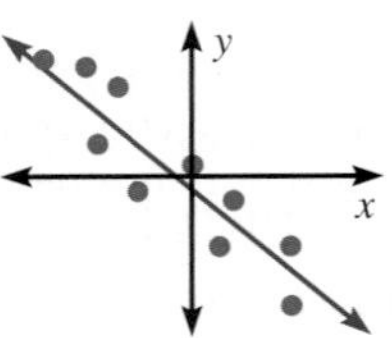

If y tends to decrease as x increases, the paired data are said to have a **negative correlation**.

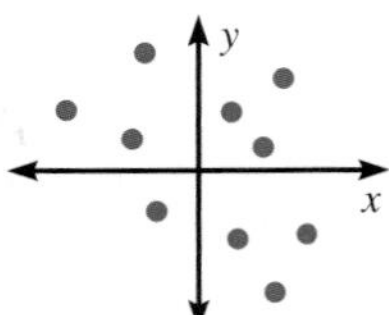

If x and y have no apparent relationship, the paired data are said to have **relatively no correlation**.

EXAMPLE 1 Describe the correlation of data

Describe **the correlation of the data graphed in the scatter plot.**

a.

y
90
70
50
0
Test scores
0 2 4 6 8 x
Hours of studying

b.

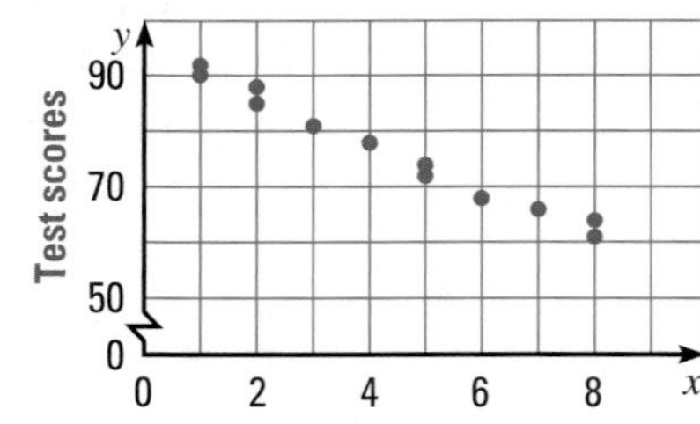

a. The scatter plot shows a positive correlation between hours of studying and test scores. This means that as the hours of studying increased, the test scores tended to increase.

b. The scatter plot shows a negative correlation between hours of television watched and test scores. This means that as the hours of television watched increased, the test scores tended to decrease.

GUIDED PRACTICE for Example 1

1. Using the scatter plots in Example 1, predict a reasonable test score for 4.5 hours of studying and 4.5 hours of television watched.

EXAMPLE 2 Make a scatter plot

SWIMMING SPEEDS The table shows the lengths (in centimeters) and swimming speeds (in centimeters per second) of six fish.

Fish	Pike	Red gurnard	Black bass	Gurnard	Norway haddock
Length (cm)	37.8	19.2	21.3	26.2	26.8
Speed (cm/sec)	148	47	88	131	98

a. Make a scatter plot of the data.

b. *Describe* the correlation of the data.

Solution

a. Treat the data as ordered pairs. Let x represent the fish length (in centimeters), and let y represent the speed (in centimeters per second). Plot the ordered pairs as points in a coordinate plane.

b. The scatter plot shows a positive correlation, which means that longer fish tend to swim faster.

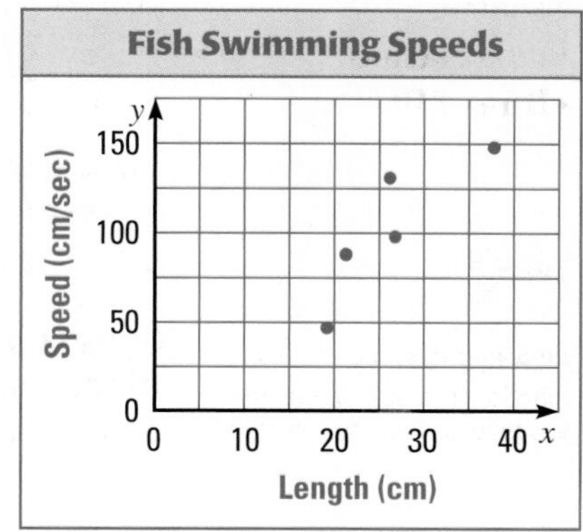

✓ GUIDED PRACTICE for Example 2

2. Make a scatter plot of the data in the table. *Describe* the correlation of the data.

x	1	1	2	3	3	4	5	5	6
y	2	3	4	4	5	5	5	7	8

MODELING DATA When data show a positive or negative correlation, you can model the trend in the data using a **line of fit**.

KEY CONCEPT *For Your Notebook*

Using a Line of Fit to Model Data

STEP 1 **Make** a scatter plot of the data.

STEP 2 **Decide** whether the data can be modeled by a line.

STEP 3 **Draw** a line that appears to fit the data closely. There should be approximately as many points above the line as below it.

STEP 4 **Write** an equation using two points on the line. The points do not have to represent actual data pairs, but they must lie on the line of fit.

EXAMPLE 3 Write an equation to model data

BIRD POPULATIONS The table shows the number of active red-cockaded woodpecker clusters in a part of the De Soto National Forest in Mississippi. Write an equation that models the number of active clusters as a function of the number of years since 1990.

Year	1992	1993	1994	1995	1996	1997	1998	1999	2000
Active clusters	22	24	27	27	34	40	42	45	51

Solution

STEP 1 **Make** a scatter plot of the data. Let x represent the number of years since 1990. Let y represent the number of active clusters.

STEP 2 **Decide** whether the data can be modeled by a line. Because the scatter plot shows a positive correlation, you can fit a line to the data.

STEP 3 **Draw** a line that appears to fit the points in the scatter plot closely.

STEP 4 **Write** an equation using two points on the line. Use (2, 20) and (8, 42).

Find the slope of the line.

$$m = \frac{y_2 - y_1}{x_2 - x_1} = \frac{42 - 20}{8 - 2} = \frac{22}{6} = \frac{11}{3}$$

Find the y-intercept of the line. Use the point (2, 20).

$y = mx + b$ **Write slope-intercept form.**

$20 = \frac{11}{3}(2) + b$ **Substitute $\frac{11}{3}$ for m, 2 for x, and 20 for y.**

$\frac{38}{3} = b$ **Solve for b.**

An equation of the line of fit is $y = \frac{11}{3}x + \frac{38}{3}$.

▶ The number y of active woodpecker clusters can be modeled by the function $y = \frac{11}{3}x + \frac{38}{3}$ where x is the number of years since 1990.

Animated Algebra at my.hrw.com

✓ GUIDED PRACTICE for Example 3

3. Use the data in the table to write an equation that models y as a function of x.

x	1	2	3	4	5	6	8
y	3	5	8	9	11	12	14

EXAMPLE 4 Interpret a model

Refer to the model for the number of woodpecker clusters in Example 3.

a. *Describe* the domain and range of the function.

b. At about what rate did the number of active woodpecker clusters change during the period 1992–2000?

Solution

a. The domain of the function is the the period from 1992 to 2000, or $2 \le x \le 10$. The range is the the number of active clusters given by the function for $2 \le x \le 10$, or $20 \le y \le 49.3$.

b. The number of active woodpecker clusters increased at a rate of $\frac{11}{3}$ or about 3.7 woodpecker clusters per year.

GUIDED PRACTICE for Example 4

4. In Guided Practice Exercise 2, at about what rate does y change with respect to x?

4.6 EXERCISES

HOMEWORK KEY

○ = See WORKED-OUT SOLUTIONS Exs. 7 and 17

★ = STANDARDIZED TEST PRACTICE Exs. 2, 8, 11, 12, and 16

SKILL PRACTICE

1. VOCABULARY Copy and complete: When data have a positive correlation, the dependent variable tends to __?__ as the independent variable increases.

2. ★ WRITING *Describe* how paired data with a positive correlation, a negative correlation, and relatively no correlation differ.

DESCRIBING CORRELATIONS **Tell whether x and y show a *positive correlation*, a *negative correlation*, or *relatively no correlation*.**

EXAMPLE 1 for Exs. 3–5, 10, 11

3.

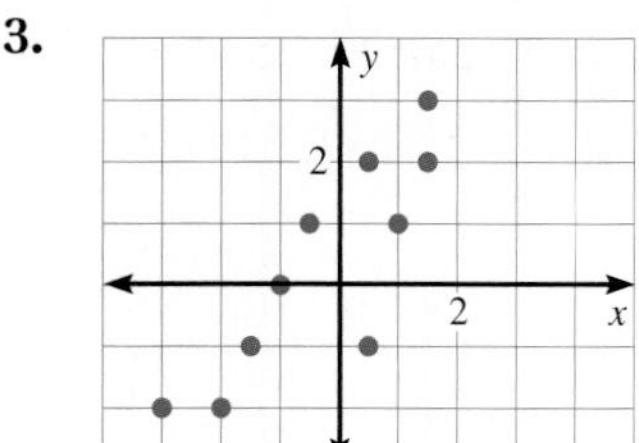

4.

y
1
1
x

5.

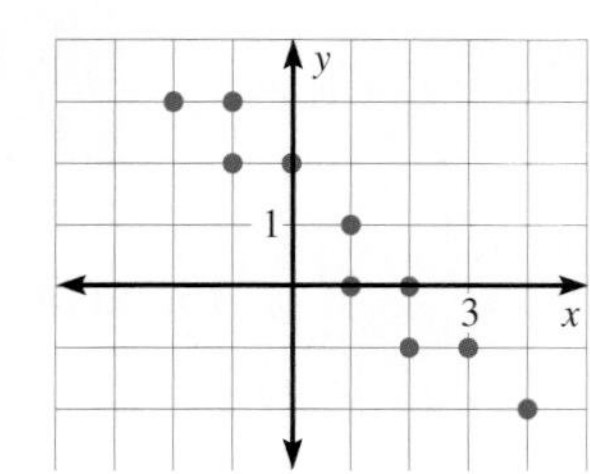

EXAMPLES 2 and 3 for Exs. 6–9

FITTING LINES TO DATA **Make a scatter plot of the data in the table. Draw a line of fit. Write an equation of the line.**

6.

x	1	1	3	4	5	6	9
y	10	12	33	46	59	70	102

7.

x	1.2	1.8	2.3	3.0	4.4	5.2
y	10	7	5	−1	−4	−8

8. ★ **MULTIPLE CHOICE** Which equation best models the data in the scatter plot?

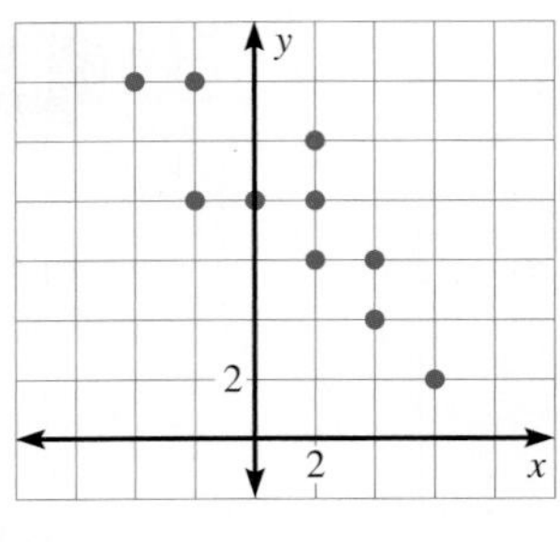

Ⓐ $y = -x - 6$ Ⓑ $y = x - 6$

Ⓒ $y = -x + 8$ Ⓓ $y = x + 8$

9. **ERROR ANALYSIS** *Describe* and correct the error in fitting the line to the data in the scatter plot.

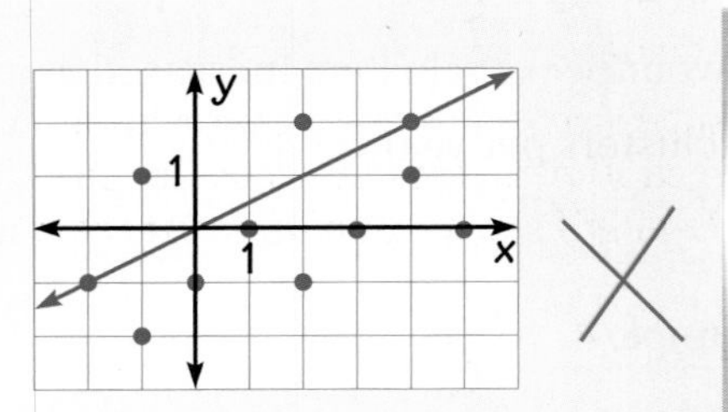

10. **ERROR ANALYSIS** *Describe* and correct the error in describing the correlation of the data in the scatter plot.

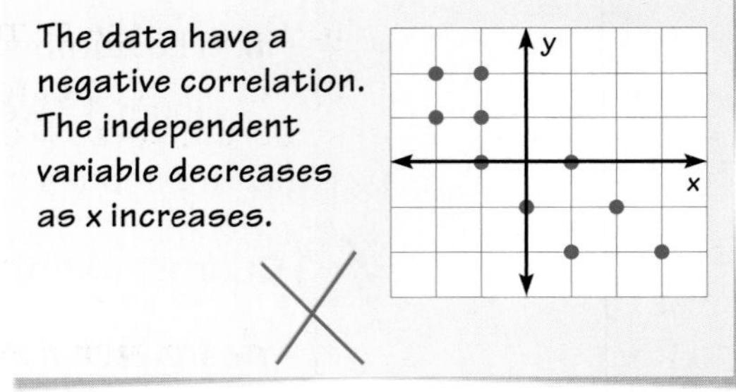

11. ★ **OPEN-ENDED** Give an example of a data set that shows a negative correlation.

12. ★ **SHORT RESPONSE** Make a scatter plot of the data. *Describe* the correlation of the data. Is it possible to fit a line to the data? If so, write an equation of the line. If not, explain why.

x	−12	−7	−4	−3	−1	2	5	6	7	9	15
y	150	50	15	10	1	5	22	37	52	90	226

MODELING DATA Make a scatter plot of the data. *Describe* the correlation of the data. If possible, fit a line to the data and write an equation of the line.

13.

x	10	12	15	20	30	45	60	99
y	−2	4	9	16	32	55	87	128

14.

x	−5	−3	−3	0	1	2	5	6
y	−4	12	10	−6	8	0	3	−9

15. **CHALLENGE** Which line shown is a better line of fit for the scatter plot? *Explain* your reasoning.

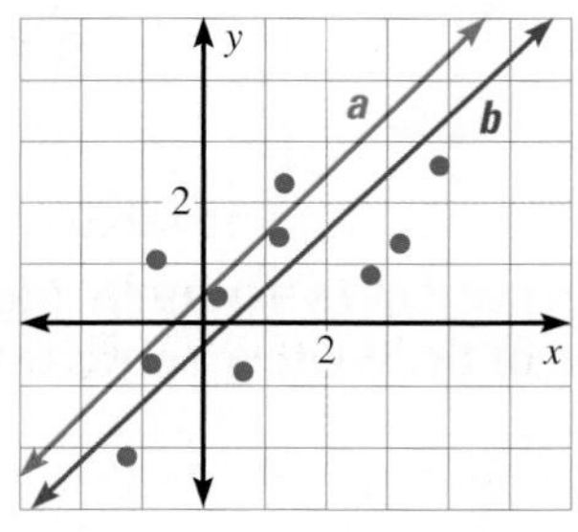

○ = See **WORKED-OUT SOLUTIONS** in Student Resoutces ★ = **STANDARDIZED TEST PRACTICE**

PROBLEM SOLVING

EXAMPLE 2
for Exs. 16

16. ★ SHORT RESPONSE The table shows the approximate home range size of big cats (members of the *Panthera* genus) in their natural habitat and the percent of time that the cats spend pacing in captivity.

Big cat (*Panthera* genus)	Lion	Jaguar	Leopard	Tiger
Home range size (km^2)	148	90	34	48
Pacing (percent of time)	48	21	11	16

a. Make a scatter plot of the data.

b. *Describe* the correlation of the data.

c. The snow leopard's home range size is about 39 square kilometers. It paces about 7% of its time in captivity. Does the snow leopard fit the pacing trend of cats in the *Panthera* genus? *Explain* your reasoning.

EXAMPLES
3 and 4
for Exs. 17–18

17. EARTH SCIENCE The mesosphere is a layer of atmosphere that lies from about 50 kilometers above Earth's surface to about 90 kilometers above Earth's surface. The diagram shows the temperature at certain altitudes in the mesosphere.

a. Make a scatter plot of the data.

b. Write an equation that models the temperature (in degrees Celsius) as a function of the altitude (in kilometers) above 50 kilometers.

c. At about what rate does the temperature change with increasing altitude in the mesosphere?

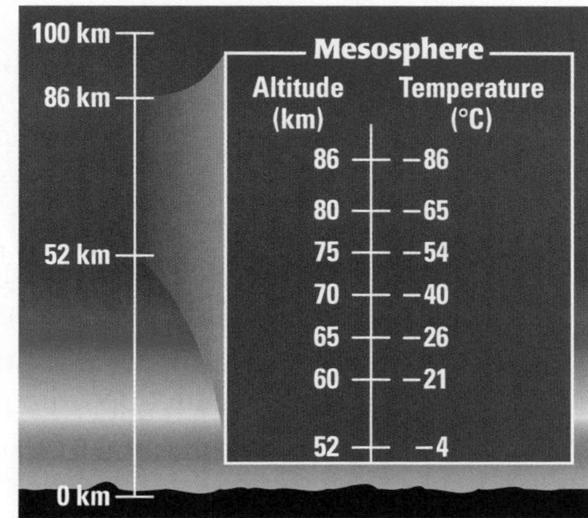

18. ALLIGATORS The table shows the weights of two alligators at various times during a feeding trial. Make two scatter plots, one for each alligator, where x is the number of weeks and y is the weight of the alligator. Draw lines of fit for both scatter plots. *Compare* the approximate growth rates.

Weeks	0	9	18	27	34	43	49
Alligator 1 weight (pounds)	6	8.6	10	13.6	15	17.2	19.8
Alligator 2 weight (pounds)	6	9.2	12.8	13.6	20.2	21.4	24.3

19. GEOLOGY The table shows the duration of several eruptions of the geyser Old Faithful and the interval between eruptions. Write an equation that models the interval as a function of an eruption's duration.

Duration (minutes)	1.5	2.0	2.5	3.0	3.5	4.0	4.5	5.0
Interval (minutes)	50	57	65	71	76	82	89	95

20. **DAYLIGHT** The table shows the number of hours and minutes of daylight in Baltimore, Maryland, for ten days in January.

Day in January	5	6	7	8	9	10	11	12	13	14
Daylight (hours and minutes)	9:30	9:31	9:32	9:34	9:35	9:36	9:37	9:38	9:40	9:41

a. Write an equation that models the hours of daylight (in minutes in excess of 9 hours) as a function of the number of days since January 5.

b. At what rate do the hours of daylight change over time in early January?

c. Do you expect the trend described by the equation to continue indefinitely? *Explain.*

21. **CHALLENGE** The table shows the estimated amount of time and the estimated amount of money the average person in the U.S. spent on the Internet each year from 1999 to 2005.

Year	1999	2000	2001	2002	2003	2004	2005
Internet time (hours)	88	107	136	154	169	182	193
Internet spending (dollars)	40.55	49.64	68.70	84.73	97.76	110.46	122.67

a. Write an equation that models the amount of time h (in hours) spent on the Internet as a function of the number of years y since 1999.

b. Write an equation that models the amount of money m spent on the Internet as a function of the time h (in hours) spent on the Internet.

c. Substitute the expression that is equal to h from part (a) in the function from part (b). What does the new function tell you?

d. Does the function from part (c) agree with the data given? *Explain.*

See **EXTRA PRACTICE** in Student Resources **ONLINE QUIZ** at my.hrw.com

Graphing Calculator ACTIVITY Use after Fit a Line to Data

my.hrw.com
Keystrokes

Perform Linear Regression

Use appropriate tools strategically.

QUESTION How can you model data with the best-fitting line?

The line that most closely follows a trend in data is the *best-fitting line*. The process of finding the best-fitting line to model a set of data is called *linear regression*. This process can be tedious to perform by hand, but you can use a graphing calculator to make a scatter plot and perform linear regression on a data set.

EXAMPLE 1 Create a scatter plot

The table shows the total sales from women's clothing stores in the United States from 1997 to 2002. Make a scatter plot of the data. *Describe* the correlation of the data.

Year	1997	1998	1999	2000	2001	2002
Sales (billions of dollars)	27.9	28.7	30.2	32.5	33.1	34.3

STEP 1 Enter data

Press STAT and select Edit. Enter years since 1997 (0, 1, 2, 3, 4, 5) into List 1 (L_1). These will be the x-values. Enter sales (in billions of dollars) into List 2 (L_2). These will be the y-values.

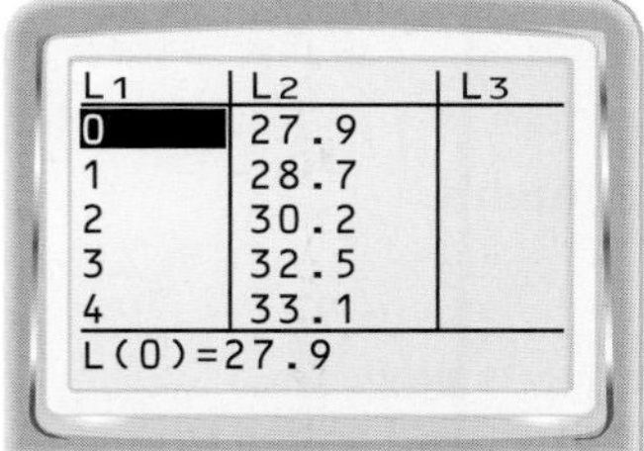

STEP 2 Choose plot settings

Press 2nd Y= and select Plot1. Turn Plot1 On. Select scatter plot as the type of display. Enter L_1 for the Xlist and L_2 for the Ylist.

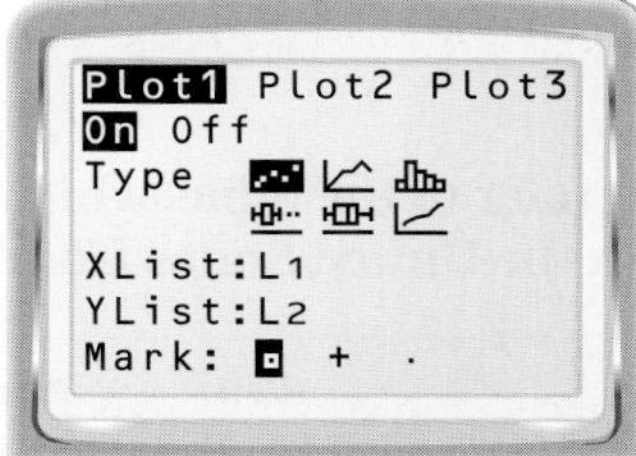

STEP 3 Make a scatter plot

Press ZOOM 9 to display the scatter plot so that the points for all data pairs are visible.

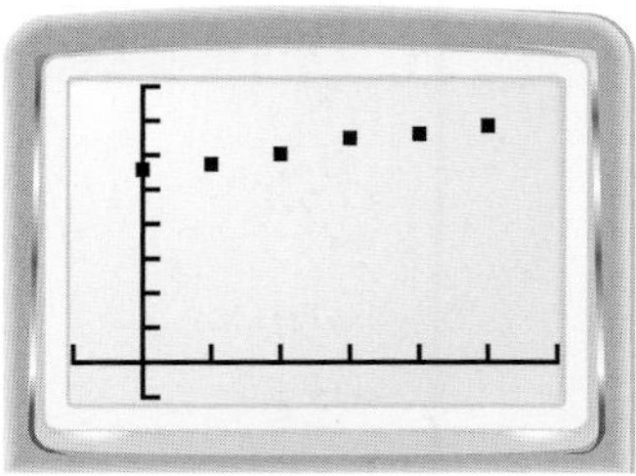

STEP 4 Describe the correlation

Describe the correlation of the data in the scatter plot.

The data have a positive correlation. This means that with each passing year, the sales of women's clothing tended to increase.

MODELING DATA The *correlation coefficient* r for a set of paired data measures how well the best-fitting line fits the data. You can use a graphing calculator to find a value for r.

For r close to 1, the data have a strong positive correlation. For r close to -1, the data have a strong negative correlation. For r close to 0, the data have relatively no correlation.

EXAMPLE 2 Find the best-fitting line

Find an equation of the best-fitting line for the scatter plot from Example 1. Determine the correlation coefficient of the data. Graph the best-fitting line.

***STEP 1* Perform regression**

Press STAT. From the CALC menu, choose LinReg(ax+b). The a- and b-values given are for an equation of the form $y = ax + b$. Rounding these values gives the equation $y = 1.36x + 27.7$. Because r is close to 1, the data have a strong positive correlation.

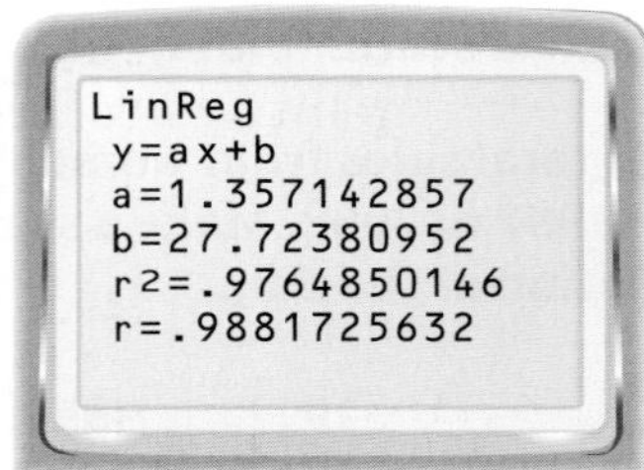

***STEP 2* Draw the best-fitting line**

Press Y= and enter $1.36x + 27.7$ for y_1.
Press GRAPH.

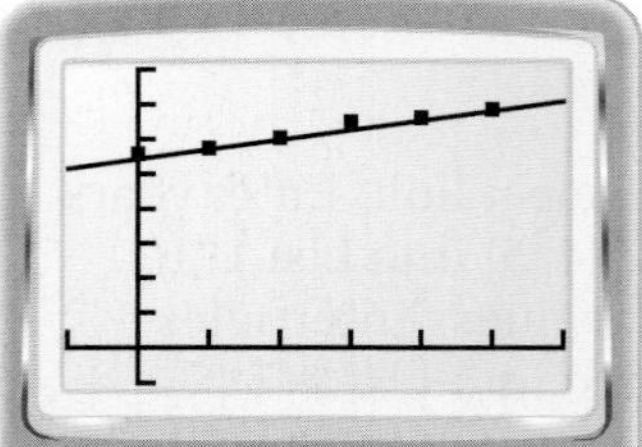

PRACTICE

In Exercises 1–5, refer to the table, which shows the total sales from men's clothing stores in the United States from 1997 to 2002.

Year	1997	1998	1999	2000	2001	2002
Sales (billions of dollars)	10.1	10.6	10.5	10.8	10.3	9.9

1. Make a scatter plot of the data. *Describe* the correlation.
2. Find the equation of the best-fitting line for the data.
3. Draw the best-fitting line for the data.

DRAW CONCLUSIONS

4. What does the value of r for the equation in Exercise 2 tell you about the correlation of the data?
5. **PREDICT** How could you use the best-fitting line to predict future sales of men's clothing? *Explain* your answer.

Extension Correlation and Causation

GOAL Understand the difference between causation and correlation.

Key Vocabulary
- **correlation**

You have seen that paired data have a strong positive correlation if the correlation coefficient r is close to 1 and a strong negative correlation if r is close to -1. But a strong correlation does not necessarily imply cause and effect, or *causation*, between the paired variables.

CC.9-12.S.ID.9 Distinguish between correlation and causation.*

EXAMPLE 1 Analyze a set of data

COMPUTERS The table shows the number (in millions) of music album downloads and the number (in millions) of individual federal income tax returns filed electronically each year from 2004 to 2008. Analyze the data in terms of correlation and causation.

Year	2004	2005	2006	2007	2008
Album downloads (millions), x	4.6	13.6	27.6	42.5	56.9
Electronic tax returns (millions), y	61.5	68.5	72.8	78.7	89.5

Solution

First, find the correlation coefficient. Because r is close to 1, there is a strong positive correlation. However, an increase in album downloads does not cause an increase in electronic tax returns. These increases are both a result of other factors, such as advances in technology and increased computer usage.

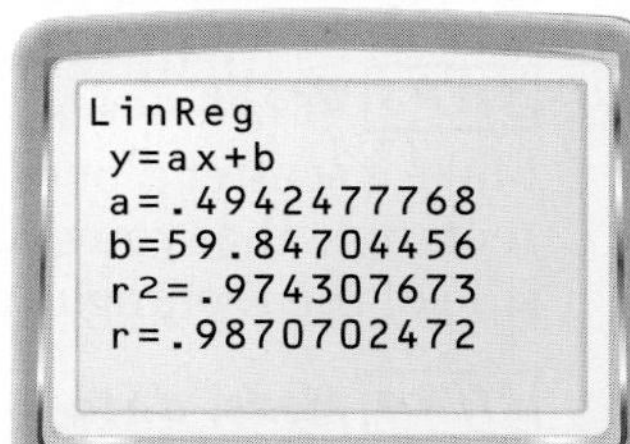

PRACTICE

EXAMPLE 1 for Exs. 1–2

In Exercises 1 and 2, analyze the data in terms of correlation and causation.

1. **BASKETBALL** The table shows the number of minutes played and the number of points scored by 6 college basketball players.

Minutes, x	30	31	33	30	25	18
Points, y	14	13	13	11	7	5

2. **SALES** The table shows the numbers of cold drinks and hot drinks sold at an outdoor concession stand from June through November.

Hot drinks, x	100	150	200	230	250	275
Cold drinks, y	300	210	175	165	140	125

3. **REASONING** You want to analyze annual data for music downloads and CD sales for the period 2000–2010 in terms of correlation and causation. What would you expect to find? *Explain.*

Collecting and Organizing Data

Model with mathematics.

MATERIALS • metric ruler

QUESTION How can you make a prediction using a line of fit?

EXPLORE Make a prediction using a line of fit

A student in your class draws a rectangle with a short side that is 4 centimeters in length. Predict the length of the long side of the rectangle.

***STEP 1* Collect data**

Ask each of 10 people to draw a rectangle. Do not let anyone drawing a rectangle see a rectangle drawn by someone else.

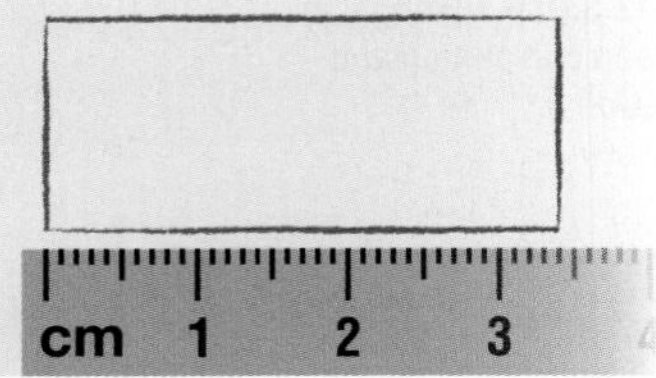

***STEP 2* Organize data**

Measure the lengths (in centimeters) of the short and long sides of the rectangles you collected. Create a table like the one shown.

Short side (cm)	2.7	2.7	1.8	2.6	1.4	1.5	1.2	0.8	3.8
Long side (cm)	4.4	6.5	3.4	6	3.4	3	2.8	1.6	6.5

***STEP 3* Graph data**

Make a scatter plot of the data where each point represents a rectangle that you collected. Let x represent the length of the short side of the rectangle, and let y represent the length of the long side.

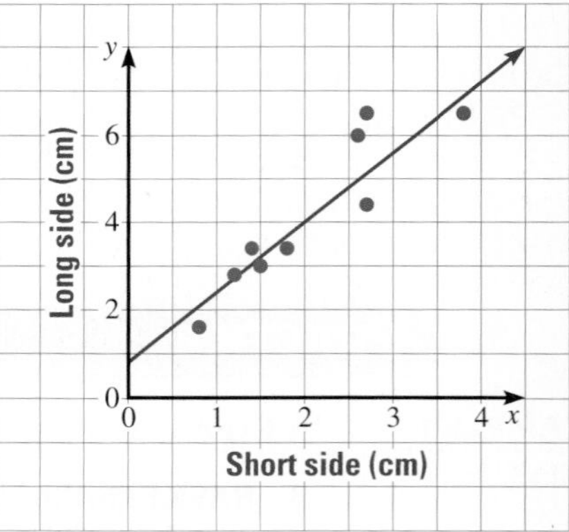

***STEP 4* Model data**

Draw a line of fit.

***STEP 5* Predict**

Use the line of fit to find the length of the long side that corresponds to a short side with a length of 4 centimeters. In this case, the long side length predicted by the line of fit has a length of about 7 centimeters.

DRAW CONCLUSIONS Use your observations to complete these exercises

1. **COMPARE** What is the slope of your line of fit? How does this slope compare with the slope of the line shown above?
2. **PREDICT** Suppose a student in your class draws a rectangle that has a long side with a length of 5 centimeters. Predict the length of the shorter side. *Explain* how you made your prediction.
3. **EXTEND** The *golden ratio* appears frequently in architectural structures, paintings, sculptures, and even in nature. This ratio of the long side of a rectangle to its short side is approximately 1.618. How does this ratio compare with the slopes of the lines you compared in Exercise 1?

4.7 Predict with Linear Models

Before You made scatter plots and wrote equations of lines of fit.

Now You will make predictions using best-fitting lines.

Why? So you can model trends, as in Ex. 21.

Key Vocabulary
- **best-fitting line**
- **linear regression**
- **interpolation**
- **extrapolation**
- **zero of a function**

The line that most closely follows a trend in data is called the **best-fitting line**. The process of finding the best-fitting line to model a set of data is called **linear regression**. You can perform linear regression using technology. Using a line or its equation to approximate a value between two known values is called **linear interpolation**.

EXAMPLE 1 Interpolate using an equation

CC.9-12.S.ID.6a Fit a function to the data; use functions fitted to data to solve problems in the context of the data.*

CD SINGLES The table shows the total number of CD singles shipped (in millions) by manufacturers for several years during the period 1993–1997.

Year	1993	1995	1996	1997
CD singles shipped (millions)	7.8	22	43	67

REVIEW REGRESSION
You may want to review performing a linear regression to find the best-fitting line.

a. Make a scatter plot of the data.

b. Find an equation that models the number of CD singles shipped (in millions) as a function of the number of years since 1993.

c. Approximate the number of CD singles shipped in 1994.

Solution

a. Enter the data into lists on a graphing calculator. Make a scatter plot, letting the number of years since 1993 be the x-values (0, 2, 3, 4) and the number of CD singles shipped be the y-values.

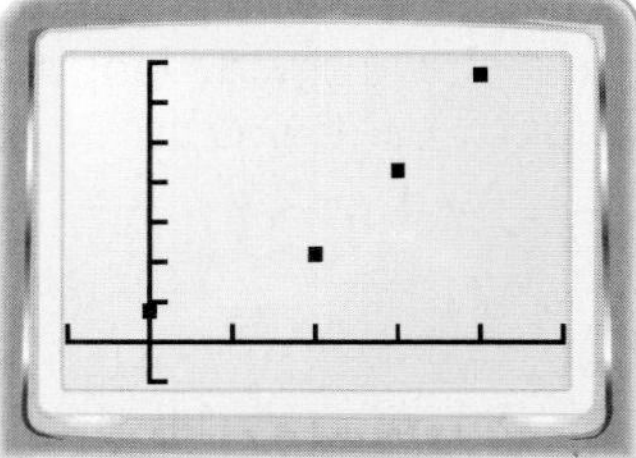

b. Perform linear regression using the paired data. The equation of the best-fitting line is approximately $y = 14x + 2.4$.

ANOTHER WAY
You can also estimate the number of CDs shipped in 1994 by evaluating $y = 14x + 2.4$ when $x = 1$.

c. Graph the best-fitting line. Use the *trace* feature and the arrow keys to find the value of the equation when $x = 1$.

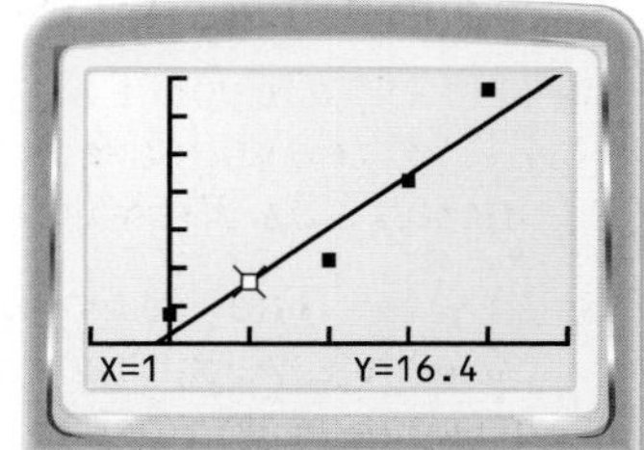

▶ About 16 million CD singles were shipped in 1994.

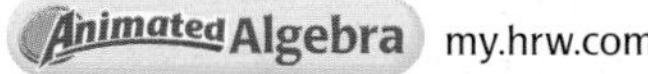

my.hrw.com

EXTRAPOLATION Using a line or its equation to approximate a value outside the range of known values is called **linear extrapolation**.

EXAMPLE 2 Extrapolate using an equation

CD SINGLES Look back at Example 1.

a. Use the equation from Example 1 to approximate the number of CD singles shipped in 1998 and in 2000.

b. In 1998 there were actually 56 million CD singles shipped. In 2000 there were actually 34 million CD singles shipped. *Describe* the accuracy of the extrapolations made in part (a).

Solution

a. Evaluate the equation of the best-fitting line from Example 1 for $x = 5$ and $x = 7$.

Y1(5)
72.4
Y1(7)
100.4

The model predicts about 72 million CD singles shipped in 1998 and about 100 million CD singles shipped in 2000.

b. The differences between the predicted number of CD singles shipped and the actual number of CD singles shipped in 1998 and 2000 are 16 million CDs and 66 million CDs, respectively. The difference in the actual and predicted numbers increased from 1998 to 2000. So, the equation of the best-fitting line gives a less accurate prediction for the year that is farther from the given years.

ACCURACY As Example 2 illustrates, the farther removed an x-value is from the known x-values, the less confidence you can have in the accuracy of the predicted y-value. This is true in general but not in every case.

✓ GUIDED PRACTICE for Examples 1 and 2

1. **HOUSE SIZE** The table shows the median floor area of new single-family houses in the United States during the period 1995–1999.

Year	1995	1996	1997	1998	1999
Median floor area (square feet)	1920	1950	1975	2000	2028

a. Find an equation that models the floor area (in square feet) of a new single-family house as a function of the number of years since 1995.

b. Predict the median floor area of a new single-family house in 2000 and in 2001.

c. Which of the predictions from part (b) would you expect to be more accurate? *Explain* your reasoning.

EXAMPLE 3 Predict using an equation

SOFTBALL The table shows the number of participants in U.S. youth softball during the period 1997–2001. Predict the year in which the number of youth softball participants reaches 1.2 million.

Year	1997	1998	1999	2000	2001
Participants (millions)	1.44	1.4	1.411	1.37	1.355

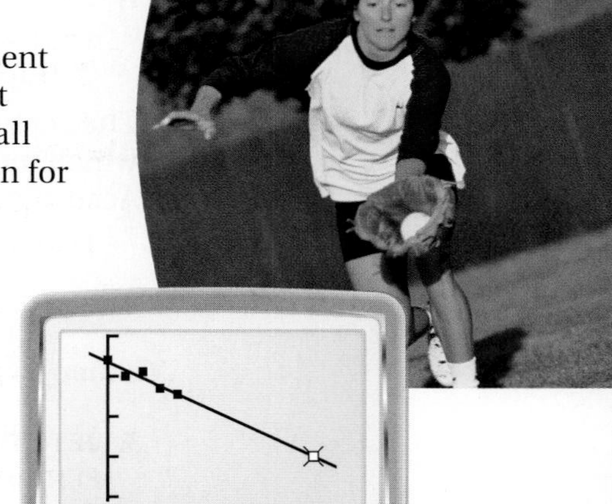

Solution

STEP 1 Perform linear regression. Let x represent the number of years since 1997, and let y represent the number of youth softball participants (in millions). The equation for the best-fitting line is approximately $y = -0.02x + 1.435$.

STEP 2 Graph the equation of the best-fitting line. Trace the line until the cursor reaches $y = 1.2$. The corresponding x-value is shown at the bottom of the calculator screen.

X=11.75 Y=1.2

▶ There will be 1.2 million participants about 12 years after 1997, or in 2009.

ANOTHER WAY

You can also predict the year by substituting 1.2 for y in the equation and solving for x:

$$y = -0.02x + 1.435$$
$$1.2 = -0.02x + 1.435$$
$$x = 11.75$$

GUIDED PRACTICE for Example 3

2. **SOFTBALL** In Example 3, in what year will there be 1.25 million youth softball participants in the U.S?

ZERO OF A FUNCTION A **zero of a function** $y = f(x)$ is an x-value for which $f(x) = 0$ (or $y = 0$). Because $y = 0$ along the x-axis of the coordinate plane, a zero of a function is an x-intercept of the function's graph.

KEY CONCEPT *For Your Notebook*

Relating Solutions of Equations, *x*-Intercepts of Graphs, and Zeros of Functions

You have learned to solve an equation like $2x - 4 = 0$:

$$2x - 4 = 0$$
$$2x = 4$$
$$x = 2$$

The solution of $2x - 4 = 0$ is 2.

You have also found the x-intercept of the graph of a function like $y = 2x - 4$:

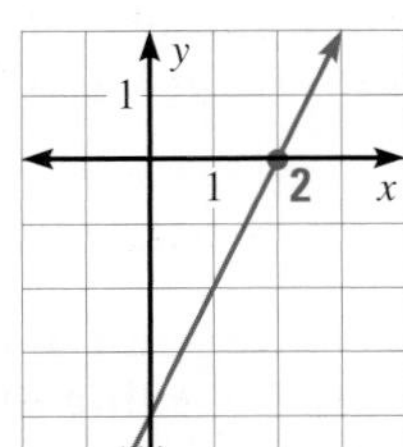

Now you are finding the zero of a function like $f(x) = 2x - 4$:

$$f(x) = 0$$
$$2x - 4 = 0$$
$$x = 2$$

The zero of $f(x) = 2x - 4$ is 2.

EXAMPLE 4 Find the zero of a function

SOFTBALL Look back at Example 3. Find the zero of the function. *Explain* what the zero means in this situation.

Solution

Substitute 0 for y in the equation of the best-fitting line and solve for x.

$y = -0.02x + 1.435$ **Write the equation.**

$0 = -0.02x + 1.435$ **Substitute 0 for y.**

$x \approx 72$ **Solve for x.**

▶ The zero of the function is about 72. The function has a negative slope, which means that the number of youth softball participants is decreasing. According to the model, there will be no youth softball participants 72 years after 1997, or in 2069.

GUIDED PRACTICE for Example 4

3. **JET BOATS** The number y (in thousands) of jet boats purchased in the U.S. can be modeled by the function $y = -1.23x + 14$ where x is the number of years since 1995. Find the zero of the function. *Explain* what the zero means in this situation.

4.7 EXERCISES

HOMEWORK KEY

○ = **See WORKED-OUT SOLUTIONS** Exs. 3 and 19

★ = **STANDARDIZED TEST PRACTICE** Exs. 2, 14, 16, and 21

◆ = **MULTIPLE REPRESENTATIONS** Exs. 22

SKILL PRACTICE

1. **VOCABULARY** Copy and complete: Using a linear function to approximate a value within a range of known data values is called __?__.

2. ★ **WRITING** *Explain* how extrapolation differs from interpolation.

EXAMPLE 1 for Exs. 3–4

LINEAR INTERPOLATION Make a scatter plot of the data. Find the equation of the best-fitting line. Approximate the value of y for $x = 5$.

3.

x	0	2	4	6	7
y	2	7	14	17	20

4.

x	2	4	6	8	10
y	6.2	22.5	40.2	55.4	72.1

EXAMPLE 2 for Exs. 5–6

LINEAR EXTRAPOLATION Make a scatter plot of the data. Find the equation of the best-fitting line. Approximate the value of y for $x = 10$.

5.

x	0	1	2	3	4
y	20	32	39	53	63

6.

x	1	3	5	7	9
y	0.4	1.4	1.9	2.3	3.2

EXAMPLE 4
for Exs. 7–13

ZERO OF A FUNCTION **Find the zero of the function.**

7. $f(x) = 7.5x - 20$ **8.** $f(x) = -x + 7$ **9.** $f(x) = \frac{1}{8}x + 2$

10. $f(x) = 17x - 68$ **11.** $f(x) = -0.5x + 0.75$ **12.** $f(x) = 5x - 7$

13. ERROR ANALYSIS *Describe* and correct the error made in finding the zero of the function $y = 2.3x - 2$.

$y = 2.3(0) - 2$
$y = -2$

14. ★ MULTIPLE CHOICE Given the function $y = 12.6x + 3$, for what x-value does $y = 66$?

(A) 0.2 (B) 5 (C) 5.5 (D) 78.6

15. ERROR ANALYSIS *Describe* and correct the error in finding an equation of the best-fitting line using a graphing calculator.

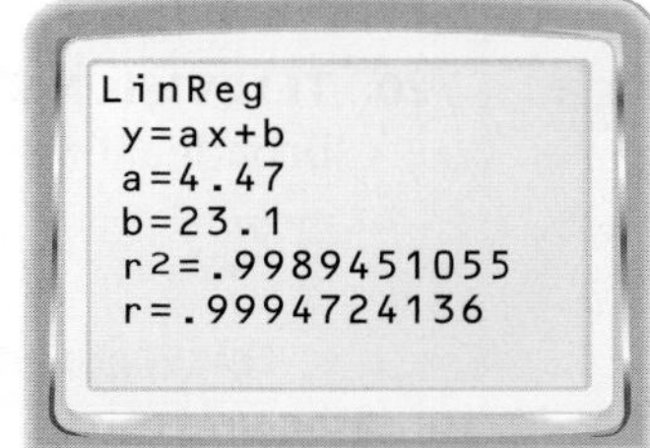

Equation of the best-fitting line is
$y = 23.1x + 4.47$.

16. ★ OPEN-ENDED Give an example of a real-life situation in which you can use linear interpolation to find the zero of a function. *Explain* what the zero means in this situation.

17. CHALLENGE A quantity increases rapidly for 10 years. During the next 10 years, the quantity decreases rapidly.

a. Can you fit a line to the data? *Explain.*

b. How could you model the data using more than one line? *Explain* the steps you could take.

PROBLEM SOLVING

EXAMPLE 1
for Ex. 18

18. SAILBOATS Your school's sailing club wants to buy a sailboat. The table shows the lengths and costs of sailboats.

Length (feet)	11	12	14	14	16	22	23
Cost (dollars)	600	500	1900	1700	3500	6500	6000

a. Make a scatter plot of the data. Let x represent the length of the sailboat. Let y represent the cost of the sailboat.

b. Find an equation that models the cost (in dollars) of a sailboat as a function of its length (in feet).

c. Approximate the cost of a sailboat that is 20 feet long.

EXAMPLE 2
for Ex. 19

19. **FARMING** The table shows the living space recommended for pigs of certain weights.

Weight (pounds)	40	60	80	100	120	150	230
Area (square feet)	2.5	3	3.5	4	5	6	8

a. Make a scatter plot of the data.

b. Write an equation that models the recommended living space (in square feet) as a function of a pig's weight (in pounds).

c. About how much living space is recommended for a pig weighing 250 pounds?

EXAMPLE 3
for Ex. 20

20. **TELEVISION STATIONS** The table shows the number of UHF and VHF broadcast television stations each year from 1996 to 2002.

Year	1996	1997	1998	1999	2000	2001	2002
Television stations	1551	1563	1583	1616	1730	1686	1714

a. Find an equation that models the number of broadcast television stations as a function of the number of years since 1996.

b. Approximate the year in which there were 1790 television stations.

EXAMPLE 4
for Exs. 21–22

21. ★ **SHORT RESPONSE** The table shows the number of people who lived in high noise areas near U.S. airports for several years during the period 1985–2000.

a. Find an equation that models the number of people (in thousands) living in high noise areas as a function of the number of years since 1985.

b. Find the zero of the function from part (a). *Explain* what the zero means in this situation. Is this reasonable?

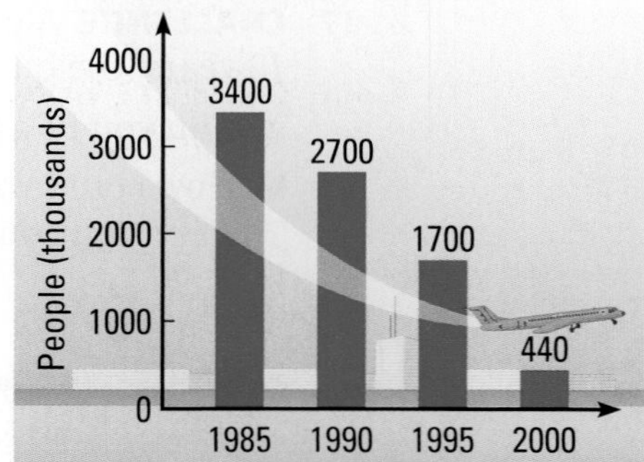

22. ◆ **MULTIPLE REPRESENTATIONS** An Internet search for used cars of a given make, model, and year in your local area found cars with different mileages and different selling prices, as shown.

Mileage (thousands of miles)	22	14	18	30	8	24
Price (thousands of dollars)	16	17	17	14	18	15

a. Making a Graph Draw two scatter plots of the data, one by hand and one using a graphing calculator.

b. Writing an Equation Draw a line of fit on your hand-drawn scatter plot. Use the line to write an equation that models the selling price as a function of the mileage. Then use a graphing calculator to find the best-fitting line. *Compare* your models.

c. Describing in Words Identify the slope and y-intercept of the best-fitting line. *Explain* their meanings in the context of the situation.

○ = See WORKED-OUT SOLUTIONS in Student Resources

★ = STANDARDIZED TEST PRACTICE

◆ = MULTIPLE REPRESENTATIONS

23. CHALLENGE The table shows the estimated populations of mallard ducks and all ducks in North America for several years during the period 1975–2000.

Year	1975	1980	1985	1990	1995	2000
Mallards (thousands)	7727	7707	4961	5452	8269	9470
All ducks (thousands)	37,790	36,220	25,640	25,080	35,870	41,840

a. Make two scatter plots where x is the number of years since 1975 and y is the number of mallards (in thousands) for one scatter plot, while y is the number of ducks (in thousands) for the other scatter plot. *Describe* the correlation of the data in each scatter plot.

b. Can you use the mallard duck population to predict the total duck population? *Explain.*

QUIZ

1. PARALLEL LINES Write an equation of the line that passes through $(-6, 8)$ and is parallel to the line $y = 3x - 15$.

PERPENDICULAR LINES Write an equation of the line that passes through the given point and is perpendicular to the given line.

2. $(5, 5)$, $y = -x + 2$

3. $(10, -3)$, $y = 2x + 24$

4. $(2, 3)$, $x + 2y = -7$

5. CASSETTE TAPES The table shows the number of audio cassette tapes shipped for several years during the period 1994–2002.

Year	1994	1996	1998	2000	2002
Tapes shipped (millions)	345	225	159	76	31

a. Write an equation that models the number of tapes shipped (in millions) as a function of the number of years since 1994.

b. At about what rate did the number of tapes shipped change over time?

c. Approximate the year in which 125 million tapes were shipped.

d. Find the zero of the function from part (a). *Explain* what the zero means in this situation.

Internet ACTIVITY *Use after Predict with Linear Models*

my.hrw.com
Keystrokes

Model Data from the Internet

MATHEMATICAL PRACTICES

Model with mathematics.

QUESTION How can you find reliable data on the Internet and use it to predict the total U.S voting-age population in 2010?

EXAMPLE 1 Collect and analyze data

Find data for the total U.S. voting-age population over several years. Use an equation that models the data to predict the total U.S. voting-age population in 2010.

STEP 1 ***Find a data source***

Reliable data about the U.S. population can be found in the online *Statistical Abstract.* Go to the address shown below. Click on a link to the most recent version of the *Statistical Abstract.*

Address http://www.census.gov

Voting-Age Population

Year	Total (mil.)
1980	157.1
1988	178.1
1990	182.1
1994	190.3
1996	193.7
1998	198.2

STEP 2 ***Find an appropriate data set***

Choose the most recent "Elections" document. In this document, find the table of data entitled "Voting-Age Population."

STEP 3 ***Find a model***

Use a graphing calculator to make a scatter plot. Let x represent the number of years since 1980. Let y represent the total U.S. voting-age population (in millions). Find an equation that models the total U.S. voting-age population (in millions) as a function of the number of years since 1980.

▶ $y = 2.23x + 159$

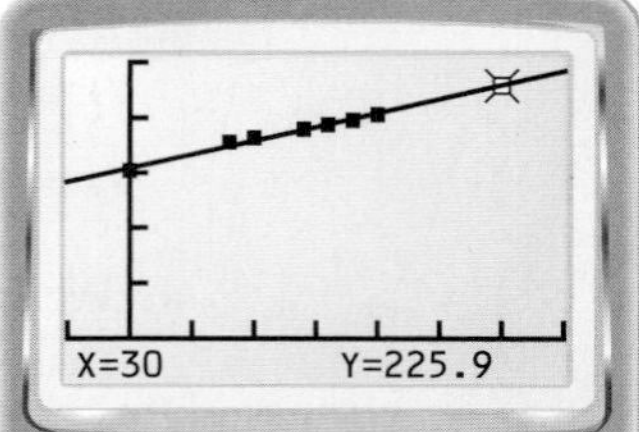

STEP 4 ***Predict***

Use the model to predict the total voting-age population in 2010. You can either evaluate the equation for $x = 30$ or trace the graph of the equation, as shown.

▶ The total U.S. voting-age population will be about 225.9 million in 2010.

DRAW CONCLUSIONS

1. In the online *Statistical Abstract,* find data for the total value of agricultural imports over several years beginning with 1990.
2. Make a scatter plot of the data you found in Exercise 1. Find an equation that models the total value of agricultural imports (in millions of dollars) as a function of the number of years since 1990.
3. Predict the year in which the total value of agricultural imports will be \$45,000 million. *Describe* the method you used.

Extension Assess the Fit of a Model

GOAL Assess the fit of a linear model by plotting and analyzing residuals.

Key Vocabulary
- **residual**

COMMON CORE

CC.9-12.S.ID.6b Informally assess the fit of a function by plotting and analyzing residuals.*

You have found lines of fit using estimation and using *linear regression.* Most lines of fit do not pass through every data point, so you can look at the *residuals* to assess whether the model is a good fit for the data.

RESIDUALS Given a set of data and a model, the difference between an actual value of the dependent variable y and the value predicted by the linear model $\hat{y}$ is called a **residual.** A *residual plot* is a scatter plot of points whose x-values are those from the data set and whose y-values are the corresponding residuals.

EXAMPLE 1 Calculate and interpret residuals

CRUISE SHIPS The table shows data for several cruise ships. Is the equation $y = 4x - 1500$ a good model for the data?

Length, x (ft)	644	720	754	781	866	915	965
Passenger capacity, y	1090	1266	1748	1440	1870	2435	1950

Solution

Make a table showing the passenger capacities predicted by the equation. Then calculate the residuals.

Length, x (ft)	644	720	754	781	866	915	965
Predicted capacity, $\hat{y}$	1076	1380	1516	1624	1964	2160	2360
Residuals, $y - \hat{y}$	14	−114	232	−184	−94	275	−410

Plot the residuals on a residual plot.

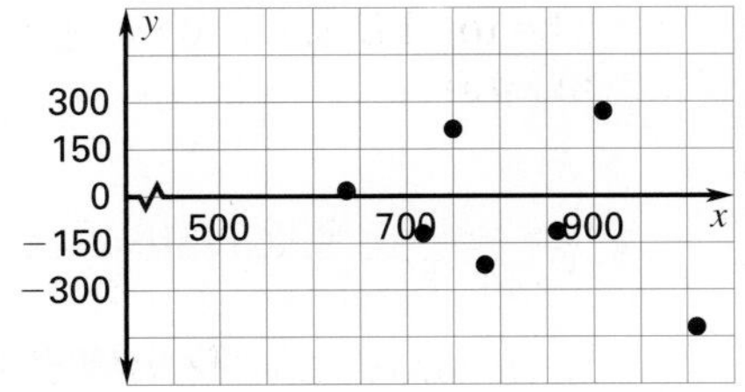

The equation $y = 4x - 1500$ models the data somewhat, but appears to predict capacity better for shorter lengths than it does for larger lengths.

GOODNESS OF FIT If a line is a good fit for a set of data, the absolute values of the residuals are relatively small and more or less evenly distributed above and below the x-axis in a residual plot. Residuals that are mostly positive or mostly negative imply that the line is in the wrong place. Residuals that are steadily increasing suggest the data is not linear, while wildly scattered residuals suggest that the data might have relatively no correlation.

EXAMPLE 2 Calculate and interpret residuals

SAFETY The table shows stopping distances for cars based on the speed being traveled. Is the equation $y = 7x - 105$ a good model for the data?

Speed, x (mi/hr)	10	20	30	40	50	60	70	80	90	100
Stopping distance, y (ft)	27	63	109	164	229	303	387	481	584	696

Solution

Create a residual plot.
The curve in the residuals suggests that a linear model may not be the best choice for this data, but for values of x between 20 and 80, this model appears to predict the actual value fairly well.

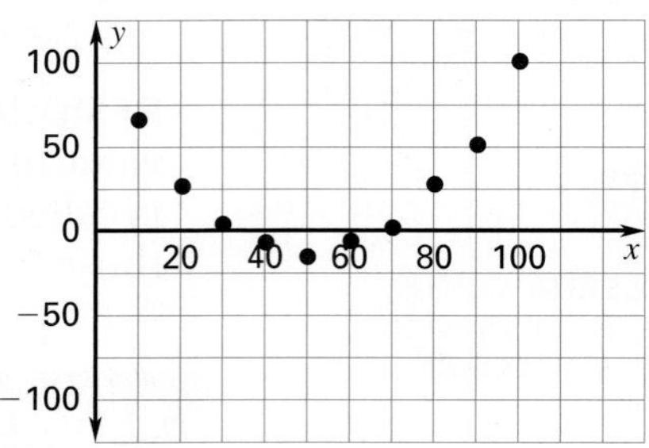

PRACTICE

For Exercises 1–4, the graph represents a residual plot for a data set and a linear model. Based on the residual plot, discuss the goodness of fit of the linear model.

1. 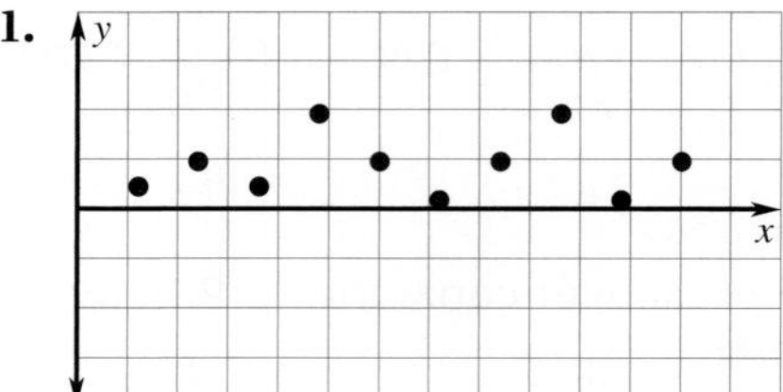

2. 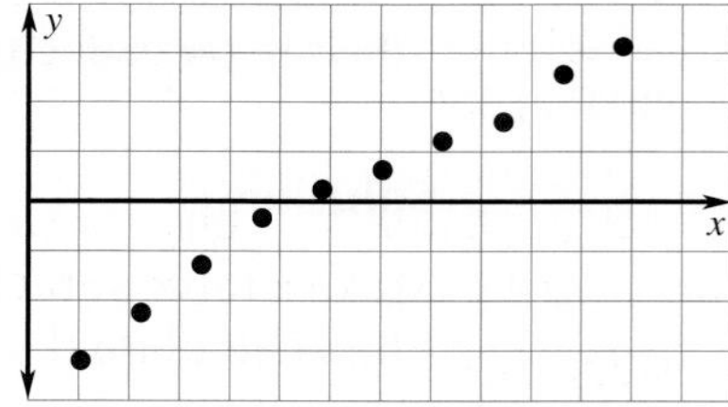

3. 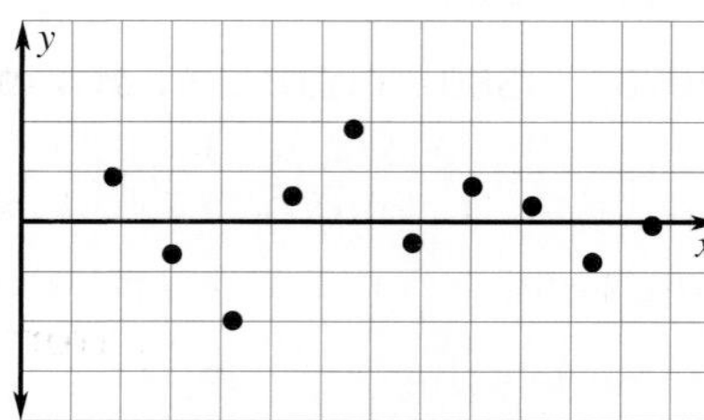

4. 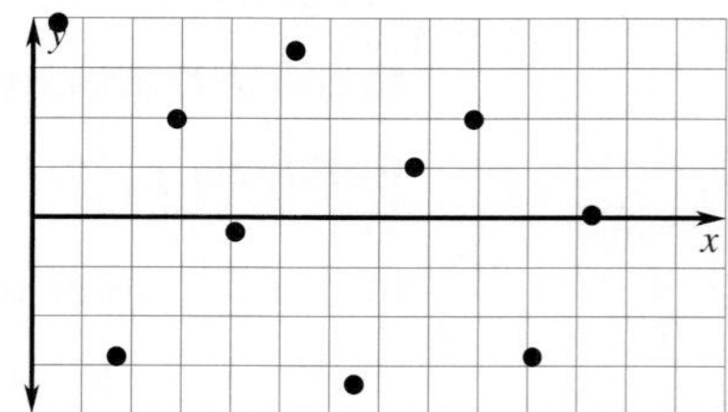

5. Create a residual plot for the data below using the model $y = 2x + 0.2$.

Time Walking, x (hr)	0	1	2	3	4	5
Distance Walked, y (mi)	0	2.1	4.3	6.1	8.6	10.1

MIXED REVIEW *of Problem Solving*

MATHEMATICAL PRACTICES Make sense of problems and persevere in solving them.

1. **MULTI-STEP PROBLEM** The table shows the value of primary and secondary schools built in the U.S. each year from 1995 to 2000.

Year	Value (millions of dollars)
1995	1245
1996	1560
1997	2032
1998	2174
1999	2420
2000	2948

   a. Make a scatter plot of the data.

   b. Write an equation that models the value (in millions of dollars) of the schools built as a function of the number of years since 1995.

   c. At approximately what rate did the value change from 1995 to 2000?

   d. In what year would you predict the value of the schools built in the U.S. to be $3,600,000,000?

2. **GRIDDED ANSWER** A map of a city shows streets as lines on a coordinate grid. State Street has a slope of $-\frac{1}{2}$. Park Street runs perpendicular to State Street. What is the slope of Park Street on the map?

3. **OPEN-ENDED** The graph represents the cost for one kayak owner for storing a kayak at a marina over time. The total cost includes a standard initial fee and a monthly storage fee. Suppose a different kayak owner pays a lower initial fee during a special promotion. Write an equation that could give the total cost as a function of the number of months of storage for this kayak owner.

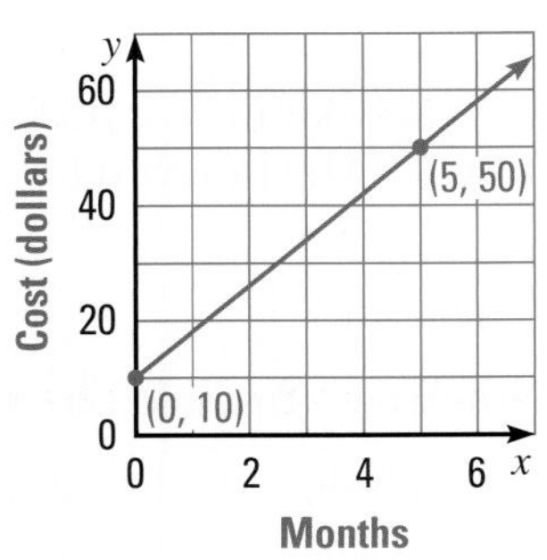

4. **SHORT RESPONSE** The table shows the heights and corresponding lengths of horses in a stable. Make a scatter plot of the data. *Describe* the correlation of the data.

Height (hands)	Length (inches)
17.0	76
16.0	72
16.2	74
15.3	71
15.1	69
16.3	75

5. **EXTENDED RESPONSE** The table shows the percent of revenue from U.S. music sales made through music clubs from 1998 through 2003.

Year	Percent of revenue
1998	9
1999	7.9
2000	7.6
2001	6.1
2002	4
2003	4.1

   a. Find an equation that models the percent of revenue from music clubs as a function of the number of years since 1998.

   b. At approximately what rate did the percent of revenue from music clubs change from 1998 to 2003?

   c. Find the zero of the function. *Explain* what the zero means in this situation.

6. **SHORT RESPONSE** The cost of bowling includes a $4.00 fee per game and a shoe rental fee. Shoes for adults cost $2.25. Shoes for children cost $1.75. Write equations that give the total cost of bowling for an adult and for a child as functions of the number of games bowled. How are the graphs of the equations related? *Explain.*

4 CHAPTER SUMMARY

BIG IDEAS For Your Notebook

Big Idea 1

Writing Linear Equations in a Variety of Forms

Using given information about a line, you can write an equation of the line in three different forms.

Form	Equation	Important information
Slope-intercept form	$y = mx + b$	• The slope of the line is m. • The y-intercept of the line is b.
Point-slope form	$y - y_1 = m(x - x_1)$	• The slope of the line is m. • The line passes through (x_1, y_1).
Standard form	$Ax + By = C$	• A, B, and C are real numbers. • A and B are not both zero.

Big Idea 2

Using Linear Models to Solve Problems

You can write a linear equation that models a situation involving a constant rate of change. Analyzing given information helps you choose a linear model.

Choosing a Linear Model	
If this is what you know . . .	**. . . then use this equation form**
constant rate of change and initial value	slope-intercept form
constant rate of change and one data pair	slope-intercept form or point-slope form
two data pairs and the fact that the rate of change is constant	slope-intercept form or point-slope form
the sum of two variable quantities is constant	standard form

Big Idea 3

Modeling Data with a Line of Fit

You can use a line of fit to model data that have a positive or negative correlation. The line or an equation of the line can be used to make predictions.

Step 1 Make a scatter plot of the data.

Step 2 Decide whether the data can be modeled by a line.

Step 3 Draw a line that appears to follow the trend in data closely.

Step 4 Write an equation using two points on the line.

Step 5 Interpolate (between known values) or extrapolate (beyond known values) using the line or its equation.

4 CHAPTER REVIEW

@HomeTutor
my.hrw.com
- Multi-Language Glossary
- Vocabulary practice

REVIEW KEY VOCABULARY

- point-slope form
- converse
- perpendicular
- scatter plot
- positive correlation, negative correlation, relatively no correlation
- line of fit
- causation
- best-fitting line
- linear regression
- interpolation
- extrapolation
- zero of a function

VOCABULARY EXERCISES

1. Copy and complete: If a best-fitting line falls from left to right, then the data have a(n) __?__ correlation.

2. Copy and complete: Using a linear function to approximate a value beyond a range of known values is called __?__.

3. **WRITING** What is the zero of a function, and how does it relate to the function's graph? *Explain.*

REVIEW EXAMPLES AND EXERCISES

Use the review examples and exercises below to check your understanding of the concepts you have learned in each lesson of this chapter.

4.1 Write Linear Equations in Slope-Intercept Form

EXAMPLE

Write an equation of the line shown.

$y = mx + b$ **Write slope-intercept form.**

$y = -\frac{2}{3}x + 4$ **Substitute $-\frac{2}{3}$ for m and 4 for b.**

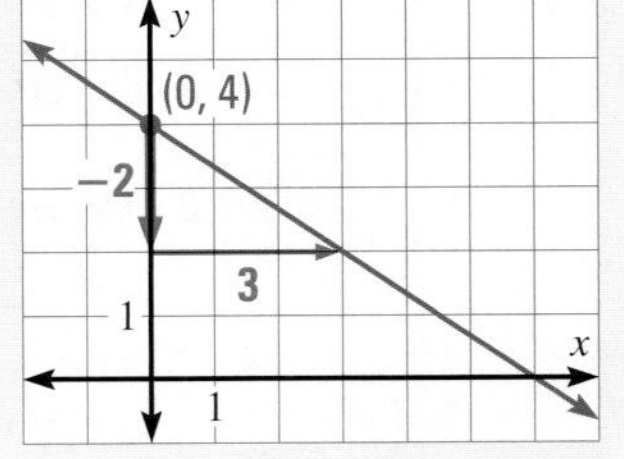

EXERCISES

EXAMPLES 1 and 5 for Exs. 4–7

Write an equation in slope-intercept form of the line with the given slope and *y*-intercept.

4. slope: 3
   y-intercept: −10

5. slope: $\frac{4}{9}$
   y-intercept: 5

6. slope: $-\frac{2}{11}$
   y-intercept: 7

7. **GIFT CARD** You have a $25 gift card for a bagel shop. A bagel costs $1.25. Write an equation that gives the amount (in dollars) that remains on the card as a function of the total number of bagels you have purchased so far. How much money is on the card after you buy 2 bagels?

4 CHAPTER REVIEW

4.2 Use Linear Equations in Slope-Intercept Form

EXAMPLE

Write an equation of the line that passes through the point (−2, −6) and has a slope of 2.

STEP 1 **Find** the y-intercept.

$y = mx + b$ **Write slope-intercept form.**

$-6 = 2(-2) + b$ **Substitute 2 for m, −2 for x, and −6 for y.**

$-2 = b$ **Solve for b.**

STEP 2 **Write** an equation of the line.

$y = mx + b$ **Write slope intercept form.**

$y = 2x - 2$ **Substitute 2 for m and −2 for b.**

EXERCISES

EXAMPLE 1 for Exs. 8–10

Write an equation in slope-intercept form of the line that passes through the given point and has the given slope m.

8. $(-3, -1)$; $m = 4$ **9.** $(-2, 1)$; $m = 1$ **10.** $(8, -4)$; $m = -3$

4.3 Write Linear Equations in Point-Slope Form

EXAMPLE

Write an equation in point-slope form of the line shown.

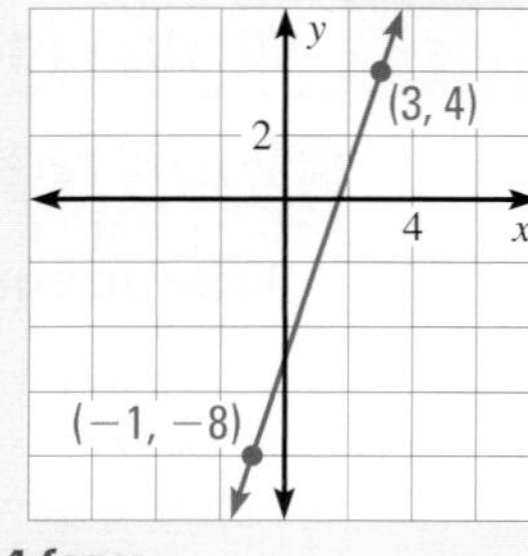

STEP 1 **Find** the slope of the line.

$$m = \frac{y_2 - y_1}{x_2 - x_1} = \frac{-8 - 4}{-1 - 3} = \frac{-12}{-4} = 3$$

STEP 2 **Write** an equation. Use (3, 4).

$y - y_1 = m(x - x_1)$ **Write point-slope form.**

$y - 4 = 3(x - 3)$ **Substitute 3 for m, 3 for x_1, and 4 for y_1.**

EXERCISES

EXAMPLES 3 and 5 for Exs. 11–14

Write an equation in point-slope form of the line that passes through the given points.

11. (4, 7), (5, 1) **12.** (9, −2), (−3, 2) **13.** (8, −8), (−3, −2)

14. BUS TRIP A bus leaves at 10 A.M. to take students on a field trip to a historic site. At 10:25 A.M., the bus is 100 miles from the site. At 11:15 A.M., the bus is 65 miles from the site. The bus travels at a constant speed. Write an equation in point-slope form that relates the distance (in miles) from the site and the time (in minutes) after 10:00 A.M. How far is the bus from the site at 11:30 A.M.?

@HomeTutor
my.hrw.com
Chapter Review Practice

4.4 Write Linear Equations in Standard Form

EXAMPLE

Write an equation in standard form of the line shown.

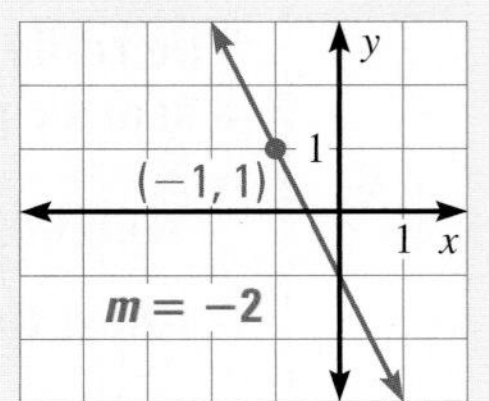

$y - y_1 = m(x - x_1)$	**Write point-slope form.**
$y - 1 = -2(x - (-1))$	**Substitute 1 for y_1, −2 for m, and −1 for x_1.**
$y - 1 = -2x - 2$	**Distributive property**
$2x + y = -1$	**Collect variable terms on one side, constants on the other.**

EXERCISES

EXAMPLES 2 and 5 for Exs. 15–17

Write an equation in standard form of the line that has the given characteristics.

15. Slope: −4; passes through (−2, 7)

16. Passes through (−1, −5) and (3, 7)

17. COSTUMES You are buying ribbon to make costumes for a school play. Organza ribbon costs \$.07 per yard. Satin ribbon costs \$.04 per yard. Write an equation to model the possible combinations of yards of organza ribbon and yards of satin ribbon you can buy for \$5. List several possible combinations.

4.5 Write Equations of Parallel and Perpendicular Lines

EXAMPLE

Write an equation of the line that passes through (−4, −2) and is perpendicular to the line $y = 4x - 7$.

The slope of the line $y = 4x - 7$ is 4. The slope of the perpendicular line through (−4, −2) is $-\frac{1}{4}$. Find the y-intercept of the perpendicular line.

$y = mx + b$	**Write slope-intercept form.**
$-2 = -\frac{1}{4}(-4) + b$	**Substitute $-\frac{1}{4}$ for m, −4 for x, and −2 for y.**
$-3 = b$	**Solve for b.**

An equation of the perpendicular line through (−4, −2) is $y = -\frac{1}{4}x - 3$.

EXERCISES

EXAMPLES 1 and 4 for Exs. 18–20

Write an equation of the line that passes through the given point and is (a) parallel to the given line and (b) perpendicular to the given line.

18. (0, 2), $y = -4x + 6$

19. (2, −3), $y = -2x - 3$

20. (6, 0), $y = \frac{3}{4}x - \frac{1}{4}$

4.6 Fit a Line to Data

EXAMPLE

The table shows the time needed to roast turkeys of different weights. Make a scatter plot of the data. *Describe* the correlation of the data.

Weight (pounds)	6	8	12	14	18	20	24
Roast time (hours)	2.75	3.00	3.50	4.00	4.25	4.75	5.25

Treat the data as ordered pairs. Let x represent the turkey weight (in pounds), and let y represent the time (in hours) it takes to roast the turkey. Plot the ordered pairs as points in a coordinate plane.

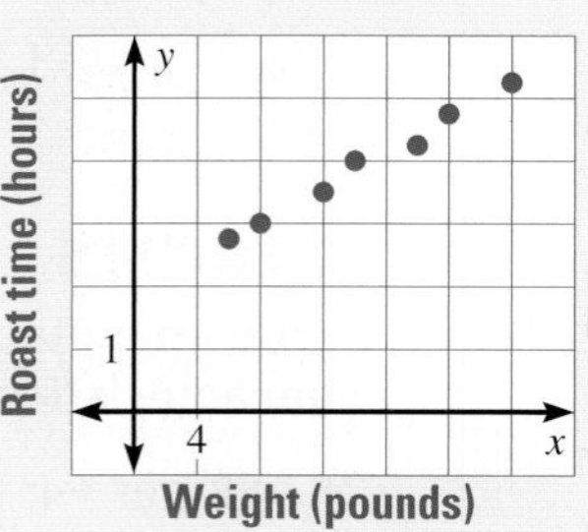

The scatter plot shows a positive correlation, which means that heavier turkeys tend to require more time to roast.

EXERCISES

EXAMPLE 2 for Ex. 21

21. **AIRPORTS** The table shows the number of airports in the Unites States for several years during the period 1990–2001. Make a scatter plot of the data. *Describe* the correlation of the data.

Years	1990	1995	1998	1999	2000	2001
Airports (thousands)	17.5	18.2	18.8	19.1	19.3	19.3

4.7 Predict with Linear Models

EXAMPLE

Use the scatter plot from the example for Lesson 5.6 above to estimate the time (in hours) it takes to roast a 10 pound turkey.

Draw a line that appears to fit the points in the scatter plot closely. There should be approximately as many points above the line as below it.

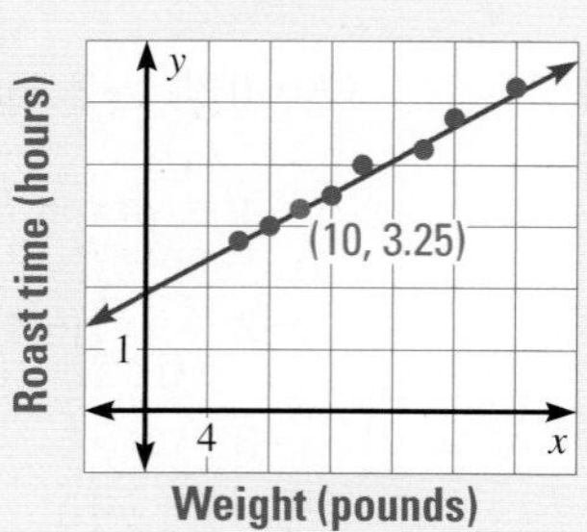

Find the point on the line whose x-coordinate is 10. At that point, you can see that the y-coordinate is about 3.25.

▶ It takes about 3.25 hours to roast a 10 pound turkey.

EXERCISES

EXAMPLE 2 for Ex. 22

22. **COOKING TIMES** Use the graph in the Example above to estimate the time (in hours) it takes to roast a turkey that weighs 30 pounds. *Explain* how you found your answer.

4 CHAPTER TEST

Write an equation in slope-intercept form of the line with the given slope and y-intercept.

1. slope: 5
   y-intercept: -7

2. slope: $\frac{2}{5}$
   y-intercept: -2

3. slope: $-\frac{4}{3}$
   y-intercept: 1

Write an equation in slope-intercept form of the line that passes through the given point and has the given slope m.

4. $(-2, -8)$; $m = 3$

5. $(1, 1)$; $m = -4$

6. $(-1, 3)$; $m = -6$

Write an equation in point-slope form of the line that passes through the given points.

7. $(4, 5), (2, 9)$

8. $(-2, 2), (8, -3)$

9. $(3, 4), (1, -6)$

Write an equation in standard form of the line with the given characteristics.

10. Slope: 10; passes through $(6, 2)$

11. Passes through $(-3, 2)$ and $(6, -1)$

Write an equation of the line that passes through the given point and is (a) parallel to the given line and (b) perpendicular to the given line.

12. $(2, 0)$, $y = -5x + 3$

13. $(-1, 4)$, $y = -x - 4$

14. $(4, -9)$, $y = \frac{1}{4}x + 2$

Make a scatter plot of the data. Draw a line of fit. Write an equation of the line.

15.

x	0	1	2	3	4
y	15	35	53	74	94

16.

x	0	2	4	8	10
y	−2	6	15	38	50

17. **FIELD TRIP** Your science class is taking a field trip to an observatory. The cost of a presentation and a tour of the telescope is $60 for the group plus an additional $3 per person. Write an equation that gives the total cost C as a function of the number of people p in the group.

18. **GOLF FACILITIES** The table shows the number of golf facilities in the United States during the period 1997–2001.

    a. Make a scatter plot of the data where x is the number of years since 1997 and y is the number of golf facilities (in thousands).

    b. Write an equation that models the number of golf facilities (in thousands) as a function of the number of years since 1997.

    c. At about what rate did the number of golf facilities change during the period 1997–2001?

    d. Use the equation from part (b) to predict the number of golf facilities in 2004.

    e. Predict the year in which the number of golf facilities reached 16,000. *Explain* how you found your answer.

Year	Golf facilities (thousands)
1997	14.6
1998	14.9
1999	15.2
2000	15.5
2001	15.7

Scoring Rubric

Full Credit
- solution is complete and correct

Partial Credit
- solution is complete but has errors,
  or
- solution is without error but incomplete

No Credit
- no solution is given,
  or
- solution makes no sense

SHORT RESPONSE QUESTIONS

PROBLEM

The average monthly cost of basic cable increased by about $1.47 each year from 1986 to 2003. In 1986 the average monthly cost of basic cable was $10.67. Write an equation that gives the monthly cost (in dollars) of basic cable as a function of the number of years since 1986. In what year was the monthly cost of basic cable $31.25? *Explain* your reasoning.

Below are sample solutions to the problem. Read each solution and the comments on the left to see why the sample represents full credit, partial credit, or no credit.

SAMPLE 1: Full credit solution

A verbal model shows how the equation is obtained.

Let y be the average monthly cost x years since 1986.

Monthly cost	=	Cost in 1986	+	Cost increase per year	•	Years since 1986
y	=	**10.67**	+	**1.47**	•	x

To find the year when the monthly cost was $31.25, substitute 31.25 for y and solve for x.

Calculations are performed correctly.

$$y = 10.67 + 1.47x$$
$$31.25 = 10.67 + 1.47x$$
$$14 = x$$

The question is answered correctly.

The monthly cost was $31.25 fourteen years after 1986, or in 2000.

SAMPLE 2: Partial credit solution

The equation is correct, and the student has explained what the variables represent.

Let y be the monthly cost. Let x be the number of years since 1986.

Monthly cost	=	Cost in 1986	+	Cost increase per year	•	Years since 1986
y	=	**10.67**	+	**1.47**	•	x

The answer is incorrect, because the student mistakenly substituted the cost for the variable that represents the years since 1986.

To find the year when the cost was $31.25, substitute 31.25 for x.

$$y = 10.67 + 1.47x$$
$$= 10.67 + 1.47(31.25) \approx 56.61$$

The cost was $31.25 about 57 years after 1986, or in 2042.

SAMPLE 3: Partial credit solution

The equation and answer are correct. There are no explanations to support the student's work.

$$y = 10.67 + 1.47x$$

$$31.25 = 10.67 + 1.47x$$

$$14 = x$$

The monthly cost was $31.25 fourteen years after 1986, or in 2000.

SAMPLE 4: No credit solution

The student's reasoning is incorrect, and the equation is incorrect. The answer is incorrect.

Year when cost is \$31.25 = \$31.25 ÷ 1.47

$$y = 31.25 \div 1.47 \approx 21.25$$

The year is about 21 years after 1986, or in 2007.

PRACTICE Apply the Scoring Rubric

Score the solution to the problem below as *full credit, partial credit,* or *no credit. Explain* your reasoning.

PROBLEM A hot air balloon is flying at an altitude of 870 feet. It descends at a rate of 15 feet per minute. Write an equation that gives the altitude (in feet) of the balloon as a function of the time (in minutes) since it began its descent. Find the time it takes the balloon to reach an altitude of 12 feet. *Explain* your reasoning.

1. Let y be the altitude (in feet) after x minutes.

Final altitude = Starting altitude + Decrease in altitude per minute • Minutes

$$y = 870 + (-15)x = 870 - 15(12) = 690$$

The balloon will take 690 minutes to reach an altitude of 12 feet.

2. Let y be the altitude (in feet) after x minutes.

Final altitude = Starting altitude + Decrease in altitude per minute • Minutes

$$y = 870 + (-15)x$$

$$12 = 870 - 15x$$

$$57.2 = x$$

The balloon will take about 57 minutes to reach an altitude of 12 feet.

3. $870 \div 15 = 58$

The balloon will take 58 minutes to reach an altitude of 12 feet.

4 ★ Standardized TEST PRACTICE

SHORT RESPONSE

1. You have \$50 to spend on pretzels and juice drinks for a school dance. A box of pretzels costs \$3.50, and a package of juice drinks costs \$5.00. Write an equation in standard form that models the possible combinations of boxes of pretzels and packages of juice drinks that you can buy. What is the greatest number of boxes of pretzels you can buy? *Explain.*

2. You and your family are traveling home in a car at an average speed of 60 miles per hour. At noon you are 180 miles from home.
   a. Write an equation that gives your distance from home (in miles) as a function of the number of hours since noon.
   b. *Explain* why the graph of this equation is a line with a negative slope.

3. Robyn needs \$2.20 to buy a bag of trail mix. Write an equation in standard form that models the possible combinations of nickels and dimes she could use to pay for the mix. How many nickels would she need if she used 14 dimes? *Explain* your reasoning.

4. On a street map, Main Street and Maple Street can be modeled by the equations $y = ax + 6$ and $x + 2y = 4$. For what value of a are the streets parallel? For what value of a are the streets perpendicular? *Justify* your answers.

5. The table shows the projected dollar amount spent per person in the U.S. on interactive television for several years during the period 1998–2006.

Year	Spending per person (dollars)
1998	0
2000	2.86
2002	6.63
2004	9.50
2006	12.85

   a. Make a scatter plot of the data.
   b. Predict the year in which spending per person in the U.S. on interactive television will reach \$20. *Explain* how you found your answer.

6. You are mountain biking on a 10 mile trail. You biked 4 miles before stopping to take a break. After your break, you bike at a rate of 9 miles per hour.
   a. Write an equation that gives the length (in miles) of the trail you have completed as a function of the number of hours since your break ended.
   b. How much time (in minutes) after your break will it take you to complete the entire trail? *Explain.*

7. A guide gives dogsled tours during the winter months. The guide charges one amount for the first hour of a tour and a different amount for each hour after the first. You paid \$55 for a 2 hour dogsled tour. Your friend paid \$70 for a 3 hour tour.
   a. *Explain* why this situation can be modeled by a linear equation.
   b. Write an equation that gives the cost (in dollars) of a dogsled tour as a function of the number of hours after the first hour of the tour.

8. The scatter plot shows the total carbon dioxide emissions throughout the world for several years during the period 1950–1995.

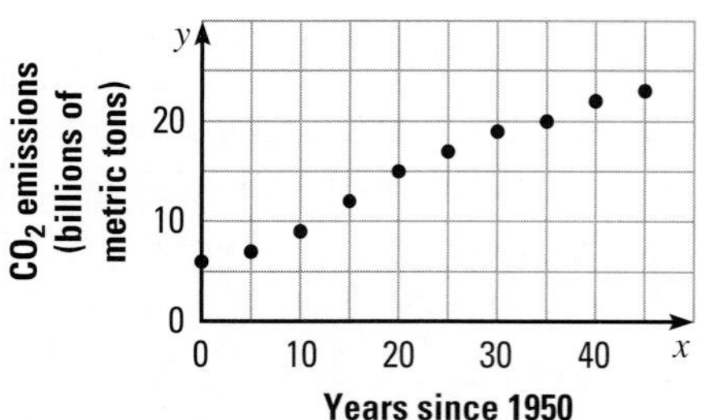

   a. Write an equation that models the carbon dioxide emissions (in billions of metric tons) as a function of the number of years since 1950.
   b. At about what rate did the amount of carbon dioxide emissions increase from 1950 to 1995? *Explain* how you found your answer.

MULTIPLE CHOICE

9. Which equation represents the line that passes through (0, 8) and (2, 0)?

Ⓐ $y = 4x + 2$ Ⓑ $y = -4x + 2$

Ⓒ $y = 4x + 8$ Ⓓ $y = -4x + 8$

10. Which equation represents the line with a slope of 5 and a *y*-intercept of 2?

Ⓐ $y = 2x + 5$ Ⓑ $y = 2x - 5$

Ⓒ $y = 5x + 2$ Ⓓ $y = 5x - 2$

11. Which function has the values $f(1) = 8$ and $f(7) = -10$?

Ⓐ $f(x) = -3x + 11$ Ⓑ $f(x) = -2x + 10$

Ⓒ $f(x) = -3x + 25$ Ⓓ $f(x) = 3x - 24$

GRIDDED ANSWER

12. What is the slope of a line that is perpendicular to the line $y = -2x - 7$?

13. What is the *y*-intercept of the line that has a slope of $\frac{1}{2}$ and passes through (5, 4)?

14. What is the *y*-intercept of the line that is parallel to the line $y = 2x - 3$ and passes through the point (6, 11)?

15. What is the zero of the function $f(x) = -\frac{4}{5}x + 9$?

16. The graph of the equation $Ax + y = 2$ is a line that passes through (−2, 8). What is the value of *A*?

EXTENDED RESPONSE

17. The table shows the time several students spent studying for an exam and each student's grade on the exam.

Study time (hours)	1.5	0.5	0.5	1	1	3	2.5	3	0
Grade	90	60	70	72	80	88	89	94	58

a. Make a scatter plot of the data.

b. Write an equation that models a student's exam grade as a function of the time (in hours) the student spent studying for the exam.

c. How many hours would you need to study in order to earn a grade of 93 on the exam? *Justify* your answer using the data above.

18. The scatter plot shows the number of FM radio stations in the United States for several years during the period 1994–2000.

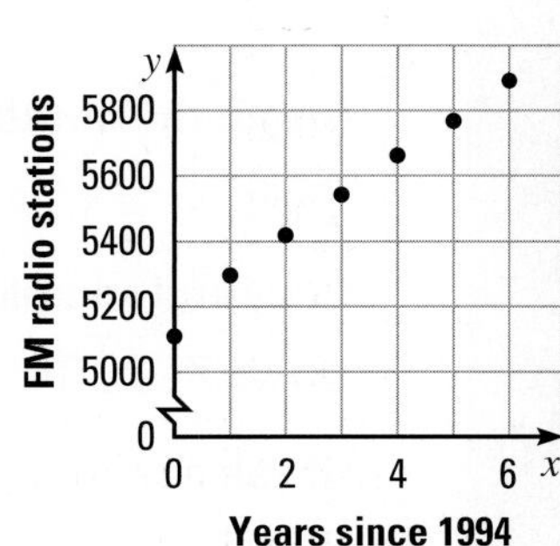

a. *Describe* the correlation of the data.

b. Write an equation that models the number of FM radio stations in the United States as a function of the number of years since 1994.

c. At about what rate did the number of radio stations change during the period 1994–2000?

d. Find the zero of the function from part (b). *Explain* what the zero means in this situation.

5 Solving and Graphing Linear Inequalities

Lesson
5.1 CC.9-12.A.REI.3
5.2 CC.9-12.A.REI.3
5.3 CC.9-12.A.REI.3
5.4 CC.9-12.A.REI.3
5.5 CC.9-12.A.CED.1*
5.6 CC.9-12.A.CED.1*
5.7 CC.9-12.A.REI.12

Before

Previously, you learned the following skills, which you'll use in this chapter: solving equations, graphing equations, and comparing rational numbers.

Prerequisite Skills

VOCABULARY CHECK

1. Identify one **ordered pair** that is a solution of $8x - 5y = -2$.
2. Are $7x - 4 = 10$ and $x = 3$ **equivalent equations**? *Explain.*
3. The **absolute value** of a number a is the distance between a and _?_ on a number line.

SKILLS CHECK

Solve the equation. Check your solution.

4. $m + 8 = -20$ 5. $7x + 3 = 38$ 6. $-9r - 4 = 25$ 7. $4t - 7t = 9$

Graph the number on a number line.

8. 6 9. −8 10. −2.1 11. 4.5

Copy and complete the statement using <, >, or =.

12. 21.7 _?_ 21 13. 13.08 _?_ 13.2 14. 0.1 _?_ 0.04 15. 0.517 _?_ 0.52

Graph the equation.

16. $y = -7x + 3$ 17. $6x + 3y = -5$ 18. $x = -8$ 19. $y = 4$

Now

In this chapter, you will apply the big ideas listed below and reviewed in the Chapter Summary. You will also use the key vocabulary listed below.

Big Ideas

1. **Applying properties of inequality**
2. **Using statements with *and* or *or***
3. **Graphing inequalities**

KEY VOCABULARY

- graph of an inequality
- equivalent inequalities
- compound inequality
- absolute value equation
- absolute deviation
- linear inequality in two variables
- graph of an inequality in two variables

Why?

You can use inequalities to solve problems in sound amplification. For example, you can solve an inequality to determine whether an amplifier provides enough amplification for a given number of people in an audience.

Animated Algebra

The animation illustrated below helps you answer a question from this chapter: Is a 2900 watt amplifier adequate for an audience of 350 people?

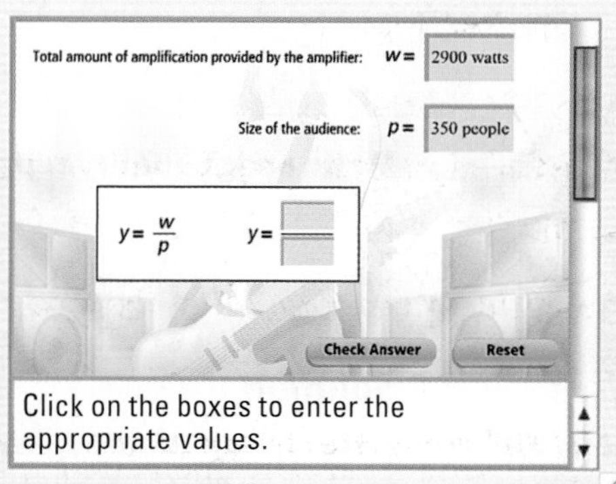

Animated Algebra at my.hrw.com

5.1 Solve Inequalities Using Addition and Subtraction

Before You solved equations using addition and subtraction.
Now You will solve inequalities using addition and subtraction.
Why So you can describe desert temperatures, as in Example 1.

Key Vocabulary
- graph of an inequality
- equivalent inequalities
- inequality
- solution of an inequality

On a number line, the **graph of an inequality** in one variable is the set of points that represent all solutions of the inequality. To graph an inequality in one variable, use an open circle for < or > and a closed circle for ≤ or ≥. The graphs of $x < 3$ and $x \geq -1$ are shown below.

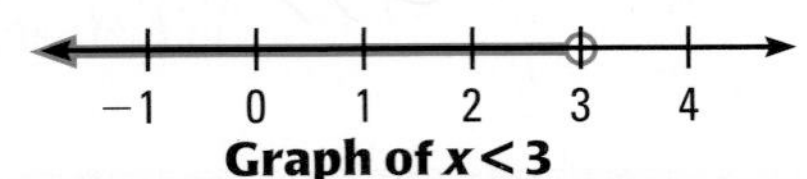

Graph of $x < 3$

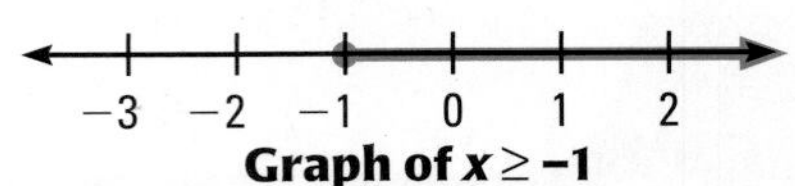

Graph of $x \geq -1$

EXAMPLE 1 Write and graph an inequality

COMMON CORE

CC.9-12.A.REI.3 Solve linear equations and inequalities in one variable, including equations with coefficients represented by letters.

DEATH VALLEY The highest temperature recorded in the United States was 134°F at Death Valley, California, in 1913. Use only this fact to write and graph an inequality that describes the temperatures in the United States.

Solution

Let T represent a temperature (in degrees Fahrenheit) in the United States. The value of T must be less than or equal to 134. So, an inequality is $T \leq 134$.

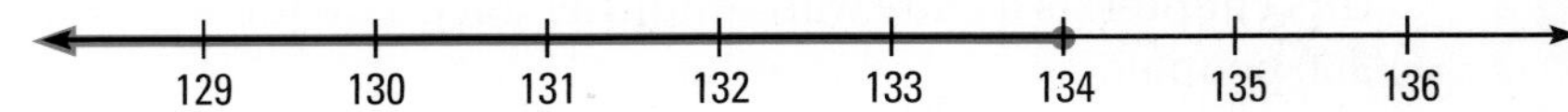

EXAMPLE 2 Write inequalities from graphs

Write an inequality represented by the graph.

a.
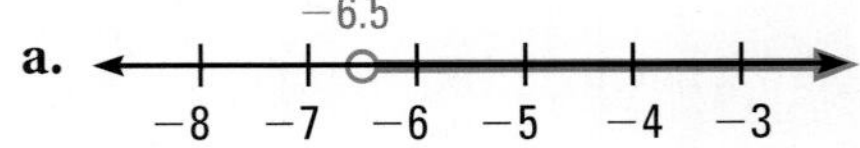

b.
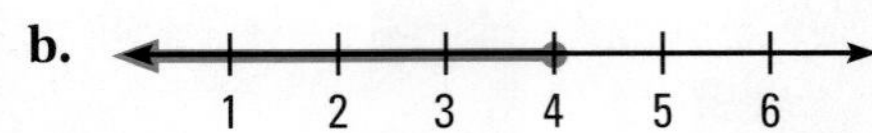

Solution

a. The open circle means that −6.5 is not a solution of the inequality. Because the arrow points to the right, all numbers greater than −6.5 are solutions.

▶ An inequality represented by the graph is $x > -6.5$.

b. The closed circle means that 4 is a solution of the inequality. Because the arrow points to the left, all numbers less than 4 are solutions.

▶ An inequality represented by the graph is $x \leq 4$.

✓ GUIDED PRACTICE for Examples 1 and 2

1. **ANTARCTICA** The lowest temperature recorded in Antarctica was −129°F at the Russian Vostok station in 1983. Use only this fact to write and graph an inequality that describes the temperatures in Antarctica.

Write an inequality represented by the graph.

2. 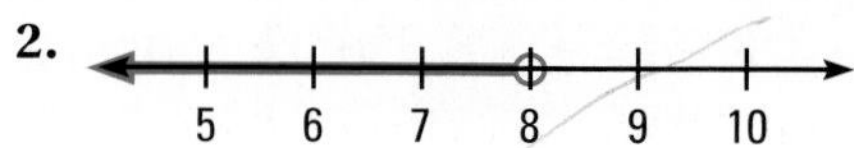

3. 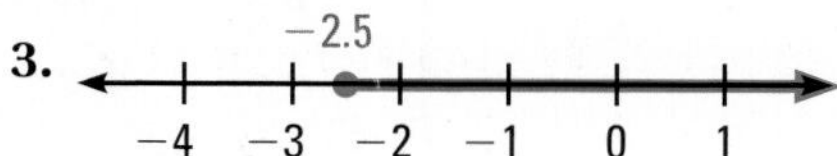

EQUIVALENT INEQUALITIES Just as you used properties of equality to produce equivalent equations, you can use properties of inequality to produce *equivalent inequalities.* **Equivalent inequalities** are inequalities that have the same solutions.

KEY CONCEPT *For Your Notebook*

Addition Property of Inequality

Words Adding the same number to each side of an inequality produces an equivalent inequality.

Algebra If $a > b$, then $a + c > b + c$. If $a \geq b$, then $a + c \geq b + c$.

If $a < b$, then $a + c < b + c$. If $a \leq b$, then $a + c \leq b + c$.

EXAMPLE 3 Solve an inequality using addition

Solve $x - 5 > -3.5$. Graph your solution.

$x - 5 > -3.5$	**Write original inequality.**
$x - 5 + 5 > -3.5 + 5$	**Add 5 to each side.**
$x > 1.5$	**Simplify.**

▶ The solutions are all real numbers greater than 1.5. Check by substituting a number greater than 1.5 for x in the original inequality.

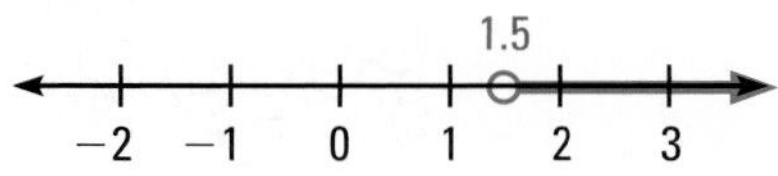

CHECK	$x - 5 > -3.5$	**Write original inequality.**
	$6 - 5 \overset{?}{>} -3.5$	**Substitute 6 for x.**
	$1 > -3.5$ ✓	**Solution checks.**

✓ GUIDED PRACTICE for Example 3

Solve the inequality. Graph your solution.

4. $x - 9 \leq 3$

5. $p - 9.2 < -5$

6. $-1 \geq m - \frac{1}{2}$

KEY CONCEPT — *For Your Notebook*

Subtraction Property of Inequality

Words Subtracting the same number from each side of an inequality produces an equivalent inequality.

Algebra If $a > b$, then $a - c > b - c$. If $a \geq b$, then $a - c \geq b - c$.

If $a < b$, then $a - c < b - c$. If $a \leq b$, then $a - c \leq b - c$.

EXAMPLE 4 Solve an inequality using subtraction

Solve $9 \geq x + 7$. Graph your solution.

$9 \geq x + 7$ **Write original inequality.**

$9 - 7 \geq x + 7 - 7$ **Subtract 7 from each side.**

$2 \geq x$ **Simplify.**

▶ You can rewrite $2 \geq x$ as $x \leq 2$. The solutions are all real numbers less than or equal to 2.

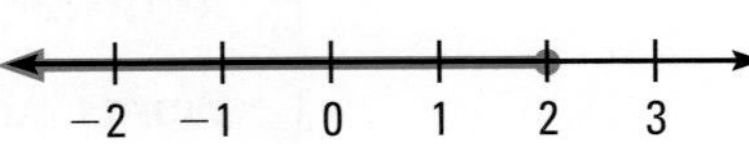

Animated Algebra at my.hrw.com

EXAMPLE 5 Solve a real-world problem

READING The phrase "no more than" indicates that you use the ≤ symbol.

LUGGAGE WEIGHTS You are checking a bag at an airport. Bags can weigh no more than 50 pounds. Your bag weighs 16.8 pounds. Find the possible weights w (in pounds) that you can add to the bag.

Solution

Write a verbal model. Then write and solve an inequality.

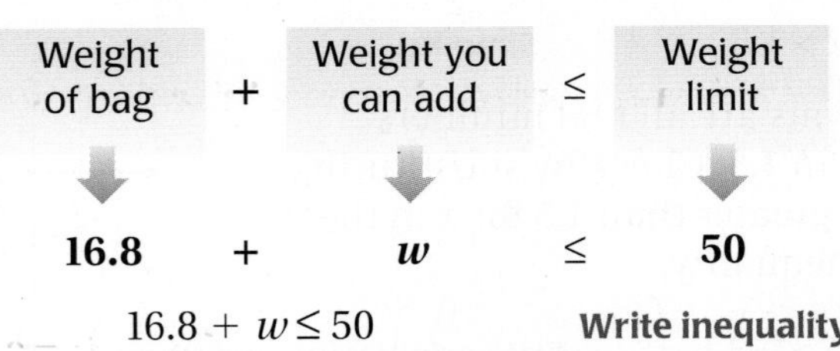

$16.8 + w \leq 50$ **Write inequality.**

$16.8 + w - 16.8 \leq 50 - 16.8$ **Subtract 16.8 from each side.**

$w \leq 33.2$ **Simplify.**

▶ You can add no more than 33.2 pounds.

✓ GUIDED PRACTICE for Examples 4 and 5

7. Solve $y + 5.5 > 6$. Graph your solution.

8. **WHAT IF?** In Example 5, suppose your bag weighs 29.1 pounds. Find the possible weights (in pounds) that you can add to the bag.

5.1 EXERCISES

HOMEWORK KEY

○ = See **WORKED-OUT SOLUTIONS** Exs. 7, 15, and 33

★ = **STANDARDIZED TEST PRACTICE** Exs. 2, 29, 34, 35, and 38

◆ = **MULTIPLE REPRESENTATIONS** Ex. 37

SKILL PRACTICE

1. VOCABULARY Copy and complete: To graph $x < -8$, you draw a(n) __?__ circle at -8, and you draw an arrow to the __?__.

2. ★ **WRITING** Are $x + 7 \geq 18$ and $x \geq 25$ equivalent inequalities? *Explain.*

EXAMPLE 1 for Exs. 3–5

WRITING AND GRAPHING INEQUALITIES Write and graph an inequality that describes the situation.

3. The speed limit on a highway is 60 miles per hour.

4. You must be at least 16 years old to go on a field trip.

5. A child must be taller than 48 inches to get on an amusement park ride.

EXAMPLE 2 for Exs. 6–9

WRITING INEQUALITIES Write an inequality represented by the graph.

6.
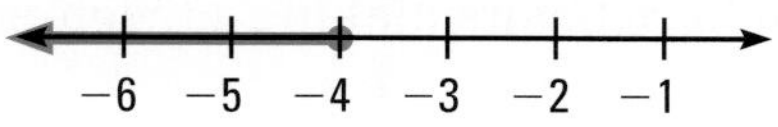

7.
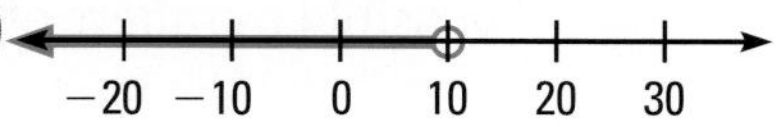

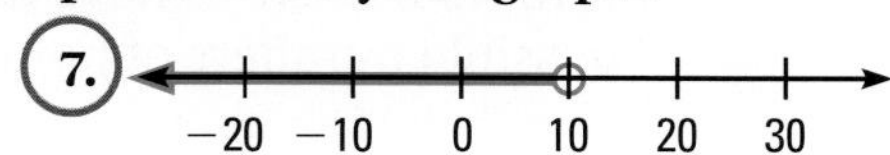

8.
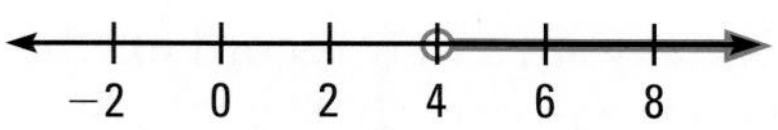

9.
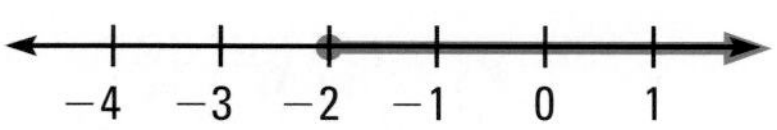

EXAMPLES 3 and 4 for Exs. 10–23

SOLVING INEQUALITIES Solve the inequality. Graph your solution.

10. $x + 4 < 5$

11. $-8 \leq 8 + y$

12. $-1\frac{1}{4} \leq m + 3$

13. $n + 17 \leq 16\frac{4}{5}$

14. $8.2 + v > -7.6$

15. $w + 14.9 > -2.7$

16. $r - 4 < -5$

17. $1 \leq s - 8$

18. $-1\frac{1}{3} \leq p - 8\frac{1}{3}$

19. $q - 1\frac{1}{3} > -2\frac{1}{2}$

20. $2.1 \geq c - 6.7$

21. $d - 1.92 > -8.76$

ERROR ANALYSIS ***Describe*** **and correct the error in solving the inequality or in graphing the solution.**

22.

$x + 8 < -3$

$x + 8 - 8 < -3 + 8$

$x < 5$

23.

$-17 \leq x - 14$

$-17 + 14 \leq x - 14 + 14$

$-3 \leq x$

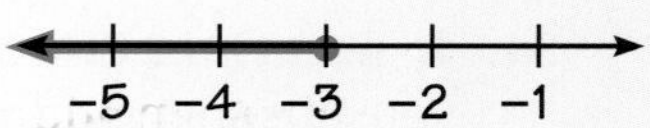

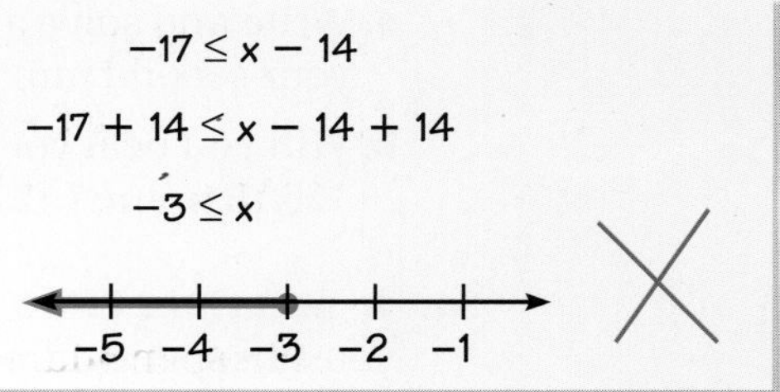

TRANSLATING SENTENCES Write the verbal sentence as an inequality. Then solve the inequality and graph your solution.

24. The sum of 11 and m is greater than -23.

25. The difference of n and 15 is less than or equal to 37.

26. The difference of c and 13 is less than -19.

GEOMETRY **Write and solve an inequality to find the possible values of x.**

27. Perimeter < 51.3 inches

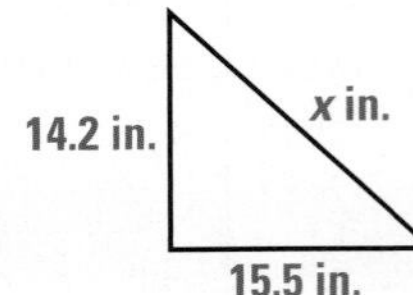

28. Perimeter ≤ 18.7 feet

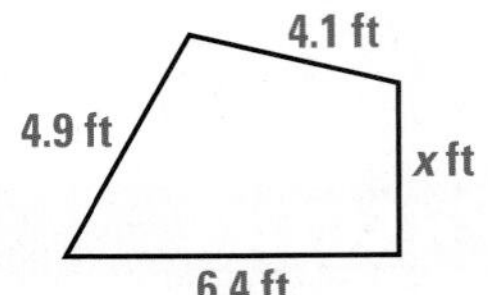

29. ★ **WRITING** Is it possible to check all the numbers that are solutions of an inequality? Does checking one solution guarantee that you have solved an inequality correctly? *Explain* your answers.

30. **CHALLENGE** Write and graph an inequality that represents the numbers that are *not* solutions of $x - 12 \geq 5.7$.

PROBLEM SOLVING

EXAMPLE 5 for Exs. 31–35

31. **INTERNET** You earn points from buying items at an Internet shopping site. You would like to redeem 2350 points to get an item for free, but you want to be sure to have more than 6000 points left over. What are the possible numbers of points you can have before making a redemption?

32. **SPORTS RECORDS** In 1982 Wayne Gretsky set a new record for the greatest number of hockey goals in one season with 92 goals. Suppose that a hockey player has 59 goals so far in a season. What are the possible numbers of additional goals that the player can make in order to match or break Wayne Gretsky's record?

33. **MULTI-STEP PROBLEM** In aerial ski competitions, athletes perform two acrobatic ski jumps, and the scores on both jumps are added together. The table shows your competitor's first and second scores and your first score.

Ski jump	Competitor's score	Your score
1	127.04	129.49
2	129.98	?

a. Write and solve an inequality to find the scores s that you can earn in your second jump in order to beat your competitor.

b. Will you beat your competitor if you earn 128.13 points? 126.78 points? 127.53 points? *Justify* your answers.

34. ★ **MULTIPLE CHOICE** You want to buy a jacket at a clothing store, and you can spend at most \$30. You have a coupon for \$3 off any item at the store. Which inequality can you use to find the original prices p of jackets that you can buy?

Ⓐ $3 + p \geq 30$ Ⓑ $30 + p \leq 3$ Ⓒ $p - 3 \leq 30$ Ⓓ $p - 30 \geq 3$

35. ★ **OPEN-ENDED** *Describe* a real-world situation that can be modeled by the inequality $x + 14 \geq 17$. *Explain* what the solution of the inequality means in this situation.

36. VEHICLE WEIGHTS According to a state law for vehicles traveling on state roads, the maximum total weight of the vehicle and its contents depends on the number of axles the vehicle has.

Maximum Total Weights

For each type of vehicle, write and solve an inequality to find the possible weights w (in pounds) of a vehicle when its contents weigh 14,200 pounds. Can a vehicle that has 2 axles and weighs 20,000 pounds hold 14,200 pounds of contents? *Explain.*

37. MULTIPLE REPRESENTATIONS Your friend is willing to spend no more than $17,000 for a new car. The car dealership offers $3000 cash back for the purchase of a new car.

a. **Making a Table** Make a table of values that gives the final price y of a car after the cash back offer is applied to the original price x. Use the following values for x: 19,459, 19,989, 20,549, 22,679, 23,999.

b. **Writing an Inequality** Write and solve an inequality to find the original prices of the cars that your friend will consider buying.

38. ★ SHORT RESPONSE A 4-member track team is trying to match or beat last year's winning time of 3 minutes 41.1 seconds for a 1600 meter relay race. The table shows the 400 meter times for the first three athletes.

Athlete	Time (sec)
1	53.34
2	56.38
3	57.46

a. **Calculate** What are the possible times that the last athlete can run 400 meters in order for the team to match or beat last year's time?

b. **Decide** So far this season the last athlete's fastest 400 meter time is 53.18 seconds, and his average 400 meter time is 53.92 seconds. In this race the last athlete expects to run faster than his slowest time this season. Is it possible for the team to fail to meet its goal? *Explain.*

39. CHALLENGE A public television station wants to raise at least $72,000 in a pledge drive. The station raised an average of $5953 per day for the first 3 days and an average of $6153 per day for the next 3 days. What are the possible additional amounts that the station can raise to meet its goal?

Investigating Algebra ACTIVITY *Use before Solve Inequalities Using Multiplication and Division*

Inequalities with Negative Coefficients

MATHEMATICAL PRACTICES

Reason abstractly and quantitatively.

MATERIALS • index cards

QUESTION How do you solve an inequality with a negative coefficient?

EXPLORE Check solutions of inequalities

STEP 1 ***Write integers*** Write the integers from -5 to 5 on index cards. Place the cards face up as shown.

−5 −4 −3 −2 −1 0 1 2 3 4 5

STEP 2 ***Check solutions*** Determine whether each integer is a solution of $4x \geq 8$. If the integer is *not* a solution, turn over the card.

2 3 4 5

STEP 3 ***Check solutions*** Turn all the cards face up. Repeat Step 2 for $-4x \geq 8$.

−5 −4 −3 −2

DRAW CONCLUSIONS Use your observations to complete these exercises

1. State an operation that you can perform on both sides of $4x \geq 8$ to obtain the solutions found in Step 2. Then solve the inequality.
2. Copy and complete the steps below for solving $-4x \geq 8$.

$-4x \geq 8$	Write original inequality.
?	Add $4x$ to each side.
?	Subtract 8 from each side.
?	Divide each side by 4.
?	Rewrite inequality with x on the left side.

3. Does dividing both sides of $-4x \geq 8$ by -4 give the solution found in Exercise 2? If not, what else must you do to the inequality when you divide by -4?
4. Do you need to change the direction of the inequality symbol when you divide each side of an inequality by a positive number? by a negative number?

Solve the inequality.

5. $20x \geq 5$ **6.** $-9x \leq 45$ **7.** $-8x > 40$ **8.** $7x < 21$

5.2 Solve Inequalities Using Multiplication and Division

Before You solved inequalities using addition and subtraction.
Now You will solve inequalities using multiplication and division.
Why? So you can find possible distances traveled, as in Ex. 40.

Key Vocabulary
- **inequality**
- **equivalent inequalities**

CC.9-12.A.REI.3 Solve linear equations and inequalities in one variable, including equations with coefficients represented by letters.

Solving an inequality using multiplication is similar to solving an equation using multiplication, but it is different in an important way.

KEY CONCEPT — *For Your Notebook*

Multiplication Property of Inequality

Words Multiplying each side of an inequality by a *positive* number produces an equivalent inequality.

Multiplying each side of an inequality by a *negative* number and *reversing the direction of the inequality symbol* produces an equivalent inequality.

Algebra If $a < b$ and $c > 0$, then $ac < bc$. If $a < b$ and $c < 0$, then $ac > bc$.

If $a > b$ and $c > 0$, then $ac > bc$. If $a > b$ and $c < 0$, then $ac < bc$.

This property is also true for inequalities involving $\le$ and $\ge$.

EXAMPLE 1 Solve an inequality using multiplication

Solve $\frac{x}{4} < 5$. Graph your solution.

$\frac{x}{4} < 5$ — **Write original inequality.**

$4 \cdot \frac{x}{4} < 4 \cdot 5$ — **Multiply each side by 4.**

$x < 20$ — **Simplify.**

▶ The solutions are all real numbers less than 20. Check by substituting a number less than 20 in the original inequality.

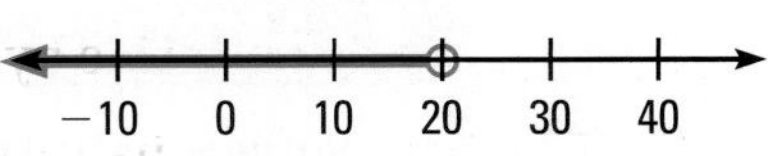

✓ GUIDED PRACTICE for Example 1

Solve the inequality. Graph your solution.

1. $\frac{x}{3} > 8$ **2.** $\frac{m}{8} \le -2$ **3.** $\frac{y}{2.5} \ge -4$

EXAMPLE 2 Solve an inequality using multiplication

Solve $\frac{x}{-6} < 7$. Graph your solution.

$\frac{x}{-6} < 7$ **Write original inequality.**

$-6 \cdot \frac{x}{-6} > -6 \cdot 7$ **Multiply each side by −6. Reverse inequality symbol.**

$x > -42$ **Simplify.**

AVOID ERRORS
Because you are multiplying by a negative number, be sure to reverse the inequality symbol.

▶ The solutions are all real numbers greater than −42. Check by substituting a number greater than −42 in the original inequality.

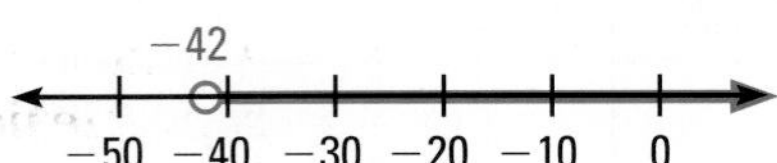

CHECK $\frac{x}{-6} < 7$ **Write original inequality.**

$\frac{0}{-6} \overset{?}{<} 7$ **Substitute 0 for *x*.**

$0 < 7$ ✓ **Solution checks.**

USING DIVISION The rules for solving an inequality using division are similar to the rules for solving an inequality using multiplication.

KEY CONCEPT *For Your Notebook*

Division Property of Inequality

Words Dividing each side of an inequality by a *positive* number produces an equivalent inequality.

Dividing each side of an inequality by a *negative* number and *reversing the direction of the inequality symbol* produces an equivalent inequality.

Algebra If $a < b$ and $c > 0$, then $\frac{a}{c} < \frac{b}{c}$. If $a < b$ and $c < 0$, then $\frac{a}{c} > \frac{b}{c}$.

If $a > b$ and $c > 0$, then $\frac{a}{c} > \frac{b}{c}$. If $a > b$ and $c < 0$, then $\frac{a}{c} < \frac{b}{c}$.

This property is also true for inequalities involving ≤ and ≥.

EXAMPLE 3 Solve an inequality using division

Solve $-3x > 24$.

$-3x > 24$ **Write original inequality.**

$\frac{-3x}{-3} < \frac{24}{-3}$ **Divide each side by −3. Reverse inequality symbol.**

$x < -8$ **Simplify.**

Animated Algebra at my.hrw.com

✓ **GUIDED PRACTICE** for Examples 2 and 3

Solve the inequality. Graph your solution.

4. $\frac{x}{-4} > 12$ **5.** $\frac{m}{-7} < 1.6$ **6.** $5v \geq 45$ **7.** $-6n < 24$

EXAMPLE 4 Standardized Test Practice

A student pilot plans to spend 80 hours on flight training to earn a private license. The student has saved $6000 for training. Which inequality can you use to find the possible hourly rates r that the student can afford to pay for training?

Ⓐ $80r \geq 6000$ Ⓑ $80r \leq 6000$ Ⓒ $6000r \geq 80$ Ⓓ $6000r \leq 80$

Solution

The total cost of training can be at most the amount of money that the student has saved. Write a verbal model for the situation. Then write an inequality.

ELIMINATE CHOICES
You need to multiply the hourly rate and the number of hours, which is 80, not 6000. So, you can eliminate choices C and D.

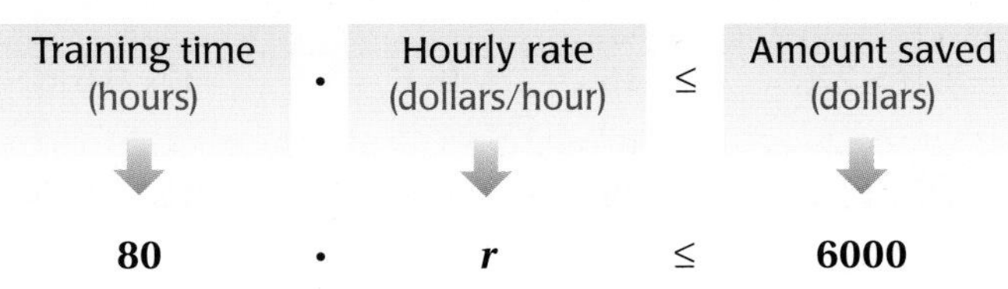

▸ The correct answer is B. Ⓐ Ⓑ Ⓒ Ⓓ

EXAMPLE 5 Solve a real-world problem

PILOTING In Example 4, what are the possible hourly rates that the student can afford to pay for training?

Solution

$80 \cdot r \leq 6000$ **Write inequality.**

$\frac{80r}{80} \leq \frac{6000}{80}$ **Divide each side by 80.**

$r \leq 75$ **Simplify.**

▸ The student can afford to pay at most $75 per hour for training.

 **GUIDED PRACTICE** for Examples 4 and 5

8. WHAT IF? In Example 5, suppose the student plans to spend 90 hours on flight training and has saved $6300. Write and solve an inequality to find the possible hourly rates that the student can afford to pay for training.

5.2 EXERCISES

HOMEWORK KEY

○ = See **WORKED-OUT SOLUTIONS** Exs. 5, 9, and 39

★ = **STANDARDIZED TEST PRACTICE** Exs. 2, 27, 34, and 41

◆ = **MULTIPLE REPRESENTATIONS** Ex. 38

SKILL PRACTICE

1. **VOCABULARY** Which property are you using when you solve $5x \geq 30$ by dividing each side by 5?

2. ★ **WRITING** Are $\frac{x}{-4} < -9$ and $x < 36$ equivalent inequalities? *Explain* your answer.

EXAMPLES 1, 2, and 3 for Exs. 3–29

SOLVING INEQUALITIES **Solve the inequality. Graph your solution.**

3. $2p \geq 14$	4. $\frac{x}{-3} < -10$	(5.) $-6y < -36$	6. $40 > \frac{w}{5}$
7. $\frac{q}{4} < 7$	8. $72 \leq 9r$	(9.) $\frac{g}{6} > -20$	10. $-11m \leq -22$
11. $-90 \geq 4t$	12. $\frac{n}{3} < -9$	13. $60 \leq -12s$	14. $\frac{v}{-4} \geq -8$
15. $-8.4f > 2.1$	16. $\frac{d}{-2} \leq 18.6$	17. $9.6 < -16c$	18. $0.07 \geq \frac{k}{7}$
19. $-1.5 \geq 6z$	20. $\frac{x}{-5} \leq -7.5$	21. $1.02 < -3j$	22. $\frac{y}{-4.5} \geq -10$
23. $\frac{r}{-30} < 1.8$	24. $1.9 \leq -5p$	25. $\frac{m}{0.6} > -40$	26. $-2t > -1.22$

27. ★ **WRITING** How is solving $ax > b$ where $a > 0$ similar to solving $ax > b$ where $a < 0$? How is it different?

ERROR ANALYSIS ***Describe*** **and correct the error in solving the inequality.**

28.
$$-15x > 45$$
$$\frac{-15x}{-15} > \frac{45}{-15}$$
$$x > -3$$
✗

29.
$$\frac{x}{9} \leq -7$$
$$9 \cdot \frac{x}{9} \leq 9 \cdot (-7)$$
$$x \geq -63$$
✗

TRANSLATING SENTENCES **In Exercises 30–33, write the verbal sentence as an inequality. Then solve the inequality and graph your solution.**

30. The product of 8 and x is greater than 50.

31. The product of -15 and y is less than or equal to 90.

32. The quotient of v and -9 is less than -18.

33. The quotient of w and 24 is greater than or equal to $-\frac{1}{6}$.

34. ★ **OPEN-ENDED** Write an inequality in the form $ax < b$ such that the solutions are all real numbers greater than 4.

35. **CHALLENGE** For the given values of a and b, tell whether the solution of $ax > b$ consists of *positive numbers, negative numbers,* or *both. Explain.*

a. $a < 0, b > 0$ **b.** $a > 0, b > 0$ **c.** $a > 0, b < 0$ **d.** $a < 0, b < 0$

PROBLEM SOLVING

EXAMPLES 4 and 5 Exs. 36–39

36. **MUSIC** You have \$90 to buy CDs for your friend's party. The CDs cost \$18 each. What are the possible numbers of CDs that you can buy?

37. **JOB SKILLS** You apply for a job that requires the ability to type 40 words per minute. You practice typing on a keyboard for 5 minutes. The average number of words you type per minute must at least meet the job requirement. What are the possible numbers of words that you can type in 5 minutes in order to meet or exceed the job requirement?

38. **MULTIPLE REPRESENTATIONS** You are stacking books on a shelf that has a height of 66 centimeters. Each book has a thickness of 4 centimeters.

a. Using a Model Use a concrete model to find the possible numbers of books that you can stack as follows: Cut strips of paper 4 centimeters wide to represent the books. Then place the strips one above the other until they form a column no taller than 66 centimeters.

b. Writing an Inequality Write and solve an inequality to find the possible numbers of books that you can stack.

c. Drawing a Graph Write and graph an equation that gives the height y of stacked books as a function of the number x of books. Then graph $y = 66$ in the same coordinate plane. To find the possible numbers of books that you can stack, identify the integer x-coordinates of the points on the first graph that lie *on or below* the graph of $y = 66$.

d. Choosing a Method Suppose the shelf has a height of 100 centimeters. Which method would you use to find the possible numbers of books, *a concrete model, solving an inequality,* or *drawing a graph*? *Explain.*

39. **MANUFACTURING** A manufacturer of architectural moldings recommends that the length of a piece be no more than 15 times its minimum width w (in inches) in order to prevent cracking. For the piece shown, what could the values of w be?

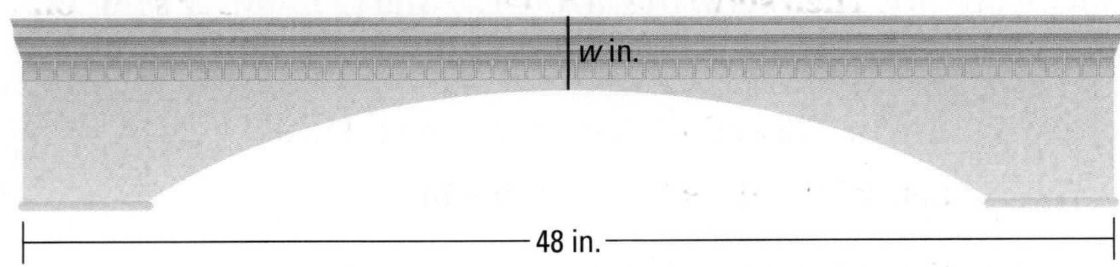

40. **RECREATION** A water-skiing instructor recommends that a boat pulling a beginning skier have a speed less than 18 miles per hour. Write and solve an inequality that you can use to find the possible distances d (in miles) that a beginner can travel in 45 minutes of practice time.

41. ★ **EXTENDED RESPONSE** A state agency that offers wild horses for adoption requires that a potential owner reserve 400 square feet of land per horse in a corral.

a. **Solve** A farmer has a rectangular corral whose length is 80 feet and whose width is 82 feet. Write and solve an inequality to find the possible numbers h of horses that the corral can hold.

b. **Explain** If the farmer increases the length and width of the corral by 20 feet each, will the corral be able to hold only 1 more horse? *Explain* your answer without calculating the new area of the corral.

c. **Calculate** The farmer decides to increase the length and width of the corral by 15 feet each. Find the possible numbers of horses that the corral can hold. Your answer should include the following:

- a calculation of the new area of the corral
- a description of your steps for solving the problem

42. **CHALLENGE** An electronics store is selling a laptop computer for $1050. You can spend no more than $900 for the laptop, so you wait for it to go on sale. Also, you plan to use a store coupon for 5% off the sale price. For which decreases in price will you consider buying the laptop?

QUIZ

Solve the inequality. Graph your solution.

1. $x + 8 \geq -5$
2. $y + 6 < 14$
3. $-8 \leq v - 5$
4. $w - 11 > 2$
5. $-40 < -5r$
6. $-93 < 3s$
7. $-2m \geq 26$
8. $\frac{n}{-4} > -7$
9. $\frac{c}{6} \leq -8$

10. **FOOD PREPARATION** You need to make at least 150 sandwiches for a charity event. You can make 3 sandwiches per minute. How long will it take you to make the number of sandwiches you need?

5.3 Solve Multi-Step Inequalities

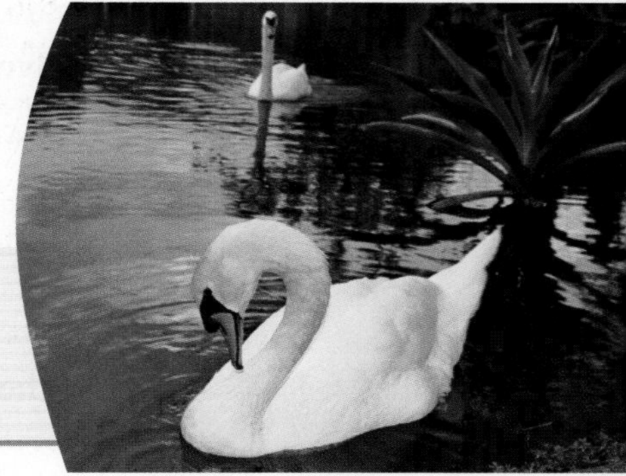

Before You solved one-step inequalities.

Now You will solve multi-step inequalities.

Why? So you can compare animal habitats, as in Ex. 39.

Key Vocabulary
- **inequality**

The steps for solving two-step and multi-step equations can be applied to linear inequalities. For inequalities, be sure to reverse the inequality symbol when multiplying or dividing by a negative number.

COMMON CORE

CC.9-12.A.REI.3 Solve linear equations and inequalities in one variable, including equations with coefficients represented by letters.

EXAMPLE 1 Solve a two-step inequality

Solve $3x - 7 < 8$. Graph your solution.

$3x - 7 < 8$	**Write original inequality.**
$3x < 15$	**Add 7 to each side.**
$x < 5$	**Divide each side by 3.**

▶ The solutions are all real numbers less than 5. Check by substituting a number less than 5 in the original inequality.

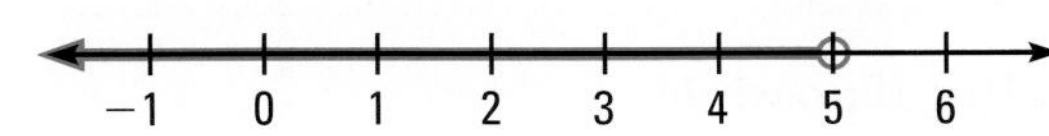

CHECK

$3x - 7 < 8$	**Write original inequality.**
$3(0) - 7 \overset{?}{<} 8$	**Substitute 0 for *x*.**
$-7 < 8$ ✓	**Solution checks.**

EXAMPLE 2 Solve a multi-step inequality

Solve $-0.6(x - 5) \le 15$.

$-0.6(x - 5) \le 15$	**Write original inequality.**
$-0.6x + 3 \le 15$	**Distributive property**
$-0.6x \le 12$	**Subtract 3 from each side.**
$x \ge -20$	**Divide each side by -0.6. Reverse inequality symbol.**

GUIDED PRACTICE for Examples 1 and 2

Solve the inequality. Graph your solution.

1. $2x - 5 \le 23$ **2.** $-6y + 5 \le -16$ **3.** $-\frac{1}{4}(p - 12) > -2$

EXAMPLE 3 Solve a multi-step inequality

ANOTHER WAY

You can also solve the inequality by subtracting 17 and $6x$ from each side, as follows:

$6x - 7 > 2x + 17$

$6x - 24 > 2x$

$-24 > -4x$

$6 < x$

The inequality $6 < x$ is equivalent to $x > 6$.

Solve $6x - 7 > 2x + 17$. Graph your solution.

$6x - 7 > 2x + 17$	**Write original inequality.**
$6x > 2x + 24$	**Add 7 to each side.**
$4x > 24$	**Subtract $2x$ from each side.**
$x > 6$	**Divide each side by 4.**

▶ The solutions are all real numbers greater than 6.

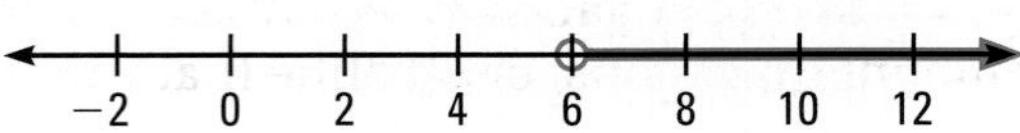

NUMBER OF SOLUTIONS If an inequality is equivalent to an inequality that is true, such as $-3 < 0$, then the solutions of the inequality are *all real numbers.* If an inequality is equivalent to an inequality that is false, such as $4 < -1$, then the inequality has *no solution.*

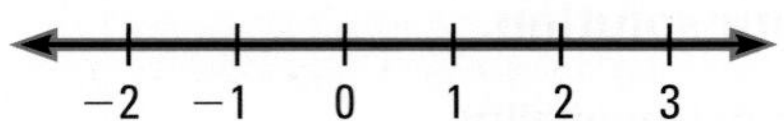

Graph of an inequality whose solutions are all real numbers

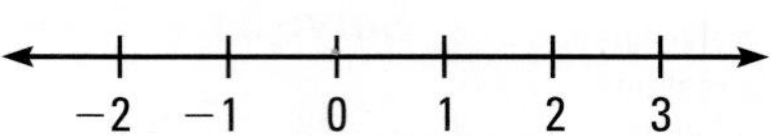

Graph of an inequality that has no solution

EXAMPLE 4 Identify the number of solutions of an inequality

Solve the inequality, if possible.

a. $14x + 5 < 7(2x - 3)$

b. $12x - 1 > 6(2x - 1)$

Solution

a. $14x + 5 < 7(2x - 3)$	**Write original inequality.**
$14x + 5 < 14x - 21$	**Distributive property**
$5 < -21$	**Subtract $14x$ from each side.**

▶ There are no solutions because $5 < -21$ is false.

b. $12x - 1 > 6(2x - 1)$	**Write original inequality.**
$12x - 1 > 12x - 6$	**Distributive property**
$-1 > -6$	**Subtract $12x$ from each side.**

▶ All real numbers are solutions because $-1 > -6$ is true.

✓ GUIDED PRACTICE for Examples 3 and 4

Solve the inequality, if possible. Graph your solution.

4. $5x - 12 \leq 3x - 4$

5. $5(m + 5) < 5m + 17$

6. $1 - 8s \leq -4(2s - 1)$

EXAMPLE 5 Solve a multi-step problem

CAR WASH Use the sign shown. A gas station charges $.10 less per gallon of gasoline if a customer also gets a car wash. What are the possible amounts (in gallons) of gasoline that you can buy if you also get a car wash and can spend at most $20?

ANOTHER WAY
For an alternative method for solving the problem in Example 5, see the **Problem Solving Workshop**.

Solution

Because you are getting a car wash, you will pay $2.09 − $.10 = $1.99 per gallon of gasoline. Let g be the amount (in gallons) of gasoline that you buy.

STEP 1 **Write** a verbal model. Then write an inequality.

Price of gasoline (dollars/gallon)	•	Amount of gasoline (gallons)	+	Price of car wash (dollars)	≤	Maximum amount (dollars)
1.99	•	g	+	**8**	≤	**20**

STEP 2 **Solve** the inequality.

$1.99g + 8 \le 20$ **Write inequality.**

$1.99g \le 12$ **Subtract 8 from each side.**

$g \le 6.03015\ldots$ **Divide each side by 1.99.**

▶ You can buy up to slightly more than 6 gallons of gasoline.

CHECK You can use a table to check the reasonableness of your answer.

The table shows that you will pay $19.94 for exactly 6 gallons of gasoline. Because $19.94 is less than $20, it is reasonable to conclude that you can buy slightly more than 6 gallons of gasoline.

Gasoline (gal)	Total amount spent (dollars)
0	8.00
1	9.99
2	11.98
3	13.97
4	15.96
5	17.95
6	19.94

✓ GUIDED PRACTICE for Example 5

7. **WHAT IF?** In Example 5, suppose that a car wash costs $9 and gasoline regularly costs $2.19 per gallon. What are the possible amounts (in gallons) of gasoline that you can buy?

8. **CAMP COSTS** You are saving money for a summer camp that costs $1800. You have saved $500 so far, and you have 14 more weeks to save the total amount. What are the possible average amounts of money that you can save per week in order to have a total of at least $1800 saved?

5.3 EXERCISES

HOMEWORK KEY

○ = See **WORKED-OUT SOLUTIONS** Exs. 5, 19, and 39

★ = **STANDARDIZED TEST PRACTICE** Exs. 2, 33, 39, 40, and 42

◆ = **MULTIPLE REPRESENTATIONS** Ex. 41

SKILL PRACTICE

1. **VOCABULARY** Copy and complete: The inequalities $3x - 1 < 11$, $3x < 12$, and $x < 4$ are called __?__.

2. ★ **WRITING** How do you know whether an inequality has no solutions? How do you know whether the solutions are all real numbers?

EXAMPLES 1, 2, and 3 for Exs. 3–16

SOLVING INEQUALITIES **Solve the inequality. Graph your solution.**

3. $2x - 3 > 7$
4. $5y + 9 \leq 4$
5. $8v - 3 \geq -11$
6. $3(w + 12) < 0$
7. $7(r - 3) \geq -13$
8. $2(s + 4) \leq 16$
9. $4 - 2m > 7 - 3m$
10. $8n - 2 > 17n + 9$
11. $-10p > 6p - 8$
12. $4 - \frac{1}{2}q \leq 33 - q$
13. $-\frac{2}{3}d - 2 < \frac{1}{3}d + 8$
14. $8 - \frac{4}{5}f > -14 - 2f$

ERROR ANALYSIS ***Describe*** **and correct the error in solving the inequality.**

15.
$17 - 3x \geq 56$
$-3x \geq 39$
$x \geq -13$

16.
$-4(2x - 3) < 28$
$-8x - 12 < 28$
$-8x < 40$
$x > -5$

EXAMPLE 4 for Exs. 17–28

SOLVING INEQUALITIES **Solve the inequality, if possible.**

17. $3p - 5 > 2p + p - 7$
18. $5d - 8d - 4 \leq -4 + 3d$
19. $3(s - 4) \geq 2(s - 6)$
20. $2(t - 3) > 2t - 8$
21. $5(b + 9) \leq 5b + 45$
22. $2(4c - 7) \geq 8(c - 3)$
23. $6(x + 3) < 5x + 18 + x$
24. $4 + 9y - 3 \geq 3(3y + 2)$
25. $2.2h + 0.4 \leq 2(1.1h - 0.1)$
26. $9.5j - 6 + 5.5j \geq 3(5j - 2)$
27. $\frac{1}{5}(4m + 10) < \frac{4}{5}m + 2$
28. $\frac{3}{4}(8n - 4) < -3(1 - 2n)$

TRANSLATING PHRASES **Translate the verbal phrase into an inequality. Then solve the inequality and graph your solution.**

29. Four more than the product of 3 and x is less than 40.
30. Twice the sum of x and 8 is greater than or equal to -36.
31. The sum of $5x$ and $2x$ is greater than the difference of $9x$ and 4.
32. The product of 6 and the difference of $6x$ and 3 is less than or equal to the product of -2 and the sum of 4 and $8x$.

33. ★ **MULTIPLE CHOICE** For which values of a and b are all the solutions of $ax + b > 0$ positive?

Ⓐ $a > 0, b > 0$ Ⓑ $a < 0, b < 0$ Ⓒ $a > 0, b < 0$ Ⓓ $a < 0, b = 0$

GEOMETRY Write and solve an inequality to find the possible values of x.

34. Area > 81 square feet

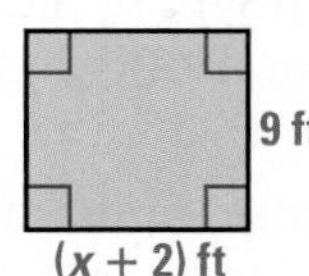

35. Area ≤ 44 square centimeters

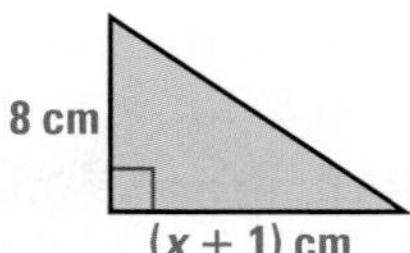

36. **CHALLENGE** For which value of a are all the solutions of $2(x - 5) \geq 3x + a$ less than or equal to 5?

PROBLEM SOLVING

EXAMPLE 5
for Exs. 37–40

37. **CD BURNING** A blank CD can hold 70 minutes of music. So far you have burned 25 minutes of music onto the CD. You estimate that each song lasts 4 minutes. What are the possible numbers of additional songs that you can burn onto the CD?

38. **BUSINESS** You spend \$46 on supplies to make wooden ornaments and plan to sell the ornaments for \$8.50 each. What are the possible numbers of ornaments that you can sell in order for your profit to be positive?

39. ★ **SHORT RESPONSE** A zookeeper is designing a rectangular habitat for swans, as shown. The zookeeper needs to reserve 500 square feet for the first 2 swans and 125 square feet for each additional swan.

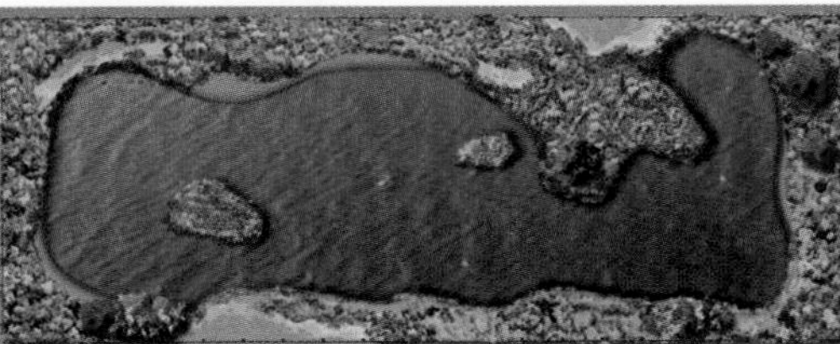

a. **Calculate** What are the possible numbers of swans that the habitat can hold? *Explain* how you got your answer.

b. **Compare** Suppose that the zookeeper increases both the length and width of the habitat by 20 feet. What are the possible numbers of additional swans that the habitat can hold?

40. ★ **MULTIPLE CHOICE** A gym is offering a trial membership for 3 months by discounting the regular monthly rate by \$50. You will consider joining the gym if the total cost of the trial membership is less than \$100. Which inequality can you use to find the possible regular monthly rates that you are willing to pay?

(A) $3x - 50 < 100$　　(B) $3x - 50 > 100$

(C) $3(x - 50) < 100$　　(D) $3(x - 50) > 100$

41. **MULTIPLE REPRESENTATIONS** A baseball pitcher makes 53 pitches in the first four innings of a game and plans to pitch in the next 3 innings.

   a. **Making a Table** Make a table that gives the total number t of pitches made if the pitcher makes an average of p pitches per inning in the next 3 innings. Use the following values for p: 15, 16, 17, 18, 19.

   b. **Writing an Inequality** The baseball coach assigns a maximum of 105 pitches to the pitcher for the game. Write and solve an inequality to find the possible average numbers of pitches that the pitcher can make in each of the next three innings.

42. ★ **EXTENDED RESPONSE** A state imposes a sales tax on items of clothing that cost more than \$175. The tax applies only to the difference of the price of the item and \$175.

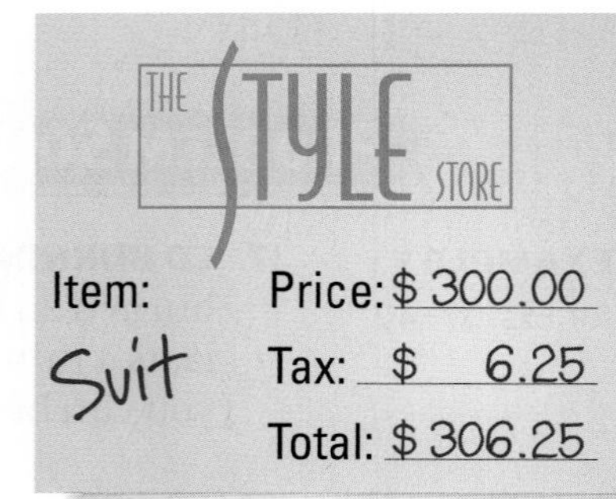

   a. **Calculate** Use the receipt shown to find the tax rate (as a percent). *Explain* how you got your answer.

   b. **Apply** A shopper has \$400 to spend on a winter coat. Write and solve an inequality to find the prices p of coats that the shopper can afford. Assume that $p \geq 175$.

   c. **Compare** Another state imposes a 4% sales tax on the entire price of an item of clothing. For which prices would paying the 4% tax be cheaper than paying the tax described above? Your answer should include the following:

   - writing and solving an inequality that describes the situation
   - checking the reasonableness of your answer using one of the solutions of the inequality

43. **CHALLENGE** Your scores in four bowling league tournaments are 157, 161, 149, and 172. After the next game, you want your average score to be at least 167. What are the possible scores that you can earn in your next tournament in order to meet your goal?

See **EXTRA PRACTICE** in Student Resources **ONLINE QUIZ** at my.hrw.com

PROBLEM SOLVING WORKSHOP
LESSON 5.3

Using ALTERNATIVE METHODS

Another Way to Solve Example 5

MATHEMATICAL PRACTICES

Make sense of problems and persevere in solving them.

MULTIPLE REPRESENTATIONS In Example 5, you saw how to solve a problem about buying gasoline using an inequality. You can also solve the problem by working backward or by using a graph.

PROBLEM

CAR WASH Use the sign shown. A gas station charges \$.10 less per gallon of gasoline if a customer also gets a car wash. What are the possible amounts (in gallons) of gasoline that you can buy if you also get a car wash and can spend at most \$20?

METHOD 1

Work backward One alternative approach is to work backward.

STEP 1 **Read** the problem. It gives you the following information:

- amount you can spend: up to \$20
- price of a car wash: \$8
- regular price per gallon of gasoline: \$2.09
- discount per gallon of gasoline when you get a car wash: \$.10

Because you are getting a car wash, gasoline costs \$2.09 − \$.10, or \$1.99, per gallon.

STEP 2 **Work** backward.

- Start with the amount you have to spend: \$20.
- Subtract the cost of a car wash: \$20 − \$8 = \$12.
- Make a table of values showing the amount of money you have left after buying various amounts of gasoline.

Gasoline (gal)	Amount of money left
0	\$12.00
1	\$10.01
2	\$8.02
3	\$6.03
4	\$4.04
5	\$2.05
6	\$.06

(Each row: − \$1.99)

▶ You can buy up to slightly more than 6 gallons of gasoline.

METHOD 2

Using a graph Another alternative approach is to use a graph.

STEP 1 **Write** a verbal model. Then write an equation that gives the total amount of money y (in dollars) that you spend as a function of the amount x (in gallons) of gasoline that you buy.

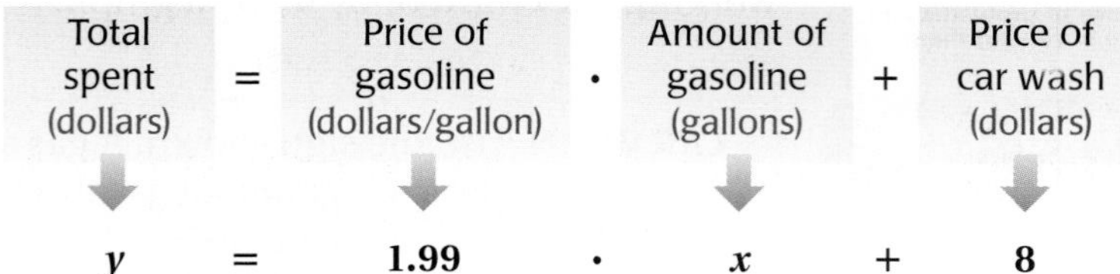

$$y = 1.99 \cdot x + 8$$

STEP 2 **Graph** $y = 1.99x + 8$.

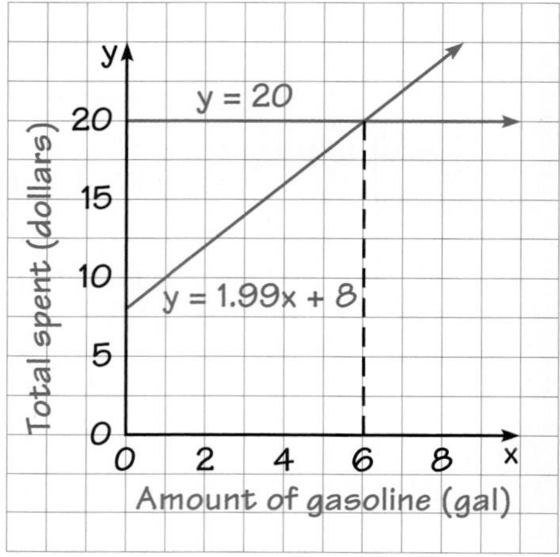

STEP 3 **Graph** $y = 20$ in the same coordinate plane. This equation gives the maximum amount of money that you can spend for gasoline and a car wash.

STEP 4 **Analyze** the graphs. The point of intersection shows that you can buy slightly more than 6 gallons of gasoline when you spend \$20. Because you can spend *at most* \$20, the solutions are the x-coordinates of the points on the graph of $y = 1.99x + 8$ that lie *on or below* the graph of $y = 20$.

▶ You can buy up to slightly more than 6 gallons of gasoline.

PRACTICE

1. **BAKING** You need to bake at least 100 cookies for a bake sale. You can bake 12 cookies per batch of dough. What are the possible numbers of batches that will allow you to bake enough cookies? Solve this problem using two different methods.

2. **VIDEO GAMES** A video game console costs \$259, and games cost \$29 each. You saved \$400 to buy a console and games. What are the possible numbers of games that you can buy? Solve this problem using two different methods.

3. **WHAT IF?** In Exercise 2, suppose that you saved \$500 and decide to buy a video game console that costs \$299. What are the possible numbers of games that you can buy?

4. **MONEY** You need to have at least \$100 in your checking account to avoid a low balance fee. You have \$247 in your account, and you make withdrawals of \$20 per week. What are the possible numbers of weeks that you can withdraw money and avoid paying the fee? Solve this problem using two different methods.

5. **RUNNING TIMES** You are running a 10 mile race. You run the first 3 miles in 24.7 minutes. Your goal is to finish the race in less than 1 hour 20 minutes. What should your average running time (in minutes per mile) be for the remaining miles?

Extension Solve Linear Inequalities by Graphing

GOAL Use graphs to solve linear inequalities.

CC.9-12.A.REI.10 Understand that the graph of an equation in two variables is the set of all its solutions plotted in the coordinate plane, often forming a curve (which could be a line).

COMPARE FUNCTION VALUES
If you think of the equation $y = ax + b$ as a function, the solutions of $ax + b > 0$ and $ax + b < 0$ tell you where the values of the function are positive or negative.

You have seen how to solve linear inequalities algebraically. You can also solve linear inequalities graphically.

KEY CONCEPT *For Your Notebook*

Solving Linear Inequalities Graphically

STEP 1 **Write** the inequality in one of the following forms: $ax + b < 0$, $ax + b \le 0$, $ax + b > 0$, or $ax + b \ge 0$.

STEP 2 **Write** the related equation $y = ax + b$.

STEP 3 **Graph** the equation $y = ax + b$.

- The solutions of $ax + b > 0$ are the x-coordinates of the points on the graph of $y = ax + b$ that lie above the x-axis.
- The solutions of $ax + b < 0$ are the x-coordinates of the points on the graph of $y = ax + b$ that lie below the x-axis.
- If the inequality symbol is $\le$ or $\ge$, then the x-intercept of the graph is also a solution.

EXAMPLE 1 Solve an inequality graphically

Solve $3x + 2 > 8$ graphically.

Solution

STEP 1 **Write** the inequality in the form $ax + b > 0$.

$3x + 2 > 8$ **Write original inequality.**

$3x - 6 > 0$ **Subtract 8 from each side.**

STEP 2 **Write** the related equation $y = 3x - 6$.

STEP 3 **Graph** the equation $y = 3x - 6$.

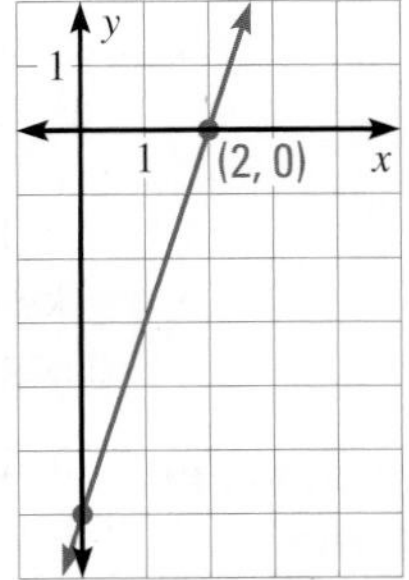

The inequality in Step 1 is in the form $ax + b > 0$, and the x-intercept of the graph in Step 3 is 2. So, $x > 2$.

▶ The solutions are all real numbers greater than 2. Check by substituting a number greater than 2 in the original inequality.

CHECK $3x + 2 > 8$ **Write original inequality.**

$3(4) + 2 \overset{?}{>} 8$ **Substitute 4 for x.**

$14 > 8$ ✓ **Solution checks.**

EXAMPLE 2 Approximate a real-world solution

CELL PHONES Your cell phone plan costs \$49.99 per month for a given number of minutes. Each additional minute or part of a minute costs \$.40. You budgeted \$55 per month for phone costs. What are the possible additional minutes x that you can afford each month?

Solution

STEP 1 **Write** a verbal model. Then write an inequality.

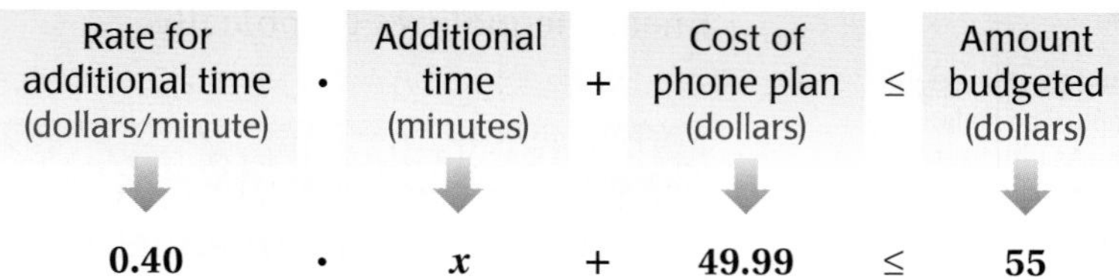

$0.40 \cdot x + 49.99 \le 55$

Write the inequality in the form $ax + b \le 0$.

$0.40x + 49.99 \le 55$ **Write original inequality.**

$0.40x - 5.01 \le 0$ **Subtract 55 from each side.**

STEP 2 **Write** the related equation $y = 0.40x - 5.01$.

STEP 3 **Graph** the equation $y = 0.40x - 5.01$ on a graphing calculator.

Use the *trace* feature of the graphing calculator to find the x-intercept of the graph.

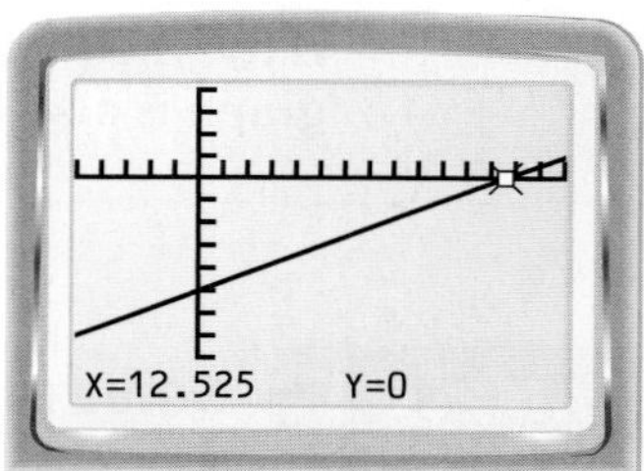

The inequality in Step 1 is in the form $ax + b \le 0$, and the x-intercept is about 12.5. Because a part of a minute costs \$.40, round 12.5 down to 12 to be sure that you stay within your budget.

▶ You can afford up to 12 additional minutes.

PRACTICE

EXAMPLES 1 and 2 for Exs. 1–4

Solve the inequality graphically.

1. $2x + 5 > 11$
2. $\frac{1}{2}x + 6 \le 13$
3. $0.2x - 15.75 < 27$
4. **CABLE COSTS** Your family has a cable television package that costs \$40.99 per month. Pay-per-view movies cost \$3.95 each. Your family budgets \$55 per month for cable television costs. What are the possible numbers of pay-per-view movies that your family can afford each month?

Investigating Algebra **ACTIVITY** *Use before Solve Compound Inequalities*

Statements with *And* and *Or*

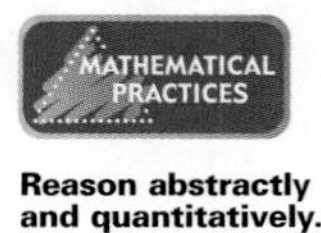

Reason abstractly and quantitatively.

MATERIALS • paper and pencil

QUESTION **What is the difference between a statement with *and* and a statement with *or*?**

EXPLORE **Use a Venn diagram to answer questions about a group**

STEP 1 ***Answer questions*** Copy the questions below and write your answers beside them.

1. Are you taking an art class?
2. Are you taking a foreign language class?

STEP 2 ***Complete a Venn diagram*** Form a group with 3 or 4 classmates. Draw a Venn diagram, like the one shown below, where set A consists of students taking an art class, and set B consists of students taking a foreign language class. Then write the name of each student in the appropriate section of the diagram.

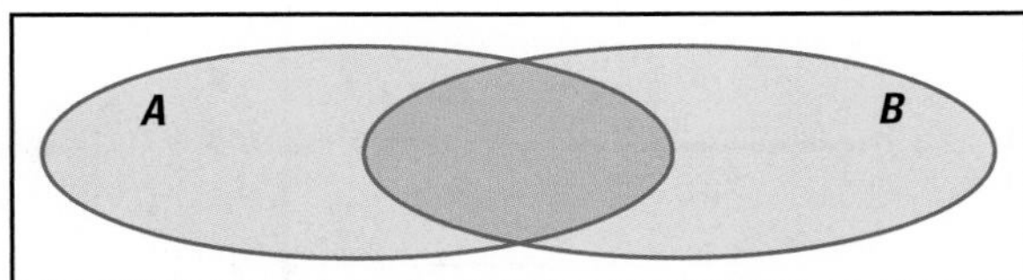

DRAW CONCLUSIONS **Use your observations to complete these exercises**

In Exercises 1–3, use your Venn diagram to list the students who belong in the given set.

1. Set A
2. Set B
3. Set A *and* set B
4. The students who belong in set A *or* set B are all of the students who belong only in set A, only in set B, or in set A *and* set B. List the students in your group who belong in set A *or* set B.
5. **OPEN-ENDED** Write a statement with *and* so that the statement is true for all students in your group.
6. **OPEN-ENDED** Write a statement with *or* so that the statement is true for all students in your group.

REASONING **Tell whether the statement is *true* or *false*.**

7. If a student belongs in set A *and* set B, then the student belongs in set A *or* set B.
8. If a student belongs in set A *or* set B, then the student belongs in set A *and* set B.

5.4 Solve Compound Inequalities

Before You solved one-step and multi-step inequalities.

Now You will solve compound inequalities.

Why? So you can describe possible heights, as in Example 2.

Key Vocabulary
- **compound inequality**

CC.9-12.A.REI.3 Solve linear equations and inequalities in one variable, including equations with coefficients represented by letters.

A **compound inequality** consists of two separate inequalities joined by *and* or *or*.

The graph of a compound inequality with *and* is the *intersection* of the graphs of the inequalities.

$x > -2$

$x \le 1$

$-2 < x$ *and* $x \le 1$
$-2 < x \le 1$

The graph of a compound inequality with *or* is the *union* of the graphs of the inequalities.

$x \ge 0$

$x < -1$

$x < -1$ *or* $x \ge 0$

EXAMPLE 1 Write and graph compound inequalities

Translate the verbal phrase into an inequality. Then graph the inequality.

a. All real numbers that are greater than −2 *and* less than 3

Inequality: $-2 < x < 3$

Graph:

b. All real numbers that are less than 0 *or* greater than or equal to 2

Inequality: $x < 0$ *or* $x \ge 2$

Graph:

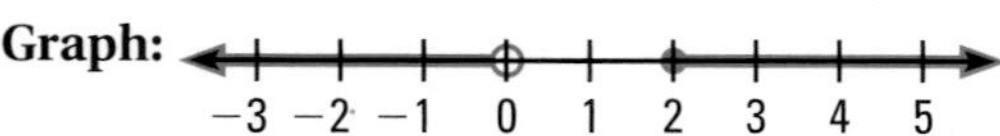

GUIDED PRACTICE for Example 1

Translate the verbal phrase into an inequality. Then graph the inequality.

1. All real numbers that are less than −1 *or* greater than or equal to 4
2. All real numbers that are greater than or equal to −3 *and* less than 5

Courtesy of www.apcamcar.com

EXAMPLE 2 Write and graph a real-world compound inequality

CAMERA CARS A crane sits on top of a camera car and faces toward the front. The crane's maximum height and minimum height above the ground are shown. Write and graph a compound inequality that describes the possible heights of the crane.

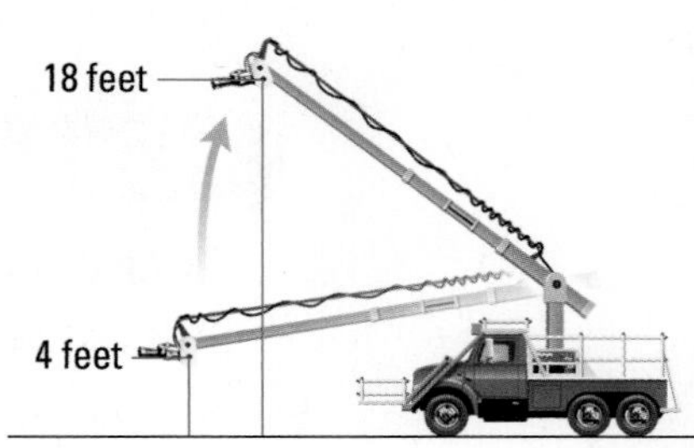

Solution

Let h represent the height (in feet) of the crane. All possible heights are greater than or equal to 4 feet *and* less than or equal to 18 feet. So, the inequality is $4 \le h \le 18$.

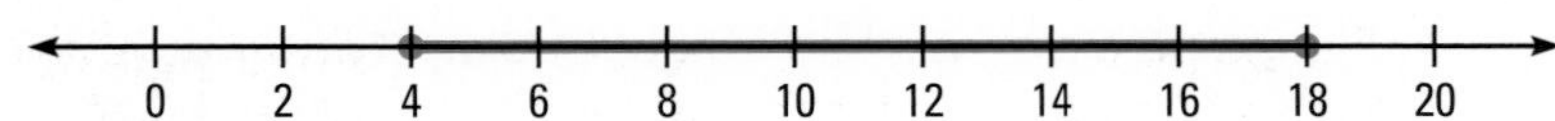

SOLVING COMPOUND INEQUALITIES A number is a solution of a compound inequality with *and* if the number is a solution of *both* inequalities. A number is a solution of a compound inequality with *or* if the number is a solution of *at least one* of the inequalities.

EXAMPLE 3 Solve a compound inequality with *and*

Solve $2 < x + 5 < 9$. Graph your solution.

Solution

Separate the compound inequality into two inequalities. Then solve each inequality separately.

$2 < x + 5$	*and*	$x + 5 < 9$	**Write two inequalities.**
$2 - 5 < x + 5 - 5$	*and*	$x + 5 - 5 < 9 - 5$	**Subtract 5 from each side.**
$-3 < x$	*and*	$x < 4$	**Simplify.**

The compound inequality can be written as $-3 < x < 4$.

▸ The solutions are all real numbers greater than -3 *and* less than 4.

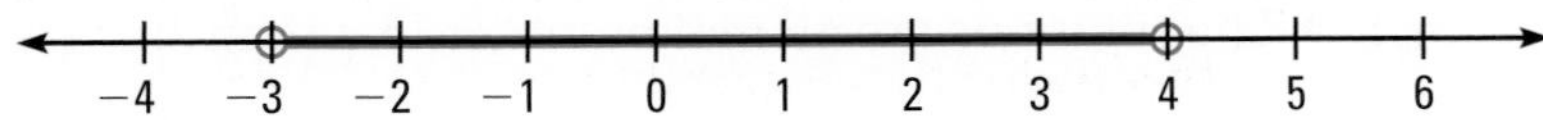

✓ GUIDED PRACTICE for Examples 2 and 3

3. **INVESTING** An investor buys shares of a stock and will sell them if the change c in value from the purchase price of a share is less than $-\$3.00$ or greater than $\$4.50$. Write and graph a compound inequality that describes the changes in value for which the shares will be sold.

Solve the inequality. Graph your solution.

4. $-7 < x - 5 < 4$
5. $10 \le 2y + 4 \le 24$
6. $-7 < -z - 1 < 3$

ANOTHER WAY In Example 3, you could solve $2 < x + 5 < 9$ by subtracting 5 from 2, $x + 5$, and 9 without first separating the compound inequality into two separate inequalities. To solve a compound inequality with *and*, you perform the same operation on each expression.

EXAMPLE 4 Solve a compound inequality with *and*

Solve $-5 \le -x - 3 \le 2$. Graph your solution.

$-5 \le -x - 3 \le 2$	Write original inequality.
$-5 + 3 \le -x - 3 + 3 \le 2 + 3$	Add 3 to each expression.
$-2 \le -x \le 5$	Simplify.
$-1(-2) \ge -1(-x) \ge -1(5)$	Multiply each expression by −1 and reverse *both* inequality symbols.
$2 \ge x \ge -5$	Simplify.
$-5 \le x \le 2$	Rewrite in the form $a \le x \le b$.

▶ The solutions are all real numbers greater than or equal to −5 *and* less than or equal to 2.

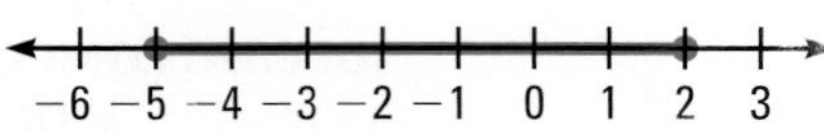

EXAMPLE 5 Solve a compound inequality with *or*

Solve $2x + 3 < 9$ *or* $3x - 6 > 12$. Graph your solution.

Solution

Solve the two inequalities separately.

$2x + 3 < 9$	*or*	$3x - 6 > 12$	Write original inequality.
$2x + 3 - 3 < 9 - 3$	*or*	$3x - 6 + 6 > 12 + 6$	Addition or subtraction property of inequality
$2x < 6$	*or*	$3x > 18$	Simplify.
$\frac{2x}{2} < \frac{6}{2}$	*or*	$\frac{3x}{3} > \frac{18}{3}$	Division property of inequality
$x < 3$	*or*	$x > 6$	Simplify.

▶ The solutions are all real numbers less than 3 *or* greater than 6.

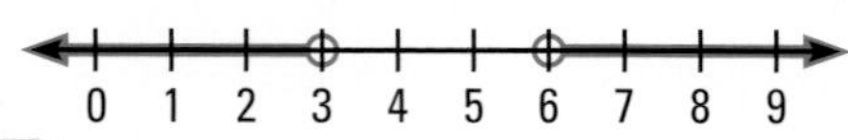

at my.hrw.com

✓ GUIDED PRACTICE for Examples 4 and 5

Solve the inequality. Graph your solution.

7. $-14 < x - 8 < -1$

8. $-1 \le -5t + 2 \le 4$

9. $3h + 1 < -5$ *or* $2h - 5 > 7$

10. $4c + 1 \le -3$ *or* $5c - 3 > 17$

EXAMPLE 6 Solve a multi-step problem

ASTRONOMY The Mars Exploration Rovers *Opportunity* and *Spirit* are robots that were sent to Mars in 2003 in order to gather geological data about the planet. The temperature at the landing sites of the robots can range from $-100°C$ to $0°C$.

- Write a compound inequality that describes the possible temperatures (in degrees Fahrenheit) at a landing site.
- Solve the inequality. Then graph your solution.
- Identify three possible temperatures (in degrees Fahrenheit) at a landing site.

Solution

Let F represent the temperature in degrees Fahrenheit, and let C represent the temperature in degrees Celsius. Use the formula $C = \frac{5}{9}(F - 32)$.

STEP 1 **Write** a compound inequality. Because the temperature at a landing site ranges from $-100°C$ to $0°C$, the lowest possible temperature is $-100°C$, and the highest possible temperature is $0°C$.

$-100 \le C \le 0$ **Write inequality using *C*.**

$-100 \le \frac{5}{9}(F - 32) \le 0$ **Substitute $\frac{5}{9}(F - 32)$ for *C*.**

STEP 2 **Solve** the inequality. Then graph your solution.

$-100 \le \frac{5}{9}(F - 32) \le 0$ **Write inequality from Step 1.**

$-180 \le F - 32 \le 0$ **Multiply each expression by $\frac{9}{5}$.**

$-148 \le F \le 32$ **Add 32 to each expression.**

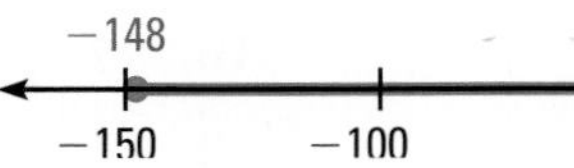

ANOTHER WAY
You can solve the compound inequality by multiplying through by 9:

$-100 \le \frac{5}{9}(F - 32) \le 0$

$-900 \le 5(F - 32) \le 0$

$-900 \le 5F - 160 \le 0$

$-740 \le 5F \le 160$

$-148 \le F \le 32$

STEP 3 **Identify** three possible temperatures.

The temperature at a landing site is greater than or equal to $-148°F$ *and* less than or equal to $32°F$. Three possible temperatures are $-115°F$, $15°F$, and $32°F$.

✓ GUIDED PRACTICE for Example 6

11. MARS Mars has a maximum temperature of $27°C$ at the equator and a minimum temperature of $-133°C$ at the winter pole.

- Write and solve a compound inequality that describes the possible temperatures (in degrees Fahrenheit) on Mars.
- Graph your solution. Then identify three possible temperatures (in degrees Fahrenheit) on Mars.

5.4 EXERCISES

HOMEWORK KEY

◯ = See **WORKED-OUT SOLUTIONS** Exs. 7, 11, and 41

★ = **STANDARDIZED TEST PRACTICE** Exs. 2, 27, 39, and 45

◆ = **MULTIPLE REPRESENTATIONS** Ex. 43

SKILL PRACTICE

1. **VOCABULARY** Copy and complete: A(n) _?_ is an inequality that consists of two inequalities joined by *and* or *or*.

2. ★ **WRITING** *Describe* the difference between the graphs of $-6 \le x \le -4$ and $x \le -6$ *or* $x \ge -4$.

EXAMPLE 1 for Exs. 3–6

TRANSLATING VERBAL PHRASES Translate the verbal phrase into an inequality. Then graph the inequality.

3. All real numbers that are less than 6 *and* greater than 2
4. All real numbers that are less than or equal to −8 *or* greater than 12
5. All real numbers that are greater than or equal to −1.5 *and* less than 9.2
6. All real numbers that are greater than or equal to $-7\frac{1}{2}$ *or* less than or equal to −10

EXAMPLE 2 for Exs. 7–8

WRITING AND GRAPHING INEQUALITIES Write and graph an inequality that describes the situation.

7. The minimum speed on a highway is 40 miles per hour, and the maximum speed is 60 miles per hour.
8. The temperature inside a room is uncomfortable if the temperature is lower than 60°F or higher than 75°F.

EXAMPLES 3, 4, and 5 for Exs. 9–22

SOLVING COMPOUND INEQUALITIES Solve the inequality. Graph your solution.

9. $6 < x + 5 \le 11$
10. $-7 > y - 8 \ge -12$
11. $-1 \le -4m \le 16$
12. $-6 < 3n + 9 < 21$
13. $-15 \le 5(3p - 2) < 20$
14. $7 > \frac{2}{3}(6q + 18) \ge -9$
15. $2r + 3 < 7$ *or* $-r + 9 \le 2$
16. $16 < -s - 6$ *or* $2s + 5 \ge 11$
17. $v + 13 < 8$ *or* $-8v < -40$
18. $-14 > w + 3$ *or* $5w - 13 > w + 7$
19. $9g - 6 > 12g + 1$ *or* $4 > -\frac{2}{5}g + 8$
20. $-2h - 7 > h + 5$ *or* $\frac{1}{4}(h + 8) \ge 9$

ERROR ANALYSIS ***Describe*** **and correct the error in solving the inequality or in graphing the solution.**

21.

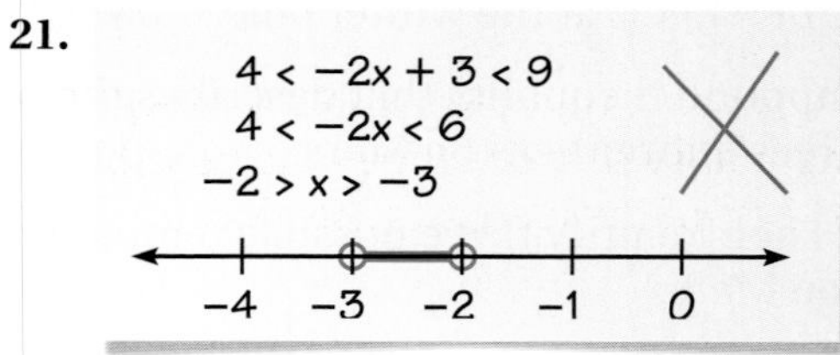

22.

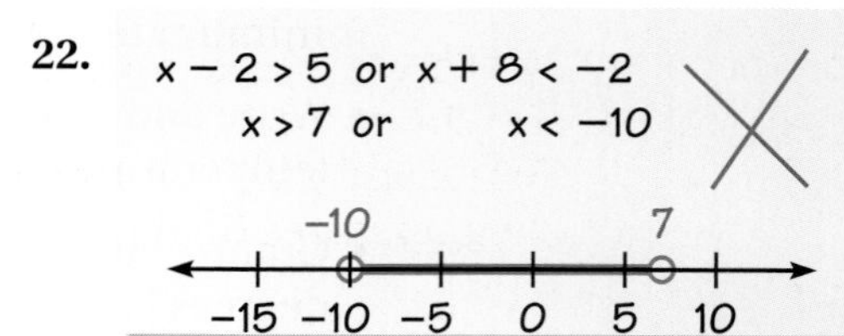

TRANSLATING SENTENCES **Write the verbal sentence as an inequality. Then solve the inequality and graph your solution.**

23. Five more than x is less than 8 *or* 3 less than x is greater than 5.

24. Three less than x is greater than -4 *and* less than -1.

25. Three times the difference of x and 4 is greater than or equal to -8 *and* less than or equal to 10.

26. The sum of $-2x$ and 8 is less than or equal to -5 *or* 6 is less than $-2x$.

27. ★ **MULTIPLE CHOICE** Consider the compound inequality $a > 3x + 8$ *or* $a > -4x - 1$. For which value of a does the solution consist of numbers greater than -6 *and* less than 5?

Ⓐ 16 Ⓑ 19 Ⓒ 23 Ⓓ 26

REASONING **In Exercises 28 and 29, tell whether the statement is *true* or *false*. If it is false, give a counterexample.**

28. If a is a solution of $x < 5$, then a is also a solution of $x < 5$ *and* $x \geq -4$.

29. If a is a solution of $x > 5$, then a is also a solution of $x > 5$ *or* $x \leq -4$.

30. Is the converse of the statement in Exercise 28 *true* or *false*? *Explain.*

31. Is the converse of the statement in Exercise 29 *true* or *false*? *Explain.*

32. **GEOMETRY** The sum of the lengths of any two sides of a triangle is greater than the length of the third side.

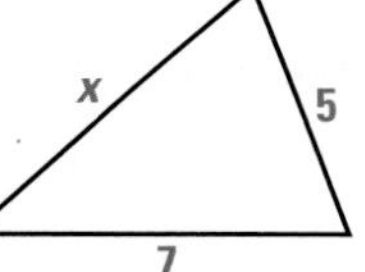

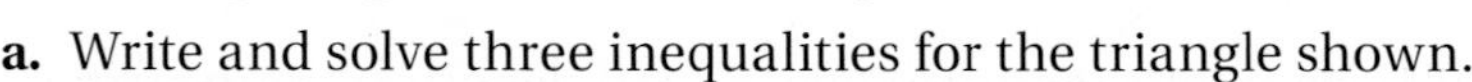

a. Write and solve three inequalities for the triangle shown.

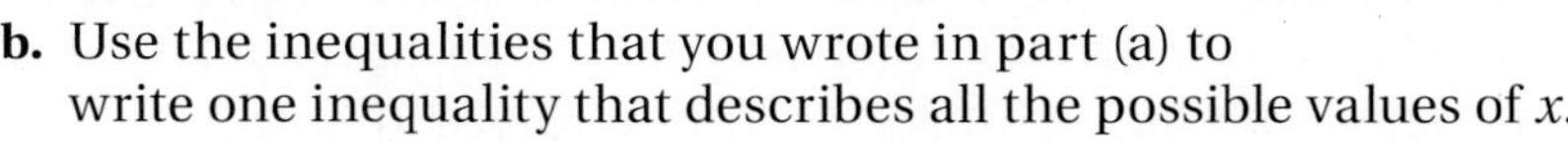

b. Use the inequalities that you wrote in part (a) to write one inequality that describes all the possible values of x.

c. Give three possible lengths for the third side of the triangle.

CHALLENGE **Solve the inequality, if possible. Graph your solution.**

33. $-18 < x - 23$ *and* $x - 16 < -22$

34. $-3y + 7 \leq 11$ *and* $y + 4 > 11$

35. $2m - 1 \geq 5$ *or* $5m > -25$

36. $n + 19 \geq 10$ *or* $-5n + 3 > 33$

PROBLEM SOLVING

EXAMPLE 2 for Exs. 37, 39, 40

37. **SLITSNAILS** Slitsnails are large mollusks that live in deep waters. Slitsnails have been found at elevations from -2600 feet to -100 feet. Write and graph a compound inequality that represents the elevations at which slitsnails have been found.

EXAMPLE 6 for Exs. 38, 41–43

38. **ICEBERGS** The temperature inside an iceberg off the coast of Newfoundland, Canada, ranges from $-20°C$ to $-15°C$. Write and graph a compound inequality that describes the possible temperatures (in degrees Fahrenheit)of the iceberg's interior.

39. ★ **MULTIPLE CHOICE** The euro is the currency in several countries in Europe. In 2003, the dollar value of one euro ranged from \$1.0361 to \$1.2597. Which inequality represents the dollar values v that the euro was *not* worth during the year?

Ⓐ $1.0361 < v < 1.2597$ Ⓑ $v < 1.0361$ *or* $v > 1.2597$

Ⓒ $1.0361 \le v \le 1.2597$ Ⓓ $v \le 1.0361$ *or* $v \ge 1.2597$

40. **CURRENCY** On October 25, 1865, the steamship *S.S. Republic* sank along with a cargo of gold and silver coins. The list gives the prices of several recovered gold coins. Use the least price and greatest price to write a compound inequality that describes the prices p of the coins.

Prices of Recovered Gold Coins

\$9,098	\$20,995	\$9,798	\$33,592	\$12,597
\$16,796	\$9,798	\$10,498	\$5,319	\$73,486
\$11,897	\$32,895	\$7,349	\$6,578	\$29,395

41. **ANIMALS** A deer can eat 2% to 4% of its body weight in food per day. The percent p of the deer's body weight eaten in food is given by the equation $p = \frac{f}{d}$ where f is the amount (in pounds) of food eaten and d is the weight (in pounds) of the deer. Find the possible amounts of food that a 160 pound deer can eat per day.

42. **SKIS** A ski shop sells recreational skis with lengths ranging from 150 centimeters to 220 centimeters. The shop recommends that recreational skis be 1.16 times the skier's height (in centimeters). For which heights of skiers does the shop *not* provide recreational skis?

43. ◆ **MULTIPLE REPRESENTATIONS** Water can exist as either a solid, a liquid, or a gas. The table shows the temperatures (in degrees Celsius) at which water can exist in each state.

State of water	Solid	Liquid	Gas
Temperatures (°C)	Less than 0	0 to 100	Greater than 100

a. **Writing an Inequality** Write and solve a compound inequality to find the temperatures (in degrees Fahrenheit) at which water is *not* a liquid.

b. **Making a Table** Make a table that gives the temperature (in degrees Celsius) when the temperature (in degrees Fahrenheit) of water is 23°F, 86°F, 140°F, 194°F, and 239°F. For which temperatures in the table is water *not* a liquid?

44. **WEATHER** Wind chill temperature describes how much colder it feels when the speed of the wind is combined with air temperature. At a wind speed of 20 miles per hour, the wind chill temperature w (in degrees Fahrenheit) can be given by the model $w = -22 + 1.3a$ where a is the air temperature (in degrees Fahrenheit). What are the possible air temperatures if the wind chill temperature ranges from −9°F to −2.5°F at a wind speed of 20 miles per hour?

45. ★ **EXTENDED RESPONSE** Some musicians use audio amplifiers so that everyone in the audience can hear the performance. The amount y of amplification per person is given by the equation $y = \frac{w}{p}$ where w is the total amount (in watts) of amplification provided by the amplifier and p is the number of people in the audience.

a. **Solve** Each person requires 8 watts to 10 watts of amplification. Write and solve an inequality to find the possible total amounts of amplification that an amplifier would need to provide for 300 people.

b. **Decide** Will an amplifier that provides 2900 watts of amplification be strong enough for an audience of 350 people? 400 people? *Explain.*

c. **Justify** Your band usually performs before an audience of 500 to 600 people. What is the least amount of amplification that your amplifier should provide? *Justify* your answer.

Animated Algebra at my.hrw.com

46. **CHALLENGE** You and three friends are planning to eat at a restaurant, and all of you agree to divide the total cost of the meals and the 15% tip equally. Each person agrees to pay at least \$10 but no more than \$20. How much can you spend altogether on meals before the tip is applied?

QUIZ

Solve the inequality, if possible. Graph your solution.

1. $-\frac{1}{5}(x - 5) > x - 9$
2. $\frac{1}{2}y - 8 \geq -2y + 3$
3. $-4r + 7 \leq r + 10$
4. $-2(s + 6) \leq -2s + 8$
5. $a - 4 \geq -1$ *or* $3a < -24$
6. $22 > -3c + 4 > 14$
7. $-27 \leq 9m \leq -18$
8. $5n + 2 > -18$ *or* $-3(n + 4) > 21$

Solve Compound Inequalities

MATHEMATICAL PRACTICES

Use appropriate tools strategically.

QUESTION How can you use a graphing calculator to display the solutions of a compound inequality?

EXAMPLE Display the solutions of a compound inequality on a graphing calculator

Display the solutions of $12 \le 3x \le 21$ on a graphing calculator.

STEP 1 Rewrite inequality

Rewrite $12 \le 3x \le 21$ as two separate inequalities joined by *and*.

$12 \le 3x \le 21$	**Write original inequality.**
$12 \le 3x$ *and* $3x \le 21$	**Write as two inequalities joined by *and*.**

STEP 2 Enter inequalities

Press Y= and enter the two inequalities, as shown. Inequality signs can be found in the TEST menu, and *and* and *or* can be found in the LOGIC menu.

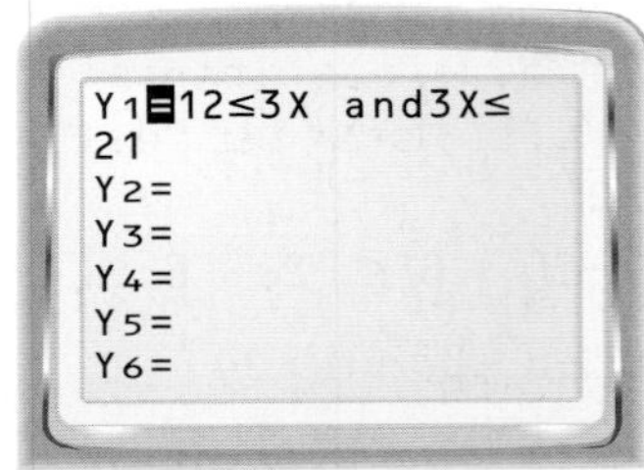

STEP 3 Display solutions

Press GRAPH to display the solutions of $12 \le 3x$ *and* $3x \le 21$. For each value of x that makes the inequality true, the calculator assigns a value of 1 to y and plots the point $(x, 1)$. For each value of x that makes the inequality false, the calculator assigns a value of 0 to y and plots the point $(x, 0)$.

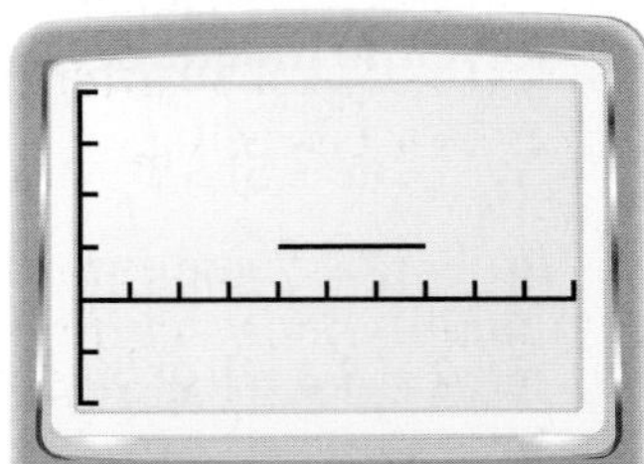

The screen in Step 3 shows the graph of $y = 1$ over the interval $4 \le x \le 7$. This suggests that the solutions are all real numbers greater than or equal to 4 *and* less than or equal to 7.

DRAW CONCLUSIONS

1. Display the solutions of $12 < 3x < 21$ on a graphing calculator. Then compare the graph of $12 < 3x < 21$ with the graph of $12 \le 3x \le 21$.
2. When displaying the solutions of an inequality on a graphing calculator, how do you know which inequality symbols you should use in your solution?

Display the solutions of the inequality on a graphing calculator.

3. $9 \le 3x \le 21$
4. $4 < 4x < 8$
5. $2 \le \frac{1}{4}x \le 12$
6. $-6x > 18$ *or* $9x > 45$
7. $4x \le 18$ *or* $5x \ge 25$
8. $8x \le 16$ *or* $3x \ge 30$

MIXED REVIEW *of Problem Solving*

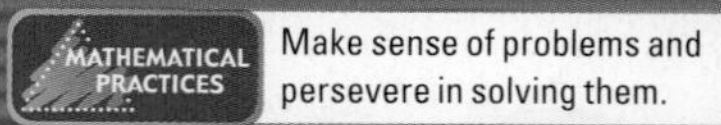

1. **MULTI-STEP PROBLEM** A nanotube thermometer is so tiny that it is invisible to the human eye. The thermometer can measure temperatures from 50°C to 500°C.
   a. Write and solve a compound inequality to find the temperatures (in degrees Fahrenheit) that the thermometer can measure.
   b. Graph your solution of the inequality.
   c. Can the thermometer measure a temperature of 1000°F? *Explain.*

2. **SHORT RESPONSE** You earned the following scores on five science tests: 75, 82, 90, 84, and 71. You want to have an average score of at least 80 after you take the sixth test.
   a. Write and solve an inequality to find the possible scores that you can earn on your sixth test in order to meet your goal.
   b. The greatest score that you can earn on a test is 100. Is it possible for you to have an average score of 90 after the sixth test? *Explain* your reasoning.

3. **GRIDDED ANSWER** You need at least 34 eggs to make enough chiffon cakes for a bake sale. Your grocery store sells cartons of eggs only by the dozen. Of all the possible numbers of cartons that you can buy, which is the least number?

4. **MULTI-STEP PROBLEM** You have a \$300 gift card to use at a sporting goods store.
   a. You want to use your card to buy 2 pairs of shoes for \$85 each and several pairs of socks. Write and solve an inequality to find the possible amounts of money that you can spend on socks using your card.
   b. Suppose that socks cost \$4.75 per pair. Write and solve an inequality to find the possible numbers of socks that you can buy using the card.

5. **OPEN-ENDED** *Describe* a real-world situation that can be modeled by the inequality $17x \leq 240$. *Explain* what the solution of the inequality means in this situation.

6. **SHORT RESPONSE** A rafting guide plans to take 6 adults on a rafting trip. The raft can hold up to 1520 pounds. The guide weighs 180 pounds and estimates that each adult will bring 10 pounds of baggage.
   a. Write and solve an inequality to find the possible average weights of an adult such that the raft will not exceed its maximum weight capacity.
   b. Suppose that the weights of the adults range from 105 pounds to 200 pounds. Can the raft accommodate all the people and the baggage at one time? *Justify* your answer.

7. **EXTENDED RESPONSE** In 1862 the United States imposed a tax on annual income in order to pay for the expenses of the Civil War. The table shows the tax rates for different incomes.

Annual income	Tax rate
\$600 to \$10,000	3% of income
Greater than \$10,000	3% of the first \$10,000 plus 5% of income over \$10,000

   a. Write a compound inequality that represents the possible taxes paid by a person whose annual income was at least \$600 but not greater than \$10,000.
   b. For people whose taxes ranged from \$400 to \$750, tell whether their annual incomes were greater than \$10,000 or less than \$10,000. *Explain* how you know. Then find the possible annual incomes of those people.
   c. Suppose that the tax rate had been 4% of the total income for people whose annual incomes were greater than \$10,000. For which incomes would paying the 4% rate have resulted in less taxes than paying the tax rate described above? *Explain.*

5.5 Solve Absolute Value Equations

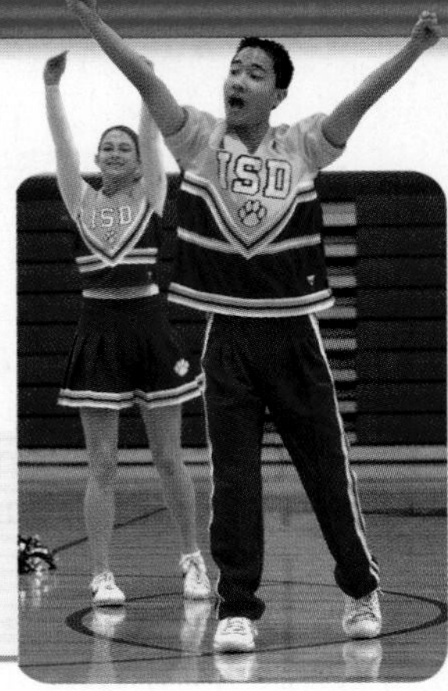

Before You solved linear equations.

Now You will solve absolute value equations.

Why? So you can analyze rules of a competition, as in Ex. 43.

Key Vocabulary
- **absolute value equation**
- **absolute deviation**
- **absolute value**

COMMON CORE

CC.9-12.A.CED.1 Create equations and inequalities in one variable and use them to solve problems. Include equations arising from linear and quadratic functions, and simple rational and exponential functions.*

The absolute value of a number a, written $|a|$, is the distance between a and 0 on a number line. An **absolute value equation**, such as $|x| = 4$, is an equation that contains an absolute value expression. The equation $|x| = 4$ means that the distance between x and 0 is 4. The solutions of the equation are 4 and -4, because they are the only numbers whose distance from 0 is 4.

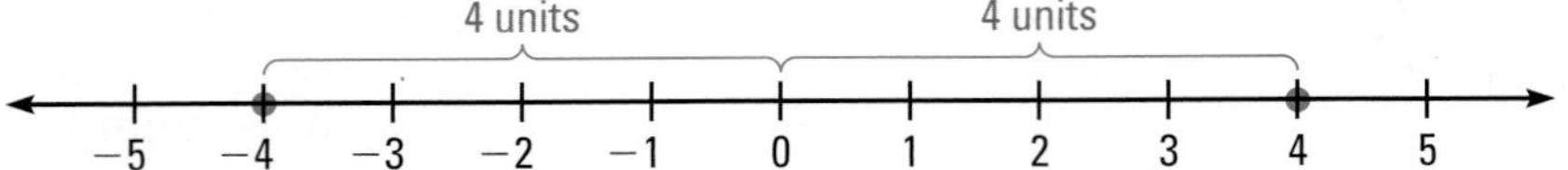

EXAMPLE 1 Solve an absolute value equation

Solve $|x| = 7$.

Solution

The distance between x and 0 is 7. So, $x = 7$ *or* $x = -7$.

▶ The solutions are 7 and -7.

Animated Algebra at my.hrw.com

✓ GUIDED PRACTICE for Example 1

1. Solve **(a)** $|x| = 3$ and **(b)** $|x| = 15$.

SOLVING ABSOLUTE VALUE EQUATIONS In Example 1, notice that the expression inside the absolute value symbols equals 7 or the opposite of 7. This suggests the following rule for solving an absolute value equation.

KEY CONCEPT *For Your Notebook*

Solving an Absolute Value Equation

The equation $|ax + b| = c$ where $c \geq 0$ is equivalent to the statement $ax + b = c$ *or* $ax + b = -c$.

EXAMPLE 2 Solve an absolute value equation

Solve $|x - 3| = 8$.

Solution

Rewrite the absolute value equation as two equations. Then solve each equation separately.

AVOID ERRORS
You cannot solve the equation $|x - 3| = 8$ by adding 3 to each side because $|x - 3| + 3 \neq |x|$.

$\lvert x - 3\rvert = 8$	**Write original equation.**
$x - 3 = 8$ *or* $x - 3 = -8$	**Rewrite as two equations.**
$x = 11$ *or* $x = -5$	**Add 3 to each side.**

▶ The solutions are 11 and −5. Check your solutions.

CHECK		
$\lvert x - 3\rvert = 8$	$\lvert x - 3\rvert = 8$	**Write original inequality.**
$\lvert 11 - 3\rvert \stackrel{?}{=} 8$	$\lvert -5 - 3\rvert \stackrel{?}{=} 8$	**Substitute for *x*.**
$\lvert 8\rvert \stackrel{?}{=} 8$	$\lvert -8\rvert \stackrel{?}{=} 8$	**Subtract.**
$8 = 8$ ✓	$8 = 8$ ✓	**Simplify. The solution checks.**

REWRITING EQUATIONS To solve an absolute value equation, you may first need to rewrite the equation in the form $|ax + b| = c$.

EXAMPLE 3 Rewrite an absolute value equation

Solve $3|2x - 7| - 5 = 4$.

Solution

First, rewrite the equation in the form $|ax + b| = c$.

$3\lvert 2x - 7\rvert - 5 = 4$	**Write original equation.**
$3\lvert 2x - 7\rvert = 9$	**Add 5 to each side.**
$\lvert 2x - 7\rvert = 3$	**Divide each side by 3.**

Next, solve the absolute value equation.

$\lvert 2x - 7\rvert = 3$	**Write absolute value equation.**
$2x - 7 = 3$ *or* $2x - 7 = -3$	**Rewrite as two equations.**
$2x = 10$ *or* $2x = 4$	**Add 7 to each side.**
$x = 5$ *or* $x = 2$	**Divide each side by 2.**

▶ The solutions are 5 and 2.

at my.hrw.com

GUIDED PRACTICE for Examples 2 and 3

Solve the equation.

2. $|r - 7| = 9$ **3.** $2|s| + 4.1 = 18.9$ **4.** $4|t + 9| - 5 = 19$

NO SOLUTIONS The absolute value of a number is never negative. So, when an absolute value expression equals a negative number, there are *no solutions.*

EXAMPLE 4 Decide if an equation has no solutions

Solve $|3x + 5| + 6 = -2$, if possible.

$|3x + 5| + 6 = -2$ **Write original equation.**

$|3x + 5| = -8$ **Subtract 6 from each side.**

▶ The absolute value of a number is never negative. So, there are no solutions.

ABSOLUTE DEVIATION The **absolute deviation** of a number x from a given value is the absolute value of the difference of x and the given value: absolute deviation $= |x - \text{given value}|$.

EXAMPLE 5 Use absolute deviation

BASKETBALLS Before the start of a professional basketball game, a basketball must be inflated to an air pressure of 8 pounds per square inch (psi) with an absolute error of 0.5 psi. (*Absolute error* is the absolute deviation of a measured value from an accepted value.) Find the minimum and maximum acceptable air pressures for the basketball.

Solution

Let p be the air pressure (in psi) of a basketball. Write a verbal model. Then write and solve an absolute value equation.

Absolute error = | Measured air pressure − Accepted air pressure |

↓ ↓ ↓

0.5 = | p − **8** |

$0.5 = |p - 8|$ **Write original equation.**

$0.5 = p - 8$ *or* $-0.5 = p - 8$ **Rewrite as two equations.**

$8.5 = p$ *or* $7.5 = p$ **Add 8 to each side.**

▶ The minimum and maximum acceptable pressures are 7.5 psi and 8.5 psi.

✓ GUIDED PRACTICE for Examples 4 and 5

Solve the equation, if possible.

5. $2|m - 5| + 4 = 2$

6. $-3|n + 2| - 7 = -10$

7. The absolute deviation of x from 7.6 is 5.2. What are the values of x that satisfy this requirement?

5.5 EXERCISES

HOMEWORK KEY

◯ = See WORKED-OUT SOLUTIONS Exs. 11, 23, and 45

★ = STANDARDIZED TEST PRACTICE Exs. 2, 32, 44, 48, and 49

SKILL PRACTICE

1. **VOCABULARY** Copy and complete: The equation $|x - 7| = 0.15$ is an example of a(n) _?_.

2. ★ **WRITING** Given $|x - 9| = 5$, describe the relationship between x, 9, and 5 using absolute deviation.

EXAMPLES 1, 2, and 3 for Exs. 3–20

SOLVING EQUATIONS Solve the equation.

3. $|x| = 5$
4. $|y| = 36$
5. $|v| = 0.7$
6. $|w| = 9.2$
7. $|r| = \frac{1}{2}$
8. $|s| = \frac{7}{4}$
9. $|m + 3| = 7$
10. $|4n - 5| = 18$
11. $|3p + 7| = 4$
12. $|q + 8| = 2$
13. $|2d + 7| = 11$
14. $|f - 8| = 14$
15. $3|13 - 2t| = 15$
16. $4|b - 1| - 7 = 17$
17. $\frac{1}{3}|2c - 5| + 3 = 7$
18. $\frac{7}{4}|3j + 5| + 1 = 15$
19. $4|2k + 3| - 2 = 6$
20. $-3|5g + 1| - 6 = -9$

ERROR ANALYSIS *Describe* and correct the error in solving the absolute value equation.

21.
$$|x + 4| = 13$$
$$x + 4 = 13$$
$$x = 9$$

22.
$$|x - 6| = -2$$
$$x - 6 = -2 \text{ or } x - 6 = 2$$
$$x = 4 \quad \text{or} \quad x = 8$$

EXAMPLE 4 for Exs. 23–31

SOLVING EQUATIONS Solve the equation, if possible.

23. $|x - 1| + 5 = 2$
24. $|y - 4| + 8 = 6$
25. $|m + 5| + 1.5 = 2$
26. $-4|8 - 5n| = 13$
27. $-3\left|1 - \frac{2}{3}v\right| = -9$
28. $-5\left|\frac{4}{5}w + 6\right| = -10$
29. $-10|14 - r| - 2 = -7$
30. $-2\left|\frac{1}{3}s - 5\right| + 3 = 8$
31. $-9|4p + 2| - 8 = -35$

32. ★ **MULTIPLE CHOICE** Which number is a solution of $|4x - 1| + 2 = 1$?

Ⓐ $-\frac{1}{2}$ Ⓑ 0 Ⓒ 1 Ⓓ There is no solution.

EXAMPLE 5 for Exs. 33–36

USING ABSOLUTE DEVIATION Find the values of x that satisfy the definition of absolute deviation for the given value and the given absolute deviation.

33. Given value: 5; absolute deviation: 8
34. Given value: 20; absolute deviation: 5
35. Given value: −9.1; absolute deviation: 1.6
36. Given value: −3.4; absolute deviation: 6.7

37. **SOLVING AN EQUATION** Interpreted geometrically, the equation $|x - a| = b$ means that the distance between x and a on a number line is b. Solve $|x - 3| = 7$ both geometrically and algebraically. *Compare* your solutions.

TRANSLATING SENTENCES In Exercises 38 and 39, write the verbal sentence as an absolute value equation. Then solve the equation.

38. Four more than the absolute deviation of x from 3 is 8.

39. Five times the absolute deviation of $2x$ from -9 is 15.

40. **REASONING** Is $a|x|$ equivalent to $|ax|$ when a is positive? when a is negative? when a is 0? Give examples to support your answers.

41. **CHALLENGE** How many solutions does the equation $a|x + b| + c = d$ have if $a > 0$ and $c = d$? if $a < 0$ and $c > d$?

PROBLEM SOLVING

EXAMPLE 5 for Exs. 42–46

42. **GUARDRAILS** A safety regulation requires that the height of a guardrail be 42 inches with an absolute deviation of 3 inches. Find the minimum and maximum heights of a guardrail.

43. **CHEERLEADING** A cheerleading team is preparing a dance program for a competition. The program must last 4 minutes with an absolute deviation of 5 seconds. Find the least and greatest possible times (in seconds) that the program can last.

44. ★ **MULTIPLE CHOICE** The diameter of a billiard ball must be 2.25 inches with an absolute error of 0.005 inch. What is the maximum possible diameter that a billiard ball can have?

Ⓐ 2.2 inches Ⓑ 2.245 inches Ⓒ 2.255 inches Ⓓ 2.3 inches

45. **SPORTS** In gymnastics meets last year, the mean of your friend's least and greatest scores was 54.675 points. The absolute deviation of his least and greatest scores from the mean was 2.213 points.

a. What were the least and greatest scores that he earned?

b. This year the mean of his least and greatest scores is 56.738 points, and the absolute deviation of the least and greatest scores from the mean is 0.45 point. How many points more than last year's greatest score is this year's greatest score?

46. **JEWELRY** A jewelry store advertisement states that a certain diamond bracelet weighs 12 carats, but the actual weight can vary by as much as 5% of the advertised weight. Find the minimum and maximum possible weights of the bracelet.

47. **CONTESTS** You currently have 450 points in an academic contest. You choose the value p of the question you want to answer. The value p represents the absolute deviation of your new score s from 450.

a. Write an absolute value equation that gives p in terms of s.

b. If you choose a question worth 150 points, what are the possible new scores that you can have after answering the question?

48. ★ **EXTENDED RESPONSE** The percent p of United States residents who were foreign born, or born outside of the United States, during the period 1910–2000 can be modeled by the equation $p = 0.165|t - 60| + 4.8$ where t is the number of years since 1910.

a. **Approximate** During the period 1910–2000, in approximately what year did foreign-born residents account for 13% of all residents?

b. **Predict** If the model holds for years after 2000, predict the year in which foreign-born residents will again account for 13% of all residents.

c. **Decide** According to the model, did foreign-born residents account for 4% of all residents at any time during the period 1910–2000? *Explain* your answer.

49. ★ **SHORT RESPONSE** A stock's average price p (in dollars) during the period February 2005 to October 2005 can be modeled by the equation $p = 2.3|m - 7| + 9.57$ where m is the number of months since February 2005.

a. **Approximate** In approximately what month and year was the average price \$16.15? If the model holds for months after October 2005, predict the month and year in which the average price will again be \$16.15.

b. **Justify** Is it possible to use the model to estimate the stock's lowest average price during this period? *Justify* your answer.

50. **CHALLENGE** In a recent Olympics, swimmers in a men's 200 meter butterfly event finished with times from 1 minute 54.04 seconds to 1 minute 57.48 seconds. Let t represent the slowest or fastest time (in seconds). Write an absolute value equation that describes the situation.

Extension Graph Absolute Value Functions

GOAL Graph absolute value functions.

Key Vocabulary
• **absolute value**

CC.9-12.F.BF.3 Identify the effect on the graph of replacing $f(x)$ by $f(x) + k$, $kf(x)$, $f(kx)$, and $f(x + k)$ for specific values of k (both positive and negative); find the value of k given the graphs. Experiment with cases and illustrate an explanation of the effects on the graph using technology.

The function $f(x) = |x|$ is an example of an *absolute value function* and is the parent function for all absolute value functions. You can graph absolute value functions by using a table of values, as shown below for $f(x) = |x|$.

KEY CONCEPT *For Your Notebook*

Graph of Parent Function for Absolute Value Functions

The domain of the parent absolute value function is all real numbers. The range is $y \geq 0$.

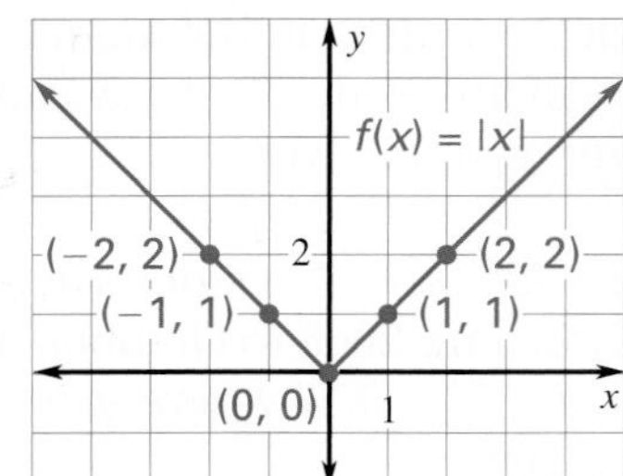

The graph consists of two rays with a common endpoint called the *vertex* of the graph. The minimum value of the function occurs at the vertex.

EXAMPLE 1 Graph $g(x) = |x - h|$ and $g(x) = |x| + k$

Graph each function. Compare the graph with the graph of $f(x) = |x|$.

a. $g(x) = |x - 2|$

STEP 1 **Make** a table of values.

x	0	1	2	3	4
$g(x)$	2	1	0	1	2

STEP 2 **Graph** the function.

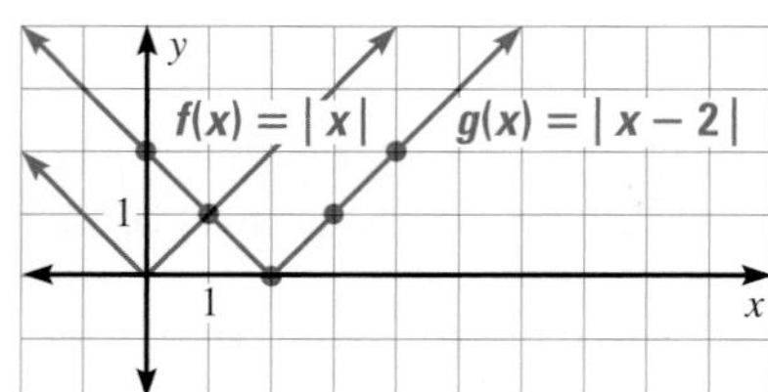

STEP 3 **Compare** the graphs of g and f. The graph of $g(x) = |x - 2|$ is 2 units to the right of the graph of $f(x) = |x|$.

b. $g(x) = |x| - 1$

STEP 1 **Make** a table of values.

x	−2	−1	0	1	2
$g(x)$	1	0	−1	0	1

STEP 2 **Graph** the function.

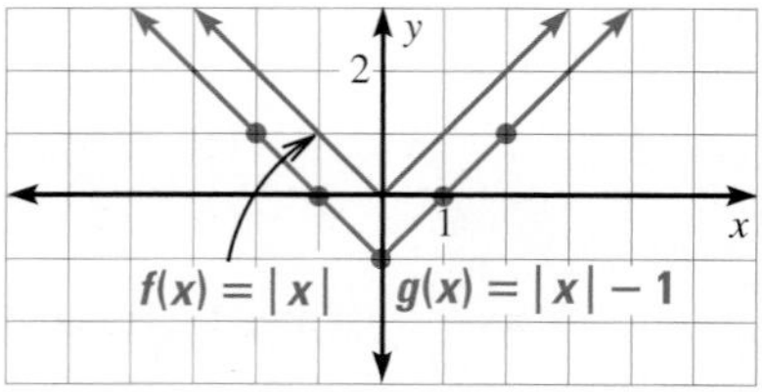

STEP 3 **Compare** the graphs of g and f. The graph of $g(x) = |x| - 1$ is 1 unit below the graph of $f(x) = |x|$.

APPLY TRANSFORMATIONS
The two graphs in Example 1 are translations of the graph of $f(x) = |x|$. The graph in part (a) is a horizontal translation. The graph in part (b) is a vertical translation.

EXAMPLE 2 Graph $g(x) = a|x|$

Graph each function. Compare the graph with the graph of $f(x) = |x|$.

a. $g(x) = 4|x|$

STEP 1 **Make** a table of values.

x	−2	−1	0	1	2
$g(x)$	8	4	0	4	8

STEP 2 **Graph** the function.

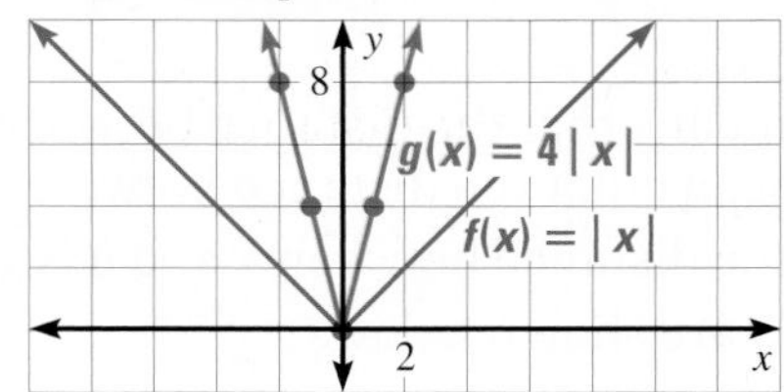

STEP 3 **Compare** the graphs of g and f. The graph of $g(x) = 4|x|$ opens up and is narrower than the graph of $f(x) = |x|$.

b. $g(x) = -0.5|x|$

STEP 1 **Make** a table of values.

x	−4	−2	0	2	4
$g(x)$	−2	−1	0	−1	−2

STEP 2 **Graph** the function.

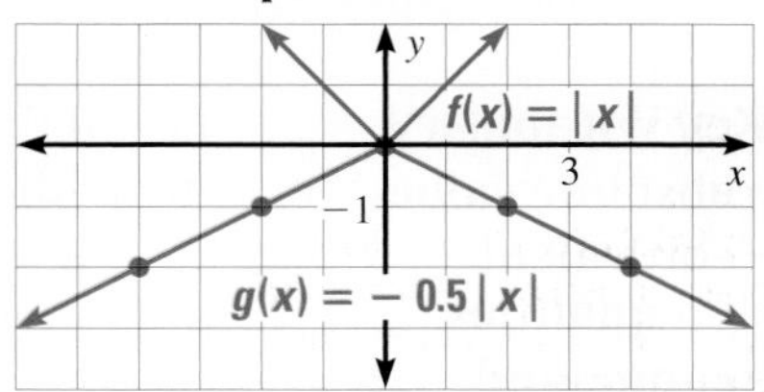

STEP 3 **Compare** the graphs of g and f. The graph of $g(x) = -0.5|x|$ opens down and is wider than the graph of $f(x) = |x|$.

APPLY TRANSFORMATIONS
The graph in part (a) of Example 2 is a vertical stretch of the graph of $f(x) = |x|$. The graph in part (b) is a vertical shrink with a reflection in the x-axis of the graph of $f(x) = |x|$.

KEY CONCEPT *For Your Notebook*

Comparing Graphs of Absolute Value Functions with the Graph of $f(x) = |x|$

$g(x) = |x - h|$

If $h > 0$, the graph of g is $|h|$ units to the right of the graph of $f(x) = |x|$.

If $h < 0$, the graph of g is $|h|$ units to the left of the graph of $f(x) = |x|$.

$g(x) = |x| + k$

If $k > 0$, the graph of g is $|k|$ units above the graph of $f(x) = |x|$.

If $k < 0$, the graph of g is $|k|$ units below the graph of $f(x) = |x|$.

$g(x) = a|x|$

If $|a| > 1$, the graph of g is narrower than the graph of $f(x) = |x|$. If $0 < |a| < 1$, the graph of g is wider.

If $a > 0$, the graph of g opens up. If $a < 0$, the graph opens down.

PRACTICE

EXAMPLES 1 and 2 for Exs. 1–6

Graph the function. *Compare* the graph with the graph of $f(x) = |x|$.

1. $g(x) = |x + 3|$
2. $g(x) = |x| + 5$
3. $g(x) = |x| - 7$
4. $g(x) = 2|x|$
5. $g(x) = 0.6|x|$
6. $g(x) = -3|x|$
7. For the absolute value function $g(x) = -|x| + 1$, identify the function's domain and range, the vertex of the function's graph, and the function's minimum or maximum value.

5.6 Solve Absolute Value Inequalities

Before You solved absolute value equations.

Now You will solve absolute value inequalities.

Why So you can analyze softball compression, as in Ex. 38.

Key Vocabulary
- **absolute value**
- **equivalent inequalities**
- **compound inequality**
- **absolute deviatio**
- **mean**

Recall that $|x| = 3$ means that the distance between x and 0 is 3. The inequality $|x| < 3$ means that the distance between x and 0 is *less than* 3, and $|x| > 3$ means that the distance between x and 0 is *greater than* 3. The graphs of $|x| < 3$ and $|x| > 3$ are shown below.

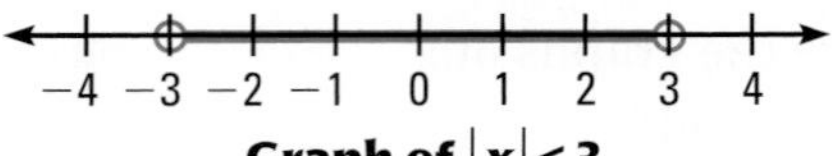

Graph of $|x| < 3$

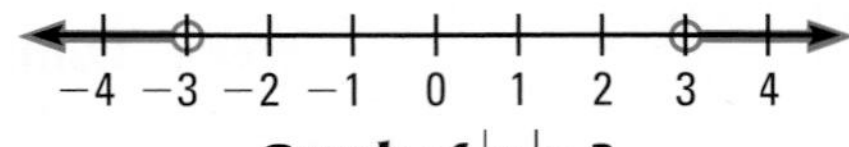

Graph of $|x| > 3$

CC.9-12.A.CED.1 Create equations and inequalities in one variable and use them to solve problems. Include equations arising from linear and quadratic functions, and simple rational and exponential functions.*

EXAMPLE 1 Solve absolute value inequalities

Solve the inequality. Graph your solution.

a. $|x| \geq 6$ **b.** $|x| \leq 0.5$

Solution

a. The distance between x and 0 is greater than or equal to 6. So, $x \leq -6$ *or* $x \geq 6$.

▶ The solutions are all real numbers less than or equal to -6 *or* greater than or equal to 6.

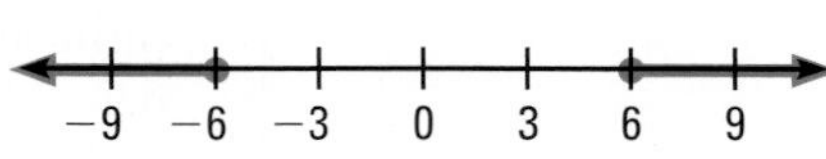

b. The distance between x and 0 is less than or equal to 0.5. So, $-0.5 \leq x \leq 0.5$.

▶ The solutions are all real numbers greater than or equal to -0.5 *and* less than or equal to 0.5.

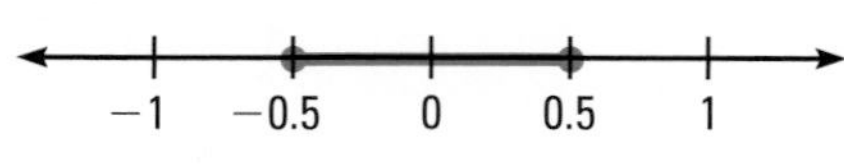

✓ GUIDED PRACTICE for Example 1

Solve the inequality. Graph your solution.

1. $|x| \leq 8$ **2.** $|u| < 3.5$ **3.** $|v| > \frac{2}{3}$

SOLVING ABSOLUTE VALUE INEQUALITIES In Example 1, the solutions of $|x| \geq 6$ and $|x| \leq 0.5$ suggest that you can rewrite an absolute value inequality as a compound inequality.

READING

You can use the words *between* and *beyond* to describe absolute value inequalites. For example, $|x| < 2$ means that x is between -2 *and* 2; $|x| > 2$ means that x is beyond -2 *or* beyond 2.

KEY CONCEPT — *For Your Notebook*

Solving Absolute Value Inequalities

- The inequality $|ax + b| < c$ where $c > 0$ is equivalent to the compound inequality $-c < ax + b < c$.
- The inequality $|ax + b| > c$ where $c > 0$ is equivalent to the compound inequality $ax + b < -c$ *or* $ax + b > c$.

In the inequalities above, $<$ can be replaced by $\le$ and $>$ can be replaced by $\ge$.

EXAMPLE 2 Solve an absolute value inequality

Solve $|x - 5| \ge 7$. Graph your solution.

$|x - 5| \ge 7$ **Write original inequality.**

$x - 5 \le -7$ *or* $x - 5 \ge 7$ **Rewrite as compound inequality.**

$x \le -2$ *or* $x \ge 12$ **Add 5 to each side.**

▶ The solutions are all real numbers less than or equal to -2 *or* greater than or equal to 12. Check several solutions in the original inequality.

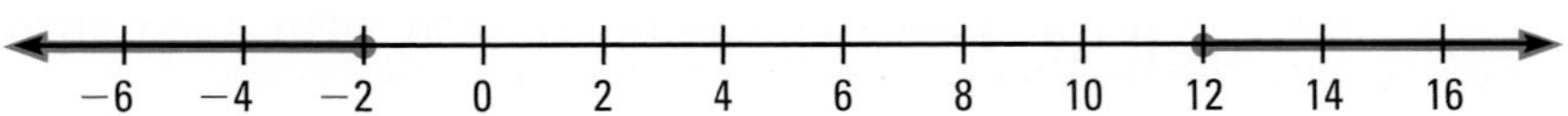

EXAMPLE 3 Solve an absolute value inequality

Solve $|-4x - 5| + 3 < 9$. Graph your solution.

$|-4x - 5| + 3 < 9$ **Write original inequality.**

$|-4x - 5| < 6$ **Subtract 3 from each side.**

$-6 < -4x - 5 < 6$ **Rewrite as compound inequality.**

$-1 < -4x < 11$ **Add 5 to each expression.**

$0.25 > x > -2.75$ **Divide each expression by -4. Reverse inequality symbol.**

$-2.75 < x < 0.25$ **Rewrite in the form $a < x < b$.**

▶ The solutions are all real numbers greater than -2.75 *and* less than 0.25.

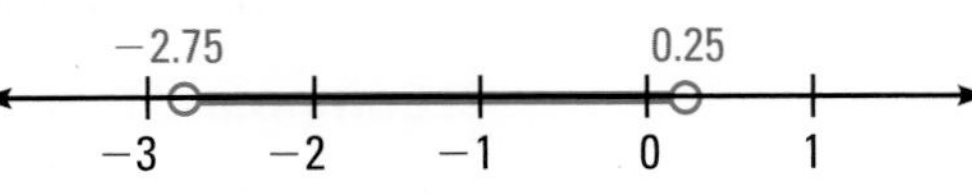

Animated Algebra at my.hrw.com

✓ GUIDED PRACTICE for Examples 2 and 3

Solve the inequality. Graph your solution.

4. $|x + 3| > 8$

5. $|2w - 1| < 11$

6. $3|5m - 6| - 8 \le 13$

EXAMPLE 4 Solve a multi-step problem

COMPUTERS You are buying a new computer and find 10 models in a store advertisement. The prices are \$890, \$750, \$650, \$370, \$660, \$670, \$450, \$650, \$725, and \$825.

- Find the mean of the computer prices.
- You are willing to pay the mean price with an absolute deviation of at most \$100. How many of the computer prices meet your condition?

Solution

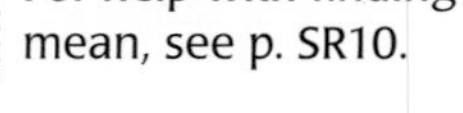

REVIEW MEAN
For help with finding a mean, see p. SR10.

STEP 1 **Find** the mean by dividing the sum of the prices by 10.

$$\text{Mean} = \frac{890 + 750 + 650 + 370 + 660 + 670 + 450 + 650 + 725 + 825}{10}$$

$$= \frac{6640}{10} = 664$$

STEP 2 **Write** and solve an inequality. An absolute deviation of at most \$100 from the mean, \$664, is given by the inequality $|x - 664| \le 100$.

$|x - 664| \le 100$ **Write absolute value inequality.**

$-100 \le x - 664 \le 100$ **Write as compound inequality.**

$564 \le x \le 764$ **Add 664 to each expression.**

▶ The prices you will consider must be at least \$564 and at most \$764. Six prices meet your condition: \$750, \$650, \$660, \$670, \$650, and \$725.

GUIDED PRACTICE for Example 4

7. **WHAT IF?** In Example 4, suppose that you are willing to pay the mean price with an absolute deviation of at most \$75. How many of the computer prices meet this condition?

CONCEPT SUMMARY *For Your Notebook*

Solving Inequalities

One-Step and Multi-Step Inequalities

- Follow the steps for solving an equation, but reverse the inequality symbol when multiplying or dividing by a negative number.

Compound Inequalities

- If necessary, rewrite the inequality as two separate inequalities. Then solve each inequality separately. Include *and* or *or* in the solution.

Absolute Value Inequalities

- If necessary, isolate the absolute value expression on one side of the inequality. Rewrite the absolute value inequality as a compound inequality. Then solve the compound inequality.

5.6 EXERCISES

HOMEWORK KEY

○ = See **WORKED-OUT SOLUTIONS** Exs. 9, 15, and 37

★ = **STANDARDIZED TEST PRACTICE** Exs. 2, 21, 22, 37, and 40

◆ = **MULTIPLE REPRESENTATIONS** Ex. 38

SKILL PRACTICE

1. **VOCABULARY** Copy and complete: The inequalities $|x| > 8$ and $x > 8$ *or* $x < -8$ are ___?___.

2. ★ **WRITING** *Describe* the difference between solving $|x| \le 5$ and solving $|x| \ge 5$.

EXAMPLES 1, 2, and 3 for Exs. 3–24

SOLVING INEQUALITIES **Solve the inequality. Graph your solution.**

3. $|x| < 4$
4. $|y| \ge 3$
5. $|h| > 4.5$
6. $|p| < 1.3$
7. $|t| \le \frac{3}{5}$
8. $|j| \ge 1\frac{3}{4}$
9. $|d + 4| \ge 3$
10. $|b - 5| < 10$
11. $|14 - m| > 6$
12. $|2s - 7| < 1$
13. $|4c + 5| \ge 7$
14. $|9 - 4n| \le 5$
15. $5\left|\frac{1}{2}r + 3\right| > 5$
16. $\left|\frac{4}{3}s - 7\right| - 8 > 3$
17. $-3\left|2 - \frac{5}{4}u\right| \le -18$
18. $2|3w + 8| - 13 < -5$
19. $2\left|\frac{1}{4}v - 5\right| - 4 > 3$
20. $\frac{2}{7}|4f + 6| - 2 \ge 10$

21. ★ **MULTIPLE CHOICE** Which inequality is equivalent to $x < 1$ *or* $x > 5$?

Ⓐ $|x + 8| - 2 > 10$　　Ⓑ $3|6 - 2x| > 12$

Ⓒ $|5x + 9| < 10$　　Ⓓ $|7 - 4x| - 9 < 8$

22. ★ **WRITING** How can you tell whether an absolute value inequality is equivalent to a compound inequality with *and* or to a compound inequality with *or*?

ERROR ANALYSIS ***Describe*** **and correct the error in solving the inequality.**

23.

$|x + 4| > 13$

$13 > x + 4 > -13$

$9 > x > -17$

24.

$|x - 5| < 20$

$x - 5 < 20$

$x < 25$

TRANSLATING SENTENCES **Write the verbal sentence as an inequality. Then solve the inequality and graph your solution.**

25. The absolute deviation of x from 6 is less than or equal to 4.
26. The absolute deviation of $2x$ from -7 is greater than or equal to 15.
27. Three more than the absolute deviation of $-4x$ from 7 is greater than 10.
28. Four times the absolute deviation of x from 9 is less than 8.

REASONING **Tell whether the statement is *true* or *false*. If it is false, give a counterexample.**

29. If a is a solution of $|x + 3| \le 8$, then a is also a solution of $x + 3 \ge -8$.

30. If a is a solution of $|x + 3| > 8$, then a is also a solution of $x + 3 > 8$.

31. If a is a solution of $|x + 3| \ge 8$, then a is also a solution of $x + 3 \le -8$.

32. If a is a solution of $x + 3 \le -8$, then a is also a solution of $|x + 3| \ge 8$.

33. **CHALLENGE** Solve $|x - 3| < 4$ *and* $|x + 2| > 8$. *Describe* your steps.

34. **CHALLENGE** If $|ax + b| < c$ where $c < 0$, what is the solution of the inequality? If $|ax + b| > c$ where $c < 0$, what is the solution of the inequality? *Explain* your answers.

PROBLEM SOLVING

EXAMPLE 4 for Exs. 35–38

35. **ESSAY CONTEST** An essay contest requires that essay entries consist of 500 words with an absolute deviation of at most 30 words. What are the possible numbers of words that the essay can have?

36. **SWIMMING POOL** The saturation index for a pool measures the balance between the acid level and the amount of minerals in pool water. Balanced water has an index value of 0. Water is highly corrosive or highly scale forming if the absolute deviation of the index value from 0 is greater than 0.5. Find the index values for which pool water is highly corrosive or highly scale forming.

37. ★ **SHORT RESPONSE** You are preheating an oven to 350°F before you bake muffins. Several minutes later, the oven thermometer reads 346°F. The measured temperature has an absolute deviation of at most 2°F. Write and solve an inequality to find the possible temperatures in the oven. Should you continue to preheat the oven, or should you start baking the muffins? *Explain* your choice.

38. ◆ **MULTIPLE REPRESENTATIONS** Softball compression measures the hardness of a softball and affects the distance that the softball can travel upon contact with a bat. A softball organization requires that the compression of a softball be 350 pounds but allows an absolute deviation of at most 50 pounds.

a. Making a Table Make a table that shows the absolute deviation from the required compression when the measured compression of a softball is p pounds. Use the following values for p: 275, 325, 375, 425, 475.

b. Writing an Inequality Write and solve an inequality to find the softball compressions that the organization will allow. Which values of p in the table are solutions of the inequality?

39. **MULTI-STEP PROBLEM** In a physics class, 7 groups of students experimentally determine the acceleration (in meters per second per second) of an object in free fall. The table below shows the value calculated by each group.

Group	1	2	3	4	5	6	7
Calculated value (m/sec^2)	10.50	9.52	9.73	9.86	9.78	10.90	9.86

a. **Calculate** Find the mean of the measured values given in the table. Round to the nearest hundredth.

b. **Solve** When writing up their lab reports, the students wanted to state that the absolute deviation of each measured value x from the mean was at most d. What is the value of d in this situation?

40. ★ **EXTENDED RESPONSE** *Relative absolute deviation* of a number from a given value is the absolute deviation expressed as a percent of the given value. A wildlife biologist estimates that the number of pronghorn antelope in Nevada is 18,000 with a relative absolute deviation of at most 20%.

a. **Calculate** Find the absolute deviation from the estimated population of pronghorn antelope by multiplying the estimated population by the relative absolute deviation.

b. **Solve** Write and solve an inequality to find the possible numbers of pronghorn antelope in Nevada.

c. **Explain** If the relative absolute deviation were 25%, could you conclude that the actual population is necessarily greater than if the relative absolute deviation were 20%? *Explain* your reasoning.

41. **CHALLENGE** According to the rules for a women's figure skating event, a skater should finish a routine in an ideal time of 3 minutes 30 seconds. The skater receives a 0.1 point penalty if the absolute deviation of the finishing time from the ideal time is greater than 10 seconds *and* less than or equal to 20 seconds. Write and solve an inequality to find the finishing times for which the skater receives a 0.1 penalty point.

Linear Inequalities in Two Variables

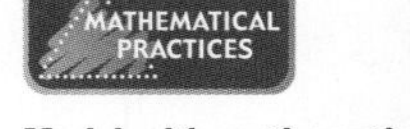

Model with mathematics.

MATERIALS • set of tangram pieces • 4 tangram puzzles • stopwatch

QUESTION How can you use inequalities to describe an overestimate or an underestimate?

EXPLORE Conduct an experiment

To solve a tangram puzzle, you use seven pieces to create a figure. Each piece must lie flat and touch at least one other piece, and the pieces cannot overlap.

STEP 1 *Predict a time*

Have your partner give you a tangram puzzle, such as the dog shown below. Predict how long it will take you to create the figure.

Predicted time: 50 seconds

STEP 2 *Create figure*

Use the tangrams to create the figure. Your partner will use a stopwatch to record the actual time it takes you to finish.

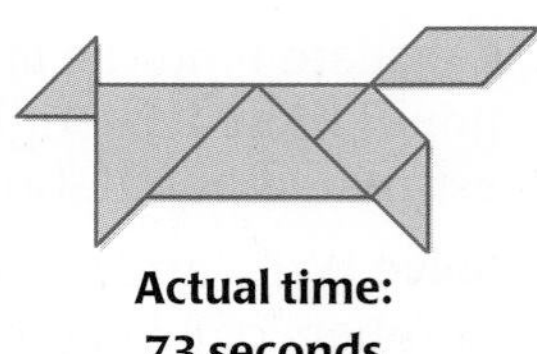

Actual time: 73 seconds

STEP 3 *Record times*

Record the actual time x and the predicted time y in a table, as below. Repeat Steps 1–3 for three more puzzles. Then switch roles with your partner.

Figure	Actual time x (sec)	Predicted time y (sec)
1	73	50
2	67	67
3	70	88
4	90	74

STEP 4 *Plot points*

Graph $y = x$ in Quadrant I. Then plot the points (x, y) from the table.

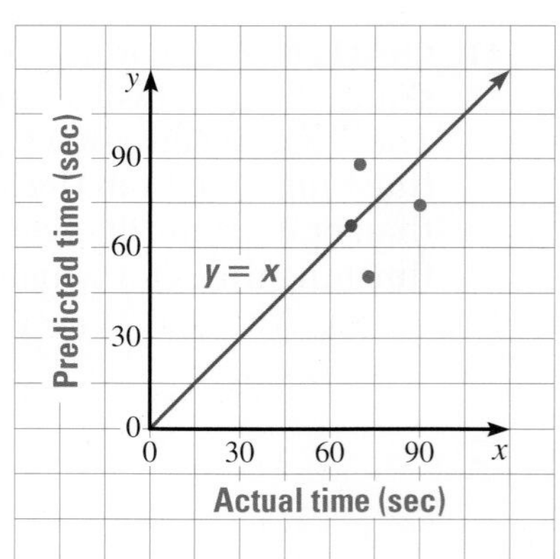

DRAW CONCLUSIONS Use your observations to complete these exercises

1. *Describe* the points that represent an *overestimate* of the actual finishing time. Then write an inequality that describes the location of the points in the coordinate plane.

2. *Describe* the points that represent an *underestimate* of the actual finishing time. Then write an inequality that describes the location of the points in the coordinate plane.

5.7 Graph Linear Inequalities in Two Variables

Before You graphed linear equations in two variables.
Now You will graph linear inequalities in two variables.
Why? So you can analyze a music competition, as in Ex. 56.

Key Vocabulary
- **linear inequality in two variables**
- **graph of an inequality in two variables**

A **linear inequality in two variables**, such as $x - 3y < 6$, is the result of replacing the = sign in a linear equation with <, ≤, >, or ≥. A **solution of an inequality in two variables** x and y is an ordered pair (x, y) that produces a true statement when the values of x and y are substituted into the inequality.

EXAMPLE 1 Standardized Test Practice

CC.9-12.A.REI.12 Graph the solutions to a linear inequality in two variables as a half-plane (excluding the boundary in the case of a strict inequality), and graph the solution set to a system of linear inequalities in two variables as the intersection of the corresponding half-planes.

Which ordered pair is *not* a solution of $x - 3y \le 6$?

Ⓐ (0, 0) Ⓑ (6, −1) Ⓒ (10, 3) Ⓓ (−1, 2)

Solution

Check whether each ordered pair is a solution of the inequality.

Test (0, 0): $x - 3y \le 6$ **Write inequality.**
$0 - 3(0) \le 6$ **Substitute 0 for x and 0 for y.**
$0 \le 6$ ✓ **Simplify.**

Test (6, −1): $x - 3y \le 6$ **Write inequality.**
$6 - 3(-1) \le 6$ **Substitute 6 for x and −1 for y.**
$9 \le 6$ ✗ **Simplify.**

So, (0, 0) is a solution of $x - 3y \le 6$ but (6, −1) is *not* a solution.

▶ The correct answer is B. Ⓐ Ⓑ Ⓒ Ⓓ

GUIDED PRACTICE for Example 1

Tell whether the ordered pair is a solution of $-x + 2y < 8$.

1. (0, 0) 2. (0, 4) 3. (3, 5)

GRAPH OF AN INEQUALITY In a coordinate plane, the **graph of an inequality in two variables** is the set of points that represent all solutions of the inequality. The *boundary line* of a linear inequality divides the coordinate plane into two **half-planes**. Only one half-plane contains the points that represent the solutions of the inequality.

KEY CONCEPT — *For Your Notebook*

Graphing a Linear Inequality in Two Variables

STEP 1 **Graph** the boundary line. Use a *dashed line* for < or >, and use a *solid line* for ≤ or ≥.

STEP 2 **Test** a point not on the boundary line by checking whether the ordered pair is a solution of the inequality.

STEP 3 **Shade** the half-plane containing the point if the ordered pair is a solution of the inequality. Shade the other half-plane if the ordered pair is *not* a solution.

EXAMPLE 2 Graph a linear inequality in two variables

Graph the inequality $y > 4x - 3$.

Solution

STEP 1 **Graph** the equation $y = 4x - 3$. The inequality is >, so use a dashed line.

STEP 2 **Test** (0, 0) in $y > 4x - 3$.

$$0 \overset{?}{>} 4(0) - 3$$

$$0 > -3 \checkmark$$

STEP 3 **Shade** the half-plane that contains (0, 0), because (0, 0) is a solution of the inequality.

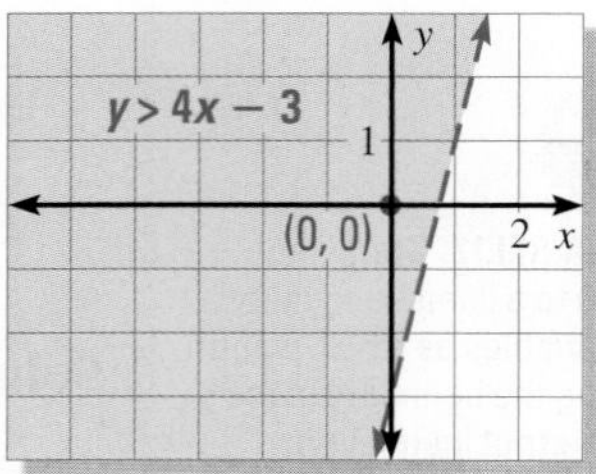

EXAMPLE 3 Graph a linear inequality in two variables

Graph the inequality $x + 2y \le 0$.

Solution

STEP 1 **Graph** the equation $x + 2y = 0$. The inequality is ≤, so use a solid line.

STEP 2 **Test** (1, 0) in $x + 2y \le 0$.

$$1 + 2(0) \overset{?}{\le} 0$$

$$1 \le 0 \text{ ✗}$$

STEP 3 **Shade** the half-plane that does not contain (1, 0), because (1, 0) is *not* a solution of the inequality.

AVOID ERRORS
Be sure to test a point that is not on the boundary line. In Example 3, you can't test (0, 0) because it lies on the boundary line $x + 2y = 0$.

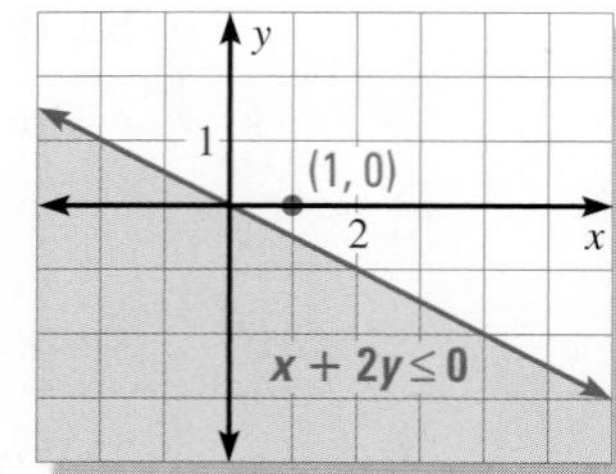

✓ **GUIDED PRACTICE** for Examples 2 and 3

4. Graph the inequality $x + 3y \ge -1$.

LINEAR INEQUALITIES IN ONE VARIABLE The steps for graphing a linear inequality in two variables can be used to graph a linear inequality in one variable in a coordinate plane.

The boundary line for an inequality in one variable is either vertical or horizontal. When testing a point to determine which half-plane to shade, do the following:

- If an inequality has only the variable x, substitute the x-coordinate of the test point into the inequality.
- If an inequality has only the variable y, substitute the y-coordinate of the test point into the inequality.

EXAMPLE 4 Graph a linear inequality in one variable

Graph the inequality $y \geq -3$.

Solution

STEP 1 **Graph** the equation $y = -3$.
The inequality is $\geq$, so use a solid line.

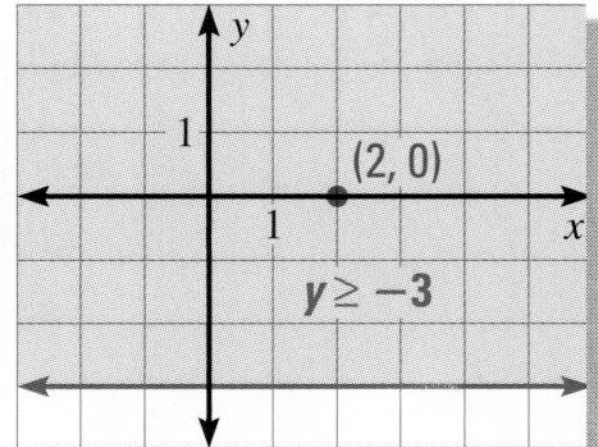

STEP 2 **Test** (2, 0) in $y \geq -3$. You substitute only the y-coordinate, because the inequality does not have the variable x.

$$0 \geq -3 \checkmark$$

STEP 3 **Shade** the half-plane that contains (2, 0), because (2, 0) is a solution of the inequality.

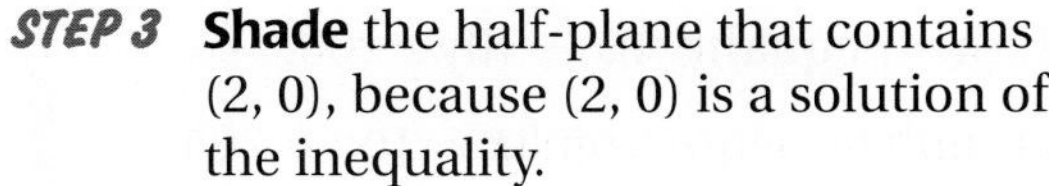

EXAMPLE 5 Graph a linear inequality in one variable

Graph the inequality $x < -1$.

Solution

STEP 1 **Graph** the equation $x = -1$.
The inequality is <, so use a dashed line.

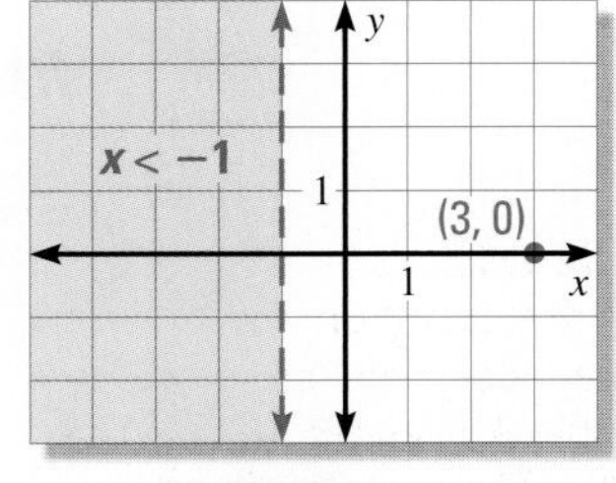

STEP 2 **Test** (3, 0) in $x < -1$. You substitute only the x-coordinate, because the inequality does not have the variable y.

$$3 < -1 \;\text{✗}$$

STEP 3 **Shade** the half-plane that does *not* contain (3, 0), because (3, 0) is not a solution of the inequality.

Animated Algebra at my.hrw.com

✓ **GUIDED PRACTICE** for Examples 4 and 5

Graph the inequality.

5. $y > 1$ **6.** $y \leq 3$ **7.** $x < -2$

EXAMPLE 6 Solve a multi-step problem

JOB EARNINGS You have two summer jobs at a youth center. You earn \$8 per hour teaching basketball and \$10 per hour teaching swimming. Let x represent the amount of time (in hours) you teach basketball each week, and let y represent the amount of time (in hours) you teach swimming each week. Your goal is to earn at least \$200 per week.

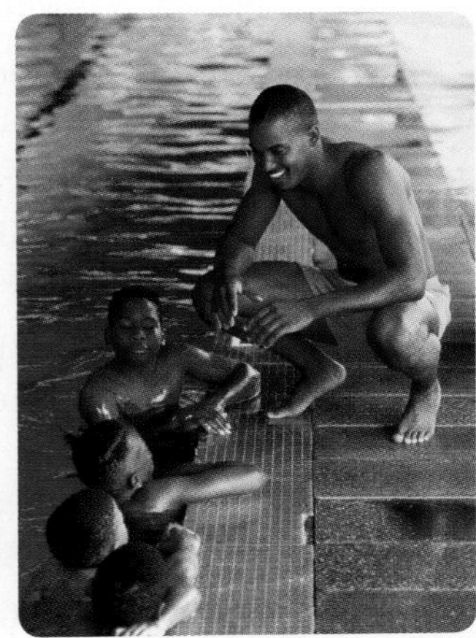

- Write an inequality that describes your goal in terms of x and y.
- Graph the inequality.
- Give three possible combinations of hours that will allow you to meet your goal.

Solution

STEP 1 **Write** a verbal model. Then write an inequality.

Basketball pay rate (dollars/hour)	$\cdot$	Basketball time (hours)	$+$	Swimming pay rate (dollars/hour)	$\cdot$	Swimming time (hours)	$\geq$	Total earnings (dollars)
8	$\cdot$	x	$+$	**10**	$\cdot$	y	$\geq$	**200**

STEP 2 **Graph** the inequality $8x + 10y \geq 200$.

AVOID ERRORS
The variables can't represent negative numbers. So, the graph of the inequality does not include points in Quadrants II, III, or IV.

First, graph the equation $8x + 10y = 200$ in Quadrant I. The inequality is $\geq$, so use a solid line.

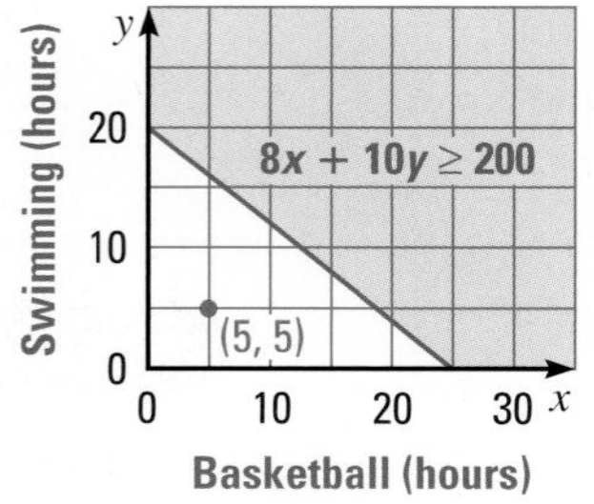

Next, test (5, 5) in $8x + 10y \geq 200$:

$$8(5) + 10(5) \geq 200$$

$$90 \geq 200 \text{ ✗}$$

Finally, shade the part of Quadrant I that does not contain (5, 5), because (5, 5) is not a solution of the inequality.

STEP 3 **Choose** three points on the graph, such as (13, 12), (14, 10), and (16, 9). The table shows the total earnings for each combination of hours.

Basketball time (hours)	13	14	16
Swimming time (hours)	12	10	9
Total earnings (dollars)	224	212	218

✓ GUIDED PRACTICE for Example 6

8. **WHAT IF?** In Example 6, suppose that next summer you earn \$9 per hour teaching basketball and \$12.50 per hour teaching swimming. Write and graph an inequality that describes your goal. Then give three possible combinations of hours that will help you meet your goal.

5.7 EXERCISES

HOMEWORK KEY

○ = See WORKED-OUT SOLUTIONS Exs. 5, 19, and 57

★ = STANDARDIZED TEST PRACTICE Exs. 2, 15, 16, 39, 56, 59, and 60

◆ = MULTIPLE REPRESENTATIONS Ex. 55

SKILL PRACTICE

1. **VOCABULARY** Copy and complete: The ordered pair $(2, -4)$ is a(n) __?__ of $3x - y > 7$.

2. ★ **WRITING** *Describe* the difference between graphing a linear inequality in two variables and graphing a linear equation in two variables.

EXAMPLE 1 for Exs. 3–15

CHECKING SOLUTIONS Tell whether the ordered pair is a solution of the inequality.

3. $x + y < -4$; $(0, 0)$
4. $x - y \le 5$; $(8, 3)$
5. $y - x > -2$; $(-1, -4)$
6. $2x + 3y \ge 14$; $(5, 2)$
7. $4x - 7y > 28$; $(-2, 4)$
8. $-3y - 2x < 12$; $(5, -6)$
9. $2.8x + 4.1y \le 1$; $(0, 0)$
10. $0.5y - 0.5x > 3.5$; $(6, 2)$
11. $x \ge -3$; $(-4, 0)$
12. $y \le 8$; $(-9, -7)$
13. $\frac{3}{4}x - \frac{1}{3}y < 6$; $(-8, 12)$
14. $\frac{2}{5}x + y \ge 2$; $(1, 2)$

15. ★ **MULTIPLE CHOICE** Which ordered pair is *not* a solution of $x + 5y < 15$?

Ⓐ $(-1, -3)$ Ⓑ $(-1, 3)$ Ⓒ $(1, 3)$ Ⓓ $(3, 2)$

EXAMPLES 2, 3, 4, and 5 for Exs. 16–38

16. ★ **MULTIPLE CHOICE** The graph of which inequality is shown?

Ⓐ $x + y \le -1$ Ⓑ $x + y \ge -1$

Ⓒ $x - y \le -1$ Ⓓ $x - y \ge -1$

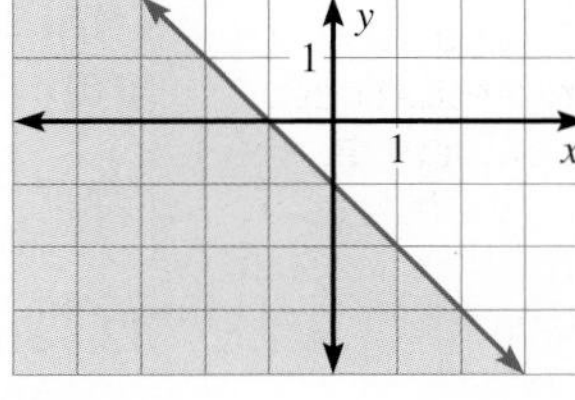

GRAPHING INEQUALITIES Graph the inequality.

17. $y > x + 3$
18. $y \le x - 2$
19. $y < 3x + 5$
20. $y \ge -2x + 8$
21. $x + y < -8$
22. $x - y \le -11$
23. $x + 8y > 16$
24. $5x - y \ge 1$
25. $2(x + 2) > 7y$
26. $y - 4 < x - 6$
27. $-4y \le 16x$
28. $6(2x) \ge -24y$
29. $y < -3$
30. $x \ge 5$
31. $x > -2$
32. $y \le 4$
33. $3(x - 2) > y + 8$
34. $x - 4 \le -2(y + 6)$
35. $\frac{1}{2}(x + 2) + 3y < 8$
36. $2(x + 1) \ge \frac{1}{4}y - 1$

ERROR ANALYSIS ***Describe*** **and correct the error in graphing the inequality.**

37. $2y - x \ge 2$

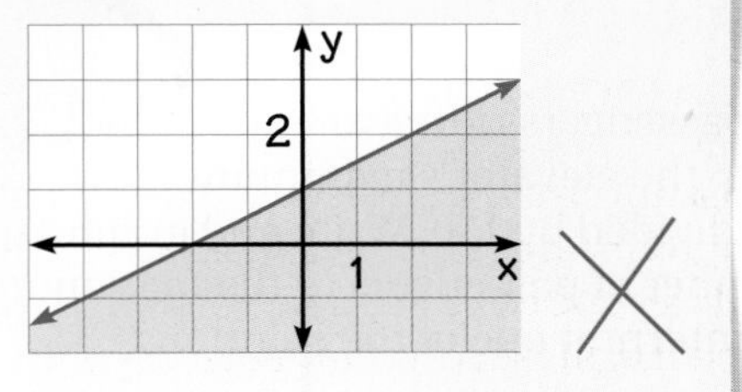

38. $x \le -3$

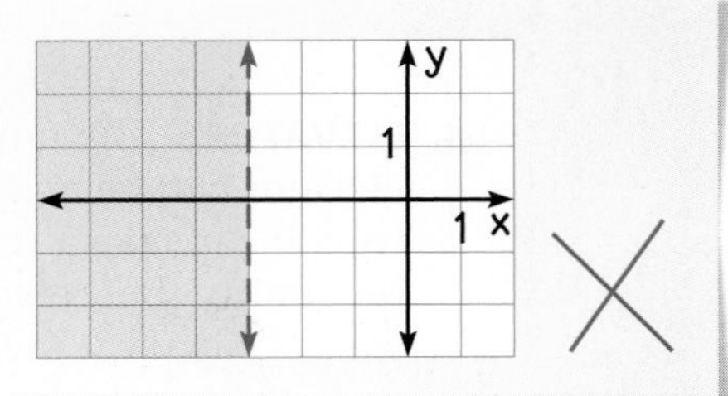

39. ★ **WRITING** Can you use (0, 0) as a test point when graphing $2x > -5y$? *Explain* your reasoning.

TRANSLATING SENTENCES **Write the verbal sentence as an inequality. Then graph the inequality.**

40. Four less than x is greater than or equal to y.

41. The product of -2 and y is less than or equal to the sum of x and 6.

42. The quotient of y and 2 is greater than the difference of 7 and x.

43. The sum of x and the product of 4 and y is less than -3.

USING A GRAPH **Write an inequality of the graph shown.**

44. 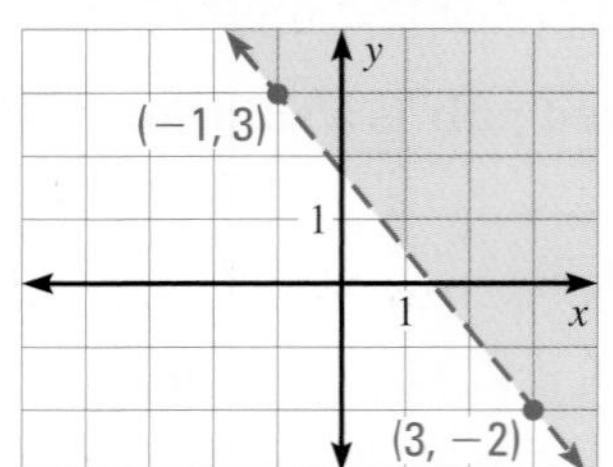

45. 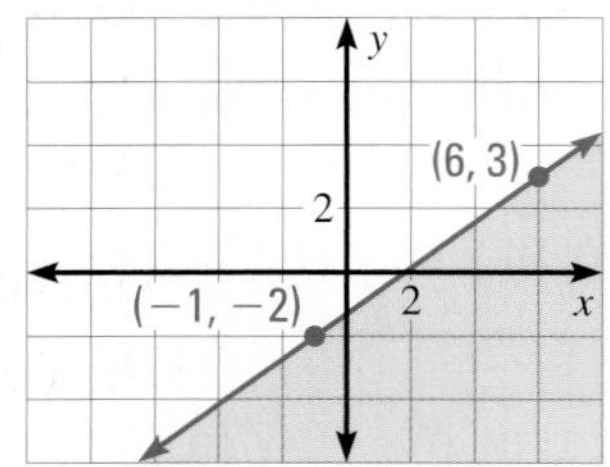

46. 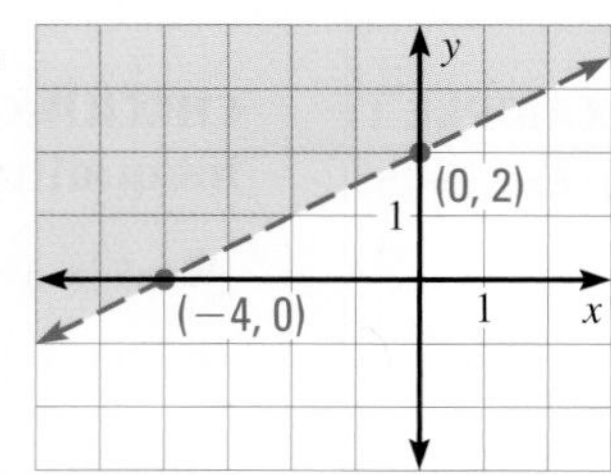

WRITING INEQUALITIES **Write an inequality whose graph contains only the points in the given quadrants.**

47. Quadrants I and II

48. Quadrants II and III

49. Quadrants III and IV

50. Quadrants I and IV

CHALLENGE **In Exercises 51 and 52, write and graph an inequality whose graph is described by the given information.**

51. The points (2, 5) and (−3, −5) lie on the boundary line. The points (6, 5) and (−2, −3) are solutions of the inequality.

52. The points (−7, −16) and (1, 8) lie on the boundary line. The points (−7, 0) and (3, 14) are *not* solutions of the inequality.

PROBLEM SOLVING

EXAMPLE 6 for Exs. 53–57

53. **BOBSLEDS** In a two-man bobsled competition, the sum of the weight x (in pounds) of the bobsled and the combined weight y (in pounds) of the athletes must not exceed 860 pounds. Write and graph an inequality that describes the possible weights of the bobsled and the athletes. Identify and interpret one of the solutions.

54. **ELEVATORS** The number y of passengers riding an elevator can be no greater than the elevator's maximum weight capacity x (in pounds) divided by 150. Write and graph an inequality that relates the number of passengers to the maximum weight capacity. Identify and interpret one of the solutions.

55. **MULTIPLE REPRESENTATIONS** You tutor Spanish for \$15 per hour and French for \$10 per hour. You want to earn at least \$100 per week.

a. **Writing an Inequality** Write an inequality that describes your goal in terms of hours spent tutoring Spanish and hours spent tutoring French.

b. **Drawing a Graph** Graph the inequality. Then give three possible combinations of hours that meet your goal.

c. **Making a Table** Make a table that gives the amount of money that you will earn for each combination of hours given in part (b).

56. ★ **MULTIPLE CHOICE** To compete in a piano competition, you need to perform two musical pieces whose combined duration is no greater than 15 minutes. Which inequality describes the possible durations x and y (in minutes) of the pieces?

(A) $x + y < 15$ (B) $x + y \leq 15$ (C) $x + y > 15$ (D) $x + y \geq 15$

57. **MULTI-STEP PROBLEM** You are making muffins and loaves of bread for a bake sale. You need $\frac{1}{6}$ batch of batter per muffin and $\frac{1}{2}$ batch of batter per loaf of bread. You have enough ingredients to make up to 12 batches of batter.

a. Write and graph an inequality that describes the possible combinations of muffins m and loaves ℓ of bread that you can make.

b. You make 4 loaves of bread. What are the possible numbers of muffins that you can make?

58. **NUTRITION** A nutritionist recommends that the fat calories y consumed per day should be at most 30% of the total calories x consumed per day.

a. Write and graph an inequality that relates the number of fat calories consumed to the total calories consumed.

b. Use the nutrition labels below. You normally consume 2000 calories per day. So far today you have eaten 6 crackers and 1 container of yogurt. What are the possible additional fat calories that you can consume today?

59. ★ **SHORT RESPONSE** You need to bring a duffel and a bedroll for a trip in the mountains. The sum of the weight x (in pounds) of the duffel and the weight y (in pounds) of the bedroll cannot exceed 30 pounds.

a. **Graph and Apply** Write and graph a linear inequality that describes the possible weights of the duffel and bedroll. Then give three possible combinations of weights of the duffel and bedroll.

b. **Interpret** Are (0, 30) and (30, 0) solutions of the inequality in part (a)? Do these ordered pairs make sense for this situation? *Explain.*

60. ★ **EXTENDED RESPONSE** A financial advisor suggests that if a person is an aggressive investor, the percent y of money that the person invests in stocks should be greater than the difference of 110 and the person's age x.

a. **Graph** Write and graph a linear inequality that relates the percent of money invested in stocks to an aggressive investor's age.

b. **Calculate** If an aggressive investor is 30 years old, what are the possible percents that the investor can invest in stocks? *Explain* your answer.

c. **Justify** Are there any ages for which none of the solutions of the inequality makes sense for this situation? *Justify* your answer.

61. **CHALLENGE** The formula $m = dV$ gives the mass m of an object in terms of the object's density d and its volume V. Water has a density of 1 gram per cubic centimeter. An object immersed in water will sink if its density is greater than the density of water. An object will float in water if its density is less than the density of water.

a. For an object that sinks, write and graph an inequality that relates its mass (in grams) to its volume (in cubic centimeters). For an object that floats, write and graph an inequality that relates its mass (in grams) to its volume (in cubic centimeters).

b. A cylindrical can has a radius of 5 centimeters, a height of 10 centimeters, and a mass of 2119.5 grams. Will the can sink or float in water? *Explain* your answer.

QUIZ

Solve the equation.

1. $|x| = 5$
2. $|c - 8| = 24$
3. $-2|r - 5| = -6$

Solve the inequality. Graph your solution.

4. $|y| > 4$
5. $|2t - 5| < 3$
6. $4|3s + 7| - 5 \geq 7$

Graph the inequality.

7. $x + y \geq 3$
8. $\frac{5}{7}x < 10$
9. $2y - x \leq 8$

See. **EXTRA PRACTICE** in Student Resources **ONLINE QUIZ** at my.hrw.com

MIXED REVIEW *of Problem Solving*

MATHEMATICAL PRACTICES Make sense of problems and persevere in solving them.

1. **MULTI-STEP PROBLEM** You gathered 36 apples from your backyard apple tree in order to make apple pies and applesauce. You use 7 apples to make one apple pie and 5 apples to make one pint of applesauce.
   - **a.** Write an inequality that describes the possible numbers of apple pies and pints of applesauce that you can make.
   - **b.** Graph the inequality.
   - **c.** Give three possible combinations of apple pies and pints of applesauce that you can make.

2. **SHORT RESPONSE** You are scooping ice cream as part of your training at an ice cream shop. The weight of a scoop must be 4 ounces with an absolute deviation of at most 0.5 ounce.
   - **a.** Write an inequality to find the possible weights (in ounces) of each scoop.
   - **b.** You make 10 scoops. You can start working at the shop if at least 80% of the scoops meet the weight requirement. The list shows the weights (in ounces) of your scoops.

     3.8, 4.2, 3.9, 4.5, 3.7, 4.6, 4.1, 3.3, 4.3, 4.2

     Can you start working at the shop? *Explain* your reasoning.

3. **GRIDDED ANSWER** You will be making a presentation in your history class. Your teacher gives you a time limit of 15 minutes with an absolute deviation of 1.5 minutes. What is the maximum possible duration (in minutes) of your presentation?

4. **OPEN-ENDED** *Describe* a real-world situation that can be modeled by the equation $|x - 50| = 10$. *Explain* what the solution of the equation means in this situation.

5. **EXTENDED RESPONSE** A tour operator recommends that a river rafter wear a protective suit under the temperature conditions described below.

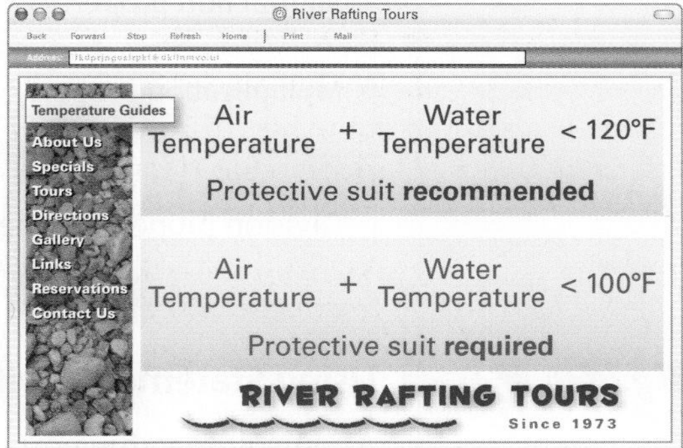

   - **a.** Write and graph an inequality that describes the possible air temperatures and water temperatures for which a protective suit is recommended.
   - **b.** If the water temperature is 40°F, for which air temperatures is a protective suit recommended?
   - **c.** How would you change the graph in part (a) in order to describe the situations in which a protective suit is required? *Explain* your answer.

6. **MULTI-STEP PROBLEM** You are buying a new cell phone and see eight phones listed on a website. The prices of the phones are shown.

   \$139, \$249, \$229, \$199, \$179, \$359, \$199, \$209

   - **a.** Find the mean price of the phones.
   - **b.** You are willing to purchase a phone that has the mean price with an absolute deviation of at most \$50. Write and solve an inequality to find the prices of phones that you will consider.
   - **c.** How many of the phones on the website will you consider buying?

5 CHAPTER SUMMARY

BIG IDEAS

For Your Notebook

Big Idea 1

Applying Properties of Inequality

You can apply the properties of inequality to solve inequalities. The properties listed below are also true for inequalities involving $\le$ and $\ge$.

Property	If $a < b$, then ...	If $a > b$, then ...
Addition property of inequality	$a + c < b + c$.	$a + c > b + c$.
Subtraction property of inequality	$a - c < b - c$.	$a - c > b - c$.
Multiplication property of inequality	$ac < bc$ if $c > 0$. $ac > bc$ if $c < 0$.	$ac > bc$ if $c > 0$. $ac < bc$ if $c < 0$.
Division property of inequality	$\frac{a}{c} < \frac{b}{c}$ if $c > 0$. $\frac{a}{c} > \frac{b}{c}$ if $c < 0$.	$\frac{a}{c} > \frac{b}{c}$ if $c > 0$. $\frac{a}{c} < \frac{b}{c}$ if $c < 0$.

Big Idea 2

Using Statements with *And* or *Or*

An absolute value equation can be rewritten as two equations joined by *or.* An absolute value inequality can be rewritten as a compound inequality with *and* or *or.* In the statements below, $<$ can be replaced by $\le$, and $>$ can be replaced by $\ge$.

Absolute value equation or inequality	Equivalent statement with *and* or *or*
$\lvert ax + b \rvert = c, c \ge 0$	$ax + b = c$ or $ax + b = -c$
$\lvert ax + b \rvert < c, c \ge 0$	$-c < ax + b < c$
$\lvert ax + b \rvert > c, c \ge 0$	$ax + b < -c$ or $ax + b > c$

Big Idea 3

Graphing Inequalities

You use a number line to graph an inequality in one variable. Similarly, you use a coordinate plane to graph a linear inequality in two variables (including cases where one of the variables has a coefficient of 0, such as $0x + y < 1$, or $y < 1$).

Graphing inequalities in one variable	Graphing linear inequalities in two variables
Graph simple inequalities: 1. Solve for the variable. 2. Draw an open circle for $<$ or $>$ and a closed circle for $\le$ or $\ge$. Draw an arrow in the appropriate direction. Graph compound inequalities: 1. Solve the compound inequality. 2. Use the union of graphs of simple inequalities for *or.* Use the intersection for *and.*	1. Graph the boundary line. Use a solid line for $\le$ or $\ge$ and a dashed line for $<$ or $>$. 2. Test a point that does not lie on the boundary line. 3. Shade the half-plane containing the point if the ordered pair is a solution of the inequality. Shade the other half-plane if the ordered pair is *not* a solution.

5 CHAPTER REVIEW

@HomeTutor
my.hrw.com
- Multi-Language Glossary
- Vocabulary practice

REVIEW KEY VOCABULARY

- graph of an inequality
- equivalent inequalities
- compound inequality
- absolute value equation
- absolute deviation
- linear inequality in two variables
- solution of an inequality in two variables
- graph of an inequality in two variables, half-plane

VOCABULARY EXERCISES

1. Translate the verbal sentence into an absolute value equation: "The absolute deviation of x from 19 is 8."
2. Identify three ordered pairs that are solutions of $2x - 3y \geq -10$.
3. **WRITING** When you graph a linear inequality in two variables, how do you know whether the boundary line is a solid line or a dashed line? How do you know which half-plane to shade?

REVIEW EXAMPLES AND EXERCISES

Use the review examples and exercises below to check your understanding of the concepts you have learned in each lesson of this chapter.

5.1 Solve Inequalities Using Addition and Subtraction

EXAMPLE

Solve $x - 2.1 \leq 1.4$. Graph your solution.

$x - 2.1 \leq 1.4$ **Write original inequality.**

$x - 2.1 + 2.1 \leq 1.4 + 2.1$ **Add 2.1 to each side.**

$x \leq 3.5$ **Simplify.**

▶ The solutions are all real numbers less than or equal to 3.5.

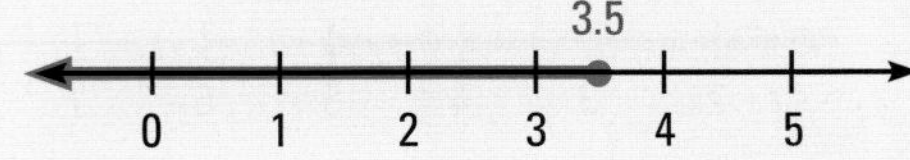

EXERCISES

EXAMPLES 1, 2, 3, and 4 for Exs. 4–7

4. **GEOGRAPHY** The lowest elevation in Mexico is −10 meters at Laguna Salada. Write and graph an inequality that describes all elevations in Mexico that are greater than the lowest elevation.

Solve the inequality. Graph your solution.

5. $x + 5 > -13$
6. $m - 9 \geq -4$
7. $s + 3.7 < 1$

5 CHAPTER REVIEW

5.2 Solve Inequalities Using Multiplication and Division

EXAMPLE

Solve $\frac{x}{-4} < 9$. Graph your solution.

$\frac{x}{-4} < 9$	**Write original inequality.**
$-4 \cdot \frac{x}{-4} > -4 \cdot 9$	**Multiply each side by −4. Reverse inequality symbol.**
$x > -36$	**Simplify.**

▸ The solutions are all real numbers greater than −36.

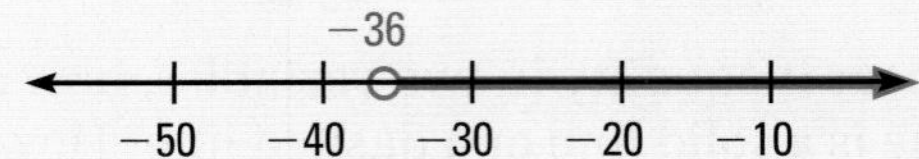

EXERCISES

EXAMPLES 1, 2, 3, 4, and 5 for Exs. 8–12

Solve the inequality. Graph your solution.

8. $\frac{p}{2} \le 5$ **9.** $\frac{n}{-4.5} < -8$ **10.** $-3x > 27$ **11.** $2y \ge 18$

12. GYMNASTICS In men's gymnastics, an athlete competes in 6 events. Suppose that an athlete's average score per event is at most 9.7 points. Write and solve an inequality to find the possible total scores for the athlete.

5.3 Solve Multi-Step Inequalities

EXAMPLE

Solve $-4x + 7 \ge -13$. Graph your solution.

$-4x + 7 \ge -13$	**Write original inequality.**
$-4x \ge -20$	**Subtract 7 from each side.**
$x \le 5$	**Divide each side by −4. Reverse inequality symbol.**

▸ The solutions are all real numbers less than or equal to 5.

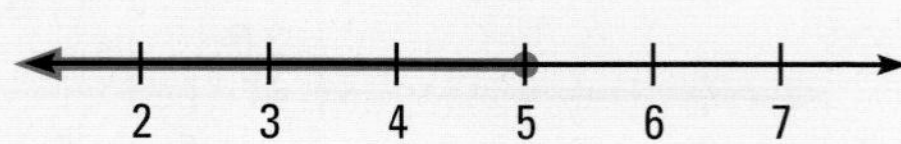

EXERCISES

EXAMPLES 1, 2, 3, and 4 for Exs. 13–19

Solve the inequality, if possible. Graph your solution.

13. $2g + 11 < 25$ **14.** $\frac{2}{3}r - 4 \ge 1$ **15.** $1 - 3x \le -14 + 2x$

16. $3(q + 1) < 3q + 7$ **17.** $8(t - 1) > -8 + 8t$ **18.** $-3(2n - 1) \ge 1 - 8n$

19. TICKET PURCHASES You can order discount movie tickets from a website for \$7 each. You must also pay a shipping fee of \$4. You want to spend no more than \$40 on movie tickets. Find the possible numbers of movie tickets that you can order.

@HomeTutor
my.hrw.com
Chapter Review Practice

5.4 Solve Compound Inequalities

EXAMPLE

Solve $-1 < -2x + 7 < 9$. Graph your solution.

$-1 < -2x + 7 < 9$	**Write original inequality.**
$-8 < -2x < 2$	**Subtract 7 from each expression.**
$4 > x > -1$	**Divide each expression by −2. Reverse both inequality symbols.**
$-1 < x < 4$	**Rewrite in the form $a < x < b$.**

▶ The solutions are all real numbers greater than −1 *and* less than 4.

EXERCISES

EXAMPLES 3, 4, and 5 for Exs. 20–23

Solve the inequality. Graph your solution.

20. $-6 \le 2t - 5 \le -3$

21. $-3 < -3x + 8 < 11$

22. $9s - 6 < 12$ *or* $3s + 1 > 13$

23. $-4w + 12 \ge 10$ *or* $5w - 14 > -4$

5.5 Solve Absolute Value Equations

EXAMPLE

Solve $4|5x - 3| + 6 = 30$.

First, rewrite the equation in the form $|ax + b| = c$.

$4|5x - 3| + 6 = 30$	**Write original equation.**
$4|5x - 3| = 24$	**Subtract 6 from each side.**
$|5x - 3| = 6$	**Divide each side by 4.**

Next, solve the absolute value equation.

$5x - 3 = 6$ *or* $5x - 3 = -6$	**Rewrite as two equations.**
$5x = 9$ *or* $5x = -3$	**Add 3 to each side.**
$x = 1.8$ *or* $x = -0.6$	**Divide each side by 5.**

▶ The solutions are −0.6 and 1.8.

EXERCISES

EXAMPLES 1, 2, 3, 4, and 5 for Exs. 24–30

Solve the equation, if possible.

24. $|r| = 7$

25. $|a + 6| = 2$

26. $|2c + 5| = 21$

27. $2|x - 3| + 1 = 5$

28. $3|2q + 1| - 5 = 1$

29. $4|3p - 2| + 5 = 11$

30. BOWLING In tenpin bowling, the height of each bowling pin must be 15 inches with an absolute deviation of 0.03125 inch. Find the minimum and maximum possible heights of a bowling pin.

5 CHAPTER REVIEW

5.6 Solve Absolute Value Inequalities

EXAMPLE

Solve $3|2x + 11| + 2 \leq 17$. Graph your solution.

$3\|2x + 11\| + 2 \leq 17$	**Write original inequality.**
$3\|2x + 11\| \leq 15$	**Subtract 2 from each side.**
$\|2x + 11\| \leq 5$	**Divide each side by 3.**
$-5 \leq 2x + 11 \leq 5$	**Rewrite as compound inequality.**
$-16 \leq 2x \leq -6$	**Subtract 11 from each expression.**
$-8 \leq x \leq -3$	**Divide each expression by 2.**

▶ The solutions are all real numbers greater than or equal to -8 *and* less than or equal to -3.

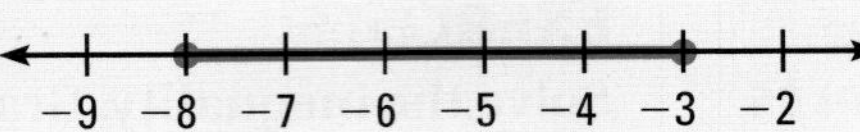

EXERCISES

EXAMPLES 1, 2, and 3 for Exs. 31–36

Solve the inequality. Graph your solution.

31. $|m| \geq 8$ **32.** $|6k + 1| \geq 2$ **33.** $|3g - 2| < 5$

34. $6|3x + 5| \leq 14$ **35.** $|2j - 9| - 2 > 10$ **36.** $5|d + 8| - 7 > 13$

5.7 Graph Linear Inequalities in Two Variables

EXAMPLE

Graph the inequality $y < 3x - 1$.

STEP 1 **Graph** the equation $y = 3x - 1$. The inequality is $<$, so use a dashed line.

STEP 2 **Test** (0, 0) in $y < 3x - 1$.

$$0 \stackrel{?}{<} 3(0) - 1$$

$$0 < -1 \text{ ✗}$$

STEP 3 **Shade** the half-plane that does not contain (0, 0), because (0, 0) is *not* a solution of the inequality.

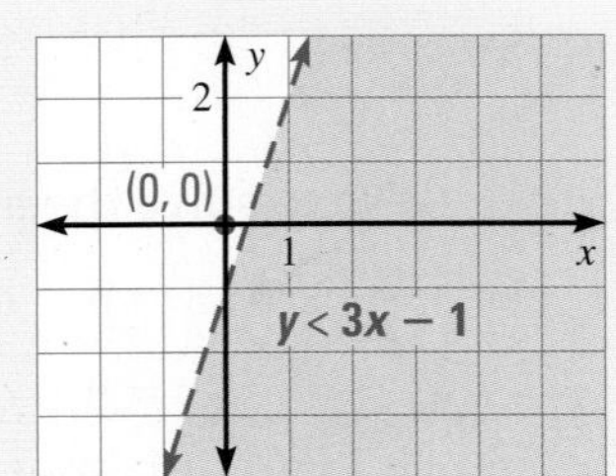

EXERCISES

EXAMPLES 1, 2, 3, 4, and 5 for Exs. 37–44

Tell whether the ordered pair is a solution of $-3x + 2y \geq 16$.

37. (−2, 8) **38.** (−1, −1) **39.** (−2, 10) **40.** (9, −5)

Graph the inequality.

41. $y > 2x + 3$ **42.** $y \leq \frac{1}{2}x - 1$ **43.** $3x - 2y < 12$ **44.** $y \geq 3$

5 CHAPTER TEST

Translate the verbal phrase into an inequality. Then graph the inequality.

1. All real numbers that are less than 5
2. All real numbers that are greater than or equal to -1
3. All real numbers that are greater than -2 *and* less than or equal to 7
4. All real numbers that are greater than 8 *or* less than -4

Solve the inequality, if possible. Graph your solution.

5. $x - 9 \geq -5$
6. $-2 > 5 + y$
7. $-0.8 \leq z + 7.7$
8. $5m \geq 35$
9. $\frac{n}{6} < -1$
10. $\frac{r}{-3} \leq 4$
11. $-4s < 6s + 1$
12. $4t - 7 \leq 13$
13. $-8 > 5 - v$
14. $3(5w + 4) < 12w - 11$
15. $4p - 3 > 2(2p + 1)$
16. $9q - 12 \geq 3(3q - 4)$
17. $-2 \leq 4 - 3a \leq 13$
18. $-7 < 2c - 1 < 10\frac{1}{2}$
19. $-5 \leq 2 - h$ *or* $6h + 5 \geq 71$
20. $|2d + 8| > 3$
21. $2|3f - 7| + 5 < 11$
22. $|j - 7| - 1 \leq 3\frac{5}{6}$

Solve the equation, if possible.

23. $-\frac{3}{4}|x - 3| = \frac{1}{4}$
24. $|3y + 1| - 6 = -2$
25. $4|2z + 5| + 9 = 5$

Check whether the ordered pair is a solution of the inequality.

26. $2x - y < 4$; $(2, -1)$
27. $y + 3x \geq -5$; $(-3, -4)$
28. $y \leq -3$; $(4, -7)$

Graph the inequality.

29. $y < x + 4$
30. $y \geq 2x - 5$
31. $y \geq -6$

32. **BUSINESS** Your friend is starting a small business baking and decorating cakes and wants to make a profit of at least \$250 for the first month. The expenses for the first month are \$155. What are the possible revenues that your friend can earn in order to meet the profit goal?

33. **BICYCLES** A manufacturer of bicycle parts requires that a bicycle chain have a width of 0.3 inch with an absolute error of at most 0.0003 inch. Find the possible widths of bicycle chains that the manufacturer will accept.

34. **HORSES** You are planning to ride a horse to a campsite. The sum of your weight x (in pounds) and the combined weight y (in pounds) of your camping supplies can be at most 20% of the weight of the horse.

    a. Suppose that the horse weighs 1000 pounds. Write and graph an inequality that describes the possible combinations of your weight and the combined weight of the camping supplies.

    b. Identify and interpret one of the solutions of the inequality in part (a).

EXTENDED RESPONSE QUESTIONS

Scoring Rubric

Full Credit
- solution is complete and correct

Partial Credit
- solution is complete but errors are made, *or*
- solution is without error but incomplete

No Credit
- no solution is given, *or*
- solution makes no sense

PROBLEM

Your school chess club is selling chess sets for \$9 each to raise funds for a regional tournament. The club wants to sell at least 100 of them. The table shows the number of chess sets sold so far by each member of the club.

Member	1	2	3	4	5	6
Chess sets sold	17	16	12	13	16	10

a. Find the possible numbers a of additional chess sets that the club can sell in order to meet its goal.

b. If the club raises more than \$1000, it will donate the amount that exceeds \$1000 to a charity. Find the possible total numbers t of chess sets that the club can sell in order to donate at least \$100 to the charity.

c. Suppose the club has 61 chess sets left to sell. Write an inequality that describes the possible amounts that the club can donate to the charity. *Explain* your answer.

Below are sample solutions to the problem. Read each solution and the comments on the left to see why the sample represents full credit, partial credit, or no credit.

SAMPLE 1: Full credit solution

The correct inequality is given. The solution is correct.

a. $17 + 16 + 12 + 13 + 16 + 10 + a \geq 100$

$$84 + a \geq 100$$

$$a \geq 16$$

The club will meet its goal if it sells at least 16 more chess sets.

The correct inequality is given. The student rounded correctly so that the answer makes sense.

b. $9t - 1000 \geq 100$

$$9t \geq 1100$$

$$t \geq 122.22\ldots$$

The club can donate only $\$9(122) - \$1000 = \$98$ if it sells 122 sets. So, the club can donate at least \$100 if it sells at least 123 sets.

The student's calculation of the least and greatest values is correct. The answer is correct.

c. If the club doesn't sell any more chess sets, it will have raised a total of $\$9(84) = \$756$. Because the club will not have raised at least \$1000, its donation to the charity would be \$0. If the club sells the remaining 61 chess sets, it will have raised a total of $\$756 + \$9(61) = \$1305$. So, the club's donation to the charity would be $\$1305 - \$1000 = \$305$. The inequality is $0 \leq d \leq 305$ where d is the donation in dollars.

SAMPLE 2: Partial credit solution

The correct inequality is given. The solution is correct.

a. $84 + a \geq 100$

$a \geq 16$

The club must sell at least 16 chess sets.

The student solved the inequality correctly but gave the wrong answer.

b. $9t - 1000 \geq 100$

$9t \geq 1100$

$t \geq 122.22...$

The club can donate at least $100 if it sells at least 122 sets.

The reasoning doesn't make sense, and the inequality is incorrect.

c. If the club doesn't sell any more chess sets, it will raise $0 more. So, the donation would be $0. If the club sells the remaining 61 sets, it will raise $9(61) = $549 more. So, the donation would be at most $549. The inequality is $0 \leq d \leq 549$ where d is the donation.

SAMPLE 3: No credit solution

The inequalities in parts (a) and (b) are incorrect, and the answers are incorrect.

a. $84 + a \leq 100$

$a \leq 16$

The club will meet its goal if it sells up to 16 chess sets.

b. $9t \geq 1000$

$t \geq 111.11...$

The club can donate at least $100 if it sells at least 112 chess sets.

The student didn't consider the number of chess sets the club can sell.

c. The donation would be $0 if the club raised up to $1000. But the donation would be greater than $0 if the club raised more than $1000. The inequality is $d \geq 0$ where d is the donation.

PRACTICE Apply the Scoring Rubric

1. A student's solution to the problem on the previous page is given below. Score the solution as *full credit, partial credit,* or *no credit. Explain* your reasoning. If you choose *partial credit* or *no credit,* explain how you would change the solution so that it earns a score of full credit.

a. Because $a \geq 100 - 84$, the club must sell at least 16 sets to meet its goal.

b. The total amount raised is 9t. In order to donate at least $100, the club needs to raise a total of at least $1100.

$9t \geq 1100$, so $t \geq 122.22...$

c. If the club sells the remaining 61 sets, then it will have raised $9(61) = $549 more. The inequality is $d \leq 549$ where d is the donation.

★ *Standardized* TEST PRACTICE

EXTENDED RESPONSE

1. You plan to work a total of 20 hours per week at two part-time jobs. The table shows the hourly wage at each job.

Job	Working at a sandwich shop	After-school tutoring
Hourly wage (dollars)	5.50	7.00

a. You want to earn from \$100 to \$120 per week. What are the possible numbers of hours that you can work at the sandwich shop so that you can meet your earnings goal?

b. Suppose you need to reduce the total number of hours you work each week to 18 hours. Can you still meet your earnings goal? If so, what are the least and greatest numbers of hours that you can work at the sandwich shop? If not, explain why not.

c. Show that it is not possible to earn more than \$150 after working 20 hours in one week by writing and solving an inequality that describes the situation and showing that the solutions do not make sense for the situation.

2. You plan to spend up to \$30 on flower bulbs for a garden. The table shows the prices of tulip bulbs and daffodil bulbs.

Flower bulb	Tulip	Daffodil
Price (dollars)	3	2

a. Write and graph an inequality that describes the possible combinations of tulip bulbs and daffodil bulbs that you can buy.

b. Give three possible combinations of tulip bulbs and daffodil bulbs that you can buy.

c. Suppose you plan to spend up to \$40 on flower bulbs. How would you change the graph in part (a) in order to describe this situation? *Explain* your answer.

3. The average number of hits h per day that your website received during the period January 2001 to February 2004 can be modeled by the equation $h = -16|m - 30| + 500$ where m is the number of months since January 2001.

a. In what month and year did your website receive an average of 100 hits per day? If the model holds for months after February 2004, predict the month and year in which your website will again receive an average of 100 hits per day.

b. According to the model, did your website receive an average of 600 hits per day at any time during the period January 2001 to February 2004? *Explain* your answer.

c. Can you use the model to find the month and year in which the average number of hits per day was the greatest? *Justify* your answer.

MULTIPLE CHOICE

4. In a piano competition, a pianist must perform a sonata that lasts no less than 8 minutes and no more than 10 minutes. Which inequality represents the durations d (in minutes) of sonatas that can be performed?

   Ⓐ $8 < d < 10$ Ⓑ $d \le 8$ *or* $d \ge 10$

   Ⓒ $8 \le d \le 10$ Ⓓ $d < 8$ *or* $d > 10$

5. Which ordered pair is a solution of the inequality $4x - y \ge 3$?

   Ⓐ (0, 0) Ⓑ (−1, 2)

   Ⓒ (1, 1) Ⓓ (0, −2)

6. You are designing an obstacle course for a dog agility event. The course includes a tunnel that must have a height of 24 inches with an absolute deviation of 2 inches. Which equation can you use to find the minimum and maximum heights of the tunnel?

   Ⓐ $|x + 24| = 2$ Ⓑ $|x - 24| = 2$

   Ⓒ $|x + 2| = 24$ Ⓓ $|x - 2| = 24$

GRIDDED ANSWER

7. You scored the following points in four basketball games: 16, 24, 32, and 22. You want to score an average of more than 25 points per game after your fifth game. Of all the possible points you can score in your fifth game in order to meet your goal, which is the least?

8. In men's weightlifting, the bar that holds the weights must have a length of 2.2 meters with an absolute deviation of 1 millimeter. Of all the possible lengths that the bar can have, which is the greatest length (in millimeters)?

9. Of all the numbers that are solutions of the inequality $\left|-\frac{1}{3}x + 4\right| \le 2$, which is the least number?

10. The perimeter of the rectangle shown is at least 47 inches and at most 52 inches. Find the greatest value of x that satisfies the condition.

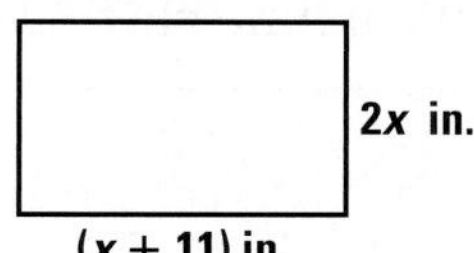

SHORT RESPONSE

11. You and 4 friends each order a three course dinner at a restaurant, and all of you agree to divide the total cost equally. The table shows the range of prices for each of the three courses.

Dinner course	Appetizer	Main course	Dessert
Price range (dollars)	2–4	12–20	3–6

   a. Find the least and greatest possible total costs C (in dollars). Then write an inequality that describes the possible total costs.

   b. Your share s (in dollars) of the total cost is given by $s = \frac{C}{5}$. You chose a \$3 appetizer, a \$15 main course, and a \$4 dessert. *Explain* why your share could be greater than or less than \$3 + \$15 + \$4 = \$22.

12. A family is planning a vacation and is willing to spend no more than \$2000 for 4 airplane tickets and 5 nights at a hotel. Write and graph an inequality that describes the combinations of prices x (in dollars) of an airplane ticket and prices y (in dollars) of a night at a hotel. If the family spends \$275 per airplane ticket, is the family willing to spend \$200 per night at a hotel? *Explain* your answer using the graph.

Systems of Equations and Inequalities

COMMON CORE

Lesson	
6.1	CC.9-12.A.REI.6
6.2	CC.9-12.A.REI.6
6.3	CC.9-12.A.REI.6
6.4	CC.9-12.A.REI.6
6.5	CC.9-12.A.REI.6
6.6	CC.9-12.A.REI.12

Before

Previously, you learned the following skills, which you'll use in this chapter: graphing linear equations, solving equations, and graphing inequalities.

Prerequisite Skills

VOCABULARY CHECK

Copy and complete the statement.

1. The least common multiple of 10 and 15 is _?_.
2. Two lines in the same plane are _?_ if they do not intersect.

SKILLS CHECK

Graph the equation.

3. $x - y = 4$ **4.** $6x - y = -1$ **5.** $4x + 5y = 20$ **6.** $3x - 2y = -12$

Solve the equation.

7. $5m + 4 - m = 20$ **8.** $10(z + 5) + z = 6$

Tell whether the graphs of the two equations are parallel lines. *Explain* your reasoning.

9. $y = 2x - 3, y + 2x = -3$ **10.** $y - 5x = -1, y - 5x = 1$

11. $y = x + 10, x - y = -9$ **12.** $6x - y = 4, 4x - y = 6$

Solve the inequality. Graph the solution.

13. $m + 4 > 9$ **14.** $-6t \geq 24$ **15.** $2x - 5 \leq 13$ **16.** $-5y + 1 < -14$

Now

In this chapter, you will apply the big ideas listed below and reviewed in the Chapter Summary. You will also use the key vocabulary listed below.

Big Ideas

1. **Solving linear systems by graphing**
2. **Solving linear systems using algebra**
3. **Solving systems of linear inequalities**

KEY VOCABULARY

- system of linear equations
- solution of a system of linear equations
- consistent independent system
- inconsistent system
- consistent dependent system
- system of linear inequalities
- solution of a system of linear inequalities
- graph of a system of linear inequalities

Why?

You can use a system of linear equations to solve problems about traveling with and against a current. For example, you can write and solve a system of linear equations to find the average speed of a kayak in still water.

Animated Algebra

The animation illustrated below helps you answer a question from this chapter: What is the average speed of the kayak in still water?

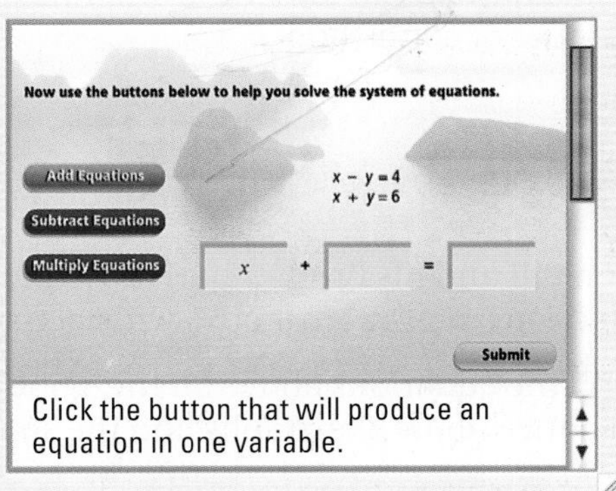

Animated Algebra at my.hrw.com

Investigating Algebra ACTIVITY *Use before Solve Linear Systems by Graphing*

Solving Linear Systems Using Tables

Model with mathematics.

MATERIALS • pencil and paper

QUESTION How can you use a table to solve a linear system?

A *system of linear equations,* or *linear system,* consists of two or more linear equations in the same variables. A *solution of a linear system* is an ordered pair that satisfies each equation in the system. You can use a table to find a solution to a linear system.

EXPLORE Solve a linear system

Bill and his brother collect comic books. Bill currently has 15 books and adds 2 books to his collection every month. His brother currently has 7 books and adds 4 books to his collection every month. Use the equations below to find the number x of months after which Bill and his brother will have the same number y of comic books in their collections.

$y = 2x + 15$ **Number of comic books in Bill's collection**

$y = 4x + 7$ **Number of comic books in his brother's collection**

STEP 1 ***Make a table***

Copy and complete the table of values shown.

STEP 2 ***Find a solution***

Find an x-value that gives the same y-value for both equations.

STEP 3 ***Interpret the solution***

Use your answer to Step 2 to find the number of months after which Bill and his brother have the same number of comic books.

x	$y = 2x + 15$	$y = 4x + 7$
0	15	7
1	?	?
2	?	?
3	?	?
4	?	?
5	?	?

DRAW CONCLUSIONS Use your observations to complete these exercises

1. When Bill and his brother have the same number of books in their collections, how many books will each of them have?

2. Graph the equations above on the same coordinate plane. What do you notice about the graphs and the solution you found above?

Use a table to solve the linear system.

3. $y = 2x + 3$
$y = -3x + 18$

4. $y = -x + 1$
$y = 2x - 5$

5. $y = -3x + 1$
$y = 5x - 31$

6.1 Solve Linear Systems by Graphing

Before You graphed linear equations.

Now You will graph and solve systems of linear equations.

Why? So you can analyze craft fair sales, as in Ex. 33.

Key Vocabulary
- **system of linear equations**
- **solution of a system of linear equations**
- **consistent independent system**

CC.9-12.A.REI.6 Solve systems of linear equations exactly and approximately (e.g., with graphs), focusing on pairs of linear equations in two variables.

A **system of linear equations,** or simply a *linear system,* consists of two or more linear equations in the same variables. An example is shown below.

$x + 2y = 7$ **Equation 1**

$3x - 2y = 5$ **Equation 2**

A **solution of a system of linear equations** in two variables is an ordered pair that satisfies each equation in the system.

One way to find the solution of a linear system is by graphing. If the lines intersect in a single point, then the coordinates of the point are the solution of the linear system. A solution found using graphical methods should be checked algebraically.

EXAMPLE 1 Check the intersection point

Use the graph to solve the system. Then check your solution algebraically.

$x + 2y = 7$ **Equation 1**

$3x - 2y = 5$ **Equation 2**

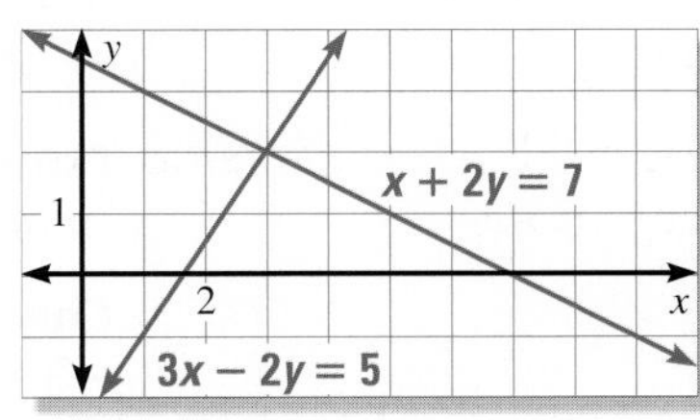

Solution

The lines appear to intersect at the point (3, 2).

CHECK Substitute 3 for x and 2 for y in each equation.

$x + 2y = 7$	$3x - 2y = 5$
$3 + 2(2) \stackrel{?}{=} 7$	$3(3) - 2(2) \stackrel{?}{=} 5$
$7 = 7$ ✓	$5 = 5$ ✓

▶ Because the ordered pair (3, 2) is a solution of each equation, it is a solution of the system.

TYPES OF LINEAR SYSTEMS In Example 1, the linear system has exactly one solution. A linear system that has exactly one solution is called a **consistent independent system** because the lines are distinct (are independent) and intersect (are consistent). You will solve consistent independent systems in this chapter and you will also consider other types of systems.

KEY CONCEPT *For Your Notebook*

Solving a Linear System Using the Graph-and-Check Method

STEP 1 **Graph** both equations in the same coordinate plane. For ease of graphing, you may want to write each equation in slope-intercept form.

STEP 2 **Estimate** the coordinates of the point of intersection.

STEP 3 **Check** the coordinates algebraically by substituting into each equation of the original linear system.

EXAMPLE 2 Use the graph-and-check method

Solve the linear system: $-x + y = -7$ **Equation 1**

$x + 4y = -8$ **Equation 2**

Solution

STEP 1 **Graph** both equations.

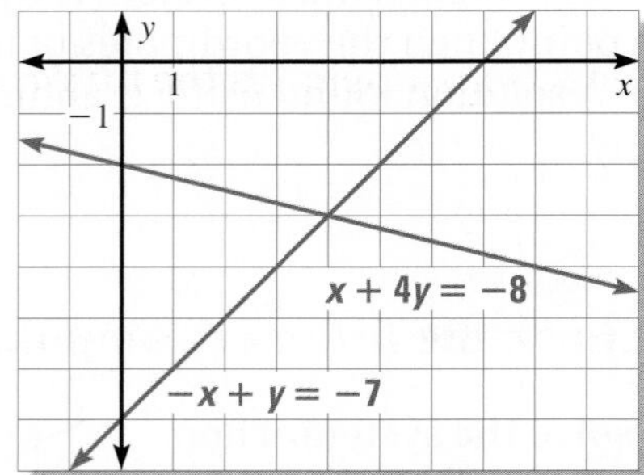

STEP 2 **Estimate** the point of intersection. The two lines appear to intersect at $(4, -3)$.

STEP 3 **Check** whether $(4, -3)$ is a solution by substituting 4 for x and -3 for y in each of the original equations.

Equation 1	**Equation 2**
$-x + y = -7$	$x + 4y = -8$
$-(4) + (-3) \stackrel{?}{=} -7$	$4 + 4(-3) \stackrel{?}{=} -8$
$-7 = -7$ ✓	$-8 = -8$ ✓

▸ Because $(4, -3)$ is a solution of each equation, it is a solution of the linear system.

 at my.hrw.com

GUIDED PRACTICE for Examples 1 and 2

Solve the linear system by graphing. Check your solution.

1. $-5x + y = 0$
$5x + y = 10$

2. $-x + 2y = 3$
$2x + y = 4$

3. $x - y = 5$
$3x + y = 3$

EXAMPLE 3 Standardized Test Practice

The parks and recreation department in your town offers a season pass for $90.

- As a season pass holder, you pay $4 per session to use the town's tennis courts.
- Without the season pass, you pay $13 per session to use the tennis courts.

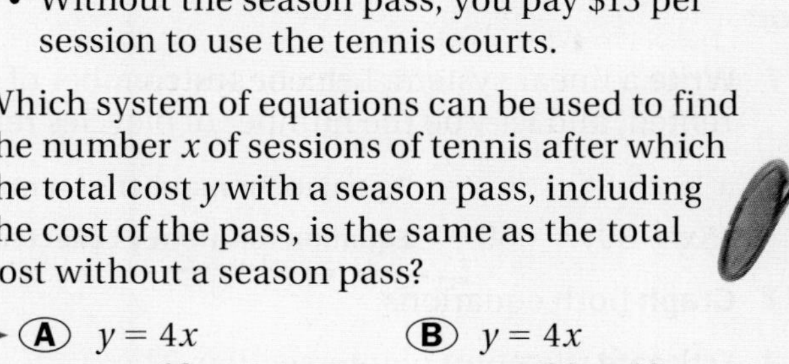

Which system of equations can be used to find the number x of sessions of tennis after which the total cost y with a season pass, including the cost of the pass, is the same as the total cost without a season pass?

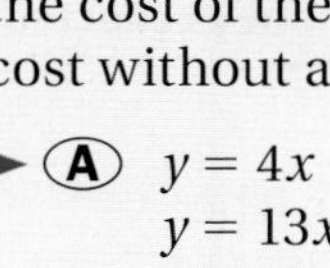

ELIMINATE CHOICES
You can eliminate choice A because neither of the equations include the cost of a season pass.

Ⓐ $y = 4x$
$y = 13x$

Ⓑ $y = 4x$
$y = 90 + 13x$

Ⓒ $y = 13x$
$y = 90 + 4x$

Ⓓ $y = 90 + 4x$
$y = 90 + 13x$

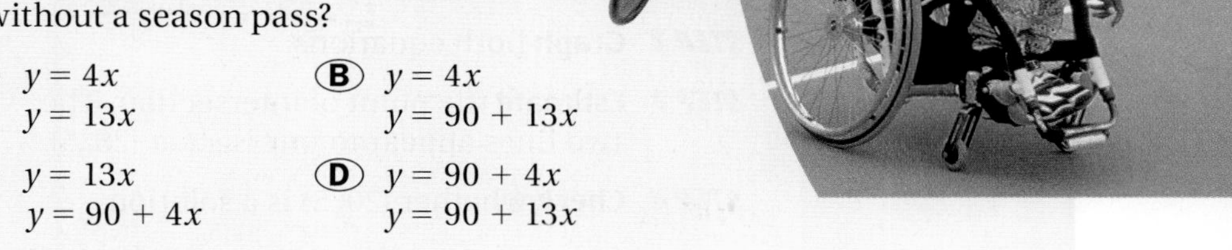

Solution

Write a system of equations where y is the total cost (in dollars) for x sessions.

EQUATION 1

Total cost (dollars)	=	Cost per session (dollars/session)	·	Number of sessions (sessions)
y	=	13	·	x

EQUATION 2

Total cost (dollars)	=	Cost for season pass (dollars)	+	Cost per session (dollars/session)	·	Number of sessions (sessions)
y	=	90	+	4	·	x

▶ The correct answer is C. Ⓐ Ⓑ Ⓒ Ⓓ

✓ GUIDED PRACTICE for Example 3

4. Solve the linear system in Example 3 to find the number of sessions after which the total cost with a season pass, including the cost of the pass, is the same as the total cost without a season pass.

5. **WHAT IF?** In Example 3, suppose a season pass costs $135. After how many sessions is the total cost with a season pass, including the cost of the pass, the same as the total cost without a season pass?

EXAMPLE 4 Solve a multi-step problem

RENTAL BUSINESS A business rents in-line skates and bicycles. During one day, the business has a total of 25 rentals and collects $450 for the rentals. Find the number of pairs of skates rented and the number of bicycles rented.

Solution

STEP 1 **Write** a linear system. Let x be the number of pairs of skates rented, and let y be the number of bicycles rented.

$x + y = 25$ **Equation for number of rentals**

$15x + 30y = 450$ **Equation for money collected from rentals**

STEP 2 **Graph** both equations.

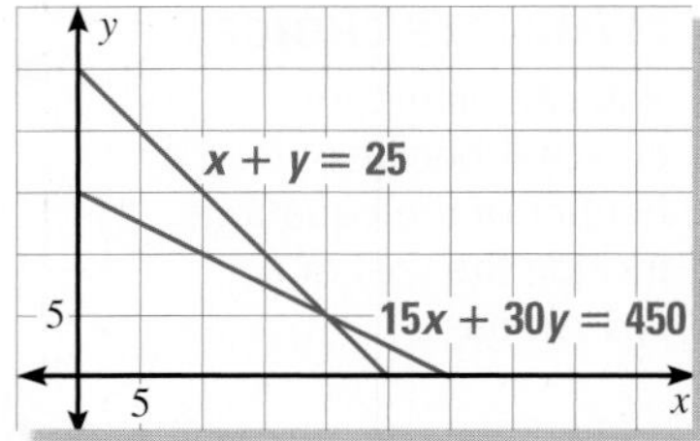

STEP 3 **Estimate** the point of intersection. The two lines appear to intersect at (20, 5).

STEP 4 **Check** whether (20, 5) is a solution.

$20 + 5 \stackrel{?}{=} 25$	$15(20) + 30(5) \stackrel{?}{=} 450$
$25 = 25$ ✓	$450 = 450$ ✓

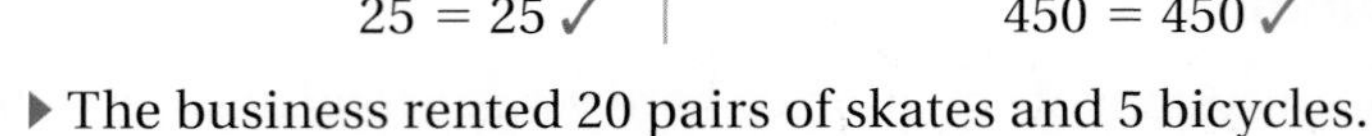

▶ The business rented 20 pairs of skates and 5 bicycles.

✓ **GUIDED PRACTICE** for Example 4

6. **WHAT IF?** In Example 4, suppose the business has a total of 20 rentals and collects $420. Find the number of bicycles rented.

6.1 EXERCISES

HOMEWORK KEY

○ = See **WORKED-OUT SOLUTIONS** Exs. 15 and 31

★ = **STANDARDIZED TEST PRACTICE** Exs. 2, 6, 7, 27, 28, 29, and 32

◆ = **MULTIPLE REPRESENTATIONS** Ex. 35

SKILL PRACTICE

1. **VOCABULARY** Copy and complete: A(n) _?_ of a system of linear equations in two variables is an ordered pair that satisfies each equation in the system.

2. ★ **WRITING** *Explain* how to use the graph-and-check method to solve a linear system of two equations in two variables.

CHECKING SOLUTIONS Tell whether the ordered pair is a solution of the linear system.

3. $(-3, 1)$;
$x + y = -2$
$x + 5y = 2$

4. $(5, 2)$;
$2x - 3y = 4$
$2x + 8y = 11$

5. $(-2, 1)$;
$6x + 5y = -7$
$x - 2y = 0$

EXAMPLE 1
for Exs. 6–11

6. ★ **MULTIPLE CHOICE** Which ordered pair is a solution of the linear system $x + y = -2$ and $7x - 4y = 8$?

Ⓐ $(-2, 0)$ Ⓑ $(0, -2)$ Ⓒ $(2, 0)$ Ⓓ $(0, 2)$

7. ★ **MULTIPLE CHOICE** Which ordered pair is a solution of the linear system $2x + 3y = 12$ and $10x + 3y = -12$?

Ⓐ $(-3, 3)$ Ⓑ $(-3, 6)$ Ⓒ $(3, 3)$ Ⓓ $(3, 6)$

SOLVING SYSTEMS GRAPHICALLY **Use the graph to solve the linear system. Check your solution.**

8. $x - y = 4$
$4x + y = 1$

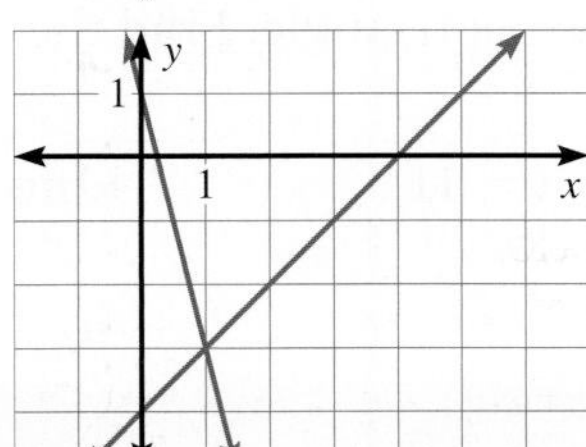

9. $-x + y = -2$
$2x - y = 6$

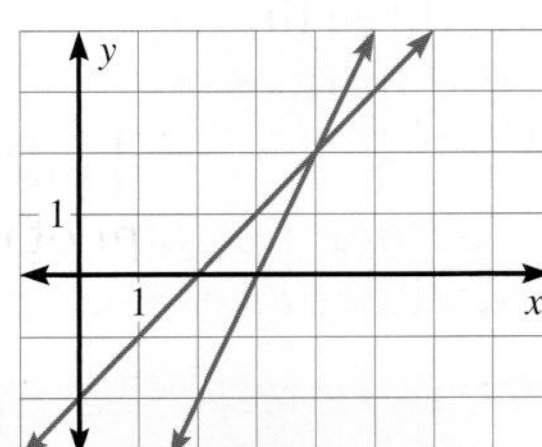

10. $x + y = 5$
$-2x + y = -4$

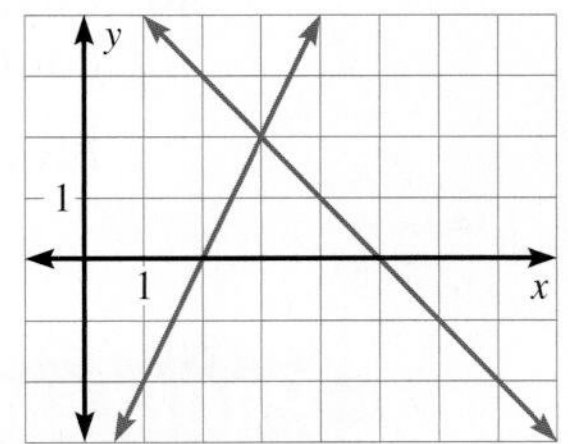

11. **ERROR ANALYSIS** *Describe* and correct the error in solving the linear system below.

$x - 3y = 6$ **Equation 1**
$2x - 3y = 3$ **Equation 2**

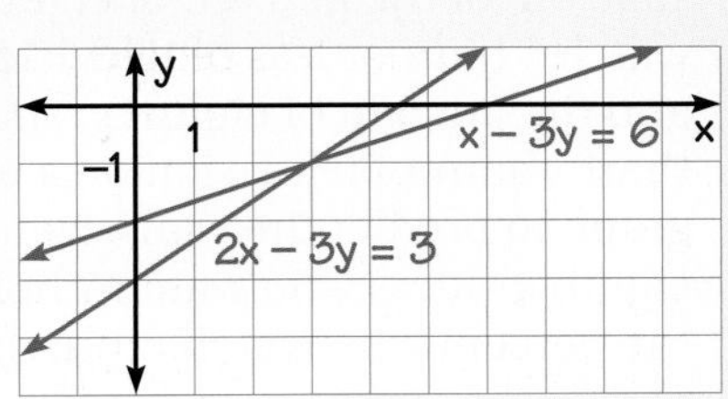

The solution is (3, −1).

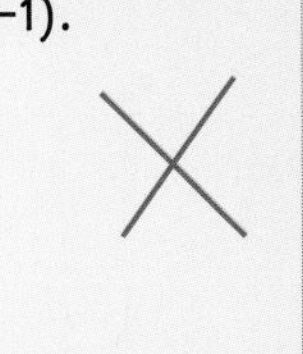

EXAMPLE 2
for Exs. 12–26

GRAPH-AND-CHECK METHOD **Solve the linear system by graphing. Check your solution.**

12. $y = -x + 3$
$y = x + 1$

13. $y = -x + 4$
$y = 2x - 8$

14. $y = 2x + 2$
$y = 4x + 6$

15. $x - y = 2$
$x + y = -8$

16. $x + 2y = 1$
$-2x + y = -4$

17. $3x + y = 15$
$y = -15$

18. $2x - 3y = -1$
$5x + 2y = 26$

19. $6x + y = 37$
$4x + 2y = 18$

20. $7x + 5y = -3$
$-9x + y = -11$

21. $6x + 12y = -6$
$2x + 5y = 0$

22. $2x + y = 9$
$2x + 3y = 15$

23. $-5x + 3y = 3$
$4x + 3y = 30$

24. $\frac{3}{4}x + \frac{1}{4}y = \frac{13}{2}$
$x - \frac{3}{4}y = \frac{13}{2}$

25. $\frac{1}{5}x - \frac{2}{5}y = -\frac{8}{5}$
$-\frac{3}{4}x + y = 3$

26. $-1.6x - 3.2y = -24$
$2.6x + 2.6y = 26$

27. ★ **OPEN-ENDED** Find values for m and b so that the system $y = \frac{3}{5}x - 1$ and $y = mx + b$ has $(5, 2)$ as a solution.

28. ★ **WRITING** Solve the linear system shown by graphing. *Explain* why it is important to check your solution.

$y = 4x - 1.5$ **Equation 1**
$y = -2x + 1.5$ **Equation 2**

29. ★ **EXTENDED RESPONSE** Consider the equation $-\frac{1}{4}x + 6 = \frac{1}{2}x + 3$.

a. Solve the equation using algebra.

b. Solve the linear system below using a graph.

$y = -\frac{1}{4}x + 6$ **Equation 1**

$y = \frac{1}{2}x + 3$ **Equation 2**

c. How is the linear system in part (b) related to the original equation?

d. *Explain* how to use a graph to solve the equation $-\frac{2}{5}x + 5 = \frac{1}{5}x + 2$.

30. **CHALLENGE** The three lines given below form a triangle. Find the coordinates of the vertices of the triangle.

Line 1: $-3x + 2y = 1$ **Line 2:** $2x + y = 11$ **Line 3:** $x + 4y = 9$

PROBLEM SOLVING

EXAMPLES 3 and 4 for Exs. 31–33

31. **TELEVISION** The graph shows a projection, from 1990 on, of the percent of eighth graders who watch 1 hour or less of television on a weekday and the percent of eighth graders who watch more than 1 hour of television on a weekday. Use the graph to predict the year when the percent of eighth graders who watch 1 hour or less will equal the percent who watch more than 1 hour.

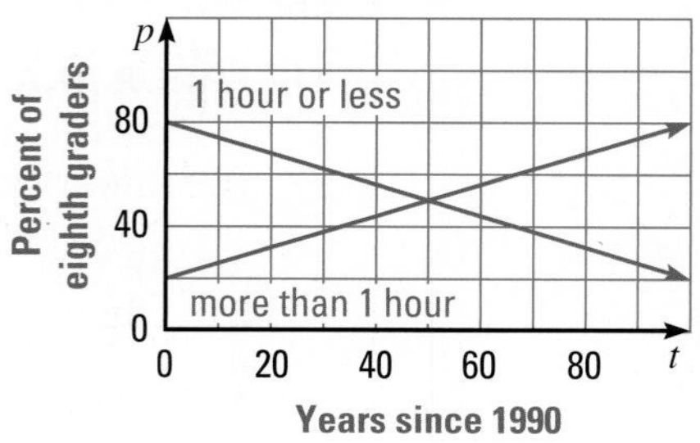

32. ★ **MULTIPLE CHOICE** A car dealership is offering interest-free car loans for one day only. During this day, a salesperson at the dealership sells two cars. One of his clients decides to pay off his \$17,424 car in 36 monthly payments of \$484. His other client decides to pay off his \$15,840 car in 48 monthly payments of \$330. Which system of equations can be used to determine the number x of months after which both clients will have the same loan balance y?

Ⓐ $y = -484x$
$y = -330x$

Ⓑ $y = -484x + 17{,}424$
$y = -330x + 15{,}840$

Ⓒ $y = -484x + 15{,}840$
$y = -330x + 17{,}424$

Ⓓ $y = 484x + 17{,}424$
$y = 330x + 15{,}840$

33. **CRAFTS** Kirigami is the Japanese art of making paper designs by folding and cutting paper. A student sells small and large greeting cards decorated with kirigami at a craft fair. The small cards cost \$3 per card, and the large cards cost \$5 per card. The student collects \$95 for selling a total of 25 cards. How many of each type of card did the student sell?

34. FITNESS You want to burn 225 calories while exercising at a gym. The number of calories that you burn per minute on different machines at the gym is shown below.

Stair machine	*Elliptical trainer*	*Stationary bike*
You burn 5 Cal/min.	You burn 8 Cal/min.	You burn 6 Cal/min.

a. Suppose you have 40 minutes to exercise at the gym and you want to use the stair machine and stationary bike. How many minutes should you spend on each machine so that you burn 225 calories?

b. Suppose you have 30 minutes to exercise at the gym and you want to use the stair machine and the elliptical trainer. How many minutes should you spend on each machine so that you burn 225 calories?

35. MULTIPLE REPRESENTATIONS It costs \$15 for a yearly membership to a movie club at a movie theater. A movie ticket costs \$5 for club members and \$8 for nonmembers.

a. Writing a System of Equations Write a system of equations that you can use to find the number x of movies viewed after which the total cost y for a club member, including the membership fee, is the same as the cost for a nonmember.

b. Making a Table Make a table of values that shows the total cost for a club member and a nonmember after paying to see 1, 2, 3, 4, 5, and 6 movies.

c. Drawing a Graph Use the table to graph the system of equations. Under what circumstances does it make sense to become a movie club member? *Explain* your answer by using the graph.

36. CHALLENGE With a minimum purchase of \$25, you can open a credit account with a clothing store. The store is offering either \$25 or 20% off of your purchase if you open a credit account. You decide to open a credit account. Should you choose \$25 or 20% off of your purchase? *Explain.*

Solving Linear Systems by Graphing

MATHEMATICAL PRACTICES

Use appropriate tools strategically.

QUESTION How can you use a graphing calculator to solve a linear system?

EXAMPLE Solve a linear system

Solve the linear system using a graphing calculator.

$5x + 2y = 6$ **Equation 1**

$x - 3y = -5$ **Equation 2**

STEP 1 Rewrite equations

Solve each equation for y.

Equation 1	Equation 2
$5x + 2y = 6$	$x - 3y = -5$
$2y = -5x + 6$	$-3y = -x - 5$
$y = -\frac{5}{2}x + 3$	$y = \frac{1}{3}x + \frac{5}{3}$

STEP 2 Enter equations

Press Y= and enter the equations.

STEP 3 Display graph

Graph the equations using a standard viewing window.

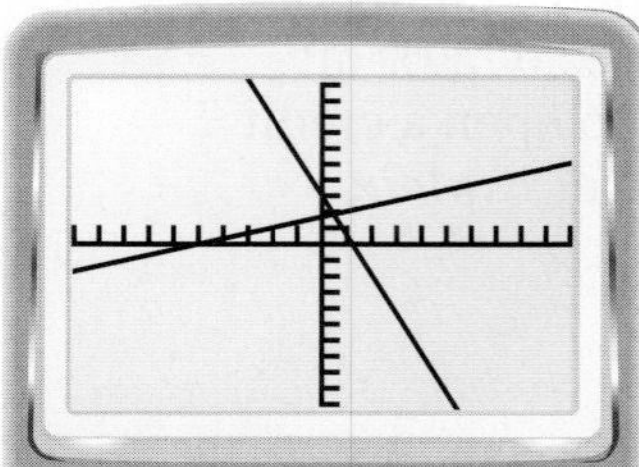

STEP 4 Find point of intersection

Use the *intersect* feature to find the point where the graphs intersect.

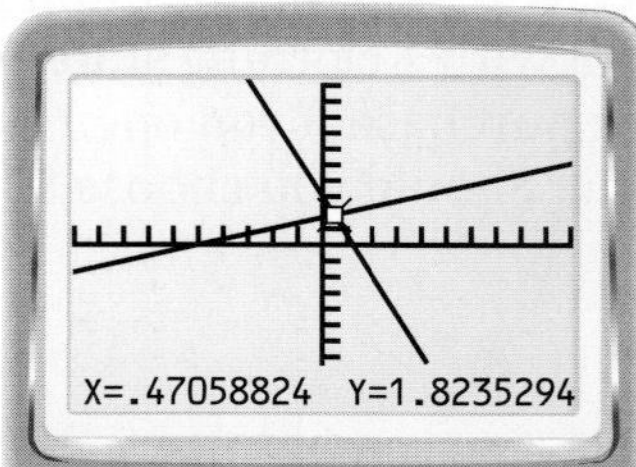

The solution is about (0.47, 1.8).

PRACTICE

Solve the linear system using a graphing calculator.

1. $y = x + 4$
   $y = -3x - 2$
2. $5x + y = -4$
   $x - y = -2$
3. $-0.45x - y = 1.35$
   $-1.8x + y = -1.8$
4. $-0.4x + 0.8y = -16$
   $1.2x + 0.4y = 1$

6.2 Solve Linear Systems by Substitution

Before You solved systems of linear equations by graphing.

Now You will solve systems of linear equations by substitution.

Why? So you can find tubing costs, as in Ex. 32.

Key Vocabulary
- **system of linear equations**

CC.9-12.A.REI.6 Solve systems of linear equations exactly and approximately (e.g., with graphs), focusing on pairs of linear equations in two variables.

KEY CONCEPT — *For Your Notebook*

Solving a Linear System Using the Substitution Method

STEP 1 **Solve** one of the equations for one of its variables. When possible, solve for a variable that has a coefficient of 1 or −1.

STEP 2 **Substitute** the expression from Step 1 into the other equation and solve for the other variable.

STEP 3 **Substitute** the value from Step 2 into the revised equation from Step 1 and solve.

EXAMPLE 1 Use the substitution method

Solve the linear system: $y = 3x + 2$ **Equation 1**
$x + 2y = 11$ **Equation 2**

Solution

STEP 1 **Solve** for y. Equation 1 is already solved for y.

STEP 2 **Substitute** $3x + 2$ for y in Equation 2 and solve for x.

$x + 2y = 11$ **Write Equation 2.**

$x + 2(3x + 2) = 11$ **Substitute 3x + 2 for y.**

$7x + 4 = 11$ **Simplify.**

$7x = 7$ **Subtract 4 from each side.**

$x = 1$ **Divide each side by 7.**

STEP 3 **Substitute** 1 for x in the original Equation 1 to find the value of y.

$y = 3x + 2 = 3(1) + 2 = 3 + 2 = 5$

▶ The solution is (1, 5).

CHECK Substitute 1 for x and 5 for y in each of the original equations.

$y = 3x + 2$	$x + 2y = 11$
$5 \stackrel{?}{=} 3(1) + 2$	$1 + 2(5) \stackrel{?}{=} 11$
$5 = 5$ ✓	$11 = 11$ ✓

Animated Algebra at my.hrw.com

EXAMPLE 2 Use the substitution method

Solve the linear system: $x - 2y = -6$ **Equation 1**
$4x + 6y = 4$ **Equation 2**

CHOOSE AN EQUATION
Equation 1 was chosen in Step 1 because x has a coefficient of 1. So, only one step is needed to solve Equation 1 for x.

Solution

STEP 1 **Solve** Equation 1 for x.

$x - 2y = -6$ **Write original Equation 1.**

$x = 2y - 6$ **Revised Equation 1**

STEP 2 **Substitute** $2y - 6$ for x in Equation 2 and solve for y.

$4x + 6y = 4$ **Write Equation 2.**

$4(2y - 6) + 6y = 4$ **Substitute $2y - 6$ for x.**

$8y - 24 + 6y = 4$ **Distributive property**

$14y - 24 = 4$ **Simplify.**

$14y = 28$ **Add 24 to each side.**

$y = 2$ **Divide each side by 14.**

STEP 3 **Substitute** 2 for y in the revised Equation 1 to find the value of x.

$x = 2y - 6$ **Revised Equation 1**

$x = 2(2) - 6$ **Substitute 2 for y.**

$x = -2$ **Simplify.**

▶ The solution is $(-2, 2)$.

CHECK Substitute -2 for x and 2 for y in each of the original equations.

Equation 1	**Equation 2**
$x - 2y = -6$	$4x + 6y = 4$
$-2 - 2(2) \stackrel{?}{=} -6$	$4(-2) + 6(2) \stackrel{?}{=} 4$
$-6 = -6$ ✓	$4 = 4$ ✓

CHECK REASONABLENESS When solving a linear system using the substitution method, you can use a graph to check the reasonableness of your solution. For example, the graph at the right verifies that $(-2, 2)$ is a solution of the linear system in Example 2.

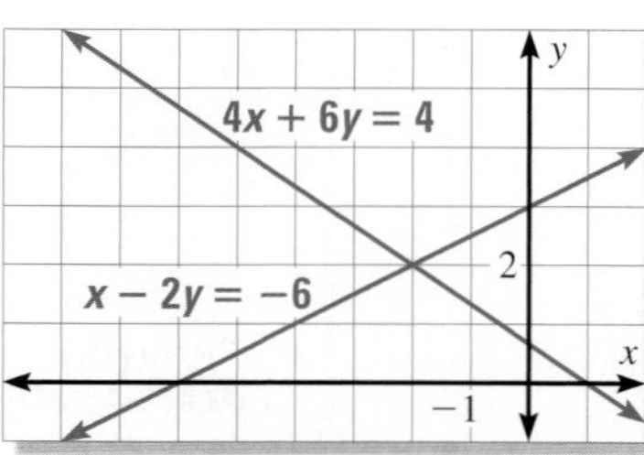

GUIDED PRACTICE for Examples 1 and 2

Solve the linear system using the substitution method.

1. $y = 2x + 5$
   $3x + y = 10$

2. $x - y = 3$
   $x + 2y = -6$

3. $3x + y = -7$
   $-2x + 4y = 0$

EXAMPLE 3 Solve a multi-step problem

ANOTHER WAY
For an alternative method for solving the problem in Example 3, see the **Problem Solving Workshop**.

WEBSITES Many businesses pay website hosting companies to store and maintain the computer files that make up their websites. Internet service providers also offer website hosting. The costs for website hosting offered by a website hosting company and an Internet service provider are shown in the table. Find the number of months after which the total cost for website hosting will be the same for both companies.

Company	Set-up fee (dollars)	Cost per month (dollars)
Internet service provider	10	21.95
Website hosting company	None	22.45

Solution

STEP 1 **Write** a system of equations. Let y be the total cost after x months.

Equation 1: Internet service provider

Total cost	=	Set-up fee	+	Cost per month	·	Number of months
y	=	**10**	+	**21.95**	·	x

Equation 2: Website hosting company

Total cost	=	Cost per month	·	Number of months
y	=	**22.45**	·	x

The system of equations is: $y = 10 + 21.95x$ **Equation 1**

$y = 22.45x$ **Equation 2**

STEP 2 **Substitute** $22.45x$ for y in Equation 1 and solve for x.

$y = 10 + 21.95x$ **Write Equation 1.**

$22.45x = 10 + 21.95x$ **Substitute 22.45*x* for *y*.**

$0.5x = 10$ **Subtract 21.95*x* from each side.**

$x = 20$ **Divide each side by 0.5.**

▶ The total cost will be the same for both companies after 20 months.

✓ GUIDED PRACTICE for Example 3

4. In Example 3, what is the total cost for website hosting for each company after 20 months?

5. **WHAT IF?** In Example 3, suppose the Internet service provider offers $5 off the set-up fee. After how many months will the total cost for website hosting be the same for both companies?

EXAMPLE 4 Solve a mixture problem

ANTIFREEZE For extremely cold temperatures, an automobile manufacturer recommends that a 70% antifreeze and 30% water mix be used in the cooling system of a car. How many quarts of pure (100%) antifreeze and a 50% antifreeze and 50% water mix should be combined to make 11 quarts of a 70% antifreeze and 30% water mix?

Solution

STEP 1 **Write** an equation for the total number of quarts and an equation for the number of quarts of antifreeze. Let x be the number of quarts of 100% antifreeze, and let y be the number of quarts of a 50% antifreeze and 50% water mix.

Equation 1: Total number of quarts

$x + y = 11$

Equation 2: Number of quarts of antifreeze

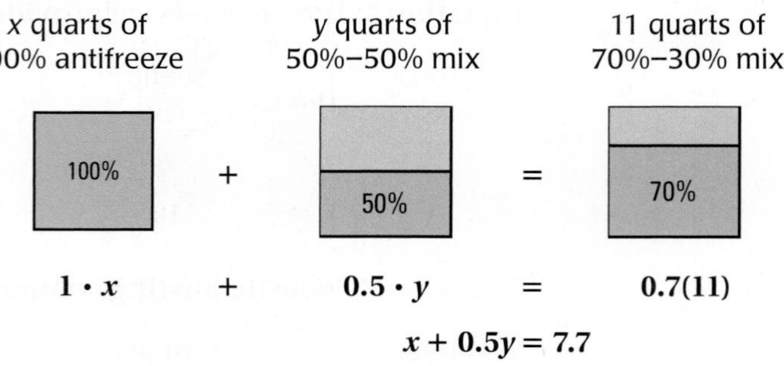

DRAW A DIAGRAM Each bar shows the liquid in each mix. The green portion shows the percent of the mix that is antifreeze.

$$1 \cdot x \quad + \quad 0.5 \cdot y \quad = \quad 0.7(11)$$

$$x + 0.5y = 7.7$$

The system of equations is: $x + y = 11$ **Equation 1**

$x + 0.5y = 7.7$ **Equation 2**

STEP 2 **Solve** Equation 1 for x.

$x + y = 11$ **Write Equation 1.**

$x = 11 - y$ **Revised Equation 1**

STEP 3 **Substitute** $11 - y$ for x in Equation 2 and solve for y.

$x + 0.5y = 7.7$ **Write Equation 2.**

$(11 - y) + 0.5y = 7.7$ **Substitute $11 - y$ for x.**

$y = 6.6$ **Solve for y.**

STEP 4 **Substitute** 6.6 for y in the revised Equation 1 to find the value of x.

$x = 11 - y = 11 - \mathbf{6.6} = 4.4$

▶ Mix 4.4 quarts of 100% antifreeze and 6.6 quarts of a 50% antifreeze and 50% water mix to get 11 quarts of a 70% antifreeze and 30% water mix.

GUIDED PRACTICE for Example 4

6. **WHAT IF?** How many quarts of 100% antifreeze and a 50% antifreeze and 50% water mix should be combined to make 16 quarts of a 70% antifreeze and 30% water mix?

6.2 EXERCISES

HOMEWORK KEY

○ = See WORKED-OUT SOLUTIONS Exs. 13 and 33

★ = STANDARDIZED TEST PRACTICE Exs. 2, 18, 29, 33, and 37

SKILL PRACTICE

1. **VOCABULARY** Give an example of a system of linear equations.

2. ★ **WRITING** If you are solving the linear system shown using the substitution method, which equation would you solve for which variable? *Explain.*

   $2x - 3y = 24$ **Equation 1**
   $2x + y = 8$ **Equation 2**

EXAMPLE 1 for Exs. 3–8

SOLVING LINEAR SYSTEMS **Solve the linear system using substitution.**

3. $x = 17 - 4y$
   $y = x - 2$

4. $y = 2x - 1$
   $2x + y = 3$

5. $x = y + 3$
   $2x - y = 5$

6. $4x - 7y = 10$
   $y = x - 7$

7. $x = 16 - 4y$
   $3x + 4y = 8$

8. $-5x + 3y = 51$
   $y = 10x - 8$

EXAMPLE 2 for Exs. 9–19

9. $2x = 12$
   $x - 5y = -29$

10. $2x - y = 23$
    $x - 9 = -1$

11. $x + y = 0$
    $x - 2y = 6$

12. $2x + y = 9$
    $4x - y = -15$

13. $5x + 2y = 9$
    $x + y = -3$

14. $5x + 4y = 32$
    $9x - y = 33$

15. $11x - 7y = -14$
    $x - 2y = -4$

16. $20x - 30y = -50$
    $x + 2y = 1$

17. $6x + y = 4$
    $x - 4y = 19$

18. ★ **MULTIPLE CHOICE** Which ordered pair is a solution of the linear system $4x - y = 17$ and $-9x + 8y = 2$?

    Ⓐ (6, 7) Ⓑ (7, 6) Ⓒ (7, 11) Ⓓ (11, 7)

19. **ERROR ANALYSIS** *Describe* and correct the error in solving the linear system $4x + 2y = 6$ and $3x + y = 9$.

Step 1	Step 2	Step 3	The solution is (6, 1).
$3x + y = 9$ $y = 9 - 3x$	$4x + 2(9 - 3x) = 6$ $4x + 18 - 6x = 6$ $-2x = -12$ $x = 6$	$y = 9 - 3x$ $6 = 9 - 3x$ $-3 = -3x$ $1 = x$	✗

SOLVING LINEAR SYSTEMS **Solve the linear system using substitution.**

20. $4.5x + 1.5y = 24$
    $x - y = 4$

21. $35x + y = 20$
    $1.5x - 0.1y = 18$

22. $3x - 2y = 8$
    $0.5x + y = 17$

23. $0.5x + 0.6y = 5.7$
    $2x - y = -1$

24. $x - 9 = 0.5y$
    $2.2x - 3.1y = -0.2$

25. $0.2x + y = -1.8$
    $1.8y + 5.5x = 27.6$

26. $\frac{1}{2}x + \frac{1}{4}y = 5$
    $x - \frac{1}{2}y = 1$

27. $x + \frac{1}{3}y = -2$
    $-8x - \frac{2}{3}y = 4$

28. $\frac{3}{8}x + \frac{3}{4}y = 12$
    $\frac{2}{3}x + \frac{1}{2}y = 13$

29. ★ **WRITING** Suppose you solve a linear system using substitution. *Explain* how you can use a graph to check your solution.

30. **CHALLENGE** Find values of a and b so that the linear system shown has a solution of $(-9, 4)$.

$ax + by = -16$ **Equation 1**

$ax - by = -56$ **Equation 2**

PROBLEM SOLVING

EXAMPLE 3 for Exs. 31–33

31. **FUNDRAISING** During a football game, the parents of the football players sell pretzels and popcorn to raise money for new uniforms. They charge \$2.50 for a bag of popcorn and \$2 for a pretzel. The parents collect \$336 in sales during the game. They sell twice as many bags of popcorn as pretzels. How many bags of popcorn do they sell? How many pretzels do they sell?

32. **TUBING COSTS** A group of friends takes a day-long tubing trip down a river. The company that offers the tubing trip charges \$15 to rent a tube for a person to use and \$7.50 to rent a "cooler" tube, which is used to carry food and water in a cooler. The friends spend \$360 to rent a total of 26 tubes. How many of each type of tube do they rent?

33. ★ **SHORT RESPONSE** In the mobile shown, objects are attached to each end of a dowel. For the dowel to balance, the following must be true:

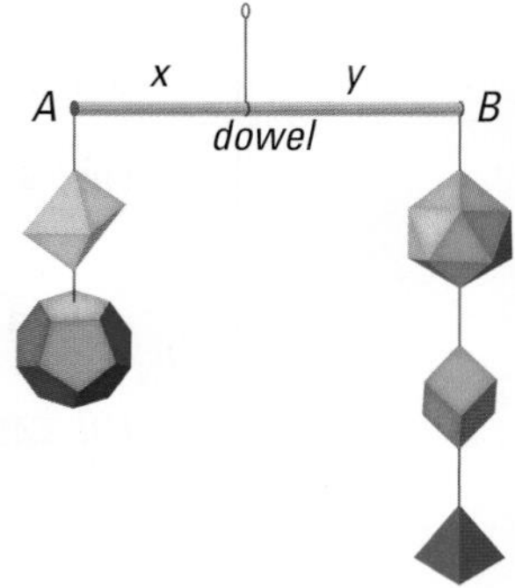

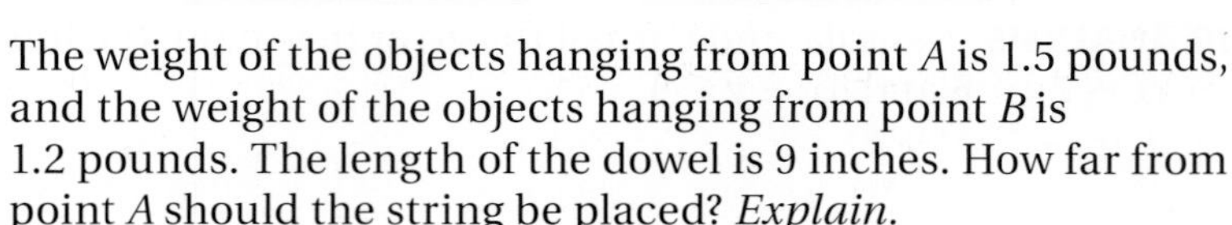

$x \cdot$ Weight hanging from point A $= y \cdot$ Weight hanging from point B

The weight of the objects hanging from point A is 1.5 pounds, and the weight of the objects hanging from point B is 1.2 pounds. The length of the dowel is 9 inches. How far from point A should the string be placed? *Explain.*

34. **MULTI-STEP PROBLEM** Two swimming teams are competing in a 400 meter medley relay. During the last leg of the race, the swimmer in lane 1 has a 1.2 second head start on the swimmer in lane 2, as shown.

a. Let t be the time since the swimmer in lane 2 started the last leg. After how many seconds into the leg will the swimmer in lane 2 catch up to the swimmer in lane 1?

b. Does the swimmer in lane 2 catch up to the swimmer in lane 1 before the race ends? *Explain.*

○ = See **WORKED-OUT SOLUTIONS** in Student Resources   ★ = **STANDARDIZED TEST PRACTICE**

EXAMPLE 4
for Ex. 35

35. CHEMISTRY In your chemistry lab, you have a bottle of 1% hydrochloric acid solution and a bottle of 5% hydrochloric acid solution. You need 100 milliliters of a 3% hydrochloric acid solution for an experiment. How many milliliters of each solution do you need to mix together?

36. MONEY Laura has \$4.50 in dimes and quarters. She has 3 more dimes than quarters. How many quarters does she have?

37. ★ SHORT RESPONSE A gazelle can run 73 feet per second for several minutes. A cheetah can run 88 feet per second, but it can sustain this speed for only 20 seconds. A gazelle is 350 feet from a cheetah when both animals start running. Can the gazelle stay ahead of the cheetah? *Explain.*

Animated Algebra at my.hrw.com

38. CHALLENGE A gardener needs 6 bushels of a potting medium of 40% peat moss and 60% vermiculite. He decides to add 100% vermiculite to his current potting medium that is 50% peat moss and 50% vermiculite. The gardener has 5 bushels of the 50% peat moss and 50% vermiculite mix. Does he have enough of the 50% peat moss and 50% vermiculite mix to make 6 bushels of the 40% peat moss and 60% vermiculite mix? *Explain.*

QUIZ

Solve the linear system by graphing. Check your solution.

1. $x + y = -2$
$-x + y = 6$

2. $x - y = 0$
$5x + 2y = -7$

3. $x - 2y = 12$
$-3x + y = -1$

Solve the linear system using substitution.

4. $y = x - 4$
$-2x + y = 18$

5. $y = 4 - 3x$
$5x - y = 22$

6. $x = y + 9$
$5x - 3y = 7$

7. $2y + x = -4$
$y - x = -5$

8. $5x - 4y = 27$
$-2x + y = 3$

9. $3x - 5y = 13$
$x + 4y = 10$

PROBLEM SOLVING WORKSHOP
LESSON 6.2

Using ALTERNATIVE METHODS

Another Way to Solve Example 3

MATHEMATICAL PRACTICES

Make sense of problems and persevere in solving them.

MULTIPLE REPRESENTATIONS In Example 3, you saw how to solve the problem about website hosting by solving a linear system algebraically. You can also solve the problem using a table.

PROBLEM

WEBSITES Many businesses pay website hosting companies to store and maintain the computer files that make up their websites. Internet service providers also offer website hosting. The costs for website hosting offered by a website hosting company and an Internet service provider are shown in the table. Find the number of months after which the total cost for website hosting will be the same for both companies.

Company	Set-up fee	Cost per month
Internet service provider	\$10	\$21.95
Website hosting company	None	\$22.45

METHOD

Making a Table An alternative approach is to make a table.

STEP 1 **Make** a table for the total cost of website hosting for both companies.

Include the set-up fee in the cost for the first month.

STEP 2 **Look** for the month in which the total cost of the service from the Internet service provider and the website hosting company is the same. This happens after 20 months.

Months	Internet service provider	Website hosting company
1	\$31.95	\$22.45
2	\$53.90	\$44.90
3	\$75.85	\$67.35
⋮	⋮	⋮
19	\$427.05	\$426.55
20	\$449.00	\$449.00
21	\$470.95	\$471.45

PRACTICE

1. **TAXIS** A taxi company charges \$2.80 for the first mile and \$1.60 for each additional mile. Another taxi company charges \$3.20 for the first mile and \$1.50 for each additional mile. After how many miles will each taxi cost the same? Use a table to solve the problem.

2. **SCHOOL PLAY** An adult ticket to a school play costs \$5 and a student ticket costs \$3. A total of \$460 was collected from the sale of 120 tickets. How many student tickets were purchased? Solve the problem using algebra. Then use a table to check your answer.

Investigating Algebra ACTIVITY *Use before Solve Linear Systems by Adding or Subtracting*

Linear Systems and Elimination

MATERIALS • algebra tiles

Use appropriate tools strategically.

QUESTION **How can you solve a linear system using algebra tiles?**

You can use the following algebra tiles to model equations.

1-tiles	**x-tiles**	**y-tiles**

EXPLORE **Solve a linear system using algebra tiles.**

Solve the linear system: $3x - y = 5$ **Equation 1**
$x + y = 3$ **Equation 2**

STEP 1 ***Model equations***

Model each equation using algebra tiles. Arrange the algebra tiles so that one equation is directly below the other equation.

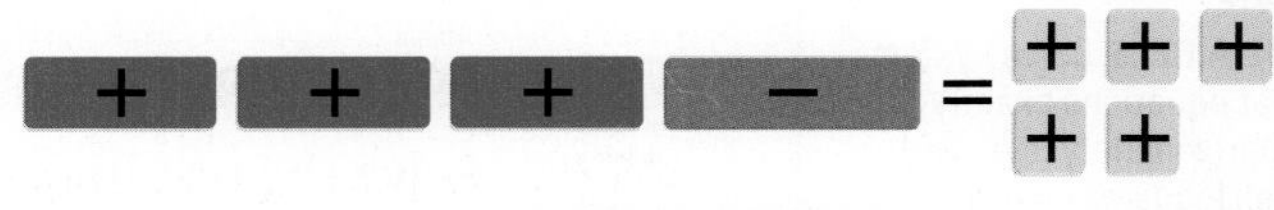

STEP 2 ***Add equations***

Combine the two equations to form one equation. Notice that the new equation has one positive y-tile and one negative y-tile. The y-tiles can be removed because the pair of y-tiles has a value of 0.

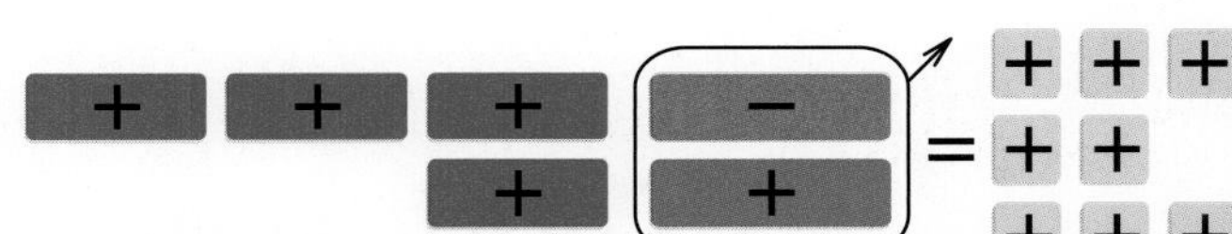

STEP 3 ***Solve for x***

Divide the remaining tiles into four equal groups. Each x-tile is equal to two 1-tiles. So, $x = 2$.

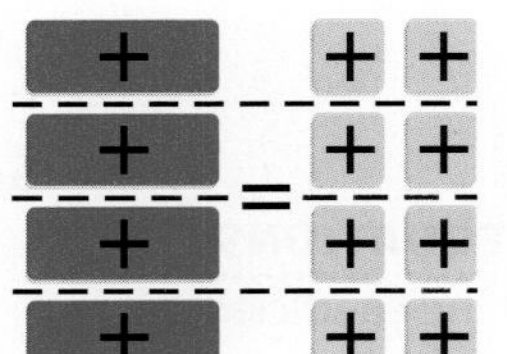

STEP 4 ***Solve for y***

To find the value of y, use the model for Equation 2. Because $x = 2$, you can replace the x-tile with two 1-tiles. Solve the new equation for y. So $y = 1$, and the solution of the system is (2, 1).

DRAW CONCLUSIONS **Use your observations to complete these exercises**

Use algebra tiles to model and solve the linear system.

1. $x + 3y = 8$
$4x - 3y = 2$

2. $2x + y = 5$
$-2x + 3y = 7$

3. $5x - 2y = -2$
$x + 2y = 14$

4. $x + 2y = 3$
$-x + 3y = 2$

5. **REASONING** Is it possible to solve the linear system $3x - 2y = 6$ and $2x + y = 11$ using the steps shown above? *Explain* your reasoning.

6.3 Solve Linear Systems by Adding or Subtracting

Before You solved linear systems by graphing and using substitution.

Now You will solve linear systems using elimination.

Why? So you can solve a problem about arranging flowers, as in Ex. 42.

Key Vocabulary
- **system of linear equations**

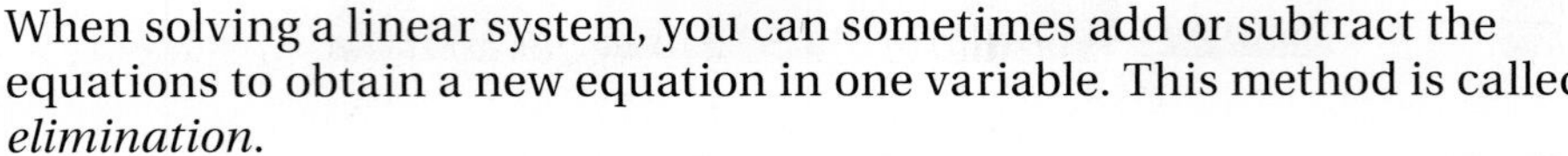

When solving a linear system, you can sometimes add or subtract the equations to obtain a new equation in one variable. This method is called *elimination.*

CC.9-12.A.REI.6 Solve systems of linear equations exactly and approximately (e.g., with graphs), focusing on pairs of linear equations in two variables.

KEY CONCEPT *For Your Notebook*

Solving a Linear System Using the Elimination Method

STEP 1 **Add or subtract** the equations to eliminate one variable.

STEP 2 **Solve** the resulting equation for the other variable.

STEP 3 **Substitute** in either original equation to find the value of the eliminated variable.

EXAMPLE 1 Use addition to eliminate a variable

Solve the linear system: $2x + 3y = 11$ **Equation 1**
$-2x + 5y = 13$ **Equation 2**

Solution

ADD EQUATIONS When the coefficients of one variable are opposites, add the equations to eliminate the variable.

STEP 1 **Add** the equations to eliminate one variable.

$$\begin{array}{r} 2x + 3y = 11 \\ -2x + 5y = 13 \\ \hline \end{array}$$

STEP 2 **Solve** for y.

$$8y = 24$$

$$y = 3$$

STEP 3 **Substitute** 3 for y in either equation and solve for x.

$2x + 3y = 11$ **Write Equation 1.**

$2x + 3(3) = 11$ **Substitute 3 for *y*.**

$x = 1$ **Solve for *x*.**

▶ The solution is (1, 3).

CHECK Substitute 1 for x and 3 for y in each of the original equations.

$2x + 3y = 11$	$-2x + 5y = 13$
$2(1) + 3(3) \stackrel{?}{=} 11$	$-2(1) + 5(3) \stackrel{?}{=} 13$
$11 = 11$ ✓	$13 = 13$ ✓

EXAMPLE 2 Use subtraction to eliminate a variable

Solve the linear system: $4x + 3y = 2$ **Equation 1**
$5x + 3y = -2$ **Equation 2**

SUBTRACT EQUATIONS
When the coefficients of one variable are the same, subtract the equations to eliminate the variable.

Solution

STEP 1 **Subtract** the equations to eliminate one variable.

$$\begin{array}{r} 4x + 3y = 2 \\ 5x + 3y = -2 \\ \hline -x \quad\quad = 4 \end{array}$$

STEP 2 **Solve** for x.

$$x = -4$$

STEP 3 **Substitute** -4 for x in either equation and solve for y.

$4x + 3y = 2$ **Write Equation 1.**

$4(-4) + 3y = 2$ **Substitute −4 for *x*.**

$y = 6$ **Solve for *y*.**

▶ The solution is $(-4, 6)$.

EXAMPLE 3 Arrange like terms

Solve the linear system: $8x - 4y = -4$ **Equation 1**
$4y = 3x + 14$ **Equation 2**

AVOID ERRORS
Make sure that the equal signs are in the same column, just as the like terms are.

Solution

STEP 1 **Rewrite** Equation 2 so that the like terms are arranged in columns.

$8x - 4y = -4$
$4y = 3x + 14$
→
$$\begin{array}{r} 8x - 4y = -4 \\ -3x + 4y = 14 \\ \hline 5x \quad\quad = 10 \end{array}$$

STEP 2 **Add** the equations.

STEP 3 **Solve** for x.

$$x = 2$$

STEP 4 **Substitute** 2 for x in either equation and solve for y.

$4y = 3x + 14$ **Write Equation 2.**

$4y = 3(2) + 14$ **Substitute 2 for *x*.**

$y = 5$ **Solve for *y*.**

▶ The solution is $(2, 5)$.

✓ GUIDED PRACTICE for Examples 1, 2, and 3

Solve the linear system.

1. $4x - 3y = 5$
$-2x + 3y = -7$

2. $-5x - 6y = 8$
$5x + 2y = 4$

3. $6x - 4y = 14$
$-3x + 4y = 1$

4. $7x - 2y = 5$
$7x - 3y = 4$

5. $3x + 4y = -6$
$2y = 3x + 6$

6. $2x + 5y = 12$
$5y = 4x + 6$

EXAMPLE 4 Write and solve a linear system

KAYAKING During a kayaking trip, a kayaker travels 12 miles upstream (against the current) and 12 miles downstream (with the current), as shown. The speed of the current remained constant during the trip. Find the average speed of the kayak in still water and the speed of the current.

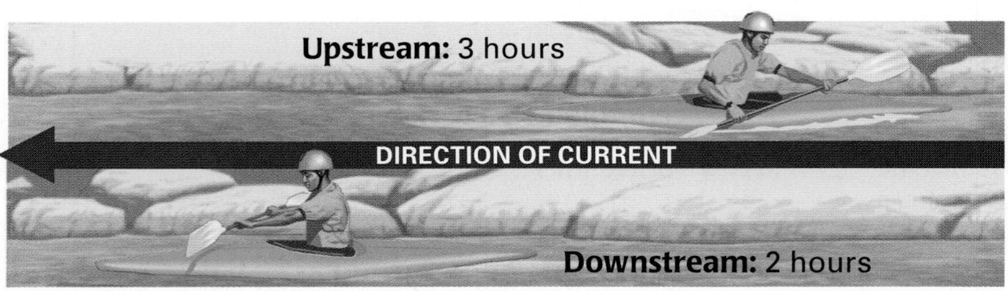

STEP 1 **Write** a system of equations. First find the speed of the kayak going upstream and the speed of the kayak going downstream.

Upstream: $d = rt$ **Downstream:** $d = rt$

$12 = r \cdot 3$ $\qquad 12 = r \cdot 2$

$4 = r$ $\qquad 6 = r$

Use the speeds to write a linear system. Let x be the average speed of the kayak in still water, and let y be the speed of the current.

COMBINE SPEEDS
When you go upstream, the speed at which you can travel in still water is decreased by the speed of the current. The opposite is true when you go downstream.

Equation 1: Going upstream

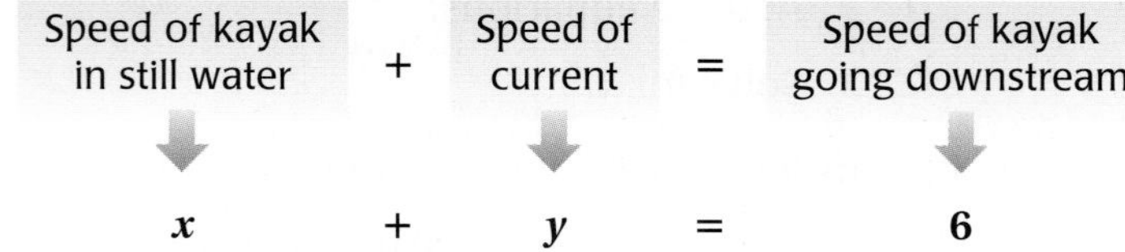

$x \quad - \quad y \quad = \quad 4$

Equation 2: Going downstream

Speed of kayak in still water + Speed of current = Speed of kayak going downstream

$x \quad + \quad y \quad = \quad 6$

STEP 2 **Solve** the system of equations.

$x - y = 4$ **Write Equation 1.**

$x + y = 6$ **Write Equation 2.**

$2x = 10$ **Add equations.**

$x = 5$ **Solve for *x*.**

Substitute 5 for x in Equation 2 and solve for y.

$5 + y = 6$ **Substitute 5 for *x* in Equation 2.**

$y = 1$ **Subtract 5 from each side.**

▶ The average speed of the kayak in still water is 5 miles per hour, and the speed of the current is 1 mile per hour.

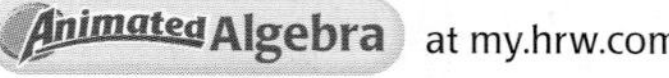 at my.hrw.com

 **GUIDED PRACTICE** for Example 4

7. **WHAT IF?** In Example 4, suppose it takes the kayaker 5 hours to travel 10 miles upstream and 2 hours to travel 10 miles downstream. The speed of the current remains constant during the trip. Find the average speed of the kayak in still water and the speed of the current.

6.3 EXERCISES

HOMEWORK KEY

○ = **See WORKED-OUT SOLUTIONS** Exs. 17 and 41

★ = **STANDARDIZED TEST PRACTICE** Exs. 2, 15, 22, 36, and 44

◆ = **MULTIPLE REPRESENTATIONS** Ex. 42

SKILL PRACTICE

1. **VOCABULARY** Give an example of a linear system in two variables that can be solved by first adding the equations to eliminate one variable.

2. ★ **WRITING** *Explain* how to solve the linear system shown using the elimination method.

$2x - y = 2$ **Equation 1**

$2x + 3y = 22$ **Equation 2**

EXAMPLE 1 for Exs. 3–8

USING ADDITION **Solve the linear system using elimination.**

3. $x + 2y = 13$
   $-x + y = 5$

4. $9x + y = 2$
   $-4x - y = -17$

5. $-3x - y = 8$
   $7x + y = -12$

6. $3x - y = 30$
   $-3x + 7y = 6$

7. $-9x + 4y = -17$
   $9x - 6y = 3$

8. $-3x - 5y = -7$
   $-4x + 5y = 14$

EXAMPLE 2 for Exs. 9–15

USING SUBTRACTION **Solve the linear system using elimination.**

9. $x + y = 1$
   $-2x + y = 4$

10. $x - y = -4$
    $x + 3y = 4$

11. $2x - y = 7$
    $2x + 7y = 31$

12. $6x + y = -10$
    $5x + y = -10$

13. $5x + 6y = 50$
    $-x + 6y = 26$

14. $4x - 9y = -21$
    $4x + 3y = -9$

15. ★ **MULTIPLE CHOICE** Which ordered pair is a solution of the linear system $4x + 9y = -2$ and $11x + 9y = 26$?

(A) $(-2, 4)$ (B) $(2, -4)$ (C) $(4, -2)$ (D) $(4, 2)$

EXAMPLE 3 for Exs. 16–22

ARRANGING LIKE TERMS **Solve the linear system using elimination.**

16. $2x - y = 32$
    $y - 5x = 13$

17. $-8y + 6x = 36$
    $6x - y = 15$

18. $2x - y = -11$
    $y = -2x - 13$

19. $-x - y = 14$
    $x = 5y - 38$

20. $11y - 3x = 18$
    $-3x = -16y + 33$

21. $-5x + y = -23$
    $-y = 3x - 9$

22. ★ **MULTIPLE CHOICE** Which ordered pair is a solution of the linear system $2x + y = 10$ and $3y = 2x + 6$?

(A) $(-3, -4)$ (B) $(3, 4)$ (C) $(-4, 3)$ (D) $(4, 3)$

ERROR ANALYSIS ***Describe*** **and correct the error in finding the value of one of the variables in the given linear system.**

23. $5x - 7y = 16$
$-x - 7y = 8$

$$\begin{array}{r} 5x - 7y = 16 \\ -x - 7y = 8 \\ \hline 4x \quad\quad = 24 \\ x = 6 \end{array}$$

24. $3x - 2y = -3$
$5y = 60 - 3x$

$$\begin{array}{r} 3x - 2y = -3 \\ -3x + 5y = 60 \\ \hline 3y = 57 \\ y = 19 \end{array}$$

SOLVING LINEAR SYSTEMS **Solve the linear system using elimination.**

25. $-x + \frac{1}{2}y = -19$
$x - y = 12$

26. $\frac{1}{4}x - \frac{2}{3}y = 7$
$\frac{1}{2}x + \frac{2}{3}y = -4$

27. $8x - \frac{1}{2}y = -38$
$\frac{1}{4}x - \frac{1}{2}y = -7$

28. $5.2x + 3.5y = 54$
$-3.6x + 3.5y = 10$

29. $1.3x - 3y = -17.6$
$-1.3x + 4.5y = 25.1$

30. $-2.6x - 3.2y = 4.8$
$1.9x - 3.2y = -4.2$

31. $\frac{4}{5}x + \frac{2}{5}y = 14$
$\frac{2}{5}y + \frac{1}{5}x = 11$

32. $2.7x + 1.5y = 36$
$3.5y = 2.7x - 6$

33. $4 - 4.8x = 1.7y$
$12.8 + 1.7y = -13.2x$

34. WRITING AN EQUATION OF A LINE Use the following steps to write an equation of the line that passes through the points (1, 2) and (−4, 12).

a. Write a system of linear equations by substituting 1 for x and 2 for y in $y = mx + b$ and −4 for x and 12 for y in $y = mx + b$.

b. Solve the system of linear equations from part (a). What is the slope of the line? What is the y-intercept?

c. Write an equation of the line that passes through (1, 2) and (−4, 12).

35. **GEOMETRY** The rectangle has a perimeter P of 14 feet, and twice its length ℓ is equal to 1 less than 4 times its width w. Write and solve a system of linear equations to find the length and the width of the rectangle.

$P = 14$ ft, w, ℓ

36. ★ **SHORT RESPONSE** Find the solution of the system of linear equations below. *Explain* your steps.

$x + 3y = 8$ **Equation 1**
$x - 6y = -19$ **Equation 2**
$5x - 3y = -14$ **Equation 3**

37. CHALLENGE For $a \neq 0$, what is the solution of the system $ax + 2y = 4$ and $ax - 3y = -6$?

38. CHALLENGE Solve for x, y, and z in the system of equations below. *Explain* your steps.

$x + 7y + 3z = 29$ **Equation 1**
$3z + x - 2y = -7$ **Equation 2**
$5y = 10 - 2x$ **Equation 3**

○ = See **WORKED-OUT SOLUTIONS** in Student Resources ★ = **STANDARDIZED TEST PRACTICE** ◆ = **MULTIPLE REPRESENTATIONS**

Problem Solving

EXAMPLE 4 for Exs. 39–41

39. **ROWING** During a practice, a 4 person crew team rows a rowing shell upstream (against the current) and then rows the same distance downstream (with the current). The shell moves upstream at a speed of 4.3 meters per second and downstream at a speed of 4.9 meters per second. The speed of the current remains constant. Use the models below to write and solve a system of equations to find the average speed of the shell in still water and the speed of the current.

Upstream

Speed of shell in still water − Speed of current = Speed of shell

Downstream

Speed of shell in still water + Speed of current = Speed of shell

40. **OIL CHANGE** Two cars get an oil change at the same service center. Each customer is charged a fee x (in dollars) for the oil change plus y dollars per quart of oil used. The oil change for the car that requires 5 quarts of oil costs \$22.45. The oil change for the car that requires 7 quarts of oil costs \$25.45. Find the fee and the cost per quart of oil.

41. **PHONES** Cellular phone ring tones can be monophonic or polyphonic. Monophonic ring tones play one tone at a time, and polyphonic ring tones play multiple tones at a time. The table shows the ring tones downloaded from a website by two customers. Use the information to find the cost of a monophonic ring tone and a polyphonic ring tone, assuming that all monophonic ring tones cost the same and all polyphonic ring tones cost the same.

Customer	Monophonic ring tones	Polyphonic ring tones	Total cost (dollars)
Julie	3	2	12.85
Tate	1	2	8.95

42. **MULTIPLE REPRESENTATIONS** For a floral arrangement class, Alicia has to create an arrangement of twigs and flowers that has a total of 9 objects. She has to pay for the twigs and flowers that she uses in her arrangement. Each twig costs \$1, and each flower costs \$3.

    a. **Writing a System** Alicia spends \$15 on the twigs and flowers. Write and solve a linear system to find the number of twigs and the number of flowers she used.

    b. **Making a Table** Make a table showing the number of twigs in the arrangement and the total cost of the arrangement when the number of flowers purchased is 0, 1, 2, 3, 4, or 5. Use the table to check your answer to part (a).

43. MULTI-STEP PROBLEM On a typical day with light winds, the 1800 mile flight from Charlotte, North Carolina, to Phoenix, Arizona, takes longer than the return trip because the plane has to fly into the wind.

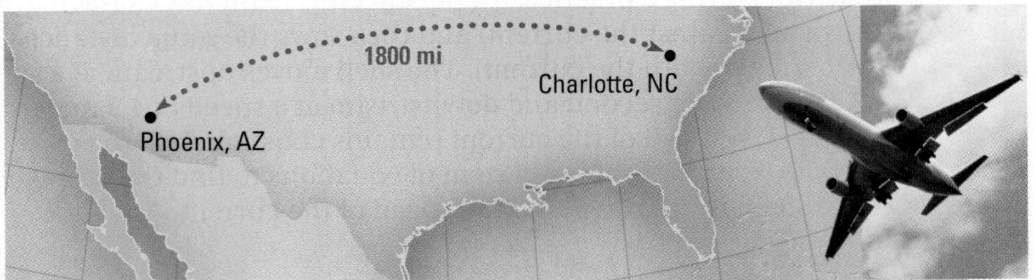

a. The flight from Charlotte to Phoenix is 4 hours 30 minutes long, and the flight from Phoenix to Charlotte is 4 hours long. Find the average speed (in miles per hour) of the airplane on the way to Phoenix and on the return trip to Charlotte.

b. Let s be the speed (in miles per hour) of the plane with no wind, and let w be the speed (in miles per hour) of the wind. Use your answer to part (a) to write and solve a system of equations to find the speed of the plane with no wind and the speed of the wind.

44. ★ SHORT RESPONSE The students in the graduating classes at the three high schools in a school district have to pay for their caps and gowns. A cap-and-gown set costs x dollars, and an extra tassel costs y dollars. At one high school, students pay \$3262 for 215 cap-and-gown sets and 72 extra tassels. At another high school, students pay \$3346 for 221 cap-and-gown sets and 72 extra tassels. How much will students at the third high school pay for 218 cap-and-gown sets and 56 extra tassels? *Explain.*

45. CHALLENGE A clothing manufacturer makes men's dress shirts. For the production process, an ideal sleeve length x (in centimeters) for each shirt size and an allowable deviation y (in centimeters) from the ideal length are established. The deviation is expressed as $\pm y$. For a specific shirt size, the minimum allowable sleeve length is 62.2 centimeters and the maximum allowable sleeve length is 64.8 centimeters. Find the ideal sleeve length and the allowable deviation.

6.4 Solve Linear Systems by Multiplying First

Before You solved linear systems by adding or subtracting.
Now You will solve linear systems by multiplying first.
Why So you can solve a problem about preparing food, as in Ex. 39.

Key Vocabulary
- **least common multiple**

CC.9-12.A.REI.6 Solve systems of linear equations exactly and approximately (e.g., with graphs), focusing on pairs of linear equations in two variables.

In a linear system like the one below, neither variable can be eliminated by adding or subtracting the equations. For systems like these, you can multiply one or both of the equations by a constant so that adding or subtracting the equations will eliminate one variable.

$5x + 2y = 16$ × 2 → $10x + 4y = 32$
$3x - 4y = 20$ → $3x - 4y = 20$

The new system is equivalent to the original system.

EXAMPLE 1 Multiply one equation, then add

Solve the linear system: $6x + 5y = 19$ **Equation 1**
$2x + 3y = 5$ **Equation 2**

Solution

STEP 1 **Multiply** Equation 2 by -3 so that the coefficients of x are opposites.

$6x + 5y = 19$ → $6x + 5y = 19$
$2x + 3y = 5$ × (−3) → $-6x - 9y = -15$

ANOTHER WAY
You can also multiply Equation 2 by 3 and subtract the equations.

STEP 2 **Add** the equations. $-4y = 4$

STEP 3 **Solve** for y. $y = -1$

STEP 4 **Substitute** -1 for y in either of the original equations and solve for x.

$2x + 3y = 5$	**Write Equation 2.**
$2x + 3(-1) = 5$	**Substitute −1 for *y*.**
$2x + (-3) = 5$	**Multiply.**
$2x = 8$	**Subtract −3 from each side.**
$x = 4$	**Divide each side by 2.**

▶ The solution is (4, −1).

CHECK Substitute 4 for x and -1 for y in each of the original equations.

Equation 1	**Equation 2**
$6x + 5y = 19$	$2x + 3y = 5$
$6(4) + 5(-1) \stackrel{?}{=} 19$	$2(4) + 3(-1) \stackrel{?}{=} 5$
$19 = 19$ ✓	$5 = 5$ ✓

MULTIPLYING BOTH EQUATIONS To eliminate one variable when adding or subtracting equations in a linear system, you may need to multiply both equations by constants. Use the least common multiple of the coefficients of one of the variables to determine the constants.

$2x - 9y = 1$ × 4 → $8x - 36y = 4$

$7x - 12y = 23$ × 3 → $21x - 36y = 69$

The least common multiple of −9 and −12 is −36.

EXAMPLE 2 Multiply both equations, then subtract

Solve the linear system: $4x + 5y = 35$ Equation 1
$2y = 3x - 9$ Equation 2

Solution

STEP 1 **Arrange** the equations so that like terms are in columns.

$4x + 5y = 35$ **Write Equation 1.**

$-3x + 2y = -9$ **Rewrite Equation 2.**

ANOTHER WAY
You can also multiply Equation 1 by 3 and Equation 2 by 4. Then add the revised equations to eliminate *x*.

STEP 2 **Multiply** Equation 1 by 2 and Equation 2 by 5 so that the coeffcient of *y* in each equation is the least common multiple of 5 and 2, or 10.

$4x + 5y = 35$ × 2 → $8x + 10y = 70$

$-3x + 2y = -9$ × 5 → $-15x + 10y = -45$

STEP 3 **Subtract** the equations. $23x = 115$

STEP 4 **Solve** for *x*. → $x = 5$

STEP 5 **Substitute** 5 for *x* in either of the original equations and solve for *y*.

$4x + 5y = 35$ **Write Equation 1.**

$4(5) + 5y = 35$ **Substitute 5 for *x*.**

$y = 3$ **Solve for *y*.**

▶ The solution is (5, 3).

CHECK Substitute 5 for *x* and 3 for *y* in each of the original equations.

Equation 1	Equation 2
$4x + 5y = 35$	$2y = 3x - 9$
$4(5) + 5(3) \stackrel{?}{=} 35$	$2(3) \stackrel{?}{=} 3(5) - 9$
$35 = 35$ ✓	$6 = 6$ ✓

Animated Algebra at my.hrw.com

✓ GUIDED PRACTICE for Examples 1 and 2

Solve the linear system using elimination.

1. $6x - 2y = 1$
$-2x + 3y = -5$

2. $2x + 5y = 3$
$3x + 10y = -3$

3. $3x - 7y = 5$
$9y = 5x + 5$

★ EXAMPLE 3 Standardized Test Practice

Darlene is making a quilt that has alternating stripes of regular quilting fabric and sateen fabric. She spends \$76 on a total of 16 yards of the two fabrics at a fabric store. Which system of equations can be used to find the amount x (in yards) of regular quilting fabric and the amount y (in yards) of sateen fabric she purchased?

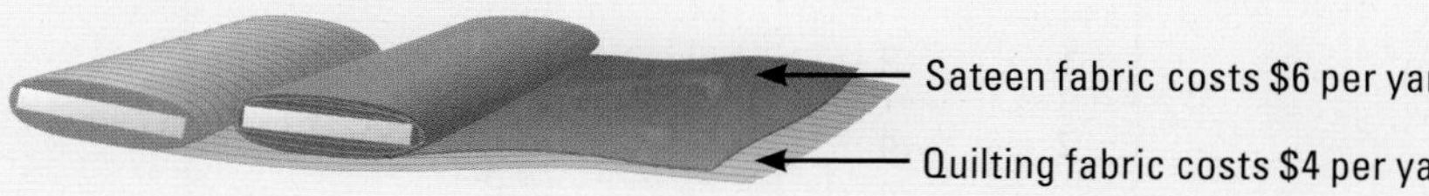

ELIMINATE CHOICES
You can eliminate choice A because $x + y$ cannot equal both 16 and 76.

Ⓐ $x + y = 16$
$x + y = 76$

Ⓑ $x + y = 16$
$4x + 6y = 76$

Ⓒ $x + y = 76$
$4x + 6y = 16$

Ⓓ $x + y = 16$
$6x + 4y = 76$

Solution

Write a system of equations where x is the number of yards of regular quilting fabric purchased and y is the number of yards of sateen fabric purchased.

Equation 1: Amount of fabric

Amount of quilting fabric + Amount of sateen fabric = Total yards of fabric

$x + y = 16$

Equation 2: Cost of fabric

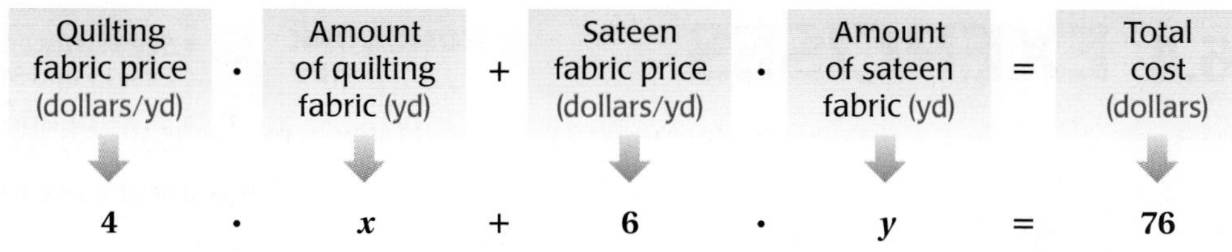

$4 \cdot x + 6 \cdot y = 76$

The system of equations is:
$x + y = 16$ **Equation 1**
$4x + 6y = 76$ **Equation 2**

▶ The correct answer is B. Ⓐ Ⓑ Ⓒ Ⓓ

✓ GUIDED PRACTICE for Example 3

4. **SOCCER** A sports equipment store is having a sale on soccer balls. A soccer coach purchases 10 soccer balls and 2 soccer ball bags for \$155. Another soccer coach purchases 12 soccer balls and 3 soccer ball bags for \$189. Find the cost of a soccer ball and the cost of a soccer ball bag.

CONCEPT SUMMARY

For Your Notebook

Methods for Solving Linear Systems

Method	Example	When to Use
Table	x / $y = 2x$ / $y = 3x - 1$: 0, 0, −1; 1, 2, 2; 2, 4, 5	When x-values are integers, so that equal values can be seen in the table
Graphing	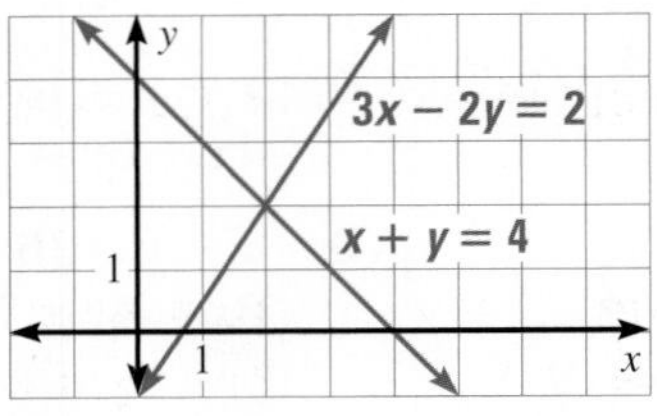	When you want to see the lines that the equations represent
Substitution	$\mathbf{y = 4 - 2x}$ $4x + 2y = 8$	When one equation is already solved for x or y
Addition	$4x + \mathbf{7y} = 15$ $6x - \mathbf{7y} = 5$	When the coefficients of one variable are opposites
Subtraction	$\mathbf{3x} + 5y = -13$ $\mathbf{3x} + y = -5$	When the coefficients of one variable are the same
Multiplication	$9x + 2y = 38$ $3x - 5y = 7$	When no corresponding coefficients are the same or opposites

Table example:

x	$y = 2x$	$y = 3x - 1$
0	0	−1
1	2	2
2	4	5

6.4 EXERCISES

HOMEWORK KEY

○ = **See WORKED-OUT SOLUTIONS** **Exs. 15 and 39**

★ = **STANDARDIZED TEST PRACTICE** **Exs. 2, 18, 34, 41, and 42**

◆ = **MULTIPLE REPRESENTATIONS** **Ex. 40**

SKILL PRACTICE

1. **VOCABULARY** What is the least common multiple of 12 and 18?

2. ★ **WRITING** *Explain* how to solve the linear system using the elimination method.
$2x - 3y = -4$ **Equation 1**
$7x + 9y = -5$ **Equation 2**

EXAMPLE 1 for Exs. 3–8

SOLVING LINEAR SYSTEMS Solve the linear system using elimination.

3. $x + y = 2$
$2x + 7y = 9$

4. $3x - 2y = 3$
$-x + y = 1$

5. $4x + 3y = 8$
$x - 2y = 13$

6. $10x - 9y = 46$
$-2x + 3y = 10$

7. $8x - 5y = 11$
$4x - 3y = 5$

8. $11x - 20y = 28$
$3x + 4y = 36$

EXAMPLE 2
Exs. 9–20

SOLVING LINEAR SYSTEMS **Solve the linear system using elimination.**

9. $4x - 3y = 8$
$5x - 2y = -11$

10. $-2x - 5y = 9$
$3x + 11y = 4$

11. $7x - 6y = -1$
$5x - 4y = 1$

12. $7x + 3y = -12$
$2x + 5y = 38$

13. $9x - 8y = 4$
$2x - 3y = -4$

14. $12x - 7y = -2$
$-8x + 11y = 14$

15. $9x + 2y = 39$
$6x + 13y = -9$

16. $-7x + 10y = 11$
$-8x + 15y = 34$

17. $-14x + 15y = 15$
$21x - 20y = -10$

18. ★ **MULTIPLE CHOICE** Which ordered pair is a solution of the linear system $15x + 8y = 6$ and $25x + 12y = 14$?

(A) $(-3, -2)$ (B) $(-3, 2)$ (C) $(-2, -3)$ (D) $(2, -3)$

ERROR ANALYSIS ***Describe*** **and correct the error when solving the linear system.**

19.

$$\begin{array}{ll} 2x - 3y = -9 \xrightarrow{\times 2} & 4x - 6y = -18 \\ 5x - 6y = -9 & 5x - 6y = -9 \\ \hline & 9x \quad = -27 \\ & x = -3 \end{array}$$

20.

$$\begin{array}{ll} 9x + 8y = 11 \xrightarrow{\times 3} & 27x + 24y = 11 \\ 7x + 6y = 9 \xrightarrow{\times 4} & 28x + 24y = 9 \\ \hline & -x \quad = 2 \\ & x = -2 \end{array}$$

SOLVING LINEAR SYSTEMS **Solve the linear system using any algebraic method.**

21. $3x + 2y = 4$
$2y = 8 - 5x$

22. $4x - 5y = 18$
$3x = y + 11$

23. $8x - 9y = -15$
$-4x = 19 + y$

24. $0.3x + 0.1y = -0.1$
$-x + y = 3$

25. $4.4x - 3.6y = 7.6$
$x - y = 1$

26. $3x - 2y = -20$
$x + 1.2y = 6.4$

27. $0.2x - 1.5y = -1$
$x - 4.5y = 1$

28. $1.5x - 3.5y = -5$
$-1.2x + 2.5y = 1$

29. $4.9x + 2.4y = 7.4$
$0.7x + 3.6y = -2.2$

30. $x + y = 0$
$\frac{1}{2}x - \frac{1}{2}y = 2$

31. $3x + y = \frac{1}{3}$
$2x - 3y = \frac{8}{3}$

32. $\frac{3}{5}x - \frac{3}{4}y = -3$
$\frac{2}{5}x + \frac{1}{3}y = 8$

33. **GEOMETRY** A rectangle has a perimeter of 18 inches. A new rectangle is formed by doubling the width w and tripling the length ℓ, as shown. The new rectangle has a perimeter P of 46 inches.

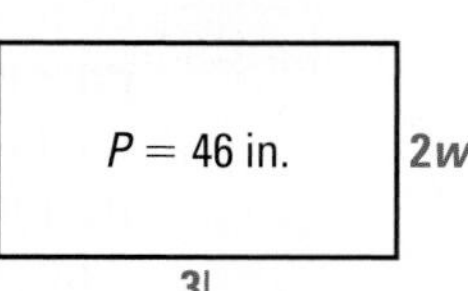

a. Write and solve a system of linear equations to find the length and width of the original rectangle.

b. Find the length and width of the new rectangle.

34. ★ **WRITING** For which values of a can you solve the linear system $ax + 3y = 2$ and $4x + 5y = 6$ without multiplying first? *Explain.*

CHALLENGE **Find the values of *a* and *b* so that the linear system has the given solution.**

$ax - by = 4$ **Equation 1**
$bx - ay = 10$ **Equation 2**

35. $(4, 2)$

36. $(2, 1)$

PROBLEM SOLVING

EXAMPLE 3
for Exs. 37–39

37. **BOOK SALE** A library is having a book sale to raise money. Hardcover books cost \$4 each and paperback books cost \$2 each. A person spends \$26 for 8 books. How many hardcover books did she purchase?

38. **MUSIC** A website allows users to download individual songs or an entire album. All individual songs cost the same to download, and all albums cost the same to download. Ryan pays \$14.94 to download 5 individual songs and 1 album. Seth pays \$22.95 to download 3 individual songs and 2 albums. How much does the website charge to download a song? an entire album?

39. **FARM PRODUCTS** The table shows the number of apples needed to make the apple pies and applesauce sold at a farm store. During a recent apple picking at the farm, 169 Granny Smith apples and 95 Golden Delicious apples were picked. How many apple pies and batches of applesauce can be made if every apple is used?

Type of apple	Granny Smith	Golden Delicious
Needed for a pie	5	3
Needed for a batch of applesauce	4	2

40. **MULTIPLE REPRESENTATIONS** Tickets for admission to a high school football game cost \$3 for students and \$5 for adults. During one game, \$2995 was collected from the sale of 729 tickets.

    a. **Writing a System** Write and solve a system of linear equations to find the number of tickets sold to students and the number of tickets sold to adults.

    b. **Drawing a Graph** Graph the system of linear equations. Use the graph to determine whether your answer to part (a) is reasonable.

41. ★ **SHORT RESPONSE** A dim sum restaurant offers two sizes of dishes: small and large. All small dishes cost the same and all large dishes cost the same. The bills show the cost of the food before the tip is included. What will 3 small and 2 large dishes cost before the tip is included? *Explain.*

42. ★ **OPEN-ENDED** *Describe* a real-world problem that can be solved using a system of linear equations. Then solve the problem and explain what the solution means in this situation.

○ = See WORKED-OUT SOLUTIONS in Student Resources ★ = STANDARDIZED TEST PRACTICE ◆ = MULTIPLE REPRESENTATIONS

43. **INVESTMENTS** Matt invested \$2000 in stocks and bonds. This year the bonds paid 8% interest, and the stocks paid 6% in dividends. Matt received a total of \$144 in interest and dividends. How much money did he invest in stocks? in bonds?

44. **CHALLENGE** You drive a car 45 miles at an average speed r (in miles per hour) to reach your destination. Due to traffic, your average speed on the return trip is $\frac{3}{4}r$. The round trip took a total of 1 hour 45 minutes. Find the average speed for each leg of your trip.

QUIZ

Solve the linear system using elimination.

1. $x + y = 4$
   $-3x + y = -8$
2. $2x - y = 2$
   $6x - y = -2$
3. $x + y = 5$
   $-x + y = -3$
4. $x + 3y = -10$
   $-x + 5y = -30$
5. $x + 3y = 10$
   $3x - y = 13$
6. $x + 7y = 10$
   $x + 2y = -8$
7. $4x - y = -2$
   $3x + 2y = 7$
8. $x + 3y = 1$
   $5x + 6y = 14$
9. $3x + y = 21$
   $x + y = 1$
10. $2x - 3y = -5$
    $5x + 2y = 16$
11. $7x + 2y = 13$
    $4x + 3y = 13$
12. $\frac{1}{3}x + 5y = -3$
    $-\frac{2}{3}x + 6y = -10$

Multiply and Then Add Equations

Use appropriate tools strategically.

QUESTION How can you see why elimination works as a method for solving linear systems?

You have used elimination to solve systems of linear equations, but you may think that it isn't obvious why this method works. You can do an algebraic proof by replacing the numbers in the system with variables, but this is complicated to do. In this activity, you will graph each equation that you get as you use elimination.

EXAMPLE 1 Solve the linear system using addition

Solve the linear system $-2x + y = 1$ Equation 1
$2x + y = 5$ Equation 2

Solution

***STEP 1* Graph the System**

Solve both equations for y.

$-2x + y = 1$ $\quad$ $2x + y = 5$

$y = 1 + 2x$ $\quad$ $y = 5 - 2x$

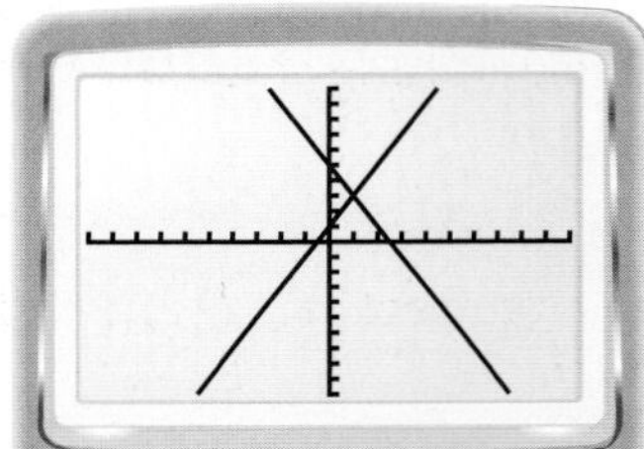

Graph the two equations using a graphing calculator. Notice that the point of intersection of the graphs is the solution of the system.

The solution is (1, 3).

***STEP 2* Graph the sum of the equations**

Add the two equations as you would if you were solving the system algebraically. Graph the resulting equation.

$-2x + y = 1$ **Equation 1**
$2x + y = 5$ **Equation 2**

$2y = 6$ **Add.**

$y = 3$ **Solve for *y*.**

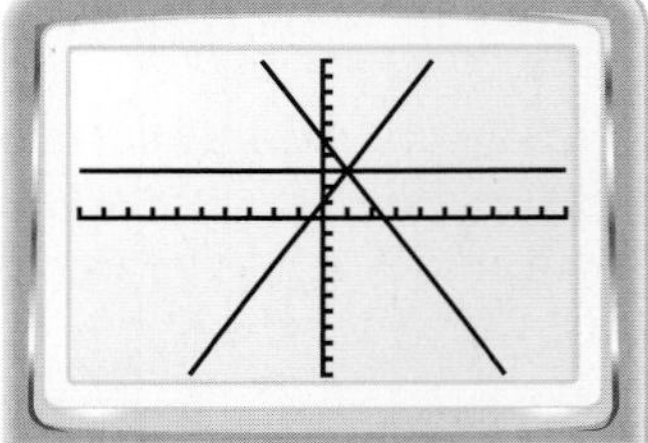

Now graph the equation $y = 3$ on the same graphing calculator screen with the two original equations.

***STEP 3* Summarize the Results**

All three equations intersect at (1, 3). So, (1, 3) is the solution of the system.

PRACTICE 1

Solve the system using elimination. Graph each resulting equation.

1. $-x + y = 9$
$x + y = 1$

2. $6x - 7y = 4$
$x + 7y = 17$

3. $2x - 3y = 4$
$8x + 3y = 1$

EXAMPLE 2 Solve a linear system using multiplication

Solve the linear system:

$$2x - y = 4 \quad \text{Equation 1}$$
$$-3x + 2y = -7 \quad \text{Equation 2}$$

STEP 1 ***Graph the System***

Solve each equation for y.

$2x - y = 4 \qquad\qquad -3x + 2y = -7$

$y = 2x - 4 \qquad\qquad y = \frac{3x - 7}{2}$

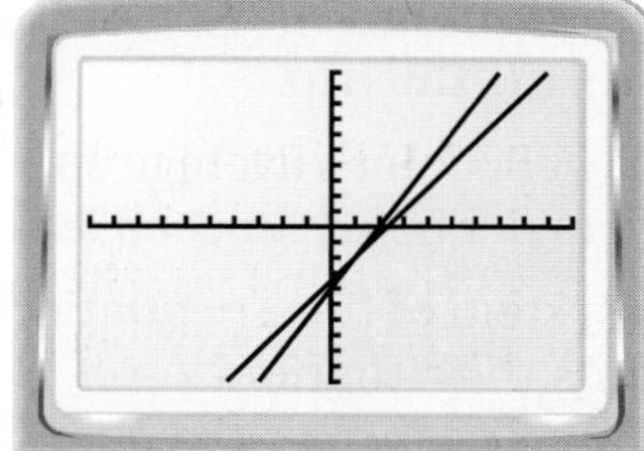

Graph the two equations. The point of intersection of the graphs is the solution of the system.

STEP 2 ***Use elimination to solve***

Multiply each equation by a constant so that you can eliminate a variable x by adding.

$2x - y = 4$	× 3	$6x - 3y = 12$	**Multiply Equation 1 by 3.**
$-3x + 2y = -7$	× 2	$-6x + 4y = -14$	**Multiply Equation 2 by 2.**
		$y = -2$	**Add.**

STEP 3 ***Graph the resulting equations***

Graph the equations $6x - 3y = 12$, $-6x + 4y = -14$, and $y = -2$ on the same graphing calculator screen with the two original equations.

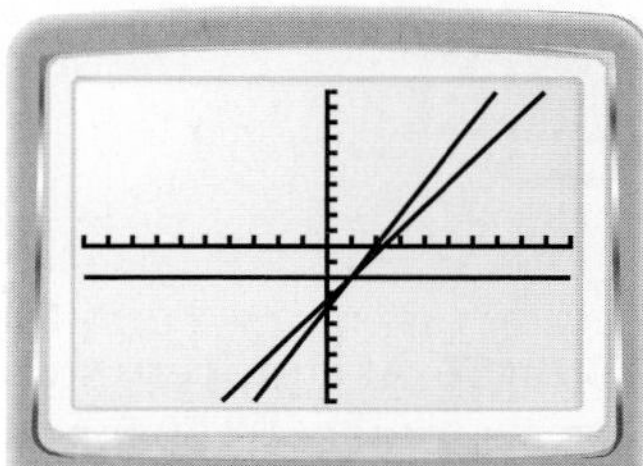

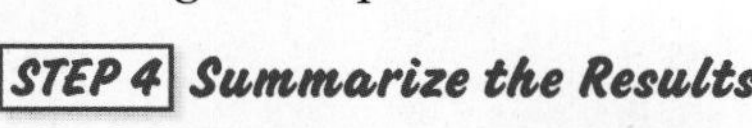

STEP 4 ***Summarize the Results***

All of the equations intersect at (1, −2). So, (1, −2) is the solution of the system.

PRACTICE

Solve the system using elimination. Graph each resulting equation.

4. $x - y = -5$
$4x + 3y = 1$

5. $2x - 5y = 3$
$-x + 2y = -2$

6. $3x + 5y = 3$
$x - y = 9$

7. Solve the linear system using a graphing calculator. Now use a linear combination on the system to eliminate the variable x. Use a linear combination on the system to eliminate the variable y. What do you notice?

$x - 2y = -6$
$2x + y = 8$

DRAW CONCLUSIONS

8. Explain how you could use this method to check whether you have correctly solved a system of linear equations by graphing?

9. Suppose you are trying to solve a system of linear equations that has no solution.

a. What happens when you use the elimination method?

b. What does the graph of the system look like?

c. Will the method of graphing the resulting equations as in Example 2 work with the system?

 MATHEMATICAL PRACTICES Make sense of problems and persevere in solving them.

1. **MULTI-STEP PROBLEM** Flying into the wind, a helicopter takes 15 minutes to travel 15 kilometers. The return flight takes 12 minutes. The wind speed remains constant during the trip.
   a. Find the helicopter's average speed (in kilometers per hour) for each leg of the trip.
   b. Write a system of linear equations that represents the situation.
   c. What is the helicopter's average speed in still air? What is the speed of the wind?

2. **SHORT RESPONSE** At a grocery store, a customer pays a total of \$9.70 for 1.8 pounds of potato salad and 1.4 pounds of coleslaw. Another customer pays a total of \$6.55 for 1 pound of potato salad and 1.2 pounds of coleslaw. How much do 2 pounds of potato salad and 2 pounds of coleslaw cost? *Explain.*

3. **GRIDDED ANSWER** During one day, two computers are sold at a computer store. The two customers each arrange payment plans with the salesperson. The graph shows the amount y of money (in dollars) paid for the computers after x months. After how many months will each customer have paid the same amount?

4. **OPEN-ENDED** *Describe* a real-world problem that can be modeled by a linear system. Then solve the system and interpret the solution in the context of the problem.

5. **SHORT RESPONSE** A hot air balloon is launched at Kirby Park, and it ascends at a rate of 7200 feet per hour. At the same time, a second hot air balloon is launched at Newman Park, and it ascends at a rate of 4000 feet per hour. Both of the balloons stop ascending after 30 minutes. The diagram shows the altitude of each park. Are the hot air balloons ever at the same height at the same time? *Explain.*

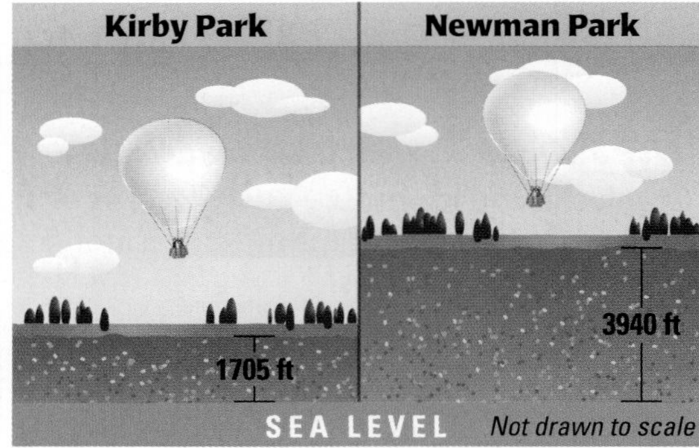

6. **EXTENDED RESPONSE** A chemist needs 500 milliliters of a 20% acid and 80% water mix for a chemistry experiment. The chemist combines x milliliters of a 10% acid and 90% water mix and y milliliters of a 30% acid and 70% water mix to make the 20% acid and 80% water mix.
   a. Write a linear system that represents the situation.
   b. How many milliliters of the 10% acid and 90% water mix and the 30% acid and 70% water mix are combined to make the 20% acid and 80% water mix?
   c. The chemist also needs 500 milliliters of a 15% acid and 85% water mix. Does the chemist need more of the 10% acid and 90% water mix than the 30% acid and 70% water mix to make this new mix? *Explain.*

6.5 Solve Special Types of Linear Systems

Before You found the solution of a linear system.

Now You will identify the number of solutions of a linear system.

Why? So you can compare distances traveled, as in Ex. 39.

Key Vocabulary
- **inconsistent system**
- **consistent dependent system**
- **system of linear equations**
- **parallel**

A linear system can have no solution or infinitely many solutions. A linear system has no solution when the graphs of the equations are parallel. A linear system with no solution is called an **inconsistent system**.

A linear system has infinitely many solutions when the graphs of the equations are the same line. A linear system with infinitely many solutions is called a **consistent dependent system**.

EXAMPLE 1 A linear system with no solution

CC.9-12.A.REI.6 Solve systems of linear equations exactly and approximately (e.g., with graphs), focusing on pairs of linear equations in two variables.

Show that the linear system has no solution.

$3x + 2y = 10$ **Equation 1**
$3x + 2y = 2$ **Equation 2**

Solution

METHOD 1 Graphing

Graph the linear system.

REVIEW GRAPHING
You may want to review graphing linear equations before graphing linear systems.

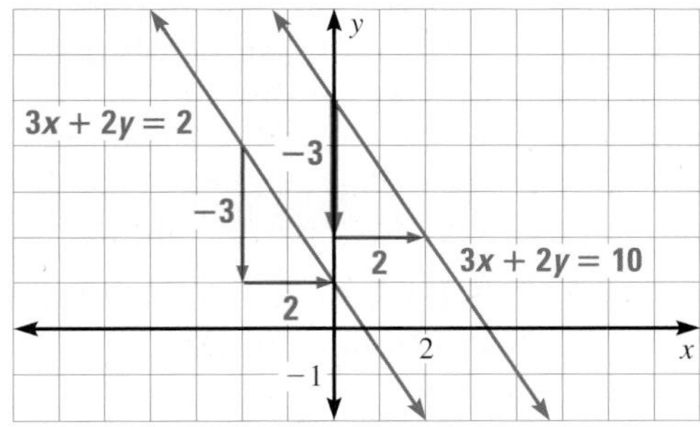

▸ The lines are parallel because they have the same slope but different y-intercepts. Parallel lines do not intersect, so the system has no solution.

METHOD 2 Elimination

Subtract the equations.

$$\begin{array}{r} 3x + 2y = 10 \\ \underline{3x + 2y = 2} \\ 0 = 8 \end{array}$$

← **This is a false statement.**

▸ The variables are eliminated and you are left with a false statement regardless of the values of x and y. This tells you that the system has no solution.

IDENTIFY TYPES OF SYSTEMS
The linear system in Example 1 is called an inconsistent system because the lines do not intersect (are not consistent).

Animated Algebra at my.hrw.com

EXAMPLE 2 A linear system with infinitely many solutions

Show that the linear system has infinitely many solutions.

$x - 2y = -4$ **Equation 1**

$y = \frac{1}{2}x + 2$ **Equation 2**

Solution

METHOD 1 Graphing

Graph the linear system.

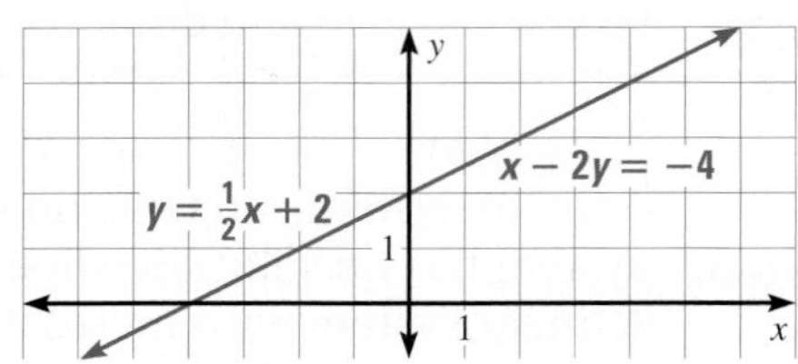

▶ The equations represent the same line, so any point on the line is a solution. So, the linear system has infinitely many solutions.

METHOD 2 Substitution

Substitute $\frac{1}{2}x + 2$ for y in Equation 1 and solve for x.

$x - 2y = -4$ **Write Equation 1.**

$x - 2\left(\frac{1}{2}x + 2\right) = -4$ **Substitute $\frac{1}{2}x + 2$ for y.**

$-4 = -4$ **Simplify.**

▶ The variables are eliminated and you are left with a statement that is true regardless of the values of x and y. This tells you that the system has infinitely many solutions.

IDENTIFY TYPES OF SYSTEMS

The linear system in Example 2 is called a consistent dependent system because the lines intersect (are consistent) and the equations are equivalent (are dependent).

✓ GUIDED PRACTICE for Examples 1 and 2

Tell whether the linear system has *no solution* or *infinitely many solutions*. *Explain.*

1. $5x + 3y = 6$
$-5x - 3y = 3$

2. $y = 2x - 4$
$-6x + 3y = -12$

IDENTIFYING THE NUMBER OF SOLUTIONS When the equations of a linear system are written in slope-intercept form, you can identify the number of solutions of the system by looking at the slopes and y-intercepts of the lines.

Number of solutions	Slopes and y-intercepts
One solution	Different slopes
No solution	Same slope Different y-intercepts
Infinitely many solutions	Same slope Same y-intercept

EXAMPLE 3 Identify the number of solutions

Without solving the linear system, tell whether the linear system has *one solution, no solution,* or *infinitely many solutions.*

a. $5x + y = -2$ Equation 1
$-10x - 2y = 4$ Equation 2

b. $6x + 2y = 3$ Equation 1
$6x + 2y = -5$ Equation 2

Solution

a. $y = -5x - 2$ Write Equation 1 in slope-intercept form.

$y = -5x - 2$ Write Equation 2 in slope-intercept form.

▶ Because the lines have the same slope and the same y-intercept, the system has infinitely many solutions.

b. $y = -3x + \frac{3}{2}$ Write Equation 1 in slope-intercept form.

$y = -3x - \frac{5}{2}$ Write Equation 2 in slope-intercept form.

▶ Because the lines have the same slope but different y-intercepts, the system has no solution.

EXAMPLE 4 Write and solve a system of linear equations

ART An artist wants to sell prints of her paintings. She orders a set of prints for each of two of her paintings. Each set contains regular prints and glossy prints, as shown in the table. Find the cost of one glossy print.

Regular	Glossy	Cost
45	30	\$465
15	10	\$155

Solution

STEP 1 **Write** a linear system. Let x be the cost (in dollars) of a regular print, and let y be the cost (in dollars) of a glossy print.

$45x + 30y = 465$ Cost of prints for one painting
$15x + 10y = 155$ Cost of prints for other painting

STEP 2 **Solve** the linear system using elimination.

$$\begin{aligned} 45x + 30y &= 465 \\ 15x + 10y &= 155 \end{aligned} \quad \xrightarrow{\times(-3)} \quad \begin{aligned} 45x + 30y &= 465 \\ -45x - 30y &= -465 \\ \hline 0 &= 0 \end{aligned}$$

▶ There are infinitely many solutions, so you cannot determine the cost of one glossy print. You need more information.

✓ GUIDED PRACTICE for Examples 3 and 4

3. Without solving the linear system, tell whether it has *one solution, no solution,* or *infinitely many solutions.*
$x - 3y = -15$ Equation 1
$2x - 3y = -18$ Equation 2

4. **WHAT IF?** In Example 4, suppose a glossy print costs \$3 more than a regular print. Find the cost of a glossy print.

CONCEPT SUMMARY

For Your Notebook

Number of Solutions of a Linear System

One solution	No solution	Infinitely many solutions
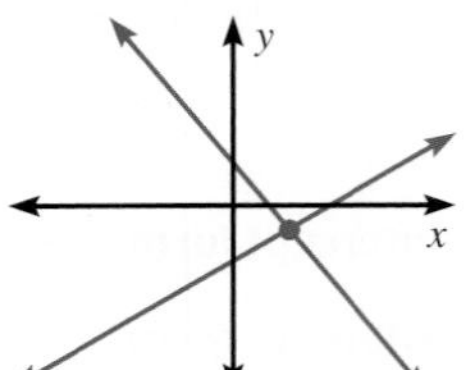	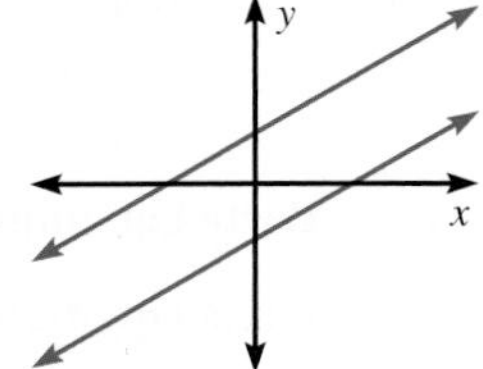	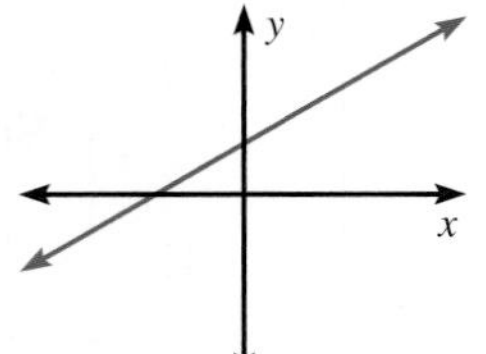
The lines intersect. The lines have different slopes.	The lines are parallel. The lines have the same slope and different y-intercepts.	The lines coincide. The lines have the same slope and the same y-intercept.

6.5 EXERCISES

HOMEWORK KEY

○ = **See WORKED-OUT SOLUTIONS** Exs. 11 and 37

★ = **STANDARDIZED TEST PRACTICE** Exs. 3, 4, 24, 25, 32, 33, and 40

SKILL PRACTICE

1. **VOCABULARY** Copy and complete: A linear system with no solution is called a(n) __?__ system.

2. **VOCABULARY** Copy and complete: A linear system with infinitely many solutions is called a(n) __?__ system.

3. ★ **WRITING** *Describe* the graph of a linear system that has no solution.

4. ★ **WRITING** *Describe* the graph of a linear system that has infinitely many solutions.

INTERPRETING GRAPHS Match the linear system with its graph. Then use the graph to tell whether the linear system has *one solution, no solution,* or *infinitely many solutions.*

5. $x - 3y = -9$
   $x - y = -1$

6. $x - y = -4$
   $-3x + 3y = 2$

7. $x + 3y = -1$
   $-2x - 6y = 2$

A. 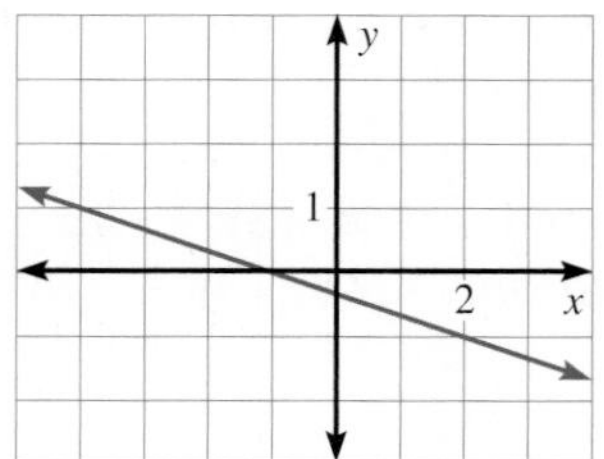

B. 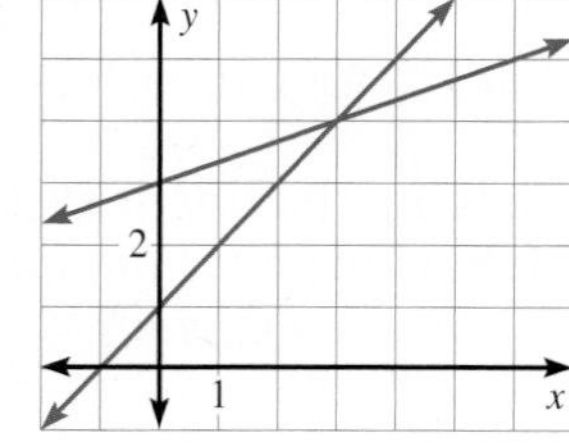

C. 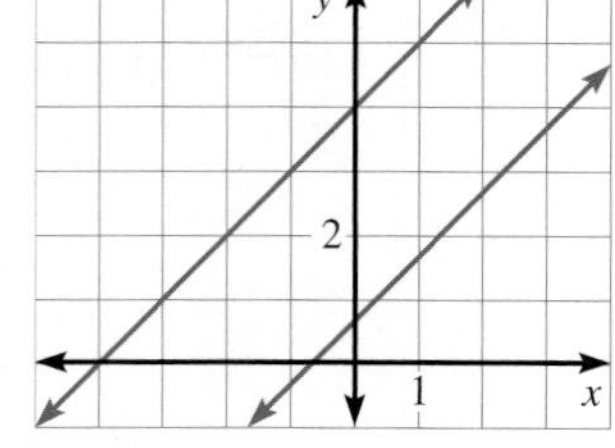

EXAMPLES 1 and 2 for Exs. 8–25

INTERPRETING GRAPHS Graph the linear system. Then use the graph to tell whether the linear system has *one solution, no solution,* or *infinitely many solutions.*

8. $x + y = -2$
   $y = -x + 5$

9. $3x - 4y = 12$
   $y = \frac{3}{4}x - 3$

10. $3x - y = -9$
    $3x + 5y = -15$

11. $-2x + 2y = -16$
    $3x - 6y = 30$

12. $-9x + 6y = 18$
    $6x - 4y = -12$

13. $-3x + 4y = 12$
    $-3x + 4y = 24$

14. **ERROR ANALYSIS** *Describe* and correct the error in solving the linear system below.

    $6x + y = 36$
    $5x - y = 8$

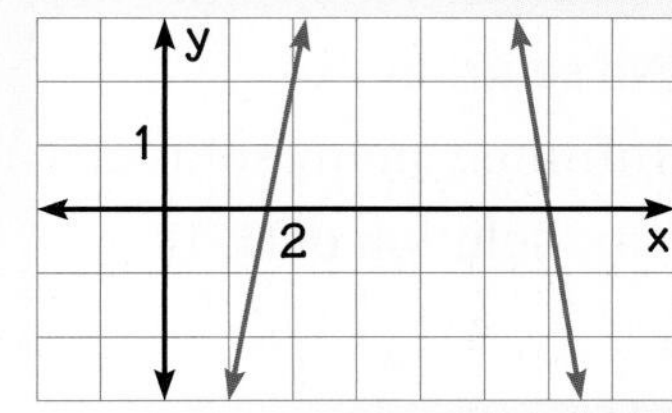

The lines do not intersect, so there is no solution.

SOLVING LINEAR SYSTEMS Solve the linear system using substitution or elimination.

15. $2x + 5y = 14$
    $6x + 7y = 10$

16. $-16x + 2y = -2$
    $y = 8x - 1$

17. $3x - 2y = -5$
    $4x + 5y = 47$

18. $5x - 5y = -3$
    $y = x + 0.6$

19. $x - y = 0$
    $5x - 2y = 6$

20. $x - 2y = 7$
    $-x + 2y = 7$

21. $-18x + 6y = 24$
    $3x - y = -2$

22. $4y + 5x = 15$
    $x = 8y + 3$

23. $6x + 3y = 9$
    $2x + 9y = 27$

24. ★ **MULTIPLE CHOICE** Which of the linear systems has *exactly* one solution?

    (A) $-x + y = 9$
        $x - y = 9$

    (B) $-x + y = 9$
        $x - y = -9$

    (C) $-x + y = 9$
        $-x - y = 9$

    (D) $x - y = -9$
        $-x + y = -9$

25. ★ **MULTIPLE CHOICE** Which of the linear systems has infinitely many solutions?

    (A) $15x + 5y = 20$
        $6x - 2y = 8$

    (B) $15x - 5y = 20$
        $6x - 2y = -8$

    (C) $15x - 5y = -20$
        $6x - 2y = 8$

    (D) $15x - 5y = 20$
        $6x - 2y = 8$

EXAMPLE 3 for Exs. 26–31

IDENTIFYING THE NUMBER OF SOLUTIONS Without solving the linear system, tell whether the linear system has *one solution, no solution,* or *infinitely many solutions.*

26. $y = -6x - 2$
    $12x + 2y = -6$

27. $y = 7x + 13$
    $-21x + 3y = 39$

28. $4x + 3y = 27$
    $4x - 3y = -27$

29. $9x - 15y = 24$
    $6x - 10y = 16$

30. $0.3x + 0.4y = 2.4$
    $0.5x - 0.6y = 0.2$

31. $0.9x - 2.1y = 12.3$
    $1.5x - 3.5y = 20.5$

32. ★ **OPEN-ENDED** Write a linear system so that it has infinitely many solutions, and one of the equations is $y = 3x + 2$.

33. ★ **OPEN-ENDED** Write a linear system so that it has no solution and one of the equations is $7x - 8y = -9$.

34. **REASONING** Give a counterexample for the following statement: If the graphs of the equations of a linear system have the same slope, then the linear system has no solution.

35. **CHALLENGE** Find values of p, q, and r that produce the solution(s).

$px + qy = r$ **Equation 1**
$2x - 3y = 5$ **Equation 2**

a. No solution

b. Infinitely many solutions

c. One solution of (4, 1)

PROBLEM SOLVING

EXAMPLE 4 for Exs. 36–38

36. **RECREATION** One admission to a roller skating rink costs x dollars and renting a pair of skates costs y dollars. A group pays $243 for admission for 36 people and 21 skate rentals. Another group pays $81 for admission for 12 people and 7 skate rentals. Is there enough information to determine the cost of one admission to the roller skating rink? *Explain.*

(37.) **TRANSPORTATION** A passenger train travels from New York City to Washington, D.C., then back to New York City. The table shows the number of coach tickets and business class tickets purchased for each leg of the trip. Is there enough information to determine the cost of one coach ticket? *Explain.*

Destination	Coach tickets	Business class tickets	Money collected (dollars)
Washington, D.C.	150	80	22,860
New York City	170	100	27,280

38. **PHOTOGRAPHY** In addition to taking pictures on your digital camera, you can record 30 second movies. All pictures use the same amount of memory, and all 30 second movies use the same amount of memory. The number of pictures and 30 second movies on 2 memory cards is shown.

a. Is there enough information given to determine the amount of memory used by a 30 second movie? *Explain.*

b. Given that a 30 second movie uses 50 times the amount of memory that a digital picture uses, can you determine the amount of memory used by a 30 second movie? *Explain.*

Size of card (megabytes)	64	256
Pictures	450	1800
Movies	7	28

◯ = See **WORKED-OUT SOLUTIONS** in Student Resources ★ = **STANDARDIZED TEST PRACTICE**

39. MULTI-STEP PROBLEM Two people are training for a speed ice-climbing event. During a practice climb, one climber starts 15 seconds after the first climber. The rates that the climbers ascend are shown.

a. Let d be the distance (in feet) traveled by a climber t seconds after the first person starts climbing. Write a linear system that models the situation.

b. Graph the linear system from part (a). Does the second climber catch up to the first climber? *Explain.*

40. ★ EXTENDED RESPONSE Two employees at a banquet facility are given the task of folding napkins. One person starts folding napkins at a rate of 5 napkins per minute. The second person starts 10 minutes after the first person and folds napkins at a rate of 4 napkins per minute.

a. **Model** Let y be the number of napkins folded x minutes after the first person starts folding. Write a linear system that models the situation.

b. **Solve** Solve the linear system.

c. **Interpret** Does the solution of the linear system make sense in the context of the problem? *Explain.*

41. CHALLENGE An airplane has an average air speed of 160 miles per hour. The airplane takes 3 hours to travel with the wind from Salem to Lancaster. The airplane has to travel against the wind on the return trip. After 3 hours into the return trip, the airplane is 120 miles from Salem. Find the distance from Salem to Lancaster. If the problem cannot be solved with the information given, *explain* why.

Extension Use Piecewise Functions

GOAL Graph and write piecewise functions.

Key Vocabulary
- **piecewise function**
- **step function**

CC.9-12.F.IF.7b Graph square root, cube root, and piecewise-defined functions, including step functions and absolute value functions.*

A **piecewise function** is defined by at least two equations, each of which applies to a different part of the function's domain. An example is given below.

$$y = \begin{cases} x + 1, & \text{if } x < 0 \\ 2x - 1, & \text{if } x \geq 0 \end{cases}$$

The expression $x + 1$ gives the value of y when x is less than 0. The expression $2x - 1$ gives the value of y when x is greater than or equal to 0.

EXAMPLE 1 Graph a piecewise function

Graph the function: $y = \begin{cases} -x - 1, & \text{if } x \leq -1 \\ 3, & \text{if } -1 < x < 2 \\ 2x - 5, & \text{if } x \geq 2 \end{cases}$

Solution

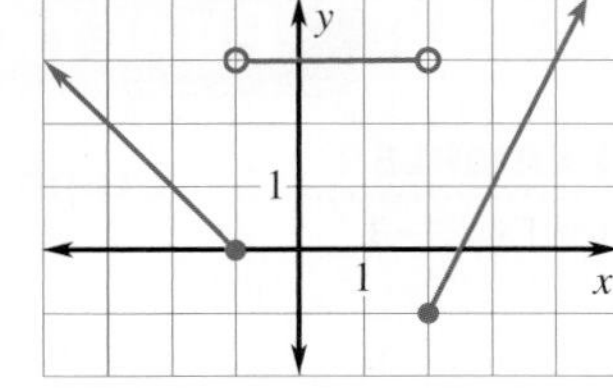

STEP 1 To the left of $x = -1$, graph $y = -x - 1$. Use a closed dot at $(-1, 0)$ because the equation applies when $x = -1$.

STEP 2 From $x = -1$ to $x = 2$, graph $y = 3$. Use open dots at $(-1, 3)$ and $(2, 3)$ because the equation does not apply when $x = -1$ or when $x = 2$.

STEP 3 To the right of $x = 2$, graph $y = 2x - 5$. Use a closed dot at $(2, -1)$ because the equation applies when $x = 2$.

EXAMPLE 2 Write a piecewise function

Write a piecewise function for the graph.

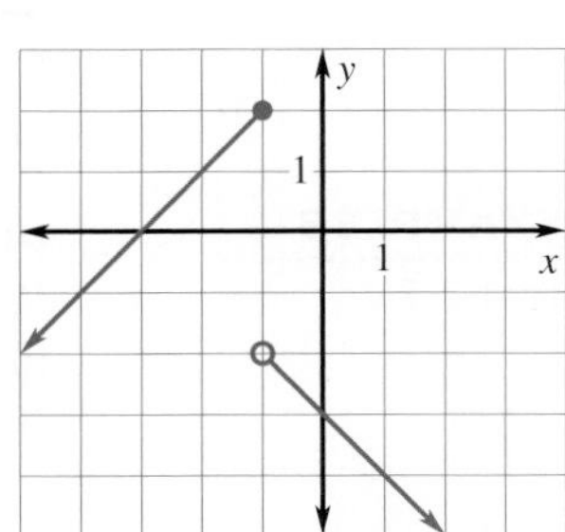

Solution

For $x \leq -1$, the graph is the line given by $y = x + 3$.

For $x > -1$, the graph is the line given by $y = -x - 3$.

▶ So, a piecewise function for the graph is as follows:

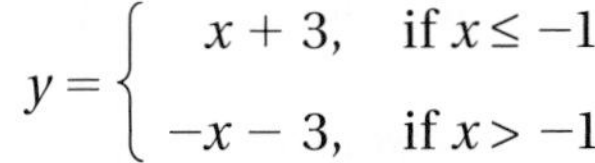

$$y = \begin{cases} x + 3, & \text{if } x \leq -1 \\ -x - 3, & \text{if } x > -1 \end{cases}$$

EXAMPLE 3 Solve a real-world problem

PARKING A parking garage charges $5.00 for each hour or fraction of an hour up to 4 hours per day. Make a table of values. Then write the cost C (in dollars) as a piecewise function of the time t (in hours) parked and graph the function. What is the cost of parking for 2 hours and 9 minutes?

Solution

Table

Time (hours)	Cost (dollars)
$0 < t \le 1$	5.00
$1 < t \le 2$	10.00
$2 < t \le 3$	15.00
$3 < t \le 4$	20.00

Function rule

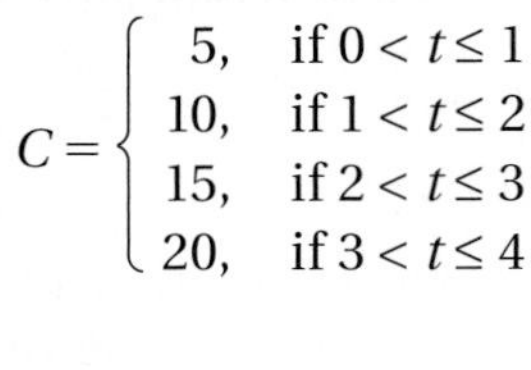

$$C = \begin{cases} 5, & \text{if } 0 < t \le 1 \\ 10, & \text{if } 1 < t \le 2 \\ 15, & \text{if } 2 < t \le 3 \\ 20, & \text{if } 3 < t \le 4 \end{cases}$$

Graph

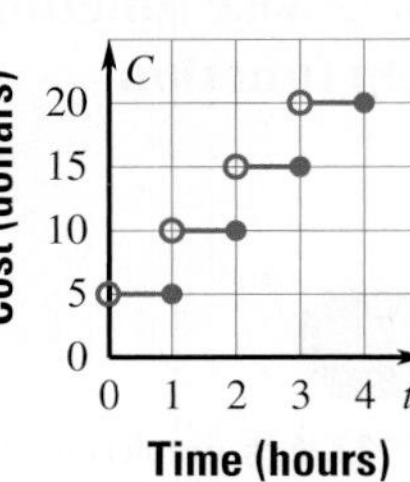

▶ Because 2 hours and 9 minutes is between 2 and 3 hours, the cost is $15.00.

STEP FUNCTIONS The function in Example 3 is called a *step function* because its graph resembles a set of stairs. A **step function** is a piecewise function that is defined by a constant value over each part of its domain.

PRACTICE

EXAMPLE 1 for Exs. 1–3

Graph the function.

1. $y = \begin{cases} x + 1, & \text{if } x < 0 \\ 0.5x - 1, & \text{if } x \ge 0 \end{cases}$

2. $y = \begin{cases} 2 + x, & \text{if } x < 0 \\ 2 - x, & \text{if } x \ge 0 \end{cases}$

3. $y = \begin{cases} 1, & \text{if } x < 0 \\ 2, & \text{if } 0 \le x < 1 \\ 3, & \text{if } x \ge 1 \end{cases}$

EXAMPLE 2 for Exs. 4–6

Write a piecewise function for the graph.

4. 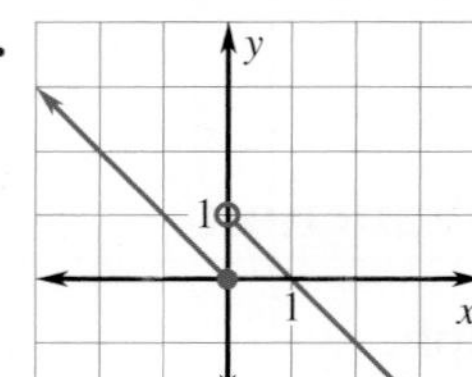

5. 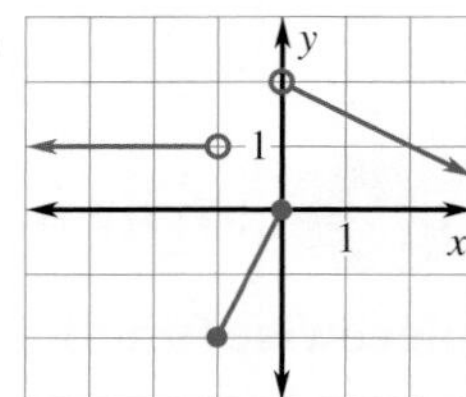

6. 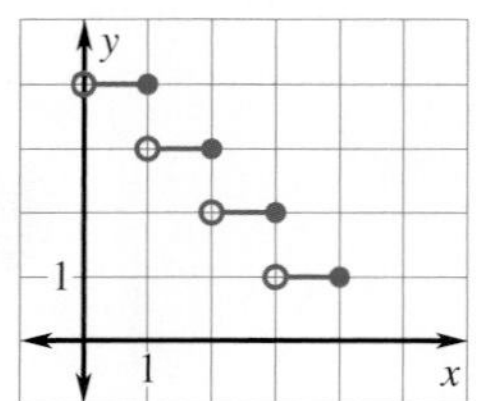

EXAMPLE 3 for Ex. 7

7. **PAY** Greg earns $20 per hour when he works 40 or fewer hours in a week. When he works more than 40 hours in a week, he earns $800 plus $30 per hour for each hour over 40. Write a piecewise function that gives his weekly pay P for working t hours. Graph the function. What is his pay for 46 hours?

8. **REASONING** *Explain* why the parent absolute value function $y = |x|$ is a piecewise function. Write a piecewise rule for the function.

9. **REASONING** The output y of the *greatest integer function* is the greatest integer less than or equal to the input value x. Graph the function for $-4 \le x < 4$. Is it a piecewise function? a step function? *Explain.*

6.6 Solve Systems of Linear Inequalities

Before You graphed linear inequalities in two variables.

Now You will solve systems of linear inequalities in two variables.

Why So you can find a marching band's competition score, as in Ex. 36.

Key Vocabulary
- **system of linear inequalities**
- **solution of a system of linear inequalities**
- **graph of a system of linear inequalities**

A **system of linear inequalities** in two variables, or simply a *system of inequalities,* consists of two or more linear inequalities in the same variables. An example is shown.

$x - y > 7$ **Inequality 1**
$2x + y < 8$ **Inequality 2**

A **solution of a system of linear inequalities** is an ordered pair that is a solution of each inequality in the system. For example, (6, −5) is a solution of the system above. The **graph of a system of linear inequalities** is the graph of all solutions of the system.

COMMON CORE

CC.9-12.A.REI.12 Graph the solutions to a linear inequality in two variables as a half-plane (excluding the boundary in the case of a strict inequality), and graph the solution set to a system of linear inequalities in two variables as the intersection of the corresponding half-planes.

KEY CONCEPT *For Your Notebook*

Graphing a System of Linear Inequalities

STEP 1 **Graph** each inequality.

STEP 2 **Find** the intersection of the half-planes. The graph of the system is this intersection.

EXAMPLE 1 Graph a system of two linear inequalities

Graph the system of inequalities. $y > -x - 2$ **Inequality 1**
$y \le 3x + 6$ **Inequality 2**

REVIEW GRAPHING INEQUALITIES
You may want to review graphing a linear inequality in two variables before graphing systems of inequalities.

Solution

Graph both inequalities in the same coordinate plane. The graph of the system is the intersection of the two half-planes, which is shown as the darker shade of blue.

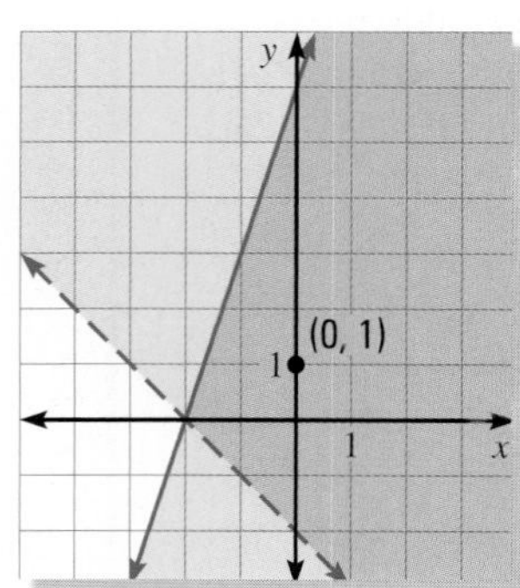

CHECK Choose a point in the dark blue region, such as (0, 1). To check this solution, substitute 0 for x and 1 for y into each inequality.

$1 \overset{?}{>} 0 - 2$ | $1 \overset{?}{\le} 0 + 6$

$1 > -2$ ✓ | $1 \le 6$ ✓

Animated Algebra at my.hrw.com

THE SOLUTION REGION In Example 1, the half-plane for each inequality is shaded, and the solution region is the intersection of the half-planes. From this point on, only the solution region will be shaded.

EXAMPLE 2 Graph a system of three linear inequalities

Graph the system of inequalities.

$y \geq -1$ **Inequality 1**
$x > -2$ **Inequality 2**
$x + 2y \leq 4$ **Inequality 3**

Solution

Graph all three inequalities in the same coordinate plane. The graph of the system is the triangular region shown.

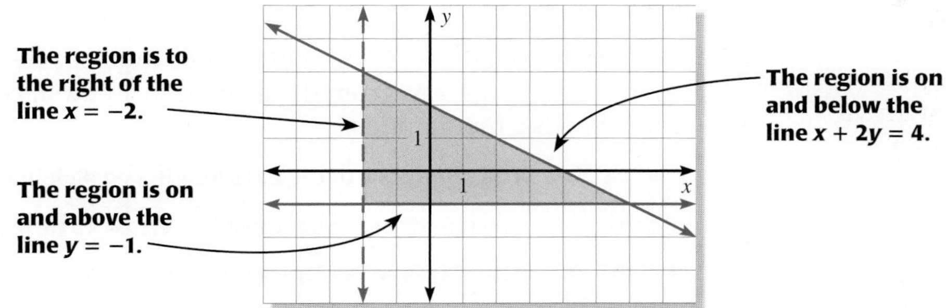

GUIDED PRACTICE for Examples 1 and 2

Graph the system of linear inequalities.

1. $y < x - 4$
   $y \geq -x + 3$

2. $y \geq -x + 2$
   $y < 4$
   $x < 3$

3. $y > -x$
   $y \geq x - 4$
   $y < 5$

EXAMPLE 3 Write a system of linear inequalities

Write a system of inequalities for the shaded region.

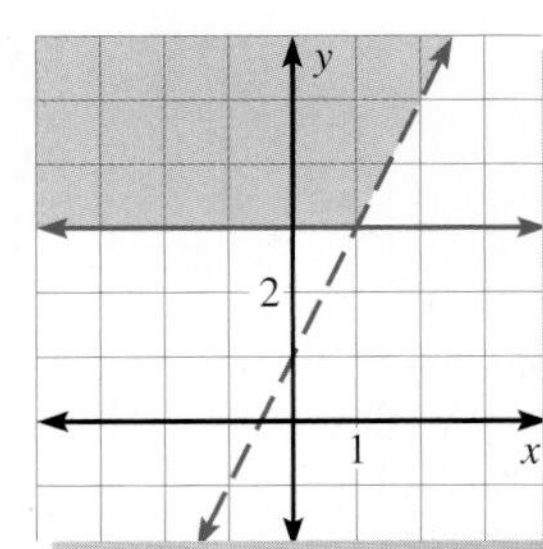

REVIEW EQUATIONS OF LINES
You may want to review writing an equation of a line before writing a system of inequalities.

Solution

INEQUALITY 1: One boundary line for the shaded region is $y = 3$. Because the shaded region is *above* the *solid* line, the inequality is $y \geq 3$.

INEQUALITY 2: Another boundary line for the shaded region has a slope of 2 and a y-intercept of 1. So, its equation is $y = 2x + 1$. Because the shaded region is *above* the *dashed* line, the inequality is $y > 2x + 1$.

▶ The system of inequalities for the shaded region is:

$y \geq 3$ **Inequality 1**
$y > 2x + 1$ **Inequality 2**

EXAMPLE 4 Write and solve a system of linear inequalities

BASEBALL The National Collegiate Athletic Association (NCAA) regulates the lengths of aluminum baseball bats used by college baseball teams. The NCAA states that the length (in inches) of the bat minus the weight (in ounces) of the bat cannot exceed 3. Bats can be purchased at lengths from 26 to 34 inches.

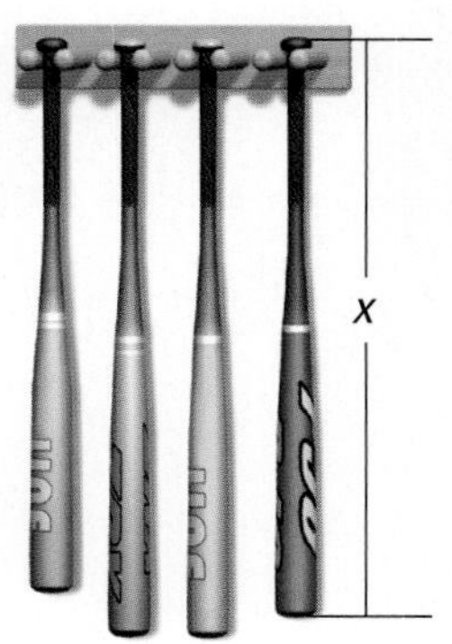

a. Write and graph a system of linear inequalities that describes the information given above.

b. A sporting goods store sells an aluminum bat that is 31 inches long and weighs 25 ounces. Use the graph to determine if this bat can be used by a player on an NCAA team.

Solution

a. Let x be the length (in inches) of the bat, and let y be the weight (in ounces) of the bat. From the given information, you can write the following inequalities:

$x - y \leq 3$ **The difference of the bat's length and weight can be at most 3.**

$x \geq 26$ **The length of the bat must be at least 26 inches.**

$x \leq 34$ **The length of the bat can be at most 34 inches.**

$y \geq 0$ **The weight of the bat cannot be a negative number.**

WRITING SYSTEMS OF INEQUALITIES
Consider the values of the variables when writing a system of inequalities. In many real-world problems, the values cannot be negative.

Graph each inequality in the system. Then identify the region that is common to all of the graphs of the inequalities. This region is shaded in the graph shown.

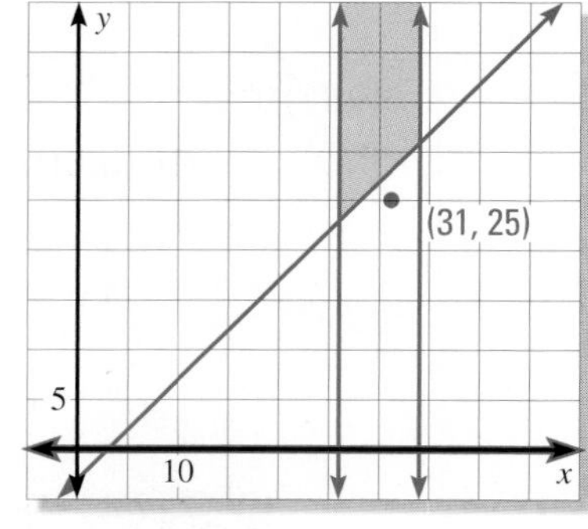

b. Graph the point that represents a bat that is 31 inches long and weighs 25 ounces.

▶ Because the point falls outside the solution region, the bat cannot be used by a player on an NCAA team.

✓ GUIDED PRACTICE for Examples 3 and 4

Write a system of inequalities that defines the shaded region.

4.

5.

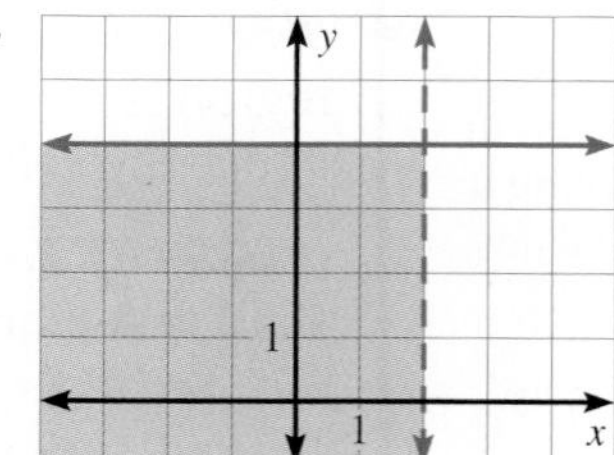

6. WHAT IF? In Example 4, suppose a Senior League (ages 10–14) player wants to buy the bat described in part (b). In Senior League, the length (in inches) of the bat minus the weight (in ounces) of the bat cannot exceed 8. Write and graph a system of inequalities to determine whether the described bat can be used by the Senior League player.

6.6 EXERCISES

HOMEWORK KEY

○ = See WORKED-OUT SOLUTIONS Exs. 13 and 39

★ = STANDARDIZED TEST PRACTICE Exs. 2, 21, 22, 33, and 40

SKILL PRACTICE

1. **VOCABULARY** Copy and complete: A(n) __?__ of a system of linear inequalities is an ordered pair that is a solution of each inequality in the system.

2. ★ **WRITING** *Describe* the steps you would take to graph the system of inequalities shown.

$x - y < 7$ **Inequality 1**
$y \geq 3$ **Inequality 2**

CHECKING A SOLUTION Tell whether the ordered pair is a solution of the system of inequalities.

3. (1, 1)

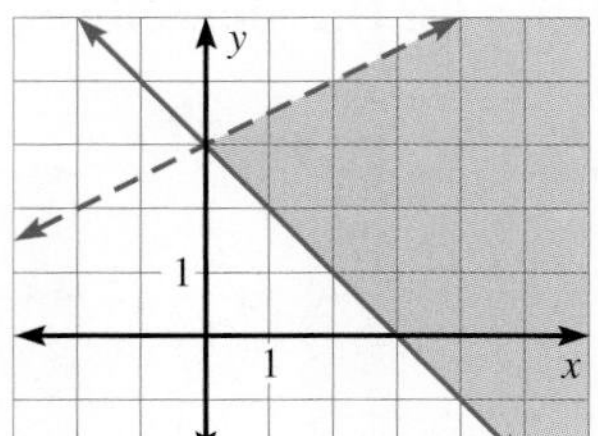

4. (0, 6)

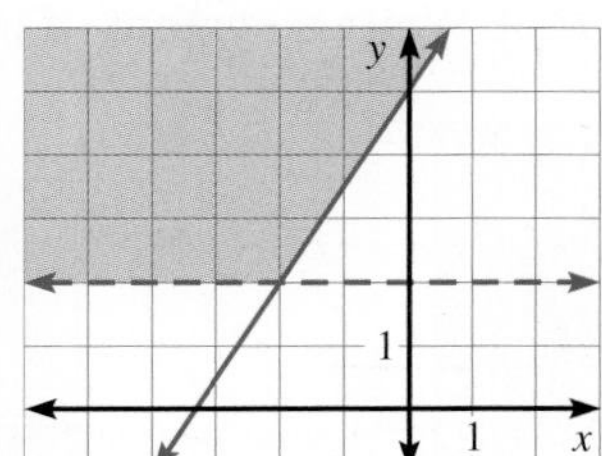

5. (3, −1)

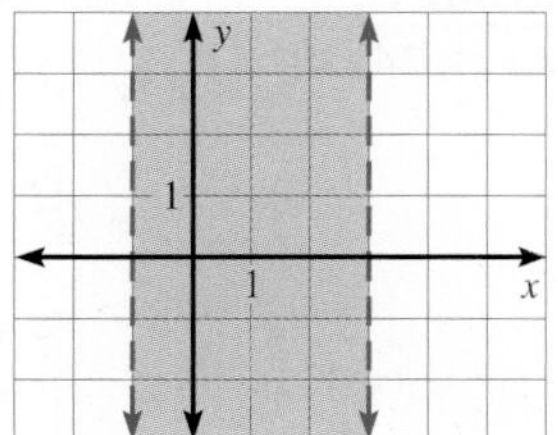

EXAMPLE 1 for Exs. 6–17

MATCHING SYSTEMS AND GRAPHS Match the system of inequalities with its graph.

6. $x - 4y > -8$
$x \geq 2$

7. 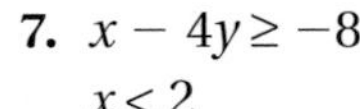 $x - 4y \geq -8$
$x < 2$

8. 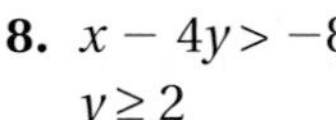 $x - 4y > -8$
$y \geq 2$

A.

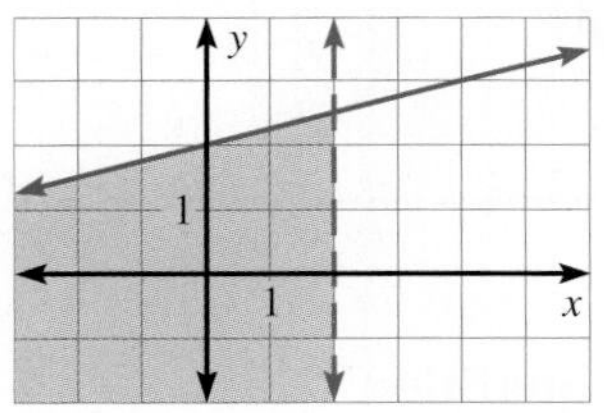

B.

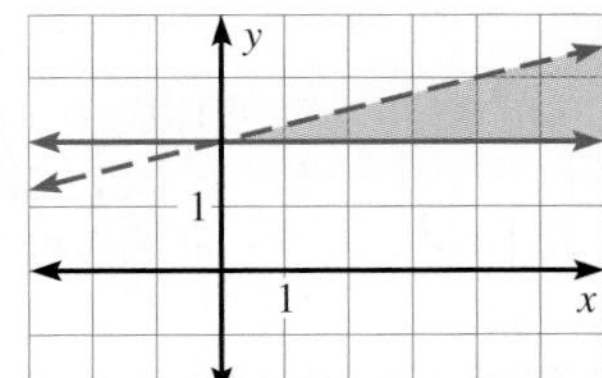

C.

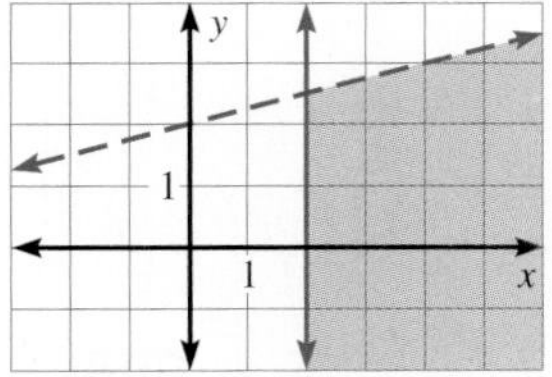

GRAPHING A SYSTEM Graph the system of inequalities.

9. $x > -5$
$x < 2$

10. $y \leq 10$
$y \geq 6$

11. $x > 3$
$y > x$

12. $y < -2x + 3$
$y \geq 4$

13. $y \geq 0$
$y < 2.5x - 1$

14. $y \geq 2x + 1$
$y < -x + 4$

15. $x < 8$
$x - 4y \leq -8$

16. $y \geq -2$
$2x + 3y > -6$

17. $y - 2x < 7$
$y + 2x > -1$

EXAMPLE 2 for Exs. 18–21

18. $x < 4$
$y > 1$
$y \geq -x + 1$

19. $x \geq 0$
$y \geq 0$
$6x - y < 12$

20. $x + y \leq 10$
$x - y \geq 2$
$y \geq 2$

21. ★ **MULTIPLE CHOICE** Which ordered pair is a solution of the system $2x - y \leq 5$ and $x + 2y > 2$?

(A) (1, −1) (B) (4, 1) (C) (2, 0) (D) (3, 2)

EXAMPLE 2
for Exs. 22–23

22. ★ **MULTIPLE CHOICE** The graph of which system of inequalities is shown?

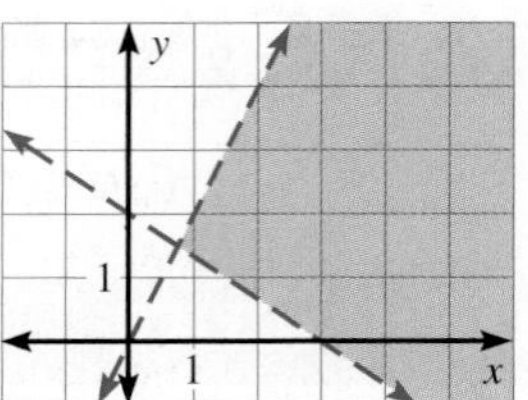

Ⓐ $y < 2x$
$2x + 3y < 6$

Ⓑ $y < 2x$
$2x + 3y > 6$

Ⓒ $y > 2x$
$2x + 3y < 6$

Ⓓ $y > 2x$
$2x + 3y > 6$

23. **ERROR ANALYSIS** *Describe* and correct the error in graphing this system of inequalities:

$x + y < 3$ **Inequality 1**
$x > -1$ **Inequality 2**
$x \leq 3$ **Inequality 3**

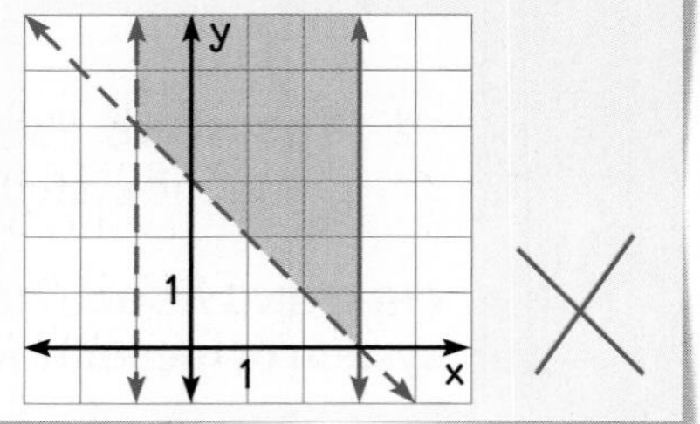

EXAMPLE 3
for Exs. 24–29

WRITING A SYSTEM Write a system of inequalities for the shaded region.

24.
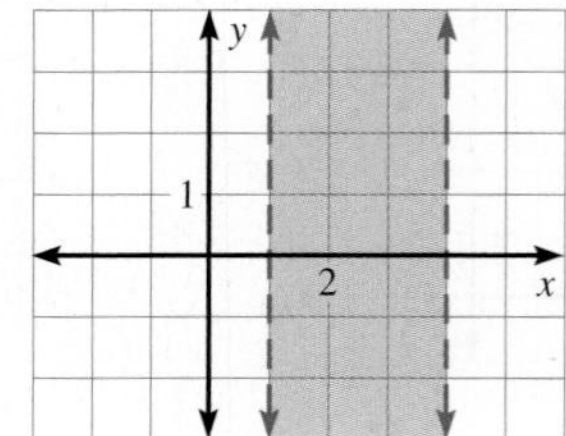

25.
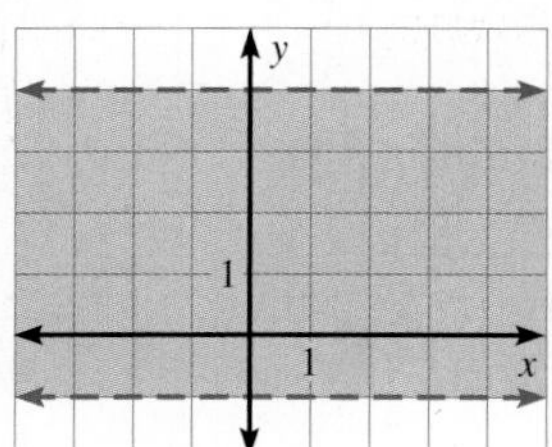

26.
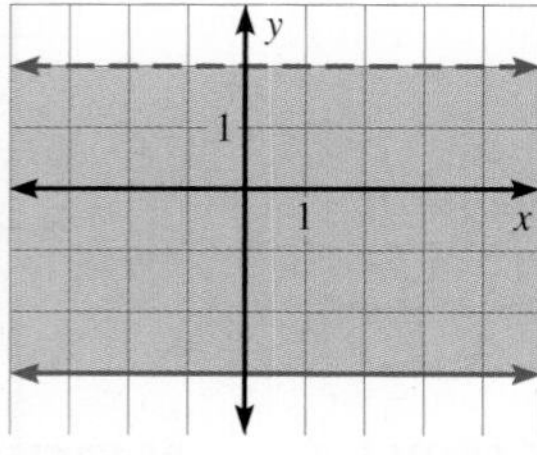

27.
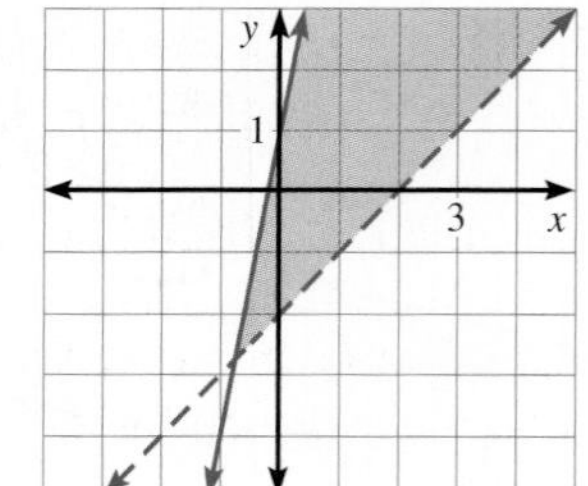

28.
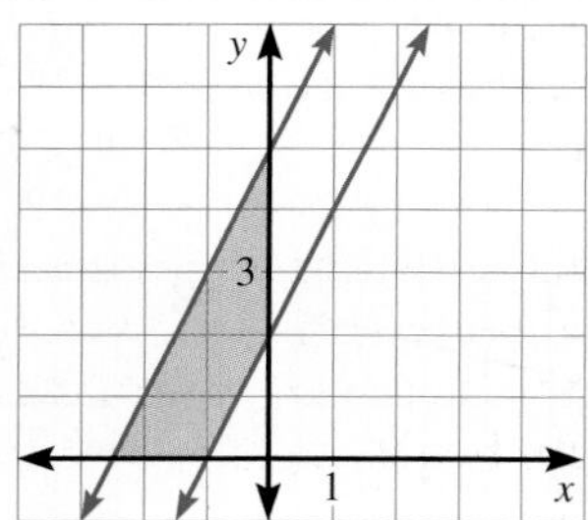

29.
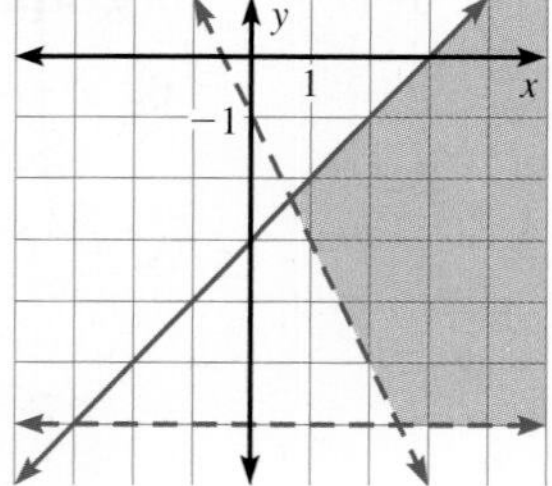

GRAPHING A SYSTEM Graph the system of inequalities.

30. $x > 4$
$x < 9$
$y \leq 2$
$y > -2$

31. $x + y < 4$
$x + y > -2$
$x - y \leq 3$
$x - y \geq -4$

32. $x \leq 10$
$3x + 2y \geq 9$
$x - 2y \leq 6$
$x + y \leq 5$

33. ★ **SHORT RESPONSE** Does the system of inequalities have any solutions? *Explain.*

$x - y > 5$ **Inequality 1**
$x - y < 1$ **Inequality 2**

CHALLENGE Write a system of inequalities for the shaded region described.

34. The shaded region is a rectangle with vertices at (2, 1), (2, 4), (6, 4), and (6, 1).

35. The shaded region is a triangle with vertices at (−3, 0), (3, 2), and (0, −2).

◯ = See WORKED-OUT SOLUTIONS in Student Resources   ★ = STANDARDIZED TEST PRACTICE

PROBLEM SOLVING

EXAMPLE 4
for Exs. 36–38

36. **COMPETITION SCORES** In a marching band competition, scoring is based on a musical evaluation and a visual evaluation. The musical evaluation score cannot exceed 60 points, the visual evaluation score cannot exceed 40 points. Write and graph a system of inequalities for the scores that a marching band can receive.

37. **NUTRITION** For a hiking trip, you are making a mix of x ounces of peanuts and y ounces of chocolate pieces. You want the mix to have less than 70 grams of fat and weigh less than 8 ounces. An ounce of peanuts has 14 grams of fat, and an ounce of chocolate pieces has 7 grams of fat. Write and graph a system of inequalities that models the situation.

38. **FISHING LIMITS** You are fishing in a marina for surfperch and rockfish, which are two species of bottomfish. Gaming laws in the marina allow you to catch no more than 15 surfperch per day, no more than 10 rockfish per day, and no more than 15 total bottomfish per day.

    a. Write and graph a system of inequalities that models the situation.

    b. Use the graph to determine whether you can catch 11 surfperch and 9 rockfish in one day.

39. **HEALTH** A person's maximum heart rate (in beats per minute) is given by $220 - x$ where x is the person's age in years ($20 \le x \le 65$). When exercising, a person should aim for a heart rate that is at least 70% of the maximum heart rate and at most 85% of the maximum heart rate.

    a. Write and graph a system of inequalities that models the situation.

    b. A 40-year-old person's heart rate varies from 104 to 120 beats per minute while exercising. Does his heart rate stay in the suggested target range for his age? *Explain.*

40. ★ **SHORT RESPONSE** A photography shop has a self-service photo center that allows you to make prints of pictures. Each sheet of printed pictures costs $8. The number of pictures that fit on each sheet is shown.

    a. You want at least 16 pictures of any size, and you are willing to spend up to $48. Write and graph a system of inequalities that models the situation.

    b. Will you be able to purchase 12 pictures that are 3 inches by 5 inches and 6 pictures that are 4 inches by 6 inches? *Explain.*

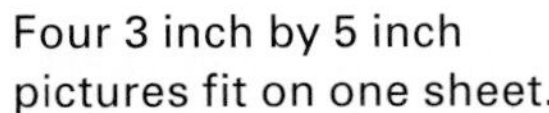
Four 3 inch by 5 inch pictures fit on one sheet.

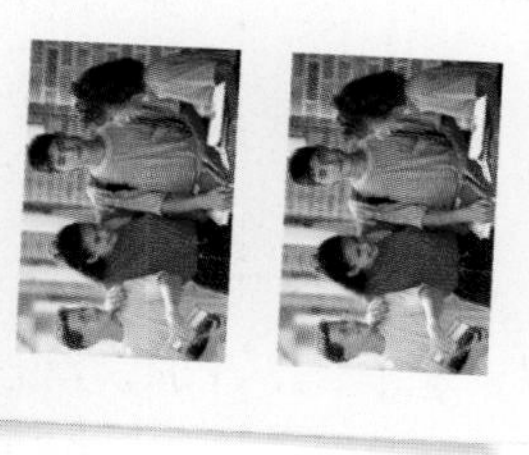
Two 4 inch by 6 inch pictures fit on one sheet.

41. **CHALLENGE** You make necklaces and keychains to sell at a craft fair. The table shows the time that it takes to make each necklace and keychain, the cost of materials for each necklace and keychain, and the time and money that you can devote to making necklaces and keychains.

	Necklace	Keychain	Available
Time to make (hours)	0.5	0.25	20
Cost to make (dollars)	2	3	120

a. Write and graph a system of inequalities for the number x of necklaces and the number y of keychains that you can make under the given constraints.

b. Find the vertices (corner points) of the graph.

c. You sell each necklace for \$10 and each keychain for \$8. The revenue R is given by the equation $R = 10x + 8y$. Find the revenue for each ordered pair in part (b). Which vertex results in the maximum revenue?

QUIZ

Graph the linear system. Then use the graph to tell whether the linear system has *one solution, no solution,* or *infinitely many solutions.*

1. $x - y = 1$
   $x - y = 6$

2. $6x + 2y = 16$
   $2x - y = 2$

3. $3x - 3y = -2$
   $-6x + 6y = 4$

Graph the system of linear inequalities.

4. $x > -3$
   $x < 7$

5. $y \leq 2$
   $y < 6x + 2$

6. $4x \geq y$
   $-x + 4y < 4$

7. $x + y < 2$
   $2x + y > -3$
   $y \geq 0$

8. $y \geq 3x - 4$
   $y \leq x$
   $y \geq -5x - 15$

9. $x > -5$
   $x < 0$
   $y \leq 2x + 7$

See **EXTRA PRACTICE** in Student Resources **ONLINE QUIZ** at my.hrw.com

MIXED REVIEW *of Problem Solving*

Make sense of problems and persevere in solving them.

1. **MULTI-STEP PROBLEM** A minimum of 600 bricks and 12 bags of sand are needed for a construction job. Each brick weighs 2 pounds, and each bag of sand weighs 50 pounds. The maximum weight that a delivery truck can carry is 3000 pounds.

   a. Let x be the number of bricks, and let y be the number of bags of sand. Write a system of linear inequalities that models the situation.

   b. Graph the system of inequalities.

   c. Use the graph to determine whether 700 bricks and 20 bags of sand can be delivered in one trip.

2. **MULTI-STEP PROBLEM** Dan decides to paint the ceiling and the walls of a room. He spends \$120 on 2 gallons of paint for the ceiling and 4 gallons of paint for the walls. Then he decides to paint the ceiling and the walls of another room using the same kinds of paint. He spends \$60 for 1 gallon of paint for the ceiling and 2 gallons of paint for the walls.

   a. Write a system of linear equations that models the situation.

   b. Is there enough information given to determine the cost of one gallon of each type of paint? *Explain.*

   c. A gallon of ceiling paint costs \$3 more than a gallon of wall paint. What is the cost of one gallon of each type of paint?

3. **SHORT RESPONSE** During a sale at a music and video store, all CDs are priced the same and all DVDs are priced the same. Karen buys 4 CDs and 2 DVDs for \$78. The next day, while the sale is still in progress, Karen goes back and buys 2 CDs and 1 DVD for \$39. Is there enough information to determine the cost of 1 CD? *Explain.*

4. **SHORT RESPONSE** Two airport shuttles, bus A and bus B, take passengers to the airport from the same bus stop. The graph shows the distance d (in miles) traveled by each bus t hours after bus A leaves the station. The distance from the bus stop to the airport is 25 miles. If bus A and bus B continue at the same rates, will bus B ever catch up to bus A? *Explain.*

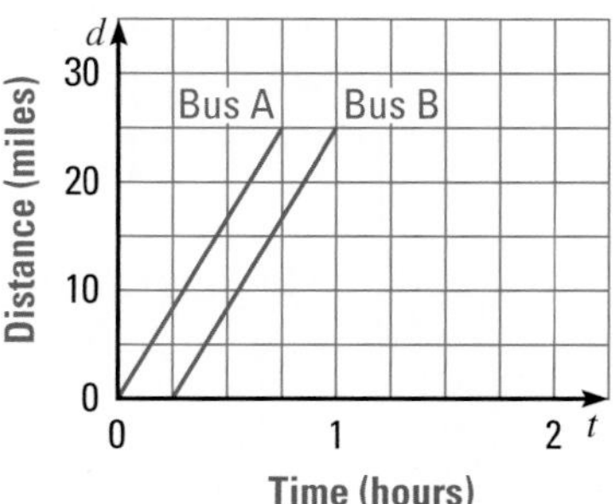

5. **EXTENDED RESPONSE** During the summer, you want to earn at least \$200 per week. You earn \$10 per hour working as a lifeguard, and you earn \$8 per hour working at a retail store. You can work at most 30 hours per week.

   a. Write and graph a system of linear inequalities that models the situation.

   b. If you work 5 hours per week as a lifeguard and 15 hours per week at the retail store, will you earn at least \$200 per week? *Explain.*

   c. You are scheduled to work 20 hours per week at the retail store. What is the range of hours you can work as a lifeguard to earn at least \$200 per week?

6. **OPEN-ENDED** *Describe* a real-world situation that can be modeled by a system of linear inequalities. Then write and graph the system of inequalities.

7. **GRIDDED ANSWER** What is the area (in square feet) of the triangular garden defined by the system of inequalities below?

$$y \geq 0$$
$$x \geq 0$$
$$4x + 5y \leq 60$$

6 CHAPTER SUMMARY

BIG IDEAS

For Your Notebook

Big Idea 1

Solving Linear Systems by Graphing

The graph of a system of two linear equations tells you how many solutions the system has.

One solution

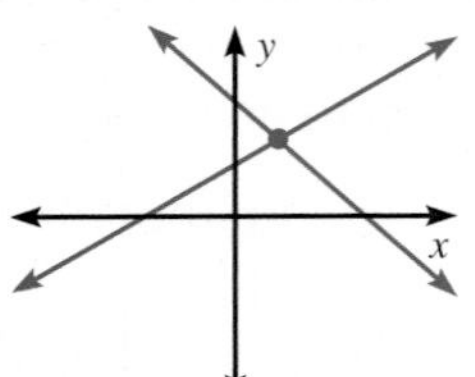

The lines intersect.

No solution

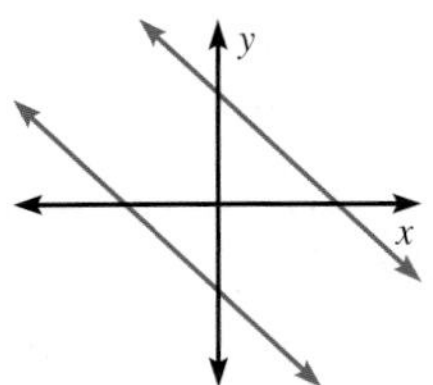

The lines are parallel.

Infinitely many solutions

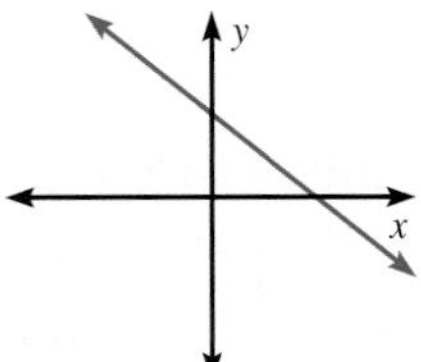

The lines coincide.

Big Idea 2

Solving Linear Systems Using Algebra

You can use any of the following algebraic methods to solve a system of linear equations. Sometimes it is easier to use one method instead of another.

Method	Procedure	When to use
Substitution	Solve one equation for x or y. Substitute the expression for x or y into the other equation.	When one equation is already solved for x or y
Addition	Add the equations to eliminate x or y.	When the coefficients of one variable are opposites
Subtraction	Subtract the equations to eliminate x or y.	When the coefficients of one variable are the same
Multiplication	Multiply one or both equations by a constant so that adding or subtracting the equations will eliminate x or y.	When no corresponding coefficients are the same or opposites

Big Idea 3

Solving Systems of Linear Inequalities

The graph of a system of linear inequalities is the intersection of the half-planes of each inequality in the system. For example, the graph of the system of inequalities below is the shaded region.

$x \le 6$ **Inequality 1**
$y < 2$ **Inequality 2**
$2x + 3y \ge 6$ **Inequality 3**

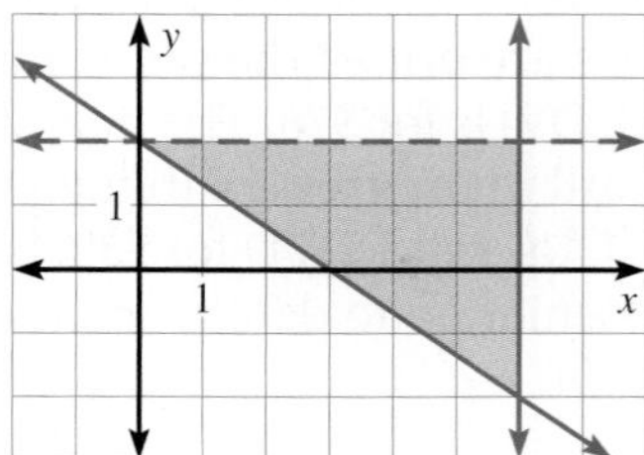

6 CHAPTER REVIEW

@HomeTutor
my.hrw.com
- Multi-Language Glossary
- Vocabulary practice

REVIEW KEY VOCABULARY

- system of linear equations
- solution of a system of linear equations
- consistent independent system
- inconsistent system
- consistent dependent system
- system of linear inequalities
- solution of a system of linear inequalities
- graph of a system of linear inequalities

VOCABULARY EXERCISES

1. Copy and complete: A(n) __?__ consists of two or more linear inequalities in the same variables.
2. Copy and complete: A(n) __?__ consists of two or more linear equations in the same variables.
3. *Describe* how you would graph a system of two linear inequalities.
4. Give an example of a consistent dependent system. *Explain* why the system is a consistent dependent system.

REVIEW EXAMPLES AND EXERCISES

Use the review examples and exercises below to check your understanding of the concepts you have learned in each lesson of this chapter.

6.1 Solve Linear Systems by Graphing

EXAMPLE

Solve the linear system by graphing. Check your solution.

$y = x - 2$ **Equation 1**
$y = -3x + 2$ **Equation 2**

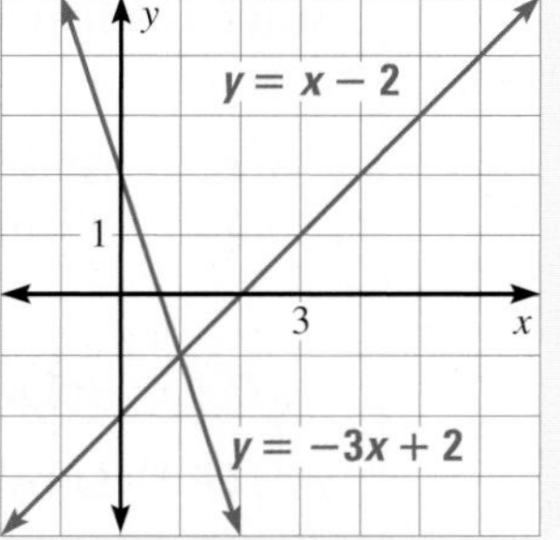

Graph both equations. The lines appear to intersect at (1, −1). Check the solution by substituting 1 for x and −1 for y in each equation.

$y = x - 2$	$y = -3x + 2$
$-1 \stackrel{?}{=} 1 - 2$	$-1 \stackrel{?}{=} -3(1) + 2$
$-1 = -1$ ✓	$-1 = -1$ ✓

EXERCISES

EXAMPLES 1 and 2 for Exs. 5–7

Solve the linear system by graphing. Check your solution.

5. $y = -3x + 1$
   $y = x - 7$
6. $y = 3x + 4$
   $y = -2x - 1$
7. $x + y = 3$
   $x - y = 5$

6 CHAPTER REVIEW

6.2 Solve Linear Systems by Substitution

EXAMPLE

Solve the linear system: $3x + y = -9$ **Equation 1**
$y = 5x + 7$ **Equation 2**

STEP 1 **Substitute** $5x + 7$ for y in Equation 1 and solve for x.

$3x + y = -9$ **Write Equation 1.**

$3x + 5x + 7 = -9$ **Substitute $5x + 7$ for y.**

$x = -2$ **Solve for x.**

STEP 2 **Substitute** -2 for x in Equation 2 to find the value of y.

$$y = 5x + 7 = 5(-2) + 7 = -10 + 7 = -3$$

▸ The solution is $(-2, -3)$. Check the solution by substituting -2 for x and -3 for y in each of the original equations.

EXERCISES

EXAMPLES 1, 2, and 3 for Exs. 8–11

Solve the linear system using substitution.

8. $y = 2x - 7$
$x + 2y = 1$

9. $x + 4y = 9$
$x - y = 4$

10. $2x + y = -15$
$y - 5x = 6$

11. ART Kara spends \$16 on tubes of paint and disposable brushes for an art project. Each tube of paint costs \$3, and each disposable brush costs \$.50. Kara purchases twice as many brushes as tubes of paint. Find the number of brushes and the number of tubes of paint that she purchases.

6.3 Solve Linear Systems by Adding or Subtracting

EXAMPLE

Solve the linear system: $5x - y = 8$ **Equation 1**
$-5x + 4y = -17$ **Equation 2**

STEP 1 **Add** the equations to eliminate one variable.

$$\begin{array}{r} 5x - y = 8 \\ -5x + 4y = -17 \\ \hline 3y = -9 \end{array}$$

STEP 2 **Solve** for y. $y = -3$

STEP 3 **Substitute** -3 for y in either equation and solve for x.

$5x - y = 8$ **Write Equation 1.**

$5x - (-3) = 8$ **Substitute -3 for y.**

$x = 1$ **Solve for x.**

▸ The solution is $(1, -3)$. Check the solution by substituting 1 for x and -3 for y in each of the original equations.

@HomeTutor
my.hrw.com
Chapter Review Practice

EXERCISES

EXAMPLES 1, 2, and 3 for Exs. 12–17

Solve the linear system using elimination.

12. $x + 2y = 13$
$x - 2y = -7$

13. $4x - 5y = 14$
$-4x + y = -6$

14. $x + 7y = 12$
$-2x + 7y = 18$

15. $9x - 2y = 34$
$5x - 2y = 10$

16. $3x = y + 1$
$2x - y = 9$

17. $4y = 11 - 3x$
$3x + 2y = -5$

6.4 Solve Linear Systems by Multiplying First

EXAMPLE

Solve the linear system: $x - 2y = -7$ **Equation 1**
$3x - y = 4$ **Equation 2**

STEP 1 **Multiply** the first equation by −3.

$x - 2y = -7$ **× (−3)** → $-3x + 6y = 21$
$3x - y = 4$ → $3x - y = 4$

STEP 2 **Add** the equations. $5y = 25$

STEP 3 **Solve** for *y*. $y = 5$

STEP 4 **Substitute** 5 for *y* in either of the original equations and solve for *x*.

$x - 2y = -7$ **Write Equation 1.**

$x - 2(5) = -7$ **Substitute 5 for *y*.**

$x = 3$ **Solve for *x*.**

▶ The solution is (3, 5).

CHECK Substitute 3 for *x* and 5 for *y* in each of the original equations.

Equation 1	Equation 2
$x - 2y = -7$	$3x - y = 4$
$3 - 2(5) \stackrel{?}{=} -7$	$3(3) - 5 \stackrel{?}{=} 4$
$-7 = -7$ ✓	$4 = 4$ ✓

EXERCISES

EXAMPLES 1 and 2 for Exs. 18–24

Solve the linear system using elimination.

18. $-x + y = -4$
$2x - 3y = 5$

19. $x + 6y = 28$
$2x - 3y = -19$

20. $3x - 5y = -7$
$-4x + 7y = 8$

21. $8x - 7y = -3$
$6x - 5y = -1$

22. $5x = 3y - 2$
$3x + 2y = 14$

23. $11x = 2y - 1$
$3y = 10 + 8x$

24. CAR MAINTENANCE You pay $24.50 for 10 gallons of gasoline and 1 quart of oil at a gas station. Your friend pays $22 for 8 gallons of the same gasoline and 2 quarts of the same oil. Find the cost of 1 quart of oil.

6 CHAPTER REVIEW

6.5 Solve Special Types of Linear Systems

EXAMPLE

Show that the linear system has no solution.

$-2x + y = -3$ **Equation 1**
$y = 2x + 1$ **Equation 2**

Graph the linear system.

The lines are parallel because they have the same slope but different y-intercepts. Parallel lines do not intersect, so the system has no solution.

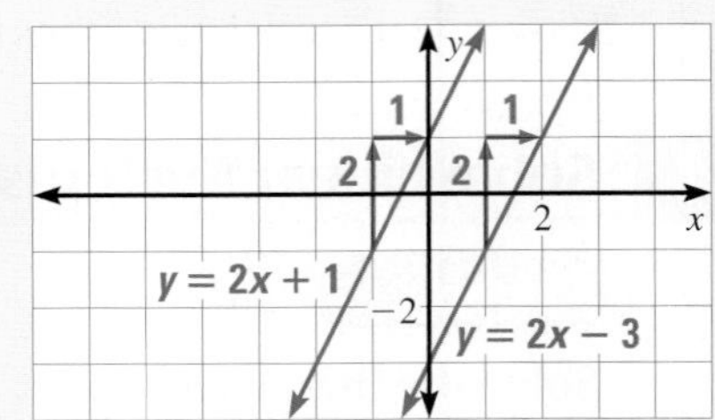

EXERCISES

EXAMPLES 1, 2, and 3 for Exs. 25–27

Tell whether the linear system has *one solution, no solution,* or *infinitely many solutions. Explain.*

25. $x = 2y - 3$
$1.5x - 3y = 0$

26. $-x + y = 8$
$x + 8 = y$

27. $4x = 2y + 6$
$4x + 2y = 10$

6.6 Solve Systems of Linear Inequalities

EXAMPLE

Graph the system of linear inequalities.

$y < -2x + 3$ **Inequality 1**
$y \geq x - 3$ **Inequality 2**

The graph of $y < -2x + 3$ is the half-plane *below* the *dashed* line $y = -2x + 3$.

The graph of $y \geq x - 3$ is the half-plane *on and above* the *solid* line $y = x - 3$.

The graph of the system is the intersection of the two half-planes shown as the darker shade of blue.

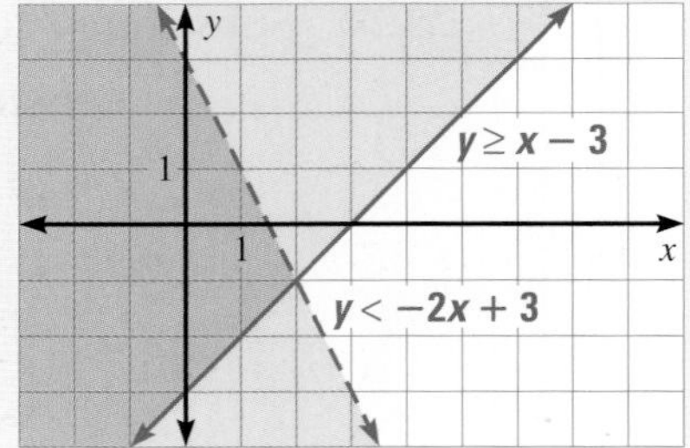

EXERCISES

EXAMPLES 1, 2, 3, and 4 for Exs. 28–31

Graph the system of linear inequalities.

28. $y < x + 3$
$y > -3x - 2$

29. $y \leq -x - 2$
$y > 4x + 1$

30. $y \geq 0$
$x \leq 2$
$y < x + 4$

31. MOVIE COSTS You receive a \$40 gift card to a movie theater. A ticket to a matinee movie costs \$5, and a ticket to an evening movie costs \$8. Write and graph a system of inequalities for the number of tickets you can purchase using the gift card.

6 CHAPTER TEST

Solve the linear system by graphing. Check your solution.

1. $3x - y = -6$
   $x + y = 2$
2. $-2x + y = 5$
   $x + y = -1$
3. $y = 4x + 4$
   $3x + 2y = 12$
4. $5x - 4y = 20$
   $x + 2y = 4$
5. $x + 3y = 9$
   $2x - y = 4$
6. $2x + 7y = 14$
   $5x + 7y = -7$

Solve the linear system using substitution.

7. $y = 5x - 7$
   $-4x + y = -1$
8. $x = y - 11$
   $x - 3y = 1$
9. $3x + y = -19$
   $x - y = 7$
10. $15x + y = 70$
    $3x - 2y = -8$
11. $3y + x = 17$
    $x + y = 8$
12. $0.5x + y = 9$
    $1.6x + 0.2y = 13$

Solve the linear system using elimination.

13. $8x + 3y = -9$
    $-8x + y = 29$
14. $x - 5y = -3$
    $3x - 5y = 11$
15. $4x + y = 17$
    $7y = 4x - 9$
16. $3x + 2y = -5$
    $x - y = 10$
17. $3y = x + 5$
    $-3x + 8y = 8$
18. $6x - 5y = 9$
    $9x - 7y = 15$

Tell whether the linear system has *one solution, no solution,* or *infinitely many solutions.*

19. $15x - 3y = 12$
    $y = 5x - 4$
20. $4x - y = -4$
    $-8x + 2y = 2$
21. $-12x + 3y = 18$
    $4x + y = -6$
22. $6x - 7y = 5$
    $-12x + 14y = 10$
23. $3x - 4y = 24$
    $3x + 4y = 24$
24. $10x - 2y = 14$
    $15x - 3y = 21$

Graph the system of linear inequalities.

25. $y < 2x + 2$
    $y \geq -x - 1$
26. $y \leq 3x - 2$
    $y > x + 4$
27. $y \leq 3$
    $x > -1$
    $y > 3x - 3$

28. **TRUCK RENTALS** Carrie and Dave each rent the same size moving truck for one day. They pay a fee of x dollars for the truck and y dollars per mile they drive. Carrie drives 150 miles and pays \$215. Dave drives 120 miles and pays \$176. Find the amount of the fee and the cost per mile.

29. **GEOMETRY** The rectangle has a perimeter P of 58 inches. The length ℓ is one more than 3 times the width w. Write and solve a system of linear equations to find the length and width of the rectangle.

$P = 58$ in.; w; ℓ

30. **COMMUNITY SERVICE** A town committee has a budget of \$75 to spend on snacks for the volunteers participating in a clean-up day. The committee chairperson decides to purchase granola bars and at least 50 bottles of water. Granola bars cost \$.50 each, and bottles of water cost \$.75 each. Write and graph a system of linear inequalities for the number of bottles of water and the number of granola bars that can be purchased.

MULTIPLE CHOICE QUESTIONS

If you have difficulty solving a multiple choice problem directly, you may be able to use another approach to eliminate incorrect answer choices and obtain the correct answer.

PROBLEM 1

Which ordered pair is the solution of the linear system $y = \frac{1}{2}x$ and $2x + 3y = -7$?

Ⓐ (2, 1) Ⓑ (1, −3) Ⓒ (−2, −1) Ⓓ (4, 2)

Method 1

SOLVE DIRECTLY Use substitution to solve the linear system.

STEP 1 **Substitute** $\frac{1}{2}x$ for y in the equation $2x + 3y = -7$ and solve for x.

$$2x + 3\mathbf{y} = -7$$

$$2x + 3\left(\frac{1}{2}\mathbf{x}\right) = -7$$

$$2x + \frac{3}{2}x = -7$$

$$\frac{7}{2}x = -7$$

$$x = -2$$

STEP 2 **Substitute** −2 for x in $y = \frac{1}{2}x$ to find the value of y.

$$y = \frac{1}{2}\mathbf{x}$$

$$= \frac{1}{2}(\mathbf{-2})$$

$$= -1$$

The solution of the system is (−2, −1).

The correct answer is C. Ⓐ Ⓑ Ⓒ Ⓓ

Method 2

ELIMINATE CHOICES Substitute the values given in each answer choice for x and y in both equations.

Choice A: (2, 1)
Substitute 2 for x and 1 for y.

$\mathbf{y} = \frac{1}{2}\mathbf{x}$ $\qquad 2\mathbf{x} + 3\mathbf{y} = -7$

$\mathbf{1} \stackrel{?}{=} \frac{1}{2}(\mathbf{2})$ $\qquad 2(\mathbf{2}) + 3(\mathbf{1}) \stackrel{?}{=} -7$

$1 = 1$ ✓ $\qquad 7 = -7$ ✗

Choice B: (1, −3)
Substitute 1 for x and −3 for y.

$\mathbf{y} = \frac{1}{2}\mathbf{x}$

$\mathbf{-3} \stackrel{?}{=} \frac{1}{2}(\mathbf{1})$

$-3 = \frac{1}{2}$ ✗

Choice C: (−2, −1)
Substitute −2 for x and −1 for y.

$\mathbf{y} = \frac{1}{2}\mathbf{x}$ $\qquad 2\mathbf{x} + 3\mathbf{y} = -7$

$\mathbf{-1} \stackrel{?}{=} \frac{1}{2}(\mathbf{-2})$ $\qquad 2(\mathbf{-2}) + 3(\mathbf{-1}) \stackrel{?}{=} -7$

$-1 = -1$ ✓ $\qquad -7 = -7$ ✓

The correct answer is C. Ⓐ Ⓑ Ⓒ Ⓓ

PROBLEM 2

The sum of two numbers is −1, and the difference of the two numbers is 5. What are the numbers?

Ⓐ −5 and 4 Ⓑ 1 and 6 Ⓒ 2 and −3 Ⓓ −2 and 3

Method 1

SOLVE DIRECTLY Write and solve a system of equations for the numbers.

STEP 1 **Write** a system of equations. Let x and y be the numbers.

$x + y = -1$ **Equation 1**
$x - y = 5$ **Equation 2**

STEP 2 **Add** the equations to eliminate one variable. Then find the value of the other variable.

$$\begin{array}{r} x + y = -1 \\ x - y = 5 \\ \hline 2x = 4, \text{ so } x = 2 \end{array}$$

STEP 3 **Substitute** 2 for x in Equation 1 and solve for y.

$2 + y = -1$, so $y = -3$

The correct answer is C. Ⓐ Ⓑ Ⓒ Ⓓ

Method 2

ELIMINATE CHOICES Find the sum and difference of each pair of numbers. Because the difference is positive, be sure to subtract the lesser number from the greater number.

Choice A: −5 and 4

Sum: $-5 + 4 = -1$ ✓

Difference: $-5 - 4 = -9$ ✗

Choice B: 1 and 6

Sum: $1 + 6 = 7$ ✗

Choice C: 2 and −3

Sum: $2 + (-3) = -1$ ✓

Difference: $2 - (-3) = 5$ ✓

The correct answer is C. Ⓐ Ⓑ Ⓒ Ⓓ

PRACTICE

Explain why you can eliminate the highlighted answer choice.

1. The sum of two numbers is –27. One number is twice the other. What are the numbers?

   Ⓐ ✗ 9 and 18 Ⓑ −3 and 24 Ⓒ −18 and −9 Ⓓ −14 and −13

2. Which ordered pair is a solution of the linear system $5x + 2y = -11$ and $x = -\frac{1}{2}y - 4$?

   Ⓐ $\left(-\frac{7}{6}, -\frac{17}{3}\right)$ Ⓑ $\left(-\frac{23}{3}, \frac{1}{3}\right)$ Ⓒ $(-3, 2)$ Ⓓ ✗ $(23, 213)$

3. Long-sleeve and short-sleeve T-shirts can be purchased at a concert. A long-sleeve T-shirt costs \$25 and a short-sleeve T-shirt costs \$15. During a concert, the T-shirt vendor collects \$8415 from the sale of 441 T-shirts. How many short-sleeve T-shirts were sold?

   Ⓐ 100 Ⓑ ✗ 180 Ⓒ 261 Ⓓ 441

6 ★ Standardized TEST PRACTICE

MULTIPLE CHOICE

1. Which ordered pair is the solution of the linear system $y = \frac{1}{2}x + 1$ and $y = \frac{3}{2}x + 4$?

   Ⓐ $\left(3, \frac{5}{2}\right)$ Ⓑ $\left(-3, -\frac{1}{2}\right)$

   Ⓒ $\left(\frac{3}{2}, \frac{7}{4}\right)$ Ⓓ $(0, 1)$

2. How many solutions does the linear system $3x + 5y = 8$ and $3x + 5y = 1$ have?

   Ⓐ 0 Ⓑ 1

   Ⓒ 2 Ⓓ Infinitely many

3. The sum of two numbers is -3, and the difference of the two numbers is 11. What are the numbers?

   Ⓐ 4 and 7 Ⓑ -3 and 8

   Ⓒ 3 and 14 Ⓓ -7 and 4

4. Which ordered pair is the solution of the system of linear equations whose graph is shown?

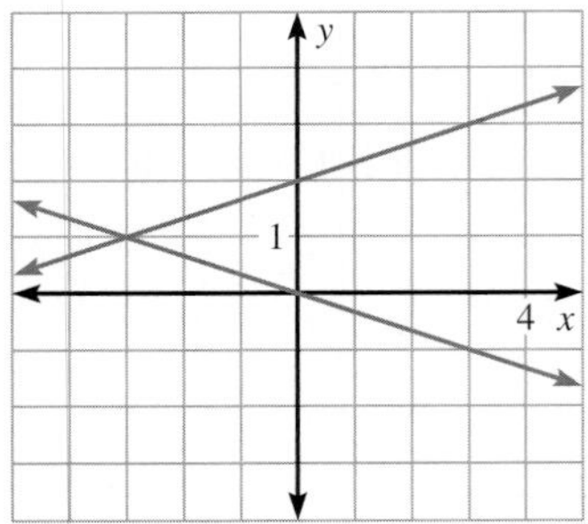

   Ⓐ $(3, -1)$ Ⓑ $(0, 0)$

   Ⓒ $(0, 2)$ Ⓓ $(-3, 1)$

5. Which ordered pair is the solution of the linear system $3x + y = -1$ and $y = -\frac{1}{2}x - \frac{7}{2}$?

   Ⓐ $\left(\frac{5}{2}, -\frac{17}{2}\right)$ Ⓑ $(1, -4)$

   Ⓒ $(-1, -3)$ Ⓓ $(0, -1)$

6. Which ordered pair is a solution of the system $x + 2y \le -2$ and $y \le -3x + 4$?

   Ⓐ $(0, 0)$ Ⓑ $(2, -2)$

   Ⓒ $(-2, 2)$ Ⓓ $(5, -4)$

7. How many solutions does the system of linear equations whose graph is shown have?

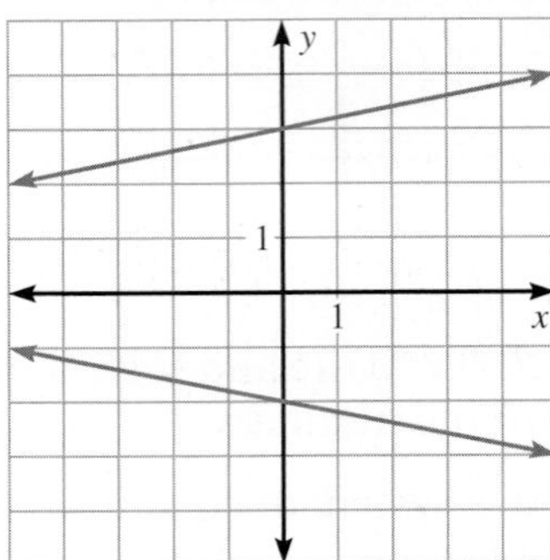

   Ⓐ 0 Ⓑ 1

   Ⓒ 2 Ⓓ Infinitely many

8. At a bakery, one customer pays \$5.67 for 3 bagels and 4 muffins. Another customer pays \$6.70 for 5 bagels and 3 muffins. Which system of equations can be used to determine the cost x (in dollars) of one bagel and the cost y (in dollars) of one muffin at the bakery?

   Ⓐ $x + y = 7$
$x + y = 8$ Ⓑ $y = 3x + 5.67$
$y = 5x + 6.7$

   Ⓒ $3x + 4y = 6.7$
$5x + 3y = 5.67$ Ⓓ $3x + 4y = 5.67$
$5x + 3y = 6.7$

9. The perimeter P (in feet) of each of the two rectangles below is given. What are the values of ℓ and w?

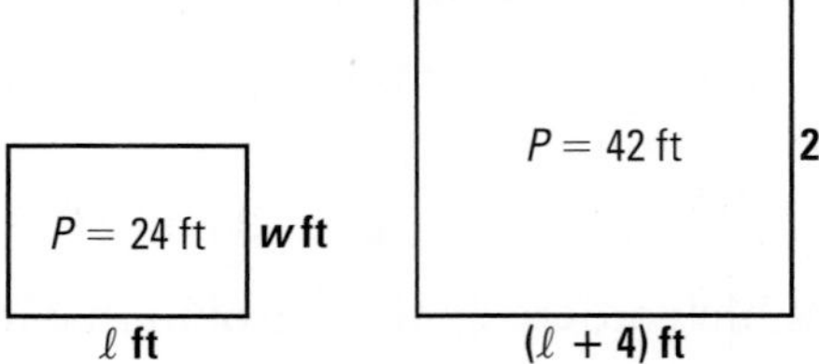

   Ⓐ $\ell = 7$ and $w = 5$

   Ⓑ $\ell = 8$ and $w = 4$

   Ⓒ $\ell = 11$ and $w = 10$

   Ⓓ $\ell = 12$ and $w = 9$

GRIDDED ANSWER

10. What is the x-coordinate of the solution of the system whose graph is shown?

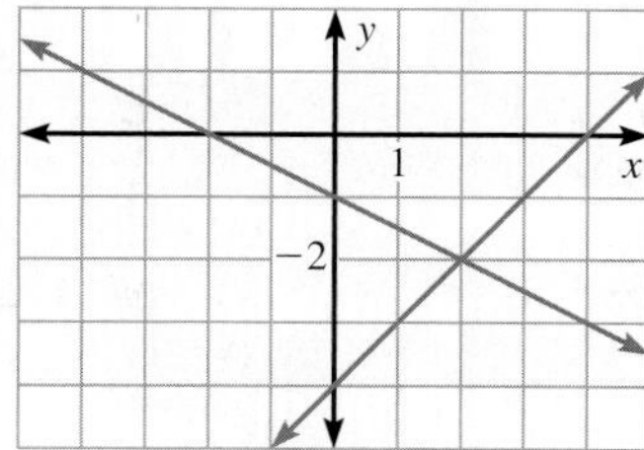

11. What is the x-coordinate of the solution of the system $y = \frac{1}{3}x + 8$ and $2x - y = 2$?

12. A science museum charges one amount for admission for an adult and a lesser amount for admission for a student. Admission to the museum for 28 students and 5 adults costs \$284. Admission for 40 students and 10 adults costs \$440. What is the admission cost (in dollars) for one student?

SHORT RESPONSE

13. Is it possible to find a value for c so that the linear system below has exactly one solution? *Explain.*

$5x + 3y = 21$ **Equation 1**

$y = -\frac{5}{3}x + c$ **Equation 2**

14. A rental car agency charges x dollars per day plus y dollars per mile to rent any of the mid-sized cars at the agency. The total costs for two customers are shown below.

Customer	Time (days)	Distance (miles)	Cost (dollars)
Jackson	3	150	217.50
Bree	2	112	148.00

How much will it cost to rent a mid-sized car for 5 days and drive 250 miles? *Explain.*

EXTENDED RESPONSE

15. A baseball player's batting average is the number of hits the player has divided by the number of at-bats. At the beginning of a game, a player has a batting average of .360. During the game, the player gets 3 hits during 5 at-bats, and his batting average changes to .375.

a. Write a system of linear equations that represents the situation.

b. How many at-bats has the player had so far this season?

c. Another player on the team has a batting average of .240 at the beginning of the same game. During the game, he gets 3 hits during 5 at-bats, and his batting average changes to .300. Has this player had more at-bats so far this season than the other player? *Explain.*

16. A gardener combines x fluid ounces of a 20% liquid fertilizer and 80% water mix with y fluid ounces of a 5% liquid fertilizer and 95% water mix to make 30 fluid ounces of a 10% liquid fertilizer and 90% water mix.

a. Write a system of linear equations that represents the situation.

b. Solve the system from part (a).

c. Suppose the gardener combines pure (100%) water and the 20% liquid fertilizer and 80% water mix to make the 30 fluid ounces of the 10% liquid fertilizer and 90% water mix. Is more of the 20% liquid fertilizer and 80% water mix used in this mix than in the original mix? *Explain.*

7 Exponents and Exponential Functions

COMMON CORE

Lesson	
7.1	CC.9-12.A.SSE.3c
7.2	CC.9-12.A.SSE.3c
7.3	CC.9-12.A.SSE.3c
7.4	CC.9-12.A.CED.2*
7.5	CC.9-12.A.CED.2*

Before

Previously, you learned the following skills, which you'll use in this chapter: using exponents, percents, and decimals, and writing function rules.

Prerequisite Skills

VOCABULARY CHECK

1. Identify the exponent and the base in the expression 13^8.
2. Copy and complete: An expression that represents repeated multiplication of the same factor is called a(n) __?__.

SKILLS CHECK

Evaluate the expression.

3. x^2 when $x = 10$ 4. a^3 when $a = 3$ 5. r^2 when $r = \frac{5}{6}$ 6. z^3 when $z = \frac{1}{2}$

Order the numbers from least to greatest.

7. 6.12, 6.2, 6.01
8. 0.073, 0.101, 0.0098

Write the percent as a decimal.

9. 4% 10. 0.5% 11. 13.8% 12. 145%

13. Write a rule for the function. Graph the function

Input	0	1	4	6	10
Output	2	3	6	8	12

Now

In this chapter, you will apply the big ideas listed below and reviewed in the Chapter Summary. You will also use the key vocabulary listed below.

Big Ideas

1. **Applying properties of exponents to simplify expressions**
2. **Writing and graphing exponential functions**

KEY VOCABULARY

- order of magnitude
- exponential function
- exponential growth
- compound interest
- exponential decay

Why?

You can use exponents to explore exponential growth and decay. For example, you can write an exponential function to find the value of a collector car over time.

Animated Algebra

The animation illustrated below helps you answer a question from this chapter: If you know the growth rate of the value of a collector car over time, can you predict what the car will sell for at an auction?

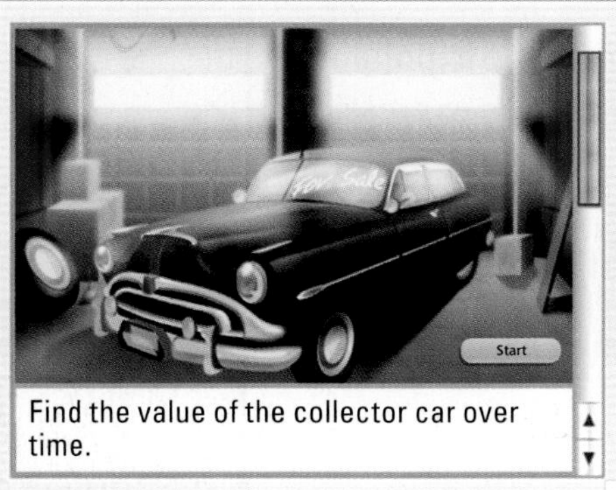

Find the value of the collector car over time.

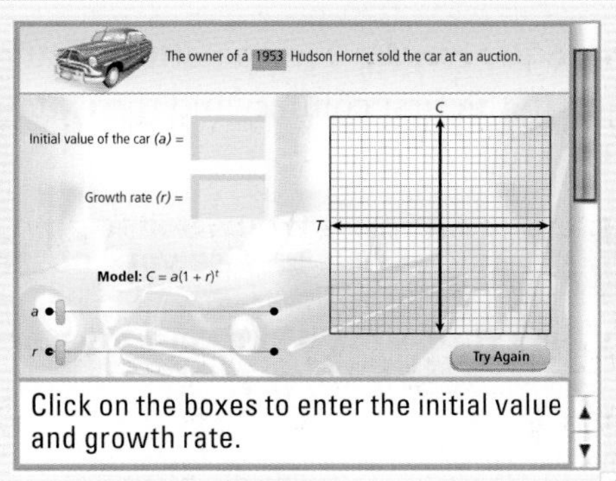

Click on the boxes to enter the initial value and growth rate.

Animated Algebra at my.hrw.com

Products and Powers

Look for and make use of structure.

MATERIALS • paper and pencil

QUESTION How can you find a product of powers and a power of a power?

EXPLORE 1 Find products of powers

STEP 1 ***Copy and complete*** Copy and complete the table.

Expression	Expression as repeated multiplication	Number of factors	Simplified expression
$7^4 \cdot 7^5$	$(7 \cdot 7 \cdot 7 \cdot 7) \cdot (7 \cdot 7 \cdot 7 \cdot 7 \cdot 7)$	9	7^9
$(-4)^2 \cdot (-4)^3$	$[(-4) \cdot (-4)] \cdot [(-4) \cdot (-4) \cdot (-4)]$	?	?
$x^1 \cdot x^5$	?	?	?

STEP 2 ***Analyze results*** Find a pattern that relates the exponents of the factors in the first column and the exponent of the expression in the last column.

EXPLORE 2 Find powers of powers

STEP 1 ***Copy and complete*** Copy and complete the table.

Expression	Expanded expression	Expression as repeated multiplication	Number of factors	Simplified expression
$(5^3)^2$	$(5^3) \cdot (5^3)$	$(5 \cdot 5 \cdot 5) \cdot (5 \cdot 5 \cdot 5)$	6	5^6
$[(-6)^2]^4$	$[(-6)^2] \cdot [(-6)^2] \cdot [(-6)^2] \cdot [(-6)^2]$	?	?	?
$(a^3)^3$	?	?	?	?

STEP 2 ***Analyze results*** Find a pattern that relates the exponents of the expression in the first column and the exponent of the expression in the last column.

DRAW CONCLUSIONS Use your observations to complete these exercises

Simplify the expression. Write your answer using exponents.

1. $5^2 \cdot 5^3$ **2.** $(-6)^1 \cdot (-6)^4$ **3.** $m^6 \cdot m^4$

4. $(10^3)^3$ **5.** $[(-2)^3]^4$ **6.** $(c^2)^6$

In Exercises 7 and 8, copy and complete the statement.

7. If a is a real number and m and n are positive integers, then $a^m \cdot a^n =$ __?__.

8. If a is a real number and m and n are positive integers, then $(a^m)^n =$ __?__.

7.1 Apply Exponent Properties Involving Products

Before You evaluated exponential expressions.

Now You will use properties of exponents involving products.

Why? So you can evaluate agricultural data, as in Example 5.

Key Vocabulary
- **order of magnitude**
- **power**
- **exponent**
- **base**

Notice what happens when you multiply two powers that have the same base.

$$a^2 \cdot a^3 = \overbrace{\underbrace{(a \cdot a)}_{\text{2 factors}} \cdot \underbrace{(a \cdot a \cdot a)}_{\text{3 factors}}}^{\text{5 factors}} = a^5 = a^{2+3}$$

The example above suggests the following property of exponents, known as the product of powers property.

CC.9-12.A.SSE.3c Use the properties of exponents to transform expressions for exponential functions.

KEY CONCEPT *For Your Notebook*

Product of Powers Property

Let a be a real number, and let m and n be positive integers.

Words To multiply powers having the same base, add the exponents.

Algebra $a^m \cdot a^n = a^{m+n}$ **Example** $5^6 \cdot 5^3 = 5^{6+3} = 5^9$

EXAMPLE 1 Use the product of powers property

SIMPLIFY EXPRESSIONS
When simplifying powers with numerical bases only, write your answers using exponents, as in parts (a), (b), and (c).

a. $7^3 \cdot 7^5 = 7^{3+5} = 7^8$

b. $9 \cdot 9^8 \cdot 9^2 = 9^1 \cdot 9^8 \cdot 9^2$
$= 9^{1+8+2}$
$= 9^{11}$

c. $(-5)(-5)^6 = (-5)^1 \cdot (-5)^6$
$= (-5)^{1+6}$
$= (-5)^7$

d. $x^4 \cdot x^3 = x^{4+3} = x^7$

✓ **GUIDED PRACTICE** for Example 1

Simplify the expression.

1. $3^2 \cdot 3^7$ **2.** $5 \cdot 5^9$ **3.** $(-7)^2(-7)$ **4.** $x^2 \cdot x^6 \cdot x$

POWER OF A POWER Notice what happens when you raise a power to a power.

$$(a^2)^3 = a^2 \cdot a^2 \cdot a^2 = (a \cdot a) \cdot (a \cdot a) \cdot (a \cdot a) = a^6 = a^{2 \cdot 3}$$

The example above suggests the following property of exponents, known as the power of a power property.

KEY CONCEPT *For Your Notebook*

Power of a Power Property

Let a be a real number, and let m and n be positive integers.

Words To find a power of a power, multiply exponents.

Algebra $(a^m)^n = a^{mn}$

Example $(3^4)^2 = 3^{4 \cdot 2} = 3^8$

EXAMPLE 2 Use the power of a power property

AVOID ERRORS
In part (d), notice that you can write $[(y+2)^6]^2$ as $(y+2)^{12}$, but you cannot write $(y+2)^{12}$ as $y^{12} + 2^{12}$.

a. $(2^5)^3 = 2^{5 \cdot 3}$
$= 2^{15}$

b. $[(-6)^2]^5 = (-6)^{2 \cdot 5}$
$= (-6)^{10}$

c. $(x^2)^4 = x^{2 \cdot 4}$
$= x^8$

d. $[(y+2)^6]^2 = (y+2)^{6 \cdot 2}$
$= (y+2)^{12}$

✓ **GUIDED PRACTICE** for Example 2

Simplify the expression.

5. $(4^2)^7$ **6.** $[(-2)^4]^5$ **7.** $(n^3)^6$ **8.** $[(m+1)^5]^4$

POWER OF A PRODUCT Notice what happens when you raise a product to a power.

$$(ab)^3 = (ab) \cdot (ab) \cdot (ab) = (a \cdot a \cdot a) \cdot (b \cdot b \cdot b) = a^3b^3$$

The example above suggests the following property of exponents, known as the power of a product property.

KEY CONCEPT *For Your Notebook*

Power of a Product Property

Let a and b be real numbers, and let m be a positive integer.

Words To find a power of a product, find the power of each factor and multiply.

Algebra $(ab)^m = a^mb^m$

Example $(23 \cdot 17)^5 = 23^5 \cdot 17^5$

EXAMPLE 3 Use the power of a product property

SIMPLIFY EXPRESSIONS
When simplifying powers with numerical *and* variable bases, be sure to evaluate the numerical power, as in parts (b), (c), and (d).

a. $(24 \cdot 13)^8 = 24^8 \cdot 13^8$

b. $(9xy)^2 = (9 \cdot x \cdot y)^2 = 9^2 \cdot x^2 \cdot y^2 = 81x^2y^2$

c. $(-4z)^2 = (-4 \cdot z)^2 = (-4)^2 \cdot z^2 = 16z^2$

d. $-(4z)^2 = -(4 \cdot z)^2 = -(4^2 \cdot z^2) = -16z^2$

EXAMPLE 4 Use all three properties

Simplify $(2x^3)^2 \cdot x^4$.

$(2x^3)^2 \cdot x^4 = 2^2 \cdot (x^3)^2 \cdot x^4$ **Power of a product property**

$= 4 \cdot x^6 \cdot x^4$ **Power of a power property**

$= 4x^{10}$ **Product of powers property**

Animated **Algebra** at my.hrw.com

ORDER OF MAGNITUDE The **order of magnitude** of a quantity can be defined as the power of 10 nearest the quantity. Order of magnitude can be used to estimate or perform rough calculations. For instance, there are about 91,000 species of insects in the United States. The power of 10 closest to 91,000 is 10^5, or 100,000. So, there are about 10^5 species of insects in the United States.

EXAMPLE 5 Solve a real-world problem

BEES In 2003 the U.S. Department of Agriculture (USDA) collected data on about 10^3 honeybee colonies. There are about 10^4 bees in an average colony during honey production season. About how many bees were in the USDA study?

Solution

To find the total number of bees, find the product of the number of colonies, 10^3, and the number of bees per colony, 10^4.

$10^3 \cdot 10^4 = 10^{3+4} = 10^7$

▶ The USDA studied about 10^7, or 10,000,000, bees.

✓ GUIDED PRACTICE for Examples 3, 4, and 5

Simplify the expression.

9. $(42 \cdot 12)^2$ **10.** $(-3n)^2$ **11.** $(9m^3n)^4$ **12.** $5 \cdot (5x^2)^4$

13. WHAT IF? In Example 5, 10^2 honeybee colonies in the study were located in Idaho. About how many bees were studied in Idaho?

7.1 EXERCISES

HOMEWORK KEY

○ = See WORKED-OUT SOLUTIONS Exs. 31 and 55

★ = STANDARDIZED TEST PRACTICE Exs. 2, 40, 41, 50, and 58

◆ = MULTIPLE REPRESENTATIONS Ex. 55

SKILL PRACTICE

1. **VOCABULARY** Copy and complete: The __?__ of the quantity 93,534,004 people is the power of 10 nearest the quantity, or 10^8 people.

2. ★ **WRITING** *Explain* when and how to use the product of powers property.

EXAMPLES 1,2,3, and 4 for Exs. 3–41

SIMPLIFYING EXPRESSIONS **Simplify the expression. Write your answer using exponents.**

3. $4^2 \cdot 4^6$
4. $8^5 \cdot 8^2$
5. $3^3 \cdot 3$
6. $9 \cdot 9^5$
7. $(-7)^4(-7)^5$
8. $(-6)^6(-6)$
9. $2^4 \cdot 2^9 \cdot 2$
10. $(-3)^2(-3)^{11}(-3)$
11. $(3^5)^2$
12. $(7^4)^3$
13. $[(-5)^3]^4$
14. $[(-8)^9]^2$
15. $(15 \cdot 29)^3$
16. $(17 \cdot 16)^4$
17. $(132 \cdot 9)^6$
18. $((-14) \cdot 22)^5$

SIMPLIFYING EXPRESSIONS **Simplify the expression.**

19. $x^4 \cdot x^2$
20. $y^9 \cdot y$
21. $z^2 \cdot z \cdot z^3$
22. $a^4 \cdot a^3 \cdot a^{10}$
23. $(x^5)^2$
24. $(y^4)^6$
25. $[(b-2)^2]^6$
26. $[(d+9)^7]^3$
27. $(-5x)^2$
28. $-(5x)^2$
29. $(7xy)^2$
30. $(5pq)^3$
31. $(-10x^6)^2 \cdot x^2$
32. $(-8m^4)^2 \cdot m^3$
33. $6d^2 \cdot (2d^5)^4$
34. $(-20x^3)^2(-x^7)$
35. $-(2p^4)^3(-1.5p^7)$
36. $\left(\frac{1}{2}y^5\right)^3(2y^2)^4$
37. $(3x^5)^3(2x^7)^2$
38. $(-10n)^2(-4n^3)^3$

39. **ERROR ANALYSIS** *Describe* and correct the error in simplifying $c \cdot c^4 \cdot c^5$.

$$c \cdot c^4 \cdot c^5 = c^1 \cdot c^4 \cdot c^5 = c^{1 \cdot 4 \cdot 5} = c^{20}$$

40. ★ **MULTIPLE CHOICE** Which expression is equivalent to $(-9)^6$?

Ⓐ $(-9)^2(-9)^3$ Ⓑ $(-9)(-9)^5$ Ⓒ $[(-9)^4]^2$ Ⓓ $[(-9)^3]^3$

41. ★ **MULTIPLE CHOICE** Which expression is equivalent to $36x^{12}$?

Ⓐ $(6x^3)^4$ Ⓑ $12x^4 \cdot 3x^3$ Ⓒ $3x^3 \cdot (4x^3)^3$ Ⓓ $(6x^5)^2 \cdot x^2$

SIMPLIFYING EXPRESSIONS **Find the missing exponent.**

42. $x^4 \cdot x^? = x^5$
43. $(y^8)^? = y^{16}$
44. $(2z^?)^3 = 8z^{15}$
45. $(3a^3)^? \cdot 2a^3 = 18a^9$

46. **POPULATION** The population of New York City in 2000 was 8,008,278. What was the order of magnitude of the population of New York City?

SIMPLIFYING EXPRESSIONS **Simplify the expression.**

47. $(-3x^2y)^3(11x^3y^5)^2$
48. $-(-xy^2z^3)^5(x^4yz)^2$
49. $(-2s)(-5r^3st)^3(-2r^4st^7)^2$

50. ★ **OPEN-ENDED** Write three expressions involving products of powers, powers of powers, or powers of products that are equivalent to $12x^8$.

51. **CHALLENGE** Show that when a and b are real numbers and n is a positive integer, $(ab)^n = a^n b^n$.

PROBLEM SOLVING

EXAMPLE 5 for Exs. 52–56

52. **ICE CREAM COMPOSITION** There are about 954,930 air bubbles in 1 cubic centimeter of ice cream. There are about 946 cubic centimeters in 1 quart. Use order of magnitude to find the approximate number of air bubbles in 1 quart of ice cream.

53. **ASTRONOMY** The order of magnitude of the radius of our solar system is 10^{13} meters. The order of magnitude of the radius of the visible universe is 10^{13} times as great. Find the approximate radius of the visible universe.

54. **COASTAL LANDSLIDE** There are about 1 billion grains of sand in 1 cubic foot of sand. In 1995 a stretch of beach at Sleeping Bear Dunes National Lakeshore in Michigan slid into Lake Michigan. Scientists believe that around 35 million cubic feet of sand fell into the lake. Use order of magnitude to find about how many grains of sand slid into the lake.

55. ◆ **MULTIPLE REPRESENTATIONS** There are about 10^{23} atoms of gold in 1 ounce of gold.

a. **Making a Table** Copy and complete the table by finding the number of atoms of gold for the given amounts of gold (in ounces).

Gold (ounces)	10	100	1000	10,000	100,000
Number of atoms	?	?	?	?	?

b. **Writing an Expression** A particular mine in California extracted about 96,000 ounces of gold in 1 year. Use order of magnitude to write an expression you can use to find the approximate number of atoms of gold extracted in the mine that year. Simplify the expression. Verify your answer using the table.

56. **MULTI-STEP PROBLEM** A microscope has two lenses, the objective lens and the eyepiece, that work together to magnify an object. The total magnification of the microscope is the product of the magnification of the objective lens and the magnification of the eyepiece.

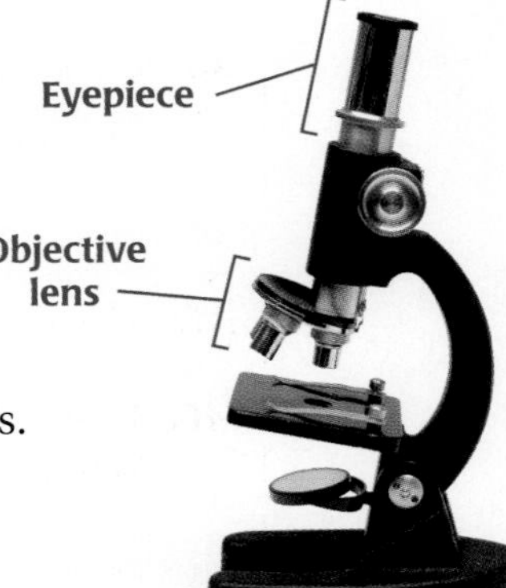

a. Your microscope's objective lens magnifies an object 10^2 times, and the eyepiece magnifies an object 10 times. What is the total magnification of your microscope?

b. You magnify an object that is 10^2 nanometers long. How long is the magnified image?

57. **VOLUME OF THE SUN** The radius of the sun is about 695,000,000 meters. The formula for the volume of a sphere, such as the sun, is $V = \frac{4}{3}\pi r^3$. Because the order of magnitude of $\frac{4}{3}\pi$ is 1, it does not contribute to the formula in a significant way. So, you can find the order of magnitude of the volume of the sun by cubing its radius. Find the order of magnitude of the volume of the sun.

58. ★ **EXTENDED RESPONSE** Rock salt can be mined from large deposits of salt called salt domes. A particular salt dome is roughly cylindrical in shape. The order of magnitude of the radius of the salt dome is 10^3 feet. The order of magnitude of the height of the salt dome is about 10 times that of its radius. The formula for the volume of a cylinder is $V = \pi r^2 h$.

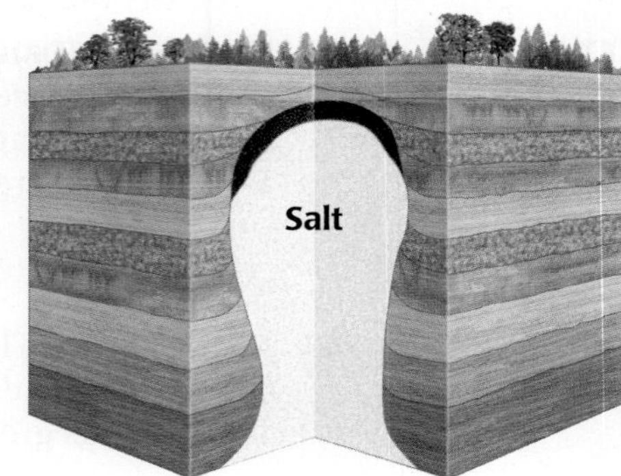

   a. **Calculate** What is the order of magnitude of the height of the salt dome?

   b. **Calculate** What is the order of magnitude of the volume of the salt dome?

   c. **Explain** The order of magnitude of the radius of a salt dome can be 10 times the radius of the salt dome described in this exercise. What effect does multiplying the order of magnitude of the radius of the salt dome by 10 have on the volume of the salt dome? *Explain.*

59. **CHALLENGE** Your school is conducting a poll that has two parts, one part that has 13 questions and a second part that has 10 questions. Students can answer the questions in either part with "agree" or "disagree." What power of 2 represents the number of ways there are to answer the questions in the first part of the poll? What power of 2 represents the number of ways there are to answer the questions in the second part of the poll? What power of 2 represents the number of ways there are to answer all of the questions on the poll?

7.2 Apply Exponent Properties Involving Quotients

Before You used properties of exponents involving products.

Now You will use properties of exponents involving quotients.

Why? So you can compare magnitudes of earthquakes, as in Ex. 53.

Key Vocabulary
- **power**
- **exponent**
- **base**

Notice what happens when you divide powers with the same base.

$$\frac{a^5}{a^3} = \frac{a \cdot a \cdot \cancel{a} \cdot \cancel{a} \cdot \cancel{a}}{\cancel{a} \cdot \cancel{a} \cdot \cancel{a}} = a \cdot a = a^2 = a^{5-3}$$

The example above suggests the following property of exponents, known as the quotient of powers property.

COMMON CORE

CC.9-12.A.SSE.3c Use the properties of exponents to transform expressions for exponential functions.

KEY CONCEPT *For Your Notebook*

Quotient of Powers Property

Let a be a nonzero real number, and let m and n be positive integers such that $m > n$.

Words To divide powers having the same base, subtract exponents.

Algebra $\frac{a^m}{a^n} = a^{m-n}, a \neq 0$ **Example** $\frac{4^7}{4^2} = 4^{7-2} = 4^5$

EXAMPLE 1 Use the quotient of powers property

SIMPLIFY EXPRESSIONS
When simplifying powers with numerical bases only, write your answers using exponents, as in parts (a), (b), and (c).

a. $\frac{8^{10}}{8^4} = 8^{10-4}$

$= 8^6$

b. $\frac{(-3)^9}{(-3)^3} = (-3)^{9-3}$

$= (-3)^6$

c. $\frac{5^4 \cdot 5^8}{5^7} = \frac{5^{12}}{5^7}$

$= 5^{12-7}$

$= 5^5$

d. $\frac{1}{x^4} \cdot x^6 = \frac{x^6}{x^4}$

$= x^{6-4}$

$= x^2$

✓ **GUIDED PRACTICE** for Example 1

Simplify the expression.

1. $\frac{6^{11}}{6^5}$ **2.** $\frac{(-4)^9}{(-4)^2}$ **3.** $\frac{9^4 \cdot 9^3}{9^2}$ **4.** $\frac{1}{y^5} \cdot y^8$

POWER OF A QUOTIENT Notice what happens when you raise a quotient to a power.

$$\left(\frac{a}{b}\right)^4 = \frac{a}{b} \cdot \frac{a}{b} \cdot \frac{a}{b} \cdot \frac{a}{b} = \frac{a \cdot a \cdot a \cdot a}{b \cdot b \cdot b \cdot b} = \frac{a^4}{b^4}$$

The example above suggests the following property of exponents, known as the power of a quotient property.

KEY CONCEPT *For Your Notebook*

Power of a Quotient Property

Let a and b be real numbers with $b \neq 0$, and let m be a positive integer.

Words To find a power of a quotient, find the power of the numerator and the power of the denominator and divide.

Algebra $\left(\frac{a}{b}\right)^m = \frac{a^m}{b^m}, b \neq 0$

Example $\left(\frac{3}{2}\right)^7 = \frac{3^7}{2^7}$

EXAMPLE 2 Use the power of a quotient property

SIMPLIFY EXPRESSIONS
When simplifying powers with numerical *and* variable bases, evaluate the numerical power, as in part (b).

a. $\left(\frac{x}{y}\right)^3 = \frac{x^3}{y^3}$

b. $\left(-\frac{7}{x}\right)^2 = \left(\frac{-7}{x}\right)^2 = \frac{(-7)^2}{x^2} = \frac{49}{x^2}$

EXAMPLE 3 Use properties of exponents

a. $\left(\frac{4x^2}{5y}\right)^3 = \frac{(4x^2)^3}{(5y)^3}$ Power of a quotient property

$= \frac{4^3 \cdot (x^2)^3}{5^3y^3}$ Power of a product property

$= \frac{64x^6}{125y^3}$ Power of a power property

b. $\left(\frac{a^2}{b}\right)^5 \cdot \frac{1}{2a^2} = \frac{(a^2)^5}{b^5} \cdot \frac{1}{2a^2}$ Power of a quotient property

$= \frac{a^{10}}{b^5} \cdot \frac{1}{2a^2}$ Power of a power property

$= \frac{a^{10}}{2a^2b^5}$ Multiply fractions.

$= \frac{a^8}{2b^5}$ Quotient of powers property

✓ GUIDED PRACTICE for Examples 2 and 3

Simplify the expression.

5. $\left(\frac{a}{b}\right)^2$

6. $\left(-\frac{5}{y}\right)^3$

7. $\left(\frac{x^2}{4y}\right)^2$

8. $\left(\frac{2s}{3t}\right)^3 \cdot \left(\frac{t^5}{16}\right)$

EXAMPLE 4 Solve a multi-step problem

FRACTAL TREE To construct what is known as a *fractal tree*, begin with a single segment (the trunk) that is 1 unit long, as in Step 0. Add three shorter segments that are $\frac{1}{2}$ unit long to form the first set of branches, as in Step 1. Then continue adding sets of successively shorter branches so that each new set of branches is half the length of the previous set, as in Steps 2 and 3.

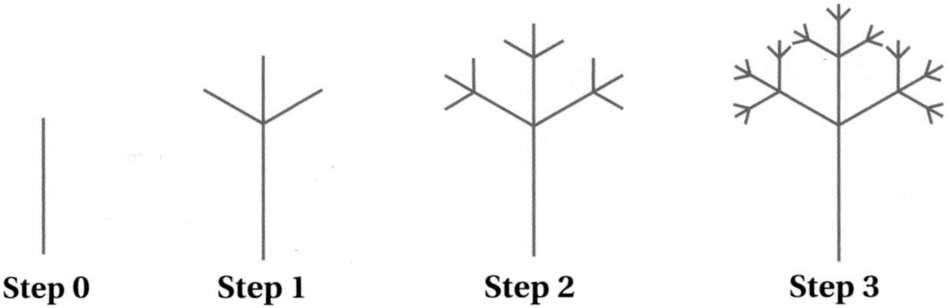

Step 0 **Step 1** **Step 2** **Step 3**

a. Make a table showing the number of new branches at each step for Steps 1–4. Write the number of new branches as a power of 3.

b. How many times greater is the number of new branches added at Step 5 than the number of new branches added at Step 2?

Solution

a.

Step	Number of new branches
1	$3 = 3^1$
2	$9 = 3^2$
3	$27 = 3^3$
4	$81 = 3^4$

b. The number of new branches added at Step 5 is 3^5. The number of new branches added at Step 2 is 3^2. So, the number of new branches added at Step 5 is $\frac{3^5}{3^2} = 3^3 = 27$ times the number of new branches added at Step 2.

✓ GUIDED PRACTICE for Example 4

9. **FRACTAL TREE** In Example 4, add a column to the table for the length of the new branches at each step. Write the lengths of the new branches as powers of $\frac{1}{2}$. What is the length of a new branch added at Step 9?

EXAMPLE 5 Solve a real-world problem

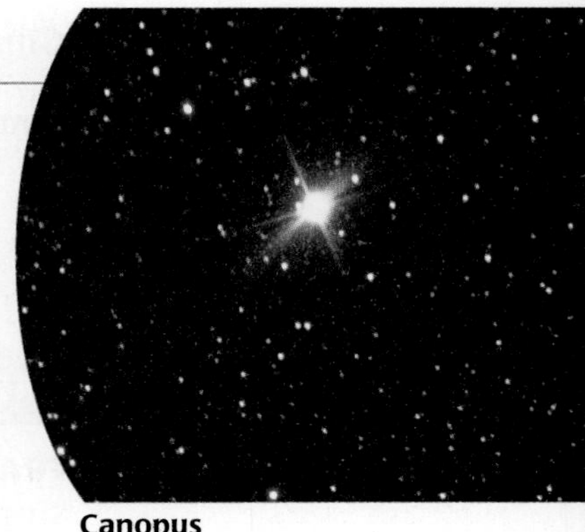
Canopus

ASTRONOMY The luminosity (in watts) of a star is the total amount of energy emitted from the star per unit of time. The order of magnitude of the luminosity of the sun is 10^{26} watts. The star Canopus is one of the brightest stars in the sky. The order of magnitude of the luminosity of Canopus is 10^{30} watts. How many times more luminous is Canopus than the sun?

Solution

$$\frac{\text{Luminosity of Canopus (watts)}}{\text{Luminosity of the sun (watts)}} = \frac{10^{30}}{10^{26}} = 10^{30-26} = 10^4$$

▶ Canopus is about 10^4 times as luminous as the sun.

GUIDED PRACTICE for Example 5

10. **WHAT IF?** Sirius is considered the brightest star in the sky. Sirius is less luminous than Canopus, but Sirius appears to be brighter because it is much closer to Earth. The order of magnitude of the luminosity of Sirius is 10^{28} watts. How many times more luminous is Canopus than Sirius?

7.2 EXERCISES

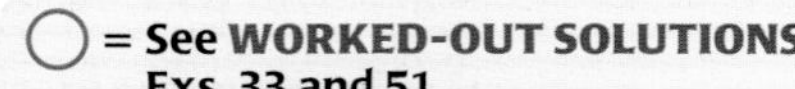

HOMEWORK KEY

○ = See WORKED-OUT SOLUTIONS Exs. 33 and 51

★ = STANDARDIZED TEST PRACTICE Exs. 2, 19, 37, 46, and 54

◆ = MULTIPLE REPRESENTATIONS Ex. 49

SKILL PRACTICE

1. **VOCABULARY** Copy and complete: In the power 4^3, 4 is the _?_ and 3 is the _?_.

2. ★ **WRITING** *Explain* when and how to use the quotient of powers property.

EXAMPLES 1 and 2 for Exs. 3–20

SIMPLIFYING EXPRESSIONS **Simplify the expression. Write your answer using exponents.**

3. $\frac{5^6}{5^2}$

4. $\frac{2^{11}}{2^6}$

5. $\frac{3^9}{3^5}$

6. $\frac{(-6)^8}{(-6)^5}$

7. $\frac{(-4)^7}{(-4)^4}$

8. $\frac{(-12)^9}{(-12)^3}$

9. $\frac{10^5 \cdot 10^5}{10^4}$

10. $\frac{6^7 \cdot 6^4}{6^6}$

11. $\left(\frac{1}{3}\right)^5$

12. $\left(\frac{3}{2}\right)^4$

13. $\left(-\frac{5}{4}\right)^4$

14. $\left(-\frac{2}{5}\right)^5$

15. $7^9 \cdot \frac{1}{7^2}$

16. $\frac{1}{9^5} \cdot 9^{11}$

17. $\left(\frac{1}{3}\right)^4 \cdot 3^{12}$

18. $4^9 \cdot \left(-\frac{1}{4}\right)^5$

19. ★ **MULTIPLE CHOICE** Which expression is equivalent to 16^6?

Ⓐ $\frac{16^4}{16^2}$ Ⓑ $\frac{16^{12}}{16^2}$ Ⓒ $\left(\frac{16^6}{16^3}\right)^2$ Ⓓ $\left(\frac{16^9}{16^6}\right)^3$

20. **ERROR ANALYSIS** *Describe* and correct the error in simplifying $\frac{9^5 \cdot 9^3}{9^4}$.

$$\frac{9^5 \cdot 9^3}{9^4} = \frac{9^8}{9^4} = 9^{12} \quad \times$$

EXAMPLES 1, 2, and 3 for Exs. 21–37

SIMPLIFYING EXPRESSIONS **Simplify the expression.**

21. $\frac{1}{y^8} \cdot y^{15}$ 22. $z^8 \cdot \frac{1}{z^7}$ 23. $\left(\frac{a}{y}\right)^9$ 24. $\left(\frac{j}{k}\right)^{11}$

25. $\left(\frac{p}{q}\right)^4$ 26. $\left(-\frac{1}{x}\right)^5$ 27. $\left(-\frac{4}{x}\right)^3$ 28. $\left(-\frac{a}{b}\right)^4$

29. $\left(\frac{4c}{d^2}\right)^3$ 30. $\left(\frac{a^7}{2b}\right)^5$ 31. $\left(\frac{x^2}{3y^3}\right)^2$ 32. $\left(\frac{3x^5}{7y^2}\right)^3$

33. $\left(\frac{3x^3}{2y}\right)^2 \cdot \frac{1}{x^2}$ 34. $\left(\frac{2x^3}{y}\right)^3 \cdot \frac{1}{6x^3}$ 35. $\frac{3}{8m^5} \cdot \left(\frac{m^4}{n^2}\right)^3$ 36. $\left(-\frac{5}{x}\right)^2 \cdot \left(\frac{2x^4}{y^3}\right)^2$

37. ★ **MULTIPLE CHOICE** Which expression is equivalent to $\left(\frac{7x^3}{2y^4}\right)^2$?

Ⓐ $\frac{7x^5}{2y^6}$ Ⓑ $\frac{7x^6}{2y^8}$ Ⓒ $\frac{49x^5}{4y^6}$ Ⓓ $\frac{49x^6}{4y^8}$

SIMPLIFYING EXPRESSIONS **Find the missing exponent.**

38. $\frac{(-8)^7}{(-8)^?} = (-8)^3$ 39. $\frac{7^? \cdot 7^2}{7^4} = 7^6$ 40. $\frac{1}{p^5} \cdot p^? = p^9$ 41. $\left(\frac{2c^3}{d^2}\right)^? = \frac{16c^{12}}{d^8}$

SIMPLIFYING EXPRESSIONS **Simplify the expression.**

42. $\left(\frac{2f^2g^3}{3fg}\right)^4$ 43. $\frac{2s^3t^3}{st^2} \cdot \frac{(3st)^3}{s^2t}$ 44. $\left(\frac{2m^5n}{4m^2}\right)^2 \cdot \left(\frac{mn^4}{5n}\right)^2$ 45. $\left(\frac{3x^3y}{x^2}\right)^3 \cdot \left(\frac{y^2x^4}{5y}\right)^2$

46. ★ **OPEN-ENDED** Write three expressions involving quotients that are equivalent to 14^7.

47. **REASONING** Name the definition or property that justifies each step to show that $\frac{a^m}{a^n} = \frac{1}{a^{n-m}}$ for $m < n$.

Let $m < n$. Given

$$\frac{a^m}{a^n} = \frac{a^m}{a^n}\left(\frac{\frac{1}{a^m}}{\frac{1}{a^m}}\right) \quad \underline{\ ?\ }$$

$$= \frac{1}{\frac{a^n}{a^m}} \quad \underline{\ ?\ }$$

$$= \frac{1}{a^{n-m}} \quad \underline{\ ?\ }$$

48. **CHALLENGE** Find the values of x and y if you know that $\frac{b^x}{b^y} = b^9$ and $\frac{b^x \cdot b^2}{b^{3y}} = b^{13}$. *Explain* how you found your answer.

PROBLEM SOLVING

EXAMPLES 4 and 5 for Exs. 49–51

49. **MULTIPLE REPRESENTATIONS** Draw a square with side lengths that are 1 unit long. Divide it into four new squares with side lengths that are one half the side length of the original square, as shown in Step 1. Keep dividing the squares into new squares, as shown in Steps 2 and 3.

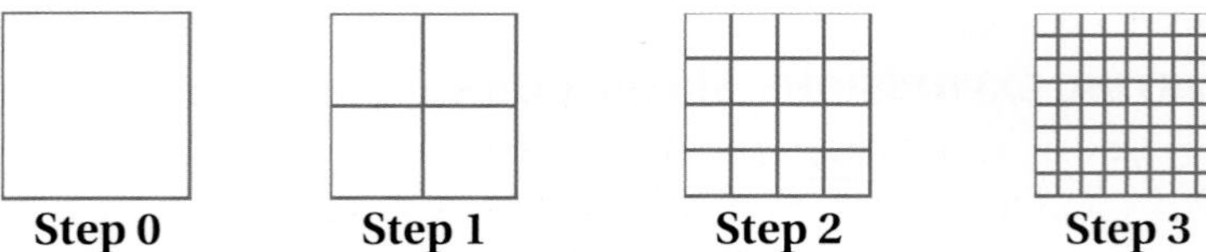

a. **Making a Table** Make a table showing the number of new squares and the side length of a new square at each step for Steps 1–4. Write the number of new squares as a power of 4. Write the side length of a new square as a power of $\frac{1}{2}$.

b. **Writing an Expression** Write and simplify an expression to find by how many times the number of new squares increased from Step 2 to Step 4.

50. **GROSS DOMESTIC PRODUCT** In 2003 the gross domestic product (GDP) for the United States was about 11 trillion dollars, and the order of magnitude of the population of the U.S. was 10^8. Use order of magnitude to find the approximate per capita (per person) GDP.

51. **SPACE TRAVEL** Alpha Centauri is the closest star system to Earth. Alpha Centauri is about 10^{13} kilometers away from Earth. A spacecraft leaves Earth and travels at an average speed of 10^4 meters per second. About how many years would it take the spacecraft to reach Alpha Centauri?

52. **ASTRONOMY** The brightness of one star relative to another star can be measured by comparing the magnitudes of the stars. For every increase in magnitude of 1, the relative brightness is diminished by a factor of 2.512. For instance, a star of magnitude 8 is 2.512 times less bright than a star of magnitude 7.

The constellation Ursa Minor (the Little Dipper) is shown. How many times less bright is Eta Ursae Minoris than Polaris?

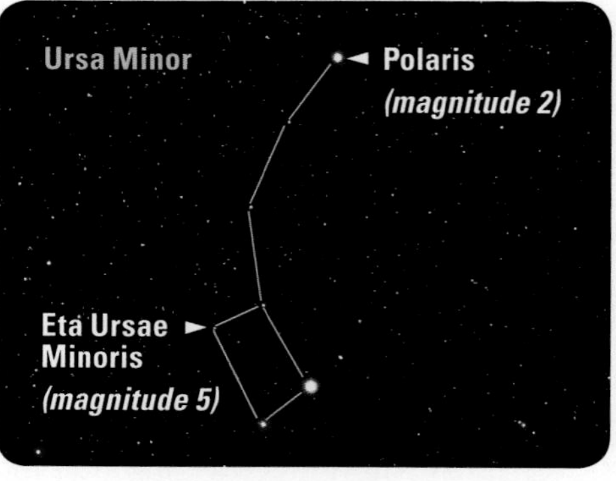

53. **EARTHQUAKES** The energy released by one earthquake relative to another earthquake can be measured by comparing the magnitudes (as determined by the Richter scale) of the earthquakes. For every increase of 1 in magnitude, the energy released is multiplied by a factor of about 31. How many times greater is the energy released by an earthquake of magnitude 7 than the energy released by an earthquake of magnitude 4?

○ = See **WORKED-OUT SOLUTIONS** in Student Resources ★ = **STANDARDIZED TEST PRACTICE** ◆ = **MULTIPLE REPRESENTATIONS**

54. ★ **EXTENDED RESPONSE** A byte is a unit used to measure computer memory. Other units are based on the number of bytes they represent. The table shows the number of bytes in certain units. For example, from the table you can calculate that 1 terabyte is equivalent to 2^{10} gigabytes.

a. **Calculate** How many kilobytes are there in 1 terabyte?

b. **Calculate** How many megabytes are there in 1 petabyte?

c. **CHALLENGE** Another unit used to measure computer memory is a bit. There are 8 bits in a byte. *Explain* how you can convert the number of bytes per unit given in the table to the number of bits per unit.

Unit	Number of bytes
Kilobyte	2^{10}
Megabyte	2^{20}
Gigabyte	2^{30}
Terabyte	2^{40}
Petabyte	2^{50}

QUIZ

Simplify the expression. Write your answer using exponents.

1. $3^2 \cdot 3^6$
2. $(5^4)^3$
3. $(32 \cdot 14)^7$
4. $7^2 \cdot 7^6 \cdot 7$
5. $(-4)(-4)^9$
6. $\frac{7^{12}}{7^4}$
7. $\frac{(-9)^9}{(-9)^7}$
8. $\frac{3^7 \cdot 3^4}{3^6}$
9. $\left(\frac{5}{4}\right)^4$

Simplify the expression.

10. $x^2 \cdot x^5$
11. $(3x^3)^2$
12. $-(7x)^2$
13. $(6x^5)^3 \cdot x$
14. $(2x^5)^3(7x^7)^2$
15. $\frac{1}{x^9} \cdot x^{21}$
16. $\left(-\frac{4}{x}\right)^3$
17. $\left(\frac{w}{v}\right)^6$
18. $\left(\frac{x^3}{4}\right)^2$

19. **AGRICULTURE** In 2004 the order of magnitude of the number of pounds of oranges produced in the United States was 10^{10}. The order of magnitude of the number of acres used for growing oranges was 10^6. About how many pounds of oranges per acre were produced in the United States in 2004?

Zero and Negative Exponents

Look for and make use of structure.

MATERIALS • paper and pencil

QUESTION How can you simplify expressions with zero or negative exponents?

EXPLORE Evaluate powers with zero and negative exponents

STEP 1 ***Find a pattern***

Copy and complete the tables for the powers of 2 and 3.

Exponent, n	Value of 2^n
4	16
3	?
2	?
1	?

Exponent, n	Value of 3^n
4	81
3	?
2	?
1	?

As you read the tables from the *bottom up*, you see that each time the exponent is increased by 1, the value of the power is multiplied by the base. What can you say about the exponents and the values of the powers as you read the table from the *top down*?

STEP 2 ***Extend the pattern***

Copy and complete the tables using the pattern you observed in Step 1.

Exponent, n	Power, 2^n
3	8
2	?
1	?
0	?
−1	?
−2	?

Exponent, n	Power, 3^n
3	27
2	?
1	?
0	?
−1	?
−2	?

DRAW CONCLUSIONS Use your observations to complete these exercises

1. Find 2^n and 3^n for $n = -3, -4,$ and -5.
2. What appears to be the value of a^0 for any nonzero number a?
3. Write each power in the tables above as a power with a positive exponent. For example, you can write 3^{-1} as $\frac{1}{3^1}$.

7.3 Define and Use Zero and Negative Exponents

Before You used properties of exponents to simplify expressions.

Now You will use zero and negative exponents.

Why? So you can compare masses, as in Ex. 52.

Key Vocabulary
- **reciprocal**

In the activity, you saw what happens when you raise a number to a zero or negative exponent. The activity suggests the following definitions.

CC.9-12.A.SSE.3c Use the properties of exponents to transform expressions for exponential functions.

KEY CONCEPT — *For Your Notebook*

Definition of Zero and Negative Exponents

Words	Algebra	Example
a to the zero power is 1.	$a^0 = 1, a \neq 0$	$5^0 = 1$
a^{-n} is the reciprocal of a^n.	$a^{-n} = \frac{1}{a^n}, a \neq 0$	$2^{-1} = \frac{1}{2}$
a^n is the reciprocal of a^{-n}.	$a^n = \frac{1}{a^{-n}}, a \neq 0$	$2 = \frac{1}{2^{-1}}$

EXAMPLE 1 Use definition of zero and negative exponents

SIMPLIFY EXPRESSIONS
In this lesson, when simplifying powers with numerical bases, evaluate the numerical power.

a. $3^{-2} = \frac{1}{3^2}$ **Definition of negative exponents**

$= \frac{1}{9}$ **Evaluate power.**

b. $(-7)^0 = 1$ **Definition of zero exponent**

c. $\left(\frac{1}{5}\right)^{-2} = \frac{1}{\left(\frac{1}{5}\right)^2}$ **Definition of negative exponents**

$= \frac{1}{\frac{1}{25}}$ **Evaluate power.**

$= 25$ **Simplify by multiplying numerator and denominator by 25.**

d. $0^{-5} = \cancel{\frac{1}{0^5}}$ (Undefined) **a^{-n} is defined only for a *nonzero* number a.**

GUIDED PRACTICE for Example 1

Evaluate the expression.

1. $\left(\frac{2}{3}\right)^0$ **2.** $(-8)^{-2}$ **3.** $\frac{1}{2^{-3}}$ **4.** $(-1)^0$

PROPERTIES OF EXPONENTS The properties of positive exponents you have already learned can be used with negative or zero exponents.

KEY CONCEPT *For Your Notebook*

Properties of Exponents

Let a and b be real numbers, and let m and n be integers.

$a^m \cdot a^n = a^{m+n}$ **Product of powers property**

$(a^m)^n = a^{mn}$ **Power of a power property**

$(ab)^m = a^m b^m$ **Power of a product property**

$\frac{a^m}{a^n} = a^{m-n}, a \neq 0$ **Quotient of powers property**

$\left(\frac{a}{b}\right)^m = \frac{a^m}{b^m}, b \neq 0$ **Power of a quotient property**

EXAMPLE 2 Evaluate exponential expressions

a. $6^{-4} \cdot 6^4 = 6^{-4+4}$ **Product of powers property**

$= 6^0$ **Add exponents.**

$= 1$ **Definition of zero exponent**

b. $(4^{-2})^2 = 4^{-2 \cdot 2}$ **Power of a power property**

$= 4^{-4}$ **Multiply exponents.**

$= \frac{1}{4^4}$ **Definition of negative exponents**

$= \frac{1}{256}$ **Evaluate power.**

c. $\frac{1}{3^{-4}} = 3^4$ **Definition of negative exponents**

$= 81$ **Evaluate power.**

d. $\frac{5^{-1}}{5^2} = 5^{-1-2}$ **Quotient of powers property**

$= 5^{-3}$ **Subtract exponents.**

$= \frac{1}{5^3}$ **Definition of negative exponents**

$= \frac{1}{125}$ **Evaluate power.**

✓ **GUIDED PRACTICE** for Example 2

Evaluate the expression.

5. $\frac{1}{4^{-3}}$ **6.** $(5^{-3})^{-1}$ **7.** $(-3)^5 \cdot (-3)^{-5}$ **8.** $\frac{6^{-2}}{6^2}$

EXAMPLE 3 Use properties of exponents

Simplify the expression. Write your answer using only positive exponents.

a. $(2xy^{-5})^3 = 2^3 \cdot x^3 \cdot (y^{-5})^3$ — **Power of a product property**

$= 8 \cdot x^3 \cdot y^{-15}$ — **Power of a power property**

$= \dfrac{8x^3}{y^{15}}$ — **Definition of negative exponents**

b. $\dfrac{(2x)^{-2}y^5}{-4x^2y^2} = \dfrac{y^5}{(2x)^2(-4x^2y^2)}$ — **Definition of negative exponents**

$= \dfrac{y^5}{(4x^2)(-4x^2y^2)}$ — **Power of a product property**

$= \dfrac{y^5}{-16x^4y^2}$ — **Product of powers property**

$= -\dfrac{y^3}{16x^4}$ — **Quotient of powers property**

Animated Algebra at my.hrw.com

EXAMPLE 4 Standardized Test Practice

The order of magnitude of the mass of a polyphemus moth larva when it hatches is 10^{-3} gram. During the first 56 days of its life, the moth larva can eat about 10^5 times its own mass in food. About how many grams of food can the moth larva eat during its first 56 days?

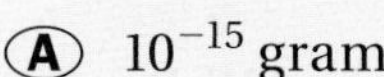
Ⓐ 10^{-15} gram Ⓑ 0.00000001 gram

Ⓒ 100 grams Ⓓ 10,000,000 grams

Not to scale

Solution

To find the amount of food the moth larva can eat in the first 56 days of its life, multiply its original mass, 10^{-3}, by 10^5.

$10^5 \cdot 10^{-3} = 10^{5+(-3)} = 10^2 = 100$

The moth larva can eat about 100 grams of food in the first 56 days of its life.

▶ The correct answer is C. Ⓐ Ⓑ Ⓒ Ⓓ

GUIDED PRACTICE for Examples 3 and 4

9. Simplify the expression $\dfrac{3xy^{-3}}{9x^3y}$. Write your answer using only positive exponents.

10. SCIENCE The order of magnitude of the mass of a proton is 10^4 times greater than the order of magnitude of the mass of an electron, which is 10^{-27} gram. Find the order of magnitude of the mass of a proton.

7.3 EXERCISES

HOMEWORK KEY

○ = See **WORKED-OUT SOLUTIONS** Exs. 11 and 53

★ = **STANDARDIZED TEST PRACTICE** Exs. 2, 44, 45, 54, and 57

◆ = **MULTIPLE REPRESENTATIONS** Ex. 55

SKILL PRACTICE

1. **VOCABULARY** Which definitions or properties would you use to simplify the expression $3^5 \cdot 3^{-5}$? *Explain.*

2. ★ **WRITING** *Explain* why the expression 0^{-4} is undefined.

EXAMPLE 1 for Exs. 3–14

EVALUATING EXPRESSIONS **Evaluate the expression.**

3. 4^{-3}
4. 7^{-3}
5. $(-3)^{-1}$
6. $(-2)^{-6}$
7. 2^0
8. $(-4)^0$
9. $\left(\frac{3}{4}\right)^0$
10. $\left(\frac{-9}{16}\right)^0$
11. $\left(\frac{2}{7}\right)^{-2}$
12. $\left(\frac{4}{3}\right)^{-3}$
13. 0^{-3}
14. 0^{-2}

EXAMPLE 2 for Exs. 15–27

15. $2^{-2} \cdot 2^{-3}$
16. $7^{-6} \cdot 7^4$
17. $(2^{-1})^5$
18. $(3^{-2})^2$
19. $\frac{1}{3^{-3}}$
20. $\frac{1}{6^{-2}}$
21. $\frac{3^{-3}}{3^2}$
22. $\frac{6^{-3}}{6^{-5}}$
23. $4\left(\frac{3}{2}\right)^{-1}$
24. $16\left(\frac{2^{-3}}{2^2}\right)$
25. $6^0 \cdot \left(\frac{1}{4^{-2}}\right)$
26. $3^{-2} \cdot \left(\frac{5}{7^0}\right)$

27. **ERROR ANALYSIS** *Describe* and correct the error in evaluating the expression $-6 \cdot 3^0$.

$$-6 \cdot 3^0 = -6 \cdot 0$$
$$= 0$$

EXAMPLE 3 for Exs. 28–43

SIMPLIFYING EXPRESSIONS **Simplify the expression. Write your answer using only positive exponents.**

28. x^{-4}
29. $2y^{-3}$
30. $(4g)^{-3}$
31. $(-11h)^{-2}$
32. x^2y^{-3}
33. $5m^{-3}n^{-4}$
34. $(6x^{-2}y^3)^{-3}$
35. $(-15fg^2)^0$
36. $\frac{r^{-2}}{s^{-4}}$
37. $\frac{x^{-5}}{y^2}$
38. $\frac{1}{8x^{-2}y^{-6}}$
39. $\frac{1}{15x^{10}y^{-8}}$
40. $\frac{1}{(-2z)^{-2}}$
41. $\frac{9}{(3d)^{-3}}$
42. $\frac{(3x)^{-3}y^4}{-x^2y^{-6}}$
43. $\frac{12x^8y^{-7}}{(4x^{-2}y^{-6})^2}$

44. ★ **MULTIPLE CHOICE** Which expression simplifies to $2x^4$?

Ⓐ $2x^{-4}$ Ⓑ $\frac{32}{(2x)^{-4}}$ Ⓒ $\frac{1}{2x^{-4}}$ Ⓓ $\frac{8}{4x^{-4}}$

45. ★ **MULTIPLE CHOICE** Which expression is equivalent to $(-4 \cdot 2^0 \cdot 3)^{-2}$?

Ⓐ -12 Ⓑ $-\frac{1}{144}$ Ⓒ 0 Ⓓ $\frac{1}{144}$

CHALLENGE In Exercises 46–48, tell whether the statement is true for all nonzero values of *a* and *b*. If it is not true, give a counterexample.

46. $\frac{a^{-3}}{a^{-4}} = \frac{1}{a}$ **47.** $\frac{a^{-1}}{b^{-1}} = \frac{b}{a}$ **48.** $a^{-1} + b^{-1} = \frac{1}{a+b}$

49. **CHALLENGE** Compare the values of a^n and a^{-n} when $n < 0$, when $n = 0$, and when $n > 0$ for **(a)** $a > 1$ and **(b)** $0 < a < 1$. *Explain* your reasoning.

PROBLEM SOLVING

EXAMPLE 4 for Exs. 50–54

50. **MASS** The mass of a grain of salt is about 10^{-4} gram. About how many grains of salt are in a box containing 100 grams of salt?

51. **MASS** The mass of a grain of a certain type of rice is about 10^{-2} gram. About how many grains of rice are in a box containing 10^3 grams of rice?

52. **BOTANY** The average mass of the fruit of the wolffia angusta plant is about 10^{-4} gram. The largest pumpkin ever recorded had a mass of about 10^4 kilograms. About how many times greater is the mass of the largest pumpkin than the mass of the fruit of the wolffia angusta plant?

53. **MEDICINE** A doctor collected about 10^{-2} liter of blood from a patient to run some tests. The doctor determined that a drop of the patient's blood, or about 10^{-6} liter, contained about 10^7 red blood cells. How many red blood cells did the entire sample contain?

54. ★ **SHORT RESPONSE** One of the smallest plant seeds comes from an orchid, and one of the largest plant seeds comes from a giant fan palm. A seed from an orchid has a mass of 10^{-9} gram and is 10^{13} times less massive than a seed from a giant fan palm. A student says that the seed from the giant fan palm has a mass of about 1 kilogram. Is the student correct? *Explain.*

Orchid

Giant fan palm

55. **MULTIPLE REPRESENTATIONS** Consider folding a piece of paper in half a number of times.

a. **Making a Table** Each time the paper is folded, record the number of folds and the fraction of the original area in a table like the one shown.

Number of folds	0	1	2	3
Fraction of original area	?	?	?	?

b. **Writing an Expression** Write an exponential expression for the fraction of the original area of the paper using a base of $\frac{1}{2}$.

56. **SCIENCE** Diffusion is the movement of molecules from one location to another. The time t (in seconds) it takes molecules to diffuse a distance of x centimeters is given by $t = \frac{x^2}{2D}$ where D is the diffusion coefficient.

   a. You can examine a cross section of a drop of ink in water to see how the ink diffuses. The diffusion coefficient for the molecules in the drop of ink is about 10^{-5} square centimeter per second. How long will it take the ink to diffuse 1 micrometer (10^{-4} centimeter)?

   b. Check your answer to part (a) using unit analysis.

57. ★ **EXTENDED RESPONSE** The intensity of sound I (in watts per square meter) can be modeled by $I = 0.08Pd^{-2}$ where P is the power (in watts) of the sound's source and d is the distance (in meters) that you are from the source of the sound.

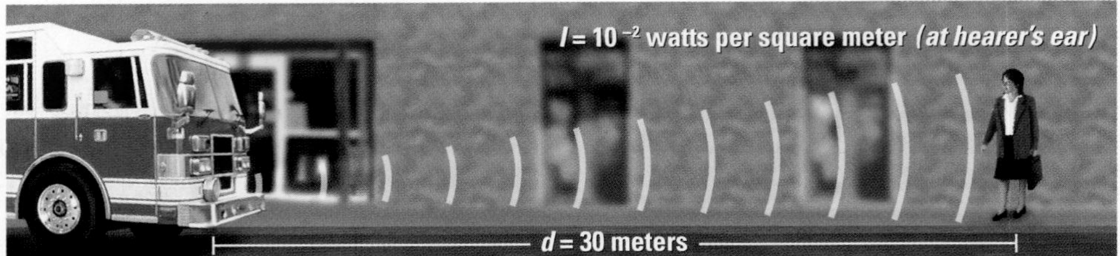

Not to scale

   a. What is the power (in watts) of the siren of the firetruck shown in the diagram?

   b. Using the power of the siren you found in part (a), simplify the formula for the intensity of sound from the siren.

   c. *Explain* what happens to the intensity of the siren when you double your distance from it.

58. **CHALLENGE** Coal can be burned to generate energy. The heat energy in 1 pound of coal is about 10^4 BTU (British Thermal Units). Suppose you have a stereo. It takes about 10 pounds of coal to create the energy needed to power the stereo for 1 year.

   a. About how many BTUs does your stereo use in 1 year?

   b. Suppose the power plant that delivers energy to your home produces 10^{-1} pound of sulfur dioxide for each 10^6 BTU of energy that it creates. How much sulfur dioxide is added to the air by generating the energy needed to power your stereo for 1 year?

See **EXTRA PRACTICE** in Student Resources **ONLINE QUIZ** at my.hrw.com

Extension Define and Use Fractional Exponents

GOAL Use fractional exponents.

Key Vocabulary
• cube root

CC.9-12.N.RN.1 Explain how the definition of the meaning of rational exponents follows from extending the properties of integer exponents to those values, allowing for a notation for radicals in terms of rational exponents.

You have learned to write the square root of a number using a radical sign. You can also write a square root of a number using exponents.

For any $a \geq 0$, suppose you want to write $\sqrt{a}$ as a^k. Recall that a number b (in this case, a^k) is a square root of a number a provided $b^2 = a$. Use this definition to find a value for k as follows.

$b^2 = a$ **Definition of square root**

$(a^k)^2 = a$ **Substitute a^k for b.**

$a^{2k} = a^1$ **Power of a power property**

Because the bases are the same in the equation $a^{2k} = a^1$, the exponents must be equal:

$2k = 1$ **Set exponents equal.**

$k = \frac{1}{2}$ **Solve for k.**

So, for a nonnegative number a, $\sqrt{a} = a^{1/2}$.

You can work with exponents of $\frac{1}{2}$ and multiples of $\frac{1}{2}$ just as you work with integer exponents.

EXAMPLE 1 Evaluate expressions involving square roots

a. $16^{1/2} = \sqrt{16}$

$= 4$

b. $25^{-1/2} = \frac{1}{25^{1/2}}$

$= \frac{1}{\sqrt{25}}$

$= \frac{1}{5}$

c. $9^{5/2} = 9^{(1/2) \cdot 5}$

$= (9^{1/2})^5$

$= (\sqrt{9})^5$

$= 3^5$

$= 243$

d. $4^{-3/2} = 4^{(1/2) \cdot (-3)}$

$= (4^{1/2})^{-3}$

$= (\sqrt{4})^{-3}$

$= 2^{-3}$

$= \frac{1}{2^3}$

$= \frac{1}{8}$

FRACTIONAL EXPONENTS You can work with other fractional exponents just as you did with $\frac{1}{2}$.

CUBE ROOTS If $b^3 = a$, then b is the **cube root** of a. For example, $2^3 = 8$, so 2 is the cube root of 8. The cube root of a can be written as $\sqrt[3]{a}$ or $a^{1/3}$.

EXAMPLE 2 Evaluate expressions involving cube roots

a. $27^{1/3} = \sqrt[3]{27}$

$= \sqrt[3]{3^3}$

$= 3$

b. $8^{-1/3} = \frac{1}{8^{1/3}}$

$= \frac{1}{\sqrt[3]{8}}$

$= \frac{1}{2}$

c. $64^{4/3} = 64^{(1/3) \cdot 4}$

$= (64^{1/3})^4$

$= (\sqrt[3]{64})^4$

$= 4^4$

$= 256$

d. $125^{-2/3} = 125^{(1/3) \cdot (-2)}$

$= (125^{1/3})^{-2}$

$= (\sqrt[3]{125})^{-2}$

$= 5^{-2}$

$= \frac{1}{5^2}$

$= \frac{1}{25}$

PROPERTIES OF EXPONENTS The properties of exponents for integer exponents also apply to fractional exponents.

EXAMPLE 3 Use properties of exponents

a. $12^{-1/2} \cdot 12^{5/2} = 12^{(-1/2) + (5/2)}$

$= 12^{4/2}$

$= 12^2$

$= 144$

b. $\frac{6^{4/3} \cdot 6}{6^{1/3}} = \frac{6^{(4/3) + 1}}{6^{1/3}}$

$= \frac{6^{7/3}}{6^{1/3}}$

$= 6^{(7/3) - (1/3)}$

$= 6^2$

$= 36$

PRACTICE

EXAMPLES 1, 2, and 3 for Exs. 1–12

Evaluate the expression.

1. $100^{3/2}$
2. $121^{-1/2}$
3. $81^{-3/2}$
4. $216^{2/3}$
5. $27^{-1/3}$
6. $343^{-2/3}$
7. $9^{7/2} \cdot 9^{-3/2}$
8. $\left(\frac{1}{16}\right)^{1/2}\left(\frac{1}{16}\right)^{-1/2}$
9. $36^{5/2} \cdot \frac{36^{-1/2}}{(36^{-1})^{-7/2}}$
10. $(27^{-1/3})^3$
11. $(-64)^{-5/3}(-64)^{4/3}$
12. $(-8)^{1/3}(-8)^{-2/3}(-8)^{1/3}$
13. **REASONING** Let $x > 0$. Compare the values of $x^{1/2}$ and $x^{-1/2}$. Give examples to support your thinking.

MIXED REVIEW of Problem Solving

MATHEMATICAL PRACTICES Make sense of problems and persevere in solving them.

1. **GRIDDED ANSWER** In 2004 the fastest computers could record about 10^9 bits per second. (A bit is the smallest unit of memory storage for computers.) Scientists believed that the speed limit at the time was about 10^{12} bits per second. About how many times more bits per second was the speed limit than the fastest computers?

2. **MULTI-STEP PROBLEM** An office supply store sells cubical containers that can be used to store paper clips, rubber bands, or other supplies.
   - **a.** One of the containers has a side length of $4\frac{1}{2}$ inches. Find the container's volume by writing the side length as an improper fraction and substituting the length into the formula for the volume of a cube.
   - **b.** Identify the property of exponents you used to find the volume in part (a).

3. **SHORT RESPONSE** Clouds contain millions of tiny spherical water droplets. The radius of one droplet is shown.

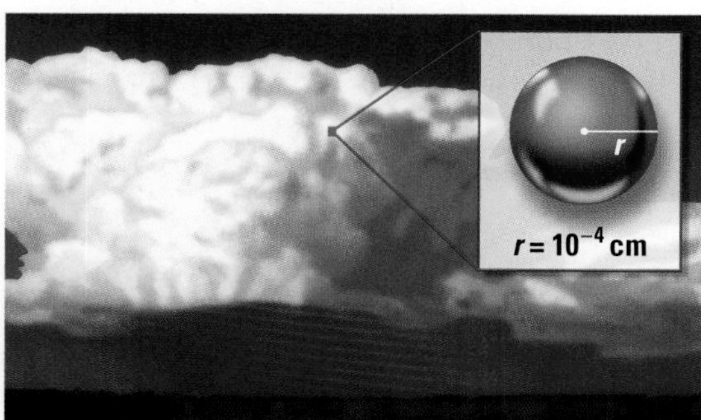

   - **a.** Find the order of magnitude of the volume of the droplet.
   - **b.** Droplets combine to form raindrops. The radius of a raindrop is about 10^2 times greater than the droplet's radius. Find the order of magnitude of the volume of the raindrop.
   - **c.** *Explain* how you can find the number of droplets that combine to form the raindrop. Then find the number of droplets and identify any properties of exponents you used.

4. **GRIDDED ANSWER** The least intense sound that is audible to the human ear has an intensity of about 10^{-12} watt per square meter. The intensity of sound from a jet engine at a distance of 30 meters is about 10^{15} times greater than the least intense sound. Find the intensity of sound from the jet engine.

5. **EXTENDED RESPONSE** For an experiment, a scientist dropped a spoonful, or about 10^{-1} cubic inch, of biodegradable olive oil into a pond to see how the oil would spread out over the surface of the pond. The scientist found that the oil spread until it covered an area of about 10^5 square inches.
   - **a.** About how thick was the layer of oil that spread out across the pond? Check your answer using unit analysis.
   - **b.** The pond has a surface area of 10^7 square inches. If the oil spreads to the same thickness as in part (a), how many cubic inches of olive oil would be needed to cover the entire surface of the pond?
   - **c.** *Explain* how you could find the amount of oil needed to cover a pond with a surface area of 10^x square inches.

6. **OPEN-ENDED** The table shows units of measurement of time and the durations of the units in seconds.

Name of unit	Duration (seconds)
Gigasecond	10^9
Megasecond	10^6
Millisecond	10^{-3}
Nanosecond	10^{-9}

   - **a.** Use the table to write a conversion problem that can be solved by applying a property of exponents involving products.
   - **b.** Use the table to write a conversion problem that can be solved by applying a property of exponents involving quotients.

7.4 Write and Graph Exponential Growth Functions

Before You wrote and graphed linear models.

Now You will write and graph exponential growth models.

Why? So you can find the value of a collector car, as in Example 4.

Key Vocabulary
- **exponential function**
- **exponential growth**
- **compound interest**

CC.9-12.A.CED.2 Create equations in two or more variables to represent relationships between quantities; graph equations on coordinate axes with labels and scales.*

An **exponential function** is a function of the form $y = ab^x$ where $a \neq 0$, $b > 0$, and $b \neq 1$. Exponential functions are *nonlinear* functions. Observe how an exponential function compares with a linear function.

Linear function: $y = 3x + 2$

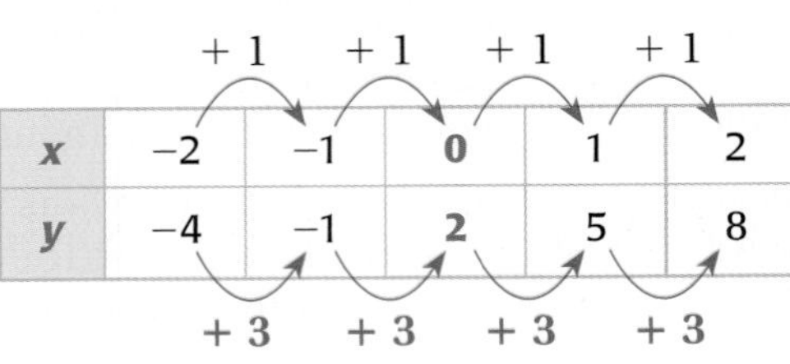

x	−2	−1	0	1	2
y	−4	−1	2	5	8

Exponential function: $y = 2 \cdot 3^x$

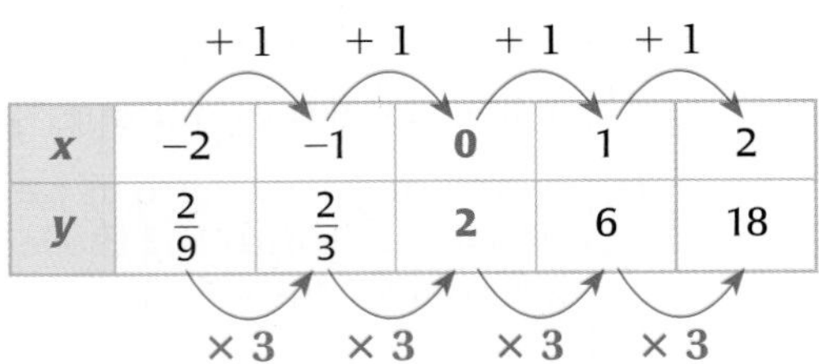

x	−2	−1	0	1	2
y	$\frac{2}{9}$	$\frac{2}{3}$	2	6	18

EXAMPLE 1 Write a function rule

Write a rule for the function.

x	−2	−1	0	1	2
y	2	4	8	16	32

Solution

STEP 1 **Tell** whether the function is exponential.

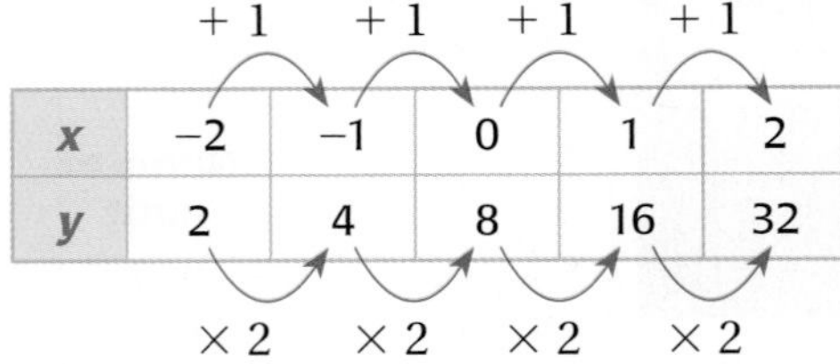

x	−2	−1	0	1	2
y	2	4	8	16	32

Here, the y-values are multiplied by 2 for each increase of 1 in x, so the table represents an exponential function of the form $y = ab^x$ where $b = 2$.

STEP 2 **Find** the value of a by finding the value of y when $x = 0$. When $x = 0$, $y = ab^0 = a \cdot 1 = a$. The value of y when $x = 0$ is 8, so $a = 8$.

STEP 3 **Write** the function rule. A rule for the function is $y = 8 \cdot 2^x$.

ANALYZE RATE OF CHANGE

Notice that for an exponential function, the rate of change in y with respect to x is not constant as it is for a linear function. For instance, $\frac{4 - 2}{-1 - (-2)} = 2$, while $\frac{8 - 4}{0 - (-1)} = 4$.

✓ GUIDED PRACTICE for Example 1

1. Write a rule for the function.

x	−2	−1	0	1	2
y	3	9	27	81	243

EXAMPLE 2 Graph an exponential function

Graph the function $y = 2^x$. Identify its domain and range.

Solution

READ A GRAPH
Notice that the graph has a y-intercept of 1 and that it gets closer to the negative x-axis as the x-values decrease.

STEP 1 **Make** a table by choosing a few values for x and finding the values of y. The domain is all real numbers.

x	-2	-1	0	1	2
y	$\frac{1}{4}$	$\frac{1}{2}$	1	2	4

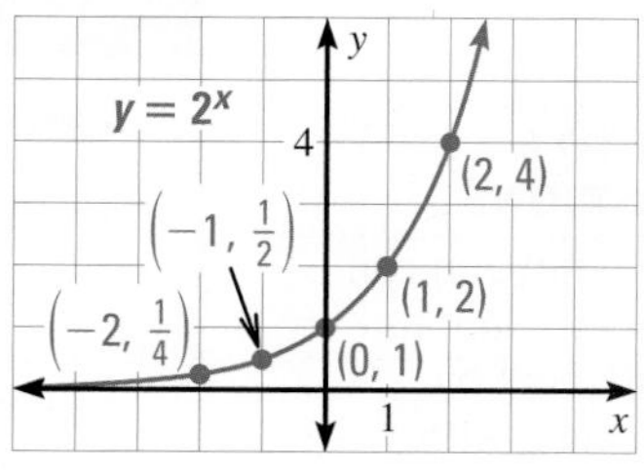

STEP 2 **Plot** the points.

STEP 3 **Draw** a smooth curve through the points. From either the table or the graph, you can see that the range is all positive real numbers.

EXAMPLE 3 Compare graphs of exponential functions

Graph the functions $y = 3 \cdot 2^x$ and $y = -3 \cdot 2^x$. Compare each graph with the graph of $y = 2^x$.

Solution

To graph each function, make a table of values, plot the points, and draw a smooth curve through the points.

DESCRIBE A FUNCTION
An exponential growth function has an unbroken graph, so the function is continuous.

x	$y = 2^x$	$y = 3 \cdot 2^x$	$y = -3 \cdot 2^x$
-2	$\frac{1}{4}$	$\frac{3}{4}$	$-\frac{3}{4}$
-1	$\frac{1}{2}$	$\frac{3}{2}$	$-\frac{3}{2}$
0	1	3	-3
1	2	6	-6
2	4	12	-12

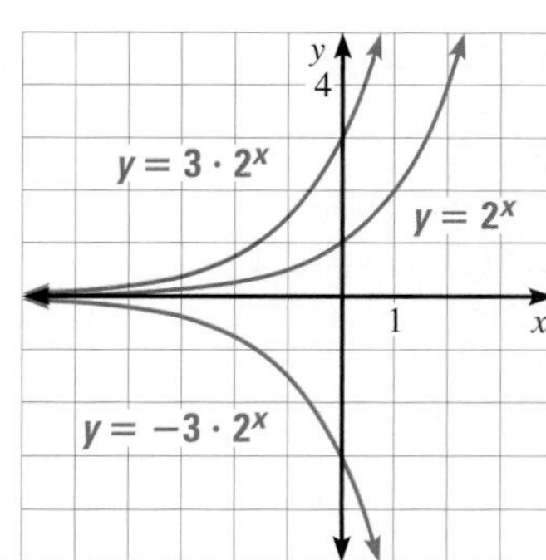

Because the y-values for $y = 3 \cdot 2^x$ are 3 times the corresponding y-values for $y = 2^x$, the graph of $y = 3 \cdot 2^x$ is a vertical stretch of the graph of $y = 2^x$.

Because the y-values for $y = -3 \cdot 2^x$ are -3 times the corresponding y-values for $y = 2^x$, the graph of $y = -3 \cdot 2^x$ is a vertical stretch with a reflection in the x-axis of the graph of $y = 2^x$.

✓ GUIDED PRACTICE for Examples 2 and 3

2. Graph $y = 5^x$ and identify its domain and range.

3. Graph $y = \frac{1}{3} \cdot 2^x$. Compare the graph with the graph of $y = 2^x$.

4. Graph $y = -\frac{1}{3} \cdot 2^x$. Compare the graph with the graph of $y = 2^x$.

EXPONENTIAL GROWTH When $a > 0$ and $b > 1$, the function $y = ab^x$ represents **exponential growth**. When a quantity grows exponentially, it increases by the same percent over equal time periods. To find the amount to which the quantity grows after t time periods, use the following model.

REWRITE EQUATIONS
Notice that you can rewrite $y = ab^x$ as $y = a(1 + r)^t$ by replacing b with $1 + r$ and x with t (for time).

KEY CONCEPT — *For Your Notebook*

Exponential Growth Model

a is the **initial amount**. r is the **growth rate**.

$$y = a(1 + r)^t$$

$1 + r$ is the **growth factor**. t is the **time period**.

Notice the relationship between the growth rate r and the growth factor $1 + r$. If the initial amount of a quantity is a units and the quantity is growing at a rate of r, then after one time period the new amount is:

$$\text{Initial amount} + \text{amount of increase} = a + r \cdot a = a(1 + r)$$

EXAMPLE 4 Solve a multi-step problem

ANOTHER WAY
For alternative methods for solving Example 4, see the **Problem Solving Workshop**.

COLLECTOR CAR The owner of a 1953 Hudson Hornet convertible sold the car at an auction. The owner bought it in 1984 when its value was $11,000. The value of the car increased at a rate of 6.9% per year.

a. Write a function that models the value of the car over time.

b. The auction took place in 2004. What was the approximate value of the car at the time of the auction? Round your answer to the nearest dollar.

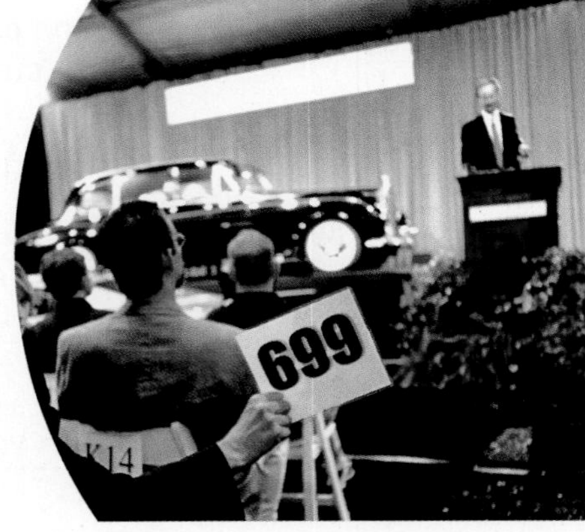

Solution

a. Let C be the value of the car (in dollars), and let t be the time (in years) since 1984. The initial value a is $11,000, and the growth rate r is 0.069.

$C = a(1 + r)^t$ — **Write exponential growth model.**

$= 11{,}000(1 + 0.069)^t$ — **Substitute 11,000 for a and 0.069 for r.**

$= 11{,}000(1.069)^t$ — **Simplify.**

AVOID ERRORS
The growth rate in this example is 6.9%, or 0.069. So, the growth factor is 1 + 0.069, or 1.069, not 0.069.

b. To find the value of the car in 2004, 20 years after 1984, substitute 20 for t.

$C = 11{,}000(1.069)^{20}$ — **Substitute 20 for t.**

$\approx 41{,}778$ — **Use a calculator.**

▶ In 2004 the value of the car was about $41,778.

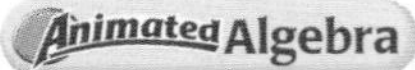 at my.hrw.com

COMPOUND INTEREST **Compound interest** is interest earned on both an initial investment and on previously earned interest. Compounding of interest can be modeled by exponential growth where a is the initial investment, r is the annual interest rate, and t is the number of years the money is invested.

EXAMPLE 5 Standardized Test Practice

You put \$250 in a savings account that earns 4% annual interest compounded yearly. You do not make any deposits or withdrawals. How much will your investment be worth in 5 years?

Ⓐ \$300 Ⓑ \$304.16 Ⓒ \$1344.56 Ⓓ \$781,250

ESTIMATE

You can use the simple interest formula, $I = prt$, to estimate the amount of interest earned: $(250)(0.04)(5) = 50$. Compounding interest will result in slightly more than \$50.

Solution

$y = a(1 + r)^t$ Write exponential growth model.

$= 250(1 + 0.04)^5$ Substitute 250 for a, 0.04 for r, and 5 for t.

$= 250(1.04)^5$ Simplify.

≈ 304.16 Use a calculator.

You will have \$304.16 in 5 years.

▶ The correct answer is B. Ⓐ Ⓑ Ⓒ Ⓓ

✓ GUIDED PRACTICE for Examples 4 and 5

5. **WHAT IF?** In Example 4, suppose the owner of the car sold it in 1994. Find the value of the car to the nearest dollar.

6. **WHAT IF?** In Example 5, suppose the annual interest rate is 3.5%. How much will your investment be worth in 5 years?

7.4 EXERCISES

HOMEWORK KEY

○ = See **WORKED-OUT SOLUTIONS** Exs. 13 and 41

★ = **STANDARDIZED TEST PRACTICE** Exs. 3, 8, 35, 42, 43, 46, and 50

◆ = **MULTIPLE REPRESENTATIONS** Exs. 34, 41

SKILL PRACTICE

1. **VOCABULARY** In the exponential growth model $y = a(1 + r)^t$, the quantity $1 + r$ is called the __?__.

2. **VOCABULARY** For what values of b does the exponential function $y = ab^x$ (where $a > 0$) represent exponential growth?

3. ★ **WRITING** How does the graph of $y = 2 \cdot 5^x$ compare with the graph of $y = 5^x$? *Explain.*

EXAMPLE 1
for Exs. 4–8

WRITING FUNCTIONS Write a rule for the function.

4.

x	−2	−1	0	1	2
y	1	2	4	8	16

5.

x	−2	−1	0	1	2
y	5	25	125	625	3125

6.

x	−2	−1	0	1	2
y	$\frac{1}{8}$	$\frac{1}{4}$	$\frac{1}{2}$	1	2

7.

x	−2	−1	0	1	2
y	$\frac{1}{81}$	$\frac{1}{27}$	$\frac{1}{9}$	$\frac{1}{3}$	1

8. ★ **WRITING** Given a table of values, describe how can you tell if the table represents a linear function or an exponential function.

EXAMPLE 2
for Exs. 9–21

GRAPHING FUNCTIONS Graph the function and identify its domain and range.

9. $y = 4^x$
10. $y = 7^x$
11. $y = 8^x$
12. $y = 9^x$
13. $y = (1.5)^x$
14. $y = (2.5)^x$
15. $y = (1.2)^x$
16. $y = (4.3)^x$
17. $y = \left(\frac{4}{3}\right)^x$
18. $y = \left(\frac{7}{2}\right)^x$
19. $y = \left(\frac{5}{3}\right)^x$
20. $y = \left(\frac{5}{4}\right)^x$

21. **ERROR ANALYSIS** The price P (in dollars) of a pound of flour was \$.27 in 1999. The price has increased by about 2% each year. Let t be the number of years since 1999. *Describe* and correct the error in finding the price of a pound of flour in 2002.

$P = a(1 + r)^t$
$= 0.27(1 + 2)^3 = 0.27(3)^3 = 7.29$
In 2002 the price of a pound of flour was \$7.29.

EXAMPLE 3
for Exs. 22–34

COMPARING GRAPHS OF FUNCTIONS Graph the function. Compare the graph with the graph of $y = 3^x$.

22. $y = 2 \cdot 3^x$
23. $y = 4 \cdot 3^x$
24. $y = \frac{1}{4} \cdot 3^x$
25. $y = \frac{2}{3} \cdot 3^x$
26. $y = 0.5 \cdot 3^x$
27. $y = 2.5 \cdot 3^x$
28. $y = -2 \cdot 3^x$
29. $y = -4 \cdot 3^x$
30. $y = -\frac{1}{4} \cdot 3^x$
31. $y = -\frac{2}{3} \cdot 3^x$
32. $y = -0.5 \cdot 3^x$
33. $y = -2.5 \cdot 3^x$

34. ◆ **MULTIPLE REPRESENTATIONS** Given the function $y = a^x$, you can find x when $y = k$ by solving the *exponential equation* $k = a^x$. Use the following methods to solve $32 = 2^x$.
    a. **Making a Table** Make a table for the function using $x = 0, 1, 2, \ldots, 6$.
    b. **Graphing Functions** Graph the functions $y = 32$ and $y = 2^x$ on the same coordinate plane. Identify the x-coordinate of the intersection point.
    c. **Using Powers** Write 32 as a power of 2. Then use the fact that powers with the same base are equal provided that their exponents are equal.

35. ★ **WRITING** If a population triples each year, what is the population's growth rate (as a percent)? *Explain.*

36. **CHALLENGE** Write a linear function and an exponential function whose graphs pass through the points (0, 2) and (1, 6).

37. **CHALLENGE** *Compare* the graphs of the functions $f(x) = 2^{x+2}$ and $g(x) = 4 \cdot 2^x$. Use properties of exponents to explain your observations.

○ = See **WORKED-OUT SOLUTIONS** in Student Resources
★ = **STANDARDIZED TEST PRACTICE**
◆ = **MULTIPLE REPRESENTATIONS**

PROBLEM SOLVING

GRAPHING CALCULATOR You may wish to use a graphing calculator to complete the following Problem Solving exercises.

EXAMPLES 4 and 5 for Exs. 38–41

38. **INVESTMENTS** You deposit \$125 in a savings account that earns 5% annual interest compounded yearly. Find the balance in the account after the given amounts of time.

    a. 1 year **b.** 2 years **c.** 5 years **d.** 20 years

39. **MULTI-STEP PROBLEM** One computer industry expert reported that there were about 600 million computers in use worldwide in 2001 and that the number was increasing at an annual rate of about 10%.

    a. Write a function that models the number of computers in use over time.

    b. Use the function to predict the number of computers that will be in use worldwide in 2009.

40. **MULTI-STEP PROBLEM** A research association reported that 3,173,000 gas grills were shipped by various manufacturers in the U.S. in 1985. Shipments increased by about 7% per year from 1985 to 2002.

    a. Write a function that models the number of gas grills shipped over time.

    b. About how many gas grills were shipped in 2002?

41. **MULTIPLE REPRESENTATIONS** A tree's cross-sectional area taken at a height of 4.5 feet from the ground is called its basal area and is measured in square inches. Tree growth can be measured by the growth of the tree's basal area. The initial basal area and annual growth rate for two particular trees are shown.

a. Writing a Model Write a function that models the basal area A of each tree over time.

b. Graphing a Function Use a graphing calculator to graph the functions from part (a) in the same coordinate plane. In about how many years will the trees have the same basal area?

42. ★ **SHORT RESPONSE** A company sells advertising blimps. The table shows the costs of advertising blimps of different lengths. Does the table represent an exponential function? *Explain.*

Length, ℓ (feet)	10	15	20	25
Cost, c (dollars)	400.00	700.00	1225.00	2143.75

43. ★ **MULTIPLE CHOICE** A weblog, or blog, refers to a website that contains a personal journal. According to one analyst, over one 18 month period, the number of blogs in existence doubled about every 6 months. The analyst estimated that there were about 600,000 blogs at the beginning of the period. How many blogs were there at the end of the period?

Ⓐ 660,000 Ⓑ 1,200,000 Ⓒ 4,800,000 Ⓓ 16,200,000

44. **TELECOMMUNICATIONS** For the period 1991–2001, the number y (in millions) of Internet users worldwide can be modeled by the function $y = 4.67(1.65)^x$ where x is the number of years since 1991.

  a. Identify the initial amount, the growth factor, and the growth rate.

  b. Graph the function. Identify its domain and range.

  c. Use your graph from part (b) to graph the line $y = 21$. Estimate the year in which the number of Internet users worldwide was about 21 million.

45. **GRAPHING CALCULATOR** The frequency (in hertz) of a note played on a piano is a function of the position of the key that creates the note. The position of some piano keys and the frequencies of the notes created by the keys are shown below. Use the exponential regression feature on a graphing calculator to find an exponential model for the frequency of piano notes. What is the frequency of the note created by the 30th key?

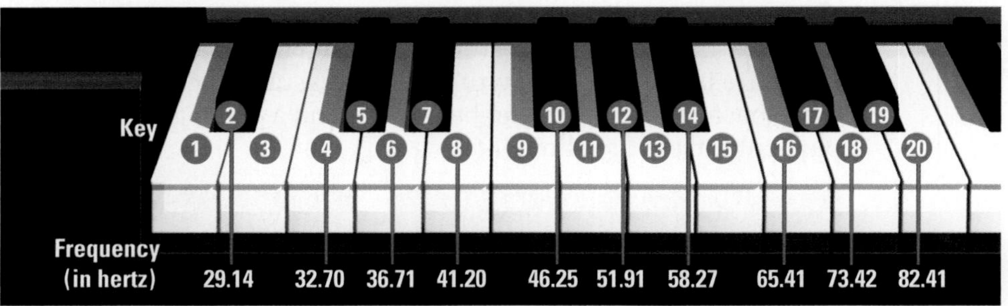

46. ★ **EXTENDED RESPONSE** In 1830, the population of the United States was 12,866,020. By 1890, the population was 62,947,714.

  a. Model Assume the population growth from 1830 to 1890 was linear. Write a linear model for the U.S. population from 1830 to 1890. By about how much did the population grow per year from 1830 to 1890?

  b. Model Assume the population growth from 1830 to 1890 was exponential. Write an exponential model for the U.S. population from 1830 to 1890. By approximately what percent did the population grow per year from 1830 to 1890?

  c. Explain The U.S. population was 23,191,876 in 1850 and 38,558,371 in 1870. Which of the models in parts (a) and (b) is a better approximation of actual U.S. population for the time period 1850–1890? *Explain.*

★ = **STANDARDIZED TEST PRACTICE**

COMPOUND INTEREST In Exercises 47–49, use the example below to find the balance of the account compounded with the given frequency.

EXAMPLE **Use the general compound interest formula**

FINANCE You deposit \$1000 in an account that pays 3% annual interest. Find the balance after 8 years if the interest is compounded monthly.

Solution

The general formula for compound interest is $A = P\left(1 + \frac{r}{n}\right)^{nt}$. In this formula, P is the initial amount, called principal, in an account that pays interest at an annual rate r and that is compounded n times per year. The amount A (in dollars) is the amount in the account after t years.

Here, the interest is compounded monthly. So, $n = 12$.

$A = P\left(1 + \frac{r}{n}\right)^{nt}$ **Write compound interest formula.**

$= 1000\left(1 + \frac{0.03}{12}\right)^{12(8)}$ **Substitute 1000 for *P*, 0.03 for *r*, 12 for *n*, and 8 for *t*.**

$= 1000(1.0025)^{96}$ **Simplify.**

≈ 1270.868467 **Use a calculator.**

▶ The account balance after 8 years will be about \$1270.87.

47. Yearly **48.** Quarterly **49.** Daily ($n = 365$)

50. ★ **WRITING** Which compounding frequency yields the highest balance in the account in the example above: monthly, yearly, quarterly, or daily? *Explain* why this is so.

51. CHALLENGE The value y (in dollars) of an investment of \$1000 is given by $y = 1000(1.05)^t$ where t is the time in years. The *doubling time* is the value of t for which the amount invested doubles, so that $1000(1.05)^t = 2000$, or $(1.05)^t = 2$. Graph the functions $y = (1.05)^t$ and $y = 2$ on a graphing calculator. Estimate the doubling time.

PROBLEM SOLVING WORKSHOP
LESSON 7.4

Using ALTERNATIVE METHODS

Another Way to Solve Example 4

MULTIPLE REPRESENTATIONS In Example 4, you saw how to solve a problem about the value of a collector car over time by using an exponential model. You can also solve the problem by using a spreadsheet.

MATHEMATICAL PRACTICES

Make sense of problems and persevere in solving them.

PROBLEM

COLLECTOR CAR The owner of a 1953 Hudson Hornet convertible sold the car at an auction. The owner bought it in 1984 when its value was $11,000. The value of the car increased at a rate of 6.9% per year.

a. Write a function that models the value of the car over time.

b. The auction took place in 2004. What was the approximate value of the car at the time of the auction? Round your answer to the nearest dollar.

METHOD

Using a Spreadsheet An alternative approach is to use a spreadsheet.

a. The model for the value of the car over time is $C = 11{,}000(1.069)^t$, as shown in Example 4.

b. You can find the value of the car in 2004 by creating a spreadsheet.

STEP 1 **Create** a table showing the years since 1984 and the value of the car. Enter the car's value in 1984. To find the value in any year after 1984, multiply the car's value in the preceding year by the growth factor, as shown in cell B3 below.

FORMAT A SPREADSHEET
Format the spreadsheet so that calculations are rounded to 2 decimal places.

	A	B
1	Years since 1984, *t*	Value, *C* (dollars)
2	0	11000
3	1	=B2*1.069

STEP 2 **Find** the value of the car in 2004 by using the *fill down* feature until you get to the desired cell.

	A	B
1	Years since 1984, *t*	Value, *C* (dollars)
2	0	11000
3	1	11759
...	...	...
21	19	39081.31
22	20	41777.92

▶ From the spreadsheet, you can see the value of the car was about $41,778 in 2004.

PROBLEM

WHAT IF? Suppose the owner decided to sell the car when it was worth about \$28,000. In what year did the owner sell the car?

METHOD

Using a Spreadsheet To solve the equation algebraically, you need to substitute 28,000 for C and solve for t, but you have not yet learned how to solve this type of equation. An alternative to the algebraic approach is using a spreadsheet.

STEP 1 **Use** the same spreadsheet as on the previous page.

STEP 2 **Find** when the value of the car is about \$28,000.

	A	B
1	Years since 1984, t	Value, C (dollars)
2	0	11000
...	...	...
15	13	26188.03
16	14	27995.01

The value of the car is about \$28,000 when $t = 14$.

▶ The owner sold the car in 1998.

PRACTICE

1. **TRANSPORTATION** In 1997 the average intercity bus fare for a particular state was \$20. For the period 1997–2000, the bus fare increased at a rate of about 12% each year.
   a. Write a function that models the intercity bus fare for the period 1997–2000.
   b. Find the intercity bus fare in 1998. Use two different methods to solve the problem.
   c. In what year was the intercity bus fare \$28.10? *Explain* how you found your answer.

2. **ERROR ANALYSIS** *Describe* and correct the error in writing the function for part (a) of Exercise 1.

   Let b be the bus fare (in dollars) and t be the number of years since 1997.
   $b = 20(0.12)^t$ ✗

3. **TECHNOLOGY** A computer's Central Processing Unit (CPU) is made up of transistors. One manufacturer released a CPU in May 1997 that had 7.5 million transistors. The number of transistors in the CPUs sold by the company increased at a rate of 3.9% per month.
   a. Write a function that models the number T (in millions) of transistors in the company's CPUs t months after May 1997.
   b. Use a spreadsheet to find the number of transistors in a CPU released by the company in November 2000.

4. **HOUSING** The value of a home in 2002 was \$150,000. The value of the home increased at a rate of about 6.5% per year.
   a. Write a function that models the value of the home over time.
   b. Use a spreadsheet to find the year in which the value of the home was about \$200,000.

Exponential Models

Reason abstractly and quantitatively.

MATERIALS • yarn • scissors

QUESTION **How can you model a situation using an exponential function?**

EXPLORE **Collect data so that you can write exponential models**

STEP 1 ***Fold and cut*** Take about 1 yard of yarn and consider it to be 1 unit long. Fold it in half and cut, as shown. You are left with two pieces of yarn, each half the length of the original piece of yarn.

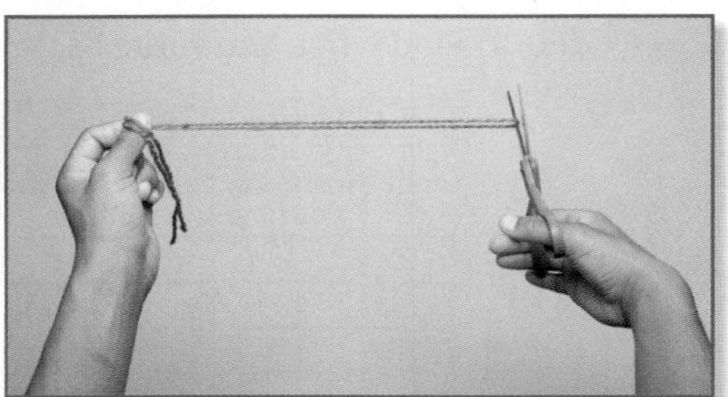

STEP 2 ***Copy and complete*** Copy the table. Notice that the row for stage 1 has the data from Step 1. For each successive stage, fold *all* the pieces of yarn in half and cut. Then record the number of new pieces and the length of each new piece until the table is complete.

Stage	Number of pieces	Length of each new piece
1	2	$\frac{1}{2}$
2	?	?
3	?	?
4	?	?
5	?	?

DRAW CONCLUSIONS **Use your observations to complete these exercises**

1. Use the data in the first and second columns of the table.
   - **a.** Do the data represent an exponential function? *Explain* how you know.
   - **b.** Write a function that models the number of pieces of yarn at stage x.
   - **c.** Use the function to find the number of pieces of yarn at stage 10.
2. Use the data in the first and third columns of the table.
   - **a.** Do the data represent an exponential function? *Explain* how you know.
   - **b.** Write a function that models the length of each new piece of yarn at stage x.
   - **c.** Use the function to find the length of each new piece of yarn at stage 10.

7.5 Write and Graph Exponential Decay Functions

Before You wrote and graphed exponential growth functions.

Now You will write and graph exponential decay functions.

Why? So you can use a graph to solve a sports problem, as in Ex. 50.

Key Vocabulary
- **exponential decay**

A table of values represents an exponential function $y = ab^x$ provided successive y-values are multiplied by b each time the x-values increase by 1.

EXAMPLE 1 Write a function rule

COMMON CORE

CC.9-12.A.CED.2 Create equations in two or more variables to represent relationships between quantities; graph equations on coordinate axes with labels and scales.*

Tell whether the table represents an exponential function. If so, write a rule for the function.

a.

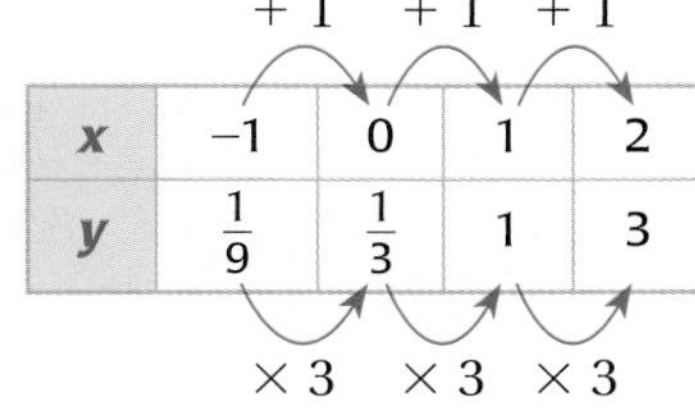

x	−1	0	1	2
y	$\frac{1}{9}$	$\frac{1}{3}$	1	3

The y-values are multiplied by 3 for each increase of 1 in x, so the table represents an exponential function of the form $y = ab^x$ with $b = 3$.

The value of y when $x = 0$ is $\frac{1}{3}$, so $a = \frac{1}{3}$.

The table represents the exponential function $y = \frac{1}{3} \cdot 3^x$.

b.

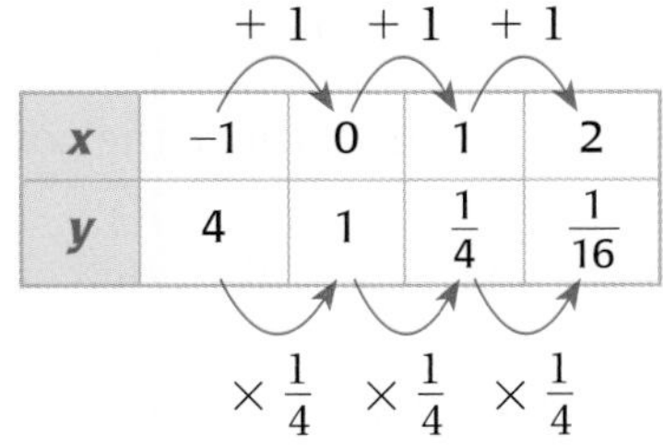

x	−1	0	1	2
y	4	1	$\frac{1}{4}$	$\frac{1}{16}$

The y-values are multiplied by $\frac{1}{4}$ for each increase of 1 in x, so the table represents an exponential function of the form $y = ab^x$ with $b = \frac{1}{4}$.

The value of y when $x = 0$ is 1, so $a = 1$.

The table represents the exponential function $y = \left(\frac{1}{4}\right)^x$.

✓ GUIDED PRACTICE for Example 1

1. Tell whether the table represents an exponential function. If so, write a rule for the function.

x	−1	0	1	2
y	5	1	$\frac{1}{5}$	$\frac{1}{25}$

EXAMPLE 2 Graph an exponential function

Graph the function $y = \left(\frac{1}{2}\right)^x$ and identify its domain and range.

Solution

READ A GRAPH
Notice that the graph has a y-intercept of 1 and that it gets closer to the positive x-axis as the x-values increase.

STEP 1 **Make** a table of values. The domain is all real numbers.

x	−2	−1	0	1	2
y	4	2	1	$\frac{1}{2}$	$\frac{1}{4}$

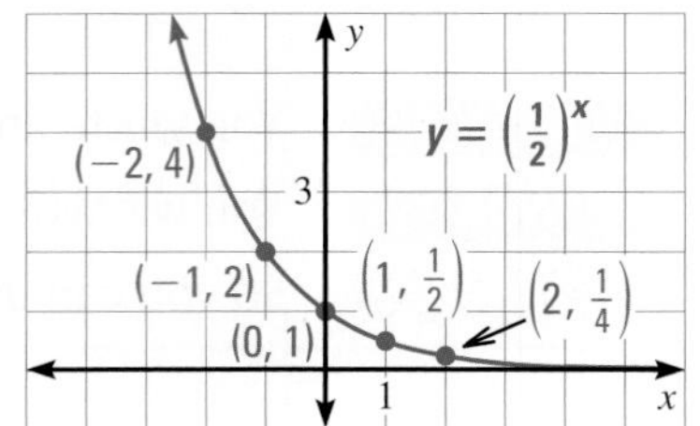

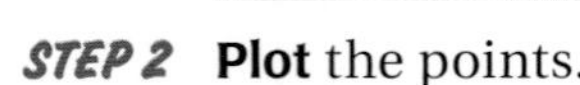

STEP 2 **Plot** the points.

STEP 3 **Draw** a smooth curve through the points. From either the table or the graph, you can see the range is all positive real numbers.

EXAMPLE 3 Compare graphs of exponential functions

Graph the functions $y = 3 \cdot \left(\frac{1}{2}\right)^x$ and $y = -\frac{1}{3} \cdot \left(\frac{1}{2}\right)^x$. Compare each graph with the graph of $y = \left(\frac{1}{2}\right)^x$.

Solution

DESCRIBE A FUNCTION
An exponential decay function has an unbroken graph, so the function is continuous.

x	$y = \left(\frac{1}{2}\right)^x$	$y = 3 \cdot \left(\frac{1}{2}\right)^x$	$y = -\frac{1}{3} \cdot \left(\frac{1}{2}\right)^x$
−2	4	12	$-\frac{4}{3}$
−1	2	6	$-\frac{2}{3}$
0	1	3	$-\frac{1}{3}$
1	$\frac{1}{2}$	$\frac{3}{2}$	$-\frac{1}{6}$
2	$\frac{1}{4}$	$\frac{3}{4}$	$-\frac{1}{12}$

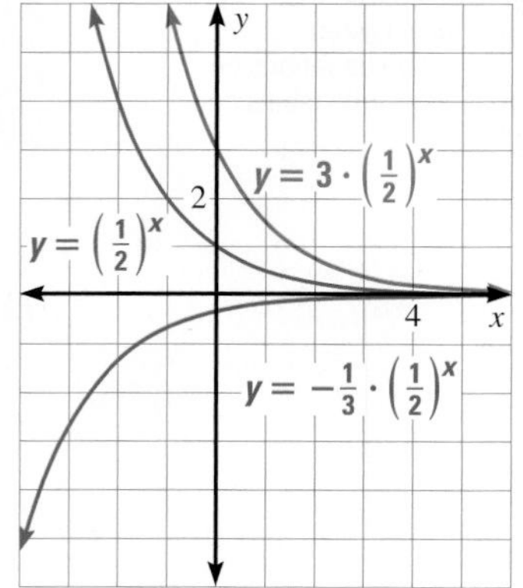

Because the y-values for $y = 3 \cdot \left(\frac{1}{2}\right)^x$ are 3 times the corresponding y-values for $y = \left(\frac{1}{2}\right)^x$, the graph of $y = 3 \cdot \left(\frac{1}{2}\right)^x$ is a vertical stretch of the graph of $y = \left(\frac{1}{2}\right)^x$.

Because the y-values for $y = -\frac{1}{3} \cdot \left(\frac{1}{2}\right)^x$ are $-\frac{1}{3}$ times the corresponding y-values for $y = \left(\frac{1}{2}\right)^x$, the graph of $y = -\frac{1}{3} \cdot \left(\frac{1}{2}\right)^x$ is a vertical shrink with reflection in the x-axis of the graph of $y = \left(\frac{1}{2}\right)^x$.

GUIDED PRACTICE for Examples 2 and 3

2. Graph $y = (0.4)^x$ and identify its domain and range.
3. Graph $y = 5 \cdot (0.4)^x$. Compare the graph with the graph of $y = (0.4)^x$.

COMPARE GRAPHS When $a > 0$ and $0 < b < 1$, the function $y = ab^x$ represents **exponential decay**. The graph of an exponential decay function falls from left to right. In comparison, the graph of an exponential growth function $y = ab^x$ where $a > 0$ and $b > 1$ rises from the left.

EXAMPLE 4 Classify and write rules for functions

Tell whether the graph represents *exponential growth* or *exponential decay*. Then write a rule for the function.

a.

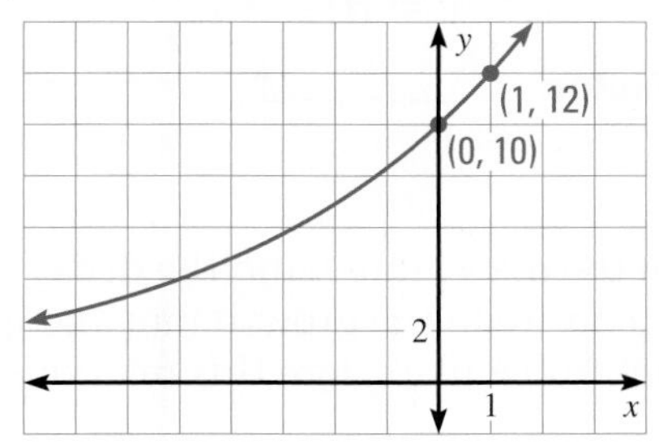

b.

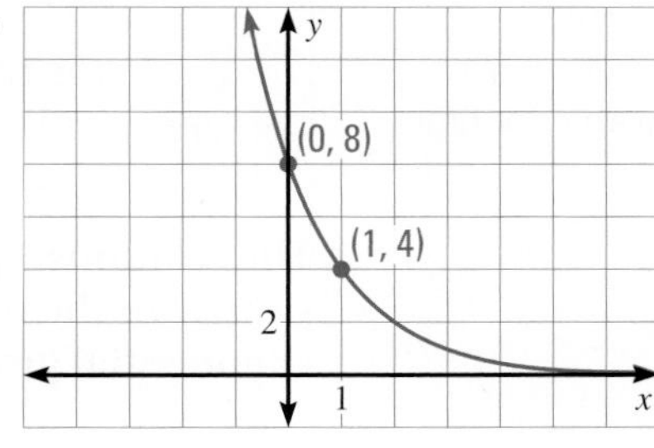

Solution

ANALYZE GRAPHS
For the function $y = ab^x$, where $x = 0$, the value of y is $y = ax^0 = a$. This means that the graph of $y = ab^x$ has a y-intercept of a.

a. The graph represents exponential growth ($y = ab^x$ where $b > 1$). The y-intercept is 10, so $a = 10$. Find the value of b by using the point (1, 12) and $a = 10$.

$y = ab^x$	**Write function.**
$12 = 10 \cdot b^1$	**Substitute.**
$1.2 = b$	**Solve.**

A function rule is $y = 10(1.2)^x$.

b. The graph represents exponential decay ($y = ab^x$ where $0 < b < 1$). The y-intercept is 8, so $a = 8$. Find the value of b by using the point (1, 4) and $a = 8$.

$y = ab^x$	**Write function.**
$4 = 8 \cdot b^1$	**Substitute.**
$0.5 = b$	**Solve.**

A function rule is $y = 8(0.5)^x$.

✓ GUIDED PRACTICE for Example 4

4. The graph of an exponential function passes through the points (0, 10) and (1, 8). Graph the function. Tell whether the graph represents *exponential growth* or *exponential decay*. Write a rule for the function.

CONCEPT SUMMARY *For Your Notebook*

Exponential Growth and Decay

Exponential Growth

$y = ab^x$, $a > 0$ and $b > 1$

y
(0, a)
x

Exponential Decay

$y = ab^x$, $a > 0$ and $0 < b < 1$

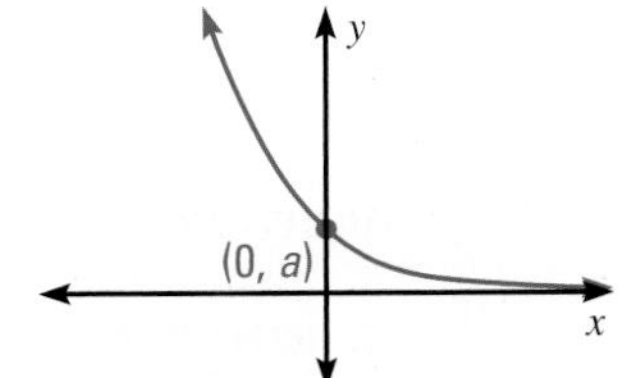

EXPONENTIAL DECAY When a quantity decays exponentially, it decreases by the same percent over equal time periods. To find the amount of the quantity left after t time periods, use the following model.

REWRITE EQUATIONS
Notice that you can rewrite $y = ab^x$ as $y = a(1 - r)^t$ by replacing b with $1 - r$ and x with t (for time).

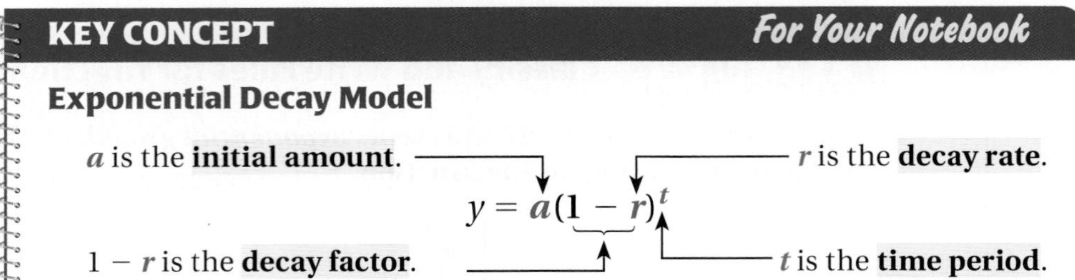

The relationship between the decay rate r and the decay factor $1 - r$ is similar to the relationship between the growth rate and growth factor in an exponential growth model. You will explore this relationship in Exercise 45.

EXAMPLE 5 Solve a multi-step problem

FORESTRY The number of acres of Ponderosa pine forests decreased in the western United States from 1963 to 2002 by 0.5% annually. In 1963 there were about 41 million acres of Ponderosa pine forests.

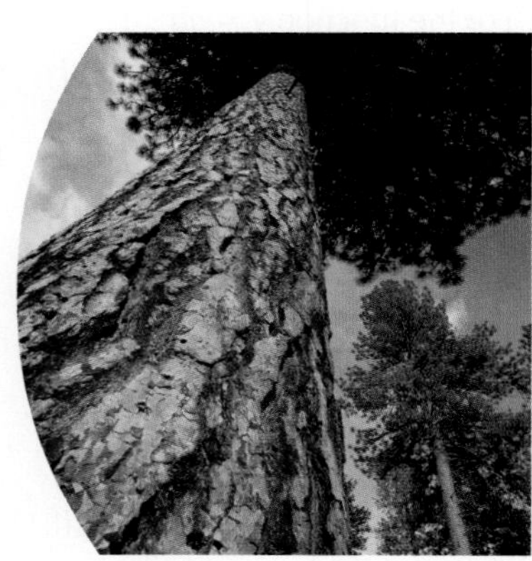

a. Write a function that models the number of acres of Ponderosa pine forests in the western United States over time.

b. To the nearest tenth, about how many million acres of Ponderosa pine forests were there in 2002?

Solution

a. Let P be the number of acres (in millions), and let t be the time (in years) since 1963. The initial value is 41, and the decay rate is 0.005.

$P = a(1 - r)^t$ **Write exponential decay model.**

$= 41(1 - 0.005)^t$ **Substitute 41 for a and 0.005 for r.**

$= 41(0.995)^t$ **Simplify.**

AVOID ERRORS
The decay rate in this example is 0.5%, or 0.005. So, the decay factor is $1 - 0.005$, or 0.995, not 0.005.

b. To find the number of acres in 2002, 39 years after 1963, substitute 39 for t.

$P = 41(0.995)^{39} \approx 33.7$ **Substitute 39 for t. Use a calculator.**

▶ There were about 33.7 million acres of Ponderosa pine forests in 2002.

Animated Algebra at my.hrw.com

✓ GUIDED PRACTICE for Example 5

5. WHAT IF? In Example 5, suppose the decay rate of the forests remains the same beyond 2002. About how many acres will be left in 2010?

7.5 EXERCISES

HOMEWORK KEY

○ = See **WORKED-OUT SOLUTIONS** Exs. 7 and 49

★ = **STANDARDIZED TEST PRACTICE** Exs. 2, 19, 36, 45, and 49

◆ = **MULTIPLE REPRESENTATIONS** Ex. 50

SKILL PRACTICE

1. **VOCABULARY** What is the decay factor in the exponential decay model $y = a(1 - r)^t$?

2. ★ **WRITING** *Explain* how you can tell if a graph represents *exponential growth* or *exponential decay.*

EXAMPLE 1 for Exs. 3–6

WRITING FUNCTIONS Tell whether the table represents an exponential function. If so, write a rule for the function.

3.

x	−1	0	1	2
y	2	8	32	128

4.

x	−1	0	1	2
y	50	10	2	0.4

5.

x	−1	0	1	2
y	6	2	$\frac{2}{3}$	$\frac{2}{9}$

6.

x	−1	0	1	2
y	−11	−7	−3	1

EXAMPLE 2 for Exs. 7–18

GRAPHING FUNCTIONS Graph the function and identify its domain and range.

7. $y = \left(\frac{1}{5}\right)^x$
8. $y = \left(\frac{1}{6}\right)^x$
9. $y = \left(\frac{2}{3}\right)^x$
10. $y = \left(\frac{3}{4}\right)^x$
11. $y = \left(\frac{4}{5}\right)^x$
12. $y = \left(\frac{3}{5}\right)^x$
13. $y = (0.3)^x$
14. $y = (0.5)^x$
15. $y = (0.1)^x$
16. $y = (0.9)^x$
17. $y = (0.7)^x$
18. $y = (0.25)^x$

EXAMPLE 3 for Exs. 19–31

19. ★ **MULTIPLE CHOICE** The graph of which function is shown?

 Ⓐ $y = (0.25)^x$ Ⓑ $y = (0.5)^x$

 Ⓒ $y = 0.25 \cdot (0.5)^x$ Ⓓ $y = 4 \cdot (0.5)^x$

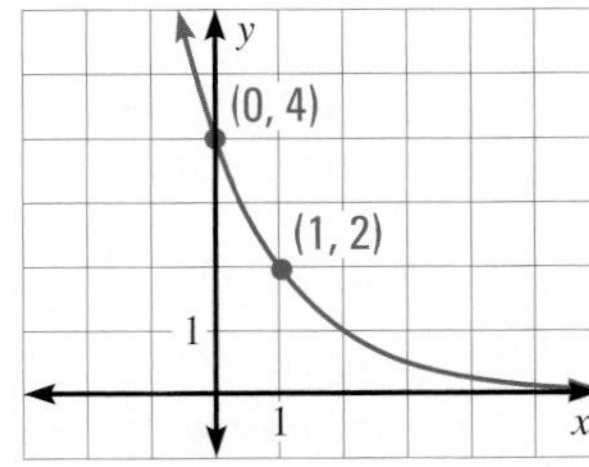

COMPARING FUNCTIONS Graph the function. Compare the graph with the graph of $y = \left(\frac{1}{4}\right)^x$.

20. $y = 5 \cdot \left(\frac{1}{4}\right)^x$
21. $y = 3 \cdot \left(\frac{1}{4}\right)^x$
22. $y = \frac{1}{2} \cdot \left(\frac{1}{4}\right)^x$
23. $y = \frac{1}{3} \cdot \left(\frac{1}{4}\right)^x$
24. $y = 0.2 \cdot \left(\frac{1}{4}\right)^x$
25. $y = 1.5 \cdot \left(\frac{1}{4}\right)^x$
26. $y = -5 \cdot \left(\frac{1}{4}\right)^x$
27. $y = -3 \cdot \left(\frac{1}{4}\right)^x$
28. $y = -\frac{1}{2} \cdot \left(\frac{1}{4}\right)^x$
29. $y = -\frac{1}{3} \cdot \left(\frac{1}{4}\right)^x$
30. $y = -0.2 \cdot \left(\frac{1}{4}\right)^x$
31. $y = -1.5 \cdot \left(\frac{1}{4}\right)^x$

MATCHING Match the function with its graph.

32. $y = (0.2)^x$

33. $y = 5(0.2)^x$

34. $y = \frac{1}{2}(0.2)^x$

A. 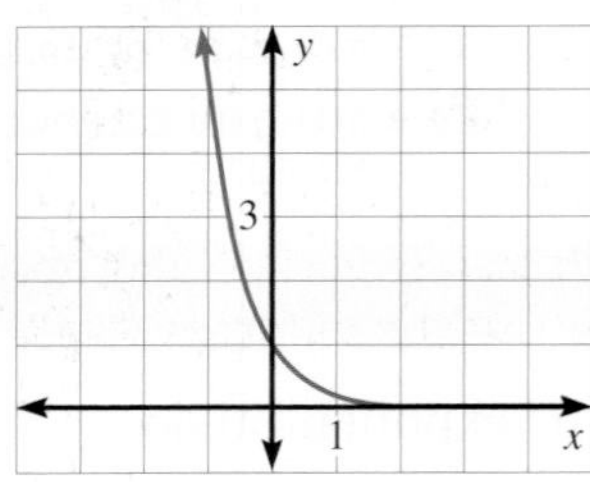

B. 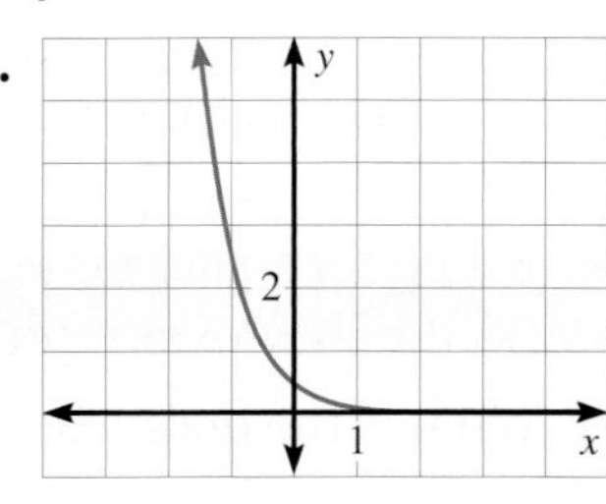

C. 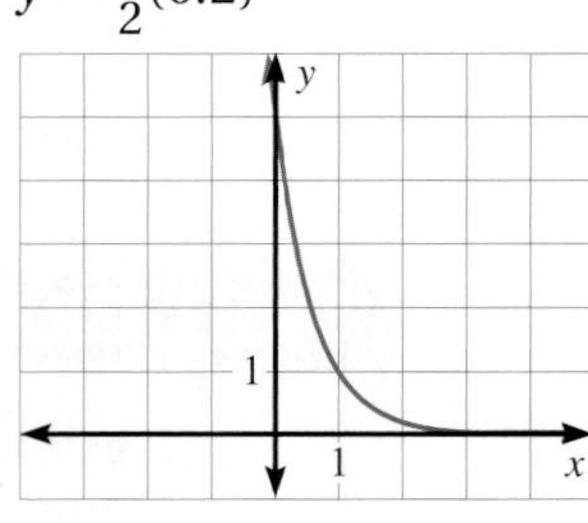

35. **POPULATION** A population of 90,000 decreases by 2.5% per year. Identify the initial amount, the decay factor, and the decay rate. Then write a function that models the population over time.

36. ★ **MULTIPLE CHOICE** What is the decay rate of the function $y = 4(0.97)^t$?

Ⓐ 4 Ⓑ 0.97 Ⓒ 0.3 Ⓓ 0.03

37. **ERROR ANALYSIS** In 2004 a person purchased a car for $25,000. The value of the car decreased by 14% annually. *Describe* and correct the error in writing a function that models the value of the car since 2004.

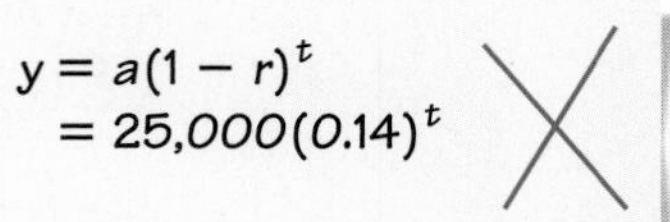

EXAMPLE 4
for Exs. 38–40

RECOGNIZING EXPONENTIAL MODELS Tell whether the graph represents *exponential growth* or *exponential decay*. Then write a rule for the function.

38. 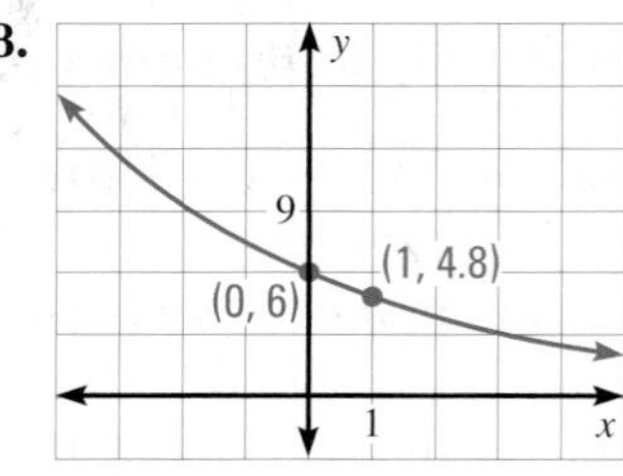

39. 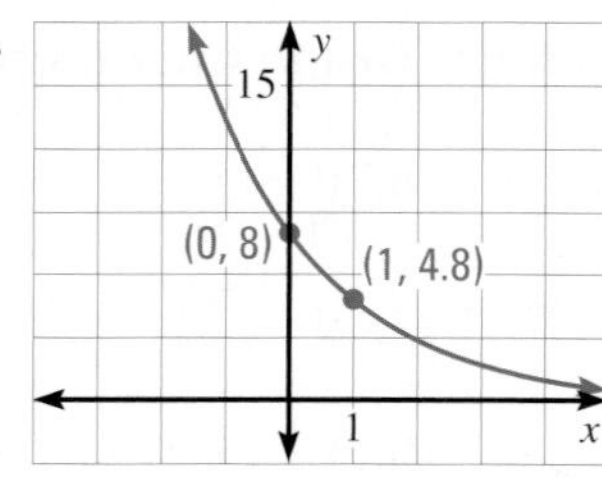

40. 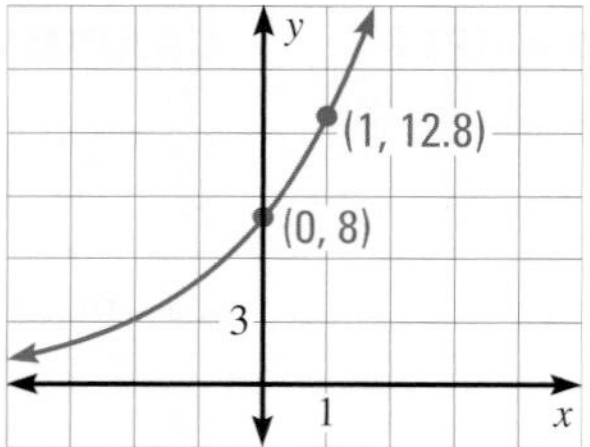

Animated Algebra at my.hrw.com

41. **REASONING** Without graphing, explain how the graphs of the given functions are related to the graph of $f(x) = (0.5)^x$.

a. $m(x) = \frac{1}{3} \cdot (0.5)^x$

b. $n(x) = -4 \cdot (0.5)^x$

c. $p(x) = (0.5)^x + 1$

CHALLENGE Write an exponential function of the form $y = ab^x$ whose graph passes through the given points.

42. $(0, 1), \left(2, \frac{1}{4}\right)$

43. $(1, 20), (2, 4)$

44. $\left(1, \frac{3}{2}\right), \left(2, \frac{3}{4}\right)$

45. ★ **WRITING** The *half-life* of a radioactive substance is the time required for half the substance to decay. The amount A (in grams) of a 100 gram sample of a radioactive substance remaining after t half-lives is given by $A = 100(0.5)^t$. Suppose the substance has a half-life of 10 days. *Explain* how to find the amount left after 40 days. Then find the amount.

46. **CHALLENGE** *Compare* the graphs of the functions $f(x) = 4^{x-2}$ and $g(x) = \frac{1}{16} \cdot 4^x$. Use properties of exponents to explain your observation.

PROBLEM SOLVING

GRAPHING CALCULATOR You may wish to use a graphing calculator to complete the following Problem Solving exercises.

EXAMPLE 5
for Exs. 47–50

47. **CELL PHONES** You purchase a cell phone for \$125. The value of the cell phone decreases by about 20% annually. Write a function that models the value of the cell phone over time. Then find the value of the cell phone after 3 years.

48. **ANIMAL POPULATION** Scientists studied the population of a species of bat in some caves in Missouri from 1983 to 2003. In 1983, there were 141,200 bats living in the caves. That number decreased by about 11% annually until 2003.

   a. Identify the initial amount, the decay factor, and the decay rate.

   b. Write a function that models the number of bats since 1983. Then find the number of bats in 2003.

49. ★ **SHORT RESPONSE** In 2003 a family bought a boat for \$4000. The boat depreciates (loses value) at a rate of 7% annually. In 2006 a person offers to buy the boat for \$3000. Should the family sell the boat? *Explain.*

50. **MULTIPLE REPRESENTATIONS** There are a total of 128 teams at the start of a citywide 3-on-3 basketball tournament. Half of the teams are eliminated after each round.

   a. **Writing a Model** Write a function for the number of teams left after x rounds.

   b. **Making a Table** Make a table for the function using $x = 0, 1, 2, \ldots, 7$.

   c. **Drawing a Graph** Use the table in part (b) to graph the function. After which round are there 4 teams left in the tournament?

51. **GUITARS** The frets on a guitar are the small metal bars that divide the fingerboard. The distance d (in inches) between the nut and the first fret or any two consecutive frets can be modeled by the function $d = 1.516(0.9439)^f$ where f is the number of the fret farthest from the nut.

   a. Identify the decay factor and the decay rate for the model.

   b. What is the distance between the nut and the first fret?

   c. The distance between the 12th and 13th frets is about half the distance between the nut and the first fret. Use this fact to find the distance between the 12th and 13th frets. Use the model to verify your answer.

52. **CHALLENGE** A college student finances a computer that costs \$1850. The financing plan states that as long as a minimum monthly payment of 2.25% of the remaining balance is made, the student does not have to pay interest for 24 months. The student makes only the minimum monthly payments until the last payment. What is the amount of the last payment if the student buys the computer without paying interest? Round your answer to the nearest cent.

53. **MULTI-STEP PROBLEM** Maximal oxygen consumption is the maximum volume of oxygen (in liters per minute) that the body uses during exercise. Maximal oxygen consumption varies from person to person and decreases with age by about 0.5% per year after age 25 for active adults.

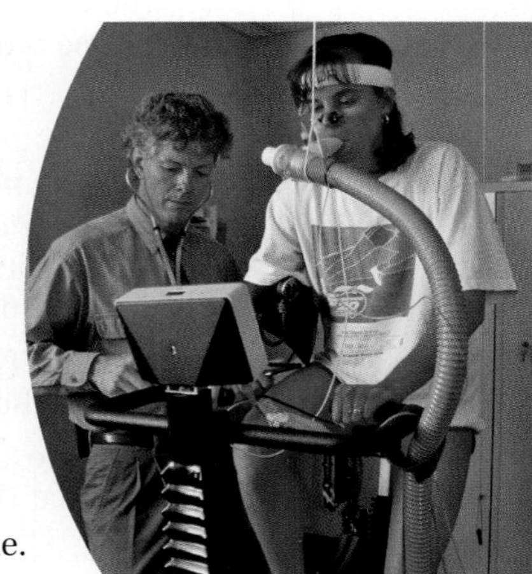

 a. **Model** A 25-year-old female athlete has a maximal oxygen consumption of 4 liters per minute. Another 25-year-old female athlete has a maximal oxygen consumption of 3.5 liters per minute. Write a function for each athlete that models the maximal consumption each year after age 25.

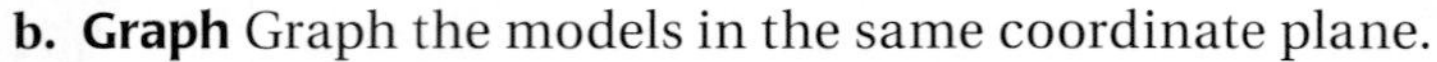

 b. **Graph** Graph the models in the same coordinate plane.

 c. **Estimate** About how old will the first athlete be when her maximal oxygen consumption is equal to what the second athlete's maximal oxygen consumption is at age 25?

QUIZ

Simplify the expression. Write your answer using only positive exponents.

1. $(-4x)^4 \cdot (-4)^{-6}$
2. $(-3x^7y^{-2})^{-3}$
3. $\frac{1}{(5z)^{-3}}$
4. $\frac{(6x)^{-2}y^5}{-x^3y^{-7}}$

Graph the function.

5. $y = \left(\frac{5}{2}\right)^x$
6. $y = 3 \cdot \left(\frac{1}{4}\right)^x$
7. $y = \frac{1}{4} \cdot 3^x$
8. $y = (0.1)^x$
9. $y = 10 \cdot 5^x$
10. $y = 7(0.4)^x$

11. **COINS** You purchase a coin from a coin collector for \$25. Each year the value of the coin increases by 8%. Write a function that models the value of the coin over time. Then find the value of the coin after 10 years. Round to the nearest cent.

See **EXTRA PRACTICE** in Student Resources **ONLINE QUIZ** at my.hrw.com

Extension Relate Geometric Sequences to Exponential Functions

GOAL Identify, graph, and write geometric sequences.

Key Vocabulary
- **geometric sequence**
- **common ratio**

In a **geometric sequence**, the ratio of any term to the previous term is constant. This constant ratio is called the **common ratio** and is denoted by r.

A geometric sequence with first term a_1 and common ratio r has the form a_1, a_1r, a_1r^2, a_1r^3, ... For instance, if $a_1 = 5$ and $r = 2$, the sequence 5, $5 \cdot 2$, $5 \cdot 2^2$, $5 \cdot 2^3$, . . . , or 5, 10, 20, 40, . . . , is geometric.

CC.9-12.F.IF.3 Recognize that sequences are functions, sometimes defined recursively, whose domain is a subset of the integers.

EXAMPLE 1 Identify a geometric sequence

Tell whether the sequence is *arithmetic* or *geometric*. Then write the next term of the sequence.

a. 3, 6, 9, 12, 15, . . . **b.** 128, 64, 32, 16, 8, . . .

Solution

a. The first term is $a_1 = 3$. Find the ratios of consecutive terms:

$\frac{a_2}{a_1} = \frac{6}{3} = 2$ $\frac{a_3}{a_2} = \frac{9}{6} = 1\frac{1}{2}$ $\frac{a_4}{a_3} = \frac{12}{9} = 1\frac{1}{3}$ $\frac{a_5}{a_4} = \frac{15}{12} = 1\frac{1}{4}$

Because the ratios are not constant, the sequence is not geometric. To see if the sequence is arithmetic, find the differences of consecutive terms.

$a_2 - a_1 = 6 - 3 = 3$ $a_3 - a_2 = 9 - 6 = 3$

$a_4 - a_3 = 12 - 9 = 3$ $a_5 - a_4 = 15 - 12 = 3$

The common difference is 3, so the sequence is arithmetic. The next term of the sequence is $a_6 = a_5 + 3 = 18$.

b. The first term is $a_1 = 128$. Find the ratios of consecutive terms:

$\frac{a_2}{a_1} = \frac{64}{128} = \frac{1}{2}$ $\frac{a_3}{a_2} = \frac{32}{64} = \frac{1}{2}$ $\frac{a_4}{a_3} = \frac{16}{32} = \frac{1}{2}$ $\frac{a_5}{a_4} = \frac{8}{16} = \frac{1}{2}$

Because the ratios are constant, the sequence is geometric. The common ratio is $\frac{1}{2}$. The next term of the sequence is $a_6 = a_5 \cdot \frac{1}{2} = 4$.

REVIEW ARITHMETIC SEQUENCES
You may want to review identifying an arithmetic sequence and finding a common difference before working with geometric sequences and common ratios.

EXAMPLE 2 Graph a geometric sequence

To graph the sequence from part (b) of Example 1, let each term's position number in the sequence be the x-value. The term is the corresponding y-value. Then make and plot the points.

Position, x	1	2	3	4	5
Term, y	128	64	32	16	8

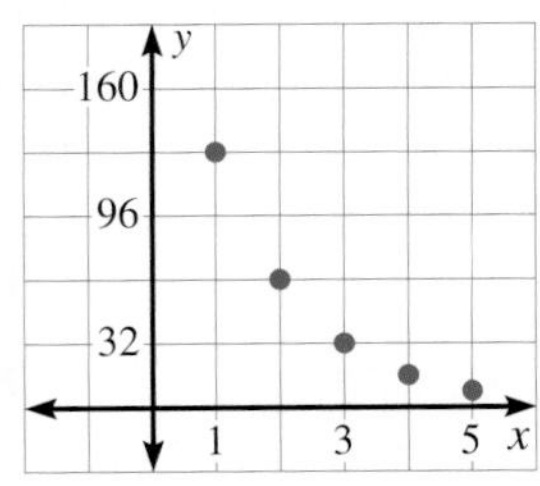

ANALYZE A GRAPH
Notice that the graph in Example 2 appears to be exponential.

USE FUNCTION NOTATION

You can write the geometric sequence with first term a_1 and common ratio r in function notation as $f(x) = a_1r^{x-1}$.

FUNCTIONS The table shows that a rule for finding the nth term of a geometric sequence is $a_n = a_1r^{n-1}$. Notice that the rule is an exponential function.

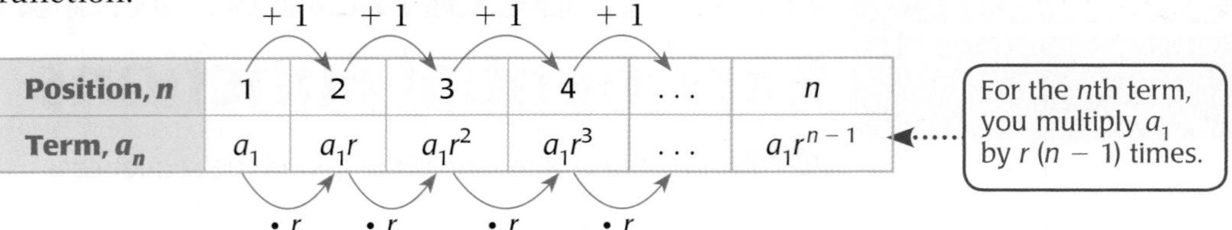

Position, n	1	2	3	4	...	n
Term, a_n	a_1	a_1r	a_1r^2	a_1r^3	...	a_1r^{n-1}

KEY CONCEPT — For Your Notebook

General Rule for a Geometric Sequence

The nth term of a geometric sequence with first term a_1 and common ratio r is given by: $a_n = a_1r^{n-1}$.

EXAMPLE 3 Write a rule for a geometric sequence

Write a rule for the nth term of the geometric sequence in Example 1. Then find a_{10}.

Solution

To write a rule for the nth term of the sequence, substitute the values for a_1 and r in the general rule $a_n = a_1r^{n-1}$. Because $a_1 = 128$ and $r = \frac{1}{2}$, $a_n = 128 \cdot \left(\frac{1}{2}\right)^{n-1}$. The 10th term of the sequence is $a_{10} = 128 \cdot \left(\frac{1}{2}\right)^{10-1} = \frac{1}{4}$.

PRACTICE

EXAMPLES 1, 2, and 3 for Exs. 1–10

Tell whether the sequence is *arithmetic* or *geometric*. Then graph the sequence.

1. 3, 12, 48, 192, . . .
2. 7, 16, 25, 34, . . .
3. 34, 28, 22, 16, . . .
4. 1024, 128, 16, 2, . . .
5. 9, −18, 36, −72, . . .
6. 29, 43, 57, 71, . . .

Write a rule for the nth term of the geometric sequence. Then find a_7.

7. 1, −5, 25, −125, . . .
8. 13, 26, 52, 104, . . .
9. 432, 72, 12, 2, . . .

10. **E-MAIL** A chain e-mail instructs the recipient to forward the e-mail to four more people. The table shows the number of rounds of sending the e-mail and the number of new e-mails generated. Write a rule for the nth term of the sequence. Then graph the first six terms of the sequence.

Number of rounds sending e-mail, n	1	2	3	4
Number of new e-mails generated, a_n	1	4	16	64

Extension Define Sequences Recursively

GOAL Write and graph recursively-defined sequences.

Key Vocabulary
- **recursive rule**

CC.9-12.F.IF.3 Recognize that sequences are functions, sometimes defined recursively, whose domain is a subset of the integers.

In previous extensions, you learned how to define arithmetic and geometric sequences *explicitly*. An explicit rule gives a_n as a function of the term's position number n in the sequence. For example, an explicit rule for the arithmetic sequence 3, 5, 7, 9, . . . is $a_n = 3 + 2(n - 1)$, or $a_n = 2n + 1$.

You can also define arithmetic and geometric sequences *recursively*. A **recursive rule** gives the beginning term(s) of a sequence and a recursive equation that tells how a_n relates to preceding terms. For example, a recursive definition for the geometric sequence 2, 6, 18, 54, . . . is $a_1 = 2$ and $a_n = 3 \cdot a_{n-1}$.

KEY CONCEPT *For Your Notebook*

Recursive Equation for an Arithmetic Sequence

$a_n = a_{n-1} + d$ where d is the common difference

Recursive Equation for a Geometric Sequence

$a_n = r \cdot a_{n-1}$ where r is the common ratio

EXAMPLE 1 Write and graph recursively-defined sequences

Write the first five terms of the sequence. Then graph the sequence.

a. $a_1 = 5,\ a_n = a_{n-1} + 5$

b. $a_1 = 1,\ a_n = 2a_{n-1}$

Solution

a. $a_1 = 5$

$a_2 = a_1 + 5 = 5 + 5 = 10$

$a_3 = a_2 + 5 = 10 + 5 = 15$

$a_4 = a_3 + 5 = 15 + 5 = 20$

$a_5 = a_4 + 5 = 20 + 5 = 25$

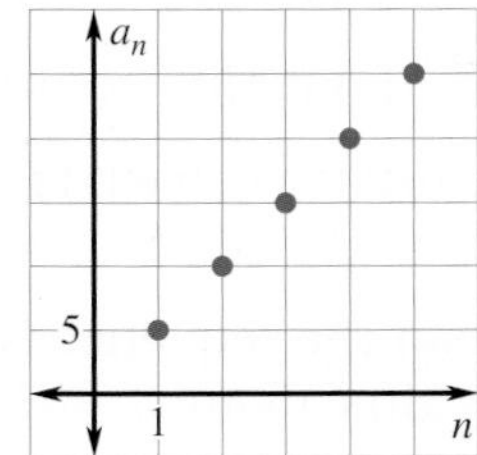

b. $a_1 = 1$

$a_2 = 2a_1 = 2(1) = 2$

$a_3 = 2a_2 = 2(2) = 4$

$a_4 = 2a_3 = 2(4) = 8$

$a_5 = 2a_4 = 2(8) = 16$

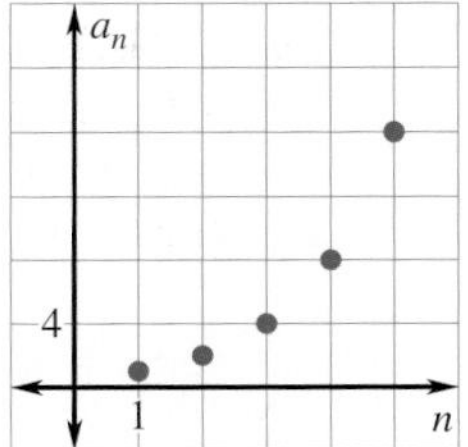

DRAW A GRAPH

A sequence is a discrete function. The points on the graph are not connected.

EXAMPLE 2 Write recursive rules for sequences

Write a recursive rule for the sequence.

a. 2, 5, 8, 11, 14, . . .   **b.** 16, 24, 36, 54, 81, . . .

Solution

AVOID ERRORS

To write a recursive *rule* for a sequence, you must give both the beginning term(s) and the recursive *equation*.

a. The sequence is arithmetic with first term $a_1 = 2$ and common difference $d = 5 - 2 = 3$.

$a_n = a_{n-1} + d$ **Recursive equation for a_n**

$a_n = a_{n-1} + 3$ **Substitute 3 for *d*.**

▶ So, a recursive rule for the sequence is $a_1 = 2$, $a_n = a_{n-1} + 3$.

b. The sequence is geometric with first term $a_1 = 16$ and common ratio $r = \frac{24}{16} = 1.5$.

$a_n = r \cdot a_{n-1}$ **Recursive equation for a_n**

$a_n = 1.5a_{n-1}$ **Substitute 1.5 for *r*.**

▶ So, a recursive rule for the sequence is $a_1 = 16$, $a_n = 1.5a_{n-1}$.

SPECIAL SEQUENCES In special cases, you may be able to write a recursive rule for a sequence that is neither arithmetic nor geometric. Consider the following sequence, called the *Fibonacci sequence*: 1, 1, 2, 3, 5, 8, 13, ... Notice that the Fibonacci sequence is neither arithmetic nor geometric.

$a_2 - a_1 = 1 - 1 = 0$, while $a_3 - a_2 = 2 - 1 = 1$.

$\frac{a_2}{a_1} = \frac{1}{1} = 1$, while $\frac{a_3}{a_2} = \frac{2}{1} = 2$.

You can still write a recursive rule for the Fibonacci sequence, as shown in Example 3.

EXAMPLE 3 Write a recursive rule for a special sequence

Write a recursive rule for the sequence 1, 1, 2, 3, 5, 8, 13, ... Identify the next two terms of the sequence.

Solution

Look at sums of consecutive pairs of terms.

$a_1 + a_2 = 1 + 1 = 2$ **2 is the third term of the sequence.**

$a_2 + a_3 = 1 + 2 = 3$ **3 is the fourth term of the sequence.**

$a_3 + a_4 = 2 + 3 = 5$ **5 is the fifth term of the sequence.**

Beginning with the third term, each term is the sum of the two previous terms.

▶ So, a recursive rule for the sequence is $a_1 = 1$, $a_2 = 1$, $a_n = a_{n-2} + a_{n-1}$. The next two terms after 13 are $8 + 13 = 21$ and $13 + 21 = 34$.

PRACTICE

EXAMPLE 1 for Exs. 1–9

Write the first five terms of the sequence. Then graph the sequence.

1. $a_1 = 0, a_n = a_{n-1} + 2$ **2.** $a_1 = 10, a_n = a_{n-1} - 5$ **3.** $a_1 = -3, a_n = a_{n-1} + 3$

4. $a_1 = 1, a_n = a_{n-1} + 1$ **5.** $a_1 = 8, a_n = a_{n-1} - 2$ **6.** $a_1 = 8, a_n = 1.5a_{n-1}$

7. $a_1 = 1, a_n = 3a_{n-1}$ **8.** $a_1 = 16, a_n = 0.5a_{n-1}$ **9.** $a_1 = -2, a_n = 2a_{n-1}$

EXAMPLE 2 for Exs. 10–18

Write a recursive rule for the sequence.

10. 8, 28, 48, 68, 88, . . . **11.** 256, 64, 16, 4, 1, . . . **12.** 0, −4, −8, −12, −16, . . .

13. 3, 7, 11, 15, 19, . . . **14.** 81, 27, 9, 3, 1, . . . **15.** −5, −3, −1, 1, 3, . . .

16. 16, 24, 36, 54, 81, . . . **17.** −2, 4, −8, 16, −32, . . . **18.** 0.5, 1.75, 3, 4.25, 5.5, . . .

EXAMPLE 3 for Exs. 19–24

Write a recursive rule for the sequence. Identify the next two terms of the sequence.

19. 1, 3, 4, 7, 11, . . . **20.** 1, 4, 4, 16, 64, . . . **21.** 1, 1, 1, 3, 5, 9, . . .

22. 10, 9, 1, 8, −7, 15, . . . **23.** 64, 16, 4, 4, 1, . . . **24.** 2, 4, 10, 24, 58, . . .

25. USING A SPREADSHEET You can use a spreadsheet to generate the terms of a sequence.

A2	=A1+2		
	A	B	C
1	3		
2	5		
3			
4			

a. To generate the terms of the sequence $a_1 = 3, a_n = a_{n-1} + 2$, enter the value of a_1, 3, into cell A1. Then enter "=A1+2" into cell A2 as shown and use the *fill down* feature to generate the first ten terms of the sequence.

b. Use a spreadsheet to generate the first ten terms of the sequence $a_1 = 3, a_n = 4a_{n-1}$. (*Hint*: Enter "=4*A1" into cell A2.)

26. BACTERIA A population of bacteria doubles every hour. After 1 hour, there are 200 bacteria. Write a recursive rule for the number a_n of bacteria after n hours. How many bacteria are there after 6 hours?

27. REASONING The explicit rule $a_n = a_1 + (n - 1)d$ defines an arithmetic sequence.

a. *Explain* why $a_{n-1} = a_1 + [(n - 1) - 1]d$.

b. *Justify* each step in showing that a recursive equation for the sequence is $a_n = a_{n-1} + d$.

$a_n = a_1 + (n - 1)d$ ____?____

$= a_1 + [(n - 1) + 0]d$ ____?____

$= a_1 + [(n - 1) - 1 + 1]d$ ____?____

$= a_1 + [((n - 1) - 1) + 1]d$ ____?____

$= a_1 + [(n - 1) - 1]d + d$ ____?____

$= a_{n-1} + d$ ____?____

MIXED REVIEW *of Problem Solving*

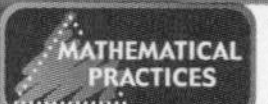

Make sense of problems and persevere in solving them.

1. **MULTI-STEP PROBLEM** The half-life of a medication is the time it takes for the medication to reduce to half of its original amount in a patient's bloodstream. A certain antibiotic has a half-life of about 8 hours.

   a. A patient is administered 500 milligrams of the medication. Write a function that models the amount of the medication in the patient's bloodstream over time.

   b. How much of the 500 milligram dose will be in the patient's bloodstream after 24 hours?

2. **SHORT RESPONSE** The graph shows the value of a truck over time.

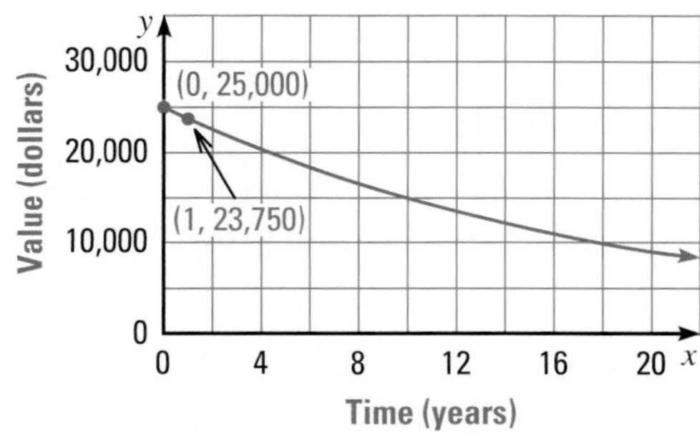

   a. Write an equation for the function whose graph is shown.

   b. At what rate is the truck losing value? *Explain.*

3. **GRIDDED ANSWER** A new laptop computer costs \$2000. The value of the computer decreases over time. The value V (in dollars) of the computer after t years is given by the function $V = 2000(0.82)^t$. What is the decay rate, written as a decimal, of the value of the computer?

4. **OPEN-ENDED** The value of a house in Iowa increased, on average, at a rate of about 4% per quarter from the first quarter in 2001 to the last quarter in 2004. Write a function that models the value of the house over time. Choose an initial value of the house and a quarter such that the value of the house is about \$275,000.

5. **EXTENDED RESPONSE** A musician is saving money to buy a new snare drum. The musician puts \$100 in a savings account that pays 3% annual interest compounded yearly.

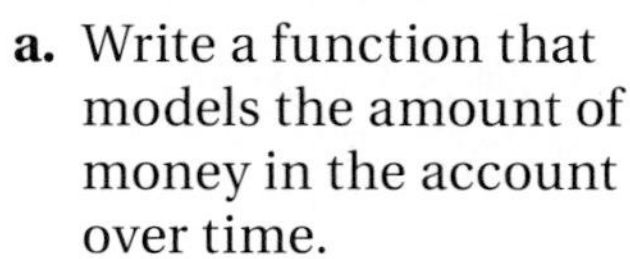

   a. Write a function that models the amount of money in the account over time.

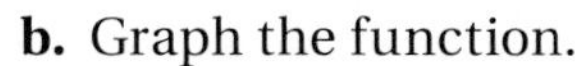

   b. Graph the function.

   c. The musician wants a drum that costs \$149.95. Will there be enough in the account after 3 years? *Explain.*

6. **MULTI-STEP PROBLEM** The graph shows the value of a business over time.

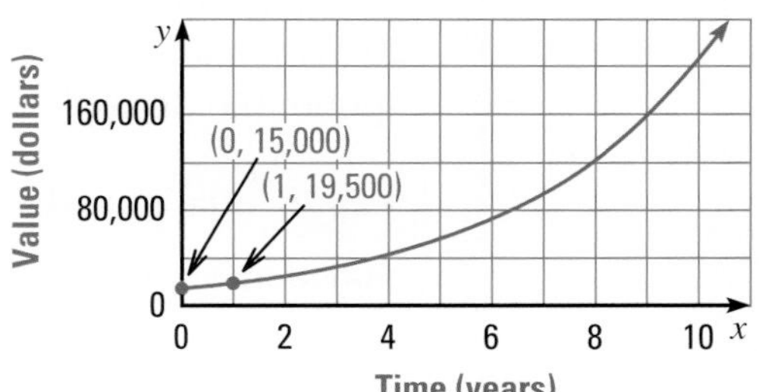

   a. Does the graph represent *exponential growth* or *exponential decay*?

   b. Write a function that models the value of the business over time.

   c. How much is the business worth after 4 years?

7 CHAPTER SUMMARY

BIG IDEAS — For Your Notebook

Big Idea 1 — Applying Properties of Exponents to Simplify Expressions

You can use the properties of exponents to simplify expressions. For the properties listed below, *a* and *b* are real numbers, and *m* and *n* are integers.

Expression	Property
$a^m \cdot a^n = a^{m+n}$	**Product of powers property**
$(a^m)^n = a^{mn}$	**Power of a power property**
$(ab)^m = a^m b^m$	**Power of a product property**
$\frac{a^m}{a^n} = a^{m-n}, a \neq 0$	**Quotient of powers property**
$\left(\frac{a}{b}\right)^m = \frac{a^m}{b^m}, b \neq 0$	**Power of a quotient property**

Big Idea 2 — Writing and Graphing Exponential Functions

You can write and graph exponential growth and decay functions. You can also model real-world situations involving exponential growth and exponential decay.

Exponential growth	Exponential decay
Function $y = ab^x$, $a > 0$ and $b > 1$	**Function** $y = ab^x$, $a > 0$ and $0 < b < 1$
Graph 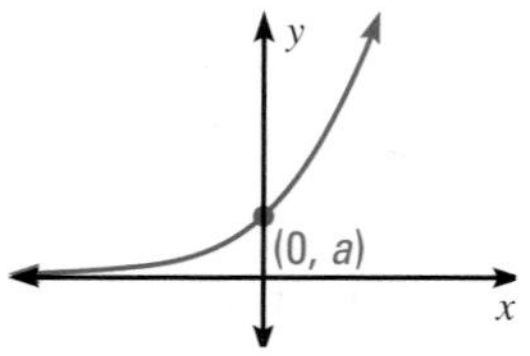	**Graph** 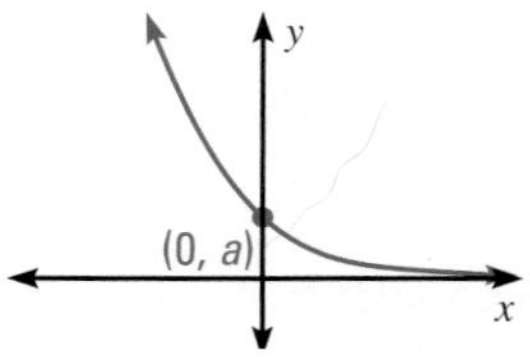
Model $y = a(1 + r)^t$	**Model** $y = a(1 - r)^t$

7 CHAPTER REVIEW

@HomeTutor
my.hrw.com
- Multi-Language Glossary
- Vocabulary practice

REVIEW KEY VOCABULARY

- order of magnitude
- zero exponent
- negative exponent
- exponential function
- exponential growth
- growth factor, growth rate
- compound interest
- exponential decay
- decay factor, decay rate

VOCABULARY EXERCISES

1. Copy and complete: The function $y = 1200(0.3)^t$ is an exponential _?_ function, and the base 0.3 is called the _?_.

2. **WRITING** *Explain* how you can tell whether a table represents a linear function or an exponential function.

Tell whether the function represents exponential growth or exponential decay. *Explain.*

3. $y = 3(0.85)^x$
4. $y = \frac{1}{2}(1.01)^x$
5. $y = 2(2.1)^x$

REVIEW EXAMPLES AND EXERCISES

Use the review examples and exercises below to check your understanding of the concepts you have learned in each lesson of this chapter.

7.1 Apply Exponent Properties Involving Products

EXAMPLE

Simplify $(3y^3)^4 \cdot y^5$.

$(3y^3)^4 \cdot y^5 = 3^4 \cdot (y^3)^4 \cdot y^5$ **Power of a product property**

$= 81 \cdot y^{12} \cdot y^5$ **Power of a power property**

$= 81y^{17}$ **Product of powers property**

EXERCISES

EXAMPLES 1, 2, 3, 4, and 5 for Exs. 6–15

Simplify the expression.

6. $4^4 \cdot 4^3$
7. $(-3)^7(-3)$
8. $z^3 \cdot z^5 \cdot z^5$
9. $(y^4)^5$
10. $[(-7)^4]^4$
11. $[(b + 2)^8]^3$
12. $(6^4 \cdot 31)^5$
13. $-(8xy)^2$
14. $(2x^2)^4 \cdot x^5$

15. **EARTH SCIENCE** The order of magnitude of the mass of Earth's atmosphere is 10^{18} kilograms. The order of magnitude of the mass of Earth's oceans is 10^3 times greater. What is the order of magnitude of the mass of Earth's oceans?

7 CHAPTER REVIEW

7.2 Apply Exponent Properties Involving Quotients

EXAMPLE

Simplify $\left(\frac{x^3}{y}\right)^4 \cdot \frac{2}{x^5}$.

$\left(\frac{x^3}{y}\right)^4 \cdot \frac{2}{x^5} = \frac{(x^3)^4}{y^4} \cdot \frac{2}{x^5}$ **Power of a quotient property**

$= \frac{x^{12}}{y^4} \cdot \frac{2}{x^5}$ **Power of a power property**

$= \frac{2x^{12}}{y^4x^5}$ **Multiply fractions.**

$= \frac{2x^7}{y^4}$ **Quotient of powers property**

EXERCISES

EXAMPLES 1, 2, and 3 for Exs. 16–24

Simplify the expression.

16. $\frac{(-3)^7}{(-3)^3}$ **17.** $\frac{5^2 \cdot 5^4}{5^3}$ **18.** $\left(\frac{m}{n}\right)^3$ **19.** $\frac{17^{12}}{17^8}$

20. $\left(-\frac{1}{x}\right)^4$ **21.** $\left(\frac{7x^5}{y^2}\right)^2$ **22.** $\frac{1}{p^2} \cdot p^6$ **23.** $\frac{6}{7r^{10}} \cdot \left(\frac{r^5}{s}\right)^5$

24. PER CAPITA INCOME The order of magnitude of the population of Montana in 2003 was 10^6 people. The order of magnitude of the total personal income (in dollars) for Montana in 2003 was 10^{10}. What was the order of magnitude of the mean personal income in Montana in 2003?

7.3 Define and Use Zero and Negative Exponents

EXAMPLE

Evaluate $(2x^0y^{-5})^3$.

$(2x^0y^{-5})^3 = 2^3 \cdot x^0 \cdot y^{-15}$ **Power of a power property**

$= 8 \cdot 1 \cdot y^{-15}$ **Definition of zero exponent**

$= \frac{8}{y^{15}}$ **Definition of negative exponents**

EXERCISES

EXAMPLES 1, 2, and 4 for Exs. 25–29

Evaluate the expression.

25. 14^0 **26.** 3^{-4} **27.** $\left(\frac{2}{3}\right)^{-3}$ **28.** $7^{-5} \cdot 7^5$

29. UNITS OF MEASURE Use the fact that 1 femtogram = 10^{-18} kilogram and 1 nanogram = 10^{-12} kilogram to complete the following statement: 1 nanogram = _?_ femtogram(s).

CHAPTER REVIEW

@HomeTutor
my.hrw.com
Chapter Review Practice

7.4 Write and Graph Exponential Growth Functions

EXAMPLE

Graph the function $y = 4^x$ and identify its domain and range.

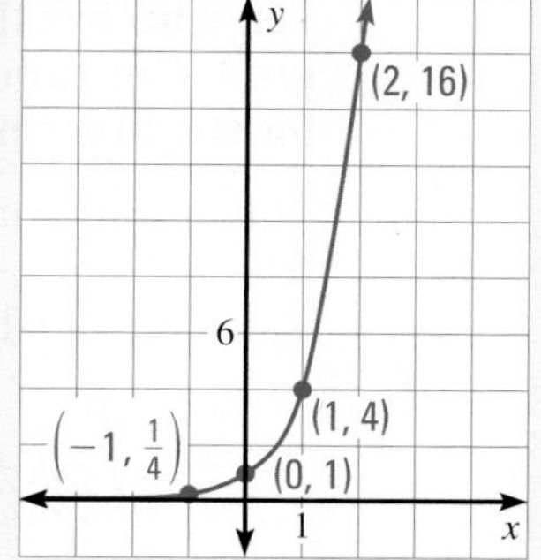

STEP 1 **Make** a table. The domain is all real numbers.

x	−1	0	1	2
y	$\frac{1}{4}$	1	4	16

STEP 2 **Plot** the points.

STEP 3 **Draw** a smooth curve through the points.

STEP 4 **Identify** the range. As you can see from the graph, the range is all positive real numbers.

EXAMPLES 2 and 3 for Exs. 30–34

EXERCISES

Graph the function and identify its domain and range.

30. $y = 6^x$ **31.** $y = (1.1)^x$ **32.** $y = (3.5)^x$ **33.** $y = \left(\frac{5}{2}\right)^x$

34. Graph the function $y = -5 \cdot 2^x$. Compare the graph with the graph of $y = 2^x$.

7.5 Write and Graph Exponential Decay Functions

EXAMPLE 1

Tell whether the graph represents *exponential growth* or *exponential decay*. Then write a rule for the function.

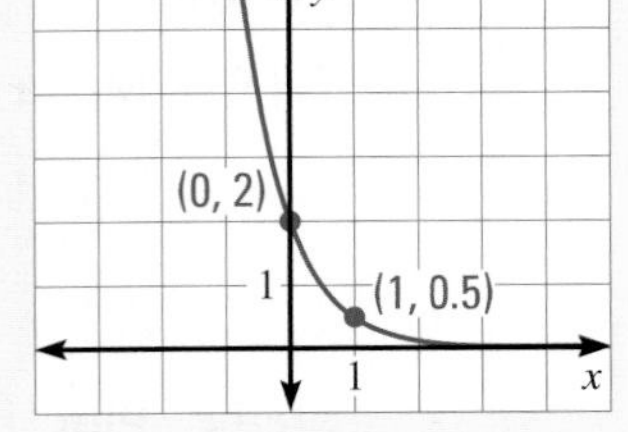

The graph represents exponential decay ($y = ab^x$ where $0 < b < 1$). The y-intercept is 2, so $a = 2$. Find the value of b by using the point (1, 0.5) and $a = 2$.

$y = ab^x$ **Write function.**

$0.5 = 2 \cdot b^1$ **Substitute.**

$0.25 = b$ **Solve for *b*.**

A function rule is $y = 2(0.25)^x$.

EXAMPLE 2

CAR VALUE A family purchases a car for $11,000. The car depreciates (loses value) at a rate of about 16% annually. Write a function that models the value of the car over time. Find the approximate value of the car in 4 years.

Let V represent the value (in dollars) of the car, and let t represent the time (in years since the car was purchased). The initial value is 11,000, and the decay rate is 0.16.

$V = a(1 - r)^t$ **Write exponential decay model.**

$= 11{,}000(1 - 0.16)^t$ **Substitute 11,000 for *a* and 0.16 for *r*.**

$= 11{,}000(0.84)^t$ **Simplify.**

To find the approximate value of the car in 4 years, substitute 4 for t.

$V = 11{,}000(0.84)^t = 11{,}000(0.84)^4 \approx \$5477$

The approximate value of the car in 4 years is $5477.

EXERCISES

EXAMPLES 4 and 5 for Exs. 35–37

Tell whether the graph represents *exponential growth* or *exponential decay*. Then write a rule for the function.

35.

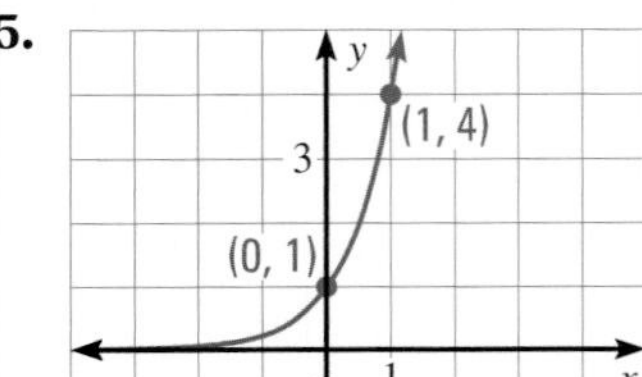

36.

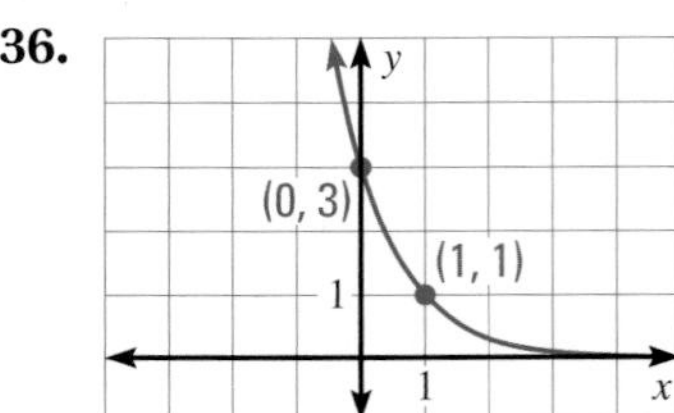

37. CAR VALUE The value of a car is $13,000. The car depreciates (loses value) at a rate of about 15% annually. Write an exponential decay model for the value of the car. Find the approximate value of the car in 4 years.

7 CHAPTER TEST

Simplify the expression. Write your answer using exponents.

1. $(62 \cdot 17)^4$

2. $(-3)(-3)^6$

3. $\frac{8^4 \cdot 8^5}{8^3}$

4. $(8^4)^3$

5. $\frac{2^{15}}{2^8}$

6. $5^3 \cdot 5^0 \cdot 5^5$

7. $[(-4)^3]^2$

8. $\frac{(-5)^{10}}{(-5)^3}$

Simplify the expression.

9. $t^2 \cdot t^6$

10. $\left(\frac{s}{t}\right)^6$

11. $\frac{1}{9^{-2}}$

12. $-(6p)^2$

13. $(5xy)^2$

14. $\frac{1}{z^7} \cdot z^9$

15. $(x^5)^3$

16. $\left(-\frac{4}{c}\right)^2$

Simplify the expression. Write your answer using only positive exponents.

17. $\left(\frac{a^{-3}}{3b}\right)^4$

18. $\frac{3}{4d} \cdot \frac{(2d)^4}{c^3}$

19. $y^0 \cdot (8x^6y^{-3})^{-2}$

20. $(5r^5)^3 \cdot r^{-2}$

21. Graph the function $y = 4^x$. Identify its domain and range.

22. Graph the function $y = \frac{1}{2} \cdot 4^x$. Compare the graph with the graph of $y = 4^x$.

23. ANIMATION About 10^7 bytes of data make up a single frame of an animated film. There are about 10^3 frames in 1 minute of a film. About how many bytes of data are there in 1 hour of an animated film?

24. SALARY A recent college graduate accepts a job at a law firm. The job has a salary of $32,000 per year. The law firm guarantees an annual pay increase of 3% of the employee's salary.

a. Write a function that models the employee's salary over time. Assume that the employee receives only the guaranteed pay increase.

b. Use the function to find the employee's salary after 5 years.

25. SCIENCE At sea level, Earth's atmosphere exerts a pressure of 1 atmosphere. Atmospheric pressure P (in atmospheres) decreases with altitude and can be modeled by $P = (0.99987)^a$ where a is the altitude (in meters).

a. Identify the initial amount, decay factor, and decay rate.

b. Use a graphing calculator to graph the function.

c. Estimate the altitude at which the atmospheric pressure is about half of what it is at sea level.

CONTEXT-BASED MULTIPLE CHOICE QUESTIONS

Some of the information you need to solve a context-based multiple choice question may appear in a table, a diagram, or a graph.

PROBLEM 1

A scientist monitors bacteria cell growth in an experiment. The scientist records the number of bacteria cells in a petri dish every 20 minutes, as shown in the table.

Number of 20 minute time periods, *t*	0	1	2	3	4
Number of bacteria cells, *c*	15	30	60	120	240

How many bacteria cells will there be after 3 hours?

Ⓐ 7.69×10^{10} Ⓑ 7680 Ⓒ 270 Ⓓ 120

Plan

INTERPRET THE TABLE Determine whether the table represents a linear or an exponential function. Use the information in the table to write a function. Then use the function to find the number of bacteria cells after 3 hours.

Solution

STEP 1 Determine whether the function is exponential.

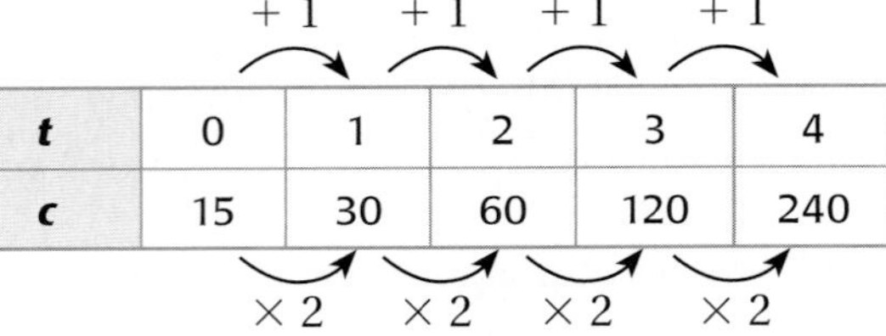

t	0	1	2	3	4
c	15	30	60	120	240

Because the *c*-values are multiplied by 2 for each increase of 1 in *t*, the table represents an exponential function of the form $c = ab^t$ where $b = 2$.

STEP 2 Write the function rule.

The value of *c* when $t = 0$ is 15, as shown in the table, so $a = 15$. Substitute the values of *a* and *b* in the function $c = ab^t$.

A function rule is $c = 15 \cdot 2^t$.

STEP 3 Find the number of cells after 3 hours.

There are 180 minutes in 3 hours. So there are nine 20 minute periods in 3 hours. Substitute 9 for *t* in the function rule you wrote in Step 2.

$c = 15 \cdot 2^t$

$= 15 \cdot 2^9$

$= 7680$

There are 7680 bacteria cells in the petri dish after 3 hours.

The correct answer is B. Ⓐ Ⓑ Ⓒ Ⓓ

PROBLEM 2

A fish tank is a rectangular prism and is partially filled with sand, as shown. The dimensions of the fish tank are given. The order of magnitude of the number of grains of sand in 1 cubic inch is 10^3. Find the order of magnitude of the total number of grains of sand in the fish tank.

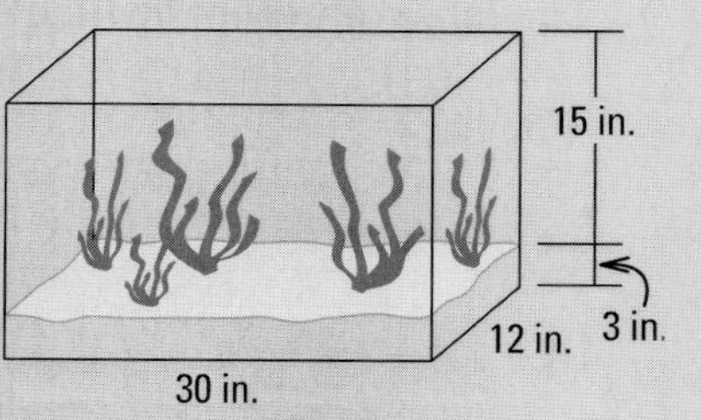

Ⓐ 10^2 grains   Ⓑ 10^3 grains   Ⓒ 10^5 grains   Ⓓ 10^6 grains

Plan

INTERPRET THE DIAGRAM Use the information in the diagram to find the order of magnitude of the volume of sand in the fish tank. Multiply the volume by the order of magnitude of the number of grains of sand in 1 cubic inch.

Solution

STEP 1 Find the order of magnitude of the volume of sand in the fish tank.

Use the formula for the volume of a rectangular prism.

$V = lwh$ **Write formula for volume of rectangular prism.**

$= 30 \cdot 12 \cdot 3$ **Substitute given values.**

$= 1080$ **Multiply.**

The order of magnitude of the volume of sand is 10^3 cubic inches.

STEP 2 Find the order of magnitude of the number of grains of sand in the fish tank.

Multiply the order of magnitude of the volume of sand in the fish tank by the order of magnitude of the grains of sand in 1 cubic inch.

$10^3 \cdot 10^3 = 10^{3+3} = 10^6$

The order of magnitude of the total number of grains of sand in the fish tank is 10^6.

The correct answer is D. Ⓐ Ⓑ Ⓒ Ⓓ

PRACTICE

1. In Problem 2, consider the section of the fish tank occupied by water only. The order of magnitude of the weight of water per cubic inch is 10^{-2} pound. The tank is filled to the top. What is the order of magnitude of the weight of the water in the fish tank?

   Ⓐ 10^{-8} pound   Ⓑ 10^{-6} pound   Ⓒ 10^2 pounds   Ⓓ 10^6 pounds

2. What is the volume of the cylinder shown?

   3x
   x

   Ⓐ $9\pi x^3$ Ⓑ $3\pi x^3$

   Ⓒ $9\pi x^2$ Ⓓ $3\pi x^2$

7 ★ Standardized TEST PRACTICE

MULTIPLE CHOICE

1. The table represents which function?

x	-2	-1	0	1	2
y	$\frac{1}{75}$	$\frac{1}{15}$	$\frac{1}{3}$	$\frac{5}{3}$	$\frac{25}{3}$

Ⓐ $y = \frac{1}{3} \cdot 5^x$ Ⓑ $y = -\frac{1}{3} \cdot 5^x$

Ⓒ $y = 3 \cdot 5^x$ Ⓓ $y = -3 \cdot 5^x$

2. What is the volume of the cube?

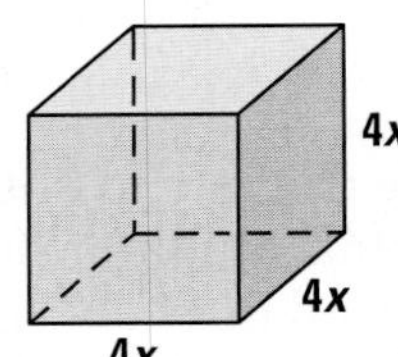

Ⓐ $4x^3$ Ⓑ $12x^3$

Ⓒ $16x^2$ Ⓓ $64x^3$

In Exercises 3 and 4, use the table below.

3. List the elements in order from least concentration to greatest concentration.

Element in Seawater	Concentration (parts per million)
Sulfur	About 10^3
Gold	About 10^{-5}
Molybdenum	About 10^{-2}
Hydrogen	About 10^5

Ⓐ Hydrogen, sulfur, gold, molybdenum

Ⓑ Sulfur, hydrogen, molybdenum, gold

Ⓒ Gold, molybdenum, hydrogen, sulfur

Ⓓ Molybdenum, gold, sulfur, hydrogen

4. About how many times greater is the concentration of molybdenum than the concentration of gold?

Ⓐ 10^{-7} Ⓑ 10^{-3}

Ⓒ 10^3 Ⓓ 10^{10}

In Exercises 5–7, use the table below.

Unit	Number of meters
Kilometer	10^3
Centimeter	10^{-2}
Millimeter	10^{-3}
Nanometer	10^{-9}

5. How many millimeters are in 1 kilometer?

Ⓐ 1 Ⓑ 10

Ⓒ 10^3 Ⓓ 10^6

6. How many nanometers are in a centimeter?

Ⓐ 10^{-11} Ⓑ 10^{-7}

Ⓒ 10^7 Ⓓ 10^{18}

7. A micrometer is 10^3 times greater than a nanometer. How many meters are in a micrometer?

Ⓐ 10^{-27} Ⓑ 10^{-12}

Ⓒ 10^{-6} Ⓓ 10^6

In Exercises 8 and 9, use the graph below.

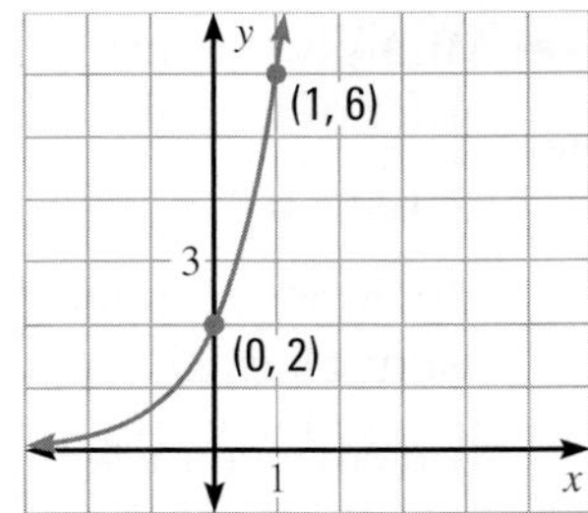

8. The graph of which exponential function is shown?

Ⓐ $y = 3^x$ Ⓑ $y = -3^x$

Ⓒ $y = -2 \cdot 3^x$ Ⓓ $y = 2 \cdot 3^x$

9. How does the graph compare with the graph of $y = 3^x$?

Ⓐ It is a vertical stretch.

Ⓑ It is a vertical shrink.

Ⓒ It is a reflection in the x-axis.

Ⓓ It is the same graph.

GRIDDED ANSWER

10. If $\left(\frac{x^{-6}}{x^{-5}}\right)^{-3} = x^n$ and $x \neq 0$, what is the value of n?

11. The table shows the values for an exponential function.

x	−2	−1	0	1	2
y	$\frac{3}{25}$	$\frac{3}{5}$	3	15	?

What is the missing value in the table?

12. An initial investment of $200 is losing value at a rate of 1.5% per year. What is the value of the investment (in dollars) after 3 years? Round your answer to the nearest cent.

13. What is the value of $(2x)^3 \cdot x^2$ when $x = \frac{1}{2}$? Write your answer as a fraction.

SHORT RESPONSE

14. A female sockeye salmon lays about 10^3 eggs in one season.

a. About how many eggs will 10^4 female sockeyes lay?

b. Suppose about 10^6 of the eggs survive to become young salmon. What percent of eggs survive? *Explain* how you found your answer.

15. You deposit $75 in a bank account that pays 3% annual interest compounded yearly. If you do not make any deposits or withdrawals, how much will your investment be worth in 3 years? *Explain.*

16. Membership in an after-school athletic club declined at a rate of 5% per year for the period 2000–2005. There were 54 members in 2000.

a. Identify the initial amount, the decay rate, and the decay factor.

b. In what year did the club have 44 members? *Explain.*

EXTENDED RESPONSE

17. Europa, one of Jupiter's moons, is roughly spherical. The equatorial radius of Europa is about 1,600,000 meters, and the mass of Europa is about 48,000,000,000,000,000,000,000 kilograms.

a. Find the order of magnitude of the radius r of Europa, and the order of magnitude of the mass m of Europa.

b. Find the order of magnitude of the volume V of Europa.

c. Use the orders of magnitude of m and V that you found in parts (a) and (b) to approximate the average density d (in kilograms per cubic meter) of Europa using the formula $d = \frac{m}{V}$.

18. A gardener is growing a water lily plant. The plant starts out with 4 lily pads and the number of lily pads increases at a rate of about 6.5% per day for the first 20 days.

a. Write a function that models the number of lily pads the plant has over the first 20 days.

b. Graph the model and identify its domain and range.

c. On about what day did the plant have 10 lily pads? *Explain* how you found your answer.

8 Polynomials and Factoring

Lesson
8.1 CC.9-12.A.APR.1
8.2 CC.9-12.A.APR.1
8.3 CC.9-12.A.APR.1
8.4 CC.9-12.A.REI.4b
8.5 CC.9-12.A.SSE.3a
8.6 CC.9-12.A.SSE.3a
8.7 CC.9-12.A.SSE.2
8.8 CC.9-12.A.SSE.3a

Before

Previously, you learned the following skills, which you'll use in this chapter: using the distributive property, combining like terms, and using the properties of exponents.

Prerequisite Skills

VOCABULARY CHECK

Copy and complete the statement.

1. Terms that have the same variable part are called _?_.
2. For a function $f(x)$, a(n) _?_ is an x-value for which $f(x) = 0$.

SKILLS CHECK

Simplify the expression.

3. $3x + (-6x)$
4. $5 + 4x + 2$
5. $4(2x - 1) + x$
6. $-(x + 4) - 6x$

Simplify the expression.

7. $(3xy)^3$
8. $xy^2 \cdot xy^3$
9. $(x^5)^3$
10. $(-x)^3$

Find the greatest common factor of the pair of numbers.

11. 121, 77
12. 96, 32
13. 81, 42
14. 12, 56

Now

In this chapter, you will apply the big ideas listed below and reviewed in the Chapter Summary. You will also use the key vocabulary listed below.

Big Ideas

1. **Adding, subtracting, and multiplying polynomials**
2. **Factoring polynomials**
3. **Writing and solving polynomial equations to solve problems**

KEY VOCABULARY

- monomial
- degree
- polynomial
- leading coefficient
- binomial
- trinomial
- roots
- vertical motion model
- perfect square trinomial
- factor by grouping
- factor completely

Why?

You can use a polynomial function to model vertical motion. For example, you can use a polynomial function to model the height of a jumping animal as a function of time.

Animated Algebra

The animation illustrated below helps you to answer a question from this chapter: How does changing the initial vertical velocity of a serval, an African cat, affect its jumping height?

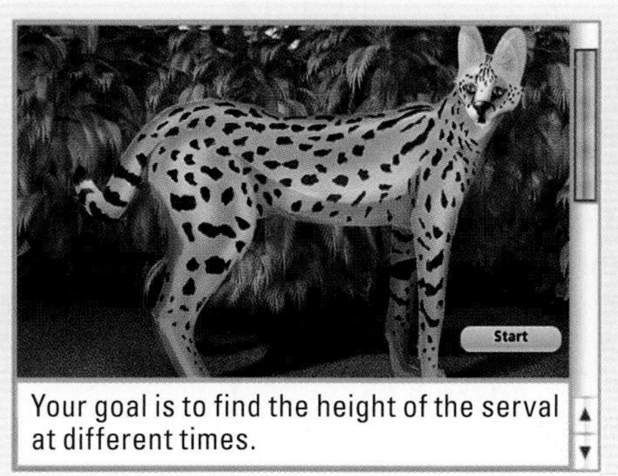

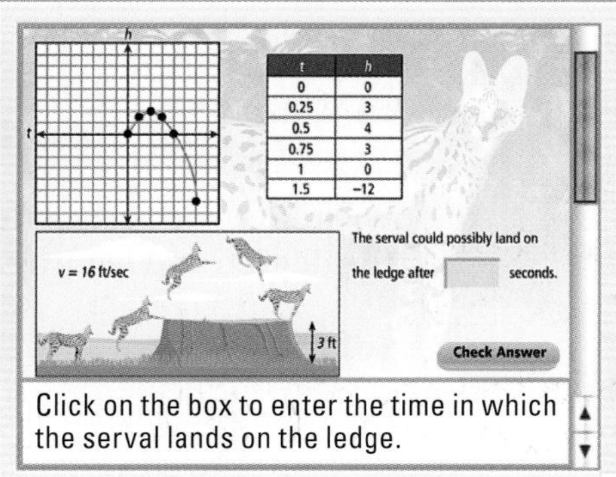

Animated Algebra at my.hrw.com

8.1 Add and Subtract Polynomials

Before You added and subtracted integers.

Now You will add and subtract polynomials.

Why? So you can model trends in recreation, as in Ex. 37.

Key Vocabulary
- monomial
- degree
- polynomial
- leading coefficient
- binomial
- trinomial

CC.9-12.A.APR.1 Understand that polynomials form a system analogous to the integers, namely, they are closed under the operations of addition, subtraction, and multiplication; add, subtract, and multiply polynomials.

A **monomial** is a number, a variable, or the product of a number and one or more variables with whole number exponents. The **degree of a monomial** is the sum of the exponents of the variables in the monomial. The degree of a nonzero constant term is 0. The constant 0 does not have a degree.

Monomial	Degree
10	0
$3x$	1
$\frac{1}{2}ab^2$	$1 + 2 = 3$
$-1.8m^5$	5

Not a monomial	Reason
$5 + x$	A sum is not a monomial.
$\frac{2}{n}$	A monomial cannot have a variable in the denominator.
4^a	A monomial cannot have a variable exponent.
x^{-1}	The variable must have a whole number exponent.

A **polynomial** is a monomial or a sum of monomials, each called a *term* of the polynomial. The **degree of a polynomial** is the greatest degree of its terms.

When a polynomial is written so that the exponents of a variable decrease from left to right, the coefficient of the first term is called the **leading coefficient**.

leading coefficient → degree → constant term

$$2x^3 + x^2 - 5x + 12$$

EXAMPLE 1 Rewrite a polynomial

Write $15x - x^3 + 3$ so that the exponents decrease from left to right. Identify the degree and leading coefficient of the polynomial.

Solution

Consider the degree of each of the polynomial's terms.

Degree is 1. Degree is 3. Degree is 0.

$$15x - x^3 + 3$$

The polynomial can be written as $-x^3 + 15x + 3$. The greatest degree is 3, so the degree of the polynomial is 3, and the leading coefficient is -1.

BINOMIALS AND TRINOMIALS A polynomial with two terms is called a **binomial**. A polynomial with three terms is called a **trinomial**.

EXAMPLE 2 Identify and classify polynomials

Tell whether the expression is a polynomial. If it is a polynomial, find its degree and classify it by the number of its terms. Otherwise, tell why it is not a polynomial.

	Expression	Is it a polynomial?	Classify by degree and number of terms
a.	9	Yes	0 degree monomial
b.	$2x^2 + x - 5$	Yes	2nd degree trinomial
c.	$6n^4 - 8^n$	No; variable exponent	
d.	$n^{-2} - 3$	No; negative exponent	
e.	$7bc^3 + 4b^4c$	Yes	5th degree binomial

ADDING POLYNOMIALS To add polynomials, add like terms. You can use a vertical or a horizontal format.

EXAMPLE 3 Add polynomials

Find the sum.

a. $(2x^3 - 5x^2 + x) + (2x^2 + x^3 - 1)$ **b.** $(3x^2 + x - 6) + (x^2 + 4x + 10)$

Solution

ALIGN TERMS
If a particular power of the variable appears in one polynomial but not the other, leave a space in that column, or write the term with a coefficient of 0.

a. Vertical format: Align like terms in vertical columns.

$$\begin{array}{rrrr} 2x^3 & - 5x^2 & + x & \\ + \quad x^3 & + 2x^2 & & - 1 \\ \hline 3x^3 & - 3x^2 & + x & - 1 \end{array}$$

b. Horizontal format: Group like terms and simplify.

$$(3x^2 + x - 6) + (x^2 + 4x + 10) = (3x^2 + x^2) + (x + 4x) + (-6 + 10)$$
$$= 4x^2 + 5x + 4$$

Animated Algebra at my.hrw.com

✓ GUIDED PRACTICE for Examples 1, 2, and 3

1. Write $5y - 2y^2 + 9$ so that the exponents decrease from left to right. Identify the degree and leading coefficient of the polynomial.
2. Tell whether $y^3 - 4y + 3$ is a polynomial. If it is a polynomial, find its degree and classify it by the number of its terms. Otherwise, tell why it is not a polynomial.
3. Find the sum $(5x^3 + 4x - 2x) + (4x^2 + 3x^3 - 6)$.

SUBTRACTING POLYNOMIALS To subtract a polynomial, add its opposite. To find the opposite of a polynomial, multiply each of its terms by -1.

EXAMPLE 4 Subtract polynomials

Find the difference.

a. $(4n^2 + 5) - (-2n^2 + 2n - 4)$ **b.** $(4x^2 - 3x + 5) - (3x^2 - x - 8)$

Solution

a.

$$\begin{array}{r} (4n^2 \quad\quad + 5) \\ -(-2n^2 + 2n - 4) \\ \hline \end{array} \longrightarrow \begin{array}{r} 4n^2 \quad\quad + 5 \\ + 2n^2 - 2n + 4 \\ \hline 6n^2 - 2n + 9 \end{array}$$

AVOID ERRORS
Remember to multiply *each* term in the polynomial by -1 when you write the subtraction as addition.

b. $(4x^2 - 3x + 5) - (3x^2 - x - 8) = 4x^2 - 3x + 5 - 3x^2 + x + 8$

$= (4x^2 - 3x^2) + (-3x + x) + (5 + 8)$

$= x^2 - 2x + 13$

EXAMPLE 5 Solve a multi-step problem

BASEBALL ATTENDANCE Major League Baseball teams are divided into two leagues. During the period 1995–2001, the attendance N and A (in thousands) at National and American League baseball games, respectively, can be modeled by

$N = -488t^2 + 5430t + 24{,}700$ and

$A = -318t^2 + 3040t + 25{,}600$

where t is the number of years since 1995. About how many people attended Major League Baseball games in 2001?

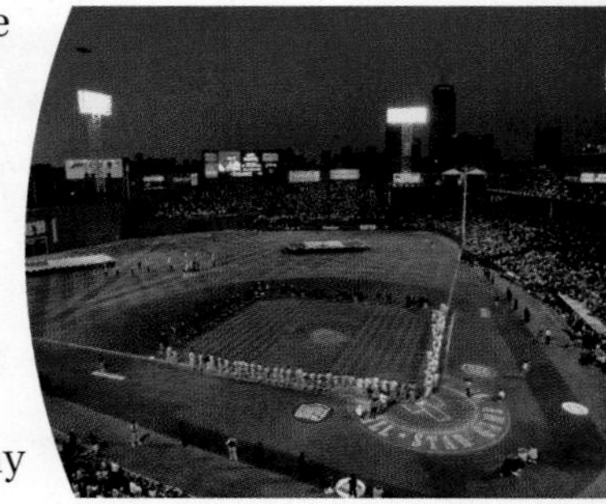

Solution

STEP 1 **Add** the models for the attendance in each league to find a model for M, the total attendance (in thousands).

$M = (-488t^2 + 5430t + 24{,}700) + (-318t^2 + 3040t + 25{,}600)$

$= (-488t^2 - 318t^2) + (5430t + 3040t) + (24{,}700 + 25{,}600)$

$= -806t^2 + 8470t + 50{,}300$

AVOID ERRORS
Because a value of M represents *thousands* of people, $M \approx 72{,}100$ represents 72,100,000 people.

STEP 2 **Substitute** 6 for t in the model, because 2001 is 6 years after 1995.

$M = -806(6)^2 + 8470(6) + 50{,}300 \approx 72{,}100$

▶ About 72,100,000 people attended Major League Baseball games in 2001.

✓ GUIDED PRACTICE for Examples 4 and 5

4. Find the difference $(4x^2 - 7x) - (5x^2 + 4x - 9)$.

5. **BASEBALL ATTENDANCE** Look back at Example 5. Find the difference in attendance at National and American League baseball games in 2001.

8.1 EXERCISES

HOMEWORK KEY

○ = See WORKED-OUT SOLUTIONS Exs. 21 and 39

★ = STANDARDIZED TEST PRACTICE Exs. 2, 9, 10, 39, and 41

SKILL PRACTICE

1. **VOCABULARY** Copy and complete: A number, a variable, or the product of one or more variables is called a(n) __?__.

2. ★ **WRITING** Is 6 a polynomial? *Explain* why or why not.

EXAMPLE 1 for Exs. 3–9

REWRITING POLYNOMIALS Write the polynomial so that the exponents decrease from left to right. Identify the degree and leading coefficient of the polynomial.

3. $9m^5$
4. $2 - 6y$
5. $2x^2y^2 - 8xy$
6. $5n^3 + 2n - 7$
7. $5z + 2z^3 - z^2 + 3z^4$
8. $-2h^2 + 2h^4 - h^6$

9. ★ **MULTIPLE CHOICE** What is the degree of $-4x^3 + 6x^4 - 1$?

(A) -4 (B) 3 (C) 4 (D) 6

EXAMPLE 2 for Exs. 10–16

10. ★ **MULTIPLE CHOICE** Which expression is *not* a monomial?

(A) $-5x^2$ (B) $0.2y^4$ (C) $3mn$ (D) $3s^{-2}$

IDENTIFYING AND CLASSIFYING POLYNOMIALS Tell whether the expression is a polynomial. If it is a polynomial, find its degree and classify it by the number of its terms. Otherwise, tell why it is not a polynomial.

11. -4^x
12. $w^{-3} + 1$
13. $3x - 5$
14. $\frac{4}{5}f^2 - \frac{1}{2}f + \frac{2}{3}$
15. $6 - n^2 + 5n^3$
16. $10y^4 - 3y^2 + 11$

EXAMPLES 3 and 4 for Exs. 17–28

ADDING AND SUBTRACTING POLYNOMIALS Find the sum or difference.

17. $(5a^2 - 3) + (8a^2 - 1)$
18. $(h^2 + 4h - 4) + (5h^2 - 8h + 2)$
19. $(4m^2 - m + 2) + (-3m^2 + 10m + 7)$
20. $(7k^2 + 2k - 6) + (3k^2 - 11k - 8)$
21. $(6c^2 + 3c + 9) - (3c - 5)$
22. $(3x^2 - 8) - (4x^3 + x^2 - 15x + 1)$
23. $(-n^2 + 2n) - (2n^3 - n^2 + n + 12)$
24. $(9b^3 - 13b^2 + b) - (-13b^2 - 5b + 14)$
25. $(4d - 6d^3 + 3d^2) - (9d^3 + 7d - 2)$
26. $(9p^2 - 6p^3 + 3 - 11p) + (7p^3 - 3p^2 + 4)$

ERROR ANALYSIS *Describe* and correct the error in finding the sum or difference of the polynomials.

27.
$$\begin{array}{r} x^3 - 4x^2 + 3 \\ + \ -3x^3 + 8x - 2 \\ \hline -2x^3 + 4x^2 + 1 \end{array}$$

28.
$$(6x^2 - 5x) - (2x^2 + 3x - 2)$$
$$= (6x^2 - 2x^2) + (-5x + 3x) - 2$$
$$= 4x^2 - 2x - 2$$

29. **ORDERING POLYNOMIALS BY DEGREE** Write the polynomials in decreasing order of *degree*: $1 - 3x + 5x^2$, $3x^5$, $x + 2x^3 + x^2$, $12x + 1$.

GEOMETRY **Write a polynomial that represents the perimeter of the figure.**

30.

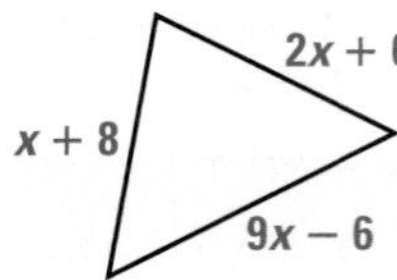

31.

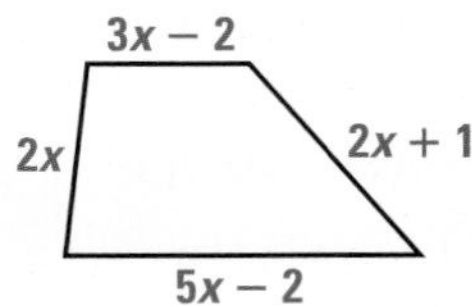

ADDING AND SUBTRACTING POLYNOMIALS **Find the sum or difference.**

32. $(3r^2s + 5rs + 3) + (-8rs^2 - 9rs - 12)$

33. $(x^2 + 11xy - 3y^2) + (-2x^2 - xy + 4y^2)$

34. $(5mn + 3m - 9n) - (13mn + 2m)$

35. $(8a^2b - 6a) - (2a^2b - 4b + 19)$

36. **CHALLENGE** Consider any integer x. The next consecutive integer can be represented by the binomial $(x + 1)$.

a. Write a polynomial for the sum of any two consecutive integers.

b. *Explain* how you can be sure that the sum of two consecutive integers is always odd. Use the polynomial from part (a) in your explanation.

PROBLEM SOLVING

EXAMPLE 5 for Exs. 37–39

37. **BACKPACKING AND CAMPING** During the period 1992–2002, the participation B (in millions of people) in backpacking and the participation C (in millions of people) in camping can be modeled by

$B = -0.0262t^3 + 0.376t^2 - 0.574t + 9.67$ and
$C = -0.0182t^3 + 0.522t^2 - 2.59t + 47$

where t is the number of years since 1992. About how many more people camped than backpacked in 2002?

38. **CAR COSTS** During the period 1990–2002, the average costs D (in dollars) for a new domestic car and the average costs I (in dollars) for a new imported car can be modeled by

$D = 442.14t + 14{,}433$ and $I = -137.63t^2 + 2705.2t + 15{,}111$

where t is the number of years since 1990. Find the difference in average costs (in dollars) for a new imported car and a new domestic car in 2002.

39. ★ **SHORT RESPONSE** During the period 1998–2002, the number A (in millions) of books for adults and the number J (in millions) of books for juveniles sold can be modeled by

$A = 9.5t^3 - 58t^2 + 66t + 500$ and $J = -15t^2 + 64t + 360$

where t is the number of years since 1998.

a. Write an equation that gives the total number (in millions) of books for adults and for juveniles sold as a function of the number of years since 1998.

b. Were more books sold in 1998 or in 2002? *Explain* your answer.

○ = See **WORKED-OUT SOLUTIONS** in Student Resources

★ = **STANDARDIZED TEST PRACTICE**

40. SCHOOL ENROLLMENT During the period 1985–2012, the projected enrollment B (in thousands of students) in public schools and the projected enrollment R (in thousands of students) in private schools can be modeled by

$$B = -18.53t^2 + 975.8t + 48{,}140 \quad \text{and} \quad R = 80.8t + 8049$$

where t is the number of years since 1985. Write an equation that models the total school enrollment (in thousands of students) as a function of the number of years since 1985. What percent of all students is expected to be enrolled in public schools in 2012?

41. ★ EXTENDED RESPONSE The award for the best pitchers in baseball is named after the pitcher Cy Young. During the period 1890–1911, the total number of Cy Young's wins W and losses L can be modeled by

$$W = -0.44t^2 + 34t + 4.7 \quad \text{and} \quad L = 15t + 15$$

where t is the number of years since 1890.

Cy Young Award

a. A game credited to a pitcher as a win or a loss is called a decision. Write an equation that models the number of decisions for Cy Young as a function of the number of years since 1890.

b. Cy Young's career in Major League Baseball lasted from 1890 to 1911. Approximately how many total decisions did Cy Young have during his career?

c. About what percent of the decisions in Cy Young's career were wins? *Explain* how you found your answer.

42. CHALLENGE In 1970 the United States produced 63.5 quadrillion BTU (British Thermal Units) of energy and consumed 67.86 quadrillion BTU. From 1970 through 2001, the total U.S. energy production increased by about 0.2813 quadrillion BTU per year, and the total U.S. energy consumption increased by about 0.912 quadrillion BTU per year.

a. Write two equations that model the total U.S. energy production and consumption (in quadrillion BTU) as functions of the number of years since 1970.

b. How much more energy was consumed than produced in the U.S. in 1970 and in 2001? What was the change in the amount of energy consumed from 1970 to 2001?

Graphing Calculator ACTIVITY *Use after Add and Subtract Polynomials*

my.hrw.com
Keystrokes

Graph Polynomial Functions

MATHEMATICAL PRACTICES

Use appropriate tools strategically.

QUESTION How can you use a graph to check your work with polynomials?

EXAMPLE Check a sum or difference of polynomials

Tell whether the sum or difference is correct.

a. $(x^2 - 2x + 3) + (2x^2 + 4x - 5) \stackrel{?}{=} 3x^2 + 2x - 2$

b. $(x^3 + x + 1) - (5x^3 - 2x + 7) \stackrel{?}{=} -4x^3 - x - 6$

STEP 1 ***Enter expressions***

Let y_1 equal the original expression.
Let y_2 equal the sum.

a.

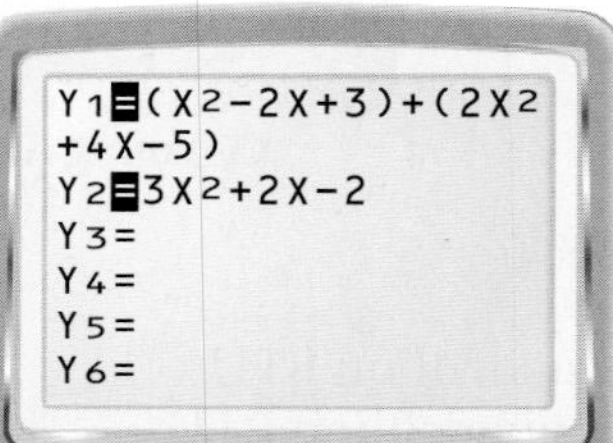

b.

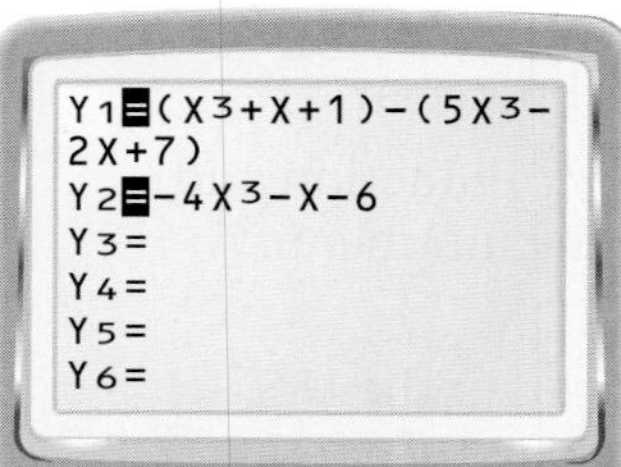

STEP 2 ***Graph expressions***

For y_1, choose a normal graph style.
For y_2, choose a thicker graph style.

a.

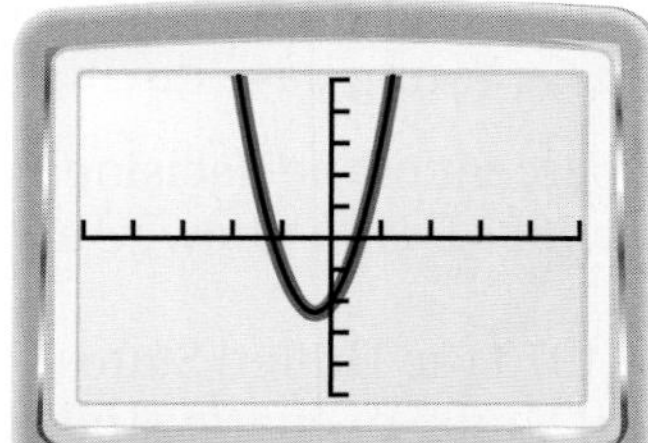

b.

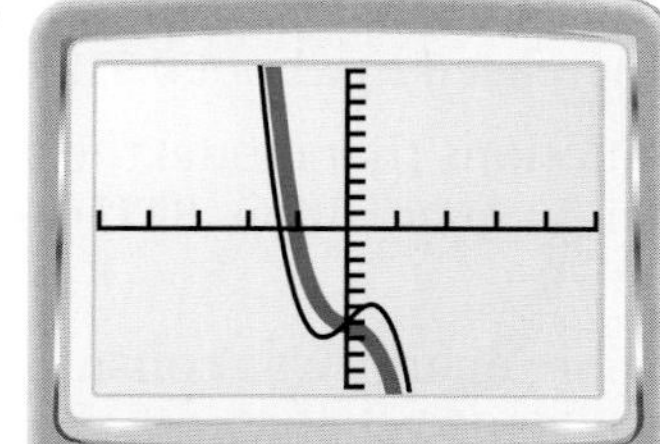

STEP 3 ***Analyze graphs***

a. The thick curve coincides with the thin curve, so the sum is correct.

b. The thick curve deviates from the thin curve, so the difference is incorrect.

PRACTICE

Find the sum or difference. Use a graphing calculator to check your answer.

1. $(6x^2 + 4x - 1) + (x^2 - 2x + 2)$ **2.** $(3x^2 - 2x + 1) - (4x^2 - 5x + 1)$

Tell whether the sum or difference is correct. Correct any incorrect answers.

3. $(3x^2 - 2x + 4) + (-x^2 + 3x + 2) \stackrel{?}{=} 2x^2 + x + 6$

4. $(-4x^2 - 5x - 1) - (-5x^2 + 6x + 3) \stackrel{?}{=} -9x^2 + x + 2$

Multiplication with Algebra Tiles

MATERIALS • algebra tiles

MATHEMATICAL PRACTICES

Use appropriate tools strategically.

QUESTION How can you multiply binomials using algebra tiles?

You can use the following algebra tiles to model polynomials. Notice that the value of each tile is the same as its area.

1-tile

x-tile

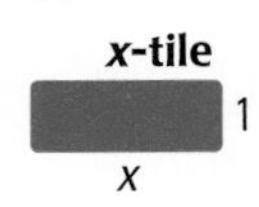

x^2-tile

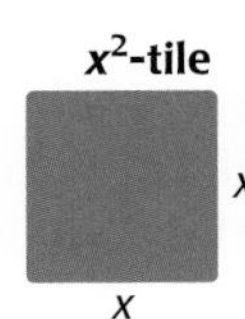

EXPLORE Multiply binomials

Find the product $(x + 3)(2x + 1)$.

STEP 1 ***Model the rectangle's dimensions***

Model each binomial with algebra tiles. Arrange the first binomial vertically and the second horizontally, as shown. These polynomials model the length and width of a rectangle.

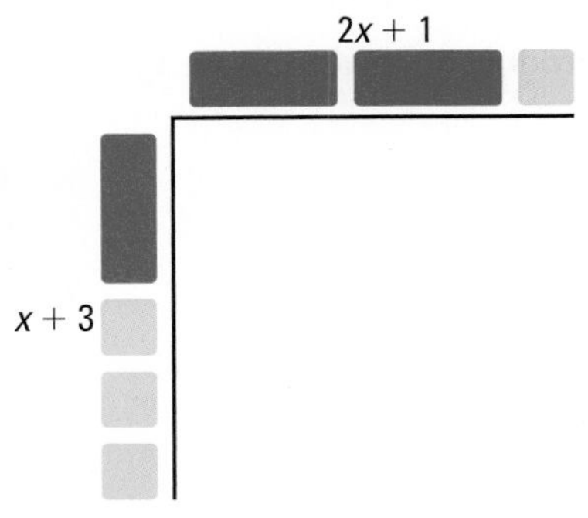

STEP 2 ***Fill in the area***

Fill in the rectangle with the appropriate algebra tiles.

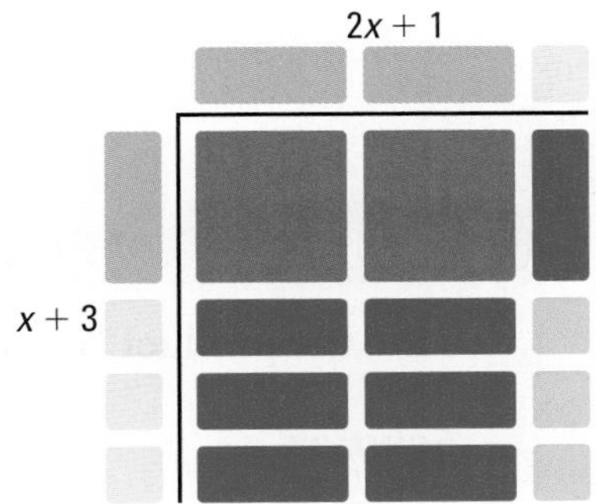

STEP 3 ***Find the product***

The rectangle you created represents the polynomial $2x^2 + 7x + 3$.
So, $(x + 3)(2x + 1) = 2x^2 + 7x + 3$.

DRAW CONCLUSIONS Use your observations to complete these exercises

Use algebra tiles to find the product. Include a drawing of your model.

1. $(x + 1)(x + 3)$
2. $(x + 5)(x + 4)$
3. $(2x + 1)(x + 2)$
4. $(3x + 2)(x + 1)$
5. $(3x + 2)(2x + 1)$
6. $(4x + 1)(2x + 3)$
7. **REASONING** Find the product $x(2x + 1)$ and the product $3(2x + 1)$. What is the sum of these two products? What do your answers suggest you can do to find the product $(x + 3)(2x + 1)$?

8.2 Multiply Polynomials

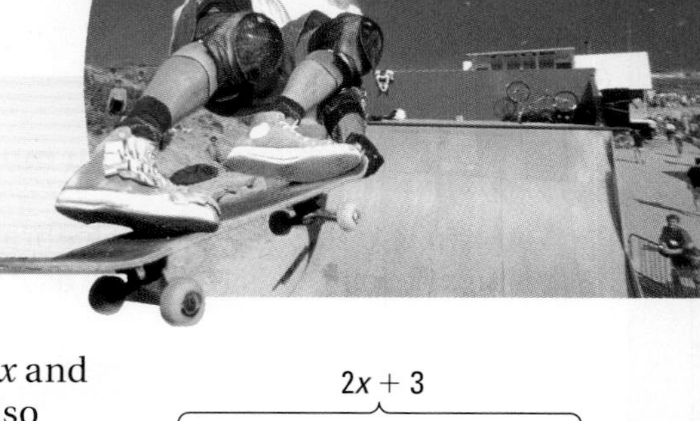

Before You added and subtracted polynomials.

Now You will multiply polynomials.

Why? So you can determine areas, as in Example 7.

Key Vocabulary
- **polynomial**
- **binomial**

The diagram shows that a rectangle with width x and length $2x + 3$ has an area of $2x^2 + 3x$. You can also find this product by using the distributive property.

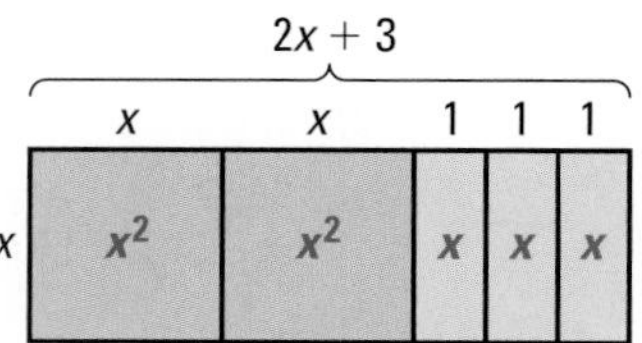

$$x(2x + 3) = x(2x) + x(3) = 2x^2 + 3x$$

In this lesson, you will learn several methods for multiplying polynomials. Each method is based on the distributive property.

REVIEW PROPERTIES OF EXPONENTS

You may want to review using the properties of exponents before multiplying polynomials.

EXAMPLE 1 Multiply a monomial and a polynomial

Find the product $2x^3(x^3 + 3x^2 - 2x + 5)$.

$2x^3(x^3 + 3x^2 - 2x + 5)$	**Write product.**
$= 2x^3(x^3) + 2x^3(3x^2) - 2x^3(2x) + 2x^3(5)$	**Distributive property**
$= 2x^6 + 6x^5 - 4x^4 + 10x^3$	**Product of powers property**

EXAMPLE 2 Multiply polynomials using a table

COMMON CORE

CC.9-12.A.APR.1 Understand that polynomials form a system analogous to the integers, namely, they are closed under the operations of addition, subtraction, and multiplication; add, subtract, and multiply polynomials.

Find the product $(x - 4)(3x + 2)$.

Solution

STEP 1 **Write** subtraction as addition in each polynomial.

$$(x - 4)(3x + 2) = [x + (-4)](3x + 2)$$

STEP 2 **Make** a table of products.

	$3x$	2
x	$3x^2$	
-4		

→

	$3x$	2
x	$3x^2$	$2x$
-4	$-12x$	-8

▶ The product is $3x^2 + 2x - 12x - 8$, or $3x^2 - 10x - 8$.

GUIDED PRACTICE for Examples 1 and 2

Find the product.

1. $x(7x^2 + 4)$
2. $(a + 3)(2a + 1)$
3. $(4n - 1)(n + 5)$

EXAMPLE 3 Multiply polynomials vertically

Find the product $(b^2 + 6b - 7)(3b - 4)$.

Solution

AVOID ERRORS
Remember that the terms of $(3b - 4)$ are $3b$ and -4. They are *not* $3b$ and 4.

STEP 1 **Multiply** by -4.

$$\begin{array}{r} b^2 + 6b - 7 \\ \times \qquad 3b - 4 \\ \hline -4b^2 - 24b + 28 \end{array}$$

STEP 2 **Multiply** by $3b$.

$$\begin{array}{r} b^2 + 6b - 7 \\ \times \qquad 3b - 4 \\ \hline -4b^2 - 24b + 28 \\ 3b^3 + 18b^2 - 21b \qquad \end{array}$$

STEP 3 **Add** products.

$$\begin{array}{r} b^2 + 6b - 7 \\ \times \qquad 3b - 4 \\ \hline -4b^2 - 24b + 28 \\ 3b^3 + 18b^2 - 21b \qquad \\ \hline 3b^3 + 14b^2 - 45b + 28 \end{array}$$

EXAMPLE 4 Multiply polynomials horizontally

Find the product $(2x^2 + 5x - 1)(4x - 3)$.

$(2x^2 + 5x - 1)(4x - 3)$	**Write product.**
$= 2x^2(4x - 3) + 5x(4x - 3) - 1(4x - 3)$	**Distributive property**
$= 8x^3 - 6x^2 + 20x^2 - 15x - 4x + 3$	**Distributive property**
$= 8x^3 + 14x^2 - 19x + 3$	**Combine like terms.**

FOIL PATTERN The letters of the word FOIL can help you to remember how to use the distributive property to multiply binomials. The letters should remind you of the words **F**irst, **O**uter, **I**nner, and **L**ast.

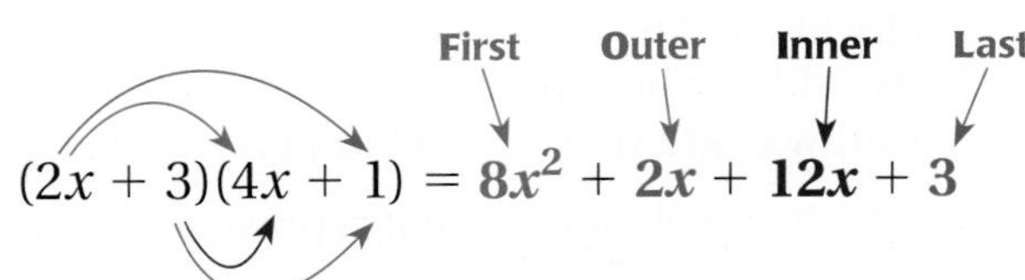

EXAMPLE 5 Multiply binomials using the FOIL pattern

Find the product $(3a + 4)(a - 2)$.

$(3a + 4)(a - 2)$	
$= (3a)(a) + (3a)(-2) + (4)(a) + (4)(-2)$	**Write products of terms.**
$= 3a^2 + (-6a) + 4a + (-8)$	**Multiply.**
$= 3a^2 - 2a - 8$	**Combine like terms.**

✓ GUIDED PRACTICE for Examples 3, 4, and 5

Find the product.

4. $(x^2 + 2x + 1)(x + 2)$ **5.** $(3y^2 - y + 5)(2y - 3)$ **6.** $(4b - 5)(b - 2)$

EXAMPLE 6 Standardized Test Practice

The dimensions of a rectangle are $x + 3$ and $x + 2$. Which expression represents the area of the rectangle?

ELIMINATE CHOICES
When you multiply $x + 3$ and $x + 2$, the product will have a constant term of $3 \cdot 2 = 6$. So, you can eliminate choice D.

(A) $x^2 + 6$ (B) $x^2 + 5x + 6$ (C) $x^2 + 6x + 6$ (D) $x^2 + 6x$

Solution

Area = length • width	**Formula for area of a rectangle**
$= (x + 3)(x + 2)$	**Substitute for length and width.**
$= x^2 + 2x + 3x + 6$	**Multiply binomials.**
$= x^2 + 5x + 6$	**Combine like terms.**

▶ The correct answer is B. (A) (B) (C) (D)

CHECK You can use a graph to check your answer. Use a graphing calculator to display the graphs of $y_1 = (x + 3)(x + 2)$ and $y_2 = x^2 + 5x + 6$ in the same viewing window. Because the graphs coincide, you know that the product of $x + 3$ and $x + 2$ is $x^2 + 5x + 6$.

EXAMPLE 7 Solve a multi-step problem

SKATEBOARDING You are designing a rectangular skateboard park on a lot that is on the corner of a city block. The park will have a walkway along two sides. The dimensions of the lot and the walkway are shown in the diagram.

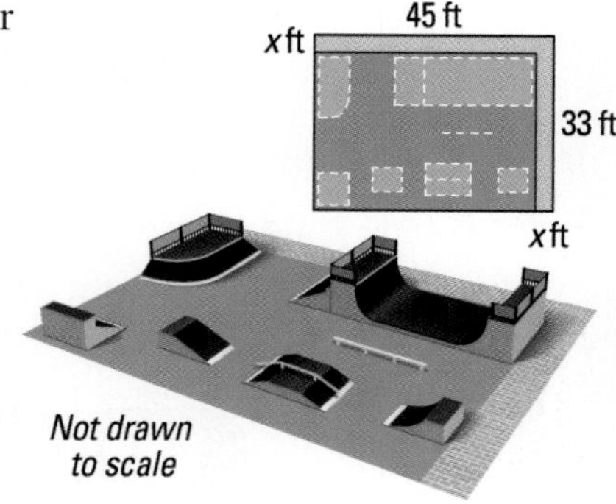

Not drawn to scale

- Write a polynomial that represents the area of the skateboard park.
- What is the area of the park if the walkway is 3 feet wide?

Solution

STEP 1 **Write** a polynomial using the formula for the area of a rectangle. The length is $45 - x$. The width is $33 - x$.

Area = length • width	**Formula for area of a rectangle**
$= (45 - x)(33 - x)$	**Substitute for length and width.**
$= 1485 - 45x - 33x + x^2$	**Multiply binomials.**
$= 1485 - 78x + x^2$	**Combine like terms.**

STEP 2 **Substitute** 3 for x and evaluate.

Area $= 1485 - 78(3) + (3)^2 = 1260$

▶ The area of the park is 1260 square feet.

GUIDED PRACTICE for Examples 6 and 7

7. The dimensions of a rectangle are $x + 5$ and $x + 9$. Which expression represents the area of the rectangle?

Ⓐ $x^2 + 45x$ Ⓑ $x^2 + 45$

Ⓒ $x^2 + 14x + 45$ Ⓓ $x^2 + 45x + 45$

8. **GARDEN DESIGN** You are planning to build a walkway that surrounds a rectangular garden, as shown. The width of the walkway around the garden is the same on every side.

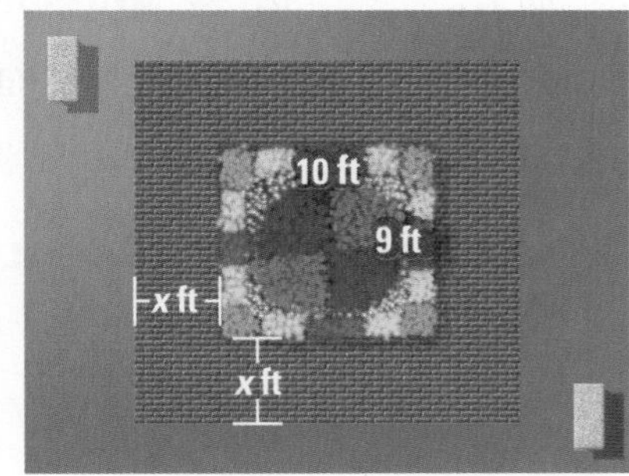

a. Write a polynomial that represents the combined area of the garden and the walkway.

b. Find the combined area when the width of the walkway is 4 feet.

8.2 EXERCISES

HOMEWORK KEY

○ = See WORKED-OUT SOLUTIONS Exs. 23 and 51

★ = STANDARDIZED TEST PRACTICE Exs. 2, 26, 44, 52, and 53

SKILL PRACTICE

1. **VOCABULARY** Copy and complete: The FOIL pattern can be used to multiply any two __?__.

2. ★ **WRITING** *Explain* how the letters of the word FOIL can help you multiply polynomials.

EXAMPLE 1 for Exs. 3–8

MULTIPLYING POLYNOMIALS Find the product.

3. $x(2x^2 - 3x + 9)$
4. $4y(-y^3 - 2y - 1)$
5. $z^2(4z^4 + z^3 - 11z^2 - 6)$
6. $3c^3(8c^4 - c^2 - 3c + 5)$
7. $-a^5(-9a^2 + 5a + 13)$
8. $-5b^3(4b^5 - 2b^3 + b - 11)$

EXAMPLE 2 for Exs. 9–15

USING TABLES Use a table to find the product.

9. $(x + 2)(x - 3)$
10. $(y - 5)(2y + 3)$
11. $(4b - 3)(b - 7)$
12. $(5s + 2)(s + 8)$
13. $(3k - 1)(4k + 9)$
14. $(8n - 5)(3n - 6)$

EXAMPLES 3 and 4 for Exs. 16–26

ERROR ANALYSIS *Describe* and correct the error in finding the product of the polynomials.

15.

$(x - 5)(3x + 1)$

	3x	1
x	$3x^2$	x
5	15x	5

$(x - 5)(3x + 1) = 3x^2 + 16x + 5$

16.

$$\begin{array}{r} 2x^2 - 3x - 4 \\ \times \qquad x + 7 \\ \hline 14x^2 - 21x - 28 \\ 2x^3 - 3x^2 - 4x \qquad \\ \hline 2x^3 + 11x^4 - 25x^2 - 28 \end{array}$$

MULTIPLYING POLYNOMIALS **Use a vertical or a horizontal format to find the product.**

17. $(y + 6)(y - 5)$
18. $(5x - 8)(2x - 5)$
19. $(7w + 5)(11w - 3)$
20. $(b - 2)(b^2 - b + 1)$
21. $(s + 4)(s^2 + 6s - 5)$
22. $(-r + 7)(2r^2 - r - 9)$
23. $(5x + 2)(-3x^2 + 4x - 1)$
24. $(y^2 + 8y - 6)(4y - 3)$
25. $(6z^2 + z - 1)(9z - 5)$

26. ★ **MULTIPLE CHOICE** What is the product of $2x - 9$ and $4x + 1$?

(A) $8x^2 - 38x - 9$ (B) $8x^2 - 34x - 9$

(C) $8x^2 + 34x - 9$ (D) $8x^2 + 38x - 9$

EXAMPLE 5 for Exs. 27–32

USING THE FOIL PATTERN **Use the FOIL pattern to find the product.**

27. $(2r - 1)(5r + 3)$
28. $(7a - 2)(3a - 4)$
29. $(4m + 9)(2m + 7)$
30. $(8t + 11)(6t - 1)$
31. $(4x - 5)(12x - 7)$
32. $(8z + 3)(5z + 4)$

SIMPLIFYING EXPRESSIONS **Simplify the expression.**

33. $p(2p - 3) + (p - 3)(p + 3)$
34. $x^2(7x + 5) - (2x + 6)(x - 1)$
35. $-3c^2(c + 11) - (4c - 5)(3c - 2)$
36. $2w^3(2w^3 - 7w - 1) + w(5w^2 + 2w)$

EXAMPLES 6 and 7 for Exs. 37–42

GEOMETRY **Write a polynomial that represents the area of the shaded region.**

37. 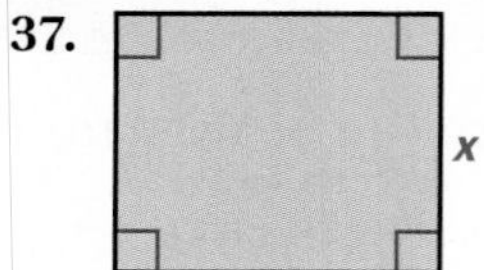

38. 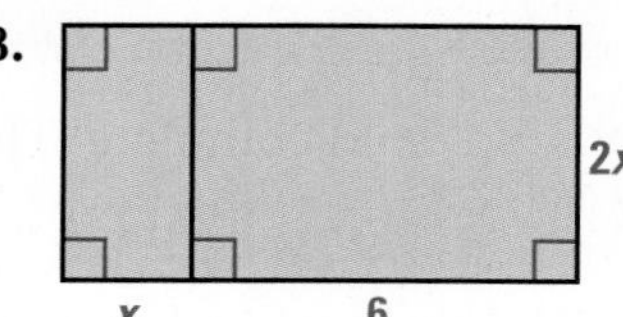

39. 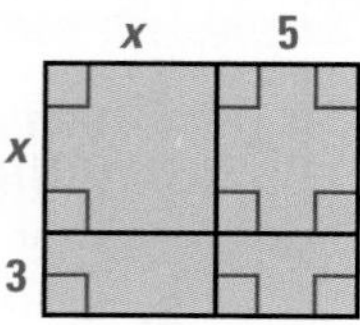

40. 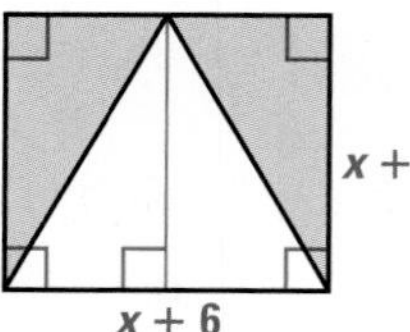

41. 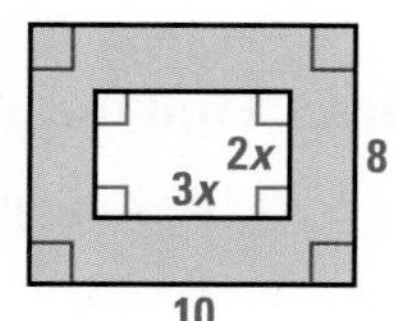

42. 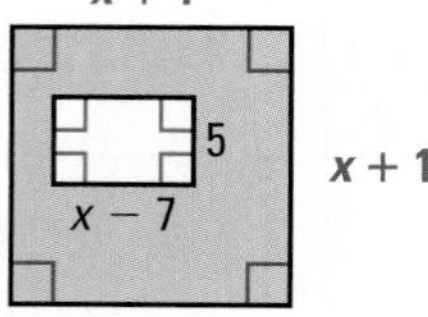

43. **POLYNOMIAL FUNCTIONS** Find the product $f(x) \cdot g(x)$ for the functions $f(x) = x - 11$ and $g(x) = 2x + 12$.

44. ★ **MULTIPLE CHOICE** Which polynomial represents $f(x) \cdot g(x)$ if $f(x) = -2x^2$ and $g(x) = x^3 - 5x^2 + 2x - 1$?

(A) $-2x^5 - 10x^4 + 4x^3 - 2x^2$ (B) $-2x^5 + 10x^4 - 4x^3 - 2x^2$

(C) $-2x^5 + 10x^4 - 4x^3 + 2x^2$ (D) $2x^5 - 10x^4 + 4x^3 - 2x^2$

45. **REASONING** Find the product $(x^2 - 7x)(2x^2 + 3x + 1)$. Show that the product is correct by using a graphing calculator. *Explain* your reasoning.

CHALLENGE **Find the product.**

46. $(x - y)(3x + 4y)$
47. $(x^2y + 9y)(2x + 3y)$
48. $(x^2 - 5xy + y^2)(4xy)$

○ = See **WORKED-OUT SOLUTIONS** in Student Resources ★ = **STANDARDIZED TEST PRACTICE**

PROBLEM SOLVING

EXAMPLE 7 for Exs. 49–50

49. **PICTURE FRAME** You are designing a frame to surround a rectangular picture. The width of the frame around the picture is the same on every side, as shown.

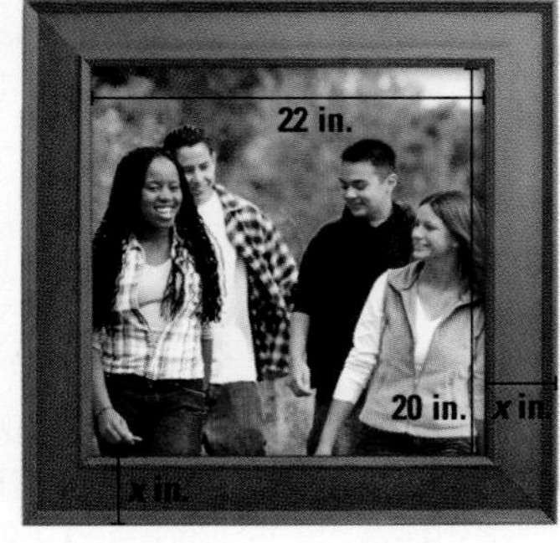

a. Write a polynomial that represents the total area of the picture and the frame.

b. Find the combined area of the picture and the frame when the width of the frame is 4 inches.

50. **SWIMMING POOL** A rectangular swimming pool is bordered on one side by a deck. A contractor is hired to build a walkway along the remaining three sides of the pool. The width of the walkway is the same on every side, as shown.

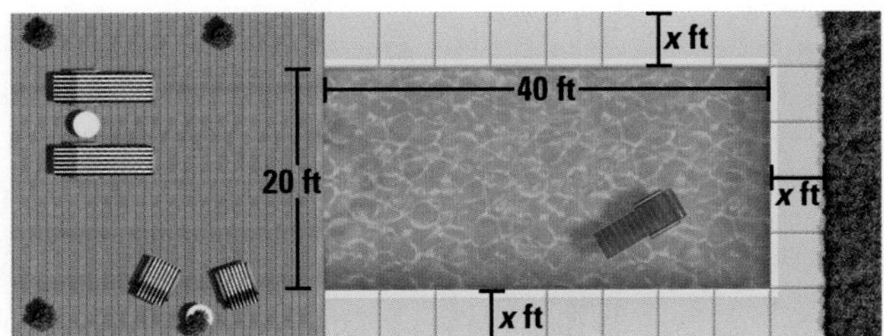

a. Write a polynomial that represents the total area of the pool and the walkway.

b. Find the combined area of the pool and the walkway when the width of the walkway is 5 feet.

51. **SOUND RECORDINGS** During the period 1997–2002, the amount of money R (in millions of dollars) spent on sound recordings in the U.S. and the percent P (in decimal form) of this amount spent by people who are between 15 and 19 years old can be modeled by

$$R = -336t^2 + 1730t + 12{,}300 \text{ and } P = 0.00351t^2 - 0.0249t + 0.171$$

where t is the number of years since 1997.

a. Find the values of R and P for $t = 0$. What does the product $R \cdot P$ mean for $t = 0$ in this situation?

b. Write an equation that models the amount spent on sound recordings by people who are between 15 and 19 years old as a function of the number of years since 1997.

c. How much money did people between 15 and 19 years old spend on sound recordings in 2002?

52. ★ **SHORT RESPONSE** During the period 1980–2002, the number H (in thousands) of housing units in the U.S. and the percent P (in decimal form) of housing units that were vacant can be modeled by

$$H = 1570t + 89{,}000 \quad \text{and} \quad P = 0.0013t + 0.094$$

where t is the number of years since 1980.

a. Write an equation that models the number (in thousands) of vacant housing units as a function of the number of years since 1980. *Explain* how you found this equation.

b. How many housing units were vacant in 2002?

53. ★ **EXTENDED RESPONSE** The bar graph shows the number of households with a television for various years during the period 1990–2001.

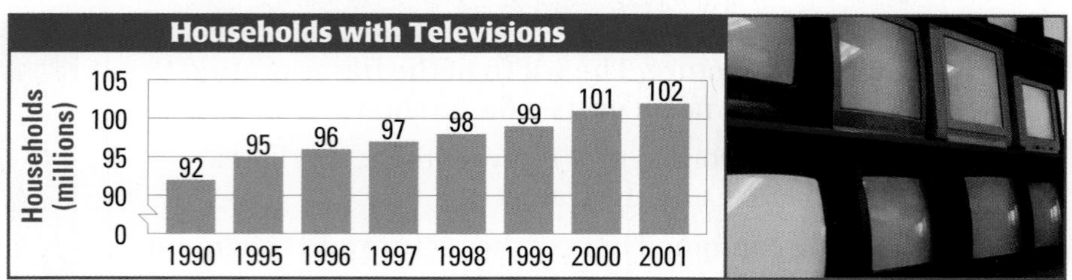

a. Find a linear equation that models the number of households T (in millions) with a television as a function of the number of years since 1990. *Explain* how you found your model.

b. During the period 1990–2001, the percent P (in decimal form) of television households that also have a VCR can be modeled by

$$P = -0.0015t^2 + 0.032t + 0.069$$

where t is the number of years since 1990. Write an equation that models the number of households V (in millions) with a VCR and a television as a function of the number of years since 1990.

c. Use the equation from part (b) to predict the number of households that had a VCR and a television in 2002 and in 2005.

54. CHALLENGE For the period 1990–2001, the total United States energy consumption C (in quadrillion British Thermal Units, or BTU) and the percent P of the total energy that was consumed in the United States for industrial purposes can be modeled by

$$C = 1.5t + 84$$
$$P = -0.05t^2 + 0.25t + 38$$

where t is the number of years since 1990.

a. Find the percent of total energy that was consumed in the United States for industrial purposes in 2000.

b. Write an equation that gives the total energy (in quadrillion BTU) consumed in the United States for industrial purposes as a function of the number of years since 1990. To write the equation, you may need to rewrite one of the given equations.

8.3 Find Special Products of Polynomials

Before You multiplied polynomials.

Now You will use special product patterns to multiply polynomials.

Why? So you can make a scientific prediction, as in Example 4.

Key Vocabulary
- **binomial**
- **trinomial**

The diagram shows a square with a side length of $(a + b)$ units. You can see that the area of the square is

$$(a + b)^2 = a^2 + 2ab + b^2.$$

	a	b
a	a^2	ab
b	ab	b^2

This is one version of a pattern called the square of a binomial. To find another version of this pattern, use algebra: replace b with $-b$.

CC.9-12.A.APR.1 Understand that polynomials form a system analogous to the integers, namely, they are closed under the operations of addition, subtraction, and multiplication; add, subtract, and multiply polynomials.

$(a + (-b))^2 = a^2 + 2a(-b) + (-b)^2$ **Replace b with $-b$ in the pattern above.**

$(a - b)^2 = a^2 - 2ab + b^2$ **Simplify.**

KEY CONCEPT — *For Your Notebook*

Square of a Binomial Pattern

Algebra	Example
$(a + b)^2 = a^2 + 2ab + b^2$	$(x + 5)^2 = x^2 + 10x + 25$
$(a - b)^2 = a^2 - 2ab + b^2$	$(2x - 3)^2 = 4x^2 - 12x + 9$

EXAMPLE 1 Use the square of a binomial pattern

USE PATTERNS
When you use special product patterns, remember that a and b can be numbers, variables, or variable expressions.

Find the product.

a. $(3x + 4)^2 = (3x)^2 + 2(3x)(4) + 4^2$ **Square of a binomial pattern**

$= 9x^2 + 24x + 16$ **Simplify.**

b. $(5x - 2y)^2 = (5x)^2 - 2(5x)(2y) + (2y)^2$ **Square of a binomial pattern**

$= 25x^2 - 20xy + 4y^2$ **Simplify.**

✓ GUIDED PRACTICE for Example 1

Find the product.

1. $(x + 3)^2$ **2.** $(2x + 1)^2$ **3.** $(4x - y)^2$ **4.** $(3m + n)^2$

SUM AND DIFFERENCE PATTERN To find the product $(x + 2)(x - 2)$, you can multiply the two binomials using the FOIL pattern.

$(x + 2)(x - 2) = x^2 - 2x + 2x - 4$ **Use FOIL pattern.**

$= x^2 - 4$ **Combine like terms.**

This suggests a pattern for the product of the sum and difference of two terms.

KEY CONCEPT *For Your Notebook*

Sum and Difference Pattern

Algebra	**Example**
$(a + b)(a - b) = a^2 - b^2$	$(x + 3)(x - 3) = x^2 - 9$

EXAMPLE 2 Use the sum and difference pattern

Find the product.

a. $(t + 5)(t - 5) = t^2 - 5^2$ **Sum and difference pattern**

$= t^2 - 25$ **Simplify.**

b. $(3x + y)(3x - y) = (3x)^2 - y^2$ **Sum and difference pattern**

$= 9x^2 - y^2$ **Simplify.**

GUIDED PRACTICE for Example 2

Find the product.

5. $(x + 10)(x - 10)$ **6.** $(2x + 1)(2x - 1)$ **7.** $(x + 3y)(x - 3y)$

SPECIAL PRODUCTS AND MENTAL MATH The special product patterns can help you use mental math to find certain products of numbers.

EXAMPLE 3 Use special products and mental math

Use special products to find the product 26 • 34.

Solution

Notice that 26 is 4 less than 30 while 34 is 4 more than 30.

$26 \cdot 34 = (30 - 4)(30 + 4)$ **Write as product of difference and sum.**

$= 30^2 - 4^2$ **Sum and difference pattern**

$= 900 - 16$ **Evaluate powers.**

$= 884$ **Simplify.**

EXAMPLE 4 Solve a multi-step problem

BORDER COLLIES The color of the dark patches of a border collie's coat is determined by a combination of two genes. An offspring inherits one patch color gene from each parent. Each parent has two color genes, and the offspring has an equal chance of inheriting either one.

The gene B is for black patches, and the gene r is for red patches. Any gene combination with a B results in black patches. Suppose each parent has the same gene combination Br. The Punnett square shows the possible gene combinations of the offspring and the resulting patch color.

- What percent of the possible gene combinations of the offspring result in black patches?
- Show how you could use a polynomial to model the possible gene combinations of the offspring.

Solution

STEP 1 **Notice** that the Punnett square shows 4 possible gene combinations of the offspring. Of these combinations, 3 result in black patches.

▶ 75% of the possible gene combinations result in black patches.

STEP 2 **Model** the gene from each parent with $0.5B + 0.5r$. There is an equal chance that the collie inherits a black or red gene from each parent.

The possible genes of the offspring can be modeled by $(0.5B + 0.5r)^2$. Notice that this product also represents the area of the Punnett square.

Expand the product to find the possible patch colors of the offspring.

$$(0.5B + 0.5r)^2 = (0.5B)^2 + 2(0.5B)(0.5r) + (0.5r)^2$$

$$= 0.25B^2 + 0.5Br + 0.25r^2$$

Consider the coefficients in the polynomial.

$$0.25B^2 + 0.5Br + 0.25r^2$$

The coefficients show that 25% + 50% = 75% of the possible gene combinations will result in black patches.

✓ GUIDED PRACTICE for Examples 3 and 4

8. *Describe* how you can use special products to find 21^2.

9. **BORDER COLLIES** Look back at Example 4. What percent of the possible gene combinations of the offspring result in red patches?

8.3 EXERCISES

HOMEWORK KEY

○ = See WORKED-OUT SOLUTIONS Exs. 11 and 41

★ = STANDARDIZED TEST PRACTICE Exs. 2, 17, 18, 42, and 44

◆ = MULTIPLE REPRESENTATIONS Ex. 41

SKILL PRACTICE

1. **VOCABULARY** Give an example of two binomials whose product you can find using the sum and difference pattern.

2. ★ **WRITING** *Explain* how to use the square of a binomial pattern.

EXAMPLE 1 for Exs. 3–10, 18

SQUARE OF A BINOMIAL Find the product.

3. $(x + 8)^2$ 4. $(a + 6)^2$ 5. $(2y + 5)^2$

6. $(t - 7)^2$ 7. $(n - 11)^2$ 8. $(6b - 1)^2$

ERROR ANALYSIS *Describe* and correct the error in multiplying.

9. $(s - 3)^2 = s^2 + 9$ ✗

10. $(2d - 10)^2 = 4d^2 - 20d + 100$ 

EXAMPLE 2 for Exs. 11–17

SUM AND DIFFERENCE PATTERN Find the product.

11. $(t + 4)(t - 4)$ 12. $(m - 6)(m + 6)$ 13. $(2x + 1)(2x - 1)$

14. $(3x - 1)(3x + 1)$ 15. $(7 + w)(7 - w)$ 16. $(3s - 8)(3s + 8)$

17. ★ **MULTIPLE CHOICE** Find the product $(7x + 3)(7x - 3)$.

Ⓐ $7x^2 - 9$ Ⓑ $49x^2 - 9$ Ⓒ $49x^2 - 21x - 9$ Ⓓ $49x^2 - 42x - 9$

18. ★ **MULTIPLE CHOICE** Find the product $(5n - 3)^2$.

Ⓐ $5n^2 - 9$ Ⓑ $25n^2 - 9$ Ⓒ $25n^2 - 15n + 9$ Ⓓ $25n^2 - 30n + 9$

EXAMPLE 3 for Exs. 19–22

MENTAL MATH *Describe* how you can use mental math to find the product.

19. $16 \cdot 24$ 20. $28 \cdot 32$ 21. 17^2 22. 44^2

SPECIAL PRODUCT PATTERNS Find the product.

23. $(r + 9s)^2$ 24. $(6x + 5)^2$ 25. $(3m + 11n)(3m - 11n)$

26. $(7a + 8b)(7a - 8b)$ 27. $(3m - 7n)^2$ 28. $(13 - 2x)^2$

29. $(3f - 9)(3f + 9)$ 30. $(9 - 4t)(9 + 4t)$ 31. $(3x + 8y)^2$

32. $(-x - 2y)^2$ 33. $(2a - 5b)(2a + 5b)$ 34. $(6x + y)(6x - y)$

MULTIPLYING FUNCTIONS Perform the indicated operation using the functions $f(x) = 3x + 0.5$ and $g(x) = 3x - 0.5$.

35. $f(x) \cdot g(x)$ 36. $(f(x))^2$ 37. $(g(x))^2$

38. **CHALLENGE** Write two binomials that have the product $x^2 - 121$. *Explain.*

39. **CHALLENGE** Write a pattern for the cube of a binomial $(a + b)^3$.

PROBLEM SOLVING

EXAMPLE 4 for Exs. 40–42

40. **PEA PLANTS** In pea plants, the gene G is for green pods, and the gene y is for yellow pods. Any gene combination with a G results in a green pod. Suppose two pea plants have the same gene combination Gy. The Punnett square shows the possible gene combinations of an offspring pea plant and the resulting pod color.

    a. What percent of possible gene combinations of the offspring plant result in a yellow pod?

    b. Show how you could use a polynomial to model the possible gene combinations of the offspring.

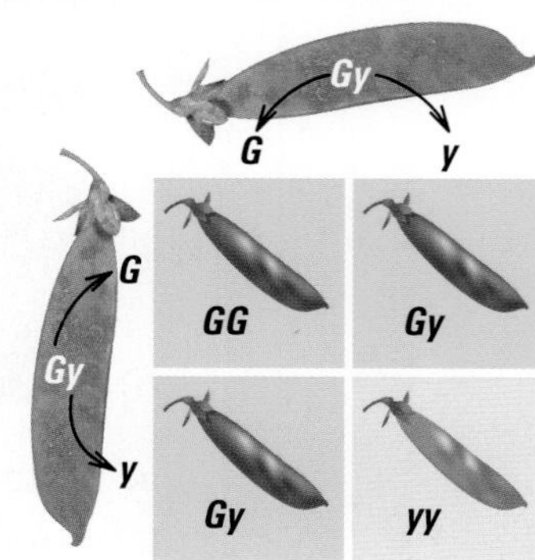

41. ◆ **MULTIPLE REPRESENTATIONS** In humans, the gene s is for straight thumbs, and the gene C is for curved thumbs. Any gene combination with a C results in a curved thumb. Suppose each parent has the same gene combination Cs.

    a. **Making a Diagram** Make a Punnett square that shows the possible gene combinations inherited by a child.

    b. **Writing a Model** Write a polynomial that models the possible gene combinations of the child.

    c. **Interpreting a Model** What percent of the possible gene combinations of the child result in a curved thumb?

42. ★ **SHORT RESPONSE** In ball pythons, the gene N is for normal coloring, and the gene a is for no coloring, or albino. Any gene combination with an N results in normal coloring. Suppose one parent python has the gene combination Na and the other parent python has the gene combination aa. What percent of the possible gene combinations of the offspring result in an albino python? *Explain* how you found your answer.

43. **FOOTBALL STATISTICS** During the 2004 regular season, the San Diego Chargers' quarterback Drew Brees completed 65.5% of the passes he attempted. The area model shows the possible outcomes of two attempted passes.

    a. What percent of the possible outcomes of two attempted passes results in Drew Brees's throwing at least one complete pass? *Explain* how you found your answer using the area model.

    b. Show how you could use a polynomial to model the possible results of two attempted passes.

Second Pass Attempt	First Pass Attempt: Complete 65.5%	First Pass Attempt: Incomplete 34.5%
Complete 65.5%	2 complete	1 complete 1 incomplete
Incomplete 34.5%	1 complete 1 incomplete	2 incomplete

44. ★ **EXTENDED RESPONSE** The iris of an eye surrounds the pupil. It regulates the amount of light entering the eye by opening and closing the pupil. For parts (a)–(c) below, leave your answers in terms of π.

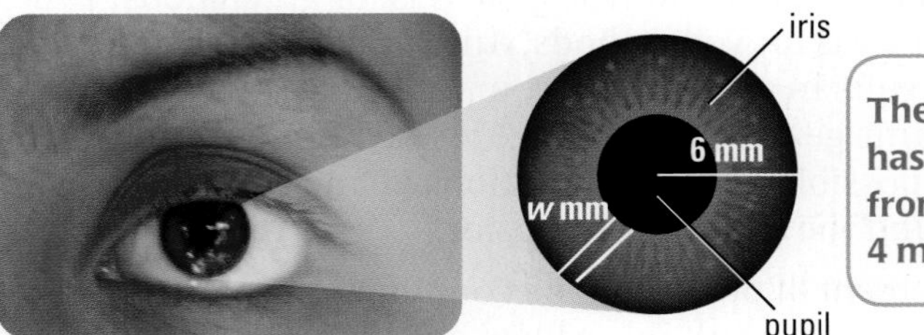

The iris of a human eye has a width w that varies from 0.5 millimeter to 4 millimeters.

a. Write a polynomial that represents the pupil's radius.

b. Write a polynomial that represents the pupil's area.

c. What is the least possible area and the greatest possible area of the pupil? *Explain* how you found your answers.

45. **CHALLENGE** You use 100 feet of fencing to form a square with a side length of 25 feet. You want to change the dimensions of the enclosed region. For every 1 foot you increase the width, you must decrease the length by 1 foot. Write a polynomial that gives the area of the rectangle after you increase the width by x feet and decrease the length by x feet. *Explain* why *any* change in dimensions results in an area less than that of the original square.

QUIZ

Find the sum, difference, or product.

1. $(x^2 - 3x + 5) + (-2x^2 + 11x + 1)$

2. $(8y^3 - 7y^2 + y) - (9y^2 - 5y + 7)$

3. $(2r + 11)(r - 6)$

4. $(m + 3)(-2m^2 + 5m - 1)$

5. $(2 + 8p)(2 - 10p)$

6. $(15 - 2s)^2$

7. $(5w + 9z)^2$

8. $(5x - 4y)(5x + 4y)$

9. **AREA** The length of a rectangular rug is 2 times its width. The rug is centered in a rectangular room. Each edge is 3 feet from the nearest wall. Write a polynomial that represents the area of the room.

8.4 Solve Polynomial Equations in Factored Form

Before You solved linear equations.

Now You will solve polynomial equations.

Why So you can analyze vertical motion, as in Ex. 55.

Key Vocabulary
- **roots**
- **vertical motion model**

CC.9-12.A.REI.4b Solve quadratic equations by inspection (e.g., for $x^2 = 49$), taking square roots, completing the square, the quadratic formula and factoring, as appropriate to the initial form of the equation. Recognize when the quadratic formula gives complex solutions and write them as $a \pm bi$ for real numbers a and b.

You have learned the property of zero: For any real number a, $a \cdot 0 = 0$. This is equivalent to saying:

For real numbers a and b, if $a = 0$ or $b = 0$, then $ab = 0$.

The converse of this statement is also true (as shown in Exercise 49), and it is called the zero-product property.

KEY CONCEPT *For Your Notebook*

Zero-Product Property

Let a and b be real numbers. If $ab = 0$, then $a = 0$ or $b = 0$.

The zero-product property is used to solve an equation when one side is zero and the other side is a product of polynomial factors. The solutions of such an equation are also called **roots**.

EXAMPLE 1 Use the zero-product property

Solve $(x - 4)(x + 2) = 0$.

$(x - 4)(x + 2) = 0$	**Write original equation.**
$x - 4 = 0$ *or* $x + 2 = 0$	**Zero-product property**
$x = 4$ *or* $x = -2$	**Solve for *x*.**

▶ The solutions of the equation are 4 and −2.

CHECK Substitute each solution into the original equation to check.

$(4 - 4)(4 + 2) \stackrel{?}{=} 0$ $\quad$ $(-2 - 4)(-2 + 2) \stackrel{?}{=} 0$

$0 \cdot 6 \stackrel{?}{=} 0$ $\quad$ $-6 \cdot 0 \stackrel{?}{=} 0$

$0 = 0$ ✓ $\quad$ $0 = 0$ ✓

GUIDED PRACTICE for Example 1

1. Solve the equation $(x - 5)(x - 1) = 0$.

REVIEW GCF
For help with finding the GCF, see p. SR2.

FACTORING To solve a polynomial equation using the zero-product property, you may need to *factor* the polynomial, or write it as a product of other polynomials. Look for the *greatest common factor* (GCF) of the polynomial's terms. This is a monomial with an integer coefficient that divides evenly into each term.

EXAMPLE 2 Find the greatest common monomial factor

Factor out the greatest common monomial factor.

a. $12x + 42y$ **b.** $4x^4 + 24x^3$

Solution

a. The GCF of 12 and 42 is 6. The variables x and y have no common factor. So, the greatest common monomial factor of the terms is 6.

▶ $12x + 42y = 6(2x + 7y)$

b. The GCF of 4 and 24 is 4. The GCF of x^4 and x^3 is x^3. So, the greatest common monomial factor of the terms is $4x^3$.

▶ $4x^4 + 24x^3 = 4x^3(x + 6)$

✓ **GUIDED PRACTICE** for Example 2

2. Factor out the greatest common monomial factor from $14m + 35n$.

EXAMPLE 3 Solve an equation by factoring

Solve $2x^2 + 8x = 0$.

$2x^2 + 8x = 0$	**Write original equation.**
$2x(x + 4) = 0$	**Factor left side.**
$2x = 0$ *or* $x + 4 = 0$	**Zero-product property**
$x = 0$ *or* $x = -4$	**Solve for *x*.**

▶ The solutions of the equation are 0 and −4.

EXAMPLE 4 Solve an equation by factoring

Solve $6n^2 = 15n$.

AVOID ERRORS
To use the zero-product property, you must write the equation so that one side is 0. For this reason, $15n$ must be subtracted from each side.

$6n^2 - 15n = 0$	**Subtract 15*n* from each side.**
$3n(2n - 5) = 0$	**Factor left side.**
$3n = 0$ *or* $2n - 5 = 0$	**Zero-product property**
$n = 0$ *or* $n = \frac{5}{2}$	**Solve for *n*.**

▶ The solutions of the equation are 0 and $\frac{5}{2}$.

✓ **GUIDED PRACTICE** for Examples 3 and 4

Solve the equation.

3. $a^2 + 5a = 0$ **4.** $3s^2 - 9s = 0$ **5.** $4x^2 = 2x$

VERTICAL MOTION A *projectile* is an object that is propelled into the air but has no power to keep itself in the air. A thrown ball is a projectile, but an airplane is not. The height of a projectile can be described by the **vertical motion model**.

UNDERSTAND THE MODEL
The vertical motion model takes into account the effect of gravity but ignores other, less significant, factors such as air resistance.

KEY CONCEPT *For Your Notebook*

Vertical Motion Model

The height h (in feet) of a projectile can be modeled by

$$h = -16t^2 + vt + s$$

where t is the time (in seconds) the object has been in the air, v is the initial vertical velocity (in feet per second), and s is the initial height (in feet).

EXAMPLE 5 Solve a multi-step problem

ARMADILLO A startled armadillo jumps straight into the air with an initial vertical velocity of 14 feet per second. After how many seconds does it land on the ground?

Solution

STEP 1 **Write** a model for the armadillo's height above the ground.

$h = -16t^2 + vt + s$ **Vertical motion model**

$h = -16t^2 + 14t + 0$ **Substitute 14 for *v* and 0 for *s*.**

$h = -16t^2 + 14t$ **Simplify.**

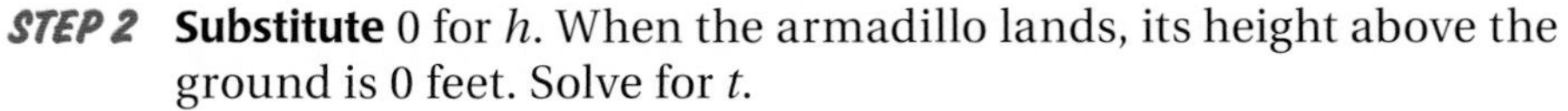

STEP 2 **Substitute** 0 for h. When the armadillo lands, its height above the ground is 0 feet. Solve for t.

$0 = -16t^2 + 14t$ **Substitute 0 for *h*.**

$0 = 2t(-8t + 7)$ **Factor right side.**

$2t = 0$ *or* $-8t + 7 = 0$ **Zero-product property**

$t = 0$ *or* $t = 0.875$ **Solve for *t*.**

▶ The armadillo lands on the ground 0.875 second after the armadillo jumps.

AVOID ERRORS
The solution $t = 0$ means that before the armadillo jumps, its height above the ground is 0 feet.

GUIDED PRACTICE for Example 5

6. WHAT IF? In Example 5, suppose the initial vertical velocity is 12 feet per second. After how many seconds does the armadillo land on the ground?

8.4 EXERCISES

HOMEWORK KEY

○ = See WORKED-OUT SOLUTIONS Exs. 3 and 55

★ = STANDARDIZED TEST PRACTICE Exs. 2, 15, 39, 53, and 56

◆ = MULTIPLE REPRESENTATIONS Ex. 58

SKILL PRACTICE

1. **VOCABULARY** What is the vertical motion model and what does each variable in the model represent?

2. ★ **WRITING** *Explain* how to use the zero-product property to find the solutions of the equation $3x(x-7)=0$.

EXAMPLE 1 for Exs. 3–16

ZERO-PRODUCT PROPERTY **Solve the equation.**

3. $(x-5)(x+3)=0$
4. $(y+9)(y-1)=0$
5. $(z-13)(z-14)=0$
6. $(c+6)(c+8)=0$
7. $(d-7)\left(d+\frac{4}{3}\right)=0$
8. $\left(g-\frac{1}{8}\right)(g+18)=0$
9. $(m-3)(4m+12)=0$
10. $(2n-14)(3n+9)=0$
11. $(3n+11)(n+1)=0$
12. $(3x+1)(x+6)=0$
13. $(2y+5)(7y-5)=0$
14. $(8z-6)(12z+14)=0$

15. ★ **MULTIPLE CHOICE** What are the roots of the equation $(y-12)(y+6)=0$?

Ⓐ -12 and -6 Ⓑ -12 and 6 Ⓒ -6 and 12 Ⓓ 6 and 12

16. **ERROR ANALYSIS** *Describe* and correct the error in solving $(z-15)(z+21)=0$.

$(z-15)(z+21)=0$
$z=-15$ or $z=21$ ✗

EXAMPLE 2 for Exs. 17–26

FACTORING EXPRESSIONS **Factor out the greatest common monomial factor.**

17. $2x+2y$
18. $6x^2-15y$
19. $3s^4+16s$
20. $5d^6+2d^5$
21. $7w^5-35w^2$
22. $9m^7-3m^2$
23. $15n^3+25n$
24. $12a^5+8a$
25. $\frac{5}{2}x^6-\frac{1}{2}x^4$

26. **ERROR ANALYSIS** *Describe* and correct the error in factoring out the greatest common monomial factor of $18x^8-9x^4-6x^3$.

$18x^8-9x^4-6x^3=3x(6x^7-3x^3-2x^2)$ ✗

EXAMPLES 3 and 4 for Exs. 27–39

SOLVING EQUATIONS **Solve the equation.**

27. $b^2+6b=0$
28. $5w^2-5w=0$
29. $-10n^2+35n=0$
30. $2x^2+15x=0$
31. $18c^2+6c=0$
32. $-32y^2-24y=0$
33. $3k^2=6k$
34. $6h^2=3h$
35. $4s^2=10s$
36. $-42z^2=14z$
37. $28m^2=-8m$
38. $-12p^2=-30p$

39. ★ **MULTIPLE CHOICE** What are the solutions of $4x^2=x$?

Ⓐ -4 and 0 Ⓑ $-\frac{1}{4}$ and 0 Ⓒ 0 and $\frac{1}{4}$ Ⓓ 0 and 4

FACTORING EXPRESSIONS **Factor out the greatest common monomial factor.**

40. $20x^2y^2 - 4xy$
41. $8a^2b - 6ab^2$
42. $18s^2t^5 - 2s^3t$
43. $v^3 - 5v^2 + 9v$
44. $-2g^4 + 14g^2 + 6g$
45. $6q^5 - 21q^4 - 15q^2$

HINT
You may want to review finding zeros of linear functions before finding zeros of quadratic functions.

FINDING ZEROS OF FUNCTIONS **Find the zeros of the function.**

46. $f(x) = x^2 - 15x$
47. $f(x) = -2x^2 + x$
48. $f(x) = 3x^2 - 27x$

49. **CHALLENGE** Consider the equation $ab = 0$. Assume that $a \neq 0$ and solve the equation for b. Then assume that $b \neq 0$ and solve the equation for a. What conclusion can you draw about the values of a and b?

50. **CHALLENGE** Consider the equation $z = x^2 - xy$. For what values of x and y does $z = 0$?

PROBLEM SOLVING

EXAMPLE 5
for Exs. 51–53

51. **MOTION** A cat leaps from the ground into the air with an initial vertical velocity of 11 feet per second. After how many seconds does the cat land on the ground?

52. **SPITTLEBUG** A spittlebug jumps into the air with an initial vertical velocity of 10 feet per second.
   a. Write an equation that gives the height of the spittlebug as a function of the time (in seconds) since it left the ground.
   b. The spittlebug reaches its maximum height after 0.3125 second. How high can it jump?

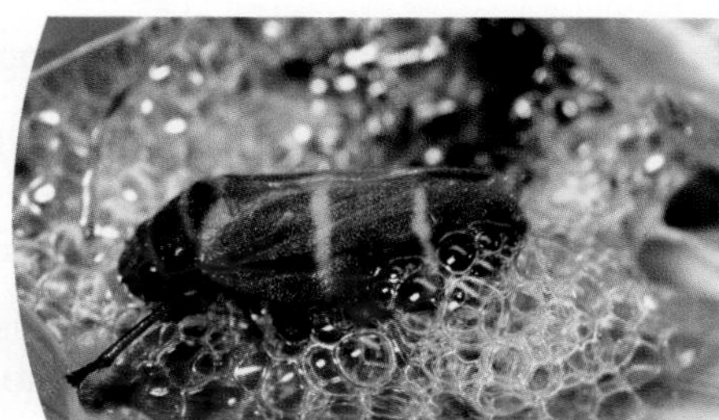

53. ★ **SHORT RESPONSE** A penguin jumps out of the water while swimming. This action is called porpoising. The height h (in feet) of the porpoising penguin can be modeled by $h = -16t^2 + 4.5t$ where t is the time (in seconds) since the penguin jumped out of the water. Find the zeros of the function. *Explain* what the zeros mean in this situation.

VERTICAL MOTION **In Exercises 54 and 55, use the information below.**

The height h (in meters) of a projectile can be modeled by $h = -4.9t^2 + vt + s$ where t is the time (in seconds) the object has been in the air, v is the initial vertical velocity (in meters per second), and s is the initial height (in meters).

54. **SOCCER** A soccer ball is kicked upward from the ground with an initial vertical velocity of 3.6 meters per second. After how many seconds does it land?

55. **RABBIT HIGH JUMP** A rabbit in a high jump competition leaves the ground with an initial vertical velocity of 4.9 meters per second.
   a. Write an equation that gives the height of the rabbit as a function of the time (in seconds) since it left the ground.
   b. What is a reasonable domain for the function? *Explain* your answer.

56. ★ **MULTIPLE CHOICE** Two rectangular rooms in a building's floor plan have different dimensions but the same area. The dimensions (in meters) are shown. What is the value of w?

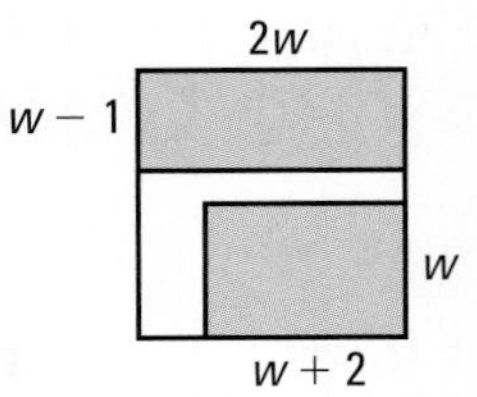

Ⓐ 3 m Ⓑ 4 m Ⓒ 6 m Ⓓ 8 m

57. TABLETOP AREAS A display in your school library sits on top of two rectangular tables arranged in an L shape, as shown. The tabletops have the same area.

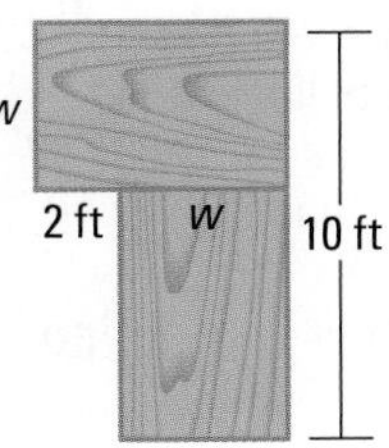

a. Write an equation that relates the areas of the tabletops.

b. Find the value of w.

c. What is the combined area of the tabletops?

58. ◆ **MULTIPLE REPRESENTATIONS** An arch frames the entrance to a garden. The shape of the arch is modeled by the graph of the equation $y = -2x^2 + 8x$ where x and y are measured in feet. On a coordinate plane, the ground is represented by the x-axis.

a. Making a Table Make a table of values that shows the height of the arch for $x = 0, 1, 2, 3,$ and 4 feet.

b. Drawing a Graph Plot the ordered pairs in the table as points in a coordinate plane. Connect the points with a smooth curve that represents the arch.

c. Interpreting a Graph How wide is the base of the arch?

59. CHALLENGE The shape of an arched doorway is modeled by the graph of the function $y = -0.5x(x - 8)$ where x and y are measured in feet. On a coordinate plane, the floor is represented by the x-axis.

a. How wide is the doorway at its base? *Justify* your answer using the zeros of the function.

b. The doorway's highest point occurs above the center of its base. How high is the highest point of the arched doorway? *Explain* how you found your answer.

MIXED REVIEW *of Problem Solving*

MATHEMATICAL PRACTICES Make sense of problems and persevere in solving them.

1. MULTI-STEP PROBLEM You are making a blanket with a fringe border of equal width on each edge, as shown.

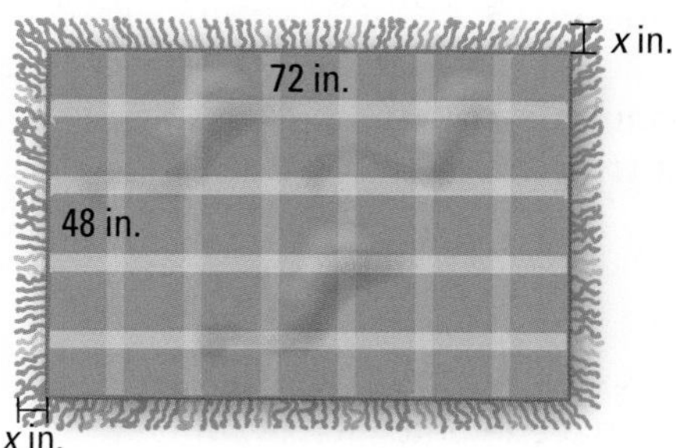

a. Write a polynomial that represents the total area of the blanket with the fringe.

b. Find the total area of the blanket with fringe when the width of the fringe is 4 inches.

2. OPEN-ENDED A horse with pinto coloring has white fur with patches of color. The gene P is for pinto coloring, and the gene s is for solid coloring. Any gene combination with a P results in pinto coloring.

a. Suppose a male horse has the gene combination *Ps*. Choose a color gene combination for a female horse. Create a Punnett square to show the possible gene combinations of the two horses' offspring.

b. What percent of the possible gene combinations of the offspring result in pinto coloring?

c. Show how you could use a polynomial to model the possible color gene combinations of the offspring.

3. SHORT RESPONSE One football is kicked into the air with an initial vertical velocity of 44 feet per second. Another football is kicked into the air with an initial vertical velocity of 40 feet per second.

a. Which football is in the air for more time?

b. *Justify* your answer to part (a).

4. GRIDDED ANSWER During the period 1996–2000, the total value T (in millions of dollars) of toys imported to the United States can be modeled by

$$T = 82.9t^3 - 848t^2 + 3030t + 9610$$

where t is the number of years since 1996. What is the degree of the polynomial that represents T?

5. EXTENDED RESPONSE During the period 1992–2000, the number C (in millions) of people participating in cross-country skiing and the number S (in millions) of people participating in snowboarding can be modeled by

$$C = 0.067t^3 - 0.107t^2 + 0.27t + 3.5$$

$$S = 0.416t + 1.24$$

where t is the number of years since 1992.

a. Write an equation that models the total number of people T (in millions) participating in cross-country skiing and snowboarding as a function of the number of years since 1992.

b. Find the total participation in these activities in 1992 and 2000.

c. What was the average rate of change in total participation from 1992 to 2000? *Explain* how you found this rate.

6. SHORT RESPONSE A circular rug has an interior circle and two rings around the circle, as shown.

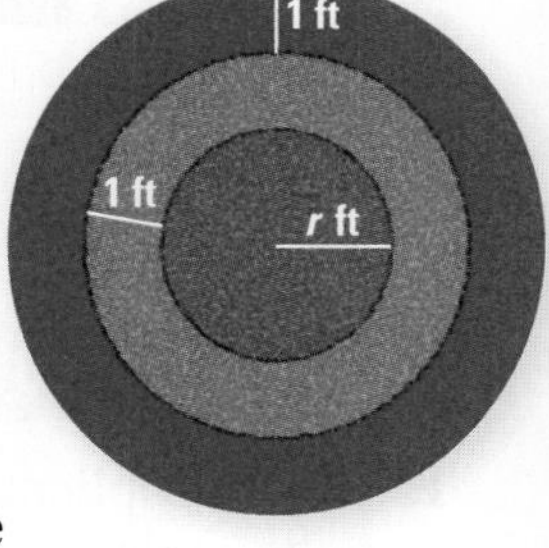

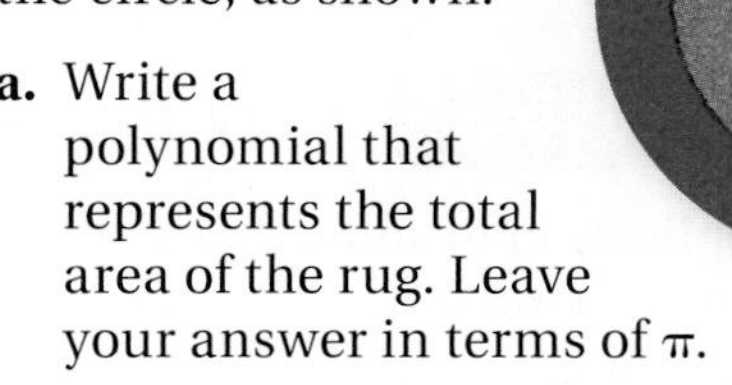

a. Write a polynomial that represents the total area of the rug. Leave your answer in terms of π.

b. The interior circle of the rug has a diameter of 3 feet. What is the area of the rug? Leave your answer in terms of π. *Explain* how you found your answer.

Factorization with Algebra Tiles

MATHEMATICAL PRACTICES

Use appropriate tools strategically.

MATERIALS • algebra tiles

QUESTION How can you factor a trinomial using algebra tiles?

You have seen that algebra tiles can be used to model polynomials and to multiply binomials. Now, you will use algebra tiles to factor trinomials.

EXPLORE Factor the trinomial $x^2 + 6x + 8$

STEP 1 *Make a rectangle*

Model the trinomial with algebra tiles. You will need one x^2-tile, six x-tiles, and eight 1-tiles. Arrange all of the tiles to form a rectangle. There can be no gaps or leftover tiles. The area of the rectangle represents the trinomial.

STEP 2 *Find the side lengths*

The side lengths of the rectangle represent the polynomials $x + 2$ and $x + 4$. So, $x^2 + 6x + 8 = (x + 2)(x + 4)$.

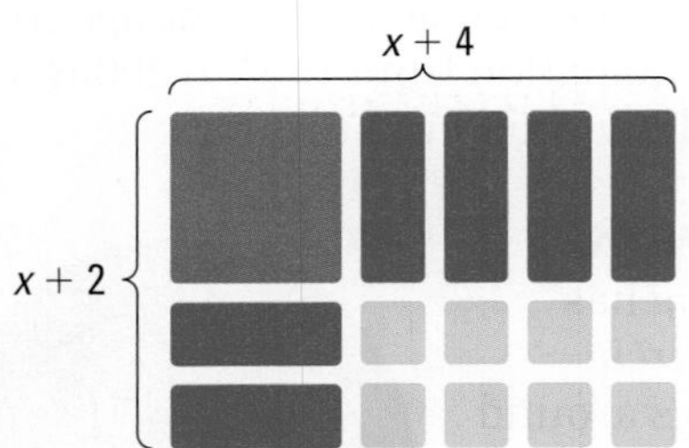

DRAW CONCLUSIONS Use your observations to complete these exercises

1. Use multiplication to show that $x + 4$ and $x + 2$ are factors of the polynomial $x^2 + 6x + 8$.

Use algebra tiles to factor the trinomial. Include a drawing of your model.

2. $x^2 + 6x + 5$
3. $x^2 + 9x + 14$
4. $x^2 + 5x + 6$
5. $x^2 + 8x + 16$
6. $x^2 + 5x + 4$
7. $x^2 + 8x + 12$
8. **REASONING** The factors of the trinomial $x^2 + 6x + 8$ have the form $x + p$ and $x + q$, as shown above. How are p and q related to 6 and 8?

8.5 Factor $x^2 + bx + c$

Before You factored out the greatest common monomial factor.
Now You will factor trinomials of the form $x^2 + bx + c$.
Why So you can find the dimensions of figures, as in Ex. 61.

Key Vocabulary
- **zero of a function**

You know from multiplying binomials that

$$(x + 3)(x + 4) = x^2 + (4 + 3)x + 4 \cdot 3 = x^2 + 7x + 12.$$

You will reverse this process to factor trinomials of the form $x^2 + bx + c$.

CC.9-12.A.SSE.3a Factor a quadratic expression to reveal the zeros of the function it defines.

KEY CONCEPT *For Your Notebook*

Factoring $x^2 + bx + c$

Algebra $x^2 + bx + c = (x + p)(x + q)$ provided $p + q = b$ and $pq = c$.

Example $x^2 + 5x + 6 = (x + 3)(x + 2)$ because $3 + 2 = 5$ and $3 \cdot 2 = 6$.

EXAMPLE 1 Factor when *b* and *c* are positive

Factor $x^2 + 11x + 18$.

Solution

Find two positive factors of 18 whose sum is 11. Make an organized list.

Factors of 18	Sum of factors	
18, 1	18 + 1 = 19	✗
9, 2	9 + 2 = 11	← Correct sum
6, 3	6 + 3 = 9	✗

The factors 9 and 2 have a sum of 11, so they are the correct values of *p* and *q*.

▶ $x^2 + 11x + 18 = (x + 9)(x + 2)$

CHECK $(x + 9)(x + 2) = x^2 + 2x + 9x + 18$ **Multiply binomials.**

$= x^2 + 11x + 18$ ✓ **Simplify.**

GUIDED PRACTICE for Example 1

Factor the trinomial.

1. $x^2 + 3x + 2$ **2.** $a^2 + 7a + 10$ **3.** $t^2 + 9t + 14$

FACTORING When factoring a trinomial, first consider the signs of p and q.

$(x + p)(x + q)$	$x^2 + bx + c$	Signs of b and c
$(x + 2)(x + 3)$	$x^2 + 5x + 6$	b is positive; c is positive.
$(x + 2)(x + (-3))$	$x^2 - x - 6$	b is negative; c is negative.
$(x + (-2))(x + 3)$	$x^2 + x - 6$	b is positive; c is negative.
$(x + (-2))(x + (-3))$	$x^2 - 5x + 6$	b is negative; c is positive.

By observing the signs of b and c in the table, you can see that:

- b and c are positive when both p and q are positive.
- b is negative and c is positive when both p and q are negative.
- c is negative when p and q have different signs.

EXAMPLE 2 Factor when b is negative and c is positive

Factor $n^2 - 6n + 8$.

Because b is negative and c is positive, p and q must both be negative.

Factors of 8	Sum of factors	
$-8, -1$	$-8 + (-1) = -9$	✗
$-4, -2$	$-4 + (-2) = -6$	← Correct sum

▶ $n^2 - 6n + 8 = (n - 4)(n - 2)$

EXAMPLE 3 Factor when b is positive and c is negative

Factor $y^2 + 2y - 15$.

Because c is negative, p and q must have different signs.

Factors of -15	Sum of factors	
$-15, 1$	$-15 + 1 = -14$	✗
$15, -1$	$15 + (-1) = 14$	✗
$-5, 3$	$-5 + 3 = -2$	✗
$5, -3$	$5 + (-3) = 2$	← Correct sum

▶ $y^2 + 2y - 15 = (y + 5)(y - 3)$

✓ GUIDED PRACTICE for Examples 2 and 3

Factor the trinomial.

4. $x^2 - 4x + 3$ **5.** $t^2 - 8t + 12$ **6.** $m^2 + m - 20$ **7.** $w^2 + 6w - 16$

EXAMPLE 4 Solve a polynomial equation

Solve the equation $x^2 + 3x = 18$.

$x^2 + 3x = 18$	**Write original equation.**
$x^2 + 3x - 18 = 0$	**Subtract 18 from each side.**
$(x + 6)(x - 3) = 0$	**Factor left side.**
$x + 6 = 0$ *or* $x - 3 = 0$	**Zero-product property**
$x = -6$ *or* $x = 3$	**Solve for *x*.**

▶ The solutions of the equation are −6 and 3.

GUIDED PRACTICE for Example 4

8. Solve the equation $s^2 - 2s = 24$.

EXAMPLE 5 Solve a multi-step problem

BANNER DIMENSIONS You are making banners to hang during school spirit week. Each banner requires 16.5 square feet of felt and will be cut as shown. Find the width of one banner.

ANOTHER WAY
For alternative methods for solving Example 5, see the **Problem Solving Workshop**.

Solution

STEP 1 **Draw** a diagram of two banners together.

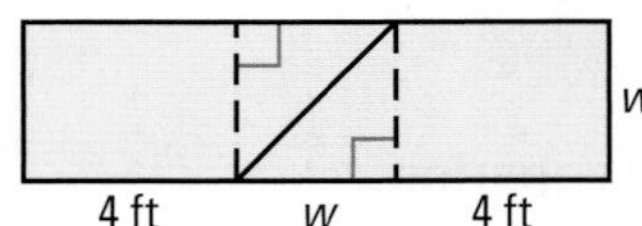

STEP 2 **Write** an equation using the fact that the area of 2 banners is $2(16.5) = 33$ square feet. Solve the equation for w.

$A = \ell \cdot w$	**Formula for area of a rectangle**
$33 = (4 + w + 4) \cdot w$	**Substitute 33 for *A* and $(4 + w + 4)$ for ℓ.**
$0 = w^2 + 8w - 33$	**Simplify and subtract 33 from each side.**
$0 = (w + 11)(w - 3)$	**Factor right side.**
$w + 11 = 0$ *or* $w - 3 = 0$	**Zero-product property**
$w = -11$ *or* $w = 3$	**Solve for *w*.**

▶ The banner cannot have a negative width, so the width is 3 feet.

GUIDED PRACTICE for Example 5

9. WHAT IF? In Example 5, suppose the area of a banner is to be 10 square feet. What is the width of one banner?

8.5 EXERCISES

HOMEWORK KEY

○ = See **WORKED-OUT SOLUTIONS** Exs. 7 and 61

★ = **STANDARDIZED TEST PRACTICE** Exs. 2, 29, 42, 61, 62, and 63

◆ = **MULTIPLE REPRESENTATIONS** Ex. 64

SKILL PRACTICE

1. **VOCABULARY** Copy and complete: The _?_ of $t^2 + 3t + 2$ are $t + 2$ and $t + 1$.

2. ★ **WRITING** If $x^2 - 8x + 12 = (x + p)(x + q)$, what are the signs of p and q? *Justify* your answer.

EXAMPLES 1, 2, and 3 for Exs. 3–19

FACTORING TRINOMIALS **Factor the trinomial.**

3. $x^2 + 4x + 3$
4. $a^2 + 6a + 8$
5. $b^2 - 17b + 72$
6. $s^2 - 10s + 16$
7. $z^2 + 8z - 48$
8. $w^2 + 18w + 56$
9. $y^2 - 7y - 18$
10. $n^2 - 9n + 14$
11. $x^2 + 3x - 70$
12. $f^2 + 4f - 32$
13. $m^2 - 7m - 120$
14. $d^2 - 20d + 99$
15. $p^2 + 20p + 64$
16. $x^2 + 6x - 72$
17. $c^2 + 15c + 44$

ERROR ANALYSIS ***Describe*** **and correct the error in factoring the trinomial.**

18. $s^2 - 17s - 60 = (s - 5)(s - 12)$

19. $m^2 - 10m + 24 = (m - 12)(m + 2)$

EXAMPLE 4 for Exs. 20–29

SOLVING EQUATIONS **Solve the equation.**

20. $x^2 - 10x + 21 = 0$
21. $n^2 - 7n - 30 = 0$
22. $w^2 - 15w + 44 = 0$
23. $a^2 + 5a = 50$
24. $r^2 + 2r = 24$
25. $t^2 + 9t = -20$
26. $y^2 - 2y - 8 = 7$
27. $m^2 + 22 = -23m$
28. $b^2 + 5 = 8b - 10$

29. ★ **MULTIPLE CHOICE** What are the solutions of the equation $x^2 - 8x = 240$?

(A) -20 and -12
(B) -20 and 12
(C) 20 and -12
(D) 12 and 20

FINDING ZEROS OF FUNCTIONS **Find the zeros of the polynomial function.**

30. $f(x) = x^2 + 11x + 18$
31. $g(x) = x^2 + 5x + 6$
32. $h(x) = x^2 - 18x + 32$
33. $f(x) = x^2 - 14x + 45$
34. $h(x) = x^2 - 5x - 24$
35. $g(x) = x^2 - 14x - 51$
36. $g(x) = x^2 + 10x - 39$
37. $f(x) = -x^2 + 16x - 28$
38. $f(x) = -x^2 + 24x + 180$

SOLVING EQUATIONS **Solve the equation.**

39. $s(s + 1) = 72$
40. $x^2 - 10(x - 1) = -11$
41. $q(q + 19) = -34$

42. ★ **SHORT RESPONSE** Write an equation of the form $x^2 + bx + c = 0$ that has the solutions -4 and 6. *Explain* how you found your answer.

GEOMETRY Find the dimensions of the rectangle or triangle that has the given area.

43. Area: 100 square inches

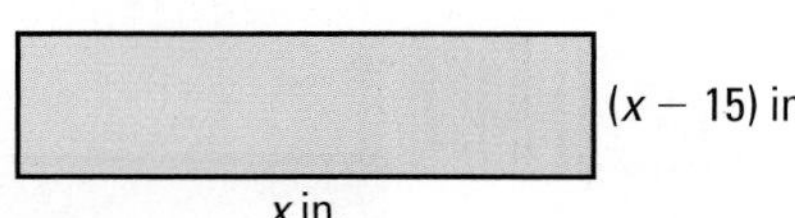

44. Area: 34 square meters

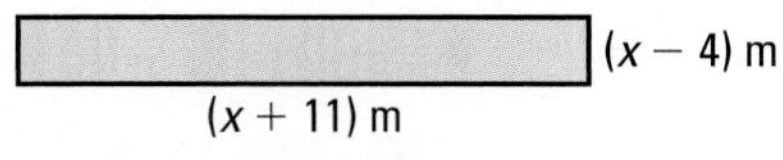

HINT In Ex. 45, convert the given area to square yards. Use the conversion factor $\frac{1 \text{ yd}^2}{9 \text{ ft}^2}$.

45. Area: 702 square feet

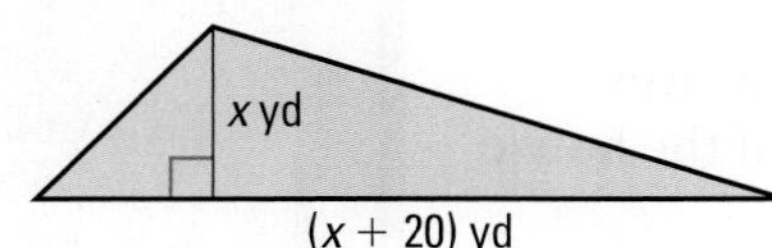

46. Area: 119 square feet

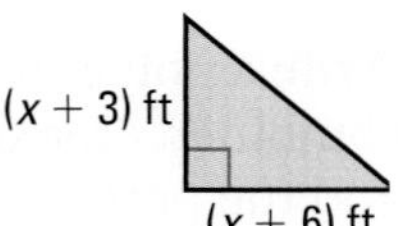

FACTORING TRINOMIALS In Exercises 47–55, use the example below to factor the trinomial.

EXAMPLE **Factor a trinomial in two variables**

Factor $x^2 + 9xy + 14y^2$.

Solution

To factor the trinomial, you must find factors of the form $x + py$ and $x + qy$.

First, consider the signs of the factors needed. In this example, b is 9, and c is 14. Because both b and c are positive, you must find two positive factors of 14 that have a sum of 9.

Factors of 14	Sum of factors	
14, 1	14 + 1 = 15	✗
7, 2	7 + 2 = 9	← Correct sum

The factors 7 and 2 have a sum of 9, so 7 and 2 are the correct values of p and q.

▸ $x^2 + 9xy + 14y^2 = (x + 7y)(x + 2y)$

47. $x^2 - 4xy + 4y^2$
48. $y^2 - 6yz + 5z^2$
49. $c^2 + 13cd + 36d^2$
50. $r^2 + 15rs + 50s^2$
51. $a^2 + 2ab - 15b^2$
52. $x^2 + 8xy - 65y^2$
53. $m^2 - mn - 42n^2$
54. $u^2 - 3uv - 108v^2$
55. $g^2 + 4gh - 60h^2$

CHALLENGE Find all integer values of b for which the trinomial has factors of the form $x + p$ and $x + q$ where p and q are integers.

56. $x^2 + bx + 15$
57. $x^2 - bx + 21$
58. $x^2 + bx - 42$

PROBLEM SOLVING

EXAMPLE 5
for Exs. 59–61

59. **CARD DESIGN** You are designing a gift card that has a border along one side, as shown. The area of the white part of the card is 30 square centimeters. What is the area of the border?

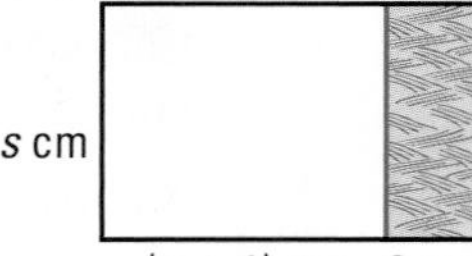

60. **CONSTRUCTION** A contractor is building a porch along two sides of a house. The house is rectangular with a width of 32 feet and a length of 50 feet. The porch will have the same width on each side of the house.

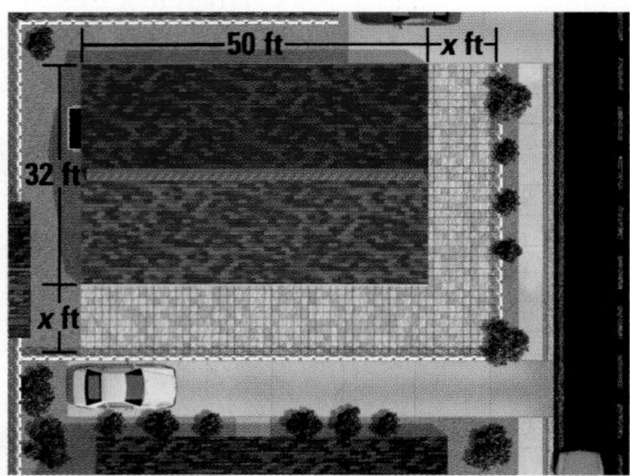

   a. Write a polynomial that represents the combined area of the first floor of the house and the porch.

   b. The owners want the combined area of the first floor and the porch to be 2320 square feet. How wide should the contractor build the porch?

61. ★ **SHORT RESPONSE** You trimmed a large square picture so that you could fit it into a frame. You trimmed 6 inches from the length and 5 inches from the width. The area of the resulting picture is 20 square inches. What was the perimeter of the original large square picture? *Explain* how you found your answer.

62. ★ **EXTENDED RESPONSE** A town has a rectangular park. The parks department is planning to install two brick paths that will intersect at right angles. One path will be 130 feet long, and the other path will be 500 feet long. The paths will have the same width.

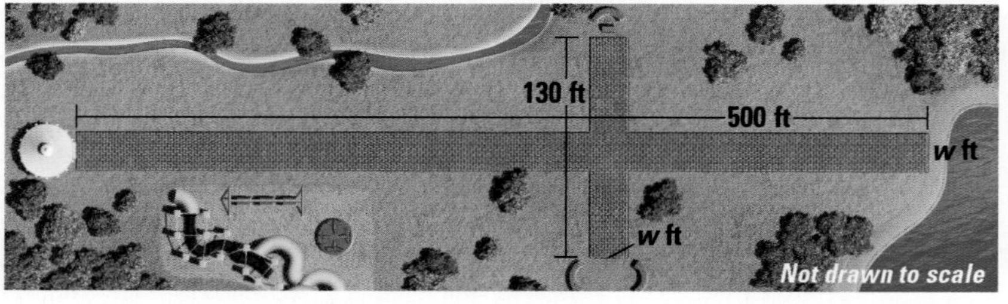

HINT
Add the path areas, but subtract the overlap, so that it is not counted twice.

   a. Write a polynomial that represents the combined area of the two paths.

   b. The parks department can afford brick for 3125 square feet of path. Write and solve an equation to find the width of the paths.

   c. In part (b) you used one solution of the equation to find your answer. *Explain* how you chose which solution to use.

○ = See **WORKED-OUT SOLUTIONS** in Student Resources ★ = **STANDARDIZED TEST PRACTICE** ◆ = **MULTIPLE REPRESENTATIONS**

63. ★ **MULTIPLE CHOICE** A square quilt has a border that is 1 foot wide on each side. The quilt has an area of 25 square feet. What is the side length of the quilt without the border?

Ⓐ 2 feet Ⓑ 3 feet Ⓒ 4 feet Ⓓ 5 feet

64. **MULTIPLE REPRESENTATIONS** You toss a set of keys to a friend who is standing at a window 20 feet above the ground in a building that is 5 feet away from where you are standing. The path of the keys can be modeled by the graph of the equation $y = -x^2 + 8x + 5$ where x and y are measured in feet. On a coordinate plane, the ground is represented by the x-axis, and you are standing at the origin.

a. **Making a Table** Make a table of values that shows the height of the keys for $x = 2, 4, 6,$ and 8 feet.

b. **Drawing a Graph** Plot the ordered pairs in the table as points in a coordinate plane. Connect the points with a smooth curve.

c. **Interpreting a Graph** Based on your graph, do you expect the keys to reach your friend? *Explain* your answer.

d. **Using an Equation** Find the value of x when $y = 20$. (You may need to factor out a -1 in order to factor the trinomial.) What do you notice? *Explain* how the x-value justifies your answer from part (c).

65. **CHALLENGE** A rectangular stage is positioned in the center of a rectangular room, as shown. The area of the stage is 120 square feet.

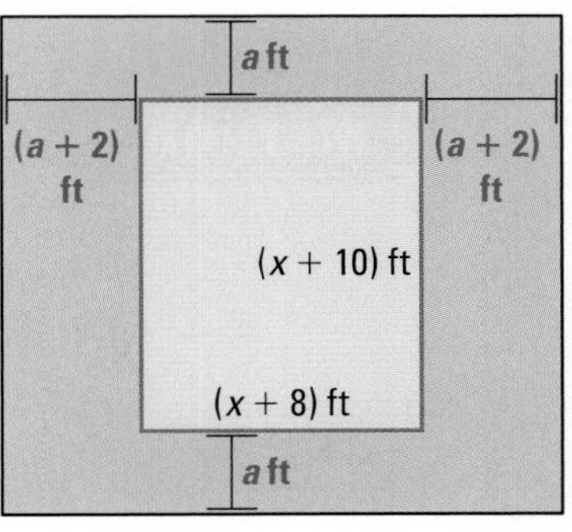

a. Use the dimensions given in the diagram to find the length and width of the stage.

b. The combined area of the stage and the surrounding floor is 360 square feet. Find the length and width of the room.

PROBLEM SOLVING WORKSHOP LESSON 8.5

Using ALTERNATIVE METHODS

Another Way to Solve Example 5

Make sense of problems and persevere in solving them.

MULTIPLE REPRESENTATIONS In Example 5, you saw how to solve the problem about a school banner by solving an equation. You can also solve the problem using a table or a graph.

PROBLEM

BANNER DIMENSIONS You are making banners to hang during school spirit week. Each banner requires 16.5 square feet of felt and will be cut as shown. Find the width of one banner.

METHOD 1

Using a Table Consider the separate geometric figures that form one banner and find their areas in terms of w. Then find the total area of the banner for different values of w until you find a value that gives a total area of 16.5 square feet. Use a table to organize your work.

STEP 1 **Write** equations for the area of the pieces and the total area.

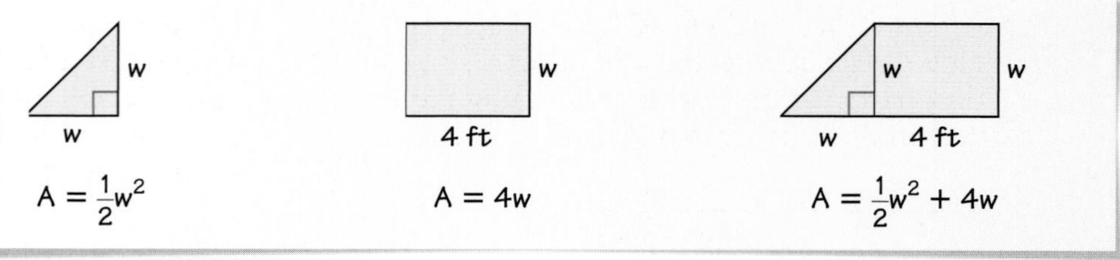

STEP 2 **Organize** your work in a table.

w	Triangle's area $\left(\frac{1}{2}w^2\right)$	Rectangle's area $(4w)$	Total area $\left(\frac{1}{2}w^2 + 4w\right)$	
1	0.5	4	4.5	← **4.5 < 16.5, so try a greater value of w.**
2	2	8	10	← **10 < 16.5, so try a greater value of w.**
3	4.5	12	16.5	← **Correct area**

▶ The width of the banner is 3 feet.

METHOD 2

Using a Graph Another approach is to use a graph.

STEP 1 **Write** an equation for the area of the banner. The area of the banner can be thought of as the area of a triangle plus the area of a rectangle.

Area of banner = Area of triangle + Area of rectangle

$$A = \frac{1}{2}w^2 + 4w$$

STEP 2 **Graph** the equation for the area of the banner using a graphing calculator. Graph $y_1 = 0.5x^2 + 4x$. Because you are looking for the value of x that gives an area of 16.5 square feet, you should display the graph of $y_2 = 16.5$ in the same viewing window.

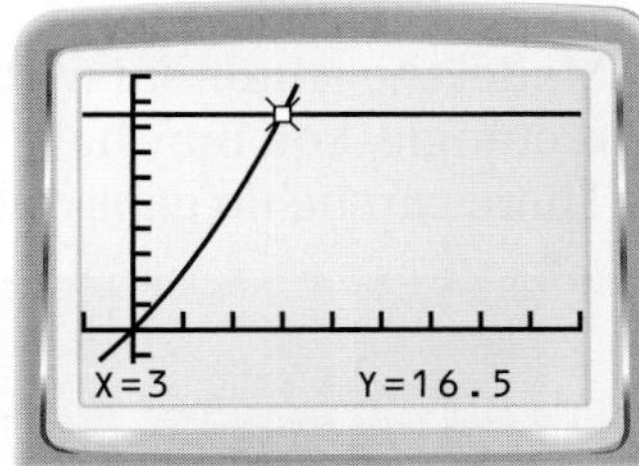

STEP 3 **Find** the intersection of the graphs by using the *intersect* feature on your calculator. The graphs intersect at (3, 16.5).

▶ The width of the banner is 3 feet.

PRACTICE

1. **COUNTER DESIGN** A contractor is building a counter in a kitchen using the diagram shown. The countertop will have an area of 12 square feet. How wide should it be? Solve this problem using two different methods.

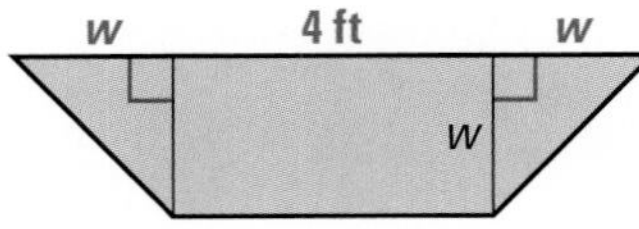

2. **ERROR ANALYSIS** *Describe* and correct the error in using an equation to solve the problem in Exercise 1.

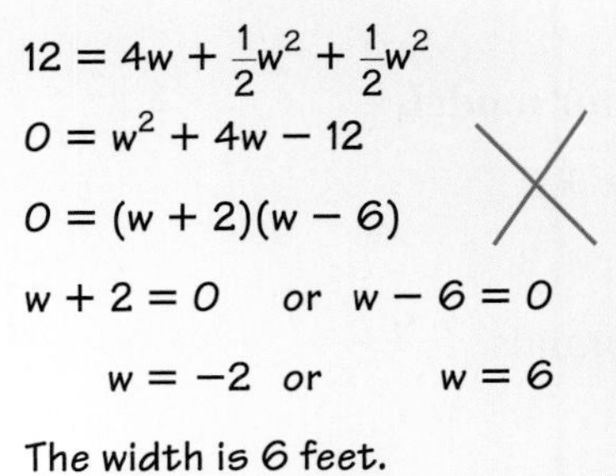

$12 = 4w + \frac{1}{2}w^2 + \frac{1}{2}w^2$

$0 = w^2 + 4w - 12$

$0 = (w + 2)(w - 6)$

$w + 2 = 0$ or $w - 6 = 0$

$w = -2$ or $w = 6$

The width is 6 feet.

3. **FOUNTAIN DESIGN** A square fountain in a city plaza is surrounded by brick patios as shown. The combined area of the fountain and brick patios is 205 square feet. What is the side length of the fountain? Solve this problem using two different methods.

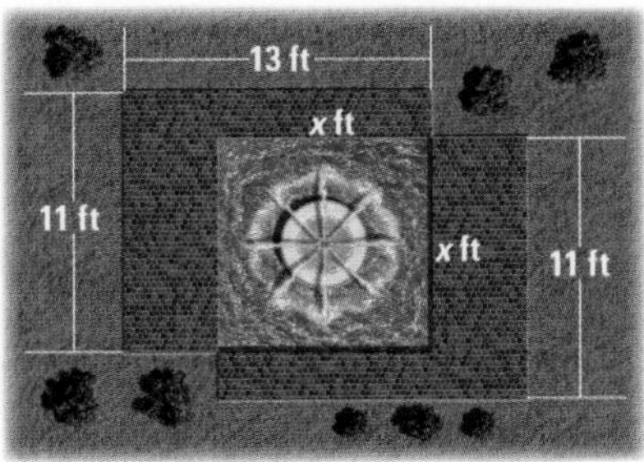

4. **WHAT IF?** You want to make a larger banner using the same pattern shown in the problem. The new banner will have an area of 24 square feet. Find the width of the new banner. *Describe* the method you used to find your answer.

More Factorization with Algebra Tiles

MATHEMATICAL PRACTICES

Use appropriate tools strategically.

MATERIALS • algebra tiles

QUESTION How can you factor a trinomial using algebra tiles?

EXPLORE Factor the trinomial $2x^2 + 7x + 3$

STEP 1 ***Make a rectangle***

Model the trinomial with algebra tiles. Arrange all of the tiles to form a rectangle. You may have to try a few arrangements to make the rectangle. There can be no gaps or leftover tiles.

STEP 2 ***Find the side lengths***

The side lengths of the rectangle represent the polynomials $x + 3$ and $2x + 1$. So $2x^2 + 7x + 3 = (x + 3)(2x + 1)$.

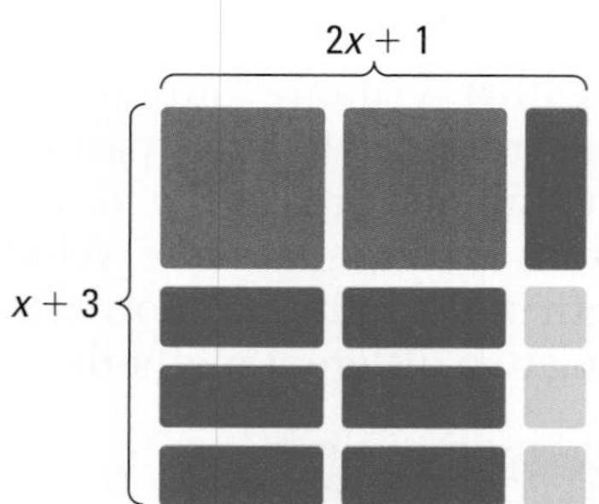

DRAW CONCLUSIONS Use your observations to complete these exercises

1. Use multiplication to show that $x + 3$ and $2x + 1$ are factors of the polynomial $2x^2 + 7x + 3$.

Use algebra tiles to factor the trinomial. Include a drawing of your model.

2. $2x^2 + 5x + 3$
3. $3x^2 + 5x + 2$
4. $4x^2 + 9x + 2$
5. $3x^2 + 13x + 4$
6. $4x^2 + 11x + 6$
7. $4x^2 + 8x + 3$
8. **REASONING** Factor the trinomial $2x^2 + 11x + 5$ into two binomials. How is the leading coefficient of the trinomial related to the leading coefficients of its binomial factors?

8.6 Factor $ax^2 + bx + c$

Before You factored trinomials of the form $x^2 + bx + c$.

Now You will factor trinomials of the form $ax^2 + bx + c$.

Why? So you can find the dimensions of a building, as in Ex. 61.

Key Vocabulary
- **trinomial**

CC.9-12.A.SSE.3a Factor a quadratic expression to reveal the zeros of the function it defines.

REVIEW FACTORING
You may want to review determining the signs of the factors of a trinomial.

When factoring a trinomial of the form $ax^2 + bx + c$, first consider the signs of b and c, as shown below. This approach works when a is positive.

EXAMPLE 1 Factor when *b* is negative and *c* is positive

Factor $2x^2 - 7x + 3$.

Solution

Because b is negative and c is positive, both factors of c must be negative. Make a table to organize your work.

You must consider the order of the factors of 3, because the x-terms of the possible factorizations are different.

Factors of 2	Factors of 3	Possible factorization	Middle term when multiplied	
1, 2	−1, −3	$(x - 1)(2x - 3)$	$-3x - 2x = -5x$	✗
1, 2	−3, −1	$(x - 3)(2x - 1)$	$-x - 6x = -7x$	← Correct

▸ $2x^2 - 7x + 3 = (x - 3)(2x - 1)$

EXAMPLE 2 Factor when *b* is positive and *c* is negative

Factor $3n^2 + 14n - 5$.

Solution

Because b is positive and c is negative, the factors of c have different signs.

Factors of 3	Factors of −5	Possible factorization	Middle term when multiplied	
1, 3	1, −5	$(n + 1)(3n - 5)$	$-5n + 3n = -2n$	✗
1, 3	−1, 5	$(n - 1)(3n + 5)$	$5n - 3n = 2n$	✗
1, 3	5, −1	$(n + 5)(3n - 1)$	$-n + 15n = 14n$	← Correct
1, 3	−5, 1	$(n - 5)(3n + 1)$	$n - 15n = -14n$	✗

▸ $3n^2 + 14n - 5 = (n + 5)(3n - 1)$

✓ GUIDED PRACTICE for Examples 1 and 2

Factor the trinomial.

1. $3t^2 + 8t + 4$ **2.** $4s^2 - 9s + 5$ **3.** $2h^2 + 13h - 7$

FACTORING WHEN *a* IS NEGATIVE To factor a trinomial of the form $ax^2 + bx + c$ when a is negative, first factor -1 from each term of the trinomial. Then factor the resulting trinomial as in the previous examples.

EXAMPLE 3 Factor when *a* is negative

Factor $-4x^2 + 12x + 7$.

Solution

STEP 1 **Factor** -1 from each term of the trinomial.

$$-4x^2 + 12x + 7 = -(4x^2 - 12x - 7)$$

STEP 2 **Factor** the trinomial $4x^2 - 12x - 7$. Because b and c are both negative, the factors of c must have different signs. As in the previous examples, use a table to organize information about the factors of a and c.

Factors of 4	Factors of −7	Possible factorization	Middle term when multiplied	
1, 4	1, −7	$(x + 1)(4x - 7)$	$-7x + 4x = -3x$	✗
1, 4	7, −1	$(x + 7)(4x - 1)$	$-x + 28x = 27x$	✗
1, 4	−1, 7	$(x - 1)(4x + 7)$	$7x - 4x = 3x$	✗
1, 4	−7, 1	$(x - 7)(4x + 1)$	$x - 28x = -27x$	✗
2, 2	1, −7	$(2x + 1)(2x - 7)$	$-14x + 2x = -12x$	← Correct
2, 2	−1, 7	$(2x - 1)(2x + 7)$	$14x - 2x = 12x$	✗

AVOID ERRORS
Remember to include the −1 that you factored out in Step 1.

▶ $-4x^2 + 12x + 7 = -(2x + 1)(2x - 7)$

CHECK You can check your factorization using a graphing calculator. Graph $y_1 = -4x^2 + 12x + 7$ and $y_2 = -(2x + 1)(2x - 7)$. Because the graphs coincide, you know that your factorization is correct.

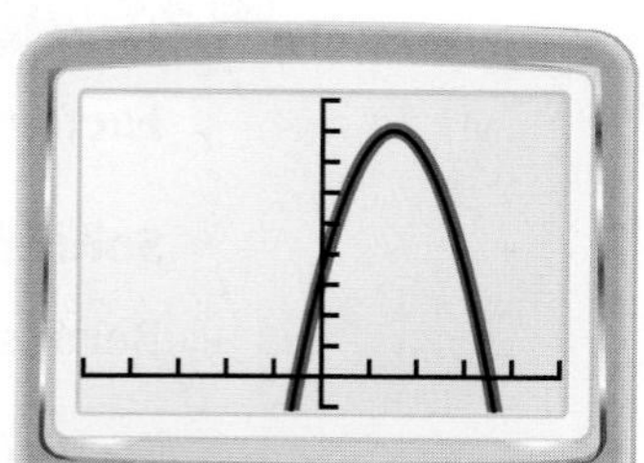

✓ GUIDED PRACTICE for Example 3

Factor the trinomial.

4. $-2y^2 - 5y - 3$ **5.** $-5m^2 + 6m - 1$ **6.** $-3x^2 - x + 2$

FINDING A COMMON FACTOR You have learned to factor out the greatest common monomial factor from the terms of a polynomial. Sometimes you may need to do this before finding two binomial factors of a trinomial.

EXAMPLE 4 Write and solve a polynomial equation

DISCUS An athlete throws a discus from an initial height of 6 feet and with an initial vertical velocity of 46 feet per second.

a. Write an equation that gives the height (in feet) of the discus as a function of the time (in seconds) since it left the athlete's hand.

b. After how many seconds does the discus hit the ground?

Solution

USE VERTICAL MOTION MODEL
You may want to review using the vertical motion model.

a. Use the vertical motion model to write an equation for the height h (in feet) of the discus. In this case, $v = 46$ and $s = 6$.

$h = -16t^2 + vt + s$	**Vertical motion model**
$h = -16t^2 + 46t + 6$	**Substitute 46 for *v* and 6 for *s*.**

b. To find the number of seconds that pass before the discus lands, find the value of t for which the height of the discus is 0. Substitute 0 for h and solve the equation for t.

$0 = -16t^2 + 46t + 6$	**Substitute 0 for *h*.**
$0 = -2(8t^2 - 23t - 3)$	**Factor out −2.**
$0 = -2(8t + 1)(t - 3)$	**Factor the trinomial. Find factors of 8 and −3 that produce a middle term with a coefficient of −23.**
$8t + 1 = 0 \quad or \; t - 3 = 0$	**Zero-product property**
$t = -\frac{1}{8} \quad or \quad t = 3$	**Solve for *t*.**

The solutions of the equation are $-\frac{1}{8}$ and 3. A negative solution does not make sense in this situation, so disregard $-\frac{1}{8}$.

▶ The discus hits the ground after 3 seconds.

✓ GUIDED PRACTICE for Example 4

7. **WHAT IF?** In Example 4, suppose another athlete throws the discus with an initial vertical velocity of 38 feet per second and releases it from a height of 5 feet. After how many seconds does the discus hit the ground?

8. **SHOT PUT** In a shot put event, an athlete throws the shot put from an initial height of 6 feet and with an initial vertical velocity of 29 feet per second. After how many seconds does the shot put hit the ground?

★ EXAMPLE 5 Standardized Test Practice

A rectangle's length is 13 meters more than 3 times its width. The area is 10 square meters. What is the width?

Ⓐ $\frac{2}{3}$ m Ⓑ 3 m Ⓒ 5 m Ⓓ 10 m

$w(3w + 13) = 10$	**Write an equation to model area.**
$3w^2 + 13w - 10 = 0$	**Simplify and subtract 10 from each side.**
$(w + 5)(3w - 2) = 0$	**Factor left side.**
$w + 5 = 0$ *or* $3w - 2 = 0$	**Zero-product property**
$w = -5$ *or* $w = \frac{2}{3}$	**Solve for *w*.**

Reject the negative width.

▶ The correct answer is A. Ⓐ Ⓑ Ⓒ Ⓓ

GUIDED PRACTICE for Example 5

9. A rectangle's length is 1 inch more than twice its width. The area is 6 square inches. What is the width?

Ⓐ $\frac{1}{2}$ in. Ⓑ $\frac{3}{2}$ in. Ⓒ 2 in. Ⓓ $\frac{5}{2}$ in.

8.6 EXERCISES

HOMEWORK KEY

○ = See WORKED-OUT SOLUTIONS Exs. 5, 25, and 61

★ = STANDARDIZED TEST PRACTICE Exs. 2, 3, 22, 41, 51, and 60

◆ = MULTIPLE REPRESENTATIONS Ex. 62

SKILL PRACTICE

1. VOCABULARY What is another word for the solutions of $x^2 + 2x + 1 = 0$?

2. ★ WRITING *Explain* how you can use a graph to check a factorization.

3. ★ WRITING *Compare* factoring $6x^2 - x - 2$ with factoring $x^2 - x - 2$.

EXAMPLES 1, 2, and 3 for Exs. 4–22

FACTORING TRINOMIALS Factor the trinomial.

4. $-x^2 + x + 20$	**5.** $-y^2 + 2y + 8$	**6.** $-a^2 + 12a - 27$
7. $5w^2 - 6w + 1$	**8.** $-3p^2 - 10p - 3$	**9.** $6s^2 - s - 5$
10. $2t^2 + 5t - 63$	**11.** $2c^2 - 7c + 3$	**12.** $3n^2 - 17n + 10$
13. $-2h^2 + 5h + 3$	**14.** $-6k^2 - 13k - 6$	**15.** $10x^2 - 3x - 27$
16. $4m^2 + 9m + 5$	**17.** $3z^2 + z - 14$	**18.** $4a^2 + 9a - 9$
19. $4n^2 + 16n + 15$	**20.** $-5b^2 + 7b - 2$	**21.** $6y^2 - 5y - 4$

22. ★ **MULTIPLE CHOICE** What is the correct factorization of $8x^2 - 10x + 3$?

Ⓐ $(2x - 3)(4x - 1)$ Ⓑ $(2x - 1)(4x - 3)$

Ⓒ $(4x + 1)(2x - 3)$ Ⓓ $(8x - 3)(x - 1)$

EXAMPLES 4 and 5 for Exs. 23–39

SOLVING EQUATIONS **Solve the equation.**

23. $2x^2 - 3x - 35 = 0$
24. $3w^2 + 22w + 7 = 0$
25. $4s^2 + 11s - 3 = 0$
26. $7a^2 + 2a = 5$
27. $8t^2 - 2t = 3$
28. $6m^2 - 5m = 14$
29. $b(20b - 3) - 2 = 0$
30. $4(3y^2 - 7y + 4) = 1$
31. $p(3p + 14) = 5$
32. $4n^2 - 2n - 90 = 0$
33. $10c^2 - 14c + 4 = 0$
34. $-16k^2 + 8k + 24 = 0$
35. $6r^2 - 15r = 99$
36. $56z^2 + 2 = 22z$
37. $30x^2 + 25x = 20$

ERROR ANALYSIS ***Describe*** **and correct the error in solving the equation.**

38.

$5x^2 + x = 4$

$x(5x + 1) = 4$

$x = 4$ *or* $5x + 1 = 4$

$x = 4$ *or* $x = \frac{3}{5}$

39.

$12x^2 + 5x - 2 = 0$

$(3x - 1)(4x + 2) = 0$

$3x - 1 = 0$ *or* $4x + 2 = 0$

$x = \frac{1}{3}$ *or* $x = -\frac{1}{2}$

40. **GEOMETRY** The length of a rectangle is 7 inches more than 5 times its width. The area of the rectangle is 6 square inches. What is the width?

41. ★ **SHORT RESPONSE** The length of a rectangle is 1 inch more than 4 times its width. The area of the rectangle is 3 square inches. What is the perimeter of the rectangle? *Explain* how you found your answer.

FINDING ZEROS OF FUNCTIONS **Find the zeros of the polynomial function.**

42. $g(x) = 2x^2 + x - 1$
43. $f(x) = -x^2 + 12x - 35$
44. $h(x) = -3x^2 + 2x + 5$
45. $f(x) = 3x^2 + x - 14$
46. $g(x) = 8x^2 - 6x - 14$
47. $f(x) = 12x^2 - 24x - 63$

SOLVING EQUATIONS **Multiply each side of the equation by an appropriate power of 10 to obtain integer coefficients. Then solve the equation.**

48. $0.3x^2 - 0.7x - 4.0 = 0$
49. $0.8x^2 - 1.8x - 0.5 = 0$
50. $0.4x^2 - 0.4x = 9.9$

51. ★ **MULTIPLE CHOICE** What are the solutions of the equation $0.4x^2 - 1.1x = 2$?

Ⓐ -12.5 and 40 Ⓑ -4 and 1.25 Ⓒ -1.25 and 4 Ⓓ -0.125 and 0.4

WRITING EQUATIONS **Write a polynomial equation that has the given solutions. The equation must have integer coefficients.** ***Explain*** **your reasoning.**

52. -3 and 2
53. $-\frac{1}{2}$ and 5
54. $-\frac{3}{4}$ and $-\frac{1}{3}$

CHALLENGE **Factor the trinomial.**

55. $2x^2 - 11xy + 5y^2$
56. $3x^2 + 2xy - 8y^2$
57. $6x^3 - 10x^2y - 56xy^2$

PROBLEM SOLVING

EXAMPLE 4 for Exs. 58, 60

58. **DIVING** A diver dives from a cliff when her center of gravity is 46 feet above the surface of the water. Her initial vertical velocity leaving the cliff is 9 feet per second. After how many seconds does her center of gravity enter the water?

EXAMPLE 5 for Exs. 59, 61

59. **SCRAPBOOK DESIGN** You plan to make a scrapbook. On the cover, you want to show three pictures with space between them, as shown. Each of the pictures is twice as long as it is wide.

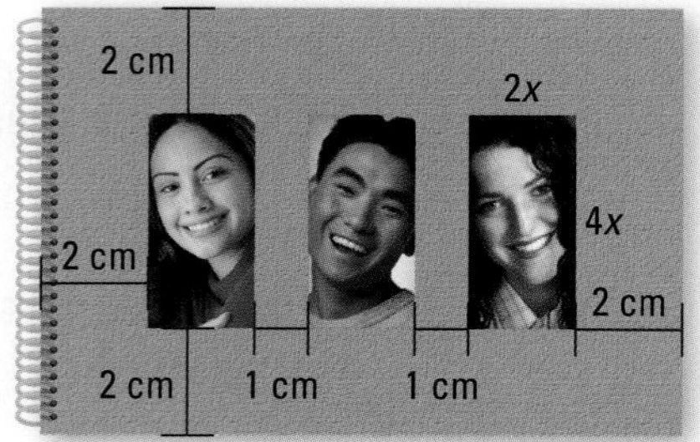

   a. Write a polynomial that represents the area of the scrapbook cover.

   b. The area of the cover will be 96 square centimeters. Find the length and width of the pictures you will use.

60. ★ **SHORT RESPONSE** You throw a ball into the air with an initial vertical velocity of 31 feet per second. The ball leaves your hand when it is 6 feet above the ground. You catch the ball when it reaches a height of 4 feet. After how many seconds do you catch the ball? *Explain* how you can use the solutions of an equation to find your answer.

61. **PARTHENON** The Parthenon in Athens, Greece, is an ancient structure that has a rectangular base. The length of the Parthenon's base is 8 meters more than twice its width. The area of the base is about 2170 square meters. Find the length and width of the Parthenon's base.

62. ◆ **MULTIPLE REPRESENTATIONS** An African cat called a serval leaps from the ground in an attempt to catch a bird. The serval's initial vertical velocity is 24 feet per second.

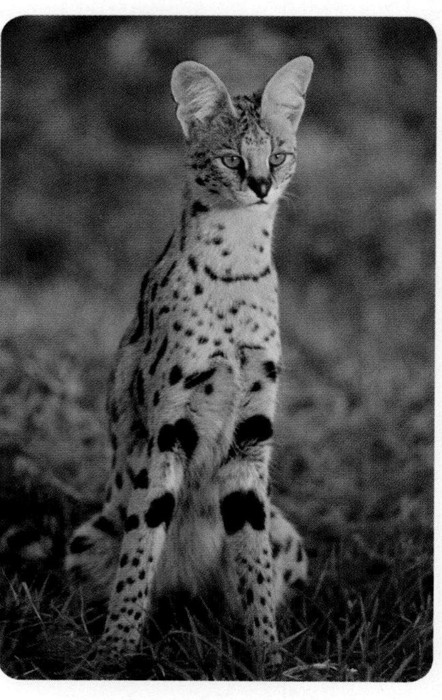

   a. **Writing an Equation** Write an equation that gives the serval's height (in feet) as a function of the time (in seconds) since it left the ground.

   b. **Making a Table** Use the equation from part (a) to make a table that shows the height of the serval for $t = 0, 0.3, 0.6, 0.9, 1.2$, and 1.5 seconds.

   c. **Drawing a Graph** Plot the ordered pairs in the table as points in a coordinate plane. Connect the points with a smooth curve. After how many seconds does the serval reach a height of 9 feet? *Justify* your answer using the equation from part (a).

   Animated **Algebra** at my.hrw.com

63. **CHALLENGE** A bush cricket jumps from the ground into the air with an initial vertical velocity of 4 feet per second.

a. Write an equation that gives the cricket's height (in feet) as a function of the time (in seconds) since it left the ground.

b. After how many seconds is the cricket 3 inches off the ground?

c. Does the cricket jump higher than 3 inches? *Explain* your reasoning using your answer from part (b).

QUIZ

Factor out the greatest common monomial factor.

1. $16a^2 - 40b$
2. $9xy^2 + 6x^2y$
3. $4n^4 - 22n^3 - 8n^2$
4. $3x^2 + 6xy - 3y^2$
5. $12abc^2 - 6a^2c$
6. $-36s^3 + 18s^2 - 54s$

Factor the trinomial.

7. $r^2 + 15r + 56$
8. $s^2 - 6s + 5$
9. $w^2 + 6w - 40$
10. $-a^2 + 9a + 22$
11. $2x^2 - 9x + 4$
12. $5m^2 + m - 6$
13. $6h^2 - 19h + 3$
14. $-7y^2 - 23y - 6$
15. $18c^2 + 12c - 6$

Solve the equation.

16. $(4p - 7)(p + 5) = 0$
17. $-8u^2 + 28u = 0$
18. $51x^2 = -17x$
19. $b^2 - 11b = -24$
20. $m^2 + 12m = -35$
21. $q^2 + 19 = -20q$
22. $3t^2 - 11t + 10 = 0$
23. $4y^2 + 31y = 8$
24. $14s^2 + 12s = 2$

25. **BASEBALL** A baseball player hits a baseball into the air with an initial vertical velocity of 72 feet per second. The player hits the ball from a height of 3 feet.

a. Write an equation that gives the baseball's height as a function of the time (in seconds) after it is hit.

b. After how many seconds is the baseball 84 feet above the ground?

8.7 Factor Special Products

Before You factored polynomials of the form $ax^2 + bx + c$.

Now You will factor special products.

Why? So you can use a scientific model, as in Ex. 48.

Key Vocabulary
- **perfect square trinomial**

CC.9-12.A.SSE.2 Use the struture of an expression to identify ways to rewrite it.

You can use the special product patterns you have learned to factor polynomials, such as the difference of two squares.

KEY CONCEPT *For Your Notebook*

Difference of Two Squares Pattern

Algebra	Example
$a^2 - b^2 = (a + b)(a - b)$	$4x^2 - 9 = (2x)^2 - 3^2 = (2x + 3)(2x - 3)$

EXAMPLE 1 Factor the difference of two squares

Factor the polynomial.

a. $y^2 - 16 = y^2 - 4^2$ — Write as $a^2 - b^2$.

$= (y + 4)(y - 4)$ — Difference of two squares pattern

b. $25m^2 - 36 = (5m)^2 - 6^2$ — Write as $a^2 - b^2$.

$= (5m + 6)(5m - 6)$ — Difference of two squares pattern

c. $x^2 - 49y^2 = x^2 - (7y)^2$ — Write as $a^2 - b^2$.

$= (x + 7y)(x - 7y)$ — Difference of two squares pattern

EXAMPLE 2 Factor the difference of two squares

Factor the polynomial $8 - 18n^2$.

$8 - 18n^2 = 2(4 - 9n^2)$ — Factor out common factor.

$= 2[2^2 - (3n)^2]$ — Write $4 - 9n^2$ as $a^2 - b^2$.

$= 2(2 + 3n)(2 - 3n)$ — Difference of two squares pattern

✓ **GUIDED PRACTICE** for Examples 1 and 2

1. Factor the polynomial $4y^2 - 64$.

PERFECT SQUARE TRINOMIALS The pattern for finding the square of a binomial gives you the pattern for factoring trinomials of the form $a^2 + 2ab + b^2$ and $a^2 - 2ab + b^2$. These are called **perfect square trinomials**.

KEY CONCEPT *For Your Notebook*

Perfect Square Trinomial Pattern

Algebra	Example
$a^2 + 2ab + b^2 = (a + b)^2$	$x^2 + 6x + 9 = x^2 + 2(x \cdot 3) + 3^2 = (x + 3)^2$
$a^2 - 2ab + b^2 = (a - b)^2$	$x^2 - 10x + 25 = x^2 - 2(x \cdot 5) + 5^2 = (x - 5)^2$

EXAMPLE 3 Factor perfect square trinomials

Factor the polynomial.

a. $n^2 - 12n + 36 = n^2 - 2(n \cdot 6) + 6^2$ — Write as $a^2 - 2ab + b^2$.

$= (n - 6)^2$ — Perfect square trinomial pattern

b. $9x^2 - 12x + 4 = (3x)^2 - 2(3x \cdot 2) + 2^2$ — Write as $a^2 - 2ab + b^2$.

$= (3x - 2)^2$ — Perfect square trinomial pattern

c. $4s^2 + 4st + t^2 = (2s)^2 + 2(2s \cdot t) + t^2$ — Write as $a^2 + 2ab + b^2$.

$= (2s + t)^2$ — Perfect square trinomial pattern

Animated Algebra at my.hrw.com

EXAMPLE 4 Factor a perfect square trinomial

Factor the polynomial $-3y^2 + 36y - 108$.

$-3y^2 + 36y - 108 = -3(y^2 - 12y + 36)$ — Factor out −3.

$= -3[y^2 - 2(y \cdot 6) + 6^2]$ — Write $y^2 - 12y + 36$ as $a^2 - 2ab + b^2$.

$= -3(y - 6)^2$ — Perfect square trinomial pattern

CHECK Check your factorization using a graphing calculator. Graph $y_1 = -3x^2 + 36x - 108$ and $y_2 = -3(x - 6)^2$. Because the graphs coincide, you know that your factorization is correct.

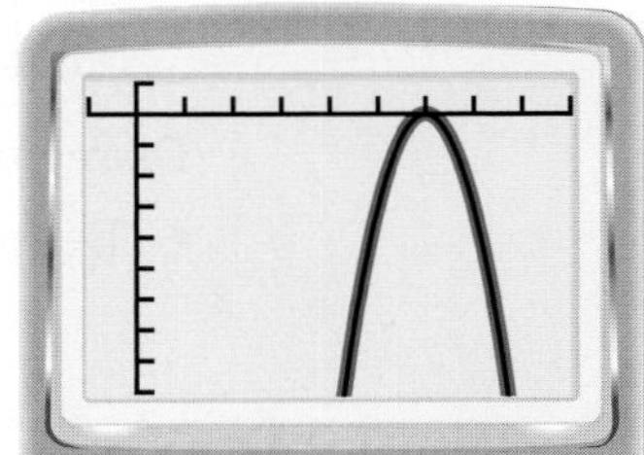

 **GUIDED PRACTICE** for Examples 3 and 4

Factor the polynomial.

2. $h^2 + 4h + 4$

3. $2y^2 - 20y + 50$

4. $3x^2 + 6xy + 3y^2$

EXAMPLE 5 Solve a polynomial equation

Solve the equation $x^2 + \frac{2}{3}x + \frac{1}{9} = 0$.

$x^2 + \frac{2}{3}x + \frac{1}{9} = 0$	**Write original equation.**
$9x^2 + 6x + 1 = 0$	**Multiply each side by 9.**
$(3x)^2 + 2(3x \cdot 1) + (1)^2 = 0$	**Write left side as $a^2 + 2ab + b^2$.**
$(3x + 1)^2 = 0$	**Perfect square trinomial pattern**
$3x + 1 = 0$	**Zero-product property**
$x = -\frac{1}{3}$	**Solve for x.**

FIND SOLUTIONS
This equation has two identical solutions, because it has two identical factors.

▶ The solution of the equation is $-\frac{1}{3}$.

EXAMPLE 6 Solve a vertical motion problem

FALLING OBJECT A window washer drops a wet sponge from a height of 64 feet. After how many seconds does the sponge land on the ground?

Solution

Use the vertical motion model to write an equation for the height h (in feet) of the sponge as a function of the time t (in seconds) after it is dropped.

The sponge was dropped, so it has no initial vertical velocity. Find the value of t for which the height is 0.

$h = -16t^2 + vt + s$	**Vertical motion model**
$0 = -16t^2 + (0)t + 64$	**Substitute 0 for h, 0 for v, and 64 for s.**
$0 = -16(t^2 - 4)$	**Factor out −16.**
$0 = -16(t - 2)(t + 2)$	**Difference of two squares pattern**
$t - 2 = 0$ *or* $t + 2 = 0$	**Zero-product property**
$t = 2$ *or* $t = -2$	**Solve for t.**

Disregard the negative solution of the equation.

▶ The sponge lands on the ground 2 seconds after it is dropped.

✓ GUIDED PRACTICE for Examples 5 and 6

Solve the equation.

5. $a^2 + 6a + 9 = 0$ **6.** $w^2 - 14w + 49 = 0$ **7.** $n^2 - 81 = 0$

8. **WHAT IF?** In Example 6, suppose the sponge is dropped from a height of 16 feet. After how many seconds does it land on the ground?

8.7 EXERCISES

HOMEWORK KEY

○ = See WORKED-OUT SOLUTIONS Exs. 11 and 49

★ = STANDARDIZED TEST PRACTICE Exs. 2, 23, 24, 49, and 50

SKILL PRACTICE

1. **VOCABULARY** Copy and complete: The polynomial $9n^2 + 6n + 1$ is called a(n) _?_ trinomial.

2. ★ **WRITING** *Explain* how to factor the difference of two squares.

EXAMPLES 1 and 2 for Exs. 3–8

DIFFERENCE OF TWO SQUARES Factor the polynomial.

3. $x^2 - 25$
4. $n^2 - 64$
5. $81c^2 - 4$
6. $49 - 121p^2$
7. $-3m^2 + 48n^2$
8. $225x^2 - 144y^2$

EXAMPLES 3 and 4 for Exs. 9–14

PERFECT SQUARE TRINOMIALS Factor the polynomial.

9. $x^2 - 4x + 4$
10. $y^2 - 10y + 25$
11. $49a^2 + 14a + 1$
12. $9t^2 - 12t + 4$
13. $m^2 + m + \frac{1}{4}$
14. $2x^2 + 12xy + 18y^2$

EXAMPLES 1, 2, 3, and 4 for Exs. 15–24

FACTORING POLYNOMIALS Factor the polynomial.

15. $4c^2 - 400$
16. $4f^2 - 36f + 81$
17. $-9r^2 + 4s^2$
18. $z^2 + 12z + 36$
19. $72 - 32y^2$
20. $45r^2 - 120rs + 80s^2$

ERROR ANALYSIS *Describe* and correct the error in factoring.

21.
$$\begin{aligned}36x^2 - 81 &= 9(4x^2 - 9)\\ &= 9((2x)^2 - 3^2)\\ &= 9(2x - 3)^2\end{aligned}$$

22.
$$\begin{aligned}y^2 - 6y + 9 &= y^2 - 2(y \cdot 3) + 3^2\\ &= (y - 3)(y + 3)\end{aligned}$$

23. ★ **MULTIPLE CHOICE** Which is the correct factorization of $-45x^2 + 20y^2$?

(A) $-5(3x + 2y)^2$
(B) $5(3x - 2y)^2$
(C) $-5(3x + 2y)(3x - 2y)$
(D) $5(3x + 2y)(3x - 2y)$

24. ★ **MULTIPLE CHOICE** Which is the correct factorization of $16m^2 - 8mn + n^2$?

(A) $(4m - n)^2$
(B) $(4m + n)^2$
(C) $(8m - n)^2$
(D) $(4m - n)(4m + n)$

EXAMPLE 5 for Exs. 25–39

SOLVING EQUATIONS Solve the equation.

25. $x^2 + 8x + 16 = 0$
26. $16a^2 - 8a + 1 = 0$
27. $4w^2 - 36 = 0$
28. $32 - 18m^2 = 0$
29. $27c^2 + 108c + 108 = 0$
30. $-2h^2 - 28h - 98 = 0$
31. $6p^2 = 864$
32. $-3t^2 = -108$
33. $8k^2 = 98$
34. $-\frac{4}{3}x + \frac{4}{9} = -x^2$
35. $y^2 - \frac{5}{3}y = -\frac{25}{36}$
36. $\frac{2}{9} = 8n^2$
37. $-9c^2 = -16$
38. $-20s - 3 = 25s^2 + 1$
39. $y^4 - 2y^3 + y^2 = 0$

CHALLENGE Determine the value(s) of k for which the expression is a perfect square trinomial.

40. $x^2 + kx + 36$

41. $4x^2 + kx + 9$

42. $16x^2 + kx + 4$

43. $25x^2 + 10x + k$

44. $49x^2 - 84x + k$

45. $4x^2 - 48x + k$

PROBLEM SOLVING

EXAMPLE 6 for Exs. 46–48

46. FALLING BRUSH While standing on a ladder, you drop a paintbrush from a height of 25 feet. After how many seconds does the paintbrush land on the ground?

47. FALLING OBJECT A hickory nut falls from a branch that is 100 feet above the ground. After how many seconds does the hickory nut land on the ground?

48. GRASSHOPPER A grasshopper jumps straight up from the ground with an initial vertical velocity of 8 feet per second.

a. Write an equation that gives the height (in feet) of the grasshopper as a function of the time (in seconds) since it leaves the ground.

b. After how many seconds is the grasshopper 1 foot off the ground?

49. ★ **SHORT RESPONSE** A ball is thrown up into the air from a height of 5 feet with an initial vertical velocity of 56 feet per second. How many times does the ball reach a height of 54 feet? *Explain* your answer.

50. ★ **EXTENDED RESPONSE** An arch of balloons decorates the stage at a high school graduation. The balloons are tied to a frame. The shape of the frame can be modeled by the graph of the equation $y = -\frac{1}{4}x^2 + 3x$ where x and y are measured in feet.

a. Make a table of values that shows the height of the balloon arch for $x = 0, 2, 5, 8$, and 11 feet.

b. For what additional values of x does the equation make sense? *Explain.*

c. At approximately what distance from the left end does the arch reach a height of 9 feet? Check your answer algebraically.

○ = See **WORKED-OUT SOLUTIONS** in Student Resources

★ = **STANDARDIZED TEST PRACTICE**

51. FRAMING A square mirror is framed with stained glass as shown. Each corner of the frame began as a square with a side length of d inches before it was cut to fit the mirror. The mirror has a side length of 3 inches. The area of the stained glass frame is 91 square inches.

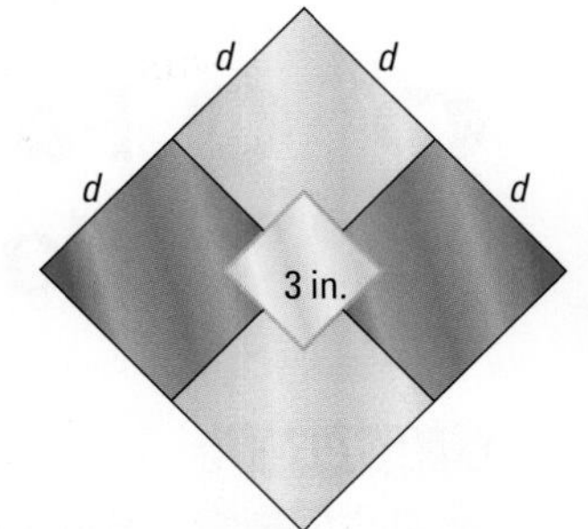

a. Write a polynomial that represents the area of the stained glass frame.

b. What is the side length of the frame?

52. CHALLENGE You have 120 folding chairs to set up in a park for an outdoor play. You want each row to have an odd number of chairs. You also want each row after the first to have 2 more chairs than the row in front of it. The first row will have 15 chairs.

a. Copy and complete the table below.

n	nth odd integer	Sum of first n odd integers	Sum as a power
1	1	1	1^2
2	3	$1 + 3 = 4$	2^2
3	5	$1 + 3 + 5 = 9$	?
4	7	?	?
5	9	?	?

b. *Describe* the relationship between n and the sum of the first n odd integers. Then find the sum of the first 10 odd integers.

c. *Explain* how to find the sum of the odd integers from 11 to 21.

d. How many rows of chairs will you need for the outdoor play? *Explain* your thinking.

8.8 Factor Polynomials Completely

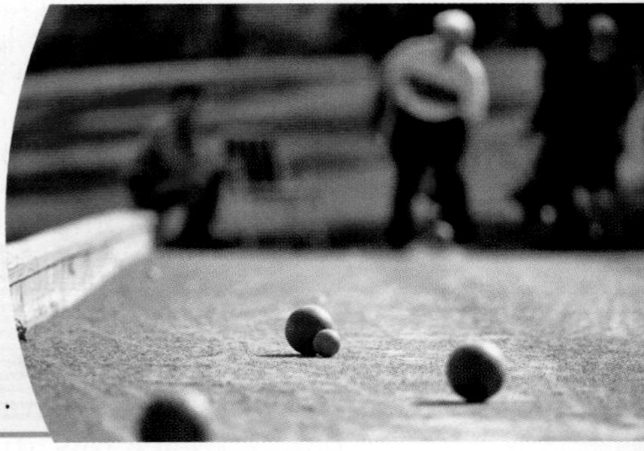

Before You factored polynomials.

Now You will factor polynomials completely.

Why? So you can model the height of a projectile, as in Ex. 71.

Key Vocabulary
- **factor by grouping**
- **factor completely**

You have used the distributive property to factor a greatest common monomial from a polynomial. Sometimes, you can factor out a common binomial.

COMMON CORE

CC.9-12.A.SSE.3a Factor a quadratic expression to reveal the zeros of the function it defines.

EXAMPLE 1 Factor out a common binomial

Factor the expression.

a. $2x(x + 4) - 3(x + 4)$

b. $3y^2(y - 2) + 5(2 - y)$

Solution

a. $2x(x + 4) - 3(x + 4) = (x + 4)(2x - 3)$

b. The binomials $y - 2$ and $2 - y$ are opposites. Factor -1 from $2 - y$ to obtain a common binomial factor.

$3y^2(y - 2) + 5(2 - y) = 3y^2(y - 2) - 5(y - 2)$ **Factor −1 from $(2 - y)$.**

$= (y - 2)(3y^2 - 5)$ **Distributive property**

GROUPING You may be able to use the distributive property to factor polynomials with four terms. Factor a common monomial from pairs of terms, then look for a common binomial factor. This is called **factor by grouping**.

EXAMPLE 2 Factor by grouping

Factor the polynomial.

a. $x^3 + 3x^2 + 5x + 15$

b. $y^2 + y + yx + x$

Solution

CHECK WORK
Remember that you can check a factorization by multiplying the factors.

a. $x^3 + 3x^2 + 5x + 15 = (x^3 + 3x^2) + (5x + 15)$ **Group terms.**

$= x^2(x + 3) + 5(x + 3)$ **Factor each group.**

$= (x + 3)(x^2 + 5)$ **Distributive property**

b. $y^2 + y + yx + x = (y^2 + y) + (yx + x)$ **Group terms.**

$= y(y + 1) + x(y + 1)$ **Factor each group.**

$= (y + 1)(y + x)$ **Distributive property**

EXAMPLE 3 Factor by grouping

Factor $x^3 - 6 + 2x - 3x^2$.

Solution

The terms x^3 and -6 have no common factor. Use the commutative property to rearrange the terms so that you can group terms with a common factor.

$x^3 - 6 + 2x - 3x^2 = x^3 - 3x^2 + 2x - 6$ **Rearrange terms.**

$= (x^3 - 3x^2) + (2x - 6)$ **Group terms.**

$= x^2(x - 3) + 2(x - 3)$ **Factor each group.**

$= (x - 3)(x^2 + 2)$ **Distributive property**

CHECK Check your factorization using a graphing calculator. Graph $y_1 = x^3 - 6 + 2x - 3x^2$ and $y_2 = (x - 3)(x^2 + 2)$. Because the graphs coincide, you know that your factorization is correct.

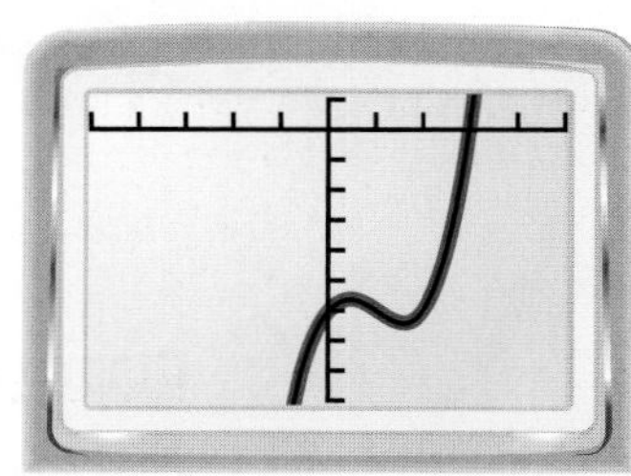

GUIDED PRACTICE for Examples 1, 2, and 3

Factor the expression.

1. $x(x - 2) + (x - 2)$ **2.** $a^3 + 3a^2 + a + 3$ **3.** $y^2 + 2x + yx + 2y$

READING

If a polynomial has two or more terms and is unfactorable, it is called a *prime polynomial.*

FACTORING COMPLETELY You have seen that the polynomial $x^2 - 1$ can be factored as $(x + 1)(x - 1)$. This polynomial is factorable. Notice that the polynomial $x^2 + 1$ cannot be written as the product of polynomials with integer coefficients. This polynomial is unfactorable. A factorable polynomial with integer coefficients is **factored completely** if it is written as a product of unfactorable polynomials with integer coefficients.

CONCEPT SUMMARY *For Your Notebook*

Guidelines for Factoring Polynomials Completely

To factor a polynomial completely, you should try each of these steps.

1. Factor out the greatest common monomial factor.	$3x^2 + 6x = 3x(x + 2)$
2. Look for a difference of two squares or a perfect square trinomial.	$x^2 + 4x + 4 = (x + 2)^2$
3. Factor a trinomial of the form $ax^2 + bx + c$ into a product of binomial factors.	$3x^2 - 5x - 2 = (3x + 1)(x - 2)$
4. Factor a polynomial with four terms by grouping.	$x^3 + x - 4x^2 - 4 = (x^2 + 1)(x - 4)$

EXAMPLE 4 Factor completely

Factor the polynomial completely.

a. $n^2 + 2n - 1$ **b.** $4x^3 - 44x^2 + 96x$ **c.** $50h^4 - 2h^2$

Solution

a. The terms of the polynomial have no common monomial factor. Also, there are no factors of -1 that have a sum of 2. This polynomial cannot be factored.

b. $4x^3 - 44x^2 + 96x = 4x(x^2 - 11x + 24)$ **Factor out $4x$.**

$= 4x(x - 3)(x - 8)$ **Find two negative factors of 24 that have a sum of -11.**

c. $50h^4 - 2h^2 = 2h^2(25h^2 - 1)$ **Factor out $2h^2$.**

$= 2h^2(5h - 1)(5h + 1)$ **Difference of two squares pattern**

GUIDED PRACTICE for Example 4

Factor the polynomial completely.

4. $3x^3 - 12x$ **5.** $2y^3 - 12y^2 + 18y$ **6.** $m^3 - 2m^2 - 8m$

EXAMPLE 5 Solve a polynomial equation

Solve $3x^3 + 18x^2 = -24x$.

$3x^3 + 18x^2 = -24x$ **Write original equation.**

$3x^3 + 18x^2 + 24x = 0$ **Add $24x$ to each side.**

$3x(x^2 + 6x + 8) = 0$ **Factor out $3x$.**

$3x(x + 2)(x + 4) = 0$ **Factor trinomial.**

$3x = 0$ *or* $x + 2 = 0$ *or* $x + 4 = 0$ **Zero-product property**

$x = 0$ $\quad x = -2$ $\quad x = -4$ **Solve for x.**

▶ The solutions of the equation are 0, -2, and -4.

CHECK Check each solution by substituting it for x in the equation. One check is shown here.

$3(-2)^3 + 18(-2)^2 \stackrel{?}{=} -24(-2)$

$-24 + 72 \stackrel{?}{=} 48$

$48 = 48$ ✓

GUIDED PRACTICE for Example 5

Solve the equation.

7. $w^3 - 8w^2 + 16w = 0$ **8.** $x^3 - 25x = 0$ **9.** $c^3 - 7c^2 + 12c = 0$

EXAMPLE 6 Solve a multi-step problem

TERRARIUM A terrarium in the shape of a rectangular prism has a volume of 4608 cubic inches. Its length is more than 10 inches. The dimensions of the terrarium are shown. Find the length, width, and height of the terrarium.

Solution

STEP 1 **Write** a verbal model. Then write an equation.

Volume (cubic inches)	=	Length (inches)	·	Width (inches)	·	Height (inches)
4608	=	$(36 - w)$	·	w	·	$(w + 4)$

STEP 2 **Solve** the equation for w.

$4608 = (36 - w)(w)(w + 4)$	**Write equation.**
$0 = 32w^2 + 144w - w^3 - 4608$	**Multiply. Subtract 4608 from each side.**
$0 = (-w^3 + 32w^2) + (144w - 4608)$	**Group terms.**
$0 = -w^2(w - 32) + 144(w - 32)$	**Factor each group.**
$0 = (w - 32)(-w^2 + 144)$	**Distributive property**
$0 = -1(w - 32)(w^2 - 144)$	**Factor −1 from $-w^2 + 144$.**
$0 = -1(w - 32)(w - 12)(w + 12)$	**Difference of two squares pattern**
$w - 32 = 0$ *or* $w - 12 = 0$ *or* $w + 12 = 0$	**Zero-product property**
$w = 32$ $\quad w = 12 \quad w = -12$	**Solve for w.**

STEP 3 **Choose** the solution of the equation that is the correct value of w. Disregard $w = -12$, because the width cannot be negative.

You know that the length is more than 10 inches. Test the solutions 12 and 32 in the expression for the length.

Length $= 36 - 12 = 24$ ✓ *or* Length $= 36 - 32 = 4$ ✗

The solution 12 gives a length of 24 inches, so 12 is the correct value of w.

STEP 4 **Find** the height.

Height $= w + 4 = 12 + 4 = 16$

▶ The width is 12 inches, the length is 24 inches, and the height is 16 inches.

GUIDED PRACTICE for Example 6

10. **DIMENSIONS OF A BOX** A box in the shape of a rectangular prism has a volume of 72 cubic feet. The box has a length of x feet, a width of $(x - 1)$ feet, and a height of $(x + 9)$ feet. Find the dimensions of the box.

8.8 EXERCISES

HOMEWORK KEY

○ = **See WORKED-OUT SOLUTIONS** Exs. 13, 23, and 71

★ = **STANDARDIZED TEST PRACTICE** Exs. 2, 12, 41, 55, 71, and 73

SKILL PRACTICE

1. **VOCABULARY** What does it mean for a polynomial to be factored completely?

2. ★ **WRITING** *Explain* how you know if a polynomial is unfactorable.

EXAMPLE 1 for Exs. 3–12

BINOMIAL FACTORS **Factor the expression.**

3. $x(x - 8) + (x - 8)$
4. $5y(y + 3) - 2(y + 3)$
5. $6z(z - 4) - 7(z - 4)$
6. $10(a - 6) - 3a(a - 6)$
7. $b^2(b + 5) - 3(b + 5)$
8. $7c^2(c + 9) + 2(c + 9)$
9. $x(13 + x) - (x + 13)$
10. $y^2(y - 4) + 5(4 - y)$
11. $12(z - 1) - 5z^2(1 - z)$

12. ★ **MULTIPLE CHOICE** Which is the correct factorization of $x^2(x - 8) + 5(8 - x)$?

   Ⓐ $(x^2 + 5)(x - 8)$ Ⓑ $(x^2 + 5)(8 - x)$

   Ⓒ $(x^2 - 5)(x - 8)$ Ⓓ $(x^2 - 5)(8 - x)$

EXAMPLES 2 and 3 for Exs. 13–22

FACTORING BY GROUPING **Factor the polynomial.**

13. $x^3 + x^2 + 2x + 2$
14. $y^3 - 9y^2 + y - 9$
15. $z^3 - 4z^2 + 3z - 12$
16. $c^3 + 7c^2 + 5c + 35$
17. $a^3 + 13a^2 - 5a - 65$
18. $2s^3 - 3s^2 + 18s - 27$
19. $5n^3 - 4n^2 + 25n - 20$
20. $x^2 + 8x - xy - 8y$
21. $y^2 + y + 5xy + 5x$

22. **ERROR ANALYSIS** *Describe* and correct the error in factoring.

$$a^3 + 8a^2 - 6a - 48 = a^2(a + 8) + 6(a + 8)$$
$$= (a + 8)(a^2 + 6)$$

EXAMPLE 4 for Exs. 23–42

FACTORING COMPLETELY **Factor the polynomial completely.**

23. $x^4 - x^2$
24. $36a^4 - 4a^2$
25. $3n^5 - 48n^3$
26. $4y^6 - 16y^4$
27. $75c^9 - 3c^7$
28. $72p - 2p^3$
29. $32s^4 - 8s^2$
30. $80z^8 - 45z^6$
31. $m^2 - 5m - 35$
32. $6g^3 - 24g^2 + 24g$
33. $3w^4 + 24w^3 + 48w^2$
34. $3r^5 + 3r^4 - 90r^3$
35. $b^3 - 5b^2 - 4b + 20$
36. $h^3 + 4h^2 - 25h - 100$
37. $9t^3 + 18t - t^2 - 2$
38. $2x^5y - 162x^3y$
39. $7a^3b^3 - 63ab^3$
40. $-4s^3t^3 + 24s^2t^2 - 36st$

41. ★ **MULTIPLE CHOICE** What is the completely factored form of $3x^6 - 75x^4$?

   Ⓐ $3x^4(x^2 - 25)$ Ⓑ $3x^4(x - 5)^2$ Ⓒ $3x^4(x + 5)^2$ Ⓓ $3x^4(x - 5)(x + 5)$

42. **ERROR ANALYSIS** *Describe* and correct the error in factoring the polynomial completely.

$$x^3 - 6x^2 - 9x + 54 = x^2(x - 6) - 9(x - 6)$$
$$= (x - 6)(x^2 - 9)$$

EXAMPLE 5
for Exs. 43–54

SOLVING EQUATIONS Solve the equation.

43. $x^3 + x^2 - 4x - 4 = 0$

44. $a^3 - 11a^2 - 9a + 99 = 0$

45. $4y^3 - 7y^2 - 16y + 28 = 0$

46. $5n^3 - 30n^2 + 40n = 0$

47. $3b^3 + 24b^2 + 45b = 0$

48. $2t^5 + 2t^4 - 144t^3 = 0$

49. $z^3 - 81z = 0$

50. $c^4 - 100c^2 = 0$

51. $12s - 3s^3 = 0$

52. $2x^3 - 10x^2 + 40 = 8x$

53. $3p + 1 = p^2 + 3p^3$

54. $m^3 - 3m^2 = 4m - 12$

55. ★ **WRITING** Is it possible to find three solutions of the equation $x^3 + 2x^2 + 3x + 6 = 0$? *Explain* why or why not.

GEOMETRY Find the length, width, and height of the rectangular prism with the given volume.

HINT
In Ex. 57, convert the given volume to cubic yards. Use the conversion factor $\frac{1 \text{ yd}^3}{27 \text{ ft}^3}$.

56. Volume = 12 cubic inches

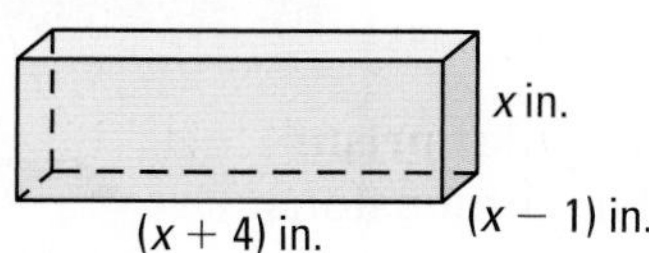

57. Volume: 2592 cubic feet

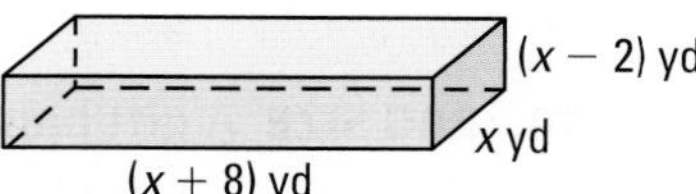

FACTORING COMPLETELY Factor the polynomial completely.

58. $x^3 + 2x^2y - x - 2y$

59. $8b^3 - 4b^2a - 18b + 9a$

60. $4s^2 - s + 12st - 3t$

FACTOR BY GROUPING In Exercises 61–66, use the example below to factor the trinomial by grouping.

EXAMPLE Factor a trinomial by grouping

Factor $8x^2 + 10x - 3$ by grouping.

Solution

Notice that the polynomial is in the form $ax^2 + bx + c$.

STEP 1 **Write** the product ac as the product of two factors that have a sum of b. In this case, the product ac is $8(-3) = -24$. Find two factors of -24 that have a sum of 10.

$-24 = 12 \cdot (-2)$ and $12 + (-2) = 10$

STEP 2 **Rewrite** the middle term as two terms with coefficients 12 and -2.

$8x^2 + 10x - 3 = 8x^2 + 12x - 2x - 3$

STEP 3 **Factor** by grouping.

$8x^2 + 12x - 2x - 3$	$= (8x^2 + 12x) + (-2x - 3)$	**Group terms.**
	$= 4x(2x + 3) - (2x + 3)$	**Factor each group.**
	$= (2x + 3)(4x - 1)$	**Distributive property**

61. $6x^2 + 5x - 4$

62. $10s^2 + 19s + 6$

63. $12n^2 - 13n + 3$

64. $16a^2 + 14a + 3$

65. $21w^2 + 8w - 4$

66. $15y^2 - 31y + 10$

67. CHALLENGE Use factoring by grouping to show that a trinomial of the form $a^2 + 2ab + b^2$ can be factored as $(a + b)^2$. *Justify* your steps.

PROBLEM SOLVING

EXAMPLE 6 for Exs. 68–70

68. CYLINDRICAL VASE A vase in the shape of a cylinder has a height of 6 inches and a volume of 24π cubic inches. What is the radius of the vase?

69. CARPENTRY You are building a birdhouse that will have a volume of 128 cubic inches. The birdhouse will have the dimensions shown.

a. Write a polynomial that represents the volume of the birdhouse.

b. What are the dimensions of the birdhouse?

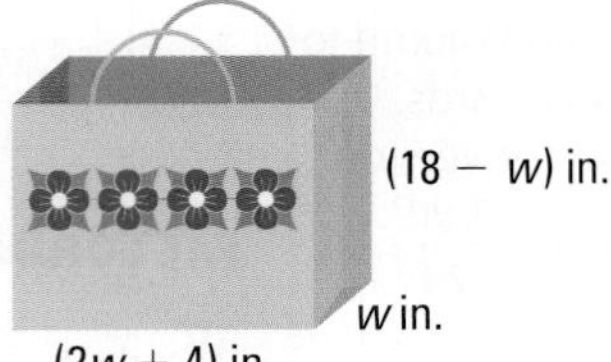

70. BAG SIZE A gift bag is shaped like a rectangular prism and has a volume of 1152 cubic inches. The dimensions of the gift bag are shown. The height is greater than the width. What are the dimensions of the gift bag?

71. ★ **SHORT RESPONSE** A pallino is the small target ball that is tossed in the air at the beginning of a game of bocce. The height h (in meters) of the pallino after you throw it can be modeled by $h = -4.9t^2 + 3.9t + 1$ where t is the time (in seconds) since you released it.

a. Find the zeros of the function.

b. Do the zeros of the function have any meaning in this situation? *Explain* your reasoning.

72. JUMPING ROBOT The path of a jumping robot can be modeled by the graph of the equation $y = -10x^2 + 30x$ where x and y are both measured in feet. On a coordinate plane, the ground is represented by the x-axis, and the robot's starting position is the origin.

a. The robot's maximum height is 22.5 feet. What is the robot's horizontal distance from its starting point when its height is 22.5 feet?

b. How far has the robot traveled horizontally when it lands on the ground? *Explain* your answer.

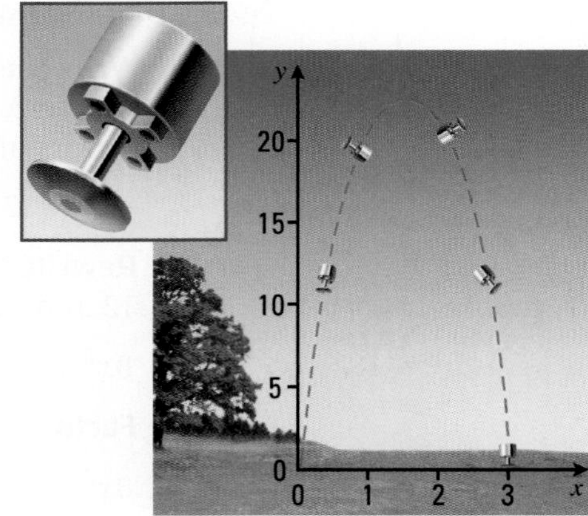

73. ★ **EXTENDED RESPONSE** The width of a box is 4 inches more than the height h. The length is the difference of 9 inches and the height.

a. Write a polynomial that represents the volume of the box.

b. The volume of the box is 180 cubic inches. What are all the possible dimensions of the box?

c. Which dimensions result in a box with the smallest possible surface area? *Explain* your reasoning.

74. **CHALLENGE** A plastic cube is used to display an autographed baseball. The cube has an outer surface area of 54 square inches.

a. What is the length of an outer edge of the cube?

b. What is the greatest volume the cube can possibly have? *Explain* why the actual volume inside of the cube may be less than the greatest possible volume.

QUIZ

Factor the polynomial.

1. $x^2 - 400$
2. $18 - 32z^2$
3. $169x^2 - 25y^2$
4. $n^2 - 6n + 9$
5. $100a^2 + 20a + 1$
6. $8r^2 - 40rs + 50s^2$

Factor the polynomial completely.

7. $3x^5 - 75x^3$
8. $72s^4 - 8s^2$
9. $3x^4y - 300x^2y$
10. $a^3 - 4a^2 - 21a$
11. $2h^4 + 28h^3 + 98h^2$
12. $z^3 - 4z^2 - 16z + 64$

Solve the equation.

13. $x^2 + 10x + 25 = 0$
14. $48 - 27m^2 = 0$
15. $w^3 - w^2 - 4w + 4 = 0$
16. $4x^3 - 28x^2 + 40x = 0$
17. $3x^5 - 6x^4 - 45x^3 = 0$
18. $x^3 - 121x = 0$

19. **VOLUME** The cylinder shown has a volume of 72π cubic inches.

a. Write a polynomial that represents the volume of the cylinder. Leave your answer in terms of π.

b. Find the radius of the cylinder.

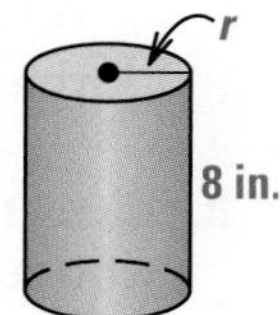

MIXED REVIEW *of Problem Solving*

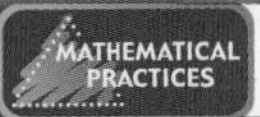

Make sense of problems and persevere in solving them.

1. **MULTI-STEP PROBLEM** A rectangular room has the dimensions shown.

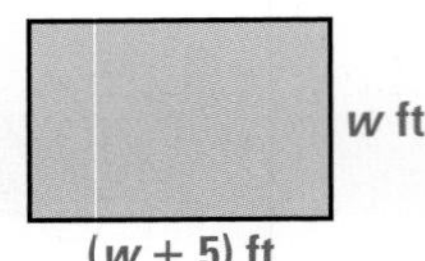

   a. Write a polynomial that represents the area of the room.

   b. The room has an area of 150 square feet. What are the length and width of the room?

2. **MULTI-STEP PROBLEM** A block of clay has the dimensions shown.

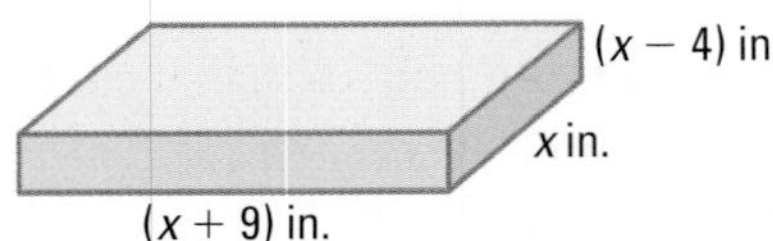

   a. Write a polynomial that represents the volume of the clay.

   b. The clay has a volume of 180 cubic inches. What are the length, width, and height of the block?

3. **MULTI-STEP PROBLEM** You are making a wooden game board. You cut a square piece of wood, as shown.

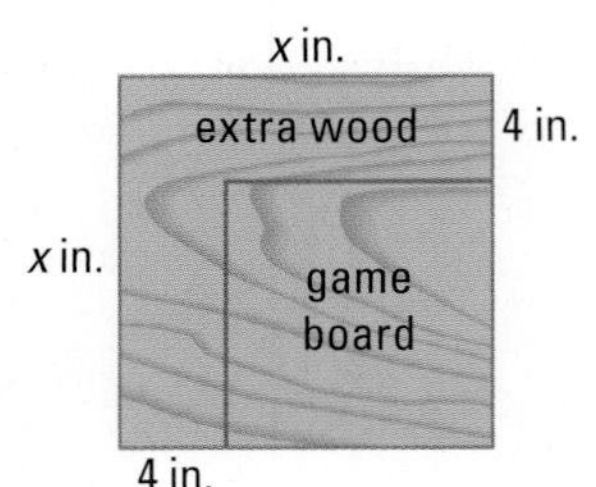

   a. Write a polynomial that represents the area of the game board.

   b. The area of the game board is 100 square inches. What was the area of the original piece of wood? *Explain* how you found your answer.

4. **OPEN-ENDED** *Describe* a situation that can be modeled using the vertical motion model $h = -16t^2 + 48t$. Then find the value of t when $h = 0$. *Explain* what this value of t means in this situation.

5. **EXTENDED RESPONSE** You hit a baseball straight up into the air. The baseball is hit with an initial vertical velocity of 80 feet per second when it is 3 feet off the ground.

   a. Write an equation that gives the height (in feet) of the baseball as a function of the time (in seconds) since it was hit.

   b. After how many seconds does the ball reach a height of 99 feet?

   c. Does the ball reach a height of 99 feet more than once? *Justify* your answer.

6. **EXTENDED RESPONSE** The length of a box is 25 inches more than its height. The width of the box is 1 inch less than its height.

   a. Draw a diagram of the box. Label its dimensions in terms of the height h.

   b. Write a polynomial that represents the volume of the box.

   c. The box has a volume of 600 cubic inches. What is the area of its top? *Explain.*

7. **SHORT RESPONSE** A tennis player hits a ball with an initial vertical velocity of 63 feet per second. Can you find the number of seconds the tennis ball is in the air? *Explain* why not or find the number of seconds.

8. **GRIDDED ANSWER** During an experiment in physics class, you drop a ball from a height of 144 feet. After how many seconds does the ball hit the ground?

9. **SHORT RESPONSE** A football is kicked toward a goal post that is 10 feet high. The path of the football is modeled by the graph of $y = -0.005x^2 + 0.6x$ where x and y are measured in feet. On a coordinate plane, the x-axis represents the ground, and the ball leaves the ground at the origin. The ball hits the goal post on the way down. How far from the goal post is the kicker? *Explain.*

8 CHAPTER SUMMARY

BIG IDEAS

For Your Notebook

Big Idea 1

Adding, Subtracting, and Multiplying Polynomials

You can perform operations with polynomials using the steps below.

Operation	Steps
Add	Group like terms and add.
Subtract	First, rewrite subtraction as addition. Second, group like terms and add.
Multiply	First, multiply terms using the distributive property. Second, combine like terms.

Big Idea 2

Factoring Polynomials

When factoring a polynomial, you should use the following checklist so that you can be sure you have factored the polynomial completely.

STEP 1 **Factor** out the greatest common monomial factor.

STEP 2 **Look** for special products to factor.

STEP 3 **Factor** a trinomial into a pair of binomials, if possible.

STEP 4 **Factor** a polynomial with four terms by grouping, if possible.

Big Idea 3

Writing and Solving Polynomial Equations to Solve Problems

You can write polynomials that model real-world situations in order to solve problems. For example, you can use the vertical motion model.

Height (in feet) of a projectile: $h = -16t^2 + vt + s$ where t is the time (in seconds) the object has been in the air, v is the initial vertical velocity (in feet per second), and s is the initial height (in feet).

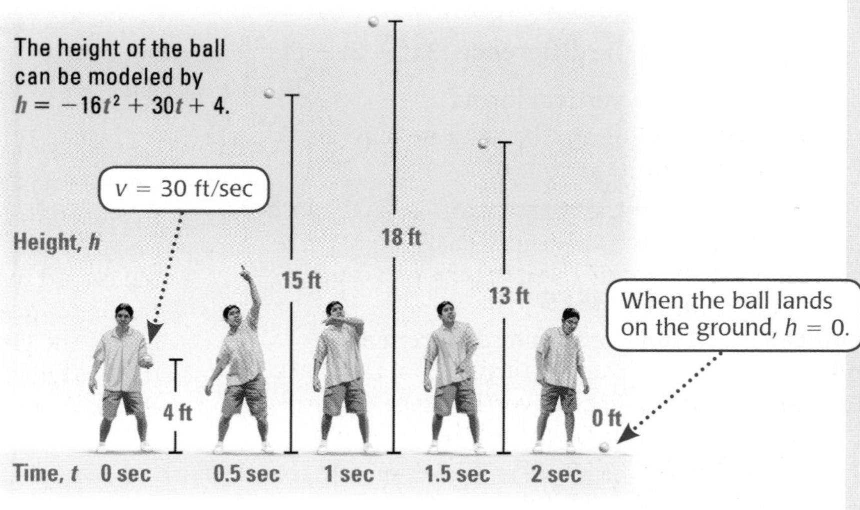

8 CHAPTER REVIEW

@HomeTutor
my.hrw.com
- Multi-Language Glossary
- Vocabulary practice

REVIEW KEY VOCABULARY

- monomial
- degree of a monomial
- polynomial
- degree of a polynomial
- leading coefficient
- binomial
- trinomial
- roots
- vertical motion model
- perfect square trinomial
- factor by grouping
- factor completely

VOCABULARY EXERCISES

1. Copy and complete: The greatest degree of the terms in a polynomial is called the __?__.

2. **WRITING** Is $2x^{-1}$ a monomial? *Explain* why or why not.

3. **WRITING** What does it mean for a polynomial to be factored completely? Give an example of a polynomial that has been factored completely.

In Exercises 4–6, match the polynomial with its classification.

4. $5x - 22$ 5. $-11x^3$ 6. $x^2 + x + 1$

A. Monomial **B.** Binomial **C.** Trinomial

REVIEW EXAMPLES AND EXERCISES

Use the review examples and exercises below to check your understanding of the concepts you have learned in each lesson of this chapter.

8.1 Add and Subtract Polynomials

EXAMPLE

Find the difference $(3x^2 + 2) - (4x^2 - x - 9)$.

Use a vertical format.

$$\begin{array}{r} 3x^2 \qquad + 2 \\ -\ (4x^2 - x - 9) \\ \hline \end{array} \quad \longrightarrow \quad \begin{array}{r} 3x^2 \qquad + 2 \\ +\ -4x^2 + x + 9 \\ \hline -x^2 + x + 11 \end{array}$$

EXERCISES

EXAMPLES 3 and 4 for Exs. 7–12

Find the sum or difference.

7. $(9x + 6x^3 - 8x^2) + (-5x^3 + 6x)$
8. $(7a^3 - 4a^2 - 2a + 1) + (a^3 - 1)$
9. $(11y^5 + 3y^2 - 4) + (y^2 - y + 1)$
10. $(3n^2 - 4n + 1) - (8n^2 - 4n + 17)$
11. $(2s^3 + 8) - (-3s^3 + 7s - 5)$
12. $(-k^2 + 7k + 5) - (2k^4 - 3k^3 - 6)$

@HomeTutor
my.hrw.com
Chapter Review Practice

8.2 Multiply Polynomials

EXAMPLE

Find the product.

a. $(x^2 + 4x - 5)(2x - 1)$

b. $(5y + 6)(y - 3)$

Solution

a. Use a horizontal format.

$(x^2 + 4x - 5)(2x - 1)$ — **Write product.**

$= x^2(2x - 1) + 4x(2x - 1) - 5(2x - 1)$ — **Distributive property**

$= 2x^3 - x^2 + 8x^2 - 4x - 10x + 5$ — **Distributive property**

$= 2x^3 + 7x^2 - 14x + 5$ — **Combine like terms.**

b. Use a vertical format.

STEP 1 **Multiply** by −3.

$$\begin{array}{r} 5y + 6 \\ \times \quad y - 3 \\ \hline -15y - 18 \end{array}$$

STEP 2 **Multiply** by y.

$$\begin{array}{r} 5y + 6 \\ \times \quad y - 3 \\ \hline -15y - 18 \\ 5y^2 + 6y \quad\quad \end{array}$$

STEP 3 **Add** products.

$$\begin{array}{r} 5y + 6 \\ \times \quad y - 3 \\ \hline -15y - 18 \\ 5y^2 + 6y \quad\quad \\ \hline 5y^2 - 9y - 18 \end{array}$$

EXERCISES

EXAMPLES 1, 2, 3, and 4 for Exs. 13–21

Find the product.

13. $(x^2 - 2x + 1)(x - 3)$ **14.** $(y^2 + 5y + 4)(3y + 2)$ **15.** $(x - 4)(x + 2)$

16. $(5b^2 - b - 7)(b + 6)$ **17.** $(z + 8)(z - 11)$ **18.** $(2a - 1)(a - 3)$

19. $(6n + 7)(3n + 1)$ **20.** $(4n - 5)(7n - 3)$ **21.** $(3x - 2)(x + 4)$

8.3 Find Special Products of Polynomials

EXAMPLE

Find the product $(3x + 2)(3x - 2)$.

$(3x + 2)(3x - 2) = (3x)^2 - 2^2$ — **Sum and difference pattern**

$= 9x^2 - 4$ — **Simplify.**

EXERCISES

EXAMPLES 1 and 2 for Exs. 22–27

Find the product.

22. $(x + 11)^2$ **23.** $(6y + 1)^2$ **24.** $(2x - y)^2$

25. $(4a - 3)^2$ **26.** $(k + 7)(k - 7)$ **27.** $(3s + 5)(3s - 5)$

8 CHAPTER REVIEW

8.4 Solve Polynomial Equations in Factored Form

EXAMPLE

Solve $6x^2 + 42x = 0$.

$6x^2 + 42x = 0$	**Write original equation.**
$6x(x + 7) = 0$	**Factor left side.**
$6x = 0$ *or* $x + 7 = 0$	**Zero-product property**
$x = 0$ *or* $x = -7$	**Solve for *x*.**

▶ The solutions of the equation are 0 and −7.

EXERCISES

EXAMPLES 3 and 4 for Exs. 28–33

Solve the equation.

28. $2a^2 + 26a = 0$ **29.** $3t^2 - 33t = 0$ **30.** $8x^2 - 4x = 0$

31. $m^2 = 9m$ **32.** $5y^2 = -50y$ **33.** $21h^2 = 7h$

8.5 Factor $x^2 + bx + c$

EXAMPLE

Factor $x^2 + 2x - 63$.

Find two factors of −63 whose sum is 2. One factor will be positive, and the other will be negative. Make an organized list of factors.

Factors of −63	Sum of factors	
1, −63	1 + (−63) = −62	✗
−1, 63	−1 + 63 = 62	✗
3, −21	3 + (−21) = −18	✗
−3, 21	−3 + 21 = 18	✗
9, −7	9 + (−7) = 2	⟵ Correct sum
−9, 7	−9 + 7 = −2	✗

▶ $x^2 + 2x - 63 = (x + 9)(x - 7)$

EXERCISES

EXAMPLES 1,2 and 3 for Exs. 34–42

Factor the trinomial.

34. $n^2 + 15n + 26$ **35.** $s^2 + 10s - 11$ **36.** $b^2 - 5b - 14$

37. $a^2 + 5a - 84$ **38.** $t^2 - 24t + 135$ **39.** $x^2 + 4x - 32$

40. $p^2 + 9p + 14$ **41.** $c^2 + 8c + 15$ **42.** $y^2 - 10y + 21$

@HomeTutor
my.hrw.com
Chapter Review Practice

8.6 Factor $ax^2 + bx + c$

EXAMPLE

THROWN BALL You throw a ball up into the air. At 4 feet above the ground, the ball leaves your hand with an initial vertical velocity of 30 feet per second.

a. Write an equation that gives the height (in feet) of the ball as a function of the time (in seconds) since it left your hand.

b. After how many seconds does the ball land on the ground?

Solution

a. Use the vertical motion model $h = -16t^2 + vt + s$ to write an equation for the height h (in feet) of the ball as a function of the time t (in seconds). In this case, $v = 30$ and $s = 4$.

$h = -16t^2 + vt + s$ **Vertical motion model**

$h = -16t^2 + 30t + 4$ **Substitute 30 for *v* and 4 for *s*.**

b. When the ball lands on the ground, its height is 0 feet. Substitute 0 for h and solve the equation for t.

$0 = -16t^2 + 30t + 4$ **Substitute 0 for *h*.**

$0 = -2(8t^2 - 15t - 2)$ **Factor out −2.**

$0 = -2(8t + 1)(t - 2)$ **Factor the trinomial. Find factors of 8 and −2 that produce a middle term with a coefficient of −15.**

$8t + 1 = 0$ *or* $t - 2 = 0$ **Zero-product property**

$t = -\frac{1}{8}$ *or* $t = 2$ **Solve for *t*.**

The solutions of the equation are $-\frac{1}{8}$ and 2. A negative solution does not make sense in this situation, so disregard $-\frac{1}{8}$.

▶ The ball lands on the ground after 2 seconds.

EXERCISES

EXAMPLES 1, 2, 3, and 4 for Exs. 43–50

Solve the equation.

43. $7x^2 - 8x = -1$

44. $4n^2 + 3 = 7n$

45. $3s^2 + 4s + 4 = 8$

46. $6z^2 + 13z = 5$

47. $-4r^2 = 18r + 18$

48. $9a^2 = 6a + 24$

49. THROWN BALL You throw a ball up into the air with an initial vertical velocity of 46 feet per second. The ball leaves your hand when it is 6 feet above the ground. After how many seconds does the ball land on the ground?

50. GEOMETRY The length of a rectangle is 1 inch less than twice the width. The area of the rectangle is 21 square inches. What is the length of the rectangle?

8 CHAPTER REVIEW

8.7 Factor Special Products

EXAMPLE

Factor the polynomial.

a. $100x^2 - y^2$

b. $4x^2 - 36x + 81$

Solution

a. $100x^2 - y^2 = (10x)^2 - y^2$ **Write as $a^2 - b^2$.**

$= (10x + y)(10x - y)$ **Difference of two squares pattern**

b. $4x^2 - 36x + 81 = (2x)^2 - 2(2x \cdot 9) + 9^2$ **Write as $a^2 - 2ab + b^2$.**

$= (2x - 9)^2$ **Perfect square trinomial pattern**

EXERCISES

EXAMPLES 1, 2, 3, 4, and 6 for Exs. 51–57

Factor the polynomial.

51. $z^2 - 225$

52. $a^2 - 16y^2$

53. $12 - 48n^2$

54. $x^2 + 20x + 100$

55. $16p^2 - 8p + 1$

56. $-2y^2 + 32y - 128$

57. DROPPED OBJECT You drop a penny from a height of 16 feet. After how many seconds does the penny land on the ground?

8.8 Factor Polynomials Completely

EXAMPLE

Factor the polynomial completely.

a. $y^3 - 4y^2 + 8y - 32$

b. $5x^3 - 40x^2 + 80x$

Solution

a. $y^3 - 4y^2 + 8y - 32 = (y^3 - 4y^2) + (8y - 32)$ **Group terms.**

$= y^2(y - 4) + 8(y - 4)$ **Factor each group.**

$= (y - 4)(y^2 + 8)$ **Distributive property**

b. $5x^3 - 40x^2 + 80x = 5x(x^2 - 8x + 16)$ **Factor out 5x.**

$= 5x(x - 4)^2$ **Perfect square trinomial pattern**

EXERCISES

EXAMPLE 4 for Exs. 58–66

Factor the polynomial completely.

58. $a^3 + 6a - 5a^2 - 30$

59. $y^2 + 3y + yx + 3x$

60. $x^3 - 11x^2 - x + 11$

61. $5s^4 - 125s^2$

62. $147n^5 - 3n^3$

63. $2z^3 + 2z^2 - 60z$

64. $x^3 + 5x^2 - x - 5$

65. $2b^3 + 3b^2 - 8b - 12$

66. $x^3 + x^2 - 6x - 6$

8 CHAPTER TEST

Find the sum or difference.

1. $(a^2 - 4a + 6) + (-3a^2 + 13a + 1)$
2. $(5x^2 - 2) + (8x^3 + 2x^2 - x + 9)$
3. $(15n^2 + 7n - 1) - (4n^2 - 3n - 8)$
4. $(9c^3 - 11c^2 + 2c) - (-6c^2 - 3c + 11)$

Find the product.

5. $(2z + 9)(z - 7)$
6. $(5m - 8)(5m - 7)$
7. $(b + 2)(-b^2 + 4b - 3)$
8. $(5 + 7y)(1 - 9y)$
9. $(2x^2 - 3x + 5)(x - 4)$
10. $(5p - 6)(5p + 6)$
11. $(12 - 3g)^2$
12. $(2s + 9t)^2$
13. $(11a - 4b)(11a + 4b)$

Factor the polynomial.

14. $x^2 + 8x + 7$
15. $2n^2 - 11n + 15$
16. $-12r^2 + 5r + 3$
17. $t^2 - 10t + 25$
18. $-3n^2 + 75$
19. $3x^2 + 29x - 44$
20. $x^2 - 49$
21. $2a^4 + 21a^3 + 49a^2$
22. $y^3 + 2y^2 - 81y - 162$

Solve the equation.

23. $25a = 10a^2$
24. $21z^2 + 85z - 26 = 0$
25. $x^2 - 22x = -121$
26. $a^2 - 11a + 24 = 0$
27. $t^2 + 7t = 60$
28. $4x^2 = 22x + 42$
29. $56b^2 + b = 1$
30. $n^3 - 121n = 0$
31. $a^3 + a^2 = 64a + 64$

32. **VERTICAL MOTION** A cricket jumps off the ground with an initial vertical velocity of 4 feet per second.
    a. Write an equation that gives the height (in feet) of the cricket as a function of the time (in seconds) since it jumps.
    b. After how many seconds does the cricket land on the ground?

33. **POSTER AREA** Two posters have the lengths and widths shown. The posters have the same area.
    a. Write an equation that relates the areas of the two posters.
    b. Find the length and width of each poster.

34. **CONSTRUCTION** A construction worker is working on the roof of a building. A drop of paint falls from a rafter that is 225 feet above the ground. After how many seconds does the paint hit the ground?

35. **BOX DIMENSIONS** A cardboard box that is a rectangular prism has the dimensions shown.
    a. Write a polynomial that represents the volume of the box.
    b. The volume of the box is 60 cubic inches. What are the length, width, and height of the box?

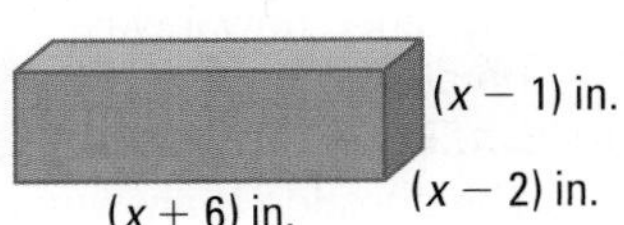

8 ★ Standardized TEST PREPARATION

Scoring Rubric

Full Credit
- solution is complete and correct

Partial Credit
- solution is complete but errors are made,

or
- solution is without error but incomplete

No Credit
- no solution is given,

or
- solution makes no sense

SHORT RESPONSE QUESTIONS

PROBLEM

A rectangular photo has an area of 24 square inches. You trim the photo so that it fits into a square frame. You trim 3 inches from the length and 1 inch from the width of the photo. Write and solve an equation to find the side length of the resulting square photo. *Explain* how you chose one solution of the equation to find the side length.

Below are sample solutions to the problem. Read each solution and the comments on the left to see why the sample represents full credit, partial credit, or no credit.

SAMPLE 1: Full credit solution

A diagram shows how the equation is obtained.

Draw a diagram. Use the formula for the area of a rectangle.

$A = \ell \cdot w$

$= (x + 3)(x + 1)$

$= x^2 + 4x + 3$

3 in. x in. x in. 1 in.

The correct calculations are performed.

Substitute 24 for A and solve.

$24 = x^2 + 4x + 3$

$0 = x^2 + 4x - 21$

$0 = (x - 3)(x + 7)$

$0 = x - 3$ *or* $0 = x + 7$

$x = 3$ *or* $x = -7$

The question is answered correctly and includes an explanation.

A solution represents the side length of the square photo. A negative side length does not make sense, so choose $x = 3$. The side length is 3 inches.

SAMPLE 2: Partial credit solution

The length of the rectangular photo is $x + 3$. The width is $x + 1$.

The equation is correct, and the student has explained how it was obtained.

$A = (x + 3)(x + 1)$

$24 = x^2 + 4x + 3$

$0 = x^2 + 4x - 21$

$0 = (x - 3)(x + 7)$

$x = 3$ *or* $x = -7$

The question is answered correctly but does not include an explanation.

The side length of the square photo is 3 inches.

SAMPLE 3: Partial credit solution

The equation and its solutions are correct, but the student found the length and width of the original photo instead of the trimmed photo.

$24 = (x + 3)(x + 1)$
$0 = x^2 + 4x - 21$
$0 = (x - 3)(x + 7)$
$x = 3 \quad or \quad x = -7$

A negative solution does not make sense in the situation. The length is $3 + 3 = 6$ inches, and the width is $3 + 1 = 4$ inches.

SAMPLE 4: No credit solution

The student's reasoning is incorrect, and the equation is incorrect. The answer is incorrect.

$(x - 3)(x - 1) = 24$
$x^2 - 4x - 21 = 0$
$(x - 3)(x + 7) = 0$

$x = -3$ or 7, so the side length of the square is 7 inches.

PRACTICE Apply the Scoring Rubric

Score the solution to the problem below as *full credit, partial credit,* or *no credit. Explain* your reasoning.

PROBLEM You are making a banner for a surprise birthday party. The banner will have the dimensions shown in the diagram. Its area will be 6 square feet. Write and solve an equation to find the length and width of the banner. *Explain* your reasoning.

Happy Birthday
$(x - 7)$ ft
$(x - 2)$ ft

1.

$6 = (x - 2)(x - 7)$
$6 = x^2 - 9x + 14$
$0 = x^2 - 9x + 8$
$0 = (x - 8)(x - 1)$
$x = 8$ or $x = 1$

In this problem, the solutions of the equation are 8 and 1. If $x = 1$, then the width of the banner is $x - 7 = -6$. A width cannot be negative, so disregard the solution $x = 1$.

The length of the banner is $8 - 2 = 6$ feet, and the width is $8 - 7 = 1$ foot.

2.

$6 = (x - 2)(x - 7)$
$6 = x^2 - 2x - 7x + 14$
$0 = x^2 - 9x + 20$
$0 = (x - 5)(x - 4)$
$x = 5$ or $x = 4$

The equation has two solutions. They are 5 and 4. So, the width of the banner is 5 feet, and the length of the banner is 4 feet.

8 ★ Standardized TEST PRACTICE

SHORT RESPONSE

1. A cat jumps straight up from the ground with an initial vertical velocity of 10 feet per second.
   a. Write an equation that gives the height of the cat (in feet) as a function of the time (in seconds) since it left the ground.
   b. Find the zeros of the function from part (a). *Explain* what the zeros mean in this situation.

2. A fish tank is shaped like a rectangular prism with a volume of 576 cubic inches. Its length is greater than 10 inches. The dimensions of the tank are shown in the diagram.

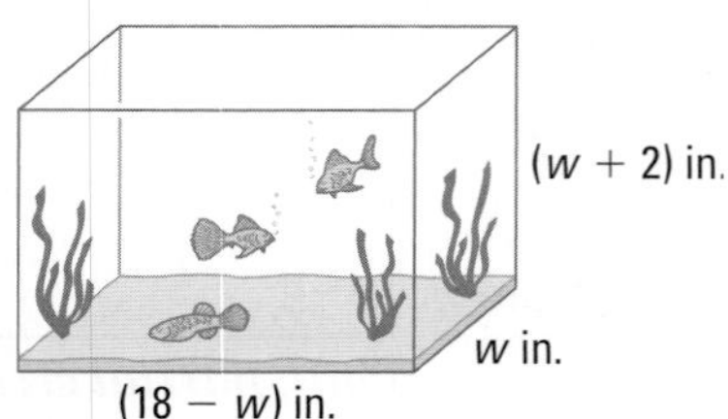

   a. Write a polynomial that represents the volume of the fish tank.
   b. Find the length, width, and height of the fish tank. *Explain* your reasoning using the solutions of the equation from part (a).

3. You throw a ball from an initial height of 5 feet and with an initial vertical velocity of 36 feet per second.
   a. Write an equation that gives the height of the ball (in feet) as a function of the time (in seconds) since it left your hand.
   b. How many times does the ball reach a height of 25 feet? *Explain* your reasoning using the function from part (a).

4. A pencil falls off a shelf with a height of 4 feet.
   a. What is the initial vertical velocity of the pencil? *Explain* your answer.
   b. After how many seconds does the pencil hit the ground?

5. During the period 1985–2000, the number S (in thousands) of students enrolled in public school in the United States and the percent p (in decimal form) of the students enrolled in public school who are also enrolled in a foreign language class can be modeled by

$$S = 27.5x^2 - 336x + 12{,}400 \text{ and}$$

$$p = 0.008x + 0.336$$

where x is the number of years since 1985.
   a. Write an equation that models the number (in thousands) of public school students in the United States enrolled in a foreign language class as a function of the number of years since 1985. *Explain* how you found this equation.
   b. How many public school students in the United States were enrolled in a foreign language class in 2000?

6. Students in an environmental club are planning a garden with four rectangular plots of land separated by stone paths, as shown. The stone paths will have the same width.

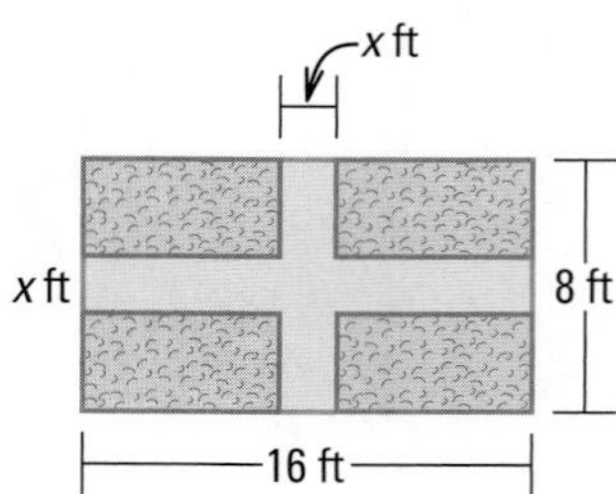

   a. The students plan to cover 80 square feet of path with stone. Write and solve an equation to find the width of the paths.
   b. In part (a) you used one solution of an equation to find your answer. *Explain* how you chose which solution to use.

7. The shape of an entrance to a tunnel can be modeled by the graph of the equation $y = -0.2x(x - 20)$ where x and y are measured in feet. On a coordinate plane, the ground is represented by the x-axis. How wide is the tunnel at its base? *Explain* how you found your answer.

MULTIPLE CHOICE

8. Which is the correct factorization of $25x^2 - 144$?

Ⓐ $(5x + 9)(5x - 16)$

Ⓑ $(5x - 12)^2$

Ⓒ $(5x + 18)(5x - 8)$

Ⓓ $(5x - 12)(5x + 12)$

9. What are the solutions of the equation $(x + 4)(x - 12) = 0$?

Ⓐ 4 and −12 Ⓑ 4 and 12

Ⓒ −4 and −12 Ⓓ −4 and 12

10. What are the solutions of the equation $x^2 - 26 = 11x$?

Ⓐ −2 and 13 Ⓑ 2 and 13

Ⓒ −2 and −13 Ⓓ 2 and −13

GRIDDED ANSWER

11. The equation $x^2 - 20x + 100 = 0$ has two identical solutions. What is the solution of the equation?

12. The square of the binomial $x + 3$ has the form $x^2 + bx + 9$. What is the value of b?

13. What is the degree of the polynomial $6x^4 - 3x^2 + 10x$?

14. The function $f(x) = 4x^2 - 36$ has two zeros. What is the greater of the two zeros?

15. The area of a rectangle is 28 square inches. The length of the rectangle is 3 inches more than its width. What is the width (in inches) of the rectangle?

16. A pine cone falls from a tree branch that is 144 feet above the ground. After how many seconds does the pine cone land on the ground?

EXTENDED RESPONSE

17. The shape of a stone arch in a park can be modeled by the graph of the equation $y = -x^2 + 6x$ where x and y are measured in feet. On a coordinate plane, the ground is represented by the x-axis.

a. Make a table of values that shows the height of the stone arch for $x = 0, 1, 2, 3, 4,$ and 5 feet.

b. Plot the ordered pairs in the table from part (a) as points in a coordinate plane. Connect the points with a smooth curve.

c. How wide is the base of the arch? *Justify* your answer using the zeros of the given function.

d. At how many points does the arch reach a height of 9 feet? *Justify* your answer algebraically.

18. A box is a rectangular prism with a volume of 768 cubic inches. The length of the box is 4 inches more than its height. Its width is the difference of 16 and its height.

a. Draw a diagram of the box and label its dimensions in terms of its height.

b. Write a polynomial that represents the volume of the box.

c. Use the polynomial from part (b) to find two sets of possible dimensions of the box.

d. Which set of dimensions results in a box with the least possible surface area? *Explain* your reasoning.

9 Quadratic Equations and Functions

Lesson

- 9.1 CC.9-12.F.BF.3
- 9.2 CC.9-12.F.IF.7a*
- 9.3 CC.9-12.F.IF.7a*
- 9.4 CC.9-12.A.REI.4b
- 9.5 CC.9-12.A.REI.4b
- 9.6 CC.9-12.A.REI.4b
- 9.7 CC.9-12.A.REI.11*
- 9.8 CC.9-12.A.CED.2*
- 9.9 CC.9-12.F.IF.4*

9.1 Graph $y = ax^2 + c$

9.2 Graph $y = ax^2 + bx + c$

9.3 Solve Quadratic Equations by Graphing

9.4 Use Square Roots to Solve Quadratic Equations

9.5 Solve Quadratic Equations by Completing the Square

9.6 Solve Quadratic Equations by the Quadratic Formula

9.7 Solve Systems with Quadratic Equations

9.8 Compare Linear, Exponential, and Quadratic Models

9.9 Model Relationships

Before

Previously, you learned the following skills, which you'll use in this chapter: reflecting points in a line and finding square roots.

Prerequisite Skills

VOCABULARY CHECK

Copy and complete the statement.

1. The x-coordinate of a point where a graph crosses the x-axis is a(n) _?_.
2. A(n) _?_ is a function of the form $y = a \cdot b^x$ where $a \neq 0$, $b > 0$, and $b \neq 1$.

SKILLS CHECK

Draw the blue figure. Then draw its image after a reflection in the red line.

3.

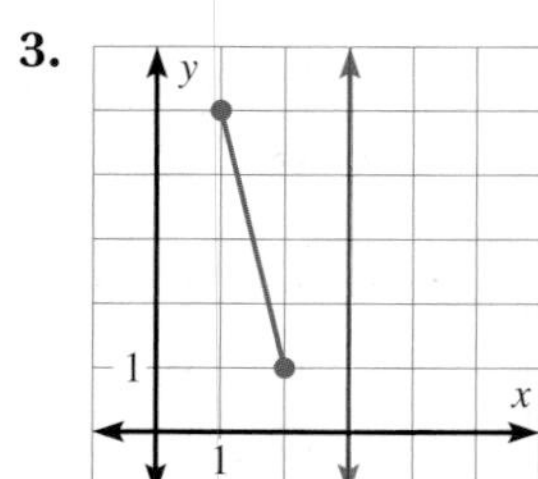

4.

5.

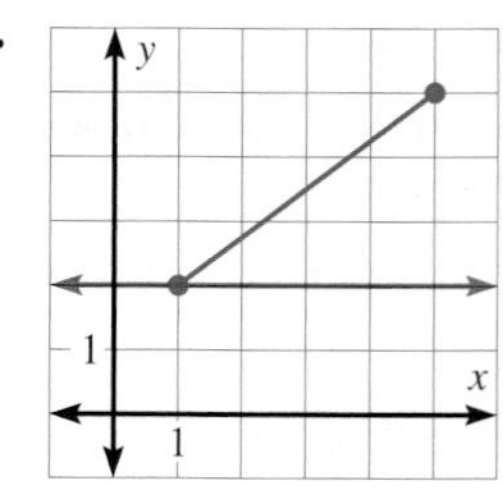

Evaluate the expression.

6. $\sqrt{81}$
7. $-\sqrt{25}$
8. $\sqrt{1}$
9. $\pm\sqrt{64}$

Now

In this chapter, you will apply the big ideas listed below and reviewed in the Chapter Summary. You will also use the key vocabulary listed below.

Big Ideas

1. **Graphing quadratic functions**
2. **Solving quadratic equations**
3. **Comparing linear, exponential, and quadratic models**

KEY VOCABULARY

- quadratic function
- parabola
- parent quadratic function
- vertex
- axis of symmetry
- minimum value
- maximum value
- quadratic equation
- completing the square
- quadratic formula

Why?

You can use a quadratic model for real-world situations involving vertical motion. For example, you can write and solve a quadratic equation to find the time a snowboarder is in the air during a jump.

Animated Algebra

The animation illustrated below helps you answer a question from this chapter: How many seconds is the snowboarder in the air during a jump?

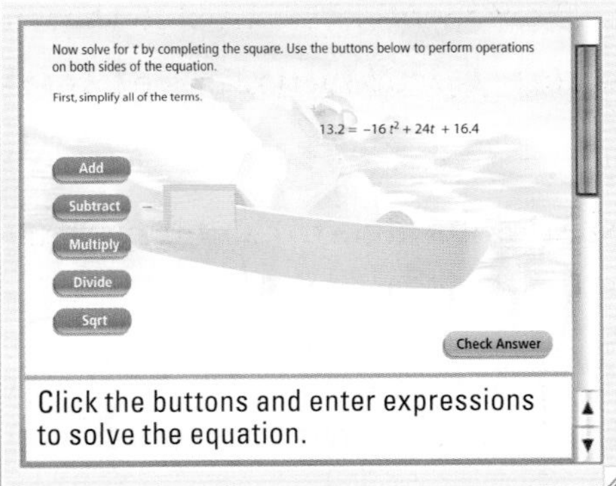

Animated Algebra at my.hrw.com

9.1 Graph $y = ax^2 + c$

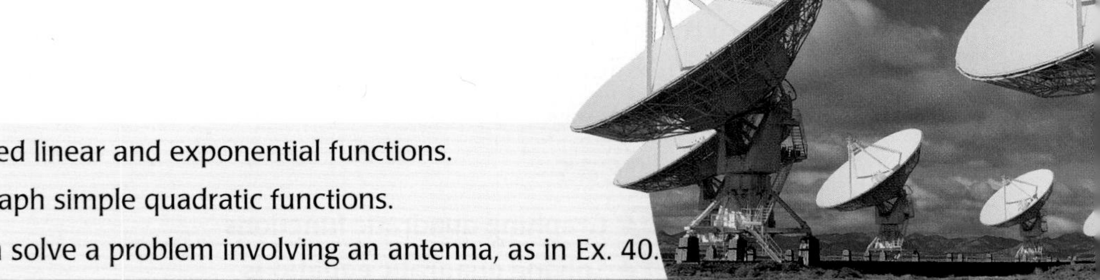

Before You graphed linear and exponential functions.

Now You will graph simple quadratic functions.

Why? So you can solve a problem involving an antenna, as in Ex. 40.

Key Vocabulary
- quadratic function
- parabola
- parent quadratic function
- vertex
- axis of symmetry

A **quadratic function** is a nonlinear function that can be written in the **standard form** $y = ax^2 + bx + c$ where $a \neq 0$. Every quadratic function has a U-shaped graph called a **parabola**. In this lesson, you will graph quadratic functions where $b = 0$.

CC.9-12.F.BF.3 Identify the effect on the graph of replacing $f(x)$ by $f(x) + k$, $kf(x)$, $f(kx)$, and $f(x + k)$ for specific values of k (both positive and negative); find the value of k given the graphs. Experiment with cases and illustrate an explanation of the effects on the graph using technology.

KEY CONCEPT *For Your Notebook*

Parent Quadratic Function

The most basic quadratic function in the family of quadratic functions, called the **parent quadratic function**, is $y = x^2$. The graph of $y = x^2$ is shown below.

The lowest or highest point on a parabola is the **vertex**. The vertex of the graph of $y = x^2$ is (0, 0).

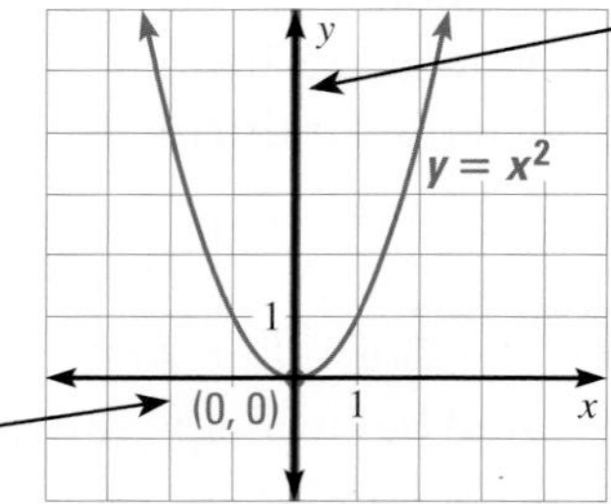

The line that passes through the vertex and divides the parabola into two symmetric parts is called the **axis of symmetry**. The axis of symmetry for the graph of $y = x^2$ is the y-axis, $x = 0$.

EXAMPLE 1 Graph $y = ax^2$ where $|a| > 1$

STEP 1 **Make** a table of values for $y = 3x^2$.

x	−2	−1	0	1	2
y	12	3	0	3	12

STEP 2 **Plot** the points from the table.

STEP 3 **Draw** a smooth curve through the points.

STEP 4 **Compare** the graphs of $y = 3x^2$ and $y = x^2$. Both graphs open up and have the same vertex, (0, 0), and axis of symmetry, $x = 0$. The graph of $y = 3x^2$ is narrower than the graph of $y = x^2$ because the graph of $y = 3x^2$ is a vertical stretch (by a factor of 3) of the graph of $y = x^2$.

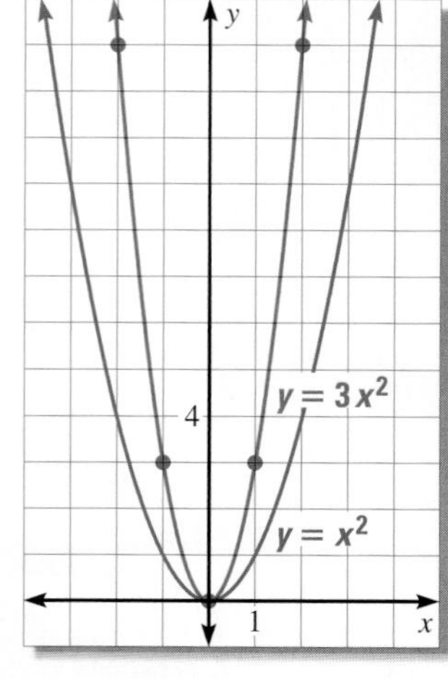

DESCRIBE A FUNCTION

A quadratic function has an unbroken graph, so the function is continuous.

© Digital Vision/Getty Images

EXAMPLE 2 Graph $y = ax^2$ where $|a| < 1$

Graph $y = -\frac{1}{4}x^2$. Compare the graph with the graph of $y = x^2$.

MAKE A TABLE
To make the calculations easier, choose values of x that are multiples of 2.

STEP 1 **Make** a table of values for $y = -\frac{1}{4}x^2$.

x	−4	−2	0	2	4
y	−4	−1	0	−1	−4

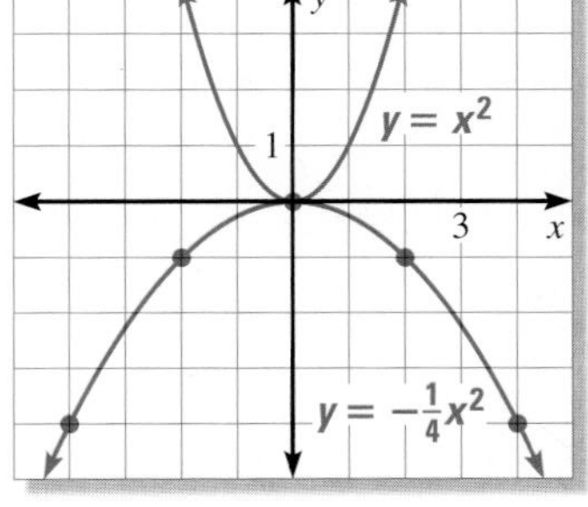

STEP 2 **Plot** the points from the table.

STEP 3 **Draw** a smooth curve through the points.

STEP 4 **Compare** the graphs of $y = -\frac{1}{4}x^2$ and $y = x^2$. Both graphs have the same vertex (0, 0), and the same axis of symmetry, $x = 0$. However, the graph of $y = -\frac{1}{4}x^2$ is wider than the graph of $y = x^2$ and it opens down. This is because the graph of $y = -\frac{1}{4}x^2$ is a vertical shrink $\left(\text{by a factor of } \frac{1}{4}\right)$ with a reflection in the x-axis of the graph of $y = x^2$.

GRAPHING QUADRATIC FUNCTIONS Examples 1 and 2 suggest the following general result: a parabola opens up when the coefficient of x^2 is positive and opens down when the coefficient of x^2 is negative.

EXAMPLE 3 Graph $y = x^2 + c$

Graph $y = x^2 + 5$. Compare the graph with the graph of $y = x^2$.

ANALYZE RATE OF CHANGE
Notice that for a quadratic function, the rate of change in y with respect to x is *not* constant as it is for a linear function. For instance, $\frac{6-9}{-1-(-2)} = -3$, while $\frac{5-6}{0-(-1)} = -1$.

STEP 1 **Make** a table of values for $y = x^2 + 5$.

x	−2	−1	0	1	2
y	9	6	5	6	9

STEP 2 **Plot** the points from the table.

STEP 3 **Draw** a smooth curve through the points.

STEP 4 **Compare** the graphs of $y = x^2 + 5$ and $y = x^2$. Both graphs open up and have the same axis of symmetry, $x = 0$. However, the vertex of the graph of $y = x^2 + 5$, (0, 5), is different than the vertex of the graph of $y = x^2$, (0, 0), because the graph of $y = x^2 + 5$ is a vertical translation (of 5 units up) of the graph of $y = x^2$.

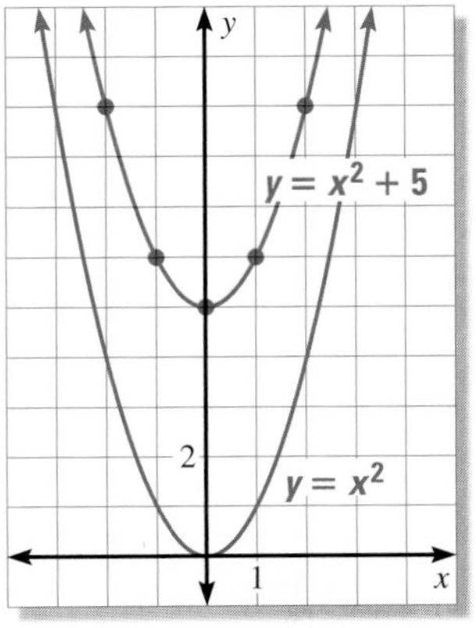

✓ GUIDED PRACTICE for Examples 1, 2, and 3

Graph the function. Compare the graph with the graph of $y = x^2$.

1. $y = -4x^2$
2. $y = \frac{1}{3}x^2$
3. $y = x^2 + 2$

EXAMPLE 4 Graph $y = ax^2 + c$

Graph $y = \frac{1}{2}x^2 - 4$. Compare the graph with the graph of $y = x^2$.

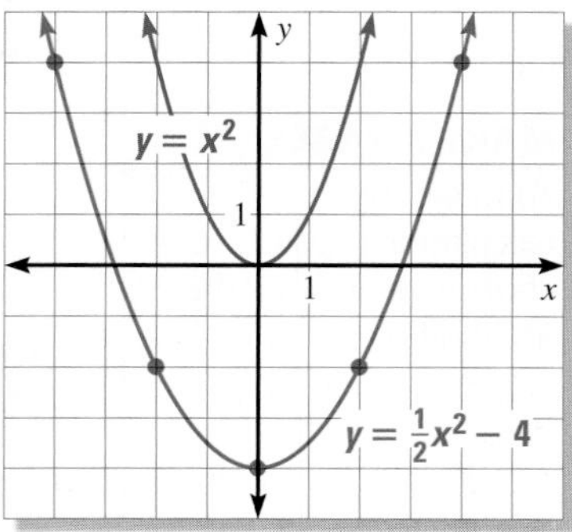

STEP 1 **Make** a table of values for $y = \frac{1}{2}x^2 - 4$.

x	−4	−2	0	2	4
y	4	−2	−4	−2	4

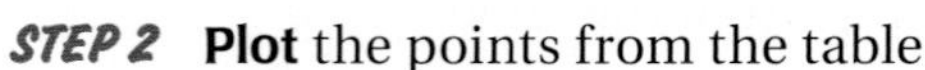

STEP 2 **Plot** the points from the table.

STEP 3 **Draw** a smooth curve through the points.

STEP 4 **Compare** the graphs of $y = \frac{1}{2}x^2 - 4$ and $y = x^2$. Both graphs open up and have the same axis of symmetry, $x = 0$. However, the graph of $y = \frac{1}{2}x^2 - 4$ is wider and has a lower vertex than the graph of $y = x^2$ because the graph of $y = \frac{1}{2}x^2 - 4$ is a vertical shrink and a vertical translation of the graph of $y = x^2$.

✓ GUIDED PRACTICE for Example 4

Graph the function. Compare the graph with the graph of $y = x^2$.

4. $y = 3x^2 - 6$

5. $y = -5x^2 + 1$

6. $y = \frac{3}{4}x^2 - 2$

KEY CONCEPT *For Your Notebook*

$y = ax^2, a > 0$

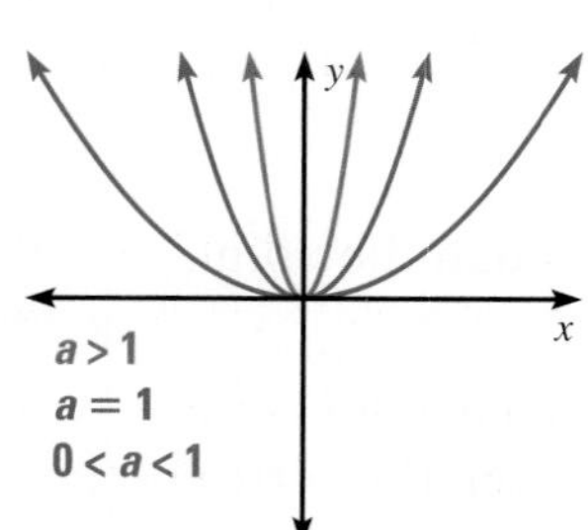

Compared with the graph of $y = x^2$, the graph of $y = ax^2$ is:

- a vertical stretch if $a > 1$,
- a vertical shrink if $0 < a < 1$.

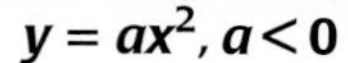

$y = ax^2, a < 0$

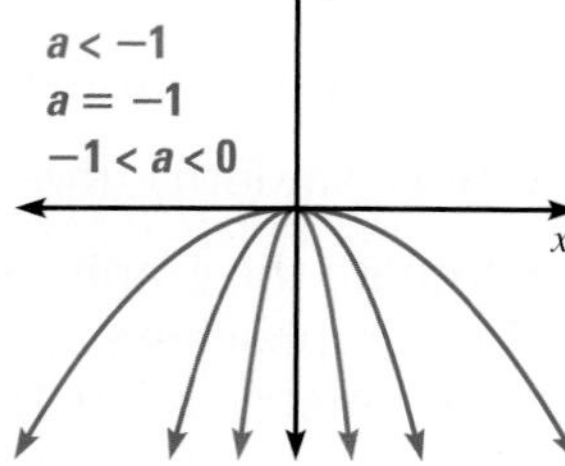

Compared with the graph of $y = x^2$, the graph of $y = ax^2$ is:

- a vertical stretch with a reflection in the x-axis if $a < -1$,
- a vertical shrink with a reflection in the x-axis if $-1 < a < 0$.

$y = x^2 + c$

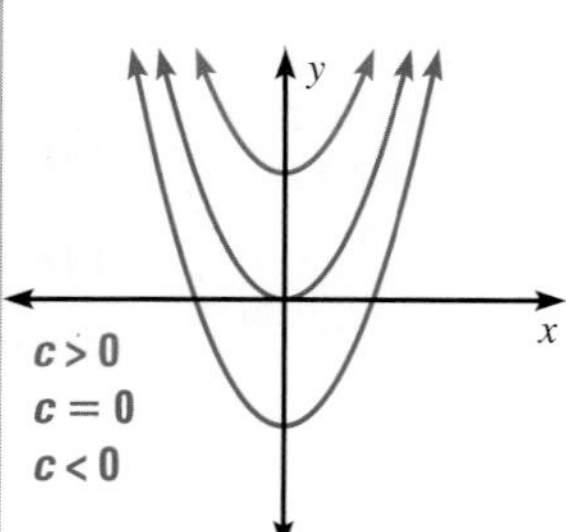

Compared with the graph of $y = x^2$, the graph of $y = x^2 + c$ is:

- an upward vertical translation if $c > 0$,
- a downward vertical translation if $c < 0$.

★ EXAMPLE 5 Standardized Test Practice

How would the graph of the function $y = x^2 + 6$ be affected if the function were changed to $y = x^2 + 2$?

Ⓐ The graph would shift 2 units up.

Ⓑ The graph would shift 4 units up.

Ⓒ The graph would shift 4 units down.

Ⓓ The graph would shift 4 units to the left.

ELIMINATE CHOICES
You can eliminate choice D because changing the value of c in a function of the form $y = x^2 + c$ translates the graph up or down.

Solution

The vertex of the graph of $y = x^2 + 6$ is 6 units above the origin, or (0, 6). The vertex of the graph of $y = x^2 + 2$ is 2 units above the origin, or (0, 2). Moving the vertex from (0, 6) to (0, 2) translates the graph 4 units down.

▶ The correct answer is C. Ⓐ Ⓑ Ⓒ Ⓓ

EXAMPLE 6 Use a graph

SOLAR ENERGY A solar trough has a reflective parabolic surface that is used to collect solar energy. The sun's rays are reflected from the surface toward a pipe that carries water. The heated water produces steam that is used to produce electricity.

ANALYZE A GRAPH
You can use the graph to estimate the range of the function. The lowest point is at the origin. The two highest points are just above the line $y = 2$. So, an estimate of the range is $0 \le y \le 2$.

The graph of the function $y = 0.09x^2$ models the cross section of the reflective surface where x and y are measured in meters. Use the graph to find the domain and range of the function in this situation.

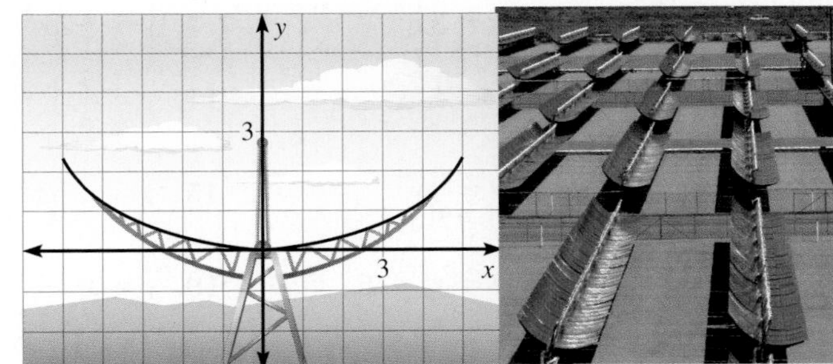

Solution

STEP 1 **Find** the domain. In the graph, the reflective surface extends 5 meters on either side of the origin. So, the domain is $-5 \le x \le 5$.

STEP 2 **Find** the range using the fact that the lowest point on the reflective surface is (0, 0) and the highest point occurs at $x = 5$ or $x = -5$.

$$y = 0.09(5)^2 = 2.25 \quad \text{Substitute 5 for } x\text{. Then simplify.}$$

The range is $0 \le y \le 2.25$.

✓ GUIDED PRACTICE for Examples 5 and 6

7. *Describe* how the graph of the function $y = x^2 + 2$ would be affected if the function were changed to $y = x^2 - 2$.

8. **WHAT IF?** In Example 6, suppose the reflective surface extends just 4 meters on either side of the origin. Find the domain and range of the function in this situation.

9.1 EXERCISES

HOMEWORK KEY

 = See **WORKED-OUT SOLUTIONS** Exs. 7 and 41

★ = **STANDARDIZED TEST PRACTICE** Exs. 2, 22, 33, 43, and 44

SKILL PRACTICE

1. **VOCABULARY** Copy and complete: Every quadratic function has a U-shaped graph called a(n) _?_.

2. ★ **WRITING** *Explain* how you can tell whether the graph of a quadratic function opens up or down.

MATCHING **Match the quadratic function with its graph.**

3. $y = \frac{1}{2}x^2 - 4$

4. $y = \frac{1}{2}x^2 - 2$

5. $y = -\frac{1}{2}x^2 + 2$

A. 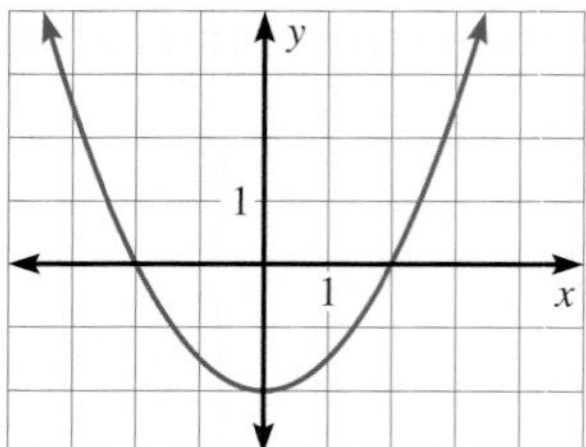

B. 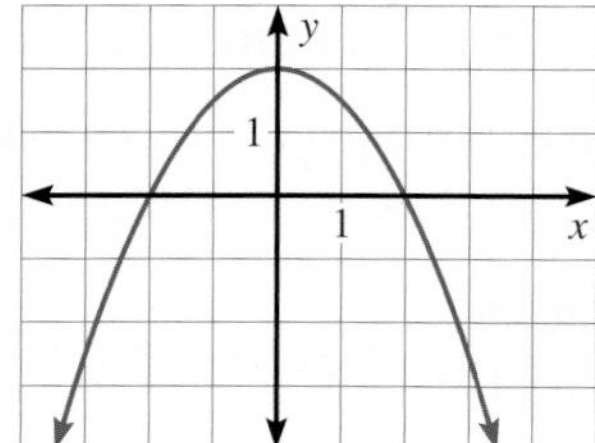

C. 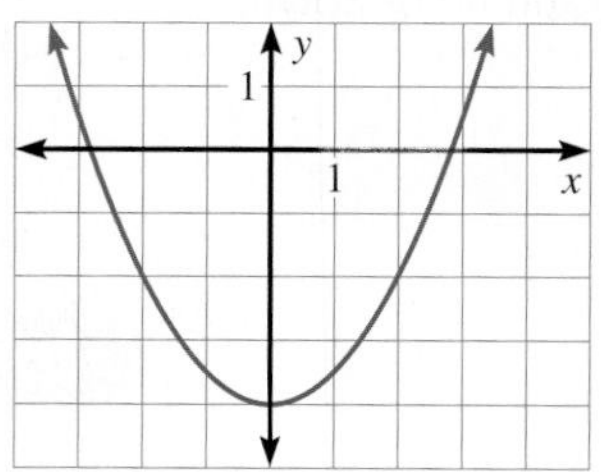

EXAMPLES 1, 2, and 3 for Exs. 6–23

GRAPHING QUADRATIC FUNCTIONS **Graph the function. Compare the graph with the graph of $y = x^2$.**

6. $y = 8x^2$

7. $y = -2x^2$

8. $y = -3x^2$

9. $y = 5x^2$

10. $y = \frac{11}{2}x^2$

11. $y = \frac{2}{3}x^2$

12. $y = -\frac{3}{4}x^2$

13. $y = -\frac{1}{9}x^2$

14. $y = \frac{3}{8}x^2$

15. $y = -\frac{1}{5}x^2$

16. $y = x^2 - 7$

17. $y = x^2 + 9$

18. $y = x^2 + 6$

19. $y = x^2 - 4$

20. $y = x^2 - 1$

21. $y = x^2 + \frac{7}{4}$

22. ★ **MULTIPLE CHOICE** What is the vertex of the graph of the function $y = -\frac{3}{4}x^2 + 7$?

Ⓐ $(-7, 0)$ Ⓑ $(0, -7)$ Ⓒ $(0, 7)$ Ⓓ $(7, 0)$

23. **ERROR ANALYSIS** *Describe* and correct the error in drawing and comparing the graphs of $y = x^2$ and $y = x^2 - 2$.

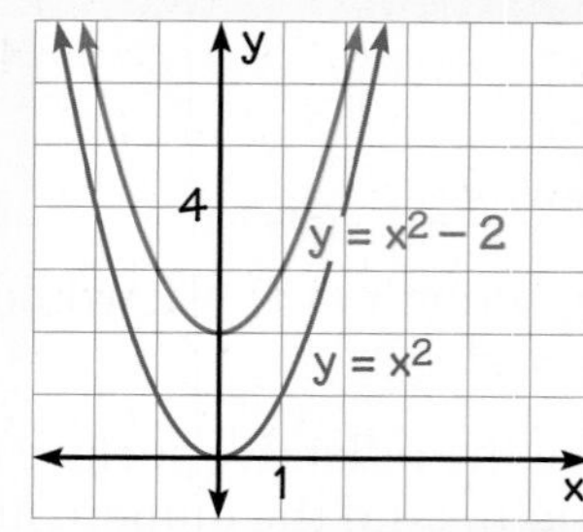

Both graphs open up and have the same axis of symmetry. However, the vertex of the graph of $y = x^2 - 2$, $(0, 2)$, is 2 units above the vertex of the graph of $y = x^2$, $(0, 0)$.

EXAMPLE 4
for Exs. 24–32

GRAPHING QUADRATIC FUNCTIONS **Graph the function. Compare the graph with the graph of $y = x^2$.**

24. $y = 7x^2 + 7$ **25.** $y = -x^2 + 5$ **26.** $y = 2x^2 - 12$

27. $y = -2x^2 - 1$ **28.** $y = -3x^2 - 2$ **29.** $y = \frac{3}{4}x^2 - 3$

30. $y = \frac{1}{5}x^2 + 10$ **31.** $y = \frac{1}{2}x^2 - 5$ **32.** $y = -\frac{2}{3}x^2 + 9$

EXAMPLE 5
for Exs. 33–36

33. ★ **MULTIPLE CHOICE** How would the graph of the function $y = x^2 + 3$ be affected if the function were changed to $y = x^2 + 9$?

Ⓐ The graph would shift 9 units to the right.

Ⓑ The graph would shift 6 units up.

Ⓒ The graph would shift 9 units up.

Ⓓ The graph would shift 6 units down.

COMPARING GRAPHS **Tell how you can obtain the graph of *g* from the graph of *f* using transformations.**

34. $f(x) = x^2 - 5$
$g(x) = x^2 + 8$

35. $f(x) = 3x^2 - 11$
$g(x) = 3x^2 - 16$

36. $f(x) = 4x^2$
$g(x) = 2x^2$

CHALLENGE **Write a function of the form $y = ax^2 + c$ whose graph passes through the two given points.**

37. $(-1, 9), (0, 3)$ **38.** $(2, 1), (5, -20)$ **39.** $(-2, -16.5), (1, 4.5)$

PROBLEM SOLVING

GRAPHING CALCULATOR **You may wish to use a graphing calculator to complete the following Problem Solving exercises.**

EXAMPLE 6
for Exs. 40–41

40. ASTRONOMY A cross section of the parabolic surface of the antenna shown can be modeled by the graph of the function $y = 0.012x^2$ where x and y are measured in meters.

a. Find the domain of the function in this situation.

b. Find the range of the function in this situation.

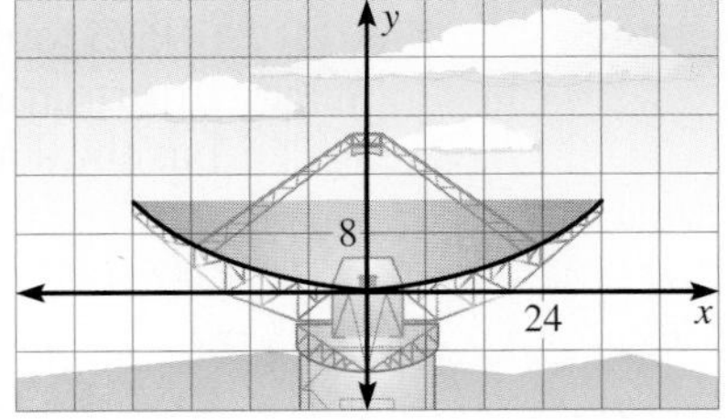

41. SAILING Sailors need to consider the speed of the wind when adjusting the sails on their boat. The force F (in pounds per square foot) on a sail when the wind is blowing perpendicular to the sail can be modeled by the function $F = 0.004v^2$ where v is the wind speed (in knots).

a. Graph the function for wind speeds from 0 knots to 50 knots.

b. Use the graph to estimate the wind speed that will produce a force of 1 pound per square foot on a sail.

c. Estimate the wind speed that will produce a force of 5 pounds per square foot on a sail.

REVIEW VERTICAL MOTION
You may want to review the vertical motion model for Ex. 42.

42. FALLING OBJECTS Two acorns drop from an oak tree. One falls 45 feet, while the other falls 32 feet.

a. For each acorn, write an equation that gives the height h (in feet) of the acorn as a function of the time t (in seconds) it has fallen.

b. *Describe* how the graphs of the two equations are related.

43. ★ SHORT RESPONSE The breaking strength w (in pounds) of a manila rope can be modeled by the function $w = 8900d^2$ where d is the diameter (in inches) of the rope.

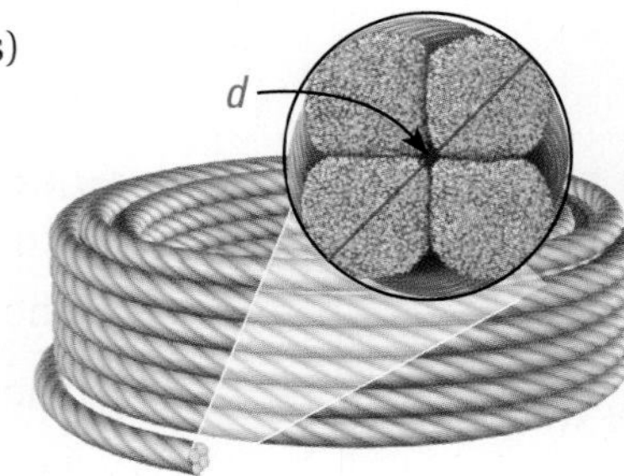

a. Graph the function.

b. If a manila rope has 4 times the breaking strength of another manila rope, does the rope have 4 times the diameter of the other rope? *Explain.*

44. ★ EXTENDED RESPONSE For an engineering contest, you have to create a container for an egg so that the container can be dropped from a height of 30 feet without breaking the egg.

a. The distance y (in feet) that the container falls is given by the function $y = 16t^2$ where t is the time (in seconds) the container has fallen. Graph the function.

b. The height y (in feet) of the dropped container is given by the function $y = -16t^2 + 30$ where t is the time (in seconds) since the container is dropped. Graph the function.

c. How are the graphs from part (a) and part (b) related? *Explain* how you can use each graph to find the number of seconds after which the container has fallen 10 feet.

Animated Algebra at my.hrw.com

45. CHALLENGE The kinetic energy E (in joules) of an object in motion is given by $E = \frac{1}{2}mv^2$ where m is the object's mass (in kilograms) and v is the object's velocity (in meters per second). Suppose a baseball has 918.75 joules of energy when traveling 35 meters per second. Use this information to write and graph an equation that gives the energy E of the baseball as a function of its velocity v.

9.2 Graph $y = ax^2 + bx + c$

Before You graphed simple quadratic functions.

Now You will graph general quadratic functions.

Why? So you can investigate a cable's height, as in Example 4.

Key Vocabulary
- **minimum value**
- **maximum value**

COMMON CORE

CC.9-12.F.IF.7a Graph linear and quadratic functions and show intercepts, maxima, and minima.*

You can use the properties below to graph any quadratic function. You will justify the formula for the axis of symmetry in Exercise 38 in this lesson.

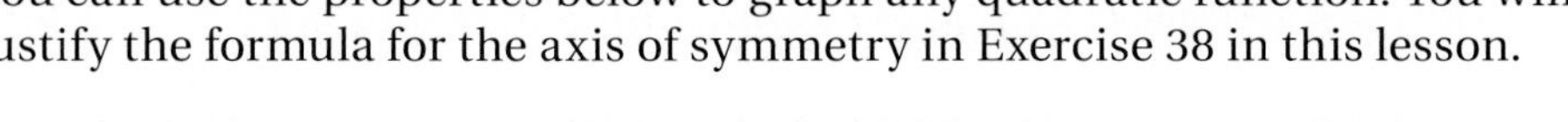

KEY CONCEPT *For Your Notebook*

Properties of the Graph of a Quadratic Function

The graph of $y = ax^2 + bx + c$ is a parabola that:

- opens up if $a > 0$ and opens down if $a < 0$.
- is narrower than the graph of $y = x^2$ if $|a| > 1$ and wider if $|a| < 1$.
- has an axis of symmetry of $x = -\frac{b}{2a}$.
- has a vertex with an x-coordinate of $-\frac{b}{2a}$.
- has a y-intercept of c. So, the point $(0, c)$ is on the parabola.

$y = ax^2 + bx + c, a > 0$

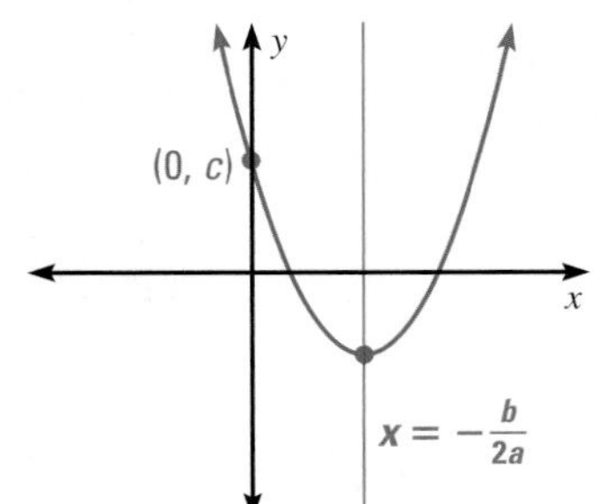

EXAMPLE 1 Find the axis of symmetry and the vertex

Consider the function $y = -2x^2 + 12x - 7$.

a. Find the axis of symmetry of the graph of the function.

b. Find the vertex of the graph of the function.

Solution

a. For the function $y = -2x^2 + 12x - 7$, $a = -2$ and $b = 12$.

$x = -\frac{b}{2a} = -\frac{12}{2(-2)} = 3$ **Substitute −2 for *a* and 12 for *b*. Then simplify.**

IDENTIFY THE VERTEX
Because the vertex lies on the axis of symmetry, x = 3, the x-coordinate of the vertex is 3.

b. The x-coordinate of the vertex is $-\frac{b}{2a}$, or 3.

To find the y-coordinate, substitute 3 for x in the function and find y.

$y = -2(3)^2 + 12(3) - 7 = 11$ **Substitute 3 for *x*. Then simplify.**

▶ The vertex is (3, 11).

EXAMPLE 2 Graph $y = ax^2 + bx + c$

Graph $y = 3x^2 - 6x + 2$.

AVOID ERRORS
Be sure to include the negative sign before the fraction when calculating the axis of symmetry.

STEP 1 **Determine** whether the parabola opens up or down. Because $a > 0$, the parabola opens up.

STEP 2 **Find** and draw the axis of symmetry: $x = -\frac{b}{2a} = -\frac{-6}{2(3)} = 1.$

STEP 3 **Find** and plot the vertex.

The x-coordinate of the vertex is $-\frac{b}{2a}$, or 1.

To find the y-coordinate, substitute 1 for x in the function and simplify.

$y = 3(1)^2 - 6(1) + 2 = -1$

So, the vertex is $(1, -1)$.

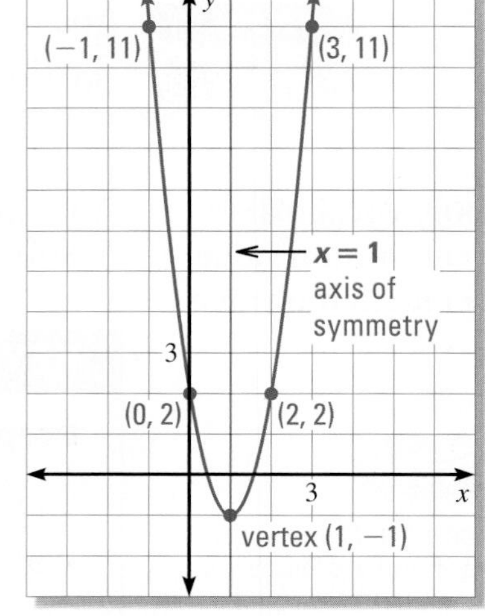

STEP 4 **Plot** two points. Choose two x-values less than the x-coordinate of the vertex. Then find the corresponding y-values.

x	0	−1
y	2	11

REVIEW REFLECTIONS
For help with reflections, see p. SR14.

STEP 5 **Reflect** the points plotted in Step 4 in the axis of symmetry.

STEP 6 **Draw** a parabola through the plotted points.

Animated Algebra at my.hrw.com

✓ GUIDED PRACTICE for Examples 1 and 2

1. Find the axis of symmetry and the vertex of the graph of the function $y = x^2 - 2x - 3$.
2. Graph the function $y = 3x^2 + 12x - 1$. Label the vertex and axis of symmetry.

KEY CONCEPT *For Your Notebook*

Minimum and Maximum Values

For $y = ax^2 + bx + c$, the y-coordinate of the vertex is the **minimum value** of the function if $a > 0$ or the **maximum value** of the function if $a < 0$.

$y = ax^2 + bx + c, a > 0$

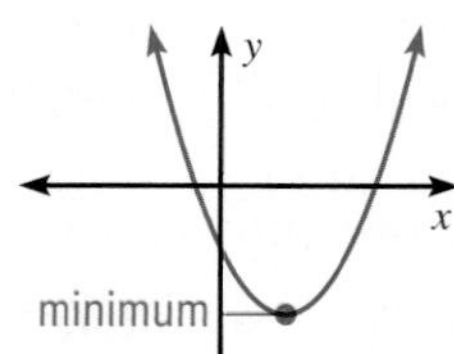

$y = ax^2 + bx + c, a < 0$

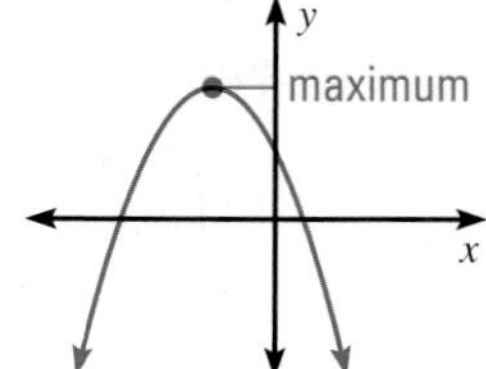

EXAMPLE 3 Find the minimum or maximum value

Tell whether the function $f(x) = -3x^2 - 12x + 10$ has a *minimum value* or a *maximum value*. Then find the minimum or maximum value.

Solution

Because $a = -3$ and $-3 < 0$, the parabola opens down and the function has a maximum value. To find the maximum value, find the vertex.

$x = -\frac{b}{2a} = -\frac{-12}{2(-3)} = -2$ **The x-coordinate is $-\frac{b}{2a}$.**

$f(-2) = -3(-2)^2 - 12(-2) + 10 = 22$ **Substitute -2 for x. Then simplify.**

▶ The maximum value of the function is $f(-2) = 22$.

EXAMPLE 4 Find the minimum value of a function

SUSPENSION BRIDGES The suspension cables between the two towers of the Mackinac Bridge in Michigan form a parabola that can be modeled by the graph of $y = 0.000097x^2 - 0.37x + 549$ where x and y are measured in feet. What is the height of the cable above the water at its lowest point?

Solution

The lowest point of the cable is at the vertex of the parabola. Find the x-coordinate of the vertex. Use $a = 0.000097$ and $b = -0.37$.

$x = -\frac{b}{2a} = -\frac{-0.37}{2(0.000097)} \approx 1910$ **Use a calculator.**

Substitute 1910 for x in the equation to find the y-coordinate of the vertex.

$y \approx 0.000097(1910)^2 - 0.37(1910) + 549 \approx 196$

▶ The cable is about 196 feet above the water at its lowest point.

✓ GUIDED PRACTICE for Examples 3 and 4

3. Tell whether the function $f(x) = 6x^2 + 18x + 13$ has a *minimum value* or a *maximum value*. Then find the minimum or maximum value.

4. **SUSPENSION BRIDGES** The cables between the two towers of the Tacoma Narrows Bridge form a parabola that can be modeled by the graph of the equation $y = 0.00014x^2 - 0.4x + 507$ where x and y are measured in feet. What is the height of the cable above the water at its lowest point? Round your answer to the nearest foot.

9.2 EXERCISES

HOMEWORK KEY

◯ = See **WORKED-OUT SOLUTIONS** Exs. 9 and 41

★ = **STANDARDIZED TEST PRACTICE** Exs. 2, 12, 27, 37, 42, and 44

SKILL PRACTICE

1. **VOCABULARY** *Explain* how you can tell whether a quadratic function has a maximum value or minimum value without graphing the function.

2. ★ **WRITING** *Describe* the steps you would take to graph a quadratic function in standard form.

EXAMPLE 1 for Exs. 3–14

FINDING AXIS OF SYMMETRY AND VERTEX Find the axis of symmetry and the vertex of the graph of the function.

3. $y = 2x^2 - 8x + 6$
4. $y = x^2 - 6x + 11$
5. $y = -3x^2 + 24x - 22$
6. $y = -x^2 - 10x$
7. $y = 6x^2 + 6x$
8. $y = 4x^2 + 7$
9. $y = -\frac{2}{3}x^2 - 1$
10. $y = \frac{1}{2}x^2 + 8x - 9$
11. $y = -\frac{1}{4}x^2 + 3x - 2$

12. ★ **MULTIPLE CHOICE** What is the vertex of the graph of the function $y = -3x^2 + 18x - 13$?

   Ⓐ (−3, −94) Ⓑ (−3, −14) Ⓒ (3, −13) Ⓓ (3, 14)

ERROR ANALYSIS ***Describe* and correct the error in finding the axis of symmetry of the graph of the given function.**

13. $y = 2x^2 + 16x - 1$

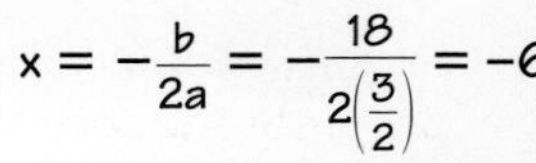

$x = \frac{b}{2a} = \frac{16}{2(2)} = 4$

The axis of symmetry is x = 4.

14. $y = -\frac{3}{2}x^2 + 18x - 5$

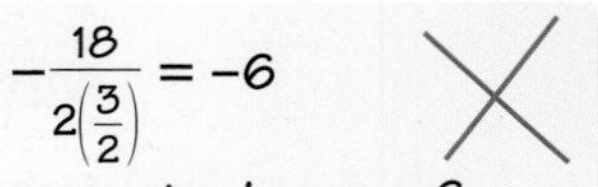

$x = -\frac{b}{2a} = -\frac{18}{2\left(\frac{3}{2}\right)} = -6$

The axis of symmetry is x = −6.

EXAMPLE 2 for Exs. 15–27

GRAPHING QUADRATIC FUNCTIONS Graph the function. Label the vertex and axis of symmetry.

15. $y = x^2 + 6x + 2$
16. $y = x^2 + 4x + 8$
17. $y = 2x^2 + 7x + 21$
18. $y = 5x^2 + 10x - 3$
19. $y = 4x^2 + x - 32$
20. $y = -4x^2 + 4x + 8$
21. $y = -3x^2 - 2x - 5$
22. $y = -8x^2 - 12x + 1$
23. $y = -x^2 + \frac{1}{4}x + \frac{1}{2}$
24. $y = \frac{1}{3}x^2 + 6x - 9$
25. $y = -\frac{1}{2}x^2 + 6x + 3$
26. $y = -\frac{1}{4}x^2 - x + 1$

27. ★ **MULTIPLE CHOICE** Which function has the graph shown?

   Ⓐ $y = -2x^2 + 8x + 3$

   Ⓑ $y = -\frac{1}{2}x^2 + 2x + 3$

   Ⓒ $y = \frac{1}{2}x^2 + 2x + 3$

   Ⓓ $y = 2x^2 + 8x + 3$

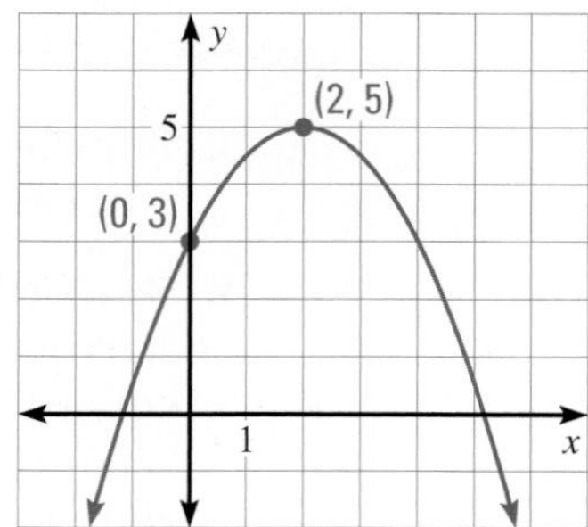

EXAMPLE 3
for Exs. 28–36

MAXIMUM AND MINIMUM VALUES Tell whether the function has a *minimum value* or a *maximum value*. Then find the minimum or maximum value.

28. $f(x) = x^2 - 6$

29. $f(x) = -5x^2 + 7$

30. $f(x) = 4x^2 + 32x$

31. $f(x) = -3x^2 + 12x - 20$

32. $f(x) = x^2 + 7x + 8$

33. $f(x) = -2x^2 - x + 10$

34. $f(x) = \frac{1}{2}x^2 - 2x + 5$

35. $f(x) = -\frac{3}{8}x^2 + 9x$

36. $f(x) = \frac{1}{4}x^2 + 7x + 11$

37. ★ **WRITING** Compare the graph of $y = x^2 + 4x + 1$ with the graph of $y = x^2 - 4x + 1$.

38. REASONING Follow the steps below to justify the equation for the axis of symmetry for the graph of $y = ax^2 + bx + c$. Because the graph of $y = ax^2 + bx + c$ is a vertical translation of the graph of $y = ax^2 + bx$, the two graphs have the same axis of symmetry. Use the function $y = ax^2 + bx$ in place of $y = ax^2 + bx + c$.

a. Find the x-intercepts of the graph of $y = ax^2 + bx$. (You can do this by finding the zeros of the function $y = ax^2 + bx$ using factoring.)

b. Because a parabola is symmetric about its axis of symmetry, the axis of symmetry passes through a point halfway between the x-intercepts of the parabola. Find the x-coordinate of this point. What is an equation of the vertical line through this point?

39. CHALLENGE Write a function of the form $y = ax^2 + bx$ whose graph contains the points (1, 6) and (3, 6).

PROBLEM SOLVING

GRAPHING CALCULATOR You may wish to use a graphing calculator to complete the following Problem Solving exercises.

EXAMPLE 4
for Exs. 40–42

40. SPIDERS Fishing spiders can propel themselves across water and leap vertically from the surface of the water. During a vertical jump, the height of the body of the spider can be modeled by the function $y = -4500x^2 + 820x + 43$ where x is the duration (in seconds) of the jump and y is the height (in millimeters) of the spider above the surface of the water. After how many seconds does the spider's body reach its maximum height? What is the maximum height?

41. ARCHITECTURE The parabolic arches that support the roof of the Dallas Convention Center can be modeled by the graph of the equation $y = -0.0019x^2 + 0.71x$ where x and y are measured in feet. What is the height h at the highest point of the arch as shown in the diagram?

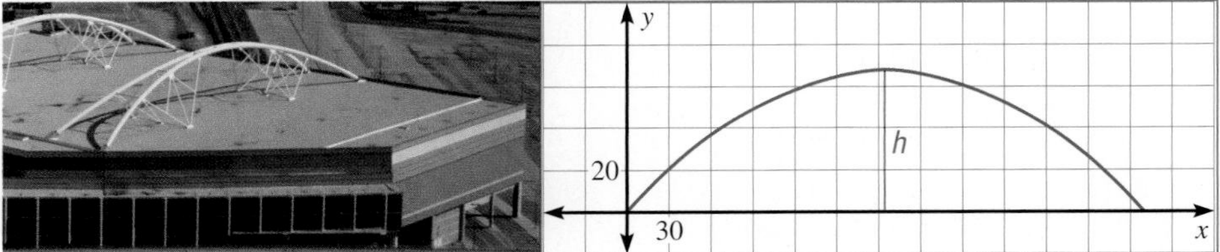

Stephen Finn/Alamy

42. ★ **EXTENDED RESPONSE** Students are selling packages of flower bulbs to raise money for a class trip. Last year, when the students charged \$5 per package, they sold 150 packages. The students want to increase the cost per package. They estimate that they will lose 10 sales for each \$1 increase in the cost per package. The sales revenue R (in dollars) generated by selling the packages is given by the function $R = (5 + n)(150 - 10n)$ where n is the number of \$1 increases.

   a. Write the function in standard form.

   b. Find the maximum value of the function.

   c. At what price should the packages be sold to generate the most sales revenue? *Explain* your reasoning.

43. **AIRCRAFT** An aircraft hangar is a large building where planes are stored. The opening of one airport hangar is a parabolic arch that can be modeled by the graph of the equation $y = -0.007x^2 + 1.7x$ where x and y are measured in feet. Graph the function. Use the graph to determine how wide the hangar is at its base.

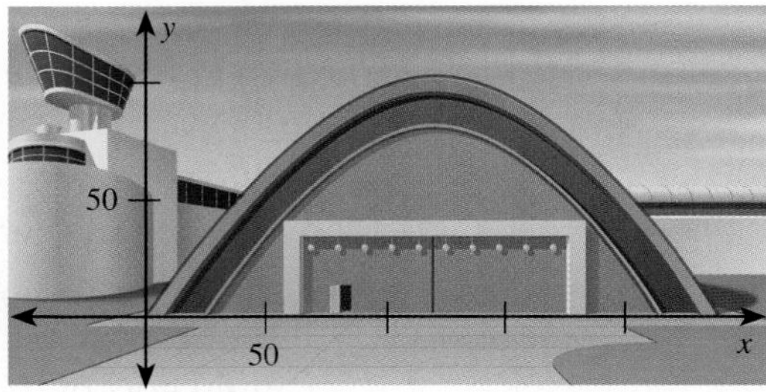

44. ★ **SHORT RESPONSE** The casts of some Broadway shows go on tour, performing their shows in cities across the United States. For the period 1990–2001, the number of tickets sold S (in millions) for Broadway road tours can be modeled by the function $S = 332 + 132t - 10.4t^2$ where t is the number of years since 1990. Was the greatest number of tickets for Broadway road tours sold in 1995? *Explain.*

45. **CHALLENGE** During an archery competition, an archer shoots an arrow from 1.5 meters off of the ground. The arrow follows the parabolic path shown and hits the ground in front of the target 90 meters away. Use the y-intercept and the points on the graph to write an equation for the graph that models the path of the arrow.

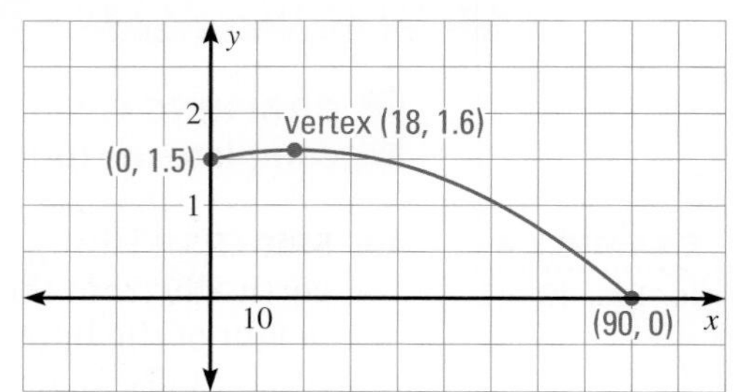

Extension Graph Quadratic Functions in Intercept Form

GOAL Graph quadratic functions in intercept form.

Key Vocabulary
- **intercept form**

You have graphed quadratic functions written in standard form. Quadratic functions can also be written in **intercept form**, $y = a(x - p)(x - q)$ where $a \neq 0$. In this form, the x-intercepts of the graph can easily be determined.

CC.9-12.F.IF.7a Graph linear and quadratic functions and show intercepts, maxima, and minima.*

KEY CONCEPT *For Your Notebook*

Graph of Intercept Form $y = a(x - p)(x - q)$

Characteristics of the graph of $y = a(x - p)(x - q)$:

- The x-intercepts are p and q.
- The axis of symmetry is halfway between $(p, 0)$ and $(q, 0)$. So, the axis of symmetry is $x = \frac{p + q}{2}$.
- The parabola opens up if $a > 0$ and opens down if $a < 0$.

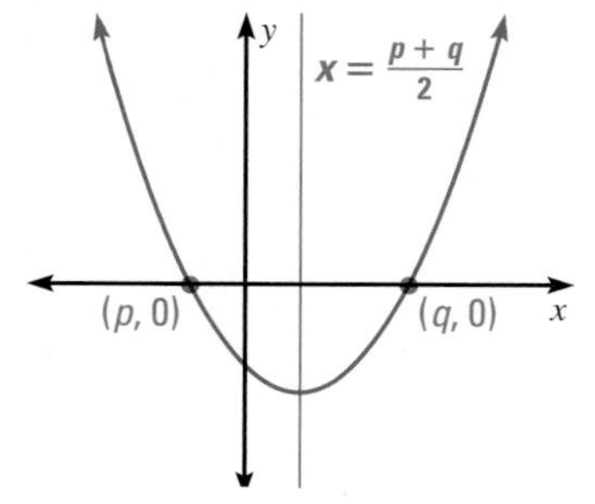

EXAMPLE 1 Graph a quadratic function in intercept form

Graph $y = -(x + 1)(x - 5)$.

Solution

FIND ZEROS OF A FUNCTION

Notice that the x-intercepts of the graph are also the zeros of the function:

$0 = -(x + 1)(x - 5)$

$x + 1 = 0$ *or* $x - 5 = 0$

$x = -1$ *or* $x = 5$

STEP 1 **Identify** and plot the x-intercepts. Because $p = -1$ and $q = 5$, the x-intercepts occur at the points $(-1, 0)$ and $(5, 0)$.

STEP 2 **Find** and draw the axis of symmetry.

$$x = \frac{p + q}{2} = \frac{-1 + 5}{2} = 2$$

STEP 3 **Find** and plot the vertex.

The x-coordinate of the vertex is 2.

To find the y-coordinate of the vertex, substitute 2 for x and simplify.

$$y = -(2 + 1)(2 - 5) = 9$$

So, the vertex is $(2, 9)$.

STEP 4 **Draw** a parabola through the vertex and the points where the x-intercepts occur.

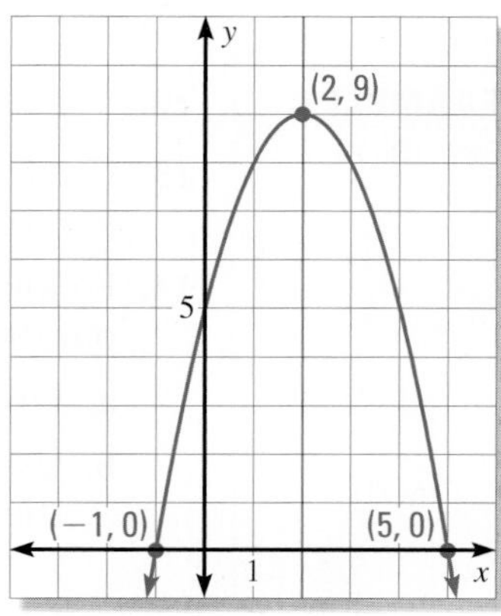

EXAMPLE 2 Graph a quadratic function

Graph $y = 2x^2 - 8$.

Solution

STEP 1 **Rewrite** the quadratic function in intercept form.

$y = 2x^2 - 8$ **Write original function.**

$= 2(x^2 - 4)$ **Factor out common factor.**

$= 2(x + 2)(x - 2)$ **Difference of two squares pattern**

STEP 2 **Identify** and plot the x-intercepts. Because $p = -2$ and $q = 2$, the x-intercepts occur at the points $(-2, 0)$ and $(2, 0)$.

STEP 3 **Find** and draw the axis of symmetry.

$$x = \frac{p + q}{2} = \frac{-2 + 2}{2} = 0$$

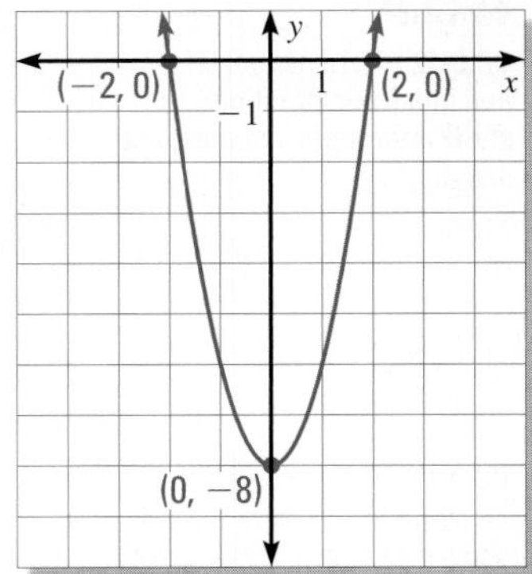

STEP 4 **Find** and plot the vertex.

The x-coordinate of the vertex is 0.

The y-coordinate of the vertex is:

$y = 2(\mathbf{0})^2 - 8 = -8$

So, the vertex is $(0, -8)$.

STEP 5 **Draw** a parabola through the vertex and the points where the x-intercepts occur.

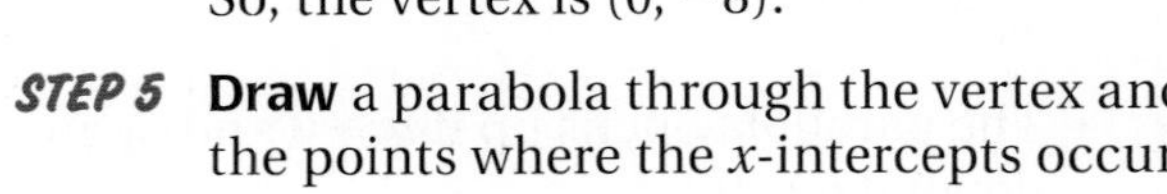

at my.hrw.com

PRACTICE

EXAMPLE 1
Exs. 1–9

Graph the quadratic function. Label the vertex, axis of symmetry, and x-intercepts.

1. $y = (x + 2)(x - 3)$
2. $y = (x + 5)(x + 2)$
3. $y = (x + 9)^2$
4. $y = -2(x - 5)(x + 1)$
5. $y = -5(x + 7)(x + 2)$
6. $y = 3(x - 6)(x - 3)$
7. $y = -\frac{1}{2}(x + 4)(x - 2)$
8. $y = (x - 7)(2x - 3)$
9. $y = 2(x + 10)(x - 3)$

EXAMPLE 2
Exs. 10–12

10. $y = -x^2 + 8x - 16$
11. $y = -x^2 - 9x - 18$
12. $y = 12x^2 - 48$
13. Use factoring to determine how many x-intercepts the graph of the function $y = 3x^2 - 12x + 12$ has.
14. Follow the steps below to write an equation of the parabola shown.
    a. Find the x-intercepts.
    b. Use the values of p and q and the coordinates of the vertex to find the value of a in the equation $y = a(x - p)(x - q)$.
    c. Write a quadratic equation in intercept form.

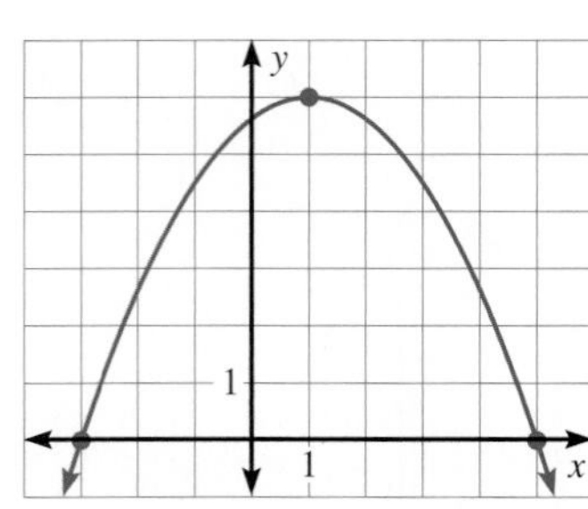

9.3 Solve Quadratic Equations by Graphing

Before You solved quadratic equations by factoring.

Now You will solve quadratic equations by graphing.

Why? So you can solve a problem about sports, as in Example 6.

Key Vocabulary
- **quadratic equation**
- ***x*-intercept**
- **roots**
- **zero of a function**

A **quadratic equation** is an equation that can be written in the **standard form** $ax^2 + bx + c = 0$ where $a \neq 0$.

You have used factoring to solve a quadratic equation. You can also use graphing to solve a quadratic equation. Notice that the solutions of the equation $ax^2 + bx + c = 0$ are the x-intercepts of the graph of the related function $y = ax^2 + bx + c$.

COMMON CORE

CC.9-12.F.IF.7a Graph linear and quadratic functions and show intercepts, maxima, and minima.*

Solve by Factoring

$$x^2 - 6x + 5 = 0$$

$$(x - 1)(x - 5) = 0$$

$$x = 1 \text{ or } x = 5$$

Solve by Graphing

To solve $x^2 - 6x + 5 = 0$, graph $y = x^2 - 6x + 5$. From the graph you can see that the x-intercepts are 1 and 5.

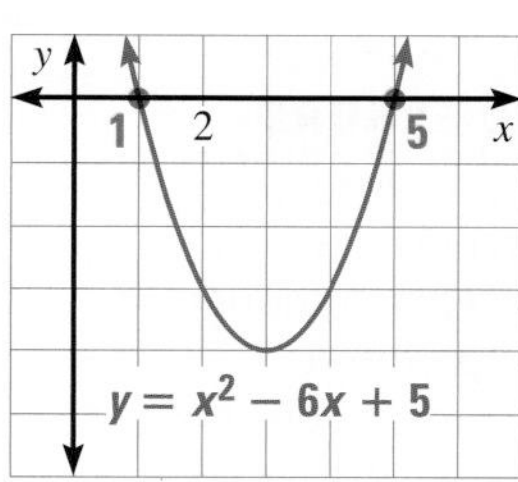

READING
In this course, *solutions* refers to real-number solutions.

To solve a quadratic equation by graphing, first write the equation in standard form, $ax^2 + bx + c = 0$. Then graph the related function $y = ax^2 + bx + c$. The x-intercepts of the graph are the solutions, or roots, of $ax^2 + bx + c = 0$.

EXAMPLE 1 Solve a quadratic equation having two solutions

Solve $x^2 - 2x = 3$ by graphing.

Solution

STEP 1 **Write** the equation in standard form.

$x^2 - 2x = 3$	**Write original equation.**
$x^2 - 2x - 3 = 0$	**Subtract 3 from each side.**

STEP 2 **Graph** the function $y = x^2 - 2x - 3$. The x-intercepts are -1 and 3.

y
1
−1
1
3
x
y = x² − 2x − 3

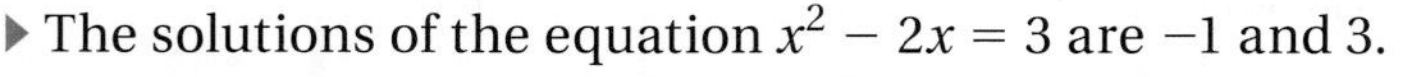

▶ The solutions of the equation $x^2 - 2x = 3$ are -1 and 3.

CHECK You can check -1 and 3 in the original equation.

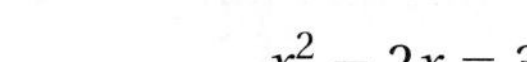

$x^2 - 2x = 3$	$x^2 - 2x = 3$	**Write original equation.**
$(-1)^2 - 2(-1) \stackrel{?}{=} 3$	$(3)^2 - 2(3) \stackrel{?}{=} 3$	**Substitute for *x*.**
$3 = 3$ ✓	$3 = 3$ ✓	**Simplify. Each solution checks.**

EXAMPLE 2 Solve a quadratic equation having one solution

Solve $-x^2 + 2x = 1$ by graphing.

Solution

STEP 1 **Write** the equation in standard form.

$-x^2 + 2x = 1$ **Write original equation.**

$-x^2 + 2x - 1 = 0$ **Subtract 1 from each side.**

STEP 2 **Graph** the function $y = -x^2 + 2x - 1$. The x-intercept is 1.

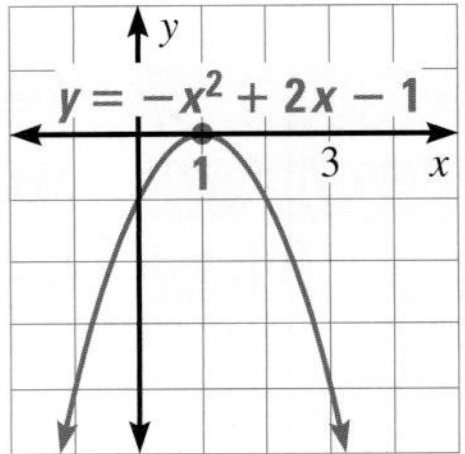

▶ The solution of the equation $-x^2 + 2x = 1$ is 1.

EXAMPLE 3 Solve a quadratic equation having no solution

Solve $x^2 + 7 = 4x$ by graphing.

Solution

STEP 1 **Write** the equation in standard form.

$x^2 + 7 = 4x$ **Write original equation.**

$x^2 - 4x + 7 = 0$ **Subtract $4x$ from each side.**

STEP 2 **Graph** the function $y = x^2 - 4x + 7$. The graph has no x-intercepts.

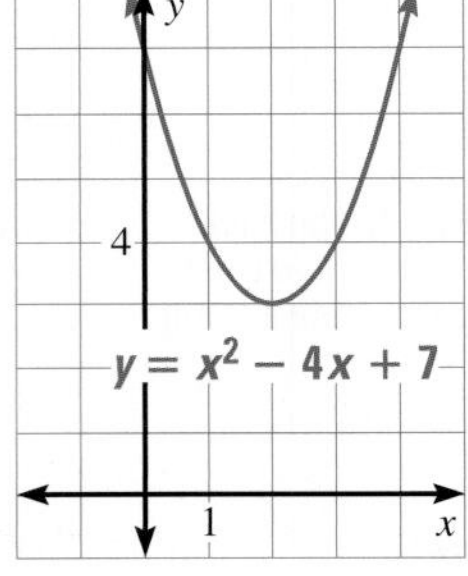

▶ The equation $x^2 + 7 = 4x$ has no solution.

AVOID ERRORS

Do not confuse y-intercepts and x-intercepts. Although the graph has a y-intercept, it does not have any x-intercepts.

✓ GUIDED PRACTICE for Examples 1, 2, and 3

Solve the equation by graphing.

1. $x^2 - 6x + 8 = 0$ **2.** $x^2 + x = -1$ **3.** $-x^2 + 6x = 9$

KEY CONCEPT *For Your Notebook*

Number of Solutions of a Quadratic Equation

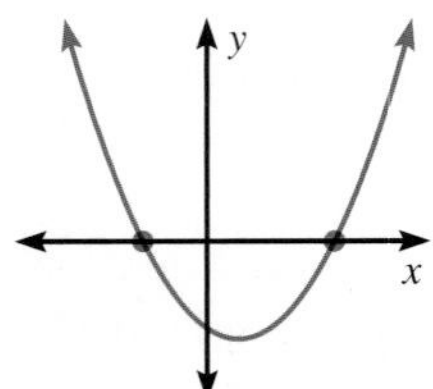

A quadratic equation has **two solutions** if the graph of its related function has **two x-intercepts.**

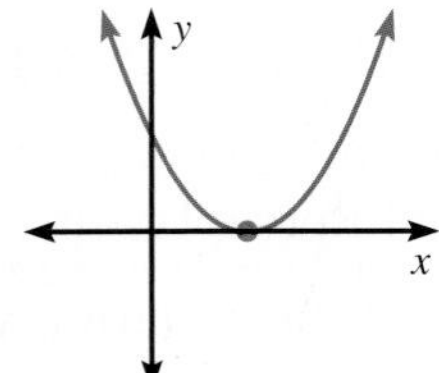

A quadratic equation has **one solution** if the graph of its related function has **one x-intercept.**

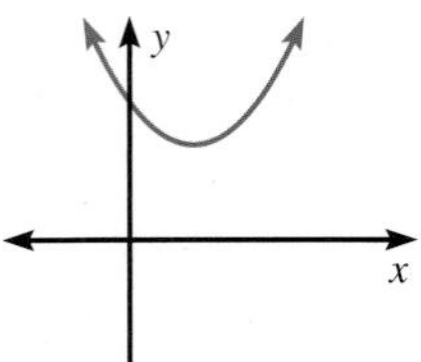

A quadratic equation has **no real solution** if the graph of its related function has **no x-intercepts.**

FINDING ZEROS Because a zero of a function is an x-intercept of the function's graph, you can use the function's graph to find the zeros of a function.

EXAMPLE 4 Find the zeros of a quadratic function

Find the zeros of $f(x) = x^2 + 6x - 7$.

ANOTHER WAY
You can find the zeros of a function by factoring:

$f(x) = x^2 + 6x - 7$
$0 = x^2 + 6x - 7$
$0 = (x + 7)(x - 1)$
$x = -7$ *or* $x = 1$

Solution

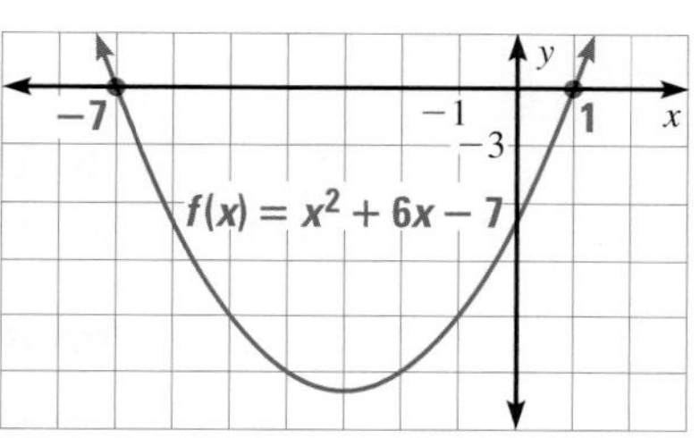

Graph the function $f(x) = x^2 + 6x - 7$. The x-intercepts are -7 and 1.

▶ The zeros of the function are -7 and 1.

CHECK Substitute -7 and 1 in the original function.

$$f(-7) = (-7)^2 + 6(-7) - 7 = 0 \checkmark$$

$$f(1) = (1)^2 + 6(1) - 7 = 0 \checkmark$$

APPROXIMATING ZEROS The zeros of a function are not necessarily integers. To approximate zeros, look at the signs of the function values. If two function values have opposite signs, then a zero falls between the x-values that correspond to the function values.

EXAMPLE 5 Approximate the zeros of a quadratic function

Approximate the zeros of $f(x) = x^2 + 4x + 1$ to the nearest tenth.

Solution

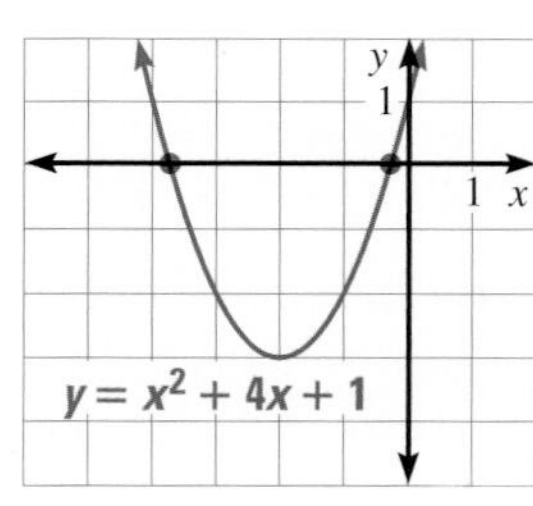

STEP 1 **Graph** the function $f(x) = x^2 + 4x + 1$. There are two x-intercepts: one between -4 and -3 and another between -1 and 0.

STEP 2 **Make** a table of values for x-values between -4 and -3 and between -1 and 0 using an increment of 0.1. Look for a change in the signs of the function values.

INTERPRET FUNCTION VALUES
The function value that is closest to 0 indicates the x-value that best approximates a zero of the function.

x	−3.9	−3.8	**−3.7**	−3.6	−3.5	−3.4	−3.3	−3.2	−3.1
$f(x)$	0.61	0.24	**−0.11**	−0.44	−0.75	−1.04	−1.31	−1.56	−1.79

x	−0.9	−0.8	−0.7	−0.6	−0.5	−0.4	**−0.3**	−0.2	−0.1
$f(x)$	−1.79	−1.56	−1.31	−1.04	−0.75	−0.44	**−0.11**	0.24	0.61

▶ In each table, the function value closest to 0 is -0.11. So, the zeros of $f(x) = x^2 + 4x + 1$ are about -3.7 and about -0.3.

✓ **GUIDED PRACTICE** for Examples 4 and 5

4. Find the zeros of $f(x) = x^2 + x - 6$.

5. Approximate the zeros of $f(x) = -x^2 + 2x + 2$ to the nearest tenth.

EXAMPLE 6 Solve a multi-step problem

SPORTS An athlete throws a shot put with an initial vertical velocity of 40 feet per second as shown.

a. Write an equation that models the height h (in feet) of the shot put as a function of the time t (in seconds) after it is thrown.

b. Use the equation to find the time that the shot put is in the air.

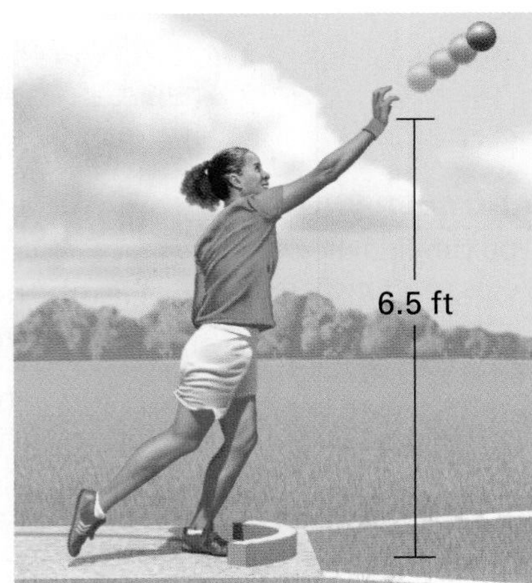

Solution

a. Use the initial vertical velocity and the release height to write a vertical motion model.

$h = -16t^2 + vt + s$ **Vertical motion model**

$h = -16t^2 + 40t + 6.5$ **Substitute 40 for v and 6.5 for s.**

b. The shot put lands when $h = 0$. To find the time t when $h = 0$, solve $0 = -16t^2 + 40t + 6.5$ for t.

USE A GRAPHING CALCULATOR
When entering $h = -16t^2 + 40t + 6.5$ in a graphing calculator, use y instead of h and x instead of t.

To solve the equation, graph the related function $h = -16t^2 + 40t + 6.5$ on a graphing calculator. Use the *trace* feature to find the t-intercepts.

▶ There is only one positive t-intercept. The shot put is in the air for about 2.6 seconds.

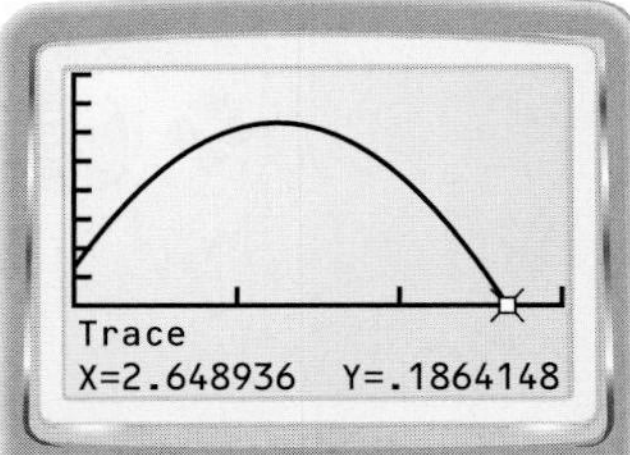

✓ GUIDED PRACTICE for Example 6

6. **WHAT IF?** In Example 6, suppose the initial vertical velocity is 30 feet per second. Find the time that the shot put is in the air.

CONCEPT SUMMARY *For Your Notebook*

Relating Solutions of Equations, *x*-Intercepts of Graphs, and Zeros of Functions

Solutions of an Equation
The solutions of the equation $-x^2 + 8x - 12 = 0$ are 2 and 6.

***x*-Intercepts of a Graph**
The x-intercepts of the graph of $y = -x^2 + 8x - 12$ occur where $y = 0$, so the x-intercepts are 2 and 6, as shown.

Zeros of a Function
The zeros of the function $f(x) = -x^2 + 8x - 12$ are the values of x for which $f(x) = 0$, so the zeros are 2 and 6.

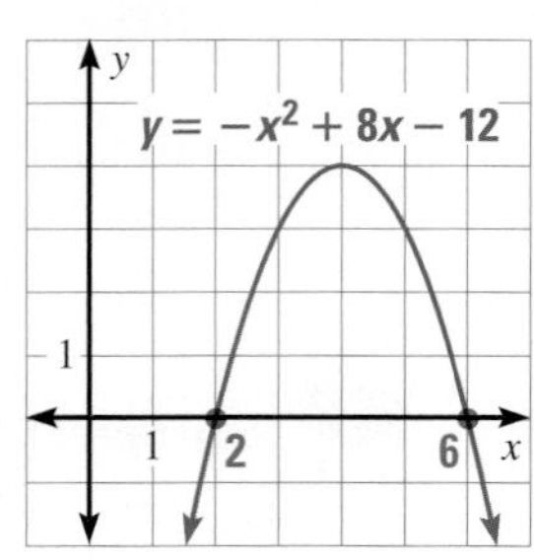

9.3 EXERCISES

HOMEWORK KEY
○ = See WORKED-OUT SOLUTIONS Exs. 5 and 51
★ = STANDARDIZED TEST PRACTICE Exs. 2, 46, 53, and 54

SKILL PRACTICE

1. **VOCABULARY** Write $2x^2 + 11 = 9x$ in standard form.

2. ★ **WRITING** Is $3x^2 - 2 = 0$ a quadratic equation? *Explain.*

SOLVING EQUATIONS Solve the equation by graphing.

EXAMPLES 1, 2, and 3 for Exs. 3–21

3. $x^2 - 5x + 4 = 0$
4. $x^2 + 5x + 6 = 0$
5. $x^2 + 6x = -8$
6. $x^2 - 4x = 5$
7. $x^2 - 16 = 6x$
8. $x^2 - 12x = -35$
9. $x^2 - 6x + 9 = 0$
10. $x^2 + 8x + 16 = 0$
11. $x^2 + 10x = -25$
12. $x^2 + 81 = 18x$
13. $-x^2 - 14x = 49$
14. $-x^2 + 16x = 64$
15. $x^2 - 5x + 7 = 0$
16. $x^2 - 2x + 3 = 0$
17. $x^2 + x = -2$
18. $\frac{1}{5}x^2 - 5 = 0$
19. $\frac{1}{2}x^2 + 2x = 6$
20. $-\frac{1}{4}x^2 - 8 = x$

21. **ERROR ANALYSIS** The graph of the function related to the equation $0 = x^2 - 4x + 4$ is shown. *Describe* and correct the error in solving the equation.

The only solution of the equation $0 = x^2 - 4x + 4$ is 4.

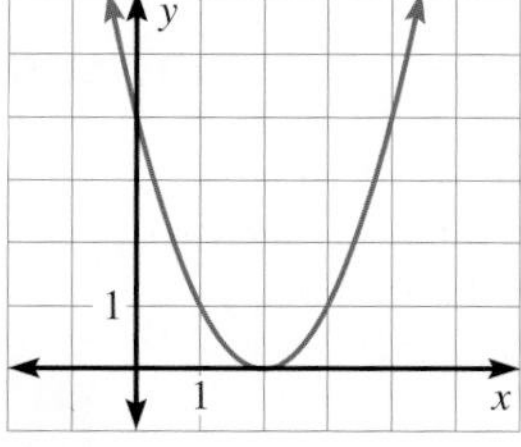

FINDING ZEROS Find the zeros of the function.

EXAMPLE 4 for Exs. 22–30

22. $f(x) = x^2 + 4x - 5$
23. $f(x) = x^2 - x - 12$
24. $f(x) = x^2 - 5x - 6$
25. $f(x) = x^2 + 3x - 10$
26. $f(x) = -x^2 + 8x + 9$
27. $f(x) = x^2 + x - 20$
28. $f(x) = -x^2 - 7x + 8$
29. $f(x) = x^2 - 12x + 11$
30. $f(x) = -x^2 + 4x + 12$

SOLVING EQUATIONS Solve the equation by graphing.

31. $2x^2 + x = 3$
32. $4x^2 - 5 = 8x$
33. $4x^2 - 4x + 1 = 0$
34. $x^2 + x = -\frac{1}{4}$
35. $3x^2 + 1 = 2x$
36. $5x^2 + x + 3 = 0$

APPROXIMATING ZEROS Approximate the zeros of the function to the nearest tenth.

EXAMPLE 5 for Exs. 37–46

37. $f(x) = x^2 + 4x + 2$
38. $f(x) = x^2 - 5x + 3$
39. $f(x) = x^2 - 2x - 5$
40. $f(x) = -x^2 - 3x + 3$
41. $f(x) = -x^2 + 7x - 5$
42. $f(x) = -x^2 - 5x - 2$
43. $f(x) = 2x^2 + x - 2$
44. $f(x) = -3x^2 + 8x - 2$
45. $f(x) = 5x^2 + 30x + 30$

46. ★ **MULTIPLE CHOICE** Which function has a zero between -3 and -2?

Ⓐ $f(x) = -3x^2 + 4x + 11$ Ⓑ $f(x) = 4x^2 - 3x - 11$

Ⓒ $f(x) = 3x^2 + 4x - 11$ Ⓓ $f(x) = 3x^2 + 11$

CHALLENGE **Use the given surface area S of the cylinder to find the radius r to the nearest tenth. (Use 3.14 for π.)**

47. $S = 251 \text{ ft}^2$

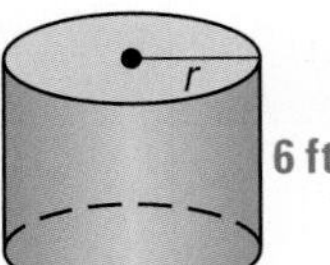

48. $S = 716 \text{ m}^2$

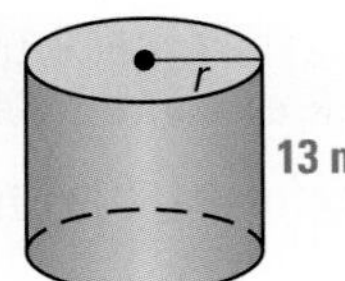

49. $S = 1074 \text{ cm}^2$

r

10 cm

PROBLEM SOLVING

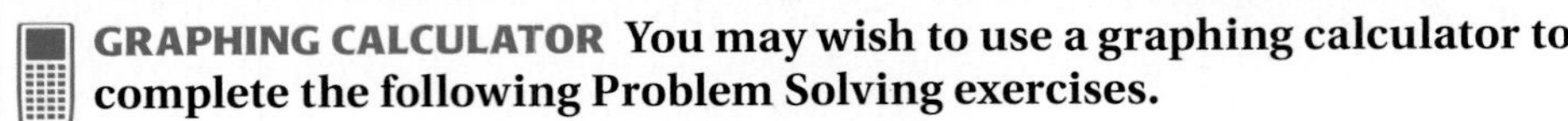

GRAPHING CALCULATOR **You may wish to use a graphing calculator to complete the following Problem Solving exercises.**

EXAMPLE 6
for Exs. 50–52

50. SOCCER The height y (in feet) of a soccer ball after it is kicked can be modeled by the graph of the equation $y = -0.04x^2 + 1.2x$ where x is the horizontal distance (in feet) that the ball travels. The ball is not touched, and it lands on the ground. Find the distance that the ball was kicked.

51. SURVEYING To keep water off a road, the road's surface is shaped like a parabola as in the cross section below. The surface of the road can be modeled by the graph of $y = -0.0017x^2 + 0.041x$ where x and y are measured in feet. Find the width of the road to the nearest tenth of a foot.

52. DIVING During a cliff diving competition, a diver begins a dive with his center of gravity 70 feet above the water. The initial vertical velocity of his dive is 8 feet per second.

a. Write an equation that models the height h (in feet) of the diver's center of gravity as a function of time t (in seconds).

b. How long after the diver begins his dive does his center of gravity reach the water?

53. ★ SHORT RESPONSE An arc of water sprayed from the nozzle of a fountain can be modeled by the graph of $y = -0.75x^2 + 6x$ where x is the horizontal distance (in feet) from the nozzle and y is the vertical distance (in feet). The diameter of the circle formed by the arcs on the surface of the water is called the display diameter. Find the display diameter of the fountain. *Explain* your reasoning.

54. ★ **EXTENDED RESPONSE** Two softball players are practicing catching fly balls. One player throws a ball to the other. She throws the ball upward from a height of 5.5 feet with an initial vertical velocity of 40 feet per second for her teammate to catch.

   a. Write an equation that models the height h (in feet) of the ball as a function of time t (in seconds) after it is thrown.

   b. If her teammate misses the ball and it lands on the ground, how long was the ball in the air?

   c. If her teammate catches the ball at a height of 5.5 feet, how long was the ball in the air? *Explain* your reasoning.

55. **CHALLENGE** A stream of water from a fire hose can be modeled by the graph of $y = -0.003x^2 + 0.58x + 3$ where x and y are measured in feet. A firefighter is holding the hose 3 feet above the ground, 137 feet from a building. Will the stream of water pass through a window if the top of the window is 26 feet above the ground? *Explain.*

QUIZ

Graph the function. Compare the graph with the graph of $y = x^2$.

1. $y = -\frac{1}{2}x^2$
2. $y = 2x^2 - 5$
3. $y = -x^2 + 3$

Graph the function. Label the vertex and axis of symmetry.

4. $y = x^2 + 5$
5. $y = -5x^2 + 1$
6. $y = x^2 + 4x - 2$
7. $y = 2x^2 - 12x + 5$
8. $y = -\frac{1}{2}x^2 + 2x - 5$
9. $y = -4x^2 - 10x + 2$

Solve the equation by graphing.

10. $x^2 - 7x = 8$
11. $x^2 + 6x + 9 = 0$
12. $x^2 + 10x = 11$
13. $x^2 - 7 = -6x$
14. $-x^2 + x - 1 = 0$
15. $x^2 - 4x + 9 = 0$

Find the zeros of the function.

16. $f(x) = x^2 + 3x - 10$
17. $f(x) = x^2 - 8x + 12$
18. $f(x) = -x^2 + 5x + 14$

Find Minimum and Maximum Values and Zeros

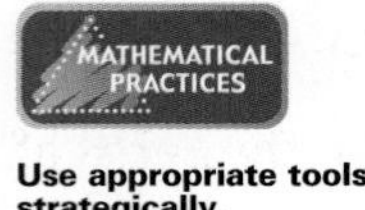

Use appropriate tools strategically.

QUESTION How can you find the minumum or maximum value and the zeros of a quadratic function using a graphing calculator?

EXAMPLE 1 Find the maximum value of a function

Find the maximum value of the function $y = -2x^2 - 6x + 7$.

STEP 1 ***Enter the function***

Press Y= and enter the function $y = -2x^2 - 6x + 7$.

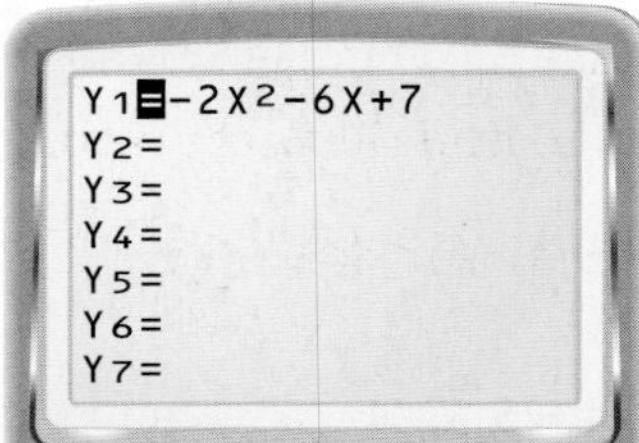

STEP 2 ***Adjust the window***

Display the graph. Adjust the viewing window as needed so that the vertex of the parabola is visible.

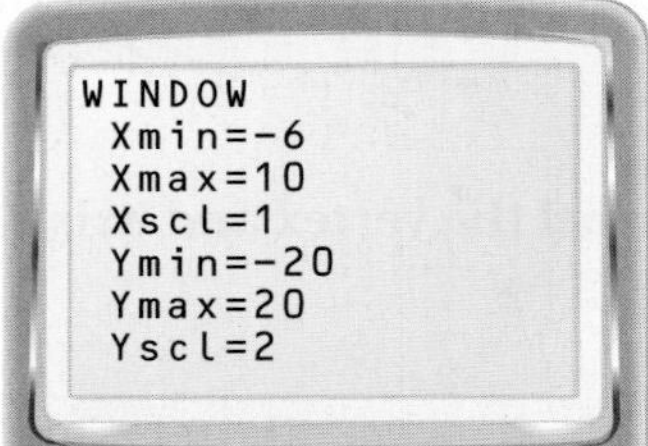

STEP 3 ***Use the maximum feature***

The *maximum* feature is located under the CALCULATE menu.

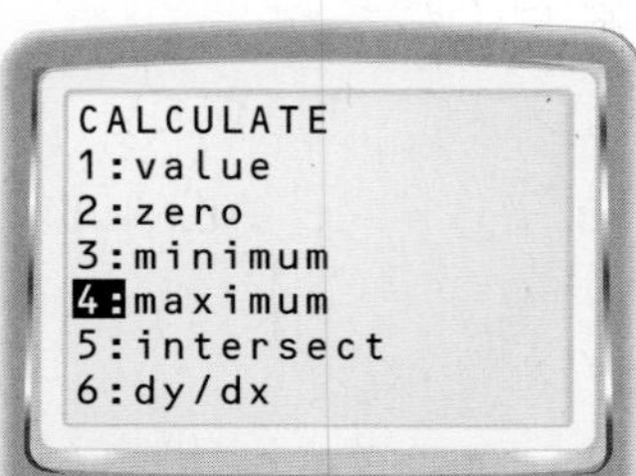

STEP 4 ***Find the maximum value***

Follow the graphing calculator's procedure to find the maximum of the function.

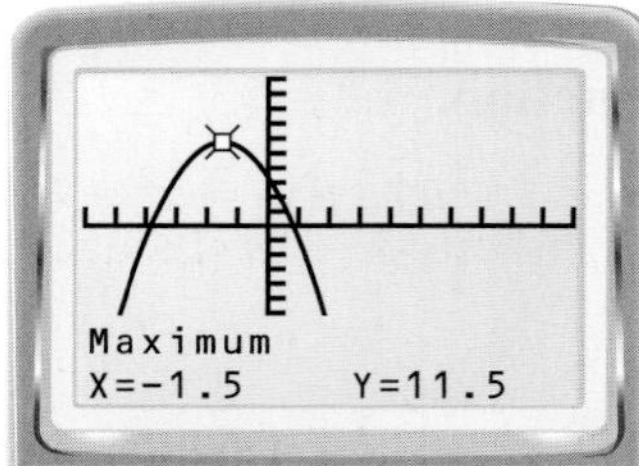

▶ The maximum value of the function $y = -2x^2 - 6x + 7$ is 11.5.

PRACTICE

Find the maximum or minimum value of the function.

1. $y = 3x^2 - 8x + 7$
2. $y = -x^2 + 3x + 10$
3. $y = -4x^2 - 6x - 6$
4. $y = 5x^2 + 10x - 8$
5. $y = -1.4x^2 + 3.8x - 6.1$
6. $y = 2.57x^2 - 8.45x - 5.04$

my.hrw.com
Keystrokes

EXAMPLE 2 Approximate the zeros of a function

Approximate the zeros of the function $y = 3x^2 + 2x - 4$.

STEP 1 ***Enter the function***
Press [Y=] and enter the function $y = 3x^2 + 2x - 4$.

```
Y1=3X2+2X-4
Y2=
Y3=
Y4=
Y5=
Y6=
Y7=
```

STEP 2 ***Adjust the window***
Display the graph. Adjust the viewing window as needed so that the x-intercepts of the parabola are visible.

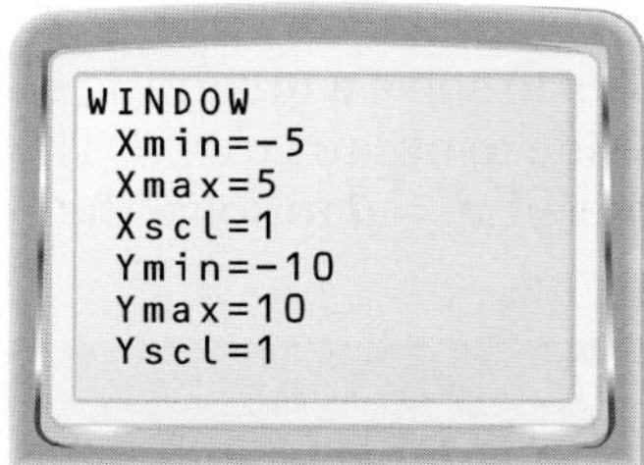

STEP 3 ***Use the zero feature***
The *zero* feature is under the CALCULATE menu.

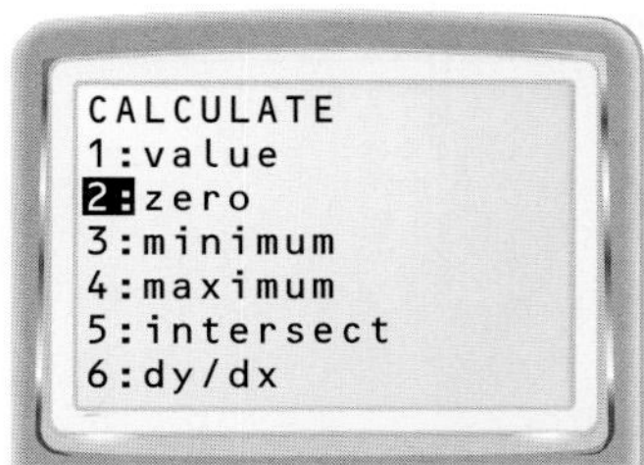

STEP 4 ***Find the zeros***
Follow the graphing calculator's procedure to find a zero of the function. Then repeat the process to find the other zero.

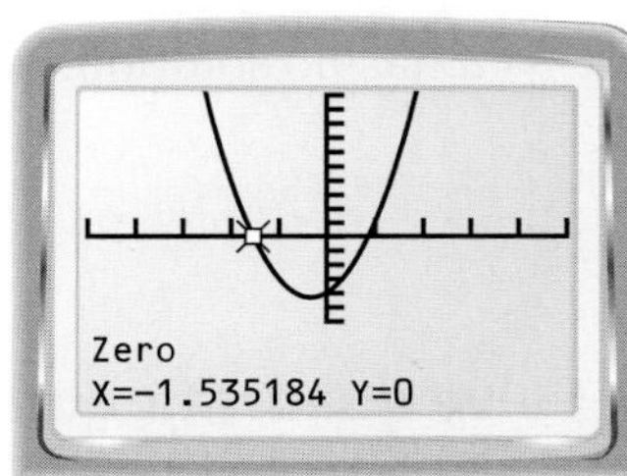

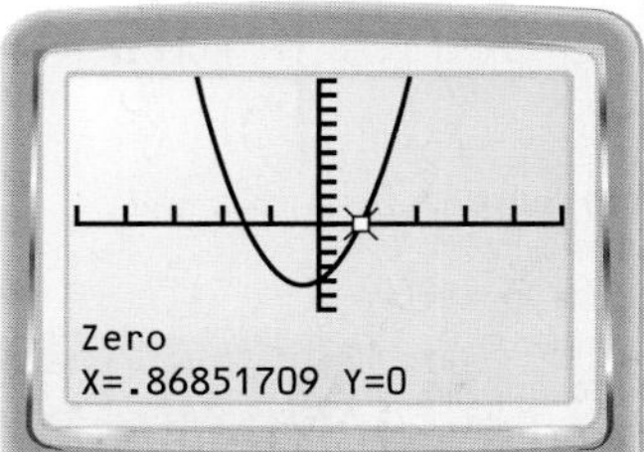

▸ The zeros are about −1.54 and about 0.87.

PRACTICE

Approximate the zeros of the quadratic function to the nearest hundredth.

7. $y = 2x^2 - 5x - 8$

8. $y = -3x^2 + 6x - 2$

9. $y = -x^2 + 4x + 9$

10. $y = 4x^2 - 7x + 1$

11. $y = -2.5x^2 + 7.7x - 4.9$

12. $y = 1.56x^2 - 5.19x - 2.25$

13. $y = -0.82x^2 - 4x + 12.4$

14. $y = 5.36x^2 + 17x + 2.67$

DRAW CONCLUSIONS

15. If a quadratic function has only one zero, what is the maximum or minimum value of the function? *Explain.*

16. If a quadratic function has a maximum value that is greater than 0, how many zeros does the function have? *Explain.*

9.4 Use Square Roots to Solve Quadratic Equations

Before You solved a quadratic equation by graphing.

Now You will solve a quadratic equation by finding square roots.

Why? So you can solve a problem about a falling object, as in Example 5.

Key Vocabulary
- **square root**
- **perfect square**

To use square roots to solve a quadratic equation of the form $ax^2 + c = 0$, first isolate x^2 on one side to obtain $x^2 = d$. Then use the following information about the solutions of $x^2 = d$ to solve the equation.

READING
Recall that in this course, *solutions* refers to real-number solutions.

KEY CONCEPT — *For Your Notebook*

Solving $x^2 = d$ by Taking Square Roots

- If $d > 0$, then $x^2 = d$ has two solutions: $x = \pm\sqrt{d}$.
- If $d = 0$, then $x^2 = d$ has one solution: $x = 0$.
- If $d < 0$, then $x^2 = d$ has no solution.

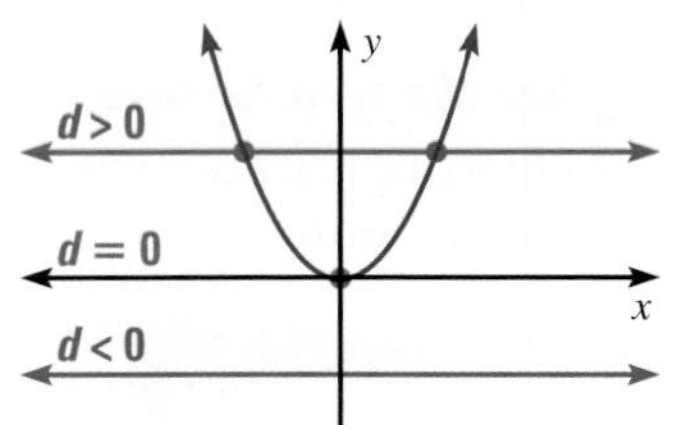

CC.9-12.A.REI.4b Solve quadratic equations by inspection (e.g., for $x^2 = 49$), taking square roots, completing the square, the quadratic formula and factoring, as appropriate to the initial form of the equation. Recognize when the quadratic formula gives complex soultions, and write them as $a \pm bi$ for real numbers a and b.

EXAMPLE 1 Solve quadratic equations

Solve the equation.

a. $2x^2 = 8$ **b.** $m^2 - 18 = -18$ **c.** $b^2 + 12 = 5$

Solution

a. $2x^2 = 8$ — **Write original equation.**

$x^2 = 4$ — **Divide each side by 2.**

$x = \pm\sqrt{4} = \pm 2$ — **Take square roots of each side. Simplify.**

▶ The solutions are −2 and 2.

ANOTHER WAY
You can also use factoring to solve $2x^2 - 8 = 0$:

$2x^2 - 8 = 0$
$2(x^2 - 4) = 0$
$2(x - 2)(x + 2) = 0$
$x = 2$ *or* $x = -2$

b. $m^2 - 18 = -18$ — **Write original equation.**

$m^2 = 0$ — **Add 18 to each side.**

$m = 0$ — **The square root of 0 is 0.**

▶ The solution is 0.

c. $b^2 + 12 = 5$ — **Write original equation.**

$b^2 = -7$ — **Subtract 12 from each side.**

▶ Negative real numbers do not have real square roots. So, there is no solution.

SIMPLIFYING SQUARE ROOTS In cases where you need to take the square root of a fraction whose numerator and denominator are perfect squares, the radical can be written as a fraction. For example, $\sqrt{\frac{16}{25}}$ can be written as $\frac{4}{5}$ because $\left(\frac{4}{5}\right)^2 = \frac{16}{25}$.

EXAMPLE 2 Take square roots of a fraction

Solve $4z^2 = 9$.

Solution

$4z^2 = 9$	**Write original equation.**
$z^2 = \frac{9}{4}$	**Divide each side by 4.**
$z = \pm\sqrt{\frac{9}{4}}$	**Take square roots of each side.**
$z = \pm\frac{3}{2}$	**Simplify.**

▶ The solutions are $-\frac{3}{2}$ and $\frac{3}{2}$.

APPROXIMATING SQUARE ROOTS In cases where d in the equation $x^2 = d$ is not a perfect square or a fraction whose numerator and denominator are not perfect squares, you need to approximate the square root. A calculator can be used to find an approximation.

EXAMPLE 3 Approximate solutions of a quadratic equation

Solve $3x^2 - 11 = 7$. Round the solutions to the nearest hundredth.

Solution

$3x^2 - 11 = 7$	**Write original equation.**
$3x^2 = 18$	**Add 11 to each side.**
$x^2 = 6$	**Divide each side by 3.**
$x = \pm\sqrt{6}$	**Take square roots of each side.**
$x \approx \pm 2.45$	**Use a calculator. Round to the nearest hundredth.**

▶ The solutions are about −2.45 and about 2.45.

✓ GUIDED PRACTICE for Examples 1, 2, and 3

Solve the equation.

1. $c^2 - 25 = 0$ **2.** $5w^2 + 12 = -8$ **3.** $2x^2 + 11 = 11$

4. $25x^2 = 16$ **5.** $9m^2 = 100$ **6.** $49b^2 + 64 = 0$

Solve the equation. Round the solutions to the nearest hundredth.

7. $x^2 + 4 = 14$ **8.** $3k^2 - 1 = 0$ **9.** $2p^2 - 7 = 2$

EXAMPLE 4 Solve a quadratic equation

Solve $6(x-4)^2 = 42$. Round the solutions to the nearest hundredth.

$6(x-4)^2 = 42$	**Write original equation.**
$(x-4)^2 = 7$	**Divide each side by 6.**
$x - 4 = \pm\sqrt{7}$	**Take square roots of each side.**
$x = 4 \pm \sqrt{7}$	**Add 4 to each side.**

▶ The solutions are $4 + \sqrt{7} \approx 6.65$ and $4 - \sqrt{7} \approx 1.35$.

CHECK To check the solutions, first write the equation so that 0 is on one side as follows: $6(x-4)^2 - 42 = 0$. Then graph the related function $y = 6(x-4)^2 - 42$. The x-intercepts appear to be about 6.6 and about 1.3. So, each solution checks.

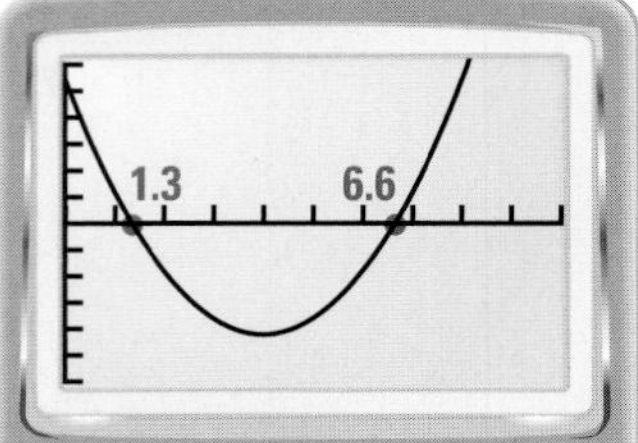

EXAMPLE 5 Solve a multi-step problem

ANOTHER WAY
For alternative methods for solving the problem in Example 5, see the **Problem Solving Workshop**.

SPORTS EVENT During an ice hockey game, a remote-controlled blimp flies above the crowd and drops a numbered table-tennis ball. The number on the ball corresponds to a prize. Use the information in the diagram to find the amount of time that the ball is in the air.

WILDCATS

45 ft

17 ft

Not drawn to scale

Solution

STEP 1 **Use** the vertical motion model to write an equation for the height h (in feet) of the ball as a function of time t (in seconds).

$h = -16t^2 + vt + s$	**Vertical motion model**
$h = -16t^2 + 0t + 45$	**Substitute for v and s.**

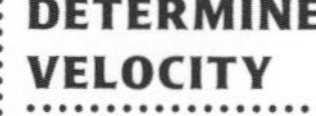

DETERMINE VELOCITY
When an object is dropped, it has an initial vertical velocity of 0 feet per second.

STEP 2 **Find** the amount of time the ball is in the air by substituting 17 for h and solving for t.

$h = -16t^2 + 45$	**Write model.**
$17 = -16t^2 + 45$	**Substitute 17 for h.**
$-28 = -16t^2$	**Subtract 45 from each side.**
$\frac{28}{16} = t^2$	**Divide each side by −16.**
$\sqrt{\frac{28}{16}} = t$	**Take positive square root.**
$1.32 \approx t$	**Use a calculator.**

INTERPRET SOLUTION
Because the time cannot be a negative number, ignore the negative square root.

▶ The ball is in the air for about 1.32 seconds.

✓ **GUIDED PRACTICE** for Examples 4 and 5

Solve the equation. Round the solutions to the nearest hundredth, if necessary.

10. $2(x - 2)^2 = 18$ **11.** $4(q - 3)^2 = 28$ **12.** $3(t + 5)^2 = 24$

13. WHAT IF? In Example 5, suppose the table-tennis ball is released 58 feet above the ground and is caught 12 feet above the ground. Find the amount of time that the ball is in the air. Round your answer to the nearest hundredth of a second.

9.4 EXERCISES

HOMEWORK KEY

○ = See **WORKED-OUT SOLUTIONS** Exs. 25 and 59

★ = **STANDARDIZED TEST PRACTICE** Exs. 2, 15, 16, 29, 51, 52, 57, and 60

◆ = **MULTIPLE REPRESENTATIONS** Ex. 62

SKILL PRACTICE

1. VOCABULARY Copy and complete: If $b^2 = a$, then b is a(n) _?_ of a.

2. ★ WRITING *Describe* two methods for solving a quadratic equation of the form $ax^2 + c = 0$.

EXAMPLES 1 and 2 for Exs. 3–16

SOLVING EQUATIONS Solve the equation.

3. $3x^2 - 3 = 0$ **4.** $2x^2 - 32 = 0$ **5.** $4x^2 - 400 = 0$

6. $2m^2 - 42 = 8$ **7.** $15d^2 = 0$ **8.** $a^2 + 8 = 3$

9. $4g^2 + 10 = 11$ **10.** $2w^2 + 13 = 11$ **11.** $9q^2 - 35 = 14$

12. $25b^2 + 11 = 15$ **13.** $3z^2 - 18 = -18$ **14.** $5n^2 - 17 = -19$

15. ★ MULTIPLE CHOICE Which of the following is a solution of the equation $61 - 3n^2 = -14$?

Ⓐ 5 Ⓑ 10 Ⓒ 25 Ⓓ 625

16. ★ MULTIPLE CHOICE Which of the following is a solution of the equation $13 - 36x^2 = -12$?

Ⓐ $-\frac{6}{5}$ Ⓑ $\frac{1}{6}$ Ⓒ $\frac{5}{6}$ Ⓓ 5

EXAMPLE 3 for Exs. 17–29

APPROXIMATING SQUARE ROOTS Solve the equation. Round the solutions to the nearest hundredth.

17. $x^2 + 6 = 13$ **18.** $x^2 + 11 = 24$ **19.** $14 - x^2 = 17$

20. $2a^2 - 9 = 11$ **21.** $4 - k^2 = 4$ **22.** $5 + 3p^2 = 38$

23. $53 = 8 + 9m^2$ **24.** $-21 = 15 - 2z^2$ **(25.)** $7c^2 = 100$

26. $5d^2 + 2 = 6$ **27.** $4b^2 - 5 = 2$ **28.** $9n^2 - 14 = -3$

29. ★ MULTIPLE CHOICE The equation $17 - \frac{1}{4}x^2 = 12$ has a solution between which two integers?

Ⓐ 1 and 2 Ⓑ 2 and 3 Ⓒ 3 and 4 Ⓓ 4 and 5

ERROR ANALYSIS ***Describe* and correct the error in solving the equation.**

30. $2x^2 - 54 = 18$

$2x^2 - 54 = 18$

$2x^2 = 72$

$x^2 = 36$

$x = \sqrt{36}$

$x = 6$

The solution is 6.

31. $7d^2 - 6 = -17$

$7d^2 - 6 = -17$

$7d^2 = -11$

$d^2 = -\frac{11}{7}$

$d \approx \pm 1.25$

The solutions are about -1.25 and about 1.25.

EXAMPLE 4 for Exs. 32–40

SOLVING EQUATIONS **Solve the equation. Round the solutions to the nearest hundredth.**

32. $(x - 7)^2 = 6$ **33.** $7(x - 3)^2 = 35$ **34.** $6(x + 4)^2 = 18$

35. $20 = 2(m + 5)^2$ **36.** $5(a - 2)^2 = 70$ **37.** $21 = 3(z + 14)^2$

38. $\frac{1}{2}(c - 8)^2 = 3$ **39.** $\frac{3}{2}(n + 1)^2 = 33$ **40.** $\frac{4}{3}(k - 6)^2 = 20$

SOLVING EQUATIONS **Solve the equation. Round the solutions to the nearest hundredth, if necessary.**

41. $3x^2 - 35 = 45 - 2x^2$ **42.** $42 = 3(x^2 + 5)$ **43.** $11x^2 + 3 = 5(4x^2 - 3)$

44. $\left(\frac{t - 5}{3}\right)^2 = 49$ **45.** $11\left(\frac{w - 7}{2}\right)^2 - 20 = 101$ **46.** $(4m^2 - 6)^2 = 81$

GEOMETRY **Use the given area *A* of the circle to find the radius *r* or the diameter *d* to the nearest hundredth.**

47. $A = 144\pi$ in.^{2}

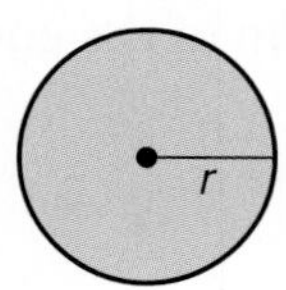

48. $A = 21\pi$ m^2

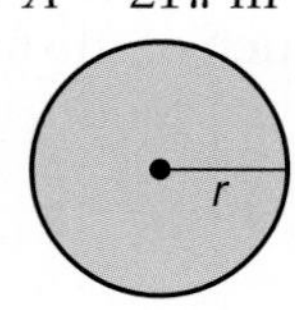

49. $A = 34\pi$ ft^2

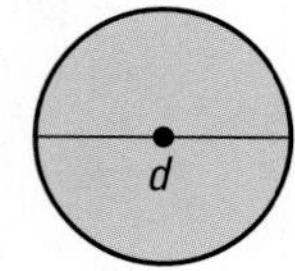

50. REASONING An equation of the graph shown is $y = \frac{1}{2}(x - 2)^2 + 1$. Two points on the parabola have y-coordinates of 9. Find the x-coordinates of these points.

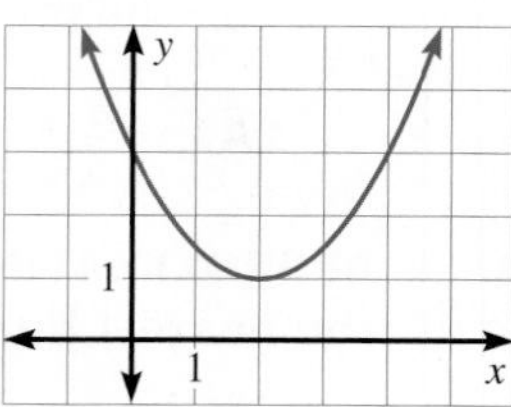

51. ★ SHORT RESPONSE Solve $x^2 = 1.44$ without using a calculator. *Explain* your reasoning.

52. ★ OPEN-ENDED Give values for a and c so that $ax^2 + c = 0$ has (a) two solutions, (b) one solution, and (c) no solution.

CHALLENGE **Solve the equation without graphing.**

53. $x^2 - 12x + 36 = 64$ **54.** $x^2 + 14x + 49 = 16$ **55.** $x^2 + 18x + 81 = 25$

○ = See WORKED-OUT SOLUTIONS in Student Resources ★ = STANDARDIZED TEST PRACTICE

PROBLEM SOLVING

EXAMPLE 5 for Exs. 56–57

56. FALLING OBJECT Fenway Park is a Major League Baseball park in Boston, Massachusetts. The park offers seats on top of the left field wall. A person sitting in one of these seats accidentally drops his sunglasses on the field. The height h (in feet) of the sunglasses can be modeled by the function $h = -16t^2 + 38$ where t is the time (in seconds) since the sunglasses were dropped. Find the time it takes for the sunglasses to reach the field. Round your answer to the nearest hundredth of a second.

57. ★ MULTIPLE CHOICE Which equation can be used to find the time it takes for an object to hit the ground after it was dropped from a height of 68 feet?

(A) $-16t^2 = 0$ (B) $-16t^2 - 68 = 0$ (C) $-16t^2 + 68 = 0$ (D) $-16t^2 = 68$

58. INTERNET USAGE For the period 1995–2001, the number y (in thousands) of Internet users worldwide can be modeled by the function $y = 12{,}697x^2 + 55{,}722$ where x is the number of years since 1995. Between which two years did the number of Internet users worldwide reach 100,000,000?

59. GEMOLOGY To find the weight w (in carats) of round faceted gems, gemologists use the formula $w = 0.0018D^2ds$ where D is the diameter (in millimeters) of the gem, d is the depth (in millimeters) of the gem, and s is the specific gravity of the gem. Find the diameter to the nearest tenth of a millimeter of each round faceted gem in the table.

	Gem	Weight (carats)	Depth (mm)	Specific gravity	Diameter (mm)
a.	Amethyst	1	4.5	2.65	?
b.	Diamond	1	4.5	3.52	?
c.	Ruby	1	4.5	4.00	?

60. ★ SHORT RESPONSE In deep water, the speed s (in meters per second) of a series of waves and the wavelength L (in meters) of the waves are related by the equation $2\pi s^2 = 9.8L$.

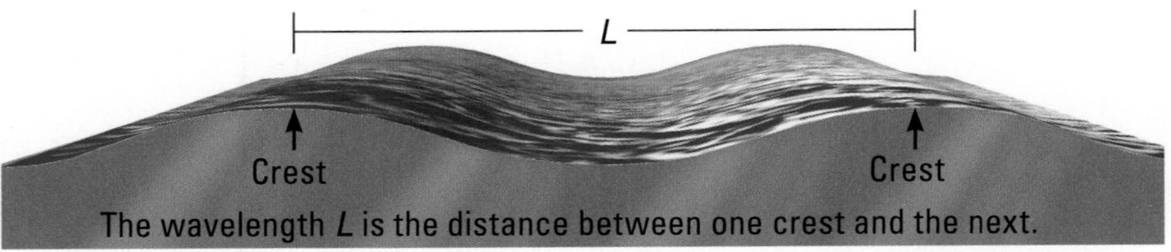

a. Find the speed to the nearest hundredth of a meter per second of a series of waves with the following wavelengths: 6 meters, 10 meters, and 25 meters. (Use 3.14 for π.)

b. Does the speed of a series of waves increase or decrease as the wavelength of the waves increases? *Explain.*

61. MULTI-STEP PROBLEM The Doyle log rule is a formula used to estimate the amount of lumber that can be sawn from logs of various sizes. The amount of lumber V (in board feet) is given by $V = \frac{L(D-4)^2}{16}$ where L is the length (in feet) of a log and D is the small-end diameter (in inches) of the log.

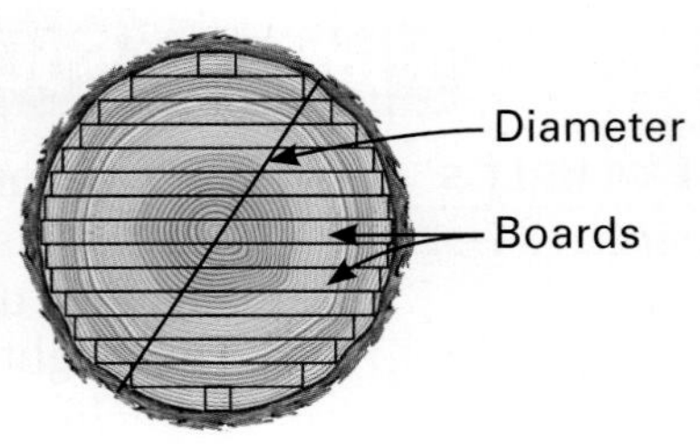

a. Solve the formula for D.

b. Use the rewritten formula to find the diameters, to the nearest tenth of an inch, of logs that will yield 50 board feet and have the following lengths: 16 feet, 18 feet, 20 feet, and 22 feet.

62. ◆ **MULTIPLE REPRESENTATIONS** A ride at an amusement park lifts seated riders 250 feet above the ground. Then the riders are dropped. They experience free fall until the brakes are activated at 105 feet above the ground.

a. Writing an Equation Use the vertical motion model to write an equation for the height h (in feet) of the riders as a function of the time t (in seconds) into the free fall.

b. Making a Table Make a table that shows the height of the riders after 0, 1, 2, 3, and 4 seconds according to the model. Use the table to estimate the amount of time the riders experience free fall.

c. Solving an Equation Use the equation to find the amount of time, to the nearest tenth of a second, that the riders experience free fall.

63. CHALLENGE The height h (in feet) of a dropped object on any planet can be modeled by $h = -\frac{g}{2}t^2 + s$ where g is the acceleration (in feet per second per second) due to the planet's gravity, t is the time (in seconds) after the object is dropped, and s is the initial height (in feet) of the object. Suppose the same object is dropped from the same height on Earth and Mars. Given that g is 32 feet per second per second on Earth and 12 feet per second per second on Mars, on which planet will the object hit the ground first? *Explain.*

PROBLEM SOLVING WORKSHOP
LESSON 9.4

Using ALTERNATIVE METHODS

Another Way to Solve Example 5

MATHEMATICAL PRACTICES

Make sense of problems and persevere in solving them.

MULTIPLE REPRESENTATIONS In Example 5, you saw how to solve a problem about a dropped table-tennis ball by using a square root. You can also solve the problem by using factoring or by using a table.

PROBLEM

SPORTS EVENT During an ice hockey game, a remote-controlled blimp flies above the crowd and drops a numbered table-tennis ball. The number on the ball corresponds to a prize. Use the information in the diagram to find the amount of time that the ball is in the air.

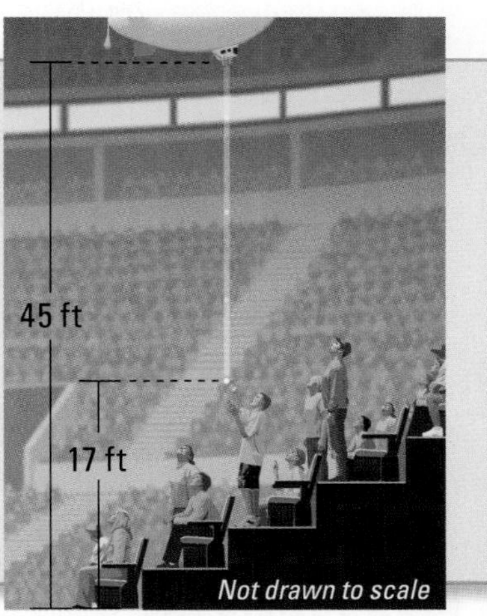

METHOD 1

Using Factoring One alternative approach is to use factoring.

STEP 1 **Write** an equation for the height h (in feet) of the ball as a function of time t (in seconds) after it is dropped using the vertical motion model.

$h = -16t^2 + vt + s$ **Vertical motion model**

$h = -16t^2 + 0t + 45$ **Substitute 0 for *v* and 45 for *s*.**

STEP 2 **Substitute** 17 for h to find the time it takes the ball to reach a height of 17 feet. Then write the equation so that 0 is on one side.

$17 = -16t^2 + 45$ **Substitute 17 for *h*.**

$0 = -16t^2 + 28$ **Subtract 17 from each side.**

STEP 3 **Solve** the equation by factoring. Replace 28 with the closest perfect square, 25, so that the right side of the equation is factorable as a difference of two squares.

USE AN APPROXIMATION
By replacing 28 with 25, you will obtain an answer that is an approximation of the amount of time that the ball is in the air.

$0 = -16t^2 + 25$ **Use 25 as an approximation for 28.**

$0 = -(16t^2 - 25)$ **Factor out −1.**

$0 = -(4t - 5)(4t + 5)$ **Difference of two squares pattern**

$4t - 5 = 0$ *or* $4t + 5 = 0$ **Zero-product property**

$t = \frac{5}{4}$ *or* $t = -\frac{5}{4}$ **Solve for *t*.**

▶ The ball is in the air about $\frac{5}{4}$, or 1.25, seconds.

METHOD 2 **Using a Table** Another approach is to make and use a table.

STEP 1 **Make** a table that shows the height h (in feet) of the ball by substituting values for time t (in seconds) in the function $h = -16t^2 + 45$. Use increments of 1 second.

Time t (seconds)	Height h (feet)
0	45
1	29
2	−19

STEP 2 **Identify** the time interval in which the height of the ball is 17 feet. This happens between 1 and 2 seconds.

STEP 3 **Make** a second table using increments of 0.1 second to get a closer approximation.

Time t (seconds)	Height h (feet)
1.0	29.00
1.1	25.64
1.2	21.96
1.3	**17.96**
1.4	13.64

▶ The ball is in the air about 1.3 seconds.

PRACTICE

1. **WHAT IF?** In the dropped-ball problem, suppose the ball is caught at a height of 10 feet. For how many seconds is the ball in the air? Solve this problem using two different methods.

2. **OPEN-ENDED** *Describe* a problem about a dropped object. Then solve the problem and explain what your solution means in this situation.

3. **GEOMETRY** The box below is a rectangular prism with the dimensions shown.

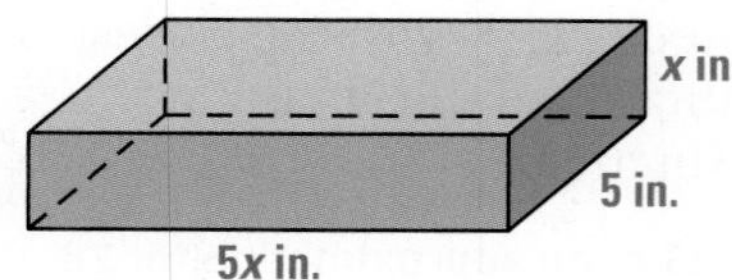

   a. Write an equation that gives the volume V (in cubic inches) of the box as a function of x.

   b. The volume of the box is 83 cubic inches. Find the dimensions of the box. Use factoring to solve the problem.

   c. Make a table to check your answer from part (b).

4. **TRAPEZE** You are learning how to perform on a trapeze. While hanging from a still trapeze bar, your shoe comes loose and falls to a safety net that is 6 feet off the ground. If your shoe falls from a height of 54 feet, how long does it take your shoe to hit the net? Choose any method for solving the problem. Show your steps.

5. **ERROR ANALYSIS** A student solved the problem in Exercise 4 as shown below. *Describe* and correct the error.

Let t be the time (in seconds) that the shoe is in the air.

$6 = -16t^2 + 54$

$0 = -16t^2 + 60$

Replace 60 with the closest perfect square, 64.

$0 = -16t^2 + 64$

$0 = -16(t - 2)(t + 2)$

$t = 2$ or $t = -2$

It takes about 2 seconds.

MIXED REVIEW of Problem Solving

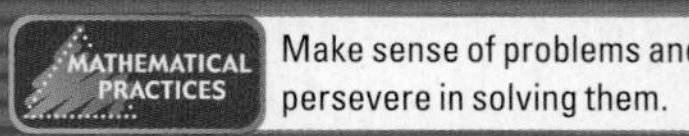

1. **MULTI-STEP PROBLEM** A company's yearly profits from 1996 to 2006 can be modeled by the function $y = x^2 - 8x + 80$ where y is the profit (in thousands of dollars) and x is the number of years since 1996.

   a. In what year did the company experience its lowest yearly profit?

   b. What was the lowest yearly profit?

2. **MULTI-STEP PROBLEM** Use the rectangle below.

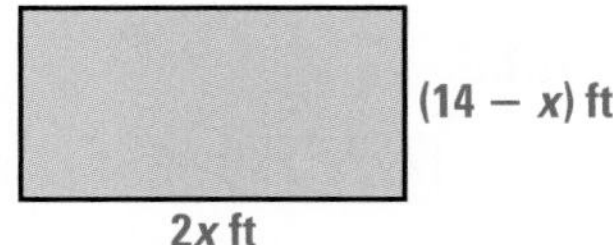

   a. Find the value of x that gives the greatest possible area of the rectangle.

   b. What is the greatest possible area of the rectangle?

3. **EXTENDED RESPONSE** You throw a lacrosse ball twice using a lacrosse stick.

   a. For your first throw, the ball is released 8 feet above the ground with an initial vertical velocity of 35 feet per second. Use the vertical motion model to write an equation for the height h (in feet) of the ball as a function of time t (in seconds).

   b. For your second throw, the ball is released 7 feet above the ground with an initial vertical velocity of 45 feet per second. Use the vertical motion model to write an equation for the height h (in feet) of the ball as a function of time t (in seconds).

   c. If no one catches either throw, for which throw is the ball in the air longer? *Explain.*

4. **OPEN-ENDED** Describe a real-world situation of an object being dropped. Then write an equation that models the height of the object as a function of time. Use the equation to determine the time it takes the object to hit the ground.

5. **SHORT RESPONSE** A football player is attempting a field goal. The path of the kicked football can be modeled by the graph of $y = -0.03x^2 + 1.8x$ where x is the horizontal distance (in yards) traveled by the football and y is the corresponding height (in feet) of the football. Will the football pass over the goal post that is 10 feet above the ground and 45 yards away? *Explain.*

6. **GRIDDED ANSWER** The force F (in newtons) a rider feels while a train goes around a curve is given by $F = \frac{mv^2}{r}$ where m is the mass (in kilograms) of the rider, v is the velocity (in meters per second) of the train, and r is the radius (in meters) of the curve. A rider with a mass of 75 kilograms experiences a force of 18,150 newtons, while going around a curve that has a radius of 8 meters. Find the velocity (in meters per second) the train travels around the curve.

7. **SHORT RESPONSE** The opening of the tunnel shown can be modeled by the graph of the equation $y = -0.18x^2 + 4.4x - 12$ where x and y are measured in feet.

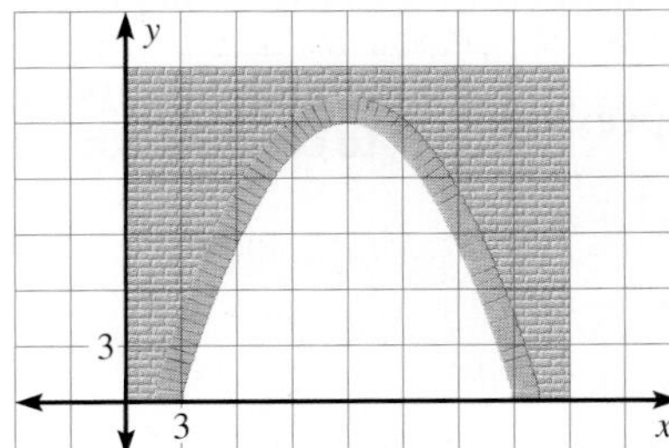

   a. Find the maximum height of the tunnel.

   b. A semi trailer is 7.5 feet wide, and the top of the trailer is 10.5 feet above the ground. Given that traffic travels one way on one lane through the center of the tunnel, will the semi trailer fit through the opening of the tunnel? *Explain.*

Completing the Square Using Algebra Tiles

MATHEMATICAL PRACTICES

Use appropriate tools strategically.

MATERIALS • algebra tiles

QUESTION How can you use algebra tiles to complete the square?

For an expression of the form $x^2 + bx$, you can add a constant c to the expression so that the expression $x^2 + bx + c$ is a perfect square trinomial. This process is called *completing the square.*

EXPLORE Complete the square

Find the value of c that makes $x^2 + 4x + c$ a perfect square trinomial.

STEP 1 ***Model expression***

Use algebra tiles to model the expression $x^2 + 4x$. You will need one x^2-tile and four x-tiles for this expression.

STEP 2 ***Rearrange tiles***

Arrange the tiles to form a square. The arrangement will be incomplete in one of the corners.

STEP 3 ***Complete the square***

Determine the number of 1-tiles needed to complete the square. The number of 1-tiles is the value of c. So, the perfect square trinomial is $x^2 + 4x + 4$ or $(x + 2)^2$.

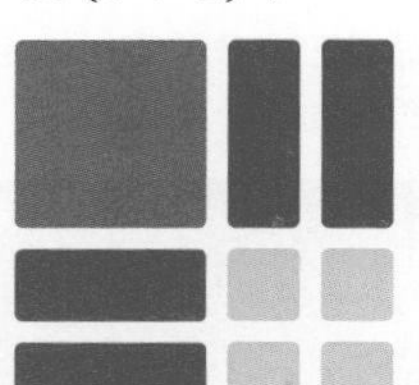

DRAW CONCLUSIONS Use your observations to complete these exercises

1. Copy and complete the table using algebra tiles.

Expression	Number of 1-tiles needed to complete the square	Expression written as a square
$x^2 + 4x$	4	$x^2 + 4x + 4 = (x + 2)^2$
$x^2 + 6x$	?	?
$x^2 + 8x$	?	?
$x^2 + 10x$	?	?

2. In the statement $x^2 + bx + c = (x + d)^2$, how are b and d related? How are c and d related?

3. Use your answer to Exercise 2 to predict the number of 1-tiles you would need to add to complete the square for the expression $x^2 + 18x$.

9.5 Solve Quadratic Equations by Completing the Square

Before You solved quadratic equations by finding square roots.

Now You will solve quadratic equations by completing the square.

Why? So you can solve a problem about snowboarding, as in Ex. 50.

Key Vocabulary
- **completing the square**
- **perfect square trinomial**

For an expression of the form $x^2 + bx$, you can add a constant c to the expression so that the expression $x^2 + bx + c$ is a perfect square trinomial. This process is called **completing the square**.

CC.9-12.A.REI.4b Solve quadratic equations by inspection (e.g., for $x^2 = 49$), taking square roots, completing the square, the quadratic formula and factoring, as appropriate to the initial form of the equation. Recognize when the quadratic formula gives complex soultions, and write them as $a \pm bi$ for real numbers a and b.

KEY CONCEPT *For Your Notebook*

Completing the Square

Words To complete the square for the expression $x^2 + bx$, add the square of half the coefficient of the term bx.

Algebra $x^2 + bx + \left(\frac{b}{2}\right)^2 = \left(x + \frac{b}{2}\right)^2$

EXAMPLE 1 Complete the square

Find the value of c that makes the expression $x^2 + 5x + c$ a perfect square trinomial. Then write the expression as the square of a binomial.

STEP 1 **Find** the value of c. For the expression to be a perfect square trinomial, c needs to be the square of half the coefficient of bx.

$c = \left(\frac{5}{2}\right)^2 = \frac{25}{4}$ — Find the square of half the coefficient of bx.

STEP 2 **Write** the expression as a perfect square trinomial. Then write the expression as the square of a binomial.

$x^2 + 5x + c = x^2 + 5x + \frac{25}{4}$ — Substitute $\frac{25}{4}$ for c.

$= \left(x + \frac{5}{2}\right)^2$ — Square of a binomial

✓ GUIDED PRACTICE for Example 1

Find the value of c that makes the expression a perfect square trinomial. Then write the expression as the square of a binomial.

1. $x^2 + 8x + c$ **2.** $x^2 - 12x + c$ **3.** $x^2 + 3x + c$

SOLVING EQUATIONS The method of completing the square can be used to solve any quadratic equation. To use completing the square to solve a quadratic equation, you must write the equation in the form $x^2 + bx = d$.

EXAMPLE 2 Solve a quadratic equation

Solve $x^2 - 16x = -15$ by completing the square.

Solution

$x^2 - 16x = -15$	**Write original equation.**
$x^2 - 16x + (-8)^2 = -15 + (-8)^2$	**Add $\left(\frac{-16}{2}\right)^2$, or $(-8)^2$, to each side.**
$(x - 8)^2 = -15 + (-8)^2$	**Write left side as the square of a binomial.**
$(x - 8)^2 = 49$	**Simplify the right side.**
$x - 8 = \pm 7$	**Take square roots of each side.**
$x = 8 \pm 7$	**Add 8 to each side.**

▶ The solutions of the equation are $8 + 7 = 15$ and $8 - 7 = 1$.

CHECK You can check the solutions in the original equation.

If $x = 15$:	**If $x = 1$:**
$(15)^2 - 16(15) \stackrel{?}{=} -15$	$(1)^2 - 16(1) \stackrel{?}{=} -15$
$-15 = -15$ ✓	$-15 = -15$ ✓

AVOID ERRORS
When completing the square to solve an equation, be sure you add the term $\left(\frac{b}{2}\right)^2$ to both sides of the equation.

EXAMPLE 3 Solve a quadratic equation in standard form

Solve $2x^2 + 20x - 8 = 0$ by completing the square.

Solution

$2x^2 + 20x - 8 = 0$	**Write original equation.**
$2x^2 + 20x = 8$	**Add 8 to each side.**
$x^2 + 10x = 4$	**Divide each side by 2.**
$x^2 + 10x + 5^2 = 4 + 5^2$	**Add $\left(\frac{10}{2}\right)^2$, or 5^2, to each side.**
$(x + 5)^2 = 29$	**Write left side as the square of a binomial.**
$x + 5 = \pm\sqrt{29}$	**Take square roots of each side.**
$x = -5 \pm \sqrt{29}$	**Subtract 5 from each side.**

▶ The solutions are $-5 + \sqrt{29} \approx 0.39$ and $-5 - \sqrt{29} \approx -10.39$.

AVOID ERRORS
Be sure that the coefficient of x^2 is 1 before you complete the square.

✓ GUIDED PRACTICE for Examples 2 and 3

Solve the equation by completing the square. Round your solutions to the nearest hundredth, if necessary.

4. $x^2 - 2x = 3$

5. $m^2 + 10m = -8$

6. $3g^2 - 24g + 27 = 0$

EXAMPLE 4 Solve a multi-step problem

CRAFTS You decide to use chalkboard paint to create a chalkboard on a door. You want the chalkboard to have a uniform border as shown. You have enough chalkboard paint to cover 6 square feet. Find the width of the border to the nearest inch.

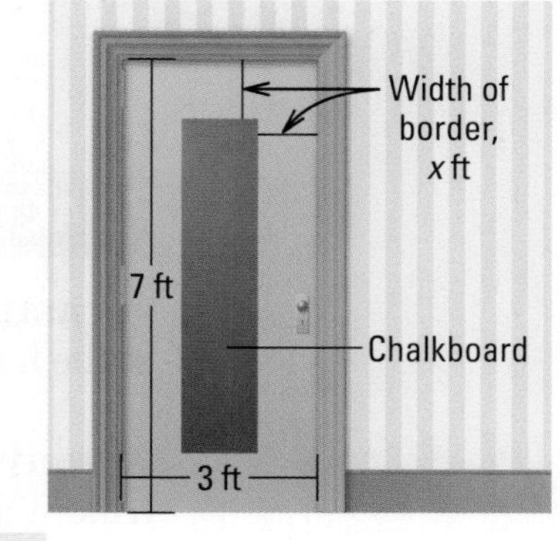

Solution

STEP 1 **Write** a verbal model. Then write an equation. Let x be the width (in feet) of the border.

Area of chalkboard (square feet)	=	Length of chalkboard (feet)	·	Width of chalkboard (feet)
6	=	**(7 − 2x)**	·	**(3 − 2x)**

WRITE EQUATION
The width of the border is subtracted twice because it is at the top and the bottom of the door, as well as at the left and the right.

STEP 2 **Solve** the equation.

$$6 = (7 - 2x)(3 - 2x)$$ **Write equation.**

$$6 = 21 - 20x + 4x^2$$ **Multiply binomials.**

$$-15 = 4x^2 - 20x$$ **Subtract 21 from each side.**

$$-\frac{15}{4} = x^2 - 5x$$ **Divide each side by 4.**

$$-\frac{15}{4} + \frac{25}{4} = x^2 - 5x + \frac{25}{4}$$ **Add $\left(-\frac{5}{2}\right)^2$, or $\frac{25}{4}$, to each side.**

$$-\frac{15}{4} + \frac{25}{4} = \left(x - \frac{5}{2}\right)^2$$ **Write right side as the square of a binomial.**

$$\frac{5}{2} = \left(x - \frac{5}{2}\right)^2$$ **Simplify left side.**

$$\pm\sqrt{\frac{5}{2}} = x - \frac{5}{2}$$ **Take square roots of each side.**

$$\frac{5}{2} \pm \sqrt{\frac{5}{2}} = x$$ **Add $\frac{5}{2}$ to each side.**

The solutions of the equation are $\frac{5}{2} + \sqrt{\frac{5}{2}} \approx 4.08$ and $\frac{5}{2} - \sqrt{\frac{5}{2}} \approx 0.92$.

It is not possible for the width of the border to be 4.08 feet because the width of the door is 3 feet. So, the width of the border is 0.92 foot. Convert 0.92 foot to inches.

$$0.92 \text{ ft} \cdot \frac{12 \text{ in.}}{1 \text{ ft}} = 11.04 \text{ in.}$$ **Multiply by conversion factor.**

▶ The width of the border should be about 11 inches.

GUIDED PRACTICE for Example 4

7. **WHAT IF?** In Example 4, suppose you have enough chalkboard paint to cover 4 square feet. Find the width of the border to the nearest inch.

9.5 EXERCISES

HOMEWORK KEY

○ = See WORKED-OUT SOLUTIONS Exs. 19 and 47

★ = STANDARDIZED TEST PRACTICE Exs. 2, 24, 25, 42, and 49

◆ = MULTIPLE REPRESENTATIONS Ex. 47

SKILL PRACTICE

1. **VOCABULARY** Copy and complete: The process of writing an expression of the form $x^2 + bx$ as a perfect square trinomial is called __?__.

2. ★ **WRITING** Give an example of an expression that is a perfect square trinomial. *Explain* why the expression is a perfect square trinomial.

EXAMPLE 1 for Exs. 3–11

COMPLETING THE SQUARE Find the value of c that makes the expression a perfect square trinomial. Then write the expression as the square of a binomial.

3. $x^2 + 6x + c$
4. $x^2 + 12x + c$
5. $x^2 - 4x + c$
6. $x^2 - 8x + c$
7. $x^2 - 3x + c$
8. $x^2 + 5x + c$
9. $x^2 + 2.4x + c$
10. $x^2 - \frac{1}{2}x + c$
11. $x^2 - \frac{4}{3}x + c$

EXAMPLES 2 and 3 for Exs. 12–27

SOLVING EQUATIONS Solve the equation by completing the square. Round your solutions to the nearest hundredth, if necessary.

12. $x^2 + 2x = 3$
13. $x^2 + 10x = 24$
14. $c^2 - 14c = 15$
15. $n^2 - 6n = 72$
16. $a^2 - 8a + 15 = 0$
17. $y^2 + 4y - 21 = 0$
18. $w^2 - 5w = \frac{11}{4}$
19. $z^2 + 11z = -\frac{21}{4}$
20. $g^2 - \frac{2}{3}g = 7$
21. $k^2 - 8k - 7 = 0$
22. $v^2 - 7v + 1 = 0$
23. $m^2 + 3m + \frac{5}{4} = 0$

24. ★ **MULTIPLE CHOICE** What are the solutions of $4x^2 + 16x = 9$?

Ⓐ $-\frac{1}{2}, -\frac{9}{2}$ Ⓑ $-\frac{1}{2}, \frac{9}{2}$ Ⓒ $\frac{1}{2}, -\frac{9}{2}$ Ⓓ $\frac{1}{2}, \frac{9}{2}$

25. ★ **MULTIPLE CHOICE** What are the solutions of $x^2 + 12x + 10 = 0$?

Ⓐ $-6 \pm \sqrt{46}$ Ⓑ $-6 \pm \sqrt{26}$ Ⓒ $6 \pm \sqrt{26}$ Ⓓ $6 \pm \sqrt{46}$

ERROR ANALYSIS ***Describe*** **and correct the error in solving the given equation.**

26. $x^2 - 14x = 11$

$$x^2 - 14x = 11$$
$$x^2 - 14x + 49 = 11$$
$$(x - 7)^2 = 11$$
$$x - 7 = \pm\sqrt{11}$$
$$x = 7 \pm \sqrt{11}$$

27. $x^2 - 2x - 4 = 0$

$$x^2 - 2x - 4 = 0$$
$$x^2 - 2x = 4$$
$$x^2 - 2x + 1 = 4 + 1$$
$$(x + 1)^2 = 5$$
$$x + 1 = \pm\sqrt{5}$$
$$x = 1 \pm \sqrt{5}$$

SOLVING EQUATIONS **Solve the equation by completing the square. Round your solutions to the nearest hundredth, if necessary.**

28. $2x^2 - 8x - 14 = 0$ **29.** $2x^2 + 24x + 10 = 0$ **30.** $3x^2 - 48x + 39 = 0$

31. $4y^2 + 4y - 7 = 0$ **32.** $9n^2 + 36n + 11 = 0$ **33.** $3w^2 - 18w - 20 = 0$

34. $3p^2 - 30p - 11 = 6p$ **35.** $3a^2 - 12a + 3 = -a^2 - 4$ **36.** $15c^2 - 51c - 30 = 9c + 15$

37. $7m^2 + 24m - 2 = m^2 - 9$ **38.** $g^2 + 2g + 0.4 = 0.9g^2 + g$ **39.** $11z^2 - 10z - 3 = -9z^2 + \frac{3}{4}$

GEOMETRY **Find the value of x. Round your answer to the nearest hundredth, if necessary.**

40. Area of triangle = 108 m^2

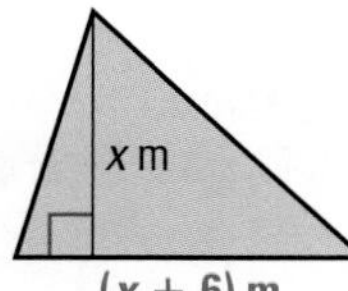

41. Area of rectangle = 288 in.^2

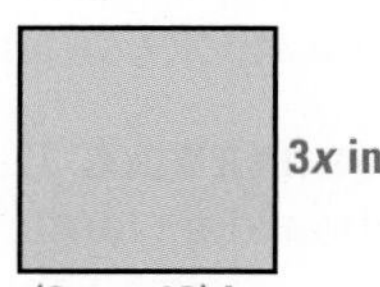

42. ★ **WRITING** How many solutions does $x^2 + bx = c$ have if $c < -\left(\frac{b}{2}\right)^2$? *Explain.*

43. **CHALLENGE** The product of two consecutive negative integers is 210. Find the integers.

44. **CHALLENGE** The product of two consecutive positive even integers is 288. Find the integers.

PROBLEM SOLVING

EXAMPLE 4 for Exs. 45–46

45. **LANDSCAPING** You are building a rectangular brick patio surrounded by crushed stone in a rectangular courtyard as shown. The crushed stone border has a uniform width x (in feet). You have enough money in your budget to purchase patio bricks to cover 140 square feet. Solve the equation $140 = (20 - 2x)(16 - 2x)$ to find the width of the border.

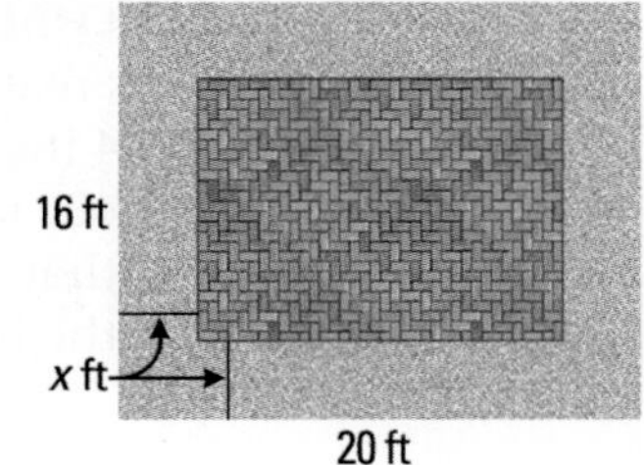

46. **TRAFFIC ENGINEERING** The distance d (in feet) that it takes a car to come to a complete stop on dry asphalt can be modeled by $d = 0.05s^2 + 1.1s$ where s is the speed of the car (in miles per hour). A car has 78 feet to come to a complete stop. Find the maximum speed at which the car can travel.

47. **MULTIPLE REPRESENTATIONS** For the period 1985–2001, the average salary y (in thousands of dollars) per season of a Major League Baseball player can be modeled by $y = 7x^2 - 4x + 392$ where x is the number of years since 1985.

a. **Solving an Equation** Write and solve an equation to find the year when the average salary was $1,904,000.

b. **Drawing a Graph** Use a graph to check your solution to part (a).

48. **MULTI-STEP PROBLEM** You have 80 feet of fencing to make a rectangular horse pasture that covers 750 square feet. A barn will be used as one side of the pasture as shown.

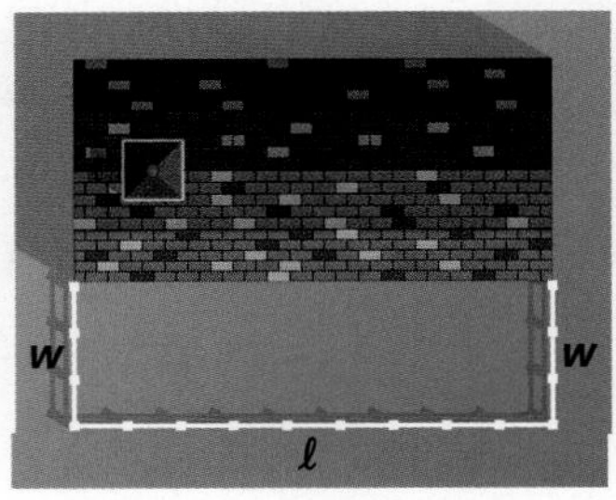

a. Write equations for the perimeter and area of the pasture.

b. Use substitution to solve the system of equations from part (a). What are the possible dimensions of the pasture?

49. ★ **SHORT RESPONSE** You purchase stock for \$16 per share, and you sell the stock 30 days later for \$23.50 per share. The price y (in dollars) of a share during the 30 day period can be modeled by $y = -0.025x^2 + x + 16$ where x is the number of days after the stock is purchased. Could you have sold the stock earlier for \$23.50 per share? *Explain.*

50. **SNOWBOARDING** During a "big air" competition, snowboarders launch themselves from a half pipe, perform tricks in the air, and land back in the half pipe.

a. **Model** Use the vertical motion model to write an equation that models the height h (in feet) of a snowboarder as a function of the time t (in seconds) she is in the air.

b. **Apply** How long is the snowboarder in the air if she lands 13.2 feet above the base of the half pipe? Round your answer to the nearest tenth of a second.

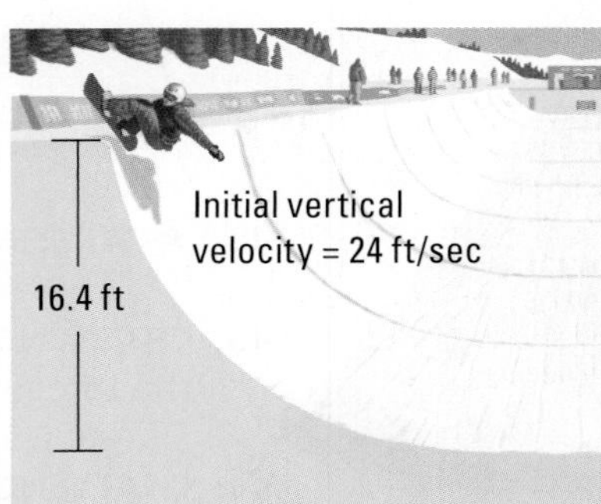

Cross section of a half pipe

Animated Algebra at my.hrw.com

51. **CHALLENGE** You are knitting a rectangular scarf. The pattern you have created will result in a scarf that has a length of 60 inches and a width of 4 inches. However, you happen to have enough yarn to cover an area of 480 square inches. You decide to increase the dimensions of the scarf so that all of your yarn will be used. If the increase in the length is 10 times the increase in the width, what will the dimensions of the scarf be?

Extension Graph Quadratic Functions in Vertex Form

GOAL Graph quadratic functions in vertex form.

Key Vocabulary
- **vertex form**

You have graphed quadratic functions in standard form. Quadratic functions can also be written in **vertex form**, $y = a(x - h)^2 + k$ where $a \neq 0$. In this form, the vertex of the graph can be easily determined.

CC.9-12.F.BF.3 Identify the effect on the graph of replacing $f(x)$ by $f(x) + k$, $kf(x)$, $f(kx)$, and $f(x + k)$ for specific values of k (both positive and negative); find the value of k given the graphs. Experiment with cases and illustrate an explanation of the effects on the graph using technology.

KEY CONCEPT *For Your Notebook*

Graph of Vertex Form $y = a(x - h)^2 + k$

The graph of $y = a(x - h)^2 + k$ is the graph of $y = ax^2$ translated h units horizontally and k units vertically.

Characteristics of the graph of $y = a(x - h)^2 + k$:

- The vertex is (h, k).
- The axis of symmetry is $x = h$.
- The graph opens up if $a > 0$, and the graph opens down if $a < 0$.

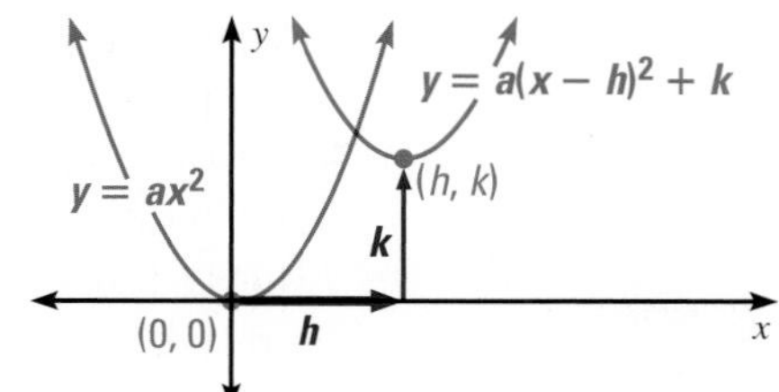

EXAMPLE 1 Graph a quadratic function in vertex form

Graph $y = -(x + 2)^2 + 3$.

Solution

STEP 1 **Identify** the values of a, h, and k: $a = -1$, $h = -2$, and $k = 3$. Because $a < 0$, the parabola opens down.

STEP 2 **Draw** the axis of symmetry, $x = -2$.

STEP 3 **Plot** the vertex $(h, k) = (-2, 3)$.

STEP 4 **Plot** four points. Evaluate the function for two x-values less than the x-coordinate of the vertex.

$\mathbf{x = -3}$: $y = -(\mathbf{-3} + 2)^2 + 3 = 2$

$\mathbf{x = -5}$: $y = -(\mathbf{-5} + 2)^2 + 3 = -6$

Plot the points $(-3, 2)$ and $(-5, -6)$ and their reflections, $(-1, 2)$ and $(1, -6)$, in the axis of symmetry.

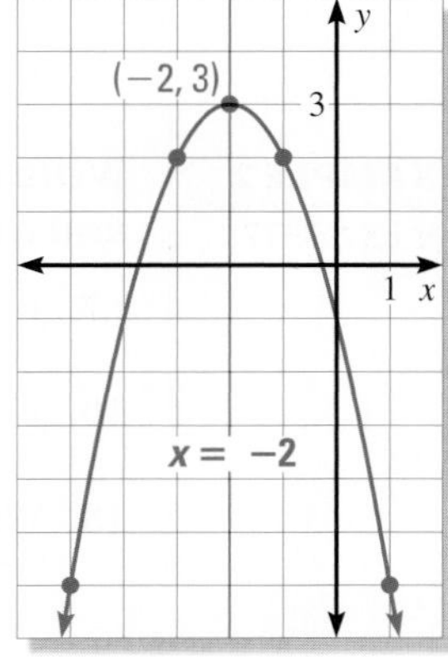

STEP 5 **Draw** a parabola through the plotted points.

EXAMPLE 2 Graph a quadratic function

Graph $y = x^2 - 8x + 11$.

Solution

STEP 1 **Write** the function in vertex form by completing the square.

$y = x^2 - 8x + 11$	**Write original function.**
$y + \square = (x^2 - 8x + \square) + 11$	**Prepare to complete the square.**
$y + 16 = (x^2 - 8x + 16) + 11$	**Add $\left(\frac{-8}{2}\right)^2 = (-4)^2 = 16$ to each side.**
$y + 16 = (x - 4)^2 + 11$	**Write $x^2 - 8x + 16$ as a square of a binomial.**
$y = (x - 4)^2 - 5$	**Subtract 16 from each side.**

STEP 2 **Identify** the values of a, h, and k: $a = 1$, $h = 4$, and $k = -5$. Because $a > 0$, the parabola opens up.

STEP 3 **Draw** the axis of symmetry, $x = 4$.

STEP 4 **Plot** the vertex $(h, k) = (4, -5)$.

STEP 5 **Plot** four more points. Evaluate the function for two x-values less than the x-coordinate of the vertex.

$x = 3$: $y = (3 - 4)^2 - 5 = -4$
$x = 1$: $y = (1 - 4)^2 - 5 = 4$

Plot the points $(3, -4)$ and $(1, 4)$ and their reflections, $(5, -4)$ and $(7, 4)$, in the axis of symmetry.

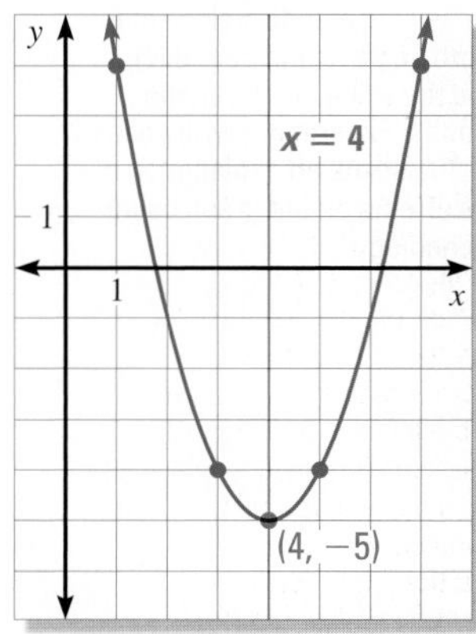

STEP 6 **Draw** a parabola through the plotted points.

PRACTICE

EXAMPLE 1 for Exs. 1–6

Graph the quadratic function. Label the vertex and axis of symmetry.

1. $y = (x + 2)^2 - 5$
2. $y = -(x - 4)^2 + 1$
3. $y = x^2 + 3$
4. $y = 3(x - 1)^2 - 2$
5. $y = -2(x + 5)^2 - 2$
6. $y = -\frac{1}{2}(x + 4)^2 + 4$

EXAMPLE 2 for Exs. 7–12

Write the function in vertex form, then graph the function. Label the vertex and axis of symmetry.

7. $y = x^2 - 12x + 36$
8. $y = x^2 + 8x + 15$
9. $y = -x^2 + 10x - 21$
10. $y = 2x^2 - 12x + 19$
11. $y = -3x^2 - 6x - 1$
12. $y = -\frac{1}{2}x^2 - 6x - 21$

13. Write an equation in vertex form of the parabola shown. Use the coordinates of the vertex and the coordinates of a point on the graph to write the equation.

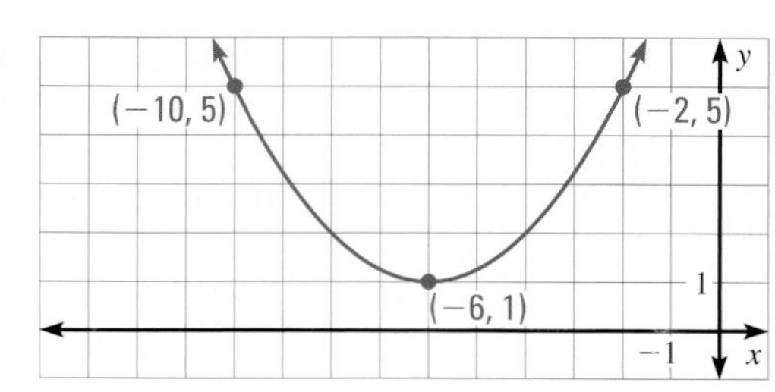

9.6 Solve Quadratic Equations by the Quadratic Formula

Before	You solved quadratic equations by completing the square.
Now	You will solve quadratic equations using the quadratic formula.
Why?	So you can solve a problem about film production, as in Example 3.

Key Vocabulary
- **quadratic formula**

By completing the square for the quadratic equation $ax^2 + bx + c = 0$, you can develop a formula that gives the solutions of any quadratic equation in standard form. This formula is called the **quadratic formula**.

COMMON CORE

CC.9-12.A.REI.4b Solve quadratic equations by inspection (e.g., for $x^2 = 49$), taking square roots, completing the square, the quadratic formula and factoring, as appropriate to the initial form of the equation. Recognize when the quadratic formula gives complex soultions, and write them as $a \pm bi$ for real numbers a and b.

KEY CONCEPT *For Your Notebook*

The Quadratic Formula

The solutions of the quadratic equation $ax^2 + bx + c = 0$ are

$x = \dfrac{-b \pm \sqrt{b^2 - 4ac}}{2a}$ where $a \neq 0$ and $b^2 - 4ac \geq 0$.

EXAMPLE 1 Standardized Test Practice

What are the solutions of $3x^2 + 5x = 8$?

Ⓐ -1 and $-\frac{8}{3}$ Ⓑ -1 and $\frac{8}{3}$ Ⓒ 1 and $-\frac{8}{3}$ Ⓓ 1 and $\frac{8}{3}$

ANOTHER WAY
Instead of solving the equation, you can check the answer choices in the equation.

Solution

$3x^2 + 5x = 8$ **Write original equation.**

$3x^2 + 5x - 8 = 0$ **Write in standard form.**

$x = \dfrac{-b \pm \sqrt{b^2 - 4ac}}{2a}$ **Quadratic formula**

$x = \dfrac{-5 \pm \sqrt{5^2 - 4(3)(-8)}}{2(3)}$ **Substitute values in the quadratic formula: $a = 3$, $b = 5$, and $c = -8$.**

$= \dfrac{-5 \pm \sqrt{121}}{6}$ **Simplify.**

$= \dfrac{-5 \pm 11}{6}$ **Simplify the square root.**

The solutions of the equation are $\frac{-5 + 11}{6} = 1$ and $\frac{-5 - 11}{6} = -\frac{8}{3}$.

▶ The correct answer is C. Ⓐ Ⓑ Ⓒ Ⓓ

EXAMPLE 2 Solve a quadratic equation

Solve $2x^2 - 7 = x$.

$2x^2 - 7 = x$ **Write original equation.**

$2x^2 - x - 7 = 0$ **Write in standard form.**

$x = \frac{-b \pm \sqrt{b^2 - 4ac}}{2a}$ **Quadratic formula**

$= \frac{-(-1) \pm \sqrt{(-1)^2 - 4(2)(-7)}}{2(2)}$ **Substitute values in the quadratic formula: $a = 2$, $b = -1$, and $c = -7$.**

$= \frac{1 \pm \sqrt{57}}{4}$ **Simplify.**

▶ The solutions are $\frac{1 + \sqrt{57}}{4} \approx 2.14$ and $\frac{1 - \sqrt{57}}{4} \approx -1.64$.

Animated Algebra at my.hrw.com

CHECK Write the equation in standard form, $2x^2 - x - 7 = 0$. Then graph the related function $y = 2x^2 - x - 7$. The x-intercepts are about -1.6 and 2.1. So, each solution checks.

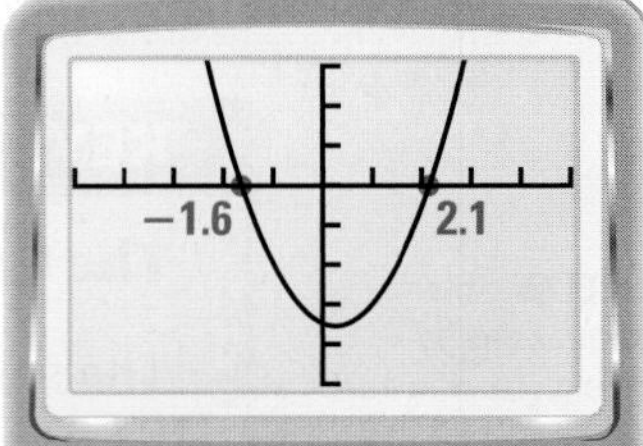

✓ GUIDED PRACTICE for Examples 1 and 2

Use the quadratic formula to solve the equation. Round your solutions to the nearest hundredth, if necessary.

1. $x^2 - 8x + 16 = 0$ **2.** $3n^2 - 5n = -1$ **3.** $4z^2 = 7z + 2$

EXAMPLE 3 Use the quadratic formula

FILM PRODUCTION For the period 1971–2001, the number y of films produced in the world can be modeled by the function $y = 10x^2 - 94x + 3900$ where x is the number of years since 1971. In what year were 4200 films produced?

Solution

$y = 10x^2 - 94x + 3900$ **Write function.**

$4200 = 10x^2 - 94x + 3900$ **Substitute 4200 for y.**

$0 = 10x^2 - 94x - 300$ **Write in standard form.**

$x = \frac{-(-94) \pm \sqrt{(-94)^2 - 4(10)(-300)}}{2(10)}$ **Substitute values in the quadratic formula: $a = 10$, $b = -94$, and $c = -300$.**

$= \frac{94 \pm \sqrt{20{,}836}}{20}$ **Simplify.**

The solutions of the equation are $\frac{94 + \sqrt{20{,}836}}{20} \approx 12$ and $\frac{94 - \sqrt{20{,}836}}{20} \approx -3$.

▶ There were 4200 films produced about 12 years after 1971, or in 1983.

INTERPRET SOLUTIONS

The solution -3 can be ignored because -3 represents the year 1968, which is not in the given time period.

GUIDED PRACTICE for Example 3

4. **WHAT IF?** In Example 3, find the year when 4750 films were produced.

CONCEPT SUMMARY *For Your Notebook*

Methods for Solving Quadratic Equations

Method	When to Use
Factoring	Use when a quadratic equation can be factored easily.
Graphing	Use when approximate solutions are adequate.
Finding square roots	Use when solving an equation that can be written in the form $x^2 = d$.
Completing the square	Can be used for *any* quadratic equation $ax^2 + bx + c = 0$ but is simplest to apply when $a = 1$ and b is an even number.
Quadratic formula	Can be used for *any* quadratic equation.

EXAMPLE 4 Choose a solution method

Tell what method you would use to solve the quadratic equation. *Explain* your choice(s).

a. $10x^2 - 7 = 0$ **b.** $x^2 + 4x = 0$ **c.** $5x^2 + 9x - 4 = 0$

Solution

a. The quadratic equation can be solved using square roots because the equation can be written in the form $x^2 = d$.

b. The equation can be solved by factoring because the expression $x^2 + 4x$ can be factored easily. Also, the equation can be solved by completing the square because the equation is of the form $ax^2 + bx + c = 0$ where $a = 1$ and b is an even number.

c. The quadratic equation cannot be factored easily, and completing the square will result in many fractions. So, the equation can be solved using the quadratic formula.

GUIDED PRACTICE for Example 4

Tell what method you would use to solve the quadratic equation. *Explain* your choice(s).

5. $x^2 + x - 6 = 0$ **6.** $x^2 - 9 = 0$ **7.** $x^2 + 6x = 5$

9.6 EXERCISES

HOMEWORK KEY

○ = See WORKED-OUT SOLUTIONS Exs. 19 and 47

★ = STANDARDIZED TEST PRACTICE Exs. 2, 12, 25, and 50

◆ = MULTIPLE REPRESENTATIONS Ex. 49

SKILL PRACTICE

1. **VOCABULARY** What formula can be used to solve any quadratic equation?

2. ★ **WRITING** What method(s) would you use to solve $-x^2 + 8x = 1$? *Explain* your choice(s).

EXAMPLES 1 and 2 for Exs. 3–27

SOLVING QUADRATIC EQUATIONS **Use the quadratic formula to find the roots of the equation. Round your solutions to the nearest hundredth, if necessary.**

3. $x^2 + 5x - 104 = 0$
4. $4x^2 - x - 18 = 0$
5. $6x^2 - 2x - 28 = 0$
6. $m^2 + 3m + 1 = 0$
7. $-z^2 + z + 14 = 0$
8. $-2n^2 - 5n + 16 = 0$
9. $4w^2 + 20w + 25 = 0$
10. $2t^2 + 3t - 11 = 0$
11. $-6g^2 + 9g + 8 = 0$

12. ★ **MULTIPLE CHOICE** What are the solutions of $10x^2 - 3x - 1 = 0$?

Ⓐ $-\frac{1}{5}$ and $-\frac{1}{2}$ Ⓑ $-\frac{1}{5}$ and $\frac{1}{2}$ Ⓒ $\frac{1}{5}$ and $-\frac{1}{2}$ Ⓓ $\frac{1}{5}$ and $\frac{1}{2}$

SOLVING QUADRATIC EQUATIONS **Use the quadratic formula to solve the equation. Round your solutions to the nearest hundredth, if necessary.**

13. $x^2 - 5x = 14$
14. $3x^2 - 4 = 11x$
15. $9 = 7x^2 - 2x$
16. $2m^2 + 9m + 7 = 3$
17. $-10 = r^2 - 10r + 12$
18. $3g^2 - 6g - 14 = 3g$
19. $6z^2 = 2z^2 + 7z + 5$
20. $8h^2 + 8 = 6 - 9h$
21. $4t^2 - 3t = 5 - 3t^2$
22. $-4y^2 - 3y + 3 = 2y + 4$
23. $7n + 5 = -3n^2 + 2$
24. $5w^2 + 4 = w + 6$

25. ★ **MULTIPLE CHOICE** What are the solutions of $x^2 + 14x = 2x - 11$?

Ⓐ −2 and −22 Ⓑ −1 and −11 Ⓒ 1 and 11 Ⓓ 2 and 22

ERROR ANALYSIS ***Describe*** **and correct the error in solving the equation.**

26. $7x^2 - 5x - 1 = 0$

$$x = \frac{-5 \pm \sqrt{(-5)^2 - 4(7)(-1)}}{2(7)}$$
$$= \frac{-5 \pm \sqrt{53}}{14}$$
$$x \approx -0.88 \text{ and } x \approx 0.16$$

27. $-2x^2 + 3x = 1$

$$x = \frac{-3 \pm \sqrt{3^2 - 4(-2)(1)}}{2(-2)}$$
$$= \frac{-3 \pm \sqrt{17}}{-4}$$
$$x \approx -0.28 \text{ and } x \approx 1.78$$

EXAMPLE 4 for Exs. 28–33

CHOOSING A METHOD **Tell what method(s) you would use to solve the quadratic equation.** ***Explain*** **your choice(s).**

28. $3x^2 - 27 = 0$
29. $5x^2 = 25$
30. $2x^2 - 12x = 0$
31. $m^2 + 5m + 6 = 0$
32. $z^2 - 4z + 1 = 0$
33. $-10g^2 + 13g = 4$

SOLVING QUADRATIC EQUATIONS **Solve the quadratic equation using any method. Round your solutions to the nearest hundredth, if necessary.**

34. $-2x^2 = -32$

35. $x^2 - 8x = -16$

36. $x^2 + 2x - 6 = 0$

37. $x^2 = 12x - 36$

38. $x^2 + 4x = 9$

39. $-4x^2 + x = -17$

40. $11x^2 - 1 = 6x^2 + 2$

41. $-2x^2 + 5 = 3x^2 - 10x$

42. $(x + 13)^2 = 25$

GEOMETRY **Use the given area A of the rectangle to find the value of x. Then give the dimensions of the rectangle.**

43. $A = 91\text{ m}^2$

(x + 2) n

(2x + 3) m

44. $A = 209\text{ ft}^2$

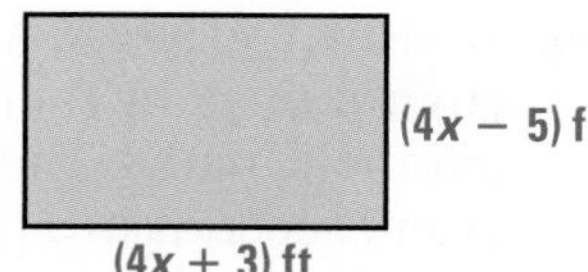

45. CHALLENGE The solutions of the quadratic equation $ax^2 + bx + c = 0$ are $x = \frac{-b + \sqrt{b^2 - 4ac}}{2a}$ and $x = \frac{-b - \sqrt{b^2 - 4ac}}{2a}$. Find the mean of the solutions. How is the mean of the solutions related to the graph of $y = ax^2 + bx + c$? *Explain.*

PROBLEM SOLVING

EXAMPLE 3 for Exs. 46–47

46. ADVERTISING For the period 1990–2000, the amount of money y (in billions of dollars) spent on advertising in the U.S. can be modeled by the function $y = 0.93x^2 + 2.2x + 130$ where x is the number of years since 1990. In what year was 164 billion dollars spent on advertising?

47. CELL PHONES For the period 1985–2001, the number y (in millions) of cell phone service subscribers in the U.S. can be modeled by the function $y = 0.7x^2 - 4.3x + 5.5$ where x is the number of years since 1985. In what year were there 16,000,000 cell phone service subscribers?

48. MULTI-STEP PROBLEM A football is punted from a height of 2.5 feet above the ground and with an initial vertical velocity of 45 feet per second.

a. Use the vertical motion model to write an equation that gives the height h (in feet) of the football as a function of the time t (in seconds) after it has been punted.

b. The football is caught 5.5 feet above the ground as shown in the diagram. Find the amount of time that the football is in the air.

49. **MULTIPLE REPRESENTATIONS** For the period 1997–2002, the number y (in thousands) of 16- and 17-year-olds employed in the United States can be modeled by the function $y = -46.7x^2 + 169x + 2650$ where x is the number of years since 1997.

   a. **Solving an Equation** Write and solve an equation to find the year during which 2,500,000 16- and 17-year-olds were employed.

   b. **Drawing a Graph** Graph the function on a graphing calculator. Use the *trace* feature to find the year when 2,500,000 16- and 17-year-olds were employed. Use the graph to check your answer from part (a).

50. ★ **SHORT RESPONSE** NASA creates a weightless environment by flying a plane in a series of parabolic paths. The height h (in feet) of a plane after t seconds in a parabolic flight path can be modeled by the graph of $h = -11t^2 + 700t + 21,000$. The passengers experience a weightless environment when the height of the plane is greater than or equal to 30,800 feet. Find the period of weightlessness on such a flight. *Explain.*

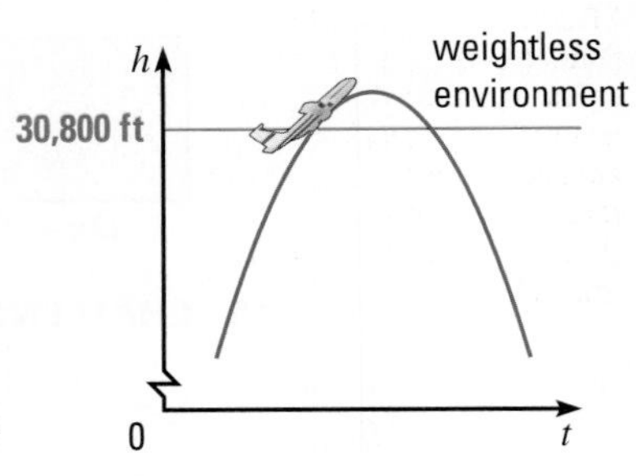

51. **CHALLENGE** Mineral deposits have formed a uniform coating that is 4 millimeters thick on the inside of a water pipe. The cross-sectional area of the pipe has decreased by 10%. What was the original diameter of the pipe (to the nearest tenth of a millimeter)?

QUIZ

Solve the equation using square roots.

1. $3x^2 - 48 = 0$
2. $-6x^2 = -24$
3. $x^2 + 5 = 16$

Solve the equation by completing the square.

4. $x^2 + 2x + 6 = 0$
5. $x^2 + 10x - 12 = 0$
6. $x^2 - 8x = -6$
7. $x^2 - 12x = 30$
8. $x^2 - 5x = -\frac{9}{4}$
9. $x^2 + x = -7.75$

Solve the equation using the quadratic formula.

10. $x^2 + 4x + 1 = 0$
11. $-3x^2 + 3x = -1$
12. $4x^2 - 11x = 3$

See **EXTRA PRACTICE** in Student Resources **ONLINE QUIZ** at my.hrw.com

Extension Derive the Quadratic Formula

GOAL Solve quadratic equations and check solutions.

COMMON CORE

CC.9-12.A.REI.4a Use the method of completing the square to transform any quadratic equation in x into an equation of the form $(x - p)^2 = q$ that has the same solutions. Derive the quadratic formula from this form.

You have learned how to find solutions of quadratic equations using the quadratic formula. You can use the method of completing the square and the quotient property of radicals to derive the quadratic formula.

$ax^2 + bx + c = 0$	**Write standard form of a quadratic equation.**
$ax^2 + bx = -c$	**Subtract c from each side.**
$x^2 + \frac{b}{a}x = -\frac{c}{a}$	**Divide each side by a, $a \neq 0$.**
$x^2 + \frac{b}{a}x + \left(\frac{b}{2a}\right)^2 = -\frac{c}{a} + \left(\frac{b}{2a}\right)^2$	**Add $\left(\frac{b}{2a}\right)^2$ to each side to complete the square.**
$\left(x + \frac{b}{2a}\right)^2 = -\frac{c}{a} + \frac{b^2}{4a^2}$	**Write left side as the square of a binomial.**
$\left(x + \frac{b}{2a}\right)^2 = \frac{b^2 - 4ac}{4a^2}$	**Simplify right side.**
$x + \frac{b}{2a} = \pm\sqrt{\frac{b^2 - 4ac}{4a^2}}$	**Take square roots of each side.**
$x + \frac{b}{2a} = \frac{\pm\sqrt{b^2 - 4ac}}{2a}$	**Quotient property of radicals**
$x = \frac{-b \pm \sqrt{b^2 - 4ac}}{2a}$	**Subtract $\frac{b}{2a}$ from each side.**

SOLVING QUADRATIC EQUATIONS You can use the quadratic formula and properties of radicals to solve quadratic equations.

EXAMPLE 1 Solve an equation

Solve $x^2 - 6x + 3 = 0$.

Solution

$x^2 - 6x + 3 = 0$	**Identify $a = 1$, $b = -6$, and $c = 3$.**
$x = \frac{-(-6) \pm \sqrt{(-6)^2 - 4(1)(3)}}{2(1)}$	**Substitute values in the quadratic formula.**
$= \frac{6 \pm \sqrt{24}}{2}$	**Simplify.**
$= \frac{6 \pm \sqrt{4 \cdot 6}}{2}$	**Product property of radicals**
$= \frac{6 \pm 2\sqrt{6}}{2} = 3 \pm \sqrt{6}$	**Simplify.**

▶ The solutions of the equation are $3 + \sqrt{6}$ and $3 - \sqrt{6}$.

EXAMPLE 2 Check the solutions of an equation

Check the solutions of the equation from Example 1.

Solution

The solutions of $x^2 - 6x + 3 = 0$ are $3 + \sqrt{6}$ and $3 - \sqrt{6}$. You can check each solution by substituting it into the original equation.

Check $x = 3 + \sqrt{6}$:

$$x^2 - 6x + 3 = 0$$ **Write original equation.**

$$(3 + \sqrt{6})^2 - 6(3 + \sqrt{6}) + 3 \stackrel{?}{=} 0$$ **Substitute $3 + \sqrt{6}$ for x.**

$$9 + 6\sqrt{6} + 6 - 18 - 6\sqrt{6} + 3 \stackrel{?}{=} 0$$ **Multiply.**

$$0 = 0 \checkmark$$ **Solution checks.**

Check $x = 3 - \sqrt{6}$:

$$x^2 - 6x + 3 = 0$$ **Write original equation.**

$$(3 - \sqrt{6})^2 - 6(3 - \sqrt{6}) + 3 \stackrel{?}{=} 0$$ **Substitute $3 - \sqrt{6}$ for x.**

$$9 - 6\sqrt{6} + 6 - 18 + 6\sqrt{6} + 3 \stackrel{?}{=} 0$$ **Multiply.**

$$0 = 0 \checkmark$$ **Solution checks.**

PRACTICE

EXAMPLES 1 and 2 for Exs. 1–18

Solve the equation using the quadratic formula. Check the solution.

1. $x^2 + 4x + 2 = 0$
2. $x^2 + 6x - 1 = 0$
3. $x^2 + 8x + 8 = 0$
4. $x^2 - 7x + 1 = 0$
5. $3x^2 + 6x - 1 = 0$
6. $2x^2 - 4x - 3 = 0$
7. $5x^2 - 2x - 2 = 0$
8. $4x^2 + 10x + 3 = 0$
9. $x^2 - x - 3 = 0$
10. $x^2 - 2x - 8 = 0$
11. $-x^2 + 7x + 3 = 0$
12. $x^2 + 3x - 9 = 0$
13. $-\frac{5}{2}x^2 + 10x - 5 = 0$
14. $\frac{1}{2}x^2 + 3x - 9 = 0$
15. $3x^2 - 2 = 0$
16. $-2x^2 - 7x = 0$
17. $3x^2 + x = 6$
18. $x^2 - 4x = -2$
19. Show that $\frac{-b + \sqrt{b^2 - 4ac}}{2a}$ and $\frac{-b - \sqrt{b^2 - 4ac}}{2a}$ are solutions of $ax^2 + bx + c = 0$ by substituting.
20. Derive a formula to find solutions of equations that have the form $ax^2 + x + c = 0$. Use your formula to find solutions of $-2x^2 + x + 8 = 0$.
21. Find the sum and product of $\frac{-b + \sqrt{b^2 - 4ac}}{2a}$ and $\frac{-b - \sqrt{b^2 - 4ac}}{2a}$. Write a quadratic expression whose solutions have a sum of 2 and a product of $\frac{1}{2}$.
22. What values can a have in the equation $ax^2 + 12x + 3 = 0$ in order for the equation to have one or two real solutions? *Explain.*

9.7 Solve Systems with Quadratic Equations

Before	You solved systems of linear equations.
Now	You will solve systems that include a quadratic equation.
Why?	So you can predict the path of a ball, as in Example 4.

You have solved systems of linear equations using the graph-and-check method and using the substitution method. You can use both of these techniques to solve a system of equations involving nonlinear equations, such as quadratic equations.

Recall that the substitution method consists of the following three steps.

STEP 1 **Solve** one of the equations for one of its variables.

STEP 2 **Substitute** the expression from Step 1 into the other equation and solve for the other variable.

STEP 3 **Substitute** the value from Step 2 into one of the original equations and solve.

COMMON CORE

CC.9-12.A.REI.11 Explain why the x-coordinates of the points where the graphs of the equations $y = f(x)$ and $y = g(x)$ intersect are the solutions of the equation $f(x) = g(x)$; find the solutions approximately, e.g., using technology to graph the functions, make tables of values, or find successive approximations. Include cases where $f(x)$ and/or $g(x)$ are linear, polynomial, rational, absolute value, exponential, and logarithmic functions.*

EXAMPLE 1 Use the substitution method

Solve the system: $y = 3x + 2$ **Equation 1**

$y = 3x^2 + 6x + 2$ **Equation 2**

Solution

STEP 1 **Solve** one of the equations for y. Equation 1 is already solved for y.

STEP 2 **Substitute** $3x + 2$ for y in Equation 2 and solve for x.

$y = 3x^2 + 6x + 2$ **Write original Equation 2.**

$3x + 2 = 3x^2 + 6x + 2$ **Substitute $3x^2 + 2$ for y.**

$0 = 3x^2 + 3x$ **Subtract $3x$ and 2 from each side.**

$0 = 3x(x + 1)$ **Factor.**

$3x = 0$ or $x + 1 = 0$ **Zero-product property**

$x = 0$ or $x = -1$ **Solve for x.**

AVOID ERRORS
Be sure to set all linear factors equal to zero when applying the zero-product property.

STEP 3 **Substitute** both 0 and −1 for x in Equation 1 and solve for y.

$y = 3x + 2$ $\quad y = 3x + 2$

$y = 3(\mathbf{0}) + 2$ $\quad y = 3(\mathbf{-1}) + 2$

$y = 2$ $\quad y = -1$

▶ The solutions are (0, 2) and (−1, −1).

POINTS OF INTERSECTION When you graph a system of equations, the graphs intersect at each solution of the system. For a system consisting of a linear equation and a quadratic equation the number of intersections, and therefore solutions, can be zero, one, or two.

KEY CONCEPT — *For Your Notebook*

Systems With One Linear Equation and One Quadratic Equation

There are three possibilities for the number of points of intersection.

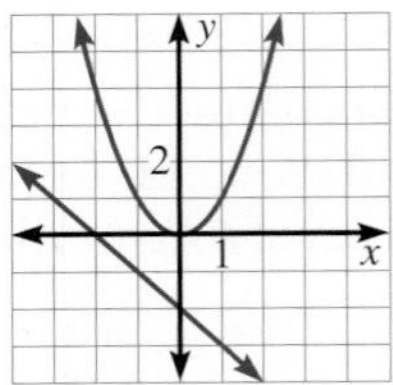

No Solution

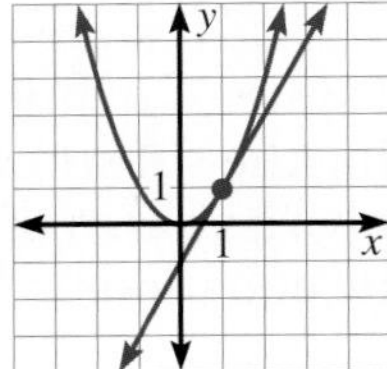

One Solution

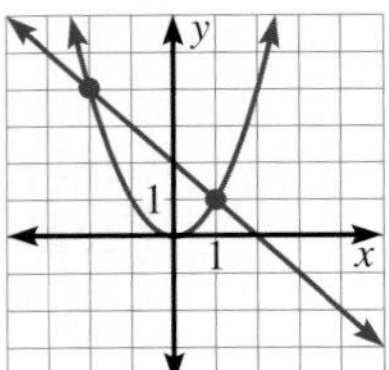

Two Solutions

EXAMPLE 2 Use a graphing calculator to solve a system

Solve the system: $y = 2x - 4$ **Equation 1**

$y = x^2 - 4x + 1$ **Equation 2**

Solution

STEP 1 Enter each equation into your graphing calculator.

Set $Y_1 = 2x - 4$ and $Y_2 = x^2 - 4x + 1$.

STEP 2 Graph the system. Set a good viewing window. For this system, a good window is $-10 \le x \le 10$ and $-10 \le y \le 10$.

STEP 3 Use the *Trace* function to find the coordinates of each point of intersection. The points of intersection are (1, −2) and (5, 6).

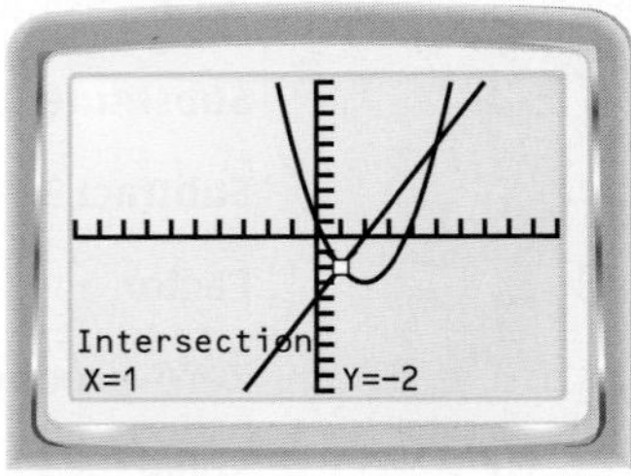

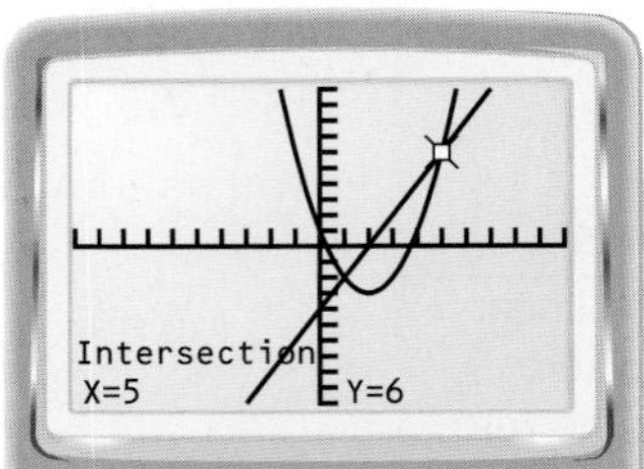

▶ The solutions are (1, −2) and (5, 6).

CHECK Check the solutions. For example, check (1, −2).

$y = 2x - 4$ $\qquad$ $y = x^2 - 4x + 1$

$-2 \stackrel{?}{=} 2(1) - 4$ $\qquad$ $-2 \stackrel{?}{=} (1)^2 - 4(1) + 1$

$-2 = -2$ ✓ $\qquad$ $-2 = -2$ ✓

GUIDED PRACTICE for Examples 1 and 2

Solve the system of equations first by using the substitution method and then by using a graphing calculator.

1. $y = x + 4$
$y = 2x^2 - 3x - 2$

2. $y = x + 1$
$y = -x^2 + 6x + 1$

3. $y = x^2 - 6x + 11$
$y = x + 1$

SOLVING EQUATIONS You can use a graph to solve an equation in one variable. Treat each side of the equation as a function. Then graph each function on the same coordinate plane. The x-value of any points of intersection will be the solutions of the equation

EXAMPLE 3 Solve an equation using a system

Solve the equation $-x^2 - 4x + 2 = -2x - 1$ using a system of equations. Check your solution(s).

Solution

STEP 1 Write a system of two equations by setting both the left and right sides of the given equation each equal to y.

$-x^2 - 4x + 2 = -2x - 1$

$y = -x^2 - 4x + 2$ **Equation 1**

$y = -2x - 1$ **Equation 2**

AVOID ERRORS

If you draw your graph on graph paper, be very neat so that you can accurately identify any points of intersection.

STEP 2 Graph Equation 1 and Equation 2 on the same coordinate plane or on a graphing calculator.

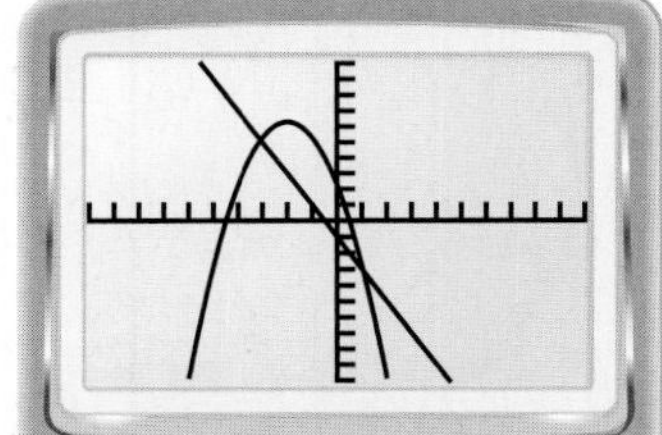

STEP 3 The x-value of each point of intersection is a solution of the original equation. The graphs intersect at $(-3, 5)$ and $(1, -3)$.

▶ The solutions of the equation are $x = -3$ and $x = 1$.

CHECK: Substitute each solution in the original equation.

$$-x^2 - 4x + 2 = -2x - 1$$
$$-(-3)^2 - 4(-3) + 2 \stackrel{?}{=} -2(-3) - 1$$
$$-9 + 12 + 2 \stackrel{?}{=} 6 - 1$$
$$5 = 5 \checkmark$$

$$-x^2 - 4x + 2 = -2x - 1$$
$$-(1)^2 - 4(1) + 2 \stackrel{?}{=} -2(1) - 1$$
$$-1 - 4 + 2 \stackrel{?}{=} -2 - 1$$
$$-3 = -3 \checkmark$$

GUIDED PRACTICE for Example 3

Solve the equation using a system of equations.

4. $x + 3 = 2x^2 + 3x - 1$

5. $x^2 + 7x + 4 = 2x + 4$

6. $8 = x^2 - 4x + 3$

7. $-x + 4 = 3^x$

EXAMPLE 4 Solve a multi-step problem

BASEBALL During practice, you hit a baseball toward the gym, which is 240 feet away.

The path of the baseball after it is hit can be modeled by the equation:

$$y = -0.004x^2 + x + 3$$

The roof of the gym can be modeled by the equation:

$$y = \frac{2}{3}x - 120$$

for values of x greater than 240 feet and less than 320 feet.

The wall of the gym can be modeled by the equation:

$$x = 240$$

for values of y between 0 feet and 40 feet.

Does the baseball hit the roof of gym?

Solution

STEP 1 Write a system of two equations for the baseball and the roof.

$y = -0.004x^2 + x + 3$ **Equation 1 (baseball)**

$y = \frac{2}{3}x - 120$ **Equation 2 (roof)**

STEP 2 Graph both equations on the same coordinate plane.

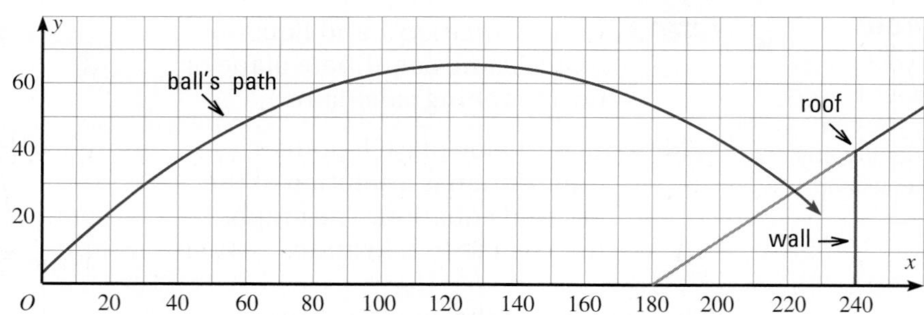

STEP 3 The x-value where the graphs intersect is between 200 feet and 230 feet which is outside the domain of the equation for the roof.

▶ The baseball does not hit the roof.

GUIDED PRACTICE for Example 4

8. **WHAT IF?** In Example 4, does the baseball hit the gym wall? If it does, how far up the wall does it hit? If it does not, how far away from the gym wall does the ball land?

9. **WHAT IF?** In Example 4, if you hit the ball so that it followed a path that had a smaller number as the coefficient of x^2, would it be *more* or *less* likely to hit the gym? *Explain.*

9.7 EXERCISES

HOMEWORK KEY
○ = See WORKED-OUT SOLUTIONS Exs. 5, 15, 19, and 23
★ = STANDARDIZED TEST PRACTICE Exs. 2, 11, 28, and 35

SKILL PRACTICE

1. **VOCABULARY** Describe how to use the substitution method to solve a system of linear equations.

2. ★ **WRITING** Describe the possible number of solutions for a system consisting of a linear equation and a quadratic equation.

EXAMPLE 1 for Exs. 3–8

SUBSTITUTION METHOD Solve the system of equations using the substitution method.

3. $y = x^2 - x + 2$
   $y = x + 5$

4. $y = -x^2 + 4x - 2$
   $y = 4x - 6$

5. $y = x^2 - x$
   $y = -\frac{5}{2}x + 1$

6. $y = 2x^2 + x - 1$
   $y = -x - 3$

7. $y = 3x^2 - 6$
   $y = -3x$

8. $y = -2x^2 - 2x + 3$
   $y = \frac{7}{2}$

9. **ERROR ANALYSIS** Describe and correct the error in the solution steps shown.

$y = 3x^2 - 6x + 4$	Equation 1
$y = 4$	Equation 2
$y = 3(4)^2 - 6(4) + 4$	Substitute.
$y = 3(16) - 24 + 4 = 28$	Simplify

10. **COPY AND COMPLETE** When a system of equations includes a linear equation and a quadratic equation, there will (*always, sometimes, never*) be an infinite number of solutions.

11. ★ **MULTIPLE CHOICE** Which equation intersects the graph of $y = x^2 - 4x + 3$ twice?

Ⓐ $y = -1$ Ⓑ $x = 2$
Ⓒ $y + 1 = x$ Ⓓ $y + x = -1$

EXAMPLE 2 for Exs. 12–17

GRAPHING CALCULATOR Use a graphing calculator to find the points of intersection, if any, of the graph of the system of equations.

12. $y = 3x^2 - 2x + 1$
    $y = x + 7$

13. $y = x^2 + 2x + 11$
    $y = -2x + 8$

14. $y = -2x^2 - 4x$
    $y = 2$

15. $y = \frac{1}{2}x^2 - 3x + 4$
    $y = x - 2$

16. $y = \frac{1}{3}x^2 + 2x - 3$
    $y = 2x$

17. $y = 4x^2 + 5x - 7$
    $y = -3x + 5$

EXAMPLE 3 for Exs. 18–21

SOLVE THE EQUATION Solve the equation using a system. Check each answer.

18. $-5x + 5 = x^2 - 4x + 3$

19. $-6 = x^2 + 2x - 5$

20. $-3 = x^2 + 5x - 3$

21. $2x^2 + 4x = 2x + 4$

GRAPHING CALCULATOR **Use a graphing calculator to find the points of intersection, if any, of the graph of the system of equations.**

22. $y = -x^2 + 4$
$y = 5$

23. $y = -1$
$y = -2^x$

24. $y = x + 6$
$y = 0.5^x$

25. $y = -x^2 + 2x$
$y = -2x + 5$

26. $y = 3x - 1$
$y = 2^x$

27. $y = -1.5x + 1$
$y = 0.4^x$

28. ★ **WRITING** Describe the possible number of solutions for a system consisting of a quadratic equation and an exponential equation.

SOLVE THE EQUATION **Solve the equation using a system.**

29. $2^x + 1 = 2x + 1$

30. $4^x = -\frac{2}{3}x + 9$

31. $-2x + 11 = 2^x - 3$

32. $3^x - 5 = 6x - 8$

33. **CHALLENGE** Using a graphing calculator, find the points of intersection, if any, of the graphs of the equations $y = x^2 - 3x + 1$ and $y = x^2 - x - 1$. What are the solutions of the system?

PROBLEM SOLVING

EXAMPLES 1 AND 2
for Exs. 34–36

34. **RECREATION** Marion and Reggie are driving boats on the same lake. Marion's chosen path can be modeled by the equation $y = -x^2 - 4x - 1$ and Reggie's path can be modeled by the equation $y = 2x + 8$. Do their paths cross each other? If so, what are the coordinates of the point(s) where the paths meet?

35. ★ **SHORT RESPONSE** Two dogs are running in a fenced dog park. One dog is following a path that can be modeled by the equation $y = 4$. Another dog is following a path that can be modeled by the equation $y = -x^2 + 3$. Will the dogs' paths cross? Explain your answer.

36. **ARCHITECTURE** The arch of the Sydney Harbor Bridge in Sydney, Australia, can be modeled by $y = -0.00211x^2 + 1.06x$ where x is the distance (in meters) from the left pylons and y is the height (in meters) of the arch above the water. The road can be modeled by the equation $y = 52$. To the nearest meter, how far from the left pylons are the two points where the road intersects the arch of the bridge?

○ = See **WORKED-OUT SOLUTIONS** in Student Resources

★ = **STANDARDIZED TEST PRACTICE**

EXAMPLES 3 AND 4 for Exs. 37–39

37. **SAVINGS** Nancy and Miranda are looking at different ways to save money. Graph the two equations. Explain what happens when the graphs intersect. When will Miranda have more money saved than Nancy?

Nancy

I will save \$15 each month.
My money will not earn interest.

A model for my savings is $y = 15x$.

x is the number of months
y is my total savings

Miranda

I will put \$200 into an account that earns 2% annually. I will not save any more money.

If the interest is compounded monthly, $y = 200(1.02)^x$ models my savings.

x is months and y is my total savings.

38. **SPACE** Suppose an asteroid and a piece of space debris are traveling in the same plane in space. The asteroid follows a path that can be modeled locally by the equation $y = 2x^2 - 3x + 1$. The space debris follows a path that can be modeled locally by the equation $y = 8x - 13$.

a. Will the paths of the two objects intersect? Is it possible for the two objects to collide? If so, what are the coordinates of the point where the paths intersect?

b. What additional information would you need to decide whether the two objects will collide? *Explain.*

39. **MULTI-STEP PROBLEM** Keno asks Miguel if the graphs of all three of the equations shown below ever intersect in a single point.

$$y = 3x + 1 \qquad y = 2x^2 - 4x + 6 \qquad y = -2x + 6$$

a. Find any points of intersection of the graphs of $y = 3x + 1$ and $y = 2x^2 - 4x + 6$.

b. Find any points of intersection of the graphs of $y = 3x + 1$ and $y = -2x + 6$.

c. Find any points of intersection of the graphs $y = 2x^2 - 4x + 6$ and $y = -2x + 6$.

d. Do the three graphs ever intersect in a single point? If so, what are the coordinates of this point of intersection?

40. **CHALLENGE** Find the point(s) of intersection, if any, for the line with equation $y = -x - 1$ and the circle with equation $x^2 + y^2 = 41$.

9.8 Compare Linear, Exponential, and Quadratic Models

Before You graphed linear, exponential, and quadratic functions.

Now You will compare linear, exponential, and quadratic models.

Why? So you can solve a problem about biology, as in Ex. 23.

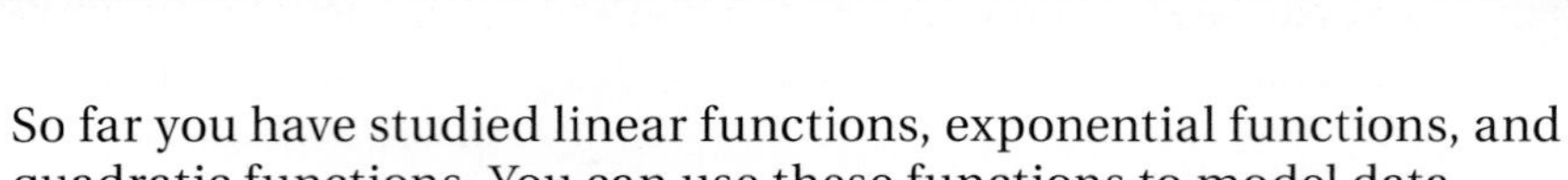

Key Vocabulary
- **linear function**
- **exponential function**
- **quadratic function**

CC.9-12.A.CED.2 Create equations in two or more variables to represent relationships between quantities; graph equations on coordinate axes with labels and scales.*

So far you have studied linear functions, exponential functions, and quadratic functions. You can use these functions to model data.

KEY CONCEPT *For Your Notebook*

Linear, Exponential, and Quadratic Functions

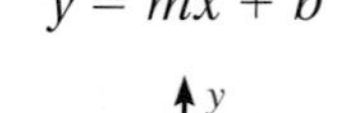

Linear Function	**Exponential Function**	**Quadratic Function**
$y = mx + b$	$y = ab^x$	$y = ax^2 + bx + c$

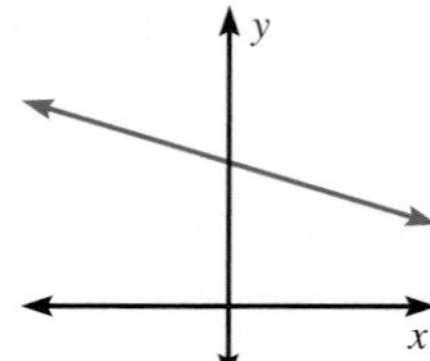

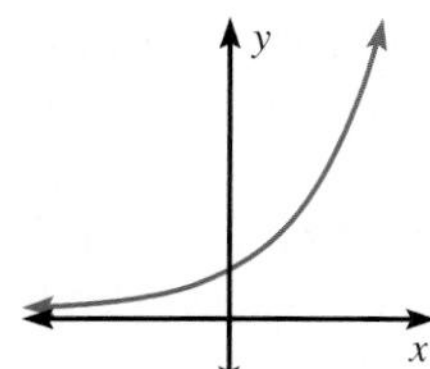

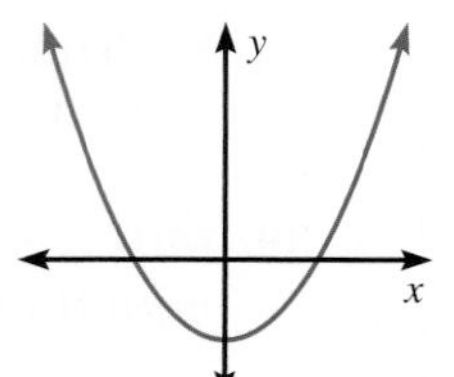

EXAMPLE 1 Choose functions using sets of ordered pairs

Use a graph to tell whether the ordered pairs represent a *linear function*, an *exponential function*, or a *quadratic function*.

a. $\left(-4, \frac{1}{32}\right), \left(-2, \frac{1}{8}\right), \left(0, \frac{1}{2}\right), (2, 2), (4, 8)$

b. $(-4, 1), (-2, 2), (0, 3), (2, 4), (4, 5)$

c. $(-4, 5), (-2, 2), (0, 1), (2, 2), (4, 5)$

Solution

a.

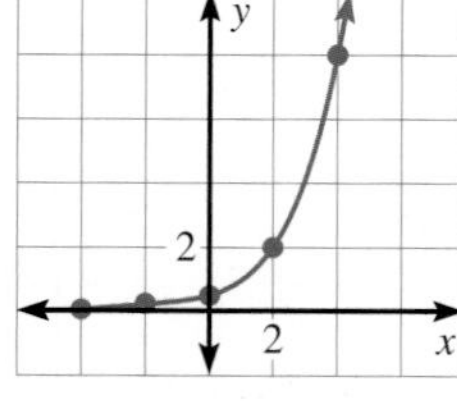

Exponential function

b.

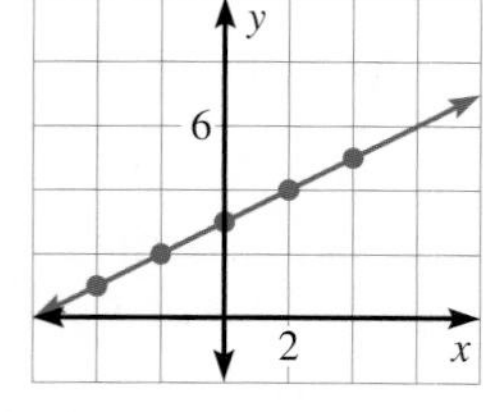

Linear function

c.

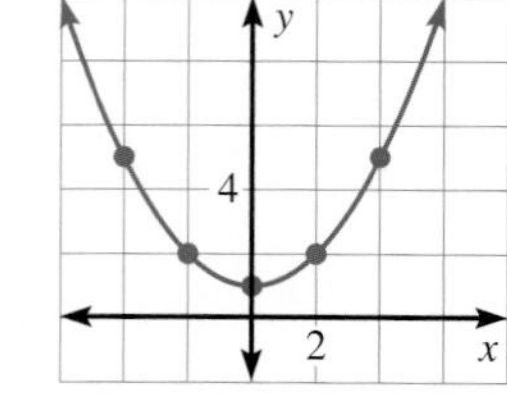

Quadratic function

Animated Algebra at my.hrw.com

DIFFERENCES AND RATIOS A table of values represents a linear function if the *differences* of successive y-values are all equal. A table of values represents an exponential function if the *ratios* of successive y-values are all equal. In both cases, the increments between successive x-values need to be equal.

Linear function: $y = 3x + 5$

x	−1	0	1	2
y	2	5	8	11

Differences: $5 - 2 = 3$ 3 3

Exponential function: $y = 0.5(2)^x$

x	−1	0	1	2
y	0.25	0.5	1	2

Ratios: $\frac{0.5}{0.25} = 2$ 2 2

ANALYZE FIRST DIFFERENCES
The first differences of a linear function are constant, which is not the case for quadratic functions or exponential functions. For instance, the first differences for the y-values shown for $y = 0.5(2)^x$ are $0.5 - 0.25 = 0.25$, $1 - 0.5 = 0.5$, and $2 - 1 = 1$.

You can use differences to tell whether a table of values represents a quadratic function, as shown.

Quadratic function: $y = x^2 - 2x + 2$

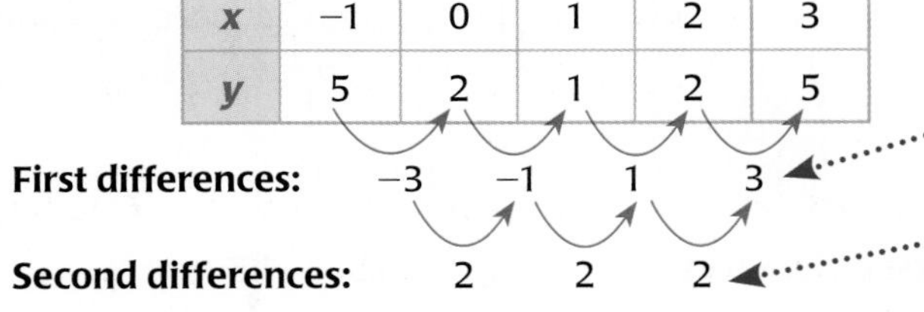

x	−1	0	1	2	3
y	5	2	1	2	5

First differences: −3 −1 1 3

Second differences: 2 2 2

First find the differences of successive y-values, or *first differences*.

Then find the differences of successive first differences, or *second differences*.

The table of values represents a quadratic function if the second differences are all equal.

EXAMPLE 2 Identify functions using differences or ratios

Use differences or ratios to tell whether the table of values represents a *linear function*, an *exponential function*, or a *quadratic function*. Extend the table to find the y-value for the next x-value.

a.

x	−2	−1	0	1	2
y	−6	−6	−4	0	6

First differences: 0 2 4 6

Second differences: 2 2 2

▶ The table of values represents a quadratic function. When $x = 3$, $y = 6 + 8 = 14$.

b.

x	−2	−1	0	1	2
y	−2	1	4	7	10

Differences: 3 3 3 3

▶ The table of values represents a linear function. When $x = 3$, $y = 10 + 3 = 13$.

✓ GUIDED PRACTICE for Examples 1 and 2

1. Tell whether the ordered pairs represent a *linear function*, an *exponential function*, or a *quadratic function*: (0, −1.5), (1, −0.5), (2, 2.5), (3, 7.5).

2. Tell whether the table of values represents a *linear function*, an *exponential function*, or a *quadratic function*.

x	−2	−1	0	1
y	0.08	0.4	2	10

WRITING AN EQUATION When you decide that a set of ordered pairs represents a linear, an exponential, or a quadratic function, you can write an equation for the function. In this lesson, when you write an equation for a quadratic function, the equation will have the form $y = ax^2$.

EXAMPLE 3 Write an equation for a function

Tell whether the table of values represents a *linear function*, an *exponential function*, or a *quadratic function*. Then write an equation for the function.

x	−2	−1	0	1	2
y	2	0.5	0	0.5	2

Solution

STEP 1 **Determine** which type of function the table of values represents.

x	−2	−1	0	1	2
y	2	0.5	0	0.5	2

First differences: −1.5 −0.5 0.5 1.5

Second differences: 1 1 1

The table of values represents a quadratic function because the second differences are equal.

STEP 2 **Write** an equation for the quadratic function. The equation has the form $y = ax^2$. Find the value of a by using the coordinates of a point that lies on the graph, such as (1, 0.5).

$y = ax^2$ **Write equation for quadratic function.**

$0.5 = a(1)^2$ **Substitute 1 for *x* and 0.5 for *y*.**

$0.5 = a$ **Solve for *a*.**

AVOID ERRORS
In Example 3, do not use (0, 0) to find the value of a, even though (0, 0) lies on the graph of $y = ax^2$. If you do, you will obtain an undefined value for a.

▸ The equation is $y = 0.5x^2$.

CHECK Plot the ordered pairs from the table. Then graph $y = 0.5x^2$ to see that the graph passes through the plotted points.

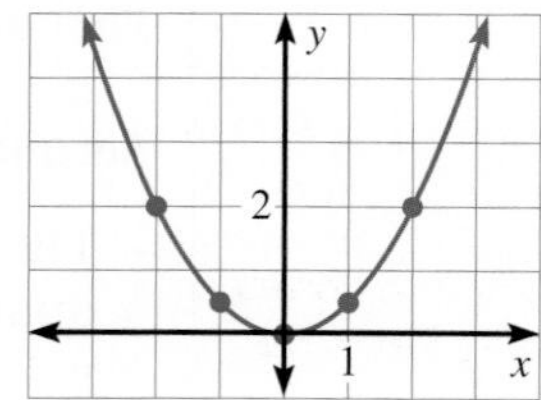

✓ GUIDED PRACTICE for Example 3

Tell whether the table of values represents a *linear function*, an *exponential function*, or a *quadratic function*. Then write an equation for the function.

3.

x	−3	−2	−1	0	1
y	−7	−5	−3	−1	1

4.

x	−2	−1	0	1	2
y	8	2	0	2	8

EXAMPLE 4 Solve a multi-step problem

CYCLING The table shows the breathing rates y (in liters of air per minute) of a cyclist traveling at different speeds x (in miles per hour). Tell whether the data can be modeled by a *linear function*, an *exponential function*, or a *quadratic function*. Then write an equation for the function.

Speed of cyclist, x (mi/h)	20	21	22	23	24	25
Breathing rate, y (L/min)	51.4	57.1	63.3	70.3	78.0	86.6

Solution

STEP 1 **Graph** the data. The graph has a slight curve. So, a linear function does not appear to model the data.

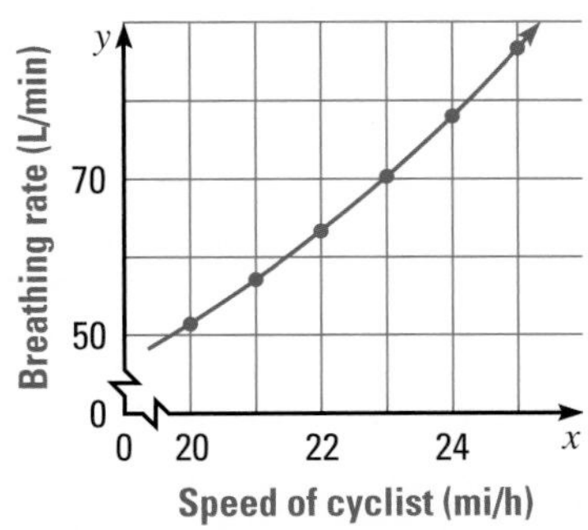

STEP 2 **Decide** which function models the data.

In the table below, notice that $\frac{57.1}{51.4} \approx 1.11$, $\frac{63.3}{57.1} \approx 1.11$, $\frac{70.3}{63.3} \approx 1.11$, $\frac{78.0}{70.3} \approx 1.11$, and $\frac{86.6}{78.0} \approx 1.11$. So, the ratios are all approximately equal. An exponential function models the data.

Speed of cyclist, x (mi/h)	20	21	22	23	24	25
Breathing rate, y (L/min)	51.4	57.1	63.3	70.3	78.0	86.6

Ratios: 1.11 1.11 1.11 1.11 1.11

STEP 3 **Write** an equation for the exponential function. The breathing rate increases by a factor of 1.11 liters per minute, so $b = 1.11$. Find the value of a by using one of the data pairs, such as (20, 51.4).

REVIEW EXPONENTIAL FUNCTIONS
You may want to review writing an equation for an exponential function.

$y = ab^x$ **Write equation for exponential function.**

$51.4 = a(1.11)^{20}$ **Substitute 1.11 for *b*, 20 for *x*, and 51.4 for *y*.**

$\frac{51.4}{(1.11)^{20}} = a$ **Solve for *a*.**

$6.38 \approx a$ **Use a calculator.**

▶ The equation is $y = 6.38(1.11)^x$.

GUIDED PRACTICE for Example 4

5. In Example 4, suppose the cyclist is traveling at 15 miles per hour. Find the breathing rate of the cyclist at this speed.

9.8 EXERCISES

HOMEWORK KEY

○ = See **WORKED-OUT SOLUTIONS** Exs. 7, 13, and 25

★ = **STANDARDIZED TEST PRACTICE** Exs. 2, 18, 26, and 27

◆ = **MULTIPLE REPRESENTATIONS** Ex. 25

SKILL PRACTICE

1. **VOCABULARY** Copy and complete: A function that is of the form $y = ab^x$ is a(n) __?__.

2. ★ **WRITING** *Describe* how you can tell whether a table of values represents a quadratic function.

EXAMPLE 1 for Exs. 3–11

MATCHING **Match the function with the graph that the function represents.**

3. Linear function
4. Exponential function
5. Quadratic function

A.

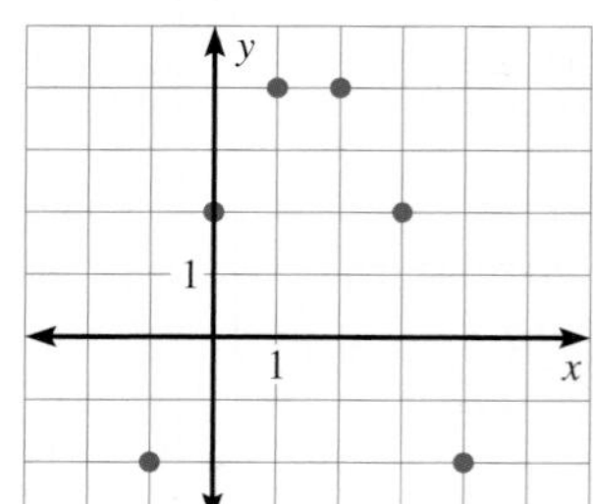

B.

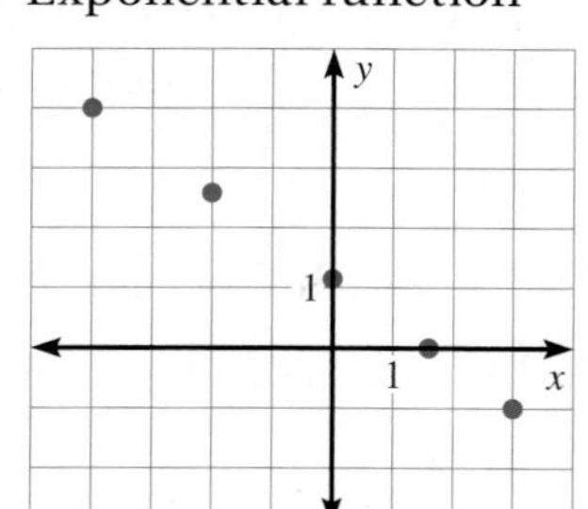

C.

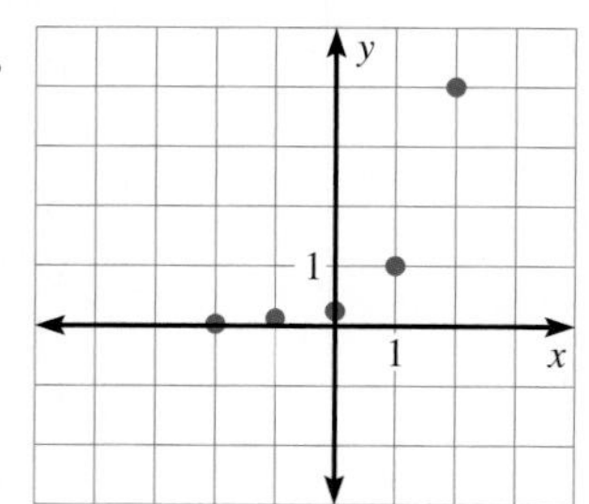

USING A GRAPH **Use a graph to tell whether the ordered pairs represent a *linear function*, an *exponential function*, or a *quadratic function*.**

6. $(-4, -7), (-2, -1), (0, 1), (2, -1), (4, -7)$
7. $(-5, -1), (-3, 0), (-1, 1), (1, 2), (3, 3)$
8. $\left(-1, \frac{1}{16}\right), \left(0, \frac{1}{4}\right), (1, 1), (2, 4), (3, 16)$
9. $(-1, 8), (1, 2), \left(3, \frac{1}{2}\right), \left(5, \frac{1}{8}\right), \left(7, \frac{1}{32}\right)$
10. $(-4, -4), (-2, -3.5), (0, -3), (2, -2.5)$
11. $(-1, 0.5), (0, -0.5), (1, 0.5), (2, 3.5)$

EXAMPLES 2 and 3 for Exs. 12–19

USING DIFFERENCES AND RATIOS **Tell whether the table of values represents a *linear function*, an *exponential function*, or a *quadratic function*. Then write an equation for the function.**

12.

x	0	1	2	3	4
y	1	0	−1	−2	−3

13.

x	−2	−1	0	1	2
y	−4	−1	0	−1	−4

14.

x	−3	−2	−1	0	1
y	13.5	6	1.5	0	1.5

15.

x	−2	−1	0	1	2
y	−5	−2	1	4	7

16.

x	−2	−1	0	1	2
y	$\frac{1}{9}$	$\frac{1}{3}$	1	3	9

17.

x	−1	0	1	2	3
y	16	4	1	$\frac{1}{4}$	$\frac{1}{16}$

18. ★ **MULTIPLE CHOICE** Which function is represented by the following ordered pairs: $(-1, 4), (0, 0), (1, 4), (2, 16), (3, 36)$?

Ⓐ $y = 0.25x^2$ Ⓑ $y = 4^x$ Ⓒ $y = 4x^2$ Ⓓ $y = 4x$

19. **ERROR ANALYSIS** *Describe* and correct the error in writing an equation for the function represented by the ordered pairs.

(0, 0), (1, 2.5), (2, 10), (3, 22.5), (4, 40)

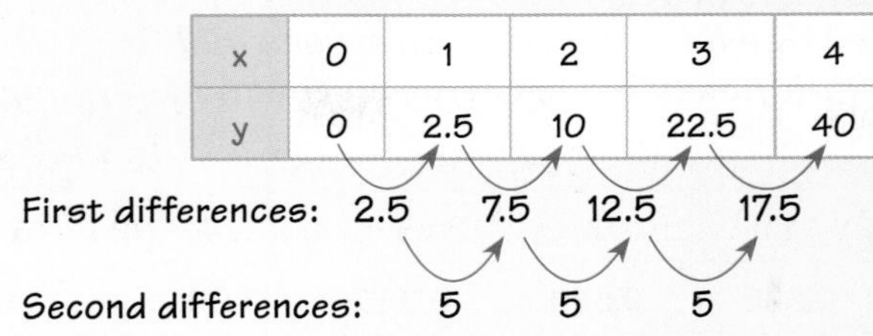

x	0	1	2	3	4
y	0	2.5	10	22.5	40

First differences: 2.5 7.5 12.5 17.5

Second differences: 5 5 5

The ordered pairs represent a quadratic function.

$y = ax^2$

$2 = a(10)^2$

$0.02 = a$

So, the equation is $y = 0.02x^2$.

20. **REASONING** Use the graph shown.

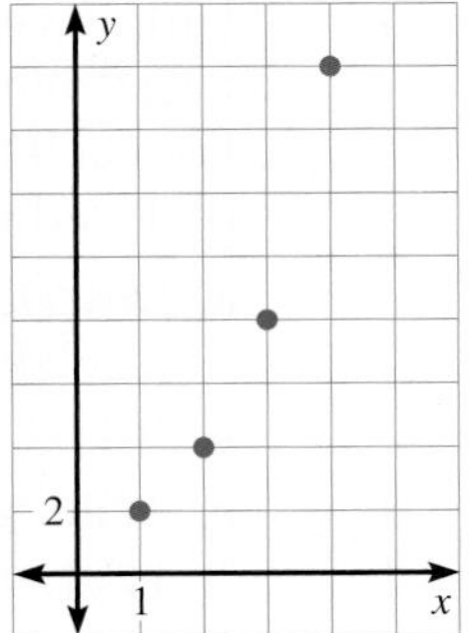

a. Tell whether the graph represents an *exponential function* or a *quadratic function* by looking at the graph.

b. Make a table of values for the points on the graph. Then use differences or ratios to check your answer in part (a).

c. Write an equation for the function that the table of values from part (b) represents.

21. **GEOMETRY** The table shows the area A (in square centimeters) of an equilateral triangle for various side lengths s (in centimeters). Write an equation for the function that the table of values represents. Then find the area of an equilateral triangle that has a side length of 10 centimeters.

Side length, *s* (cm)	1	2	3	4	5
Area, *A* (cm²)	$0.25\sqrt{3}$	$\sqrt{3}$	$2.25\sqrt{3}$	$4\sqrt{3}$	$6.25\sqrt{3}$

22. **CHALLENGE** In the ordered pairs below, the y-values are given in terms of m. Tell whether the ordered pairs represent a *linear function*, an *exponential function*, or a *quadratic function*.

$(1, 3m - 1), (2, 10m + 2), (3, 26m), (4, 51m - 7), (5, 85m - 19)$

PROBLEM SOLVING

EXAMPLE 4 for Exs. 23–25

23. **LIZARDS** The table shows the body temperature B (in degrees Celsius) of a desert spiny lizard at various air temperatures A (in degrees Celsius). Tell whether the data can be modeled by a *linear function*, an *exponential function*, or a *quadratic function*. Then write an equation for the function.

Air temperature, *A* (°C)	26	27	28	29	30
Body temperature, *B* (°C)	33.44	33.78	34.12	34.46	34.80

24. **NAUTILUS** A chambered nautilus is a marine animal that lives in the outermost chamber of its shell. When the nautilus outgrows a chamber, it adds a new, larger chamber to its shell. The table shows the volumes (in cubic centimeters) of consecutive chambers of a nautilus. Tell whether the data can be modeled by a *linear function*, an *exponential function*, or a *quadratic function*. Then write an equation for the function.

Chamber	1	2	3	4	5	6
Volume (cm^3)	0.836	0.889	0.945	1.005	1.068	1.135

(25) **MULTIPLE REPRESENTATIONS** In 1970, the populations of Troy and Union were each 3000. From 1970 to 2010, the population of Troy doubled every decade. The population of Union increased by 3000 every decade. For each town, consider the set of data pairs (n, P) where n is the number of decades since 1970 and P is the population.

a. **Describing in Words** Tell whether the data for each town can be modeled by a *linear function*, an *exponential function*, or a *quadratic function*. *Explain* your reasoning.

b. **Making a Table** Make a table for each town. Use the tables to justify your answers in part (a).

c. **Writing a Model** For each town, do the following: Write an equation for the function that models the data. Suppose that the growth pattern continues. *Predict* the population in 2030.

26. ★ **MULTIPLE CHOICE** The table shows the cost of a custom circular rug for various diameters (in feet). What is the approximate cost of a custom circular rug that has a diameter of 8 feet?

Diameter (ft)	2	3	4	5	6
Cost (dollars)	28.40	63.90	113.60	177.50	255.60

(A) \$333.70 (B) \$411.80 (C) \$454.40 (D) \$908.80

27. ★ **EXTENDED RESPONSE** The time it takes for a clock's pendulum to swing from one side to the other and back again, as shown in the back view of the clock, is called the pendulum's period. The table shows the period t (in seconds) of a pendulum of length ℓ (in feet).

Period, t (sec)	1	2	3	4	5
Length, ℓ (ft)	0.82	3.28	7.38	13.12	20.5

a. **Model** Tell whether the data can be modeled by a *linear function*, an *exponential function*, or a *quadratic function*. Then write an equation for the function.

b. **Apply** Find the length of a pendulum that has a period of 0.5 second.

c. **Analyze** How does decreasing the length of the pendulum by 50% change the period? *Justify* your answer using several examples.

○ = See **WORKED-OUT SOLUTIONS** in Student Resources ★ = **STANDARDIZED TEST PRACTICE** ◆ = **MULTIPLE REPRESENTATIONS**

28. CHALLENGE The table shows the height h (in feet) that a pole vaulter's center of gravity reaches for various running speeds s (in feet per second) at the moment the pole vaulter launches himself into the air.

Running speed, s (ft/sec)	30	31	32	33	34
Height of center of gravity, h (ft)	$14\frac{1}{16}$	$15\frac{1}{64}$	16	$17\frac{1}{64}$	$18\frac{1}{16}$

a. A pole vaulter is running at $31\frac{1}{2}$ feet per second when he launches himself into the air. Find the height that the pole vaulter's center of gravity reaches.

b. Find the speed at which the pole vaulter needs to be running when he launches himself into the air in order for his center of gravity to reach a height of 19 feet. Round your answer to the nearest foot per second.

Perform Regressions

Use appropriate tools strategically.

QUESTION How can you use a graphing calculator to find models for data?

You have used a graphing calculator to perform linear regression on data to find a linear model for the data. A graphing calculator can also be used to perform exponential regression and quadratic regression.

EXAMPLE 1 Use exponential regression to find a model

The table shows the sales (in millions of dollars) of organic milk, organic half and half, and organic cream in the U.S. each year for the period 1996–2000. Find an exponential model for the data.

Year	1996	1997	1998	1999	2000
Sales (millions of dollars)	15.8	30.7	46	75.7	104

STEP 1 ***Enter data***

Enter the data into two lists. Let $x = 0$ represent 1996.

```
L1 | L2   | L3
0  | 15.8 |
1  | 30.7 |
2  | 46   |
3  | 75.7 |
4  | 104  |
L2(4)=104
```

STEP 2 ***Make scatter plot***

Make a scatter plot of the data. Notice that the points show an exponential trend.

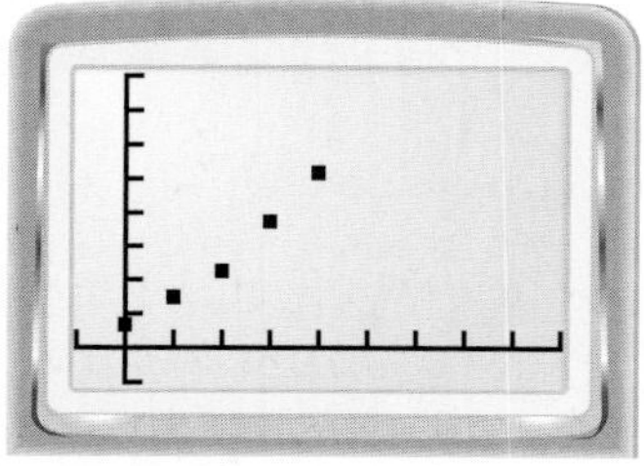

STEP 3 ***Perform regression***

Use the exponential regression feature to obtain the model $y = 17.5(1.6)^x$.

STEP 4 ***Check model***

Check how well the model fits the data by graphing the model and the data.

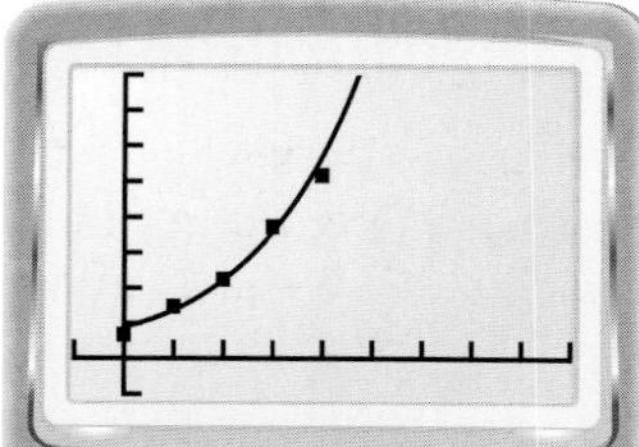

PRACTICE

1. The table shows the value of a car over time. Find an exponential model for the data. Use the model to estimate the value of the car after 7 years.

Age of car (years)	0	1	2	3	4	5
Value (dollars)	15,600	13,510	11,700	10,132	8774	7598

my.hrw.com
Keystrokes

EXAMPLE 2 Use quadratic regression to find a model

The table shows the number of subscribers to the first U.S. digital satellite radio service for various months after its launch. Find a quadratic model for the data.

Months after launch	0	3	6	9	12	15
Subscribers	500	31,000	76,000	135,500	201,500	360,000

STEP 1 *Make scatter plot*
Enter the data into two lists and make a scatter plot. Notice the quadratic trend in the data.

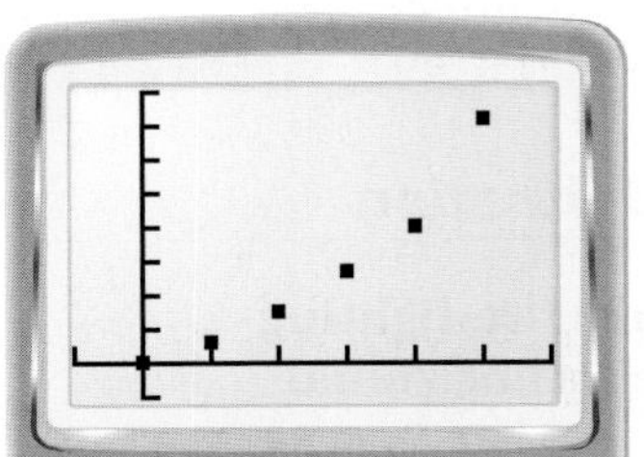

STEP 2 *Perform regression*
Use the quadratic regression feature to obtain the model $y = 1440x^2 + 1010x + 8000$.

STEP 3 *Check model*
Check how well the model fits the data by graphing the model and the data.

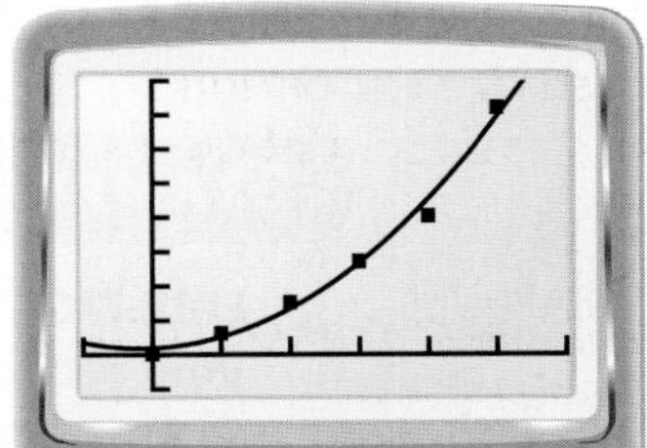

PRACTICE

2. The table shows the maximum weight that can be supported by a 16 foot floor beam of different depths. Find a quadratic model for the data.

Depth (inches)	6	7.5	9	10.5	12	13.5
Weight (pounds)	68	137	242	389	586	838

DRAW CONCLUSIONS

3. The table shows the temperature (in degrees Fahrenheit) of a cup of hot chocolate over time. Find an exponential model and a quadratic model for the data. Make a scatter plot of the data and graph both models. Which model fits the data better? *Explain.*

Time (minutes)	0	10	20	30	40	50	60
Temperature (°F)	200	157	128	109	99	92	90

4. **DATA COLLECTION** For this exercise, you will need a collection of pennies. Use a compass to draw 7 or 8 circles with diameters d ranging in size from 8 centimeters to 20 centimeters. Count the number n of pennies you need to (**a**) surround each circle completely and (**b**) cover each circle completely. For each set of ordered pairs (d, n), find a linear model, an exponential model, and a quadratic model, and tell which model fits the data best.

9.9 Model Relationships

Before You studied linear, exponential, and quadratic functions.
Now You will compare representations of these functions.
Why So you can model the height of water, as in Example 1.

Key Vocabulary
- verbal model
- slope
- vertex

Sometimes you will find it helpful to model a function with a graph even if you don't have enough information to write an equation to model the function.

Sketching a graph based on a description of a situation can help you understand the situation and identify key features of the model.

COMMON CORE

CC.9-12.F.IF.4 For a function that models a relationship between two quantities, interpret key features of graphs and tables in terms of the quantities, and sketch graphs showing key features given a verbal description of the relationship.*

EXAMPLE 1 Sketch a graph of a real-world situation

FIRE-FIGHTING The water from one water cannon on a fire-fighting boat reaches a maximum height of 25 feet and travels a horizontal distance of about 140 feet.

a. What type of function should you use to represent the path of the water? Sketch a graph of the path of the water.

b. In the context of the given situation, what do the intercepts and maximum point represent?

Solution

a. The path of the water can be modeled by a parabola. Let x represent the horizontal distance in feet and let y represent the vertical distance in feet.

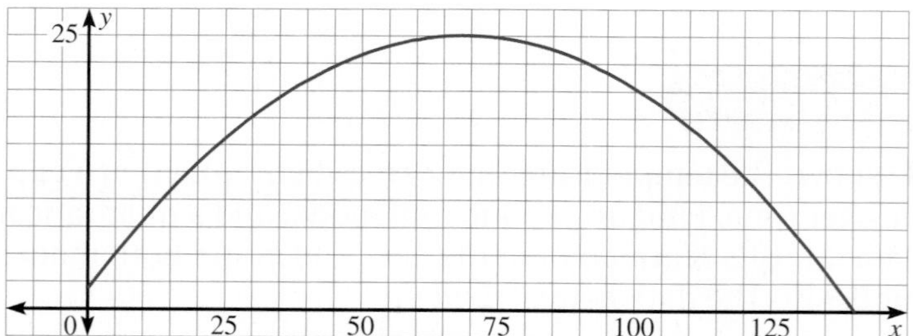

b. Because the water cannon is on a boat, the graph has only one x-intercept where the water reaches the surface of the water or ground. The maximum point of the graph is where the water reaches its maximum height, about 70 feet from the boat.

✓ **GUIDED PRACTICE for Example 1**

1. Using the graph in Example 1, describe the intervals in which the function is increasing and decreasing. Explain what the intervals mean in the given situation.

EXAMPLE 2 Compare properties of two linear functions

Decide which linear function is increasing at a greater rate.

- Linear Function 1 has an x-intercept of 4 and a y-intercept of -2.
- Linear Function 2 includes the points in the table below.

x	−2	−1	0	1	2	3
y	−11	−6	−1	4	9	14

Solution

AVOID ERRORS
In calculating the slope of a linear function, remember to divide the change in y by the change in x.

The slope of a linear equation indicates how rapidly a linear function is increasing or decreasing. The points (4, 0) and (0, −2) are on the graph of Linear Function 1, so its slope is $\frac{0-(-2)}{4-0} = \frac{1}{2}$.

The table for Linear Function 2 shows that for each increase of 1 in the value of x there is an increase of 5 in the value of y, so its slope is $\frac{5}{1} = 5$.

▶ Linear Function 2 is increasing more rapidly.

EXAMPLE 3 Compare properties of two quadratic functions

Use the given information to decide which quadratic function has the lesser minimum value.

- Quadratic Function 1: The function whose equation is $y = 3x^2 - 12x + 1$.
- Quadratic Function 2: The function whose graph is shown at the right.

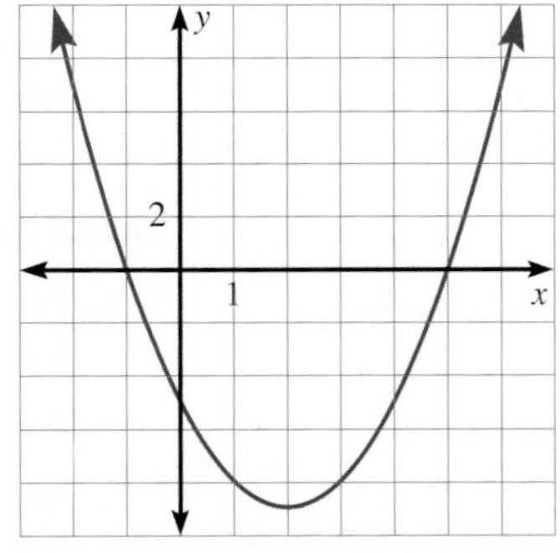

STUDY HELP
Review the lesson *Graph* $y = ax^2 + bx + c$ for information on finding the coordinates of the minimum value of a quadratic function.

Solution

The minimum value of Quadratic Function 1 is the y-value of the vertex of its parabola. The x-coordinate of the vertex is $-\left(\frac{b}{2a}\right) = -\frac{-12}{2(3)} = \frac{12}{6} = 2$. When $x = 2$, $y = 3(2)^2 - 12(2) + 1 = 12 - 24 + 1 = -11$. So the vertex is (2, −11) and the minimum value is − 11.

The minimum value of Quadratic Function 2 can be seen on the graph of the function; it is −9.

▶ Quadratic Function 1 has the lesser minimum value.

✓ **GUIDED PRACTICE** for Examples 2 and 3

2. **COMPARE** Compare the rates of change in the linear functions $y = 4x + 5$ and $y = 3 - 4x$.

3. **WHAT IF?** In Example 3, replace the equation for Quadratic Function 1 with $y = x^2 - 6x - 7$. Which function now has the lesser minimum value?

EXAMPLE 4 Choose a model for a real-world situation

BUSINESS The table shows the revenue generated by a company during each of the previous five years. Based on the change per unit interval, choose an appropriate type of function to model the situation.

Year	2008	2009	2010	2011	2012
Revenue ($)	50,000	51,500	53,045	54,636	56,275

Solution

The revenue is increasing each year by about 3%. Because the quantity grows by a constant percent rate per unit interval, you should use an exponential growth model for the situation.

EXAMPLE 5 Choose a model for a real-world situation

FURNITURE You are a furniture salesperson and earn $200 a week plus a 5% commission on the total value of all sales you make during the week.

a. Based on the given information, choose an appropriate type of function to model your potential weekly earnings as a function of sales.

b. Sketch a graph representing your potential earnings for any given week as a function of sales. Identify the function's intercept(s) and interpret the meaning of each intercept in the context of the given situation.

Solution

a. For every $100 of sales, your earnings increase by $5. Earnings are increasing by a constant rate. Use a linear function.

b. Let x represent the weekly sales and let y represent total earnings. The y-intercept is 200 and represents your weekly salary when you do not sell any furniture during that week. The function only makes sense for $x \geq 0$, so there is no x-intercept.

STUDY HELP
Remember that the graph of a real-world function does not necessarily have both an x-intercept and a y-intercept.

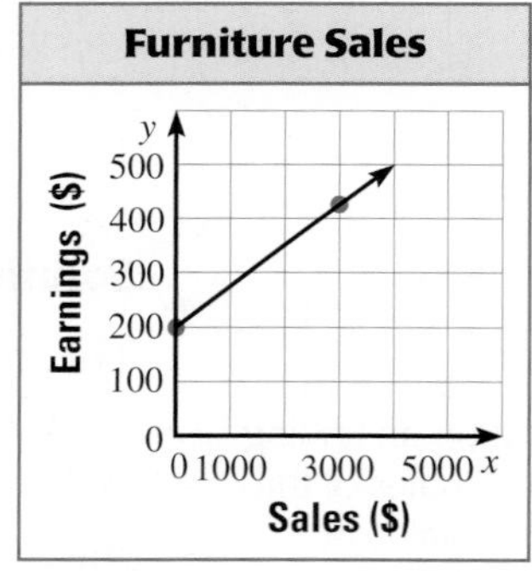

✓ GUIDED PRACTICE for Examples 4 and 5

4. RUNNING The table shows the distance that Juan covered per hour in the first four hours of a triathlon. Based on the change per unit interval, choose an appropriate function to model the situation.

Hour	1	2	3	4
Miles	6	5.4	4.86	4.374

9.9 EXERCISES

HOMEWORK KEY

◯ = **See WORKED-OUT SOLUTIONS** Exs. 3, 5, 11, and 15

★ = **STANDARDIZED TEST PRACTICE** Exs. 2, 6, 11, 18, and 19

SKILL PRACTICE

1. **VOCABULARY** Copy and complete: A __?__ describes a real-world situation using words as labels and using math symbols to relate the words.

2. ★ **WRITING** Explain the relationship between the slope of a linear function and the concept of an increasing/decreasing linear function.

EXAMPLE 1 for Exs. 3–5

3. **CHOOSE A MODEL** A hot air balloon has already risen 20 feet above the ground. At this point in time it begins to rise at a steady rate of 2 feet per second.

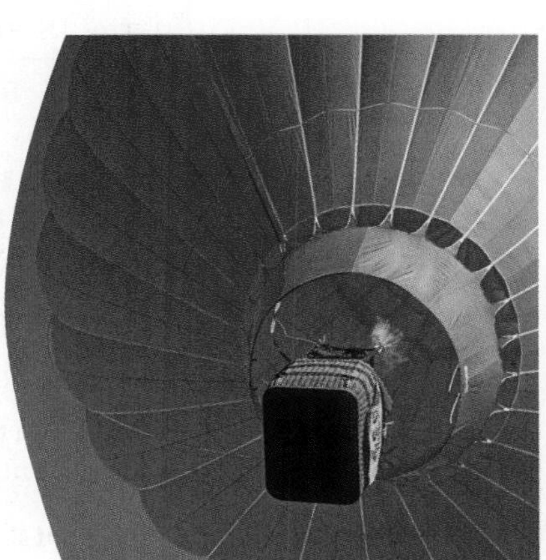

   a. What type of function would be a good model for this situation?

   b. Sketch a graph representing the balloon's altitude y in terms of the time x since it resumed its ascent.

   c. Identify the intervals on which the graph is increasing or decreasing and explain what these intervals mean in the context of the situation.

4. **CHOOSE A MODEL** During a weekend trip riding his motorcycle, Neil plans to average 55 miles per hour.

   a. What type of function would be a good model for this situation?

   b. Sketch a graph representing the distance he will travel y in terms of the number of hours x that he rides.

   c. Use the graph to identify the intercept(s) and interpret the meaning of each intercept in the context of the situation.

5. **CHOOSE A MODEL** A juggler throws a ball into the air. It reaches a maximum height of about 25 feet, and the juggler catches it again after 2.5 seconds.

   a. What type of function would be a good model for this situation?

   b. Sketch the graph of an equation that could model the height of the ball as a function of time.

   c. Identify the intervals on which the graph is increasing or decreasing and explain what these intervals mean in the context of the situation.

6. ★ **MULTIPLE CHOICE** Marvin is making a rectangular quilt. Suppose the width of the quilt is x meters and length of the quilt is $(3 - x)$ meters. Which type of function should you use to model the area y of the quilt in terms of its width?

   (A) linear (B) quadratic

   (C) exponential growth (D) exponential decay

ERROR ANALYSIS In Exercises 7 and 8, *describe* and correct the error in the model.

7. A student uses a quadratic function to model a population that is increasing by 4% per year.

8. A student uses an exponential decay function to model the distance traveled over time of a car traveling at a steady speed of 50 miles per hour.

EXAMPLES 2 and 3 for Exs. 9–10

9. **LINEAR FUNCTIONS** Use the given information to decide which linear function is decreasing more rapidly.
   - Linear Function 1 has a y-intercept of -3 and a slope of -1.
   - The table shows the coordinates of six points found on the line representing Linear Function 2.

x	-4	-2	0	2	4	6
y	8	4	0	-4	-8	-12

10. **QUADRATIC FUNCTIONS** Use the given information to decide which quadratic function has the greater maximum value.
    - Quadratic Function 1: The function whose equation is $y = -x^2 + 4x + 2$.
    - Quadratic Function 2: The function whose graph is shown at the right.

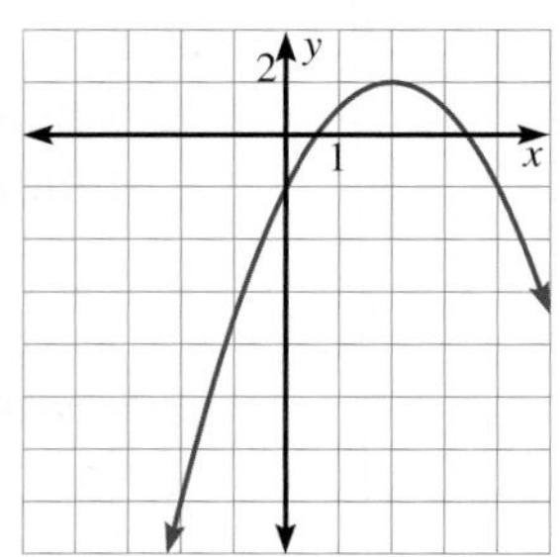

EXAMPLES 4 and 5 for Exs. 11–12

11. ★ **MULTIPLE CHOICE** Decide which relationship grows by a constant percent rate per unit interval.

Ⓐ

Hours	1	2	3	4
Miles	5	10	15	20

Ⓑ

Year	1	2	3	4
Revenue ($)	2000	1500	1125	843.75

Ⓒ

Days	1	2	3	4
Windows Installed	2	4	8	16

Ⓓ

Minutes	1	2	3	4
Pancakes Made	27	9	3	1

12. **CHALLENGE** In 2010, the United States Census Bureau estimated that there were approximately 310 million people in the United States. By some estimates the population is growing by about 0.9% per year.

    a. Sketch a graph relating the population y at any time x. Let $x = 0$ represent the year 2010. What type of function will be a good model?

    b. Interpret the meaning of the x- and y-intercepts, if they exist, in terms of the context of this situation.

    c. Is the graph of the function increasing or decreasing? *Explain.*

○ = See **WORKED-OUT SOLUTIONS** in Student Resources

★ = **STANDARDIZED TEST PRACTICE**

PROBLEM SOLVING

EXAMPLES 3 and 4 for Exs. 13–15

13. **MUSIC** Celia has already downloaded 14 songs to her cell phone. In the future she intends to download 2 songs per week. Her friend Connie has already downloaded 12 songs to her cell phone and she plans to download songs based on the table below. Which girl's playlist is growing faster?

Week	1	2	3	4
Total Number of Songs on Connie's Cell Phone	17	22	27	32

14. **BASEBALL** Tim threw a baseball in the air. Suppose the ball's height in feet can be modeled by the equation $y = -16x^2 + 40x + 5$. Matt threw the same baseball in the air. The graph models the height in feet of Matt's ball as a function of time. Which ball reached a greater height?

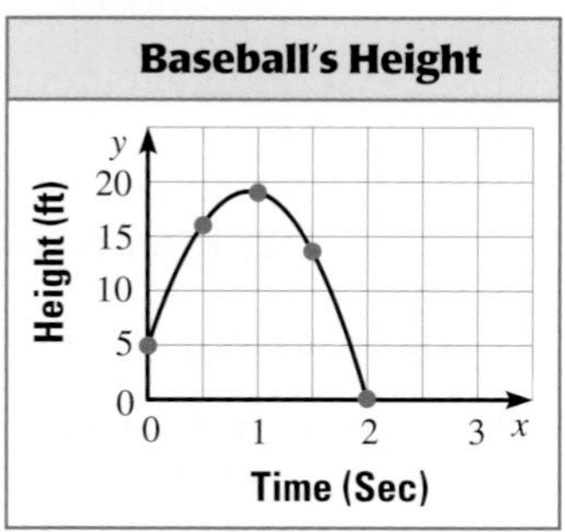

15. **SCIENCE** Tanya placed mold spores in a Petri dish. The table shows the number of spores in the dish at the end of each hour. Indicate whether the number of spores in the Petri dish represents *growth, decay,* or *neither.* Identify the growth or decay rate, if it exists, expressing it as a percent.

Hour	1	2	3	4
Number of Spores	16	24	36	54

16. **CHICKENS** You have 100 meters of fencing to build a chicken pen.

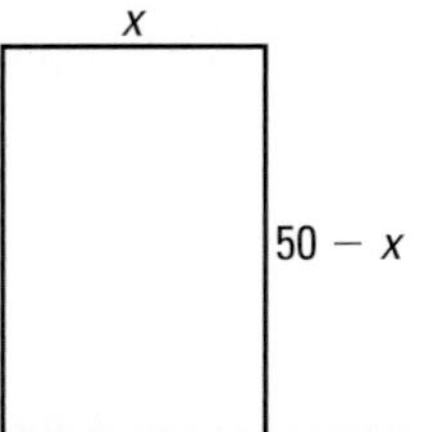

 a. Use the diagram to help sketch a graph representing the area y of the pen in terms of the width x of the pen.

 b. Use the graph to identify the intercept(s) and interpret the meaning of each intercept in the context of the situation.

17. **ROWING** The table shows the distance in miles that a rowing crew covered during each 15-minute interval in the first hour of practice. Based on the change per unit interval, choose an appropriate function to model the situation.

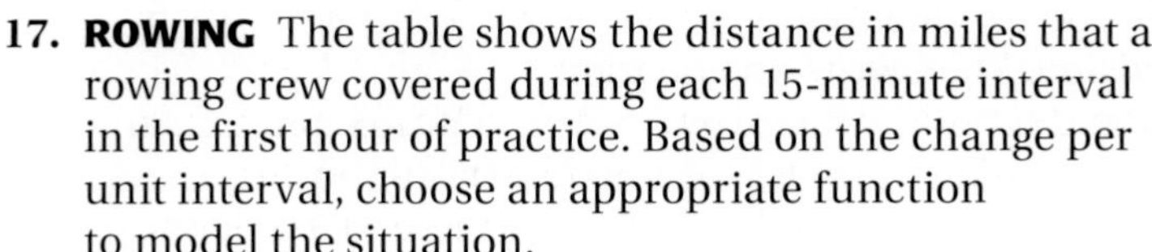

Minutes	15	30	45	60
Miles	2	1.6	1.28	1.024

18. ★ **MULTIPLE CHOICE** Choose the situation in which one quantity changes by a constant amount per unit interval relative to a second quantity.

(A) Michael rented tables and chairs for a party. The cost for the rental was $10 for the first day. If he keeps them for more than one day the cost per day is double the preceding day.

(B) Alexi's stamp collection already contains 12 stamps. Each time he goes to the post office he will buy 2 stamps to add to his collection.

(C) Sue has an ant farm. The number of ants can be modeled by the equation $y = 100(1.05)^x$, where y is the number of ants on any given day and x is the number of days since she started the farm.

(D) Pam accidently dropped her watch from her tree house. The equation $y = -16x^2 + 37$ models the height of the watch as it is falling to the ground. The variable y represents the height of the watch and x represents the time in seconds since Pam dropped the watch.

19. ★ **EXTENDED RESPONSE** Use the information to answer each question.

a. Graphs Using a single coordinate system, graph the functions $y = 2x$, $y = x^2$, and $y = 2^x$. Which function eventually has the greatest y-value for a given value of x?

b. Tables Complete a table similar to the one below for each of the three given functions. Which function eventually has the greatest y-value for a given value of x?

Linear Function: $y = 3x + 1$
Quadratic Function: $y = 3x^2 + 1$
Exponential Function: $y = 3^x + 1$

x	−1	0	2	4	6	8	10
y	?	?	?	?	?	?	?

c. CHALLENGE Given any quantity that can be modeled by a linear function, any quantity that can be modeled by a quadratic function, and any quantity that can be modeled by an exponential growth function, can you predict which quantity will eventually exceed the other two? *Explain.*

QUIZ

1. Tell whether the table of values represents a *linear function*, an exponential *function*, or a *quadratic function*. Then write an equation for the function.

x	1	2	3	4	5
y	5	1	$\frac{1}{5}$	$\frac{1}{25}$	$\frac{1}{125}$

2. Solve the system shown. $y = x^2 - 4x - 11$
$y = x - 5$

3. **EXERCISE** You ride your bicycle 2 miles to a local park and join friends for a hike. You walk at a rate of 3 miles per hour. Sketch a graph that relates total distance y traveled to time x walking. Identify the intercept(s). Interpret them in the context of the situation.

See EXTRA PRACTICE in Student Resources

Graphing Calculator **ACTIVITY** *Use after Model Relationships*

Average Rate of Change

MATHEMATICAL PRACTICES

Use appropriate tools strategically.

QUESTION What is the average rate of change between two points?

The *average rate of change* is useful for some real-world situations, like finding the average growth rate of a tree over a 20-year period. You can use the slope formula to find the average rate of change between two points on the graph of a non-linear function.

EXAMPLE Find an average rate of change

Find the average rate of change between points on the graph of $y = 2x^2 - 3x - 1$. How does the choice of the points impact the average rate of change?

STEP 1 *Graph the function*

Graph the function on a graphing calculator. Then use the *Trace* feature to identify the coordinates of points on the graph. Record four pairs of points in a table like the one shown.

STEP 2 *Calculate average rate of change*

Calculate the average rate of change between the points in each pair by calculating the slope of the line through the two points. Record the results. Add a column for the absolute values of the average rates of change.

Points	Average Rate of Change	Absolute Value of the Average Rate of Change
(2, 1), (3, 8)	7	7
(0, −1), (0.5, −2)	−2	2

Depending on the pair of points chosen for an interval, notice that the average rate of change can be positive or negative, and either very large or very small.

DRAW CONCLUSIONS

In Exercises 1–4, repeat Steps 1 and 2 for the given function.

1. $y = 2x - 3$
2. $y = -4x^2 + 2x - 1$
3. $y = 10 \cdot 2^x$
4. $y = 2\left(\frac{1}{3}\right)^x$

5. Graph the functions given in the table below. Estimate the average rate of change for each graph. Copy and complete the table. Generalize the results.

Function	$\frac{f(10) - f(0)}{10 - 0}$	$\frac{f(100) - f(10)}{100 - 10}$	$\frac{f(1000) - f(100)}{1000 - 100}$	$\frac{f(10{,}000) - f(1000)}{10{,}000 - 1000}$
$y = x + 1$	1	1	?	?
$y = x^2 + 1$	10	110	?	?
$y = 2^x$	102.3	?	?	?

 MATHEMATICAL PRACTICES Make sense of problems and persevere in solving them.

1. **MULTI-STEP PROBLEM** Different masses (in kilograms) are hung from a spring. The distances (in centimeters) that the spring stretches are shown in the table.

Mass (kilograms)	Distance (centimeters)
1	2.6
2	5.2
3	7.8
4	10.4
5	13.0

   a. Tell whether the data can be modeled by a *linear function*, an *exponential function*, or a *quadratic function*.

   b. Write an equation for the function.

2. **MULTI-STEP PROBLEM** In slow-pitch softball, the ball is pitched in an underhand motion. A batter in a softball game is pitched a ball that has an initial height of 2 feet above the ground and an initial vertical velocity of 35 feet per second.

   a. Write an equation for the height h (in feet) of the ball as a function of the time t (in seconds) after it is pitched.

   b. The batter hits the ball when it is 2.5 feet above the ground. How long after the ball is pitched is the ball hit? Round your answer to the nearest tenth of a second.

3. **SHORT RESPONSE** Part of a cheerleading routine involves throwing a flyer straight up into the air and catching her on the way down. The flyer begins this stunt with her center of gravity 4.5 feet above the ground, and she is thrown with an initial vertical velocity of 30 feet per second. Will her center of gravity reach a height of 20 feet? *Explain.*

4. **OPEN-ENDED** In Exercise 3, suppose the flyer wants to have her center of gravity reach a height of at least 25 feet above the ground. Give an initial vertical velocity that will accomplish this.

5. **SHORT RESPONSE** For the period 1990–2000, the sales y (in billions of dollars) of computers, computer accessories, and computer software can be modeled by the function $y = -0.05x^2 + 2.2x + 7$ where x is the number of years since 1990.

   a. Write and graph a system of equations to determine the number of values of x that correspond to $y = 24$.

   b. Were there any years during the period 1990–2000 in which the sales reached 24 billion dollars? *Explain.*

6. **GRIDDED ANSWER** The trapezoid below has an area of 54 square inches. What is the value of x?

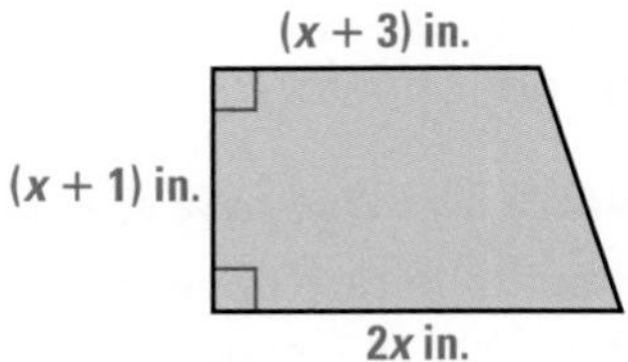

7. **SHORT RESPONSE** You have 24 feet of fencing that you are using to make a rectangular dog pen. You want the dog pen to enclose 150 square feet. Is it possible for the 24 feet of fencing to enclose a rectangular area of 150 square feet? *Explain.*

8. **EXTENDED RESPONSE** You are making a tiled tabletop with a uniform mosaic tile border as shown.

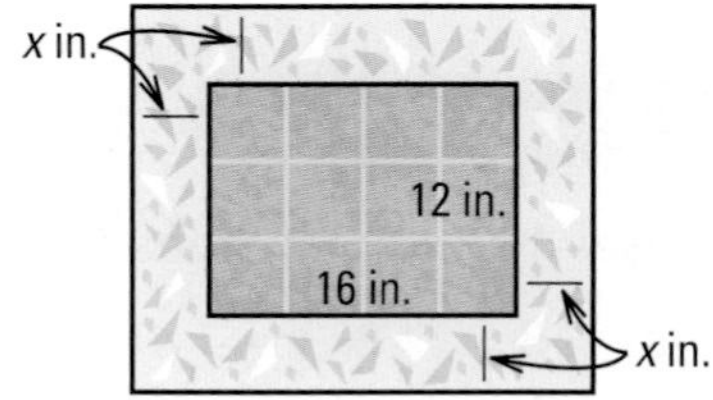

   a. Write an equation for the area A (in square inches) of the border.

   b. You have enough mosaic tiles to cover 130 square inches. What should the width of the border be? Round your answer to the nearest inch.

   c. *Explain* why you could ignore one of the values of x in part (b).

9 CHAPTER SUMMARY

Animated Algebra
my.hrw.com
Electronic Function Library

BIG IDEAS

For Your Notebook

Big Idea 1

Graphing Quadratic Functions

You can use the properties below to graph any quadratic function.

The graph of $y = ax^2 + bx + c$ is a parabola that:

- opens up if $a > 0$ and opens down if $a < 0$.
- is narrower than the graph of $y = x^2$ if $|a| > 1$ and wider if $|a| < 1$.
- has an axis of symmetry of $x = -\frac{b}{2a}$.
- has a vertex with an x-coordinate of $-\frac{b}{2a}$.
- has a y-intercept of c. So, the point $(0, c)$ is on the parabola.

$y = ax^2 + bx + c, a > 0$

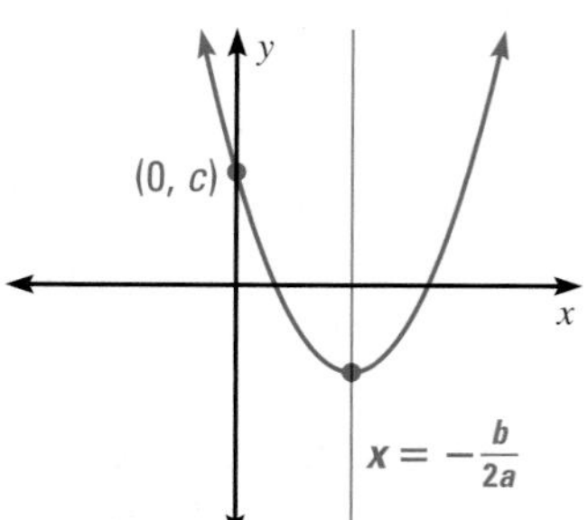

Big Idea 2

Solving Quadratic Equations

You can use the following methods to solve a quadratic equation. Sometimes it is easier to use one method instead of another.

Method	When to use
Graphing	Use when approximate solutions are adequate.
Finding square roots	Use when solving an equation that can be written in the form $x^2 = d$.
Completing the square	Can be used for *any* quadratic equation $y = ax^2 + bx + c$ but is simplest to apply when $a = 1$ and b is an even number.
Quadratic formula	Can be used for *any* quadratic equation

Big Idea 3

Comparing Linear, Exponential, and Quadratic Models

You can use linear, exponential, and quadratic functions to model data.

Function	Example	x- and y-values
Linear	$y = 5x + 1$	If the increments between successive x-values are equal, the differences of successive y-values are all equal.
Exponential	$y = 3(2)^x$	If the increments between successive x-values are equal, the ratios of successive y-values are all equal.
Quadratic	$y = x^2 - 4x + 6$	If the increments between successive x-values are equal, the differences of successive first differences of y-values are all equal.

9 CHAPTER REVIEW

@HomeTutor
my.hrw.com
• Multi-Language Glossary
• Vocabulary practice

REVIEW KEY VOCABULARY

- quadratic function
- standard form of a quadratic function
- parabola
- parent quadratic function
- vertex of a parabola
- axis of symmetry
- minimum value
- maximum value
- intercept form of a quadratic function
- quadratic equation
- standard form of a quadratic equation
- completing the square
- vertex form of a quadratic function
- quadratic formula

VOCABULARY EXERCISES

1. Copy and complete: The line that passes through the vertex and divides a parabola into two symmetric parts is called the __?__.

Tell whether the function has a *minimum value* or a *maximum value*.

2. $f(x) = 5x^2 - 4x$
3. $f(x) = -x^2 + 6x + 2$
4. $f(x) = 0.3x^2 - 7.7x + 1.8$

REVIEW EXAMPLES AND EXERCISES

Use the review examples and exercises below to check your understanding of the concepts you have learned in each lesson of this chapter.

9.1 Graph $y = ax^2 + c$

EXAMPLE

Graph $y = -x^2 + 3$. Compare the graph with the graph of $y = x^2$.

Make a table of values for $y = -x^2 + 3$. Then plot the points from the table and draw a smooth curve through the points.

x	−2	−1	0	1	2
y	−1	2	3	2	−1

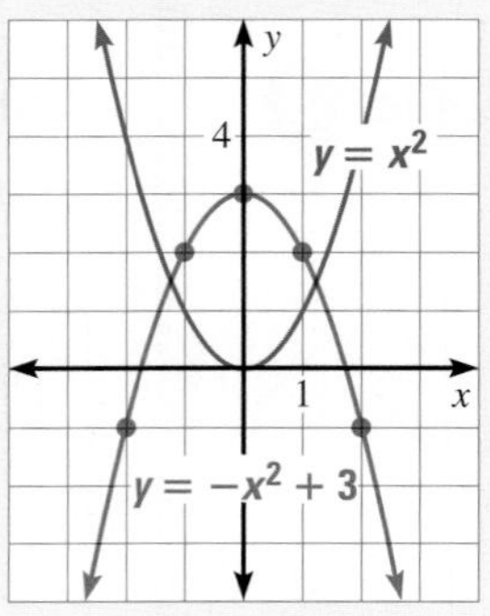

Both graphs have the same axis of symmetry, $x = 0$. However, the graph of $y = -x^2 + 3$ has a different vertex than the graph of $y = x^2$, and it opens down. This is because the graph of $y = -x^2 + 3$ is a vertical translation (of 3 units up) and a reflection in the x-axis of the graph of $y = x^2$.

EXAMPLES 1, 2, and 4 for Exs. 5–7

EXERCISES

Graph the function. Compare the graph with the graph of $y = x^2$.

5. $y = -4x^2$
6. $y = \frac{1}{3}x^2$
7. $y = 2x^2 - 1$

@HomeTutor
my.hrw.com
Chapter Review Practice

9.2 Graph $y = ax^2 + bx + c$

EXAMPLE

Graph $y = -x^2 + 2x + 1$.

STEP 1 **Determine** whether the parabola opens up or down. Because $a < 0$, the parabola opens down.

STEP 2 **Find** and draw the axis of symmetry:

$$x = -\frac{b}{2a} = -\frac{2}{2(-1)} = 1$$

STEP 3 **Find** and plot the vertex. The x-coordinate of the vertex is $-\frac{b}{2a}$, or 1. The y-coordinate of the vertex is $y = -(1)^2 + 2(1) + 1 = 2$.

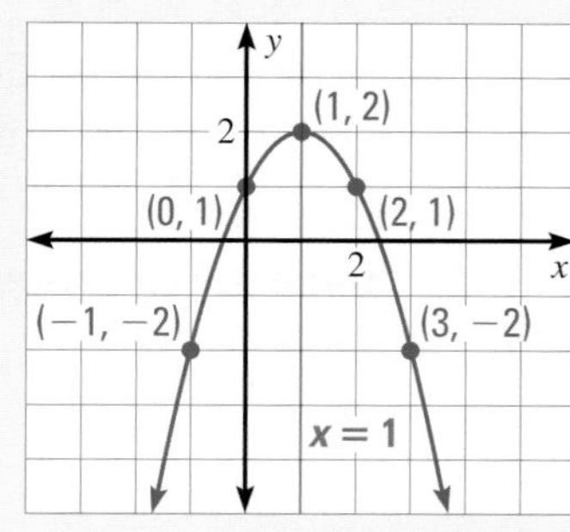

STEP 4 **Plot** four more points. Evaluating the function for $x = 0$ and $x = -1$ gives the points (0, 1) and (−1, −2). Plot these points and their reflections in the axis of symmetry.

STEP 5 **Draw** a parabola through the plotted points.

EXERCISES

EXAMPLE 2 for Exs. 8–10

Graph the function. Label the vertex and axis of symmetry.

8. $y = x^2 + 4x + 1$ **9.** $y = 2x^2 - 4x - 3$ **10.** $y = -2x^2 + 8x + 5$

9.3 Solve Quadratic Equations by Graphing

EXAMPLE

Solve $x^2 - 7x = -12$ by graphing.

STEP 1 **Write** the equation in standard form.

$x^2 - 7x = -12$ **Write original equation.**

$x^2 - 7x + 12 = 0$ **Add 12 to each side.**

STEP 2 **Graph** the related function $y = x^2 - 7x + 12$. The x-intercepts of the graph are 3 and 4.

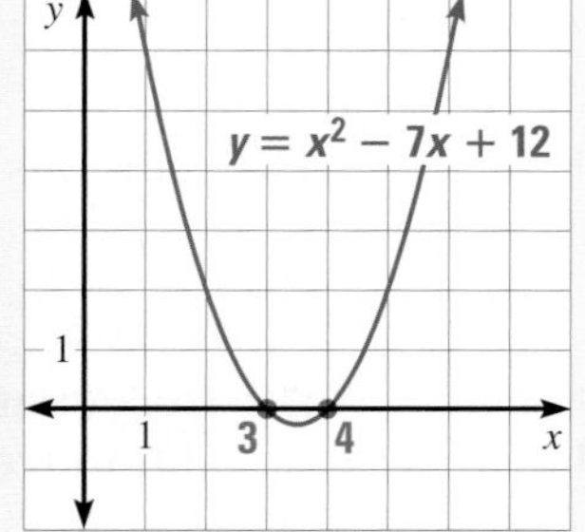

▶ The solutions of the equation $x^2 - 7x + 12 = 0$ are 3 and 4.

EXERCISES

EXAMPLES 1, 2, and 3 for Exs. 11–13

Solve the equation by graphing.

11. $4x^2 + x + 3 = 0$ **12.** $x^2 + 2x = -1$ **13.** $-x^2 + 8 = 7x$

9 CHAPTER REVIEW

9.4 Use Square Roots to Solve Quadratic Equations

EXAMPLE

Solve $5(x - 6)^2 = 30$. Round the solutions to the nearest hundredth.

$5(x - 6)^2 = 30$	Write original equation.
$(x - 6)^2 = 6$	Divide each side by 5.
$x - 6 = \pm\sqrt{6}$	Take square roots of each side.
$x = 6 \pm \sqrt{6}$	Add 6 to each side.

▶ The solutions of the equation are $6 + \sqrt{6} \approx 8.45$ and $6 - \sqrt{6} \approx 3.55$.

EXERCISES

EXAMPLES 1–4 for Exs. 14–19

Solve the equation. Round your solutions to the nearest hundredth, if necessary.

14. $6x^2 - 54 = 0$ **15.** $3x^2 + 7 = 4$ **16.** $g^2 + 11 = 24$

17. $7n^2 + 5 = 9$ **18.** $2(a + 7)^2 = 34$ **19.** $3(w - 4)^2 = 5$

9.5 Solve Quadratic Equations by Completing the Square

EXAMPLE

Solve $3x^2 + 12x = 18$ by completing the square.

$3x^2 + 12x = 18$	Write original equation.
$x^2 + 4x = 6$	Divide each side by 3.
$x^2 + 4x + 2^2 = 6 + 2^2$	Add $\left(\frac{4}{2}\right)^2$, or 2^2, to each side.
$(x + 2)^2 = 10$	Write left side as the square of a binomial.
$x + 2 = \pm\sqrt{10}$	Take square roots of each side.
$x = -2 \pm \sqrt{10}$	Subtract 2 from each side.

▶ The solutions of the equation are $-2 + \sqrt{10} \approx 1.16$ and $-2 - \sqrt{10} \approx -5.16$.

EXERCISES

EXAMPLES 2 and 3 for Exs. 20–23

Solve the equation by completing the square. Round your solutions to the nearest hundredth, if necessary.

20. $x^2 - 14x = 51$ **21.** $2a^2 + 12a - 4 = 0$

22. $2n^2 + 4n + 1 = 10n + 9$ **23.** $5g^2 - 3g + 6 = 2g^2 + 9$

9.6 Solve Quadratic Equations by the Quadratic Formula

EXAMPLE

Solve $4x^2 + 3x = 1$.

$4x^2 + 3x = 1$ — **Write original equation.**

$4x^2 + 3x - 1 = 0$ — **Write in standard form.**

$x = \frac{-b \pm \sqrt{b^2 - 4ac}}{2a}$ — **Quadratic formula**

$= \frac{-3 \pm \sqrt{3^2 - 4(4)(-1)}}{2(4)}$ — **Substitute values in the quadratic formula: $a = 4$, $b = 3$, and $c = -1$.**

$= \frac{-3 \pm \sqrt{25}}{8} = \frac{-3 \pm 5}{8}$ — **Simplify.**

▶ The solutions of the equation are $\frac{-3+5}{8} = \frac{1}{4}$ and $\frac{-3-5}{8} = -1$.

EXERCISES

EXAMPLES 1–3 for Exs. 24–29

Use the quadratic formula to solve the equation. Round your solutions to the nearest hundredth, if necessary.

24. $x^2 - 2x - 15 = 0$

25. $2m^2 + 7m - 3 = 0$

26. $-w^2 + 5w = 3$

27. $5n^2 - 7n = -1$

28. $t^2 - 4 = 6t + 8$

29. $2h - 1 = 10 - 9h^2$

9.7 Solve Systems with Quadratic Equations

EXAMPLE

Solve the system using substitution: $y = x + 10$ — **Equation 1**

$y = x^2 + x + 1$ — **Equation 2**

STEP 1 **Solve** one of the equations for y. Equation 1 is already solved for y.

STEP 2 **Substitute** $x + 10$ for y in Equation 2 and solve for x.

$y = x^2 + x + 1$ — **Write original equation 2.**

$x + 10 = x^2 + x + 1$ — **Substitute $x + 10$ for y.**

$9 = x^2$ — **Solve for x^2**

$x = -3$ or $x = 3$ — **Solve for x**

STEP 3 **Substitute** both -3 and 3 for y in Equation 1

$y = -3 + 7 = 4$ and $y = 3 + 7 = 10$

▶ The solutions of the system are $(-3, 4)$ and $(3, 10)$.

EXERCISES

EXAMPLES 1–3 for Exs. 30–33

Solve the system using the substitution method or a graphing calculator.

30. $y = x + 8$
$y = x^2 + 2x + 2$

31. $x + y = 0$
$y = 2x^2 - 3x - 4$

32. $2x + y = 1$
$y = 3x^2 - x - 1$

33. Solve $4x^2 - 2x - 1 = 2x + 2$ using a system of equations.

9 CHAPTER REVIEW

9.8 Compare Linear, Exponential, and Quadratic Models

EXAMPLE

Use differences or ratios to tell whether the table of values represents a *linear function*, an *exponential function*, or a *quadratic function*.

a.

x	−1	0	1	2
y	5	3	1	−1

Differences: −2 −2 −2

▸ The table of values represents a linear function.

b.

x	−1	0	1	2
y	4	5	4	1

First differences: 1 −1 −3

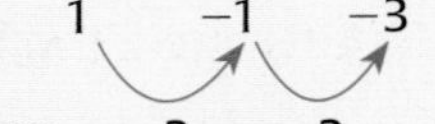

Second differences: −2 −2

▸ The table of values represents a quadratic function.

EXERCISES

EXAMPLE 2
for Exs. 34–35

Tell whether the table of values represents a *linear function*, an *exponential function*, or a *quadratic function*.

34.

x	1	2	3	4	5	6
y	1	2	4	8	16	32

35.

x	−2	−1	0	1	2	3
y	0	3	6	9	12	15

9.9 Model Relationships

EXAMPLE

Decide which function is increasing more rapidly.

Linear Function 1 has an x-intercept of −3 and a y-intercept of 2.

Linear Function 2 includes the points in the table below.

x	−2	−1	0	1	2
y	−3	−2.5	−2	−1.5	−1

The points (−3, 0) and (0, 2) are on the graph of Linear Function 1, so its slope is $\frac{2-0}{0-(-3)} = \frac{2}{3}$. The table for Linear Function 2 shows that for each increase of 1 in the value of x, there is an increase of 0.5 in the value of y. The slope of the graph of Linear Function 2 is $= \frac{0.5}{1} = \frac{1}{2}$. So, Linear Function 1 is increasing more rapidly.

EXERCISES

EXAMPLES 1–2
for Exs. 36–37

36. Linear Function 1 has a y-intercept of 3 and a slope of –1. Linear Function 2 has an x-intercept of 4 and a y-intercept of 3. Which linear function is decreasing more rapidly?

37. The population of a city is increasing at a rate of 2.5% per decade. What type of function would be a good model for this situation?

9 CHAPTER TEST

Match the quadratic function with its graph.

1. $y = x^2 - 2$
2. $y = x^2 + 2$
3. $y = -2x^2$

A.

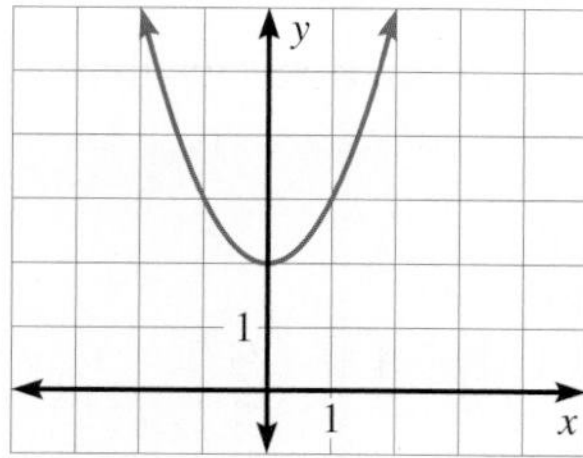

B.

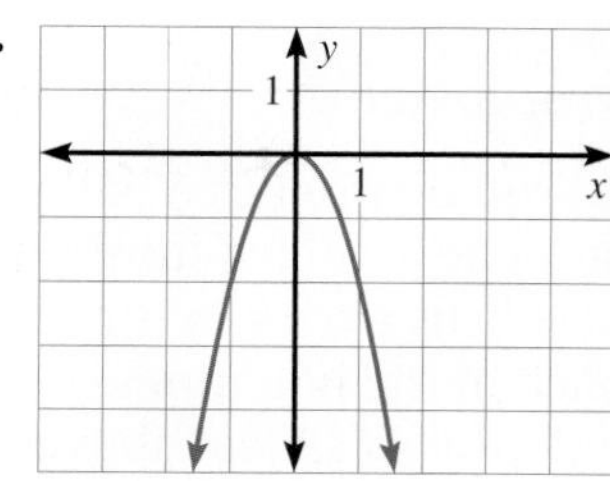

C.

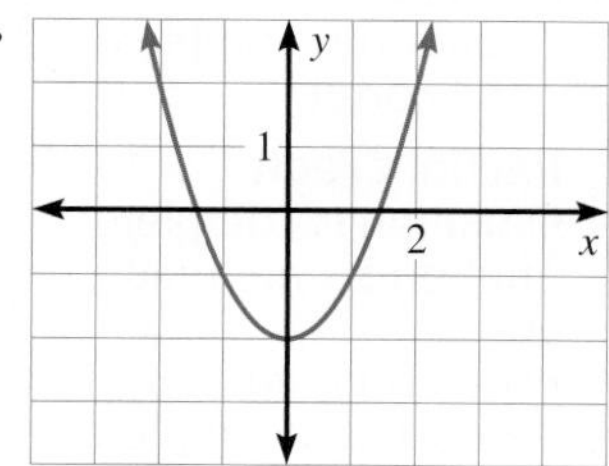

Graph the function. Label the vertex and axis of symmetry.

4. $y = 2x^2 + 6x - 5$
5. $y = -4x^2 - 8x + 25$
6. $y = \frac{1}{4}x^2 - x - 7$

Approximate the zeros of the function to the nearest tenth.

7. $f(x) = x^2 + 5x + 1$
8. $f(x) = x^2 - 8x + 3$
9. $f(x) = -3x^2 - 2x + 5$

Solve the equation. Round your solutions to the nearest hundredth, if necessary.

10. $3x^2 = 108$
11. $-5w^2 + 51 = 6$
12. $-p^2 + 2p + 3 = 0$
13. $-2t^2 + 6t + 9 = 0$
14. $5m^2 - m = 5$
15. $2x^2 - 12x - 1 = -7x + 6$

Solve the system using the substitution method or a graphing calculator.

16. $y = 3x - 2$
    $y = -x^2 + 2x + 4$
17. $x + y = -3$
    $y = 2x^2 + x - 7$
18. $2x - y = 2$
    $y = -2x^2 - 4x + 6$

Tell whether the table of values represents a *linear function*, an *exponential function*, or a *quadratic function*. Then write an equation for the function.

19.

x	−3	−2	−1	0	1	2
y	18	8	2	0	2	8

20.

x	−4	0	4	8	12	16
y	1	2	3	4	5	6

21. **TENNIS** In a tennis match, a player hits the ball and the opponent fails to return it. The ball reaches a maximum height of 20 feet and hits the ground at a horizontal distance of 50 feet from where it was hit.
    a. What type of function should you use to represent the path of the ball? Sketch a graph of the path of the ball.
    b. In the context of the given situation what do the intercepts and maximum point represent?

Scoring Rubric

Full Credit
- solution is complete and correct

Partial Credit
- solution is complete but errors are made,

or
- solution is without error but incomplete

No Credit
- no solution is given,

or
- solution makes no sense

EXTENDED RESPONSE QUESTIONS

PROBLEM

A skateboarder in a half pipe launches himself from the half pipe, performs a trick in the air, and lands back in the half pipe. The top of the half pipe is 12 feet above the base of the half pipe as shown.

a. During his first run, the skateboarder leaves the half pipe with an initial vertical velocity of 17 feet per second. Write an equation that models the height h (in feet) of a skateboarder as a function of the time t (in seconds) after leaving the half pipe.

b. How long is the skateboarder in the air if he lands 5 feet above the base of the half pipe? Round your answer to the nearest hundredth of a second.

c. During his second run, the skateboarder leaves the half pipe with an initial vertical velocity that is greater than his initial vertical velocity during his first run. He again lands 5 feet above the base of the half pipe. During which run is his time spent in the air greater? *Explain.*

Below are sample solutions to the problem. Read each solution and the comments on the left to see why the sample represents full credit, partial credit, or no credit.

SAMPLE 1: Full credit solution

The correct equation is given.

a. $h = -16t^2 + 17t + 12$

b. $5 = -16t^2 + 17t + 12$

$0 = -16t^2 + 17t + 7$

$t = \dfrac{-17 \pm \sqrt{17^2 - 4(-16)(7)}}{2(-16)} \approx -0.32 \text{ or } 1.38$

The correct equation is given, and the answer that makes sense is given.

The skateboarder is in the air for about 1.38 seconds.

c. $5 = -16t^2 + 18t + 12$ | $5 = -16t^2 + 20t + 12$

$0 = -16t^2 + 18t + 7$ | $0 = -16t^2 + 20t + 7$

$t = \dfrac{-18 \pm \sqrt{18^2 - 4(-16)(7)}}{2(-16)}$ | $t = \dfrac{-20 \pm \sqrt{20^2 - 4(-16)(7)}}{2(-16)}$

$t \approx -0.31$ (crossed out) or $t \approx 1.43$ | $t \approx -0.29$ (crossed out) or $t \approx 1.54$

The answer is correct, and it includes an explanation.

The examples above show that the time the skateboarder spends in the air increases as the initial vertical velocity increases and the landing height remains constant. So, the skateboarder spends more time in the air during his second run.

SAMPLE 2: Partial credit solution

The correct equation is given.

In parts (b) and (c), the reasoning is correct but errors are made in calculating the values of *t*. So, the answers are incorrect.

a. $h = -16t^2 + 17t + 12$

b. $0 = -16t^2 + 17t + 7$

$$t = \frac{-17 \pm \sqrt{17^2 - 4(-16)(7)}}{2(-16)} \approx -1.38 \text{ or } 0.32$$

The skateboarder is in the air for about 0.32 second.

c. $0 = -16t^2 + 19t + 7$

$$t = \frac{-19 \pm \sqrt{19^2 - 4(-16)(7)}}{2(-16)} \approx -1.48 \text{ or } 0.3$$

With an initial vertical velocity of 19 feet per second, the skateboarder is in the air for about 0.3 second, which is less than 0.32 second. So, the skateboarder spends more time in the air during his first run.

SAMPLE 3: No credit solution

The equation is incorrect.

In parts (b) and (c), the incorrect equations are solved, and no answers are given.

a. $h = -16t^2 + 12t + 17$

b. $0 = -16t^2 + 12t + 17$

$$t = \frac{-12 \pm \sqrt{12^2 - 4(-16)(17)}}{2(-16)} \approx -0.72 \text{ or } 1.47$$

c. $0 = -16t^2 + 15t + 17$

$$t = \frac{-15 \pm \sqrt{15^2 - 4(-16)(17)}}{2(-16)} \approx -0.66 \text{ or } 1.6$$

PRACTICE Apply Scoring Rubric

1. A student's solution to the problem on the previous page is given below. Score the solution as *full credit, partial credit,* or *no credit. Explain* your reasoning. If you choose *partial credit* or *no credit,* explain how you would change the solution so that it earns a score of full credit.

a. $h = -16t^2 + 17t + 12$

b. $0 = -16t^2 + 17t + 7$

$$t = \frac{-17 \pm \sqrt{17^2 - 4(-16)(7)}}{2(-16)} \approx 0.32$$

The skateboarder is in the air for about 0.32 second.

c. A greater initial vertical velocity means that the skateboarder will go higher. This means that he will be in the air longer. So, the skateboarder will be in the air longer during his second run.

9 ★ Standardized TEST PRACTICE

EXTENDED RESPONSE

1. A community garden is being planned in the town-owned field behind the housing development where you live. The rectangular garden will border the development and extend into the field. Each household that joins the project will have a rectangular plot that is 20 feet wide. The town has already permitted the plots to extend 10 feet into the field, and promised another foot for every household that reserves a plot.

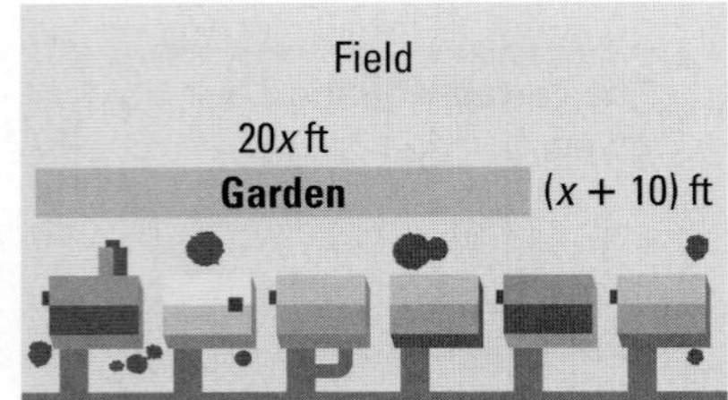

   a. Write an equation that gives the area A (in square feet) of the community garden as a function of the number x of households that reserve a plot.

   b. The housing association decides that the entire area of the garden cannot exceed 4000 square feet. What is the maximum number of plots there can be? *Explain.*

   c. The maximum number of plots is used. One of the residents decides to plant a uniform border of wildflowers around all four sides of her plot. She has enough wildflower seeds to cover 111 square feet. How wide should the border be? *Explain.*

2. During a water-polo practice, a player positioned directly in front of the goal throws the ball at the goal. The ball follows a parabolic path that can be modeled by the graph of the equation $y = -0.018x^2 + 0.25x + 0.7$ where y is the height (in feet) of the ball above the surface of the water x feet from the player.

   a. What is the maximum height of the ball to the nearest tenth of a foot?

   b. The ball goes into the goal. The goal is bounded by the surface of the water and a crossbar that is 3 feet high above the surface of the water. Give a possible distance that the player is from the goal. *Explain.*

   c. Describe all possible distances that the player can be from the goal in order for the ball to go into the goal. *Explain.*

3. A farm machine called a planter plants multiple rows of seeds while being pulled by a tractor. Planters can be purchased in various sizes. The operation costs of a 6 row, 8 row, 12 row, 16 row, and 24 row planter are analyzed. The operation cost y (in dollars per acre) for a planter that plants x rows at once for two different sizes of fields is shown in the table.

   a. Which planter costs the least per acre to operate for planting 400 acres?

   b. Which planter costs the least per acre to operate for planting 800 acres?

Acres planted	Operation cost (dollars per acre), y
400	$y = 0.071x^2 - 1.1x + 17$
800	$y = 0.062x^2 - 1.6x + 20$

   c. A farmer who is planting 800 acres uses the planter that costs the least per acre to operate. The operation cost function takes into account that a tractor operator is paid \$.82 per acre to drive the tractor pulling the planter. The farmer drives the tractor, so he doesn't have to pay for labor. Does his planter still cost the least per acre to operate? *Explain.*

MULTIPLE CHOICE

4. How would the graph of the function $y = -3x^2 + 6$ be affected if the function were changed to $y = -3x^2 - 1$?

   Ⓐ The graph would shift 5 units up.

   Ⓑ The graph would shift 5 units down.

   Ⓒ The graph would shift 7 units up.

   Ⓓ The graph would shift 7 units down.

5. A volleyball player serves the ball from a height of 6.5 feet above the ground with an initial vertical velocity of 21 feet per second. Which function models the height h (in feet) of the ball t seconds after it is served?

   Ⓐ $h = 21t - t^2 + 6.5$

   Ⓑ $h = -16t^2 + 6.5$

   Ⓒ $h = 16t^2 + 21t + 6.5$

   Ⓓ $h = 6.5 + 21t - 16t^2$

GRIDDED ANSWER

6. The area of the rectangle below is 170 square meters. What is the value of x?

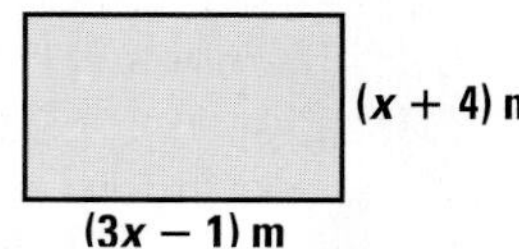

7. A cross section of the glass lamp shade below can be modeled by the graph of the equation $y = -0.625x^2 + 5x$ where x and y are measured in inches. How tall (in inches) is the shade?

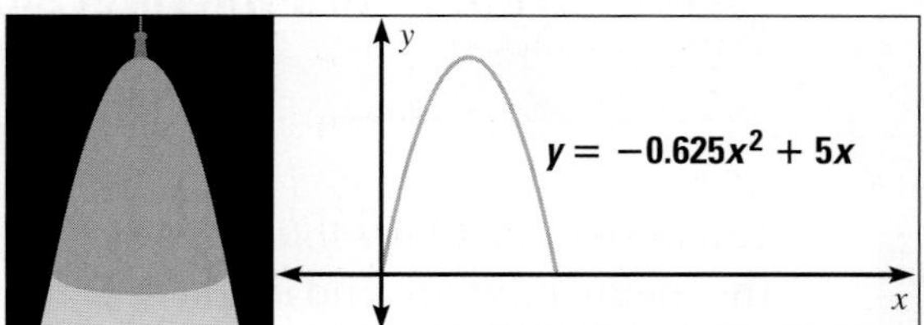

SHORT RESPONSE

8. From January to May in 2003, the monthly snowfall y (in inches) recorded at the observatory at Mount Washington in New Hampshire can be modeled by the function $y = -5.34x^2 + 17.4x + 21.2$ where x is the number of months since January. Did the greatest monthly snowfall during the given time period occur in January? *Explain.*

9. You throw a tennis ball upward from a height of 4 feet with an initial vertical velocity of 36 feet per second.

   a. Write an equation that models the height h (in feet) of the tennis ball as a function of the time t (in seconds) after it is thrown.

   b. Does the ball reach a height of 30 feet? *Explain.*

10. A band wants to have customized stickers printed. The table shows the cost y (in dollars) for x customized stickers.

Stickers, x	1000	2000	3000	4000
Cost (dollars), y	199	239	279	319

   a. Tell whether the data can be modeled by a *linear function*, an *exponential function*, or a *quadratic function*. Then write an equation for the function.

   b. If the number of stickers printed is doubled, does the price double? *Explain.*

10 Data Analysis

Lesson
10.1 CC.9-12.S.IC.1*
10.2 CC.9-12.S.ID.2*
10.3 CC.9-12.S.ID.5*
10.4 CC.9-12.S.ID.1*
10.5 CC.9-12.S.ID.1*

Before

You have learned the following skills, which you'll use in this chapter: finding the mean, median, and mode(s) of data, finding absolute values, and finding square roots.

Prerequisite Skills

VOCABULARY CHECK

1. Copy and complete: The _?_ of a numerical data set is the middle number when the values are written in numerical order.

SKILLS CHECK

Find the mean, median, and mode(s) of the data.

2. 0.2, 1.3, 0.9, 1.5, 2.1, 1.8, 0.6

3. 103, 121, 111, 194, 99, 160, 134, 160

Evaluate the expression.

4. $|2.65|$ **5.** $|-1.3|$ **6.** $|0.7|$ **7.** $|-54.01|$

Evaluate the expression.

8. $\sqrt{289}$ **9.** $\sqrt{121}$ **10.** $\sqrt{6.25}$ **11.** $\sqrt{1.44}$

Use a calculator to approximate the square root to the nearest hundredth.

12. $\sqrt{80}$ **13.** $\sqrt{13}$ **14.** $\sqrt{25.7}$ **15.** $\sqrt{0.89}$

Radius Images/Alamy Images

Now

In this chapter, you will apply the big ideas listed below and reviewed in the Chapter Summary. You will also use the key vocabulary listed below.

Big Ideas

1. **Analyzing sets of data**
2. **Making and interpreting data displays**

KEY VOCABULARY

- survey
- sample
- measure of dispersion
- range
- marginal frequency
- joint frequency
- stem-and-leaf plot
- frequency
- histogram
- box-and-whisker plot
- interquartile range
- outlier

Why?

You can use data analysis and data displays to represent both how data cluster around measures of central tendency and how data are spread out.

Animated Algebra

The animation illustrated below helps you to create a box-and-whisker plot to represent data, such as how the lengths of songs on a music CD, are distributed.

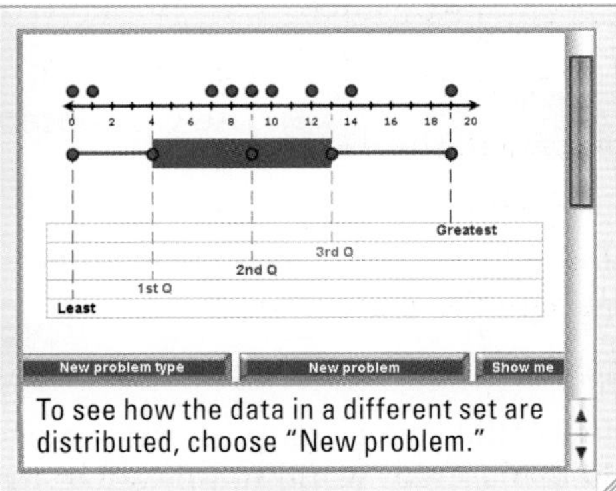

Animated Algebra at my.hrw.com

Investigating Samples

MATERIALS • red beans, pinto beans, container

Construct viable arguments and critique the reasoning of others.

QUESTION How well do different samples represent a situation?

EXPLORE Select a sample

STEP 1 ***Create the population*** Drop 80 pinto beans into a container. Place 20 red beans directly on top of the pinto beans. Then out of 100 beans in the jar, twenty percent of the beans are red beans.

STEP 2 ***Take a sample*** Without stirring, reach in and pull a handful of beans out of the jar. Count the number of red beans and the total number of beans in your handful. Record your results in a table like the one below. Return the beans to the jar.

STEP 3 ***Take a second sample*** Stir the jar thoroughly. Pull a handful of beans out of the jar. Record your results of this sample in your table. Return the beans to the jar.

STEP 4 ***Take a third sample*** Stir the jar thoroughly. Pull a handful of beans out of the jar. Add your results to your table.

Sample	Number of red beans, b	Total number of beans, T	Percent that is red (b/T)
one handful, not stirred	?	?	?
one handful, stirred	?	?	?
two handfuls, stirred	?	?	?

DRAW CONCLUSIONS Use your observations to complete these exercises

1. Compare the first two samples.
   a. How does stirring affect the results?
   b. Which sample seems to be more representative of the beans in the jar? Why do you think this occurred?
   c. How could you accomplish the same effect as stirring the beans when choosing a real-world sample for a survey or study?
2. Compare the last two samples. Which of these samples seems to be more representative of the beans in the jar? *Explain.*
3. You would like to perform a fourth trial. Which of the samples below do you think would produce the most representative sample? *Explain* your reasoning.

   Ⓐ 20 beans poured out, unstirred Ⓑ two handfuls, stirred
   Ⓒ three handfuls, stirred Ⓓ three handfuls, unstirred

10.1 Analyze Surveys and Samples

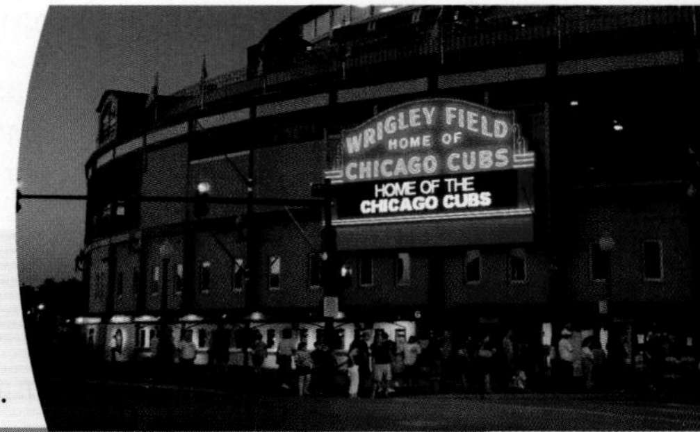

Before You found experimental probabilities.
Now You will identify populations and sampling methods.
Why? So you can analyze surveys of sports fans, as in Ex. 15.

Key Vocabulary
- survey
- population
- sample
- biased sample
- biased question

CC.9-12.S.IC.1 Understand statistics as a process for making inferences about population parameters based on a random sample from that population.*

A **survey** is a study of one or more characteristics of a group. The entire group you want information about is called a **population**. A survey of an entire population is called a *census*. When it is difficult to perform a census, you can survey a **sample**, which is a part of the population.

KEY CONCEPT *For Your Notebook*

Sampling Methods

In a **random sample**, every member of the population has an equal chance of being selected.

In a **stratified random sample**, the population is divided into distinct groups. Members are selected at random from each group.

In a **systematic sample**, a rule is used to select members of the population.

In a **convenience sample**, only members of the population who are easily accessible are selected.

In a **self-selected sample**, members of the population select themselves by volunteering.

EXAMPLE 1 Classify a sampling method

EMPLOYEE SAFETY The owners of a company with several factories conduct a survey to determine whether employees are informed about safety regulations. At each factory, 50 employees are chosen at random to complete the survey. Identify the population and classify the sampling method.

Solution

The population is all company employees. Because the population is divided into distinct groups (individual factories), with employees chosen at random from each group, the sample is a stratified random sample.

GUIDED PRACTICE for Example 1

1. **WHAT IF?** In Example 1, suppose the owners survey each employee whose last name begins with M. Classify the sampling method.

BIASED SAMPLES A sample chosen for a survey should be representative of the population. A **biased sample** is a sample that is not representative. In a biased sample, parts of the population may be over-represented or under-represented.

Random samples and stratified random samples (as in Example 1) are the most likely types of samples to be representative. A systematic sample may be representative if the rule used to choose individuals is not biased.

EXAMPLE 2 Identify a potentially biased sample

In Example 1, suppose the owners question 50 workers chosen at random from one factory. Is the method likely to result in a biased sample?

Solution

Workers at other factories may hold significantly different opinions, so the method may result in a biased sample.

BIASED QUESTIONS A question that encourages a particular response is a **biased question**. Survey questions should be worded to avoid bias.

EXAMPLE 3 Identify potentially biased questions

Tell whether the question is potentially biased. Explain your answer. If the question is potentially biased, rewrite it so that it is not.

a. Don't you agree that the voting age should be lowered to 16 because many 16-year-olds are responsible and informed?

b. Do you think the city should risk an increase in pollution by allowing expansion of the Northern Industrial Park?

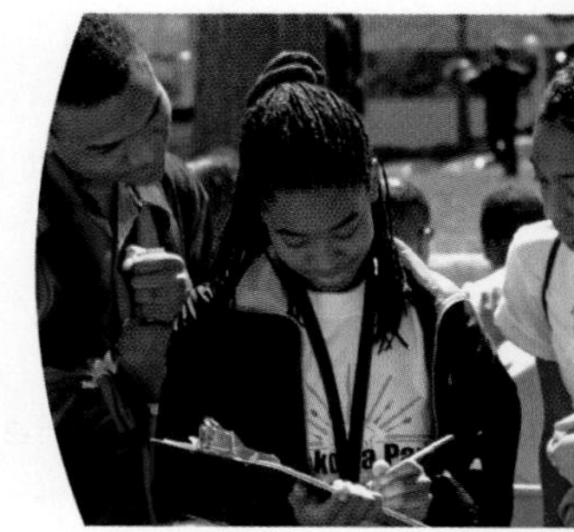

Solution

a. This question is biased because it suggests that lowering the voting age is a good thing to do. An unbiased question is "Do you think the voting age should be lowered to 16?"

b. This question is biased because it suggests that the proposed expansion will be bad for the environment. An unbiased question is "Do you think the city should allow expansion of the Northern Industrial Park?"

✓ GUIDED PRACTICE for Examples 2 and 3

2. **SOCCER** In a survey about Americans' interest in soccer, the first 25 people admitted to a high school soccer game were asked, "How interested are you in the world's most popular sport, soccer?"

   a. Is the sampling method likely to result in a biased sample? *Explain.*

   b. Is the question potentially biased? *Explain* your answer. If the question is potentially biased, rewrite it so that it is not.

10.1 EXERCISES

HOMEWORK KEY

○ = See **WORKED-OUT SOLUTIONS** Exs. 3 and 15

★ = **STANDARDIZED TEST PRACTICE** Exs. 2, 6, and 17

SKILL PRACTICE

1. **VOCABULARY** Copy and complete: In a(n) __?__ sample, participants are chosen using a rule.

2. ★ **WRITING** *Describe* the difference between a census and a sample.

POPULATIONS AND SAMPLES In Exercises 3–5, identify the population and classify the sampling method.

EXAMPLE 1 for Exs. 3–6

3. **RESTAURANT SERVICE** A restaurant manager wants to evaluate the restaurant's quality of service. Diners are given mail-in comment cards.

4. **EXTRACURRICULAR ACTIVITIES** Your school wants to know if students are satisfied with the school's extracurricular activities. In each grade, every tenth student on an alphabetized list is surveyed.

5. **CUSTOMER SATISFACTION** An airline wants to gather information on passenger satisfaction during a flight. A computer randomly selects 30 passengers to complete a survey.

6. ★ **MULTIPLE CHOICE** Scientists wanted to gather information about the birds in a particular region. They chose observation sites and asked bird watchers at those sites to record the number and types of birds they saw in 3 minutes. What population was being studied?

   (A) Birds (B) Sites (C) Scientists (D) Bird watchers

EXAMPLE 2 for Exs. 7–8

BIASED SAMPLES Tell whether the sampling method used is likely to result in a biased sample. *Explain*.

7. **NEIGHBORHOOD WATCH** A family wants to gather information from other residents on their street about forming a neighborhood watch. They survey every third house on both sides of the street.

8. **NURSE SURVEY** The American Nurses Association wanted to gather information about the working environment for nurses in hospitals. A survey for nurses was posted on the association's website.

EXAMPLE 3 for Exs. 9–11

BIASED QUESTIONS In Exercises 9 and 10, tell whether the question is potentially biased. *Explain* your answer.

9. Do you support the incumbent's tax plan or the challenger's tax plan?

10. Do you prefer the ease of shopping online or the fun of going to a mall?

11. **ERROR ANALYSIS** *Describe* and correct the error in revising the survey question "Don't you think the minimum driving age should be lower?" so that it is not biased.

   Not biased:
   Is the minimum driving age too high or too low?

12. **CHALLENGE** Two toothpaste manufacturers each claim that 4 out of every 5 dentists use their brand exclusively. Both manufacturers can support their claims with survey results. *Explain* how this is possible.

PROBLEM SOLVING

EXAMPLES 2 and 3 for Exs. 13–16

***Explain* why the question is biased. Then rewrite it so that it is not.**

13. Don't you agree that the school needs a new athletic field more than a new science lab?

14. Would you pay even higher concert ticket prices to finance a new arena?

15. **BASEBALL** Each baseball season, Major League Baseball (MLB) fans cast ballots to choose players for the MLB All-Star Game. Do the ballots cast necessarily represent the opinions of all baseball fans? *Explain.*

16. **WATER SAMPLING** Scientists designed a project in which students performed tests on local water sources each day. Students from 18 countries participated in the project. The results of the survey were used to assess the quality of the world's fresh water. Is the sample likely to be biased? *Explain.*

17. ★ **SHORT RESPONSE** You plan to report on the academic performance of students in your school for your school newspaper. *Describe* how you could choose a representative sample. Then write an unbiased question you could use to collect information on how many hours each day a student studies. *Explain* why your question is unbiased.

18. **CHALLENGE** The results of two five-year studies of a possible link between exercise and decreased risk of heart attack in men appear in a newspaper. The studies involve two different groups of 1000 men over the age of 40 who have never had a heart attack. In the *randomized experiment,* half of the 1000 men are chosen at random to take part in a supervised exercise program, while the other half continue their usual routines. In the *observational study,* the men are divided into two groups, those who exercise regularly and those who do not, and their health status is observed. Which study's results would you expect to be more reliable? *Explain.*

See **EXTRA PRACTICE** in Student Resources **ONLINE QUIZ** at my.hrw.com

10.2 Use Measures of Central Tendency and Dispersion

Before You analyzed surveys and samples.
Now You will compare measures of central tendency and dispersion.
Why? So you can analyze and compare data, as in Example 1.

Key Vocabulary
- **measure of dispersion**
- **range**
- **mean absolute deviation**

CC.9-12.S.ID.2 Use statistics appropriate to the shape of the data distribution to compare center (median, mean) and spread (interquartile range, standard deviation) of two or more different data sets.*

KEY CONCEPT *For Your Notebook*

Measures of Central Tendency

The **mean**, or *average*, of a numerical data set is denoted by $\overline{x}$, which is read as "x-bar." For the data set $x_1, x_2, \ldots, x_n$, the mean is $\overline{x} = \frac{x_1 + x_2 + \ldots + x_n}{n}$.

The **median** of a numerical data set is the middle number when the values are written in numerical order. If the data set has an even number of values, the median is the mean of the two middle values.

The **mode** of a data set is the value that occurs most frequently. There may be one mode, no mode, or more than one mode.

EXAMPLE 1 Compare measures of central tendency

The heights (in feet) of 8 waterfalls in the state of Washington are listed below. Which measure of central tendency best represents the data?

1000, 1000, 1181, 1191, 1200, 1268, 1328, 2584

Solution

$$\overline{x} = \frac{1000 + 1000 + 1181 + 1191 + 1200 + 1268 + 1328 + 2584}{8} = \frac{10{,}752}{8} = 1344$$

The median is the mean of the two middle values, 1191 and 1200, or 1195.5.

The mode is 1000.

▶ The median best represents the data. The mode is significantly less than most of the data, and the mean is significantly greater than most of the data.

Animated Algebra at my.hrw.com

✓ **GUIDED PRACTICE** for Example 1

1. **WHAT IF?** In Example 1, suppose you eliminate the greatest data value, 2584. Which measure of central tendency best represents the remaining data? *Explain* your reasoning.

MEASURES OF DISPERSION A **measure of dispersion** describes the dispersion, or spread, of data. Two such measures are the *range*, which gives the length of the interval containing the data, and the *mean absolute deviation*, which gives the average variation of the data from the mean.

REVIEW ABSOLUTE VALUE

You may want to review finding an absolute value.

KEY CONCEPT *For Your Notebook*

Measures of Dispersion

The **range** of a numerical data set is the difference of the greatest value and the least value.

The **mean absolute deviation** of the data set $x_1, x_2, \ldots, x_n$ is given by:

$$\text{Mean absolute deviation} = \frac{|x_1 - \bar{x}| + |x_2 - \bar{x}| + \ldots + |x_n - \bar{x}|}{n}$$

EXAMPLE 2 Compare measures of dispersion

RUNNING The top 10 finishing times (in seconds) for runners in two men's races are given. The times in a 100 meter dash are in set A, and the times in a 200 meter dash are in set B. Compare the spread of the data for the two sets using (**a**) the range and (**b**) the mean absolute deviation.

A: 10.62, 10.94, 10.94, 10.98, 11.05, 11.13, 11.15, 11.28, 11.29, 11.32

B: 21.37, 21.40, 22.23, 22.23, 22.34, 22.34, 22.36, 22.60, 22.66, 22.73

Solution

a. A: $11.32 - 10.62 = 0.7$ B: $22.73 - 21.37 = 1.36$

▶ The range of set B is greater than the range of set A. So, the data in B cover a wider interval than the data in A.

b. The mean of set A is 11.07, so the mean absolute deviation is:

$$\frac{|10.62 - 11.07| + |10.94 - 11.07| + \ldots + |11.32 - 11.07|}{10} = 0.164$$

The mean of set B is 22.226, so the mean absolute deviation is:

$$\frac{|21.37 - 22.226| + |21.40 - 22.226| + \ldots + |22.73 - 22.226|}{10} = 0.3364$$

▶ The mean absolute deviation of set B is greater, so the average variation from the mean is greater for the data in B than for the data in A.

REVIEW NEGATIVE NUMBERS

When using the formula for mean absolute deviation, you will encounter negative numbers.

✓ **GUIDED PRACTICE** for Example 2

2. **RUNNING** The top 10 finishing times (in seconds) for runners in a men's 400 meter dash are 46.89, 47.65, 48.15, 49.05, 49.19, 49.50, 49.68, 51.09, 53.31, and 53.68. *Compare* the spread of the data with that of set A in Example 2 using (**a**) the range and (**b**) the mean absolute deviation.

10.2 EXERCISES

HOMEWORK KEY

○ = See WORKED-OUT SOLUTIONS Exs. 7 and 19

★ = STANDARDIZED TEST PRACTICE Exs. 2, 9, 17, 19, and 22

SKILL PRACTICE

1. **VOCABULARY** Copy and complete: The value that occurs most frequently in a data set is called the _?_ of the data.

2. ★ **WRITING** How are measures of central tendency and measures of dispersion used to compare data?

EXAMPLE 1 for Exs. 3–10

MEASURES OF CENTRAL TENDENCY Find the mean, median, and mode(s) of the data.

3. 1, 1, 1, 2, 3, 3, 5, 5, 6

4. 9, 10, 12, 15, 16

5. 13, 16, 19, 20, 22, 25, 30, 31

6. 14, 15, 15, 14, 14, 16, 18, 15

7. 5.52, 5.44, 3.60, 5.76, 3.80, 7.22

8. 300, 320, 341, 348, 360, 333

9. ★ **MULTIPLE CHOICE** What is the median of the data set?

0.7, 0.3, 0.7, 0.8, 0.9, 0.4, 1.0, 1.6, 1.2

Ⓐ 0.7 Ⓑ 0.8 Ⓒ 0.9 Ⓓ 1.0

10. **ERROR ANALYSIS** *Describe* and correct the error in finding the median of the data set.

7 4 6 2 4 6 8 8 3

The median is 4.

EXAMPLE 2 for Exs. 11–16

MEASURES OF DISPERSION Find the range and mean absolute deviation of the data. Round to the nearest hundredth, if necessary.

11. 30, 35, 20, 85, 60

12. 111, 135, 115, 120, 145, 130

13. 30, 45, 52, 48, 100, 45, 42, 45

14. 505, 510, 480, 550, 495, 500

15. 1.25, 1.50, 1.70, 0.85, 1.00, 1.25

16. 38.2, 80.1, 2.6, 84.2, 2.5, 5.5

17. ★ **WRITING** *Explain* why the mean absolute deviation of a data set is generally a better measure of dispersion than the range.

18. **CHALLENGE** Suppose you **(a)** add the same constant to each value in a data set or **(b)** multiply each value by the same nonzero constant. *Describe* the effect on the mean, median, mode, range, and mean absolute deviation.

PROBLEM SOLVING

EXAMPLE 1 for Exs. 19–20

19. ★ **SHORT RESPONSE** The weights (in pounds) of ten pumpkins are 22, 21, 24, 24, 5, 24, 5, 23, 24, and 24.
    a. What is the range of the pumpkin weights?
    b. Find the mean, median, and mode(s) of the pumpkin weights.
    c. Which measure of central tendency best represents the data? *Explain.*

20. **POPULATION** The population densities (in people per square mile) for each of the 10 most densely populated states in 2003 were 719.0, 418.5, 315.6, 563.6, 820.6, 1164.6, 406.5, 279.3, 275.9, and 1029.9.

   a. Find the mean, median, and mode(s) of the data set.

   b. Which measure of central tendency best represents the data? *Explain.*

EXAMPLE 2 for Ex. 21

21. **BOWLING** The average scores of the bowlers on two different bowling teams are given. *Compare* the spreads of the data sets using (**a**) the range and (**b**) the mean absolute deviation.

   Team 1: 162, 150, 173, 202 **Team 2:** 140, 153, 187, 196

22. ★ **EXTENDED RESPONSE** Use the information in the article about the sediment discharges of U.S. rivers. For parts (a)–(c), round your answers to the nearest whole number, if necessary.

   a. Find the mean and the median of the data for all seven rivers. Which measure represents the data better? *Explain.*

   b. Find the mean of the data for the other six rivers, excluding the Mississippi River. Does this mean represent the data better than the mean you found in part (a)? *Explain.*

   c. Find the range and mean absolute deviation of the data for all seven rivers. *Describe* what the measures tell you about the dispersion of the data.

Sunday Edition

MISSISSIPPI RIVER DOMINATES AS SEDIMENT MOVER

The Mississippi River discharges an average of 230 million tons of sediment per year. Other U.S. rivers with the greatest average sediment discharges (in millions of tons per year) are the Copper (80), Yukon (65), Columbia (40), Susitna (25), Eel (15), and Brazos (11) rivers.

23. **CHALLENGE** A student asked 12 friends how many sisters and brothers they have. The line plot shows the results.

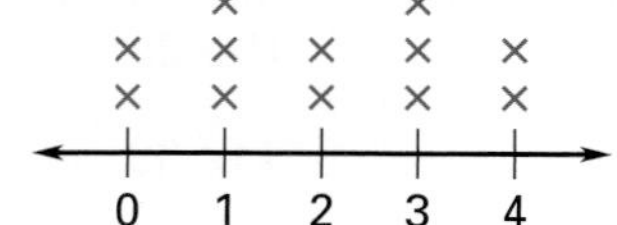

   a. *Describe* how you would find the mean, median, and mode of the data. Then calculate each value.

   b. The *weight* of a distinct data value is the quotient of its frequency and the total number of data values. Compute the *weighted average* of the data by taking the sum of the products of the distinct values and their weights. *Explain* why the weighted average of the data is simply the mean.

QUIZ

1. **HOTEL SURVEY** A hotel manager leaves guest comment cards in each room. Identify the population and classify the sampling method.

In Exercises 2 and 3, find the range and mean absolute deviation of the data. Round to the nearest hundredth, if necessary.

2. 62, 63, 70, 40, 50, 60

3. 14, 18, 22, 14, 14, 6, 17

Extension Calculate Variance and Standard Deviation

GOAL Find the variance and standard deviation of a data set.

Key Vocabulary
- **variance**
- **standard deviation**

In addition to range and mean absolute deviation, *variance* and *standard deviation* are also measures of dispersion that can be used to describe the spread of a set of data.

CC.9-12.S.ID.3 Interpret differences in shape, center, and spread in the context of the data sets, accounting for possible effects of extreme data points (outliers).*

KEY CONCEPT *For Your Notebook*

Variance and Standard Deviation

The **variance** of a numerical data set is denoted by σ^2, which is read as "sigma squared." For the data set $x_1, x_2, \ldots, x_n$, the variance is given by:

$$\sigma^2 = \frac{(x_1 - \overline{x})^2 + (x_2 - \overline{x})^2 + \ldots + (x_n - \overline{x})^2}{n}$$

The **standard deviation** of a numerical data set is denoted by σ, which is read as "sigma." For the data set $x_1, x_2, \ldots, x_n$, the standard deviation is the square root of the variance and is given by:

$$\sigma = \sqrt{\frac{(x_1 - \overline{x})^2 + (x_2 - \overline{x})^2 + \ldots + (x_n - \overline{x})^2}{n}}$$

EXAMPLE 1 Find variance and standard deviation

E-MAIL SIZES The sizes of e-mails (in kilobytes) in your inbox are 1, 2, 2, 7, 4, 1, 10, 3, and 6. Find the variance and standard deviation of the data.

Solution

IMPROVE ACCURACY
The more accurate the value of σ^2 you use to calculate σ, the more accurate the value of σ you obtain. In the final answer, both results are rounded.

STEP 1 **Find** the mean.

$$\overline{x} = \frac{1 + 2 + 2 + 7 + 4 + 1 + 10 + 3 + 6}{9} = \frac{36}{9} = 4$$

STEP 2 **Find** the variance.

$$\sigma^2 = \frac{(1 - 4)^2 + (2 - 4)^2 + \ldots + (6 - 4)^2}{9} = \frac{76}{9} = 8.444\ldots$$

STEP 3 **Find** the standard deviation.

$$\sigma = \sqrt{\sigma^2} = \sqrt{8.444\ldots} \approx 2.9$$

▶ The variance is about 8.4, and the standard deviation is about 2.9.

USING A CALCULATOR You can use a graphing calculator to find the standard deviation of a data set.

EXAMPLE 2 Find standard deviation

HOUSEHOLDS In 2000 the numbers (in thousands) of households in the 13 states with Atlantic Ocean coastline are given. Find the standard deviation of the data.

299 6338 3006 518 1981 2444 475 3065
7057 3132 408 1534 2699

Solution

STEP 1 **Enter** the data into a graphing calculator. Press STAT and select Edit. Enter the data into List 1 (L_1).

STEP 2 **Calculate** the standard deviation. Press STAT. From the CALC menu select 1-Var Stats.

On this screen, σ_x stands for standard deviation.

▶ The standard deviation of the data is about 2056.

PRACTICE

EXAMPLE 1 for Exs. 1–3

Use the formulas for variance and standard deviation to find the variance and standard deviation of the data. Round to the nearest tenth, if necessary.

1. 4, 5, 3, 2, 4, 7, 8, 9, 4, 6, 7, 8, 9, 1
2. 14, 16, 19, 20, 28, 7, 24, 15, 16, 30, 33, 24
3. 110, 205, 322, 608, 1100, 240, 185, 552, 418, 300

EXAMPLE 2 for Exs. 4–7

In Exercises 4–6, use a graphing calculator to find the standard deviation of the data. Round to the nearest tenth, if necessary.

4. 3.5, 3.8, 4.1, 3.0, 3.8, 3.6, 3.3, 4.0, 3.8, 3.9, 3.2, 3.0, 3.3, 4.2, 3.0
5. 66, 43, 9, 28, 7, 5, 90, 9, 78, 6, 69, 55, 28, 43, 10, 54, 13, 88, 21, 4
6. 1002, 1540, 480, 290, 2663, 3800, 690, 1301, 1750, 2222, 4040, 800

7. **REASONING** The heights (in feet) of 9 pecan trees are 72, 84, 81, 78, 80, 86, 70, 80, and 88. For parts (a)–(c) below, round your answers to the nearest tenth.
   a. Find the standard deviation of the data.
   b. Suppose you include a pecan tree with a height of 136 feet. *Predict* the effect of the additional data on the standard deviation of the data set.
   c. Find the standard deviation of the new data set in part (b). *Compare* the results to your prediction in part (b).

MIXED REVIEW of Problem Solving

MATHEMATICAL PRACTICES Make sense of problems and persevere in solving them.

1. **MULTI-STEP PROBLEM** A doctor would like to extend her office hours to better accommodate her patients. She asks each patient who visits her office on Tuesday which day the patient thinks the hours should be extended.

   a. Identify the population and classify the sampling method.

   b. Tell whether the survey method used is likely to result in a biased sample.

2. **GRIDDED ANSWER** The average lengths (in hours) of several morning commutes are listed below. How many minutes is the mean commute?

   0.25, 0.20, 0.50, 0.50, 0.50, 0.05, 0.65, 1.00, 1.50, 0.75, 0.50, 1.10, 0.60, 0.80, 1.00, 0.10

3. **EXTENDED RESPONSE** The prices (in dollars) of portable DVD players at two different stores are listed below.

   Store A: 280, 200, 260, 230, 200, 150, 300, 260, 500, 190

   Store B: 350, 190, 230, 250, 400, 200, 200, 220, 185, 150

   a. Find the mean, median, and mode(s) of each data set. Which measure of central tendency best represents each data set? *Explain* your reasoning.

   b. Find the range and mean absolute deviation of each data set. Which store's prices are more spread out? *Explain.*

   c. Can any of the prices of the portable DVD players be considered outliers? *Explain* your reasoning.

4. **OPEN-ENDED** A clothing store sells several different styles of jeans. The mean price of the jeans is $27. The median price of the jeans is $27.50. The mode of the prices is $20. Make a list of prices of jeans that has these measures of central tendency.

5. **SHORT RESPONSE** A group of students plans to lobby their town officials to enact conservation rules protecting the habitat of a species of turtle in their area. First, the students will conduct a survey to determine whether there is voter support for such rules. *Describe* how the students might choose a representative sample for their survey.

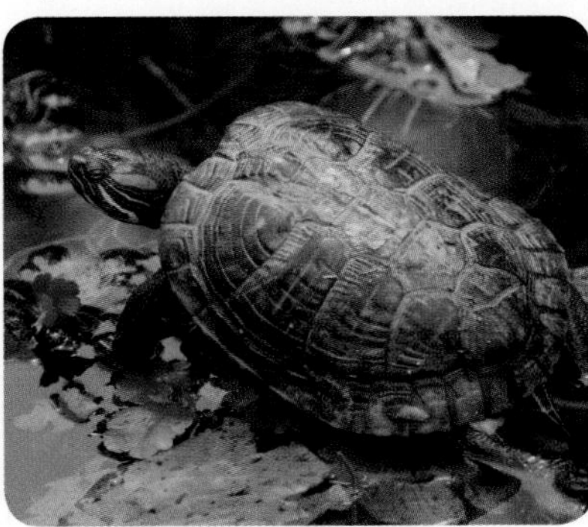

6. **GRIDDED ANSWER** A commuter records the length of time (in minutes) that she waits for a morning subway train each day for two work weeks. The times are listed below.

   5, 4, 10, 6, 12, 9, 3, 8, 5, 2

   What is the standard deviation of the times to the nearest tenth?

10.3 Analyze Data

Before You found measures of central tendency.

Now You will find frequencies in a two-way frequency table.

Why? So you can use data about dogs in a store in Exercise 3.

Key Vocabulary
- **marginal frequency**
- **joint frequency**

A two-way frequency table shows the number of items in various categories. Every element in the sample must fit into one of the categories and there must be no overlap between categories.

CC.9-12.S.ID.5 Recognize and explain the concepts of conditional probability and independence in everyday language and everyday situations.*

KEY CONCEPT *For Your Notebook*

Two-way frequency table

A two-way frequency table divides the data into categories across the top and down the side.

	Apples	Oranges	Total
Boys	15	18	33
Girls	21	16	37
Total	36	34	70

The body of the table gives the **joint frequencies**.

The row and column totals give the **marginal frequencies**.

EXAMPLE 1 Read information from a two-way frequency table

The table shows the results of students naming their favorite subject.

	Math	Science	English	Total
Miss Bailey's homeroom	8	6	5	19
Mr. Cole's homeroom	4	7	9	20
Total	12	13	14	39

a. How many students in Miss Bailey's homeroom prefer math?

b. How many students from both homerooms prefer science?

Solution

a. The cell in the row for Miss Bailey's homeroom and in the column for Math contains 8, so 8 students in her homeroom prefer math.

b. The cell in the total row and in the column for Science contains 13, so 13 students prefer Science.

EXAMPLE 2 Make a two-way frequency table

Make a two-way frequency table for the following data.

There are 175 freshmen taking a foreign language. Of these, 88 take Spanish, 46 take French, and the rest take German. No one takes more than one language. There are 42 boys taking Spanish, 31 girls taking French, and a total of 89 girls taking a language.

Solution

The categories are Spanish, French, German, boys, and girls. Fill in the given information. Then look for ways to calculate the missing values.

For example, the number of girls taking Spanish is $88 - 42 = 46$. The number of boys taking a foreign language is $175 - 89 = 86$. The total number of students taking German is $175 - (88 + 46)$.

AVOID ERRORS
Be sure to enter the given information in the correct cells of the table.

	Spanish	French	German	Total
Boys	42	15	29	86
Girls	46	31	12	89
Total	88	46	41	175

GUIDED PRACTICE for Examples 1 and 2

1. Using the table in Example 1, tell whether more students in Mr. Cole's homeroom prefer science or English.

2. There are 152 students who play golf, basketball, or soccer. No one plays more than one of these sports. There are 22 who play golf, 50 who play basketball, and the rest play soccer. There are 10 boys who play golf, 26 girls who play basketball, and a total of 80 boys who play one of these sports. Make a two-way frequency table for the data.

EXAMPLE 3 Analyze a situation in a two-way table

The table shows where students at a university live.

	Live on Campus	Live off Campus	Total
Men	3216	4010	7226
Women	3824	3758	7582
Total	7040	7768	14,808

a. Do more students live on campus or off campus?

b. Is it also true that more women live off campus than on campus?

Solution

a. Look at the marginal frequencies in the Total row. More students live off campus.

b. No. Even though the marginal frequencies show that more students live off campus, looking at just the row for women, you can see that more women live on campus than off campus.

10.3 EXERCISES

HOMEWORK KEY

○ = **See WORKED-OUT SOLUTIONS** Exs, 3, 7, and 15

★ = **STANDARDIZED TEST PRACTICE** Exs. 2, 8, 15, and 18

SKILL PRACTICE

1. **VOCABULARY** copy and complete: The body of a two-way frequency table gives the _?_ of the categories involved.

2. ★ **WRITING** Explain how you find the marginal frequency of a category in a two-way frequency table. Give an example.

EXAMPLE 1 for Exs. 3–5

READING A TWO-WAY TABLE Answer the questions based on the table showing the number of different kinds of puppies at a pet store.

	Labradors	Poodles	Yorkies	Total
Males	7	5	3	15
Females	4	8	6	18
Total	11	13	9	33

3. How many male poodles does the pet store have?

4. How many female puppies does the pet store have?

5. How many more labradors than yorkies does the pet store have?

EXAMPLE 2 for Exs. 6–7

6. **COPY AND COMPLETE** Copy and complete the two-way table showing data about cars sold.

	2 door	4 door	Total
6 cylinder	586	?	?
8 cylinder	?	840	?
Total	?	1564	2465

7. **MAKING A TWO-WAY TABLE** You surveyed 82 students in your grade and found that twenty-three have 2 brothers and twenty-eight have 1 brother. Nine students are only children, ten have only 1 sister, seven have only 1 brother, six have 2 sisters and 1 brother, twenty-two have 2 sisters, twenty-seven have no sisters, and eight have 1 sister and 2 brothers. Make a two-way frequency table of the given information.

8. ★ **MULTIPLE CHOICE** Use this two-way table to find how many 4 bedroom houses with 3 baths are for sale.

	3 Bedroom	4 Bedroom	Total
1 Bath	10	1	11
2 Bath	68	47	115
3 Bath	31	75	106
Total	109	122	232

Ⓐ 31 Ⓑ 47 Ⓒ 68 Ⓓ 75

EXAMPLE 3
for Exs. 9–11

ANALYZING A TWO-WAY TABLE **The table shows the number of votes each student received from the various classes in the Student Government President Election.**

	Freshmen	Sophomores	Juniors	Seniors	Total
Matt	92	86	110	110	359
Olivia	77	99	82	71	326
Katy	115	94	90	149	448
Total	284	279	282	288	1133

9. If Matt received the most votes from the students in his class, what year student is Matt?

10. Did any candidate have the most votes from more than one class? If so, who and which classes? *Explain.*

11. Which student won the election?

12. **CHALLENGE** Create a two-way table from the given information. Water and iced tea come in 12-ounce and 16-ounce bottles. The number of 16-ounce bottles is one less than the number of 12-ounce bottles. There are 11 more bottles of iced tea than water. There are 16 bottles of water and the number of 12-ounce bottles of water is 2 less than twice the number of 16-ounce bottles of water.

PROBLEM SOLVING

In Exercises 13–15, use the given two-way table showing sandwiches sold at a deli to answer the questions.

	Ham	Chicken	Salami	Total
White bread	65	41	37	143
Wheat bread	97	75	62	234
Total	162	116	99	377

EXAMPLE 1
for Exs. 13–15

13. **SANDWICHES** How many more ham sandwiches on wheat bread were sold than chicken sandwiches on white bread?

14. **PREDICT** If you choose one sandwich at random would it be more likely to be chicken on wheat bread or ham on white bread? *Explain.*

15. ★ **SHORT RESPONSE** If you know that a customer is going to order a sandwich on wheat bread, what is the most likely type of sandwich that customer will order? *Explain.*

16. **MUSIC** There are 33 students in choir and 74 in band. No one is in both. Twenty-three of these students are less than 5 feet tall and 24 are more than 6 feet tall. Six choir members are less than 5 feet tall while twenty-two choir members are between 5 and 6 feet tall.

a. How many students in the choir are more than 6 feet tall?

b. How many students in the band are between 5 and 6 feet tall?

c. If you choose a student at random from the choir and from the band, which student is more likely to be between 5 and 6 feet tall? *Explain.*

○ = See **WORKED-OUT SOLUTIONS** in Student Resources

★ = **STANDARDIZED TEST PRACTICE**

17. **VEGETABLES** A gardener planted two tomato and green pepper plants in each of two types of soil to test fertilizers. The table shows the number of tomatoes and green peppers harvested from each set of plants. Which type of soil seems better for each vegetable?

	Tomatoes	Green Peppers	Total
Fertilizer- fortified soil	56	37	93
Soil fertilized every 2 weeks	65	19	84
Total	121	56	77

a. Does one treatment appear to better for tomatoes?

b. Does one treatment appear to better for green peppers?

c. Looking at just the totals, which treatment appears to be better? Is this the best choice for both types of plants? *Explain.*

18. ★ **EXTENDED RESPONSE** Sangee, Tom, and Maleho have classical and rock CDs. They have a total of 141 CDs, of which 47 are classical. Sangee has 19 rock CDs and 26 classical CDs, Tom has 38 rock CDs, and Maleho has 49 CDs.

a. **Model** Make a two-way table to display this data.

b. **Calculate** If Sangee bought a classical CD, how would his classical CD total compare to Maleho's rock CD total?

c. **Analyze** If a CD is chosen at random from those owned by these three boys, would it be more likely to be classical or rock?

19. **CHALLENGE** There were 1809 tickets sold to a play, of which 800 were for the main floor. These tickets consisted of $2x + y$ adult tickets on the main floor, $x - 40$ child tickets on the main floor, $x + 2y$ adult tickets in the balcony, and $3x - y - 80$ child tickets in the balcony.

a. Find the values of x and y.

b. Find the number of adult balcony tickets sold.

c. Find the number of child main floor tickets sold.

Investigate Dot Plots

Model with mathematics.

MATERIALS • ruler, graph paper

QUESTION How do you represent data in a dot plot?

Data can be represented by dots in a display called a dot plot. A dot plot shows the frequency of data and how the data are distributed.

EXPLORE Draw a dot plot

STEP 1 *Collect data*

Look up the low temperature for a city in the northern United States for each day in January of last year.

STEP 2 *Make a dot plot*

Use graph paper to draw a horizontal axis. Label it Temperatures and number it using a reasonable scale. Place a dot above the appropriate temperature to represent the low temperature for each day in January. For example, put a dot over the temperature 4 to indicate that the low temperature on one day was 4°F. The sample graph shows that it was 4°F on two days and −3°F on one day.

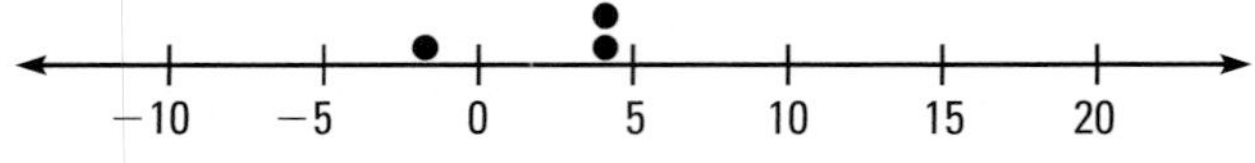

DRAW CONCLUSIONS Use your observations to complete these exercises

1. Examine your dot plot. What is the range of the data values?
2. Are the data tightly clustered or spread apart?
3. Is there a value that occurs more often than the others? If so, what does this mean in the context of the data?
4. If you were to add the temperature for February 1st to your dot plot, what would you expect it to be? Explain your reasoning. What types of values would be surprising? Why?
5. How would your dot plot change if you collected temperatures from a summer month rather than from January?
6. Compare the data in the dot plots.

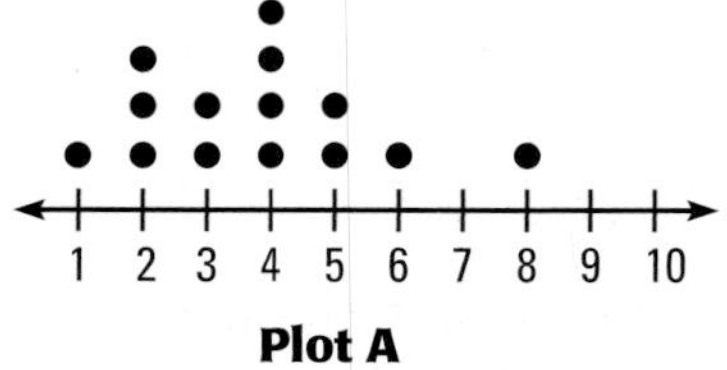

Plot A

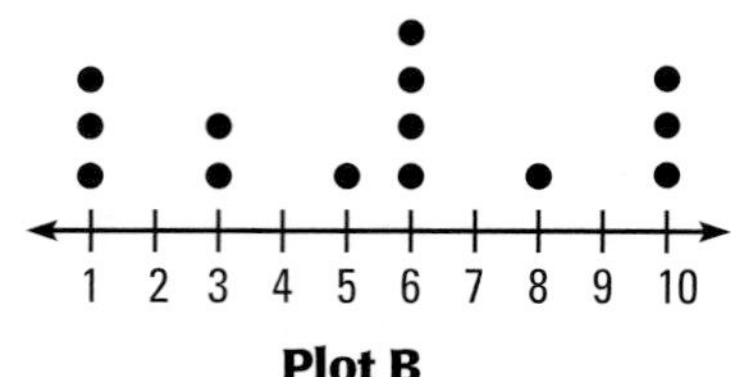

Plot B

10.4 Interpret Stem-and-Leaf Plots and Histograms

Before You found measures of central tendency and dispersion.

Now You will make stem-and-leaf plots and histograms.

Why? So you can analyze historical data, as in Ex. 20.

Key Vocabulary
- **stem-and-leaf plot**
- **frequency**
- **frequency table**
- **histogram**

A **stem-and-leaf plot** is a data display that organizes data based on their digits. Each value is separated into a *stem* (the leading digit(s)) and a *leaf* (the last digit). A stem-and-leaf plot has a key that tells you how to read the data. A stem-and-leaf plot shows how the data are distributed.

EXAMPLE 1 Make a stem-and-leaf plot

CC.9-12.S.ID.1 Represent data with plots on the real number line (dot plots, histograms, and box plots).*

BASEBALL The number of home runs hit by the 20 baseball players with the best single-season batting averages in Major League Baseball since 1900 are listed below. Make a stem-and-leaf plot of the data.

14, 25, 8, 8, 7, 7, 19, 37, 39, 18, 42, 23, 4, 32, 14, 21, 3, 12, 19, 41

Solution

STEP 1 **Separate** the data into stems and leaves.

Home Runs

Stem	Leaves
0	8 8 7 7 4 3
1	4 9 8 4 2 9
2	5 3 1
3	7 9 2
4	2 1

Key: 1 | 4 = 14 home runs

STEP 2 **Write** the leaves in increasing order.

Home Runs

Stem	Leaves
0	3 4 7 7 8 8
1	2 4 4 8 9 9
2	1 3 5
3	2 7 9
4	1 2

Key: 1 | 4 = 14 home runs

INTERPRET INTERVALS
Each stem in a stem-and-leaf plot defines an interval. For instance, the stem 2 represents the interval 20–29. The data values in this interval are 21, 23, and 25.

✓ GUIDED PRACTICE for Example 1

1. **U.S. HISTORY** The years in which each of the first 20 states were admitted to the Union are listed below. Make a stem-and-leaf plot of the years.

   1788, 1787, 1788, 1816, 1792, 1812, 1788, 1788, 1817, 1788,
   1787, 1788, 1789, 1803, 1787, 1790, 1788, 1796, 1791, 1788

2. **REASONING** In Example 1, describe the distribution of the data on the intervals represented by the stems. Are the data clustered together in a noticeable way? *Explain.*

EXAMPLE 2 Interpret a stem-and-leaf plot

GYMNASTICS The back-to-back stem-and-leaf plot shows the ages of members of the U.S men's and women's 2004 Olympic gymnastics teams. Compare the ages of the gymnasts on the two teams.

2004 Olympic Gymnast Ages

Men	Stem	Women
	1	6 6 8 8
7 4 3 1 1	2	5 6
0	3	

Key: 1 | 2 | 5 = 21, 25

Solution

Consider the distribution of the data. The interval for 10–19 years old contains more than half of the female gymnasts. The interval for 20–29 years old contains more than half of the male gymnasts. The clustering of the data shows that the men's team was generally older than the women's team.

FREQUENCY The **frequency** of an interval is the number of data values in that interval. A stem-and-leaf plot shows the frequencies of intervals determined by the stems. A **frequency table** is also used to group data values into equal intervals, with no gaps between intervals and no intervals overlapping.

A **histogram** is a bar graph that displays data from a frequency table. Each bar represents an interval. Because intervals have equal size, the bars have equal width. A bar's length indicates the frequency. There is no space between bars.

EXAMPLE 3 Make a histogram

SANDWICH PRICES The prices (in dollars) of sandwiches at a restaurant are listed below. Make a histogram of the data.

4.00, 4.00, 4.25, 4.50, 4.75, 4.25, 5.95, 5.50, 5.50, 5.75

Solution

CHOOSE AN INTERVAL SIZE
To choose the interval size for a frequency table, divide the range of the data by the number of intervals you want the table to have. Use the quotient as an approximate interval size.

STEP 1 **Choose** intervals of equal size that cover all of the data values. Organize the data using a frequency table.

Prices	Sandwiches
\$4.00–4.49	||||
\$4.50–4.99	||
\$5.00–5.49	
\$5.50–5.99	||||

STEP 2 **Draw** the bars of the histogram using the intervals from the frequency table.

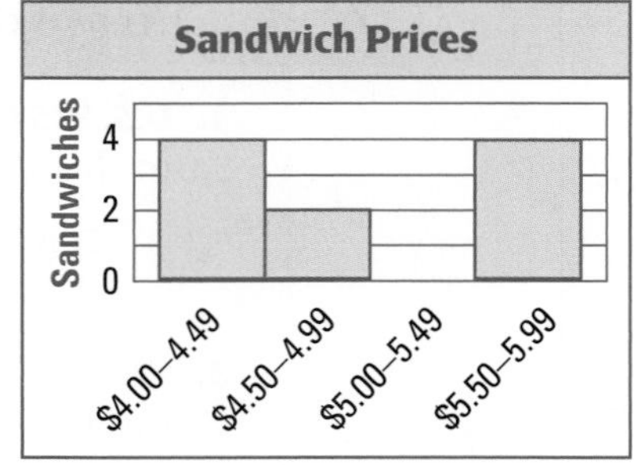

 **GUIDED PRACTICE** for Examples 2 and 3

3. **TELEVISION** The back-to-back stem-and-leaf plot shows the percents of students in 24 countries who report watching television for 4 or more hours each day. *Compare* the data for female and male students.

Female		Male
9 9 9 8 8 8 6 6 5 4	1	7 8 9
6 6 5 4 3 3 0 0	2	0 1 2 2 4 5 5 6 6 7 7 8
8 3 2 2 1	3	4 6 6 8 8 9
1	4	0 6 6

Key: 4 | 1 | 7 = 14%, 17%

4. **PRECIPITATION** The average number of days each month with precipitation of 0.01 inch or more in Buffalo, New York, are 20, 17, 16, 14, 13, 11, 10, 10, 11, 12, 16, and 19. Make a histogram of the data.

10.4 EXERCISES

HOMEWORK KEY
○ = See **WORKED-OUT SOLUTIONS** Exs. 3 and 19
★ = **STANDARDIZED TEST PRACTICE** Exs. 2, 8, 9, 15, and 20

SKILL PRACTICE

1. **VOCABULARY** Copy and complete: The number of data values in an interval is the __?__ of that interval.

2. ★ **WRITING** *Explain* how a histogram differs from a bar graph.

EXAMPLE 1 for Exs. 3–7

STEM-AND-LEAF PLOTS Make a stem-and-leaf plot of the data.

3. 17, 31, 42, 33, 38, 20, 24, 30, 39, 38, 35, 20, 55

4. 2, 8, 17, 7, 14, 20, 32, 5, 33, 6, 6, 8, 11, 9

5. 121, 124, 133, 111, 109, 182, 105, 127, 156, 179, 142

6. 1.23, 1.05, 1.11, 1.29, 1.31, 1.19, 1.45, 1.22, 1.19, 1.35

7. **ERROR ANALYSIS** *Describe* and correct the error in making a stem-and-leaf plot of the following data: 18, 19, 18, 19, 20, 20, 21, 22, 18, 19, 20, 21, 23, 21.

STEM-AND-LEAF PLOT In Exercises 8 and 9, consider the back-to-back stem-and-leaf plot that shows data sets *A* and *B*.

Set *A*		Set *B*
1 1 1	2	
4 3 3 2	3	1 2 2
2 0	4	1 1 3 4
	5	0 1

Key: 2 | 3 | 1 = 32, 31

8. ★ **MULTIPLE CHOICE** What is the median of data set *A*?

Ⓐ 21 Ⓑ 32 Ⓒ 33 Ⓓ 34

9. ★ **MULTIPLE CHOICE** What is the range of data set *B*?

Ⓐ 18 Ⓑ 19 Ⓒ 20 Ⓓ 21

EXAMPLE 3
for Exs. 10–14

10. **ERROR ANALYSIS** *Describe* and correct the error in creating a histogram using the frequency table below.

Ages	0–9	10–19	20–29	30–39
Frequency	|||	~~||||~~ |		||||

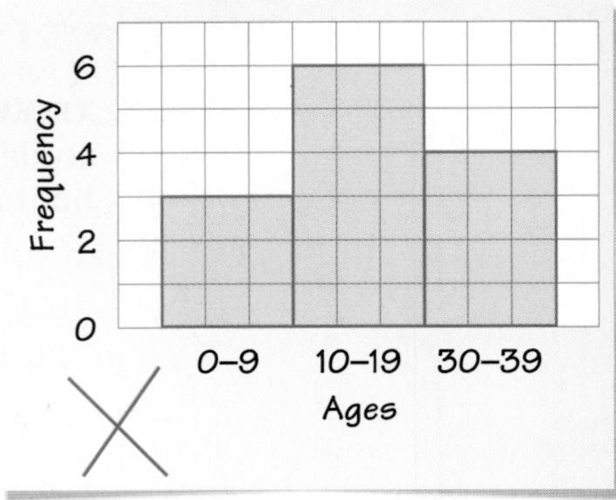

HISTOGRAMS **Make a histogram of the data.**

11. 55, 82, 94, 75, 61, 69, 77, 98, 81, 83, 75, 90, 51

12. 12, 0, 22, 31, 14, 7, 7, 45, 31, 28, 21, 25, 25, 18

13. 0.01, 0.13, 0.09, 1.10, 1.33, 0.99, 0.50, 0.95, 1.05, 1.50, 0.75, 1.01

14. 111, 109, 224, 657, 284, 120, 119, 415, 180, 105, 208, 108

15. ★ **WRITING** *Explain* why a histogram can show the distribution of the data below better than a stem-and-leaf plot.

15, 21, 18, 10, 12, 11, 17, 18, 16, 12, 20, 12, 17, 16

16. **CHALLENGE** Create a stem-and-leaf plot that has the same distribution of data as the histogram shown. *Explain* the steps you took to create the stem-and-leaf plot.

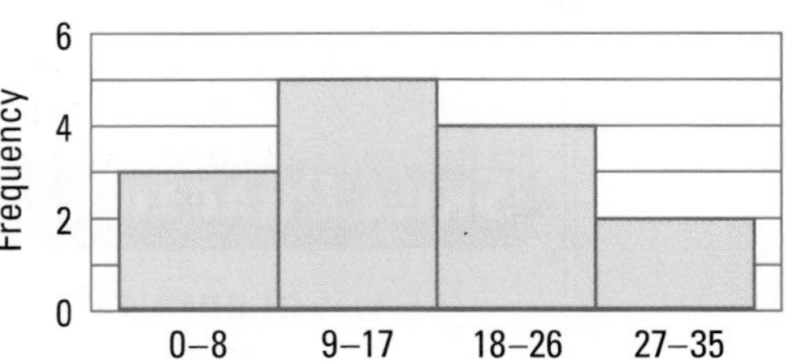

PROBLEM SOLVING

EXAMPLE 1
for Ex. 17

17. **HEIGHTS** The heights (in inches) of players on a boys' basketball team are as follows: 80, 76, 81, 69, 81, 78, 74, 68, 78, 74, 81, 72, 69, 81, 70. Make a stem-and-leaf plot of the heights.

EXAMPLE 3
for Exs. 18–19

18. **SURVEY** A survey asked people how many 8 ounce glasses of water they drink in one day. The results are below. Make a histogram of the data.

3, 0, 9, 1, 4, 2, 11, 5, 3, 6, 0, 5, 7, 8, 5, 2, 9, 6, 10, 2, 4

19. **MEMORY** A survey asked people how many phone numbers they have memorized. The results are shown in the table.

Phone numbers	1–5	6–10	11–15	16–20	21–25
Frequency	88	85	50	28	14

a. Make a histogram of the data.

b. What is the probability that a person surveyed, chosen at random, has 11–25 phone numbers memorized?

◯ = See WORKED-OUT SOLUTIONS in Student Resources

★ = STANDARDIZED TEST PRACTICE

EXAMPLE 2
for Ex. 20

20. ★ EXTENDED RESPONSE The back-to-back stem-and-leaf plot shows the numbers of days the House of Representatives and the Senate spent in session each year from 1996 to 2004.

Days in Session

House		Senate
9 0	11	
3 2	12	
7 5 3 2	13	2 3
2	14	1 3 9
	15	3
	16	2 7
	17	3

Key: 2 | 14 | 1 = 142, 141

a. What was the median number of days the House of Representatives spent in session? the Senate?

b. What is the range of the number of days the House of Representatives spent in session? the Senate?

c. *Compare* the data for the House of Representatives and the Senate. What does the distribution of the data tell you?

21. MAYFLOWER The known ages (in years) of adult male passengers on the *Mayflower* at the time of its departure are listed below.

21, 34, 29, 38, 30, 54, 39, 20, 35, 64, 37, 45, 21, 25, 55, 45, 40, 38, 38, 21, 21, 20, 34, 38, 50, 41, 48, 18, 32, 21, 32, 49, 30, 42, 30, 25, 38, 25, 20

a. Make a stem-and-leaf plot of the ages.

b. Find the median age and range of the ages.

c. According to one source, the age of passenger Thomas English was unknown at the time of the *Mayflower's* departure. What is the probability that he was 18–29 years old? *Explain* your reasoning.

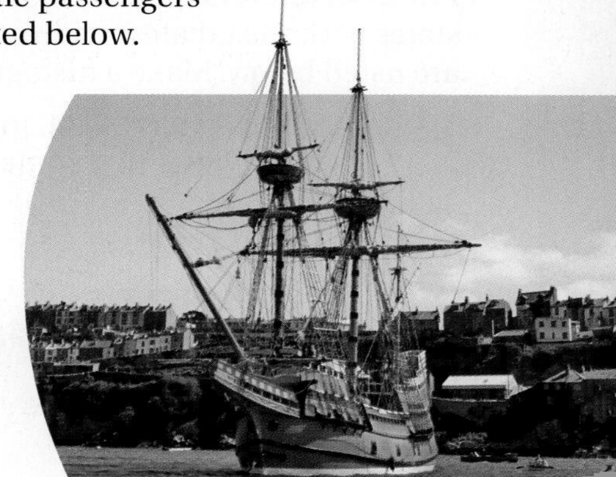

Replica of the *Mayflower*

22. CHALLENGE The first two rows of a *cumulative frequency table* for the data in Exercise 21 are shown. The *cumulative frequency* for a given interval is the sum of the current frequency and all preceding frequencies. A histogram constructed from a cumulative frequency table is called a *cumulative frequency histogram.* Copy and complete the table. Then make a cumulative frequency histogram for the data.

Ages	Frequency	Cumulative frequency
15–24	9	9
25–34	11	9 + 11 = 20
?	?	?

my.hrw.com
Keystrokes

Draw Histograms

Use appropriate tools strategically.

QUESTION How can you use a graphing calculator to make a histogram?

EXAMPLE Make a histogram

POPULATION The populations (in thousands) of metropolitan areas in the states with the greatest metropolitan populations in the United States in 2000 are listed below. Make a histogram of the data.

4527 32,750 14,837 5667 10,542 4390 4911 6101 8169 3795 8414
17,473 5437 9214 10,392 3862 17,692 5528 4899 3640

STEP 1 ***Enter the data***

Go to the STAT menu and choose Edit. Enter the data into List 1.

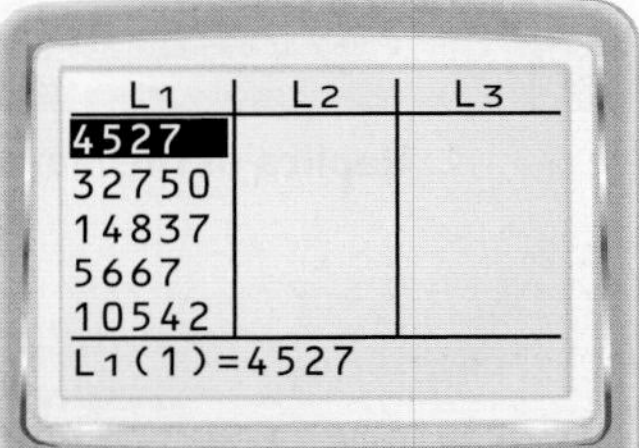

STEP 2 ***Select histogram***

Go to the STAT PLOT screen. Select Plot 1. Use the settings shown below.

STEP 3 ***Set the viewing window***

Go to the WINDOW screen. Use the settings shown below.

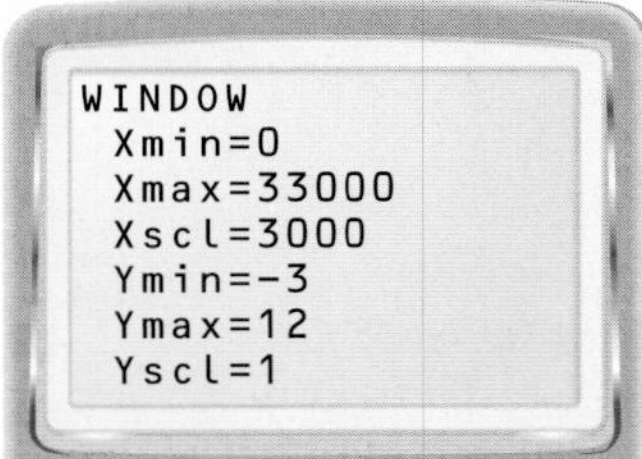

STEP 4 ***Graph***

Press GRAPH. Use the *trace* feature to move from bar to bar.

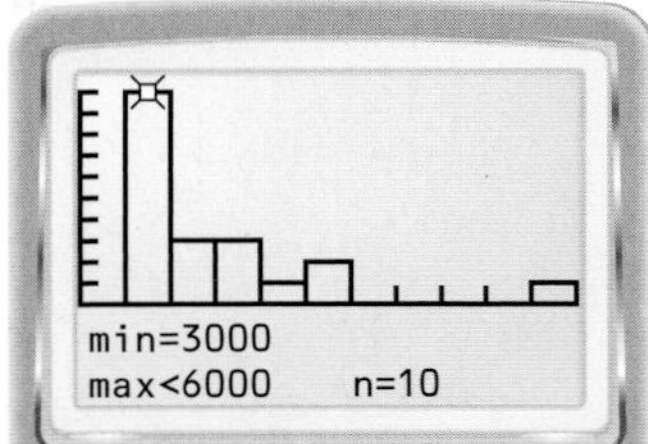

DRAW CONCLUSIONS

1. *Describe* the distribution of the population data in the example above.
2. **BOWLING** Use a graphing calculator to make a histogram of the following bowling scores: 200, 210, 105, 300, 180, 175, 162, 110, 140, 300, 152, 165, 175, 115, 250, 270, 145, 182, 164, 122, 141, 135, 189, 170, 151, 158.

10.5 Interpret Box-and-Whisker Plots

Before	You made stem-and-leaf plots and histograms.
Now	You will make and interpret box-and-whisker plots.
Why?	So you can compare sets of scientific data, as in Ex. 19.

Key Vocabulary
- **box-and-whisker plot**
- **quartile**
- **interquartile range**
- **outlier**

A **box-and-whisker plot** organizes data values into four groups. Ordered data are divided into lower and upper halves by the median. The median of the lower half is the **lower quartile**. The median of the upper half is the **upper quartile**.

COMMON CORE

CC.9-12.S.ID.1 Represent data with plots on the real number line (dot plots, histograms, and box plots).*

EXAMPLE 1 Make a box-and-whisker plot

SONG LENGTHS The lengths of songs (in seconds) on a CD are listed below. Make a box-and-whisker plot of the song lengths.

173, 206, 179, 257, 198, 251, 239, 246, 295, 181, 261

Solution

STEP 1 **Order** the data. Then find the median and the quartiles.

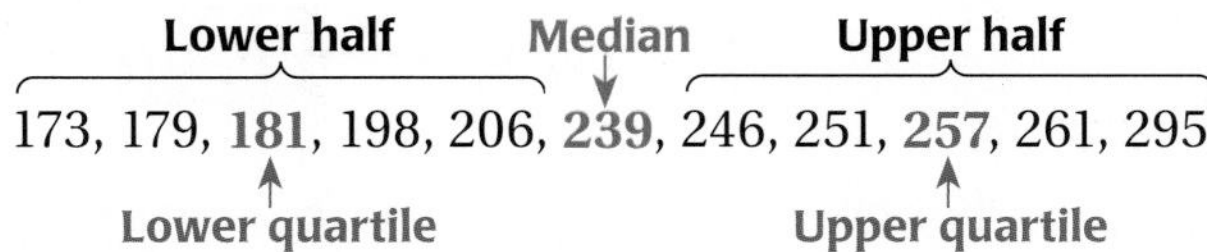

STEP 2 **Plot** the median, the quartiles, the maximum value, and the minimum value below a number line.

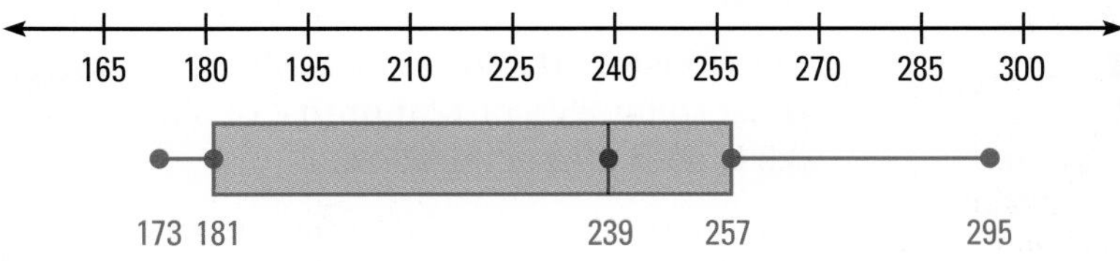

STEP 3 **Draw** a box from the lower quartile to the upper quartile. Draw a vertical line through the median. Draw a line segment (a "whisker") from the box to the maximum and another from the box to the minimum.

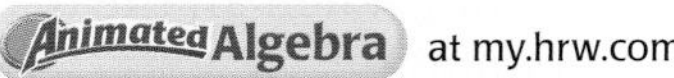

at my.hrw.com

✓ **GUIDED PRACTICE** for Example 1

1. Make a box-and-whisker plot of the ages of eight family members: 60, 15, 25, 20, 55, 70, 40, 30.

INTERPRET A BOX-AND-WHISKER PLOT A box-and-whisker plot separates data into four groups: the two parts of the box and the two whiskers. Each part contains approximately the same number of data values.

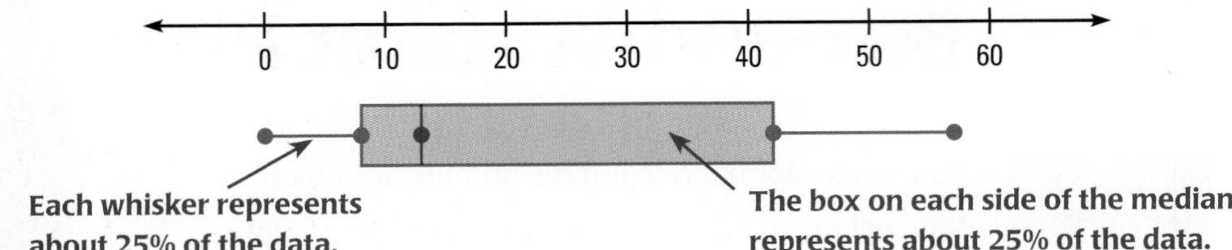

INTERPRET VARIATION

The interquartile range measures the variation in the middle half of the data and ignores the extreme values, whose variation may not be representative of the data.

You know that the range of a data set is the difference of the maximum value and the minimum value. The **interquartile range** of a data set is the difference of the upper quartile and the lower quartile.

EXAMPLE 2 Interpret a box-and-whisker plot

PRECIPITATION The box-and-whisker plots below show the normal precipitation (in inches) each month in Dallas and in Houston, Texas.

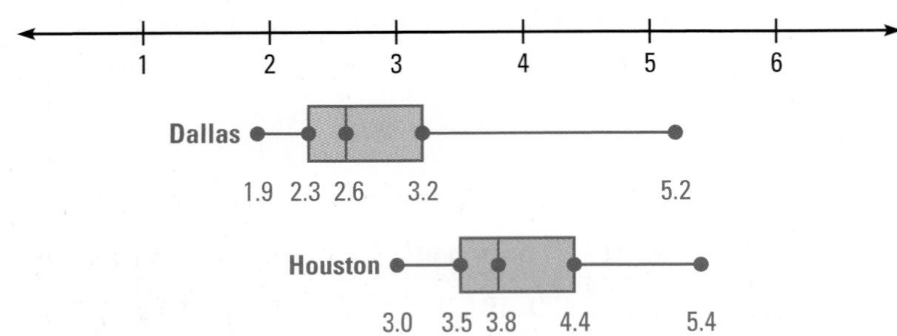

a. For how many months is Houston's precipitation less than 3.5 inches?

b. Compare the precipitation in Dallas with the precipitation in Houston.

Solution

a. For Houston, the lower quartile is 3.5. A whisker represents 25% of the data, so for 25% of 12 months, or 3 months, Houston has less than 3.5 inches of precipitation.

b. The median precipitation for a month in Dallas is 2.6 inches. The median for Houston is 3.8 inches. In general, Houston has more precipitation.

For Dallas, the interquartile range is $3.2 - 2.3$, or 0.9 inch. For Houston, the interquartile range is $4.4 - 3.5 = 0.9$ inch. So, the cities have the same variation in the middle 50% of the data. The range for Dallas is greater than the range for Houson. When all the data are considered, Dallas has more variation in precipitation.

INTERPRET QUARTILES

When the number of data values is a multiple of 4, the median and quartiles will divide the data into four groups of *exactly* the same size.

✓ **GUIDED PRACTICE** for Example 2

2. **PRECIPITATION** In Example 2, for how many months was the precipitation in Dallas more than 2.6 inches?

OUTLIERS A value that is widely separated from the rest of the data in a data set is called an **outlier**. Typically, a data value is considered to be an outlier if it is greater than the upper quartile by more than 1.5 times the interquartile range or if it is less than the lower quartile by more than 1.5 times the interquartile range.

EXAMPLE 3 Standardized Test Practice

The normal monthly amounts of precipitation (in inches) in Dallas are: 1.9, 2.4, 3.1, 3.2, 5.2, 3.2, 2.1, 2.0, 2.4, 4.1, 2.6, 2.6. These data were used to create the box-and-whisker plot in Example 2. Which value, if any, is an outlier?

Ⓐ 1.9 Ⓑ 5.2 Ⓒ 1.9 and 5.2 Ⓓ No outlier

Solution

From Example 2, you know the interquartile range of the data is 0.9 inch. Find 1.5 times the interquartile range: $1.5(0.9) = 1.35$.

From Example 2, you also know that the lower quartile is 2.3 and the upper quartile is 3.2. A value less than $2.3 - 1.35 = 0.95$ is an outlier. A value greater than $3.2 + 1.35 = 4.55$, is an outlier. Notice that $5.2 > 4.55$.

▸ The correct answer is B. Ⓐ Ⓑ Ⓒ Ⓓ

✓ GUIDED PRACTICE for Example 3

3. Which value, if any, is an outlier in the data set?

3.7, 3.0, 3.4, 3.6, 5.2, 5.4, 3.2, 3.8, 4.3, 4.5, 4.2, 3.7

Ⓐ 3.0 Ⓑ 5.4 Ⓒ 3.0 and 5.4 Ⓓ No outlier

10.5 EXERCISES

HOMEWORK KEY
○ = See **WORKED-OUT SOLUTIONS** Exs. 3 and 17
★ = **STANDARDIZED TEST PRACTICE** Exs. 2, 8, 9, 18, and 19

SKILL PRACTICE

1. VOCABULARY What is the interquartile range of a data set?

2. ★ **WRITING** *Explain* how you can identify an outlier in a data set.

EXAMPLE 1
for Exs. 3–7

BOX-AND-WHISKER PLOTS Make a box-and-whisker plot of the data.

3. 1, 7, 0, 7, 2, 6, 3, 6, 0, 7, 8

4. 10, 1, 7, 5, 1, 8, 5, 4, 6, 5, 9, 12

5. 52, 20, 24, 45, 35, 32, 39, 42, 23, 64

6. 0.8, 0.4, 0.3, 0.6, 0.7, 0.2, 0.7, 0.9

7. **ERROR ANALYSIS** *Describe* and correct the error in creating a box-and-whisker plot of the data 0, 2, 4, 0, 6, 10, 8, 12, 5.

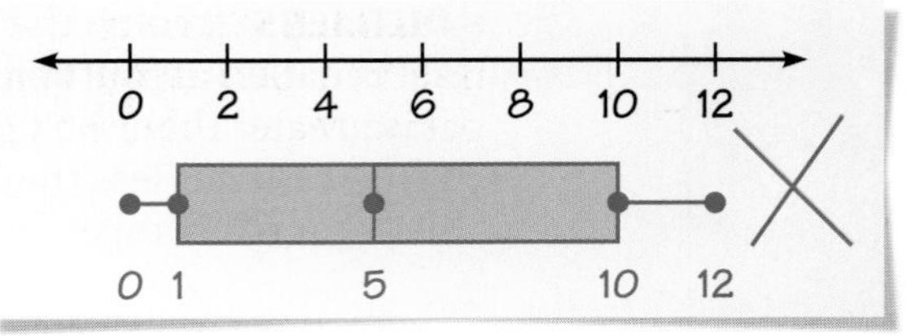

BOX-AND-WHISKER PLOT **In Exercises 8–10, use the box-and-whisker plot.**

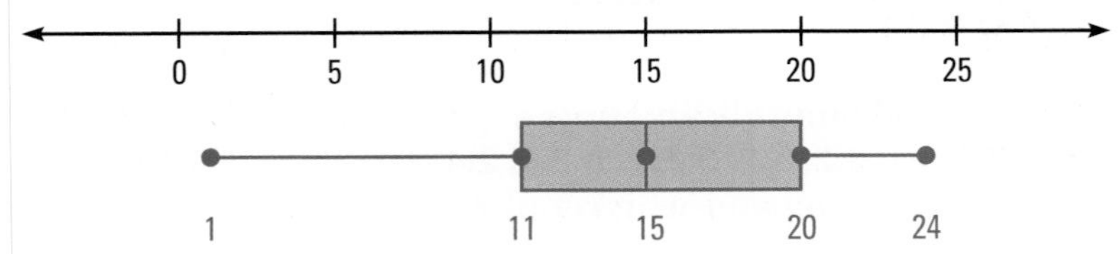

EXAMPLE 2
for Exs. 8–10

8. ★ **MULTIPLE CHOICE** About what percent of the data are greater than 20?

Ⓐ 25% Ⓑ 50% Ⓒ 75% Ⓓ 100%

9. ★ **MULTIPLE CHOICE** About what percent of the data are less than 15?

Ⓐ 25% Ⓑ 50% Ⓒ 75% Ⓓ 100%

10. **ERROR ANALYSIS** *Describe* and correct the error in interpreting the box-and-whisker plot.

About 25% of the data values lie between 11 and 20.

EXAMPLES 1 and 3
for Exs. 11–13

OUTLIERS **Make a box-and-whisker plot of the data. Identify any outliers.**

11. Hours worked per week: 15, 15, 10, 12, 22, 10, 8, 14, 18, 22, 18, 15, 12, 11, 10

12. Prices of MP3 players: \$124, \$95, \$105, \$110, \$95, \$124, \$300, \$190, \$114

13. Annual salaries: \$30,000, \$35,000, \$48,000, \$68,500, \$32,000, \$38,000

14. **CHALLENGE** Two data sets have the same mean, the same interquartile range, and the same range. Is it possible for the box-and-whisker plots of such data sets to be different? *Justify* your answer by creating data sets that fit the situation.

PROBLEM SOLVING

EXAMPLE 1
for Exs. 15–16

15. **SEAWAY** The average sailing times to the Atlantic Ocean from several ports on the St. Lawrence Seaway are shown on the map. Make a box-and-whisker plot of the sailing times.

○ = See **WORKED-OUT SOLUTIONS** in Student Resources ★ = **STANDARDIZED TEST PRACTICE**

16. **BASEBALL STATISTICS** In 2004, Ichiro Suzuki scored 101 runs. The numbers of runs he scored against different opposing teams are listed below. Make a box-and-whisker plot of the numbers of runs scored.

Runs scored: 18, 8, 4, 8, 2, 8, 0, 9, 0, 4, 2, 5, 9, 1, 2, 1, 2, 11, 7

EXAMPLES 1 and 3 for Exs. 17–18

17. **RETAIL SALES** The retail sales (in billions of dollars) of the nine U.S. states with the highest retail sales in 2002 are listed below.

California: $153.1	Florida: $118.2	Georgia: $38.4
Illinois: $52.4	New Jersey: $35.8	New York: $54.7
Ohio: $50.7	Pennsylvania: $49.9	Texas: $107.0

a. Make a box-and-whisker plot of the retail sales.

b. Which states, if any, had retail sales in 2002 that can be considered outliers?

18. ★ **SHORT RESPONSE** The stem-and-leaf plot shows the ages of the first 43 presidents of the United States when they first took the oath of office.

Stem	Leaves
4	2 3 6 6 7 8 9 9
5	0 0 1 1 1 1 2 2 4 4 4 4 4 5 5 5 5 6 6 6 7 7 7 7 8
6	0 1 1 1 2 4 4 5 8 9

Key: 4 | 2 = 42 years

a. Make a box-and-whisker plot of the ages.

b. Ronald Reagan was the oldest United States president, and Theodore Roosevelt was the youngest. Can either of these presidents' ages be considered outliers? *Explain* why or why not.

EXAMPLE 2 for Ex. 19

19. ★ **EXTENDED RESPONSE** The box-and-whisker plots show the diameters (in kilometers) of craters on Jupiter's moons Callisto and Ganymede.

0 200 400 600 800 1000

Callisto: 38, 58.5, 74.5, 121.5, 980

Ganymede: 16, 50, 62, 93, 588

Callisto

a. *Compare* the diameters of craters on Callisto with the diameters of craters on Ganymede.

b. The largest crater in the United States is the Chesapeake Bay in Virginia, with a diameter of 90 kilometers. *Compare* the diameter of the Chesapeake Bay with diameters of craters on Callisto and Ganymede.

c. The largest crater on Earth is Vredefort in South Africa, with a diameter of 300 kilometers. *Compare* the diameter of Vredefort with the diameter of craters on Callisto and Ganymede.

20. **CHALLENGE** The box-and-whisker plots show the heights (in inches) of singers in a chorus, according to their voice parts. A soprano part has the highest pitch, followed by alto, tenor, and bass, respectively. Draw a conclusion about voice parts and heights. *Justify* your conclusion.

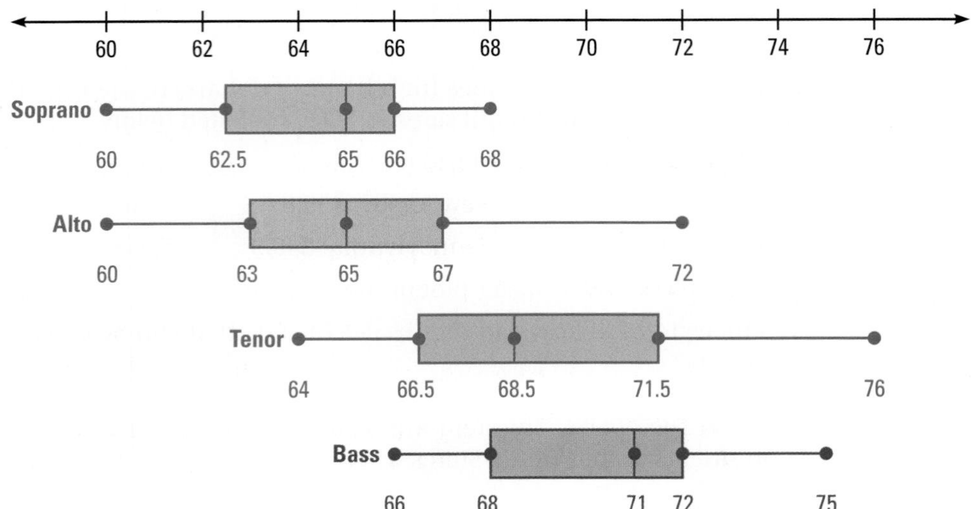

QUIZ

The table shows the number of girls and boys in the ninth grade at Jefferson High School who expressed interest in playing on a soccer team or on a lacrosse team. Use the table for Exercises 1 and 2.

	Soccer	Lacrosse	Total
Girls	64	52	116
Boys	58	60	118
Total	122	112	234

1. Are more ninth graders interested in playing on a soccer team or on a lacrosse team?
2. Did more boys or more girls express interest in playing on a lacrosse team?
3. Make a histogram of the data: 44, 52, 60, 47, 65, 40, 49, 45, 32, 68, 39.
4. Make a stem-and-leaf plot of the data: 1.8, 2.2, 1.2, 2.8, 3.6, 3.3, 1.8, 2.2.
5. **TEST SCORES** The scores on a math exam are given below. Make a box-and-whisker plot of the data. Identify any outliers.

   76, 55, 88, 92, 79, 85, 90, 88, 85, 92, 100, 91, 90, 86, 88

See **EXTRA PRACTICE** in Student Resources **ONLINE QUIZ** at my.hrw.com

Using ALTERNATIVE METHODS

Another Way to Solve Example 1

Use appropriate tools strategically.

MULTIPLE REPRESENTATIONS In Example 1, you saw how to analyze the lengths of songs on a CD by drawing a box-and-whisker plot. You can also solve the problem by using a graphing calculator.

PROBLEM

SONG LENGTH The lengths of the songs (in seconds) on a CD are listed below. Make a box-and-whisker plot of the song lengths.

173, 206, 179, 257, 198, 251, 239, 246, 295, 181, 261

METHOD 1

Using a Graphing Calculator An alternative approach is to use a graphing calculator.

STEP 1 **Enter** the data into List 1.

STEP 2 **Go to** the STAT PLOT screen and select the box-and-whisker plot for Plot 1. The Xlist for Plot 1 should be L_1, so that it displays the data from List 1. Make sure Plot 1 is on.

STEP 3 **Press** ZOOM 9 to set the window so that it shows all of the data.

STEP 4 **Press** GRAPH. Use the trace feature to examine the box-and-whisker plot more closely. Notice that the graphing calculator refers to the lower quartile as Q_1 and the upper quartile as Q_3.

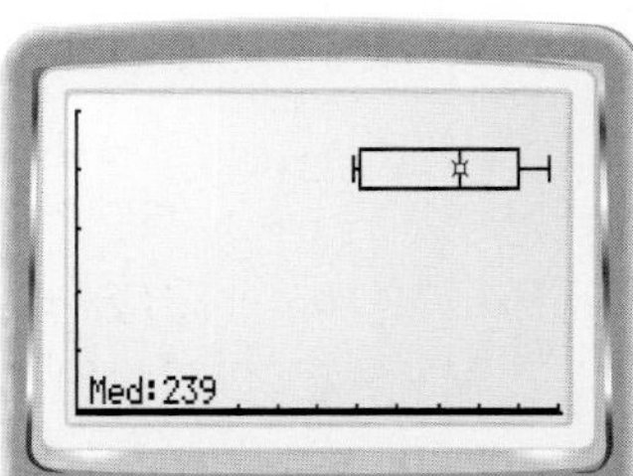

PRACTICE

In Exercises 1 and 2, use a graphing calculator to make a box-and-whisker plot of the data.

1. **REPTILE SPECIES** The number of known reptile species per 10,000 square kilometers in the countries of Asia (excluding the Middle East): 36, 26, 49, 11, 32, 35, 27, 58, 91, 26, 8, 8, 12, 12, 23, 110, 4, 51, 41, 41, 62, 350, 77, 18, 81, 23, 18, 59

2. **BIRD SPECIES** The number of threatened bird species per 10,000 square kilometers in the countries of North and South America: 5, 50, 41, 27, 103, 18, 64, 53, 3, 26, 64, 2, 11, 22

Extension Analyze Data Distribution

GOAL Choose an appropriate display, measure of central tendency, and measure of spread based on the shape of a data distribution.

CC.9-12.S.ID.3 Interpret differences in shape, center, and spread in the context of the data sets, accounting for possible effects of extreme data points (outliers).*

When you are presenting a set of data, you should consider the distribution of the data before deciding what type of measure of central tendency and graph to use for the data.

DATA THAT ARE CLOSELY GROUPED Use a histogram to display the data. Use the mean as a measure of central tendency. Use standard deviation as a measure of the spread.

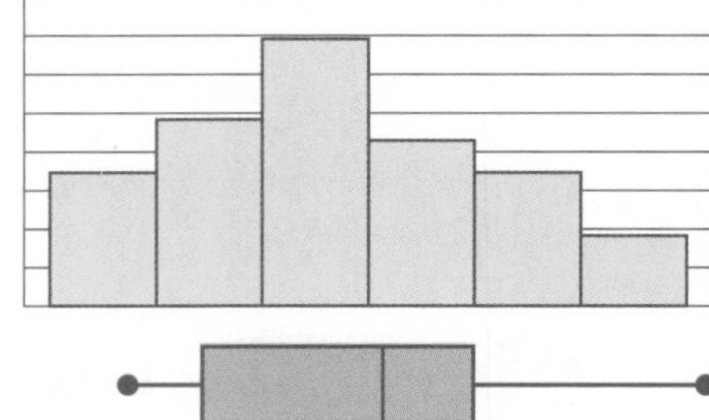

DATA VALUES THAT ARE SPREAD OUT Use a box-and-whisker plot to display the data. Use the median as a measure of central tendency. Use the interquartile range as a measure of the spread.

EXAMPLE 1 Choose a display for data

A used car dealer has 21 cars for sale at the prices shown in the table. Choose an appropriate display, measure of central tendency, and measure of spread for this data set.

\$2150	\$2800	\$3500	\$5100	\$6050	\$7100	\$7250
\$8000	\$8850	\$9100	\$9225	\$9900	\$10,200	\$10,800
\$11,750	\$12,200	\$12,640	\$13,020	\$14,700	\$15,500	\$16,400

Solution

The data are close together with no outliers. Use a histogram. The center of the data can be represented by the mean, which is \$9,345. The spread can be represented by the standard deviation, which is about \$3946.

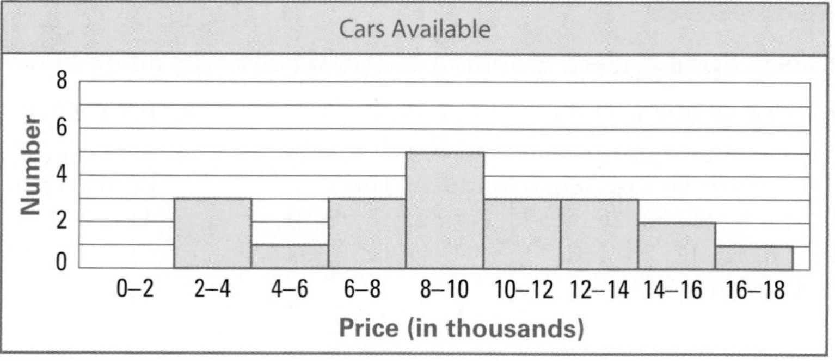

EXAMPLE 2 Choose a display for data

Another used car dealer has 24 cars for sale at the prices shown in the table. Choose an appropriate display, measure of central tendency, and measure of spread for this data set.

$3,800	$5,100	$7,100	$7,250	$8,850	$9,225	$9,900	$10,200
$10,500	$10,800	$11,400	$11,750	$12,200	$12,350	$12,640	$13,020
$13,890	$14,700	$15,500	$15,990	$17,000	$17,800	$22,900	$38,775

Solution

The data value $38,775 appears to be an outlier. Use a box-and-whisker plot to display the data. The outlier will affect the mean and standard deviation, so they do not represent the data well. The median is $11,975. The interquartile range is $5537.50.

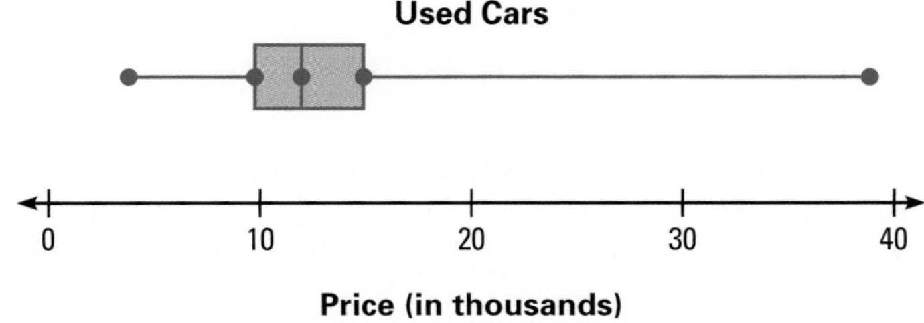

PRACTICE

For Exercises 1–6, choose an appropriate display, measure of central tendency, and measure of spread for the data set. Explain your reasoning.

1. **QUIZ SCORES** The scores on the first quiz in Mr. Stuart's math class were 6, 9, 10, 12, 12, 13, 14, 14, 15, 15, 15, 16, 16, 17, 17, 17, 17, 18, 18, 18, 19, 19, 19, 20, and 20.

2. **FOOTBALL** The points scored by twenty of the top 25 college football teams on Saturday, September 25, 2010 were 24, 73, 37, 42, 17, 31, 70, 35, 10, 20, 37, 65, 22, 31, 20, 24, 12, 27, 14, and 34.

3. **RUNNING** The time (in minutes) it took twenty freshmen to run the mile in physical education class were 7, 7.5, 8, 8, 8.2, 8.4, 8.5, 9, 9, 9, 9.6, 9.8, 10, 10.5, 10.5, 10.8, 11.2, 11.5, 11.7, and 12 minutes.

4. **HOMEWORK** The numbers of hours that twenty-five students spent doing homework last week were 1, 8, 8, 8.5, 9, 9.5, 9.5, 10, 10, 10, 10, 10, 10.5, 10.5, 10.5, 11, 11, 11, 11, 11.5, 11.5, 12, 12, 12, and 12.

5. **COOKIES** The numbers of cookies in 20 boxes at a bake sale are 16, 16, 18, 18, 20, 20, 24, 24, 24, 24, 26, 28, 28, 30, 30, 30, 30, 36, 36, and 36.

6. **BASEBALL** The attendance at a professional baseball team's home games during September are shown in the table.

39,555	31,424	40,788	31,647	31,596	33,623
36,364	37,285	34,481	36,553	39,316	38,057

MIXED REVIEW *of Problem Solving*

MATHEMATICAL PRACTICES Make sense of problems and persevere in solving them.

1. **MULTI-STEP PROBLEM** The ages of people who attended an opening reception for a theater production are listed below.

   54, 25, 28, 64, 30, 42, 33, 50, 27, 35, 40, 39, 41, 52, 49, 48, 56, 60, 58, 37, 56, 45, 57, 62

   a. Make a frequency table of the data.

   b. Make a histogram of the data.

2. **SHORT RESPONSE** Students collected fish of two species, blue gill and largemouth bass, from the same pond for a science fair project. The lengths (in millimeters) of the fish they collected are listed below.

   Blue gill: 186, 171, 171, 176, 183, 182, 172, 172, 173, 184

   Largemouth bass: 354, 297, 300, 344, 317, 360, 432, 457, 392, 395

   a. Make a box-and-whisker plot for the data.

   b. Based on the fish the students collected, which of the species has more variation in length? *Explain* your reasoning.

3. **MULTI-STEP PROBLEM** Jo and her friend Abe sold tickets for the Homecoming football game. The table shows the number of student tickets and adult tickets each person sold.

	Student	Adult	Total
Jo	178	215	393
Abe	201	188	389
Total	379	403	782

   a. How many adult tickets did Jo sell?

   b. How many tickets did Jo and Abe sell altogether?

   c. Who sold more student tickets?

4. **SHORT RESPONSE** The back-to-back stem-and-leaf plot below shows the lengths (in meters) of the eight best men's and women's final long jump results from the 2004 Olympics. *Compare* the lengths of the jumps by men with those by women.

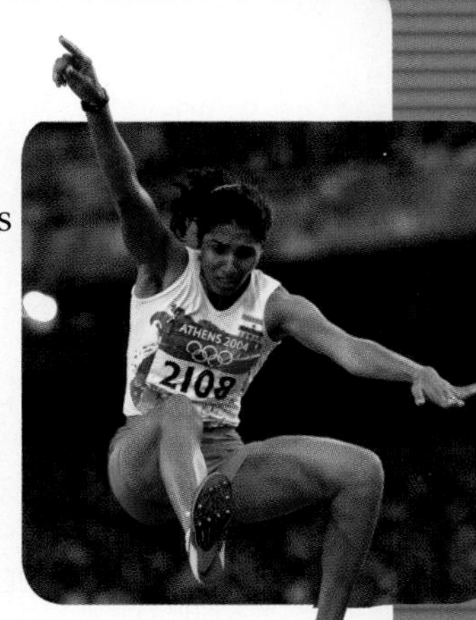

Lengths (in meters) of Long Jump

Men		Women
	6	7 8 8 9
	7	0 0 0 1
6 5 3 3 2 2 2 0	8	

Key: 0 | 7 | 1 = 7.0 m, 7.1 m

5. **SHORT RESPONSE** The stem-and-leaf plot shows the number of games lost by 15 NCAA football coaches with the greatest career winning percentages after at least 10 years of coaching.

Stem	Leaves
1	1 2 3 6 7 7 8
2	1 3 3 4 5 9
3	6
4	9

Key: 2 | 1 = 21 games

   a. Make a box-and-whisker plot of the data.

   b. Tom Osborne had a winning percentage of 83.6% over his career and lost 49 games. Can the number of games lost by Tom Osborne be considered an outlier? *Explain* your reasoning.

10 CHAPTER SUMMARY

BIG IDEAS

For Your Notebook

Big Idea 1

Analyzing Sets of Data

You can find values that represent a typical data value using the following measures of central tendency:

mean, median, and mode

You can find values that describe the spread of data using the following measures of dispersion:

range, mean absolute deviation, and interquartile range

Big Idea 2

Making and Interpreting Data Displays

Use an appropriate display to show the distribution of a set of numerical data.

A **stem-and-leaf plot** organizes data based on their digits.

Stem	Leaves
1	0 1 1 2 3
2	0 0 0 2

Key: 1 | 0 = 10

A **histogram** shows the frequency of data on intervals of equal size, with no gaps or overlaps.

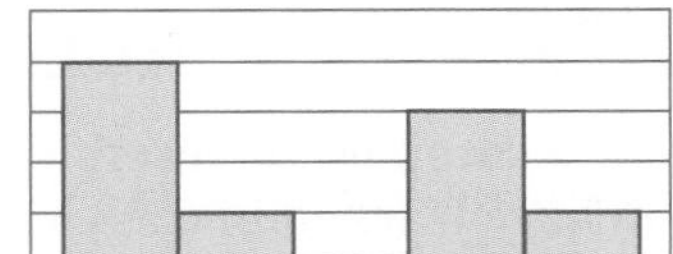

A **box-and-whisker plot** organizes data into four groups of approximately equal size.

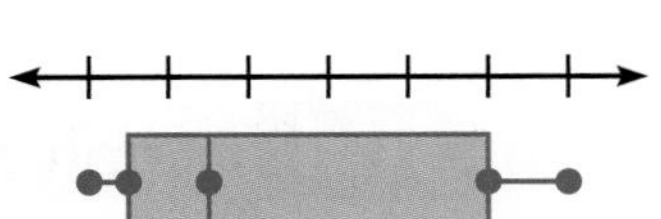

10 CHAPTER REVIEW

@HomeTutor
my.hrw.com
- Multi-Language Glossary
- Vocabulary Practice

REVIEW KEY VOCABULARY

- survey
- population
- sample: random, stratified random, systematic, convenience, self-selected
- biased sample
- biased question
- mean, median, mode
- measure of dispersion
- range
- mean absolute deviation
- variance
- standard deviation
- marginal frequency
- joint frequency
- stem-and-leaf plot
- frequency, frequency table
- histogram
- box-and-whisker plot
- lower quartile, upper quartile
- interquartile range
- outlier

VOCABULARY EXERCISES

Copy and complete the statement.

1. In a _?_ sample, a rule is used to select members of the population.
2. In a two-way frequency table, the row and column totals give the _?_.
3. **WRITING** *Explain* what the "box" and the "whiskers" represent on a box-and-whisker plot.

REVIEW EXAMPLES AND EXERCISES

Use the review examples and exercises below to check your understanding of the concepts you have learned in each lesson of this chapter.

10.1 Analyze Surveys and Samples

EXAMPLE

You create a survey to determine what type of music is the favorite of students in your grade. You ask each surveyed student, "What is your favorite type of music, classical or country?"

Tell whether the question is potentially biased. Explain your answer. If the question is potentially biased, rewrite it so that it is not.

The question is biased, because it does not allow students to choose a type of music other than classical or country. An unbiased question is "What is your favorite type of music?"

EXERCISES

EXAMPLE 1
for Ex. 4

4. **SURVEY** In the example above, suppose you create a questionnaire and distribute one to every student in your grade. There is a box in the cafeteria where students can drop off completed questionnaires during lunch. Identify the sampling method.

@HomeTutor
my.hrw.com
Chapter Review Practice

10.2 Use Measures of Central Tendency and Dispersion

EXAMPLE

The amounts of snowfall (in inches) in one town for 8 months of the year are listed below. Find the mean, median, and mode(s) of the data. Which measure of central tendency best represents the data?

0.5, 0.5, 1.5, 2.0, 3.5, 4.5, 16.5, 30.5

$$\bar{x} = \frac{0.5 + 0.5 + 1.5 + 2.0 + 3.5 + 4.5 + 16.5 + 30.5}{8} = \frac{59.5}{8} = 7.4375 \text{ inches}$$

The median is the mean of the two middle values, 2.0 and 3.5, or 2.75 inches.

The mode is 0.5 inch.

The median best represents the data. The mean is greater than most of the data values. The mode is less than most of the data values.

EXERCISES

EXAMPLES 1 and 2 for Ex. 5

5. **BASEBALL STATISTICS** The numbers of home runs hit by baseball player Manny Ramirez against several different opposing teams over 3 seasons are 5, 1, 10, 5, 5, 4, 1, 0, 7, 2, 1, 1, 1, 9, 6, 1, 2, 6, 2, 19, 6, and 17.
   a. Find the mean, median, and mode(s) of the data.
   b. Which measure of central tendency best represents the data? *Explain.*

10.3 Analyze Data

EXAMPLE

There are 212 students in a tutoring program for younger students. Of these, 131 tutor math and 81 tutor science. No one tutors both. There are 78 girls tutoring math, 42 boys tutoring science, and a total of 117 girls tutoring. Make a two-way frequency table for the data.

The categories are math, science, girls, and boys. Fill in the given information.
Girls tutoring science: $117 - 78 = 39$
Boys tutoring math: $131 - 78 = 53$
Boys tutoring: $42 + 53 = 95$

	Math	Science	Total
Girls	78	39	117
Boys	53	42	95
Total	131	81	212

EXERCISES

EXAMPLE 2 for Ex. 6

6. In the example above, suppose that last year, 198 students tutored in all. Of those, 122 students (including 86 boys) tutored math, and 43 girls tutored science. Make a two-way frequency table for the data.

10 CHAPTER REVIEW

10.4 Interpret Stem-and-Leaf Plots and Histograms

EXAMPLE

The prices (in dollars) of several books are listed below. Make a stem-and-leaf plot of the prices.

14, 15, 9, 19, 21, 29, 12, 25, 10, 8, 15, 13, 15, 20

STEP 1 **Separate** the data into stems and leaves.

Book Prices

Stem	Leaves
0	9 8
1	4 5 9 2 0 5 3 5
2	1 9 0 5

Key: 1 | 4 = $14

STEP 2 **Write** the leaves in increasing order.

Book Prices

Stem	Leaves
0	8 9
1	0 2 3 4 5 5 5 9
2	0 1 5 9

Key: 1 | 4 = $14

EXERCISES

EXAMPLE 1 for Ex. 7

7. **EXERCISING** The minutes per day that the students in a class spend exercising are listed below. Make a stem-and-leaf plot of the data.

20, 25, 0, 10, 0, 30, 35, 20, 45, 25, 40, 0, 0, 0, 5, 10, 20, 15, 20, 30

10.5 Interpret Box-and-Whisker Plots

EXAMPLE

Make a box-and-whisker plot of the book prices in the example above.

Order the data. Then find the median and quartiles.

Upper quartile → 12   **Median** = 15   **Lower quartile** → 20

8 9 10 **12** 13 14 15 15 15 19 **20** 21 25 29

Plot the median, the quartiles, the maximum value, and the minimum value below a number line. Draw the box and the whiskers.

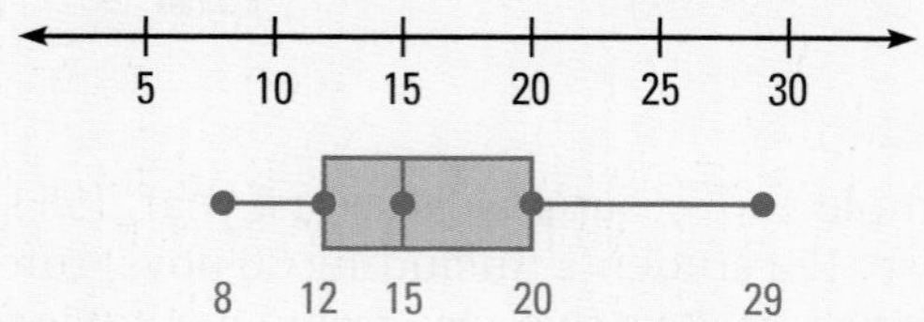

EXERCISES

EXAMPLE 1 for Ex. 8

8. **EXERCISING** Use the data in Exercise 7 to make a box-and-whisker plot of the minutes per day that the students in the class spend exercising.

10 CHAPTER TEST

Find the mean, median, and mode(s) of the data.

1. 55, 42, 51, 66, 88, 102, 86
2. 12.5, 22, 18.5, 16.2, 12.8, 18.5

Find the range and mean absolute deviation of the data. Round to the nearest hundredth, if necessary.

3. 20, 45, 50, 40, 35
4. 1200, 1150, 950, 900, 800, 1000

The table shows the numbers of people enrolled in weekend art classes at an artists' workshop. No person is enrolled in more than one class. Use the table for Exercises 5–8.

	Oil Painting	Water Color	Charcoal Sketching	Total
Students	78	56	39	173
Adults	92	88	34	214
Total	170	144	73	387

5. How many adults are enrolled in oil painting classes?
6. How many students are enrolled altogether?
7. How many people altogether are enrolled in water color classes?
8. How many students are enrolled in either oil painting or water color classes?
9. **GOVERNMENT PROJECT** City officials want to know whether residents will support construction of a new library. This question appears on the ballot in the citywide election: "Do you support a tax increase to replace the old, deteriorating library with a brand new one?"Is the question potentially biased? *Explain* your answer. If the question is potentially biased, rewrite it so that it is not.
10. **BASKETBALL** The back-to-back stem-and-leaf plot shows the heights (in inches) of the players on a high school's basketball teams.

Basketball Players' Heights

Girls		Boys
9 7 7 6 6 5 3 3	6	9 9 9
3 2 1 1 0	7	0 0 0 2 4 4 6 6 7 7 7 8

Key: 3 | 6 | 9 = 63 in., 69 in.

a. Find the mean, median, and mode(s) of each data set. Which measure of central tendency best represents each data set? *Explain.*

b. Find the range and mean absolute deviation of each data set. Which team's heights are more spread out? *Explain.*

c. Make a box-and-whisker plot of each data set.

d. *Compare* the boys' heights with the girls' heights.

10 ★ Standardized TEST PREPARATION

Scoring Rubric

Full Credit
- solution is complete and correct

Partial Credit
- solution is complete but has errors,
or
- solution is without error but incomplete

No Credit
- no solution is given,
or
- solution makes no sense

SHORT RESPONSE QUESTIONS

PROBLEM

The lengths (in inches) of several goldfish are listed below. Make a box-and-whisker plot of the lengths. Can any of the goldfish lengths be considered outliers? *Explain* why or why not.

8, 5, 4, 5, 4, 5, 4, 3, 4, 8

Below are sample solutions to the problem. Read each solution and the comments on the left to see why the sample represents full credit, partial credit, or no credit.

SAMPLE 1: Full credit solution

First, order the lengths from least to greatest.

3, 4, 4, 4, 4, 5, 5, 5, 8, 8

Then, plot the median, the quartiles, the maximum value, and the minimum value below a number line. Draw the box and whiskers.

The box-and-whisker plot is correct, and the student explained how it was drawn.

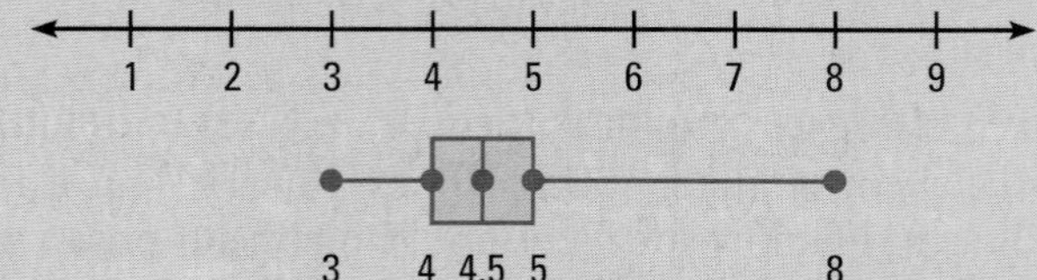

The interquartile range of the goldfish lengths is $5 - 4 = 1$, and 1.5 times the interquartile range is $1.5 \cdot 1 = 1.5$.

The question is answered correctly and includes an explanation.

A length that is less than $4 - 1.5 = 2.5$ would be an outlier. A length that is greater than $5 + 1.5 = 6.5$ would also an outlier. So, the two fish lengths of 8 inches are outliers.

SAMPLE 2: Partial credit solution

The box-and-whisker plot is incorrect. The student has not identified the median.

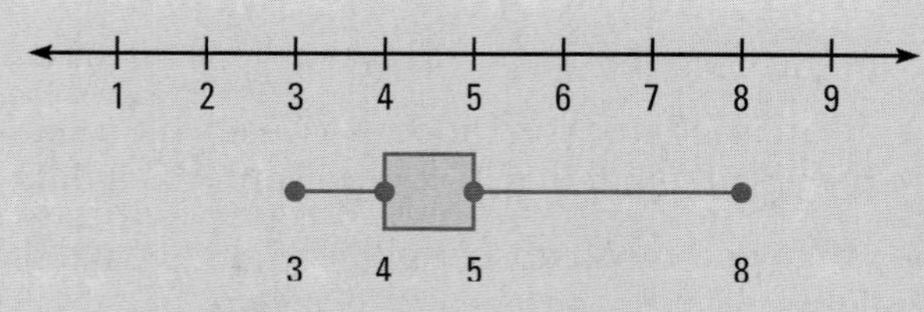

The answer and reasoning are correct.

The interquartile range of the lengths is $5 - 4 = 1$, and $1 \cdot 1.5 = 1.5$.

A length that is less than $4 - 1.5 = 2.5$ is an outlier. A length that is greater than $5 + 1.5 = 6.5$ is an outlier. So, the two fish lengths of 8 inches are outliers.

SAMPLE 3: Partial credit solution

The box-and-whisker plot is correct.

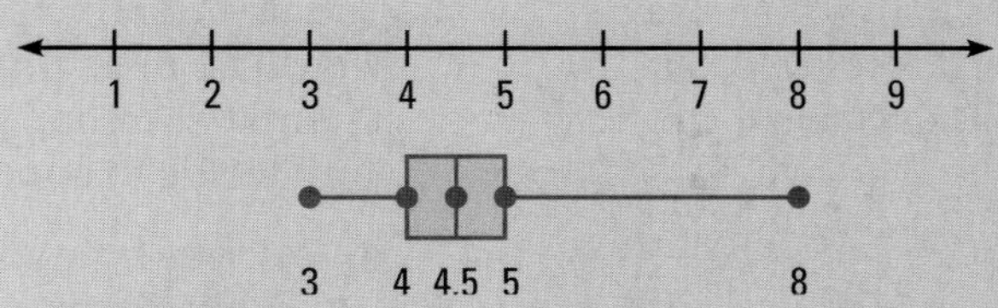

The answer is correct, but the reasoning is incorrect.

The interquartile range of the goldfish lengths is $5 - 4 = 1$.

A length that is less than $4 - 1 = 3$ is an outlier. A length that is greater than $5 + 1 = 6$ is an outlier. So, the two fish lengths of 8 inches are outliers.

SAMPLE 4: No credit solution

There is no box-and-whisker plot. The answer is incorrect.

The value 3 is an outlier because it is a very small goldfish.

PRACTICE Apply the Scoring Rubric

Score the solution to the problem below as *full credit, partial credit,* or *no credit. Explain* your reasoning.

PROBLEM The number of runs scored by 13 players on a baseball team are listed below. Make a box-and-whisker plot of the data. Can any of the values be considered outliers? *Explain* why or why not.

24, 20, 20, 11, 17, 6, 16, 16, 6, 5, 1, 5, 4

1.

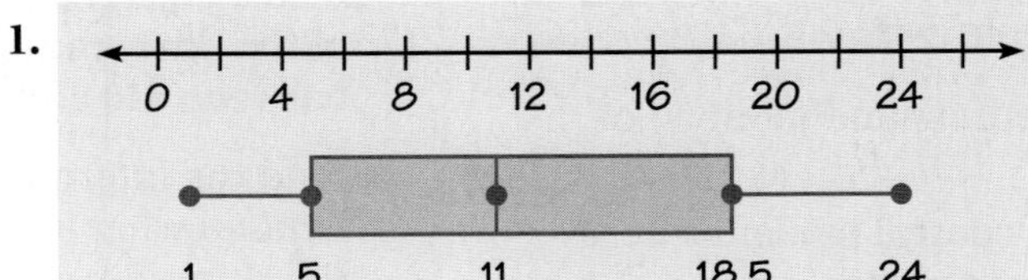

There are no outliers in the data set.

2.

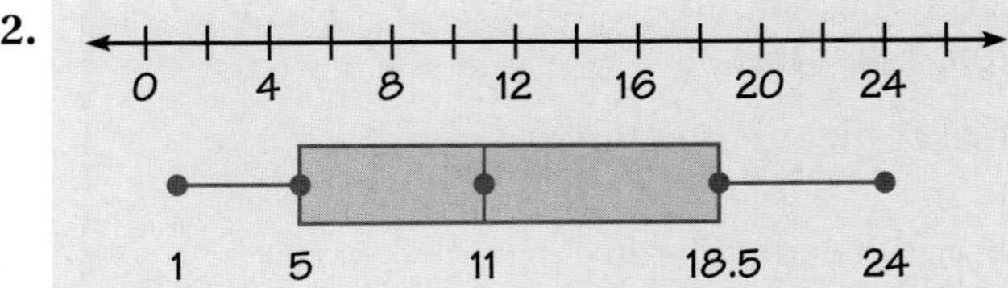

The interquartile range is 13.5, and $1.5 \cdot 13.5 = 20.25$. No values are less than $5 - 20.25 = -15.25$ or greater than $18.5 + 20.25 = 38.75$. So, there are no outliers.

10 ★ *Standardized* TEST PRACTICE

SHORT RESPONSE

1. Estrella is using glass tiles to make a mosaic. Among the many tiles she has collected are square tiles as described in the table below.

	Blue	White	Total
Small	112	96	208
Large	86	100	186
Total	198	196	394

   a. How many of the small tiles are white? How many of the tiles are blue?

   b. Part of Estrella's pattern calls for two squares, one made of all small blue squares, 10 tiles on a side. The other calls for all large white squares, 10 tiles on a side. Can Estrella complete that part of the pattern? *Explain.*

2. The median ages (in years) of residents of 13 towns in a county are listed below.

   39, 35, 34, 40, 33, 30, 37,
   27, 33, 29, 33, 31, 35

   a. Make a box-and-whisker plot of the ages.

   b. Can any of the ages be considered outliers? *Explain* why or why not.

3. The lengths (in seconds) of songs on one CD are listed below.

   136, 249, 434, 136, 299,
   227, 270, 270, 46, 254

   a. Find the mean, median, and mode(s) of the song lengths.

   b. Which measure of central tendency best represents the data? *Explain.*

4. The prices (in dollars) of several mobile phones sold by one retailer are listed below.

   350, 395, 429, 300, 569, 200, 500, 10,
   234, 245, 440, 50, 800, 390, 440, 338

   a. Make a box-and-whisker plot of the mobile phone prices.

   b. Which prices, if any, can be considered outliers? *Explain.*

5. You want to find out what kinds of food items would be most popular to sell to people who attend basketball games at your high school. You decide to conduct a survey.

   a. *Describe* how you could choose a representative sample.

   b. Write an unbiased question that you could use to collect information on what kinds of food items people would be most likely to purchase during a basketball game. *Explain* why your question is unbiased.

The back-to-back stem-and-leaf plot shows the prices (in dollars) of 15 dinners at two competing restaurants. Use the stem-and-leaf plot in Exercises 6 and 7.

Dinner Prices

Restaurant A		Restaurant B
9 9 9 8	0	
7 7 5 5 2 2 1 0	1	0 2 2 3 5 6 6 8
1 0 0	2	1 2 4 4 5 5 5

Key: 0 | 2 | 1 = $20, $21

6. *Compare* the prices at the two restaurants.

7. **a.** Make a box-and-whisker plot of the data. What percent of the dinners at Restaurant A cost between $8 and $12? What percent of the dinners at Restaurant B cost between $10 and $13?

   b. Find the interquartile range of the data. *Explain* what it means in the context of the situation, and describe the overall variation in the prices of the dinners at the two restaurants.

MULTIPLE CHOICE

The two-way frequency table gives some information about two friends' card collections. Use the table in Exercises 8–10.

	Football	Baseball	Total
Ann	145	297	342
Carl	?	189	517
Total	473	486	859

8. Which number is *not* a marginal frequency in the table?

Ⓐ 145 Ⓑ 189
Ⓒ 297 Ⓓ 342

9. Which number belongs in the blank cell?

Ⓐ 152 Ⓑ 328
Ⓒ 442 Ⓓ 618

10. About what percent of the cards are Ann's?

Ⓐ 31% Ⓑ 40%
Ⓒ 61% Ⓓ 66%

GRIDDED ANSWER

11. What is the mean of the data set?

32, 20, 18, 12, 7, 16, 9, 10

12. What is the range of the given data set?

32, 41, 29, 28, 40, 78, 56, 23, 61, 30

13. The stem-and-leaf plot shows the ages (in years) of members of one family. What is the median age (in years)?

Stem	Leaves
0	8 9
1	0 4 6 7
2	0
3	9
4	2 3 3 4 5
5	
6	8 9

Key: 0 | 8 = 8 years

EXTENDED RESPONSE

14. A survey asked 500 teenagers where they would like to live. Of those surveyed, 150 teenagers would like to live in a large city. A participant in this survey is chosen at random.

a. What is the probability that the participant would like to live in a large city?

b. What are the odds in favor of the participant's wanting to live in a large city?

c. *Explain* how the probability in part (a) and odds in part (b) are related.

15. The histogram shows the diameters (in kilometers) of Jupiter's ten largest moons.

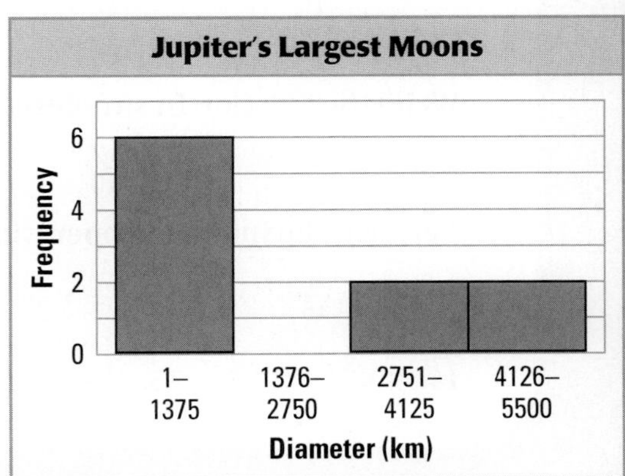

a. *Describe* the distribution of the data in the histogram. In your description, mention whether the data appear to be spread out or clumped in a certain way.

b. The diameters (in kilometers) of Saturn's ten largest moons are listed below.

97, 209, 256, 536, 560, 764, 2575, 180, 718, 110

Make a histogram of the diameters.

c. *Compare* the distribution of diameters of Jupiter's moons with the distribution of diameters of Saturn's moons.

11 Probability

Lesson
11.1 CC.9-12.S.CP.1*
11.2 CC.9-12.S.CP.9(+)*
11.3 CC.9-12.S.CP.9(+)*
11.4 CC.9-12.S.CP.1*
11.5 CC.9-12.S.CP.2*

Before

In previous courses, you learned the following skills, which you'll use in this chapter: writing fractions as decimals, simplifying fractions, and performing operations with fractions.

Prerequisite Skills

VOCABULARY CHECK

1. Copy and complete: A _?_ uses shapes to show how sets are related.

SKILLS CHECK

Write the fraction as a decimal. Round to the nearest hundredth, if necessary.

2. $\frac{17}{40}$ **3.** $\frac{10}{25}$ **4.** $\frac{14}{35}$ **5.** $\frac{2}{15}$

Write the fraction in simplest form.

6. $\frac{16}{24}$ **7.** $\frac{12}{40}$ **8.** $\frac{16}{36}$ **9.** $\frac{12}{50}$

Perform the indicated operation.

10. $\frac{4}{15} + \frac{8}{15}$ **11.** $\frac{7}{27} + \frac{11}{27}$ **12.** $\frac{15}{32} - \frac{7}{32}$ **13.** $\frac{19}{28} - \frac{5}{28}$

14. $\frac{2}{3} \cdot \frac{3}{4}$ **15.** $\frac{3}{8} \cdot \frac{4}{5}$ **16.** $\frac{9}{20} \cdot \frac{5}{12}$ **17.** $\frac{14}{26} \cdot \frac{13}{25}$

Now

In this chapter, you will apply the big ideas listed below and reviewed in the Chapter Summary. You will also use the key vocabulary listed below.

Big Ideas

1. **Finding probabilities of simple events**
2. **Finding probabilities of compound events**

KEY VOCABULARY

- outcome
- event
- probability
- odds
- permutation
- combination
- compound events
- overlapping events
- disjoint events
- independent events
- dependent events
- conditional probability

Why?

You can use probability and data analysis to make predictions. For example, you can use data about a kicker's past successes in football games to find the chance of his success in the future.

Animated Algebra

The animation illustrated below helps you to answer a question from this chapter: What is the probability that the kicker makes an attempted field goal?

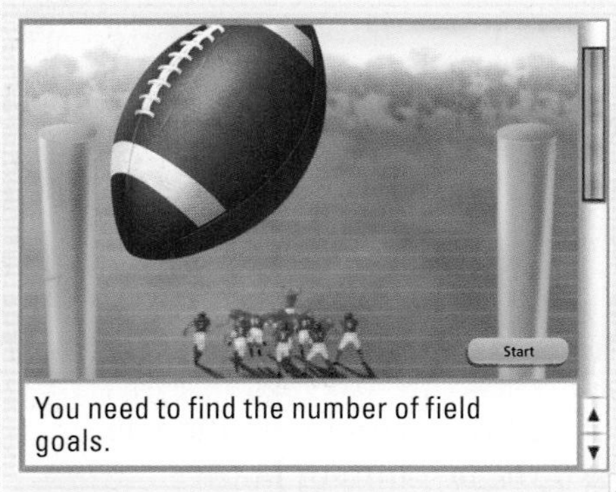

You need to find the number of field goals.

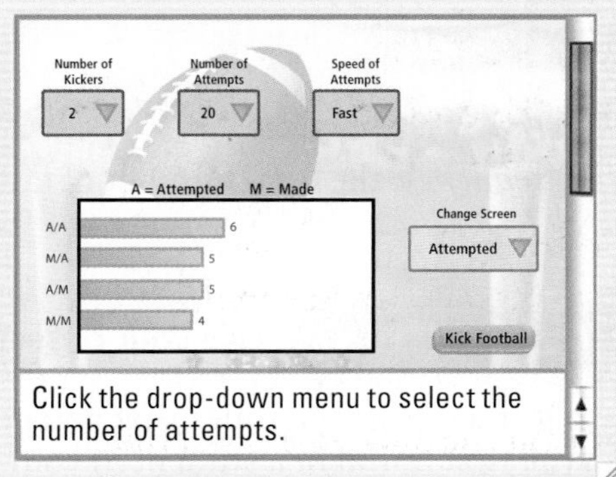

Click the drop-down menu to select the number of attempts.

Animated Algebra at my.hrw.com

Find a Probability

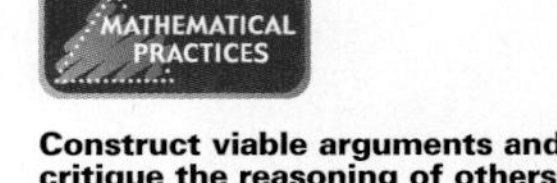

Construct viable arguments and critique the reasoning of others.

MATERIALS • paper bag

QUESTION **What is the chance that you would select the initials of a student in your class from a bag of letters?**

You can perform an experiment and record the results to approximate the likelihood of selecting the initials of a student in your class.

EXPLORE Perform an experiment

STEP 1 ***Select letters***

Write each of the 26 letters of the alphabet on separate pieces of paper. Put all of the letters into a bag. Select a letter at random (without looking into the bag). Replace the letter and select a second letter at random.

STEP 2 ***Record the results***

Record the results of the selections in a table like the one shown.

- If the first letter is the first initial of any student in your class, put a tally mark in the "first initial" column.
- If the second letter is the last initial of any student in your class, put a tally mark in the "last initial" column.
- If the two letters are the first and last initials of any student in your class, put a tally mark in the "both initials" column, but do not put a tally mark in the other columns.

Perform this experiment 30 times.

	First initial	Last initial	Both initials
Tally	卌	卌 II	I
Frequency	?	?	?

STEP 3 ***Record the frequencies***

Record the *frequency*, the total number of tally marks, of each possible result.

DRAW CONCLUSIONS Use your observations to complete these excercises

1. For what fraction of the times that you performed the experiment did you select the first initial of a student in your class? the last initial? both?
2. Which of these results do you think is least likely to happen if you repeat the experiment 30 more times? *Explain* your choice.
3. **REASONING** You perform the experiment 90 times. How many times do you expect to select both the first and last initials of a student in your class? *Explain* how you made your prediction.

11.1 Find Probabilities and Odds

Before You made organized lists and tree diagrams.

Now You will find sample spaces and probabilities.

Why? So you can find the likelihood of an event, as in Example 2.

Key Vocabulary
- **outcome**
- **event**
- **sample space**
- **probability**
- **odds**

A possible result of an experiment is an **outcome**. For instance, when you roll a number cube there are 6 possible outcomes: a 1, 2, 3, 4, 5, or 6. An **event** is an outcome or a collection of outcomes, such as rolling an odd number. The set of all possible outcomes is called a **sample space**.

EXAMPLE 1 Find a sample space

You flip a coin and roll a number cube. How many possible outcomes are in the sample space? List the possible outcomes.

REVIEW TREE DIAGRAMS
For help with tree diagrams, see p. SR22.

CC.9-12.S.CP.1 Describe events as subsets of a sample space (the set of outcomes) using characteristics (or categories) of the outcomes, or as unions, intersections, or complements of other events ("or," "and," "not").*

Solution

Use a tree diagram to find the outcomes in the sample space.

Coin flip Heads Tails

Number cube roll 1 2 3 4 5 6 1 2 3 4 5 6

The sample space has 12 possible outcomes. They are listed below.

Heads, 1	Heads, 2	Heads, 3	Heads, 4	Heads, 5	Heads, 6
Tails, 1	Tails, 2	Tails, 3	Tails, 4	Tails, 5	Tails, 6

✓ GUIDED PRACTICE for Example 1

1. You flip 2 coins and roll a number cube. How many possible outcomes are in the sample space? List the possible outcomes.

PROBABILITY The **probability of an event** is a measure of the likelihood, or chance, that the event will occur. Probability is a number from 0 to 1 and can be expressed as a decimal, fraction, or percent.

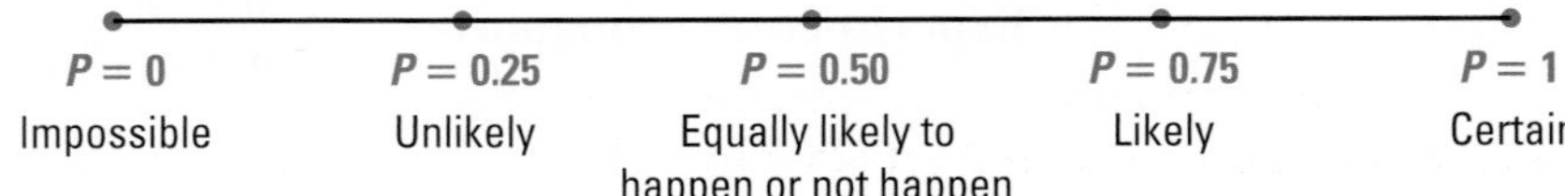

THEORETICAL PROBABILITY The outcomes for a specified event are called *favorable outcomes*. When all outcomes are equally likely, the **theoretical probability** of the event can be found using the following:

$$\textbf{Theoretical probability} = \frac{\textbf{Number of favorable outcomes}}{\textbf{Total number of outcomes}}$$

The probability of event A is written as $P(A)$.

EXAMPLE 2 Find a theoretical probability

T-SHIRTS You and your friends designed T-shirts with silk screened emblems, and you are selling the T-shirts to raise money. The table below shows the number of T-shirts you have in each design. A student chooses a T-shirt at random. What is the probability that the student chooses a red T-shirt?

	Gold emblem	Silver emblem
Green T-shirt	10	8
Red T-shirt	6	6

Solution

You and your friends have a total of $10 + 6 + 8 + 6 = 30$ T-shirts. So, there are 30 possible outcomes. Of all the T-shirts, 12 T-shirts are red. There are 12 favorable outcomes.

$$P(\text{red T-shirt}) = \frac{\text{Number of favorable outcomes}}{\text{Total number of outcomes}}$$

$$= \frac{\text{Number of red T-shirts}}{\text{Total number of T-shirts}}$$

$$= \frac{12}{30}$$

$$= \frac{2}{5}$$

GUIDED PRACTICE for Example 2

2. **T-SHIRTS** In Example 2, what is the probability that the student chooses a T-shirt with a gold emblem?
3. You toss a coin and roll a number cube. What is the probability that the coin shows tails and the number cube shows 4?

EXPERIMENTAL PROBABILITY An **experimental probability** is based on repeated *trials* of an experiment. The number of trials is the number of times the experiment is performed. Each trial in which a favorable outcome occurs is called a *success*.

$$\textbf{Experimental probability} = \frac{\textbf{Number of successes}}{\textbf{Number of trials}}$$

★ EXAMPLE 3 Standardized Test Practice

Each section of the spinner shown has the same area. The spinner was spun 20 times. The table shows the results. For which color is the experimental probability of stopping on the color the same as the theoretical probability?

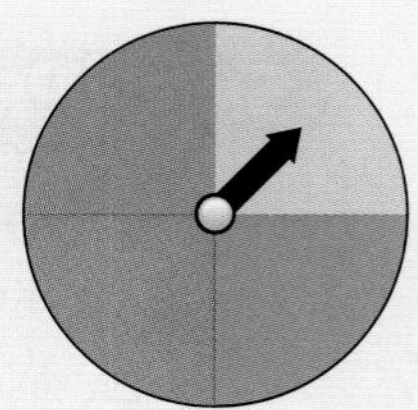

Spinner Results			
Red	Green	Blue	Yellow
5	9	3	3

Ⓐ Red Ⓑ Green Ⓒ Blue Ⓓ Yellow

Solution

The theoretical probability of stopping on each of the four colors is $\frac{1}{4}$. Use the outcomes in the table to find the experimental probabilities.

$P(\text{red}) = \frac{5}{20} = \frac{1}{4}$ $P(\text{green}) = \frac{9}{20}$ $P(\text{blue}) = \frac{3}{20}$ $P(\text{yellow}) = \frac{3}{20}$

▶ The correct answer is A. Ⓐ Ⓑ Ⓒ Ⓓ

Animated Algebra at my.hrw.com

ODDS The odds of an event compare the number of favorable and unfavorable outcomes when all outcomes are equally likely.

$$\textbf{Odds in favor} = \frac{\text{Number of favorable outcomes}}{\text{Number of unfavorable outcomes}}$$

$$\textbf{Odds against} = \frac{\text{Number of unfavorable outcomes}}{\text{Number of favorable outcomes}}$$

EXAMPLE 4 Find the odds

READING
Odds are read as the ratio of one number to another. For instance, the odds  $\frac{3}{1}$ are read as "three to one." Odds are usually written as *a* : *b*.

SPINNER In Example 3, find the odds against stopping on green.

Solution

The 4 possible outcomes are all equally likely. Green is the 1 favorable outcome. The other 3 colors are unfavorable outcomes.

$$\text{Odds against green} = \frac{\text{Number of unfavorable outcomes}}{\text{Number of favorable outcomes}} = \frac{3}{1} \text{ or } 3 : 1.$$

✓ GUIDED PRACTICE for Examples 3 and 4

4. In Example 3, for which color is the experimental probability of stopping on the color greater than the theoretical probability?

5. In Example 3, what are the odds in favor of stopping on blue?

11.1 EXERCISES

HOMEWORK KEY

○ = See **WORKED-OUT SOLUTIONS** Exs. 3 and 21

★ = **STANDARDIZED TEST PRACTICE** Exs. 2, 14–16, 21, and 22

SKILL PRACTICE

1. **VOCABULARY** Copy and complete: A number that describes the likelihood of an event is the __?__ of the event.

2. ★ **WRITING** *Explain* how the probability of an event differs from the odds in favor of the event when all outcomes are equally likely.

EXAMPLE 1 for Exs. 3–6

SAMPLE SPACE In Exercises 3–6, find the number of possible outcomes in the sample space. Then list the possible outcomes.

3. A bag contains 4 red cards numbered 1–4, 4 white cards numbered 1–4, and 4 black cards numbered 1–4. You choose a card at random.

4. You toss two coins.

5. You roll a number cube and toss three coins.

6. You roll two number cubes.

EXAMPLE 2 for Exs. 7–8

PROBABILITY AND ODDS In Exercises 7–13, refer to the spinner shown. The spinner is divided into sections with the same area.

7. What is the probability that the spinner stops on a multiple of 3?

8. **ERROR ANALYSIS** *Describe* and correct the error in finding the probability of stopping on a multiple of 9.

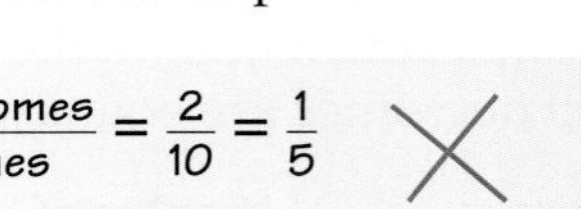

$$\frac{\text{Number of favorable outcomes}}{\text{Total number of outcomes}} = \frac{2}{10} = \frac{1}{5}$$

EXAMPLE 3 for Exs. 9–10

9. You spin the spinner 30 times. It stops on 12 three times. What is the experimental probability of stopping on 12?

10. You spin the spinner 10 times. It stops on an even number 6 times. What is the experimental probability of stopping on an even number?

EXAMPLE 4 for Exs. 11–14

11. What are the odds in favor of stopping on a multiple of 4?

12. What are the odds against stopping on a number less than 12?

13. **ERROR ANALYSIS** *Describe* and correct the error in finding the odds in favor of stopping on a multiple of 3.

$$\text{Odds in favor of a multiple of 3} = \frac{\text{Number of favorable outcomes}}{\text{Total number of outcomes}} = \frac{9}{10} \text{ or } 9:10$$

14. ★ **MULTIPLE CHOICE** The odds in favor of an event are 5 : 8. What are the odds against the event?

Ⓐ 3 : 8 Ⓑ 8 : 3 Ⓒ 5 : 8 Ⓓ 8 : 5

15. ★ **WRITING** A manufacturer tests 1200 computers and finds that 1191 of them have no defects. Find the probability that a computer chosen at random has no defects. *Predict* the number of computers without defects in a shipment of 15,000 computers. *Explain* your reasoning.

16. ★ **MULTIPLE CHOICE** According to a meteorologist, there is a 40% chance that it will rain today. What are the odds in favor of rain?

Ⓐ 2 : 5 Ⓑ 2 : 3 Ⓒ 3 : 2 Ⓓ 4 : 1

17. **DECISION MAKING** A driver wants to determine which of two possible routes to work he should choose. For 60 work days he recorded which route he took and whether or not he encountered heavy traffic. On 28 days he took route A, and on 7 of those days he encountered heavy traffic. On 32 days he took route B, and on 12 of those days he encountered heavy traffic. Which route would you suggest he choose? *Explain* your answer using experimental probabilities.

18. **CHALLENGE** You randomly draw a marble from a bag containing white, red, and blue marbles. The odds against drawing a white marble are 47 : 3.
   a. There are fewer than 100 marbles in the bag. How many marbles are in the bag? *Justify* your answer.
   b. The probability of drawing a red marble is 0.5. What is the probability of drawing a blue marble? *Explain* how you found your answer.

PROBLEM SOLVING

EXAMPLE 2 for Exs. 19–20

19. **MUSIC PROGRAM** You have created a playlist of 7 songs on your MP3 player. You play these songs in a random shuffle, where each song has an equally likely chance of being played. What is the probability that the second song on the list will be played first?

20. **SURVEY** A survey asked a total of 600 students (100 male students and 100 female students who were 11, 13, and 15 years old) about their exercise habits. The table shows the numbers of students who said they exercise 2 hours or more each week.

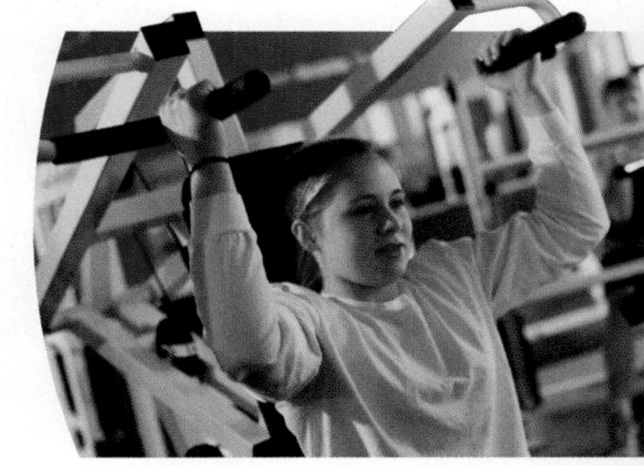

	11 years	13 years	15 years
Female	53	57	51
Male	65	68	67

   a. What is the probability that a randomly selected female student who participated in this survey exercises 2 hours or more each week?
   b. What is the probability that a randomly selected 15-year-old student who participated in this survey exercises 2 hours or more each week?
   c. What is the probability that a randomly selected student who participated in this survey exercises 2 hours or more each week?

EXAMPLES 2 and 4 for Ex. 21

21. ★ **SHORT RESPONSE** Suppose there are 15 girls and 12 boys in your homeroom. The teacher chooses one student representative at random. What is the probability that a boy is chosen? What are the odds in favor of choosing a boy? *Explain* how the probablity and odds are related.

22. ★ **EXTENDED RESPONSE** The table shows the 2003 regular season field goal statistics for kicker Adam Vinatieri.

	Point difference at end of game		
	0–7 points	8–14 points	≥ 15 points
Field goals attempted	20	11	3
Field goals made	16	7	2

a. During the 2003 regular season, what was the probability that Adam Vinatieri would make an attempted field goal, regardless of the point difference?

b. Find the probabilities that Vinatieri made an attempted field goal when the point difference at the end of the game was 0–7 points, 8–14 points, and at least 15 points.

c. During what kinds of games was Adam Vinatieri most likely to make attempted field goals? *Justify* your answer.

Animated Algebra at my.hrw.com

23. **CHALLENGE** The table shows the results of Congressional elections that involved incumbent candidates (representatives or senators who ran for re-election) during the period 1980–2000.

	Incumbent representatives		Incumbent senators	
	Ran	Re-elected	Ran	Re-elected
Presidential election year	2373	2235	163	130
Midterm election year	1984	1873	145	130

a. Did a representative or a senator have a better chance of being re-elected? *Justify* your answer using the data in the table.

b. Did a member of Congress have a better chance of being re-elected during a presidential election year than during a midterm election year? *Justify* your answer.

Extension Perform Simulations

GOAL Perform simulations to make predictions.

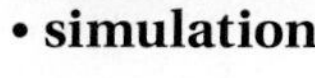

Key Vocabulary
- **simulation**

CC.9-12.S.IC.1 Understand statistics as a process for making inferences about population parameters based on a random sample from that population.*

A **simulation** is an experiment that you can perform to make predictions about real-world situations.

EXAMPLE 1 Perform a simulation

CONCESSION PRIZES Each time you buy an item from the concession stand at a baseball stadium, you receive a prize coupon, chosen at random. There is an equal chance of winning each prize from the following list: hot dog, popcorn, peanuts, pretzel, ice cream, and small drink. About how many times must you buy an item from the concession stand before you win each prize at least once?

Solution

You can perform a simulation to answer the question.

STEP 1 **Write** each prize on a separate piece of paper. Put the pieces of paper in a container.

STEP 2 **Draw** a piece of paper from the container at random. Record the result in a table like the one shown. Put the piece of paper back in the container. Repeat until you put a tally mark in the last empty cell of the table.

Prize	Hot dog	Popcorn	Peanuts	Pretzel	Ice cream	Small drink
Tally	I	IIII	II	𝍸	𝍸 I	II

The sum of all of the tally marks is the number of times you must buy an item from the concession stand before you win each prize at least once.

▶ In this simulation, you must buy an item from the concession stand 20 times.

USING A GRAPHING CALCULATOR You can also use the random integer generator on a graphing calculator to perform simulations.

The random integer generator is found by pressing the MATH key and selecting the PRB menu. It is the fifth item on the list and is displayed as randInt(.

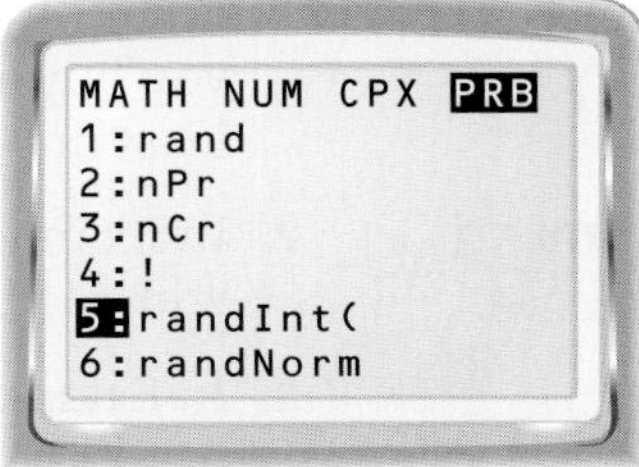

EXAMPLE 2 Perform a simulation using technology

GAME CARDS You receive a game card with every purchase at a sandwich shop. Each card has two circles to scratch. One circle reveals a prize, and the other says "Not a Winner." You cannot claim a prize if you scratch both circles. There is a $\frac{1}{6}$ chance that a card is for a CD, a $\frac{1}{2}$ chance that it is for a drink, and a $\frac{1}{3}$ chance that it is for a sandwich. About how many game cards must you scratch before you win a CD?

Solution

STEP 1 **Use** List 1 to show whether you scratch the circle with the prize. Generate a list of 50 random 1s and 0s. Each 1 means that you scratch the circle with the prize, and each 0 means that you scratch "Not a Winner."

Press STAT and select Edit. Highlight L_1. Enter randInt(0,1,50).

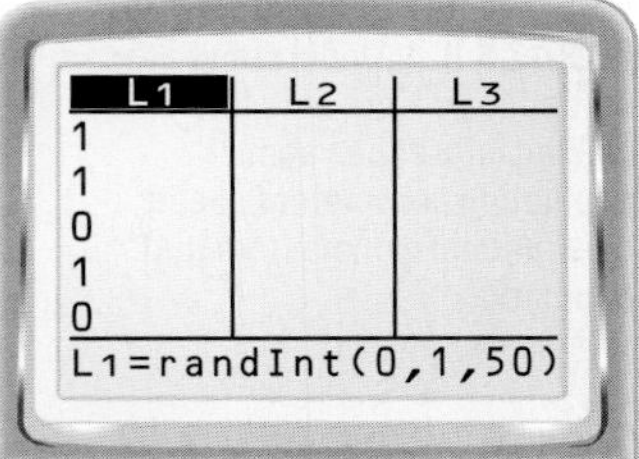

STEP 2 **Use** List 2 to show whether your game card contains the CD as the prize. Generate a list of 50 random integers from 1 to 6. Each 1 represents a prize card with a CD.

Highlight L_2. Enter randInt(1,6,50).

STEP 3 **Compare** the results of your two lists using List 3. Multiply the numbers from List 1 and List 2. Each 0 in List 3 means that you chose the wrong circle, so the prize does not matter. Because $1 \cdot 1 = 1$, you chose the correct circle *and* your card contains the CD prize when you see a 1 in L_3.

Highlight L_3. Enter $L_1 * L_2$.

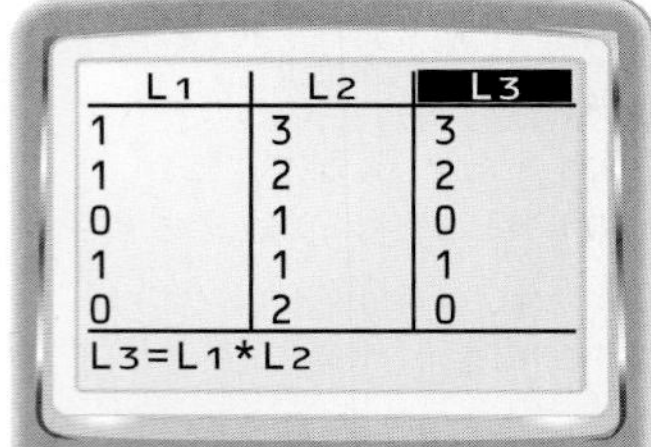

STEP 4 **Find** the first occurrence of a 1 in List 3. In this simulation, you can see that the first occurrence of a 1 in List 3 happens after 4 trials.

▶ For this simulation, you must scratch 4 game cards before you win a CD.

PRACTICE

EXAMPLE 1 for Exs. 1–3

1. In Example 1, suppose you can receive a prize coupon for nachos in addition to the items listed in the example. About how many times must you buy an item from the concession stand before you win each prize at least once? *Explain* how you found your answer.

EXAMPLE 2 for Exs. 2–3

2. In Example 2, about how many game cards must you scratch before you win one of each prize? *Explain* how you found your answer.

3. In Example 2, there are 3 prizes. *Explain* why the results of the simulation would be inaccurate if you generated random integers from 1 to 3.

11.2 Find Probabilities Using Permutations

Before You used the counting principle.

Now You will use the formula for the number of permutations.

Why? So you can find the number of possible arrangements, as in Ex. 38.

Key Vocabulary
- **permutation**
- ***n* factorial**

A **permutation** is an arrangement of objects in which order is important. For instance, the 6 possible permutations of the letters A, B, and C are shown.

ABC ACB BAC BCA CAB CBA

CC.9-12.S.CP.9(+) Use permutations and combinations to compute probabilities of compound events and solve problems.*

REVIEW COUNTING PRINCIPLE
For help with using the counting principle, see p. SR22.

EXAMPLE 1 Count permutations

Consider the number of permutations of the letters in the word JULY.

a. In how many ways can you arrange all of the letters?

b. In how many ways can you arrange 2 of the letters?

Solution

a. Use the counting principle to find the number of permutations of the letters in the word JULY.

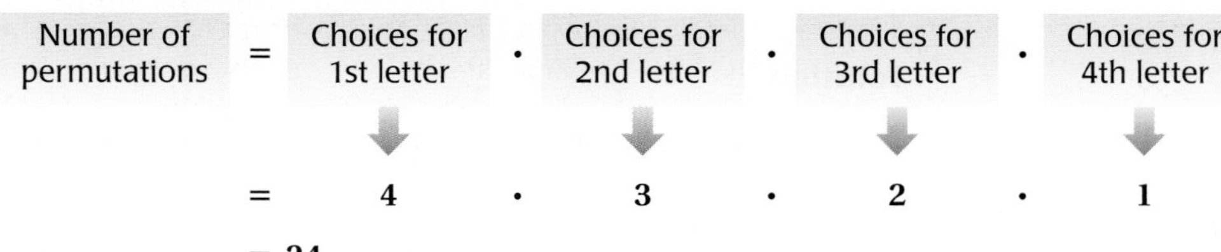

$= 4 \cdot 3 \cdot 2 \cdot 1$

$= 24$

▶ There are 24 ways you can arrange all of the letters in the word JULY.

b. When arranging 2 letters of the word JULY, you have 4 choices for the first letter and 3 choices for the second letter.

Number of permutations = Choices for 1st letter • Choices for 2nd letter

$= 4 \cdot 3$

$= 12$

▶ There are 12 ways you can arrange 2 of the letters in the word JULY.

✓ GUIDED PRACTICE for Example 1

1. In how many ways can you arrange the letters in the word MOUSE?

2. In how many ways can you arrange 3 of the letters in the word ORANGE?

FACTORIAL In Example 1, you evaluated the expression $4 \cdot 3 \cdot 2 \cdot 1$. This expression can be written as 4! and is read "4 *factorial*." For any positive integer n, the product of the integers from 1 to n is called ***n* factorial** and is written as $n!$. The value of 0! is defined to be 1.

$$n! = n \cdot (n-1) \cdot (n-2) \cdot \ldots \cdot 3 \cdot 2 \cdot 1 \text{ and } 0! = 1$$

In Example 1, you also found the permutations of four objects taken two at a time. You can find the number of permutations using the formulas below.

KEY CONCEPT ***For Your Notebook***

Permutations

Formulas	Examples
The number of permutations of n objects is given by: $_nP_n = n!$	The number of permutations of 4 objects is: $_4P_4 = 4! = 4 \cdot 3 \cdot 2 \cdot 1 = 24$
The number of permutations of n objects taken r at a time, where $r \le n$, is given by: $_nP_r = \frac{n!}{(n-r)!}$	The number of permutations of 4 objects taken 2 at a time is: $_4P_2 = \frac{4!}{(4-2)!} = \frac{4 \cdot 3 \cdot \cancel{2!}}{\cancel{2!}} = 12$

EXAMPLE 2 Use a permutations formula

CD RECORDING Your band has written 12 songs and plans to record 9 of them for a CD. In how many ways can you arrange the songs on the CD?

Solution

To find the number of permutations of 9 songs chosen from 12, find $_{12}P_9$.

$_{12}P_9 = \frac{12!}{(12-9)!}$ **Permutations formula**

$= \frac{12!}{3!}$ **Subtract.**

$= \frac{12 \cdot 11 \cdot 10 \cdot 9 \cdot 8 \cdot 7 \cdot 6 \cdot 5 \cdot 4 \cdot \cancel{3!}}{\cancel{3!}}$ **Expand factorials. Divide out common factor, 3!.**

$= 79{,}833{,}600$ **Multiply.**

▶ There are 79,833,600 ways to arrange 9 songs out of 12.

DIVIDE COMMON FACTORS
When you divide out common factors, remember that 3! is a factor of 12!.

✓ **GUIDED PRACTICE** for Example 2

3. **WHAT IF?** In Example 2, suppose your band has written 15 songs. You will record 9 of them for a CD. In how many ways can you arrange the songs on the CD?

EXAMPLE 3 Find a probability using permutations

PARADE For a town parade, you will ride on a float with your soccer team. There are 12 floats in the parade, and their order is chosen at random. Find the probability that your float is first and the float with the school chorus is second.

Solution

STEP 1 **Write** the number of possible outcomes as the number of permutations of the 12 floats in the parade. This is ${}_{12}P_{12} = 12!$.

STEP 2 **Write** the number of favorable outcomes as the number of permutations of the other floats, given that the soccer team is first and the chorus is second. This is ${}_{10}P_{10} = 10!$.

STEP 3 **Calculate** the probability.

$$P\left(\begin{array}{c}\text{soccer team is first}\\ \text{chorus is second}\end{array}\right) = \frac{10!}{12!}$$ **Form a ratio of favorable to possible outcomes.**

$$= \frac{\cancel{10!}}{12 \cdot 11 \cdot \cancel{10!}}$$ **Expand factorials. Divide out common factor, 10!.**

$$= \frac{1}{132}$$ **Simplify.**

 **GUIDED PRACTICE** for Example 3

4. **WHAT IF?** In Example 3, suppose there are 14 floats in the parade. Find the probability that the soccer team is first and the chorus is second.

11.2 EXERCISES

HOMEWORK KEY

○ = **See WORKED-OUT SOLUTIONS Exs. 21 and 35**

★ = **STANDARDIZED TEST PRACTICE Exs. 2, 11, 30, 33, and 35**

◆ = **MULTIPLE REPRESENTATIONS Ex. 34**

SKILL PRACTICE

1. **VOCABULARY** Copy and complete: An arrangement of objects in which order is important is called a(n) _?_.

2. ★ **WRITING** *Explain* what the notation ${}_9P_2$ means. What is the value of this expression?

EXAMPLES 1 and 2 for Exs. 3–11

COUNTING PERMUTATIONS Find the number of ways you can arrange (a) all of the letters in the given word and (b) 2 of the letters in the word.

3. AT
4. TRY
5. GAME
6. CAT
7. WATER
8. ROCK
9. APRIL
10. FAMILY

11. ★ **OPEN-ENDED** *Describe* a real-world situation where the number of possibilities is given by ${}_5P_2$.

EXAMPLE 2
for Exs. 12–30

FACTORIALS AND PERMUTATIONS **Evaluate the expression.**

12. 1!
13. 3!
14. 0!
15. 5!
16. 8!
17. 10!
18. 12!
19. 13!
20. ${}_5P_2$
21. ${}_7P_3$
22. ${}_9P_1$
23. ${}_6P_5$
24. ${}_8P_8$
25. ${}_{12}P_0$
26. ${}_{30}P_2$
27. ${}_{25}P_5$

ERROR ANALYSIS ***Describe*** **and correct the error in evaluating the expression.**

28. $${}_{11}P_7 = \frac{11!}{(11-7)} = \frac{11!}{4} = 9{,}979{,}200 \quad \times$$

29. $${}_5P_3 = \frac{5!}{3!} = \frac{5 \cdot 4 \cdot \cancel{3!}}{\cancel{3!}} = 20 \quad \times$$

30. ★ **MULTIPLE CHOICE** The judges in an art contest award prizes for first, second, and third place out of 11 entries. Which expression gives the number of ways the judges can award first, second, and third place?

Ⓐ $\frac{3!}{11!}$ Ⓑ $\frac{8!}{11!}$ Ⓒ $\frac{11!}{8!}$ Ⓓ $\frac{11!}{3!}$

31. **CHALLENGE** Consider a set of 4 objects and a set of n objects.

a. Are there more permutations of all 4 of the objects or of 3 of the 4 objects? *Justify* your answer using an organized list.

b. In general, are there more permutations of n objects taken n at a time or of n objects taken $n - 1$ at a time? *Justify* your answer using the formula for the number of permutations.

PROBLEM SOLVING

EXAMPLE 2
for Exs. 32–33

32. **MOVIES** Six friends go to a movie theater. In how many different ways can they sit together in a row of 6 empty seats?

33. ★ **MULTIPLE CHOICE** You plan to visit 4 stores during a shopping trip. In how many orders can you visit these stores?

Ⓐ 4 Ⓑ 16 Ⓒ 24 Ⓓ 256

EXAMPLE 3
for Exs. 34–38

34. ◆ **MULTIPLE REPRESENTATIONS** You and your friend are two of 4 servers working a shift in a restaurant. The host assigns tables of new diners to the servers in a particular order. This order remains the same, so that all servers are likely to wait on the same number of tables by the end of the shift.

a. Making a List List all the possible orders in which the host can assign tables to the servers.

b. Using a Formula Use the formula for permutations to find the number of ways in which the host can assign tables to the servers.

c. Describe in Words What is the likelihood that you and your friend are assigned the first 2 tables? *Explain* your answer using probability.

○ = See **WORKED-OUT SOLUTIONS** in Student Resources ★ = **STANDARDIZED TEST PRACTICE** ◆ = **MULTIPLE REPRESENTATIONS**

35. ★ **SHORT RESPONSE** Every student in your history class is required to present a project in front of the class. Each day, 4 students make their presentations in an order chosen at random by the teacher. You make your presentation on the first day.

a. What is the probability that you are chosen to be the first or second presenter on the first day? *Explain* how you found your answer.

b. What is the probability that you are chosen to be the second or third presenter on the first day? *Compare* your answer with that in part (a).

36. **HISTORY EXAM** On an exam, you are asked to list 5 historical events in the order in which they occurred. You guess the order of the events at random. What is the probability that you choose the correct order?

37. **SPIRIT** You make 6 posters to hold up at a basketball game. Each poster has a letter of the word TIGERS. You and 5 friends sit next to each other in a row. The posters are distributed at random. What is the probability that TIGERS is spelled correctly when you hold up the posters?

38. **BAND COMPETITION** Seven marching bands will perform at a competition. The order of the performances is determined at random. What is the probability that your school band will perform first, followed by the band from the one other high school in your town?

39. **CHALLENGE** You are one of 10 students performing in a school talent show. The order of the performances is determined at random. The first five performers go on stage before the intermission, while the remaining five performers go on stage after the intermission.

a. What is the probability that you are the last performer before the intermission and your rival performs immediately before you?

b. What is the probability that you are *not* the first performer?

QUIZ

1. **MARBLES** A bag contains 16 red marbles and 8 white marbles. You select a marble at random.

a. What is the probability that you select a red marble?

b. What are the odds in favor of selecting a red marble?

2. **PASSWORD** The password for an e-mail account is the word FISH followed by a 3-digit number. The 3-digit number contains the digits 1, 2, and 3. How many different passwords are possible?

11.3 Find Probabilities Using Combinations

Before You used permutations to count possibilities.
Now You will use combinations to count possibilities.
Why? So you can find the probability of an event, as in Example 3.

Key Vocabulary
- **combination**

A **combination** is a selection of objects in which order is *not* important. For instance, in a drawing for 3 identical prizes, you would use combinations, because the order of the winners would not matter. If the prizes were different, you would use permutations, because the order would matter.

CC.9-12.S.CP.9(+) Use permutations and combinations to compute probabilities of compound events and solve problems.*

EXAMPLE 1 Count combinations

Count the combinations of two letters from the list A, B, C, D.

Solution

List all of the permutations of two letters in the list A, B, C, D. Because order is not important in a combination, cross out any duplicate pairs.

AB	AC	AD	~~BA~~	BC	BD
~~CA~~	~~CB~~	CD	~~DA~~	~~DB~~	~~DC~~

BD and DB are the same pair.

▶ There are 6 possible combinations of 2 letters from the list A, B, C, D.

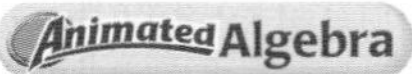 at my.hrw.com

GUIDED PRACTICE for Example 1

1. Count the combinations of 3 letters from the list A, B, C, D, E.

COMBINATIONS In Example 1, you found the number of combinations of objects by making an organized list. You can also find the number of combinations using the following formula.

KEY CONCEPT *For Your Notebook*

Combinations

Formula

The number of combinations of n objects taken r at a time, where $r \le n$, is given by:

$${}_nC_r = \frac{n!}{(n-r)! \cdot r!}$$

Example

The number of combinations of 4 objects taken 2 at a time is:

$${}_4C_2 = \frac{4!}{(4-2)! \cdot 2!} = \frac{4 \cdot 3 \cdot \cancel{2!}}{\cancel{2!} \cdot (2 \cdot 1)} = 6$$

EXAMPLE 2 Use the combinations formula

LUNCH MENU You order a sandwich at a restaurant. You can choose 2 side dishes from a list of 8. How many combinations of side dishes are possible?

Solution

The order in which you choose the side dishes is not important. So, to find the number of combinations of 8 side dishes taken 2 at a time, find ${}_8C_2$.

$${}_8C_2 = \frac{8!}{(8-2)! \cdot 2!}$$ **Combinations formula**

$$= \frac{8!}{6! \cdot 2!}$$ **Subtract.**

$$= \frac{8 \cdot 7 \cdot \cancel{6!}}{\cancel{6!} \cdot (2 \cdot 1)}$$ **Expand factorials. Divide out common factor, 6!.**

$$= 28$$ **Simplify.**

▶ There are 28 different combinations of side dishes you can order.

EXAMPLE 3 Find a probability using combinations

PHOTOGRAPHY A yearbook editor has selected 14 photos, including one of you and one of your friend, to use in a collage for the yearbook. The photos are placed at random. There is room for 2 photos at the top of the page. What is the probability that your photo and your friend's photo are the two placed at the top of the page?

Solution

STEP 1 **Write** the number of possible outcomes as the number of combinations of 14 photos taken 2 at a time, or ${}_{14}C_2$, because the order in which the photos are chosen is not important.

$${}_{14}C_2 = \frac{14!}{(14-2)! \cdot 2!} = \frac{14!}{12! \cdot 2!} = \frac{14 \cdot 13 \cdot \cancel{12!}}{\cancel{12!} \cdot (2 \cdot 1)} = 91$$

STEP 2 **Find** the number of favorable outcomes. Only one of the possible combinations includes your photo and your friend's photo.

STEP 3 **Calculate** the probability.

$P(\text{your photo and your friend's photos are chosen}) = \frac{1}{91}$

GUIDED PRACTICE for Examples 2 and 3

2. **WHAT IF?** In Example 2, suppose you can choose 3 side dishes out of the list of 8 side dishes. How many combinations are possible?

3. **WHAT IF?** In Example 3, suppose there are 20 photos in the collage. Find the probability that your photo and your friend's photo are the two placed at the top of the page.

11.3 EXERCISES

HOMEWORK KEY

○ = See **WORKED-OUT SOLUTIONS** Exs. 7 and 25

★ = **STANDARDIZED TEST PRACTICE** Exs. 2, 14–20, and 25

SKILL PRACTICE

1. **VOCABULARY** Copy and complete: A(n) __?__ is a selection of objects in which order is not important.

2. ★ **WRITING** *Explain* how a combination differs from a permutation.

EXAMPLE 1 for Exs. 3, 4

3. **COMBINATIONS** How many combinations of 3 letters from the list A, B, C, D, E, F are possible?

4. **ERROR ANALYSIS** *Describe* and correct the error in listing all of the possible combinations of 2 letters from the list A, B, C.

AB	BA	CA
AC	BC	CB

EXAMPLE 2 for Exs. 5–15

5. **ERROR ANALYSIS** *Describe* and correct the error in evaluating ${}_9C_4$.

$${}_9C_4 = \frac{9!}{(9-4)!} = \frac{9!}{5!} = 3024$$

COMBINATIONS Evaluate the expression.

6. ${}_5C_1$ 7. ${}_8C_5$ 8. ${}_9C_9$ 9. ${}_8C_6$

10. ${}_{12}C_3$ 11. ${}_{11}C_4$ 12. ${}_{15}C_8$ 13. ${}_{20}C_5$

14. ★ **MULTIPLE CHOICE** What is the value of ${}_{10}C_6$?

Ⓐ 7 Ⓑ 60 Ⓒ 210 Ⓓ 151,200

15. ★ **MULTIPLE CHOICE** You have the first season of your favorite television show on a set of DVDs. The set contains 13 episodes. You have time to watch 3 episodes. How many combinations of 3 episodes can you watch?

Ⓐ 286 Ⓑ 572 Ⓒ 1716 Ⓓ 589,680

★ **SHORT RESPONSE In Exercises 16–19, tell whether the question can be answered using *combinations* or *permutations*. *Explain* your choice, then answer the question.**

16. Four students from your class of 120 students will be selected to organize a fundraiser. How many groups of 4 students are possible?

17. Ten students are auditioning for 3 different roles in a play. In how many ways can the 3 roles be filled?

18. To complete an exam, you must answer 8 questions from a list of 10 questions. In how many ways can you complete the exam?

19. In how many ways can 5 people sit in a car that holds 5 passengers?

20. ★ **WRITING** Which is greater, ${}_6P_r$ or ${}_6C_r$? *Justify* your answer.

21. **REASONING** Write an equation that relates ${}_nP_r$ and ${}_nC_r$. *Explain* your reasoning.

22. **CHALLENGE** Prove that ${}_nC_r = {}_nC_{n-r}$. *Explain* why this makes sense.

PROBLEM SOLVING

EXAMPLE 2 for Ex. 23

23. **RESTAURANT** You are ordering a burrito with 2 main ingredients and 3 toppings. The menu below shows the possible choices. How many different burritos are possible?

EXAMPLE 3 for Exs. 24–26

24. **WORK SCHEDULE** You work 3 evenings each week at a bookstore. Your supervisor assigns you 3 evenings at random from the 7 possibilities. What is the probability that your schedule this week includes working on Friday?

25. ★ **SHORT RESPONSE** On a television game show, 9 members of the studio audience are randomly selected to be eligible contestants.

   a. Six of the 9 eligible contestants are randomly chosen to play a game on the stage. How many combinations of 6 players from the group of eligible contestants are possible?

   b. You and your two friends are part of the group of 9 eligible contestants. What is the probability that all three of you are chosen to play the game on stage? *Explain* how you found your answer.

26. **REPRESENTATIVES** Your teacher chooses 2 students at random to represent your homeroom. The homeroom has a total of 30 students, including your best friend. What is the probability that you and your best friend are chosen? What is the probability that you are chosen first and your best friend is chosen second? Which event is more likely to occur?

27. **CHALLENGE** There are 30 students in your class. Your science teacher will choose 5 students at random to complete a group project. Find the probability that you and your 2 best friends in the science class are chosen to work in the group. *Explain* how you found your answer.

Graphing Calculator ACTIVITY Use after Find Probabilities Using Combinations

my.hrw.com
Keystrokes

Find Permutations and Combinations

MATHEMATICAL PRACTICES

Use appropriate tools strategically.

QUESTION How can you find combinations and permutations using a graphing calculator?

EXAMPLE 1 Find the number of combinations

STARTERS There are 15 players on your softball team, but only 9 of them can be the starting players in one game. How many combinations of starting players are possible?

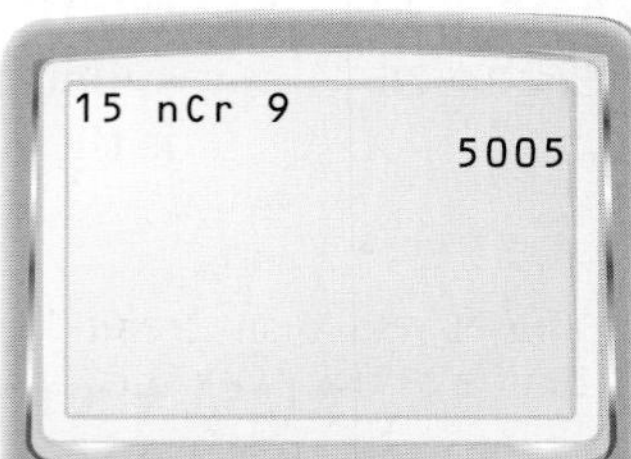

Solution

You are finding ${}_nC_r$ where $n = 15$ and $r = 9$. Enter 15 for n.

Press MATH. Go to the PRB menu and select ${}_nC_r$.
Then enter 9 for r.

▶ There are 5005 possible combinations of starting players.

EXAMPLE 2 Find the number of permutations

BATTING ORDER Before each softball game, your coach announces the batting order of the 9 starting players. This is the order in which the starting players will bat. How many batting orders can be formed using 9 players on your team of 15 players?

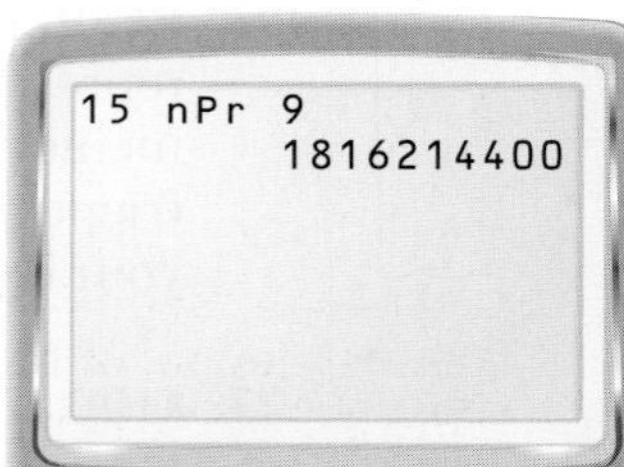

Solution

You are finding ${}_nP_r$ where $n = 15$ and $r = 9$. Enter 15 for n.

Press MATH. Go to the PRB menu and select ${}_nP_r$.
Then enter 9 for r.

▶ There are 1,816,214,400 possible batting orders.

PRACTICE

Evaluate the expression.

1. ${}_7C_4$ **2.** ${}_6C_6$ **3.** ${}_{10}C_3$ **4.** ${}_{16}C_8$

5. ${}_9P_5$ **6.** ${}_7P_6$ **7.** ${}_{11}P_8$ **8.** ${}_{12}P_5$

9. GROUP PROJECT Your teacher selects 3 students from a class of 28 students to work on a project in a group. Within the group, one member must be the writer, one must be the researcher, and one must be the presenter.

a. How many different groups of 3 can your teacher select?

b. After the group is formed, in how many ways can the roles in the group be assigned?

MIXED REVIEW of Problem Solving

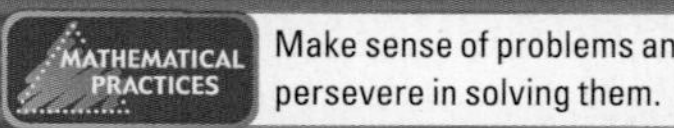

1. **MULTI-STEP PROBLEM** There are 5743 known amphibian species in the world. Of these, 1856 species are judged to be at risk of extinction, and another 113 species may already be extinct.

   a. Find the probability that an amphibian species chosen at random is at risk of extinction.

   b. Find the probability that an amphibian species chosen at random may already be extinct.

The Puerto Rican crested toad is at risk of extinction.

2. **MULTI-STEP PROBLEM** You are ordering an omelet with two ingredients. You can choose from the following list: cheese, mushrooms, onions, tomatoes, peppers, sausage, ham, and steak.

   a. Make an organized list of all the possible omelets that you can order.

   b. Use a permutation or combination formula to find the number of possible omelets.

3. **MULTI-STEP PROBLEM** In NCAA women's basketball tournaments from 1982 to 2003, teams seeded, or ranked, number one have won 283 games and lost 71 games in the tournament. Suppose a team is chosen at random from all those that have been seeded number one.

   a. What is the probability that the team won a game in the tournament?

   b. What are the odds in favor of the team's having won a game in the tournament?

4. **SHORT RESPONSE** A meteorologist reports that there is a 15% chance of snow tomorrow. What are the odds in favor of snow tomorrow? *Explain* how you found your answer.

5. **OPEN-ENDED** *Describe* a real-world situation in which the number of possible arrangements is given by ${}_{10}P_2$.

6. **EXTENDED RESPONSE** A survey asked a total of 400 students, 100 male students and 100 female students who were 13 and 15 years old, about their eating habits. The table shows the numbers of students who said that they eat fruit every day.

	13 years old	15 years old
Male	60	53
Female	61	58

   a. Find the probability that a female student, chosen at random from the students surveyed, eats fruit every day.

   b. Find the probability that a 15-year-old student, chosen at random from the students surveyed, eats fruit every day.

   c. You select a student at random from the students surveyed. Find the odds against the student's eating fruit every day. *Explain* your reasoning.

7. **GRIDDED ANSWER** A music club gives you 6 free CDs for joining. You would like to own 11 of the free CDs that are offered. How many combinations of 6 CDs from the 11 CDs can you choose?

Investigating Algebra ACTIVITY *Use before Find Probabilities of Disjoint and Overlapping Events*

Find Probabilities Using Venn Diagrams

Construct viable arguments and critique the reasoning of others.

QUESTION How can you use a Venn diagram to find probabilities involving two events?

You have learned how to compute the probability of one event. In some situations, however, you might be interested in the probability that two events will occur simultaneously. You also might be interested in the probability that at least one of two events will occur. This activity demonstrates how a Venn diagram is useful for computing such probabilities.

EXPLORE Use a Venn diagram to collect data

STEP 1 *Complete a Venn diagram*

Copy the Venn diagram shown below. Ask the members of your class if they have a sister, have a brother, have both, or have neither. Write their names in the appropriate part of the Venn diagram.

No sister or brother

Have a sister

Have a brother

STEP 2 *Complete a table*

Copy and complete the frequency table. When determining the frequency for a category, be sure to include all the students who are in the category. Note that a student can belong to more than one category.

Category	Number of students
Have a sister	?
Have a brother	?
Have both a sister and brother	?
Do not have a sister or brother	?

DRAW CONCLUSIONS Use your data to complete these exercises

1. A student from your class is selected at random. Find the probability of each event. *Explain* how you found your answers.
   - **a.** The student has a sister.
   - **b.** The student has a brother.
   - **c.** The student has a sister and a brother.
   - **d.** The student does not have a sister or a brother.
2. Find the probability that a randomly selected student from your class has either a sister or a brother. *Explain* how you found your answer.
3. How could you calculate the answer to Exercise 2 using your answers from Exercise 1?

11.4 Find Probabilities of Disjoint and Overlapping Events

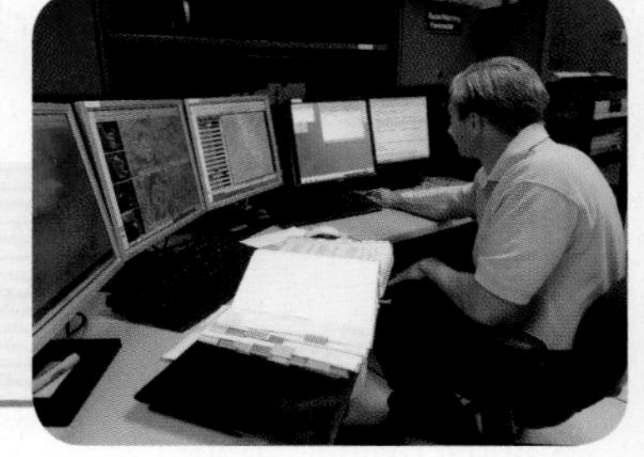

Before You found probabilities of simple events.

Now You will find probabilities of compound events.

Why? So you can solve problems about meteorology, as in Ex. 44.

Key Vocabulary
- **compound event**
- **overlapping events**
- **disjoint or mutually exclusive events**

CC.9-12.S.CP.1 Describe events as subsets of a sample space (the set of outcomes) using characteristics (or categories) of the outcomes, or as unions, intersections, or complements of other events ("or," "and," "not").*

When you consider all the outcomes for either of two events A and B, you form the *union* of A and B. When you consider only the outcomes shared by both A and B, you form the *intersection* of A and B. The union or intersection of two events is called a **compound event**.

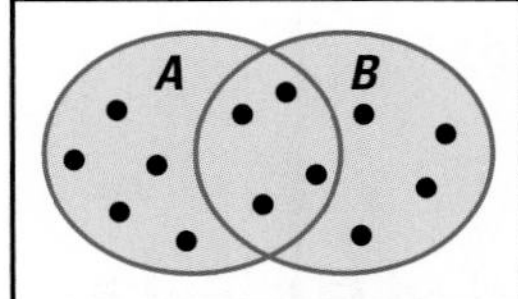

Union of A and B

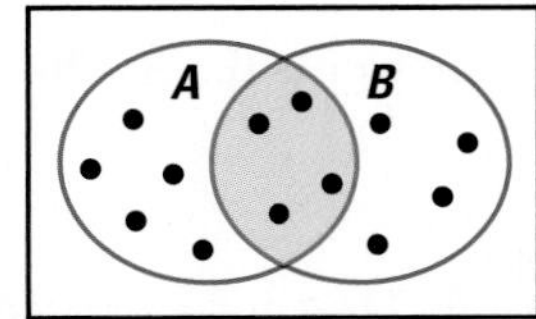

Intersection of A and B

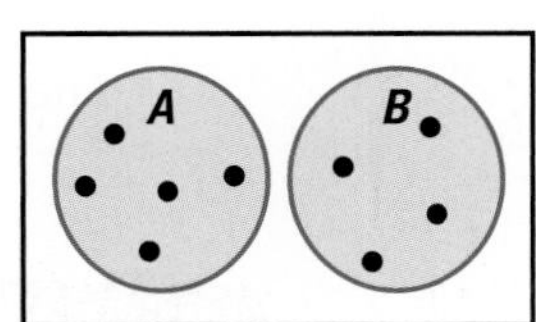

Intersection of A and B is empty.

To find $P(A \text{ or } B)$ you must consider what outcomes, if any, are in the intersection of A and B. Two events are **overlapping** if they have one or more outcomes in common, as shown in the first diagram. Two events are **disjoint**, or **mutually exclusive**, if they have no outcomes in common, as shown in the third diagram.

KEY CONCEPT *For Your Notebook*

Probability of Compound Events

If A and B are any two events, then the probability of A or B is:

$$P(A \text{ or } B) = P(A) + P(B) - P(A \text{ and } B)$$

If A and B are disjoint events, then the probability of A or B is:

$$P(A \text{ or } B) = P(A) + P(B)$$

EXAMPLE 1 Find probability of disjoint events

A card is randomly selected from a standard deck of 52 cards. What is the probability that it is a 10 *or* a face card?

Solution

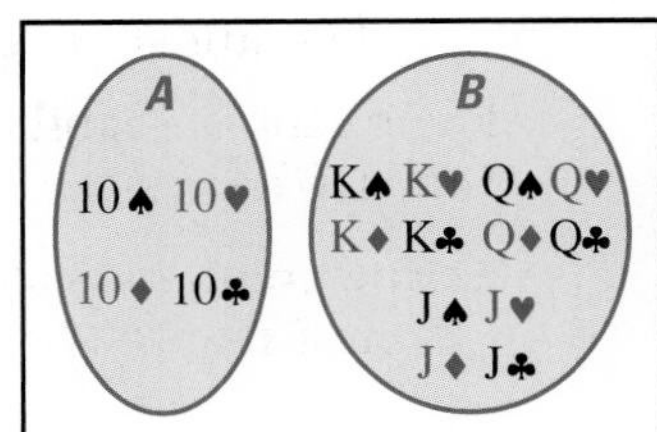

Let event A be selecting a 10 and event B be selecting a face card. A has 4 outcomes and B has 12 outcomes. Because A and B are disjoint, the probability is:

$$P(A \text{ or } B) = P(A) + P(B) = \frac{4}{52} + \frac{12}{52} = \frac{16}{52} = \frac{4}{13} \approx 0.308$$

dmac/Alamy

EXAMPLE 2 Standardized Test Practice

A card is randomly selected from a standard deck of 52 cards. What is the probability that it is a face card *or* a spade?

Ⓐ $\frac{3}{52}$ Ⓑ $\frac{11}{26}$ Ⓒ $\frac{25}{52}$ Ⓓ $\frac{7}{13}$

Solution

AVOID ERRORS
When two events *A* and *B* overlap, as in Example 2, *P*(*A* or *B*) does not equal *P*(*A*) + *P*(*B*).

Let event *A* be selecting a face card and event *B* be selecting a spade. *A* has 12 outcomes and *B* has 13 outcomes. Of these, 3 outcomes are common to *A* and *B*. So, the probability of selecting a face card *or* a spade is:

A: K♥ Q♥ J♥ K♦ Q♦ J♦ K♣ Q♣ J♣
A and B: K♠ Q♠ J♠
B: 10♠ 9♠ 8♠ 7♠ 6♠ 5♠ 4♠ 3♠ 2♠ A♠

$$P(A \text{ or } B) = P(A) + P(B) - P(A \text{ and } B) = \frac{12}{52} + \frac{13}{52} - \frac{3}{52} = \frac{22}{52} = \frac{11}{26}$$

▶ The correct answer is B. Ⓐ Ⓑ Ⓒ Ⓓ

EXAMPLE 3 Use a formula to find *P*(*A* and *B*)

SENIOR CLASS Out of 200 students in a senior class, 113 students are either varsity athletes *or* on the honor roll. There are 74 seniors who are varsity athletes and 51 seniors who are on the honor roll. What is the probability that a randomly selected senior is both a varsity athlete *and* on the honor roll?

Solution

Let event *A* be selecting a senior who is a varsity athlete and event *B* be selecting a senior on the honor roll. From the given information you know that $P(A) = \frac{74}{200}$, $P(B) = \frac{51}{200}$, and $P(A \text{ or } B) = \frac{113}{200}$. Find $P(A \text{ and } B)$.

$P(A \text{ or } B) = P(A) + P(B) - P(A \text{ and } B)$ **Write general formula.**

$\frac{113}{200} = \frac{74}{200} + \frac{51}{200} - P(A \text{ and } B)$ **Substitute known probabilities.**

$P(A \text{ and } B) = \frac{74}{200} + \frac{51}{200} - \frac{113}{200}$ **Solve for *P*(*A* and *B*).**

$P(A \text{ and } B) = \frac{12}{200} = \frac{3}{50} = 0.06$ **Simplify.**

✓ GUIDED PRACTICE for Examples 1, 2, and 3

A card is randomly selected from a standard deck of 52 cards. Find the probability of the given event.

1. Selecting an ace *or* an eight
2. Selecting a 10 *or* a diamond
3. **WHAT IF?** In Example 3, suppose 32 seniors are in the band and 64 seniors are in the band *or* on the honor roll. What is the probability that a randomly selected senior is both in the band *and* on the honor roll?

COMPLEMENTS The event $\overline{A}$, called the *complement* of event A, consists of all outcomes that are not in A. The notation $\overline{A}$ is read as "A bar."

KEY CONCEPT *For Your Notebook*

Probability of the Complement of an Event

The probability of the complement of A is $P(\overline{A}) = 1 - P(A)$.

EXAMPLE 4 Find probabilities of complements

ANOTHER WAY
For an alternative method for solving the problem in Example 4, see the **Problem Solving Workshop**.

DICE When two six-sided dice are rolled, there are 36 possible outcomes, as shown. Find the probability of the given event.

a. The sum is not 6.

b. The sum is less than or equal to 9.

Solution

a. $P(\text{sum is not } 6) = 1 - P(\text{sum is } 6) = 1 - \frac{5}{36} = \frac{31}{36} \approx 0.861$

b. $P(\text{sum} \le 9) = 1 - P(\text{sum} > 9) = 1 - \frac{6}{36} = \frac{30}{36} = \frac{5}{6} \approx 0.833$

EXAMPLE 5 Use a complement in real life

FORTUNE COOKIES A restaurant gives a free fortune cookie to every guest. The restaurant claims there are 500 different messages hidden inside the fortune cookies. What is the probability that a group of 5 people receive at least 2 fortune cookies with the same message inside?

Solution

The number of ways to give messages to the 5 people is 500^5. The number of ways to give *different* messages to the 5 people is $500 \cdot 499 \cdot 498 \cdot 497 \cdot 496$. So, the probability that at least 2 of the 5 people have the same message is:

$$P(\text{at least 2 are the same}) = 1 - P(\text{none are the same})$$

$$= 1 - \frac{500 \cdot 499 \cdot 498 \cdot 497 \cdot 496}{500^5}$$

$$\approx 0.0199$$

GUIDED PRACTICE for Examples 4 and 5

Find $P(\overline{A})$.

4. $P(A) = 0.45$

5. $P(A) = \frac{1}{4}$

6. $P(A) = 1$

7. $P(A) = 0.03$

8. WHAT IF? In Example 5, how does the answer change if there are only 100 different messages hidden inside the fortune cookies?

11.4 EXERCISES

HOMEWORK KEY

○ = See **WORKED-OUT SOLUTIONS** Exs. 11, 21, and 45

★ = **STANDARDIZED TEST PRACTICE** Exs. 2, 15, 34, 39, 40, 44, and 47

SKILL PRACTICE

1. **VOCABULARY** Copy and complete: The union or intersection of two events is called a(n) _?_.

2. ★ **WRITING** Are the events A and $\overline{A}$ disjoint? *Explain.* Then give an example of a real-life event and its complement.

EXAMPLE 1 for Exs. 3–8

DISJOINT EVENTS Events A and B are disjoint. Find $P(A \text{ or } B)$.

3. $P(A) = 0.3, P(B) = 0.1$
4. $P(A) = 0.55, P(B) = 0.2$
5. $P(A) = 0.41, P(B) = 0.24$
6. $P(A) = \frac{2}{5}, P(B) = \frac{3}{5}$
7. $P(A) = \frac{1}{3}, P(B) = \frac{1}{4}$
8. $P(A) = \frac{2}{3}, P(B) = \frac{1}{5}$

EXAMPLES 2 and 3 for Exs. 9–15

OVERLAPPING EVENTS Find the indicated probability.

9. $P(A) = 0.5, P(B) = 0.35$
   $P(A \text{ and } B) = 0.2$
   $P(A \text{ or } B) =$ _?_
10. $P(A) = 0.6, P(B) = 0.2$
   $P(A \text{ or } B) = 0.7$
   $P(A \text{ and } B) =$ _?_
11. $P(A) = 0.28, P(B) = 0.64$
   $P(A \text{ or } B) = 0.71$
   $P(A \text{ and } B) =$ _?_
12. $P(A) = 0.46, P(B) = 0.37$
   $P(A \text{ and } B) = 0.31$
   $P(A \text{ or } B) =$ _?_
13. $P(A) = \frac{2}{7}, P(B) = \frac{4}{7}$
   $P(A \text{ and } B) = \frac{1}{7}$
   $P(A \text{ or } B) =$ _?_
14. $P(A) = \frac{6}{11}, P(B) = \frac{3}{11}$
   $P(A \text{ or } B) = \frac{7}{11}$
   $P(A \text{ and } B) =$ _?_

15. ★ **MULTIPLE CHOICE** What is $P(A \text{ or } B)$ if $P(A) = 0.41$, $P(B) = 0.53$, and $P(A \text{ and } B) = 0.27$?

   Ⓐ 0.12   Ⓑ 0.67   Ⓒ 0.80   Ⓓ 0.94

EXAMPLE 4 for Exs. 16–19

FINDING PROBABILITIES OF COMPLEMENTS Find $P(\overline{A})$.

16. $P(A) = 0.5$
17. $P(A) = 0$
18. $P(A) = \frac{1}{3}$
19. $P(A) = \frac{5}{8}$

CHOOSING CARDS A card is randomly selected from a standard deck of 52 cards. Find the probability of drawing the given card.

20. A king *and* a diamond
21. A king *or* a diamond
22. A spade *or* a club
23. A 4 *or* a 5
24. A 6 *and* a face card
25. *Not* a heart

ERROR ANALYSIS *Describe* and correct the error in finding the probability of randomly drawing the given card from a standard deck of 52 cards.

26.
P(heart or face card)
$= P(\text{heart}) + P(\text{face card})$
$= \frac{13}{52} + \frac{12}{52}$
$= \frac{25}{52}$
✗

27.
P(club or 9)
$= P(\text{club}) + P(9) + P(\text{club and } 9)$
$= \frac{13}{52} + \frac{4}{52} + \frac{1}{52}$
$= \frac{9}{26}$
✗

FINDING PROBABILITIES **Find the indicated probability. State whether A and B are disjoint events.**

28. $P(A) = 0.25$
$P(B) = 0.4$
$P(A \text{ or } B) = 0.50$
$P(A \text{ and } B) = \underline{\ ?\ }$

29. $P(A) = 0.6$
$P(B) = 0.32$
$P(A \text{ or } B) = \underline{\ ?\ }$
$P(A \text{ and } B) = 0.25$

30. $P(A) = \underline{\ ?\ }$
$P(B) = 0.38$
$P(A \text{ or } B) = 0.65$
$P(A \text{ and } B) = 0$

31. $P(A) = \frac{8}{15}$
$P(B) = \underline{\ ?\ }$
$P(A \text{ or } B) = \frac{3}{5}$
$P(A \text{ and } B) = \frac{2}{15}$

32. $P(A) = \frac{1}{2}$
$P(B) = \frac{1}{6}$
$P(A \text{ or } B) = \frac{2}{3}$
$P(A \text{ and } B) = \underline{\ ?\ }$

33. $P(A) = 16\%$
$P(B) = \underline{\ ?\ }$
$P(A \text{ or } B) = 32\%$
$P(A \text{ and } B) = 8\%$

34. ★ **OPEN-ENDED MATH** *Describe* a real-life situation that involves two disjoint events A and B. Then describe a real-life situation that involves two overlapping events C and D.

ROLLING DICE **Two six-sided dice are rolled. Find the probability of the given event. (Refer to Example 4 for the possible outcomes.)**

35. The sum is 3 or 4.

36. The sum is not 7.

37. The sum is greater than or equal to 5.

38. The sum is less than 8 or greater than 11.

39. ★ **MULTIPLE CHOICE** Two six-sided dice are rolled. What is the probability that the sum is a prime number?

Ⓐ $\frac{13}{36}$ Ⓑ $\frac{7}{18}$ Ⓒ $\frac{5}{12}$ Ⓓ $\frac{5}{11}$

40. ★ **SHORT RESPONSE** Use the first diagram at the right to explain why this equation is true:

$$P(A) + P(B) = P(A \text{ or } B) + P(A \text{ and } B)$$

41. **CHALLENGE** Use the second diagram at the right to derive a formula for $P(A \text{ or } B \text{ or } C)$.

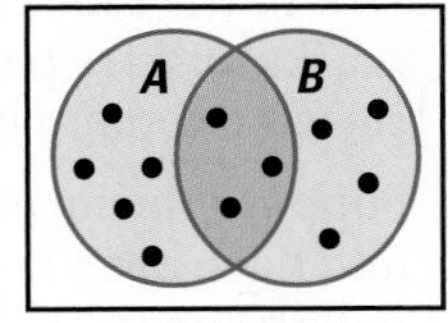

Ex. 40

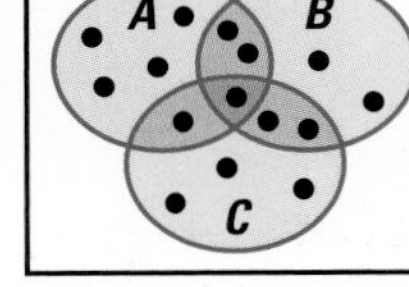

Ex. 41

PROBLEM SOLVING

EXAMPLES 1, 2, and 3 for Exs. 42–44

42. **CLASS ELECTIONS** You and your best friend are among several candidates running for class president. You estimate that there is a 45% chance you will win and a 25% chance your best friend will win. What is the probability that either you or your best friend win the election?

43. **BIOLOGY** You are performing an experiment to determine how well plants grow under different light sources. Out of the 30 plants in the experiment, 12 receive visible light, 15 receive ultraviolet light, and 6 receive both visible and ultraviolet light. What is the probability that a plant in the experiment receives either visible light or ultraviolet light?

Animated Algebra at my.hrw.com

EXAMPLES 4 and 5 for Exs. 44–46

44. ★ **MULTIPLE CHOICE** Refer to the chart below. Which of the following probabilities is greatest?

Ⓐ P(rains on Sunday) Ⓑ P(does not rain on Saturday)

Ⓒ P(rains on Monday) Ⓓ P(does not rain on Friday)

Four Day Forecast

Friday	Saturday	Sunday	Monday
Chance of Rain **5%**	Chance of Rain **30%**	Chance of Rain **80%**	Chance of Rain **90%**

45. **DRAMA CLUB** The organizer of a cast party for a drama club asks each of 6 cast members to bring one food item from a list of 10 items. What is the probability that at least 2 of the 6 cast members bring the same item?

46. **HOME ELECTRONICS** A development has 6 houses with the same model of garage door opener. Each opener has 4096 possible transmitter codes. What is the probability that at least 2 of the 6 houses have the same code?

47. ★ **EXTENDED RESPONSE** Use the given information about a farmer's tomato crop to complete parts (a)–(c).

a. 40% of the tomatoes are partially rotten, 30% of the tomatoes have been fed on by insects, and 12% are partially rotten *and* have been fed on by insects. What is the probability that a randomly selected tomato is partially rotten *or* has been fed on by insects?

b. 20% of the tomatoes have bite marks from a chipmunk and 7% have bite marks *and* are partially rotten. What is the probability that a randomly selected tomato has bite marks *or* is partially rotten?

c. Suppose the farmer finds out that 6% of the tomatoes have bite marks *and* have been fed on by insects. Do you have enough information to determine the probability that a randomly selected tomato has been fed on by insects *or* is partially rotten *or* has bite marks from a chipmunk? If not, what other information do you require?

48. **MULTI-STEP PROBLEM** Follow the steps below to explore a famous probability problem called the *birthday problem.* (Assume that there are 365 possible birthdays.)

a. Calculate Suppose that 6 people are chosen at random. Find the probability that at least 2 of the people share the same birthday.

b. Calculate Suppose that 10 people are chosen at random. Find the probability that at least 2 of the people share the same birthday.

c. Model Generalize the results from parts (a) and (b) by writing a formula for the probability $P(x)$ that at least 2 people in a group of x people share the same birthday. (*Hint:* Use ${}_nP_r$ notation in your formula.)

d. Analyze Enter the formula from part (c) into a graphing calculator. Use the *table* feature to make a table of values. For what group size does the probability that at least 2 people share the same birthday first exceed 50%?

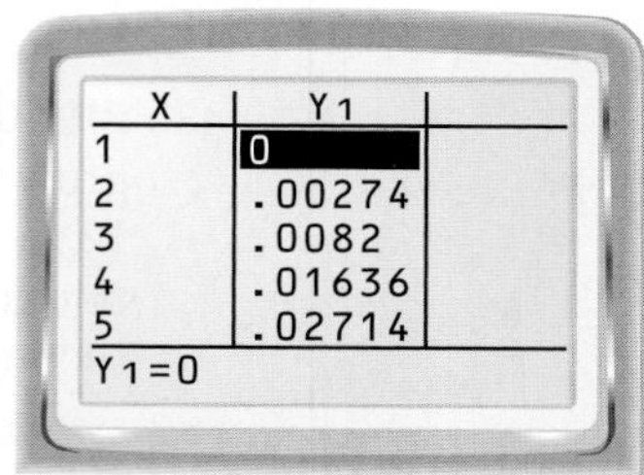

○ = See WORKED-OUT SOLUTIONS in Student Resources ★ = STANDARDIZED TEST PRACTICE

49. PET STORE A pet store has 8 black Labrador retriever puppies (5 females and 3 males) and 12 yellow Labrador retriever puppies (4 females and 8 males). You randomly choose one of the Labrador retriever puppies. What is the probability that it is a female or a yellow Labrador retriever?

50. CHALLENGE You own 50 DVDs consisting of 25 comedies, 15 dramas, and 10 thrillers. You randomly pick 4 movies to watch during a long train ride. What is the probability that you pick at least one DVD of each type of movie?

PROBLEM SOLVING WORKSHOP
LESSON 11.4

Using ALTERNATIVE METHODS

Another Way to Solve Example 4

Use appropriate tools strategically.

MULTIPLE REPRESENTATIONS In Example 4, you found theoretical probabilities involving the sum of two dice. You can also perform a *simulation* to estimate these probabilities.

PROBLEM

DICE When two six-sided dice are rolled, there are 36 possible outcomes. Find the probability of the given event.

a. The sum is not 6. **b.** The sum is less than or equal to 9.

METHOD

Using a Simulation An alternative approach is to use the random number feature of a graphing calculator to simulate rolling two dice. You can then use the results of the simulation to find the experimental probabilities for the problem.

STEP 1 **Generate** two lists of 120 random integers from 1 to 6 by entering randInt(1,6,120) into lists L_1 and L_2. Define list L_3 to be the sum of lists L_1 and L_2.

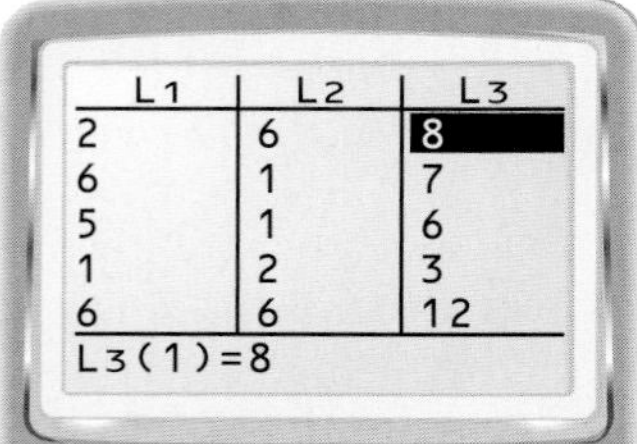

STEP 2 **Sort** the sums in list L_3 in ascending order using the command SortA(L_3). Scroll through the list and count the frequency of each sum.

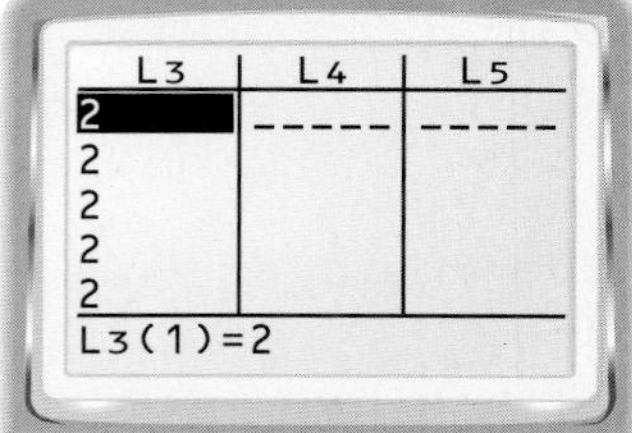

STEP 3 **Find** the probabilities.

a. Divide the number of times the sum was 6 by the total number of simulated rolls, then subtract the result from 1.

b. Divide the number of times the sum was greater than 9 by the total number of simulated rolls, then subtract the result from 1.

PRACTICE

1. **WRITING** *Compare* the probabilities found in the simulation above with the theoretical probabilities found in Example 4.

2. **SIMULATIONS** Use the results of the simulation above to find the experimental probability that the sum is greater than or equal to 4. *Compare* this to the theoretical probability of the event.

3. **SIMULATIONS** Use the results of the simulation above to find the experimental probability that the sum is not 8 or 9. *Compare* this to the theoretical probability of the event.

4. **REASONING** How could you change the simulation above so that the results would be closer to the theoretical probabilities of the events? *Explain.*

11.5 Find Probabilities of Independent and Dependent Events

Before You found probabilities of compound events.
Now You will examine independent and dependent events.
Why? So you can formulate coaching strategies, as in Ex. 37.

Key Vocabulary
- **independent events**
- **dependent events**
- **conditional probability**

Two events are **independent events** if the occurrence of one event does not affect the occurrence of the other. Two events are **dependent events** if the occurrence of one event *does* affect the occurrence of the other.

EXAMPLE 1 Identify independent and dependent events

CC.9-12.S.CP.2 Understand that two events *A* and *B* are independent if the probability of *A* and *B* occurring together is the product of their probabilities, and use this characterization to determine if they are independent.*

A jar contains red and blue marbles. You randomly choose a marble from the jar, and you do not replace it. Then you randomly choose another marble. Tell whether the events are *independent* or *dependent*.

Event A: The first marble you choose is red.
Event B: The second marble you choose is blue.

Solution

After you choose a red marble, fewer marbles remain in the jar. This affects the probability that the second marble is blue. So, the events are dependent.

CONDITIONAL PROBABILITIES
The conditional probability of B given A can be greater than, less than, or equal to the probability of B.

The probability that event B occurs given that event A has occurred is called the **conditional probability** of B given A and is written $P(B|A)$. Note that A and B are independent events if and only if $P(B) = P(B|A)$ since the probability of event B does not depend on the occurrence of event A.

KEY CONCEPT *For Your Notebook*

Probabilities of Independent and Dependent Events

Independent Events

For two independent events A and B, the probability that both events occur is the product of the probabilities of the events.

$P(A \text{ and } B) = P(A) \cdot P(B)$ *Events A and B are independent.*

Dependent Events

For two dependent events A and B, the probability that both occur is the product of the probability of the first event and the conditional probability of the second event given the first event.

$P(A \text{ and } B) = P(A) \cdot P(B|A)$ *Events A and B are dependent.*

The formulas for finding the probabilities of independent and dependent events can be extended to three or more events.

EXAMPLE 2 Find probability of independent events

As part of a board game, you need to spin the spinner at the right, which is divided into equal parts. Find the probability that you get 25 on your first spin and 50 on your second spin.

Solution

Let event A be "get 25 on first spin" and let event B be "get 50 on second spin." Find the probability of each event. Then multiply the probabilities.

$P(A) = \frac{2}{8}$ "25" appears twice.

$P(B) = \frac{1}{8}$ "50" appears once.

$$P(A \text{ and } B) = P(A) \cdot P(B) = \frac{2}{8} \cdot \frac{1}{8} = \frac{2}{64} \approx 0.031$$

▶ The probability that you get 25 on your first spin and 50 on your second spin is about 3.1%.

EXAMPLE 3 Find probability of dependent events

A bowl contains 36 green grapes and 14 purple grapes. You randomly choose a grape, eat it, and randomly choose another grape. Find the probability that both events *A* and *B* will occur.

Event *A*: The first grape is green.
Event *B*: The second grape is green.

Solution

Find $P(A)$ and $P(B|A)$. Then multiply the probabilities.

$P(A) = \frac{36}{50}$ Of the 50 grapes, 36 are green.

$P(B|A) = \frac{35}{49}$ Of the 49 remaining grapes, 35 are green.

$$P(A \text{ and } B) = P(A) \cdot P(B|A) = \frac{36}{50} \cdot \frac{35}{49} = \frac{1260}{2450} \approx 0.514$$

▶ The probability that both of the grapes are green is about 51.4%.

GUIDED PRACTICE for Examples 1, 2, and 3

Tell whether the situation describes *independent* or *dependent* events. Then answer the question.

1. **CLOTHING** A drawer contains 12 white socks and 8 black socks. You randomly choose one sock, and you do not replace it. Then you randomly choose another sock. What is the probability that both socks chosen are white?
2. **COIN FLIPS** Suppose you flip a coin twice. What is the probability that you get tails on the first flip and tails on the second flip?

CONDITIONAL PROBABILITY You can rewrite the formula for dependent events from the first page of this lesson to give a rule for finding conditional probabilities. Dividing both sides of the formula by $P(A)$ gives the following.

$$P(B|A) = \frac{P(A \text{ and } B)}{P(A)}$$

EXAMPLE 4 Find a conditional probability

WEATHER The table shows the numbers of tropical cyclones that formed during the hurricane seasons from 1988 to 2004. Use the table to estimate **(a)** the probability that a future tropical cyclone in the Northern Hemisphere is a hurricane, and **(b)** the probability that a hurricane is in the Northern Hemisphere.

Type of Tropical Cyclone	Northern Hemisphere	Southern Hemisphere
Tropical depression	199	18
Tropical storm	398	200
Hurricane	545	215

Solution

a. $P(\text{hurricane}|\text{Northern Hemisphere})$

$$= \frac{\text{Number of hurricanes in Northern Hemisphere}}{\text{Total number of cyclones in Northern Hemisphere}} = \frac{545}{1142} \approx 0.477$$

b. $P(\text{Northern Hemisphere}|\text{hurricane})$

$$= \frac{\text{Number of hurricanes in Northern Hemisphere}}{\text{Total number of hurricanes}} = \frac{545}{760} \approx 0.717$$

EXAMPLE 5 Compare independent and dependent events

SELECTING CARDS You randomly select two cards from a standard deck of 52 cards. What is the probability that the first card is not a heart and the second is a heart if **(a)** you replace the first card before selecting the second, and **(b)** you do not replace the first card?

Solution

Let A be "the first card is not a heart" and B be "the second card is a heart."

AVOID ERRORS
It is important first to determine whether A and B are independent or dependent in order to calculate $P(A \text{ and } B)$ correctly.

a. If you replace the first card before selecting the second card, then A and B are independent events. So, the probability is:

$$P(A \text{ and } B) = P(A) \cdot P(B) = \frac{39}{52} \cdot \frac{13}{52} = \frac{3}{16} \approx 0.188$$

b. If you do not replace the first card before selecting the second card, then A and B are dependent events. So, the probability is:

$$P(A \text{ and } B) = P(A) \cdot P(B|A) = \frac{39}{52} \cdot \frac{13}{51} = \frac{13}{68} \approx 0.191$$

GUIDED PRACTICE for Examples 4 and 5

3. **WHAT IF?** Use the information in Example 4 to find **(a)** the probability that a future tropical cyclone is a tropical storm and **(b)** the probability that a future tropical cyclone in the Southern Hemisphere is a tropical storm.

Find the probability of drawing the given cards from a standard deck of 52 cards (a) with replacement and (b) without replacement.

4. A spade, then a club
5. A jack, then another jack

EXAMPLE 6 Solve a multi-step problem

SAFETY Using observations made of drivers arriving at a certain high school, a study reports that 69% of adults wear seat belts while driving. A high school student also in the car wears a seat belt 66% of the time when the adult wears a seat belt, and 26% of the time when the adult does not wear a seat belt. What is the probability that a high school student in the study wears a seat belt?

Solution

A probability tree diagram, where the probabilities are given along the branches, can help you solve the problem. Notice that the probabilities for all branches from the same point must sum to 1.

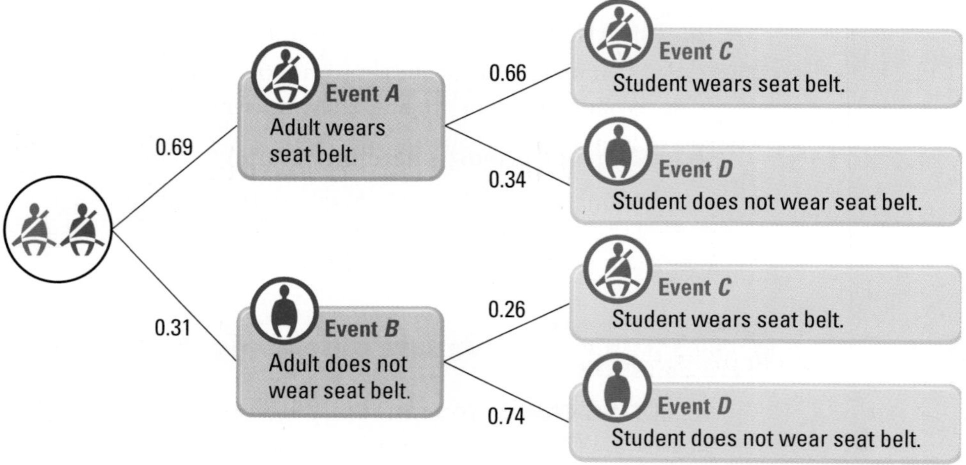

So, the probability that a high school student wears a seat belt is:

$$P(C) = P(A \text{ and } C) + P(B \text{ and } C)$$
$$= P(A) \cdot P(C|A) + P(B) \cdot P(C|B)$$
$$= (0.69)(0.66) + (0.31)(0.26) = 0.536$$

GUIDED PRACTICE for Example 6

6. **BASKETBALL** A high school basketball team leads at halftime in 60% of the games in a season. The team wins 80% of the time when they have the halftime lead, but only 10% of the time when they do not. What is the probability that the team wins a particular game during the season?

11.5 EXERCISES

HOMEWORK KEY

○ = See **WORKED-OUT SOLUTIONS** Exs. 18 and 35

★ = **STANDARDIZED TEST PRACTICE** Exs. 2, 10, 28, 29, and 37

SKILL PRACTICE

1. **VOCABULARY** Copy and complete: The probability that B will occur given that A has occurred is called the _?_ of B given A.

2. ★ **WRITING** *Explain* the difference between dependent events and independent events, and give an example of each.

EXAMPLE 1 for Exs. 3–6

INDEPENDENT AND DEPENDENT EVENTS **Tell whether the events are *independent* or *dependent*.**

3. A box of energy bars contains an assortment of flavors. You randomly choose an energy bar and eat it. Then you randomly choose another bar.

   Event *A*: You choose a honey-peanut bar first.
   Event *B*: You choose a chocolate chip bar second.

4. You roll a number cube and flip a coin.

   Event *A*: You get a 4 when rolling the number cube.
   Event *B*: You get tails when flipping the coin.

5. Your CD collection contains hip-hop and rock CDs. You randomly choose a CD, then choose another without replacing the first CD.

   Event *A*: You choose a hip-hop CD first.
   Event *B*: You choose a rock CD second.

6. There are 22 volumes of an encyclopedia on a shelf. You randomly choose a volume and put it back. Then you randomly choose another volume.

   Event *A*: You choose volume 7 first.
   Event *B*: You choose volume 5 second.

EXAMPLE 2 for Exs. 7–11

INDEPENDENT EVENTS **Events *A* and *B* are independent. Find the missing probability.**

7. $P(A) = 0.7$
   $P(B) = 0.3$
   $P(A \text{ and } B) = \underline{?}$

8. $P(A) = 0.22$
   $P(B) = \underline{?}$
   $P(A \text{ and } B) = 0.11$

9. $P(A) = \underline{?}$
   $P(B) = 0.4$
   $P(A \text{ and } B) = 0.13$

10. ★ **MULTIPLE CHOICE** Events A and B are independent. What is $P(A \text{ and } B)$ if $P(A) = 0.3$ and $P(B) = 0.2$?

    (A) 0.06 (B) 0.1 (C) 0.5 (D) 0.6

11. **REASONING** Let $P(A) = 0.3$, $P(B) = 0.2$, and $P(A \text{ and } B) = 0.06$. Find $P(A|B)$ and $P(B|A)$. Tell if A and B are dependent or independent. *Explain.*

EXAMPLE 3 for Exs. 12–14

DEPENDENT EVENTS **Events *A* and *B* are dependent. Find the missing probability.**

12. $P(A) = 0.5$
    $P(B|A) = 0.4$
    $P(A \text{ and } B) = \underline{?}$

13. $P(A) = 0.9$
    $P(B|A) = \underline{?}$
    $P(A \text{ and } B) = 0.72$

14. $P(A) = \underline{?}$
    $P(B|A) = 0.6$
    $P(A \text{ and } B) = 0.15$

EXAMPLE 4
for Exs. 15–18

CONDITIONAL PROBABILITY Let n be a randomly selected integer from 1 to 20. Find the indicated probability.

15. n is 2 given that it is even

16. n is 5 given that it is less than 8

17. n is prime given that it has 2 digits

18. n is odd given that it is prime

EXAMPLE 5
for Exs. 19–26

DRAWING CARDS Find the probability of drawing the given cards from a standard deck of 52 cards (a) with replacement and (b) without replacement.

19. A club, then a spade

20. A queen, then an ace

21. A face card, then a 6

22. A 10, then a 2

23. A king, then a queen, then a jack

24. A spade, then a club, then another spade

25. REASONING You are playing a game that involves spinning the wheel shown. Find **(a)** the probability of spinning blue and **(b)** the probability of first spinning green and then spinning blue. Are the events of spinning green and then blue dependent or independent? *Explain.*

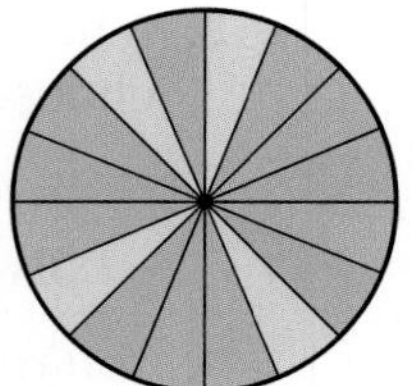

26. ★ MULTIPLE CHOICE What is the approximate probability of drawing 3 consecutive hearts from a standard deck of 52 cards without replacement?

Ⓐ 0.0122 Ⓑ 0.0129 Ⓒ 0.0156 Ⓓ 0.0166

27. ERROR ANALYSIS Events A and B are independent. *Describe* and correct the error in finding $P(A \text{ and } B)$.

P(A) = 0.4, P(B) = 0.5
P(A and B) = 0.4 + 0.5 = 0.9

28. ★ OPEN-ENDED MATH Flip a set of 3 coins and record the number of coins that come up heads. Repeat until you have a total of 10 trials.

a. What is the experimental probability that a trial results in 2 heads?

b. *Compare* your answer from part (a) with the theoretical probability that a trial results in 2 heads.

29. ★ SHORT RESPONSE A basket contains bottles of apple juice and orange juice in two sizes. The number of each type of bottle is shown in the table.

	6 oz	8 oz
Apple	4	8
Orange	6	9

a. What is the probability that a randomly chosen bottle of juice is a 6-ounce bottle given that the bottle contains apple juice?

b. What is the probability that a randomly chosen 6-ounce bottle contains orange juice?

c. What is the probability that a randomly chosen bottle of orange juice is a 6-ounce bottle?

d. Explain the difference between parts (b) and (c).

30. REASONING Let A and B be independent events. What is the relationship between $P(B)$ and $P(B|A)$? *Explain.*

○ = See **WORKED-OUT SOLUTIONS** in Student Resources ★ = **STANDARDIZED TEST PRACTICE**

31. **CHALLENGE** Bayes's Theorem states that $P(A|B) = \frac{P(B|A) \cdot P(A)}{P(B)}$. Prove it by using the formula for the probability of dependent events and another version of it in which A and B are swapped.

PROBLEM SOLVING

EXAMPLE 4 for Exs. 32–34

32. **ENVIRONMENT** The table shows the numbers of species in the United States listed as endangered or threatened a few years ago. Find **(a)** the probability that a listed animal is a bird, **(b)** the probability that an endangered animal is a bird, and **(c)** the probability that a bird is endangered.

	Endangered	Threatened
Mammals	69	9
Birds	77	14
Reptiles	14	22
Amphibians	11	10
Other	219	74

In Exercises 33 and 34, use the following information.

TRANSPORTATION All the students at Allen High School were surveyed to find out how they get to school each day. The table shows the number of students at each grade level who walk, bike, or take the bus to school.

	Walk	Bike	Bus	Total
Freshman	52	16	72	140
Sophomore	41	18	61	120
Junior	43	35	72	150
Senior	28	40	52	120
Total	164	109	257	530

33. **a.** What is the probability that a randomly chosen student is a senior?

    b. What is the probability that a randomly chosen student is a senior given that the student bikes to school?

    c. Are the events "student is a senior" and "student bikes to school" independent events? Why or why not?

34. **a.** What is the probability that a randomly chosen student takes the bus given that the student is a junior?

    b. What is the probability that a randomly chosen student who takes the bus is a junior?

    c. ★ **WRITING** Discuss the difference between the probabilities in parts (a) and (b).

EXAMPLE 6 for Ex. 35

35. **TENNIS** A tennis player wins a match 55% of the time when she serves first and 47% of the time when her opponent serves first. The player who serves first is determined by a coin toss before the match. What is the probability that the player wins a given match?

EXAMPLE 6
for Exs. 36–37

36. **MEDICAL TESTING** Suppose 1% of the population is known to have a medical condition. There is a test for the condition, and 80% of people with the condition test positive for it. Also, 10% of people without the condition test positive for it. Follow these steps to find the probability that a person actually has the condition given that he or she tests positive.

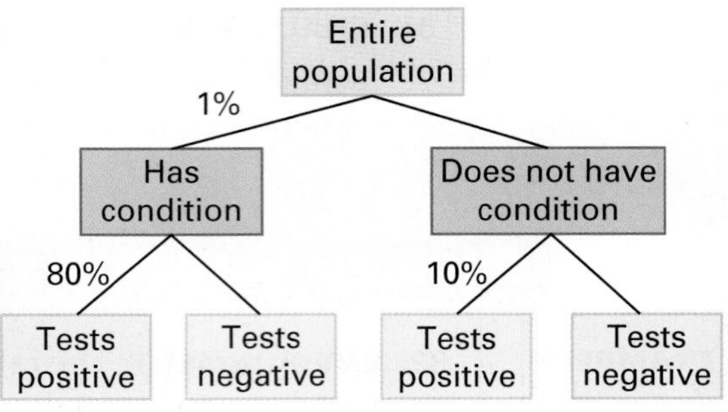

a. Let A be the event that a person has the condition and let B be the event that the person tests positive. What are $P(B|A)$ and $P(A)$?

b. Find $P(B)$. (*Hint:* Consider the portion of the population with the condition that tests positive and the portion of the population without the condition that tests positive.)

c. Use parts (a) and (b) and Bayes's Theorem to find the probability that a person has the condition given that he or she tests positive.

Bayes's Theorem: $P(A|B) = \frac{P(B|A) \cdot P(A)}{P(B)}$

37. ★ **EXTENDED RESPONSE** A football team is losing by 14 points near the end of a game. The team scores two touchdowns (worth 6 points each) before the end of the game. After each touchdown, the coach must decide whether to go for 1 point with a kick (which is successful 99% of the time) or 2 points with a run or pass (which is successful 45% of the time).

a. **Calculate** If the team goes for 1 point after each touchdown, what is the probability that the coach's team wins? loses? ties?

b. **Calculate** If the team goes for 2 points after each touchdown, what is the probability that the coach's team wins? loses? ties?

c. **Reasoning** Can you develop a strategy so that the coach's team has a probability of winning the game that is greater than the probability of losing? If so, explain your strategy and calculate the probabilities of winning and losing using your strategy.

QUIZ

Find the indicated probability.

1. $P(A) = 0.6$
   $P(B) = 0.35$
   $P(A \text{ or } B) = ?$
   $P(A \text{ and } B) = 0.2$

2. $P(A) = ?$
   $P(B) = 0.44$
   $P(A \text{ or } B) = 0.56$
   $P(A \text{ and } B) = 0.12$

3. $P(A) = 0.75$
   $P(B) = ?$
   $P(A \text{ or } B) = 0.83$
   $P(A \text{ and } B) = 0.25$

Find the probability of randomly drawing the given marbles from a bag of 6 red, 9 green, and 5 blue marbles (a) with replacement and (b) without replacement.

4. red, then green
5. blue, then red
6. green, then green

See **EXTRA PRACTICE** in Student Resources

Extension Make and Analyze Decisions

CC.9-12.S.MD.6(+) Use probabilities to make fair decisions (e.g., drawing by lots, using a random number generator).*

Probabilities can help in making fair decisions, as when using a process with equally likely outcomes to select a contest winner. Probabilities also underlie all kinds of real-world decisions in business, science, agriculture, and so on.

EXAMPLE 1 Use probability to make a decision

Twenty students, including Noe, volunteer to present the "Best Teacher" award at a school banquet. Describe a process that gives Noe a fair chance to be chosen, and find the probability, if (a) "fair" means equally likely, and (b) "fair" means proportional to how many banquet prep hours the volunteer worked. Each volunteer worked at least one hour, Noe worked four hours, and, in all, the 20 students worked 45 hours.

Solution

a. Write the names on slips of paper, place them in a box, and draw a slip at random. The probability is 1 out of 20, or 5%.

b. Write the names on slips of paper, but for each hour more than one that a student worked, write their name on an extra slip. Then draw as in part (a). The probability is 4 out of 45, or about 8.9%.

EXAMPLE 2 Use probability to make a decision

Your company must produce 50,000 non-defective cell phones using a component from one of the suppliers below.

	Price per 1000	*P*(defective)	*P*(working)
Supplier *X*	$740.00	4.0%	96.0%
Supplier *Y*	$800.00	1.9%	98.1%

Each defective component bought results in $2.20 in extra cost to your company. From which supplier should you buy?

Solution

Use the probability that a component is defective to estimate the total cost.

$$\text{Total cost} = \begin{matrix}\text{Cost to get 50,000} \\ \text{working components}\end{matrix} + \begin{matrix}\text{Extra cost from} \\ \text{defective components}\end{matrix}$$

X: Solving $0.96x = 50{,}000$ gives $x = 52{,}083$. You must buy 53,000 components.
Total cost = 53,000($.74) + (0.04)(53,000)($2.20) = $39,220 + $4664 = $43,884

Y: Solving $0.981y = 50{,}000$ gives $y = 50{,}968$. You must buy 51,000 components.
Total cost = 51,000($.80) + (0.019)(51,000)($2.20) = $40,800 + $2132 = $42,932

▶ For the lowest total cost, you should buy from supplier Y.

PRACTICE

EXAMPLE 1
for Ex. 1

1. A teacher tells students, "For each puzzler you complete, I will assign you a prize entry." In all, 10 students complete 53 puzzlers. Leon completed 7. To award the prize, the teacher sets a calculator to generate a random integer from 1 to 53. Leon is assigned 18 to 24 as "winners." Is this fair to Leon according to the original instructions? *Explain.*

EXAMPLE 2
for Exs. 2–4

2. A company creates a new brand of a snack, N, and tests it against the current market leader, L. The table shows the results.

	Prefer L	Prefer N
Current L consumer	72	46
Not current L consumer	52	114

Use probability to explain how the company's decisions about whether to try to improve the snack before marketing it and to which consumers it should aim its marketing might differ if the total size of the snack's market is expected to (a) change very little, and (b) expand very rapidly.

3. The Redbirds trail the Bluebirds by 1 goal with 1 minute left in the hockey game. The coach must decide whether to remove the goalie and add a frontline player. The only way the Redbirds can tie the game is for them to score and for the Bluebirds not to score. The probabilities are shown below.

	Goalie	No Goalie
Redbirds score	0.1	0.3
Bluebirds score	0.1	0.6

a. Find the probability that the Redbirds score and the Bluebirds do not score if the coach leaves the goalie in.

b. Find the probability that the Redbirds score and the Bluebirds do not score if the coach takes the goalie out.

c. Based on parts (a) and (b), what should the coach do?

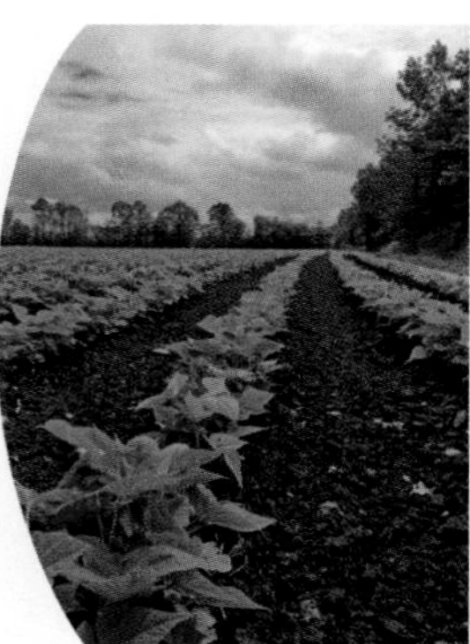

4. A farmer is offered a contract that guarantees him $11.00 per bushel for his entire soybean crop when it is harvested in three months. Below are predictions for the market price *m* per of soybeans in three months.

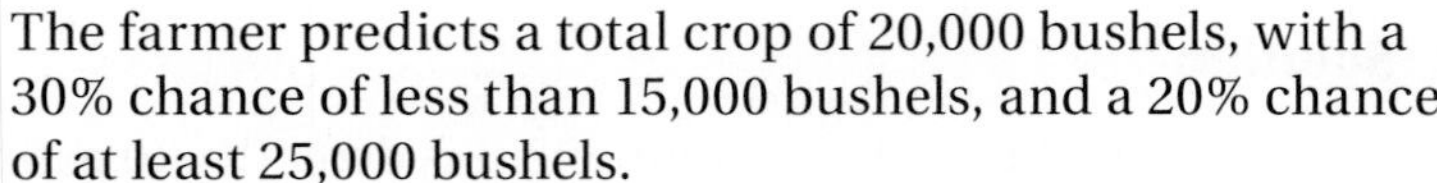

$P(m \le \$9.00) = 10\%$ $\quad P(m \ge \$10.50) = 50\%$
$P(m \ge \$12.50) = 20\%$

The farmer predicts a total crop of 20,000 bushels, with a 30% chance of less than 15,000 bushels, and a 20% chance of at least 25,000 bushels.

a. Find the probability and income range for (i) the best case: the farmer declines the contract, the price is highest, and the harvest is largest; and (ii) the worst case: he declines the contract, the price is lowest, and the harvest is smallest. (Assume harvest size and price are independent.)

b. How much will the farmer make if he accepts the contract and his total crop prediction is accurate? How might this and the answers to part (a) affect the decision of whether or not to accept the contract?

MIXED REVIEW *of Problem Solving*

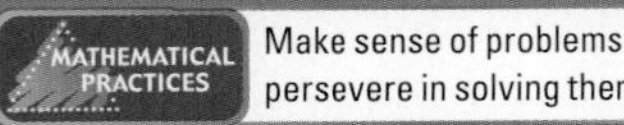

Make sense of problems and persevere in solving them.

1. **MULTI-STEP PROBLEM** You and a friend are playing a word game that involves lettered tiles. The distribution of letters is shown below.

Letter	Count	Letter	Count	Letter	Count	Letter	Count
A	9	H	2	O	8	V	2
B	2	I	9	P	2	W	2
C	2	J	1	Q	1	X	1
D	4	K	1	R	6	Y	2
E	12	L	4	S	4	Z	1
F	2	M	2	T	6	Blank	2
G	3	N	6	U	4		

   a. You randomly draw 1 tile. What is the probability of getting a vowel? (Assume that Y is a consonant.)

   b. You randomly draw 2 tiles without replacement. What is the probability of getting 2 vowels?

   c. At the start of the game, you randomly choose 7 tiles without replacement. What is the probability that all of the tiles are vowels?

2. **SHORT RESPONSE** A manufacturer makes briefcases with numbered locks. The locks can be set so that any one of 1000 different codes will open the briefcase. Four friends have briefcases from this manufacturer. What is the probability that at least 2 of the 4 briefcases have the same code? If two more friends buy the same briefcase, how does the probability that at least 2 of the briefcases have the same code change?

3. **OPEN-ENDED** Write a real-life problem that you can solve using a tree diagram and conditional probabilities. Draw the tree diagram and show how to solve the problem.

4. **EXTENDED RESPONSE** The owner of a lawn mowing business owns three old and unreliable riding mowers. As long as one of the mowers is working, the owner can stay productive. From past experience, one of the mowers is unusable 10% of the time, one is unusable 8% of the time, and one is unusable 18% of the time.

   a. Find the probability that all three mowers are unusable on a given day.

   b. Find the probability that at least one of the mowers is usable on a given day.

   c. Suppose the least reliable mower stops working completely. How does this affect the probability that the lawn mowing business can be productive on a given day?

5. **SHORT RESPONSE** In the United States there are 21 states (not including Washington, D.C.) with teams in the National Football League and 17 states with Major League Baseball teams. There are 15 states that have both types of teams. Suppose a state is chosen at random.

   a. Find the probability that the state has either a National Football League team or a Major League Baseball team.

   b. There are 21 states that have a team in the National Basketball Association. What additional information would you need in order to find the probability that the state chosen at random has either a team in the National Basketball Association or a Major League Baseball team? *Explain* your reasoning.

11 CHAPTER SUMMARY

BIG IDEAS

For Your Notebook

Big Idea 1

Finding Probabilities of Simple Events

To find $P(A)$ when...	
all outcomes are equally likely, use $P(A) = \frac{\text{Number of favorable outcomes}}{\text{Number of possible outcomes}}$	you perform an experiment, use $P(A) = \frac{\text{Number of successes}}{\text{Number of trials}}$

Big Idea 2

Finding Probabilities of Compound Events

To find $P(A \text{ or } B)$ when...	...use this formula
events A and B are disjoint or mutually exclusive, that is, when events A and B have no common outcomes	$P(A \text{ or } B) = P(A) + P(B)$
events A and B are overlapping, that is, when events A and B have at least one common outcome	$P(A \text{ or } B) = P(A) + P(B) - P(A \text{ and } B)$

To find $P(A \text{ and } B)$ when...	...use this formula
events A and B are independent	$P(A \text{ and } B) = P(A) \cdot P(B)$
events A and B are dependent	$P(A \text{ and } B) = P(A) \cdot P(B \text{ given } A)$

11 CHAPTER REVIEW

@HomeTutor
my.hrw.com
- Multi-Language Glossary
- Vocabulary Practice

REVIEW KEY VOCABULARY

- outcome, event
- sample space
- probability of an event
- theoretical, experimental probability
- odds in favor, odds against
- permutation
- *n* factorial
- combination
- compound events
- overlapping events
- disjoint or mutually exclusive events
- independent events
- dependent events
- conditional probability

VOCABULARY EXERCISES

Copy and complete the statement.

1. An event that combines two or more events is a(n) _?_.
2. A possible result of an experiment is a(n) _?_.
3. **WRITING** *Compare* theoretical probability and experimental probability.

REVIEW EXAMPLES AND EXERCISES

Use the review examples and exercises below to check your understanding of the concepts you have learned in each lesson of this chapter.

11.1 Find Probabilities and Odds

EXAMPLE

A bag contains 15 red checkers and 15 black checkers. You choose a checker at random. Find the probability that you choose a black checker.

$$P(\text{black checker}) = \frac{\text{Number of black checkers}}{\text{Total number of checkers}} = \frac{15}{30} = \frac{1}{2}$$

EXERCISES

EXAMPLE 2 for Exs. 4–5

4. **CHECKERS** In the example above, suppose an extra red checker is added to the bag. Find the probability of randomly choosing a black checker.
5. **BAG OF LETTERS** A bag contains tiles. Each tile has one letter from the word HAPPINESS on it. You choose a tile at random. What is the probability that you choose a tile with the letter S?

@HomeTutor
my.hrw.com
Chapter Review Practice

11.2 Find Probabilities Using Permutations

EXAMPLE

You need to enter a 4 digit code in order to enter the building where you work. The digits are 4 different numbers from 1 to 5. You forgot the code and try to guess it. Find the probability that you guess correctly.

STEP 1 **Write** the number of possible outcomes as the number of permutations of 4 out of the 5 possible digits. This is ${}_5P_4$.

$${}_5P_4 = \frac{5!}{(5-4)!} = \frac{5!}{1!} = 5! = 5 \cdot 4 \cdot 3 \cdot 2 \cdot 1 = 120$$

STEP 2 **Find** the probability. Because only one of the permutations is the correct code, the probability that you guess the correct code is $\frac{1}{120}$.

EXERCISES

EXAMPLE 2
for Exs. 6–10

Evaluate the expression.

6. ${}_7P_6$ **7.** ${}_6P_2$ **8.** ${}_8P_5$ **9.** ${}_{13}P_{10}$

10. MUSIC You downloaded 6 songs. You randomly choose 4 of these songs to play. Find the probability that you play the first 4 songs you downloaded in the order in which you downloaded them.

11.3 Find Probabilities Using Combinations

EXAMPLE

For your government class, you must choose 3 states in the United States to research. You may choose your states from the 6 New England states. How many combinations of states are possible?

The order in which you choose the states is not important. So, to find the number of combinations of 6 states taken 3 at a time, find ${}_6C_3$.

$${}_6C_3 = \frac{6!}{(6-3)! \cdot 3!}$$ **Combinations formula**

$$= \frac{6 \cdot 5 \cdot 4 \cdot \cancel{3!}}{\cancel{3!} \cdot (3 \cdot 2 \cdot 1)}$$ **Expand factorials. Divide out common factor, 3!.**

$$= 20$$ **Simplify.**

EXERCISES

EXAMPLE 2
for Exs. 11–15

Evaluate the expression.

11. ${}_7C_6$ **12.** ${}_6C_2$ **13.** ${}_8C_5$ **14.** ${}_{13}C_{10}$

15. TICKETS You win 5 tickets to a concert. In how many ways can you choose 4 friends out of a group of 9 to take with you to the concert?

11 CHAPTER REVIEW

11.4 Probabilities of Disjoint and Overlapping Events

EXAMPLE

Let A and B be events such that $P(A) = \frac{2}{3}$, $P(B) = \frac{1}{2}$, and $P(A \text{ and } B) = \frac{1}{3}$. Find $P(A \text{ or } B)$.

$$P(A \text{ or } B) = P(A) + P(B) - P(A \text{ and } B) = \frac{2}{3} + \frac{1}{2} - \frac{1}{3} = \frac{5}{6}$$

EXERCISES

EXAMPLES 2 and 4 for Exs. 16–18

Let A and B be events such that $P(A) = 0.32$, $P(B) = 0.48$, and $P(A \text{ and } B) = 0.12$. Find the indicated probability.

16. $P(A \text{ or } B)$

17. $P(\overline{A})$

18. $P(\overline{B})$

11.5 Probabilities of Independent and Dependent Events

EXAMPLE

Find the probability of selecting a club and then another club from a standard deck of 52 cards if (a) you replace the first card before selecting the second, and (b) you do *not* replace the first card.

Let event A be "the first card is a club" and B be "the second card is a club."

a. $P(A \text{ and } B) = P(A) \cdot P(B) = \frac{13}{52} \cdot \frac{13}{52} = \frac{1}{16} = 0.0625$

b. $P(A \text{ and } B) = P(A) \cdot P(B|A) = \frac{13}{52} \cdot \frac{12}{51} = \frac{1}{17} \approx 0.0588$

EXERCISES

EXAMPLE 5 for Exs. 19–21

Find the probability of randomly selecting the given marbles from a bag of 5 red, 8 green, and 3 blue marbles if (a) you replace the first marble before drawing the second and (b) you do *not* replace the first marble.

19. red, then green

20. blue, then red

21. green, then green

11 CHAPTER TEST

You roll a number cube. Find (a) the probability that the number rolled is as described and (b) the odds in favor of rolling such a number.

1. a 4
2. an even number
3. a number less than 5
4. a multiple of 3

Evaluate the expression.

5. ${}_7P_2$
6. ${}_8P_3$
7. ${}_6C_3$
8. ${}_{12}C_7$

Tell whether the question can be answered using *combinations* or *permutations*. *Explain* your choice, then answer the question.

9. Eight swimmers participate in a race. In how many ways can the swimmers finish in first, second, and third place?

10. A restaurant offers 7 different side dishes. In how many different ways can you choose 2 side dishes?

In Exercises 11 and 12, refer to a bag containing 12 tiles numbered 1–12.

11. You choose a tile at random. What is the probability that you choose a number less than 10 or an odd number?

12. You choose a tile at random, replace it, and choose a second tile at random. What is the probability that you choose a number greater than 3, then an odd number?

Find the indicated probability.

13. $P(A) = 0.3$
    $P(B) = 0.6$
    $P(A \text{ or } B) = \underline{\ ?\ }$
    $P(A \text{ and } B) = 0.1$

14. $P(A) = 35\%$
    $P(B) = \underline{\ ?\ }$
    $P(A \text{ or } B) = 80\%$
    $P(A \text{ and } B) = 20\%$

15. $P(A) = \underline{\ ?\ }$
    $P(\overline{A}) = \frac{2}{5}$

16. A and B are independent.
    $P(A) = 0.15$
    $P(B) = 0.6$
    $P(A \text{ and } B) = \underline{\ ?\ }$

17. A and B are dependent.
    $P(A) = 60\%$
    $P(B|A) = \underline{\ ?\ }$
    $P(A \text{ and } B) = 25\%$

18. A and B are dependent.
    $P(A) = \underline{\ ?\ }$
    $P(B|A) = 0.4$
    $P(A \text{ and } B) = 0.36$

19. **EDUCATION** A high school has an enrollment of 1800 students. There are 1050 females enrolled in the school. The high school has 1200 students who are involved in an after-school activity, 725 of whom are female. What is the probability that a randomly selected student at the school is a female who is not involved in an after-school activity?

SHORT RESPONSE QUESTIONS

Scoring Rubric

Full Credit
- solution is complete and correct

Partial Credit
- solution is complete but has errors,
  or
- solution is without error but incomplete

No Credit
- no solution is given,
  or
- solution makes no sense

PROBLEM

A survey of 887 households found that 270 households have a dog, 327 have a cat, and 82 have both. One of the households surveyed is chosen at random. Which is greater, the probability that the household has either a dog *or* a cat, or that the household has neither?

Below are sample solutions to the problem. Read each solution and the comments on the left to see why the sample represents full credit, partial credit, or no credit.

SAMPLE 1: Full credit solution

Because some households have both a cat and a dog, having a dog and having a cat are overlapping events.

The student correctly identified and used language and formulas.

So, $P(\text{dog or cat}) = P(\text{dog}) + P(\text{cat}) - P(\text{dog and cat})$.

$P(\text{dog}) = \frac{271}{887} \approx 0.306$ and $P(\text{cat}) = \frac{327}{887} \approx 0.369$

$P(\text{dog and cat}) = \frac{82}{887} \approx 0.092$

$P(\text{dog or cat}) \approx 0.306 + 0.369 - 0.092 = 0.583$

$P(\text{neither}) = \frac{887 - ((270 + 327) - 82)}{887} = \frac{372}{887} \approx 0.419$

The answer is correct and clearly stated in a sentence.

The probability that the household has a dog or a cat, about 0.583, is greater than the probability that the household has neither, 0.419.

SAMPLE 2: Partial credit solution

The events "having a dog" and "having a cat" are overlapping.

$P(\text{dog or cat}) = P(\text{dog}) + P(\text{cat}) - P(\text{dog and cat})$.

The reasoning is complete but has errors

$P(\text{dog}) = \frac{271}{877} \approx 0.309$ and $P(\text{cat}) = \frac{326{,}591}{877{,}403} \approx 0.373$

$P(\text{dog and cat}) = \frac{82}{877} \approx 0.094$

$P(\text{dog or cat}) \approx 0.309 + 0.373 - 0.094 = 0.588$

$P(\text{neither}) = \frac{877 - ((270 + 327) - 82)}{877} \approx 0.413$

$P(\text{dog or cat}) > P(\text{neither})$

SAMPLE 3: Partial credit solution

The solution is correct, but incomplete. No explanation is provided.

$P(\text{dog or cat}) = \approx 0.306 + 0.369 - 0.092 = 0.583$

$P(\text{dog or cat}) > P(\text{neither})$

SAMPLE 4: No credit solution

The reasoning and the answer are both incorrect.

The probability that a household has a dog or a cat is the sum of the probability that the household has a dog and the probability that it has a cat, which is about 0.369 + 0.306, or 0.675. The probability that the household has neither is $\frac{887 - 82}{887} \approx 0.908$, so the probability that the household has neither is greater.

PRACTICE Apply the Scoring Rubric

Score the solution to the problem below as *full credit, partial credit,* or *no credit. Explain* your reasoning.

PROBLEM A survey of 1200 high school students found that 650 of the students have a paid part-time job, 340 have a volunteer job, and 115 have both. One of the students surveyed is chosen at random. Which is greater, the probability that the student has either a paid part-time job or a volunteer job, or the probability that the student has neither?

1. The number of students who have either a paid part-time job, a volunteer job, or both is 1105, so the probability the student chosen at random has either is $\frac{1105}{1200} \approx 0.921$. To check, notice that 1105 is close to 1200, so $\frac{1105}{1200} \approx 1$.

The number of students who have neither is $1200 - (650 + 340 + 115) = 95$, so the probability the student has neither is $\frac{95}{1200} \approx 0.079$. To check, notice that $\frac{95}{1000} \approx \frac{100}{1000} = 0.1$.

Then the probability that the student has either a paid part-time job or a volunteer job is greater than the probability that the student has neither.

2. I made a Venn diagram to display the data.

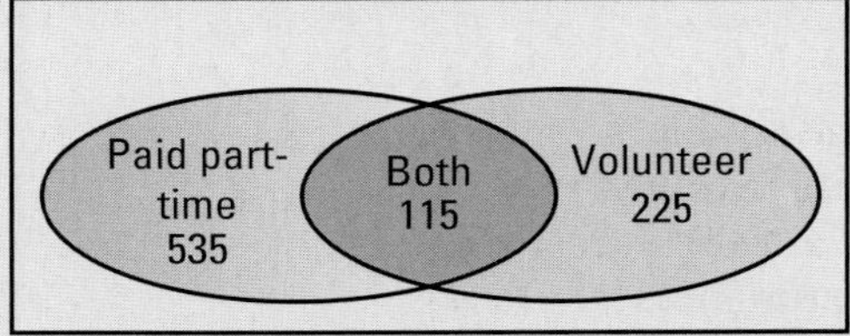

Because there are 115 students with both a paid part-time job and a volunteer job, there are 650 − 115 students with a paid part-time job only and 340 − 115 = 225 students with a volunteer job only. So, the number of students with either is 535 + 115 + 225 = 875. The probability that the student has either a paid part-time job or a volunteer job is $\frac{875}{1200} \approx 0.729$.

The number of students with neither is 1200 − 875 = 325. The probability that the student has neither is $\frac{325}{1200} \approx 0.271$.

The probability that the student has either a paid part-time job or a volunteer job is greater than the probability that the student has neither a paid part-time job nor a volunteer job.

11 ★ *Standardized* TEST PRACTICE

SHORT RESPONSE

1. Your English teacher gives you a list of 5 books that you are required to read over summer vacation. You read the books in a random order.
   a. In how many different ways can you read the 5 books?
   b. What is the probability that you read the longest book first or second? *Explain* how you found this probability.

2. You are ordering a pizza with 3 toppings. There are 8 toppings available.
   a. How many possible pizzas with 3 toppings can you order?
   b. Did you answer the question in part (a) using combinations or permutations? *Explain* your choice.

3. You must choose a password for an online account. The password must have between 4 and 6 characters, consisting of letters or digits. The letters or digits may repeat. How many passwords are possible? *Explain* how you found your answer.

4. A meteorologist claims that there is a 70% chance of rain. Brett knows that if it rains, there is a 75% chance that his softball game will be rescheduled. Is it *more likely* or *less likely* that the game will be rescheduled? *Explain* your reasoning.

5. In one high school, 40% of the students are involved in sports, 25% are involved in community service clubs, and 15% are involved in both. Suppose a student is selected at random. *Compare* the following probabilities: the probability that a student is on a sports team, given that the student is in a service club, and the probability that a student is in a service club given that the student is on a sports team.

6. A stock market analyst predicts that the probability that a company's stock will rise next week is about 20%. The analyst also predicts that if the stock *does* rise next week, the probability that it will rise the following week is 50%. How likely is it that the stock will rise both weeks? *Explain.*

7. Of the 8 members of a math club, 2 are being chosen to compete as a team for a statewide competition. To choose the team, the team adviser plans to observe each possible pair of club members working together for 20 minutes to solve problems, then choose the pair that works best together. How long will the observations take altogether?

8. In a game, player A thinks of a number from 1 to 10, and player B (knowing the number is from 1 to 10) guesses what it is. Player A then tells player B whether the guess was correct, or whether or not the actual number is higher or lower than the guess. Player B gets one more chance to guess the number.
   a. Find the probability that player B guesses correctly on the first try.
   b. Given that player B guesses "5" on the first try and is wrong, find the probability that player B wins the game.

MULTIPLE CHOICE

9. The odds in favor of an event are 3 : 4. What is the probability of the event?

   (A) $\frac{1}{4}$ (B) $\frac{3}{7}$

   (C) 75% (D) $\frac{3}{4}$

10. A bag contains 4 red marbles, 3 green marbles, and 5 blue marbles. You randomly choose a marble from the bag. What is the probability that you choose a blue marble?

    (A) $\frac{1}{5}$ (B) $\frac{5}{12}$

    (C) $\frac{5}{11}$ (D) $\frac{5}{7}$

11. You roll a number cube. What is the probability that you roll a multiple of 2 or a multiple of 3?

    (A) $\frac{1}{6}$ (B) $\frac{1}{3}$

    (C) $\frac{2}{3}$ (D) $\frac{5}{6}$

GRIDDED ANSWER

12. What is the value of ${}_4P_3$?

13. In how many ways can you arrange the letters in the word BEACH?

14. In how many ways can a president, vice president, and treasurer be chosen from among the 10 members of a club?

15. Given that *A* and *B* are dependent events, and that $P(A \text{ and } B) = 0.4$ and $P(B \mid A) = 0.8$, what is $P(A)$?

16. There are 13 girls and 12 boys in a class. What is the probability that a student selected at random is a girl?

17. You draw a marble from a bag containing 6 green marbles and 4 red marbles, replace it, and draw a second marble. What is the probability that both marbles you drew are green?

EXTENDED RESPONSE

18. A computer software company is performing a market test on two designs, A and B, for its new software program. Out of 250 people who view the designs, 85 like design A, 135 like design B, and 45 like both designs.

    a. Copy and complete the Venn diagram.

    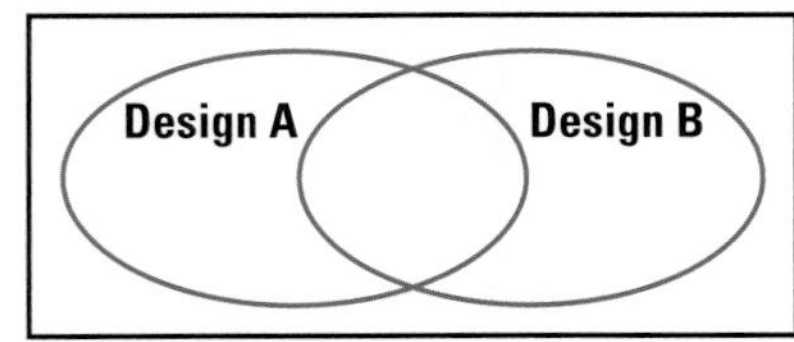

    b. What is the probability that a person likes design A or design B?

    c. What is the probability that a person does not like either design?

    d. *Explain* how you can calculate the probability from part (c) if you know the probability from part (b).

Contents of Student Resources

Comparing and Ordering Decimals

A **number line** is a line whose points are associated with numbers. You can use a number line to compare and order decimals. From left to right, the numbers on a number line appear in order from least to greatest.

EXAMPLE **Copy and complete the statement using <, >, or =.**

a. 9.67 __?__ 9.59

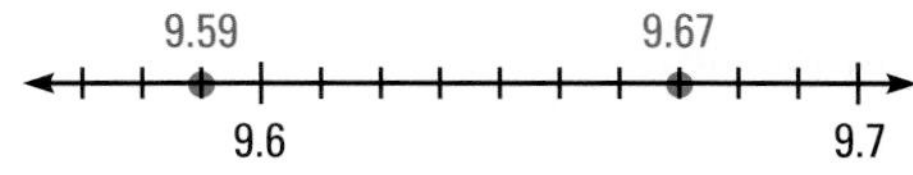

9.67 is to the right of 9.59, so 9.67 is greater than 9.59.

▶ 9.67 > 9.59

b. 0.08 __?__ 0.12

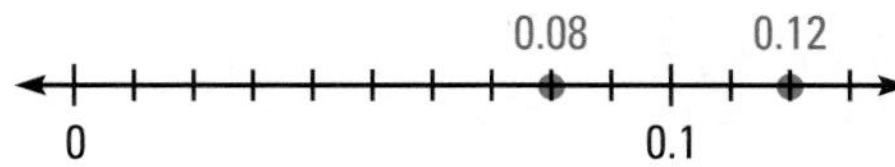

0.08 is to the left of 0.12, so 0.08 is less than 0.12.

▶ 0.08 < 0.12

EXAMPLE **Order the numbers 0.4, 0.56, 0.48, and 0.515 from least to greatest.**

Graph all the numbers on a number line.

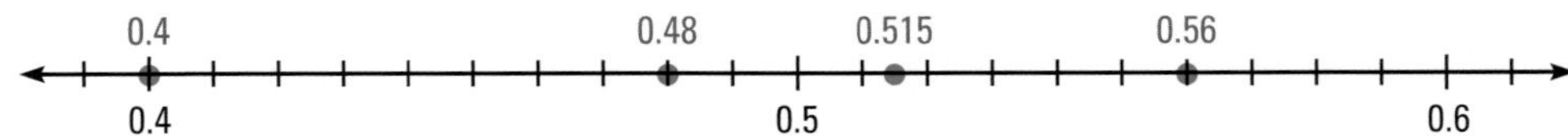

Write the numbers as they appear on the number line from left to right.

▶ The numbers in order from least to greatest are 0.4, 0.48, 0.515, and 0.56.

PRACTICE

Copy and complete the statement using <, >, or =.

1. 1.48 __?__ 1.413
2. 0.809 __?__ 0.81
3. 5.47 __?__ 5.43
4. 0.01 __?__ 0.005
5. 35.2 __?__ 35
6. 6.24 __?__ 6.2
7. 1.674 __?__ 1.678
8. 20.05 __?__ 20.3
9. 9.018 __?__ 9.017

Order the numbers from least to greatest.

10. 2.5, 2.3, 2.45, 2.38
11. 7.01, 7.13, 7.3, 7.03
12. 10.19, 10.2, 10, 10.4
13. 0.3, 0.47, 0.9, 0.15
14. 1.3, 1.05, 1.11, 1.0
15. 12.6, 10.9, 11, 11.9
16. 6.1, 6.89, 7.25, 7
17. 3.1, 3.3, 0.3, 1.33
18. 5.46, 5.4, 5.64, 5.6

Factors and Multiples

A **prime number** is a whole number that is greater than 1 and has exactly two whole number factors, 1 and itself. A **composite number** is a whole number that is greater than 1 and has more than two whole number factors. The table below shows that the first five prime numbers are 2, 3, 5, 7, and 11.

Number	Product(s)	Factor(s)	Prime or composite?
1	1 • 1	1	Neither
2	1 • 2	1, 2	Prime
3	1 • 3	1, 3	Prime
4	1 • 4, 2 • 2	1, 2, 4	Composite
5	1 • 5	1, 5	Prime
6	1 • 6, 2 • 3	1, 2, 3, 6	Composite
7	1 • 7	1, 7	Prime
8	1 • 8, 2 • 4	1, 2, 4, 8	Composite
9	1 • 9, 3 • 3	1, 3, 9	Composite
10	1 • 10, 2 • 5	1, 2, 5, 10	Composite
11	1 • 11	1, 11	Prime
12	1 • 12, 2 • 6, 3 • 4	1, 2, 3, 4, 6, 12	Composite

When you write a composite number as a product of prime numbers, you are writing its **prime factorization**. You can use a **factor tree** to write the prime factorization of a number.

EXAMPLE **Write the prime factorization of 120.**

Write 120 at the top of your factor tree. Draw two branches and write 120 as the product of two factors. Continue to draw branches until all the factors are prime numbers (shown in red). Here are two possible factor trees for 120.

Start with $120 = 2 \cdot 60$.

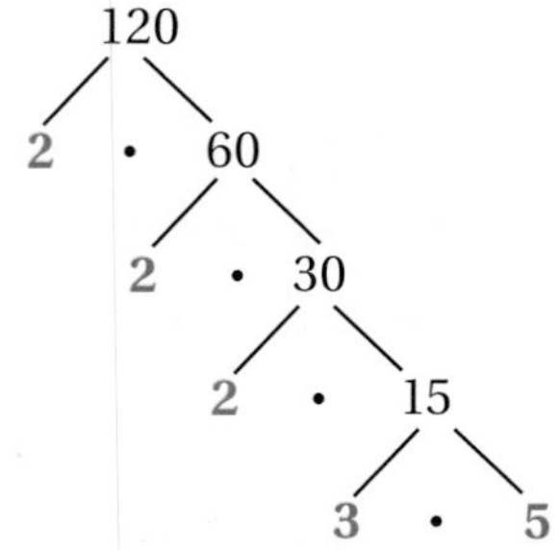

Start with $120 = 10 \cdot 12$.

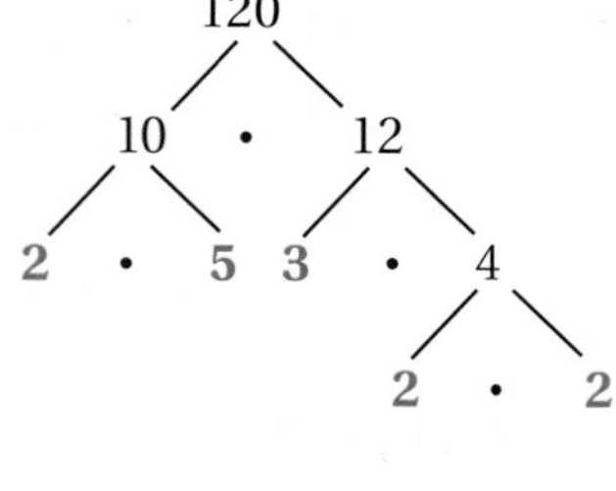

Both factor trees show that $120 = 2 \cdot 2 \cdot 2 \cdot 3 \cdot 5$, or $120 = 2^3 \cdot 3 \cdot 5$.

▸ The prime factorization of 120 is $2^3 \cdot 3 \cdot 5$.

For two or more nonzero whole numbers, a **common factor** is a whole number that is a factor of each number. The **greatest common factor (GCF)** of two or more nonzero whole numbers is the greatest of their common factors.

EXAMPLE **Find the greatest common factor of 30 and 42.**

Write the prime factorization of each number. The greatest common factor is the product of the common prime factors.

$30 = 2 \cdot 3 \cdot 5$ and $42 = 2 \cdot 3 \cdot 7$

The common prime factors are 2 and 3. The GCF is the product $2 \cdot 3 = 6$.

▶ The greatest common factor of 30 and 42 is 6.

A **multiple** of a whole number is the product of the number and any nonzero whole number. A **common multiple** of two or more whole numbers is a multiple of each number. The **least common multiple (LCM)** of two or more whole numbers is the least of their common multiples.

EXAMPLE **Find the least common multiple of 10 and 15.**

Write the prime factorization of each number. The least common multiple is the product of the factors, using each common prime factor only once.

$10 = 2 \cdot 5$ and $15 = 3 \cdot 5$

The common prime factor is 5. The LCM is the product $2 \cdot 3 \cdot 5 = 30$.

▶ The least common multiple of 10 and 15 is 30.

PRACTICE

Write the prime factorization of the number if it is not a prime number. If the number is prime, write *prime*.

1. 28 **2.** 16 **3.** 11 **4.** 100
5. 81 **6.** 49 **7.** 60 **8.** 53
9. 180 **10.** 19 **11.** 51 **12.** 72

Find the greatest common factor of the pair of numbers.

13. 4, 8 **14.** 5, 6 **15.** 60, 18 **16.** 2, 10
17. 36, 27 **18.** 15, 21 **19.** 12, 16 **20.** 24, 108
21. 48, 88 **22.** 8, 12 **23.** 20, 28 **24.** 3, 5

Find the least common multiple of the pair of numbers.

25. 6, 9 **26.** 3, 8 **27.** 5, 45 **28.** 16, 20
29. 10, 65 **30.** 12, 15 **31.** 9, 30 **32.** 8, 9
33. 2, 14 **34.** 28, 32 **35.** 7, 49 **36.** 4, 6

Finding Equivalent Fractions and Simplifying Fractions

A **fraction** is a number of the form $\frac{a}{b}$ where a is the **numerator** and b is the **denominator**. The value of b cannot be 0.

The number lines show the graphs of two fractions, $\frac{1}{2}$ and $\frac{2}{4}$.

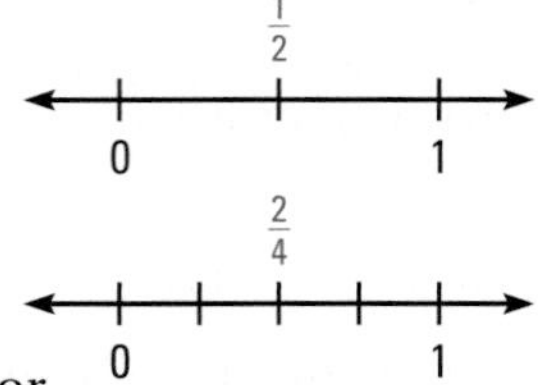

These fractions represent the same number. Two fractions that represent the same number are called **equivalent fractions**.

To write equivalent fractions, you can multiply or divide the numerator and the denominator by the same nonzero number.

EXAMPLE **Write two fractions that are equivalent to $\frac{6}{8}$.**

Multiply the numerator and denominator by 3.

$\frac{6}{8} = \frac{6 \times 3}{8 \times 3} = \frac{18}{24}$ **Equivalent fraction**

Divide the numerator and denominator by 2.

$\frac{6}{8} = \frac{6 \div 2}{8 \div 2} = \frac{3}{4}$ **Equivalent fraction**

A fraction is in **simplest form** when its numerator and its denominator have no common factors besides 1.

EXAMPLE **Write the fraction $\frac{10}{15}$ in simplest form.**

Divide the numerator and denominator by 5, the greatest common factor of 10 and 15.

$\frac{10}{15} = \frac{10 \div 5}{15 \div 5} = \frac{2}{3}$ **Simplest form**

PRACTICE

Write two fractions that are equivalent to the given fraction.

1. $\frac{9}{12}$ **2.** $\frac{4}{6}$ **3.** $\frac{1}{2}$ **4.** $\frac{2}{5}$ **5.** $\frac{10}{14}$

Write the fraction in simplest form.

6. $\frac{16}{24}$ **7.** $\frac{3}{12}$ **8.** $\frac{30}{48}$ **9.** $\frac{5}{40}$ **10.** $\frac{8}{20}$

11. $\frac{4}{16}$ **12.** $\frac{64}{72}$ **13.** $\frac{35}{100}$ **14.** $\frac{21}{81}$ **15.** $\frac{44}{55}$

16. $\frac{15}{20}$ **17.** $\frac{12}{28}$ **18.** $\frac{15}{39}$ **19.** $\frac{24}{78}$ **20.** $\frac{60}{96}$

Mixed Numbers and Improper Fractions

SKILLS REVIEW HANDBOOK

A **mixed number** is the sum of a whole number and a fraction. An **improper fraction** is a fraction with a numerator that is greater than or equal to the denominator.

The shaded part of the model at the right represents the mixed number $2\frac{1}{4}$ and the improper fraction $\frac{9}{4}$.

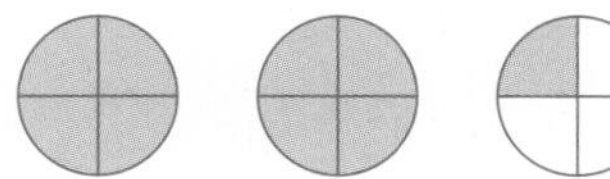

EXAMPLE **Write $5\frac{7}{8}$ as an improper fraction.**

$5\frac{7}{8} = 5 + \frac{7}{8}$ — **Definition of mixed number**

$= \frac{40}{8} + \frac{7}{8}$ — **1 whole = $\frac{8}{8}$, so 5 wholes = $\frac{40}{8}$.**

$= \frac{47}{8}$ — **Add.**

EXAMPLE **Write $\frac{17}{5}$ as a mixed number.**

$$\begin{array}{r} 3 \\ 5\overline{)17} \\ \underline{15} \\ 2 \end{array}$$

Divide the numerator by the denominator: 17 ÷ 5.
The quotient is 3 and the remainder is 2.

▶ $\frac{17}{5} = 3\frac{2}{5}$ — **Write the remainder as a fraction, $\frac{\text{remainder}}{\text{divisor}}$.**

PRACTICE

Write the mixed number as an improper fraction.

1. $1\frac{2}{3}$ **2.** $3\frac{1}{4}$ **3.** $10\frac{3}{10}$ **4.** $2\frac{3}{5}$ **5.** $4\frac{1}{2}$

6. $9\frac{1}{3}$ **7.** $1\frac{11}{12}$ **8.** $2\frac{3}{4}$ **9.** $6\frac{5}{8}$ **10.** $5\frac{9}{16}$

11. $8\frac{1}{8}$ **12.** $6\frac{3}{5}$ **13.** $7\frac{2}{9}$ **14.** $2\frac{3}{13}$ **15.** $12\frac{2}{3}$

Write the improper fraction as a mixed number.

16. $\frac{5}{2}$ **17.** $\frac{12}{5}$ **18.** $\frac{15}{8}$ **19.** $\frac{25}{4}$ **20.** $\frac{37}{3}$

21. $\frac{7}{4}$ **22.** $\frac{27}{8}$ **23.** $\frac{29}{10}$ **24.** $\frac{69}{16}$ **25.** $\frac{54}{5}$

26. $\frac{31}{4}$ **27.** $\frac{22}{5}$ **28.** $\frac{13}{3}$ **29.** $\frac{43}{9}$ **30.** $\frac{35}{11}$

Adding and Subtracting Fractions

To add or subtract two fractions with the same denominator, write the sum or difference of the numerators over the denominator.

Sum and Difference Rules ($c \neq 0$)	
$\frac{a}{c} + \frac{b}{c} = \frac{a+b}{c}$	$\frac{a}{c} - \frac{b}{c} = \frac{a-b}{c}$

EXAMPLE **Add or subtract: a.** $\frac{1}{10} + \frac{3}{10}$ **b.** $\frac{7}{8} - \frac{3}{8}$

a. $\frac{1}{10} + \frac{3}{10} = \frac{4}{10}$ **Add numerators.**

$= \frac{2}{5}$ **Simplify.**

b. $\frac{7}{8} - \frac{3}{8} = \frac{4}{8}$ **Subtract numerators.**

$= \frac{1}{2}$ **Simplify.**

The **least common denominator (LCD)** of two fractions is the least common multiple of the denominators. To add or subtract two fractions with different denominators, use the LCD of the fractions to write equivalent fractions that have the same denominator.

EXAMPLE **Add:** $\frac{1}{4} + \frac{5}{6}$

The LCD of the fractions is 12, so write $\frac{1}{4}$ as $\frac{1 \times 3}{4 \times 3} = \frac{3}{12}$ and $\frac{5}{6}$ as $\frac{5 \times 2}{6 \times 2} = \frac{10}{12}$.

$\frac{1}{4} + \frac{5}{6} = \frac{3}{12} + \frac{10}{12}$ **Write equivalent fractions.**

$= \frac{13}{12}$ **Add.**

$= 1\frac{1}{12}$ **Write as a mixed number.**

PRACTICE

Add or subtract.

1. $\frac{1}{16} + \frac{3}{16}$ **2.** $\frac{1}{5} + \frac{2}{5}$ **3.** $\frac{7}{12} - \frac{5}{12}$ **4.** $\frac{2}{3} - \frac{1}{3}$ **5.** $\frac{5}{8} + \frac{3}{8}$

6. $\frac{3}{4} + \frac{3}{4}$ **7.** $\frac{7}{8} - \frac{3}{8}$ **8.** $\frac{17}{20} + \frac{9}{20}$ **9.** $\frac{7}{10} + \frac{1}{2}$ **10.** $\frac{3}{10} + \frac{3}{5}$

11. $\frac{3}{8} - \frac{3}{16}$ **12.** $\frac{1}{3} + \frac{1}{10}$ **13.** $\frac{7}{12} - \frac{1}{16}$ **14.** $\frac{2}{3} - \frac{1}{4}$ **15.** $\frac{5}{6} + \frac{7}{8}$

16. $\frac{3}{4} - \frac{5}{8}$ **17.** $\frac{3}{4} - \frac{1}{5}$ **18.** $\frac{5}{12} + \frac{2}{3}$ **19.** $1 - \frac{1}{5}$ **20.** $4 - \frac{3}{16}$

21. $2\frac{5}{8} + 4\frac{1}{8}$ **22.** $2\frac{9}{10} - 1\frac{7}{10}$ **23.** $1\frac{5}{6} + 3\frac{1}{6}$ **24.** $2\frac{1}{2} + 2\frac{3}{8}$ **25.** $1\frac{3}{4} - \frac{11}{16}$

Multiplying and Dividing Fractions

To multiply two fractions, write the product of the numerators over the product of the denominators.

Product Rule ($b, d \neq 0$)

$$\frac{a}{b} \times \frac{c}{d} = \frac{ac}{bd}$$

EXAMPLE **Multiply:** $\frac{3}{5} \times \frac{7}{8}$

$\frac{3}{5} \times \frac{7}{8} = \frac{3 \times 7}{5 \times 8}$ **Use product rule.**

$= \frac{21}{40}$ **Simplify.**

Two nonzero numbers whose product is 1 are **reciprocals**. For example, 6 and $\frac{1}{6}$ are reciprocals because $6 \times \frac{1}{6} = 1$. Every number except 0 has a reciprocal.

To divide by a fraction, multiply by its reciprocal.

Quotient Rule ($b, c, d \neq 0$)

$$\frac{a}{b} \div \frac{c}{d} = \frac{a}{b} \times \frac{d}{c}$$

EXAMPLE **Divide:** $\frac{5}{7} \div \frac{3}{4}$

The reciprocal of $\frac{3}{4}$ is $\frac{4}{3}$ because $\frac{3}{4} \times \frac{4}{3} = 1$, so multiply $\frac{5}{7}$ by $\frac{4}{3}$.

$\frac{5}{7} \div \frac{3}{4} = \frac{5}{7} \times \frac{4}{3}$ **Use quotient rule.**

$= \frac{20}{21}$ **Use product rule.**

PRACTICE

Multiply or divide.

1. $\frac{3}{4} \times \frac{2}{3}$ **2.** $\frac{1}{5} \times \frac{5}{8}$ **3.** $\frac{1}{6} \div \frac{1}{3}$ **4.** $\frac{2}{3} \div \frac{2}{3}$ **5.** $\frac{9}{10} \div \frac{4}{5}$

6. $\frac{1}{12} \times \frac{3}{4}$ **7.** $\frac{3}{8} \times \frac{1}{8}$ **8.** $\frac{5}{6} \div \frac{1}{4}$ **9.** $\frac{1}{2} \times \frac{1}{4}$ **10.** $\frac{7}{10} \div \frac{5}{8}$

11. $\frac{3}{4} \div \frac{1}{2}$ **12.** $\frac{5}{6} \times \frac{3}{10}$ **13.** $\frac{2}{5} \div \frac{4}{5}$ **14.** $\frac{9}{10} \times \frac{1}{3}$ **15.** $\frac{1}{4} \div \frac{7}{8}$

16. $\frac{3}{16} \times \frac{2}{5}$ **17.** $\frac{2}{5} \div 20$ **18.** $18 \times \frac{1}{3}$ **19.** $\frac{1}{10} \times 6$ **20.** $24 \div \frac{3}{8}$

21. $5\frac{1}{2} \times \frac{9}{16}$ **22.** $8\frac{1}{4} \div \frac{3}{10}$ **23.** $1\frac{7}{8} \times 2\frac{1}{3}$ **24.** $3\frac{3}{4} \div 6\frac{1}{2}$ **25.** $2\frac{1}{2} \div 1\frac{7}{8}$

Fractions, Decimals, and Percents

A **percent** is a fraction whose denominator is 100. The symbol for percent is %. In the model at the right, there are 100 squares in all, and 49 of the 100 squares are shaded. You can write the shaded part of the model as a fraction, a decimal, or a percent.

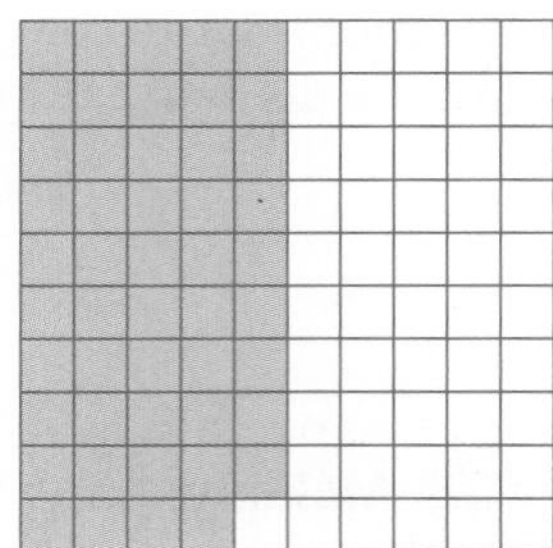

Fraction: forty-nine out of one hundred, or $\frac{49}{100}$

Decimal: forty-nine hundredths, or 0.49

Percent: forty-nine percent, or 49%

EXAMPLE **Write the fraction as a decimal: a. $\frac{1}{8}$ b. $\frac{5}{12}$**

a. $8\overline{)1.000}$ with quotient 0.125 **Divide.**

▶ $\frac{1}{8} = 0.125$

b. $12\overline{)5.00000...}$ with quotient 0.41666. . . **Divide.**

▶ $\frac{5}{12} = 0.41666... = 0.41\overline{6}$

EXAMPLE **Write the decimal as a fraction: a. 0.7 b. 0.32**

a. $0.7 = \text{seven tenths}$

$= \frac{7}{10}$

b. $0.32 = \text{thirty-two hundredths}$

$= \frac{32}{100}$

$= \frac{8}{25}$

To write a percent as a decimal, move the decimal point two places to the left and remove the percent sign.

EXAMPLE **Write the percent as a decimal: a. 16% b. 5%**

a. 16% = 16%

= 0.16

b. 5% = 05%

= 0.05

To write a decimal as a percent, move the decimal point two places to the right and write a percent sign.

EXAMPLE **Write the decimal as a percent: a. 0.83 b. 0.195**

a. 0.83 = 0.83

= 83%

b. 0.195 = 0.195

= 19.5%

EXAMPLE Write the percent as a fraction: **a.** 98% **b.** 5%

a. $98\% = \frac{98}{100}$ Definition of percent

$= \frac{49}{50}$ Simplify.

b. $5\% = \frac{5}{100}$ Definition of percent

$= \frac{1}{20}$ Simplify.

To write a fraction as a percent, you may be able to rewrite the fraction using a denominator of 100. If the denominator of the fraction is not a factor of 100, you can first write the fraction as a decimal and then as a percent.

EXAMPLE Write the fraction as a percent: **a.** $\frac{2}{5}$ **b.** $\frac{5}{8}$

a. $\frac{2}{5} = \frac{2(20)}{5(20)}$ Write as a fraction with denominator 100.

$= \frac{40}{100} = 40\%$ Write as a percent.

b. $\frac{5}{8} = 0.625$ Write as a decimal.

$= 62.5\%$ Write as a percent.

The table below gives commonly used fractions, decimals, and percents written in increasing order.

$\frac{1}{100} = 0.01 = 1\%$	$\frac{1}{16} = 0.0625 = 6.25\%$	$\frac{1}{10} = 0.1 = 10\%$	$\frac{1}{8} = 0.125 = 12.5\%$
$\frac{1}{5} = 0.2 = 20\%$	$\frac{1}{4} = 0.25 = 25\%$	$\frac{1}{3} = 0.\overline{3} \approx 33.3\%$	$\frac{3}{8} = 0.375 = 37.5\%$
$\frac{2}{5} = 0.4 = 40\%$	$\frac{1}{2} = 0.5 = 50\%$	$\frac{3}{5} = 0.6 = 60\%$	$\frac{5}{8} = 0.625 = 62.5\%$
$\frac{2}{3} = 0.\overline{6} \approx 66.7\%$	$\frac{3}{4} = 0.75 = 75\%$	$\frac{4}{5} = 0.8 = 80\%$	$\frac{7}{8} = 0.875 = 87.5\%$

PRACTICE

Write the percent as a decimal and as a fraction.

1. 70% **2.** 12% **3.** 3% **4.** 55% **5.** 35%

6. 9% **7.** 110% **8.** 225% **9.** 0.3% **10.** 0.5%

Write the decimal as a fraction and as a percent.

11. 0.28 **12.** 0.13 **13.** 0.05 **14.** 0.36 **15.** 0.52

16. 0.004 **17.** 0.025 **18.** 4 **19.** 1.5 **20.** 2.3

Write the fraction as a decimal and as a percent. Round decimals to the nearest thousandth. Round percents to the nearest tenth of a percent.

21. $\frac{3}{16}$ **22.** $\frac{1}{9}$ **23.** $\frac{61}{100}$ **24.** $\frac{3}{20}$ **25.** $\frac{19}{100}$

26. $\frac{17}{25}$ **27.** $\frac{9}{25}$ **28.** $\frac{5}{6}$ **29.** $\frac{4}{7}$ **30.** $\frac{5}{12}$

Mean, Median, and Mode

Three measures of central tendency are mean, median, and mode.

The **mean** of a data set is the sum of the values divided by the number of values.	The **median** of a data set is the middle value when the values are written in numerical order. If a data set has an even number of values, the median is the mean of the two middle values.	The **mode** of a data set is the value that occurs most often. A data set can have no mode, one mode, or more than one mode.

EXAMPLE **Find the mean, median, and mode(s) of the data in the table.**

Lengths of School Years	
Country	School year (days)
China	251
Korea	222
Taiwan	222
Japan	220
Israel	215
Switzerland	207
Canada	188
United States	178

Mean

Add the values. Then divide by 8, the number of values.

$$\text{Sum} = 251 + 222 + 222 + 220 + 215 + 207 + 188 + 178 = 1703$$

▸ $\text{Mean} = \frac{1703}{8} = 212.875$

Median

Write the values in order from least to greatest. Then find the middle value(s).

178, 188, 207, **215**, **220**, 222, 222, 251

Find the mean of the two middle values.

▸ $\text{Median} = \frac{215 + 220}{2} = \frac{435}{2} = 217.5$

Mode

Find the value that occurs most often.

▸ Mode = 222

PRACTICE

Find the mean, median, and mode(s) of the data.

1. Test scores: 90, 88, 95, 94, 87, 85, 92, 99, 100, 94
2. Daily high temperatures (°F) for a week: 68, 70, 67, 68, 75, 75, 74
3. Ages of employees: 24, 52, 21, 55, 39, 49, 28, 33, 52, 41, 30, 64, 45
4. Numbers of students in classes: 21, 24, 27, 28, 25, 18, 22, 25, 26, 22, 27, 20
5. Movie ticket prices: $6.75, $7.50, $7.25, $6.75, $6.25, $7.50, $7.25, $6.75, $7
6. Hourly rates of pay: $14.50, $8.75, $7, $11, $16.50, $18, $12, $10.25
7. Numbers of children in families: 0, 0, 1, 1, 1, 2, 2, 2, 2, 2, 3, 3, 4, 4, 4, 5
8. Ages of students in a high school class: 3 sixteen-year-olds, 10 seventeen-year-olds, and 7 eighteen-year-olds

The Coordinate Plane

Just as you use a number line to graph numbers, you use a *coordinate plane* to graph *ordered pairs* of numbers.

A **coordinate plane** has a horizontal ***x*-axis** and a vertical ***y*-axis** that intersect at a point called the **origin**. The origin is labeled *O*.

In an **ordered pair**, the first number is the ***x*-coordinate** and the second number is the ***y*-coordinate**. The coordinates of the origin are (0, 0). The ordered pair (4, 5) is graphed at the right.

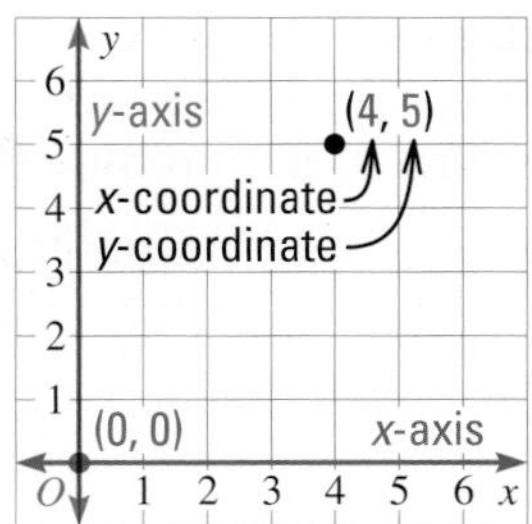

EXAMPLE **Give the coordinates of points *A* and *B*.**

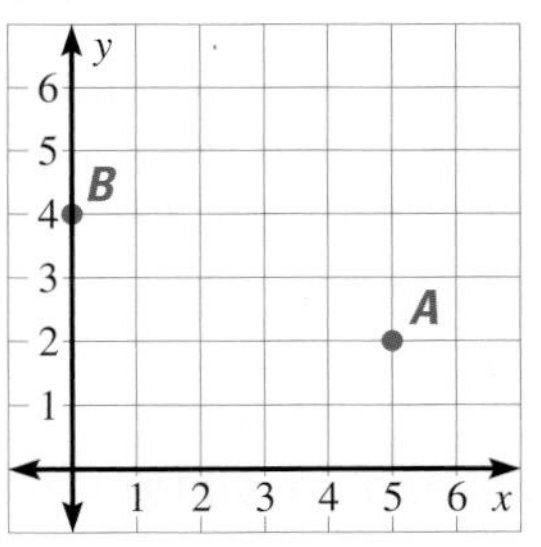

Point *A* is 5 units to the right of the origin and 2 units up, so the *x*-coordinate is 5 and the *y*-coordinate is 2.

▶ The coordinates of point *A* are (5, 2).

Point *B* is 0 units to the right or left of the origin and 4 units up, so the *x*-coordinate is 0 and the *y*-coordinate is 4.

▶ The coordinates of point *B* are (0, 4).

EXAMPLE **Plot the points *C*(1, 3) and *D*(3, 0) in a coordinate plane.**

To plot the point *C*(1, 3), begin at the origin and move 1 unit to the right, then 3 units up.

To plot the point *D*(3, 0), begin at the origin and move 3 units right, then 0 units up.

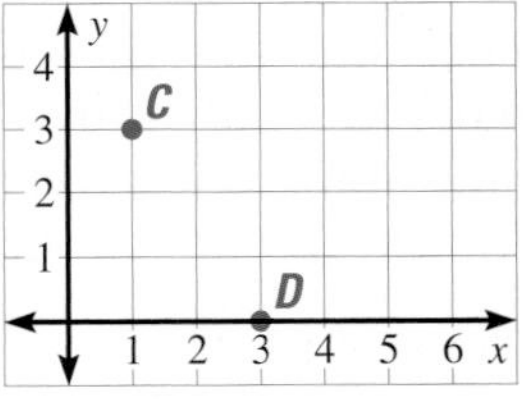

PRACTICE

Give the coordinates of the point.

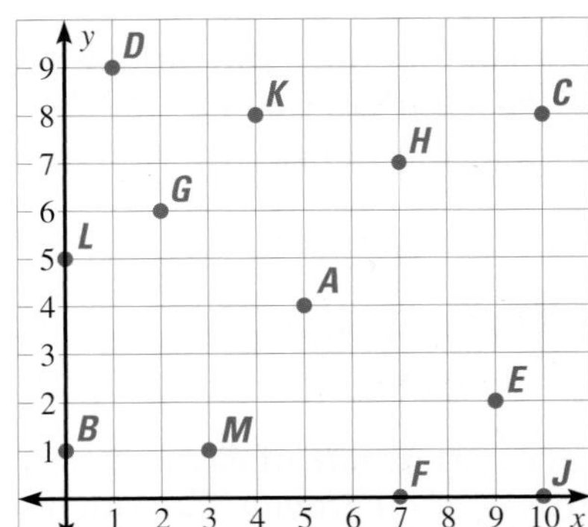

1. *A* **2.** *B* **3.** *C*

4. *D* **5.** *E* **6.** *F*

7. *G* **8.** *H* **9.** *J*

10. *K* **11.** *L* **12.** *M*

Plot the point in a coordinate plane.

13. *M*(1, 7) **14.** *N*(2, 1) **15.** *P*(4, 4)

16. *Q*(0, 3) **17.** *R*(4, 0) **18.** *S*(6, 8)

19. *T*(3, 6) **20.** *U*(8, 4) **21.** *V*(7, 0)

22. *W*(0, 8) **23.** *X*(3, 5) **24.** *Z*(5, 6)

Transformations

A **transformation** is a change made to the location, size, or shape of a figure. The new figure formed by a transformation is called an **image**. In this book, original figures are shown in blue and images in red.

A **translation** is a transformation in which each point of a figure moves the same distance in the same direction. A figure and its translated image are identical in size and shape.

EXAMPLE **Translate the triangle 4 units to the right and 1 unit up.**

From each vertex of the triangle, move 4 units to the right and 1 unit up to plot the image of the vertex. Draw segments connecting the images of the vertices.

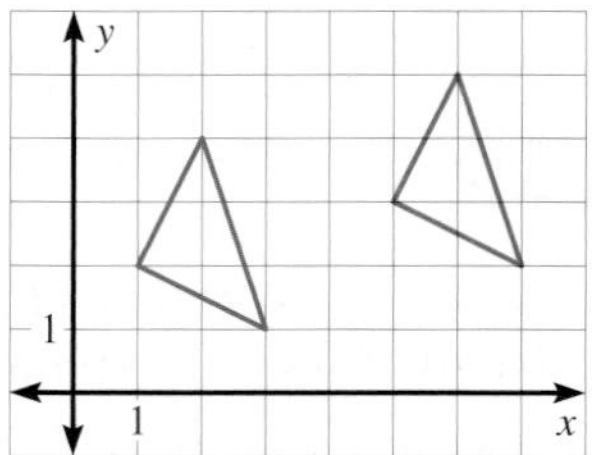

A **reflection** is a transformation in which a figure is reflected, or flipped, in a line, called the *line of reflection*. A figure and its reflected image are identical in size and shape.

EXAMPLE **Reflect the line segment in the given line.**

For each endpoint, find the distance from the endpoint to the line of reflection. Move the same distance on the opposite side of the line of reflection and plot the image point. Draw a segment connecting the image points.

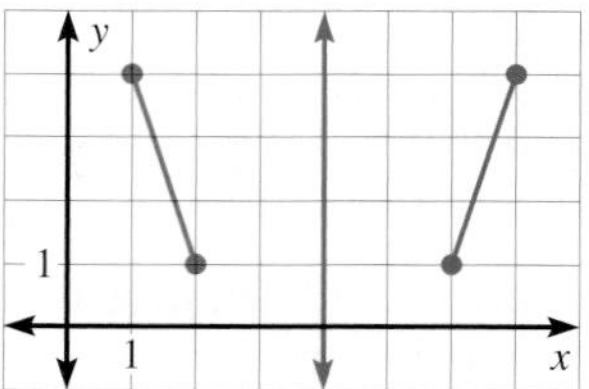

A **dilation** is a transformation in which a figure stretches or shrinks with respect to a fixed point called the *center of dilation*. (The examples and exercises below all have the origin as the center of dilation.) A figure and its dilated image have the same shape.

The **scale factor** of a dilation is the ratio of a side length of the image to the corresponding side length of the original figure. A figure *stretches* if its scale factor is greater than 1. A figure *shrinks* if its scale factor is between 0 and 1.

EXAMPLE **Dilate the rectangle using a scale factor of 3.**

Multiply each coordinate of each vertex by 3 to find the coordinates of the image. Plot the image of each vertex. Connect the image points to form a rectangle.

(1, 1) → (3, 3)   (1, 2) → (3, 6)

(3, 2) → (9, 6)   (3, 1) → (9, 3)

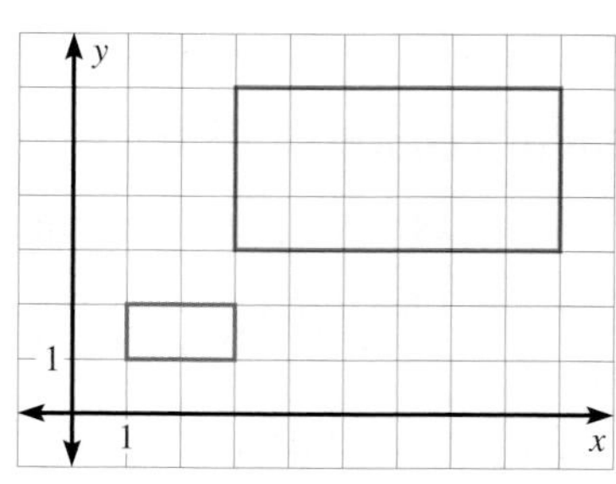

EXAMPLE **Dilate the triangle using a scale factor of $\frac{1}{2}$.**

Multiply each coordinate of each vertex by $\frac{1}{2}$ to find the coordinates of the image. Plot the image of each vertex. Connect the image points to form a triangle.

(2, 6) → (1, 3)

(2, 2) → (1, 1)

(6, 4) → (3, 2)

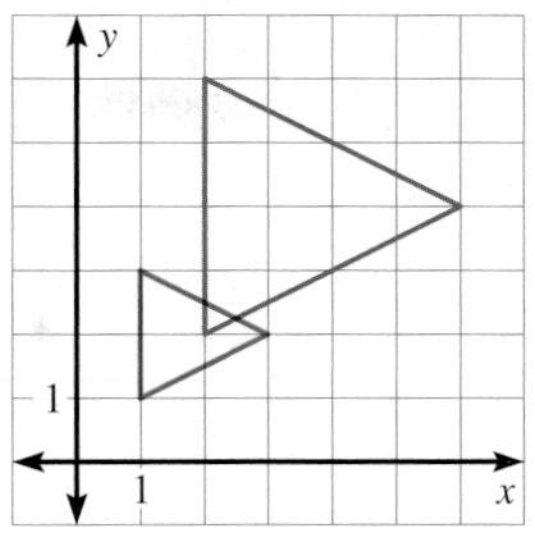

PRACTICE

The coordinates of the vertices of a polygon are given. Draw the polygon. Then find the coordinates of the vertices of the image after the specified translation, and draw the image.

1. (1, 5), (3, 4), (3, 1); translate 3 units to the right and 2 units up
2. (5, 0), (7, 0), (7, 2), (5, 2); translate 4 units to the left and 5 units up
3. (4, 4), (6, 4), (6, 7); translate 3 units to the left and 3 units down
4. (2, 1), (4, 1), (4, 6), (2, 6); translate 5 units to the right
5. (4, 5), (7, 2), (3, 3); translate 1 unit down

For the figure shown, find the coordinates of the vertices of the image after a reflection in the given line. Then draw the image.

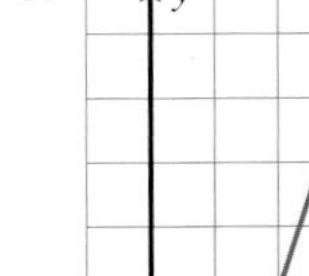

6.

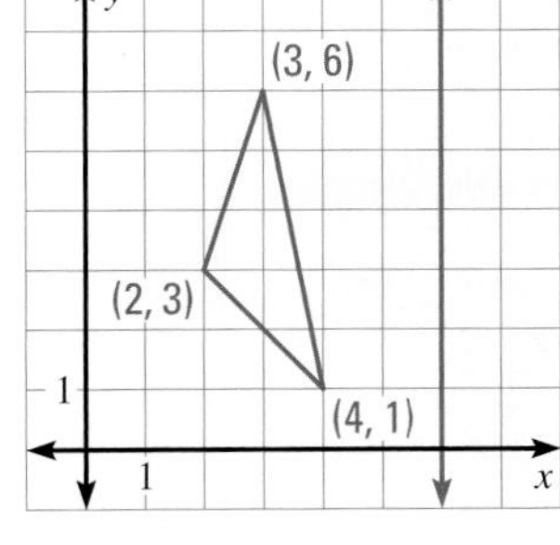

7.

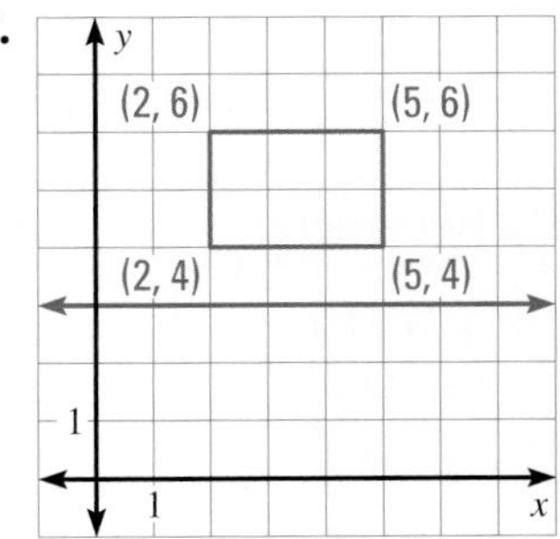

8.

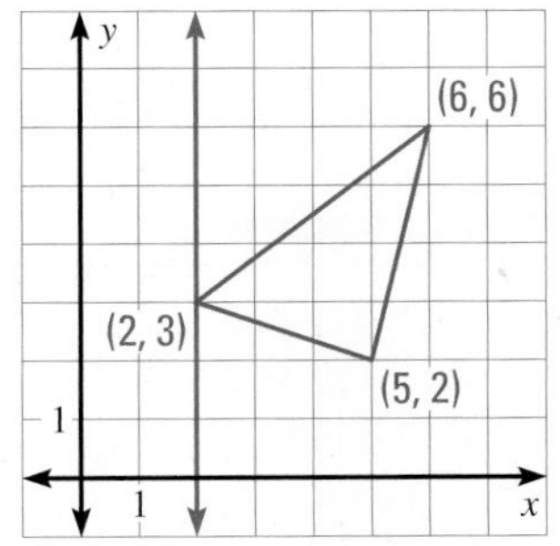

The coordinates of the vertices of a polygon are given. Draw the polygon. Then find the coordinates of the vertices of the image after the specified dilation, and draw the image.

9. (1, 2), (2, 4), (5, 3); dilate using a scale factor of 2
10. (2, 6), (6, 6), (6, 2), (2, 2); dilate using a scale factor of $\frac{1}{2}$
11. (1, 3), (3, 3), (3, 1), (1, 1); dilate using a scale factor of 4
12. (3, 9), (6, 9), (6, 3); dilate using a scale factor of $\frac{1}{3}$
13. (0, 2), (4, 4), (6, 0); dilate using a scale factor of $1\frac{1}{2}$

Perimeter and Area

The **perimeter** P of a figure is the distance around it.

Perimeter of a Square

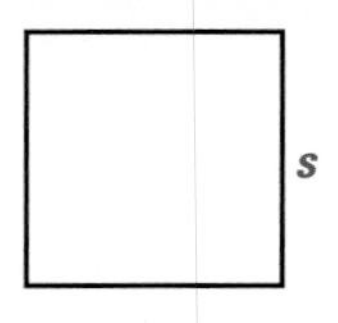

$P = s + s + s + s$
$= 4s$

Perimeter of a Rectangle

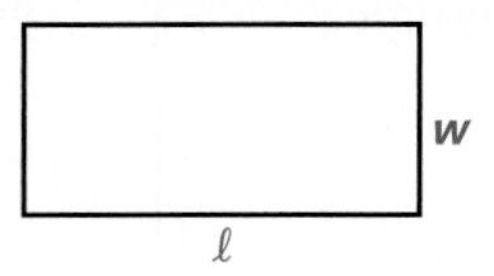

$P = \ell + w + \ell + w$
$= 2\ell + 2w$

Perimeter of a Triangle

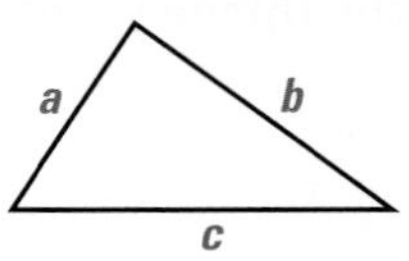

$P = a + b + c$

EXAMPLE **Find the perimeter of the figure.**

a. Square

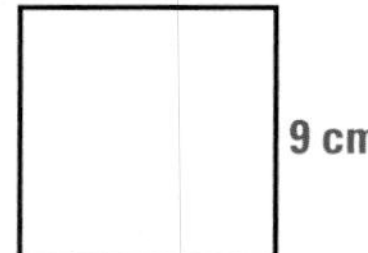

$P = 4s$
$= 4(9)$
$= 36$ cm

b. Rectangle

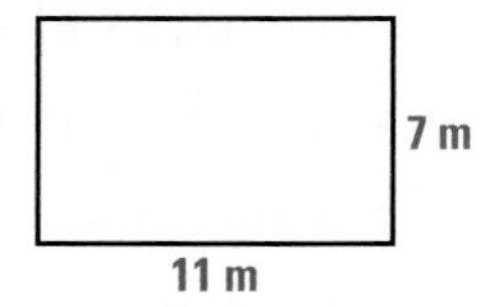

$P = 2\ell + 2w$
$= 2(11) + 2(7)$
$= 22 + 14 = 36$ m

c. Triangle

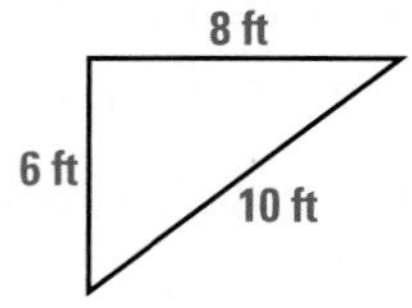

$P = a + b + c$
$= 6 + 8 + 10$
$= 24$ ft

The **area** A of a figure is the number of square units enclosed by the figure.

Area of a Square

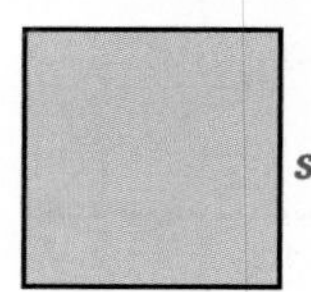

$A = s^2$

Area of a Rectangle

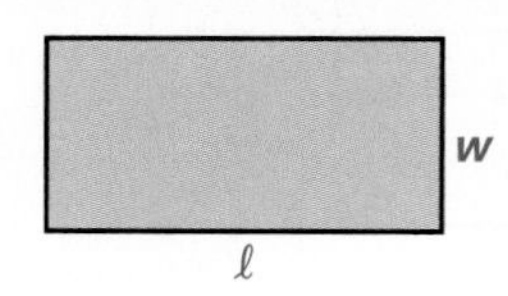

$A = \ell w$

Area of a Parallelogram

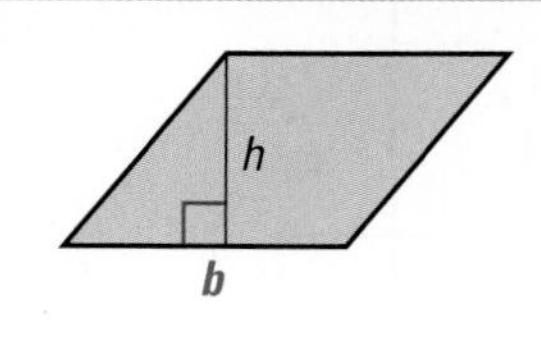

$A = bh$

Area of a Triangle

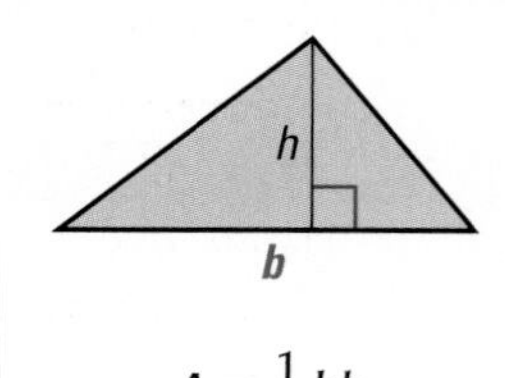

$A = \frac{1}{2}bh$

Area of a Trapezoid

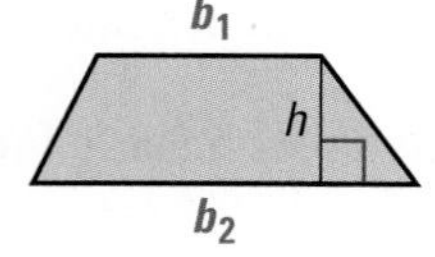

$P = \frac{1}{2}(b_1 + b_2)h$

EXAMPLE **Find the area of the figure.**

a. Rectangle

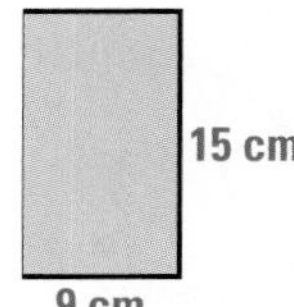

$A = \ell w$

$= 9(15)$

$= 135 \text{ cm}^2$

b. Triangle

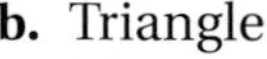
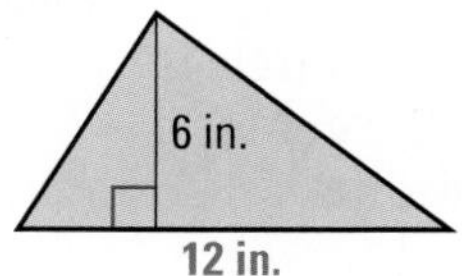

$A = \frac{1}{2}bh$

$= \frac{1}{2}(12)(6)$

$= 36 \text{ in.}^2$

c. Parallelogram

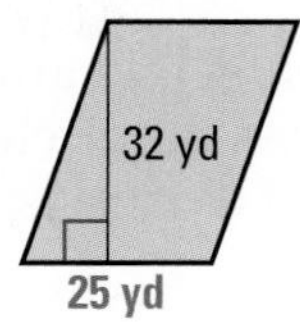

$A = bh$

$= 25(32)$

$= 800 \text{ yd}^2$

PRACTICE

Find the perimeter of the figure.

1. Square

2. Rectangle

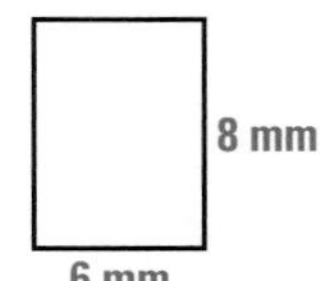

3. Triangle

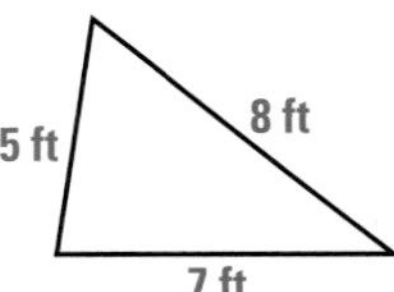

Find the area of the figure.

4. Square

5. Rectangle

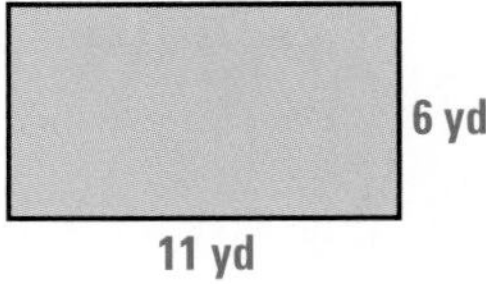

6. Triangle

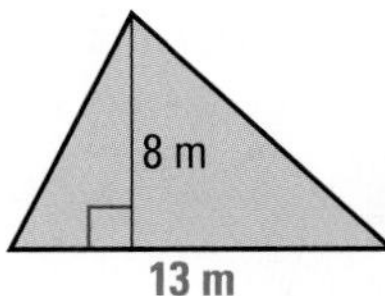

7. Parallelogram

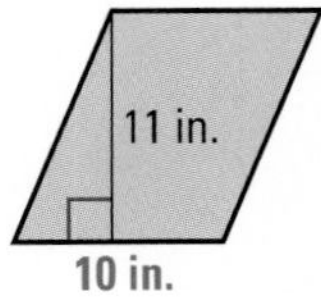

8. Trapezoid

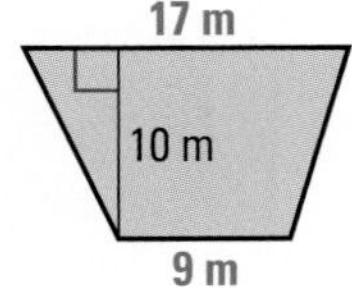

9. Parallelogram

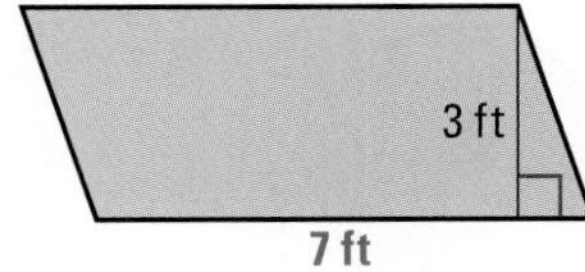

10. Trapezoid

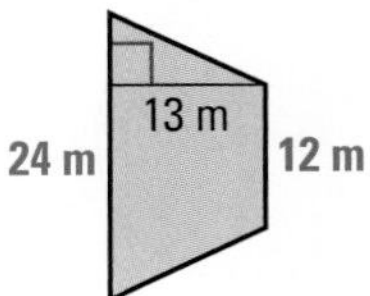

11. Triangle

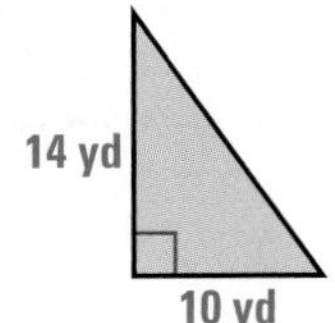

12. Rectangle

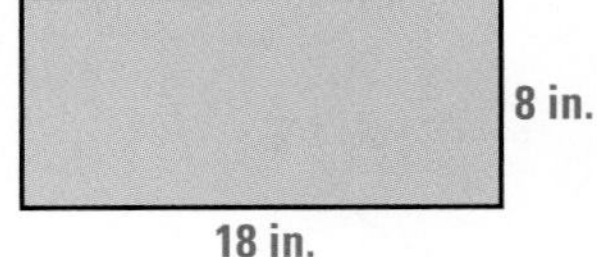

Circumference and Area of a Circle

A circle consists of all points in a plane that are the same distance from a fixed point called the **center**.

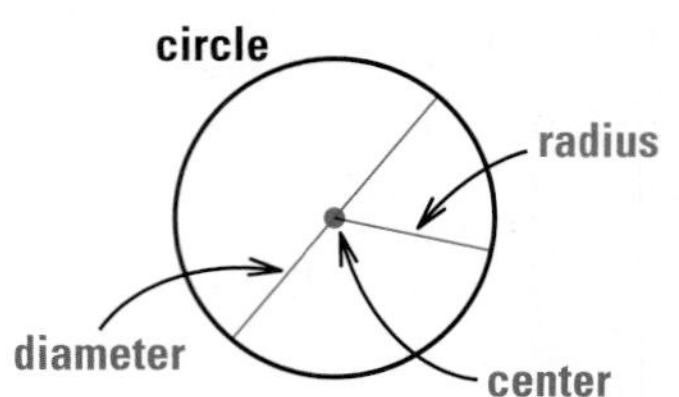

The distance between the center and any point on the circle is the **radius**. The distance across the circle through the center is the **diameter**. The diameter of a circle is twice its radius.

The **circumference** of a circle is the distance around the circle. For any circle, the ratio of its circumference to its diameter is π (pi), a number that is approximately equal to 3.14 or $\frac{22}{7}$.

Circumference and Area of a Circle

To find the circumference C of a circle with radius r or diameter d, use the formula $C = 2\pi r$ or $C = \pi d$.

To find the area A of a circle with radius r, use the formula $A = \pi r^2$.

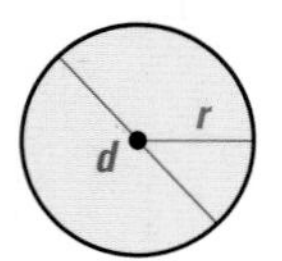

EXAMPLE **Find the circumference and area of the circle. Give your answers in terms of π and as decimals rounded to the nearest tenth.**

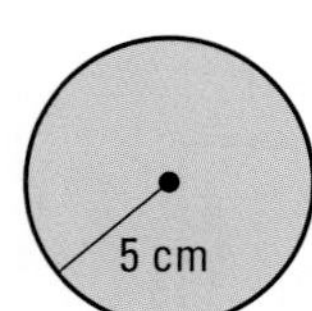

Circumference

$C = 2\pi r$

$= 2\pi(5)$

$= 10\pi$ cm **Exact answer**

$\approx 10(3.14)$

$= 31.4$ cm **Decimal approximation**

Area

$A = \pi r^2$

$= \pi(5^2)$

$= 25\pi \text{ cm}^2$ **Exact answer**

$\approx 25(3.14)$

$= 78.5 \text{ cm}^2$ **Decimal approximation**

PRACTICE

Find the circumference and area of the circle. Give your answers in terms of π and as decimals rounded to the nearest tenth.

1.

2.
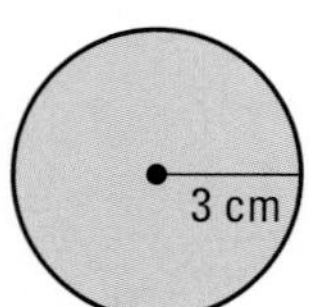

3.
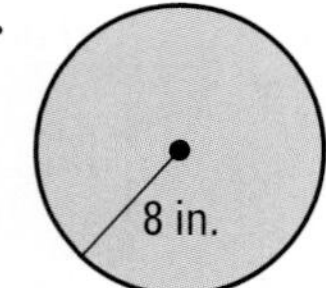

4.
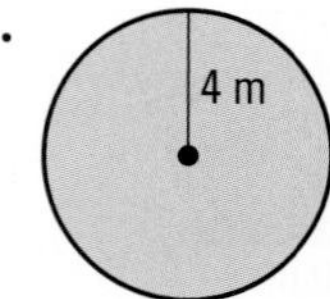

5.
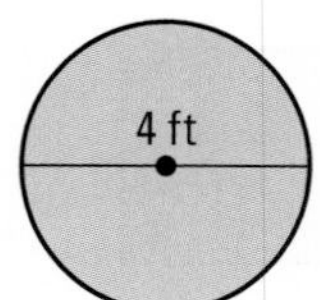

6.
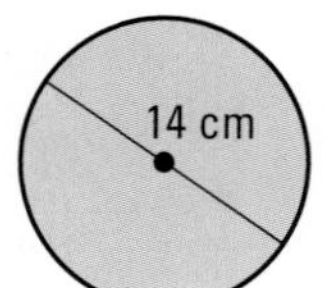

7.
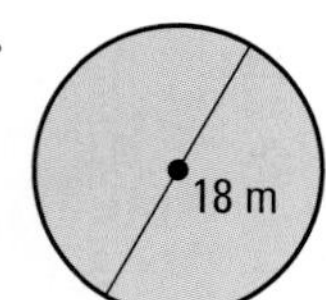

8.
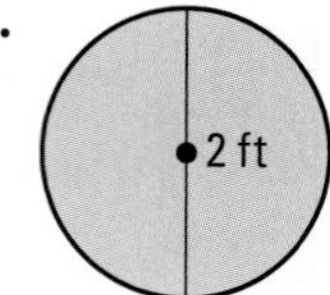

Surface Area and Volume

A **solid** is a three-dimensional figure that encloses part of space. The **surface area** S of a solid is the sum of the areas of all of its surfaces. The **volume** V of a solid is the amount of space that the solid occupies. In the formulas for surface area and volume, the number π (pi) is approximately equal to 3.14 or $\frac{22}{7}$.

Right Rectangular Prism

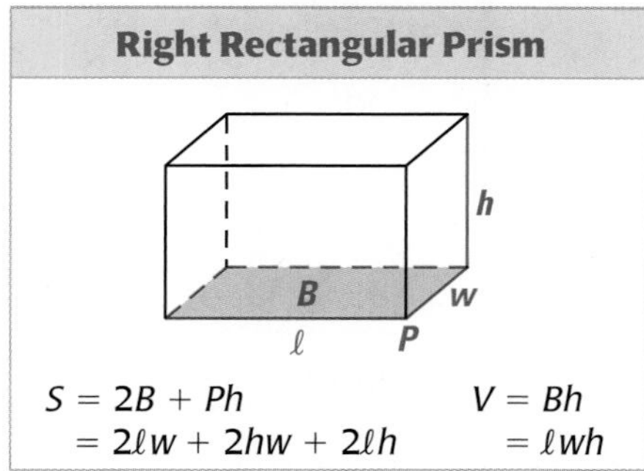

$S = 2B + Ph$
$= 2\ell w + 2hw + 2\ell h$

$V = Bh$
$= \ell wh$

Right Circular Cylinder

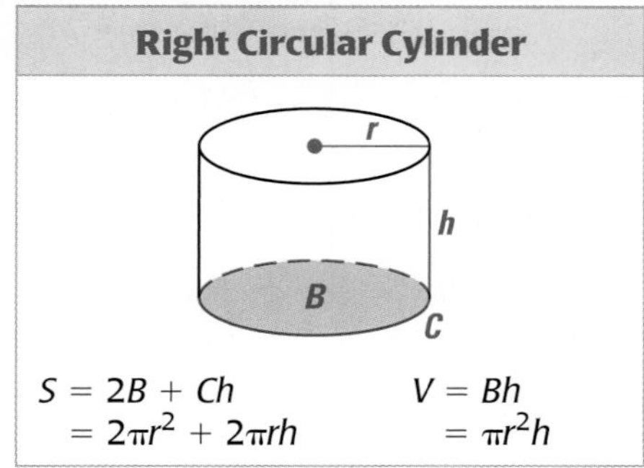

$S = 2B + Ch$
$= 2\pi r^2 + 2\pi rh$

$V = Bh$
$= \pi r^2 h$

Regular Pyramid

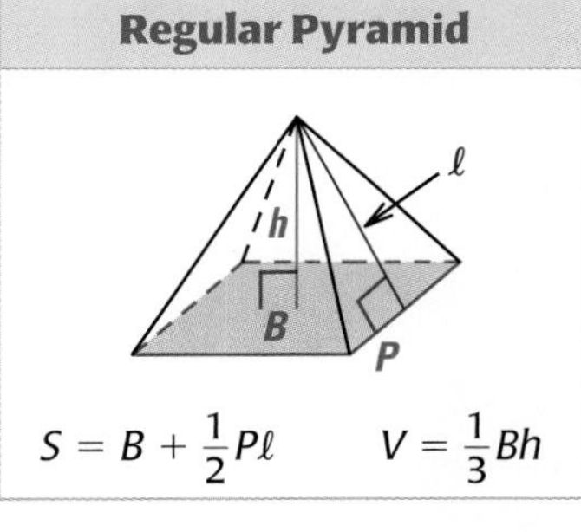

$S = B + \frac{1}{2}P\ell$

$V = \frac{1}{3}Bh$

Right Circular Cone

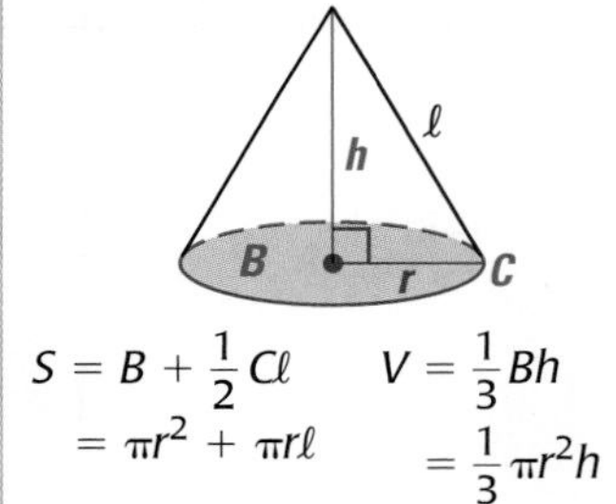

$S = B + \frac{1}{2}C\ell$
$= \pi r^2 + \pi r\ell$

$V = \frac{1}{3}Bh$
$= \frac{1}{3}\pi r^2 h$

Sphere

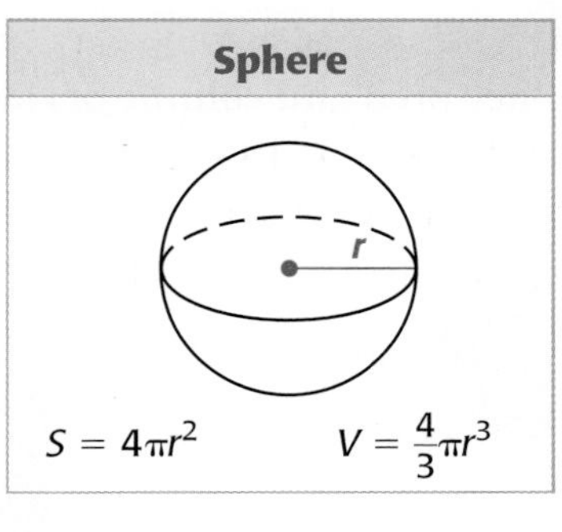

$S = 4\pi r^2$

$V = \frac{4}{3}\pi r^3$

In this book, the adjectives *right* and *circular* will be assumed and therefore will not be used in naming solids.

EXAMPLE **Find the surface area of the solid.**

a. Sphere

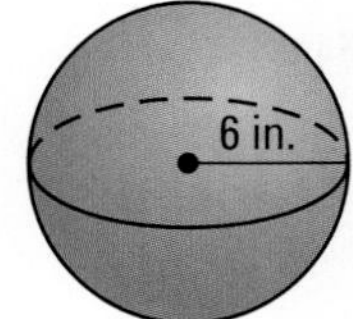

$S = 4\pi r^2$
$= 4\pi(6^2)$
$= 144\pi \text{ in.}^2$
$\approx 144(3.14)$
$\approx 452.2 \text{ in.}^2$

b. Cylinder

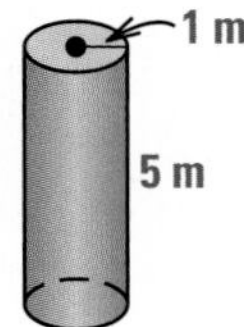

$S = 2\pi r^2 + 2\pi rh$
$= 2\pi(1^2) + 2\pi(1)(5)$
$= 2\pi + 10\pi$
$= 12\pi \text{ m}^2$
$\approx 12(3.14) \approx 37.7 \text{ m}^2$

c. Cone

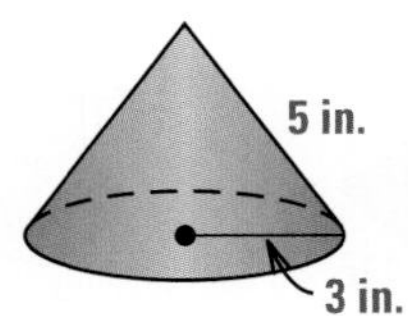

$S = \pi r^2 + \pi r\ell$
$= \pi(3^2) + \pi(3)(5)$
$= 9\pi + 15\pi$
$= 24\pi \text{ in.}^2$
$\approx 24(3.14) \approx 75.4 \text{ in.}^2$

EXAMPLE **Find the volume of the solid.**

a. Rectangular prism

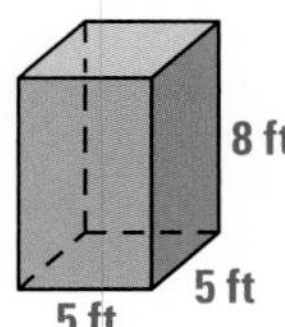

$V = Bh$

$= 25(8)$

$= 200 \text{ ft}^3$

b. Regular pyramid

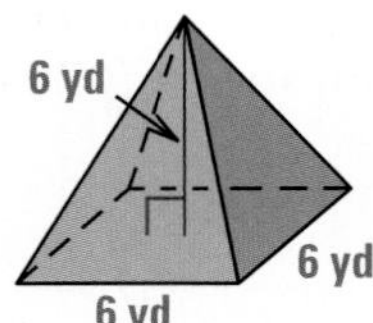

$V = \frac{1}{3}Bh$

$= \frac{1}{3}(36)6$

$= 72 \text{ yd}^3$

c. Cone

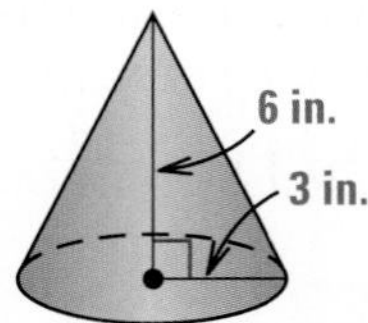

$V = \frac{1}{3}Bh$

$= \frac{1}{3}\pi(3^2)(6)$

$= 18\pi \text{ in.}^3$

$\approx 18(3.14) \approx 56.5 \text{ in.}^3$

PRACTICE

Find the surface area and volume of the solid. For spheres, cylinders, and cones, give your answers in terms of π and as decimals rounded to the nearest tenth.

1. Rectangular prism

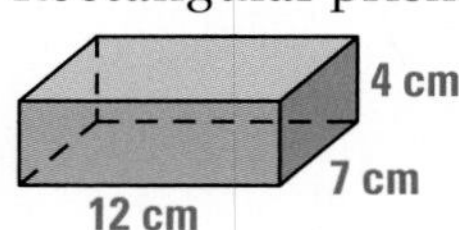

2. Cylinder

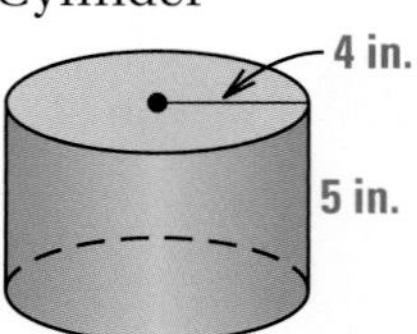

3. Sphere

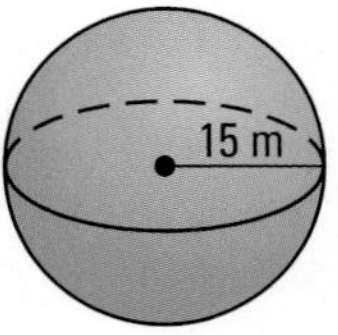
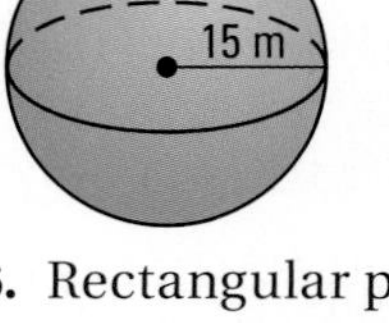

4. Cylinder

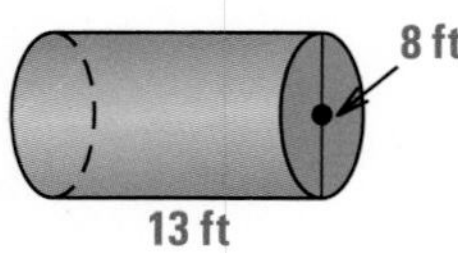

5. Cone

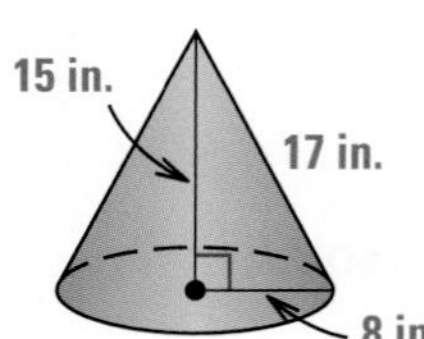

6. Rectangular prism

7. Regular pyramid

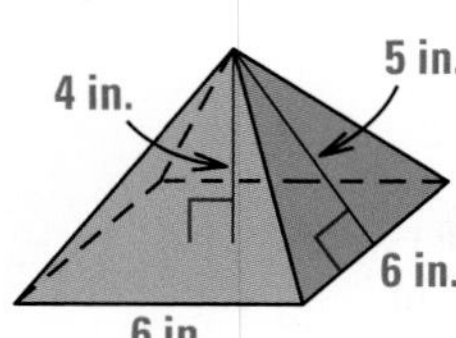

8. Sphere

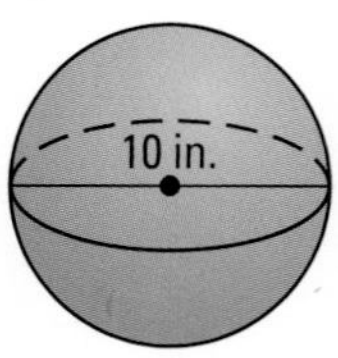
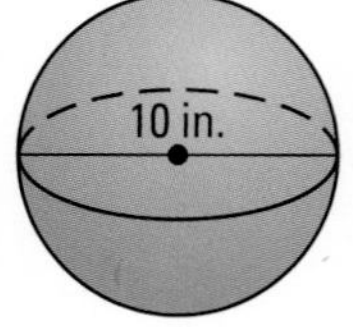

9. Cylinder

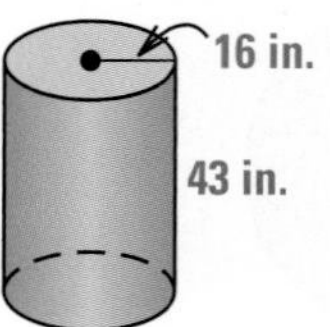
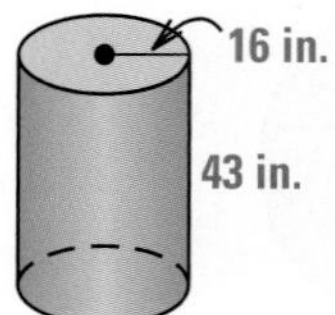

10. Rectangular prism

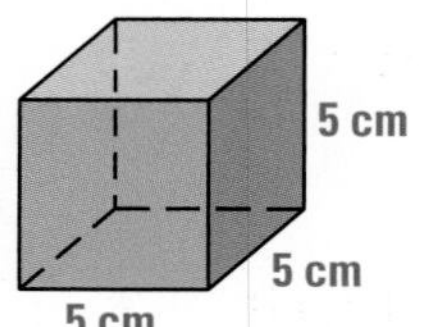

11. Cone

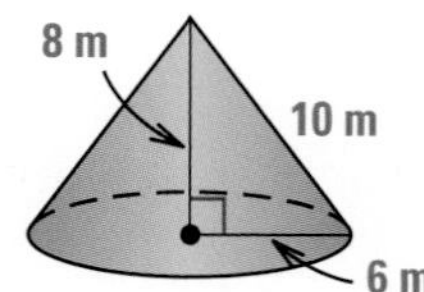

12. Regular pyramid

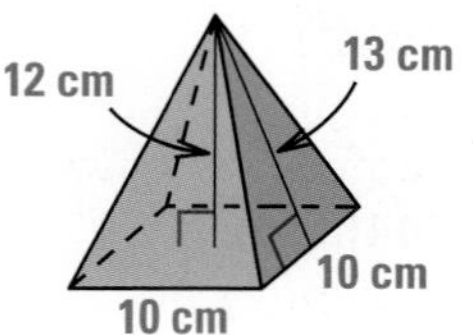

Converting Units of Measurement

The Table of Measures on page T6 gives many statements of equivalent measures. You can write two different conversion factors for each statement, as shown below. Each conversion factor is equal to 1.

Statement of Equivalent Measures	Conversion Factors	
100 cm = 1 m	$\frac{100 \text{ cm}}{1 \text{ m}} = 1$	$\frac{1 \text{ m}}{100 \text{ cm}} = 1$

To convert from one unit of measurement to another, multiply by a conversion factor that will eliminate the starting unit and result in the desired unit.

Convert meters to centimeters:

Use $\frac{100 \text{ cm}}{1 \text{ m}}$.

$3 \cancel{\text{m}} \times \frac{100 \text{ cm}}{1 \cancel{\text{m}}} = 300 \text{ cm}$

Convert centimeters to meters:

Use $\frac{1 \text{ m}}{100 \text{ cm}}$.

$400 \cancel{\text{cm}} \times \frac{1 \text{ m}}{100 \cancel{\text{cm}}} = 4 \text{ m}$

Sometimes you need to use more than one conversion factor.

EXAMPLE **Copy and complete: 2 d = _?_ sec**

STEP 1 **Find** the appropriate statements of equivalent measures.

24 h = 1 d, 60 min = 1 h, and 60 sec = 1 min

STEP 2 **Write** the appropriate conversion factors: $\frac{24 \text{ h}}{1 \text{ d}}$, $\frac{60 \text{ min}}{1 \text{ h}}$, and $\frac{60 \text{ sec}}{1 \text{ min}}$

STEP 3 **Multiply** by the conversion factors:

$$2 \cancel{\text{d}} \times \frac{24 \cancel{\text{h}}}{1 \cancel{\text{d}}} \times \frac{60 \cancel{\text{min}}}{1 \cancel{\text{h}}} \times \frac{60 \text{ sec}}{1 \cancel{\text{min}}} = 172{,}800 \text{ sec}$$

▶ 2 d = 172,800 sec

PRACTICE

Copy and complete.

1. 300 sec = _?_ min
2. 2.6 g = _?_ kg
3. 64 oz = _?_ lb
4. 4 gal = _?_ qt
5. 72 in. = _?_ ft
6. 94 mm = _?_ cm
7. 42 ft = _?_ yd
8. 5 d = _?_ h
9. 3 m = _?_ cm
10. 2 yd = _?_ in.
11. 70 L = _?_ mL
12. 10 mi = _?_ ft
13. 1.5 ton = _?_ lb
14. 4500 mL = _?_ L
15. 15,000 mg = _?_ g

Convert to common units as necessary and perform the indicated operation.

16. 42 g − 500 mg
17. $3\frac{2}{3}$ yd + 33 ft
18. $2\frac{1}{4}$ mi − 3960 ft

Converting Between Systems

To convert between metric and customary units, use the approximate relationships shown in the table. The symbol ≈ means is *approximately equal to.*

Length	Capacity	Weight
1 mm ≈ 0.0394 in.	1 mL ≈ 0.0338 fl oz	1 g ≈ 0.0353 oz
1 m ≈ 3.28 ft	1 L ≈ 1.06 qt	1 kg ≈ 2.2 lb
1 km ≈ 0.621 mi	1 kL ≈ 264 gal	

EXAMPLE **Copy and complete: 131 km ≈ __?__ mi. Round to the nearest whole number.**

STEP 1 **Find** the appropriate statement of equivalent measures: 1 km ≈ 0.621 mi

STEP 2 **Write** the appropriate conversion factor: $\frac{0.621 \text{ mi}}{1 \text{ km}}$

STEP 3 **Multiply** by the conversion factor:

$$131 \text{ km} \times \frac{0.621 \text{ mi}}{1 \text{ km}} = 81.351 \text{ mi} \approx 81 \text{ mi}$$

▶ 131 km ≈ 81 mi

EXAMPLE **Copy and complete: 124 lb ≈ __?__ kg. Round to the nearest whole number.**

STEP 1 **Find** the appropriate statement of equivalent measures: 1 kg ≈ 2.2 lb

STEP 2 **Write** the appropriate conversion factor: $\frac{1 \text{ kg}}{2.2 \text{ lb}}$

STEP 3 **Multiply** by the conversion factor:

$$124 \text{ lb} \times \frac{1 \text{ kg}}{2.2 \text{ lb}} = 56.\overline{36} \text{ kg} \approx 56 \text{ kg}$$

▶ 124 lb ≈ 56 kg

PRACTICE

Copy and complete the statement. Round to the nearest whole number.

1. 3.2 kL ≈ __?__ gal
2. 25 mm ≈ __?__ in.
3. 180 g ≈ __?__ oz
4. 10 qt ≈ __?__ L
5. 35 km ≈ __?__ mi
6. 85 kg ≈ __?__ lb
7. 12 ft ≈ __?__ m
8. 14 oz ≈ __?__ g
9. 30 L ≈ __?__ qt
10. 15 m ≈ __?__ ft
11. 2.5 mi ≈ __?__ km
12. 8 fl oz ≈ __?__ ml
13. 42 mm ≈ __?__ in.
14. 39 mL ≈ __?__ fl oz
15. 1300 gal ≈ __?__ kL

Venn Diagrams and Logical Reasoning

A **Venn diagram** uses shapes to show how sets are related.

EXAMPLE **Draw a Venn diagram of the whole numbers less than 10 where set *A* consists of prime numbers and set *B* consists of even numbers.**

Whole numbers less than 10:
0, 1, 2, 3, 4, 5, 6, 7, 8, 9

Set *A*: 2, 3, 5, 7

Set *B*: 0, 2, 4, 6, 8

Both set *A* and set *B*: 2

Neither set *A* nor set *B*: 1, 9

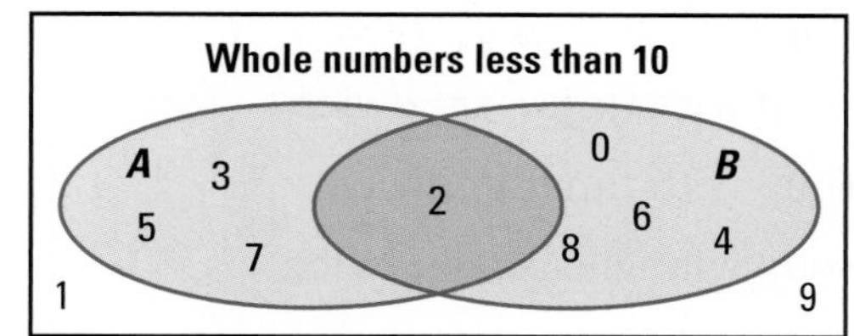

You can use a Venn diagram to answer questions about sets.

EXAMPLE **Use the Venn diagram above to answer the question.**

a. Is the statement below *true* or *false*? Explain.

No whole number less than 10 is prime.

▶ False. The whole number 2 is less than 10 and is prime.

b. Is the statement below *always, sometimes,* or *never* true? Explain.

A whole number less than 10 is either even or prime.

▶ Sometimes. Each of the numbers 0, 2, 3, 4, 5, 6, 7, and 8 are either even or prime, but the numbers 1 and 9 are not even and not prime.

PRACTICE

Draw a Venn diagram of the sets described.

1. Of the whole numbers less than 10, set *A* consists of factors of 10 and set *B* consists of odd numbers.
2. Of the whole numbers less than 10, set *A* consists of factors of 6 and set *B* consists of even numbers.

Use the Venn diagrams you drew in Exercises 1 and 2 to answer the question.

3. Are the following statements *true* or *false*? Explain.
   a. *If a whole number less than 10 is odd, then it must be a factor of 10.*
   b. *A whole number less than 10 that is a factor of 10 must be odd.*
4. Are the following statements *always, sometimes,* or *never* true? Explain.
   a. *A whole number that is even and less than 10 is a factor of 6.*
   b. *A factor of 6 that is less than 10 is even.*

Counting Methods

There are several methods for counting the number of possibilities in a situation.

EXAMPLE **Make a list to find the number of possible lunch specials.**

Lunch Special $6.95	
Choose 1 soup and 1 sandwich.	
Soups	**Sandwiches**
Chicken	Turkey
Tomato	Tuna
	Cheese

Pair each soup with each sandwich.

Chicken soup with turkey sandwich

Chicken soup with tuna sandwich

Chicken soup with cheese sandwich

Tomato soup with turkey sandwich

Tomato soup with tuna sandwich

Tomato soup with cheese sandwich

Count the number of lunch specials in the list.

▶ There are 6 possible lunch specials.

EXAMPLE **Draw a tree diagram to find the number of possible lunch specials given the choices in the example above.**

Arrange the soups and sandwiches in a tree diagram.

Soup	Sandwich	Lunch
Chicken	Turkey	Chicken soup, turkey sandwich
	Tuna	Chicken soup, tuna sandwich
	Cheese	Chicken soup, cheese sandwich
Tomato	Turkey	Tomato soup, turkey sandwich
	Tuna	Tomato soup, tuna sandwich
	Cheese	Tomato soup, cheese sandwich

▶ There are 6 possible lunch specials.

Another way to count the number of possible lunch specials described in the examples above is to multiply. Since there are 2 choices of soup and 3 choices of sandwich, there are $2 \times 3 = 6$ possible lunch specials. This method uses the counting principle.

The Counting Principle

If one event can occur in m ways, and for each of these ways a second event can occur in n ways, then the number of ways that the two events can occur together is $m \cdot n$.

The counting principle can be extended to three or more events.

EXAMPLE **Greta must choose a 4-digit password for her cell phone mailbox. Use the counting principle to find the number of possible 4-digit passwords.**

For each of the 4 digits in the password, there are 10 choices: 0, 1, 2, 3, 4, 5, 6, 7, 8, and 9.

10 choices for first digit	×	10 choices for second digit	×	10 choices for third digit	×	10 choices for fourth digit

$10 \times 10 \times 10 \times 10 = 10{,}000$

▶ There are 10,000 possible 4-digit passwords.

PRACTICE

In Exercises 1–3, use the indicated counting method to answer the question.

1. Andrew, Bettina, and Carl are triplets. In how many different ways can the triplets stand in a row for a photo? (Make a list.)
2. The sign at the right shows the color and size choices for school T-shirts. How many different types of school T-shirts are available? (Draw a tree diagram.)
3. A 3-letter monogram consists of the first letter of a person's first name, middle name, and last name. For example, Matthew David Weaver's monogram is MDW. How many different 3-letter monograms are possible? (Use the counting principle.)

School T-Shirts $9.99

Choose 1 color and 1 size.

Colors:	Sizes:
Black, Gold, or White	S, M, L, or XL

In Exercises 4–8, answer the question using any counting method you choose.

4. How many different pizzas with 2 different toppings are available for the large pizza special advertised at the right?
5. Lance must choose 4 characters for his computer password. Each character can be any letter A–Z or any digit 0–9. How many different computer passwords are possible?
6. Mia must choose 3 whole numbers less than 50 for her locker combination. The numbers may be repeated. How many different locker combinations are possible?
7. A restaurant offers a dinner special. You can choose a main course, a vegetable, and a salad from a choice of 6 main courses, 4 vegetables, and 3 salads. How many different dinners are available?
8. Each day Scott walks, rides the bus, or gets a ride to school. He has each of the same possibilities for getting home each day. How many combinations of travel to and from school does Scott have?

Large Pizza Special

Any 2 toppings for $12.49

Pepperoni	Black olive
Sausage	Green pepper
Ground beef	Red onion
Extra cheese	Mushroom

Bar Graphs

You can use a **bar graph** to display and compare data that are in categories.

EXAMPLE **Use the bar graph, which shows the medals won by the United States in the 2004 Summer Olympics. (a) Did the United States win more gold medals, silver medals, or bronze medals? (b) How many more silver medals than bronze medals did the United States win?**

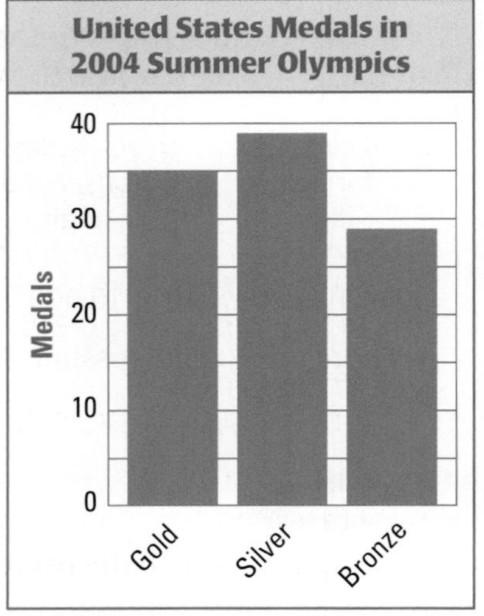

a. The longest bar on the graph is for silver medals won.

▶ The United States won more silver medals than any other type.

b. The bar for silver medals shows 39 silver medals won. The bar for bronze medals shows 29 bronze medals won.

$39 - 29 = 10$

▶ The United States won 10 more silver medals than bronze medals.

PRACTICE

In Exercises 1–3, use the bar graph above.

1. The United States won fewer of which type of medal than any other type?
2. How many more silver medals than gold medals did the United States win?
3. How many medals did the United States win altogether?

In Exercises 4–11, use the bar graph below, which shows the top medal-winning countries in the 2002 Winter Olympics.

4. Which country won the most medals? How many medals did it win?
5. How many medals did Norway win?
6. Which two countries won 17 medals each?
7. Which country won the same number of medals as France?
8. How many countries won more than 15 medals?
9. Which country won twice as many medals as Austria?
10. How many medals did Russia and Italy win altogether?
11. How many medals did the top 3 medal-winning countries win?

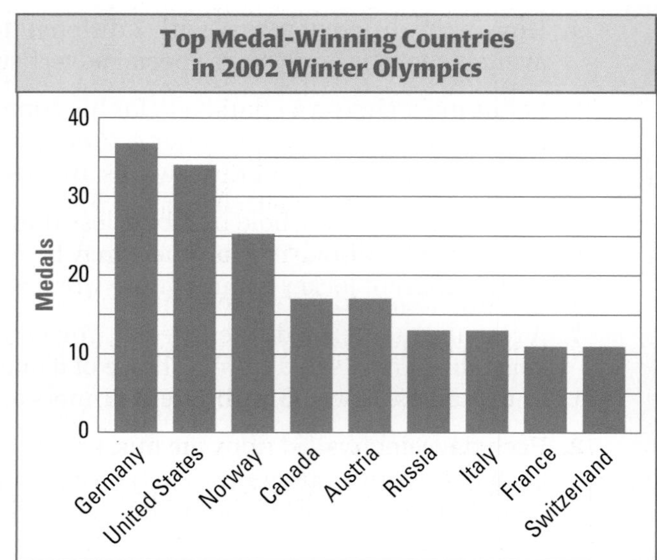

Line Graphs

You can use a **line graph** to show how numerical data change over time.

EXAMPLE **Use the line graph, which shows Charlie's weight from birth to 5 years old. (a) How much weight did Charlie gain in 5 years? (b) At what age did Charlie weigh 30 pounds? (c) In which year did Charlie gain the most weight?**

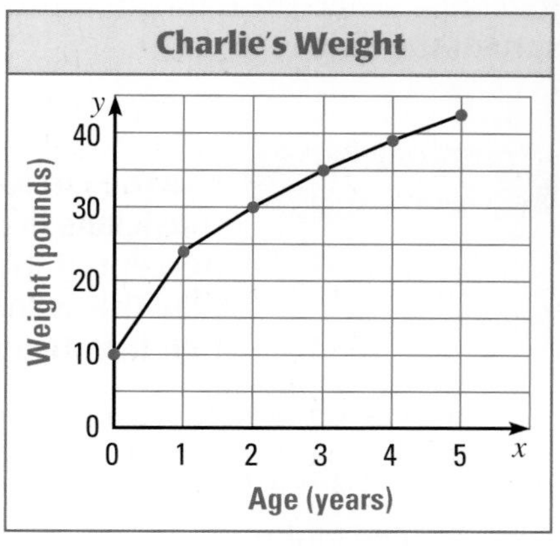

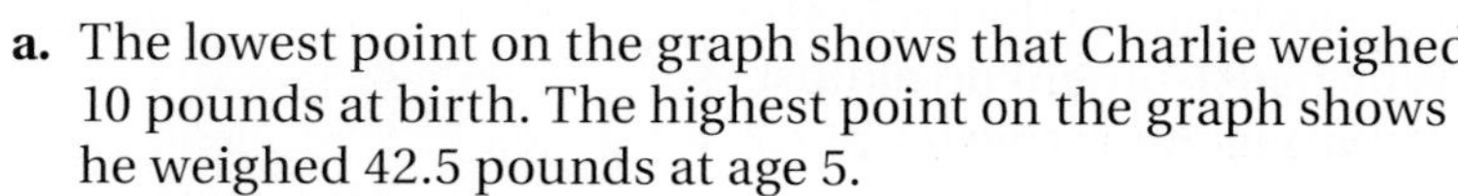

a. The lowest point on the graph shows that Charlie weighed 10 pounds at birth. The highest point on the graph shows he weighed 42.5 pounds at age 5.

$42.5 - 10 = 32.5$

▶ Charlie gained 32.5 pounds in 5 years.

b. The point on the graph to the right of 30 on the weight axis corresponds to an age of 2.

▶ Charlie weighed 30 pounds at age 2.

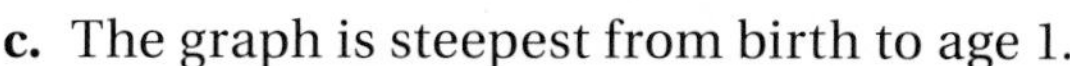

c. The graph is steepest from birth to age 1.

▶ Charlie gained the most weight in his first year.

PRACTICE

In Exercises 1–5, use the line graph above.

1. How much did Charlie weigh on his first birthday?
2. How old was Charlie when he weighed 40 pounds?
3. In which year did Charlie gain the least weight?
4. How much weight did Charlie gain his first year?
5. How much weight did Charlie gain from age 1 to age 4?

In Exercises 6–14, use the line graph, which shows Abby's height from birth to 4 years old.

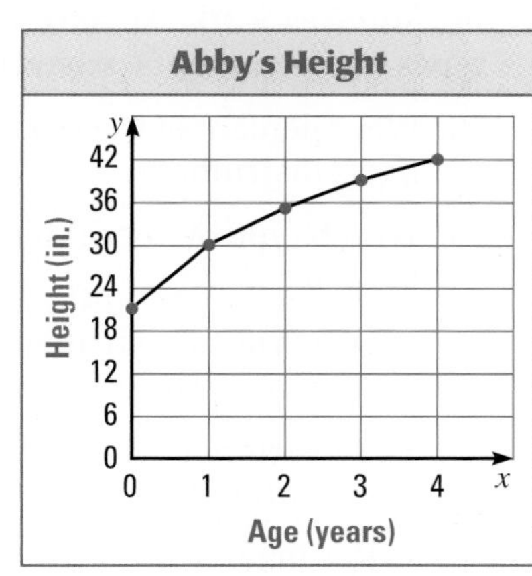

6. How tall was Abby when she was born?
7. How old was Abby when she was 35 inches tall?
8. In which year did Abby grow the most?
9. In which year did Abby grow the least?
10. How many inches did Abby grow from age 3 to age 4?
11. In which year did Abby grow 5 inches?
12. How many inches did Abby grow in 4 years?
13. At what age was Abby's height double her height at birth?
14. If Abby maintains the same growth rate from age 4 to age 5 that she had from age 3 to age 4, how tall will she be when she is 5?

Circle Graphs

You can use a **circle graph** to display data as sections of a circle. The entire circle represents all of the data. The sections of the circle may be labeled using the actual data or the data expressed as fractions, decimals, or percents. When the data are expressed as fractions, decimals, or percents, the sum of the data is 1.

EXAMPLE **Use the circle graph, which shows the string musicians in a college orchestra. (a) What percent of the string musicians in the orchestra play the cello? (b) Which instrument do almost half the string musicians in the orchestra play?**

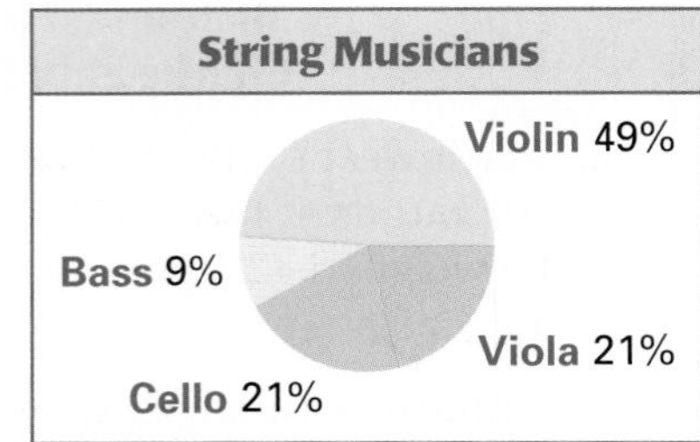

a. The cello section of the circle is labeled 21%.

▸ Of the string musicians in the orchestra, 21% play cello.

b. The violin section of the circle is labeled 49%, which is almost 50%. Also, the violin section of the circle is almost half the total area of the circle.

▸ Almost half of the string musicians in the orchestra play the violin.

PRACTICE

In Exercises 1–4, use the circle graph above.

1. What percent of the string musicians in the orchestra play the bass?
2. How does the number of string musicians who play the viola compare with the number of string musicians who play the cello?
3. The violinists are divided evenly into two groups, first violin and second violin. What percent of the string musicians are in each of these groups?
4. If there are 57 string musicians in the orchestra, how many musicians play each type of instrument?

In Exercises 5–10, use the circle graph, which shows the types of instruments played by musicians in a college band.

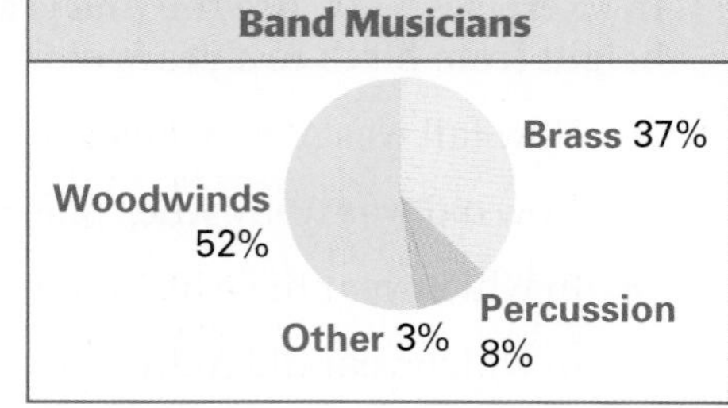

5. What percent of the musicians in the band play a brass instrument?
6. Which type of instrument do 8% of the musicians in the band play?
7. Which type of instrument do more than half of the musicians in the band play?
8. The instruments in the “Other” category are harp, string bass, and keyboard. What percent of the band musicians play one of these instruments?
9. In this band, which type of instrument is played by about 5 times as many musicians as play percussion instruments?
10. There are 91 musicians in the band. How many more musicians play a woodwind than play a percussion instrument?

Misleading Data Displays

Data displays may be misleading because of the way in which they are drawn.

EXAMPLE ***Explain*** **why the data display may be misleading.**

a.

b.

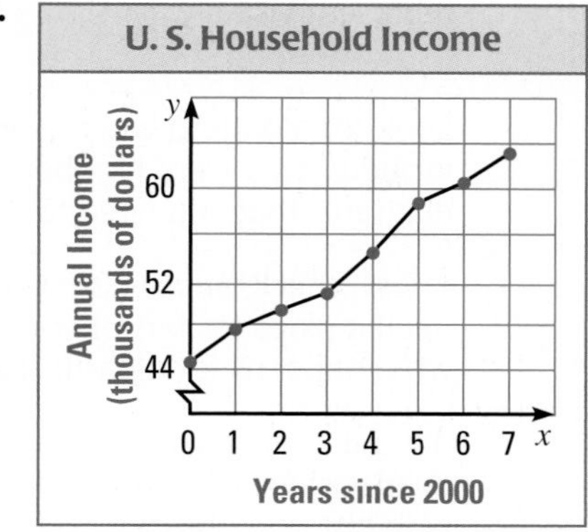

a. The large increments on the y-axis flatten the graph and make the increases seem insignificant.

b. The break in the y-axis stretches the graph and exaggerates the increases.

PRACTICE

Explain **why the data display may be misleading.**

1.

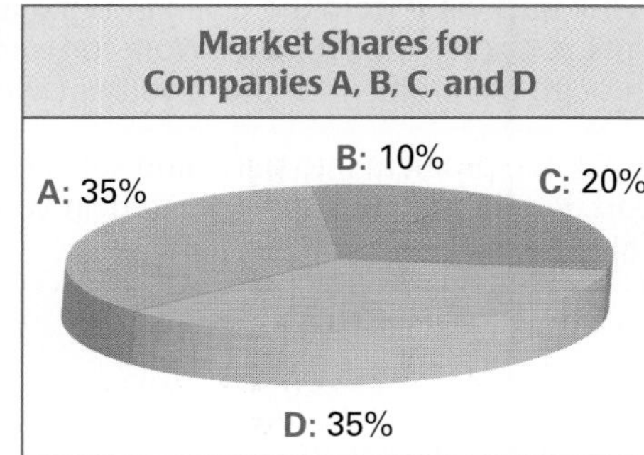

2.

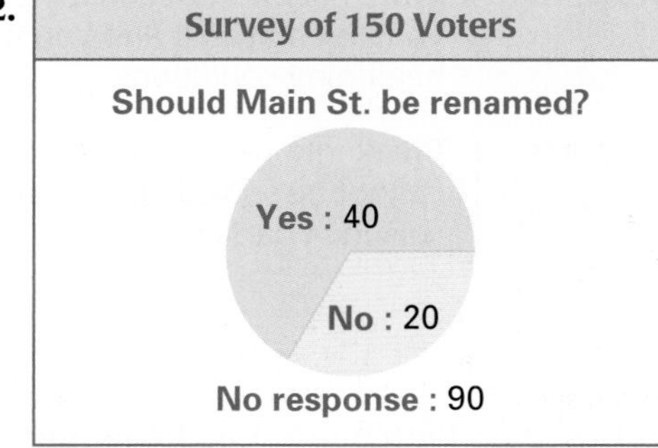

3.

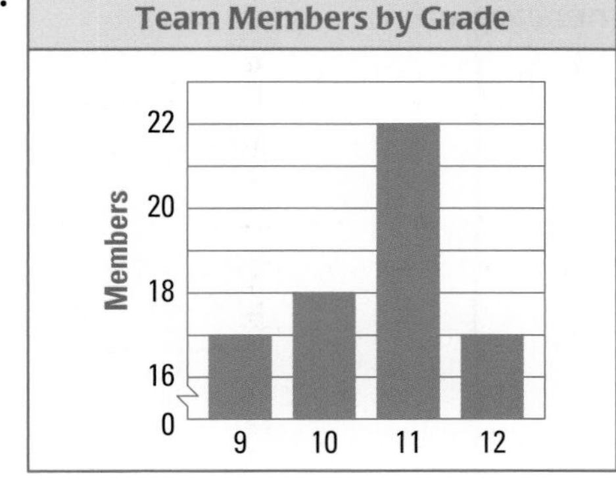

4.

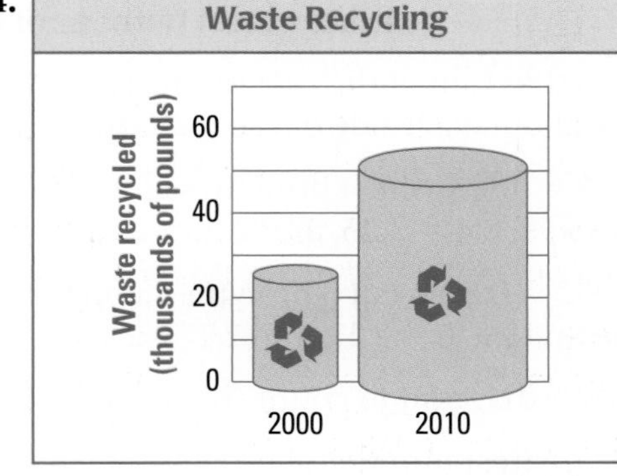

Problem Solving Strategies

The following are strategies that you can use to solve problems.

Strategy	When to use	How to use
Draw a diagram	Draw a diagram when a problem involves any relationships that you can represent visually.	Draw a diagram that shows the given information. Label any unknowns in your diagram and look for relationships between givens and unknowns.
Look for a pattern	Look for a pattern when a problem includes a series of numbers or diagrams that you need to analyze.	Look for a pattern in any given information. Apply, extend, or generalize the pattern to help you solve the problem.
Guess, check, and revise	Guess, check, and revise when you need a place to start or you want to see what happens for a particular number.	Make a reasonable guess. Check to see if your guess solves the problem. If it does not, revise your guess and check again.
Act it out	Act out a problem that involves any relationships that you can represent with physical objects and movement.	Act out the problem, using objects described in the problem or other items that represent those objects.
Make a list or table	Make a list or table when you need to record, generate, or organize information.	Generate a list systematically, accounting for all possibilities. Look for relationships across rows or down columns within a table.
Solve a simpler or related problem	Solve a simpler or related problem when a problem seems difficult and can be made easier by using simpler numbers or conditions.	Think of a way to make the problem easier. Solve the simpler or related problem. Use what you learned to help you solve the original problem.
Work backward	Work backward when a problem gives you an end result and you need to find beginning conditions.	Work backward from the given information until you solve the problem. Work forward through the problem to check your answer.
Break into parts	Break into parts when a problem cannot be solved all at once, but can be solved in parts or stages.	Break the problem into parts and solve each part. Put the answers together to help you solve the original problem.

EXAMPLE **Fletcher baked brownies in a rectangular pan that measures 9 inches by 13 inches. He wants to cut rectangular brownies that are at least 2 inches on each side, with all brownies the same size. What is the greatest number of brownies Fletcher can cut?**

Draw a diagram of the rectangular pan. Label the sides with their lengths. Think about each side of the rectangle.

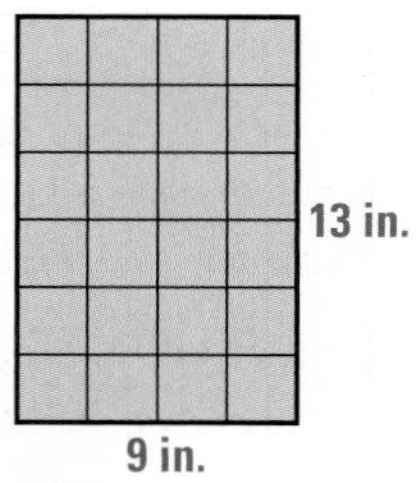

$9 \div 2 = 4.5$, so cut 4 brownies along the 9 inch side.
Check: $9 \div 4 = 2.25$, and $2.25 > 2$.

$13 \div 2 = 6.5$, so cut 6 brownies along the 13 inch side.
Check: $13 \div 6 \approx 2.17$, and $2.17 > 2$.

Use your diagram to count the brownies: $4 \times 6 = 24$.

▶ The greatest number of brownies Fletcher can cut is 24.

PRACTICE

1. Four friends hosted a party. The table shows the amount of money each friend spent. The friends want to share the party expenses equally, and Pam will pay the entire amount she owes to one person. Who owes money to whom?

Person	Party expenses
Barb	$11 for drinks
Bonnie	$15 for food
Pam	$6 for invitations
Holly	$8 for decorations

2. Six people can be seated at a rectangular table, with one person at each end. How many people can be seated at five of these tables if they are placed end to end?

3. Bob is 55 years old. In 5 years, Bob will be twice as old as his son. How old is Bob's son?

4. Maddie and Rob are sharing a pack of 25 pens. Maddie offers to let Rob have 3 pens for every 2 pens she gets. If they use the entire package of pens, how many pens will each person get?

5. In how many different ways can you make $.50 in change using quarters, dimes, and nickels?

6. The diagram shows two cuts through the center of a pizza. How many cuts through the center are needed to divide a pizza into 12 equal pieces?

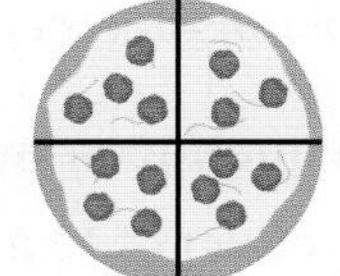

7. Deb is flying to Seattle. Her flight leaves at 4:15 P.M. She wants to arrive at the airport 2 hours early to check in and get through security. The taxi ride from her office to the airport takes about 30 minutes. What time should Deb ask the taxi driver to pick her up at the office?

8. Dan wants to enclose a rectangular area with a fence. He has 12 fence posts to use, and the fence posts will be placed 10 feet apart. The diagram shows a possible shape for the area. Find another shape that would use all the fence posts, placed 10 feet apart, and would increase the area by 100 square feet.

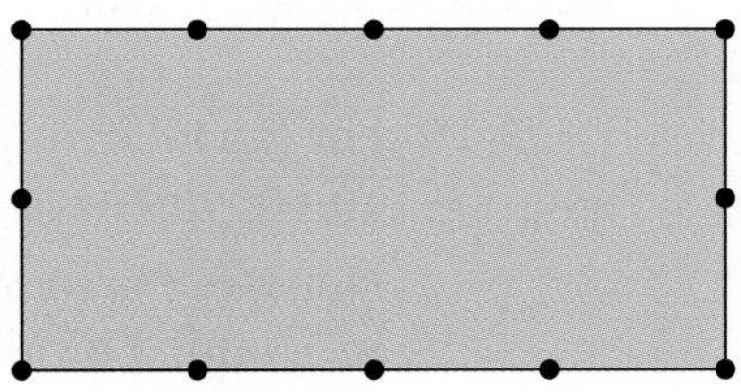

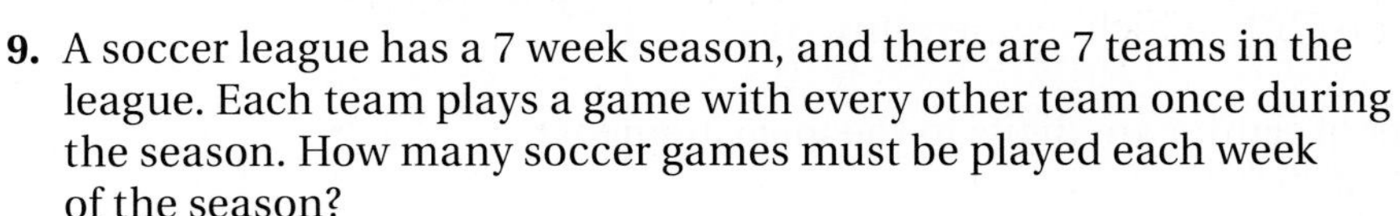

9. A soccer league has a 7 week season, and there are 7 teams in the league. Each team plays a game with every other team once during the season. How many soccer games must be played each week of the season?

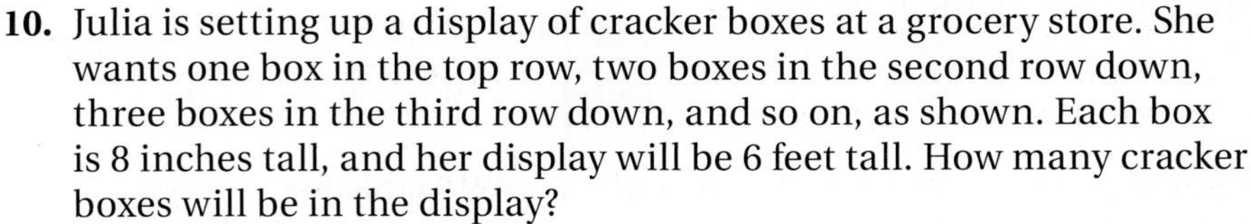

10. Julia is setting up a display of cracker boxes at a grocery store. She wants one box in the top row, two boxes in the second row down, three boxes in the third row down, and so on, as shown. Each box is 8 inches tall, and her display will be 6 feet tall. How many cracker boxes will be in the display?

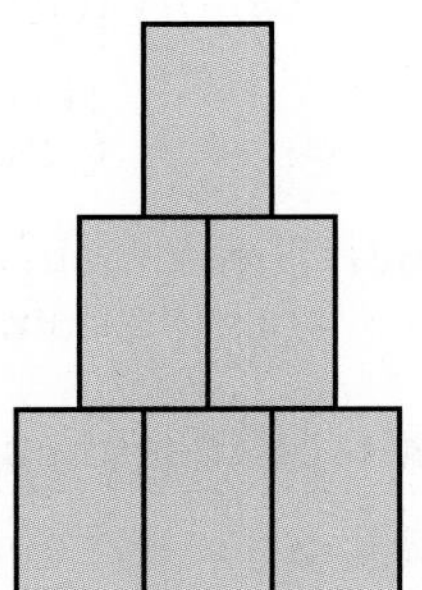

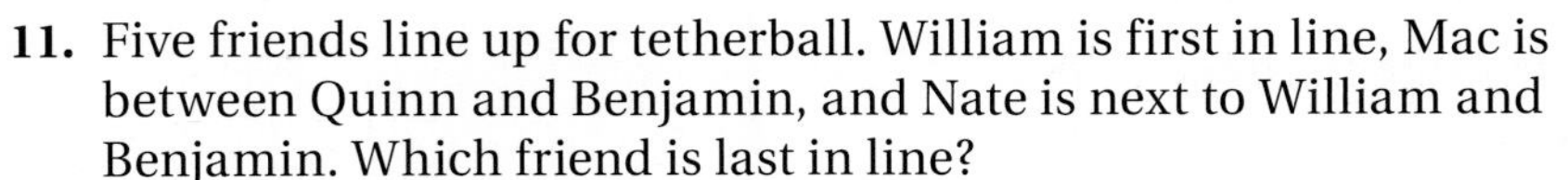

11. Five friends line up for tetherball. William is first in line, Mac is between Quinn and Benjamin, and Nate is next to William and Benjamin. Which friend is last in line?

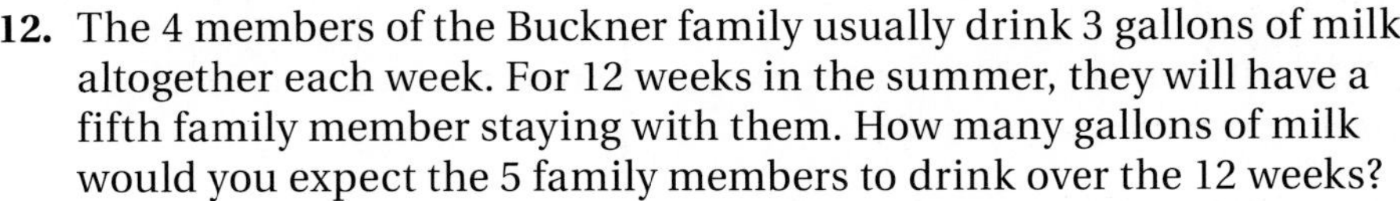

12. The 4 members of the Buckner family usually drink 3 gallons of milk altogether each week. For 12 weeks in the summer, they will have a fifth family member staying with them. How many gallons of milk would you expect the 5 family members to drink over the 12 weeks?

Extra Practice

Chapter 1

Evaluate the expression.

1.1 **1.** $k + 9$ when $k = 7$ **2.** $21 - x$ when $x = 3$ **3.** $3.5 + t$ when $t = 0.9$ **4.** $y - \frac{3}{8}$ when $y = \frac{7}{12}$

5. $\frac{m}{4}$ when $m = 9.6$ **6.** $1.5t$ when $t = 2.3$ **7.** z^3 when $z = \frac{2}{3}$ **8.** p^4 when $p = 0.2$

1.2 **9.** $25 - 7 + 8$ **10.** $67 - 3 \cdot 4$ **11.** $8^2 \div 4 + 12$ **12.** $9 + 6 \div 3$

13. $\frac{3^3 - 7}{2}$ **14.** $\frac{1}{3}(7 - 5.5)^2$ **15.** $3 + 4(3 + 24)$ **16.** $\frac{3}{5}[27 - (2 + 5)]^2$

1.3 **Translate the verbal phrase into an expression.**

17. $\frac{3}{4}$ of a number m **18.** the quotient of a number x and 7

19. the difference of a number y and 3 **20.** 6 more than 3 times a number n

1.3 **Write an expression for the situation.**

21. Number of minutes left in a 45 minute class after m minutes have gone by

22. Number of meters in c centimeters

1.4 **Write an equation or an inequality.**

23. The product of 12 and the difference of a number r and 4 is 72.

24. The difference of a number q and 18 is greater than 10 and less than 15.

1.4 **Solve the equation using mental math.**

25. $d - 13 = 25$ **26.** $12z = 96$ **27.** $23 - m = 7$ **28.** $\frac{k}{6} = 12$

1.5 **29.** For the following, identify what you know and what you need to find out. You do *not* need to solve the problem.

One day the temperature in Quito, Ecuador, was 20°C. The temperature in Miami, Florida was 75°F. Which temperature was higher?

1.6 **30.** Identify the number of significant digits in the measurements **(a)** 25.03 m and **(b)** 1.620 ft.

1.7 **31.** Identify the domain and range of the function.

Input	3	4	5	6
Output	9	11	13	15

1.7 **32.** The domain of the function $y = 1.25x + 5$ is 2, 4, 6, and 8. Make a table for the function. Identify the range of the function.

1.8 **Graph the function.**

33. $y = x + 2$; domain: 0, 1, 2, and 3 **34.** $y = 3x - 3$; domain: 1, 2, 3, and 4

35. $y = 1.5x$; domain: 0, 20, 40, and 60 **36.** $y = \frac{1}{4}x + 2$; domain: 0, 4, 8, and 12

Extra Practice

Chapter 2

2.1 Evaluate the expression.

1. $-\sqrt{36}$ **2.** $\pm\sqrt{400}$ **3.** $\sqrt{6400}$ **4.** $\pm\sqrt{144}$

2.1 Approximate the square root to the nearest integer.

5. $\sqrt{135}$ **6.** $-\sqrt{75}$ **7.** $-\sqrt{160}$ **8.** $\sqrt{250}$

Solve the equation. Check your solution.

2.2 **9.** $x + 4 = 20$ **10.** $8 = m - 13$ **11.** $t + 2 = -10$ **12.** $z - 8 = -7$

13. $7h = 63$ **14.** $-4t = -44$ **15.** $\frac{b}{4} = 13$ **16.** $\frac{y}{-3} = 8$

2.3 **17.** $4x + 3 = 27$ **18.** $6m - 4 = 14$ **19.** $50 = 7y - 6$

20. $\frac{t}{4} - 3 = 9$ **21.** $\frac{x}{7} + 3 = -2$ **22.** $6p - 2p = 28$

2.4 **23.** $6x + 3x + 8 = 35$ **24.** $12w - 5 - 3w = 40$ **25.** $4d - 3 - 2d = -15$

26. $7m + 3(m + 2) = -24$ **27.** $5x - 3(x - 5) = 13$ **28.** $\frac{3}{4}(2y - 8) = 6$

2.5 **29.** $8x - 4 = 3x + 6$ **30.** $10 - 2x = 3x - 20$ **31.** $5 - 5x = 14 - 8x$

32. $3(2y - 5) = 4y - 7$ **33.** $9 + 4y = 2(3 - y)$ **34.** $3x - 3 = \frac{3}{4}(2x + 12)$

2.6 Solve the proportion. Check your solution.

35. $\frac{7}{2} = \frac{x}{16}$ **36.** $\frac{m}{9} = \frac{6}{27}$ **37.** $\frac{z}{4} = \frac{48}{12}$ **38.** $\frac{30}{50} = \frac{t}{10}$

2.6 Write the sentence as a proportion. Then solve the proportion.

39. 5 is to 7 as 15 is to x. **40.** 9 is to 3 as x is to 12.

41. g is to 9 as 16 is to 12. **42.** 6 is to 18 as y is to 3.

2.7 Solve the proportion. Check your solution.

43. $\frac{12}{x} = \frac{6}{7}$ **44.** $\frac{6x}{4} = \frac{18}{12}$ **45.** $\frac{7}{x + 13} = \frac{4}{12}$ **46.** $\frac{y + 5}{y} = \frac{10}{8}$

47. $\frac{2x + 6}{x} = \frac{7}{2}$ **48.** $\frac{3b}{5b - 7} = \frac{8}{11}$ **49.** $\frac{8}{2x + 12} = \frac{6}{x + 8}$ **50.** $\frac{4.8 - 2x}{8} = \frac{0.4 + x}{10}$

2.8 Solve the literal equation for *x*. Then use the solution to solve the specific equation.

51. $ax - b = c$; $6x - 5 = 25$ **52.** $a(b - x) = c$; $2(8 - x) = -6$

2.8 Write the equation so that *y* is a function of *x*.

53. $5x + y = 10$ **54.** $8x - 2y = 16$ **55.** $7x + 3y = 6 - 5x$ **56.** $21 = 6x + 7y$

Extra Practice

Chapter 3

3.1 Plot the point in a coordinate plane. *Describe* the location of the point.

1. $K(-4, -2)$
2. $L(5, 0)$
3. $M(3, -1)$
4. $N(-2, 2)$
5. $P(0, 4)$
6. $Q(-3.5, 5)$
7. $R(2.5, 6)$
8. $S(-1, -1.5)$

3.1 Graph the function with the given domain. Then identify the range of the function.

9. $y = -2x + 2$; domain: $-2, -1, 0, 1, 2$
10. $y = \frac{1}{2}x - 3$; domain: $-4, -2, 0, 2, 4$

3.2 Graph the equation.

11. $y - x = 3$
12. $y + 3x = 5$
13. $y - 4x = 10$
14. $y = 4$
15. $2x - y = 0$
16. $3x + y = 0$
17. $3x + 2y = -6$
18. $x = 0.5$

3.3 Find the x-intercept and the y-intercept of the graph of the equation.

19. $2x - y = 12$
20. $-5x - 2y = 20$
21. $-4x + 1.5y = 4$
22. $y = \frac{3}{4}x - 15$

3.3 Graph the equation. Label the points where the line crosses the axes.

23. $y = 3x - 6$
24. $4x + 5y = -20$
25. $\frac{2}{3}x + \frac{1}{2}y = 10$
26. $0.3x - y = 6$

3.4 Find the slope of the line that passes through the points.

27. $(4, 2)$ and $(6, 8)$
28. $(-3, 0)$ and $(2, -5)$
29. $(-5, 3)$ and $(-8, 10)$
30. $(9, 4)$ and $(0, 1)$
31. $(-2, 5)$ and $(-2, 10)$
32. $(6, -4)$ and $(4, -4)$

3.5 Identify the slope and y-intercept of the line with the given equation.

33. $y = 7x + 8$
34. $y = 10x - 6$
35. $y = 3 - 4x$
36. $y = x$

3.5 Rewrite the equation in slope-intercept form. Then identify the slope and the y-intercept of the line.

37. $2x + y = 8$
38. $10x - y = 20$
39. $5x + 2y = 10$
40. $-2x - y = 3$

3.6 Graph the equation.

41. $y = 2x - 4$
42. $y = -\frac{3}{4}x + 1$
43. $2x + y = 1$
44. $-2x + 3y = -9$

3.6 Graph the direct variation equation.

45. $y = 2x$
46. $y = -x$
47. $y = 4x$
48. $5x + y = 0$
49. $x - 2y = 0$
50. $3x + y = 0$
51. $2y = 9x$
52. $y - \frac{5}{4}x = 0$

3.7 Find the value of x so that the function has the given value.

53. $f(x) = -7x - 3$; -17
54. $g(x) = 5x - 4$; 12
55. $t(x) = 3x + 1$; -11

3.7 Graph the function. Compare the graph with the graph of $f(x) = x$.

56. $m(x) = x - 2$
57. $t(x) = x + 4$
58. $z(x) = 6x$
59. $h(x) = -2x$

Extra Practice

Chapter 4

4.1 Write an equation of the line with the given slope and y-intercept.

1. slope: 3
   y-intercept: 6
2. slope: -2
   y-intercept: 4
3. slope: 5
   y-intercept: -1
4. slope: -1
   y-intercept: -3
5. slope: $\frac{1}{2}$
   y-intercept: -5
6. slope: $-\frac{7}{10}$
   y-intercept: 8

4.2 Write an equation of the line that passes through the given point and has the given slope m.

7. $(3, 8)$; $m = 2$
8. $(-1, 5)$; $m = -4$
9. $(-6, 3)$; $m = \frac{2}{3}$

4.2 Write an equation of the line that passes through the given points.

10. $(2, 4)$, $(5, 13)$
11. $(1, -2)$, $(-2, 13)$
12. $\left(2, \frac{1}{3}\right)$, $(6, 3)$

4.3 Graph the equation.

13. $y - 3 = -3(x + 4)$
14. $y + 5 = -2(x - 1)$
15. $y - 6 = \frac{2}{3}(x - 3)$

4.3 Write an equation in point-slope form of the line that passes through the given points.

16. $(-4, 2)$, $(-2, 16)$
17. $(3, 9)$, $(-7, 4)$
18. $(10, -2)$, $(12, -6)$

4.4 Write an equation in standard form of the line that passes through the given point and has the given slope m or that passes through the two given points.

19. $(2, 7)$, $m = -4$
20. $(5, 11)$, $m = 3$
21. $(1, -2)$, $(-2, 4)$

4.5 Write an equation of the line that passes through the given point and is parallel to the given line.

22. $(5, 4)$, $y = 3x + 5$
23. $(-3, -7)$, $y = -5x - 2$
24. $(8, -3)$, $y = \frac{3}{4}x + 5$

4.5 Write an equation of the line that passes through the given point and is perpendicular to the given line.

25. $(-12, -2)$, $y = 3x + 2$
26. $(15, -11)$, $y = \frac{3}{5}x - 8$
27. $(7, -6)$, $4x + 6y = 7$

4.6 Make a scatter plot of the data in the table. Draw a line of fit. Write an equation of the line.

28.

x	1	2	3	3.5	4	4.5	5
y	20	35	40	55	60	45	60

29.

x	10	20	30	40	50	60
y	55	45	45	40	35	20

4.7 Make a scatter plot of the data. Find the equation of the best-fitting line. Approximate the value of y for $x = 7$.

30.

x	0	2	4	6	8
y	0.5	3	4	5.5	7

31.

x	0	1	3	6	8
y	5	8	12	15	14

Extra Practice

Chapter 5

Solve the inequality. Graph your solution.

5.1

1. $y - 2 > 3$ **2.** $5 + x \leq 2$ **3.** $4 \geq x - 3$ **4.** $m + 3 < 2$

5. $2 + n \leq 4\frac{1}{2}$ **6.** $2\frac{3}{4} + n < -3\frac{5}{8}$ **7.** $1\frac{7}{8} > 6\frac{3}{4} + z$ **8.** $3\frac{2}{5} \geq 1\frac{1}{3} + k$

9. $-8.5 \leq t - 10$ **10.** $r + 4 < -0.7$ **11.** $-6.9 > -1.4 + y$ **12.** $1.48 - m \geq -3.13$

5.2

13. $3p \leq 27$ **14.** $-13t > 26$ **15.** $\frac{x}{3} \geq 2$ **16.** $\frac{y}{-2} < 5$

17. $-6m \geq -9$ **18.** $-3 \geq \frac{n}{2}$ **19.** $0.3z \leq 2.4$ **20.** $25 > -2.5s$

21. $4.8z \leq 3.2$ **22.** $0.09d < -1.8$ **23.** $\frac{y}{0.3} > -15$ **24.** $-1.8t < 9$

5.3 Solve the inequality, if possible. Graph your solution.

25. $3x + 5 \geq 20$ **26.** $6z - 5 < 13$ **27.** $8(t + 4) > -8$

28. $7 - 8n \leq 4n - 17$ **29.** $8(m + 2) < 4(5 + 2m)$ **30.** $6d - 4 - 3d \geq 14$

31. $\frac{2}{3}y + 28 > 20 + 2y$ **32.** $6(-5 + 3p) \geq 3(6p - 10)$ **33.** $\frac{5}{6}(12z - 24) > \frac{2}{5}(25z - 25)$

5.4 Solve the inequality. Graph your solution.

34. $2 \leq y - 4 < 7$ **35.** $-27 < 9x < 27$ **36.** $2 < 6z - 10 < 20$

37. $15 < \frac{5}{9}(18a - 9) \leq 30$ **38.** $2v > 12$ *or* $v + 2 < 6$ **39.** $3r + 7 < -5$ *or* $32 \leq 7r + 46$

40. $-4m < 8$ *or* $2m - 2 < -12$ **41.** $9t - 20 \geq 4t$ *or* $4 < \frac{1}{-2}t$ **42.** $-n - 1 > 1$ *or* $2n + 8 > n + 8$

5.5 Solve the equation, if possible.

43. $|x| = 8$ **44.** $|y| = -10$ **45.** $|m + 6| = 5$ **46.** $|4z - 2| = 14$

47. $|t - 7| = 21$ **48.** $6|z - 4| = 36$ **49.** $4|6s + 11| = -52$ **50.** $|r + 3| - 16 = -4$

51. $|5r| + 10 = 15$ **52.** $2|3s + 4| = 14$ **53.** $-4|7v + 2| = 32$ **54.** $12\left|\frac{5}{6}w - 4\right| - 4 = 8$

5.6 Solve the inequality. Graph your solution.

55. $|x| \leq 3$ **56.** $|y| \geq 5$ **57.** $|s| > 1.2$ **58.** $|q| < \frac{2}{5}$

59. $|x + 2| > 6$ **60.** $|y + 3| \leq 5$ **61.** $|8 - m| < 3$ **62.** $|4n - 1| \geq 7$

63. $3|p - 3| \leq 12$ **64.** $|3q + 2| - 3 \geq 8$ **65.** $2|5a - 1| + 3 \leq 11$ **66.** $4\left|\frac{2}{3}c + 2\right| < 64$

5.7 Graph the inequality.

67. $y \geq x + 5$ **68.** $y < x - 1$ **69.** $4x + y > 3$ **70.** $x \leq -5$

71. $3(x - 8) \leq 6y$ **72.** $2x - y \geq -2$ **73.** $y > 8$ **74.** $2(x - 1) \geq 1 - y$

75. $x - 8 \leq y + 2$ **76.** $2x \geq -2y$ **77.** $3(y - 8) > x - 9$ **78.** $2(-x - 1) \geq 4 + y$

Extra Practice

Chapter 6

6.1 Solve the linear system by graphing. Check your solution.

1. $y = x - 1$
$y = -x + 5$

2. $y = 3x + 12$
$y = -4x - 2$

3. $x - y = 4$
$x + y = -2$

4. $4x - y = 10$
$x = 4$

5. $3x - 2y = -5$
$4x + 3y = -18$

6. $\frac{2}{3}x + \frac{1}{3}y = \frac{16}{3}$
$-\frac{2}{5}x + y = \frac{8}{5}$

6.2 Solve the linear system using substitution.

7. $y = 2x + 6$
$x = y - 3$

8. $y = 3x + 5$
$x + y = -1$

9. $x = 2y - 5$
$2x - y = 11$

10. $2x - y = 0$
$x + 3y = -56$

11. $1.5x - 2.5y = 22$
$x - y = 10$

12. $\frac{1}{2}x + \frac{3}{4}y = 5$
$x - \frac{1}{2}y = 6$

Solve the linear system using elimination.

6.3

13. $x + 2y = 2$
$-x + 3y = 13$

14. $3x - 4y = -16$
$x - 4y = -40$

15. $3x + 2y = -31$
$5x + 2y = -49$

16. $5x + 4y = 6$
$7x + 4y = 14$

17. $10y - 3x = -41$
$3x - 5y = 16$

18. $4x - 3y = 39$
$7y = 4x - 79$

6.4

19. $x + y = -3$
$5x + 7y = -9$

20. $5x + 2y = -19$
$10x - 7y = -16$

21. $8x - 3y = 61$
$2x - 5y = -23$

22. $4x - 3y = -2$
$6x + 4y = 31$

23. $5x - 2y = 53$
$2x + 6y = 11$

24. $15x - 8y = 6$
$25x - 12y = 16$

6.5 Graph the linear system. Then use the graph to tell whether the linear system has *one solution*, *no solution*, or *infinitely many solutions*.

25. $2x + y = -3$
$y = -2x + 5$

26. $2y - 4x = 10$
$-2y - 2x = 8$

27. $10x + 5y = -15$
$y = -2x - 3$

6.5 Solve the linear system using substitution or elimination.

28. $y - 3x = 5$
$x = y - 5$

29. $2y - 3x = 36$
$y = 3x - 12$

30. $5x + 5y = -32$
$3x + 3y = 14$

31. $4x + 6y = 11$
$y = -\frac{2}{3}x + 7$

32. $3y - 3x = 12$
$y = x - 4$

33. $x + 2y = -30$
$y = \frac{1}{2}x + 15$

6.6 Graph the system of inequalities.

34. $y \geq -5$
$y \leq -2$

35. $x \geq -3$
$y < 1$

36. $y < -2x - 3$
$x - y > -4$

37. $x + 4y \geq -8$
$y - 4x < 8$
$x > -1$

38. $x > 3$
$x < 5$
$y > -2$
$y \leq 0$

39. $x + y > 3$
$x - y > 5$
$x + 2y \leq 8$
$x - 5y > 10$

Extra Practice

Chapter 7

Simplify the expression. In exercises involving numerical bases only, write your answer using exponents.

7.1

1. $5^3 \cdot 5^4$
2. $6 \cdot 6^7$
3. $(-2)^3 \cdot (-2)^6$
4. $(2^8)^2$
5. $[(-4)^3]^2$
6. $(8 \cdot 4)^5$
7. $m^5 \cdot m^2$
8. $n^2 \cdot n^4 \cdot n^5$
9. $(y^3)^5$
10. $(-2x)^3$
11. $(3d^2)^3 \cdot 2d^2$
12. $(-4s^2)^3(2s^3)^6$

7.2

13. $\frac{8^7}{8^2}$
14. $\frac{4^6 \cdot 4^2}{4^3}$
15. $\left(-\frac{2}{3}\right)^5$
16. $10^{12} \cdot \frac{1}{10^7}$
17. $7^9 \cdot \left(\frac{1}{7}\right)^4$
18. $\frac{1}{t^9} \cdot t^{13}$
19. $\left(\frac{p}{q}\right)^7$
20. $\left(\frac{6x^9}{3y^4}\right)^2$
21. $\left(\frac{4y^5}{3}\right)^3 \cdot \frac{1}{y^6}$
22. $\left(\frac{2}{u^2}\right)^3 \cdot \left(\frac{3u^4}{z^2}\right)^4$
23. $\left(\frac{5x^3y^4}{2x^2y}\right)^2$
24. $\frac{6a^4b^5}{ab} \cdot \left(\frac{2ab}{a^2b^2}\right)^3$

7.3 Evaluate the expression.

25. 3^{-4}
26. $(-5)^{-3}$
27. 7^0
28. $4^{-5} \cdot 4^3$
29. $\left(\frac{1}{2}\right)^{-3}$
30. $(3^{-2})^3$
31. $\frac{1}{2^{-5}}$
32. $\frac{8^{-4}}{8^{-6}}$

7.3 Simplify the expression. Write your answer using only positive exponents.

33. y^{-10}
34. $(3c)^{-4}$
35. $10b^{-3}c^5$
36. $(2d^5e^{-2})^{-3}$
37. $\frac{x^{-4}}{y^{-5}}$
38. $\frac{1}{6t^{-5}u^3}$
39. $\frac{3}{(-2z)^{-5}}$
40. $\frac{(2e)^{-4}g^5}{e^5g^{-3}}$

Graph the function.

7.4

41. $y = 3^x$
42. $y = 1.25^x$
43. $y = \left(\frac{9}{4}\right)^x$
44. $y = 5 \cdot 2^x$
45. $y = \frac{1}{3} \cdot 2^x$
46. $y = -\frac{1}{2} \cdot 5^x$
47. $y = -5 \cdot 2^x$
48. $y = -\frac{1}{3} \cdot 4^x$

7.5

49. $y = \left(\frac{1}{3}\right)^x$
50. $y = (0.2)^x$
51. $y = 3 \cdot (0.2)^x$
52. $y = 2 \cdot \left(\frac{1}{3}\right)^x$
53. $y = 4 \cdot \left(\frac{1}{3}\right)^x$
54. $y = \frac{1}{2} \cdot \left(\frac{1}{3}\right)^x$
55. $y = -2 \cdot \left(\frac{1}{3}\right)^x$
56. $y = -\frac{3}{4} \cdot \left(\frac{1}{3}\right)^x$

7.5 Tell whether the table represents an exponential function. If so, write a rule for the function.

57.

x	−1	0	1	2	3
y	$\frac{5}{2}$	5	10	20	40

58.

x	−1	0	1	2	3
y	80	40	20	10	5

59.

x	−1	0	1	2	3
y	1	0	1	4	9

60.

x	−1	0	1	2	3
y	48	36	27	$20\frac{1}{4}$	$15\frac{3}{16}$

Extra Practice

Chapter 8

Find the sum or difference.

8.1

1. $(6x^2 + 7) + (x^2 - 9)$
2. $(8y^2 - 3y - 10) + (-11y^2 + 2y - 7)$
3. $(10m^2 - 7m + 2) - (3m^2 - 2m + 5)$
4. $(2t^3 - 3t^2 + 5t) - (6t^3 + 3t^2 - 5t)$
5. $(6b^3 + 12b^2 - b) - (15b^2 + 7b - 8)$
6. $(r^2 - 8 + 4r^3 + 5r) - (7r^3 - 3r^2 + 5)$

Find the product.

8.2

7. $5x^4(2x^3 - 3x^2 + 5x - 1)$
8. $(x^2 + 4x + 2)(x + 7)$
9. $(2x + 3)(4x + 2)$
10. $(2x^2 - 5x + 6)(3x - 2)$
11. $(3x - 7)(x + 5)$
12. $(9t - 2)(2t - 3)$

8.3

13. $(x + 10)^2$
14. $(m + 8)(m - 8)$
15. $(4x - 2)(4x + 2)$
16. $(3x - 4y)(3x + 4y)$
17. $(6 - 3t)(6 + 3t)$
18. $(-11x - 4y)^2$

8.4 Solve the equation.

19. $(m + 8)(m - 2) = 0$
20. $(2y - 6)(y + 3) = 0$
21. $(5y - 3)(2y - 4) = 0$
22. $3b^2 + 9b = 0$
23. $-12m^2 - 3m = 0$
24. $14k^2 = 28k$

8.5 Factor the trinomial.

25. $y^2 + 7y + 12$
26. $x^2 - 12x + 35$
27. $x^2 + 5x - 36$
28. $q^2 + 3q - 40$
29. $m^2 - 29m + 100$
30. $y^2 + 14y - 72$

8.5 Solve the equation.

31. $m^2 - 7m + 10 = 0$
32. $p^2 - 7p = 18$
33. $z^2 - 13z + 24 = -12$
34. $n^2 + 8 = 6n$
35. $r^2 - 15r = -8r - 10$
36. $c^2 - 8 = -13c + 6$

8.6 Factor the trinomial.

37. $-x^2 + 5x - 6$
38. $3k^2 - 10k + 8$
39. $4k^2 - 12k + 5$
40. $6t^2 - 5t - 6$
41. $-3s^2 - 7s - 2$
42. $2v^2 - 5v + 3$

8.6 Solve the equation.

43. $-3x^2 + 14x - 8 = 0$
44. $8t^2 + 6t = 9$
45. $2x^2 + 3x - 2 = 0$
46. $3p^2 - 28 = 17p$
47. $16m^2 - 1 = -15m$
48. $t(6t - 7) = 3$

8.7 Factor the polynomial.

49. $y^2 - 36$
50. $9y^2 - 49$
51. $12y^2 - 27$
52. $x^2 - 8x + 16$
53. $4x^2 - 12x + 9$
54. $27x^2 - 36x + 12$
55. $g^2 + 10g + 25$
56. $9b^2 + 24b + 16$
57. $4w^2 + 28w + 49$

8.8 Factor the polynomial completely.

58. $2x^2 + 8x + 6$
59. $3z^2 - 16z + 5$
60. $5m^2 - 23m + 12$
61. $3y^3 + 15y^2 + 2y + 10$
62. $30z^3 - 14z^2 - 8z$
63. $98m^3 - 18m$
64. $8h^2k - 32k$
65. $2h^3 - 3h^2 - 18h + 27$
66. $-12z^3 + 12z^2 - 3z$

Extra Practice

Chapter 9

9.1 Graph the function. Compare the graph with the graph of $y = x^2$.

1. $y = 4x^2$
2. $y = -5x^2$
3. $y = \frac{1}{2}x^2$
4. $y = -\frac{2}{5}x^2$
5. $y = x^2 + 3$
6. $y = x^2 - 2$
7. $y = 3x^2 + 4$
8. $y = -4x^2 - 3$

9.2 Graph the function. Label the vertex and axis of symmetry.

9. $y = x^2 + 4x + 4$
10. $y = -x^2 - 2x + 3$
11. $y = 2x^2 - 6x + 5$
12. $y = 3x^2 + 12x + 8$
13. $y = -2x^2 + 6$
14. $y = \frac{3}{4}x^2 - 3x$

9.3 Solve the equation by graphing.

15. $x^2 + 3x - 10 = 0$
16. $x^2 + 14 = 9x$
17. $-x^2 + 3x = -18$
18. $2x^2 + 3x - 20 = 0$
19. $2x^2 + x = 6$
20. $\frac{1}{2}x^2 - x = 12$

9.4 Solve the equation. Round the solutions to the nearest hundredth, if necessary.

21. $2x^2 - 20 = 78$
22. $3y^2 + 16 = 4$
23. $16y^2 - 6 = 3$
24. $48 - x^2 = -52$
25. $5m^2 - 5 = 10$
26. $2 - 5t^2 = 4$

9.5 Solve the equation by completing the square. Round the solutions to the nearest hundredth, if necessary.

27. $x^2 + 4x - 21 = 0$
28. $g^2 - 10g = 24$
29. $4m^2 + 8m - 7 = 0$

9.6 Use the quadratic formula to solve the equation. Round the solutions to the nearest hundredth, if necessary.

30. $h^2 + 6h - 72 = 0$
31. $3x^2 - 7x + 2 = 0$
32. $2k^2 - 5k + 2 = 0$
33. $n^2 + 1 = 5n$
34. $2z + 4 = 3z^2$
35. $5x^2 - 4x = 2$

9.7 Solve the system.

36. $y = -x^2 + 5x - 4$
    $y = 2x - 4$
37. $y = \frac{2}{3}x^2 - 3x - 1$
    $y = -x - 1$
38. $y = -2x^2 + 4x - 1$
    $y = -4x - 7$

9.8 Tell whether the table of values represents a *linear function*, an *exponential function*, or a *quadratic function*. Then write an equation for the function.

39.

x	−1	0	1	2	3
y	3	0	3	12	27

40.

x	0	1	2	3	4
y	−5	−2	1	4	7

41.

x	1	2	3	4	5
y	1	2	4	8	16

42.

x	−2	−1	0	1	2
y	18	14	10	6	2

9.9 43. Linear Function 1 has equation $2x - 5y = -12$. The graph of Linear Function 2 contains $(-3, -3)$, $(0, 2)$, $(3, 7)$, and $(6, 12)$. Which function is increasing more rapidly?

Chapter 10

10.1 In Exercises 1–3, use the following information.

Some parents want to gather information about updating the sound system in the high school auditorium. They obtain a list of high school students and call the parents or guardians of every 20th student on the list. The question they ask is "Don't you think the sound system in the high school auditorium needs updating?"

1. Identify the population and classify the sampling method.
2. Is the sampling method used likely to result in a biased sample? *Explain*.
3. Tell whether the question is potentially biased. *Explain* your answer.

10.2 4. The numbers of stories in ten of the world's tallest buildings are given below. Find the mean, median, mode(s), range, and mean absolute deviation of the data. Round to the nearest hundredth, if necessary.
101, 88, 88, 108, 88, 88, 80, 69, 102, 78

10.3 In Exercises 5 and 6, use the given two-way table showing the side dish chosen with the lunch plate and supper plate at a diner on one day.

	Salad	Fries	Broccoli	Total
Lunch	26	47	9	82
Supper	42	29	34	105
Total	68	76	43	187

5. What was the most popular side at lunch? at dinner? overall?
6. About what percent of the total number of sides were salad or broccoli?

In Exercises 7 and 8, use the data in Exercise 4, above.

10.4 7. Make a histogram and a stem-and-leaf plot of the data.

10.5 8. Make a box-and-whisker plot of the data. Identify any outliers.

10.5 In Exercises 9 and 10, use the following information.

The box-and-whisker plot shows the maximum elevations (in thousands of feet) in the top 13 U.S. states ranked by maximum elevation.

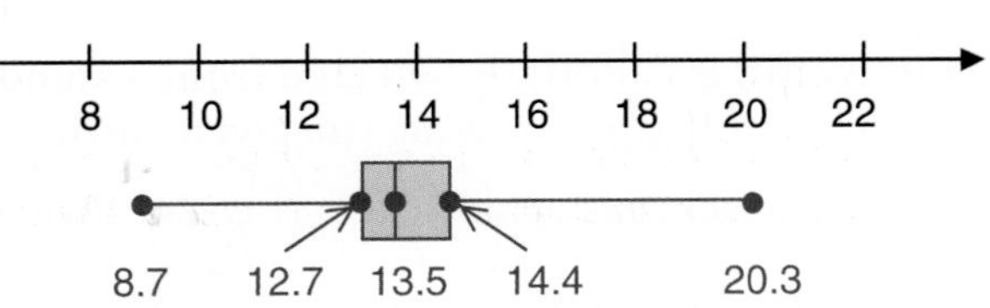

9. What is the median of the maximum elevations in these states?
10. What is the interquartile range of the maximum elevations in these states?

Extra Practice

Chapter 11

11.1 In Exercises 1 and 2, use the following information. A bag contains 3 red, 3 blue, and 3 yellow marbles. You toss a coin and then draw a marble out of the bag at random.

1. Find the number of possible outcomes in the sample space. Then list the possible outcomes.

2. What is the probability that the coin shows tails and the marble is blue?

11.1 **3.** You toss a coin 3 times. What are the odds against the coin's showing heads twice and tails once?

11.2 **4.** In how many ways can you arrange the letters in the word SPRING?

5. In how many ways can you arrange 3 of the letters in the word TULIP?

11.2 Evaluate the expression.

6. 7! **7.** ${}_8P_3$ **8.** ${}_{10}P_3$ **9.** ${}_5P_5$

11.3 **10.** You can choose 3 books from a list of 5 books to read for English class. How many combinations of 3 books are possible?

11. You are making a snack tray. You plan to choose 3 of 5 available types of bread and 3 of 6 available types of cheese. How many different combinations of bread and cheese are possible?

11.3 Evaluate the expression.

12. ${}_6C_2$ **13.** ${}_7C_3$ **14.** ${}_{10}C_4$ **15.** ${}_{20}C_{15}$

11.4 Events *A* and *B* are disjoint. Find *P*(*A* or *B*).

16. $P(A) = 0.4$, $P(B) = 0.15$ **17.** $P(A) = 0.3$, $P(B) = 0.5$ **18.** $P(A) = 0.7$, $P(B) = 0.21$

11.4 Find the indicated probability. State whether *A* and *B* are disjoint events.

19. $P(A) = 0.25$
$P(B) = 0.55$
$P(A \text{ or } B) = \underline{\ ?\ }$
$P(A \text{ and } B) = 0.2$

20. $P(A) = 0.52$
$P(B) = 0.15$
$P(A \text{ or } B) = 0.67$
$P(A \text{ and } B) = \underline{\ ?\ }$

21. $P(A) = 0.54$
$P(B) = 0.28$
$P(A \text{ or } B) = 0.65$
$P(A \text{ and } B) = \underline{\ ?\ }$

22. $P(A) = 0.5$
$P(B) = 0.4$
$P(A \text{ or } B) = \underline{\ ?\ }$
$P(A \text{ and } B) = 0.3$

11.4 A card is randomly selected from a standard deck of 52 cards. Find the probability of drawing the given card.

23. a jack *and* a club **24.** an ace *or* a 10 **25.** a queen *or* a heart

11.5 Events *A* and *B* are independent. Find the missing probability.

26. $P(A) = 0.8$
$P(B) = 0.25$
$P(A \text{ and } B) = \underline{\ ?\ }$

27. $P(A) = \underline{\ ?\ }$
$P(B) = 0.4$
$P(A \text{ and } B) = 0.05$

28. $P(A) = 0.9$
$P(B) = \underline{\ ?\ }$
$P(A \text{ and } B) = 0.27$

11.5 Events *A* and *B* are dependent. Find the missing probability.

29. $P(A) = 0.4$
$P(B \mid A) = 0.6$
$P(A \text{ and } B) = \underline{\ ?\ }$

30. $P(A) = \underline{\ ?\ }$
$P(B \mid A) = 0.75$
$P(A \text{ and } B) = 0.3$

31. $P(A) = 0.15$
$P(B \mid A) = \underline{\ ?\ }$
$P(A \text{ and } B) = 0.03$

Symbols

Symbol	Meaning
$3 \cdot x$ $3x \quad 3(x)$	3 times x
$\frac{a}{b}$	a divided by b, $b \neq 0$
a^4	the fourth power of a, or $a \cdot a \cdot a \cdot a$
( )	parentheses—a grouping symbol
[ ]	brackets—a grouping symbol
$=$	is equal to
$<$	is less than
$>$	is greater than
$\leq$	is less than or equal to
$\geq$	is greater than or equal to
$\stackrel{?}{=}$	is equal to?
(x, y)	ordered pair
$\ldots$	continues on
$-a$	the opposite of a
$\|a\|$	the absolute value of a
$\begin{bmatrix} 1 & 0 \\ 0 & 1 \end{bmatrix}$	matrix
$\frac{1}{a}$	the reciprocal of a, $a \neq 0$
$\neq$	is not equal to
$\sqrt{a}$	the nonnegative square root of a, $a \geq 0$
$\pm$	plus or minus
$\approx$	is approximately equal to
$a:b$	the ratio of a to b

Symbol	Meaning
$\cong$	is congruent to
$\sim$	is similar to
A'	the image of point A
m	slope
b	y-intercept
a	constant of variation
$f(x)$	the value of the function f at x
a^{-n}	$\frac{1}{a^n}$, $a \neq 0$
$\sqrt[3]{a}$	the cube root of a
$c \times 10^n$	scientific notation, $1 \leq c < 10$ and n is an integer
$P(A)$	the probability of an event A
$n!$	n factorial, or $n \cdot (n-1) \cdot \ldots \cdot 2 \cdot 1$, n is a nonnegative integer
${}_nP_r$	the number of permutations of n objects taken r at a time, $r \leq n$
${}_nC_r$	the number of combinations of n objects taken r at a time, $r \leq n$
$\overline{x}$	x bar, the mean of numerical data
σ^2	variance, the square of standard deviation
σ	standard deviation, the nonnegative square root of variance

Geometric Formulas

Pythagorean Theorem

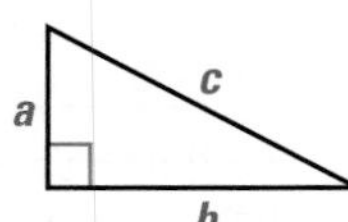

In a right triangle, $a^2 + b^2 = c^2$ where a and b are the lengths of the legs and c is the length of the hypotenuse.

Square

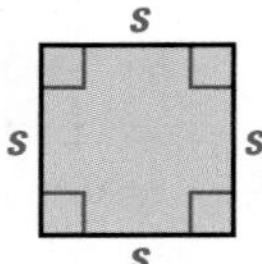

Area
$A = s^2$

Perimeter
$P = 4s$

Rectangle

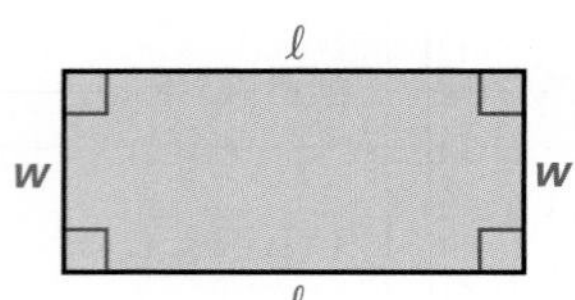

Area
$A = \ell w$

Perimeter
$P = 2\ell + 2w$

Parallelogram

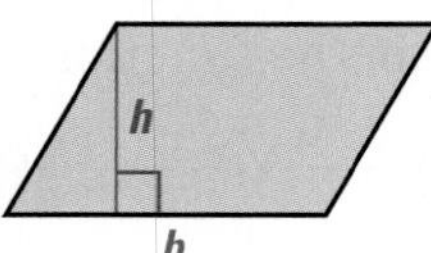

Area
$A = bh$

Triangle

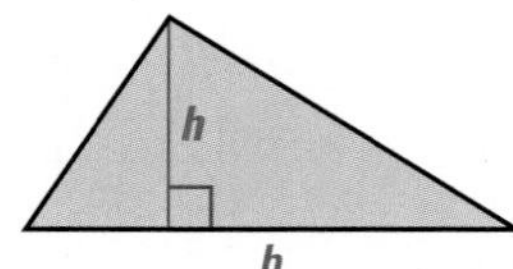

Area
$A = \frac{1}{2}bh$

Trapezoid

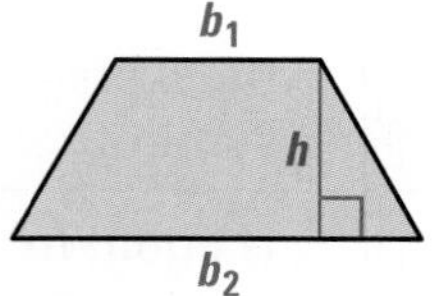

Area
$A = \frac{1}{2}(b_1 + b_2)h$

Circle

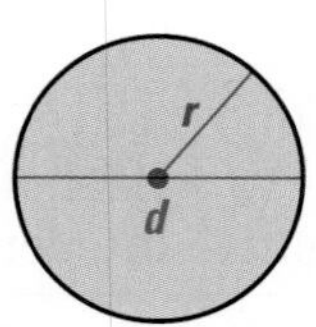

Circumference
$C = \pi d$ or
$C = 2\pi r$

Area
$A = \pi r^2$

Prism

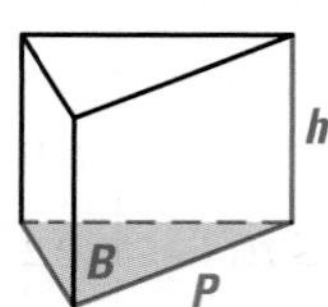

Surface Area
$S = 2B + Ph$

Volume
$V = Bh$

Cylinder

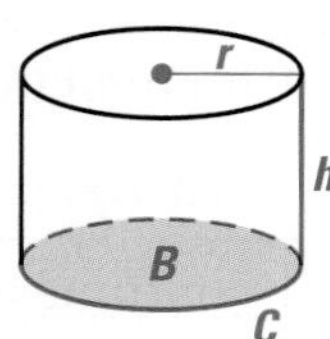

Surface Area
$S = 2B + Ch$
$= 2\pi r^2 + 2\pi rh$

Volume
$V = Bh$
$= \pi r^2 h$

Pyramid

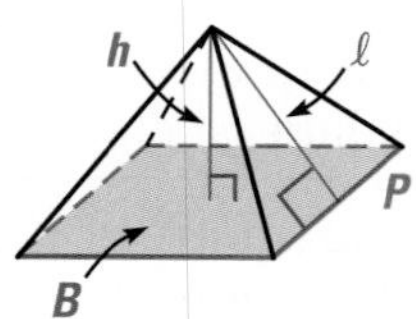

Surface Area
$S = B + \frac{1}{2}P\ell$

Volume
$V = \frac{1}{3}Bh$

Cone

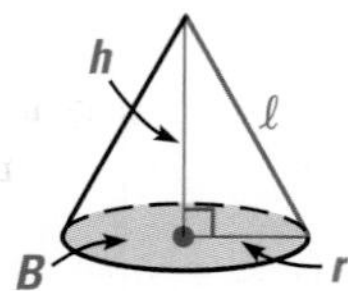

Surface Area
$S = B + \frac{1}{2}C\ell$
$= \pi r^2 + \pi r\ell$

Volume
$V = \frac{1}{3}Bh$
$= \frac{1}{3}\pi r^2 h$

Sphere

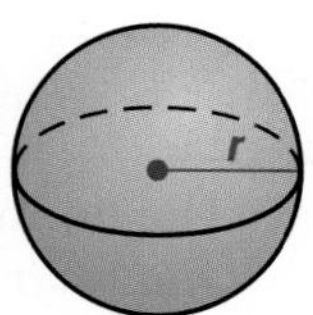

Surface Area
$S = 4\pi r^2$

Volume
$V = \frac{4}{3}\pi r^3$

TABLES

Other Formulas

Slope	The slope m of a nonvertical line passing through the two points (x_1, y_1) and (x_2, y_2) is $m = \frac{y_2 - y_1}{x_2 - x_1}$.
Compound interest	$y = a(1 + r)^t$ where y is the account balance, a is the initial investment, r is the annual interest rate (in decimal form), and t is the time in years.
Quadratic formula	The real-number solutions of the quadratic equation $ax^2 + bx + c = 0$ are $x = \frac{-b \pm \sqrt{b^2 - 4ac}}{2a}$ where $a \neq 0$ and $b^2 - 4ac \geq 0$.
Distance formula	The distance d between any two points (x_1, y_1) and (x_2, y_2) is $d = \sqrt{(x_2 - x_1)^2 + (y_2 - y_1)^2}$.
Midpoint formula	The midpoint M of the line segment with endpoints $A(x_1, y_1)$ and $B(x_2, y_2)$ is $M\left(\frac{x_1 + x_2}{2}, \frac{y_1 + y_2}{2}\right)$.
Theoretical probability	The probability of an event when all the outcomes are equally likely is $P(\text{event}) = \frac{\text{Number of favorable outcomes}}{\text{Total number of outcomes}}$.
Experimental probability	For repeated trials of an experiment, the probability of an event is $P(\text{event}) = \frac{\text{Number of successes}}{\text{Number of trials}}$.
Permutations	The number of permutations of n objects taken r at a time, where $r \leq n$, is given by ${}_nP_r = \frac{n!}{(n - r)!}$.
Combinations	The number of combinations of n objects taken r at a time, where $r \leq n$, is given by ${}_nC_r = \frac{n!}{(n - r)! \cdot r!}$.
Probability of mutually exclusive or overlapping events	If A and B are mutually exclusive events, then $P(A \text{ or } B) = P(A) + P(B)$. If A and B are overlapping events, then $P(A \text{ or } B) = P(A) + P(B) - P(A \text{ and } B)$.
Probability of independent or dependent events	If A and B are independent events, then $P(A \text{ and } B) = P(A) \cdot P(B)$. If A and B are dependent events, then $P(A \text{ and } B) = P(A) \cdot P(B \text{ given } A)$.

TABLES

Properties

Properties of Addition and Multiplication

Commutative Properties The order in which you add two numbers does not change the sum.	$a + b = b + a$
The order in which you multiply two numbers does not change the product.	$a \cdot b = b \cdot a$
Associative Properties The way you group three numbers in a sum does not change the sum.	$(a + b) + c = a + (b + c)$
The way you group three numbers in a product does not change the product.	$(a \cdot b) \cdot c = a \cdot (b \cdot c)$
Identity Properties The sum of a number and the additive identity, 0, is the number.	$a + 0 = 0 + a = a$
The product of a number and the multiplicative identity, 1, is the number.	$a \cdot 1 = 1 \cdot a = a$
Inverse Properties The sum of a number and its additive inverse, or opposite, is 0.	$a + (-a) = -a + a = 0$
The product of a nonzero number and its multiplicative inverse, or reciprocal, is 1.	$a \cdot \frac{1}{a} = \frac{1}{a} \cdot a = 1\ (a \neq 0)$
Distributive Property You can multiply a number and a sum by multiplying each term of the sum by the number and then adding these products. The same property applies to the product of a number and a difference.	$a(b + c) = ab + ac$ $(b + c)a = ba + ca$ $a(b - c) = ab - ac$ $(b - c)a = ba - ca$

TABLES

Properties of Equality

Addition Property of Equality Adding the same number to each side of an equation produces an equivalent equation.	If $x - a = b$, then $x - a + a = b + a$, or $x = b + a$.
Subtraction Property of Equality Subtracting the same number from each side of an equation produces an equivalent equation.	If $x + a = b$, then $x + a - a = b - a$, or $x = b - a$.
Multiplication Property of Equality Multiplying each side of an equation by the same nonzero number produces an equivalent equation.	If $\frac{x}{a} = b$ and $a \neq 0$, then $a \cdot \frac{x}{a} = a \cdot b$, or $x = ab$.
Division Property of Equality Dividing each side of an equation by the same nonzero number produces an equivalent equation.	If $ax = b$ and $a \neq 0$, then $\frac{ax}{a} = \frac{b}{a}$, or $x = \frac{b}{a}$.

Properties of Inequality

Addition and Subtraction Properties of Inequality Adding or subtracting the same number on each side of an inequality produces an equivalent inequality.	If $a < b$, then $a + c < b + c$ and $a - c < b - c$. If $a > b$, then $a + c > b + c$ and $a - c > b - c$.
Multiplication and Division Properties of Inequality Multiplying or dividing each side of an inequality by a *positive* number produces an equivalent inequality. Multiplying or dividing each side of an inequality by a *negative* number and *reversing the direction of the inequality symbol* produces an equivalent inequality.	If $a < b$ and $c > 0$, then $ac < bc$ and $\frac{a}{c} < \frac{b}{c}$. If $a < b$ and $c < 0$, then $ac > bc$ and $\frac{a}{c} > \frac{b}{c}$.

Properties of Exponents

Product of Powers Property To multiply powers having the same base, add the exponents.	$a^m \cdot a^n = a^{m+n}$
Power of a Power Property To find a power of a power, multiply exponents.	$(a^m)^n = a^{mn}$
Power of a Product Property To find a power of a product, find the power of each factor and multiply.	$(ab)^m = a^m b^m$
Quotient of Powers Property To divide powers having the same nonzero base, subtract exponents.	$\frac{a^m}{a^n} = a^{m-n}, a \neq 0$
Power of a Quotient Property To find a power of a quotient, find the power of the numerator and the power of the denominator and divide.	$\left(\frac{a}{b}\right)^m = \frac{a^m}{b^m}, b \neq 0$

Other Properties

Cross Products Property The cross products of a proportion are equal.	If $\frac{a}{b} = \frac{c}{d}$ $(b, d \neq 0)$, then $ad = bc$.
Product Property of Radicals The square root of a product equals the product of the square roots of the factors.	$\sqrt{ab} = \sqrt{a} \cdot \sqrt{b}, a \geq 0$ and $b \geq 0$
Quotient Properties of Radicals The square root of a quotient equals the quotient of the square roots of the numerator and denominator.	$\sqrt{\frac{a}{b}} = \frac{\sqrt{a}}{\sqrt{b}}, a \geq 0$ and $b > 0$

TABLES

Measures

Time	
60 seconds (sec) = 1 minute (min) 60 minutes = 1 hour (h) 24 hours = 1 day 7 days = 1 week 4 weeks (approx.) = 1 month	365 days, 52 weeks (approx.), 12 months = 1 year 10 years = 1 decade 100 years = 1 century

Metric	United States Customary
Length 10 millimeters (mm) = 1 centimeter (cm) 100 cm, 1000 mm = 1 meter (m) 1000 m = 1 kilometer (km)	**Length** 12 inches (in.) = 1 foot (ft) 36 in., 3 ft = 1 yard (yd) 5280 ft, 1760 yd = 1 mile (mi)
Area 100 square millimeters (mm^2) = 1 square centimeter (cm^2) 10,000 cm^2 = 1 square meter (m^2) 10,000 m^2 = 1 hectare (ha)	**Area** 144 square inches ($in.^2$) = 1 square foot (ft^2) 9 ft^2 = 1 square yard (yd^2) 43,560 ft^2, 4840 yd^2 = 1 acre (A)
Volume 1000 cubic millimeters (mm^3) = 1 cubic centimeter (cm^3) 1,000,000 cm^3 = 1 cubic meter (m^3)	**Volume** 1728 cubic inches ($in.^3$) = 1 cubic foot (ft^3) 27 ft^3 = 1 cubic yard (yd^3)
Liquid Capacity 1000 milliliters (mL), 1000 cubic centimeters (cm^3) = 1 liter (L) 1000 L = 1 kiloliter (kL)	**Liquid Capacity** 8 fluid ounces (fl oz) = 1 cup (c) 2 c = 1 pint (pt) 2 pt = 1 quart (qt) 4 qt = 1 gallon (gal)
Mass 1000 milligrams (mg) = 1 gram (g) 1000 g = 1 kilogram (kg) 1000 kg = 1 metric ton (t)	**Weight** 16 ounces (oz) = 1 pound (lb) 2000 lb = 1 ton
Temperature Degrees Celsius (°C) 0°C = freezing point of water 37°C = normal body temperature 100°C = boiling point of water	**Temperature Degrees Fahrenheit (°F)** 32°F = freezing point of water 98.6°F = normal body temperature 212°F = boiling point of water

TABLES

Squares and Square Roots

No.	Square	Sq. Root
1	1	1.000
2	4	1.414
3	9	1.732
4	16	2.000
5	25	2.236
6	36	2.449
7	49	2.646
8	64	2.828
9	81	3.000
10	100	3.162
11	121	3.317
12	144	3.464
13	169	3.606
14	196	3.742
15	225	3.873
16	256	4.000
17	289	4.123
18	324	4.243
19	361	4.359
20	400	4.472
21	441	4.583
22	484	4.690
23	529	4.796
24	576	4.899
25	625	5.000
26	676	5.099
27	729	5.196
28	784	5.292
29	841	5.385
30	900	5.477
31	961	5.568
32	1024	5.657
33	1089	5.745
34	1156	5.831
35	1225	5.916
36	1296	6.000
37	1369	6.083
38	1444	6.164
39	1521	6.245
40	1600	6.325
41	1681	6.403
42	1764	6.481
43	1849	6.557
44	1936	6.633
45	2025	6.708
46	2116	6.782
47	2209	6.856
48	2304	6.928
49	2401	7.000
50	2500	7.071

No.	Square	Sq. Root
51	2601	7.141
52	2704	7.211
53	2809	7.280
54	2916	7.348
55	3025	7.416
56	3136	7.483
57	3249	7.550
58	3364	7.616
59	3481	7.681
60	3600	7.746
61	3721	7.810
62	3844	7.874
63	3969	7.937
64	4096	8.000
65	4225	8.062
66	4356	8.124
67	4489	8.185
68	4624	8.246
69	4761	8.307
70	4900	8.367
71	5041	8.426
72	5184	8.485
73	5329	8.544
74	5476	8.602
75	5625	8.660
76	5776	8.718
77	5929	8.775
78	6084	8.832
79	6241	8.888
80	6400	8.944
81	6561	9.000
82	6724	9.055
83	6889	9.110
84	7056	9.165
85	7225	9.220
86	7396	9.274
87	7569	9.327
88	7744	9.381
89	7921	9.434
90	8100	9.487
91	8281	9.539
92	8464	9.592
93	8649	9.644
94	8836	9.695
95	9025	9.747
96	9216	9.798
97	9409	9.849
98	9604	9.899
99	9801	9.950
100	10,000	10.000

No.	Square	Sq. Root
101	10,201	10.050
102	10,404	10.100
103	10,609	10.149
104	10,816	10.198
105	11,025	10.247
106	11,236	10.296
107	11,449	10.344
108	11,664	10.392
109	11,881	10.440
110	12,100	10.488
111	12,321	10.536
112	12,544	10.583
113	12,769	10.630
114	12,996	10.677
115	13,225	10.724
116	13,456	10.770
117	13,689	10.817
118	13,924	10.863
119	14,161	10.909
120	14,400	10.954
121	14,641	11.000
122	14,884	11.045
123	15,129	11.091
124	15,376	11.136
125	15,625	11.180
126	15,876	11.225
127	16,129	11.269
128	16,384	11.314
129	16,641	11.358
130	16,900	11.402
131	17,161	11.446
132	17,424	11.489
133	17,689	11.533
134	17,956	11.576
135	18,225	11.619
136	18,496	11.662
137	18,769	11.705
138	19,044	11.747
139	19,321	11.790
140	19,600	11.832
141	19,881	11.874
142	20,164	11.916
143	20,449	11.958
144	20,736	12.000
145	21,025	12.042
146	21,316	12.083
147	21,609	12.124
148	21,904	12.166
149	22,201	12.207
150	22,500	12.247

English–Spanish Glossary

A

absolute deviation The absolute deviation of a number x from a given value is the absolute value of the difference of x and the given value:

$$\text{absolute deviation} = |x - \text{given value}|$$

If the absolute deviation of x from 2 is 3, then $|x - 2| = 3$.

desviación absoluta La desviación absoluta de un número x con respecto a un valor dado es el valor absoluto de la diferencia entre x y el valor dado:

$$\text{desviación absoluta} = |x - \text{valor dado}|$$

Si la desviación absoluta de x con respecto a 2 es 3, entonces $|x - 2| = 3$.

absolute value The absolute value of a number a is the distance between a and 0 on a number line. The symbol $|a|$ represents the absolute value of a.

$|2| = 2$, $|-5| = 5$, and $|0| = 0$

valor absoluto El valor absoluto de un número a es la distancia entre a y 0 en una recta numérica. El símbolo $|a|$ representa el valor absoluto de a.

$|2| = 2$, $|-5| = 5$, y $|0| = 0$

absolute value equation An equation that contains an absolute value expression.

$|x + 2| = 3$ is an absolute value equation.

ecuación de valor absoluto Ecuación que contiene una expresión de valor absoluto.

$|x + 2| = 3$ es una ecuación de valor absoluto.

additive identity The number 0 is the additive identity, because the sum of any number and 0 is the number: $a + 0 = 0 + a = a$.

identidad aditiva El número 0 es la identidad aditiva ya que la suma de cualquier número y 0 es ese número: $a + 0 = 0 + a = a$.

$-2 + 0 = -2, 0 + \frac{3}{4} = \frac{3}{4}$

additive inverse The additive inverse of a number a is its opposite, $-a$. The sum of a number and its additive inverse is 0: $a + (-a) = -a + a = 0$.

The additive inverse of -5 is 5, and $-5 + 5 = 0$.

inverso aditivo El inverso aditivo de un número a es su opuesto, $-a$. La suma de un número y su inverso aditivo es 0: $a + (-a) = -a + a = 0$.

El inverso aditivo de -5 es 5, y $-5 + 5 = 0$.

algebraic expression An expression that includes at least one variable. Also called *variable expression.*

$5n$, $\frac{14}{y}$, $6 + c$, and $8 - x$ are algebraic expressions.

expresión algebraica Expresión que incluye por lo menos una variable.

$5n$, $\frac{14}{y}$, $6 + c$ y $8 - x$ son expresiones algebraicas.

arithmetic sequence A sequence in which the difference between consecutive terms is constant. **progresión aritmética** Progresión en la que la diferencia entre los términos consecutivos es constante.	**2, 8, 14, 20, 26, . . . is an arithmetic sequence in which the difference between consecutive terms is 6.** **2, 8, 14, 20, 26, . . . es una progresión aritmética en la que la diferencia entre los términos consecutivos es 6.**
asymptotes of a hyperbola Lines that a hyperbola approaches but does not intersect. **asíntotas de una hipérbola** Rectas a las que la hipérbola se acerca pero sin cortarlas.	***See* hyperbola.** ***Ver* hipérbola.**
axis of symmetry The line that passes through the vertex and divides the parabola into two symmetric parts. **eje de simetría** La recta que pasa por el vértice y divide a la parábola en dos partes simétricas.	$y = -x^2 + 2x + 1$ $x = 1$ **The axis of symmetry of the graph of $y = -x^2 + 2x + 1$ is the line $x = 1$.** **El eje de simetría de la gráfica de $y = -x^2 + 2x + 1$ es la recta $x = 1$.**

B

base of a power The number or expression that is used as a factor in a repeated multiplication. **base de una potencia** El número o la expresión que se usa como factor en la multiplicación repetida.	**In the power 3^4, the base is 3.** **En la potencia 3^4, la base es 3.**
best-fitting line The line that most closely follows a trend in data, found using technology. **mejor recta de regresión** La recta que se ajusta más a la tendencia de los datos y que se encuentra mediante tecnología.	**The graph shows the best-fitting line for the data in the scatter plot.** **La gráfica muestra la mejor recta de regresión para los datos del diagrama de dispersión.**

biased question A question that encourages a particular response.

"Don't you agree that the voting age should be lowered to 16 because many 16-year-olds are responsible and informed?" is a biased question.

pregunta capciosa Pregunta que impulsa a dar una respuesta determinada.

"¿No estás de acuerdo en que se debe bajar la edad para votar a los 16 años ya que muchos jóvenes de 16 años son responsables y están bien informados?" es una pregunta capciosa.

---

biased sample A sample that is not representative of the population.

The members of a school's basketball team would form a biased sample for a survey about whether to build a new gym.

muestra sesgada Muestra que no es representativa de la población.

Los miembros del equipo de baloncesto de una escuela formarían una muestra sesgada si participaran en una encuesta sobre si quieren que se construya un nuevo gimnasio.

---

binomial A polynomial with two terms.

$t^3 - 4t$ and $2x + 5$ are binomials.

binomio Polinomio con dos términos.

$t^3 - 4t$ y $2x + 5$ son binomios.

---

box-and-whisker plot A data display that organizes data values into four groups using the minimum value, lower quartile, median, upper quartile, and maximum value.

gráfica de frecuencias acumuladas Presentación de datos que organiza los valores de los datos en cuatro grupos usando el valor mínimo, el cuartil inferior, la mediana, el cuartil superior y el valor máximo.

0 10 20 30 40 50

8 19 26 37 45

C

closure A set has closure when an operation performed on two numbers in that set results in a number that is part of the original set.

Multiplication is closed over whole numbers because the product of any two whole numbers is also a whole number.

cerradura Un conjunto tiene cerradura cuando el resultado de una operación entre dos números cualesquiera del conjunto también está en el conjunto.

Multiplicación es cerrado por los números cabales porque el producto de cualquiera dos números cabales también es un numero cabal.

---

coefficient The number part of a term with a variable part.

The coefficient of $-6x$ is -6.

coeficiente La parte numérica de un término que tiene una variable.

El coeficiente de $-6x$ es -6.

---

combination A selection of objects in which order is *not* important.

There are 6 combinations of two of the letters from the list A, B, C, D: AB, AC, AD, BC, BD, and CD.

combinación Selección de objetos en la que el orden *no* es importante.

Hay 6 combinaciones de dos de las letras de la lista A, B, C, D: AB, AC, AD, BC, BD y CD.

common difference The constant difference between consecutive terms of an arithmetic sequence. **diferencia común** La diferencia constante entre los términos consecutivos de una progresión aritmética.	**2, 8, 14, 20, 26, . . . is an arithmetic sequence with a common difference of 6.** **2, 8, 14, 20, 26, . . . es una progresión aritmética con una diferencia común de 6.**
common ratio The ratio of any term of a geometric sequence to the previous term of the sequence. **razón común** La razón entre cualquier término de una progresión geométrica y el término anterior de la progresión.	**The sequence 5, 10, 20, 40, . . . is a geometric sequence with common ratio 2.** **La progresión 5, 10, 20, 40, . . . es una progresión geométrica con una razón común de 2.**
completing the square The process of rewriting a quadratic expression so that it is a perfect square trinomial. **completar el cuadrado** El proceso de escribir una expresión cuadrática de manera que sea un trinomio cuadrado perfecto.	**To write $x^2 - 16x$ as a perfect square trinomial, add $\left(\frac{-16}{2}\right)^2$, or $(-8)^2$. This gives $x^2 - 16x + (-8)^2 = (x - 8)^2$.** **Para escribir $x^2 - 16x$ como trinomio cuadrado perfecto, suma $\left(\frac{-16}{2}\right)^2$, o $(-8)^2$. Así resulta $x^2 - 16x + (-8)^2 = (x - 8)^2$.**
complex fraction A fraction that contains a fraction in its numerator, denominator, or both. **fracción compleja** Fracción que contiene una fracción en su numerador, en su denominador o en ambos.	**$\frac{\frac{3x}{2}}{-6x^3}$ and $\frac{x^2-1}{\frac{x+1}{x-1}}$ are complex fractions.** **$\frac{\frac{3x}{2}}{-6x^3}$ y $\frac{x^2-1}{\frac{x+1}{x-1}}$ son fracciones complejas.**
compound event An event that combines two or more events, using the word *and* or the word *or*. **suceso compuesto** Suceso que combina dos o más sucesos usando la palabra *y* o la palabra *o*.	**When you roll a number cube, the event "roll a 2 or an odd number" is a compound event.** **Cuando lanzas un cubo numerado, el suceso "salir el 2 ó número impar" es un suceso compuesto.**
compound inequality Two inequalities joined by *and* or *or*. **desigualdad compuesta** Dos desigualdades unidas por *y* u *o*.	**$-2 < x$ *and* $x < 1$, which can be written as $-2 < x < 1$, is a compound inequality, as is $x < -1$ *or* $x > 0$.** **$-2 < x$ *y* $x < 1$, que puede escribirse $-2 < x < 1$, es una desigualdad compuesta, al igual que $x < -1$ *ó* $x > 0$.**
compound interest Interest that is earned on both an initial investment and on previously earned interest. **interés compuesto** Interés obtenido tanto sobre la inversión inicial como sobre el interés conseguido anteriormente.	**You deposit \$250 in an account that earns 4% interest compounded yearly. After 5 years, your account balance is $y = 250(1 + 0.04)^5 \approx$ \$304.16.** **Depositas \$250 en una cuenta al 4% anual de interés compuesto. Después de 5 años, el balance de la cuenta es $y = 250(1 + 0.04)^5 \approx$ \$304.16.**

ENGLISH-SPANISH GLOSSARY

conditional statement A statement with a hypothesis and a conclusion.

enunciado condicional Enunciado que tiene una hipótesis y una conclusión.

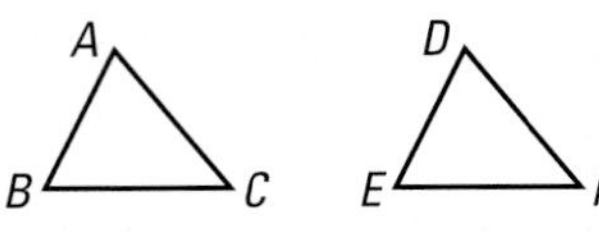

congruent figures Figures that have the same size and shape. The symbol ≅ indicates congruence.

figuras congruentes Figuras que tienen igual tamaño y forma. El símbolo ≅ indica la congruencia.

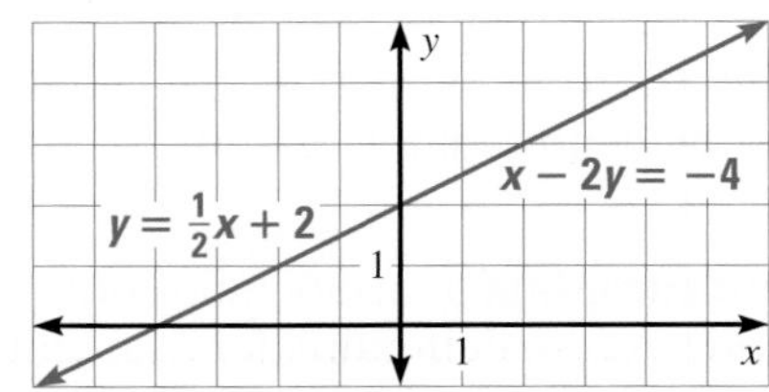

conjecture A statement that is believed to be true but not yet shown to be true.

conjetura Enunciado que se considera verdadero sin que haya sido demostrado todavía.

A conclusion reached using inductive reasoning is a conjecture.

Una conclusión que se saca mediante el razonamiento inductivo es una conjetura.

consistent dependent system A linear system with infinitely many solutions. The graphs of the equations of a consistent dependent system coincide.

sistema dependiente compatible Sistema lineal con infinitas soluciones. Las gráficas de las ecuaciones de un sistema dependiente compatible coinciden.

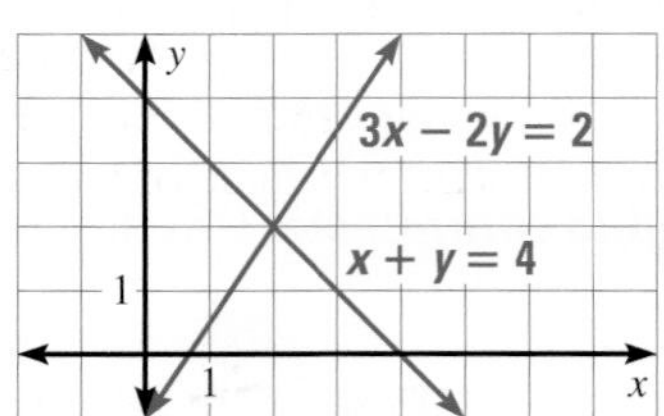

The linear system $x - 2y = -4$ and $y = \frac{1}{2}x + 2$ is a consistent dependent system because the graphs of the equations coincide.

El sistema lineal $x - 2y = -4$ e $y = \frac{1}{2}x + 2$ es un sistema dependiente compatible ya que las gráficas de las ecuaciones coinciden.

consistent independent system A linear system with exactly one solution. The graphs of the equations of a consistent independent system intersect.

sistema independiente compatible Sistema lineal con una sola solución. Las gráficas de las ecuaciones de un sistema independiente compatible se cortan.

$3x - 2y = 2$

$x + y = 4$

The linear system $3x - 2y = 2$ and $x + y = 4$ is a consistent independent system because the graphs of the equations intersect.

El sistema lineal $3x - 2y = 2$ y $x + y = 4$ es un sistema independiente compatible ya que las gráficas de las ecuaciones se cortan.

constant of variation The nonzero constant a in a direct variation equation $y = ax$ or in an inverse variation equation $y = \frac{a}{x}$. **constante de variación** La constante a distinta de cero de una ecuación de variación directa $y = ax$ o de una ecuación de variación inversa $y = \frac{a}{x}$.	The constant of variation in the direct variation equation $y = \frac{2}{3}x$ is $\frac{2}{3}$, and the constant of variation in the inverse variation equation $y = \frac{-1}{x}$ is -1. **La constante de variación de la ecuación de variación directa $y = \frac{2}{3}x$ es $\frac{2}{3}$, y la constante de variación de la ecuación de variación inversa $y = \frac{-1}{x}$ es -1.**
constant term A term with a number part but no variable part. **término constante** Término que tiene una parte numérica sin variable.	In the expression $3x + (-4) + (-6x) + 2$, the constant terms are -4 and 2. **En la expresión $3x + (-4) + (-6x) + 2$, los términos constantes son -4 y 2.**
continuous function A function with a graph that is unbroken. **función continua** Función con una gráfica no interrumpida.	y x
convenience sample A sample in which only members of a population who are easily accessible are selected. **muestra de conveniencia** Muestra en la que se selecciona sólo a los miembros de una población fácilmente accesibles.	You can select a convenience sample of a school's student population by choosing only students who are in your classes. **Para seleccionar una muestra de conveniencia de la población de estudiantes de una escuela, puedes escoger sólo a los estudiantes que están en tus clases.**
converse of a conditional A statement formed by interchanging the hypothesis and the conclusion of the conditional. The converse of a true statement is not necessarily true. **recíproco de un condicional** Enunciado formado al intercambiar la hipótesis y la conclusión del condicional. El recíproco de un enunciado verdadero no es necesariamente verdadero.	The converse of the statement "If $x = 5$, then $\lvert x \rvert = 5$" is "If $\lvert x \rvert = 5$, then $x = 5$." The original statement is true, but the converse is false. **El recíproco del enunciado "Si $x = 5$, entonces $\lvert x \rvert = 5$" es "Si $\lvert x \rvert = 5$, entonces $x = 5$". El enunciado original es verdadero, pero el recíproco es falso.**

correlation The relationship between paired data. The paired data have *positive correlation* if y tends to increase as x increases, *negative correlation* if y tends to decrease as x increases, and *relatively no correlation* if x and y have no apparent relationship.

correlación La relación entre los pares de datos. Los pares de datos presentan una *correlación positiva* si y tiende a aumentar al aumentar x, una *correlación negativa* si y tiende a disminuir al aumentar x y una *correlación nula* si x e y no tienen ninguna relación aparente.

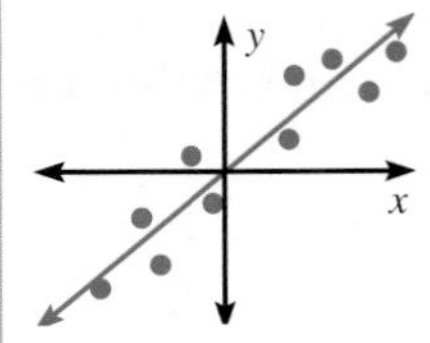

Positive correlation
Correlación positiva

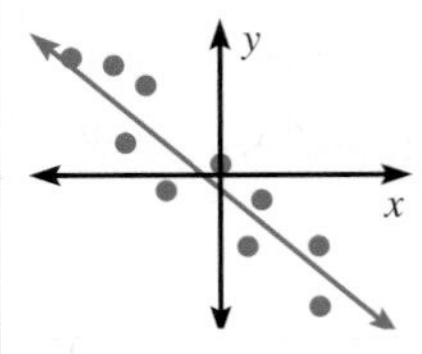

Negative correlation
Correlación negativa

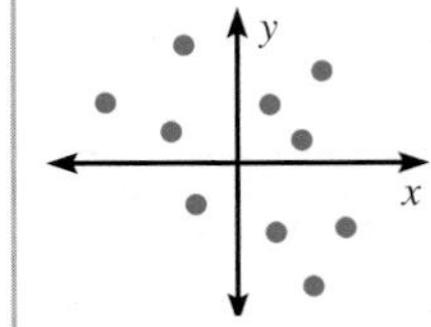

Relatively no correlation
Correlación nula

corresponding parts A pair of sides or angles that have the same relative position in two figures.

partes correspondientes Par de lados o ángulos que tienen la misma posición relativa en dos figuras.

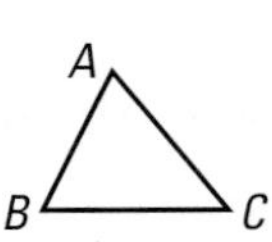

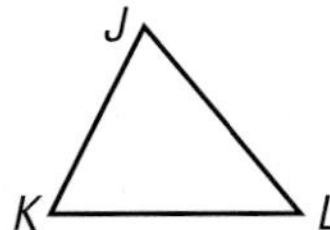

$\angle A$ and $\angle J$ are corresponding angles.
$\overline{AB}$ and $\overline{JK}$ are corresponding sides.

$\angle A$ y $\angle J$ son ángulos correspondientes.
$\overline{AB}$ y $\overline{JK}$ son lados correspondientes.

counterexample An example used to show that an if-then statement is false.

contraejemplo Ejemplo utilizado para demostrar que un enunciado de "si…, entonces…" es falso.

The statement "If a number is a whole number, then the number is positive" is false because 0 is a whole number that is not a positive number.

El enunciado "Si un número es un número natural, entonces es positivo" es falso ya que 0 es un número natural que no es positivo.

cross product In a proportion, a cross product is the product of the numerator of one ratio and the denominator of the other ratio. The cross products of a proportion are equal.

producto cruzado En una proporción, un producto cruzado es el producto del numerador de una de las razones y el denominador de la otra razón. Los productos cruzados de una proporción son iguales.

The cross products of the proportion $\frac{3}{4} = \frac{6}{8}$ are $3 \cdot 8 = 24$ and $4 \cdot 6 = 24$.

Los productos cruzados de la proporción $\frac{3}{4} = \frac{6}{8}$ son $3 \cdot 8 = 24$ y $4 \cdot 6 = 24$.

cube root If $b^3 = a$, then b is the cube root of a.

raíz cúbica Si $b^3 = a$, entonces b es la raíz cúbica de a.

2 is the cube root of 8 because $2^3 = 8$.

2 es la raíz cúbica de 8 ya que $2^3 = 8$.

D

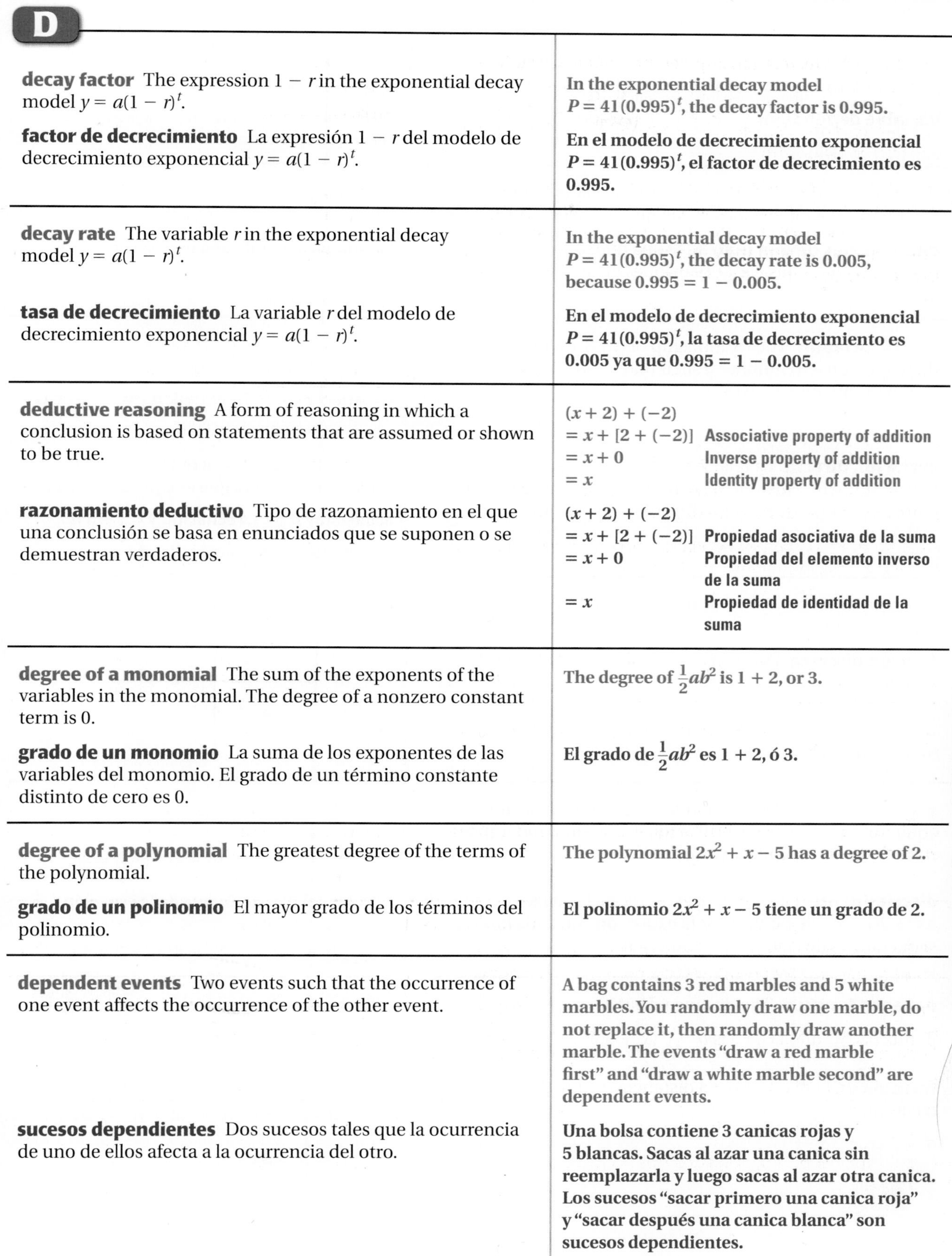

decay factor The expression $1 - r$ in the exponential decay model $y = a(1 - r)^t$. **factor de decrecimiento** La expresión $1 - r$ del modelo de decrecimiento exponencial $y = a(1 - r)^t$.	In the exponential decay model $P = 41(0.995)^t$, the decay factor is 0.995. En el modelo de decrecimiento exponencial $P = 41(0.995)^t$, el factor de decrecimiento es 0.995.
decay rate The variable r in the exponential decay model $y = a(1 - r)^t$. **tasa de decrecimiento** La variable r del modelo de decrecimiento exponencial $y = a(1 - r)^t$.	In the exponential decay model $P = 41(0.995)^t$, the decay rate is 0.005, because $0.995 = 1 - 0.005$. En el modelo de decrecimiento exponencial $P = 41(0.995)^t$, la tasa de decrecimiento es 0.005 ya que $0.995 = 1 - 0.005$.
deductive reasoning A form of reasoning in which a conclusion is based on statements that are assumed or shown to be true. **razonamiento deductivo** Tipo de razonamiento en el que una conclusión se basa en enunciados que se suponen o se demuestran verdaderos.	$(x + 2) + (-2)$ $= x + [2 + (-2)]$ Associative property of addition $= x + 0$ Inverse property of addition $= x$ Identity property of addition $(x + 2) + (-2)$ $= x + [2 + (-2)]$ Propiedad asociativa de la suma $= x + 0$ Propiedad del elemento inverso de la suma $= x$ Propiedad de identidad de la suma
degree of a monomial The sum of the exponents of the variables in the monomial. The degree of a nonzero constant term is 0. **grado de un monomio** La suma de los exponentes de las variables del monomio. El grado de un término constante distinto de cero es 0.	The degree of $\frac{1}{2}ab^2$ is $1 + 2$, or 3. El grado de $\frac{1}{2}ab^2$ es $1 + 2$, ó 3.
degree of a polynomial The greatest degree of the terms of the polynomial. **grado de un polinomio** El mayor grado de los términos del polinomio.	The polynomial $2x^2 + x - 5$ has a degree of 2. El polinomio $2x^2 + x - 5$ tiene un grado de 2.
dependent events Two events such that the occurrence of one event affects the occurrence of the other event. **sucesos dependientes** Dos sucesos tales que la ocurrencia de uno de ellos afecta a la ocurrencia del otro.	A bag contains 3 red marbles and 5 white marbles. You randomly draw one marble, do not replace it, then randomly draw another marble. The events "draw a red marble first" and "draw a white marble second" are dependent events. Una bolsa contiene 3 canicas rojas y 5 blancas. Sacas al azar una canica sin reemplazarla y luego sacas al azar otra canica. Los sucesos "sacar primero una canica roja" y "sacar después una canica blanca" son sucesos dependientes.

dependent variable The output variable of a function. **variable dependiente** La variable de salida de una función.	**In the function equation $y = x + 3$, y is the dependent variable.** **En la ecuación de función $y = x + 3$, y es la variable dependiente.**
dimensions of a matrix If a matrix has m rows and n columns, the dimensions of the matrix are written as $m \times n$. **dimensiones de una matriz** Si una matriz tiene m filas y n columnas, las dimensiones de la matriz se escriben $m \times n$.	**The dimensions of a matrix with 2 rows and 3 columns are 2×3 ("2 by 3").** **Las dimensiones de una matriz con 2 filas y 3 columnas son 2×3 ("2 por 3").**
direct variation The relationship of two variables x and y if there is a nonzero number a such that $y = ax$. If $y = ax$, then y is said to vary directly with x. **variación directa** La relación entre dos variables x e y si hay un número a distinto de cero tal que $y = ax$. Si $y = ax$, entonces se dice que y varía directamente con x.	**The equation $2x - 3y = 0$ represents direct variation because it is equivalent to the equation $y = \frac{2}{3}x$. The equation $y = x + 5$ does *not* represent direct variation.** **La ecuación $2x - 3y = 0$ representa una variación directa ya que es equivalente a la ecuación $y = \frac{2}{3}x$. La ecuación $y = x + 5$ *no* representa una variación directa.**
discrete function A function with a graph that consists of isolated points. **función discreta** Función cuya gráfica consta de puntos aislados.	
discriminant The expression $b^2 - 4ac$ of the assciated equation $ax^2 + bx + c = 0$; also the expression under the radical sign in the quadratic formula. **discriminante** La expresión $b^2 - 4ac$ de la ecuación asociada $ax^2 + bx + c = 0$; también es la expresión colocada bajo el signo radical de la fórmula cuadrática.	**The value of the discriminant of the equation $3x^2 - 2x - 7 = 0$ is:** $b^2 - 4ac = (-2)^2 - 4(3)(-7) = 88$ **El valor del discriminante de la ecuación $3x^2 - 2x - 7 = 0$ es:** $b^2 - 4ac = (-2)^2 - 4(3)(-7) = 88$
distance formula The distance d between any two points (x_1, y_1) and (x_2, y_2) is $d = \sqrt{(x_2 - x_1)^2 + (y_2 - y_1)^2}$. **fórmula de la distancia** La distancia d entre dos puntos cualesquiera (x_1, y_1) y (x_2, y_2) es $d = \sqrt{(x_2 - x_1)^2 + (y_2 - y_1)^2}$.	**The distance d between $(-1, 3)$ and $(5, 2)$ is:** $d = \sqrt{(5 - (-1))^2 + (2 - 3)^2} = \sqrt{37}$ **La distancia d entre $(-1, 3)$ y $(5, 2)$ es:** $d = \sqrt{(5 - (-1))^2 + (2 - 3)^2} = \sqrt{37}$

distributive property A property that can be used to find the product of a number and a sum or difference: $a(b + c) = ab + ac$ $(b + c)a = ba + ca$ $a(b - c) = ab - ac$ $(b - c)a = ba - ca$ **propiedad distributiva** Propiedad que sirve para hallar el producto de un número y una suma o una diferencia: $a(b + c) = ab + ac$ $(b + c)a = ba + ca$ $a(b - c) = ab - ac$ $(b - c)a = ba - ca$	**$3(4 + 2) = 3(4) + 3(2)$, $(8 - 6)4 = (8)4 - (6)4$**
domain of a function The set of all inputs of a function. **dominio de una función** El conjunto de todas las entradas de una función.	***See* function.** ***Ver* función.**

E

element of a matrix Each number in a matrix. **elemento de una matriz** Cada número de la matriz.	***See* matrix.** ***Ver* matriz.**
element of a set Each object in a set. Also called a *member* of a set. **elemento de un conjunto** Cada objeto de un conjunto; llamado también *miembro* de un conjunto.	**5 is an element of the set of whole numbers, $W = \{0, 1, 2, 3, \ldots\}$.** **5 es un elemento del conjunto de los números naturales, $W = \{0, 1, 2, 3, \ldots\}$.**
empty set The set with no elements, written as Ø. **conjunto vacío** El conjunto que no tiene ningún elemento, escrito Ø.	**The set of negative whole numbers = Ø.** **El conjunto de los números naturales negativos = Ø.**
equation A mathematical sentence formed by placing the symbol = between two expressions. **ecuación** Enunciado matemático formado al colocar el símbolo = entre dos expresiones.	**$2k - 8 = 12$ is an equation.** **$2k - 8 = 12$ es una ecuación.**
equivalent equations Equations that have the same solution(s). **ecuaciones equivalentes** Ecuaciones que tienen la misma solución o soluciones.	**$x + 7 = 4$ and $x = -3$ are equivalent equations.** **$x + 7 = 4$ y $x = -3$ son ecuaciones equivalentes.**

ENGLISH-SPANISH GLOSSARY

equivalent expressions Two expressions that have the same value for all values of the variable. **expresiones equivalentes** Dos expresiones que tienen el mismo valor para todos los valores de la variable.	$3(x + 2) + x$ and $4x + 6$ are equivalent expressions. $3(x + 2) + x$ y $4x + 6$ son expresiones equivalentes.
equivalent inequalities Inequalities that have the same solutions. **desigualdades equivalentes** Desigualdades con las mismas soluciones.	$2t < 4$ and $t < 2$ are equivalent inequalities, because the solutions of both inequalities are all real numbers less than 2. $2t < 4$ y $t < 2$ son desigualdades equivalentes ya que las soluciones de ambas son todos los números reales menores que 2.
evaluate an algebraic expression To find the value of an algebraic expression by substituting a number for each variable and performing the operation(s). **evaluar una expresión algebraica** Hallar el valor de una expresión algebraica sustituyendo cada variable por un número y realizando la operación o operaciones.	The value of $n - 1$ when $n = 3$ is $3 - 1 = 2$. El valor de $n - 1$ cuando $n = 3$ es $3 - 1 = 2$.
event An outcome or a collection of outcomes. **suceso** Caso o colección de casos.	When you roll a number cube, "roll an odd number" is an event. Cuando lanzas un cubo numerado, "salir número impar" es un suceso.
excluded value A number that makes a rational expression undefined. **valor excluido** Número que hace que una expresión racional sea indefinida.	3 is an excluded value of the expression $\frac{2}{x-3}$ because 3 makes the value of the denominator 0. 3 es un valor excluido de la expresión $\frac{2}{x-3}$ ya que 3 hace que el valor del denominador sea 0.
experimental probability A probability based on repeated trials of an experiment. The experimental probability of an event is the ratio of the number of successes (trials in which a favorable outcome occurs) to the number of trials. **probabilidad experimental** Probabilidad basada en la realización repetida de las pruebas de un experimento. La probabilidad experimental de un suceso es la razón entre el número de resultados deseados (pruebas en las que se produce un caso favorable) y el número de pruebas.	You spin a spinner 20 times and it stops on yellow 3 times. The experimental probability that the spinner stops on yellow is $\frac{3}{20}$, 15%, or 0.15. Giras una ruleta 20 veces y ésta se detiene en el amarillo 3 veces. La probabilidad experimental de que la ruleta se detenga en el amarillo es $\frac{3}{20}$, 15% ó 0.15.
exponent The number or variable that represents the number of times the base of a power is used as a factor. **exponente** El número o la variable que representa la cantidad de veces que se usa la base de una potencia como factor.	In the power 3^4, the exponent is 4. En la potencia 3^4, el exponente es 4.

ENGLISH-SPANISH GLOSSARY

exponential decay When $a > 0$ and $0 < b < 1$, the function $y = ab^x$ represents exponential decay. When a quantity decays exponentially, it decreases by the same percent over equal time periods. The exponential decay model is $y = a(1 - r)^t$. **decrecimiento exponencial** Cuando $a > 0$ y $0 < b < 1$, la función $y = ab^x$ representa el decrecimiento exponencial. Cuando una cantidad decrece de forma exponencial, disminuye en el mismo porcentaje durante períodos de tiempo iguales. El modelo de decrecimiento exponencial es $y = a(1 - r)^t$.	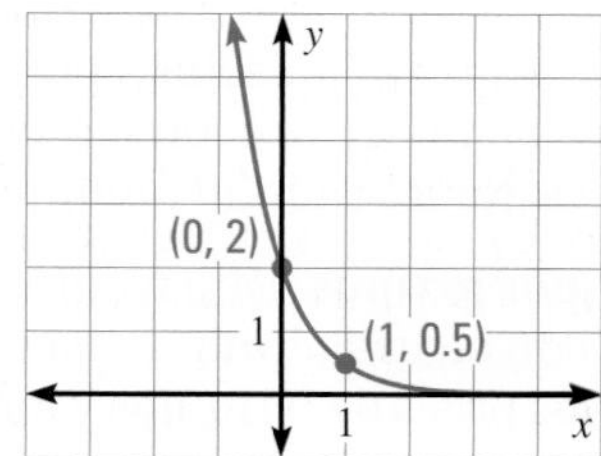 The function $y = 2(0.25)^x$ represents exponential decay. *See also* decay rate *and* decay factor. La función $y = 2(0.25)^x$ representa el decrecimiento exponencial. *Ver también* tasa de decrecimiento *y* factor de decrecimiento.
exponential function A function of the form $y = ab^x$ where $a \neq 0$, $b > 0$, and $b \neq 1$. **función exponencial** Función de la forma $y = ab^x$, donde $a \neq 0$, $b > 0$ y $b \neq 1$.	The functions $y = 2 \cdot 3^x$ and $y = -2 \cdot \left(\frac{1}{2}\right)^x$ are exponential functions. *See also* exponential growth *and* exponential decay. Las funciones $y = 2 \cdot 3^x$ e $y = -2 \cdot \left(\frac{1}{2}\right)^x$ son funciones exponenciales. *Ver también* crecimiento exponencial *y* decrecimiento exponencial.
exponential growth When $a > 0$ and $b > 1$, the function $y = ab^x$ represents exponential growth. When a quantity grows exponentially, it increases by the same percent over equal time periods. The exponential growth model is $y = a(1 + r)^t$. **crecimiento exponencial** Cuando $a > 0$ y $b > 1$, la función $y = ab^x$ representa el crecimiento exponencial. Cuando una cantidad crece de forma exponencial, aumenta en el mismo porcentaje durante períodos de tiempo iguales. El modelo de crecimiento exponencial es $y = a(1 + r)^t$.	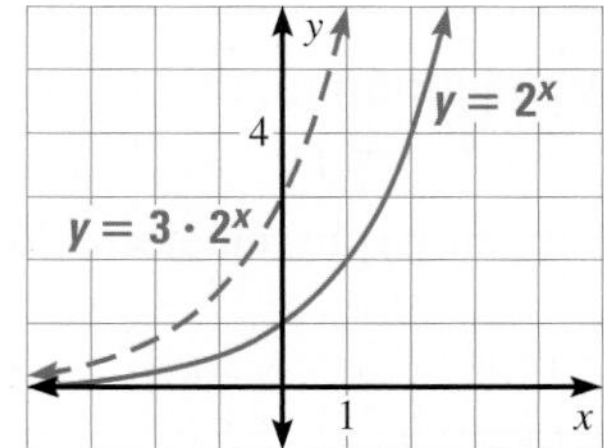 The functions $y = 3 \cdot 2^x$ and $y = 2^x$ represent exponential growth. *See also* growth rate *and* growth factor. Las funciones $y = 3 \cdot 2^x$ e $y = 2^x$ representan el crecimiento exponencial. *Ver también* tasa de crecimiento *y* factor de crecimiento.
extraneous solution A solution of a transformed equation that is not a solution of the original equation. **solución extraña** Solución de una ecuación transformada que no es solución de la ecuación original.	When you square both sides of the radical equation $\sqrt{6 - x} = x$, the resulting equation has two solutions, 2 and -3, but -3 is an extraneous solution because it does not satisfy the original equation $\sqrt{6 - x} = x$. Al elevar al cuadrado ambos miembros de la ecuación radical $\sqrt{6 - x} = x$, la ecuación resultante tiene dos soluciones, 2 y -3, pero -3 es una solución extraña ya que no satisface la ecuación original $\sqrt{6 - x} = x$.

ENGLISH-SPANISH GLOSSARY

F

factor by grouping To factor a polynomial with four terms by grouping, factor a common monomial from pairs of terms, and then look for a common binomial factor. **factorizar por grupos** Para factorizar por grupos un polinomio con cuatro términos, factoriza un monomio común a partir de los pares de términos y luego busca un factor binómico común.	$x^3 + 3x^2 + 5x + 15 = (x^3 + 3x^2) + (5x + 15)$ $= x^2(x + 3) + 5(x + 3)$ $= (x + 3)(x^2 + 5)$
factor completely A factorable polynomial with integer coefficients is factored completely if it is written as a product of unfactorable polynomials with integer coefficients. **factorizar completamente** Un polinomio que puede descomponerse en factores y que tiene coeficientes enteros está completamente factorizado si está escrito como producto de polinomios que no pueden descomponerse en factores y que tienen coeficientes enteros.	The polynomial $x^3 - x$ is *not* factored completely when written as $x(x^2 - 1)$ but is factored completely when written as $x(x + 1)(x - 1)$. El polinomio $x^3 - x$ *no* está completamente factorizado cuando se escribe $x(x^2 - 1)$, pero sí está completamente factorizado cuando se escribe $x(x + 1)(x - 1)$.
family of functions A group of functions with similar characteristics. **familia de funciones** Grupo de funciones con características similares.	Functions that have the form $f(x) = mx + b$ constitute the family of linear functions. Las funciones que tienen la forma $f(x) = mx + b$ constituyen la familia de las funciones lineales.
formula An equation that relates two or more quantities. **fórmula** Ecuación que relaciona dos o más cantidades.	The formula $d = rt$ relates the distance traveled to the rate of speed and travel time. La fórmula $d = rt$ relaciona la distancia recorrida con la velocidad y el tiempo transcurrido.
frequency The frequency of an interval is the number of data values in that interval. **frecuencia** La frecuencia de un intervalo es el número de datos de valores que hay en ese intervalo.	*See* frequency table *and* histogram. *Ver* tabla de frecuencias *e* histograma.
frequency table A data display that groups data into equal intervals with no gaps between intervals and no intervals overlapping. **tabla de frecuencias** Presentación de datos en la que se agrupan los datos en intervalos iguales sin que haya interrupciones entre los intervalos y sin intervalos superpuestos.	(see table below)

Prices Precios	Sandwiches Sándwiches
\$4.00–4.49	||||
\$4.50–4.99	||
\$5.00–5.49	
\$5.50–5.99	||||

function A function consists of:

- A set called the domain containing numbers called inputs, and a set called the range containing numbers called outputs.
- A pairing of inputs with outputs such that each input is paired with exactly one output.

función Una función consta de:

- Un conjunto llamado dominio que contiene los números conocidos como entradas, y otro conjunto llamado rango que contiene los números conocidos como salidas.
- Una correspondencia entre las entradas y las salidas tal que a cada entrada le corresponde una sola salida.

The pairing in the table below is a function, because each input is paired with exactly one output.

La correspondencia que aparece en la tabla de abajo es una función ya que a cada entrada le corresponde una sola salida.

Input, x Entrada, x	0	1	2	3	4
Output, y Salida, y	3	4	5	6	7

The domain is the set of inputs: 0, 1, 2, 3, and 4.
The range is the set of outputs: 3, 4, 5, 6, and 7.

El dominio es el conjunto de entradas: 0, 1, 2, 3 y 4.
El rango es el conjunto de salidas: 3, 4, 5, 6 y 7.

function notation A way to name a function using the symbol $f(x)$ instead of y. The symbol $f(x)$ is read as "the value of f at x" or as "f of x."

notación de función Forma de nombrar una función usando el símbolo $f(x)$ en lugar de y. El símbolo $f(x)$ se lee "el valor de f en x" o "f de x".

The function $y = 2x - 9$ can be written in function notation as $f(x) = 2x - 9$.

La función $y = 2x - 9$ escrita en notación de función es $f(x) = 2x - 9$.

G

geometric sequence A sequence in which the ratio of any term to the previous term is constant. The constant ratio is called the common ratio.

progresión geométrica Progresión en la que la razón entre cualquier término y el término anterior es constante. La razón constante se llama razón común.

The sequence 5, 10, 20, 40, . . . is a geometric sequence with common ratio 2.

La progresión 5, 10, 20, 40, . . . es una progresión geométrica cuya razón común es 2.

graph of an equation in two variables The set of points in a coordinate plane that represent all solutions of the equation.

gráfica de una ecuación con dos variables El conjunto de puntos de un plano de coordenadas que representa todas las soluciones de la ecuación.

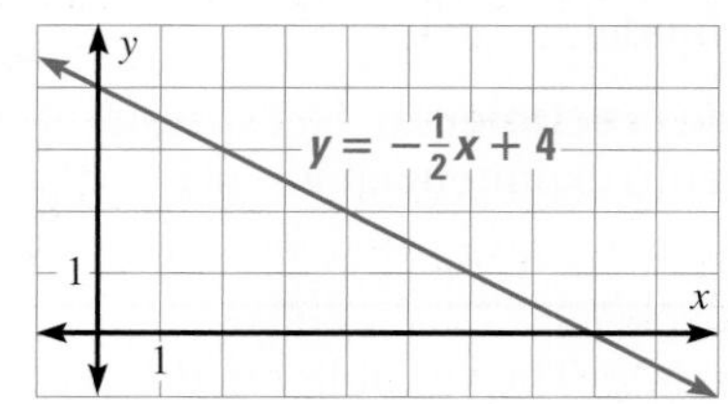

The line is the graph of the equation $y = -\frac{1}{2}x + 4$.

La recta es la gráfica de la ecuación $y = -\frac{1}{2}x + 4$.

ENGLISH-SPANISH GLOSSARY

graph of an inequality in one variable On a number line, the set of points that represent all solutions of the inequality.

gráfica de una desigualdad con una variable En una recta numérica, el conjunto de puntos que representa todas las soluciones de la desigualdad.

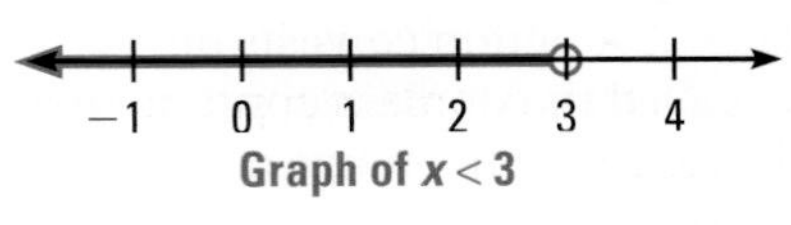

Graph of $x < 3$

Gráfica de $x < 3$

graph of an inequality in two variables In a coordinate plane, the set of points that represent all solutions of the inequality.

gráfica de una desigualdad con dos variables En un plano de coordenadas, el conjunto de puntos que representa todas las soluciones de la desigualdad.

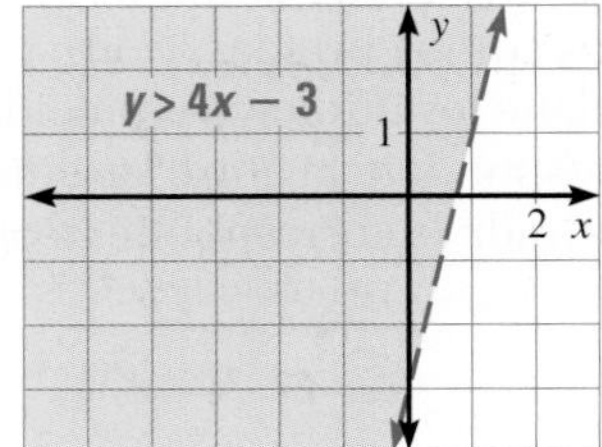

The graph of $y > 4x - 3$ is the shaded half-plane.

La gráfica de $y > 4x - 3$ es el semiplano sombreado.

graph of a system of linear inequalities The graph of all solutions of the system.

gráfica de un sistema de desigualdades lineales La gráfica de todas las soluciones del sistema.

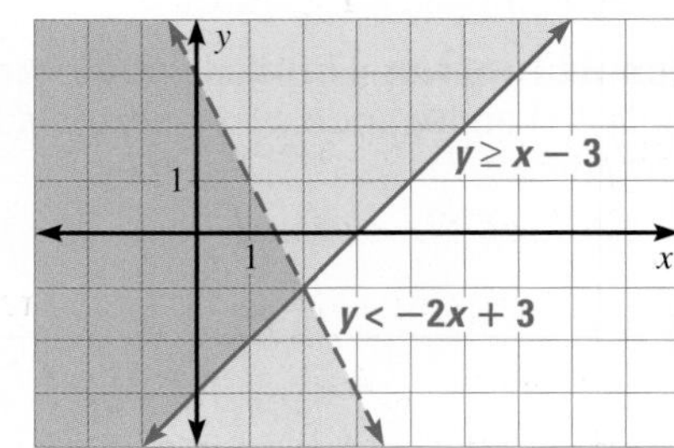

The graph of the system $y < -2x + 3$ and $y \geq x - 3$ is the intersection of the half-planes.

La gráfica del sistema $y < -2x + 3$ e $y \geq x - 3$ es la intersección de los semiplanos.

growth factor The expression $1 + r$ in the exponential growth model $y = a(1 + r)^t$.

factor de crecimiento La expresión $1 + r$ del modelo de crecimiento exponencial $y = a(1 + r)^t$.

In the exponential growth model $C = 11{,}000(1.069)^t$, the growth factor is 1.069.

En el modelo de crecimiento exponencial $C = 11{,}000(1.069)^t$, el factor de crecimiento es 1.069.

growth rate The variable r in the exponential growth model $y = a(1 + r)^t$.

tasa de crecimiento La variable r del modelo de crecimiento exponencial $y = a(1 + r)^t$.

In the exponential growth model $C = 11{,}000(1.069)^t$, the growth rate is 0.069.

En el modelo de crecimiento exponencial $C = 11{,}000(1.069)^t$, la tasa de crecimiento es 0.069.

half-plane In a coordinate plane, the region on either side of a boundary line.

See **graph of an inequality in two variables.**

semiplano En un plano de coordenadas, la región situada a cada lado de una recta límite.

Ver **gráfica de una desigualdad con dos variables.**

histogram A bar graph that displays data from a frequency table. Each bar represents an interval, and the length of each bar indicates the frequency.

histograma Gráfica de barras que presenta los datos de una tabla de frecuencias. Cada barra representa un intervalo, y la longitud de cada barra indica la frecuencia.

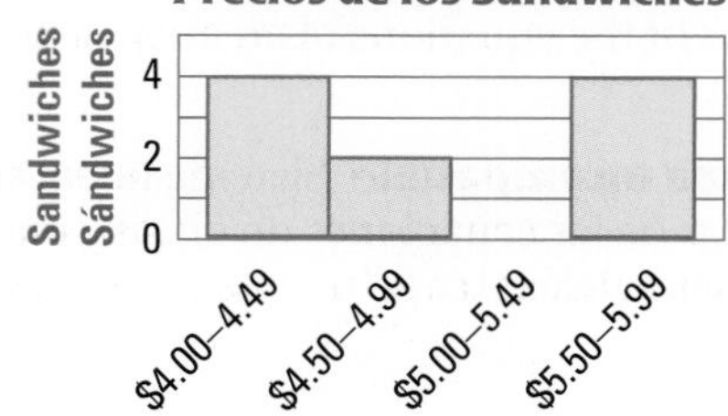

hyperbola The graph of the inverse variation equation $y = \frac{a}{x}$ $(a \neq 0)$ or the graph of a rational function of the form $y = \frac{a}{x - h} + k$ $(a \neq 0)$. A hyperbola has two symmetrical parts called branches. A hyperbola approaches but doesn't intersect lines called asymptotes.

hipérbola La gráfica de la ecuación de variación inversa $y = \frac{a}{x}$ $(a \neq 0)$ o la gráfica de una función racional de la forma $y = \frac{a}{x - h} + k$ $(a \neq 0)$. La hipérbola tiene dos partes simétricas llamadas ramas. La hipérbola se acerca a las rectas llamadas asíntotas pero sin cortarlas.

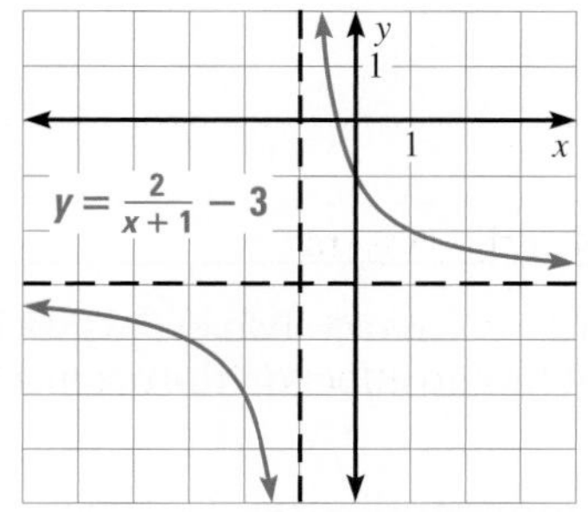

The graph of $y = \frac{2}{x+1} - 3$ is a hyperbola. The asymptotes of the hyperbola are the lines $x = -1$ and $y = -3$.

La gráfica de $y = \frac{2}{x+1} - 3$ es una hipérbola. Las asíntotas de la hipérbola son las rectas $x = -1$ e $y = -3$.

hypotenuse The hypotenuse of a right triangle is the side opposite the right angle.

hipotenusa La hipotenusa de un triángulo rectángulo es el lado opuesto al ángulo recto.

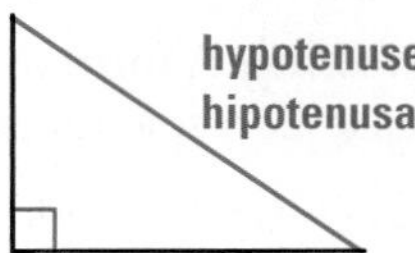

identity An equation that is true for all values of the variable.

The equation $2x + 10 = 2(x + 5)$ is an identity.

identidad Ecuación que es verdadera para todos los valores de la variable.

La ecuación $2x + 10 = 2(x + 5)$ es una identidad.

if-then statement A conditional statement with an *if* part and a *then* part. The *if* part contains the hypothesis, and the *then* part contains the conclusion. **enunciado de "si..., entonces..."** Enunciado condicional con una parte de *si* y otra de *entonces*. La parte de *si* contiene la hipótesis, y la parte de *entonces* contiene la conclusión.	If $a = -1$, then $\|a\| = 1$. The hypothesis is $a = -1$. The conclusion is $\|a\| = 1$. **Si $a = -1$, entonces $\|a\| = 1$.** **La hipótesis es $a = -1$.** **La conclusión es $\|a\| = 1$.**
inconsistent system A linear system with no solution. The graphs of the equations of an inconsistent system are parallel lines. **sistema incompatible** Sistema lineal sin solución. Las gráficas de las ecuaciones de un sistema incompatible son rectas paralelas.	 The linear system $y = 2x + 1$ and $y = 2x - 3$ is inconsistent because the graphs of the equations are parallel lines. **El sistema lineal $y = 2x + 1$ e $y = 2x - 3$ es incompatible ya que las gráficas de las ecuaciones son rectas paralelas.**
independent events Two events such that the occurrence of one event has no effect on the occurrence of the other event. **sucesos independientes** Dos sucesos tales que la ocurrencia de uno de ellos no afecta a la ocurrencia del otro.	You roll a number cube twice. The events "roll a 3 first" and "roll a 6 second" are independent events. **Lanzas un cubo numerado dos veces. Los sucesos "salir primero el 3" y "salir después el 6" son sucesos independientes.**
independent variable The input variable of a function. **variable independiente** La variable de entrada de una función.	In the function equation $y = x + 3$, x is the independent variable. **En la ecuación de función $y = x + 3$, x es la variable independiente.**
inductive reasoning A form of reasoning in which a conclusion is based on several examples. **razonamiento inductivo** Tipo de razonamiento en el que la conclusión se basa en varios ejemplos.	You add several pairs of odd numbers and notice that the sum is even. You conclude that the sum of any two odd numbers is even. **Sumas varias parejas de números impares y observas que la suma es par. Sacas la conclusión de que la suma de dos números impares cualesquiera es par.**
inequality A mathematical sentence formed by placing one of the symbols $<$, $\leq$, $>$, or $\geq$ between two expressions. **desigualdad** Enunciado matemático formado al colocar uno de les siguentes símbolos entre dos expresiones: $<$, $\leq$, $>$ o $\geq$.	$6n \geq 24$ and $x - 2 < 7$ are inequalities. **$6n \geq 24$ y $x - 2 < 7$ son desigualdades.**

ENGLISH-SPANISH GLOSSARY

input A number in the domain of a function. **entrada** Número del dominio de una función.	***See*** **function.** ***Ver*** **función.**
integers The numbers . . . , −3, −2, −1, 0, 1, 2, 3, . . . , consisting of the negative integers, zero, and the positive integers. **números enteros** Los números . . . , −3, −2, −1, 0, 1, 2, 3, . . . , que constan de los números enteros negativos, cero y los números enteros positivos.	**−8 and 46 are integers.** **$-8\frac{1}{2}$ and 46.2 are *not* integers.** **−8 y 46 son números enteros.** **$-8\frac{1}{2}$ y 46.2 *no* son números enteros.**
intercept form of a quadratic function A quadratic function in the form $y = a(x - p)(x - q)$ where $a \neq 0$. The x-intercepts of the graph of the function are p and q. **forma de intercepto de una función cuadrática** Función cuadrática de la forma $y = a(x - p)(x - q)$, donde $a \neq 0$. Los interceptos en x de la gráfica de la función son p y q.	**The quadratic function $y = -(x + 1)(x - 5)$ is in intercept form. The intercepts of the graph of the function are −1 and 5.** **La función cuadrática $y = -(x + 1)(x - 5)$ está en la forma de intercepto. Los interceptos de la gráfica de la función son −1 y 5.**
interquartile range The difference of the upper and the lower quartiles of a data set. **rango intercuartílico** La diferencia entre el cuartil superior y el cuartil inferior de un conjunto de datos.	**The interquartile range of the data set below is 23 − 10 = 13.** **lower quartile ↓ upper quartile ↓** **8 10 14 17 20 23 50** **El rango intercuartílico del siguiente conjunto de datos es 23 − 10 = 13.** **cuartil inferior ↓ cuartil superior ↓** **8 10 14 17 20 23 50**
intersection The intersection of two sets A and B is the set of all elements in *both* A and B. The intersection of A and B is written as $A \cap B$. **intersección** La intersección de dos conjuntos A y B es el conjunto de todos los elementos *tanto* de A *como* de B. La intersección de A y B se escribe $A \cap B$.	U A B 4 6 8 2 3 5 7 1 9 $A \cap B = \{2\}$
inverse operations Two operations that undo each other. **operaciones inversas** Dos operaciones que se anulan entre sí.	**Addition and subtraction are inverse operations. Multiplication and division are also inverse operations.** **La suma y la resta son operaciones inversas. La multiplicación y la división también son operaciones inversas.**

ENGLISH-SPANISH GLOSSARY

inverse variation The relationship of two variables x and y if there is a nonzero number a such that $y = \frac{a}{x}$. If $y = \frac{a}{x}$, then y is said to vary inversely with x.

variación inversa La relación entre dos variables x e y si hay un número a distinto de cero tal que $y = \frac{a}{x}$. Si $y = \frac{a}{x}$, entonces se dice que y varía inversamente con x.

The equations $xy = 4$ and $y = \frac{-1}{x}$ represent inverse variation.

Las ecuaciones $xy = 4$ e $y = \frac{-1}{x}$ representan una variación inversa.

irrational number A number that cannot be written as the quotient of two integers. The decimal form of an irrational number neither terminates nor repeats.

número irracional Número que no puede escribirse como cociente de dos números enteros. La forma decimal de un número irracional no termina ni se repite.

$\sqrt{945} = 30.74085\ldots$ is an irrational number. $1.666\ldots$ is *not* an irrational number.

$\sqrt{945} = 30.74085\ldots$ es un número irracional. $1.666\ldots$ *no* es un número irracional.

leading coefficient When a polynomial is written so that the exponents of a variable decrease from left to right, the coefficient of the first term is the leading coefficient.

coeficiente inicial Cuando un polinomio se escribe de tal manera que los exponentes de una variable disminuyen de izquierda a derecha, el coeficiente del primer término es el coeficiente inicial.

The leading coefficient of the polynomial $2x^3 + x^2 - 5x + 12$ is 2.

El coeficiente inicial del polinomio $2x^3 + x^2 - 5x + 12$ es 2.

least common denominator (LCD) of rational expressions The product of the factors of the denominators of the rational expressions with each common factor used only once.

mínimo común denominador (m.c.d.) de las expresiones racionales El producto de los factores de los denominadores de las expresiones racionales usando cada factor común una sola vez.

The LCD of $\frac{5}{(x-3)^2}$ and $\frac{3x+4}{(x-3)(x+2)}$ is $(x-3)^2(x+2)$.

El m.c.d. de $\frac{5}{(x-3)^2}$ y $\frac{3x+4}{(x-3)(x+2)}$ es $(x-3)^2(x+2)$.

legs of a right triangle The two sides that form the right angle.

catetos de un triángulo rectángulo Los dos lados que forman el ángulo recto.

leg
cateto
leg
cateto

like terms Terms that have the same variable parts. Constant terms are also like terms.

términos semejantes Términos que tienen las mismas variables. Los términos constantes también son términos semejantes.

In the expression $3x + (-4) + (-6x) + 2$, $3x$ and $-6x$ are like terms, and -4 and 2 are like terms.

En la expresión $3x + (-4) + (-6x) + 2$, $3x$ y $-6x$ son términos semejantes, y -4 y 2 también son términos semejantes.

line of fit A line used to model the trend in data having a positive or negative correlation.

recta de regresión Recta utilizada para representar la tendencia de los datos que presentan una correlación positiva o negativa.

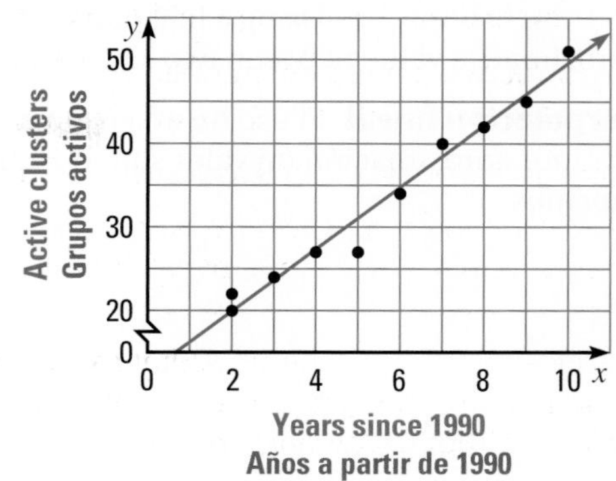

The graph shows a line of fit for the data in the scatter plot.

La gráfica muestra una recta de regresión para los datos del diagrama de dispersión.

linear equation An equation whose graph is a line.

ecuación lineal Ecuación cuya gráfica es una recta.

See standard form of a linear equation.

***Ver* forma general de una ecuación lineal.**

linear extrapolation Using a line or its equation to approximate a value outside the range of known values.

extrapolación lineal El uso de una recta o su ecuación para hallar por aproximación un valor situado fuera del rango de los valores conocidos.

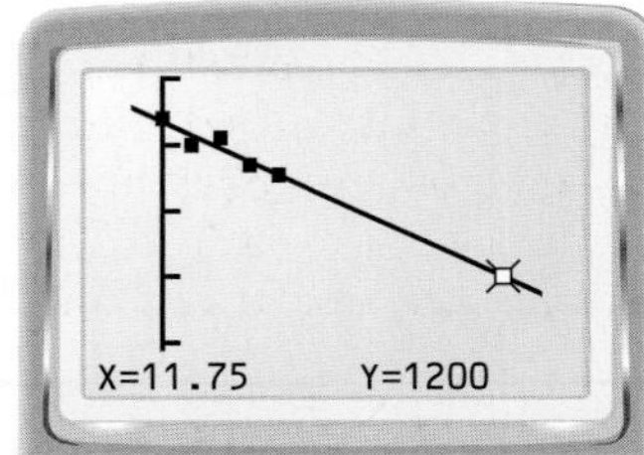

The best-fitting line can be used to estimate that when $y = 1200$, $x \approx 11.75$.

La mejor recta de regresión puede utilizarse para estimar que cuando $y = 1200$, $x \approx 11.75$.

linear function The equation $Ax + By = C$ represents a linear function provided $B \neq 0$.

función lineal La ecuación $Ax + By = C$ representa una función lineal siempre que $B \neq 0$.

The equation $2x - y = 3$ represents a linear function. The equation $x = 3$ does *not* represent a function.

La ecuación $2x - y = 3$ representa una función lineal. La ecuación $x = 3$ *no* representa una función.

linear inequality in two variables An inequality that is the result of replacing the = sign in a linear equation with $<$, $\leq$, $>$, or $\geq$.

desigualdad lineal con dos variables Desigualdad que se obtiene al reemplazar el símbolo = de la ecuación lineal por $<$, $\leq$, $>$ o $\geq$.

$x - 3y < 6$ is a linear inequality in two variables, x and y.

$x - 3y < 6$ es una desigualdad lineal con dos variables, x e y.

linear interpolation Using a line or its equation to approximate a value between two known values. **interpolación lineal** El uso de una recta o su ecuación para hallar por aproximación un valor situado entre dos valores conocidos.	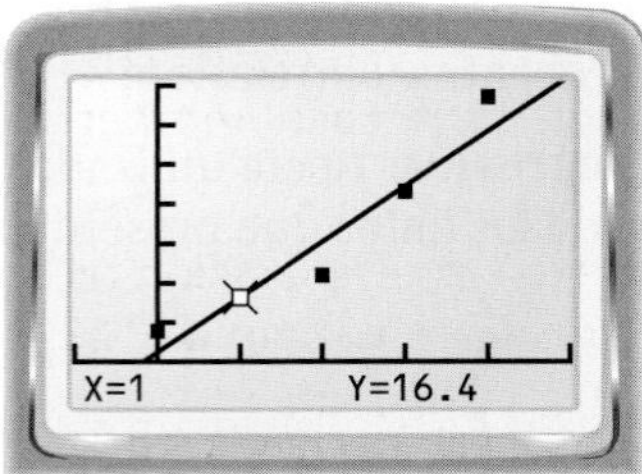 **The best-fitting line can be used to estimate that when $x = 1$, $y \approx 16.4$.** **La mejor recta de regresión puede utilizarse para estimar que cuando $x = 1$, $y \approx 16.4$.**
linear regression The process of finding the best-fitting line to model a set of data. **regresión lineal** El proceso de hallar la mejor recta de regresión para representar un conjunto de datos.	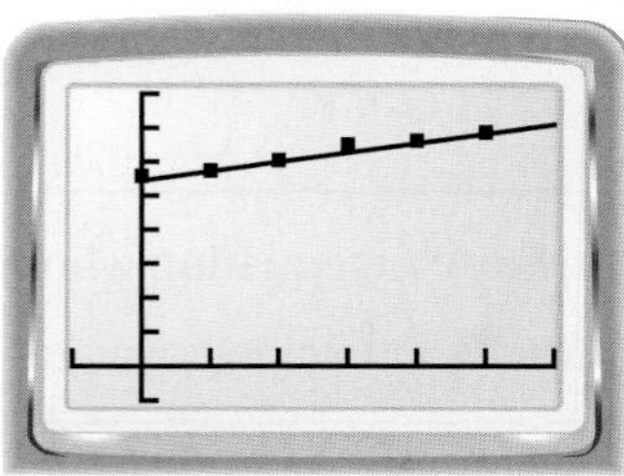 **You can use a graphing calculator to perform linear regression on a data set.** **Puedes usar una calculadora de gráficas para realizar una regresión lineal a un conjunto de datos.**
literal equation An equation in which letters are used to replace the coefficients and constants of another equation. **ecuación literal** Ecuación en la que se usan letras para reemplazar los coeficientes y las constantes de otra ecuación.	**The equation $5(x + 3) = 20$ can be written as the literal equation $a(x + b) = c$.** **La ecuación $5(x + 3) = 20$ puede escribirse como la ecuación literal $a(x + b) = c$.**
lower quartile The median of the lower half of an ordered data set. **cuartil inferior** La mediana de la mitad inferior de un conjunto de datos ordenados.	**The lower quartile of the data set below is 10.** **lower quartile ↓ median ↓** **8 10 14 17 20 23 50** **El cuartil inferior del siguiente conjunto de datos es 10.** **cuartil inferior ↓ mediana ↓** **8 10 14 17 20 23 50**

ENGLISH-SPANISH GLOSSARY

M

matrix, matrices A rectangular arrangement of numbers in rows and columns. Each number in a matrix is an element, or *entry.*

matriz, matrices Disposición rectangular de números colocados en filas y columnas. Cada número de la matriz es un elemento, o *entrada.*

$$A = \begin{bmatrix} 0 & 4 & -1 \\ -3 & 2 & 5 \end{bmatrix}$$ 2 rows / 2 filas

3 columns
3 columnas

Matrix *A* has 2 rows and 3 columns. The element in the first row and second column is 4.

La matriz *A* tiene 2 filas y 3 columnas. El elemento de la primera fila y la segunda columna es 4.

maximum value For $y = ax^2 + bx + c$ where $a < 0$, the y-coordinate of the vertex is the maximum value of the function.

valor máximo Para $y = ax^2 + bx + c$ donde $a < 0$, la coordenada y del vértice es el valor máximo de la función.

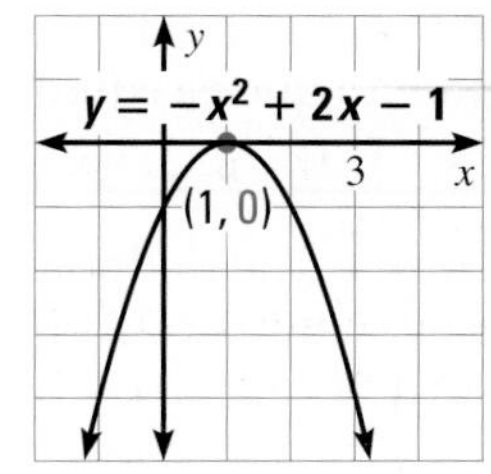

The maximum value of the function $y = -x^2 + 2x - 1$ is 0.

El valor máximo de la función $y = -x^2 + 2x - 1$ es 0.

mean For the numerical data set $x_1, x_2, \ldots, x_n$, the mean, or average, is:

$$\overline{x} = \frac{x_1 + x_2 + \ldots + x_n}{n}$$

media Para el conjunto de datos numéricos $x_1, x_2, \ldots, x_n$, la media, o el promedio, es:

$$\overline{x} = \frac{x_1 + x_2 + \ldots + x_n}{n}$$

The mean of 5, 9, 14, 23 is $\frac{5 + 9 + 14 + 23}{4} = \frac{51}{4} = 12.75$.

La media de 5, 9, 14, 23 es $\frac{5 + 9 + 14 + 23}{4} = \frac{51}{4} = 12.75$.

mean absolute deviation The mean absolute deviation of the data set $x_1, x_2, \ldots, x_n$ is a measure of dispersion given by:

$$\frac{|x_1 - \overline{x}| + |x_2 - \overline{x}| + \ldots + |x_n - \overline{x}|}{n}$$

desviación absoluta media La desviación absoluta media del conjunto de datos $x_1, x_2, \ldots, x_n$ es una medida de dispersión dada por:

$$\frac{|x_1 - \overline{x}| + |x_2 - \overline{x}| + \ldots + |x_n - \overline{x}|}{n}$$

The mean absolute deviation of the data set 3, 9, 13, 23 (with mean = 12) is:

$$\frac{|3 - 12| + |9 - 12| + |13 - 12| + |23 - 12|}{4} = 6$$

La desviación absoluta media del conjunto de datos 3, 9, 13, 23 (con media = 12)es:

$$\frac{|3 - 12| + |9 - 12| + |13 - 12| + |23 - 12|}{4} = 6$$

measure of dispersion A measure that describes the dispersion, or spread, of data.

medida de dispersión Medida que describe la dispersión, o extensión, de los datos.

***See* range *and* mean absolute deviation.**

***Ver* rango *y* desviación absoluta media.**

ENGLISH-SPANISH GLOSSARY

median The median of a numerical data set is the middle number when the values are written in numerical order. If the data set has an even number of values, the median is the mean of the two middle values.

mediana La mediana de un conjunto de datos numéricos es el número central cuando los valores se escriben en orden numérico. Si el conjunto de datos tiene un número par de valores, la mediana es la media de los dos valores centrales.

The median of 5, 9, 14, 23 is the mean of 9 and 14, or $\frac{9 + 14}{2} = 11.5$.

La mediana de 5, 9, 14, 23 es la media de 9 y 14, ó $\frac{9 + 14}{2} = 11.5$.

midpoint The midpoint of a line segment is the point on the segment that is equidistant from the endpoints.

punto medio El punto medio de un segmento de recta es el punto del segmento que es equidistante de los extremos.

***M* is the midpoint of $\overline{AB}$.**

***M* en el punto medio de $\overline{AB}$.**

midpoint formula The midpoint M of the line segment with endpoints $A(x_1, y_1)$ and $B(x_2, y_2)$ is $M\left(\frac{x_1 + x_2}{2}, \frac{y_1 + y_2}{2}\right)$.

fórmula del punto medio El punto medio M del segmento de recta cuyos extremos son $A(x_1, y_1)$ y $B(x_2, y_2)$ es $M\left(\frac{x_1 + x_2}{2}, \frac{y_1 + y_2}{2}\right)$.

The midpoint M of the line segment with endpoints $(-1, -2)$ and $(3, -4)$ is:

$$\left(\frac{-1 + 3}{2}, \frac{-2 + (-4)}{2}\right) = (1, -3)$$

El punto medio M del segmento de recta cuyos extremos son $(-1, -2)$ y $(3, -4)$ es:

$$\left(\frac{-1 + 3}{2}, \frac{-2 + (-4)}{2}\right) = (1, -3)$$

minimum value For $y = ax^2 + bx + c$ where $a > 0$, the y-coordinate of the vertex is the minimum value of the function.

valor mínimo Para $y = ax^2 + bx + c$ donde $a > 0$, la coordenada y del vértice es el valor mínimo de la función.

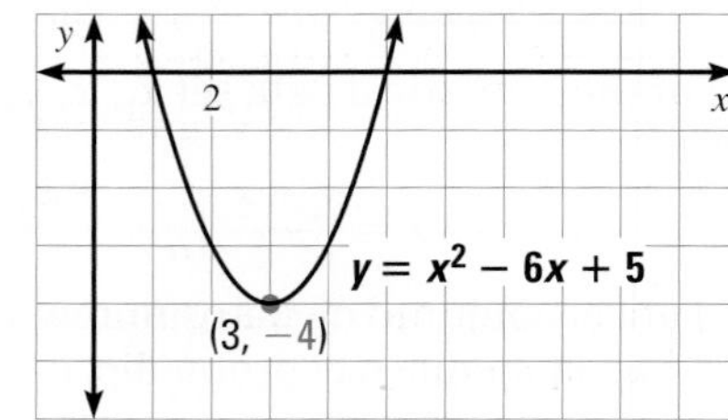

The minimum value of the function $y = x^2 - 6x + 5$ is -4.

El valor mínimo de la función $y = x^2 - 6x + 5$ es -4.

mode The mode of a data set is the value that occurs most frequently. There may be one mode, no mode, or more than one mode.

moda La moda de un conjunto de datos es el valor que ocurre más veces. Puede haber una moda, más de una moda o ninguna moda.

The mode of the data set 4, 7, 9, 11, 11, 12, 18 is 11.

La moda del conjunto de datos 4, 7, 9, 11, 11, 12, 18 es 11.

monomial A number, variable, or the product of a number and one or more variables with whole number exponents. **monomio** Un número, una variable o el producto de un número y una o más variables que tienen exponentes expresados por números naturales.	**10, $3x$, $\frac{1}{2}ab^2$, and $-1.8m^5$ are monomials.** **10, $3x$, $\frac{1}{2}ab^2$ y $-1.8m^5$ son monomios.**
multiplicative identity The number 1 is the multiplicative identity, because the product of any number and 1 is the number: $a \cdot 1 = 1 \cdot a = a$. **identidad multiplicativa** El número 1 es la identidad multiplicativa ya que el producto de cualquier número y 1 es ese número: $a \cdot 1 = 1 \cdot a = a$.	**$3.6(1) = 3.6$, $1(-7) = -7$**
multiplicative inverse The multiplicative inverse of a nonzero number a is its reciprocal, $\frac{1}{a}$. The product of a nonzero number and its multiplicative inverse is 1: $a \cdot \frac{1}{a} = \frac{1}{a} \cdot a = 1, a \neq 0$. **inverso multiplicativo** El inverso multiplicativo de un número a distinto de cero es su recíproco, $\frac{1}{a}$. El producto de un número distinto de cero y su inverso multiplicativo es 1: $a \cdot \frac{1}{a} = \frac{1}{a} \cdot a = 1, a \neq 0$.	**The multiplicative inverse of $-\frac{1}{5}$ is -5 because $-\frac{1}{5} \cdot (-5) = 1$.** **El inverso multiplicativo de $-\frac{1}{5}$ es -5 ya que $-\frac{1}{5} \cdot (-5) = 1$.**
mutually exclusive events Events that have no common outcome. **sucesos mutuamente excluyentes** Sucesos que no tienen ningún caso en común.	**When you roll a number cube, "roll a 3" and "roll an even number" are mutually exclusive events.** **Cuando lanzas un cubo numerado, "salir el 3" y "salir número par" son sucesos mutuamente excluyentes.**

N

n* factorial** For any positive integer n, n factorial, written $n!$, is the product of the integers from 1 to n; $0! = 1$. **factorial de *n Para cualquier número entero positivo n, el factorial de n, escrito $n!$, es el producto de los números enteros de 1 a n; $0! = 1$.	**$5! = 5 \cdot 4 \cdot 3 \cdot 2 \cdot 1 = 120$**
negative exponent If $a \neq 0$, then a^{-n} is the reciprocal of a^n; $a^{-n} = \frac{1}{a^n}$. **exponente negativo** Si $a \neq 0$, entonces a^{-n} es el recíproco de a^n; $a^{-n} = \frac{1}{a^n}$.	**$3^{-2} = \frac{1}{3^2} = \frac{1}{9}$**

negative integers The integers that are less than 0. **números enteros negativos** Los números enteros menores que 0.	$-1, -2, -3, -4, \ldots$

O

odds against When all outcomes are equally likely, the odds against an event is the ratio of the number of unfavorable outcomes to the number of favorable outcomes. **probabilidad en contra** Cuando todos los casos son igualmente posibles, la probabilidad en contra de que ocurra un suceso es la razón entre el número de casos desfavorables y el número de casos favorables.	When you roll a number cube, the odds against rolling a number less than 5 is $\frac{2}{4} = \frac{1}{2}$, or 1 : 2. Cuando lanzas un cubo numerado, la probabilidad en contra de que salga un número menor que 5 es $\frac{2}{4} = \frac{1}{2}$, ó 1 : 2.
odds in favor When all outcomes are equally likely, the odds in favor of an event is the ratio of the number of favorable outcomes to the number of unfavorable outcomes. **probabilidad a favor** Cuando todos los casos son igualmente posibles, la probabilidad a favor de que ocurra un suceso es la razón entre el número de casos favorables y el número de casos desfavorables.	When you roll a number cube, the odds in favor of rolling a number less than 5 is $\frac{4}{2} = \frac{2}{1}$, or 2 : 1. Cuando lanzas un cubo numerado, la probabilidad a favor de que salga un número menor que 5 es $\frac{4}{2} = \frac{2}{1}$, ó 2 : 1.
open sentence An equation or an equality that contains an algebraic expression. **enunciado con variables** Ecuación o desigualdad que contiene una expresión algebraica.	$2k - 8 = 12$ and $6n \geq 24$ are open sentences. $2k - 8 = 12$ y $6n \geq 24$ son enunciados con variables.
opposites Two numbers that are the same distance from 0 on a number line but are on opposite sides of 0. **opuestos** En una recta numérica, dos números que están a la misma distancia de 0 pero en lados opuestos de 0.	4 units 4 units 4 unidades 4 unidades −6 −4 −2 0 2 4 6 4 and −4 are opposites. 4 y −4 son opuestos.
order of magnitude of a quantity The power of 10 nearest the quantity. **orden de magnitud de una cantidad** La potencia de 10 más próxima a la cantidad.	The order of magnitude of 91,000 is 10^5, or 100,000. El orden de magnitud de 91,000 es 10^5, ó 100,000.

ENGLISH-SPANISH GLOSSARY

order of operations Rules for evaluating an expression involving more than one operation. **orden de operaciones** Reglas para evaluar una expresión relacionada con más de una operación.	**To evaluate $24 - (3^2 + 1)$, evaluate the power, then add within the parentheses, and then subtract:** $24 - (3^2 + 1) = 24 - (9 + 1) = 24 - 10 = 14$ **Para evaluar $24 - (3^2 + 1)$, evalúa la potencia, suma las cantidades entre paréntesis y después resta:** $24 - (3^2 + 1) = 24 - (9 + 1) = 24 - 10 = 14$
outcome A possible result of an experiment. **caso** Resultado posible de un experimento.	**When you roll a number cube, there are 6 possible outcomes: a 1, 2, 3, 4, 5, or 6.** **Cuando lanzas un cubo numerado, hay 6 casos posibles: 1, 2, 3, 4, 5 ó 6.**
outlier A value that is widely separated from the rest of the data in a data set. Typically, a value that is greater than the upper quartile by more than 1.5 times the interquartile range or is less than the lower quartile by more than 1.5 times the interquartile range. **valor extremo** En un conjunto de datos, valor muy alejado del resto de los datos. Generalmente, un valor mayor que el cuartil superior en más de 1.5 veces el rango intercuartílico o menor que el cuartil inferior en más de 1.5 veces el rango intercuartílico.	**The interquartile range of the data set below is $23 - 10 = 13$.** **lower quartile ↓ upper quartile ↓** **8 10 14 17 20 23 50** **The data value 50 is greater than $23 + 1.5(13) = 42.5$, so it is an outlier.** **El rango intercuartílico del siguiente conjunto de datos es $23 - 10 = 13$.** **cuartil inferior ↓ cuartil superior ↓** **8 10 14 17 20 23 50** **El valor 50 es mayor que $23 + 1.5(13) = 42.5$, por lo que es un valor extremo.**
output A number in the range of a function. **salida** Número que pertenece al rango de una función.	***See* function.** ***Ver* función.**
overlapping events Events that have at least one common outcome. **sucesos de intersección** Sucesos que tienen al menos un caso en común.	**When you roll a number cube, "roll a 3" and "roll an odd number" are overlapping events.** **Cuando lanzas un cubo numerado, "salir el 3" y "salir número impar" son sucesos de intersección.**

parabola The U-shaped graph of a quadratic function.

parábola La gráfica en forma de U de una función cuadrática.

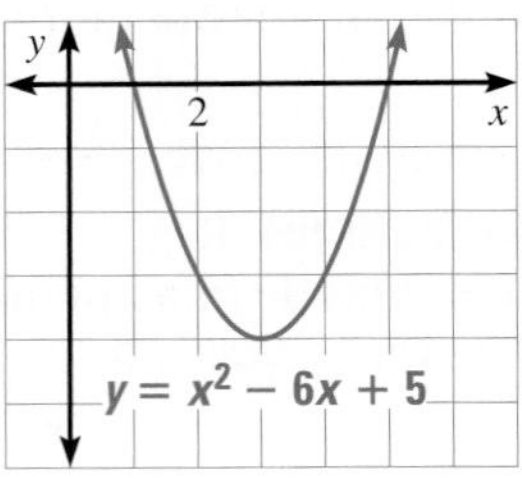

The graph of $y = x^2 - 6x + 5$ is a parabola.

La gráfica de $y = x^2 - 6x + 5$ es una parábola.

parallel lines Two lines in the same plane that do not intersect.

rectas paralelas Dos rectas del mismo plano que no se cortan.

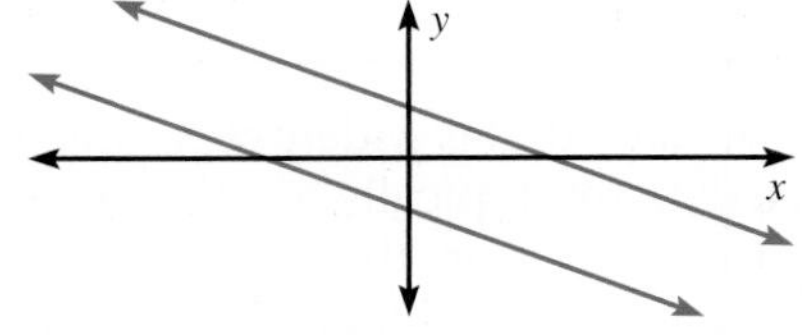

parent linear function The function $f(x) = x$, which is the most basic function in the family of linear functions.

función lineal básica La función $f(x) = x$, que es la más básica de la familia de las funciones lineales.

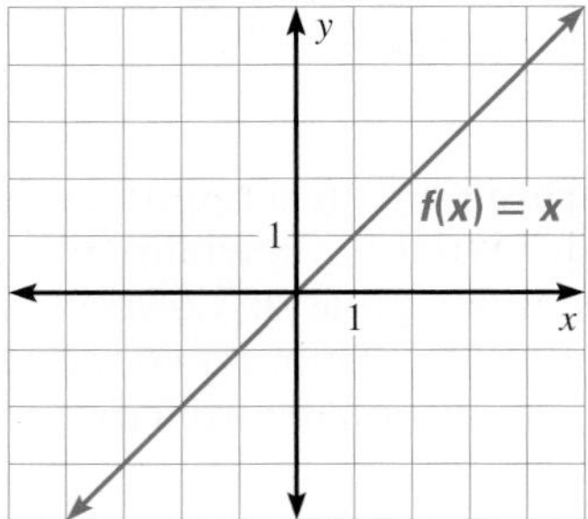

parent quadratic function The function $y = x^2$, which is the most basic function in the family of quadratic functions.

función cuadrática básica La función $y = x^2$, que es la más básica de la familia de las funciones cuadráticas.

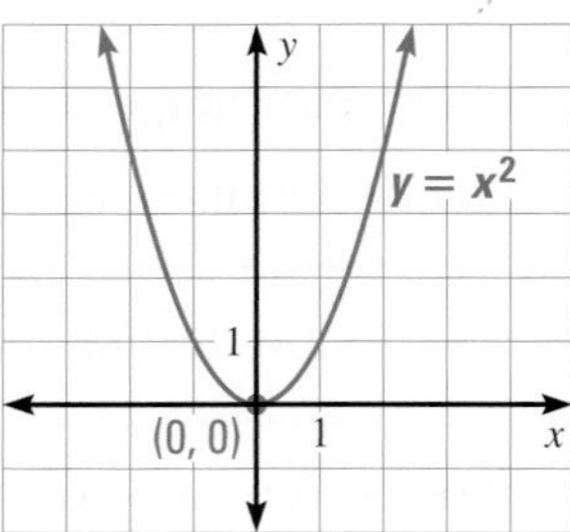

parent square root function The function $y = \sqrt{x}$, which is the most basic function in the family of square root functions.

función con raíz cuadrada básica La función $y = \sqrt{x}$, que es la más básica de la familia de las funciones con raíz cuadrada.

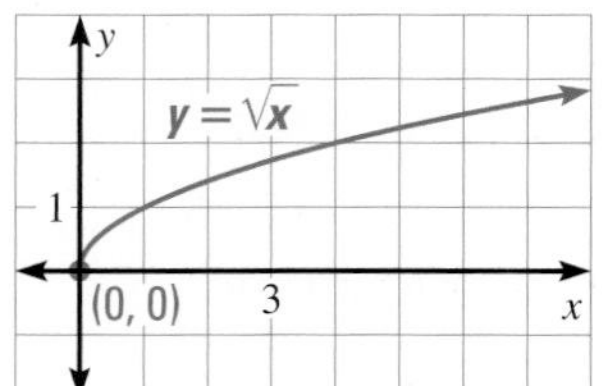

percent of change A percent that indicates how much a quantity increases or decreases with respect to the original amount. Percent of change, $p\% = \frac{\text{Amount of increase or decrease}}{\text{Original amount}}$ **porcentaje de cambio** Porcentaje que indica cuánto aumenta o disminuye una cantidad con respecto a la cantidad original. Porcentaje de cambio, $p\% = \frac{\text{Cantidad de aumento o disminución}}{\text{Cantidad original}}$	The percent of change, $p\%$, from 140 to 189 is: $p\% = \frac{189 - 140}{140} = \frac{49}{140} = 0.35 = 35\%$ El porcentaje de cambio, $p\%$, de 140 a 189 es: $p\% = \frac{189 - 140}{140} = \frac{49}{140} = 0.35 = 35\%$
percent of decrease The percent of change in a quantity when the new amount of the quantity is less than the original amount. **porcentaje de disminución** El porcentaje de cambio de una cantidad cuando la nueva cantidad es menor que la cantidad original.	*See* percent of change. *Ver* porcentaje de cambio.
percent of increase The percent of change in a quantity when the new amount of the quantity is greater than the original amount. **porcentaje de aumento** El porcentaje de cambio de una cantidad cuando la nueva cantidad es mayor que la cantidad original.	*See* percent of change. *Ver* porcentaje de cambio.
perfect square A number that is the square of an integer. **cuadrado perfecto** Número que es el cuadrado de un número entero.	49 is a perfect square, because $49 = 7^2$. 49 es un cuadrado perfecto ya que $49 = 7^2$.
perfect square trinomials Trinomials of the form $a^2 + 2ab + b^2$ and $a^2 - 2ab + b^2$. **trinomios cuadrados perfectos** Trinomios de la forma $a^2 + 2ab + b^2$ y $a^2 - 2ab + b^2$.	$x^2 + 6x + 9$ and $x^2 - 10x + 25$ are perfect square trinomials. $x^2 + 6x + 9$ y $x^2 - 10x + 25$ son trinomios cuadrados perfectos.
permutation An arrangement of objects in which order is important. **permutación** Disposición de objetos en la que el orden es importante.	There are 6 permutations of the numbers 1, 2, and 3: 123, 132, 213, 231, 312, and 321. Existen 6 permutaciones de los números 1, 2 y 3: 123, 132, 213, 231, 312 y 321.
perpendicular lines Two lines in the same plane that intersect to form a right angle. **rectas perpendiculares** Dos rectas del mismo plano que al cortarse forman un ángulo recto.	Horizontal and vertical lines are perpendicular to each other. Las rectas horizontales y verticales son perpendiculares entre sí.

ENGLISH-SPANISH GLOSSARY

point-slope form An equation of a nonvertical line written in the form $y - y_1 = m(x - x_1)$ where the line passes through a given point (x_1, y_1) and has a slope of m. **forma punto-pendiente** Ecuación de una recta no vertical escrita en la forma $y - y_1 = m(x - x_1)$, donde la recta pasa por un punto dado (x_1, y_1) y tiene pendiente m.	The equation $y + 3 = 2(x - 4)$ is in point-slope form. The graph of the equation is a line that passes through the point $(4, -3)$ and has a slope of 2. **La ecuación $y + 3 = 2(x - 4)$ está en la forma punto-pendiente. La gráfica de la ecuación es una recta que pasa por el punto $(4, -3)$ y tiene pendiente 2.**
polynomial A monomial or a sum of monomials, each called a term of the polynomial. **polinomio** Monomio o suma de monomios; cada uno se llama término del polinomio.	9, $2x^2 + x - 5$, and $7bc^3 + 4b^4c$ are polynomials. **9, $2x^2 + x - 5$ y $7bc^3 + 4b^4c$ son polinomios.**
population The entire group that you want information about. **población** El grupo entero sobre el que se desea información.	A magazine invites its readers to mail in answers to a questionnaire rating the magazine. The population consists of all the magazine's readers. **Una revista invita a sus lectores a enviar por correo las respuestas a un cuestionario sobre la calidad de la revista. La población está formada por todos los lectores de la revista.**
power An expression that represents repeated multiplication of the same factor. **potencia** Expresión que representa la multiplicación repetida del mismo factor.	81 is a power of 3, because $81 = 3 \cdot 3 \cdot 3 \cdot 3 = 3^4$. **81 es una potencia de 3 ya que $81 = 3 \cdot 3 \cdot 3 \cdot 3 = 3^4$.**
precision The level of detail that an instrument can measure. **precisión** Detalle de una medición, determinado por la unidad de medida.	The level of precision of a ruler is 1 mm. **El nivel de precisión de una regla es 1 mm.**
probability of an event A number from 0 to 1 that measures the likelihood, or chance, that the event will occur. **probabilidad de un suceso** Número de 0 a 1 que mide la posibilidad de que ocurra un suceso.	*See* experimental probability *and* theoretical probability. ***Ver* probabilidad experimental *y* probabilidad teórica.**
proportion An equation that states that two ratios are equivalent: $\frac{a}{b} = \frac{c}{d}$ where $b \neq 0$ and $d \neq 0$. **proporción** Ecuación que establece que dos razones son equivalentes: $\frac{a}{b} = \frac{c}{d}$ donde $b \neq 0$ y $d \neq 0$.	$\frac{3}{4} = \frac{6}{8}$ and $\frac{11}{6} = \frac{x}{30}$ are proportions. **$\frac{3}{4} = \frac{6}{8}$ y $\frac{11}{6} = \frac{x}{30}$ son proporciones.**

ENGLISH-SPANISH GLOSSARY

Pythagorean theorem If a triangle is a right triangle, then the sum of the squares of the lengths a and b of the legs equals the square of the length c of the hypotenuse: $a^2 + b^2 = c^2$.

teorema de Pitágoras Si un triángulo es rectángulo, entonces la suma de los cuadrados de las longitudes a y b de los catetos es igual al cuadrado de la longitud c de la hipotenusa: $a^2 + b^2 = c^2$.

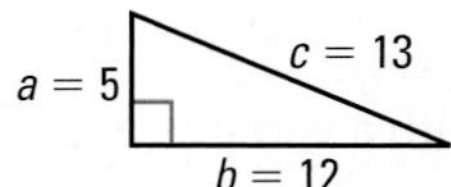

$5^2 + 12^2 = 13^2$

Q

quadrants The four regions into which the coordinate plane is divided by the x-axis and the y-axis.

cuadrantes Las cuatro regiones en las que el eje de x y el eje de y dividen al plano de coordenadas.

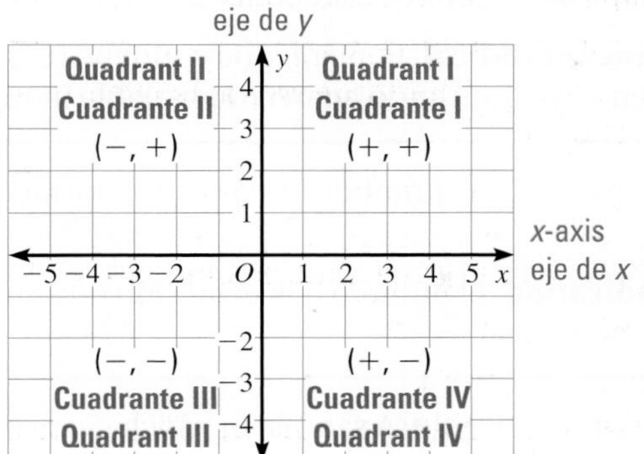

quadratic equation An equation that can be written in the standard form $ax^2 + bx + c = 0$ where $a \neq 0$.

ecuación cuadrática Ecuación que puede escribirse en la forma general $ax^2 + bx + c = 0$, donde $a \neq 0$.

The equations $x^2 - 2x = 3$ and $0.1x^2 = 40$ are quadratic equations.

$x^2 - 2x = 3$ y $0.1x^2 = 40$ son ecuaciones cuadráticas.

quadratic formula The formula below that can be used to find the solutions of the quadratic equation $ax^2 + bx + c = 0$ where $a \neq 0$ and $b^2 - 4ac \geq 0$:

$$x = \frac{-b \pm \sqrt{b^2 - 4ac}}{2a}$$

fórmula cuadrática La fórmula de abajo puede utilizarse para hallar las soluciones de la ecuación cuadrática $ax^2 + bx + c = 0$ donde $a \neq 0$ y $b^2 - 4ac \geq 0$:

$$x = \frac{-b \pm \sqrt{b^2 - 4ac}}{2a}$$

To solve $3x^2 + 5x - 8 = 0$, substitute 3 for a, 5 for b, and −8 for c in the quadratic formula:

$$x = \frac{-5 \pm \sqrt{5^2 - 4(3)(-8)}}{2(3)}$$

$x = 1$ **or** $x = -\frac{8}{3}$

Para resolver $3x^2 + 5x - 8 = 0$, sustituye a por 3, b por 5 y c por −8 en la fórmula cuadrática:

$$x = \frac{-5 \pm \sqrt{5^2 - 4(3)(-8)}}{2(3)}$$

$x = 1$ **ó** $x = -\frac{8}{3}$

quadratic function A nonlinear function that can be written in the standard form $y = ax^2 + bx + c$ where $a \neq 0$.

función cuadrática Función no lineal que puede escribirse en la forma general $y = ax^2 + bx + c$, donde $a \neq 0$.

$y = 2x^2 + 5x - 3$ is a quadratic function.

$y = 2x^2 + 5x - 3$ es una función cuadrática.

R

radical equation An equation that contains a radical expression with a variable in the radicand. **ecuación radical** Ecuación que contiene una expresión radical en cuyo radicando aparece una variable.	$2\sqrt{x} - 8 = 0$ and $\sqrt{3x - 17} = \sqrt{x + 21}$ are radical equations. $2\sqrt{x} - 8 = 0$ y $\sqrt{3x - 17} = \sqrt{x + 21}$ son ecuaciones radicales.
radical expression An expression that contains a radical, such as a square root, cube root, or other root. **expresión radical** Expresión que contiene un radical, como una raíz cuadrada, una raíz cúbica u otra raíz.	$3\sqrt{2x}$ and $\sqrt[3]{x - 1}$ are radical expressions. $3\sqrt{2x}$ y $\sqrt[3]{x - 1}$ son expresiones radicales.
radical function A function that contains a radical expression with the independent variable in the radicand. **función radical** Función que contiene una expresión radical y en cuyo radicando aparece la variable independiente.	$y = \sqrt[3]{2x}$ and $y = \sqrt{x + 2}$ are radical functions. $y = \sqrt[3]{2x}$ e $y = \sqrt{x + 2}$ son funciones radicales.
radicand The number or expression inside a radical symbol. **radicando** El número o la expresión que aparece bajo el signo radical.	The radicand of $\sqrt{9}$ and $-\sqrt{9}$ is 9. El radicando de $\sqrt{9}$ y $-\sqrt{9}$ es 9.
random sample A sample in which every member of the population has an equal chance of being selected. **muestra aleatoria** Muestra en la que cada miembro de la población tiene igual probabilidad de ser seleccionado.	You can select a random sample of a school's student population by having a computer randomly choose 100 student identification numbers. Para seleccionar una muestra aleatoria de la población de estudiantes de una escuela, puedes usar la computadora para elegir al azar 100 números de identificación estudiantil.
range of a data set The range of a numerical data set is a measure of dispersion. It is the difference of the greatest value and the least value. **rango de un conjunto de datos** El rango de un conjunto de datos numéricos es una medida de dispersión. Es la diferencia entre los valores mayor y menor.	The range of the data set 4, 7, 9, 11, 11, 12, 18 is $18 - 4 = 14$. El rango del conjunto de datos 4, 7, 9, 11, 11, 12, 18 es $18 - 4 = 14$.
range of a function The set of all outputs of a function. **rango de una función** El conjunto de todas las salidas de una función.	*See* function. *Ver* función.

ENGLISH-SPANISH GLOSSARY

rate A fraction that compares two quantities measured in different units. **relación** Fracción que compara dos cantidades medidas en unidades diferentes.	$\frac{110 \text{ miles}}{2 \text{ hours}}$ and $\frac{55 \text{ miles}}{1 \text{ hour}}$ are rates. $\frac{110 \text{ millas}}{2 \text{ horas}}$ y $\frac{55 \text{ millas}}{1 \text{ hora}}$ son relaciones.
rate of change A comparison of a change in one quantity with a change in another quantity. In real-world situations, you can interpret the slope of a line as a rate of change. **relación de cambio** Comparación entre el cambio producido en una cantidad y el cambio producido en otra cantidad. En situaciones de la vida real, se puede interpretar la pendiente de una recta como una relación de cambio.	You pay \$7 for 2 hours of computer use and \$14 for 4 hours of computer use. The rate of change is $\frac{\text{change in cost}}{\text{change in time}} = \frac{14-7}{4-2} = 3.5$, or \$3.50 per hour. Pagas \$7 por usar la computadora 2 horas y \$14 por usarla 4 horas. La relación de cambio es $\frac{\text{cambio en el costo}}{\text{cambio en el tiempo}} = \frac{14-7}{4-2} = 3.5$, o \$3.50 por hora.
ratio A comparison of two numbers using division. The ratio of a and b, where $b \neq 0$, can be written as a to b, as $a : b$, or as $\frac{a}{b}$. **razón** Comparacion de dos números mediante la división. La razón entre a y b, donde $b \neq 0$, puede escribirse a a b, $a : b$ o $\frac{a}{b}$.	The ratio of 5 wins to 2 losses can be written as 5 to 2, as 5 : 2, or as $\frac{5}{2}$. La razón de 5 victorias a 2 derrotas puede escribirse 5 a 2, 5 : 2 ó $\frac{5}{2}$.
rational equation An equation that contains one or more rational expressions. **ecuación racional** Ecuación que contiene una o más expresiones racionales.	The equations $\frac{6}{x+4} = \frac{x}{2}$ and $\frac{x}{x-2} + \frac{1}{5} = \frac{2}{x-2}$ are rational equations. $\frac{6}{x+4} = \frac{x}{2}$ y $\frac{x}{x-2} + \frac{1}{5} = \frac{2}{x-2}$ son ecuaciones racionales.
rational expression An expression that can be written as a ratio of two polynomials where the denominator is not 0. **expresión racional** Expresión que puede escribirse como razón de dos polinomios, donde el denominador no es 0.	$\frac{x+8}{10x}$ and $\frac{5}{x^2-1}$ are rational expressions. $\frac{x+8}{10x}$ y $\frac{5}{x^2-1}$ son expresiones racionales.
rational function A function whose rule is given by a fraction whose numerator and denominator are polynomials and whose denominator is not 0. **función racional** Función cuya regla viene dada por una fracción cuyo numerador y denominador son polinomios y cuyo denominador no es 0.	The equations $y = \frac{-1}{x}$ and $y = \frac{2x-1}{x-2}$ are rational functions. Las ecuaciones $y = \frac{-1}{x}$ e $y = \frac{2x-1}{x-2}$ son funciones racionales.

rationalizing the denominator The process of eliminating a radical from an expression's denominator by multiplying the expression by an appropriate form of 1.

To rationalize the denominator of $\frac{5}{\sqrt{7}}$, multiply the expression by $\frac{\sqrt{7}}{\sqrt{7}}$:

$$\frac{5}{\sqrt{7}} = \frac{5}{\sqrt{7}} \cdot \frac{\sqrt{7}}{\sqrt{7}} = \frac{5\sqrt{7}}{\sqrt{49}} = \frac{5\sqrt{7}}{7}$$

racionalizar el denominador El proceso de eliminar el radical del denominador de una expresión multiplicando la expresión por la forma apropiada de 1.

Para racionalizar el denominador de $\frac{5}{\sqrt{7}}$, multiplica la expresión por $\frac{\sqrt{7}}{\sqrt{7}}$:

$$\frac{5}{\sqrt{7}} = \frac{5}{\sqrt{7}} \cdot \frac{\sqrt{7}}{\sqrt{7}} = \frac{5\sqrt{7}}{\sqrt{49}} = \frac{5\sqrt{7}}{7}$$

---

real numbers The set of all rational and irrational numbers.

$8, -6.2, \frac{6}{7}, \pi$, and $\sqrt{2}$ are real numbers.

números reales El conjunto de todos los números racionales e irracionales.

$8, -6.2, \frac{6}{7}, \pi$ y $\sqrt{2}$ son números reales.

---

reflection A reflection flips a figure in a line.

reflexión Una reflexión vuelca una figura en una recta.

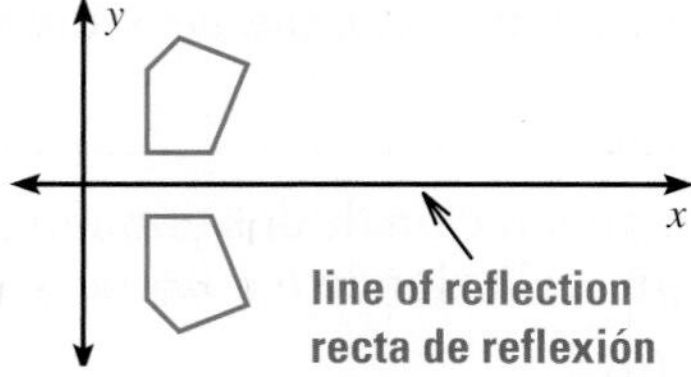

---

relation Any pairing of a set of inputs with a set of outputs.

relación Cualquier correspondencia establecida entre un conjunto de entradas y un conjunto de salidas.

The pairing in the table below is a relation, but it is *not* a function.

La correspondencia en la tabla de abajo es una relación, pero *no* es una función.

Input Entrada	4	4	5	6	7
Output Salida	0	1	2	3	4

---

residual The signed vertical distance between a data point and a line of fit.

residuo La diferencia vertical entre un dato y una línea de ajuste.

---

roots The solutions of an equation in which one side is zero and other side is a product of polynomial factors.

raíces Las soluciones de una ecuación en la que un lado es cero y el otro lado es el producto de factores polinómicos.

The roots of the equation $(x - 4)(x + 2) = 0$ are 4 and -2.

Las raíces de la ecuación $(x - 4)(x + 2) = 0$ son 4 y -2.

S

sample A part of a population. **muestra** Parte de una población.	To predict the results of an election, a survey is given to a sample of voters. **Para predecir los resultados de una elección, se realiza una encuesta entre una muestra de votantes.**
sample space The set of all possible outcomes. **espacio muestral** El conjunto de todos los casos posibles.	When you toss two coins, the sample space is heads, heads; heads, tails; tails, heads; and tails, tails. **Cuando lanzas al aire dos monedas, el espacio muestral es cara, cara; cara, cruz; cruz, cara; y cruz, cruz.**
scalar A real number by which you multiply a matrix. **escalar** Número real por el que se multiplica una matriz.	*See* scalar multiplication. ***Ver* multiplicación escalar.**
scalar multiplication Multiplication of each element in a matrix by a real number, called a scalar. **multiplicación escalar** Multiplicación de cada elemento de una matriz por un número real llamado escalar.	The matrix is multiplied by the scalar 3. $3\begin{bmatrix}1 & 2\\0 & -1\end{bmatrix}=\begin{bmatrix}3 & 6\\0 & -3\end{bmatrix}$ **La matriz se multiplica por el escalar 3.** $3\begin{bmatrix}1 & 2\\0 & -1\end{bmatrix}=\begin{bmatrix}3 & 6\\0 & -3\end{bmatrix}$
scale A ratio that relates the dimensions of a scale drawing or scale model and the actual dimensions. **escala** Razón que relaciona las dimensiones de un dibujo a escala o un modelo a escala con las dimensiones reales.	The scale 1 in. : 12 ft on a floor plan means that 1 inch in the floor plan represents an actual distance of 12 feet. **La escala 1 pulg : 12 pies en un diagrama de planta significa que 1 pulgada en el diagrama de planta representa una distancia real de 12 pies.**
scale drawing A two-dimensional drawing of an object in which the dimensions of the drawing are in proportion to the dimensions of the object. **dibujo a escala** Dibujo bidimensional de un objeto en el que las dimensiones del dibujo guardan proporción con las dimensiones del objeto.	A floor plan of a house is a scale drawing. **El diagrama de planta de una casa es un dibujo a escala.**
scale model A three-dimensional model of an object in which the dimensions of the model are in proportion to the dimensions of the object. **modelo a escala** Modelo tridimensional de un objeto en el que las dimensiones del modelo guardan proporción con las dimensiones del objeto.	A globe is a scale model of Earth. **El globo terráqueo es un modelo a escala de la Tierra.**

scatter plot A graph used to determine whether there is a relationship or trend between paired data. **diagrama de dispersión** Gráfica utilizada para determinar si hay una relación o tendencia entre los pares de datos.	
scientific notation A number is written in scientific notation when it is of the form $c \times 10^n$ where $1 \le c < 10$ and n is an integer. **notación científica** Un número está escrito en notación científica cuando es de la forma $c \times 10^n$, donde $1 \le c < 10$ y n es un número entero.	Two million is written in scientific notation as 2×10^6, and 0.547 is written in scientific notation as 5.47×10^{-1}. El número dos millones escrito en notación científica es 2×10^6, y 0.547 escrito en notación científica es 5.47×10^{-1}.
self-selected sample A sample in which members of the population select themselves by volunteering. **muestra autoseleccionada** Muestra en la que los miembros de la población se seleccionan a sí mismos ofreciéndose a participar.	You can obtain a self-selected sample of a school's student population by asking students to return surveys to a collection box. Para obtener una muestra autoseleccionada de la población de estudiantes de una escuela, puedes pedir a los estudiantes que hagan la encuesta que la depositen en un recipiente de recogida.
sequence An ordered list of numbers. **progresión** Lista ordenada de números.	−4, 1, 6, 11, 16, . . . is a sequence. −4, 1, 6, 11, 16, . . . es una progresión.
set A collection of distinct objects. **conjunto** Colección de objetos diferenciados.	The set of whole numbers is $W = \{0, 1, 2, 3, \ldots\}$. El conjunto de los números naturales es $W = \{0, 1, 2, 3, \ldots\}$.
significant digits The digits used to express the precision of a measurement. **dígitos significativos** Dígitos usados para expresar la precisión de una medida.	The number 3.5 has two significant digits. El numero 3.5 tiene dos digitos significados.

simplest form of a radical expression A radical expression that has no perfect square factors other than 1 in the radicand, no fractions in the radicand, and no radicals appearing in the denominator of a fraction.

In simplest form, $\sqrt{32}$ is written as $4\sqrt{2}$, and $\frac{5}{\sqrt{7}}$ is written as $\frac{5\sqrt{7}}{7}$.

forma más simple de una expresión radical Expresión radical que no tiene en el radicando fracciones ni factores cuadrados perfectos distintos de 1 y que no tiene radicales en el denominador de las fracciones.

En la forma más simple, $\sqrt{32}$ se escribe $4\sqrt{2}$, y $\frac{5}{\sqrt{7}}$ se escribe $\frac{5\sqrt{7}}{7}$.

simplest form of a rational expression A rational expression whose numerator and denominator have no factors in common other than 1.

The simplest form of $\frac{2x}{x(x-3)}$ is $\frac{2}{x-3}$.

forma más simple de una expresión racional Expresión racional cuyo numerador y denominador no tienen más factores en común que el 1.

La forma más simple de $\frac{2x}{x(x-3)}$ es $\frac{2}{x-3}$.

simulation An experiment that you can perform to make predictions about real-world situations.

Each box of Oaties contains 1 of 6 prizes. The probability of getting each prize is $\frac{1}{6}$. To predict the number of boxes of cereal you must buy to win all 6 prizes, you can roll a number cube 1 time for each box of cereal you buy. Keep rolling until you have rolled all 6 numbers.

simulación Experimento que se puede realizar para hacer predicciones sobre situaciones de la vida real.

Cada paquete de Oaties contiene 1 de un total de 6 premios. La probabilidad de obtener cada premio es $\frac{1}{6}$. Para predecir el número de paquetes de cereales que debes comprar para poder conseguir los 6 premios, puedes lanzar un cubo numerado 1 vez por cada paquete de cereales que compres. Sigue lanzando el cubo hasta obtener los 6 números.

slope The slope m of a nonvertical line is the ratio of the vertical change (the *rise*) to the horizontal change (the *run*) between any two points (x_1, y_1) and (x_2, y_2) on the line: $m = \frac{y_2 - y_1}{x_2 - x_1}$.

pendiente La pendiente m de una recta no vertical es la razón del cambio vertical (*distancia vertical*) al cambio horizontal (*distancia horizontal*) entre dos puntos cualesquiera (x_1, y_1) y (x_2, y_2) de la recta: $m = \frac{y_2 - y_1}{x_2 - x_1}$.

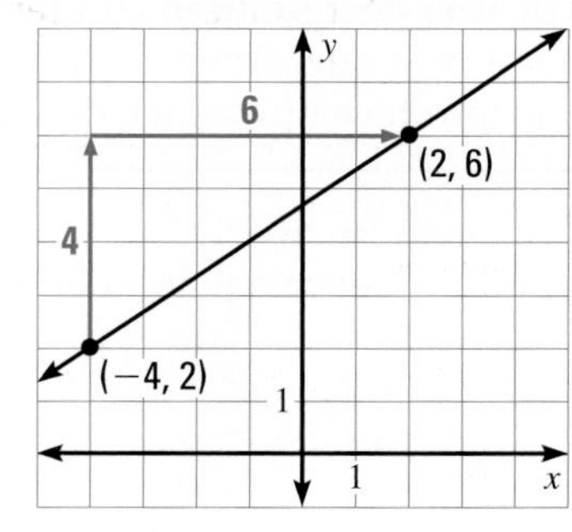

The slope of the line shown is $\frac{4}{6}$, or $\frac{2}{3}$.

La pendiente de la recta indicada es $\frac{4}{6}$, ó $\frac{2}{3}$.

slope-intercept form A linear equation written in the form $y = mx + b$ where m is the slope and b is the y-intercept of the equation's graph.	$y = 3x + 4$ is in slope-intercept form. The slope of the line is 3, and the y-intercept is 4.
forma pendiente-intercepto Ecuación lineal escrita en la forma $y = mx + b$, donde m es la pendiente y b es el intercepto en y de la gráfica de la ecuación.	**$y = 3x + 4$ está en la forma pendiente-intercepto. La pendiente de la recta es 3, y el intercepto en y es 4.**
solution of an equation in one variable A number that produces a true statement when substituted for the variable in an equation.	The number 3 is a solution of the equation $8 - 2x = 2$, because $8 - 2(3) = 2$.
solución de una ecuación con una variable Número que, al sustituirse por la variable de la ecuación, produce un enunciado verdadero.	**El número 3 es una solución de la ecuación $8 - 2x = 2$ ya que $8 - 2(3) = 2$.**
solution of an equation in two variables An ordered pair that produces a true statement when the coordinates of the ordered pair are substituted for the variables in the equation.	$(1, -4)$ is a solution of $3x - y = 7$, because $3(1) - (-4) = 7$.
solución de una ecuación con dos variables Par ordenado que, al ser sustituidas sus coordenadas por las variables de la ecuación, produce un enunciado verdadero.	**$(1, -4)$ es una solución de $3x - y = 7$ ya que $3(1) - (-4) = 7$.**
solution of an inequality in one variable A number that produces a true statement when substituted for the variable in an inequality.	The number 3 is a solution of the inequality $5 + 3n \leq 20$, because $5 + 3(3) = 14$ and $14 \leq 20$.
solución de una desigualdad con una variable Número que, al sustituirse por la variable de la desigualdad, produce un enunciado verdadero.	**El número 3 es una solución de la desigualdad $5 + 3n \leq 20$ ya que $5 + 3(3) = 14$ y $14 \leq 20$.**
solution of an inequality in two variables x and y An ordered pair (x, y) that produces a true statement when the values of x and y are substituted into the inequality.	$(-1, 2)$ is a solution of the inequality $x - 3y < 6$ because $-1 - 3(2) = -7$ and $-7 < 6$.
solución de una desigualdad con las dos variables x e y Par ordenado (x, y) que, al sustitutirse los valores de x e y en la desigualdad, produce un enunciado verdadero.	**$(-1, 2)$ es una solución de la desigualdad $x - 3y < 6$ ya que $-1 - 3(2) = -7$ y $-7 < 6$.**
solution of a system of linear equations An ordered pair that is a solution of each equation in the system.	$(3, 2)$ is a solution of the system of linear equations $x + 2y = 7$, $3x - 2y = 5$ because each equation is a true statement when 3 is substituted for x and 2 is substituted for y.
solución de un sistema de ecuaciones lineales Par ordenado que es una solución de cada ecuación del sistema.	**$(3, 2)$ es una solución del sistema de ecuaciones lineales $x + 2y = 7$, $3x - 2y = 5$ ya que cada ecuación es un enunciado verdadero cuando x se sustituye por 3 e y se sustituye por 2.**

solution of a system of linear inequalities An ordered pair that is a solution of each inequality in the system. **solución de un sistema de desigualdades lineales** Par ordenado que es una solución de cada desigualdad del sistema.	**(6, −5) is a solution of the system of inequalities $x - y > 7$, $2x + y < 8$ because each inequality is a true statement when 6 is substituted for x and −5 is substituted for y.** **(6, −5) es una solución del sistema de desigualdades $x - y > 7$, $2x + y < 8$ ya que cada desigualdad es un enunciado verdadero cuando x se sustituye por 6 e y se sustituye por −5.**
square root If $b^2 = a$, then b is a square root of a. The radical symbol $\sqrt{\ }$ represents a nonnegative square root. **raíz cuadrada** Si $b^2 = a$, entonces b es una raíz cuadrada de a. El signo radical $\sqrt{\ }$ representa una raíz cuadrada no negativa.	**The square roots of 9 are 3 and −3, because $3^2 = 9$ and $(-3)^2 = 9$. So, $\sqrt{9} = 3$ and $-\sqrt{9} = -3$.** **Las raíces cuadradas de 9 son 3 y −3 ya que $3^2 = 9$ y $(-3)^2 = 9$. Así pues, $\sqrt{9} = 3$ y $-\sqrt{9} = -3$.**
square root function A radical function whose equation contains a square root with the independent variable in the radicand. **función con raíz cuadrada** Función radical representada por una ecuación con una raíz cuadrada en cuyo radicando aparece la variable independiente.	**$y = 2\sqrt{x+2}$ and $y = \sqrt{x} + 3$ are square root functions.** **$y = 2\sqrt{x+2}$ e $y = \sqrt{x} + 3$ son funciones con raíz cuadrada.**
standard deviation The standard deviation of a numerical data set $x_1, x_2, \ldots, x_n$ is a measure of dispersion denoted by σ and computed as the square root of the variance. $\sigma = \sqrt{\frac{(x_1 - \overline{x})^2 + (x_2 - \overline{x})^2 + \ldots + (x_n - \overline{x})^2}{n}}$ **desviación típica** La desviación típica de un conjunto de datos numéricos $x_1, x_2, \ldots, x_n$ es una medida de dispersión designada por σ y calculada como raíz cuadrada de la varianza. $\sigma = \sqrt{\frac{(x_1 - \overline{x})^2 + (x_2 - \overline{x})^2 + \ldots + (x_n - \overline{x})^2}{n}}$	**The standard deviation of the data set 3, 9, 13, 23 (with mean = 12) is:** $\sigma = \sqrt{\frac{(3-12)^2 + (9-12)^2 + (13-12)^2 + (23-12)^2}{4}} = \sqrt{53} \approx 7.3$ **La desviación típica del conjunto de datos 3, 9, 13, 23 (con media = 12) es:** $\sigma = \sqrt{\frac{(3-12)^2 + (9-12)^2 + (13-12)^2 + (23-12)^2}{4}} = \sqrt{53} \approx 7.3$
standard form of a linear equation $Ax + By = C$, where A, B, and C are real numbers and A and B are not both zero. **forma general de una ecuación lineal** $Ax + By = C$, donde A, B y C son números reales, y A y B no son ambos cero.	**The linear equation $y = 2x - 3$ can be written in standard form as $2x - y = 3$.** **La ecuación lineal $y = 2x - 3$ puede escribirse en la forma general como $2x - y = 3$.**

ENGLISH-SPANISH GLOSSARY

standard form of a quadratic equation A quadratic equation in the form $ax^2 + bx + c = 0$ where $a \neq 0$. **forma general de una ecuación cuadrática** Ecuación cuadrática de la forma $ax^2 + bx + c = 0$, donde $a \neq 0$.	The quadratic equation $x^2 - 2x - 3 = 0$ is in standard form. La ecuación cuadrática $x^2 - 2x - 3 = 0$ está en la forma general.
standard form of a quadratic function A quadratic function in the form $y = ax^2 + bx + c$ where $a \neq 0$. **forma general de una función cuadrática** Función cuadrática de la forma $y = ax^2 + bx + c$, donde $a \neq 0$.	The quadratic function $y = 2x^2 + 5x - 3$ is in standard form. La función cuadrática $y = 2x^2 + 5x - 3$ está en la forma general.
stem-and-leaf plot A data display that organizes data based on their digits. **tabla arborescente** Presentación de datos que organiza los datos basándose en sus dígitos.	Stem / Raíces | Leaves / Hojas 0 | 8 9 1 | 0 2 3 4 5 5 5 9 2 | 1 1 5 9 Key: / Clave: 1 | 9 = $19
stratified random sample A sample in which a population is divided into distinct groups, and members are selected at random from each group. **muestra aleatoria estratificada** Muestra en la que la población está dividida en grupos diferenciados, y los miembros de cada grupo se seleccionan al azar.	You can select a stratified random sample of a school's student population by having a computer randomly choose 25 students from each grade level. Para seleccionar una muestra aleatoria estratificada de la población de estudiantes de una escuela, puedes usar la computadora para elegir al azar a 25 estudiantes de cada grado.
survey A study of one or more characteristics of a group. **encuesta** Estudio de una o más características de un grupo.	A magazine invites its readers to mail in answers to a questionnaire rating the magazine. Una revista invita a sus lectores a enviar por correo las respuestas a un cuestionario sobre la calidad de la revista.
system of linear equations Two or more linear equations in the same variables; also called a *linear system.* **sistema de ecuaciones lineales** Dos o más ecuaciones lineales con las mismas variables; llamado también *sistema lineal.*	The equations below form a system of linear equations: $x + 2y = 7$ $3x - 2y = 5$ Las siguientes ecuaciones forman un sistema de ecuaciones lineales: $x + 2y = 7$ $3x - 2y = 5$

system of linear inequalities in two variables Two or more linear inequalities in the same variables; also called a *system of inequalities.*

The inequalities below form a system of linear inequalities in two variables:

$$x - y > 7$$
$$2x + y < 8$$

sistema de desigualdades lineales con dos variables Dos o más desigualdades lineales con las mismas variables; llamado también *sistema de desigualdades.*

Las siguientes desigualdades forman un sistema de desigualdades lineales con dos variables:

$$x - y > 7$$
$$2x + y < 8$$

---

systematic sample A sample in which a rule is used to select members of the population.

You can select a systematic sample of a school's student population by choosing every tenth student on an alphabetical list of all students at the school.

muestra sistemática Muestra en la que se usa una regla para seleccionar a los miembros de la población.

Para seleccionar una muestra sistemática de la población de estudiantes de una escuela, puedes elegir a cada décimo estudiante de una lista ordenada alfabéticamente de todos los estudiantes de la escuela.

terms of an expression The parts of an expression that are added together.

The terms of the expression $3x + (-4) + (-6x) + 2$ are $3x$, -4, $-6x$, and 2.

términos de una expresión Las partes de una expresión que se suman.

Los términos de la expresión $3x + (-4) + (-6x) + 2$ son $3x$, -4, $-6x$ y 2.

---

theoretical probability When all outcomes are equally likely, the theoretical probability of an event is the ratio of the number of favorable outcomes to the total number of possible outcomes. The probability of event *A* is written as *P*(*A*).

A bag of 20 marbles contains 8 red marbles. The theoretical probability of randomly choosing a red marble from the bag is $\frac{8}{20} = \frac{2}{5}$, 40%, or 0.4.

probabilidad teórica Cuando todos los casos son igualmente posibles, la probabilidad teórica de un suceso es la razón entre el número de casos favorables y el número total de casos posibles. La probabilidad del suceso *A* se escribe *P*(*A*).

Una bolsa de 20 canicas contiene 8 canicas rojas. La probabilidad teórica de sacar al azar una canica roja de la bolsa es $\frac{8}{20} = \frac{2}{5}$, 40% ó 0.4.

---

transformation For a given set of points, a transformation produces an image by applying a rule to the coordinates of the points.

Translations, vertical stretches, vertical shrinks, and reflections are transformations.

transformación Para un conjunto dado de puntos, una transformación produce una imagen al aplicar una regla a las coordenadas de los puntos.

Las traslaciones, las expansiones verticales, las contracciones verticales y las reflexiones son transformaciones.

translation A translation moves every point in a figure the same distance in the same direction.

traslación Una traslación desplaza cada punto de una figura la misma distancia en la misma dirección.

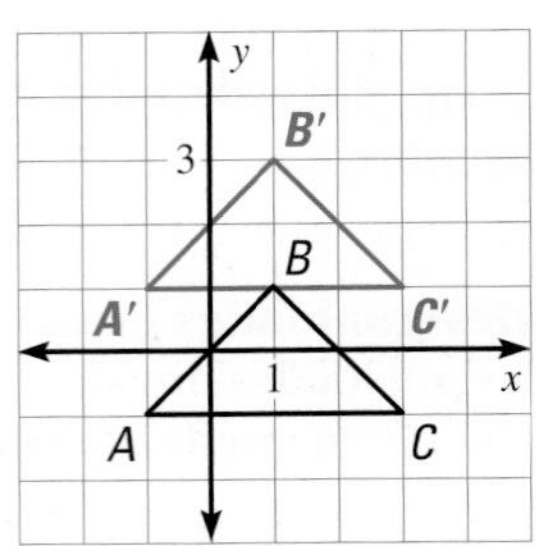

△*ABC* is translated up 2 units.

△*ABC* es trasladada 2 unidades hacia arriba.

trinomial A polynomial with three terms.

trinomio Polinomio con tres términos.

$2x^2 + x - 5$ is a trinomial.

$2x^2 + x - 5$ es un trinomio.

union The union of two sets *A* and *B* is the set of all elements in *either A* or *B*. The union of *A* and *B* is written as $A \cup B$.

unión La unión de dos conjuntos *A* y *B* es el conjunto de todos los elementos en *A o B*. La unión de *A* y *B* se escribe $A \cup B$.

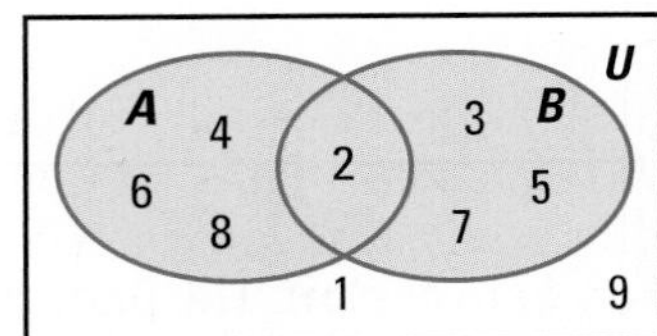

$A \cup B = \{2, 3, 4, 5, 6, 7, 8\}$

unit rate A rate in which the denominator of the fraction is 1 unit.

relación unitaria Relación en la que el denominador de la fracción es 1 unidad.

$\frac{55 \text{ miles}}{1 \text{ hour}}$, or 55 mi/h, is a unit rate.

$\frac{55 \text{ millas}}{1 \text{ hora}}$, ó 55 mi/h, es una relación unitaria.

universal set The set of all elements under consideration, written as *U*.

conjunto universal El conjunto de todos los elementos en cuestión, escrito *U*.

If the universal set is the set of positive integers, then $U = \{1, 2, 3, \ldots\}$.

Si el conjunto universal es el conjunto de los números enteros positivos, entonces $U = \{1, 2, 3, \ldots\}$.

upper quartile The median of the upper half of an ordered data set.

The upper quartile of the data set below is 23.

median ↓ (17), upper quartile ↓ (23)

8 10 14 17 20 23 50

cuartil superior La mediana de la mitad superior de un conjunto de datos ordenados.

El cuartil superior del siguiente conjunto de datos es 23.

mediana ↓ (17), cuartil superior ↓ (23)

8 10 14 17 20 23 50

V

variable A letter that is used to represent one or more numbers.

variable Letra que sirve para representar uno o más números.

In the expressions $5n$, $n + 1$, and $8 - n$, the letter n is the variable.

En las expresiones $5n$, $n + 1$ y $8 - n$, la letra n es la variable.

variance The variance of a numerical data set $x_1, x_2, \ldots, x_n$ is a measure of dispersion denoted by σ^2 and given by:

$$\sigma^2 = \frac{(x_1 - \overline{x})^2 + (x_2 - \overline{x})^2 + \ldots + (x_n - \overline{x})^2}{n}$$

varianza La varianza de un conjunto de datos numéricos $x_1, x_2, \ldots, x_n$ es una medida de dispersión designada por σ^2 y dada por:

$$\sigma^2 = \frac{(x_1 - \overline{x})^2 + (x_2 - \overline{x})^2 + \ldots + (x_n - \overline{x})^2}{n}$$

The variance of the data set 3, 9, 13, 23 (with mean = 12) is:

$$\sigma^2 = \frac{(3-12)^2 + (9-12)^2 + (13-12)^2 + (23-12)^2}{4}$$
$$= 53$$

La varianza del conjunto de datos 3, 9, 13, 23 (con media = 12) es:

$$\sigma^2 = \frac{(3-12)^2 + (9-12)^2 + (13-12)^2 + (23-12)^2}{4}$$
$$= 53$$

verbal model A verbal model describes a real-world situation using words as labels and using math symbols to relate the words.

modelo verbal Un modelo verbal describe una situación de la vida real mediante palabras que la exponen y símbolos matemáticos que relacionan esas palabras.

A verbal model and algebraic expression for dividing a dollars in a tip jar among 6 people:

Un modelo verbal y una expresión algebraica utilizados para dividir entre 6 personas a dólares del recipiente de las propinas:

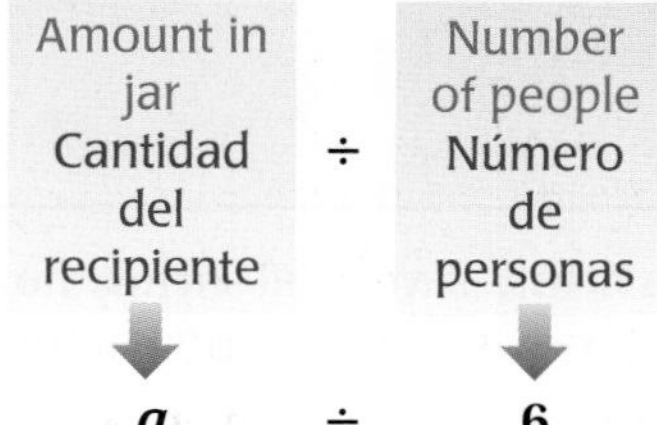

vertex form of a quadratic function A quadratic function in the form $y = a(x - h)^2 + k$ where $a \neq 0$. The vertex of the graph of the function is (h, k).

forma de vértice de una función cuadrática Función cuadrática de la forma $y = a(x - h)^2 + k$, donde $a \neq 0$. El vértice de la gráfica de la función es (h, k).

The quadratic function $y = -2(x + 1)^2 - 5$ is in vertex form. The vertex of the graph of the function is $(-1, -5)$.

La función cuadrática $y = -2(x + 1)^2 - 5$ está en la forma de vértice. El vértice de la gráfica de la función es $(-1, -5)$.

vertex of a parabola The lowest or highest point on a parabola.

vértice de una parábola El punto más bajo o más alto de la parábola.

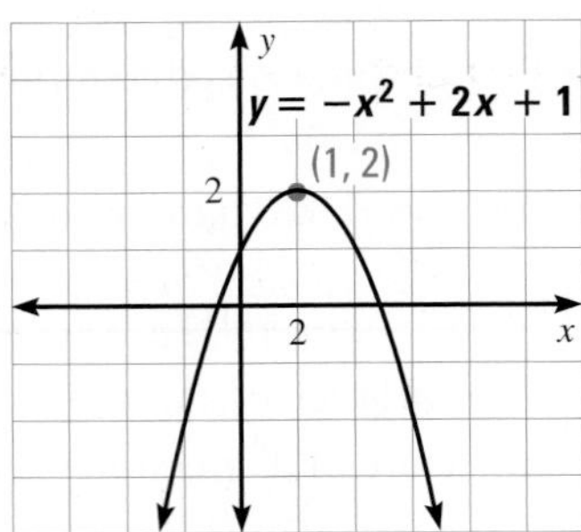

The vertex of the graph of $y = -x^2 + 2x + 1$ is the point (1, 2).

El vértice de la gráfica de $y = -x^2 + 2x + 1$ es el punto (1, 2).

vertical motion model A model for the height of an object that is propelled into the air but has no power to keep itself in the air.

modelo de movimiento vertical Modelo para representar la altura de un objeto que es lanzado hacia arriba pero que no tiene potencia para mantenerse en el aire.

The vertical motion model for an object thrown upward with an initial vertical velocity of 20 feet per second from an initial height of 8 feet is $h = -16t^2 + 20t + 8$ where h is the height (in feet) of the object t seconds after it is thrown.

El modelo de movimiento vertical de un objeto lanzado hacia arriba con una velocidad vertical inicial de 20 pies por segundo desde una altura inicial de 8 pies es $h = -16t^2 + 20t + 8$, donde h es la altura (en pies) del objeto t segundos después del lanzamiento.

vertical shrink A vertical shrink moves every point in a figure toward the x-axis, while points on the x-axis remain fixed.

contracción vertical La contracción vertical desplaza cada punto de una figura en dirección del eje de x, mientras los puntos del eje de x permanecen fijos.

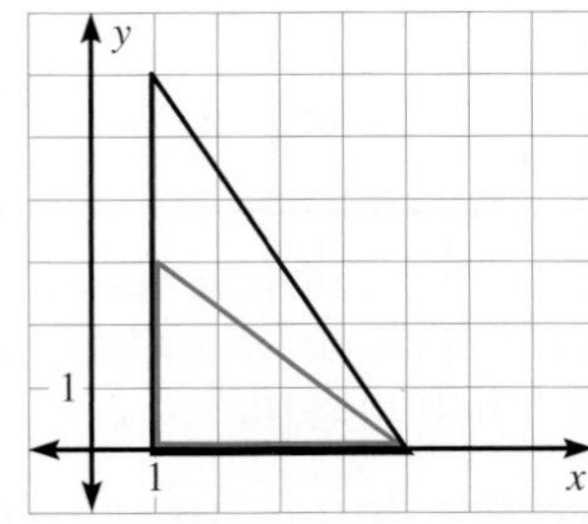

The black triangle is shrunk vertically to the green triangle.

El triángulo negro se contrae verticalmente hacia el triángulo verde.

vertical stretch A vertical stretch moves every point in a figure away from the x-axis, while points on the x-axis remain fixed.

expansión vertical La expansión vertical desplaza cada punto de una figura alejándose del eje de x, mientras los puntos del eje de x permanecen fijos.

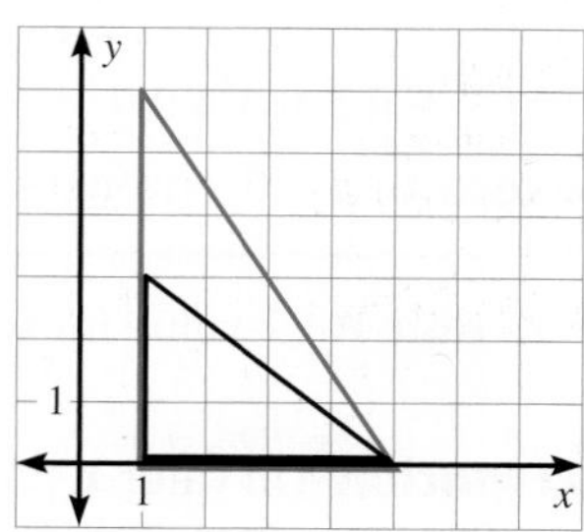

The black triangle is stretched vertically to the green triangle.

El triángulo negro se expande verticalmente hacia el triángulo verde.

whole numbers The numbers 0, 1, 2, 3, ...

números naturales Los números 0, 1, 2, 3, ...

0, 8, and 106 are whole numbers.
−1 and 0.6 are *not* whole numbers.

0, 8 y 106 son números naturales.
−1 y 0.6 *no* son números naturales.

x-intercept The x-coordinate of a point where a graph crosses the x-axis.

intercepto en x La coordenada x de un punto donde la gráfica corta al eje de x.

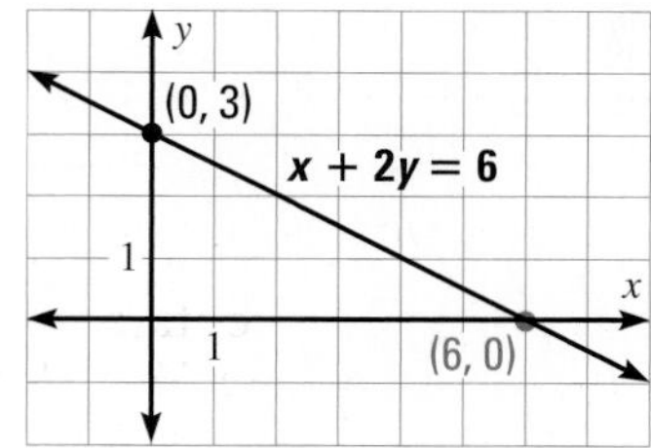

The x-intercept is 6.

El intercepto en x es 6.

y-intercept The y-coordinate of a point where a graph crosses the y-axis.

intercepto en y La coordenada y de un punto donde la gráfica corta al eje de y.

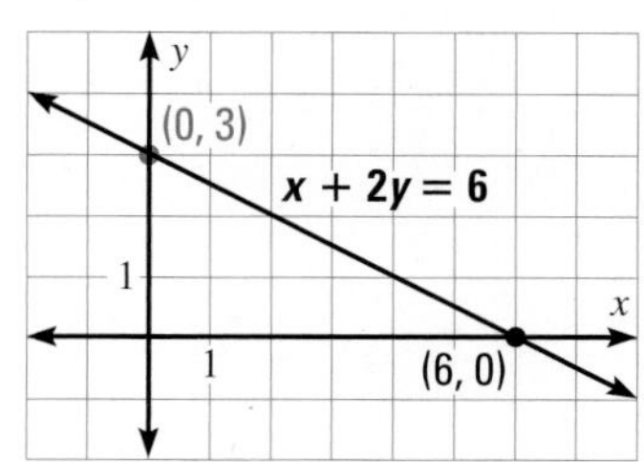

The y-intercept is 3.

El intercepto en y es 3.

ENGLISH-SPANISH GLOSSARY

Z

zero exponent If $a \neq 0$, then $a^0 = 1$. **exponente cero** Si $a \neq 0$, entonces $a^0 = 1$.	$(-7)^0 = 1$
zero of a function An x-value for which $f(x) = 0$ (or $y = 0$). **cero de una función** Un valor x para el que $f(x) = 0$ (o $y = 0$).	The zero of $f(x) = 2x - 4$ is 2 because $f(2) = 0$. El cero de $f(x) = 2x - 4$ es 2 ya que $f(2) = 0$.

Index

B

C

INDEX

D

INDEX

E

INDEX

INDEX

Q

R

S

T

U

V

INDEX

INDEX

Worked-Out Solutions

This section of the book provides step-by-step solutions to exercises with circled exercise numbers. These solutions provide models that can help guide your work with the homework exercises.

The separate **Selected Answers** section follows this section. It provides numerous answers that you can use to check your own answers.

Chapter 1

Lesson 1.1

19. three tenths to the fourth power; $(0.3)^4 = 0.3 \cdot 0.3 \cdot 0.3 \cdot 0.3$

35. $\left(\frac{3}{5}\right)^3 = \frac{3}{5} \cdot \frac{3}{5} \cdot \frac{3}{5} = \frac{27}{125}$

51. a. Total length $= 3.5 + 5.5 + 3 = 12$

The total length is 12 inches.

b. Evaluate $12f$ for $f = 12$: $12(12) = 144$

The area of water surface needed is 144 square inches.

Lesson 1.2

16. $\frac{1}{6}(6 + 18) - 2^2 = \frac{1}{6}(24) - 2^2$

$= \frac{1}{6}(24) - 4$

$= 4 - 4 = 0$

35. a. Total cost $= 3 \cdot 0.99 + 2 \cdot 9.95$

$= 2.97 + 19.90 = 22.87$

The total cost is \$22.87.

b. Amount of money left $= 25 - 22.87 = 2.13$

The amount you have left is \$2.13.

Lesson 1.3

11. 7 less than twice a number k

Less than is subtraction after the next term, and twice a number is two times a number. The expression is $2k - 7$.

21. [Number of months in y years] = [Number of months in one year] • [Number of years]

$= 12y$

The number of months is $12y$.

33. a. 48 ounce container:

$\frac{\$2.64}{48 \text{ ounces}} = \frac{\$2.64 \div 48}{48 \text{ ounces} \div 48} = \frac{\$.055}{1 \text{ ounce}}$

The unit rate is \$.055 per ounce.

64 ounce container:

$\frac{\$3.84}{64 \text{ ounces}} = \frac{\$3.84 \div 64}{64 \text{ ounces} \div 64} = \frac{\$.06}{1 \text{ ounce}}$

The unit rate is \$.06 per ounce.

b. Since \$.055 is less than \$.06, the 48 ounce container costs less per ounce.

c. Write a verbal model and an expression. Let n be the number of ounces.

[Savings] = [Unit rate for 64 ounce container] • [Number of ounces] − [Unit rate for 48 ounce container] • [Number of ounces]

$= 0.06n - 0.055n$

Evaluate the expression when $n = 192$.

$0.06(192) - 0.055(192) = 0.96$

The amount of money you save is \$.96.

Lesson 1.4

7. 5 more than a number t is written as $t + 5$.

The product of 9 and the quantity 5 more than a number t is written as $9(t + 5)$.

The product of 9 and the quantity 5 more than a number t is less than 6 is written as $9(t + 5) < 6$.

Worked-Out Solutions

41. Write a verbal model. Then write an equation. Let w be the winning team's time.

U.S. team's time	$-$	Winning team's time	$=$	Difference in time

$173 - w = 6$

Use mental math to solve the equation. Think: 173 less what number is 6?

Because $173 - 167 = 6$, the solution is 167 hours.

Lesson 1.5

5. You know that the temperature in Rome, Italy, is 30°C, and the temperature in Dallas, Texas, is 83°F.

You want to find out which temperature is higher.

17. Step 1: You know the total weight of your backpack and its contents is $13\frac{3}{8}$ pounds. The total weight you want to carry is no more than 15 pounds. The weight of each bottle of water is $\frac{3}{4}$ pound. You want to find out how many extra bottles of water you can add to your backpack. First find the additional weight you can add to your backpack.

Step 2: Write a verbal model that represents what you want to find out. Then write an equation and solve it.

Step 3: Let w be the additional weight (in pounds) you can add to your backpack.

Desired weight of backpack	$-$	Current weight of backpack	$=$	Additional weight possible

$$15 - 13\frac{3}{8} = w$$

$$1\frac{5}{8} = w$$

You can carry an additional $1\frac{5}{8}$ pounds, and each bottle weighs $\frac{3}{4}$ pound.

$$1\frac{5}{8} \div \frac{3}{4} = \frac{13}{8} \times \frac{4}{3} = \frac{52}{24} = 2\frac{1}{6}$$

Since you cannot carry a fraction of a bottle, round down to 2 bottles.

Step 4: You know that 2 is a solution; check to see if 3 could be a solution. The additional bottle of water weighs $\frac{3}{4}$ pound. Since $14\frac{7}{8}$ pounds is only $\frac{1}{8}$ pound less than the maximum of 15 pounds, and $\frac{3}{4} > \frac{1}{8}$, adding another bottle weighing $\frac{3}{4}$ pound would make the total weight more than 15 pounds. Therefore, the number of extra bottles of water you can add to your backpack is 2 bottles.

Lesson 1.6

3. The units are the same. Because tenths are smaller than ones, 14.2 gallons is more precise.

11. None of the digits are zero, so each digit is significant. There are 4 significant digits.

21.
$$\begin{array}{r} 1 \\ 97.\not{2}0 \\ -16.04 \\ \hline 81.16 \end{array}$$

33. The units are the same. Hundredths are smaller than tenths, so 8.05 is more precise; Justine.

Lesson 1.7

7. The pairing is not a function because the input $\frac{3}{4}$ is paired with two outputs, 3 and 5.

23. You have 10 quarters that you can use for a parking meter.

a. Each time you put 1 quarter in the meter, you have 1 less quarter, so <u>the number of quarters left</u> is a function of <u>the number of quarters used</u>.

b. Let y represent the number of quarters you have left.

Number of quarters you have left	$=$	Total number of quarters	$-$	Number of quarters you have used so far

$y = 10 - x$

The domain of the function is: 0, 1, 2, 3, 4, 5, 6, 7, 8, 9, and 10.

c. Make a table of inputs, x, and use $y = 10 - x$ to find the corresponding outputs.

Input, *x*	0	1	2	3	4	5
Output, *y*	10	9	8	7	6	5

Input, *x*	6	7	8	9	10
Output, *y*	4	3	2	1	0

The range of the function is: 0, 1, 2, 3, 4, 5, 6, 7, 8, 9, and 10.

Lesson 1.8

3. Make an input-output table using the given domain values.

x	0	1	2	3	4	5
y	3	4	5	6	7	8

Plot a point for each ordered pair (x, y).

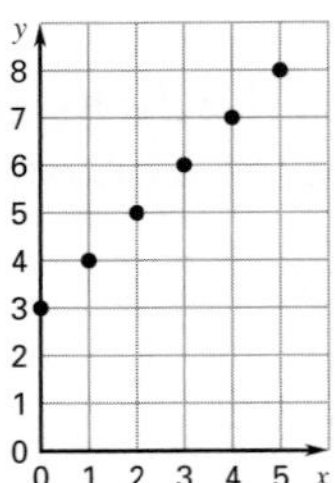

17. Number of voters v as a function of time t in years since 1984.

Years since 1984	Voters	Voters (millions)
0	92,652,680	93
4	91,594,693	92
8	104,405,155	104
12	96,456,345	96
16	105,586,274	106

The t-values range from 0 to 16, so label the t-axis from 0 to 18 in increments of 2 units. The v-values (in millions) range from 93 to 106, so label the v-axis from 90 to 114 in increments of 4 units.

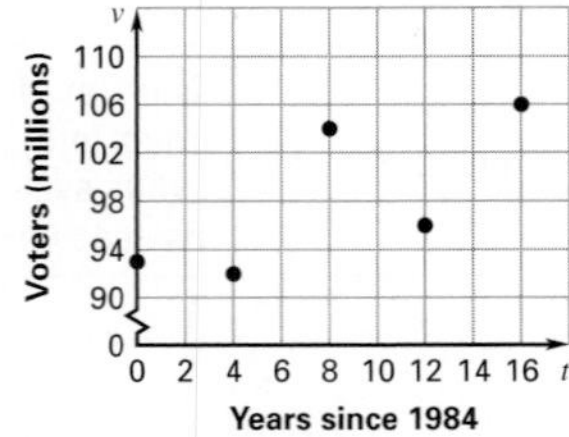

Worked-Out Solutions

This section of the book provides step-by-step solutions to exercises with circled exercise numbers. These solutions provide models that can help guide your work with the homework exercises.

The separate **Selected Answers** section follows this section. It provides numerous answers that you can use to check your own answers.

Chapter 2

Lesson 2.1

9. Since $50^2 = 2500$, $\pm\sqrt{2500} = \pm 50$.

19. Write a compound inequality that compares $-\sqrt{86}$ with both $-\sqrt{100}$ and $-\sqrt{81}$.

$-\sqrt{100} < -\sqrt{86} < -\sqrt{81}$

Take the square root of each number.

$-10 < -\sqrt{86} < -9$

Because 86 is closer to 81 than to 100, $-\sqrt{86}$ is closer to -9 than to -10. So $-\sqrt{86}$ is about -9.

47. You need to find the side length s of the mazes such that s^2 is the given area in square feet, so s is the positive square root of the area. Then identify the side length as rational or irrational.

Dallas: $s^2 = 1225$, $s = 35$; rational

San Francisco: $s^2 = 576$, $s = 24$; rational

Corona: $s^2 = 2304$, $s = 48$; rational

Waterville: $s^2 = 900$, $s = 30$; rational

The side lengths are 35 feet, 24 feet, 48 feet, and 30 feet. All the lengths are rational numbers.

Lesson 2.2

13.
$$-2 = n - 6$$
$$-2 + 6 = n - 6 + 6$$
$$4 = n$$

55. Let w represent the width of the trampoline.

$$A = \ell \cdot w$$
$$187 = 17 \cdot w$$
$$\frac{187}{17} = \frac{17w}{17}$$
$$11 = w$$

The width of the trampoline is 11 feet.

Lesson 2.3

13.
$$7 = \frac{5}{6}c - 8$$
$$7 + 8 = \frac{5}{6}c - 8 + 8$$
$$15 = \frac{5}{6}c$$
$$\frac{6}{5} \cdot 15 = \frac{6}{5} \cdot \frac{5}{6}c$$
$$18 = c$$

19.
$$-32 = -5k + 13k$$
$$-32 = 8k$$
$$\frac{-32}{8} = \frac{8k}{8}$$
$$-4 = k$$

39. Write a verbal model. Then write an equation. Let h be the number of half-side advertisements.

[Total budget] = [Cost per month] • [Number of full bus wrap advertisements] + [Cost per month] • [Number of half-side advertisements]

$$6000 = 2000(1) + 800h$$
$$6000 = 2000 + 800h$$

Solve the equation.

$$6000 = 2000 + 800h$$
$$6000 - 2000 = 2000 - 2000 + 800h$$
$$4000 = 800h$$
$$\frac{4000}{800} = \frac{800h}{800}$$
$$5 = h$$

The museum can have 5 half-side advertisements.

Lesson 2.4

17.

$$-3 = 12y - 5(2y - 7)$$
$$-3 = 12y - 10y + 35$$
$$-3 = 2y + 35$$
$$-3 - 35 = 2y + 35 - 35$$
$$-38 = 2y$$
$$\frac{-38}{2} = \frac{2y}{2}$$
$$-19 = y$$

39. Let x be the amount of space you should leave between posters (in feet).

[Total wall space] = [Width of poster] • [Number of posters] + 2 • [Space at end of wall] + [Amount of space between posters] • [Number of spaces between posters]

$$13.5 = 2(3) + 2(3) + x(2)$$
$$13.5 = 6 + 6 + 2x$$
$$13.5 = 12 + 2x$$
$$13.5 - 12 = 12 - 12 + 2x$$
$$1.5 = 2x$$
$$0.75 = x$$

You should leave 0.75 foot between each poster.

Lesson 2.5

13.

$$40 + 14j = 2(-4j - 13)$$
$$40 + 14j = -8j - 26$$
$$40 + 14j + 8j = -8j + 8j - 26$$
$$40 + 22j = -26$$
$$40 - 40 + 22j = -26 - 40$$
$$22j = -66$$
$$j = -3$$

51. Let x represent the number of years. So $33x$ represents the increase in the number of students taking Spanish, and $2x$ represents the decreased number of students who are taking French.

[Number of students taking Spanish this year] + [Number of additional students each year] • [Number of years] = 3 • ([Number of students taking French this year] − [Number of students each year] • [Number of years])

$$555 + 33x = 3(230 - 2x)$$
$$555 + 33x = 690 - 6x$$
$$555 + 33x + 6x = 690 - 6x + 6x$$
$$555 + 39x = 690$$
$$555 - 555 + 39x = 690 - 555$$
$$39x = 135$$
$$x \approx 3.5$$

So it will be after 3 more school years, or in about 4 years, when the number of students taking Spanish will be 3 times the number of students taking French.

Lesson 2.6

17.

$$\frac{16}{48} = \frac{n}{36}$$
$$36 \cdot \frac{16}{48} = 36 \cdot \frac{n}{36}$$
$$\frac{576}{48} = n$$
$$12 = n$$

49. Find the total number of pizzas: $96 + 144 + 240 = 480$.

The ratio of large pizzas to all pizzas is $\frac{\text{number of large pizzas}}{\text{total number of pizzas}} = \frac{240}{480} = \frac{1}{2}$.

Lesson 2.7

13. $$\frac{11}{w} = \frac{33}{w + 24}$$

$$11(w + 24) = 33w$$

$$11w + 264 = 33w$$

$$11w - 11w + 264 = 33w - 11w$$

$$264 = 22w$$

$$12 = w$$

39. The ratio of model to height is $\frac{\text{height of model}}{\text{actual height}}$. Write and solve a proportion.

$$\frac{1}{25} = \frac{x}{443.2}$$

$$443.2 = 25x$$

$$17.728 = x$$

The height of the model is 17.728 meters.

Lesson 2.8

17. $$30 = 9x - 5y$$

$$30 + 5y = 9x - 5y + 5y$$

$$30 + 5y = 9x$$

$$30 - 30 + 5y = 9x - 30$$

$$5y = 9x - 30$$

$$y = \frac{9}{5}x - 6$$

33. a. $C = 12x + 25$

$$C - 25 = 12x + 25 - 25$$

$$C - 25 = 12x$$

$$\frac{C - 25}{12} = x$$

b. \$145: $\frac{C - 25}{12} = x$

$$\frac{145 - 25}{12} = x$$

$$10 = x$$

For \$145, you bowled 10 league nights.

\$181: $\frac{C - 25}{12} = x$

$$\frac{181 - 25}{12} = x$$

$$13 = x$$

For \$181, you bowled 13 league nights.

\$205: $\frac{C - 25}{12} = x$

$$\frac{205 - 25}{12} = x$$

$$15 = x$$

For \$205, you bowled 15 league nights.

Worked-Out Solutions

This section of the book provides step-by-step solutions to exercises with circled exercise numbers. These solutions provide models that can help guide your work with the homework exercises.

The separate **Selected Answers** section follows this section. It provides numerous answers that you can use to check your own answers.

Chapter 3

Lesson 3.1

15. To plot $Q(-1, 5)$, begin at the origin. First move 1 unit to the left, then 5 units up. Point Q is in Quadrant II.

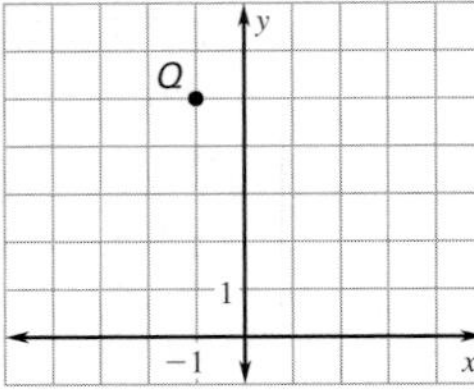

25. First create a table of values by substituting the domain values into the function.

x	$y = 2x - 5$
−2	$y = 2(-2) - 5 = -9$
−1	$y = 2(-1) - 5 = -7$
0	$y = 2(0) - 5 = -5$
1	$y = 2(1) - 5 = -3$
2	$y = 2(2) - 5 = -1$

The table gives the ordered pairs $(-2, -9)$, $(-1, -7)$, $(0, -5)$, $(1, -3)$, and $(2, -1)$.

Graph the function by plotting these points. The range of the function is the y-values from the table: $-9, -7, -5, -3, -1$.

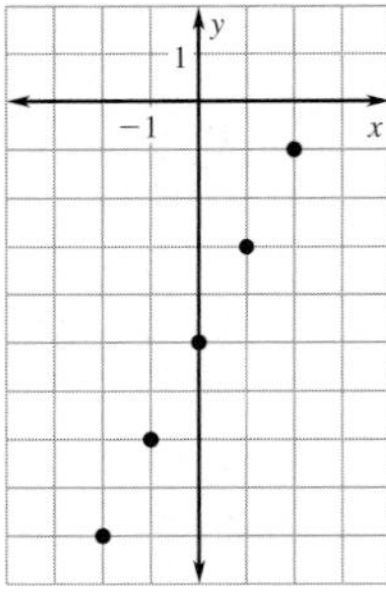

37. The table represents a function because there is exactly one low temperature for each day in the first week of February.

To graph the data, plot the ordered pairs (day, record low).

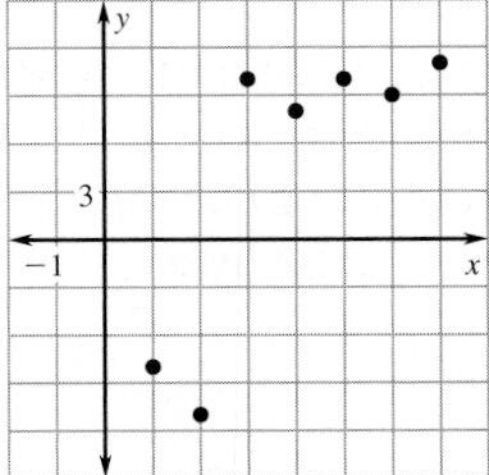

Lesson 3.2

3. Test $(-2, 3)$:

$$2y + x = 4$$

$$2(3) + (-2) \stackrel{?}{=} 4 \quad \text{Substitute } -2 \text{ for } x \text{ and } 3 \text{ for } y.$$

$$6 + (-2) \stackrel{?}{=} 4$$

$$4 = 4 \checkmark$$

So, $(-2, 3)$ is a solution of $2y + x = 4$.

11. First, solve the equation for y.

$$y + x = 2$$

$$y + x - x = 2 - x$$

$$y = 2 - x$$

Use this equation to create a table of values.

x	−2	−1	0	1	2
y	4	3	2	1	0

Plot at least three of the points whose ordered pairs (x, y) are indicated by the table. Draw a line through the plotted points.

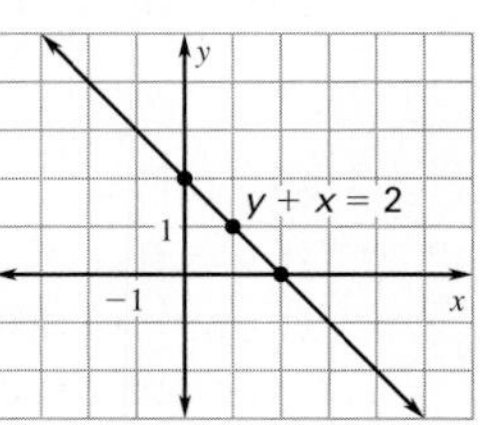

37. a. 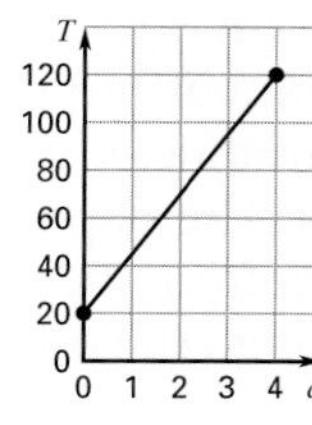
Since the scientist is studying the organisms in the first 4 kilometers of Earth's crust, the domain of the function is $0 \le d \le 4$. The range of the function is $20 \le T \le 120$. The temperature 4 kilometers from the surface is 120°C.

b. Notice in the table for part (a) that the temperatures between 20°C and 95°C occur when the distance from the surface is between 0 kilometers and 3 kilometers.

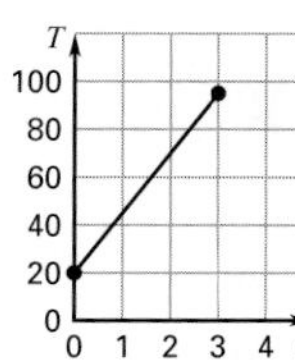
The domain of the function is now $0 \le d \le 3$ and the range is $20 \le T \le 95$. So this section of crust is 3 kilometers deep.

Lesson 3.3

21. Substitute 0 for y in $y = -4x + 3$ and solve for x.

$0 = -4x + 3$

$-3 = -4x$

$\frac{3}{4} = x$

The x-intercept is $\frac{3}{4}$.

Substitute 0 for x in $y = -4x + 3$ and solve for y.

$y = -4(0) + 3 = 0 + 3 = 3$

The y-intercept is 3.

Plot the two points that correspond to the intercepts and draw a line through them.

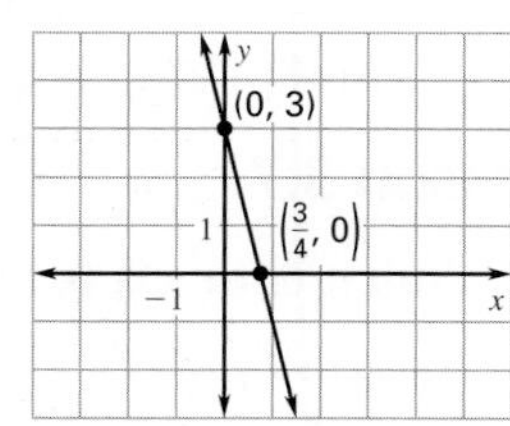

47. a. If $v = 0$ in the function $f = 180 - 1.5v$, then $f = 180 - 1.5(0)$, and $f = 180$. This is the intercept on the vertical axis, and it represents the area (in square feet) available for flowers when no vegetables are planted.

Letting $f = 0$ gives $0 = 180 - 1.5v$, $1.5v = 180$, and $v = 120$. This is the intercept on the horizontal axis, and it represents the area (in square feet) available for vegetables when no flowers are planted.

b. 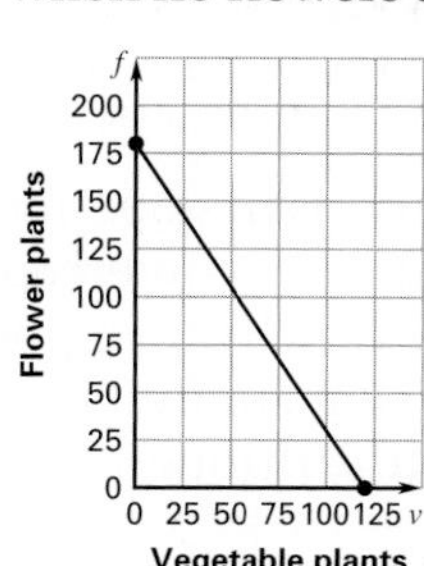

The domain is $0 \le v \le 120$. The range is $0 \le f \le 180$.

c. $f = 180 - 1.5(80)$ Substitute 80 for v.

$= 180 - 120 = 60$

There are 60 square feet left to plant flowers.

Lesson 3.4

11. Let $(x_1, y_1) = (1, 3)$ and $(x_2, y_2) = (3, -2)$.

$m = \frac{y_2 - y_1}{x_2 - x_1} = \frac{-2 - 3}{3 - 1} = \frac{-5}{2}$ or $-\frac{5}{2}$

37. a. rate of change $= \frac{\text{change in temperature}}{\text{change in time}}$

0–1.5 hours:
$\frac{1000 - 250}{1.5 - 0} = \frac{750}{1.5} = 500$ degrees per hour

1.5–2.5 hours:
$\frac{1300 - 1000}{2.5 - 1.5} = \frac{300}{1} = 300$ degrees per hour

2.5–4.65 hours:
$\frac{1680 - 1300}{4.65 - 2.5} = \frac{380}{2.15} \approx 177$ degrees per hour

4.65–8.95 hours:
$\frac{1920 - 1680}{8.95 - 4.65} = \frac{240}{4.3} \approx 56$ degrees per hour

The time interval with the greatest rate of change was from 0 hours to 1.5 hours.

b. The time interval that showed the least rate of change was from 4.65 hours to 8.95 hours.

Lesson 3.5

11.

$$4x + y = 1$$
$$4x - 4x + y = 1 - 4x$$
$$y = -4x + 1$$

The slope is -4 and the y-intercept is 1.

21. The equation $y = -6x + 1$ is in slope-intercept form. The slope is -6 and the y-intercept is 1. Locate the point (0, 1), which corresponds to the intercept. Use the slope to find a second point, (1, -5). Draw a line through the points.

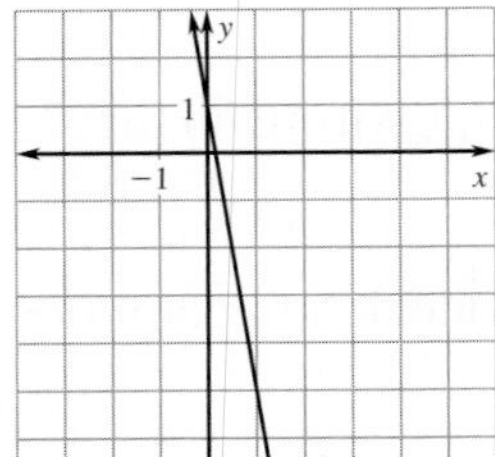

41. a.

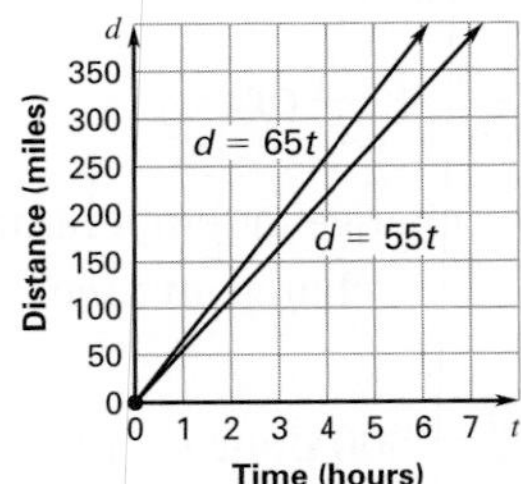

b. On the graph, the vertical distance between the lines is about 30 when $t = 3$. To verify this estimate, substitute 3 in $d = 55t$: $d = 55(3) = 165$. Now substitute 3 in $d = 65t$: $d = 65(3) = 195$. Subtract: $195 - 165 = 30$. Driving at the maximum speed limit, a driver could travel 30 miles farther after 1995 than before 1995.

Lesson 3.6

7. Solve the equation for y: $8x + 2y = 0$

$$2y = -8x$$
$$y = -4x$$

Because $8x + 2y = 0$ can be written in the form $y = ax$, it does represent direct variation. The constant of variation is -4.

21. When solved for y, the equation is $y = -4x$. The slope of the line is the constant of variation, -4. The graph of a direct variation equation always passes through (0, 0). The slope can be used to locate a second point from the origin, like (1, -4). Draw a line through the points.

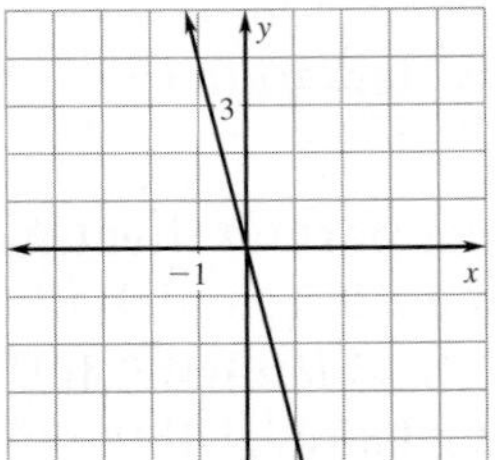

43. a. Compare the ratio $\frac{f}{w}$ for all three data pairs:

$$\frac{2.50}{10} = 0.25, \frac{3.75}{15} = 0.25, \frac{7.50}{30} = 0.25$$

Because the ratios are all equal, f varies directly with w.

b. Since $\frac{f}{w} = 0.25$, multiply both sides by w to obtain the direct variation equation $f = 0.25w$; the constant 0.25 represents $.25 per pound.

The computer weighs 18 pounds, so substitute 18 for w.

$f = 0.25(18) = 4.50$

The printer weighs 10 pounds, so substitute 10 for w.

$f = 0.25(10) = 2.50$

The total recycling fee for the computer and printer is $4.50 + $2.50 = $7.00.

Lesson 3.7

3. Substitute -2, 0, and 3 for x.

$f(-2) = 12(-2) + 1 = -24 + 1 = -23$

$f(0) = 12(0) + 1 = 0 + 1 = 1$

$f(3) = 12(3) + 1 = 36 + 1 = 37$

17. Substitute -13 for $j(x)$.

$$-13 = 4x + 11$$
$$-13 - 11 = 4x + 11 - 11$$
$$-24 = 4x$$
$$\frac{-24}{4} = \frac{4x}{4}$$
$$-6 = x$$

39. a. Create a table of values for the function.

x	$f(x)$
0	$0.10(0) + 2.75 = 2.75$
5	$0.10(5) + 2.75 = 3.25$
10	$0.10(10) + 2.75 = 3.75$
15	$0.10(15) + 2.75 = 4.25$
20	$0.10(20) + 2.75 = 4.75$

Use the ordered pairs given by the table to graph the function.

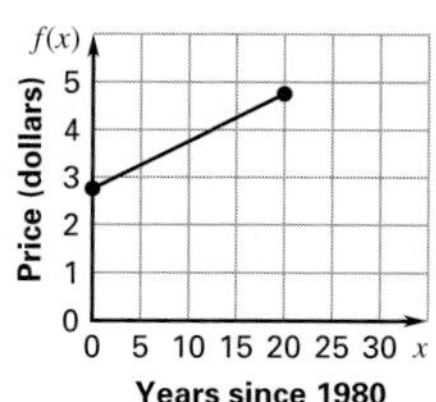

The domain of the function is $0 \le x \le 20$ and the range is $2.75 \le f(x) \le 4.75$.

b. Substitute 4.55 for $f(x)$.

$$4.55 = 0.10x + 2.75$$

$$4.55 - 2.75 = 0.10x + 2.75 - 2.75$$

$$1.8 = 0.10x$$

$$\frac{1.8}{0.10} = \frac{0.10x}{0.10}$$

$$18 = x$$

When $x = 18$, $f(x) = 4.55$. In 1998, 18 years after 1980, the average price of a movie ticket was $4.55.

Worked-Out Solutions

This section of the book provides step-by-step solutions to exercises with circled exercise numbers. These solutions provide models that can help guide your work with the homework exercises.

The separate **Selected Answers** section follows this section. It provides numerous answers that you can use to check your own answers.

Chapter 4

Lesson 4.1

11. Determine the slope: $m = \frac{\text{rise}}{\text{run}} = \frac{-1}{2} = \text{or } -\frac{1}{2}$.

The line crosses the y-axis at (0, 0), so the y-intercept is 0.

Substitute $-\frac{1}{2}$ for m and 0 for b in the slope-intercept form $y = mx + b$: $y = -\frac{1}{2}x$.

19. Calculate the slope:
$m = \frac{y_2 - y_1}{x_2 - x_1} = \frac{4 - 0}{0 - (-1)} = \frac{4}{1} = 4$.

The line crosses the y-axis at (0, 4), so the y-intercept is 4.

Substitute 4 for m and 4 for b in the slope-intercept form $y = mx + b$: $y = 4x + 4$.

47. Let C be the cost of a visit to the aquarium and t be the time parked there. The total cost C is given by the function $C = 3h + 30$, where h is the number of hours parked at the aquarium.

Evaluate the function for $h = 4$:
$C = 3(4) + 30 = 12 + 30 = 42$

The total cost is $42.

Lesson 4.2

5. The slope is given. To find the y-intercept, substitute the slope, -5, and the coordinates of the given point $(-4, 7)$ into the equation $y = mx + b$, and solve for b.

$y = mx + b$

$7 = -5(-4) + b$

$7 = 20 + b$

$-13 = b$

The equation of the line is $y = -5x - 13$.

11. Calculate the slope:
$m = \frac{y_2 - y_1}{x_2 - x_1} = \frac{7 - 4}{2 - 1} = \frac{3}{1} = 3$.

To find the y-intercept, substitute the slope, 3, and the coordinates of either given point into the equation $y = mx + b$, and solve for b. Using (1, 4),

$y = mx + b$

$4 = 3(1) + b$

$4 = 3 + b$

$1 = b$

The equation of the line is $y = 3x + 1$.

49. Let T be the total time (in minutes) for cooking a roast that weighs p pounds and t be the extra time needed (in minutes). The equation $T = 30p + t$ models the situation.

For a 2 pound roast, the total time was 1 hour 25 minutes, or 85 minutes. Find the extra time t needed by substituting 85 for T and 2 for p, and solving for t.

$85 = 30(2) + t$

$85 = 60 + t$

$25 = t$

Find the value of T for a 3 pound roast by substituting 3 for p.

$T = 30(3) + 25 = 90 + 25 = 115$

You need 115 minutes, or 1 hour 55 minutes, to cook a 3 pound roast.

Lesson 4.3

3. Substitute 2 for x_1, 1 for y_1, and 2 for m in the point-slope form $y - y_1 = m(x - x_1)$:
$y - 1 = 2(x - 2)$.

39. The rate of change is given as $10,000 per year. Let y be the annual sales (in dollars) and x be the number of years since 1994. From the given information about 1997, one data pair is (3, 97000). Use the point-slope form of an equation.

$$y - y_1 = m(x - x_1)$$

$$y - 97000 = 10000(x - 3)$$

$$y - 97000 = 10000x - 30000$$

$$y = 10000x + 67000$$

To find the sales in 2000, use the equation above with $x = 2000 - 1994$, or 6.

$$y = 10000(6) + 67000$$

$$= 60000 + 67000 = 127000$$

The annual sales in 2000 were $127,000.

Lesson 4.4

17. Calculate the slope:
$m = \frac{y_2 - y_1}{x_2 - x_1} = \frac{-4 - 4}{4 - (-8)} = \frac{-8}{12}$ or $-\frac{2}{3}$.

Use either point to write an equation in point-slope form. Using (−8, 4):

$$y - y_1 = m(x - x_1)$$

$$y - 4 = -\frac{2}{3}[x - (-8)]$$

$$y - 4 = -\frac{2}{3}(x + 8)$$

Rewrite the equation in standard form.

$$y - 4 = -\frac{2}{3}x - \frac{16}{3}$$

$$\frac{2}{3}x + y - 4 = -\frac{16}{3}$$

$$\frac{2}{3}x + y = -\frac{4}{3} \text{ (or } 2x + 3y = -4)$$

39. a. Let n be the number of ounces in a box of wheat cereal.

Amount of snack mix (ounces)	=	Number of boxes of corn cereal	•	Number of ounces per box	+
		Number of boxes of wheat cereal	•	Number of ounces per box	

$$120 = 5 \cdot 12 + 4 \cdot n$$

$$120 = 60 + 4n$$

$$60 = 4n$$

$$15 = n$$

There are 15 ounces in a box of wheat cereal.

b. Let c be the number of boxes of corn cereal and let w be the number of boxes of wheat cereal you use. Use the verbal model from part (a).

$$120 = c \cdot 12 + w \cdot 15$$

$$120 = 12c + 15w \text{ or } 12c + 15w = 120$$

c. Substitute different values for c and w in the equation for part (b).

If $c = 0$, then $12(0) + 15w = 120$, and $w = 8$; you can use 0 boxes of corn cereal and 8 boxes of wheat cereal.

If $c = 5$, then $12(5) + 15w = 120$, and $w = 4$; you can use 5 boxes of corn cereal and 4 boxes of wheat cereal.

If $c = 10$, then $12(10) + 15w = 120$, and $w = 0$; you can use 10 boxes of corn cereal and 0 boxes of wheat cereal.

Lesson 4.5

19. The slope of the line $y = 3x - 12$ is 3, so the slope of the perpendicular line is $-\frac{1}{3}$.

Use the slope $-\frac{1}{3}$ and the point (−9, 2) to find the y-intercept of the line.

$$y = mx + b$$

$$2 = -\frac{1}{3}(-9) + b$$

$$2 = 3 + b$$

$$-1 = b$$

The equation of the line through (−9, 2) that is perpendicular to the line $y = 3x - 12$ is $y = -\frac{1}{3}x - 1$.

33. a. Let w represent the weight of the blue whale calves and let d represent the number of days since birth.

The rate of change is 200 pounds per day. Use this value and the birth weights to write an equation for each calf.

First calf: $w_1 = 200d + 6000$
Second calf: $w_2 = 200d + 6250$

b. Substitute 30 for d in each equation from part (a).

$w_1 = 200(30) + 6000 = 12{,}000$

After 30 days, the first calf weighs 12,000 pounds.

$w_2 = 200(30) + 6250 = 12{,}250$

After 30 days, the second calf weighs 12,250 pounds.

c. The graphs of the equations in part (a) are parallel, since the two equations have the same slope, 200. The w-intercept of the second line is 250 greater than the w-intercept of the first line.

Lesson 4.6

7. The ordered pairs from the table are (1.2, 10), (1.8, 7), (2.3, 5), (3.0, −1), (4.4, −4), and (5.2, −8).

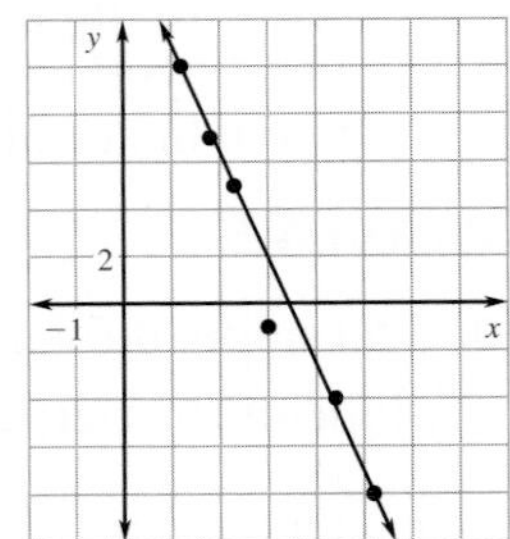

Use the points (1.2, 10) and (5.2, −8) to find the slope of the line of fit.

$$m = \frac{y_2 - y_1}{x_2 - x_1} = \frac{-8 - 10}{5.2 - 1.2} = \frac{-18}{4} = -4.5.$$

Use the slope −4.5 and the point (5.2, −8) to find the y-intercept of the line.

$$y = mx + b$$
$$-8 = -4.5(5.2) + b$$
$$-8 = -23.4 + b$$
$$15.4 = b$$

A line of fit is $y = -4.5x + 15.4$.

17. a. The ordered pairs from the diagram are (86, −86), (80, −65), (75, −54), (70, −40), (65, −26), (60, −21), and (52, −4).

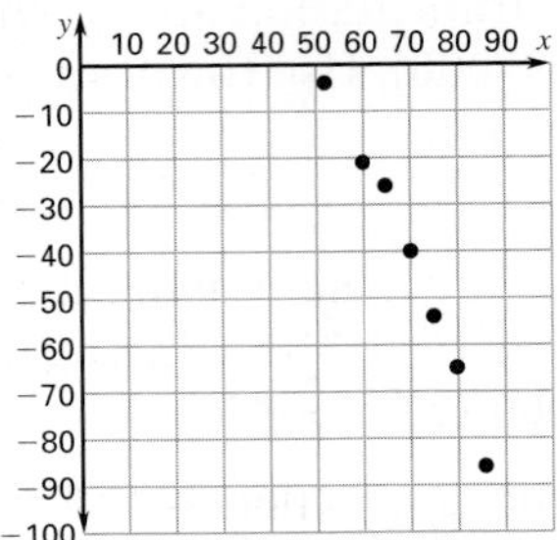

b. Draw a line that appears to fit the points.
Sample:

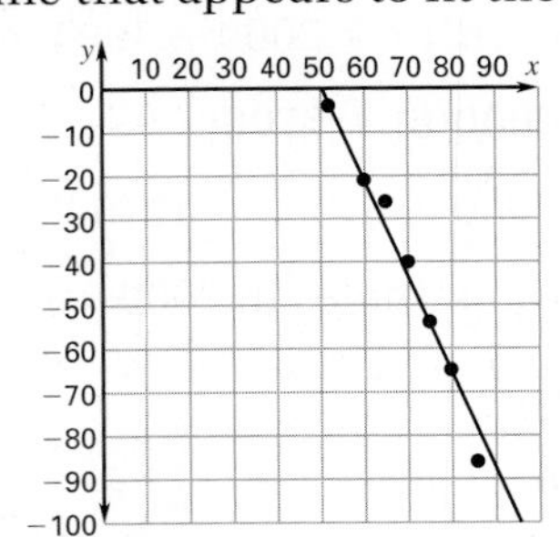

Use the points (60, −21) and (80, −65) to find the slope of the line of fit.

$$m = \frac{y_2 - y_1}{x_2 - x_1} = \frac{-21 - (-65)}{60 - 80} = \frac{44}{-20} = -2.2$$

Use the slope −2.2 and the point (80, −65) to find the y-intercept of the line.

$$y = mx + b$$
$$-65 = -2.2(80) + b$$
$$-65 = -176 + b$$
$$111 = b$$

A line of fit is $y = -2.2x + 111$.

c. The slope of the line of fit models the rate of change. So the temperature changes at an approximate rate of −2.2°C per kilometer of increasing altitude.

Lesson 4.7

3. Enter the data list on a graphing calculator. Create a scatter plot.

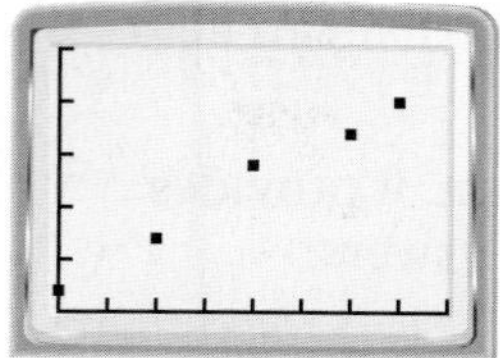

Perform a linear regression using the paired data. An equation of the best-fitting line is approximately $y = 2.6x + 2.5$.

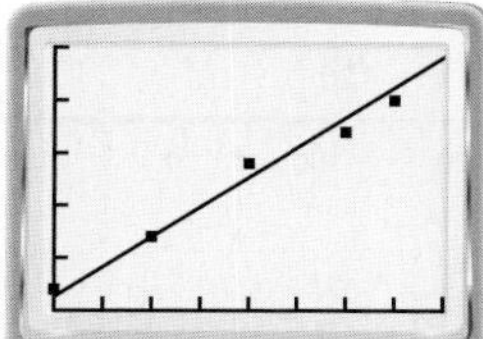

Graph the best-fitting line. Use the trace feature and arrow keys to find the value of y when $x = 5$. For $x = 5$, $y = 15.5$.

19. a. Enter the data list on a graphing calculator. Make a scatter plot.

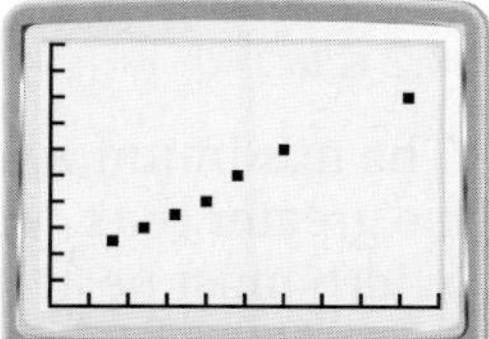

b. Perform a linear regression using the paired data. An equation of the best-fitting line is approximately $y = 0.03x + 1.23$ where y is the recommended space (in square feet) and x is a pig's weight (in pounds).

c. Evaluate $y = 0.03x + 1.23$ for $x = 250$.

$y = 0.03(250) + 1.23 = 7.5 + 1.23 = 8.73$

The model predicts that about 8.73 square feet of space is needed for a pig weighing 250 pounds.

Worked-Out Solutions

This section of the book provides step-by-step solutions to exercises with circled exercise numbers. These solutions provide models that can help guide your work with the homework exercises.

The separate **Selected Answers** section follows this section. It provides numerous answers that you can use to check your own answers.

Chapter 5

Lesson 5.1

7. The open circle means that 10 is not a solution of the inequality. Because the arrow points to the left, all numbers less than 10 are solutions. An inequality represented by the graph is $x < 10$.

15.

$$w + 14.9 > -2.7$$
$$w + 14.9 - 14.9 > -2.7 - 14.9$$
$$w > -17.6$$

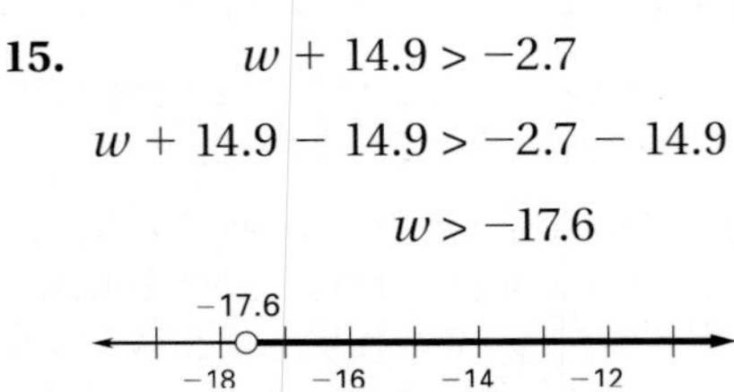

33. a. Let s represent score you can earn.

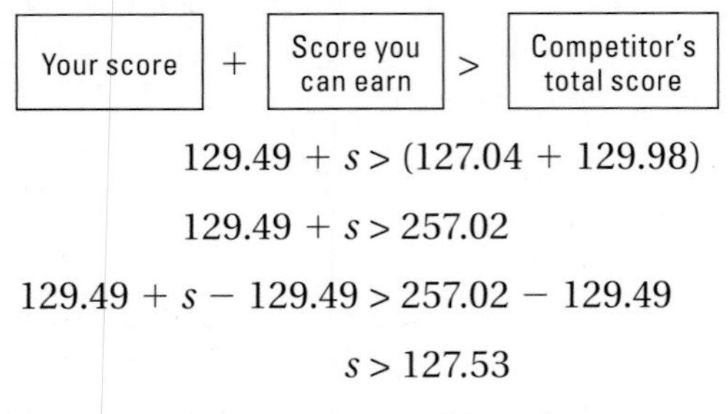

$$129.49 + s > (127.04 + 129.98)$$
$$129.49 + s > 257.02$$
$$129.49 + s - 129.49 > 257.02 - 129.49$$
$$s > 127.53$$

The score you can earn must be greater than 127.53.

b. Yes; since $128.13 > 127.53$, you will beat your competitor.

No; since $126.78 < 127.53$, you will not beat your competitor.

No; when your score is 127.53, you and your competitor will tie.

Lesson 5.2

5. $-6y < -36$

$\frac{-6y}{-6} > \frac{-36}{-6}$ Reverse the inequality symbol when dividing by −6.

$y > 6$

9.

$$\frac{g}{6} > -20$$
$$6 \cdot \frac{g}{6} > 6 \cdot (-20)$$
$$g > -120$$

39. $48 \le 15 \cdot w$

$$\frac{48}{15} \le \frac{15w}{15}$$
$$3.2 \le w$$

The minimum width of the molding must be greater than or equal to 3.2 inches, or the width must be at least 3.2 inches.

Lesson 5.3

5.

$$8v - 3 \ge -11$$
$$8v \ge -8$$
$$v \ge -1$$

19.

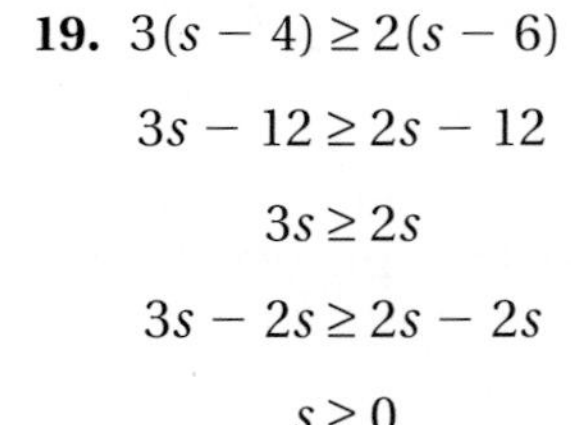

$$3(s - 4) \ge 2(s - 6)$$
$$3s - 12 \ge 2s - 12$$
$$3s \ge 2s$$
$$3s - 2s \ge 2s - 2s$$
$$s \ge 0$$

39. a. The area of the habitat is (20 feet)(50 feet) = 1000 square feet. Since 500 square feet are needed for the first two swans, 1000 − 500 = 500 square feet are left for the other swans. 500 square feet can hold up to 500 ÷ 125 = 4 more swans; so, the maximum number of swans is 2 + 4 = 6 swans.

b. The area of the new habitat is $[(20 + 20) \text{ feet}][(50 + 20) \text{ feet}] = (40 \text{ feet})(70 \text{ feet}) = 2800$ square feet. Since $2800 - 1000 = 1800$, the additional area is 1800 square feet. 1800 square feet can hold up to $1800 \div 125 = 14.4$ more swans; so the possible number of additional swans is at most 14 swans. The habitat can hold at most 14 more swans.

Lesson 5.4

7. Let s be the speed of a vehicle that is traveling within the posted speed limits.

$40 \le s \le 60$

11. Separate the compound inequality $-1 \le -4m \le 16$ into two inequalities.

$-1 \le -4m$ *and* $-4m \le 16$

$\frac{-1}{-4} \ge \frac{-4m}{-4}$ *and* $\frac{-4m}{-4} \ge \frac{16}{-4}$

$\frac{1}{4} \ge m$ *and* $m \ge -4$

The inequality can be written as $-4 \le m \le \frac{1}{4}$.

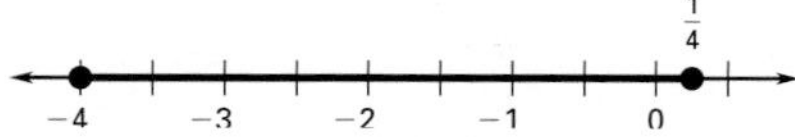

41. An inequality representing values for p is $0.02 \le p \le 0.04$.

$0.02 \le \frac{f}{d} \le 0.04$ Substitute $\frac{f}{d}$ for p.

$0.02 \le \frac{f}{160} \le 0.04$ Substitute 160 for w.

$3.2 \le f \le 6.4$

The possible amounts of food f eaten per day by a deer is greater or equal to 3.2 pounds and less than or equal to 6.4 pounds.

Lesson 5.5

11. Rewrite the absolute value equation $|3p + 7| = 4$ as two equations.

$3p + 7 = 4$ *or* $3p + 7 = -4$

$3p = -3$ *or* $3p = -11$

$p = -1$ *or* $p = -3\frac{2}{3}$

The solutions are -1 and $-3\frac{2}{3}$.

23. $|x - 1| + 5 = 2$

$|x - 1| = -3$

The absolute value of a number is never negative. So, there are no solutions.

45. a. Let s represent your friend's scores last year.

Absolute deviation = | Score − Mean score |

$2.213 = |s - 54.675|$

$2.213 = s - 54.675$

$56.888 = s$

or $-2.213 = s - 54.675$

$52.462 = s$

His least score earned was 52.462, and his greatest score was 56.888 points.

b. Let t represent your friend's scores this year. Find his greatest score for this year. Then find the difference between this year's greatest score and last year's greatest score.

$0.45 = |t - 56.738|$

$0.45 = t - 56.738$

$57.188 = t$

or $-0.45 = t - 56.738$

$56.288 = t$

His greatest score was 57.188 points. This score is $57.188 - 56.888$, or 0.3 point more than his greatest score last year.

Lesson 5.6

9. Rewrite $|d + 4| \ge 3$ as a compound inequality.

$d + 4 \le -3$ *or* $d + 4 \ge 3$

$d \le -7$ *or* $d \ge -1$

15. $5\left|\frac{1}{2}r + 3\right| > 5$

$\left|\frac{1}{2}r + 3\right| > 1$

$\frac{1}{2}r + 3 < -1$ *or* $\frac{1}{2}r + 3 > 1$

$\frac{1}{2}r < -4$ *or* $\frac{1}{2}r > -2$

$r < -8$ *or* $r > -4$

−14 −10 −6 −2 2

37. Let t represent the oven temperature.

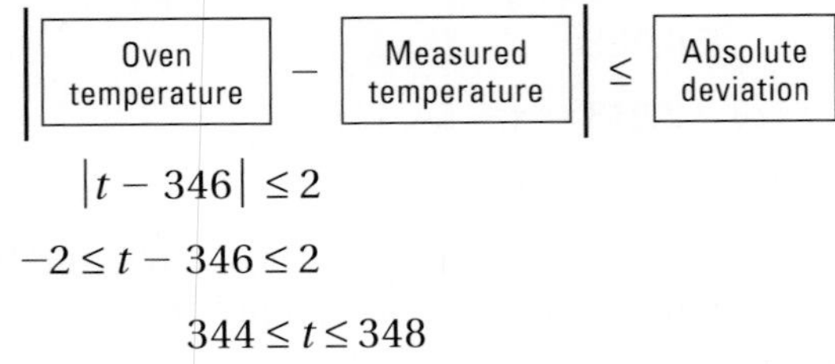

$|t - 346| \le 2$

$-2 \le t - 346 \le 2$

$344 \le t \le 348$

The temperature is at least 344°F and at most 348°F. You should continue to preheat; the temperature is still below 350°F.

Lesson 5.7

5. Substitute −1 for x and −4 for y in the inequality $y - x > -2$.

$-4 - (-1) > -2$

$-3 > -2$ ✘

Since −3 is not greater than −2, the ordered pair (−1, −4) is not a solution.

19. Graph the equation $y = 3x + 5$. The symbol of the given inequality is <, so use a dashed line. Since the line does not pass through the origin, test the ordered pair (0, 0) in $y < 3x + 5$.

$0 < 3(0) + 5$

$0 < 5$ ✓

Shade the half-plane that contains (0, 0) because (0, 0) is a solution of the inequality.

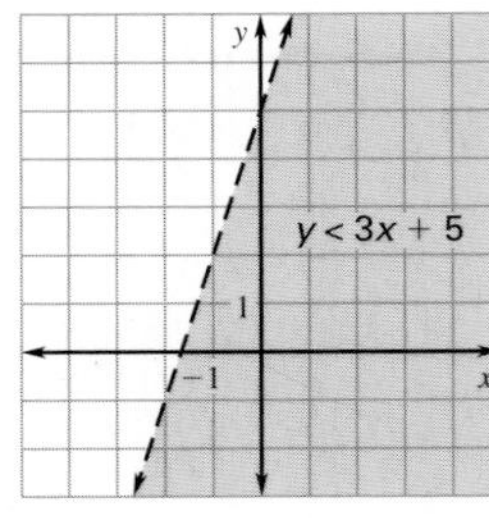

57. a. Let m be the number of muffins and let ℓ be the number of loaves of bread. An inequality modeling this situation is $\frac{1}{6}m + \frac{1}{2}\ell \le 12$.

To graph $\frac{1}{6}m + \frac{1}{2}\ell \le 12$, first graph the equation $\frac{1}{6}m + \frac{1}{2}\ell = 12$ in Quadrant I; the inequality symbol is ≤, so use a solid line.

Next, test (12, 12) in $\frac{1}{6}m + \frac{1}{2}\ell \le 12$.

$\frac{1}{6}(12) + \frac{1}{2}(12) \le 12$

$2 + 6 \le 12$ ✓

Finally, shade the part of Quadrant I that contains (12, 12), because (12, 12) is a solution of the inequality.

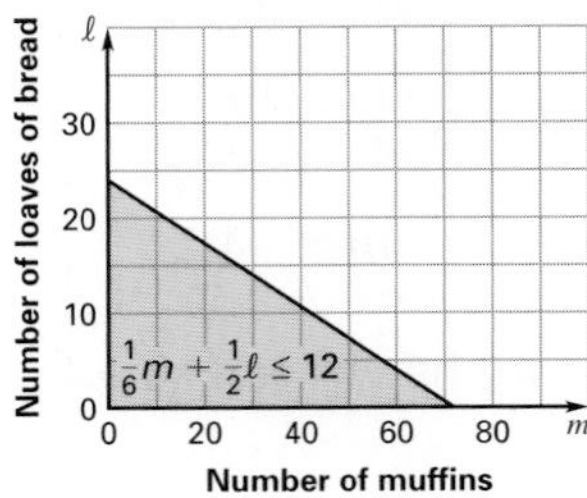

b. $\frac{1}{6}m + \frac{1}{2}(4) \le 12$ Substitute 4 for ℓ.

$\frac{1}{6}m + 2 \le 12$

$\frac{1}{6}m \le 10$

$m \le 60$

You can make up to 60 muffins.

Worked-Out Solutions

This section of the book provides step-by-step solutions to exercises with circled exercise numbers. These solutions provide models that can help guide your work with the homework exercises.

The separate **Selected Answers** section follows this section. It provides numerous answers that you can use to check your own answers.

Chapter 6

Lesson 6.1

15. Graph both equations.

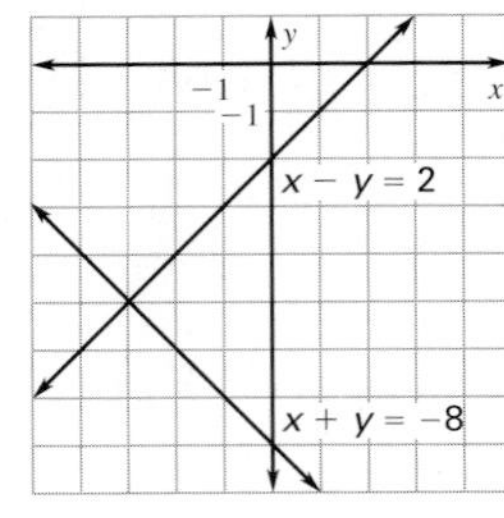

The lines appear to intersect at (−3, −5).

Check: Substitute −3 for x and −5 for y in each equation.

$$x - y = 2 \qquad x + y = -8$$
$$-3 - (-5) = 2 \qquad -3 + (-5) = -8$$
$$2 = 2 \checkmark \qquad -8 = -8 \checkmark$$

So, (−3, −5) is the solution of the system.

31. The two lines appear to intersect at (50, 50). If the value of t is 50, then the year is 1990 + 50, or 2040. So, the percent of eighth graders who watch 1 hour or less of television will equal the percent of eighth graders who watch 1 hour or more of television in the year 2040.

Lesson 6.2

13. Solve $x + y = -3$ for x: $x = -y - 3$.

Substitute $-y - 3$ for x in the other equation and solve for y.

$$5(-y - 3) + 2y = 9$$
$$-5y - 15 + 2y = 9$$
$$-3y - 15 = 9$$
$$-3y = 24$$
$$y = -8$$

Substitute −8 for y in the equation $x = -y - 3$.

$x = -(-8) - 3 = 5$

The solution of the linear system is (5, −8).

33. a. Write a system of two linear equations.

Use the given verbal model to write the first equation: $x \cdot 1.5 = y \cdot 1.2$, or $1.5x = 1.2y$.

Since the length of the dowel is 9 inches, the second equation is $x + y = 9$.

Solve $x + y = 9$ for x: $x = -y + 9$.

Substitute $-y + 9$ for x in the equation $1.5x = 1.2y$ and solve for y.

$$1.5x = 1.2y$$
$$1.5(-y + 9) = 1.2y$$
$$-1.5y + 13.5 = 1.2y$$
$$13.5 = 2.7y$$
$$5 = y$$

Substitute 5 for y in the equation $x = -y + 9$.

$x = -5 + 9 = 4$

The solution is (4, 5). So the string should be placed 4 inches from point A.

Lesson 6.3

17. Rewrite the first equation so that the x-term is first. Subtract the equations to eliminate the variable x, then solve for y.

$$\begin{array}{r} 6x - 8y = 36 \\ \underline{6x - y = 15} \\ -7y = 21 \\ y = -3 \end{array}$$

Substitute −3 for y in either equation.

$$6x - (-3) = 15$$
$$6x + 3 = 15$$
$$6x = 12$$
$$x = 2$$

The solution of the linear system is (2, −3).

41. Write a system of equations. Let x be the cost of a monophonic ring tone and let y be the cost of a polyphonic ring tone.

$3 \cdot x + 2 \cdot y = 12.85$ ← Julie's total cost

$1 \cdot x + 2 \cdot y = 8.95$ ← Tate's total cost

Subtract the equations to eliminate y.

$$3x + 2y = 12.85$$
$$x + 2y = 8.95$$
$$2x = 3.90$$
$$x = 1.95$$

Substitute 1.95 for x in either equation.

$$1.95 + 2y = 8.95$$
$$2y = 7.00$$
$$y = 3.50$$

The solution of the linear system is (1.95, 3.50). The cost of a monophonic ring tone is \$1.95 and the cost of a polyphonic ring tone is \$3.50.

Lesson 6.4

15. Begin by multiplying $9x + 2y = 39$ by 2 and $6x + 13y = -9$ by 3 so that the coefficient of x is the same in both equations. Then subtract the equations to eliminate x. Solve for y.

$9x + 2y = 39$ [×2] $18x + 4y = 78$

$6x + 13y = -9$ [×3] $18x + 39y = -27$

$$-35y = 105$$
$$y = -3$$

Substitute −3 for y in either original equations.

$9x + 2(-3) = 39$ Use the equation $9x + 2y = 39$.

$$9x - 6 = 39$$
$$9x = 45$$

$x = 5$ The solution is (5, −3).

39. Let x be the number of pies and y be the number of batches of applesauce.

$5x + 4y = 169$ ← Granny Smith apples

$3x + 2y = 95$ ← Golden Delicious apples

Now begin to solve the system by multiplying $5x + 4y = 169$ by 3 and $3x + 2y = 95$ by 5 so that the coefficient of x is the same in both equations. Then subtract the equations to eliminate x. Solve for y.

$5x + 4y = 169$ [×3] $15x + 12y = 507$

$3x + 2y = 95$ [×5] $15x + 10y = 475$

$$2y = 32$$
$$y = 16$$

Substitute 16 for y in either original equations.

$$3x + 2(16) = 95$$
$$3x + 32 = 95$$
$$3x = 63$$
$$x = 21$$

The solution is (21, 16). The apples can be used to make 21 pies and 16 batches of applesauce.

Lesson 6.5

11.

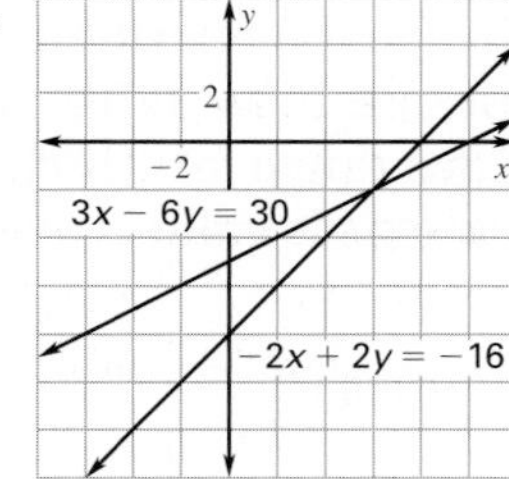

The lines intersect, so the linear system has one solution.

37. Write a system of equations. Let x be the cost of a coach ticket and let y be the cost of a business class ticket.

$150x + 80y = 22{,}860$ ← Washington, D.C.

$170x + 100y = 27{,}280$ ← New York City

Solve the linear system using elimination. Multiply the Washington, D.C. equation by 5 and the New York City equation by 4.

$$750x + 400y = 114{,}300$$
$$680x + 400y = 109{,}120$$
$$70x = 5180$$
$$x = 74$$

Substitute 74 for x in either original equations.

$$170(74) + 100y = 27{,}280$$
$$12{,}580 + 100y = 27{,}280$$
$$100y = 14{,}700$$
$$y = 147$$

The solution is (74, 147). Since there is one solution to the system, there is enough information to determine the cost of one coach ticket.

Lesson 6.6

13. The graph of the system is the intersection of the two half-planes when both inequalities are graphed in the same coordinate plane.

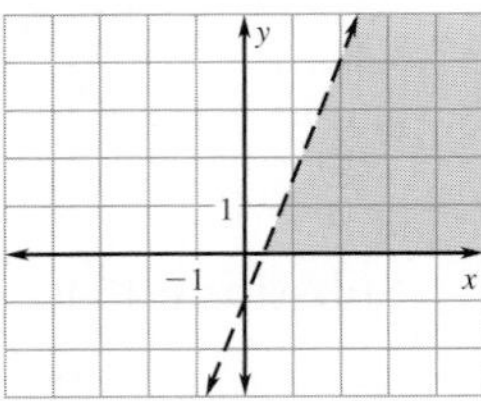

39. a. Let x be the person's age in years and let y be the target heart rate (in beats per minute). A person's maximum heart rate is given by $220 - x$, so 70% of this value is $0.7(220 - x)$ and 85% of this value is $0.85(220 - x)$. So the range for the target heart rate is given by the compound inequality $0.7(220 - x) \le y \le 0.85(220 - x)$, or $154 - 0.70x \le y \le 187 - 0.85x$. This compound inequality can be rewritten as the two inequalities $y \ge 154 - 0.70x$ and $y \le 187 - 0.85x$. The age range for which the heart rate calculations is valid is given as $20 \le x \le 65$.

The system of inequalities is:

$y \ge 154 - 0.70x$
$y \le 187 - 0.85x$
$20 \le x \le 65$

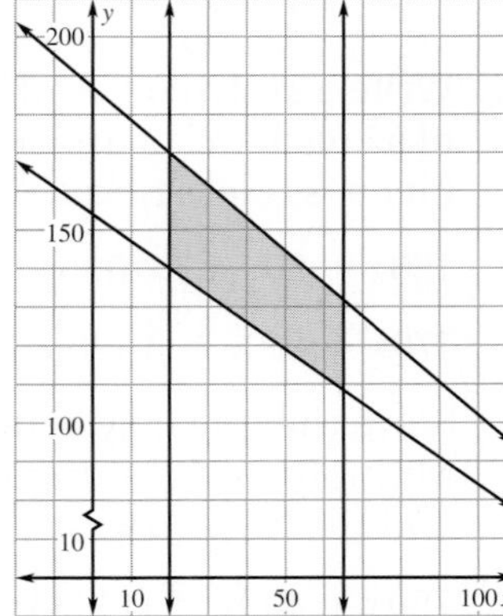

b. No; substituting 40 for x in the inequality $0.70(220 - x) \le y \le 0.85(220 - x)$ gives a range of $126 \le y \le 153$. Since 104 and 120 are both less than 126, his heart rate stays below 70% of the maximum heart rate and is not in the target range for his age.

Worked-Out Solutions

This section of the book provides step-by-step solutions to exercises with circled exercise numbers. These solutions provide models that can help guide your work with the homework exercises.

The separate **Selected Answers** section follows this section. It provides numerous answers that you can use to check your own answers.

Chapter 7

Lesson 7.1

31. $(-10x^6)^2 \cdot x^2 = (-10 \cdot x^6)^2 \cdot x^2$

$= (-10)^2 \cdot (x^6)^2 \cdot x^2$

$= 100 \cdot x^{6 \cdot 2} \cdot x^2$

$= 100 \cdot x^{12} \cdot x^2$

$= 100 \cdot x^{12+2}$

$= 100x^{14}$

55. a. For 10 ounces of gold, there are $10^1 \cdot 10^{23} = 10^{1+23}$, or 10^{24} atoms of gold; for 100 ounces of gold, there are $10^2 \cdot 10^{23} = 10^{25}$ atoms of gold; for 1000 ounces of gold, there are $10^3 \cdot 10^{23} = 10^{26}$ atoms of gold; for 10,000 ounces of gold, there are $10^4 \cdot 10^{23} = 10^{27}$ atoms of gold; and for 100,000 ounces of gold, there are $10^5 \cdot 10^{23} = 10^{28}$ atoms of gold.

b. The power of 10 closest to 96,000 is 10^5, or 100,000. So there were about $10^5 \cdot 10^{23} = 10^{5+23}$, or 10^{28} atoms of gold extracted from the mine.

Lesson 7.2

33. $\left(\frac{3x^3}{2y}\right)^2 \cdot \frac{1}{x^2} = \frac{(3x^3)^2}{(2y)^2} \cdot \frac{1}{x^2}$

$= \frac{3^2 \cdot (x^3)^2}{2^2 \cdot y^2} \cdot \frac{1}{x^2}$

$= \frac{9x^6}{4y^2} \cdot \frac{1}{x^2}$

$= \frac{9x^6}{4x^2y^2}$

$= \frac{9x^4}{4y^2}$

51. Convert the speed of the spacecraft to kilometers per second.

$\frac{10^4 \text{ m}}{1 \text{ sec}} \cdot \frac{1 \text{ km}}{10^3 \text{ m}} = \frac{10^{4-3} \text{ km}}{1 \text{ sec}} = \frac{10^1 \text{ km}}{1 \text{ sec}}$

So the speed of the spacecraft is 10 kilometers per second.

Use the quotient of powers property to calculate the number of seconds it would take to make the trip.

$\frac{10^{13} \text{ km}}{10^1 \text{ km/sec}} = 10^{13-1} \text{ sec} = 10^{12} \text{ sec}$

Calculate the number of seconds in a year (using 365 days = 1 year).

$\frac{60 \text{ sec}}{1 \text{ min}} \cdot \frac{60 \text{ min}}{1 \text{ h}} \cdot \frac{24 \text{ h}}{1 \text{ day}} \cdot \frac{365 \text{ day}}{1 \text{ yr}} = \frac{31{,}356{,}000 \text{ sec}}{1 \text{ yr}}$

Now convert the trip time, 10^{12} seconds, to years.

$10^{12} \text{ sec} \div \frac{31{,}536{,}000 \text{ sec}}{1 \text{ yr}} \approx 31{,}710 \text{ yr}$

It would take about 31,710 years for the spacecraft to reach Alpha Centauri.

Lesson 7.3

11. $\left(\frac{2}{7}\right)^{-2} = \frac{1}{\left(\frac{2}{7}\right)^2} = \frac{1}{\frac{4}{49}} = \frac{49}{4}$

53. To find the number of red blood cells in the entire sample, multiply the sample size, 10^{-2} liter, by the ratio 10^7 red blood cells per 10^{-6} liter.

$10^{-2} \text{ L} \cdot \frac{10^7 \text{ red blood cells}}{10^{-6} \text{ L}}$

$= \frac{10^{-2} \cdot 10^7}{10^{-6}}$ red blood cells

$= 10^{-2+7-(-6)}$ red blood cells

$= 10^{11}$ red blood cells

The entire sample would contain about 10^{11} red blood cells.

Lesson 7.4

13. Make a table of values by choosing values for x and finding the corresponding values for y. The domain of the function is all real numbers.

x	−2	−1	0	1	2	3
y	$0.\overline{4}$	$0.\overline{6}$	1	1.5	2.25	3.375

Plot the points from the table and draw a smooth curve through them.

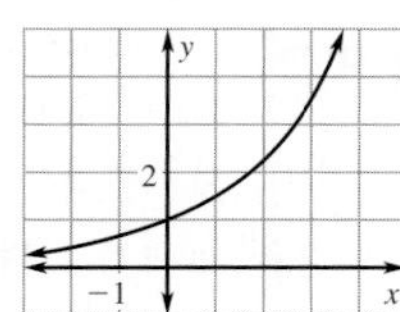

The table and the graph show that the range of the function is all positive real numbers.

41. a. Use the exponential growth model, $y = a(1 + r)^t$.

For tree 1 (with 6% = 0.06), substitute A for y, 154 for a, and 0.06 for r.

$A = 154(1 + 0.06)^t = 154(1.06)^t$

For tree 2 (with 10% = 0.1), substitute A for y, 113 for a, and 0.1 for r.

$A = 113(1 + 0.1)^t = 113(1.1)^t$

The functions are $A = 154(1.06)^t$ for tree 1 and $A = 113(1.1)^t$ for tree 2.

b. 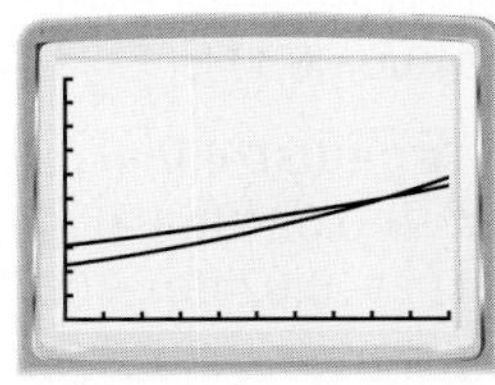

Using the *intersect* feature of the graphing calculator, the graphs intersect at about the point (8.4, 250.6). So, the trees will be the same height in about 8.4 years.

Lesson 7.5

7. Make a table of values by choosing values for x and finding the corresponding values for y. The domain of the function is all real numbers.

x	−2	−1	0	1	2
y	25	5	1	$\frac{1}{5}$	$\frac{1}{25}$

Plot the points from the table and draw a smooth curve through them.

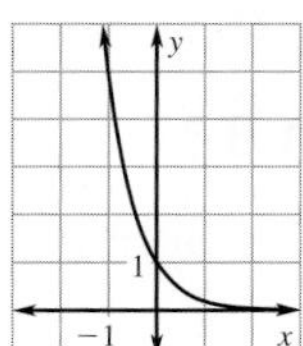

The table and the graph show that the range of the function is all positive real numbers.

49. Let V be the value of the boat (in dollars) and let t be the time (in years since 2003).

Use the exponential decay model, $y = a(1 - r)^t$, to write a function for the value of the boat over time. Substitute V for y, 4000 for a, and 0.07 for r.

$V = 4000(1 - 0.07)^t$

$= 4000(0.93)^t$

In 2006, the value of t is 2006 − 2003, or 3.

$V = 4000(0.93)^3 \approx \$3217.43$

The value of the boat in 2006 is about \$3217. The family should not sell the boat, since the \$3000 offer is less than the value of the boat.

Worked-Out Solutions

This section of the book provides step-by-step solutions to exercises with circled exercise numbers. These solutions provide models that can help guide your work with the homework exercises.

The separate **Selected Answers** section follows this section. It provides numerous answers that you can use to check your own answers.

Chapter 8

Lesson 8.1

21. $(6c^2 + 3c + 9) - (3c - 5)$

$= 6c^2 + 3c + 9 - 3c + 5$

$= 6c^2 + (3c - 3c) + (9 + 5)$

$= 6c^2 + 14$

39. a. Add the models for the number of books of each type sold to find a model T for the total number (in millions) of books sold.

$T = A + J$

$= (9.5t^3 - 58t^2 + 66t + 500) + (-15t^2 + 64t + 360)$

$= 9.5t^3 + (-58t^2 - 15t^2) + (66t + 64t) + (500 + 360)$

$= 9.5t^3 - 73t^2 + 130t + 860$

b. To find the total number (in millions) of books sold in the years 1998 and 2002, substitute the number of years since 1998 for t in the model. Then compare the results.

For 1998, $t = 1998 - 1998 = 0$:

$M = 9.5(0)^3 - 73(0)^2 + 130(0) + 860 = 860$

There were 860 million books sold in 1998.

For 2002, $t = 2002 - 1998 = 4$:

$M = 9.5(4)^3 - 73(4)^2 + 130(4) + 860$

$= 9.5(64) - 73(16) + 130(4) + 860$

$= 608 - 1168 + 520 + 860$

$= 820$

There were 820 million books sold in 2002.

More books were sold in 1998 than in 2002.

Lesson 8.2

23. $(5x + 2)(-3x^2 + 4x - 1)$

$= 5x(-3x^2 + 4x - 1) + 2(-3x^2 + 4x - 1)$

$= -15x^3 + 20x^2 - 5x - 6x^2 + 8x - 2$

$= -15x^3 + (20x^2 - 6x^2) + (-5x + 8x) - 2$

$= -15x^3 + 14x^2 + 3x - 2$

51. a. Substitute 0 for t in each function:

$R = -336(0)^2 + 1730(0) + 12{,}300 = 12{,}300$

$P = 0.00351(0)^2 - 0.0249(0) + 0.171 = 0.171$

Since t is the number of years since 1997, the product $R \cdot P$ when $t = 0$ represents the amount (in million of dollars) spent in 1997 on sound recordings in the U.S. by people between 15 and 19 years old.

b. $R \cdot P = (-336t^2 + 1730t + 12{,}300) \cdot (0.00351t^2 - 0.0249t + 0.171)$

$= -336t^2(0.00351t^2 - 0.0249t + 0.171) + 1730t(0.00351t^2 - 0.0249t + 0.171) + 12{,}300(0.00351t^2 - 0.0249t + 0.171)$

$= -1.17936t^4 + 8.3664t^3 - 57.456t^2 + 6.0723t^3 - 43.077t^2 + 295.83t + 43.173t^2 - 306.27t + 2103.3$

$= -1.17936t^4 + (8.3664t^3 + 6.0723t^3) + (-57.456t^2 - 43.077t^2 + 43.173t^2) + (295.83t - 306.27t) + 2103.3$

$= -1.17936t^4 + 14.4387t^3 - 57.36t^2 - 10.44t + 2103.3$

So, $R \cdot P \approx -1.18t^4 + 14.4t^3 - 57.4t^2 - 10.4t + 2100$.

c. For 2002, $t = 2002 - 1997 = 5$. Substitute 5 for t in the equation for part (b).

$R \cdot P \approx -1.18(5)^4 + 14.4(5)^3 - 57.4(5)^2 - 10.4(5) + 2100$

$\approx -1.18(625) + 14.4(125) - 57.4(25) - 10.4(5) + 2100$

$\approx -737.50 + 1800 - 1435 - 52 + 2100$

≈ 1675.5

In 2002, people between the ages of 15 and 19 years old spent about 1680 million dollars (or $1,680,000,000) on sound recordings.

Lesson 8.3

11. $(t + 4)(t - 4) = t^2 - 4^2 = t^2 - 16$

41. a.

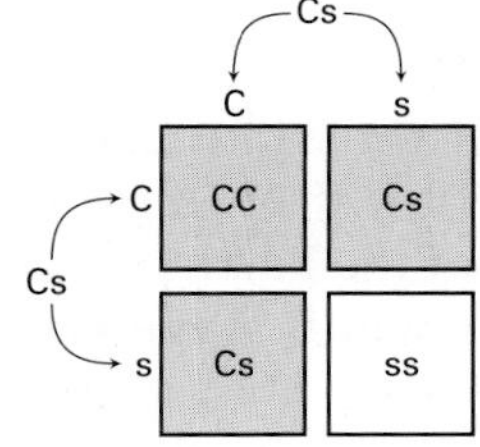

b. Model the gene from each parent with $0.5C + 0.5s$. There is an equal chance that the child inherits a straight thumb gene or a curved thumb gene from each parent. The possible gene combinations of the child can be modeled by $(0.5C + 0.5s)^2$, or

$(0.5C)^2 + 2(0.5C)(0.5s) + (0.5s)^2$

$= 0.25C^2 + 0.5Cs + 0.25s^2$

c. Consider the coefficients in the polynomial found in part (b). The coefficients show that 25% + 50% = 75% of the possible gene combinations will contain a C, and thus result in a child with a curved thumb.

Lesson 8.4

3. $(x - 5)(x + 3) = 0$

$x - 5 = 0$ *or* $x + 3 = 0$

$x = 5$ *or* $x = -3$

The solutions of the equation are 5 and -3.

55. a. The initial vertical velocity is given as 4.9 meters per second and the rabbit starts from the ground, so $v = 4.9$ and $s = 0$ in the vertical motion model.

$h = -4.9t^2 + vt + s$

$= -4.9t^2 + 4.9t + 0$

$= -4.9t^2 + 4.9t$

b. When the rabbit lands, its height above the ground is 0 meters. A reasonable domain for t can be found by substituting 0 for h and solving for t.

$0 = -4.9t^2 + 4.9t$

$0 = 4.9t(-t + 1)$

$4.9t = 0$ *or* $-t + 1 = 0$

$t = 0$ *or* $t = 1$

Since a height of 0 represents when the rabbit is on the ground, $t = 1$ second represents how long it takes for the rabbit to land back on the ground after jumping at $t = 0$ seconds. So, a reasonable domain is all real numbers greater than or equal to 0 and less than or equal to 1, or $0 \le t \le 1$.

Lesson 8.5

7. In $z^2 + 8z - 48$, $c = -48$. Since c is negative, p and q must have different signs.

Factors of −48	Sum of factors	
−48, 1	−48 + 1 = −47	✗
48, −1	48 + (−1) = 47	✗
−24, 2	−24 + 2 = −22	✗
24, −2	24 + (−2) = 22	✗
−16, 3	−16 + 3 = −13	✗
16, −3	16 + (−3) = 13	✗
−12, 4	−12 + 4 = −8	✗
12, −4	12 + (−4) = 8	← Correct

So, $z^2 + 8z - 48 = (z + 12)(z - 4)$.

61. Let x be the original length of the sides of the square photo. Then the length of the trimmed photo is $(x - 6)$ inches and its width is $(x - 5)$ inches. The formula $A = \ell \cdot w$ models the area of the trimmed photo which is 20 square inches.

$$A = \ell \cdot w$$
$$20 = (x - 6)(x - 5)$$
$$20 = x^2 - 11x + 30$$
$$0 = x^2 - 11x + 10$$
$$0 = (x - 10)(x - 1)$$
$$x - 10 = 0 \quad or \quad x - 1 = 0$$
$$x = 10 \quad or \quad x = 1$$

So, the original square photo had a side length of 10 inches or 1 inch. But an original length of 1 inch does not make sense in this situation, so the side length of the original square photo was 10 inches. Therefore, the perimeter of the original square photo was 4(10), or 40 inches.

Lesson 8.6

5. Factor −1 from each term of the trinomial: $-y^2 + 2y + 8 = -(y^2 - 2y - 8)$.

In $y^2 - 2y - 8$, $c = -8$. Since c is negative, the factors of c must have different signs.

Factors of −8	Possible factorization	Middle term when multiplied	
−8, 1	$(y - 8)(y + 1)$	$y - 8y = -7y$	✗
8, −1	$(y + 8)(y - 1)$	$-y + 8y = 7y$	✗
−4, 2	$(y - 4)(y + 2)$	$2y - 4y = -2y$	← Correct
4, −2	$(y + 4)(y - 2)$	$-2y + 4y = 2y$	✗

So, $y^2 - 2y - 8 = (y - 4)(y + 2)$. Therefore,

$$-y^2 + 2y + 8 = -(y^2 - 2y - 8)$$
$$= -(y - 4)(y + 2)$$

25. $4s^2 + 11s - 3 = 0$

$$(4s - 1)(s + 3) = 0$$
$$4s - 1 = 0 \quad or \quad s + 3 = 0$$
$$s = \frac{1}{4} \quad or \quad s = -3$$

61. Let w be the width of the Parthenon's base. Then $2w + 8$ is the length of the base. The formula $A = \ell \cdot w$ models the area of the rectangular base which is 2170 square meters.

$$A = \ell \cdot w$$
$$2170 = (2w + 8) \cdot w$$
$$2170 = 2w^2 + 8w$$
$$0 = 2w^2 + 8w - 2170$$
$$0 = 2(w^2 + 4w - 1085)$$
$$0 = 2(w + 35)(w - 31)$$
$$w + 35 = 0 \quad or \quad w - 31 = 0$$
$$w = -35 \quad or \quad w = 31$$

The solutions are −35 and 31.

Since the width cannot be negative, reject −35 as a solution. So, the width is 31 meters and the length is 2(31) + 8, or 70 meters. Therefore, the base of the Parthenon has length 70 meters and width 31 meters.

Lesson 8.7

11. $49a^2 + 14a + 1 = (7a)^2 + 2(7a \cdot 1) + 1^2$

$$= (7a + 1)^2$$

49. Use the vertical motion model with $h = 54$, $v = 56$, and $s = 5$.

$$h = -16t^2 + vt + s$$
$$54 = -16t^2 + 56t + 5$$
$$0 = -16t^2 + 56t - 49$$
$$0 = -(16t^2 - 56t + 49)$$
$$0 = -[(4t)^2 - 2(4t \cdot 7) + 7^2]$$
$$0 = -(4t - 7)^2$$
$$0 = (4t - 7)^2$$
$$4t - 7 = 0$$
$$t = 1.75$$

The ball reaches a height of 54 feet in 1.75 seconds. Since there is one solution for t, the ball reaches a height of 54 feet just once.

Lesson 8.8

13. $x^3 + x^2 + 2x + 2 = (x^3 + x^2) + (2x + 2)$

$= x^2(x + 1) + 2(x + 1)$

$= (x + 1)(x^2 + 2)$

23. $x^4 - x^2 = x^2(x^2 - 1) = x^2(x - 1)(x + 1)$

71. a. Substitute 0 for h in $h = -4.9t^2 + 3.9t + 1$.

$0 = -4.9t^2 + 3.9t + 1$

$0 = -(4.9t^2 - 3.9t - 1)$

$0 = -(4.9t + 1)(t - 1)$

$4.9t + 1 = 0$ *or* $t - 1 = 0$

$t \approx -0.20$ *or* $t = 1$

The zeros are 1 and about -0.2.

b. The zero $t \approx -0.2$ has no meaning in this situation because t represents time which cannot be negative. The zero $t = 1$ means that the pallino hits the ground (where $h = 0$) 1 second after it is thrown.

Worked-Out Solutions

This section of the book provides step-by-step solutions to exercises with circled exercise numbers. These solutions provide models that can help guide your work with the homework exercises.

The separate **Selected Answers** section follows this section. It provides numerous answers that you can use to check your own answers.

Chapter 9

Lesson 9.1

7. Make a table of values for $y = -2x^2$.

x	-2	-1	0	1	2
y	-8	-2	0	-2	-8

Plot the points from the table. Draw a smooth curve through the points.

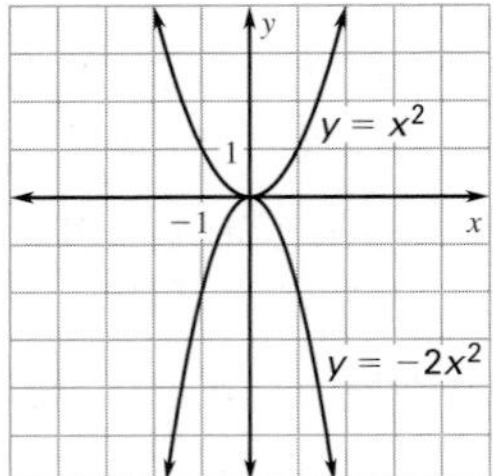

The graphs of $y = -2x^2$ and $y = x^2$ have the same vertex, (0, 0), and the same axis of symmetry, $x = 0$. However, the graph of $-2x^2$ is narrower than the graph of $y = x^2$, and it opens down. This is because the graph of $y = -2x^2$ is a vertical stretch (by a factor of 2) with a reflection in the x-axis of the graph of $y = x^2$.

41. a.

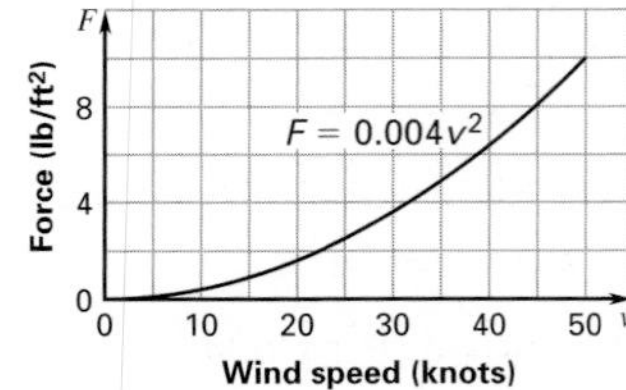

b. From the graph, the wind speed that will produce a force of 1 pound per square foot on a sail is about 16 knots. Using the function to check: $F = 0.004(16)^2 = 1.024$.

c. From the graph, the wind speed that will produce a force of 5 pounds per square foot on a sail is about 35 knots. Using the function to check: $F = 0.004(35)^2 = 4.9$.

Lesson 9.2

9. For $y = -\frac{2}{3}x^2 - 1$, $a = -\frac{2}{3}$ and $b = 0$.

$$x = -\frac{b}{2a} = \frac{0}{2\left(-\frac{2}{3}\right)} = 0$$

The axis of symmetry is $x = 0$.

The x-coordinate of the vertex, $-\frac{b}{2a}$, is 0. To find the y-coordinate, substitute 0 for x in the function and find y: $y = -\frac{2}{3}(0)^2 - 1 = -1$. The vertex is $(0, -1)$.

41. The highest point of each parabolic arch is at the vertex of the parabola. The height h is the y-coordinate of the vertex.

To find the x-coordinate of the vertex, use $x = -\frac{b}{2a}$ with $a = -0.0019$ and $b = 0.71$.

$$x = -\frac{b}{2a} = -\frac{0.71}{2(-0.0019)} \approx 187$$

Substitute 187 for x in the given equation to find the y-coordinate of the vertex.

$$y = -0.0019(187)^2 + 0.71(187) \approx 66.3$$

The height h at the highest point of the arch is about 66 feet.

Lesson 9.3

5. Write the equation $x^2 + 6x = -8$ in standard form: $x^2 + 6x + 8 = 0$.

Graph the function $y = x^2 + 6x + 8$.

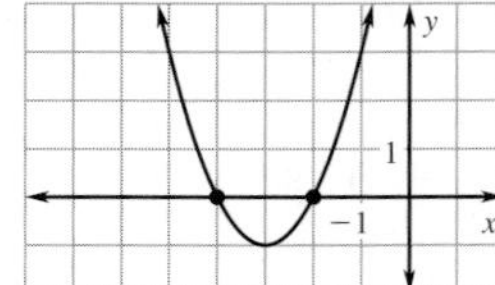

The x-intercepts are -4 and -2.

So, the solutions of $x^2 + 6x = -8$ are -4 and -2.

51. The width of the road can be found by finding the distance between the x-intercepts of the graph $y = -0.0017x^2 + 0.041x$.

Graph the function $y = -0.0017x^2 + 0.041x$ on a graphing calculator.

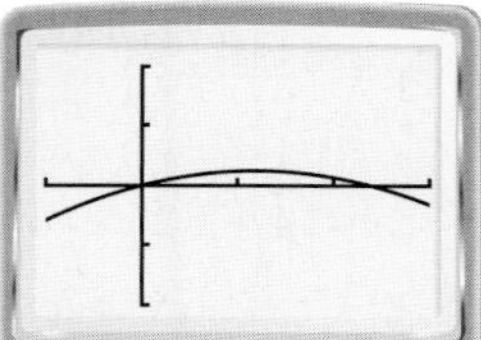

Use the *trace* feature of the graphing calculator to find the x-intercepts. There are two x-intercepts, one at 0 and one at approximately 24.12.

To the nearest tenth of a foot, the width of the road is 24.1 feet.

Lesson 9.4

25. $7c^2 = 100$

$c^2 = \frac{100}{7}$

$c = \pm\sqrt{\frac{100}{7}}$

$c \approx \pm 3.78$ Use a calculator.

59. First, solve the formula for D: $D = \pm\sqrt{\frac{w}{0.0018ds}}$.

Since D cannot be negative in this situation, use the positive square root only.

a. For amethyst, substitute 1 for w, 4.5 for d, and 2.65 for s.

$$D = \sqrt{\frac{1}{0.0018(4.5)(2.65)}} \approx 6.83$$

The diameter is about 6.8 millimeters.

b. For diamond, substitute 1 for w, 4.5 for d, and 3.52 for s.

$$D = \sqrt{\frac{1}{0.0018(4.5)(3.52)}} \approx 5.92$$

The diameter is about 5.9 millimeters.

c. For ruby, substitute 1 for w, 4.5 for d, and 4.00 for s.

$$D = \sqrt{\frac{1}{0.0018(4.5)(4.00)}} \approx 5.55$$

The diameter is about 5.6 millimeters.

Lesson 9.5

19.
$$z^2 + 11z = -\frac{21}{4}$$
$$z^2 + 11z + \left(\frac{11}{2}\right)^2 = -\frac{21}{4} + \left(\frac{11}{2}\right)^2$$
$$\left(z + \frac{11}{2}\right)^2 = -\frac{21}{4} + \frac{121}{4}$$
$$\left(z + \frac{11}{2}\right)^2 = 25$$
$$z + \frac{11}{2} = \pm 5$$
$$z = -\frac{11}{2} \pm 5$$

The solutions of the equation are $-\frac{11}{2} + 5 = -0.5$ and $-\frac{11}{2} - 5 = -10.5$.

47. a. Convert \$1,904,000 to thousands of dollars: $1{,}904{,}000 \div 1000 = 1904$.

Substitute 1904 for y in $y = 7x^2 - 4x + 392$: $1904 = 7x^2 - 4x + 392$.

$$7x^2 - 4x + 392 = 1904$$
$$7x^2 - 4x = 1512$$
$$x^2 - \frac{4}{7}x = 216$$
$$x^2 - \frac{4}{7}x + \left(\frac{2}{7}\right)^2 = 216 + \left(\frac{2}{7}\right)^2$$
$$\left(x - \frac{2}{7}\right)^2 = 216\frac{4}{49}$$
$$x - \frac{2}{7} = \pm\sqrt{216\frac{4}{49}}$$
$$x = \frac{2}{7} \pm \sqrt{216\frac{4}{49}}$$

Using a calculator, the solutions are about 14.99 and about −14.41.

The negative value does not make sense in this situation because the function does not model the years prior to 1985. So, the year when the average salary was \$1,904,000 was 1985 + 15, or 2000.

b. First, graph the function $y = 7x^2 - 4x + 392$ for $x \geq 0$. Then draw a dashed line at about $y = 1904$ until it intersects the curve. Draw a dashed line from this point down to the x-axis. The x-value here is about 15. So, the year when the average salary was \$1,904,000 is about 1985 + 15, or 2000.

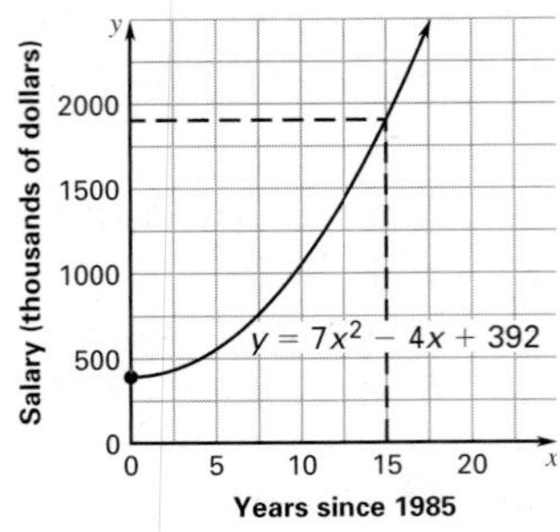

Lesson 9.6

19. Write $6z^2 = 2z^2 + 7z + 5$ in standard form: $4z^2 - 7z - 5 = 0$.

Use the quadratic formula, with $a = 4$, $b = -7$, and $c = -5$.

$$z = \frac{-(-7) \pm \sqrt{(-7)^2 - 4(4)(-5)}}{2(4)} = \frac{7 \pm \sqrt{129}}{8}$$

Using a calculator, the solutions are about 2.29 and about −0.54.

47. For 16,000,000 subscribers, $y = 16$ in the function.

$$16 = 0.7x^2 - 4.3x + 5.5$$

$$0 = 0.7x^2 - 4.3x - 10.5$$

Use the quadratic formula, with $a = 0.7$, $b = -4.3$, and $c = -10.5$.

$$x = \frac{-(-4.3) \pm \sqrt{(-4.3)^2 - 4(0.7)(-10.5)}}{2(0.7)}$$

$$= \frac{4.3 \pm \sqrt{47.89}}{1.4} \quad \text{Use a calculator.}$$

The solutions are about 8.01 and about −1.87.

The negative value does not make sense in this situation because the function does not model the years prior to 1985. So, the year when the number of subscribers was 16,000,000 was 1985 + 8, or 1993.

Lesson 9.7

5. Solve one of the equations for y. Equation 2 is already solved for y. Substitute $-\frac{5}{2}x + 1$ for y in Equation 1. Solve for x.

$$-\frac{5}{2}x + 1 = x^2 - x$$

$$-5x + 2 = 2x^2 - 2x$$

$$0 = 2x^2 + 3x - 2$$

$$0 = (2x - 1)(x + 2)$$

$$x = \frac{1}{2} \text{ or } x = -2$$

Substitute each value for x in one of the original equations.

$y = x^2 - x$	$y = x^2 - x$
$y = \left(\frac{1}{2}\right)^2 - \frac{1}{2}$	$y = (-2)^2 - (-2)$
$y = \left(\frac{1}{4}\right) - \frac{1}{2}$	$y = 4 + 2$
$y = -\frac{1}{4}$	$y = 6$

The solutions are $\left(\frac{1}{2}, -\frac{1}{4}\right)$ and $(-2, 6)$.

15. Graph the equations and use the *Intersect* feature to find the solutions.

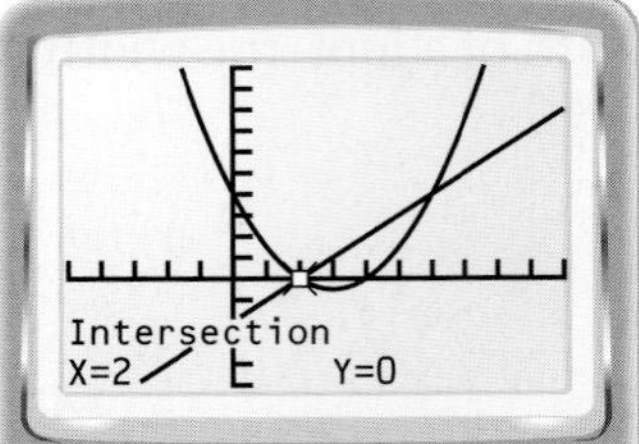

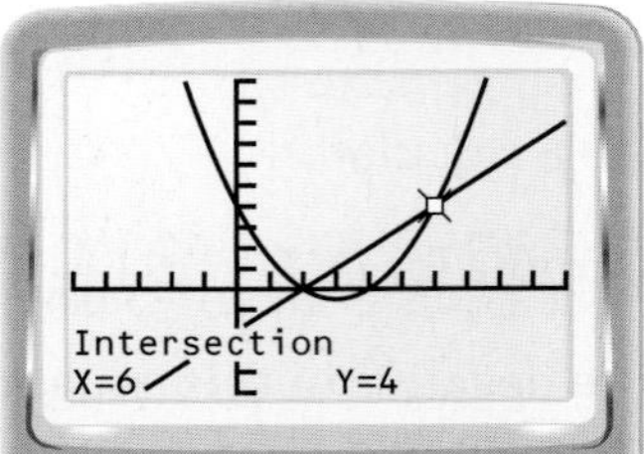

19. Set each side of the equation equal to y. Then graph each equation.

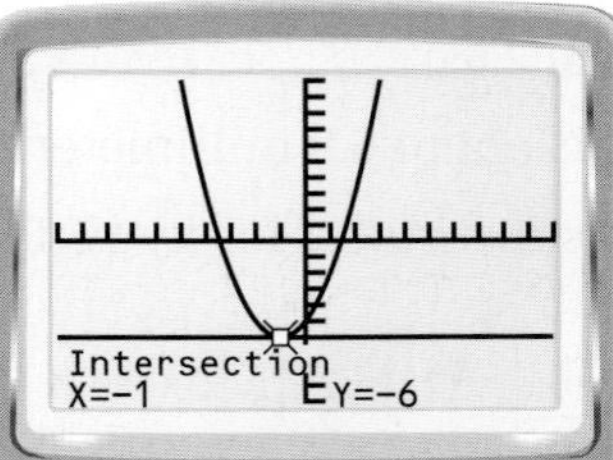

There appears to be one intersection at (−6, −1), so −1 is the only solution. Check this solution in the original equation.

$$-6 = x^2 + 2x - 5$$

$$-6 \stackrel{?}{=} (-1)^2 + 2(-1) - 5$$

$$-6 \stackrel{?}{=} 1 - 2 - 5$$

$$-6 = -6 \checkmark$$

23. Graph each equation.

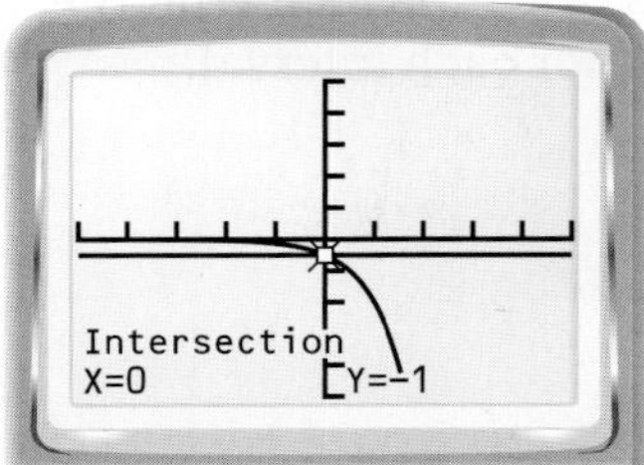

The graphs intersect at one point: $(0, -1)$.

Lesson 9.8

7. 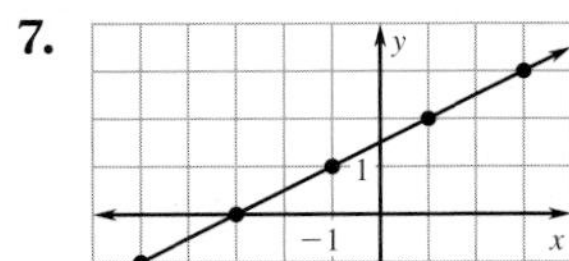

linear function

13.

x	−2	−1	0	1	2
y	−4	−1	0	−1	−4

First differences: +3 +1 −1 −3

Second differences: −2 −2 −2

The second differences are equal, so the table of values represents a quadratic function.

The equation has the form $y = ax^2$. Find the value of a by using the coordinates of a point (other than the origin) that lies on the graph, such as $(-1, -1)$.

$$y = ax^2$$
$$-1 = a(-1)^2$$
$$-1 = a$$

An equation for the function is $y = -x^2$.

25. a. Troy: The population doubled every decade, so the data can be modeled by an exponential function. Union: The population increased by a fixed amount every decade, so the data can be modeled by a linear function.

b.

Decades since 1970	Troy's pop.
0	3000
1	6000
2	12,000
3	24,000
4	48,000

Decades since 1970	Union's pop.
0	3000
1	6000
2	9000
3	12,000
4	15,000

Troy: Ratios of successive y-values are equal. Union: First differences are constant.

c. Let P = population and n = number of decades since 1970. For 2030, $n = 6$. Troy: The population doubles, so $b = 2$. Use a data pair such as (1, 6000) to find a. Because $6000 = a(2^1)$, $a = 3000$. Then $P = 3000 \cdot 2^n$, and $P(6) = 3000 \cdot 2^6 = 192{,}000$. Union: The initial value is 3000 and the rate of change is 3000, so the linear function is $P = 3000n + 3000$, and $P(6) = 3000(6) + 3000 = 21{,}000$.

Lesson 9.9

3. a. The balloon rises at a *constant* rate, so use a linear model.

b.

Balloon's Height

Height (ft)

Time (seconds)

c. The graph is always increasing, so this model works for the period of time when the balloon is rising.

5. a. The juggler is throwing the balls, so use a quadratic model.

b.

Height (feet)

Time (seconds)

c. The graph increases from time 0 to about 1.25 seconds, which is when the height of the ball is increasing. The graph decreases from time 1.25 seconds to time 2.5 seconds, which is when the height of the ball is decreasing.

11. Look for the relationships that are increasing: A and C. A is increasing by a constant rate of 5 per unit interval, so A is a linear relationship. C is doubling per unit interval, which means it is increasing by a constant rate of 100% per unit interval. The solution is C.

15. The number of spores increases each hour, so it is either *growth* or *neither*. Find the percent increase for each interval.

$$\frac{24 - 16}{16} = \frac{1}{2} = 50\%$$

$$\frac{36 - 24}{24} = \frac{1}{2} = 50\%$$

$$\frac{54 - 36}{36} = \frac{1}{2} = 50\%$$

The percent increase is constant, so the relationship represents *growth* with a growth rate of 50%.

Worked-Out Solutions

This section of the book provides step-by-step solutions to exercises with circled exercise numbers. These solutions provide models that can help guide your work with the homework exercises.

The separate **Selected Answers** section follows this section. It provides numerous answers that you can use to check your own answers.

Chapter 10

Lesson 10.1

3. The population is all persons who dine at the restaurant. Because the diners ultimately decide whether or not to take part in the survey by mailing their comment cards, this is a self-selected sample.

15. No. *Sample answer:* The sample may be biased. It does not include fans who only listen to or watch games broadcast on radio or television. The sample is also self-selected. Fans in attendance have to choose to turn in their surveys in order to be counted.

Lesson 10.2

7. Mean:

$$\bar{x} = \frac{5.52 + 5.44 + 3.60 + 5.76 + 3.80 + 7.22}{6}$$

$$= \frac{31.34}{6} = 5.2233...$$

So, the mean of the data is $5.22\overline{3}$.

Median: The ordered list of numbers is: 3.60, 3.80, 5.44, 5.52, 5.76, 7.22. There are two middle values, 5.44 and 5.52. Therefore, the median is $\frac{5.44 + 5.52}{2} = 5.48$.

Each data value appears just once, so there is no mode.

19. a. The range of the pumpkin weights is the difference of the greatest value and the least value; $24 - 5 = 19$ pounds.

b. Mean: $\bar{x} =$

$$\frac{22 + 21 + 24 + 24 + 5 + 24 + 5 + 23 + 24 + 24}{10}$$

$$= \frac{196}{10} = 19.6$$

The mean of the pumpkin weights is 19.6 pounds.

Median: The ordered list of weights is: 5, 5, 21, 22, 23, 24, 24, 24, 24, 24. There are two middle values, 23 and 24. So, the median is 23.5 pounds.

Mode: The weight that occurs most frequently is 24 pounds.

c. The median best represents the data. *Sample answer:* The mode is the greatest data value and the mean is less than 8 of the 10 data values.

Lesson 10.3

3. Look at the number in the cell that is in both the *Males* row and the *Poodles* column. The pet store has 5 male poodles.

7. Set up a table and fill in the given information.

	0 B	1 B	2 B	Total
0 S	9	7		27
1 S	10		8	
2 S		7		22
Total		28	23	82

Using B for brothers and S for sisters:

2 B and 0 S: $27 - (9 + 7) = 11$

1 B and 2 S: $28 - (6 + 7) = 15$

1 S Total: $10 + 15 + 8 = 33$

0 B Total: $82 - (28 + 23) = 31$

0 B and 2 S: $31 - (10 + 9) = 12$

2 B and 2 S: $23 - (11 + 8) = 4$

Use these calculated values to complete the table.

	0 B	1 B	2 B	Total
0 S	9	7	11	27
1 S	10	15	8	33
2 S	12	6	4	22
Total	31	28	23	82

15. Look for the largest number in the *Wheat Bread* row. The answer is *Ham*, because the number of ham sandwiches is higher than the numbers of other types of sandwiches on whole wheat bread.

Lesson 10.4

3. First, separate the data into stems and leaves.

Stem	Leaves
1	7
2	0 4 0
3	1 3 8 0 9 8 5
4	2
5	5

Key: 1 | 7 = 17

Now rewrite the leaves in increasing order.

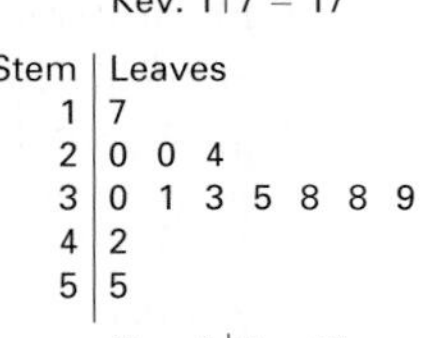

Stem	Leaves
1	7
2	0 0 4
3	0 1 3 5 8 8 9
4	2
5	5

Key: 1 | 7 = 17

19. a. Draw the bars of the histogram using the intervals from the frequency table.

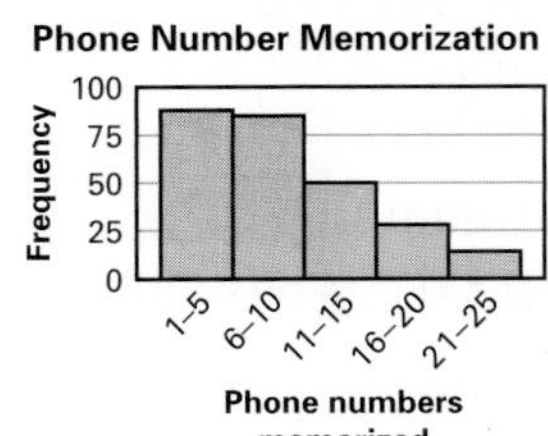

b. Use the table to determine the total number of people surveyed: 88 + 85 + 50 + 28 + 14 = 265.

Determine the number of favorable outcomes. This number is the sum of the number of people in the 11–15 range, the 16–20 range, and the 21–25 range.

$$P(11\text{–}25) = \frac{\text{Number of favorable outcomes}}{\text{Total number of outcomes}}$$

$$= \frac{50 + 28 + 14}{265} = \frac{92}{265}$$

Lesson 10.5

3. Write the data in order from least to greatest. Find the median and the quartiles.

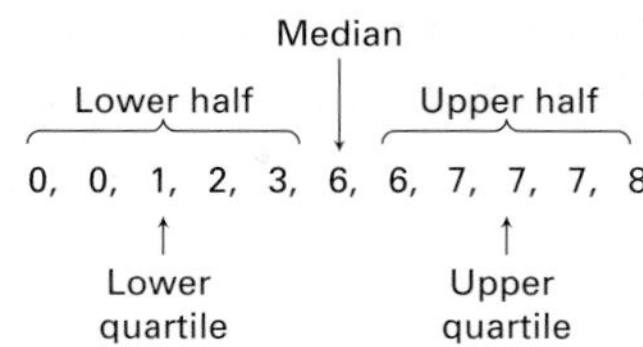

Plot the median, the quartiles, the maximum value, and the minimum value below a number line. Draw a box from the lower quartile to the upper quartile. Draw a vertical line through the median. Draw a line segment from the side of the box to the maximum value and another from the other side of the box to the minimum value.

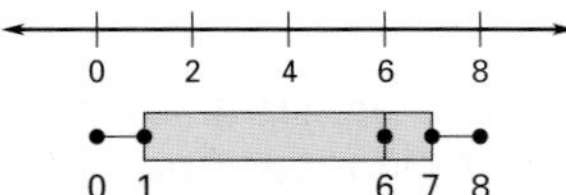

17. a. Order the data, and then find the median and the quartiles.

lower quartile: $\frac{\$38.4 + \$49.9}{2} = \$44.15$

median: \$52.4

upper quartile: $\frac{\$107.0 + \$118.2}{2} = \$112.60$

Use the median, the quartiles, the maximum value, and the minimum value to draw the box-and-whisker plot.

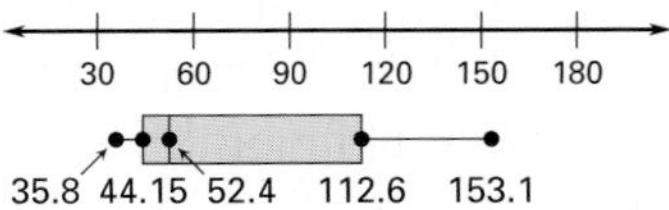

b. To check if any of the data are outliers, find the inner quartile range: 112.6 − 44.15 = 68.45. An outlier would be any value greater than 1.5(68.45) + 112.6 = 215.275 or less than 44.15 − 1.5(68.45) = −58.525. Since all the data values are within these two values, there are no outliers. So, none of the states had retail sales that can be considered outliers.

Worked-Out Solutions

This section of the book provides step-by-step solutions to exercises with circled exercise numbers. These solutions provide models that can help guide your work with the homework exercises.

The separate **Selected Answers** section follows this section. It provides numerous answers that you can use to check your own answers.

Chapter 11

Lesson 11.1

3. Use a tree diagram to find the possible outcomes in the sample space.

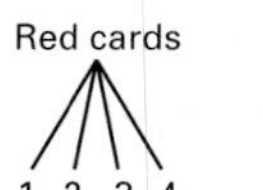

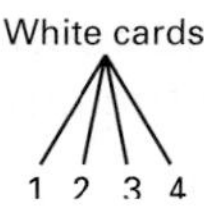

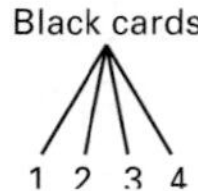

The sample space has 12 possible outcomes. The outcomes are: Red 1, Red 2, Red 3, Red 4, White 1, White 2, White 3, White 4, Black 1, Black 2, Black 3, Black 4.

21. Since there are 15 girls and 12 boys, there are a total of 27 students. So there are 27 possible outcomes.

$P(\text{boy}) = \dfrac{\text{Number of boys}}{\text{Total number of students}} = \dfrac{12}{27} = \dfrac{4}{9}$

Odds in favor of choosing a boy

$= \dfrac{\text{Number of boys}}{\text{Number of girls}} = \dfrac{12}{15} = \dfrac{4}{5}$

Sample answer: The probability and odds of choosing a boy are related because they each compare the number of favorable outcomes to another number. The probability of choosing a boy compares the number of boys to the total number of outcomes possible, while the odds of choosing a boy compare the number of boys to the total number of outcomes less the number of boys.

Lesson 11.2

21. ${}_7P_3 = \dfrac{7!}{(7-3)!} = \dfrac{7!}{4!} = \dfrac{7 \cdot 6 \cdot 5 \cdot \cancel{4!}}{\cancel{4!}} = 210$

35. a. The total number of possible outcomes for the order on the first day is the number of permutations of the 4 student presenters on that day: ${}_4P_4 = 4!$.

The number of favorable outcomes (being chosen to be the first or second presenter) is the number of permutations of the 3 other presenters, given that you are chosen to be the first or second presenter. This is ${}_3P_3 = 3!$ if you are the first presenter and also ${}_3P_3 = 3!$ if you are the second presenter.

$P(\text{1st or 2nd presenter})$
$= P(\text{1st presenter}) + P(\text{2nd presenter})$

$= \dfrac{3!}{4!} + \dfrac{3!}{4!} = \dfrac{1}{4} + \dfrac{1}{4}, \text{ or } \dfrac{1}{2}$

The probability that you are the first or the second presenter is $\frac{1}{2}$.

b. The number of possible outcomes is still 4!. The number of favorable outcomes is again ${}_3P_3 = 3!$ for you being the second presenter and ${}_3P_3 = 3!$ for you being the third presenter.

$P(\text{2nd or 3rd presenter})$
$= P(\text{2nd presenter}) + P(\text{3rd presenter})$

$= \dfrac{3!}{4!} + \dfrac{3!}{4!} = \dfrac{1}{4} + \dfrac{1}{4}, \text{ or } \dfrac{1}{2}$

The probability that you are the second or the third presenter is $\frac{1}{2}$.

This answer is the same as the answer in part (a).

Lesson 11.3

7. ${}_8C_5 = \dfrac{8!}{(8-5)!5!} = \dfrac{8!}{3!5!} = \dfrac{8 \cdot 7 \cdot 6 \cdot \cancel{5!}}{3! \cdot \cancel{5!}} = 56$

25. a. The number of possible outcomes is the number of combinations of the 9 contestants taken 6 at a time, or ${}_9C_6$, because the order in which the contestants are chosen is not important.

$${}_9C_6 = \frac{9!}{(9-6)!6!} = \frac{9!}{3!6!} = \frac{9 \cdot 8 \cdot 7 \cdot \cancel{6!}}{3! \cdot \cancel{6!}} = 84$$

There are 84 possible combinations of 6 players from the group of eligible contestants.

b. Find the number of favorable outcomes, those where you and your two friends are 3 of the 6 contestants selected to play. The order of the selections is not important. The favorable outcomes are those where only 3 of the other 6 eligible contestants are chosen. So the number of favorable combinations is ${}_6C_3 = 20$. Therefore, the probability that you and your friends are chosen is $\frac{20}{84}$, or $\frac{5}{21}$.

Lesson 11.4

11. $P(A \text{ or } B) = P(A) + P(B) - P(A \text{ and } B)$

$0.71 = 0.28 + 0.64 - P(A \text{ and } B)$

$-0.21 = -P(A \text{ and } B) \rightarrow P(A \text{ and } B) = 0.21$

21. $P(\text{K or } \blacklozenge) = P(\text{K}) + P(\blacklozenge) - P(\text{K and } \blacklozenge)$

$= \left(\frac{4}{52}\right) + \left(\frac{13}{52}\right) - \left(\frac{1}{52}\right) = \frac{4}{13}$

45. The number of combinations of 6 food items is 10^6. The number of combinations of 6 different food items is $10 \cdot 9 \cdot 8 \cdot 7 \cdot 6 \cdot 5$. So, the probability that at least 2 bring the same item is $P = 1 - P(\text{none are the same}) =$

$1 - \frac{10 \cdot 9 \cdot 8 \cdot 7 \cdot 6 \cdot 5}{10^6} = 0.8488.$

Lesson 11.5

18. Primes from 1 to 20: 2, 3, 5, 7, 11, 13, 17, 19.

$$P(\text{odd} \mid \text{prime}) = \frac{\text{number of odd primes}}{\text{number of primes}} = \frac{7}{8}$$

35.

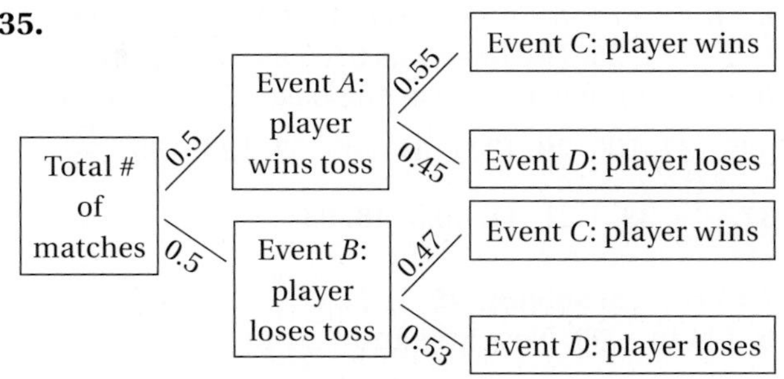

$P(C) = P(A \text{ and } C) + P(B \text{ and } C)$

$= P(A) \cdot P(C \mid A) + P(B) \cdot P(C \mid B)$

$= (0.5)(0.55) + (0.5)(0.47) = 0.51$

Selected Answers

Chapter 1

1.1 Skill Practice **1.** exponent: 12, base: 6 **3.** 60 **5.** 12 **7.** 12 **9.** 3 **11.** 10 **13.** $\frac{1}{3}$ **17.** seven to the third power, $7 \cdot 7 \cdot 7$ **19.** three tenths to the fourth power, $0.3 \cdot 0.3 \cdot 0.3 \cdot 0.3$ **21.** n to the seventh power, $n \cdot n \cdot n \cdot n \cdot n \cdot n \cdot n$ **23.** t to the fourth power, $t \cdot t \cdot t \cdot t$ **25.** The base was used as the exponent and the exponent was used as the base; $5^4 = 5 \cdot 5 \cdot 5 \cdot 5 = 625$. **27.** 100 **29.** 1331 **31.** 243 **33.** 1296 **35.** $\frac{27}{125}$ **37.** $\frac{1}{216}$ **39.** 1.21 **41.** 40.5 **43.** 9.6

1.1 Problem Solving **49.** 162.5 cm **51. a.** 12 in. **b.** 144 in.^{2} **53.** New England Patriots

1.2 Skill Practice **1.** Square 4. **3.** 8 **5.** 14 **7.** $3\frac{3}{5}$ **9.** $63\frac{3}{4}$ **11.** 21 **13.** 73.5 **15.** $12\frac{1}{2}$ **17.** 48 **21.** $\frac{1}{2}$ was multiplied by 6 before squaring 6; $20 - \frac{1}{2} \cdot 6^2 = 20 - \frac{1}{2} \cdot 36 = 20 - 18 = 2$. **23.** 29 **25.** 126 **27.** 0.75 **29.** 3 **33.** $(2 \times 2 + 3)^2 - (4 + 3) \times 5$

1.2 Problem Solving **35. a.** \$22.87 **b.** \$2.13 **37.** *Sample answer:* $(3 \times 4) + 5$ **39. a.** \$380, \$237.99; \$142.01 **b.** *Sample answer:* You could write an expression showing the difference of your income and expenses as $10s - (4.50m + 12.99)$.

1.2 Graphing Calculator Activity **1.** 5 **3.** 0.429 **5.** 0.188 **7.** 40.9 BMI units

1.3 Skill Practice **1.** rate **3.** $x + 8$ **5.** $\frac{1}{2}m$ **7.** $7 - n$ **9.** $\frac{2t}{12}$ **11.** $2k - 7$ **15.** $4v$ **17.** $\frac{16}{p}$ **19.** $7 - d$ **21.** $12y$ **23.** 0.2 ft/sec **25.** 83.6 ft/sec **27.** Feet should cancel out; \$54. **29.** \$19.50 for 1 h

1.3 Problem Solving **31.** $19.95t + 3$; \$102.75 **33. a.** \$.055, \$.06 **b.** 48 oz container **c.** \$.96 **35.** \$500 **37. a.** $12g + h + \frac{1}{4}c$ **b.** 247; 376.75; 242

1.4 Skill Practice **1.** *Sample answer:* $3x + 5 = 20$ **3.** $42 + n = 51$ **5.** $9 - \frac{t}{6} = 5$ **7.** $9(t + 5) < 6$ **9.** $8 < b + 3 < 12$ **11.** $10 < t - 7 < 20$ **13.** $p \geq 12.99$ **15.** The wrong inequality symbol is used; $\frac{t}{4.2} \leq 15$. **17.** solution **19.** not a solution **21.** not a solution **23.** solution **25.** solution **27.** not a solution **29.** 5 **31.** 12 **33.** 9 **35.** $3x - 2 = x + 5$; solution

1.4 Problem Solving **39.** 7.5 mi **41.** 167 h **43.** \$100 **45. a.** $6r + 5(10 - r) \geq 55$ **b.** Yes; you will earn \$30 running errands and \$25 walking dogs; $30 + 25 = 55$. **c.** Yes; if you work 10 hours running errands, you will earn \$60. You will not meet your goal if you work all 10 hours walking dogs.

1.5 Skill Practice **1.** *Sample answer:* $d = rt$ **3.** You know the cost of materials and the amount you hope to make. You need to find the amount you should charge for each collar. You need to know the number of collars you made, which is missing. **5.** You know the temperature in Rome and the temperature in Dallas. You know the formula to convert Fahrenheit temperatures to Celsius temperatures. You need to find the higher temperature. **7.** The formula for perimeter should be used, not area; $P = 2\ell + 2w$; $P = 2(200) + 2(150) = 700$; $\$10(700) = \$7000$. **9.** $P = I - E$

1.5 Problem Solving **15.** 46.25 in.^{2} **17.** 2 water bottles **19. a.** 960 ft **b.** 480 ft **21. a.**

Room size (feet)	1 by 1	2 by 2	3 by 3	4 by 4	5 by 5
Remaining area (square feet)	431	428	423	416	407

b. $1 \leq s \leq 5$; 5 ft

1.5 Problem Solving Workshop
1. 9 pieces of cake; Equation: Let c be the number of pieces of cake; $9c = 99$, $c = 11$. Diagram: Draw a diagram of a 9 inch by 11 inch pan and cut the cake into 3 inch by 3 inch pieces. From the diagram you see that you can cut 9 such pieces. The diagram shows that you cannot actually cut 11 square pieces because of the shape of the pan.

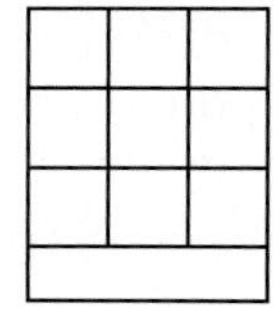

3. The equation should be $3x + 6 = 12$ because there are only 3 spaces between the 4 floats; $3(2) + 6 = 12$.

1.6 Skill Practice **1.** precision **3.** 14.2 gal **5.** 71 in. **7.** 29.3 cm **9.** Minutes are a smaller unit of measure than hours, therefore 85 minutes is more precise than 1.5 hours. **11.** 4 **13.** 2 **15.** 3 **17.** 3 **19.** 7 **21.** 81.2 m **23.** 110 **25.** 48.2 mm **27.** 227 kg **29.** The area must have the same number of significant digits as the least precise measurement. The value 20 is less precise than 8.2, having one significant digit. Therefore the area of the rectangle should be given with just one significant digit.

Selected Answers

1.6 Problem Solving **33.** Justine **35.** Chandra **37.** No. *Sample answer:* Both 426 miles and 19.3 gallons are measurements with 3 significant digits, so Brian's answer should have 3 significant digits. He should say that his car gets 22.1 miles per gallon. **39.** 118.5 lb; because tenths are smaller units than ones, 118.5 pounds is more precise than 118 pounds.
41. 13.2 mi **43.** *Sample answer:* 22,000 cm
45. *Sample answer:* 4020 m^2 **47.** 24 in. **49.** 1800 ft^2

1.7 Skill Practice **1.** input; output
3. domain: 0, 1, 2, and 3, range: 5, 7, 15, and 44
5. domain: 6, 12, 21, and 42, range: 5, 7, 10, and 17
7. not a function **9.** The pairing is a function. Each input is paired with only one output.
11. *Sample:*

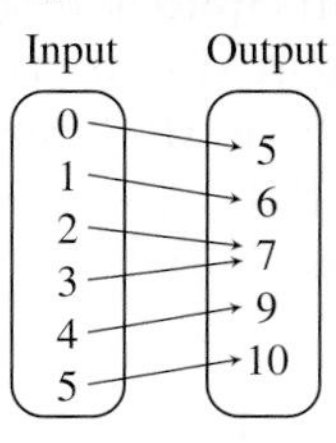

Input	Output
0	5
1	6
2	7
3	7
4	9
5	10

15.

Input	4	5	7	8	12
Output	7.5	8.5	10.5	11.5	15.5

range: 7.5, 8.5, 10.5, 11.5, and 15.5

17.

Input	4	6	9	11
Output	5	6	7.5	8.5

range: 5, 6, 7.5, and 8.5

19.

Input	0	2	4	6
Output	$\frac{1}{2}$	1	$1\frac{1}{2}$	2

range: $\frac{1}{2}$, 1, $1\frac{1}{2}$, and 2

21. $y = x - 8$

1.7 Problem Solving **23. a.** the number of quarters left; the number of quarters used
b. $y = 10 - x$; domain: 0, 1, 2, 3, 4, 5, 6, 7, 8, 9, and 10
c.

Input	0	1	2	3	4	5	6	7	8	9	10
Output	10	9	8	7	6	5	4	3	2	1	0

range: 0, 1, 2, 3, 4, 5, 6, 7, 8, 9, and 10
25. $y = 100 + 20m$; independent variable: m, the number of months; dependent variable: y, the amount of money saved; domain: $m > 0$, range: $y \geq 100$; $340

27. a.

2	3	4	5
A, B, C	D, E, F	G, H, I	J, K, L

6	7	8	9
M, N, O	P, Q, R, S	T, U, V	W, X, Y, Z

No; because there is more than one output for each input.

b.

A	B	C	D	E	F	G	H	I	J	K	L
2	2	2	3	3	3	4	4	4	5	5	5

M	N	O	P	Q	R	S	T	U	V	W	X	Y	Z
6	6	6	7	7	7	7	8	8	8	9	9	9	9

Yes; because there is only one output for each input.

1.7 Graphing Calculator Activity **1.** 50°F; scroll down until you see the output 10, look to see that the input is 50.

3.

Input	0	1	2	3
Output	5	5.75	6.5	7.25

5.

Input	1	2	3	4
Output	7	14.5	22	29.5

1.8 Skill Practice **1.** domain; range

3.

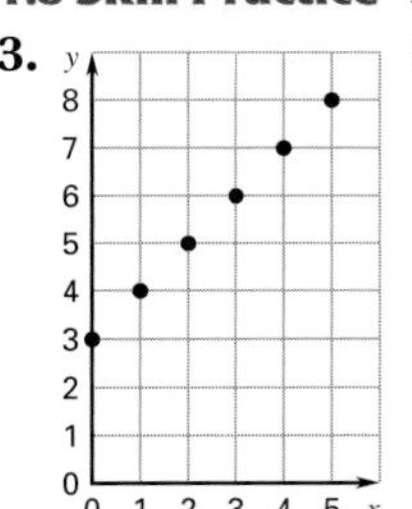

5.

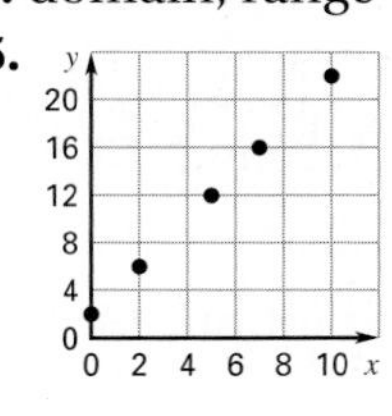

7.

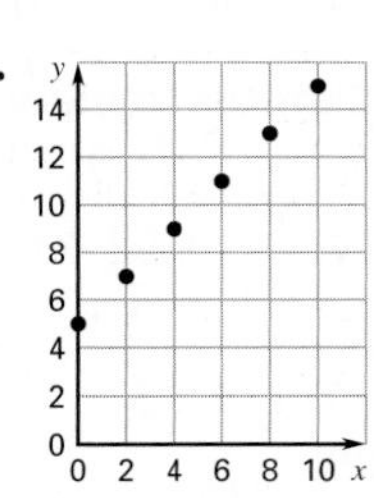

9. The domain and range are graphed backwards.

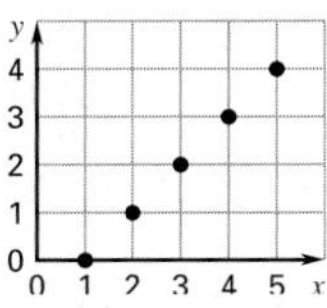

11. $y = 2x - 2$; domain: 1, 2, 3, and 4, range: 0, 2, 4, and 6

1.8 Problem Solving

15.

Cost (millions of dollars)

Years since 1997

17.

Years since 1984	Voters	Voters (millions)
0	92,652,680	93
4	91,594,693	92
8	104,405,155	104
12	96,456,345	96
16	105,586,274	106

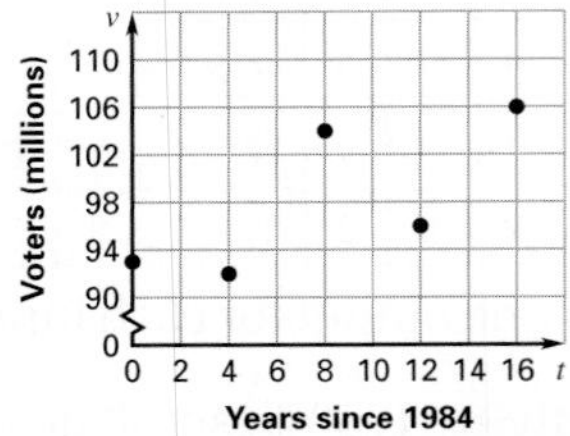

19. a. increases **b.** Yes; 27.5 grams is between the mass of an egg that is just under 38 millimeters long and an egg that is just over 38 millimeters long.

Extension **1.** function **3.** not a function **5.** function **7.** Not a function. *Sample answer:* There could be many students whose first names have 4 letters, for instance, but their last names could all have a different number of letters. **9.** Function; for each of your birthdays, you have only one height.

Chapter Review **1.** 7, 12 **3.** algebraic expression **5.** 16 **7.** 10 **9.** 400 **11.** 25 in.^{2} **13.** 9 **15.** 8 **17.** $\frac{1}{3}$ **19.** 52 **21.** 18 **23.** $z - 5$ **25.** $3x^2$ **27.** $2.95n + 2.19$ **29.** $13 + t \geq 24$ **31.** solution **33.** 240 ft^2 **35.** 4 **37.** 2

39.

Input	10	12	15	20	21
Output	5	7	10	15	16

range: 5, 7, 10, 15, and 16

41. $y = x + 4$ **43.**

Chapter 1 Extra Practice

1. 16 **3.** 4.4 **5.** 2.4 **7.** $\frac{8}{27}$ **9.** 26 **11.** 28 **13.** 10 **15.** 111 **17.** $\frac{3}{4}m$ **19.** $y - 3$ **21.** $45 - m$ **23.** $12 \cdot (r - 4) = 72$ **25.** 38 **27.** 16 **29.** *Sample answer:* You know the temperature in Quito in degrees Celsius and the temperature in Miami in degrees Fahrenheit. You need to find out which one is greater. **31.** domain: 3, 4, 5, 6; range: 9, 11, 13, 15

33.

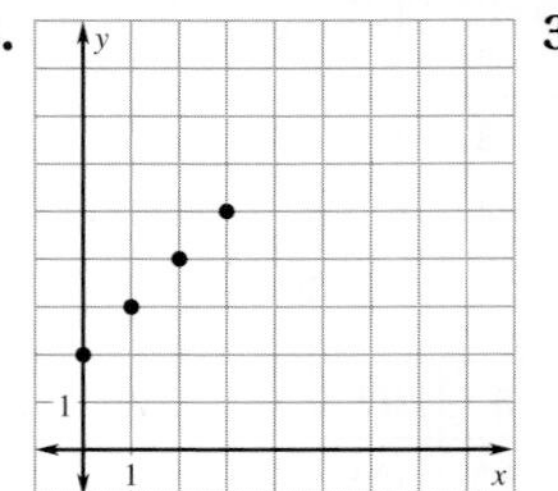

35.

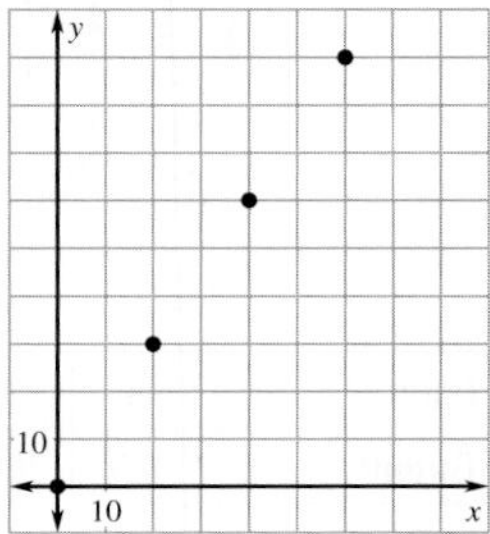

Selected Answers

Chapter 2

2.1 Skill Practice **1.** real numbers **3.** 2 **5.** −3 **7.** 14 **9.** ±50 **11.** −15 **13.** ±13 **15.** 3 **17.** −2 **19.** −9 **21.** 14 **25.** $-\sqrt{12}$: real number, irrational number, −3.7: real number, rational number, $\sqrt{9}$: real number, rational number, integer, whole number, 2.9: real number, rational number; −3.7, $-\sqrt{12}$, 2.9, $\sqrt{9}$ **27.** $\sqrt{8}$: real number, irrational number, $-\frac{2}{5}$: real number, rational number, −1: real number, rational number, integer, 0.6: real number, rational number, $\sqrt{6}$: real number, irrational number; −1, $-\frac{2}{5}$, 0.6, $\sqrt{6}$, $\sqrt{8}$ **29.** −8.3: real number, rational number, $-\sqrt{80}$: real number, irrational number, $-\frac{17}{2}$: real number, rational number, −8.25: real number, rational number, $-\sqrt{100}$: real number, rational number, integer; $-\sqrt{100}$, $-\sqrt{80}$, $-\frac{17}{2}$, −8.3, −8.25 **31.** If a number is a real number, then it is an irrational number; false. *Sample answer:* 3 is a real number and a rational number. **33.** If a number is an irrational number, then it is not a whole number; true. **35.** 2 **37.** −42 **39.** 63 **41.** B

2.1 Problem Solving **45.** 60 in. **47.** 35 ft **49.** 2.2 ft **51. a.** 144 tiles **b.** 16 ft. *Sample answer:* If the homeowner can buy 144 tiles that are each 256 square inches, then the total area is (144 tiles)(256 square inches per tile) = 36,864 square inches. Divide 36,864 square inches by 144 square inches to find the number of square feet, 256 square feet. If the area of the square is 256 square feet, take the square root of 256 to find the side length, 16 feet.

Extension **1.** Let x and y be two rational numbers. By definition $x = \frac{a}{b}$ and $y = \frac{c}{d}$ where a, b, c, and d are integers with $b \neq 0$ and $d \neq 0$; $xy = \frac{a}{b} \bullet \frac{c}{d} = \frac{ac}{bd}$. Because the set of integers is closed under the operation of multiplication, the expressions ac and bd are both integers. Therefore, the product xy is equal to the ratio of two integers. So by definition, this product is a rational number. **3.** Let x be a rational number and y be an irrational number. By definition, $x = \frac{a}{b}$ where a and b are integers with $b \neq 0$. Now assume that the sum $x + y$ is a rational number. Therefore $x + y$ can be written as the quotient of integers c and d with $d \neq 0$; $x + y = \frac{c}{d}$; $\frac{a}{b} + y = \frac{c}{d}$; $\frac{a}{b} + y - \frac{a}{b} = \frac{c}{d} - \frac{a}{b}$; $y = \frac{bc - ad}{bd}$. Because the set of integers is closed under the operations of subtraction and multiplication, the expression $bc - ad$ is an integer. So by definition $\frac{bc - ad}{bd}$ is a rational number, which means that y must be rational. But y is an irrational number, meaning the assumption that $x + y$ is rational must be false. Therefore, $x + y$ is an irrational number.

2.2 Skill Practice **1.** inverse operations **3.** 3 **5.** 5 **7.** −3 **9.** 7 **11.** 17 **13.** 4 **17.** 4 **19.** 6 **21.** −15 **23.** 15 **25.** 48 **27.** 22 **29.** The student multiplied x by 100 to produce a number with a decimal part identical to the decimal part of x. When the student subtracted, the result was a whole number. **35.** −2.05 **37.** $\frac{5}{8}$ **39.** 0.06 **41.** 96 **43.** 12 **45.** −56 **47.** $\frac{3}{5}$ **49.** $54 = 12x$; 4.5 in.

2.2 Problem Solving **53.** 1046.6 ft **55.** 11 ft **57. a.** $\frac{4}{7}x = 200$ **b.** Plants; if you solve the equation in part (a) you find that there are 350 species of birds.

59. a.

t	d
1	6.5
2	13
3	19.5
4	26
5	32.5

b. 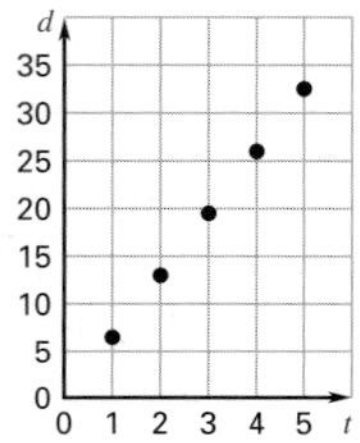 4 sec

c. $26 = 6.5t$; 4 sec **61. a.** 171 hits **b.** 215 hits **c.** No; if Mueller had fewer hits than Wells but had a higher batting average, he must have had fewer at bats than Wells.

2.3 Skill Practice **1.** like terms **3.** 4 **5.** 2 **7.** −3 **9.** 6 **11.** 40 **13.** 18 **15.** 4 **17.** 9 **19.** −4 **23.** The division of $-2x + x$ by −2 is done incorrectly. *Sample answer:* If like terms are combined as the first step, the second line would be $-x = 10$ and the final result would be $x = -10$. **25.** $y = 2x + 4$; −7 **27.** 4 **29.** 5 **31.** 0.5 **33.** 15.9 **35.** 6.9

2.3 Problem Solving **37.** 28 classes **39.** 5 half-side advertisements **41.** Yes; the equation \$542 = \$50 + 6x gives the monthly cost of a guitar that costs \$542. Solving the equation gives x = \$82 per month, so you can afford the guitar. **43. a.** $y = 12x$

b.

x (hours)	Marissa	Ryan	Total
1	5	7	12
2	10	14	24
3	15	21	36
4	20	28	48
5	25	35	60

c. 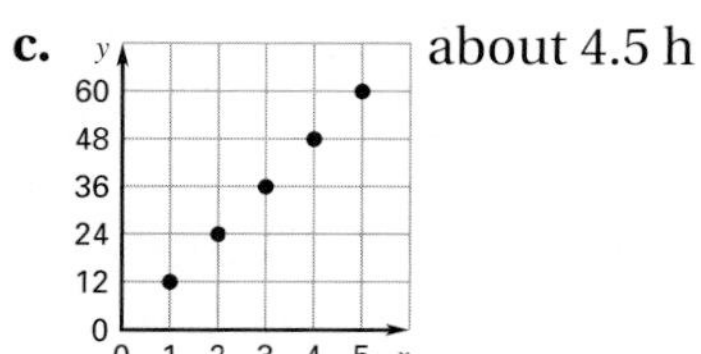 about 4.5 h

2.3 Problem Solving Workshop
1. 7 players **3.** 4 chairs

2.4 Skill Practice **1.** $\frac{5}{3}$ **3.** 3 **5.** 6 **7.** -2 **9.** -8 **11.** -8 **13.** 4 **15.** -9 **17.** -19 **19.** 12 **21.** -2 **23.** -9 **25.** -3 times -6 is 18, not -18; $5x - 3x + 18 = 2$, $2x + 18 = 2$, $2x = -16$, $x = -8$. **27.** 2 **29.** 3 **31.** -5 **33.** 2 **35.** 9.5 in., 6 in.; if you use the perimeter formula $P = 2\ell + 2w$ and substitute $3.5 + w$ for ℓ, the solution is $w = 6$.

2.4 Problem Solving **39.** 0.75 ft **41. a.** 34 mo **b.** 307 ft per mo **c.** After the work crews merged; before the work crews merged they were working at a rate of $115 + 137 = 252$ feet per month, and after merging at a rate of 307 feet per month.

2.5 Skill Practice **1.** identity **3.** -2 **5.** -4 **7.** -7 **9.** 8 **11.** -4 **13.** -3 **17.** *Sample answer:* Distribute the 3 to get $6z - 15 = 2z + 13$, then subtract $2z$ from each side to get $4z - 15 = 13$, next add 15 to each side to get $4z = 28$, finally divide each side by 4 to get $z = 7$. **19.** 2 **21.** -7 **23.** no solution **25.** no solution **27.** The 3 was not distributed to both terms; $3x + 15 = 3x + 15$, $15 = 15$, so the equation is an identity. **29.** *Sample answer:* $5x + 4 = 5x$; the number $5x$ cannot be equal to 4 more than itself. **31.** 2 **33.** -4 **35.** 6 **37.** identity **39.** 2 **41.** 10 **43.** identity **45.** 60

2.5 Problem Solving **49.** 9 nights **51.** about 4 yr **53. a.** $23.4t = 24(t - 0.3)$; 12 sec **b.** about 4.4 sec **c.** No; it would take 12 seconds for the sheepdog to catch up to the collie and it only takes 4.4 seconds for the collie to complete the last leg.

2.5 Spreadsheet Activity **1.** 2 **3.** 4

Extension **1.** Subt. Prop. of Equality; Add. Prop. of Equality; Div. Prop. of Equality **3.** $5x - 10 = -40$ (Given); $5x = -30$ (Add. Prop. of Equality); $x = -6$ (Div. Prop. of Equality) **5.** $5 - x = 17$ (Given); $-x = 12$ (Subt. Prop. of Equality); $x = -12$ (Div. Prop. of Equality) **7.** $19 - 2x = -17$ (Given); $-2x = -36$ (Subt. Prop. of Equality); $x = 18$ (Div. Prop. of Equality) **9.** $5(3x - 20) = -10$ (Given); $15x - 100 = -10$ (Dist. Prop.); $15x = 90$ (Add. Prop. of Equality); $x = 6$ (Div. Prop. of Equality) **11.** $2(-x - 5) = 12$ (Given); $-2x - 10 = 12$ (Dist. Prop.); $-2x = 22$ (Add. Prop. of Equality); $x = -11$ (Div. Prop. of Equality) **13.** $13 - x = -2(x + 3)$ (Given); $13 - x = -2x - 6$ (Dist. Prop.); $13 + x = -6$ (Add. Prop. of Equality); $x = -19$ (Subt. Prop. of Equality) **15.** In the initial step, x should have been subtracted from each side, not added. The second line should be $6x = 24$ and its reason should be the Subtraction Property of Equality. The third line should then begin with $x = 4$.

2.6 Skill Practice **1.** ratios **3.** no; 7 to 9 **5.** yes **7.** $\frac{6}{5}$ **9.** 22 **11.** 48 **13.** 15 **15.** 40 **17.** 12 **21.** Multiply each side by 6, not $\frac{1}{6}$; $6 \cdot \frac{3}{4} = 6 \cdot \frac{x}{6}$, $4\frac{1}{2} = x$. **23.** $\frac{3}{8} = \frac{x}{32}$; 12 **25.** $\frac{x}{4} = \frac{8}{16}$; 2 **27.** $\frac{b}{10} = \frac{7}{2}$; 35 **29.** $\frac{12}{18} = \frac{d}{27}$; 18 **31.** 1.8 **33.** 2.4 **35.** 4 **37.** 4 **39.** 2 **41.** 3.5 **43.** Yes. *Sample answer:* $\frac{3}{6} = \frac{4}{8}$

2.6 Problem Solving **45.** $\frac{2}{145}$ **47.** $\frac{2}{5}$ **49.** $\frac{1}{2}$ **51.** 45 goals **53. a.** $\frac{10}{23}$ **b.** 110 lift tickets **c.** 40 snowboarders

2.7 Skill Practice **1.** cross product **3.** 6 **5.** 24 **7.** 1 **9.** -49 **11.** 2 **13.** 12 **17.** Use the cross products property to multiply 4 by x and 16 by 3; $4 \cdot x = 3 \cdot 16$, $4x = 48$, $x = 12$. **19.** 15 **21.** 10 **23.** 5.5 **25.** -3.4 **27.** 4.2 **29.** -5.9 **31. a.** Multiplication property of equality **b.** Multiply **c.** Simplify

2.7 Problem Solving **33.** 5 c **35.** 90 km **37.** 7.5 km **39.** 17.728 m **41.** 80 yd; find the actual length of the field by using the ratio 1 in.: 20 yd, then use that number to find the width of the soccer field by using the ratio 3 : 2.

2.8 Skill Practice **1.** literal equation **3.** $x = \frac{c}{b - a}$; -2 **5.** $x = bc - a$; 9 **7.** $x = a(c - b)$; 28 **9.** b should have been subtracted from both sides, not added; $ax = -b$, $x = -\frac{b}{a}$. **11.** $y = 7 - 2x$ **13.** $4 - 3x = y$ **15.** $2 + \frac{6}{7}x = y$ **17.** $\frac{9}{5}x - 6 = y$ **19.** $y = \frac{1}{2}x + \frac{1}{3}$ **21.** $h = \frac{S - 2B}{P}$ **25.** $y = 18 - 5x$ **27.** $\ell = \frac{S}{\pi r} - r$; 13.03 cm **29.** *Sample answer:* You want to find how long it will take to drive 150 miles if you drive at an average rate of 55 miles per hour.

2.8 Problem Solving **33. a.** $x = \frac{C - 25}{12}$ **b.** 10 nights; 13 nights; 15 nights **35.** Divide each side by the total bill, b, to get $\frac{a}{b} = p\%$.

Chapter Review **1.** scale drawing **3.** If you collect like terms you get $10x = 10x$, so any value of x will make it true. **5.** Subtract $6x$ from each side, then divide each side by -2 **7.** -6 **9.** ± 15 **11.** -7 **13.** 17 **15.** $-\sqrt{4}$, -0.3, 0, 1.25, $\sqrt{11}$ **17.** 13 **19.** -15 **21.** -36 **23.** 2 **25.** 18 **27.** 5 **29.** 2 **31.** -6 **33.** 14 **35.** 1 **37.** -4 **39.** 1 **41.** -4 **43.** -5 **45.** identity **47.** 7 **49.** 26 **51.** 15 **53.** 2.5 gal **55.** 2.5 **57.** -4 **59.** -13 **61.** $y = \frac{-x}{7}$ **63.** $y = \frac{1}{5}x + 4$

Chapter 2
Extra Practice

1. -6 **3.** 80 **5.** 12 **7.** -13 **9.** 16 **11.** -12 **13.** 9 **15.** 52 **17.** 6 **19.** 8 **21.** -35 **23.** 3 **25.** -6 **27.** -1 **29.** 2 **31.** 3 **33.** $-\frac{1}{2}$ **35.** 56 **37.** 16 **39.** $\frac{5}{7} = \frac{15}{x}$; 21 **41.** $\frac{g}{9} = \frac{16}{12}$; 12 **43.** 14 **45.** 8 **47.** 4 **49.** -2 **51.** $x = \frac{c + b}{a}$; 5 **53.** $y = -5x + 10$ **55.** $y = -4x + 2$

Chapter 3

3.1 Skill Practice **1.** 5; −3 **3.** (3, −2) **5.** (4, 4) **7.** (4, −1) **9.** (−5, 4) **11.** (−4, −1)

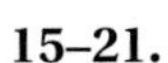

15–21.

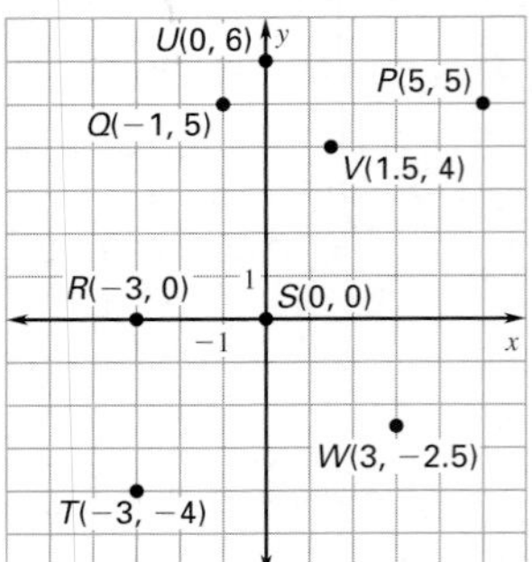

15. Quadrant II
17. origin
19. y-axis
21. Quadrant IV

25. −9, −7, −5, −3, −1

27.

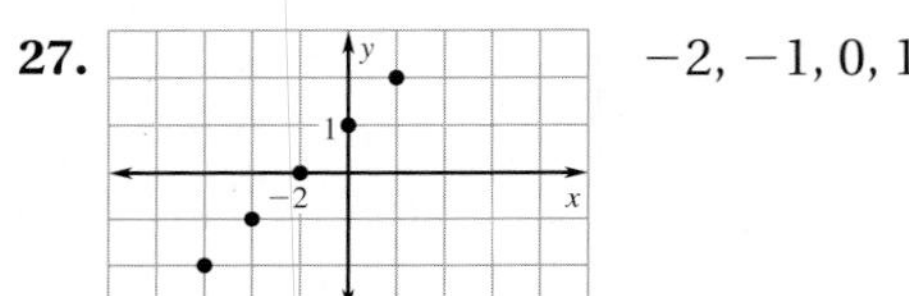

−2, −1, 0, 1, 2

29. Quadrant IV; the x-coordinate is positive and the y-coordinate is negative so the point is in Quadrant IV. **31.** Quadrant II; the x-coordinate is negative and the y-coordinate is positive so the point is in Quadrant II. **33.** If the x-coordinate is 0, then the point is on the y-axis. If the y-coordinate is 0, then the point is on the x-axis.

3.1 Problem Solving

37. There is exactly one low temperature for each day in February.

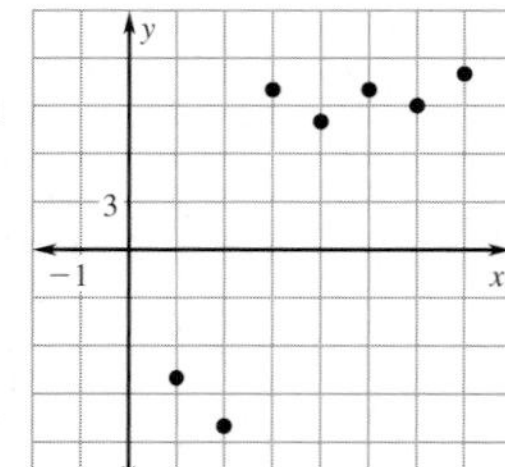

39. a.

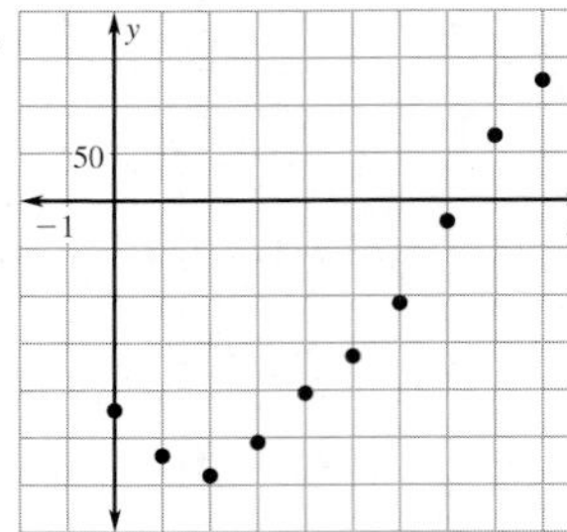

b. *Sample answer:* From 1992 to 1999 the federal deficit was decreasing.

41. a.

Height (in.)		
Reported	Measured	Difference
70	68	2
70	67.5	2.5
78.5	77.5	1
68	69	−1
71	72	−1
70	70	0

Weight (lb)		
Reported	Measured	Difference
154	146	8
141	143	−2
165	168	−3
146	143	3
220	223	−3
176	176	0

b. (2, 8), (2.5, −2), (1, −3), (−1, 3), (−1, −3), (0, 0)

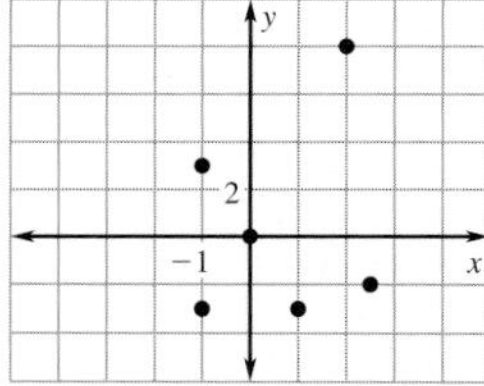

3.2 Skill Practice **1.** linear function **3.** solution **5.** solution **7.** not a solution **9.** The 8 should be substituted for x and 11 for y, $11 - 8 \neq -3$, so (8, 11) is not a solution.

11.

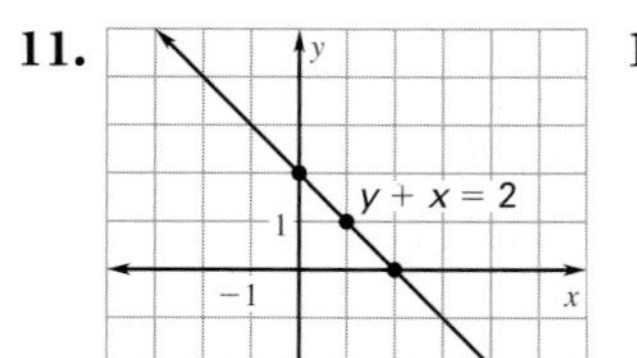

13.

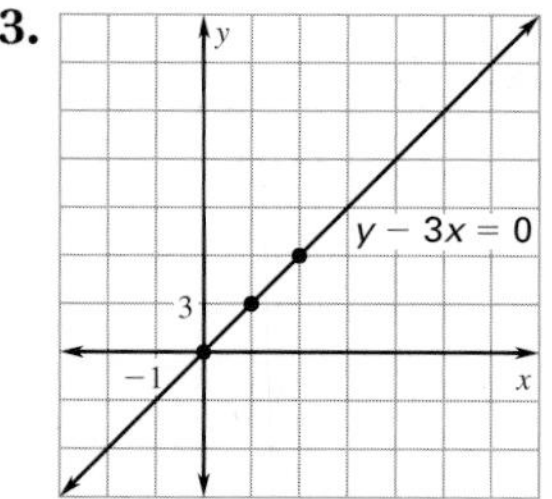

15.

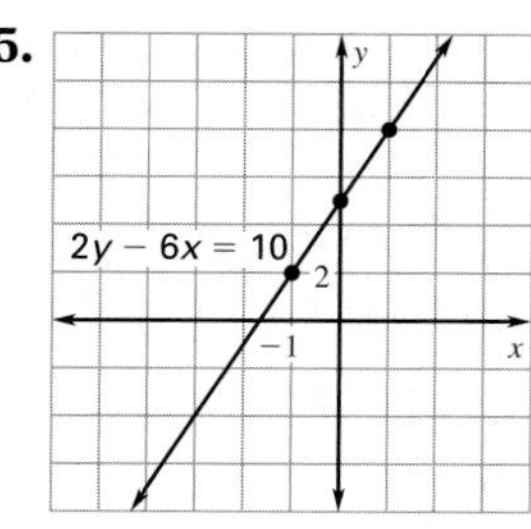

17.

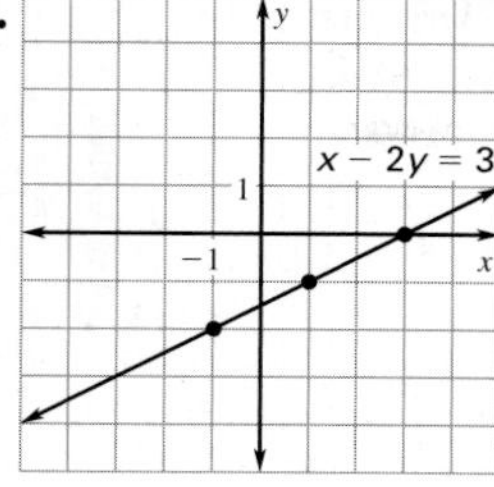

19.

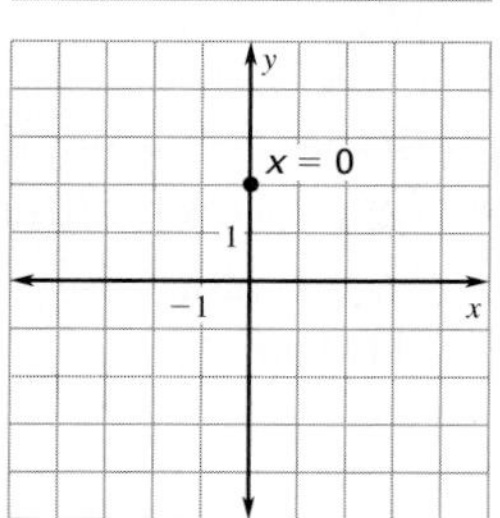

21.

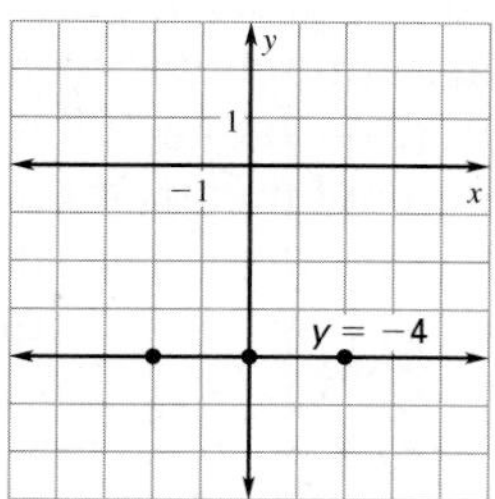

23. C **25.** B

27.

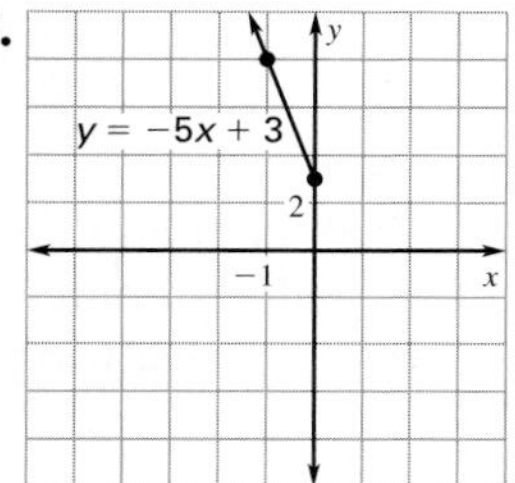

$y \geq 3$

29.

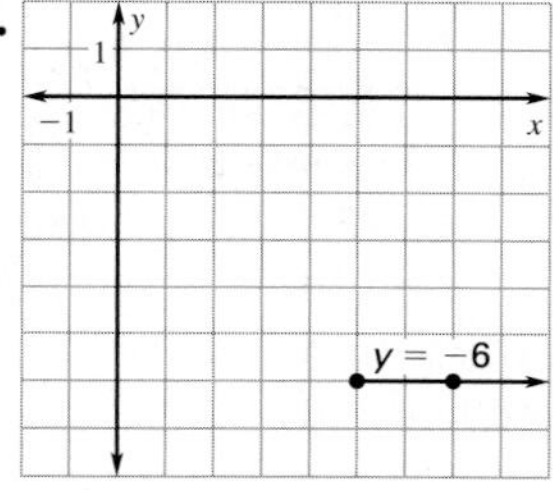

$y = -6$

31.

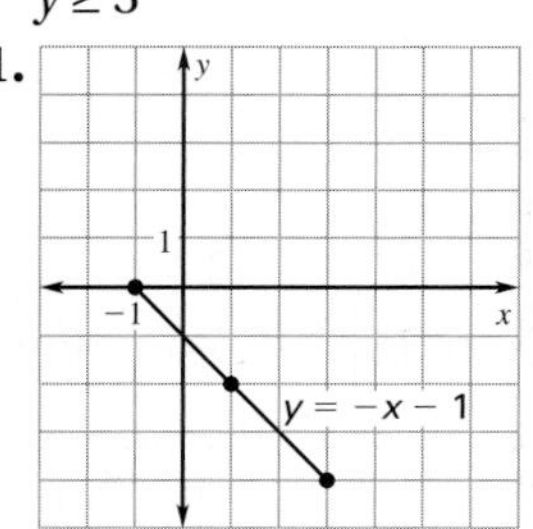

$-4 \leq y \leq 0$

3.2 Problem Solving

35.

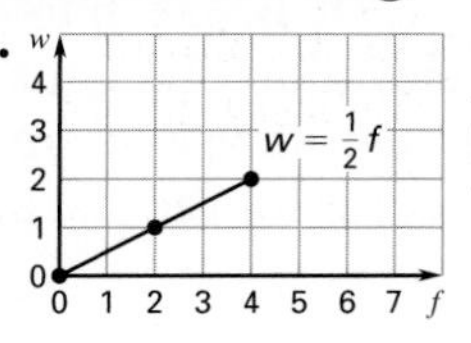

domain: $0 \leq f \leq 4$, range: $0 \leq w \leq 2$; 2 lb

37. a.

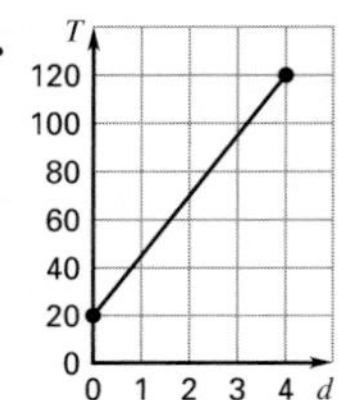

domain: $0 \leq d \leq 4$, range: $20 \leq T \leq 120$; 120°C

b.

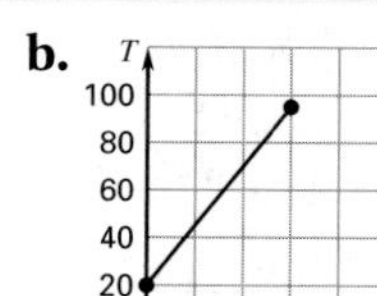

domain: $0 \leq d \leq 3$, range: $20 \leq T \leq 95$; 3 km

39. a.

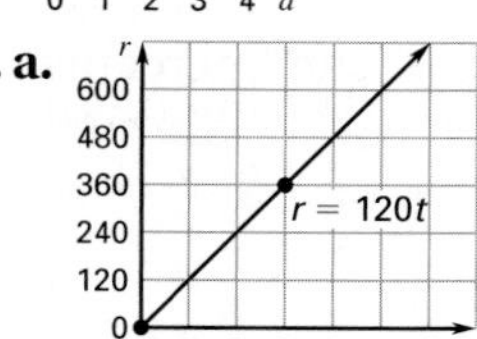

domain: $t \geq 0$, range: $r \geq 0$

b. Domain: $0 \leq t \leq 4$, range: $0 \leq r \leq 480$; the graph was a ray, but is now a segment.

41. a.

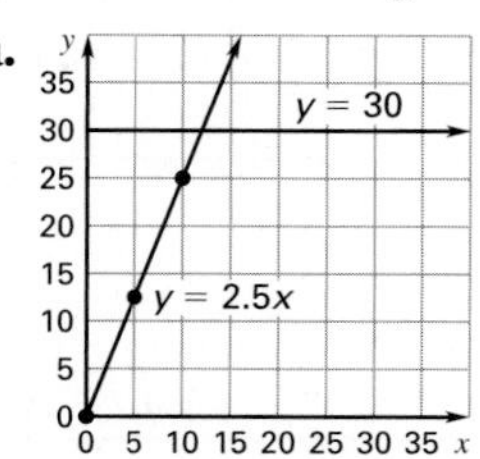

3.2 Graphing Calculator Activity **1.** 5.6 **3.** −5.3

Extension

1. discrete

3.

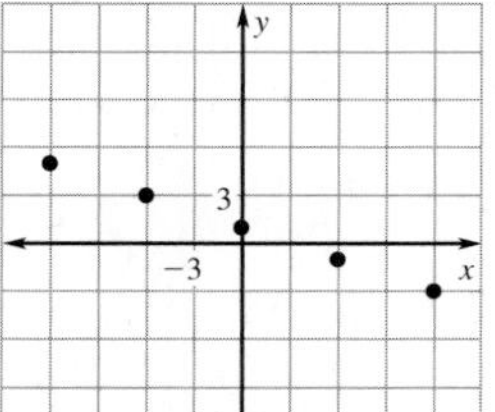

discrete

5. continuous

7. Discrete; you can only rent a whole number of DVDs.

9. Continuous; it makes sense to talk about the weight of water for any volume of water.

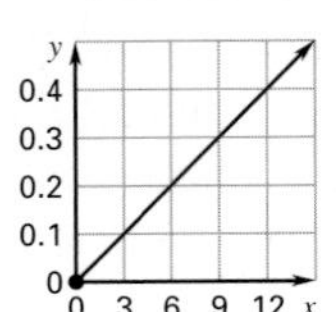

about 0.12

3.3 Skill Practice **1.** x-intercept **3.** The intercepts are switched around; the x-intercept is -2, and the y-intercept is 1. **5.** 3, -3 **7.** 1, 4 **9.** 12, -3 **11.** 64, 4 **13.** $\frac{1}{2}$, 7 **15.** 20, -12

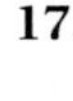

17.

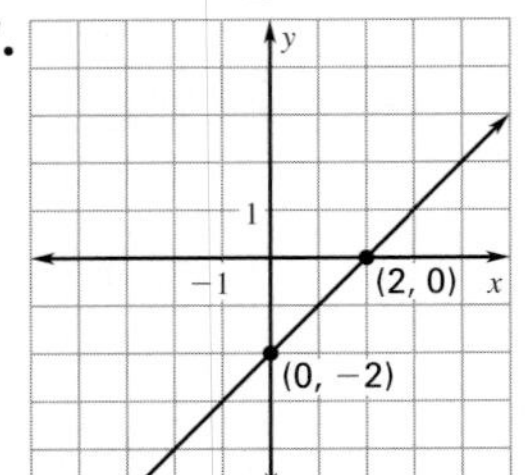

19.

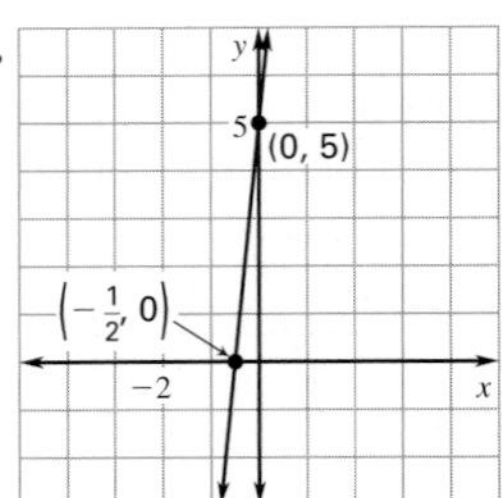

21.

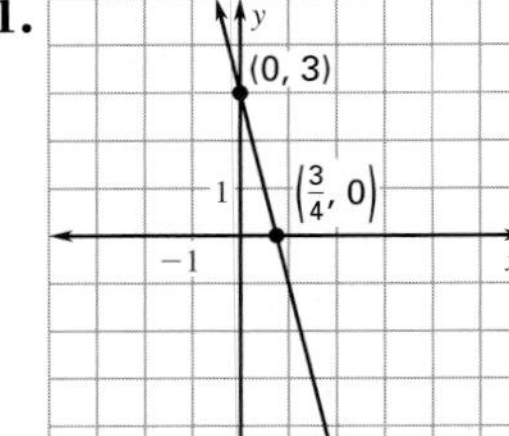

23.

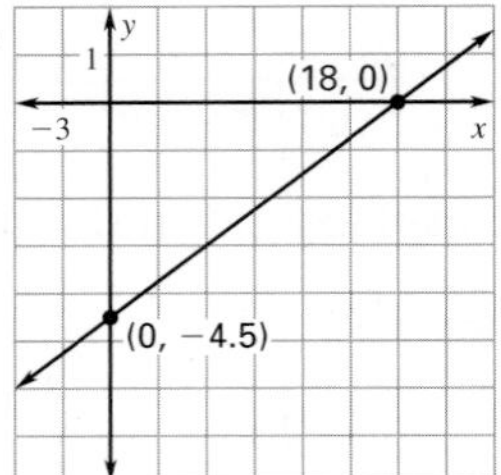

25.

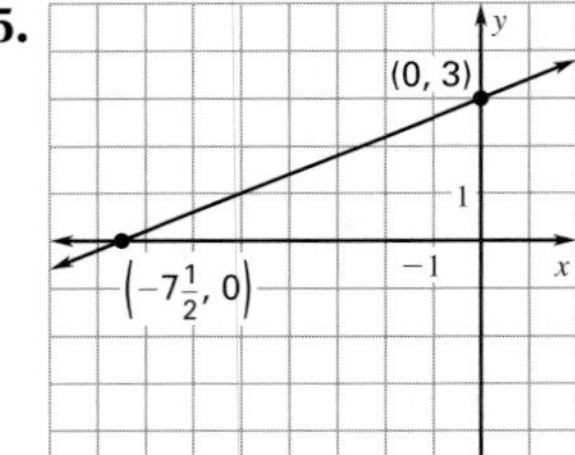

27.

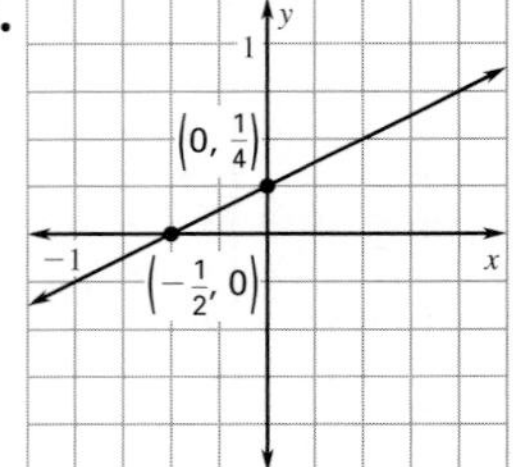

29. 3, -2

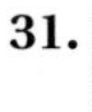

31.

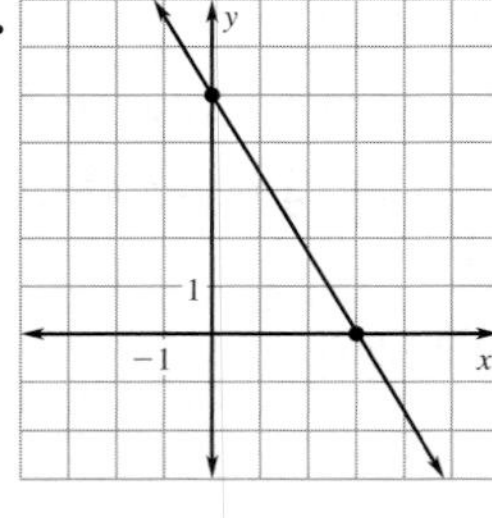

33.

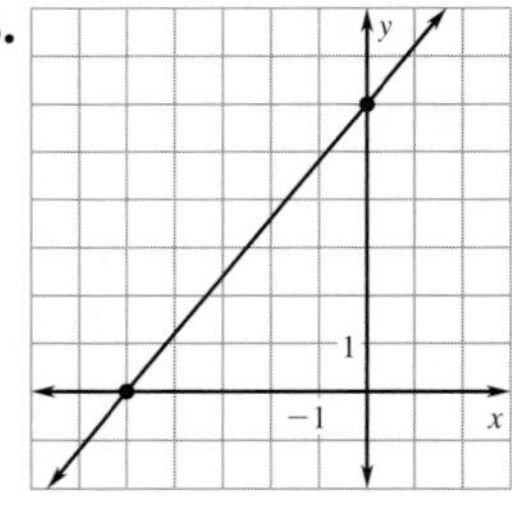

35.

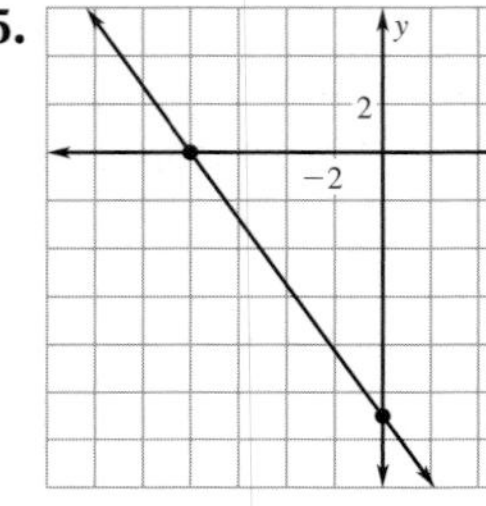

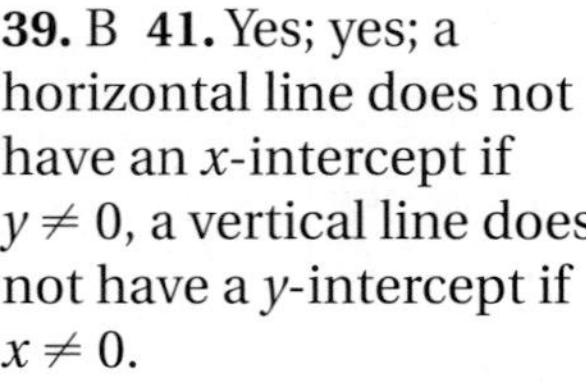

39. B **41.** Yes; yes; a horizontal line does not have an x-intercept if $y \neq 0$, a vertical line does not have a y-intercept if $x \neq 0$.

3.3 Problem Solving

45. a. $x = 14$, $y = 7$

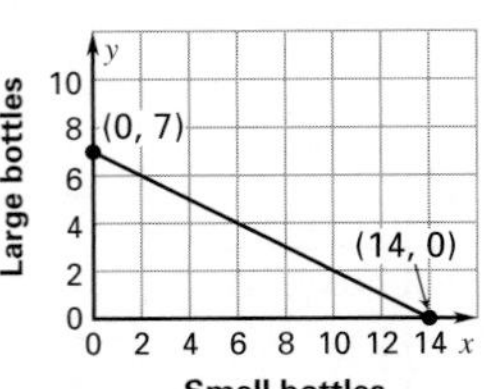

b. *Sample answer:* 2 and 6, 4 and 5, 6 and 4 **47. a.** v-intercept: 120, f-intercept: 180; the v-intercept means there are no flowers planted, the f-intercept means there are no vegetables planted.

b.

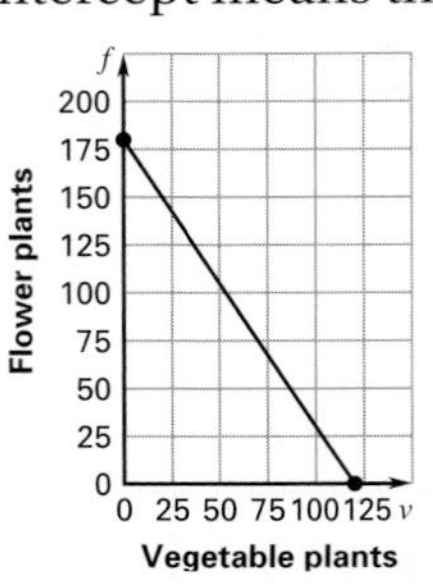

domain: $0 \leq v \leq 120$, range: $0 \leq f \leq 180$

c. 60 ft^2 **49.** 12.5 h. *Sample answer:* Since the tank will be empty when it needs to be refilled, replace w in the function with 0 and then solve the resulting equation for t.

3.4 Skill Practice **1.** slope **3.** The denominator should be $2 - 5$, not $5 - 2$; $m = \frac{6-3}{2-5} = \frac{3}{-3} = -1$. **5.** undefined **7.** The slope was calculated using $\frac{\text{run}}{\text{rise}}$, not $\frac{\text{rise}}{\text{run}}$; $m = \frac{0-3}{12-6} = \frac{-3}{6} = -\frac{1}{2}$. **9.** undefined **11.** $-\frac{5}{2}$ **13.** 1 **15.** 0 **19.** \$2.25 per day; it costs \$2.25 per day to rent a movie. **21.** 0.3 **23.** 0.1 **25.** -15 **27.** -2 **29.** -3 **31.** -15 **33.** Yes; the slope of the line containing both points is -3.

3.4 Problem Solving **37. a.** 0 h to 1.5 h **b.** 4.65 h to 8.95 h **39.** *Sample answer:* The elevation of the hiker increases for about 60 minutes, then stays the same for about 30 minutes, then decreases for the last 60 minutes.

3.5 Skill Practice **1.** parallel **3.** 2, 1 **5.** -3, 6 **7.** $\frac{2}{3}$, -1 **11.** $y = -4x + 1$; -4, 1 **13.** $y = 2x + 3$; 2, 3 **15.** $y = -\frac{2}{5}x - 2$; $-\frac{2}{5}$, -2 **17.** B **19.** C

21.

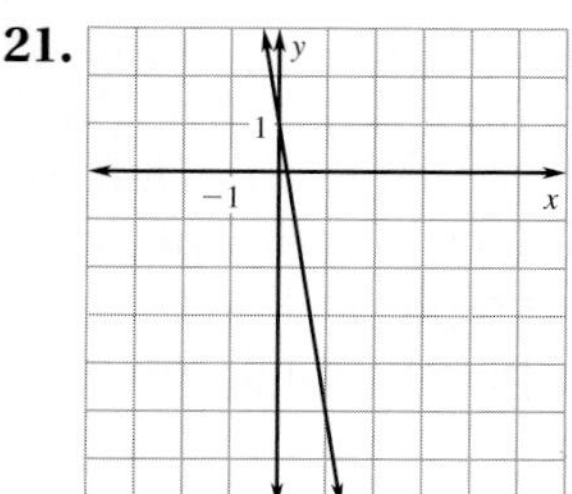

23.

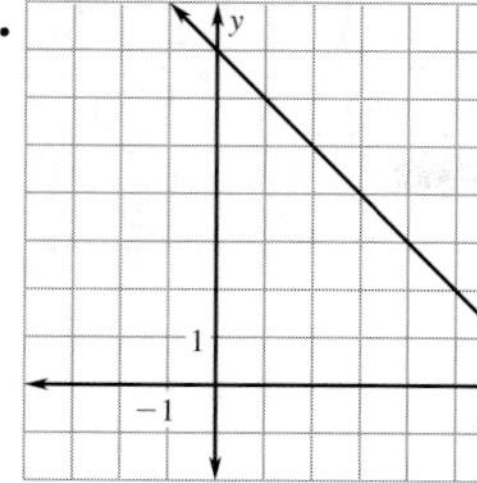

25.

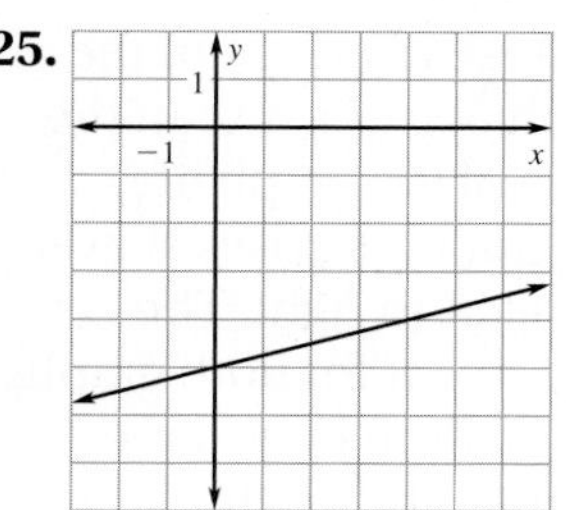

27.

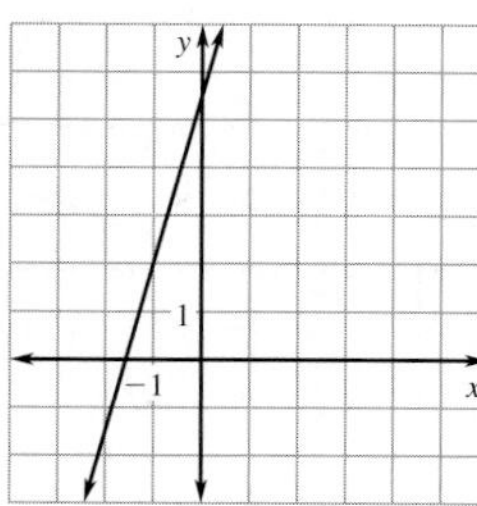

29.

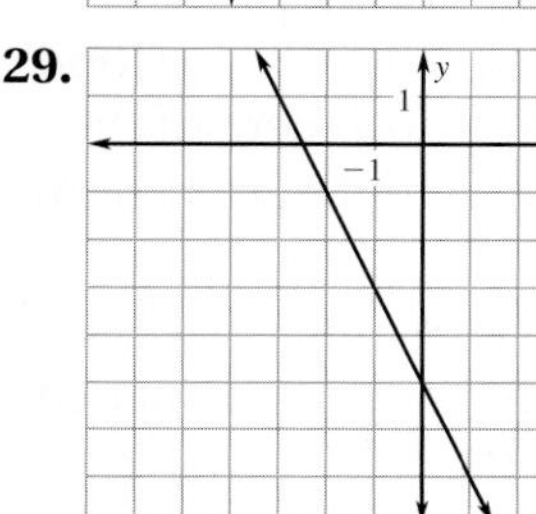

31. red, blue, and green **33.** Parallel; the slopes are both 3. **35.** Not parallel; the slopes are -4 and $-\frac{1}{4}$. **37.** -2

3.5 Problem Solving

41. a.

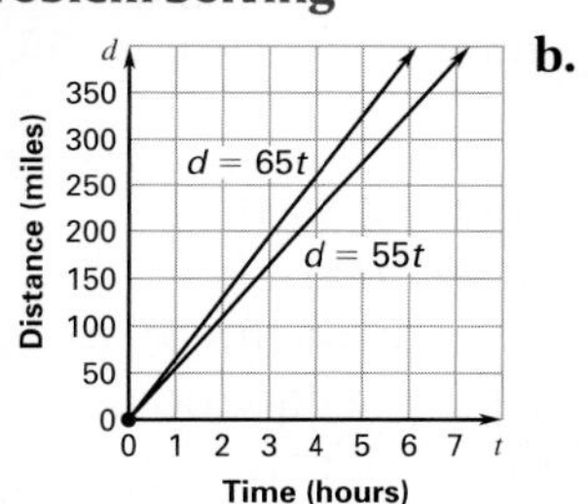

b. 30 mi

43. a.

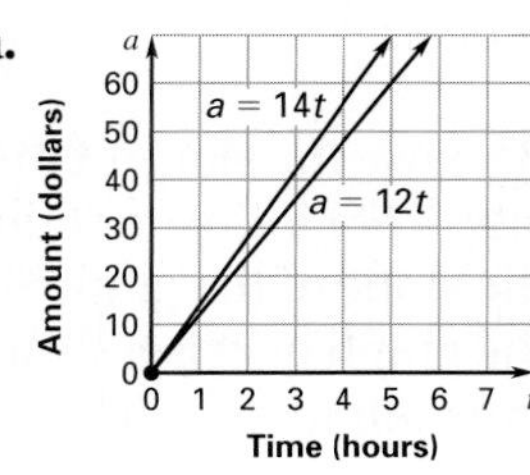

The slopes are the amount of money earned per hour, the a-intercepts show the amount of money made at 0 hours. **b.** \$80

Extension **1.** -2 **3.** -4 **5.** $\frac{1}{2}$ **7.** 2000 **9.** 2000

3.6 Skill Practice **1.** direct variation **3.** direct variation; 1 **5.** not direct variation **7.** direct variation; -4

11.

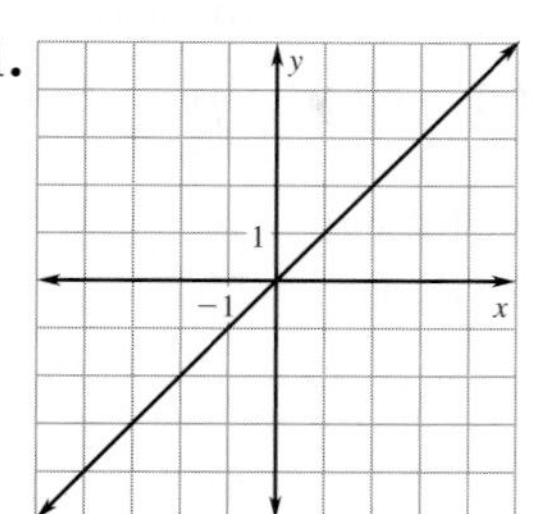

13.

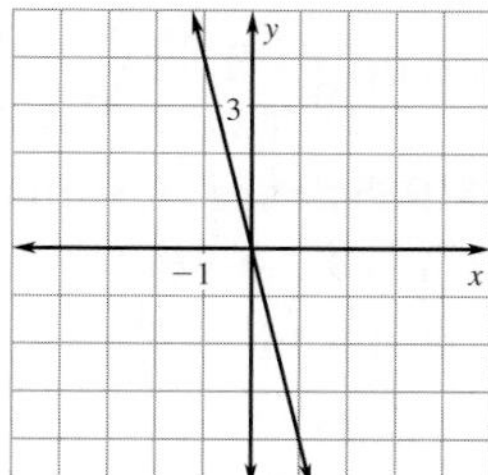

15.

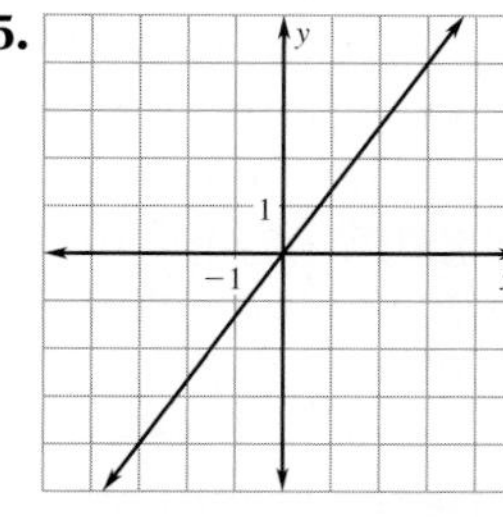

17.

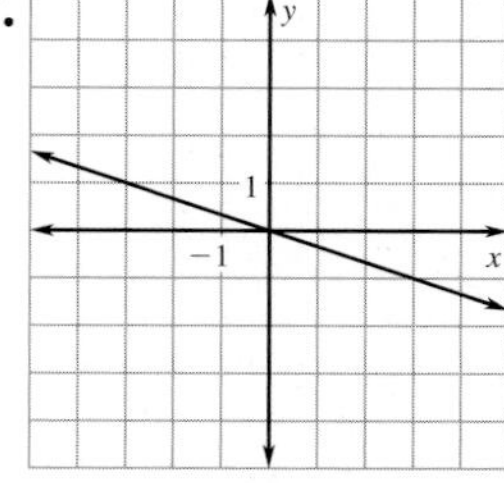

19.

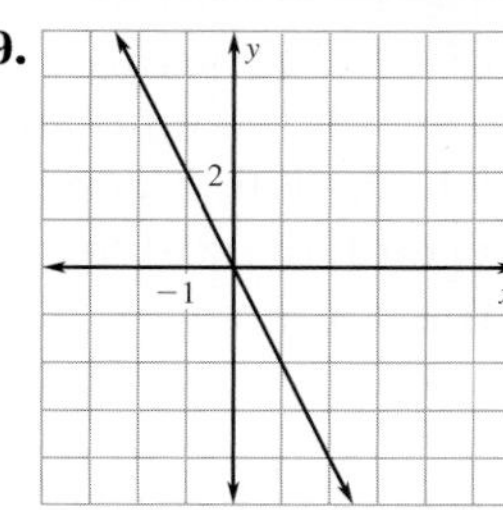

21.

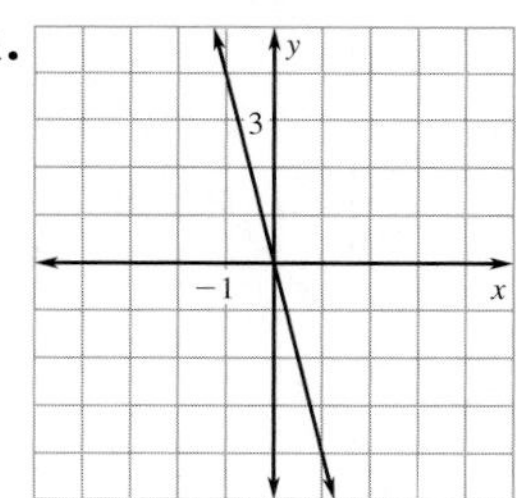

23. $y = -x$; -8 **25.** $y = -\frac{3}{4}x$; -6 **27.** not direct variation **29.** $y = 3x$ **31.** $y = \frac{1}{2}x$ **33.** $y = x$ **35.** $y = 4x$ **37.** $y = -\frac{7}{26}x$

3.6 Problem Solving **41. a.** $v = \frac{3}{2}t$ **b.** 12 h

43. a. Compare the ratios, $\frac{f}{w}$, for all data pairs (w, f). Since the ratios all equal 0.25, f varies directly with w. **b.** $f = 0.25w$; \$.25 per pound; \$7

45. a. *Sample answer:*

d	C (dollars)
1	1.5
2	3
3	4.5

b. Cost (dollars) vs. Number of days graph

c. $C = 1.5d$; yes; it is in the form $y = ax$; \$33.

3.6 Problem Solving Workshop **1.** 110 tbsp. *Sample answer:* Use the proportion $\frac{20}{100} = \frac{22}{x}$. **3.** Because 7 is half of 14, you can take half of 5.88 to find 7 words cost \$2.94. Because 21 is 3 times 7, multiply \$2.94 by 3 to get \$8.82. **5.** The proportion should be $\frac{6}{96} = \frac{10}{x}$; $\frac{6}{96} = \frac{10}{x}$, $960 = 6x$, $x = 160$.

3.7 Skill Practice **1.** function notation **3.** $-23, 1, 37$ **5.** $14, -2, -26$ **7.** $13, 0, -19.5$ **9.** $2\frac{1}{5}, 3, 4\frac{1}{5}$ **11.** $-7\frac{1}{2}, -6, -3\frac{3}{4}$ **15.** 3 **17.** -6 **19.** -7.5 **21.** 3.5

23. 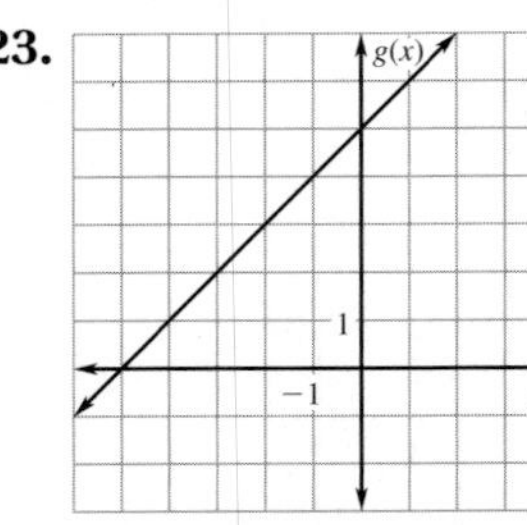

Because the graphs of g and f have the same slope, $m = 1$, the lines are parallel. The y-intercept of the graph of g is 5 more than the y-intercept of the graph of f.

25. 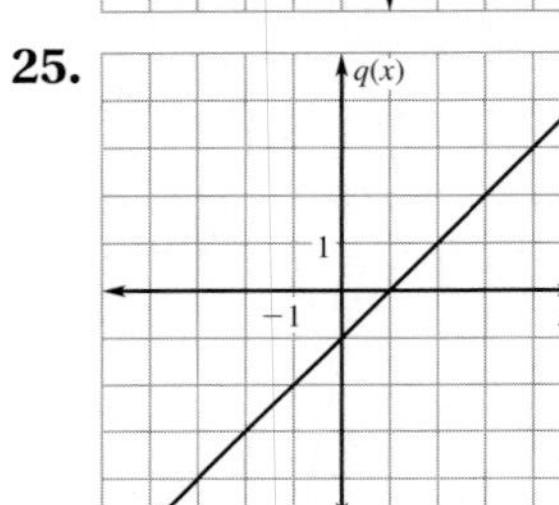

Because the graphs of q and f have the same slope, $m = 1$, the lines are parallel. The y-intercept of the graph of q is 1 less than the y-intercept of the graph of f.

27. 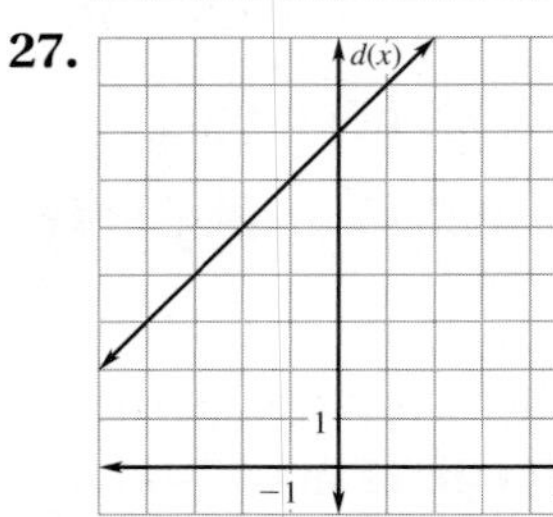

Because the graphs of d and f have the same slope, $m = 1$, the lines are parallel. The y-intercept of the graph of d is 7 more than the y-intercept of the graph of f.

29. 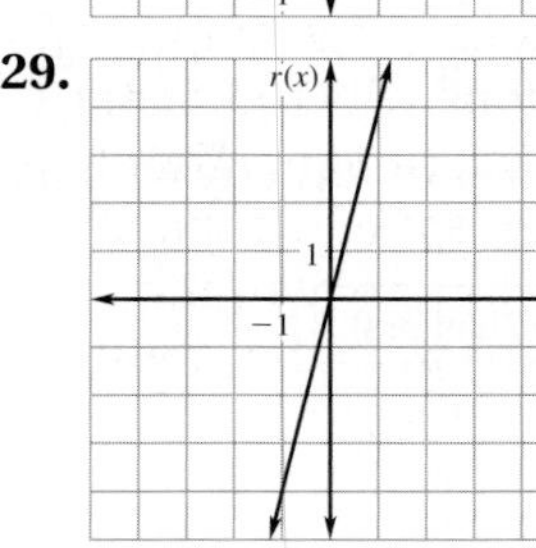

Because the slope of the graph of r is greater than the slope of the graph of f, the graph of r rises faster from left to right. The y-intercept for both graphs is 0, so both lines pass through the origin.

31. 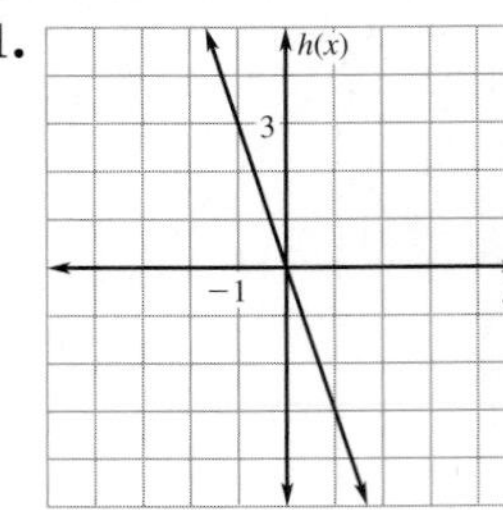

Because the slope of the graph of h is negative, the graph of h falls from left to right. The y-intercept for both graphs is 0, so both lines pass through the origin.

33. 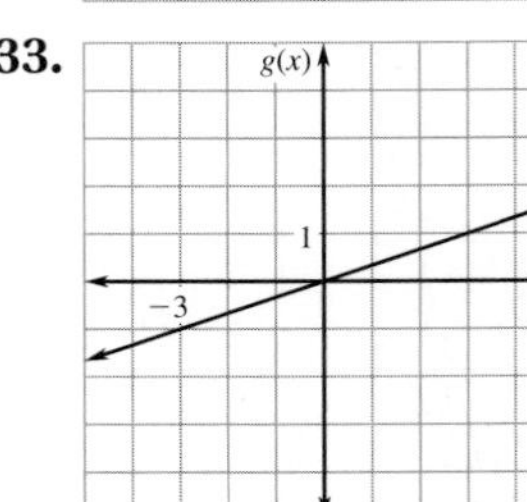

Because the slope of the graph of g is less than the slope of the graph of f, the graph of g rises slower from left to right. The y-intercept for both graphs is 0, so both lines pass through the origin.

37. Since the graphs of g and h have the same slope, $m = 0$, the lines are parallel. The y-intercept of the graph of h is 2 less than the y-intercept of the graph of g.

3.7 Problem Solving

39. a. 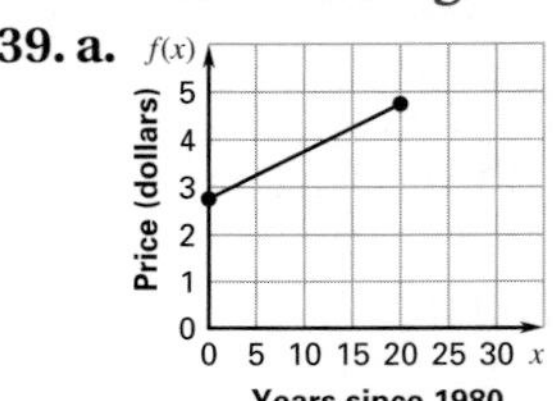

domain: $0 \le x \le 20$, range: $2.75 \le f(x) \le 4.75$ **b.** 18; in 1998, 18 years after 1980, the price of a movie ticket was \$4.55.

41. 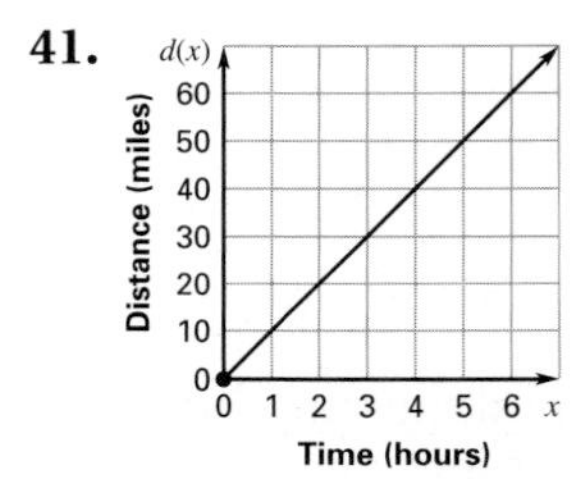

Domain: $x \ge 0$, range: $d(x) \ge 0$; 1.5 h; substitute 15 for $d(x)$ to get the equation $15 = 10x$, solve for x.

43. 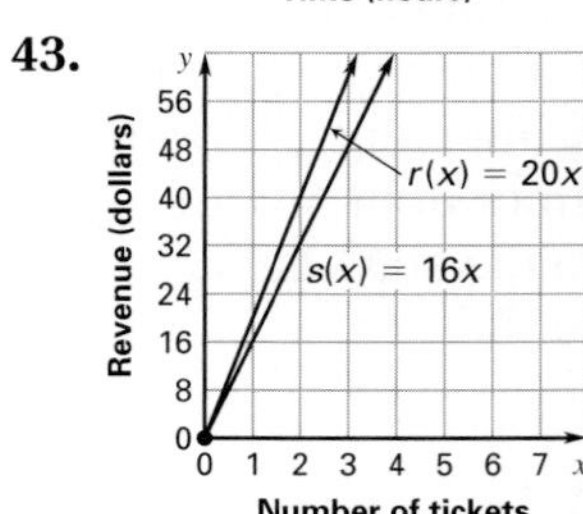

Because the slope of the graph of r is greater than the slope of the graph of s, the graph of r rises faster from left to right. The y-intercept for both graphs is 0, so both lines pass through the origin.

45. a. See graph in part (b); domain: $1 \le x \le 31$, range: $11.53 \le \ell(x) \le 12.43$.

Selected Answers

b.

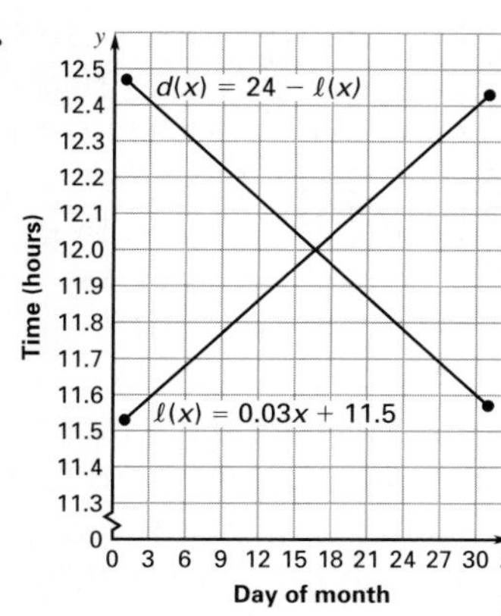

domain: $11.53 \le \ell(x) \le 12.43$, range: $11.57 \le d(x) \le 12.47$

3.7 Graphing Calculator Activity **1.** $x = 4$ **3.** $q = -3$ **5.** $c = -6$ **7.** $x = 1$ **9.** $x = -3$ **11.** $x = -18$ **13.** *Sample answer:* Set each side of the equation equal to y to create two functions. Graph each function and look for the intersection. The solution is the x-value of the point of intersection.

Chapter Review **1.** slope **3.** *Sample answer:* Make a table, use intercepts, and use the slope and y-intercept.

5–7.

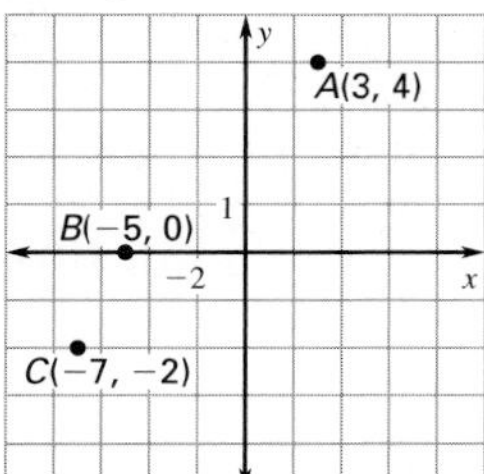

5. Quadrant I **7.** Quadrant III

9.

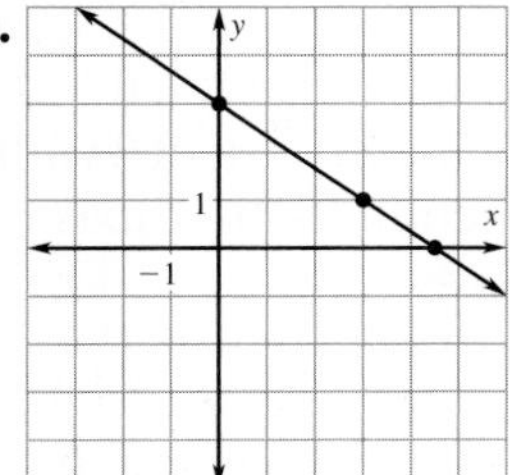

11.

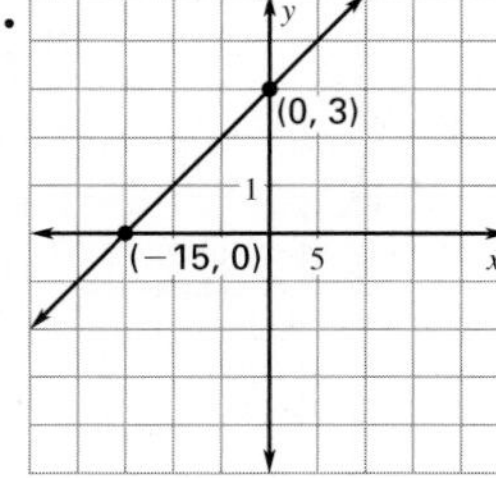

13.

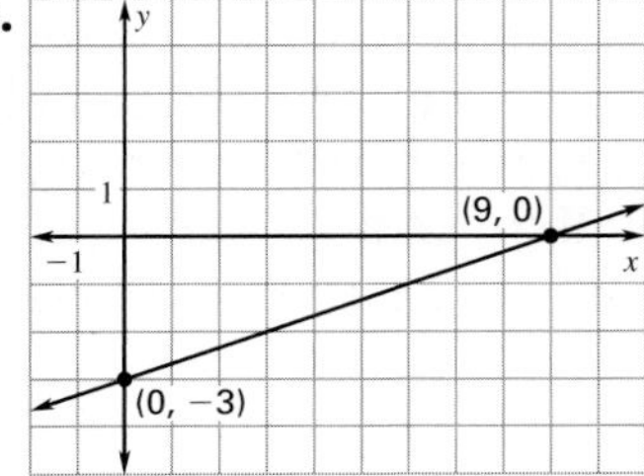

15. $-\frac{1}{3}$ **17.** -2

19.

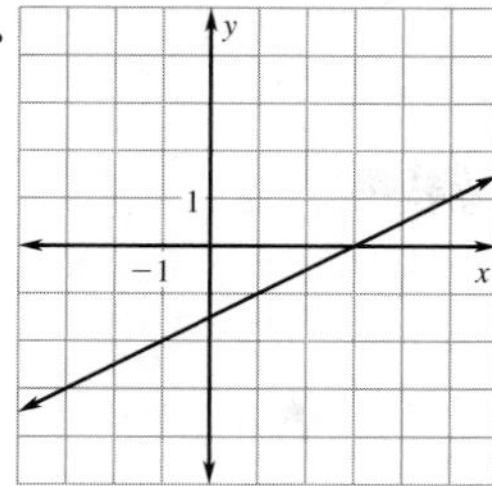

21.

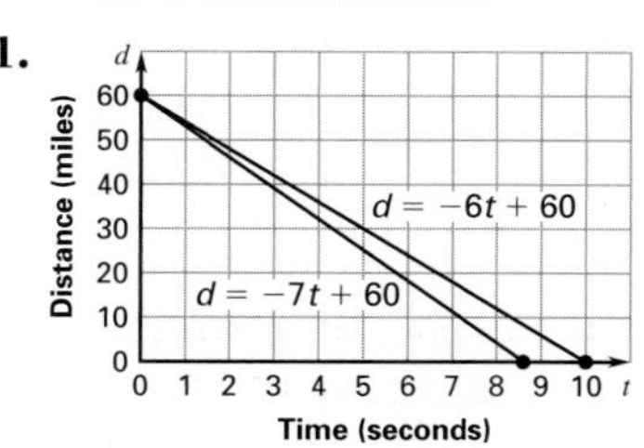

about 1.4 sec

23. direct variation; $-\frac{1}{2}$

25.

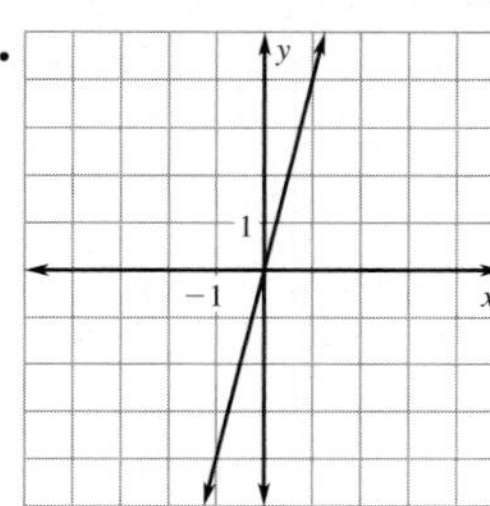

27.

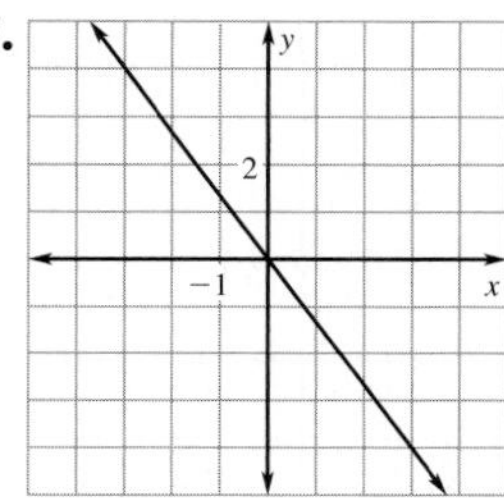

29. 11

31.

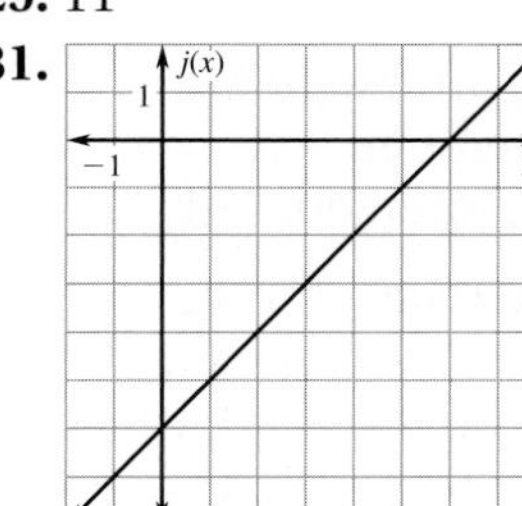

Because the graphs of j and f have the same slope, $m = 1$, the lines are parallel. The y-intercept of the graph of j is 6 less than the y-intercept of the graph of f.

33.

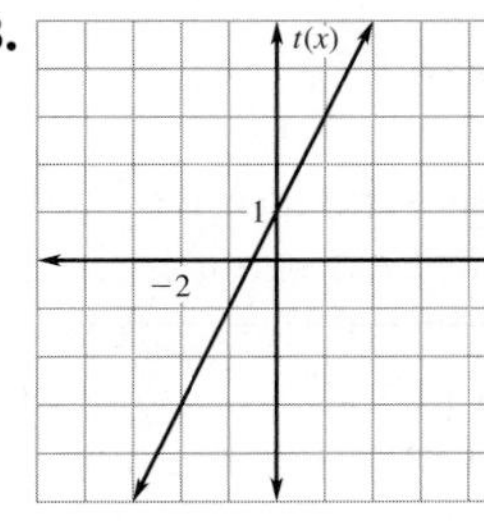

Because the slope of the graph of t is greater than the slope of the graph of f, the graph of t rises faster from left to right. The y-intercept of the graph of t is 1 more than the y-intercept of the graph of f.

Chapter 3
Extra Practice

1. 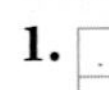

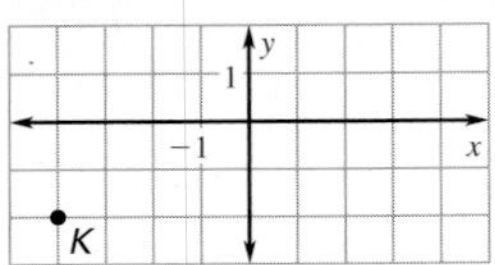

Quadrant III

3. 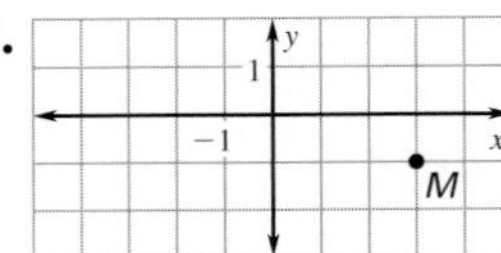

Quadrant IV

5. 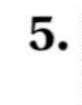

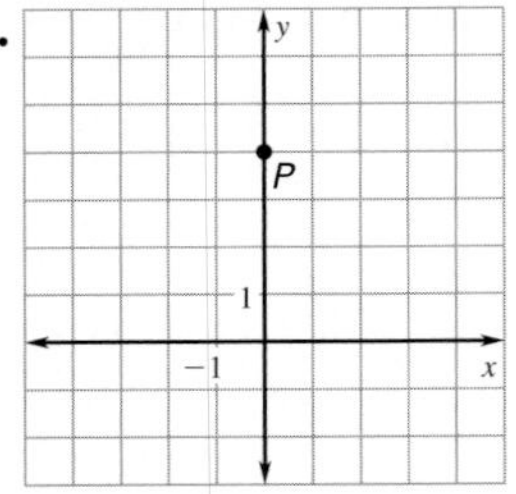

on the y-axis

7. 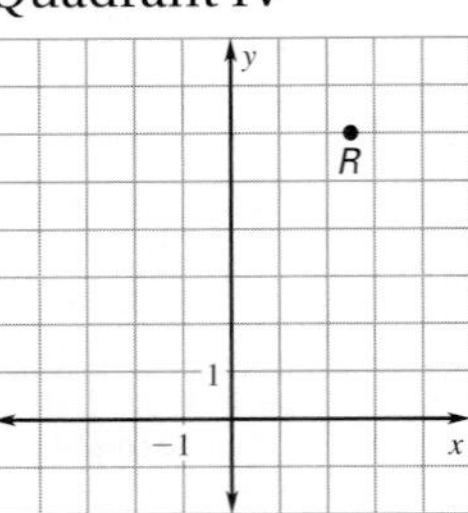

Quadrant I

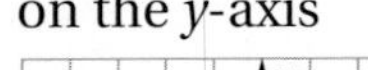

9. 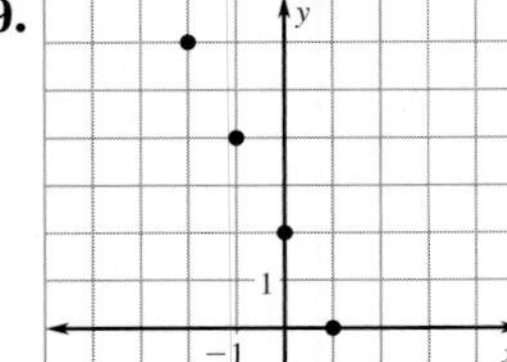

range: $-2, 0, 2, 4, 6$

11. 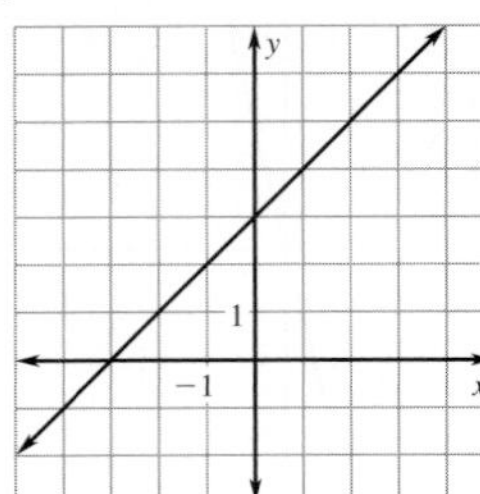

17. 

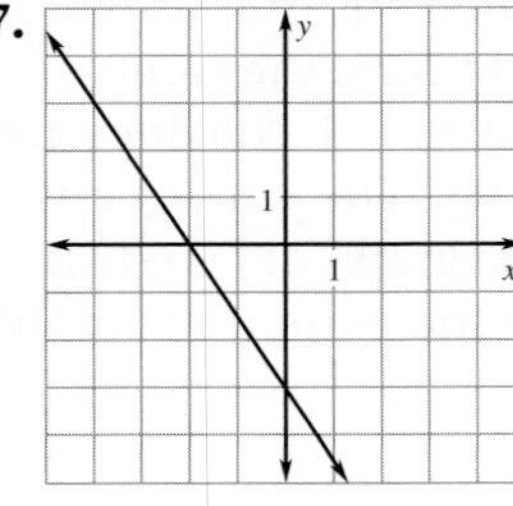

19. x-intercept: 6, y-intercept: -12 **21.** x-intercept: -1, y-intercept: $\frac{8}{3}$

23. 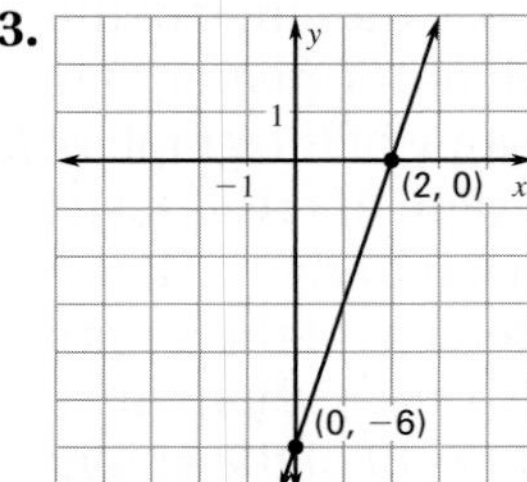

25. 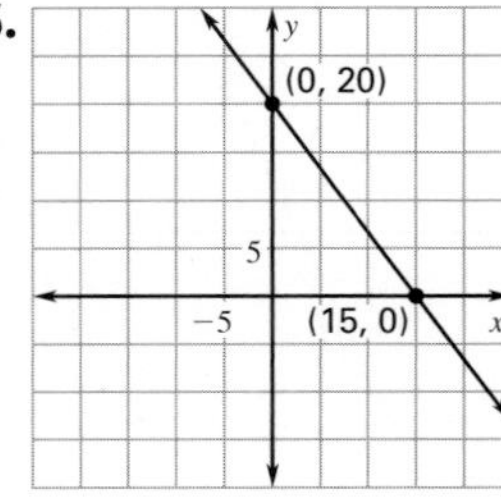

27. 3 **29.** $-\frac{7}{3}$ **31.** no slope **33.** slope: 7, y-intercept: 8 **35.** slope: -4, y-intercept: 3 **37.** $y = -2x + 8$; slope: -2, y-intercept: 8 **39.** $y = -\frac{5}{2}x + 5$; slope: $-\frac{5}{2}$, y-intercept: 5

41. 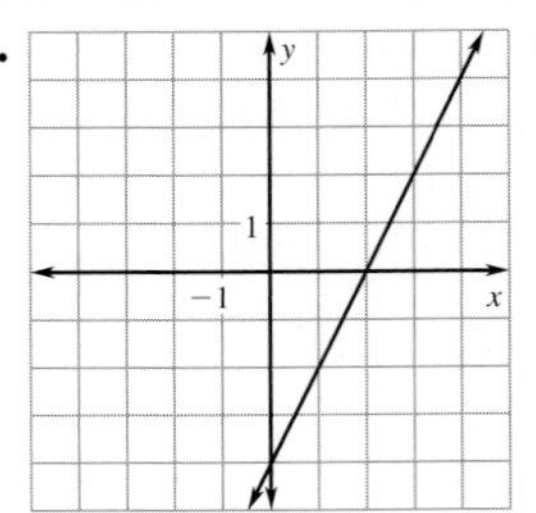

43. 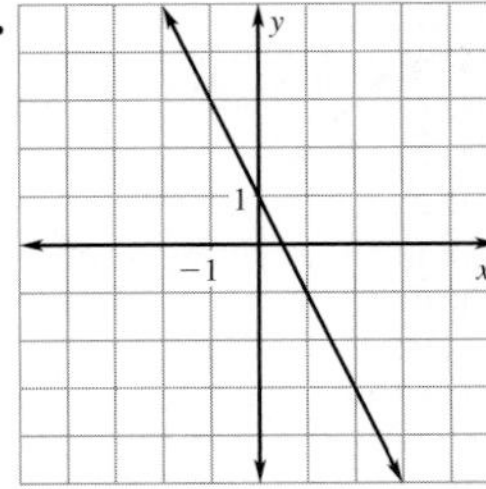

45. 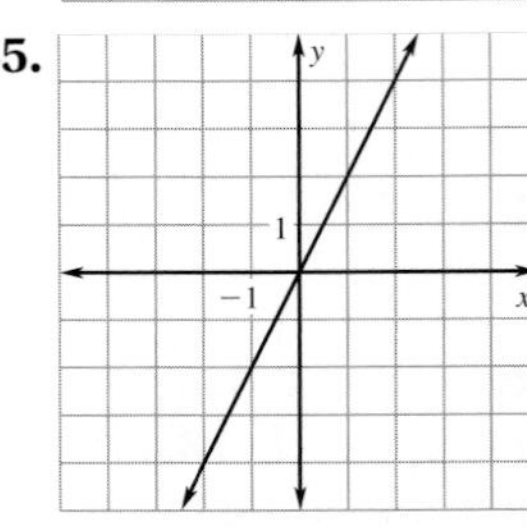

47. 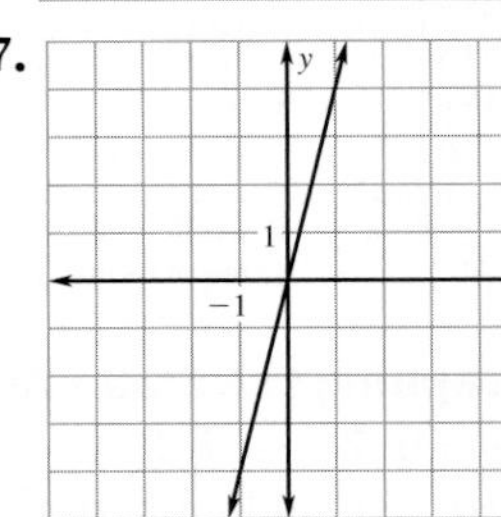

49. 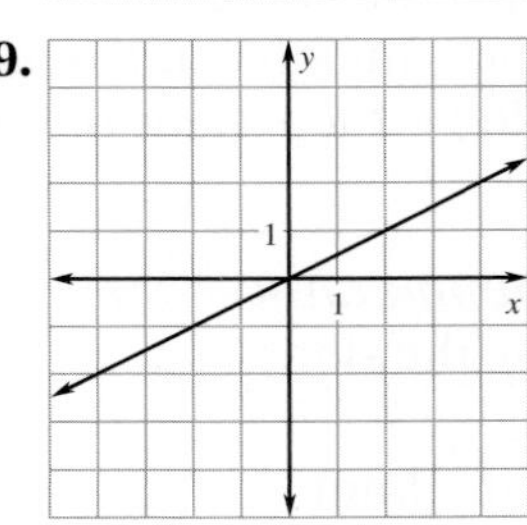

51. 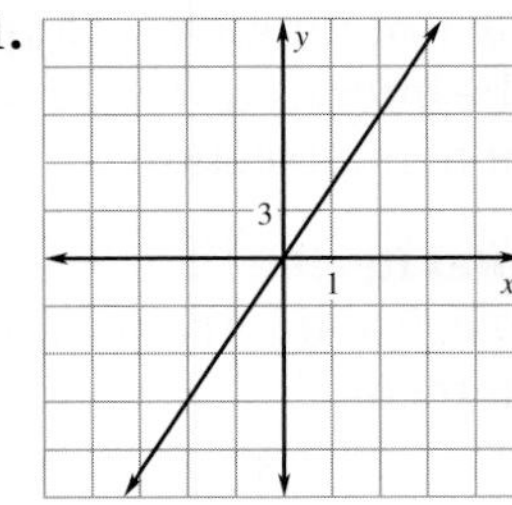

53. 2 **55.** -4

57. 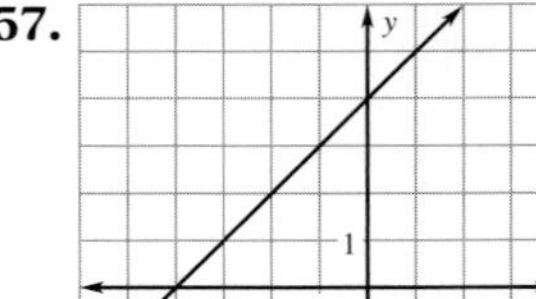

The graph is a vertical translation 4 units up of $f(x) = x$.

59. 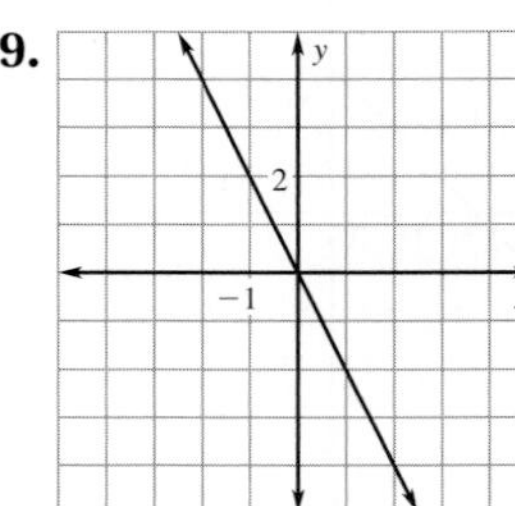

The graph is a vertical stretch by a factor of 2 with a reflection in the x-axis of $f(x) = x$.

Chapter 4

4.1 Skill Practice **1.** slope **3.** $y = 2x + 9$ **5.** $y = -3x$ **7.** $y = \frac{2}{3}x - 9$ **11.** $y = -\frac{1}{2}x$ **13.** $y = \frac{2}{3}x - 8$ **15.** $y = -2x - 2$ **17.** The slope should be $\frac{0-4}{5-0}$, $y = -\frac{4}{5}x + 4$. **19.** $y = 4x + 4$ **21.** $y = -\frac{4}{3}x$ **23.** $y = 2x - 2$ **25.** $y = -x - 5$ **27.** $y = -0.0625x + 4$ **29.** $y = -4x - 24$ **31.** $y = -2x + 7$ **33.** $y = -\frac{4}{5}x - 1$ **35.** $y = \frac{2}{3}x + 3$ **37.** $y = -3x + 9$ **39.** m changed from 2 to $-\frac{1}{3}$, and b changed from -1 to 1. **41.** $y = -2x + 1$ **43.** No; the slope of the line is undefined, the equation is $x = 3$, which is not in slope-intercept form.

4.1 Problem Solving **45. a.** $C = 44m + 48$ **b.** \$312 **47.** $C = 3h + 30$; \$42

49. a.

x (years since 1970)	y (km²)
0	5.2
10	4.1
20	3.0
30	1.9

b.

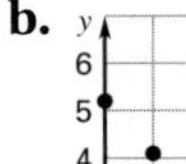
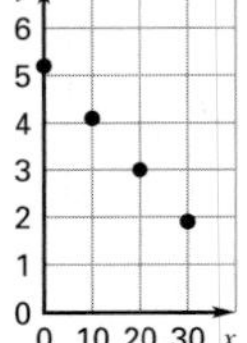

The area of the glaciers changed -1.1 square kilometers between every 10 year interval. **c.** $y = -0.11x + 5.2$; -0.11 km^2

51. a. $t = 0.7d + 2$ **b.** 16 min

4.1 Graphing Calculator Activity
1. $y = -2x + 5$ **3.** $y = 2x + 1.5$ **5.** $y = 1.5x + 2$ **7.** $y = 4x - 3$ **9.** $y = 0.5x + 1$; substitute 2 for x, 2 for y, and solve for b.

4.2 Skill Practice **1.** y-intercept **3.** $y = 3x - 2$ **5.** $y = -5x - 13$ **7.** $y = -\frac{3}{4}x + 2$ **9.** -3 was substituted for x instead of y and 6 was substituted for y instead of x, $-3 = -2(6) + b$, $-3 = -12 + b$, $9 = b$. **11.** $y = 3x + 1$ **13.** $y = -\frac{2}{5}x - 1$ **15.** $y = -\frac{3}{4}x + \frac{35}{8}$ **17.** $y = 4x - 15$ **19.** $y = -\frac{1}{2}x + \frac{1}{2}$ **21.** $y = \frac{1}{3}x - \frac{4}{3}$ **23.** $y = -2x + 11$ **25.** $y = -\frac{1}{2}x + 8$ **27.** $y = x - 2$ **31.** $y = -\frac{2}{3}x + 6$ **33.** $y = 6x - 4$ **35.** Yes; you can substitute m and the coordinates of the point in $y = mx + b$, solve for b, and write the equation. **37.** Yes; you can find the slope of the line, then substitute the y-intercept for b, and write the equation. **39.** $y = \frac{9}{2}x - \frac{1}{2}$ **41.** The lines $y = \frac{3}{2}x - \frac{1}{2}$ and $y = \frac{9}{2}x - \frac{1}{2}$ and the lines $y = \frac{9}{2}x - \frac{1}{2}$ and $y = \frac{3}{2}x + \frac{11}{2}$ intersect because they have different slopes; the lines $y = \frac{3}{2}x - \frac{1}{2}$ and $y = \frac{3}{2}x + \frac{11}{2}$ will not intersect because they have the same slope, so they are parallel. **43.** The three points do not lie on the same line. If you find the equation of the line between two of the points and then check to see that the third point is a solution, you can see they do not lie on the same line. **45.** The three points do not lie on the same line. If you find the equation of the line between two of the points and then check to see that the third point is a solution, you can see they do not lie on the same line.

4.2 Problem Solving **47.** $\frac{3}{4}$ ft/yr; 6 ft **49.** 115 min or 1 h 55 min; substitute 30 for m, 2 for x, and 85 for y into the equation $y = mx + b$ to find $b = 25$. Then substitute 3 for x into the equation $y = 30x + 25$ to solve for y. **51. a.** about 584 newspapers **b.** $y = 11.8x + 584$ **c.** about 938 newspapers **53. a.** $d = -18t + 234$

b.

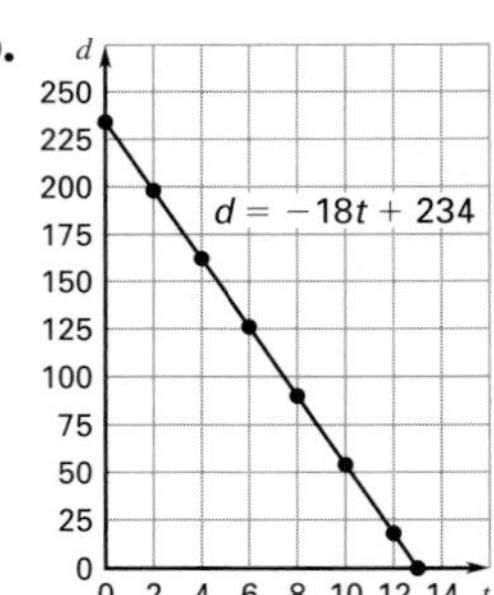

The slope is the rate that the hurricane is traveling, the y-intercept represents the distance from the town at 12 P.M.

c. 1 A.M.; find the t-intercept to find the value of t when the distance to the town is 0; substitute 0 for d and solve for t; $t = 13$, so you need to add 13 hours to 12 P.M. to get 1 A.M.

4.2 Problem Solving Workshop **1.** \$5; \$19 **3.** No; if the cost of the 60 inch bookshelf changes, the cost no longer increases at a constant rate. **5.** The student assumes that there is no fixed fee by using a proportion; $93 - 57 = 36$, $36 \div 2 = 18$, $57 + 18 = 75$.

4.3 Skill Practice **1.** -2; $(-5, 5)$ **3.** $y - 1 = 2(x - 2)$ **5.** $y + 1 = -6(x - 7)$ **7.** $y - 2 = 5(x + 8)$ **9.** $y + 3 = -9(x + 11)$ **11.** $y + 12 = -\frac{2}{5}(x - 5)$ **13.** The form is $y - y_1$, so the left side should be $y - (-5)$ or $y + 5$; $y + 5 = -2(x - 1)$.

15. 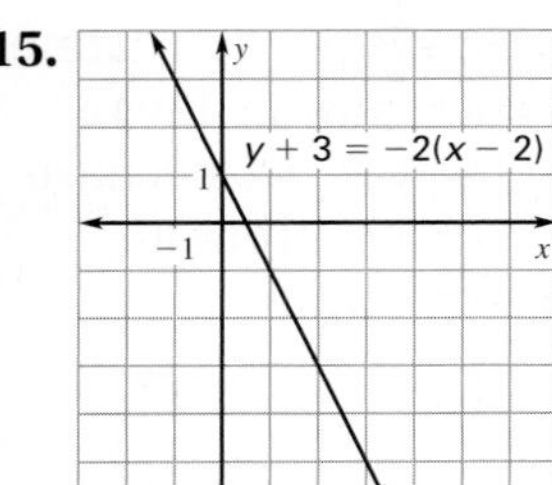

17. 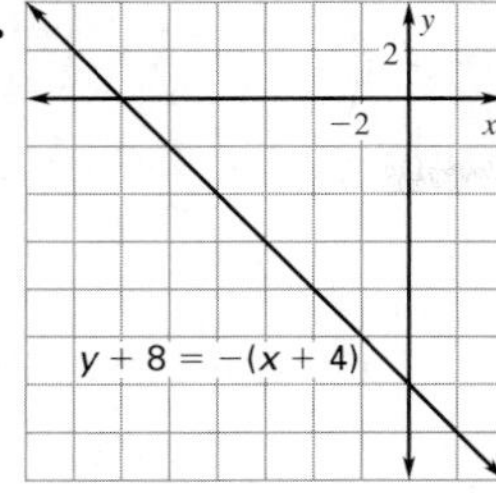

19. 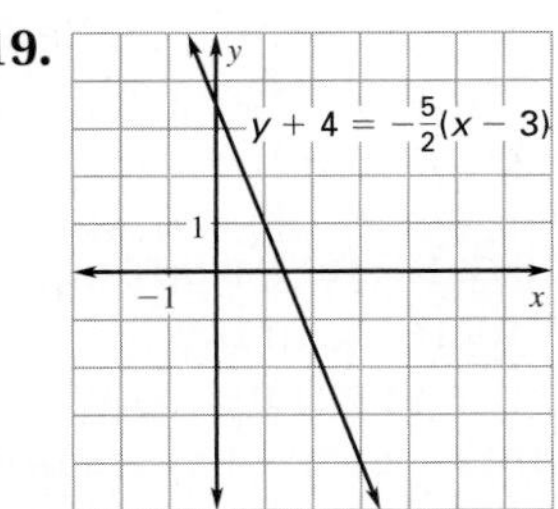

21. $y - 4 = (x - 1)$ or $y - 1 = (x + 2)$ **23.** $y - 2 = -2(x - 7)$ or $y - 12 = -2(x - 2)$ **25.** $y + 1 = -\frac{3}{5}(x + 4)$ or $y + 7 = -\frac{3}{5}(x - 6)$

27. $y + 20 = 8(x + 3)$ or $y - 36 = 8(x - 4)$ **29.** A point was not substituted into the equation, the y-coordinates of the two points were substituted; $y - 2 = \frac{2}{3}(x - 1)$. **31.** No; because the increase is not at a constant rate, the situation cannot be modeled by a linear equation. **33.** No; because the increase is not at a constant rate, the situation cannot be modeled by a linear equation.

4.3 Problem Solving **37. a.** $y = 130x + 530$ **b.** \$1570 **39.** $y = 10000x + 67000$; \$127,000 **41. a.** Since the cost increases at a constant rate of \$.49 per print, the situation can be modeled by a linear equation. **b.** *Sample answer:* $y - 1.98 = 0.49(x - 1)$ **c.** \$1.49 **d.** \$1.79 **43. a.** $y - 17.6 = -0.06(x - 60)$ **b.** 16.4 ft/sec

Extension **1.** yes; 2, −1 **3.** yes; −43, −50

5. 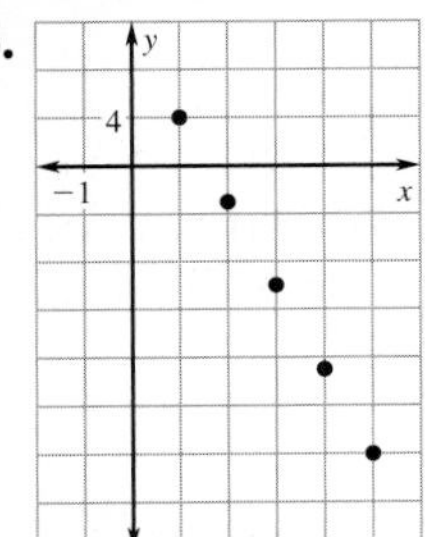

7. 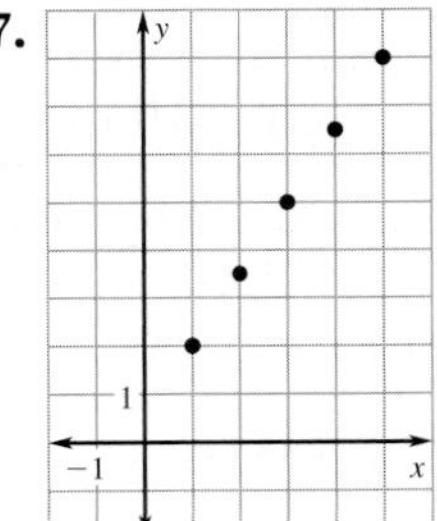

9. 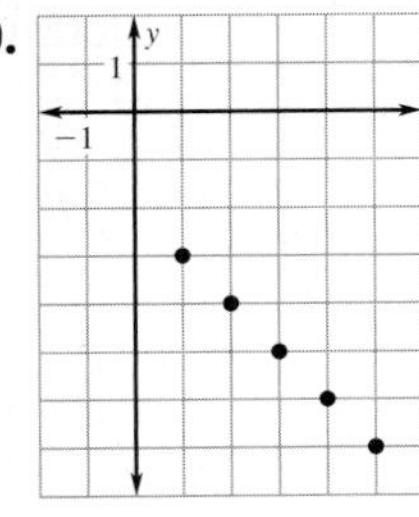

11. $a_n = 51 + (n - 1)21$; 2130 **13.** $a_n = \frac{1}{4} + (n - 1)\frac{1}{8}$; $12\frac{5}{8}$ **15.** $a_n = 1 + (n - 1)\frac{1}{3}$; 34

4.4 Skill Practice **1.** standard form **3.** point-slope form **5–9.** Sample answers are given. **5.** $2x + 2y = -20$, $3x + 3y = -30$ **7.** $x - 2y = -9$, $-2x + 4y = 18$ **9.** $3x - y = -4$, $6x - 2y = -8$ **11.** $-x + y = 5$ **13.** $2x + y = 5$ **15.** $\frac{3}{2}x + y = -10$ **17.** $\frac{2}{3}x + y = -\frac{4}{3}$ **19.** $-\frac{4}{3}x + y = -1$ **21.** $-\frac{1}{2}x + y = 1$ **23.** $y = 2$, $x = 3$ **25.** $y = 3$, $x = -1$ **27.** $y = 4$, $x = -1$ **29.** (1, −4) was substituted incorrectly, 1 should be substituted for x and −4 substituted for y, $A(1) - 3(-4) = 5$, $A + 12 = 5$, $A = -7$. **31.** 4; $4x + 3y = 5$ **33.** −4; $-x - 4y = 10$ **35.** −5; $-5x - 3y = -5$

4.4 Problem Solving **39. a.** 15 oz **b.** $12c + 15w = 120$ **c.** 10 corn, 0 wheat; 5 corn, 4 wheat; 0 corn, 8 wheat **41. a.** $100\ell + 40s = 1600$

b. 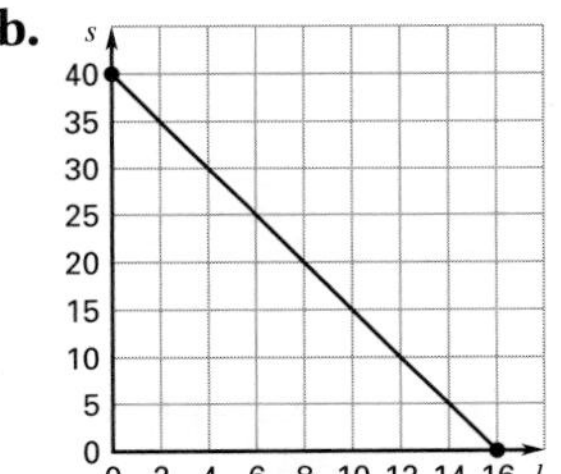

c.

Large rafts	Small rafts
16	0
14	5
12	10
10	15
8	20
6	25
4	30
2	35
0	40

4.5 Skill Practice **1.** perpendicular **3.** $y = 2x + 5$ **5.** $y = -\frac{3}{5}x + 2$ **7.** $y = 6x + 1$ **9.** $y = 2x + 9$ **11.** $y = 3x + 30$ **13.** parallel: a and b; perpendicular: none **15.** parallel: none; perpendicular: a and b **17.** The line through points (6, 4) and (4, 1) is perpendicular to the line through points (1, 3) and (4, 1); the slope of the line through the points (6, 4) and (4, 1) is $\frac{3}{2}$, the slope of the line through the points (1, 3) and (4, 1) is $-\frac{2}{3}$. The slopes are negative reciprocals, so the lines are perpendicular. **19.** $y = -\frac{1}{3}x - 1$ **21.** $y = -2x + 24$ **23.** $y = -\frac{3}{4}x - 4$ **25.** $y = -\frac{1}{2}x - \frac{1}{2}$ **27.** (2, 1) was substituted incorrectly, 2 should be substituted for x, and 1 should be substituted for y; $1 = 2(2) + b$, $1 = 4 + b$, $-3 = b$.

4.5 Problem Solving **33. a.** $w = 200d + 6000$; $w = 200d + 6250$ **b.** 12,000 lb; 12,250 lb **c.** The graphs of the lines are parallel because they have the same slope, 200. The w-intercept of the second line is 250 more than the w-intercept of the first line. **35.** Different registration fees; because the lines are parallel, the rate of change, the monthly fee, for each must be equal. Therefore, the students paid different registration fees.

4.6 Skill Practice **1.** increase **3.** positive correlation **5.** negative correlation

7. 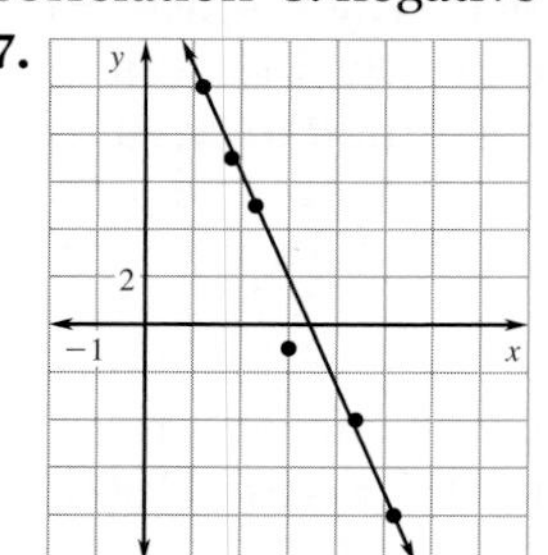 *Sample answer:* $y = -4.5x + 15.4$

9. The line does not have approximately half the data above it and half below it. 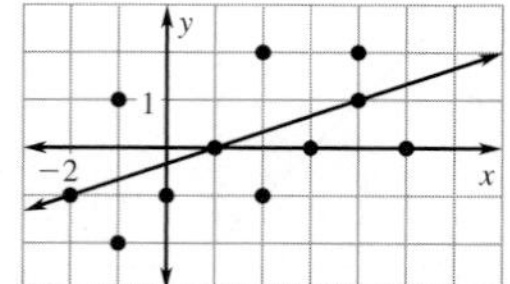

11. *Sample answer:* The amount of time driving a car and the amount of gas left in the gas tank

13. 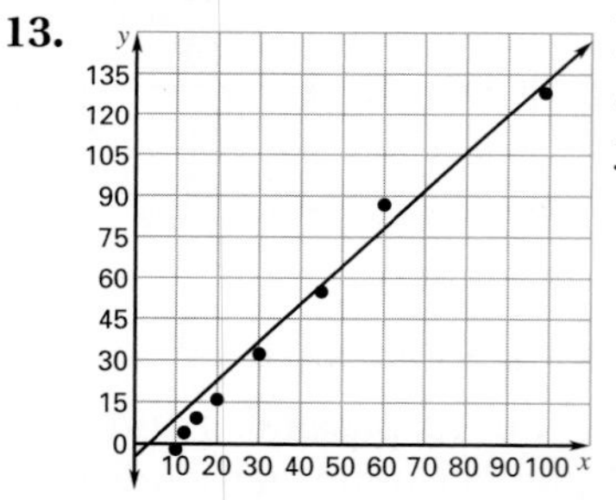 Positive correlation. *Sample answer:* $y = 1.49x - 13$

4.6 Problem Solving

17. a. 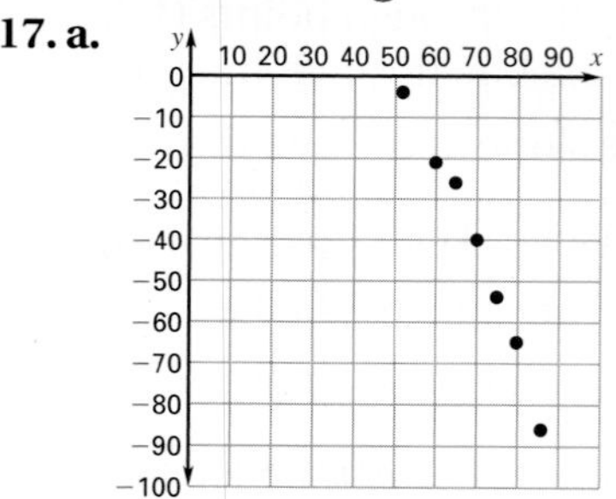 **b.** *Sample answer:* $y = -2.2x + 111$ **c.** *Sample answer:* -2.2 degrees per kilometer

19. *Sample answer:* $y = 12.6x + 32$

4.6 Graphing Calculator Activity **1.** See art in Exercise 3; negative correlation.

3. 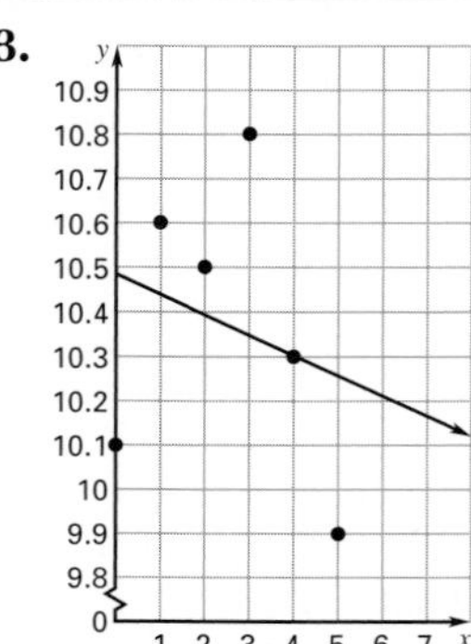

5. *Sample answer:* You cannot use the best-fitting line to predict future sales because the data do not show a strong correlation.

Extension **1.** about 0.927; The data show a strong positive correlation. While an increase in the number of minutes played may contribute to an increase in the number of points scored, there is not causation. The number of minutes played and the number of points scored may both be a result of the ability of the player. **3.** *Sample answer:* I think that as music downloads increase, sales of CDs decrease, so I would expect a strong negative correlation. The increase in the number of music downloads causes the decline in CD sales as users find downloading a more convenient way to obtain music.

4.7 Skill Practice **1.** linear interpolation

3. 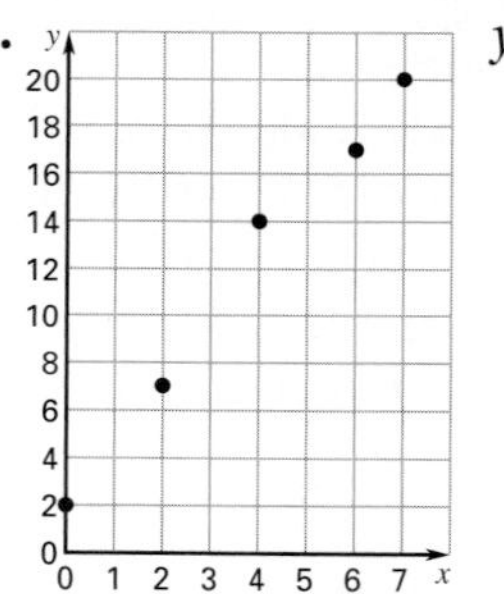 $y = 2.6x + 2.3$; 15.3

5. $y = 10.7x + 20$; 127

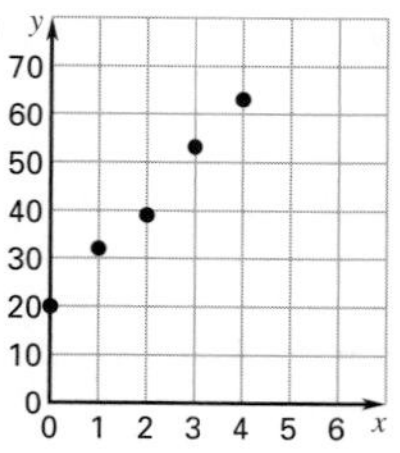

7. $2\frac{2}{3}$ **9.** -16 **11.** 1.5 **13.** To find the zero of a function, substitute 0 for y, not x; $0 = 2.3x - 2$, $2 = 2.3x$, $x = \frac{20}{23}$. **15.** a and b were not substituted correctly; $y = 4.47x + 23.1$.

4.7 Problem Solving

19. a.

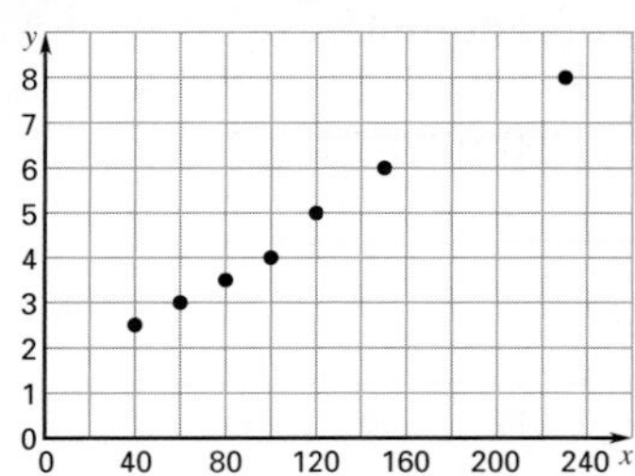

b. $y = 0.03x + 1.23$ **c.** about 8.73 ft^2
21. a. $y = -197.6x + 3542$ **b.** about 17.9; 17.9 years from 1985, or 2002, the number of people living in high noise areas will be 0; no.

4.7 Internet Activity
1. Answers may vary. **3.** Answers may vary.

Extension 1. The residuals are consistently positive; this implies that the line is in the wrong place. **3.** The distances between the points and the x-axis appear to be relatively small and the points are more or less evenly distributed above and below the x-axis. The linear model is a good fit. **5.** The residuals are -0.2, -0.1, 0.1, -0.1, 0.4, and -0.1.

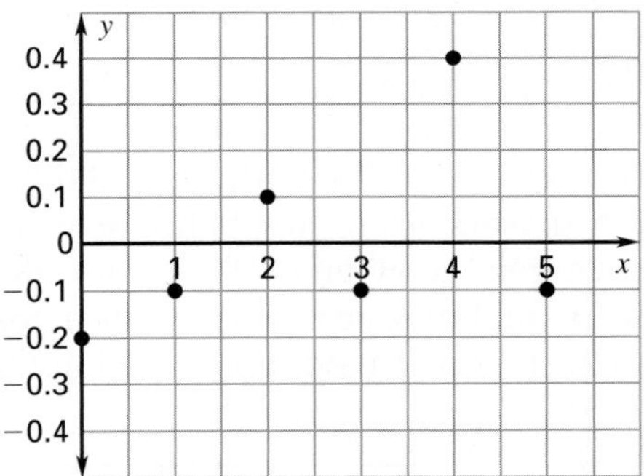

Chapter Review 1. negative **3.** The zero of a function is the x-value of the function when $y = 0$; it is the x-intercept of the graph. **5.** $y = \frac{4}{9}x + 5$ **7.** $y = -1.25x + 25$; \$22.50 **9.** $y = x + 3$ **11.** $y - 7 = -6(x - 4)$ or $y - 1 = -6(x - 5)$ **13.** $y + 2 = -\frac{6}{11}(x + 3)$ or $y + 8 = -\frac{6}{11}(x - 8)$ **15.** $4x + y = -1$ **17.** $0.07r + 0.04s = 5$. *Sample answer:* 4 organza, 118 satin; 8 organza, 111 satin; 12 organza, 104 satin

19. a. $y = -2x + 1$ **b.** $y = \frac{1}{2}x - 4$

21.

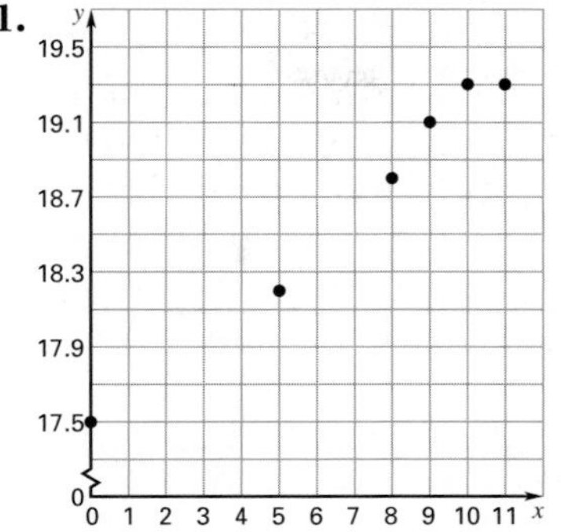

positive correlation

Chapter 4 Extra Practice

1. $y = 3x + 6$ **3.** $y = 5x - 1$ **5.** $y = \frac{1}{2}x - 5$ **7.** $y = 2x + 2$ **9.** $y = \frac{2}{3}x + 7$ **11.** $y = -5x + 3$

13.

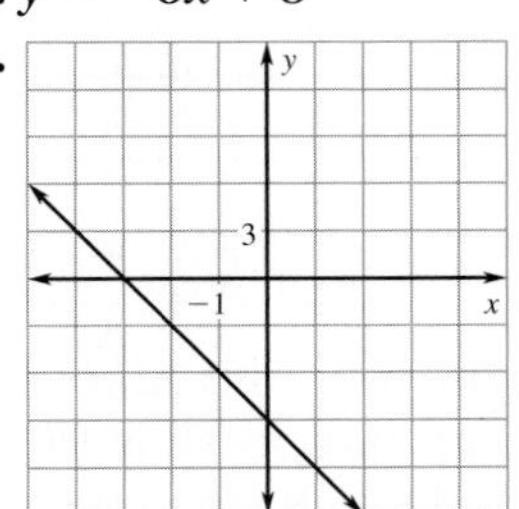

15.

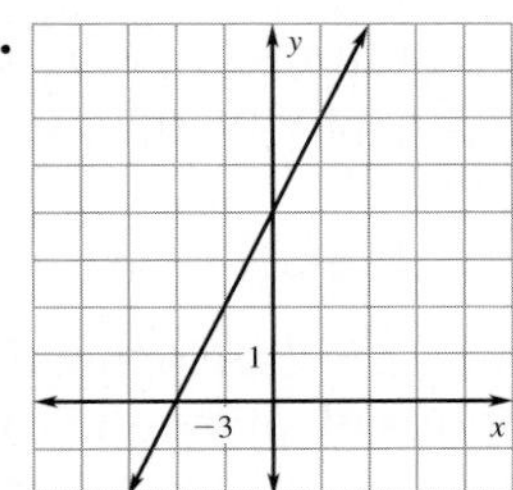

17. *Sample answer:* $y - 9 = \frac{1}{2}(x - 3)$ **19.** $4x + y = 15$ **21.** $2x + y = 0$ **23.** $y = -5x - 22$ **25.** $y = -\frac{1}{3}x - 6$ **27.** $y = \frac{3}{2}x - \frac{33}{2}$

29.

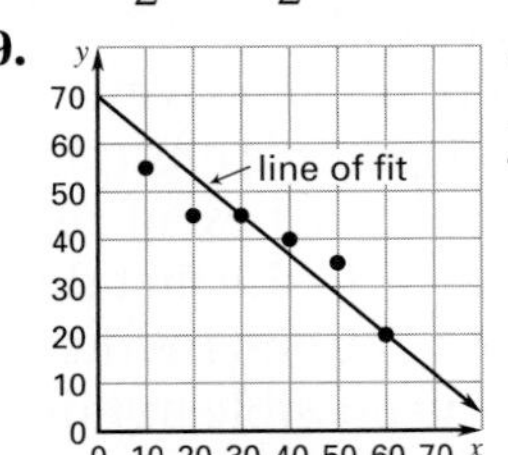

Sample answer: $y = -\frac{5}{6}x + 70$

31. $y = 1.1x + 6.7$; 14.4

Selected Answers

Chapter 5

5.1 Skill Practice **1.** open, left of -8

3. $s \le 60$

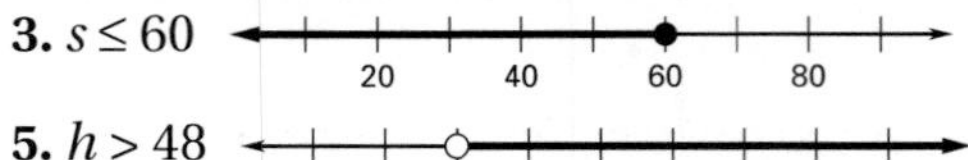

5. $h > 48$

7. $x < 10$ **9.** $x \ge -2$

11. $y \ge -16$

13. $n \le -\frac{1}{5}$

15. $w > -17.6$

17. $s \ge 9$

19. $q > -1\frac{1}{6}$

21. $d > -6.84$

23. The number line should be shaded to the right of -3, not the left.

25. $n - 15 \le 37$; $n \le 52$

27. $x < 21.6$ **29.** No; no; there are infinitely many solutions of an inequality, so it is not possible to check them all. One solution might check in the inequality while another does not. For example, if you incorrectly solve $x + 7 > 10$ as $x > 2$, the solution $x = 4$ checks in the original inequality.

5.1 Problem Solving **31.** more than 8350 points **33. a.** $s > 127.53$ **b.** Yes; no; no; $128.13 > 127.53$; $126.78 < 127.53$; when your score is 127.53, you and your competitor will tie. **35.** *Sample answer:* You want to improve on your personal best of 16 points scored in a basketball game. In the first three quarters of the game, you scored 14 points. Write and solve an inequality to find the possible numbers of points that you can score in the fourth quarter to give yourself a new personal best; $x \ge 3$, if you score at least 3 points in the fourth quarter, you will have a new personal best.

37. a.

Original price, x ($)	19,459	19,989	20,549	22,679	23,999
Final price, y ($)	16,459	16,989	17,549	19,679	20,999

b. $x - 3000 \le 17{,}000$, $x \le 20{,}000$

5.2 Skill Practice

1. Division property of inequality

3. $p \ge 7$

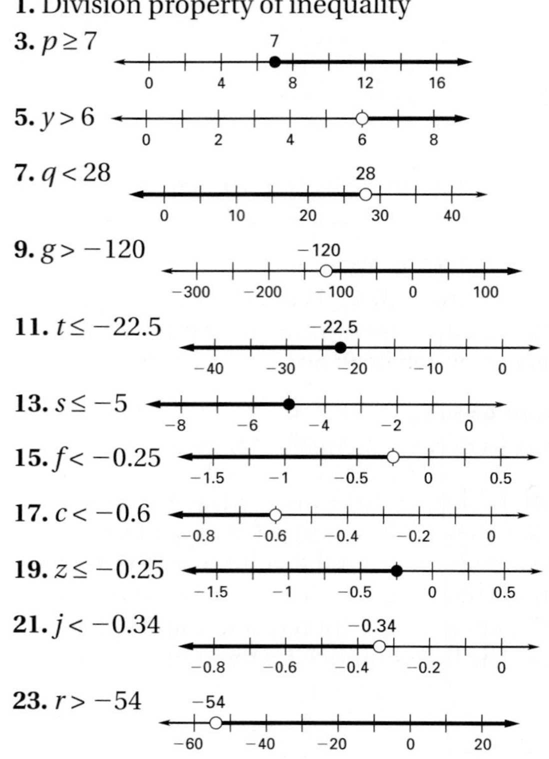

5. $y > 6$

7. $q < 28$

9. $g > -120$

11. $t \le -22.5$

13. $s \le -5$

15. $f < -0.25$

17. $c < -0.6$

19. $z \le -0.25$

21. $j < -0.34$

23. $r > -54$

25. $m > -24$

27. In both cases, you divide both sides of the inequality by a; when $a > 0$, you do not reverse the inequality symbol, but when $a < 0$, you do. **29.** Both sides of the inequality were multiplied by a positive number, so the inequality symbol should not have been reversed; $x \le -63$.

31. $-15y \le 90$; $y \ge -6$

33. $\frac{w}{24} \ge -\frac{1}{6}$; $w \ge -4$

5.2 Problem Solving **37.** at least 200 words **39.** at least 3.2 **41. a.** $400h \le 6560$, $h \le 16.4$, no more than 16 horses **b.** No; the area added by increasing both the length and the width by 20 feet can be divided into 2 rectangles (80 feet by 20 feet and 82 feet by 20 feet) and 1 square (20 feet by 20 feet). The 400 square feet of the square is large enough to hold one horse, and the rectangular areas will be able to hold additional horses. **c.** no more than 23 horses; the area of the new corral is $(80 + 15)(82 + 15) = 9215$ square feet. Find the possible numbers of horses h the corral can hold by solving the inequality $9215 \ge 400h$; $h \le 23.04$.

5.3 Skill Practice

1. equivalent inequalities

3. $x > 5$

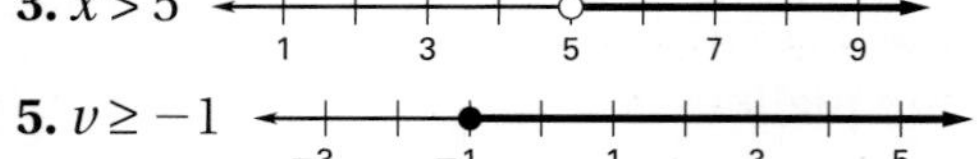

5. $v \geq -1$

7. $r \geq 1\frac{1}{7}$

9. $m > 3$

11. $p < \frac{1}{2}$

13. $d > -10$

15. The inequality symbol was not reversed when dividing both sides by -3; $x \leq -13$. **17.** all real numbers **19.** $s \geq 0$ **21.** all real numbers **23.** no solution **25.** no solution **27.** no solution

29. $3x + 4 < 40$; $x < 12$

31. $5x + 2x > 9x - 4$; $x < 2$

35. $\frac{1}{2} \cdot 8(x + 1) \leq 44$; $x \leq 10$

5.3 Problem Solving **37.** at most 11 songs

39. a. Up to 6 swans; the area of the habitat is (20 feet)(50 feet) = 1000 square feet. 500 square feet are needed for the first two swans and the remaining 1000 − 500 = 500 square feet can hold up to 500 ÷ 125 = 4 more swans; so, the maximum number of swans is 2 + 4 = 6 swans. **b.** at most 14 more swans

41. a.

Pitches per inning, p	15	16	17	18	19
Total number of pitches, t	98	101	104	107	110

b. $53 + 3p \leq 105$, $p \leq 17\frac{1}{3}$, at most 17 pitches

5.3 Problem Solving Workshop **1.** at least 9 batches **3.** at most 6 games **5.** less than 7.9 min/mi

Extension **1.** $x > 3$ **3.** $x < 213.75$

5.4 Skill Practice

1. compound inequality

3. $2 < x < 6$

5. $-1.5 \leq x < 9.2$

7. $40 \leq s \leq 60$

9. $1 < x \leq 6$

11. $-4 \leq m \leq \frac{1}{4}$

13. $-\frac{1}{3} \leq p < 2$

15. $r < 2$ or $r \geq 7$

17. $v < -5$ or $v > 5$

19. $g < -2\frac{1}{3}$ or $g > 10$

21. 3 was subtracted from only two of the three expressions of the inequality; $1 < -2x < 6$, $-\frac{1}{2} > x > -3$.

23. $x + 5 < 8$ or $x - 3 > 5$; $x < 3$ or $x > 8$

25. $-8 \leq 3(x - 4) \leq 10$; $1\frac{1}{3} \leq x \leq 7\frac{1}{3}$

29. true **31.** False. *Sample answer:* $a = -4$ is a solution of $x > 5$ or $x \leq -4$, but it is not a solution of $x > 5$.

5.4 Problem Solving

37. $-2600 \leq e \leq -100$

41. 3.2 lb $\leq f \leq$ 6.4 lb **43. a.** $\frac{5}{9}(F - 32) < 0$ or $\frac{5}{9}(F - 32) > 100$, $F < 32°F$ or $F > 212°F$

b.

°F	23	86	140	194	239
°C	−5	30	60	90	115

23°F, 239°F

45. a. $8 \leq \frac{w}{300} \leq 10$, $2400 \leq w \leq 3000$; 2400 watts to 3000 watts **b.** Yes; no; the amplification per person for 350 people is $\frac{2900}{350} \approx 8.3$ watts, which is between 8 watts and 10 watts, the amplification per person for 400 people is $\frac{2900}{400} = 7.25$ watts, which is not between 8 watts and 10 watts. **c.** 4800 watts; because each person requires at least 8 watts of amplification, and you want to be sure to provide enough amplification for 600 people, you need at least 8(600) = 4800 watts of amplification.

Selected Answers

5.4 Graphing Calculator Activity **1.** $4 < x < 7$; the graphs are the same. **3–7.** Displays should show the graphs of the following inequalities. **3.** $3 \le x \le 7$ **5.** $8 \le x \le 48$ **7.** $x \le 4\frac{1}{2}$ or $x \ge 5$

5.5 Skill Practice **1.** absolute value equation **3.** 5, −5 **5.** 0.7, −0.7 **7.** $\frac{1}{2}$, $-\frac{1}{2}$ **9.** 4, −10 **11.** −1, $-3\frac{2}{3}$ **13.** 2, −9 **15.** 4, 9 **17.** $8\frac{1}{2}$, $-3\frac{1}{2}$ **19.** $-\frac{1}{2}$, $-2\frac{1}{2}$ **21.** The absolute value symbol was removed without writing the second equation, $x + 4 = -13$; $x = 9$ or $x = -17$. **23.** no solution **25.** −4.5, −5.5 **27.** −3, 6 **29.** $13\frac{1}{2}$, $14\frac{1}{2}$ **31.** $\frac{1}{4}$, $-1\frac{1}{4}$ **33.** 13, −3 **35.** −7.5, −10.7 **37.** The distance between x and 3 is 7, 10, −4; $x - 3 = 7$ *or* $x - 3 = -7$, 10, −4; the solutions are the same. **39.** $5|2x + 9| = 15$; −3, −6

5.5 Problem Solving **43.** 235 sec, 245 sec **45. a.** 52.462 points, 56.888 points **b.** 0.3 point **47. a.** $p = |s - 450|$ **b.** 300 points, 600 points **49. a.** June 2005; November 2005 **b.** Yes; make a table of values for (m, p) using integer values of m from 0 to 8. Look for the lowest value of p in the table.

Extension

1.

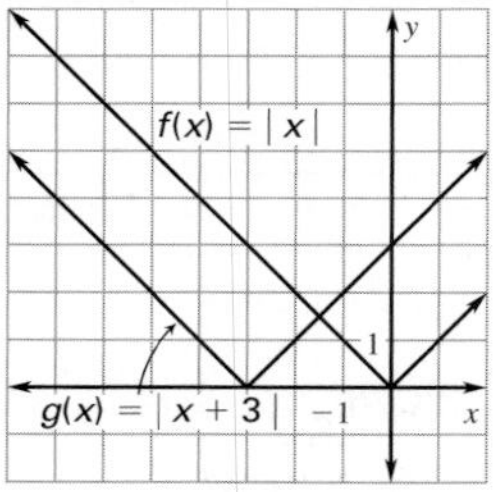

The graph of g is 3 units to the left of the graph of f.

3.

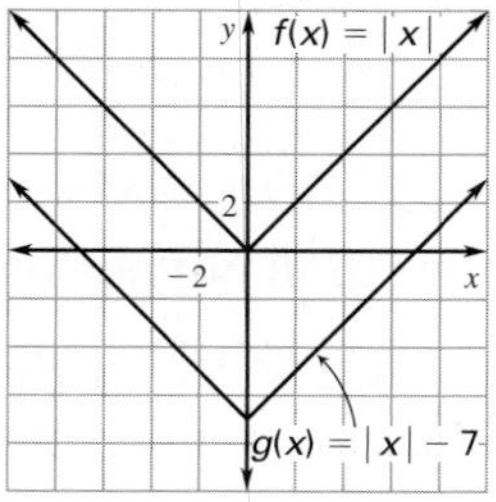

The graph of g is 7 units below the graph of f.

5.

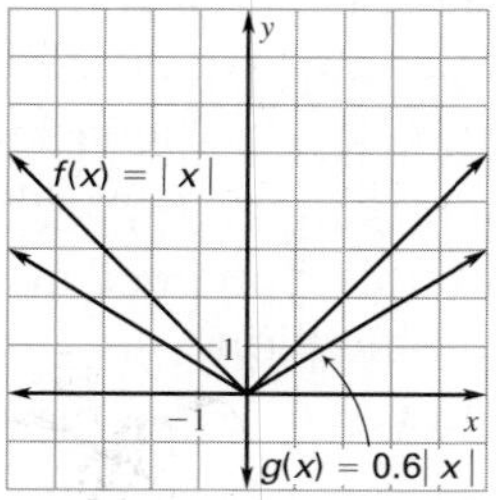

The graph of g opens up and is wider than the graph of f.

7. domain: all real numbers, range: $y \le 1$; (0, 1); maximum value: 1

5.6 Skill Practice

1. equivalent inequalities

3. $-4 < x < 4$

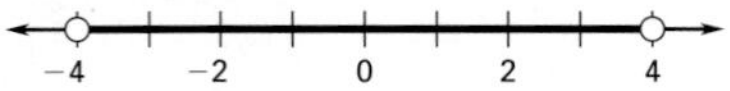

5. $h < -4.5$ or $h > 4.5$

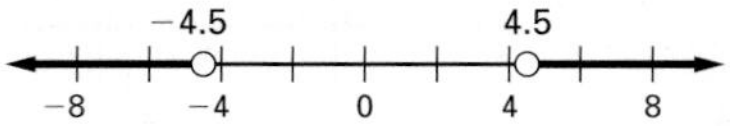

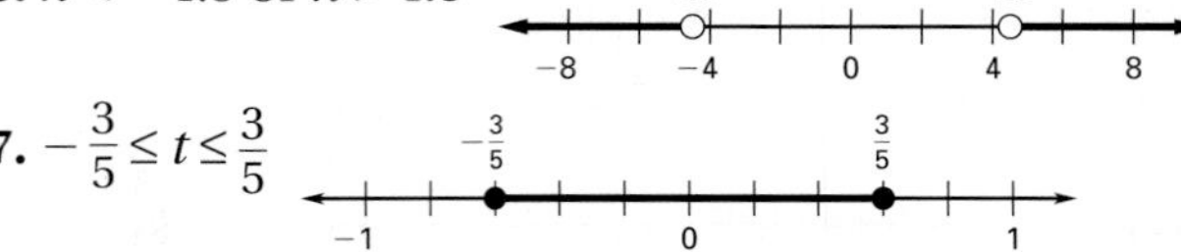

7. $-\frac{3}{5} \le t \le \frac{3}{5}$

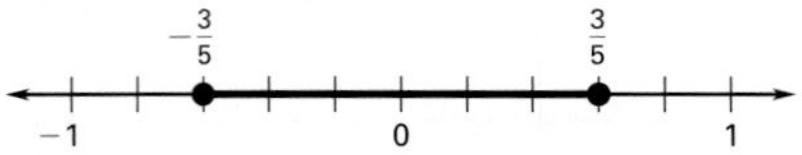

9. $d \le -7$ or $d \ge -1$

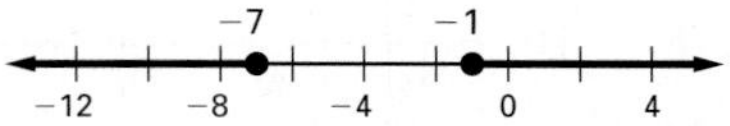

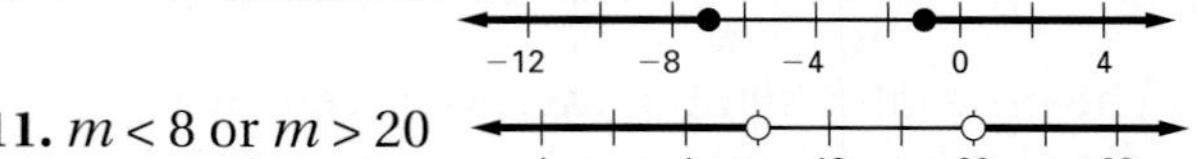

11. $m < 8$ or $m > 20$

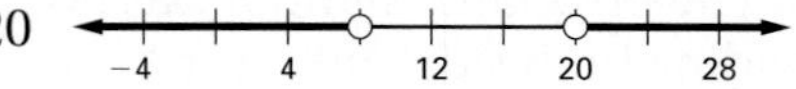

13. $c \le -3$ or $c \ge \frac{1}{2}$

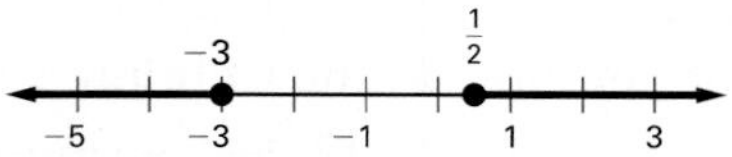

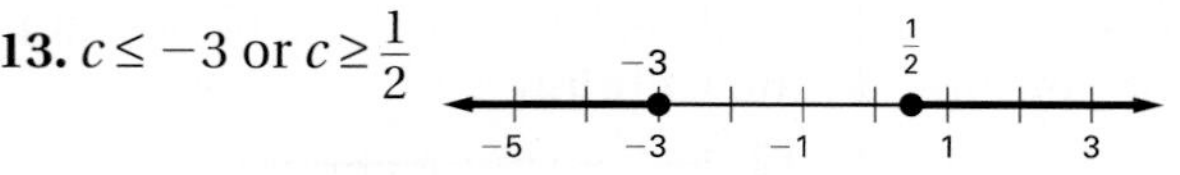

15. $r < -8$ or $r > -4$

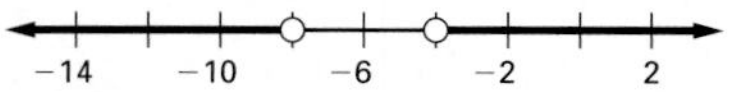

17. $u \le -3\frac{1}{5}$ or $u \ge 6\frac{2}{5}$

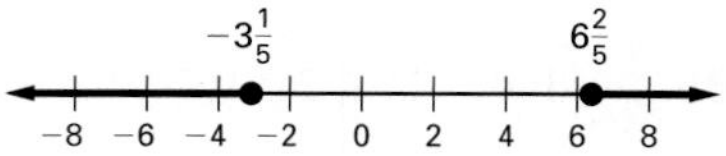

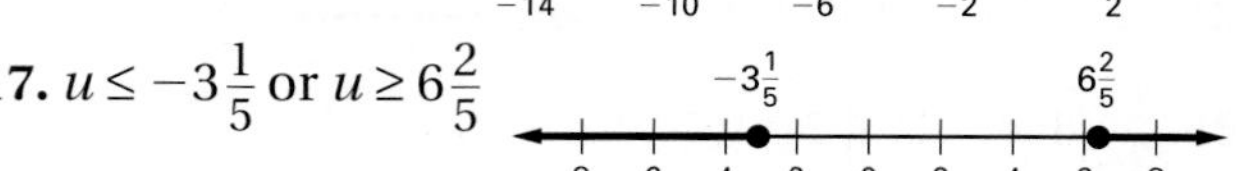

19. $v < 6$ or $v > 34$

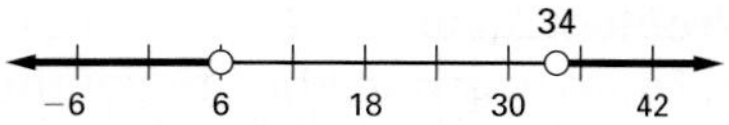

23. The compound inequality should use *or*: $x + 4 > 13$ *or* $x + 4 < -13$; $x > 9$ *or* $x < -17$.

25. $|x - 6| \le 4$; $2 \le x \le 10$

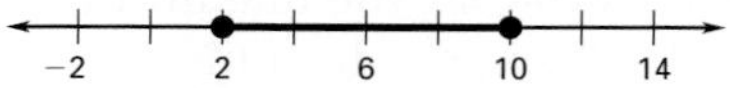

27. $|-4x - 7| + 3 > 10$; $x < -3.5$ *or* $x > 0$

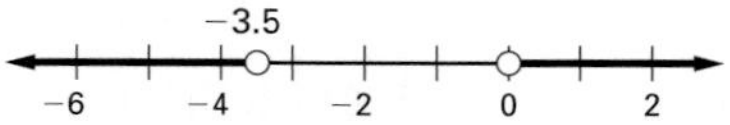

29. true **31.** False. *Sample answer:* 20

5.6 Problem Solving **35.** at least 470 words and at most 530 words **37.** $|t - 346| \le 2$, at least 344°F and at most 348°F; continue to preheat; the temperature is still below 350°F. **39. a.** 10.02 m/sec^2 **b.** 0.88 m/sec^2

5.7 Skill Practice **1.** solution **3.** not a solution **5.** not a solution **7.** not a solution **9.** solution **11.** not a solution **13.** solution

17.

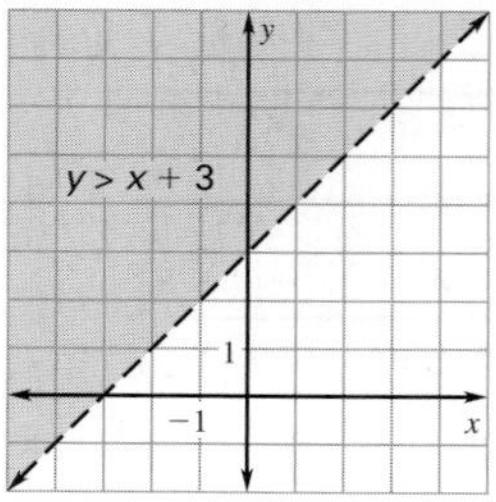

19.

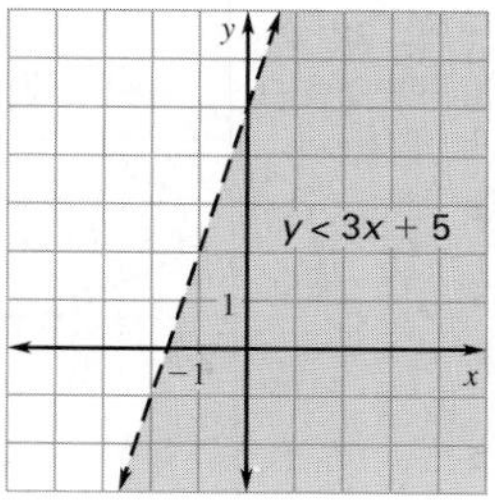

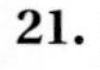

21.
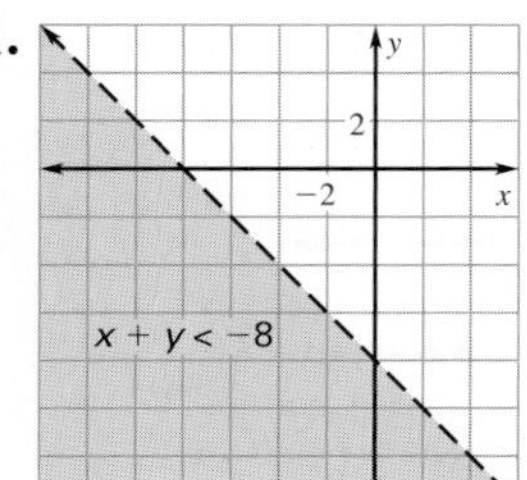

23.
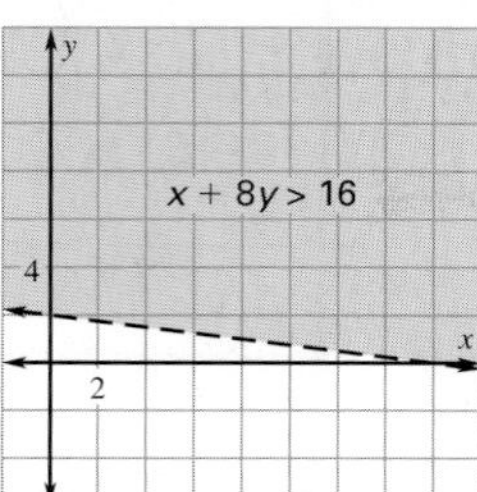

25.
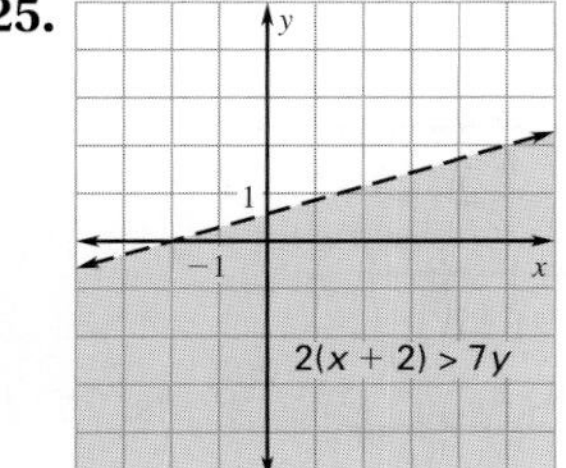

27.
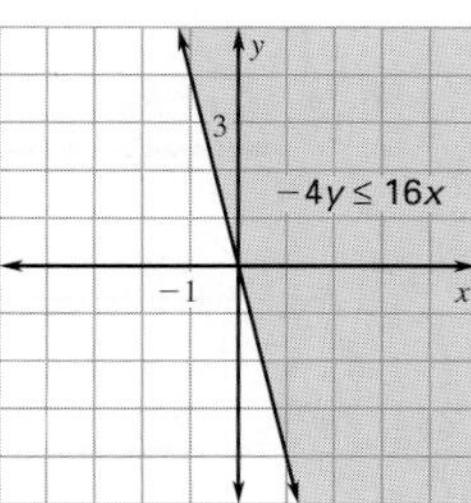

29.
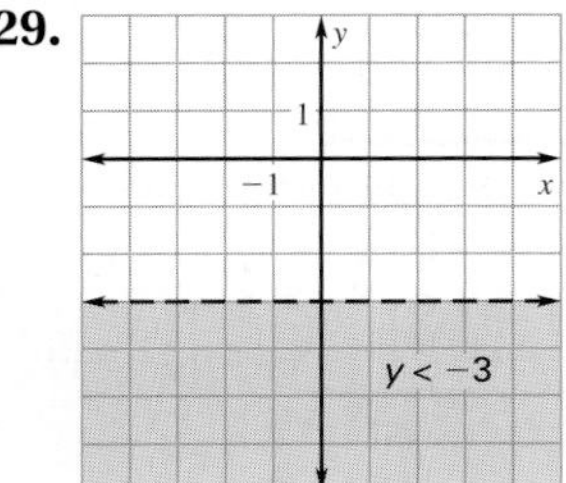

31.
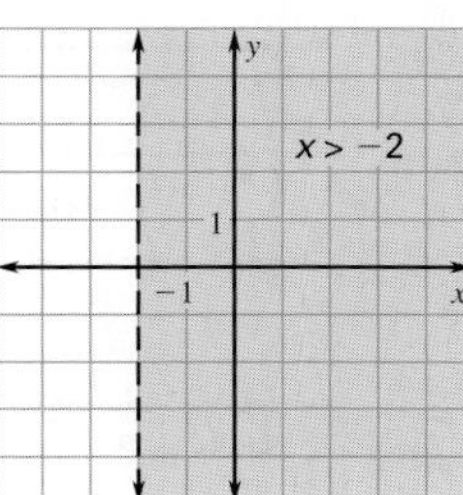

33.
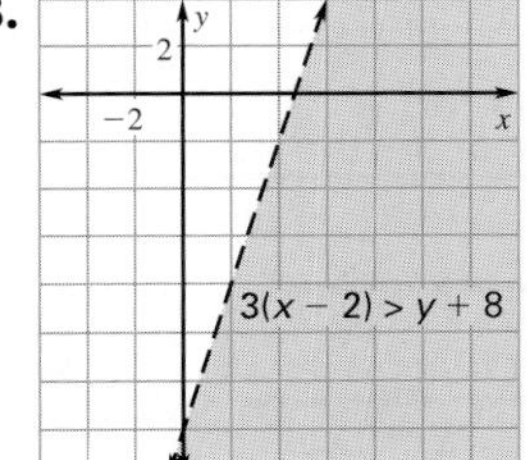

35.
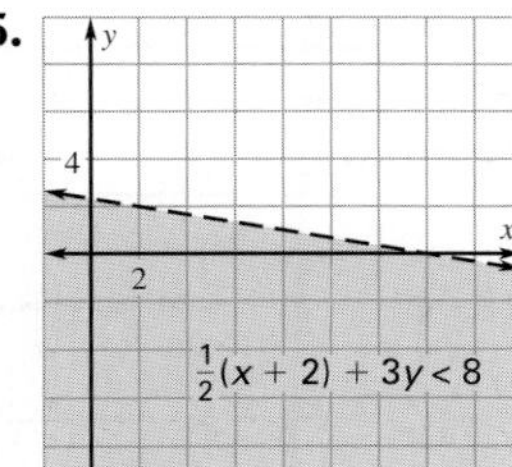

37. The wrong half-plane is shaded.

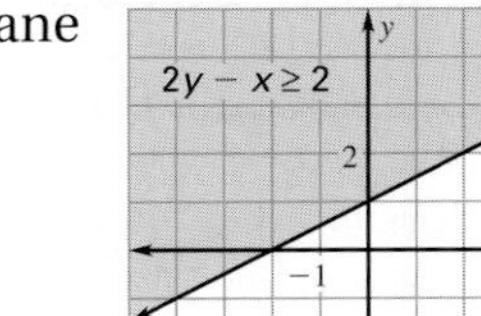

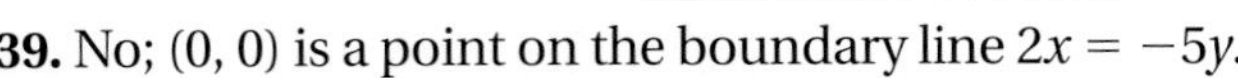

39. No; (0, 0) is a point on the boundary line $2x = -5y$.

41. $-2y \leq x + 6$ **43.** $x + 4y < -3$

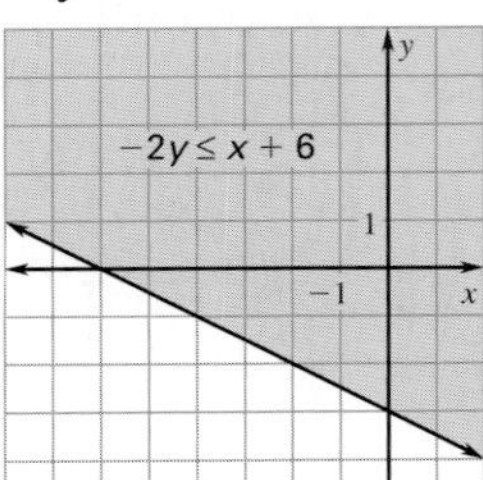

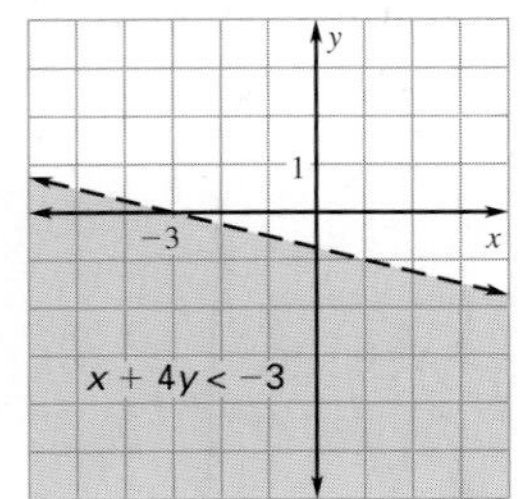

45. $y \leq \frac{5}{7}x - \frac{9}{7}$ **47.** $y > 0$ **49.** $y < 0$

5.7 Problem Solving

53.

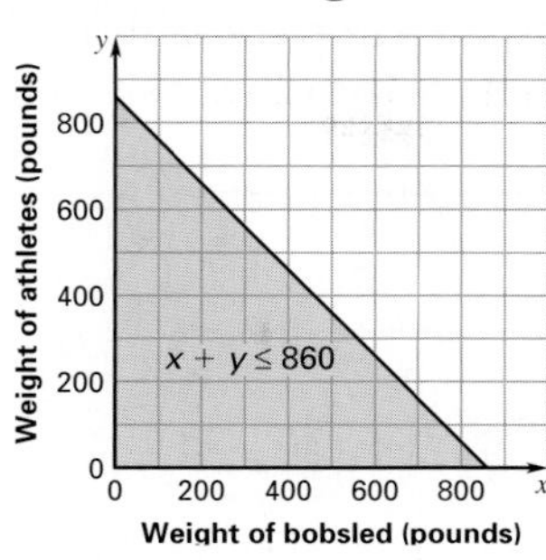

Sample answer: The solution (450, 400) means that the bobsled can weigh 450 pounds when the combined weight of the athletes is 400 pounds.

55. a. $15x + 10y \geq 100$

b.

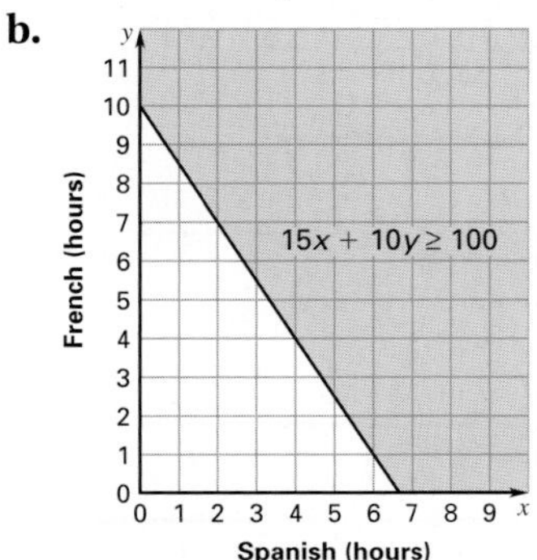

Sample answer: (4, 8), (5, 3), (6, 1)

c. *Sample answer:*

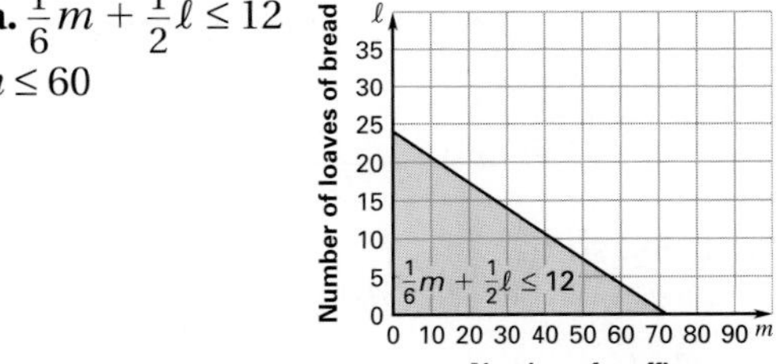

Spanish time (hours)	4	5	6
French time (hours)	8	3	1
Total earnings (dollars)	140	105	100

57. a. $\frac{1}{6}m + \frac{1}{2}\ell \leq 12$
b. $m \leq 60$

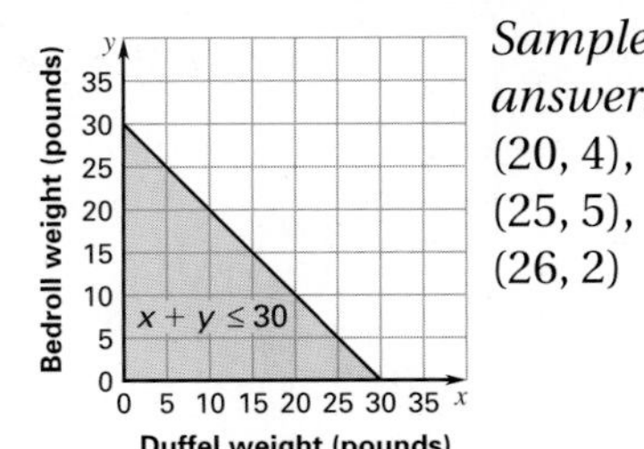

59. a. $x + y \leq 30$

Sample answer: (20, 4), (25, 5), (26, 2)

b. Yes; no; (0, 30) means that you do not take a duffel and have a 30 pound bedroll, while (30, 0) means you take a 30 pound duffel and do not take a bedroll. You need to bring both a duffel and a bedroll.

Chapter Review 1. $|x - 19| = 8$ **3.** The boundary line is solid if the inequality symbol is ≤ or ≥, the boundary line is dashed if the inequality symbol is < or >; choose a test point that is not on the boundary line. If the ordered pair is a solution to the inequality, shade the half-plane that contains the test point; if it not a solution, shade the other half-plane.

5. $x > -18$

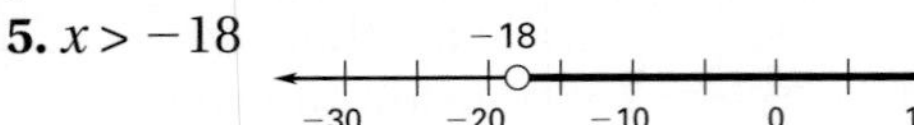

7. $s < -2.7$

9. $n > 36$

11. $y \geq 9$

13. $g < 7$

15. $x \geq 3$

17. no solution

19. at most 5 tickets

21. $-1 < x < 3\frac{2}{3}$

23. $w \leq \frac{1}{2}$ or $w > 2$

25. $-4, -8$ **27.** 5, 1 **29.** $1\frac{1}{6}, \frac{1}{6}$

31. $m \leq -8$ or $m \geq 8$

33. $-1 < g < 2\frac{1}{3}$

35. $j < -1\frac{1}{2}$ or $j > 10\frac{1}{2}$

37. solution **39.** solution

41.

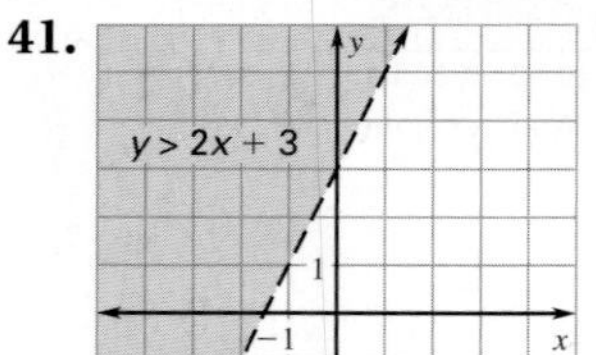

43.

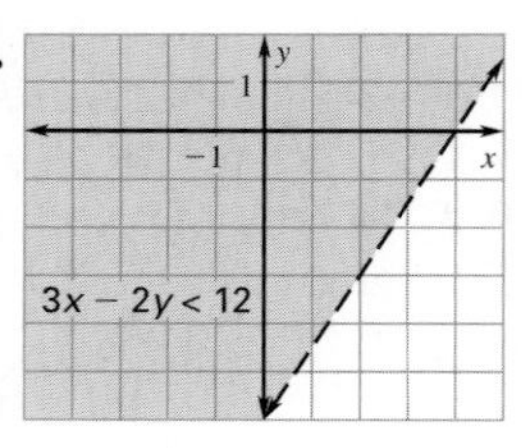

Chapter 5 Extra Practice

1. $y > 5$

3. $x \leq 7$

5. $n \leq 2\frac{1}{2}$

7. $z < -4\frac{7}{8}$

9. $t \geq 1.5$

11. $y < -5.5$

13. $p \leq 9$

15. $x \geq 6$

17. $m \leq \frac{3}{2}$

19. $z \leq 8$

21. $z \leq \frac{2}{3}$

23. $y > -4.5$

25. $x \geq 5$

27. $t > -5$

29. all real numbers

31. $y < 6$

33. no solution

35. $-3 < x < 3$

37. $2 < a \leq 3.5$

39. $r < -4$ or $r \geq -2$

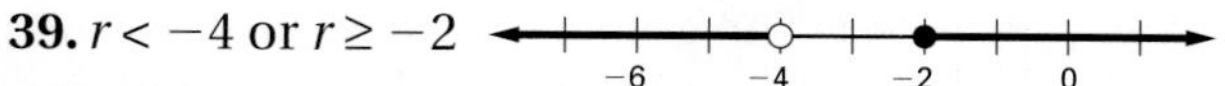

41. $t \geq 4$ or $t < -8$

43. ± 8 **45.** $-11, -1$ **47.** $-14, 28$ **49.** no solution
51. $-1, 1$ **53.** no solution

55. $-3 \leq x \leq 3$

57. $s < -1.2$ or $s > 1.2$

59. $x < -8$ or $x > 4$

61. $5 < m < 11$

63. $-1 \leq p \leq 7$

65. $-\frac{3}{5} \leq a \leq 1$

67. **69.**

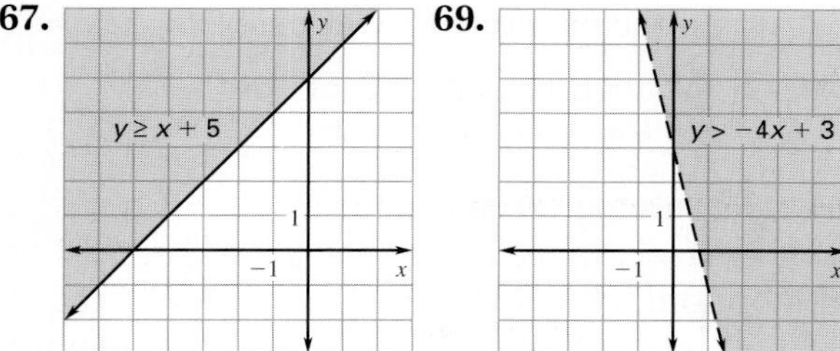

71. **73.**

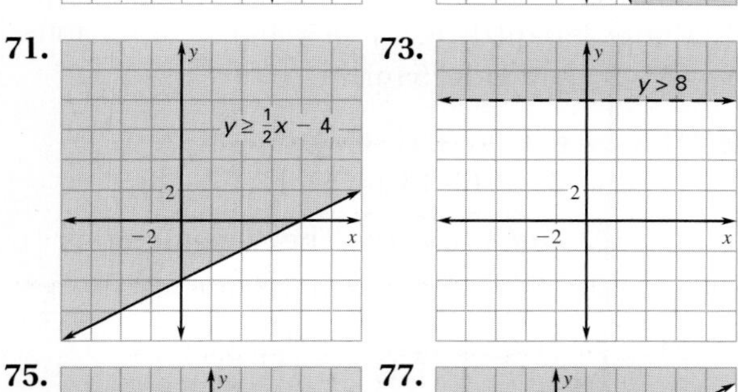

75. **77.**

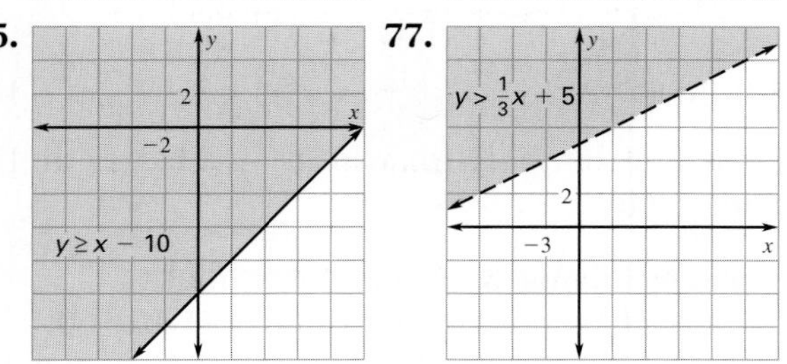

Chapter 6

6.1 Skill Practice **1.** solution **3.** solution **5.** not a solution **9.** (4, 2) **11.** The solution (3, −1) does not satisfy Equation 2. The graph of Equation 2 is incorrect; if properly graphed, the lines would intersect at (−3, −3).

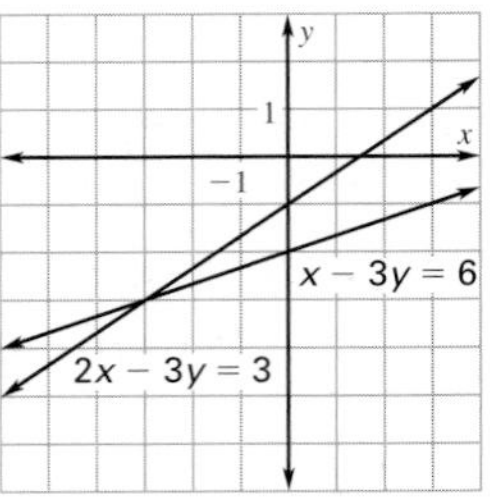

13. (4, 0) **15.** (−3, −5) **17.** (10, −15) **19.** (7, −5) **21.** (−5, 2) **23.** (3, 6) **25.** (4, 6) **27.** *Sample answer:* $m = 0$ and $b = 2$ **29. a.** 4 **b.** (4, 5) **c.** *Sample answer:* Each side of the equation is set equal to *y*. **d.** *Sample answer:* Set each side of the equation equal to *y* to create a system of two equations. Then solve the system using the graph-and-check method. The *x*-coordinate of the system's solution is the solution of the original equation.

6.1 Problem Solving **31.** 2040 **33.** 15 small cards and 10 large cards **35. a.** $y = 5x + 15$, $y = 8x$

b.

Tickets	Cost for members	Cost for nonmembers
1	$20	$8
2	$25	$16
3	$30	$24
4	$35	$32
5	$40	$40
6	$45	$48

c.

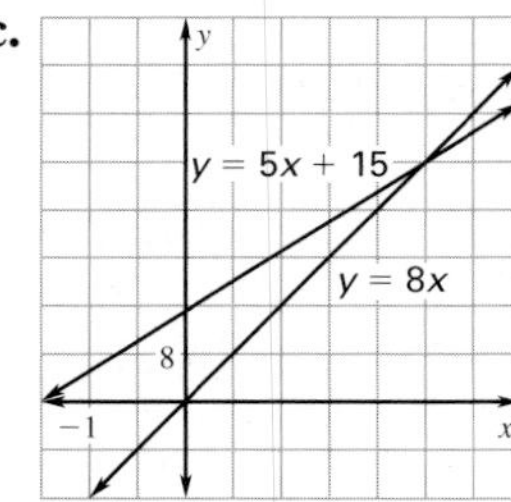

When you view 6 or more movies. *Sample answer:* The graph for a non-member is below the graph for a member up through 4 movies. For 5 movies, the cost is the same. The graph for members is lower than the graph for nonmembers for 6 or more movies.

6.1 Graphing Calculator Activity **1.** (−1.5, 2.5) **3.** (0.2, −1.44)

6.2 Skill Practice **1.** *Sample answer:* $y = x + 1$, $y = 2x + 1$ **3.** (5, 3) **5.** (2, −1) **7.** (−4, 5) **9.** (6, 7) **11.** (2, −2) **13.** (5, −8) **15.** (0, 2) **17.** (1.4, −4.4) **19.** *Sample answer:* In Step 3, 6 is substituted for *y* instead of *x*; $y = 9 - 3(6)$, $y = -9$, the solution is (6, −9). **21.** (4, −120) **23.** (3, 7) **25.** (6, −3) **27.** (0, −6) **29.** *Sample answer:* The graphs of the equations should intersect at the solution you found using the substitution method.

6.2 Problem Solving **31.** 96 bags of popcorn; 48 pretzels **33.** 4 in. *Sample answer:* (4, 5) is the solution to the appropriate linear system, so *x* should equal 4. **35.** 50 milliliters of 1% hydrochloric acid solution and 50 milliliters of 5% hydrochloric acid solution **37.** Yes. *Sample answer:* The cheetah would have to run at 88 feet per second for 23.3 seconds to catch the gazelle.

6.2 Problem Solving Workshop **1.** 5 mi

6.3 Skill Practice **1.** *Sample answer:* $x + y = 10$, $x - y = 5$ **3.** (1, 6) **5.** (−1, −5) **7.** (5, 7) **9.** (−1, 2) **11.** (5, 3) **13.** (4, 5) **17.** (2, −3) **19.** (−18, 4) **21.** (4, −3) **23.** *Sample answer:* The two equations should be subtracted rather than added; $6x = 8$, $x = \frac{4}{3}$. **25.** (26, 14) **27.** (−4, 12) **29.** (−2, 5) **31.** (5, 25) **33.** (−2, 8) **35.** $\ell = 4.5$ ft, $w = 2.5$ ft

6.3 Problem Solving **39.** speed in still water: 4.6 m/sec, speed of current: 0.3 m/sec **41.** monophonic ring tone: $1.95, polyphonic ring tone: $3.50 **43. a.** flight to Phoenix: 400 mi/h, flight to Charlotte: 450 mi/h **b.** $s + w = 450$, $s - w = 400$; plane: 425 mi/h, wind: 25 mi/h

6.4 Skill Practice **1.** 36 **3.** (1, 1) **5.** (5, −4) **7.** (2, 1) **9.** (−7, −12) **11.** (5, 6) **13.** (4, 4) **15.** (5, −3) **17.** $\left(4\frac{2}{7}, 5\right)$ **19.** *Sample answer:* The two equations should be subtracted rather than added; $-x = -9$, $x = 9$. **21.** (2, −1) **23.** $\left(-4\frac{5}{22}, -2\frac{1}{11}\right)$ **25.** (5, 4) **27.** (10, 2) **29.** (2, −1) **31.** $\left(\frac{1}{3}, -\frac{2}{3}\right)$ **33. a.** $2\ell + 2w = 18$, $6\ell + 4w = 46$; length: 5 in., width: 4 in. **b.** length: 15 in., width: 8 in.

6.4 Problem Solving **37.** 5 hardcover books **39.** 21 pies, 16 batches of applesauce **41.** $16.50; a small costs $2.90, and a large costs $3.90; 3(2.90) + 2(3.90) = 16.50. **43.** $800; $1200

Graphing Calculator Activity **1.** (–2, 3) **3.** (6, –3) **5.** (4, 1) **7.** The solution (2, 4) found using the graphing calculator has coordinates that are given by the equations resulting from using linear combinations to eliminate one of the variables from the original system. **9.a.** You get a false equation such as 5 = 3. **b.** The lines are parallel. **c.** When you add the equations, you don't get an equation that can be graphed, so the method does not work.

6.5 Skill Practice **1.** inconsistent **3.** *Sample answer:* The lines have the same slope but different y-intercepts. **5.** B; one solution **7.** A; infinitely many solutions

9.

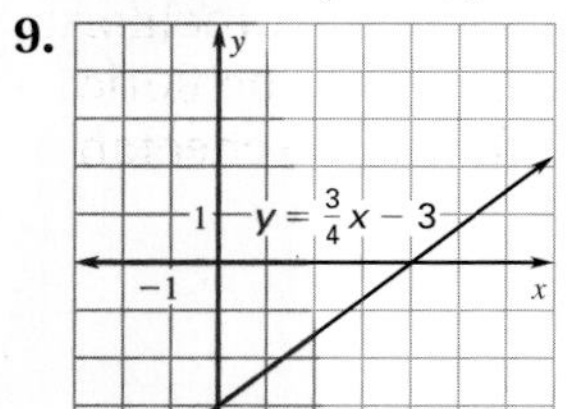
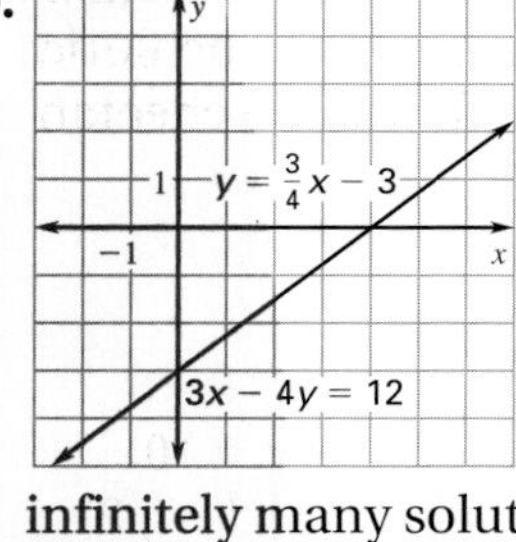

11.

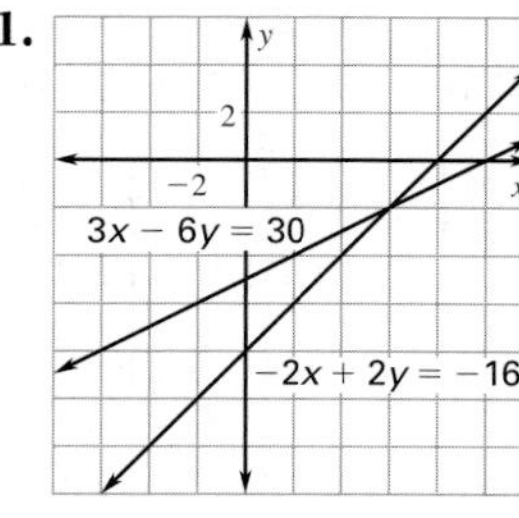

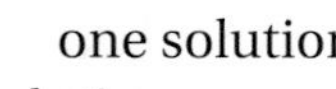

infinitely many solutions one solution

13.

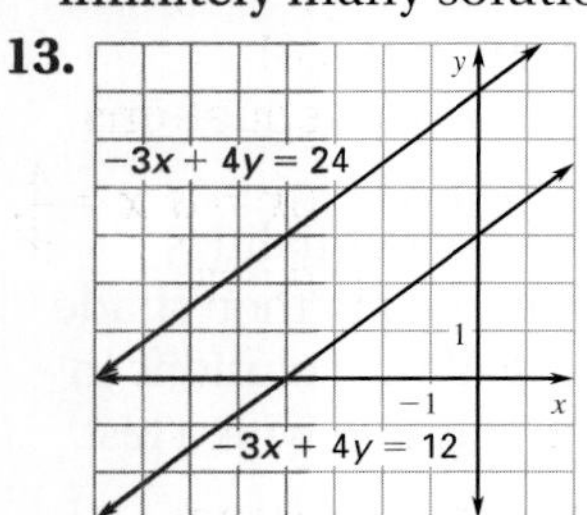

no solution

15. $(-3, 4)$ **17.** $(3, 7)$ **19.** $(2, 2)$ **21.** no solution **23.** $(0, 3)$ **27.** infinitely many solutions **29.** infinitely many solutions **31.** infinitely many solutions **33.** *Sample answer:* $7x - 8y = -9$, $7x - 8y = 4$

6.5 Problem Solving **37.** Yes. *Sample answer:* There is one solution to the resulting linear system.

39. a. $d = \frac{t}{3}$, $d = \frac{t}{3} - 5$

b.

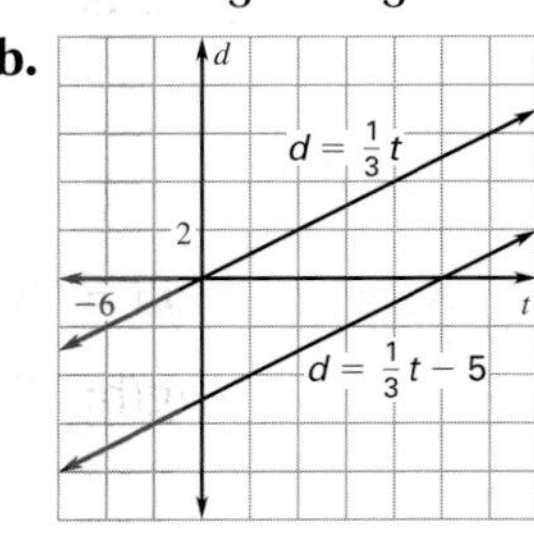

Sample answer: No, since the lines are parallel, the two climbers will never be at the same distance at the same time.

Extension **1.**

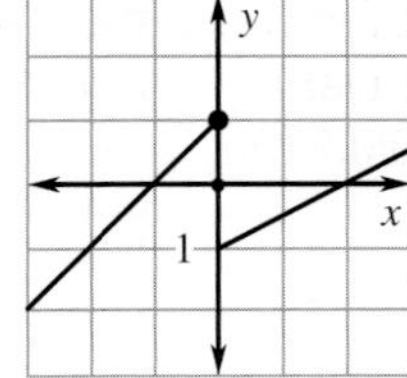

3.

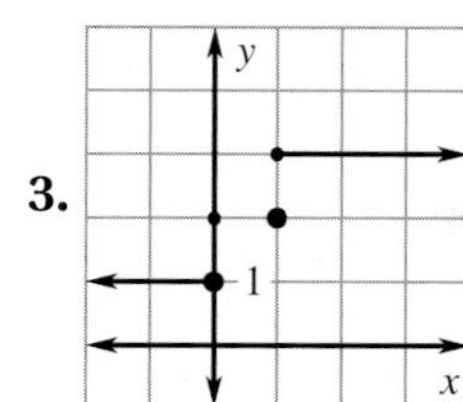

5. $y = \begin{cases} 1, \text{ if } x < -1 \\ 2x, \text{ if } x - 1 \le 0 \\ -\frac{1}{2}x + 2, \text{ if } x > 2 \end{cases}$

7. $P = \begin{cases} 20t, \text{ if } 0 \le t \ge 40 \\ 30(t-40) + 800, \text{ if } t > 40 \end{cases}$

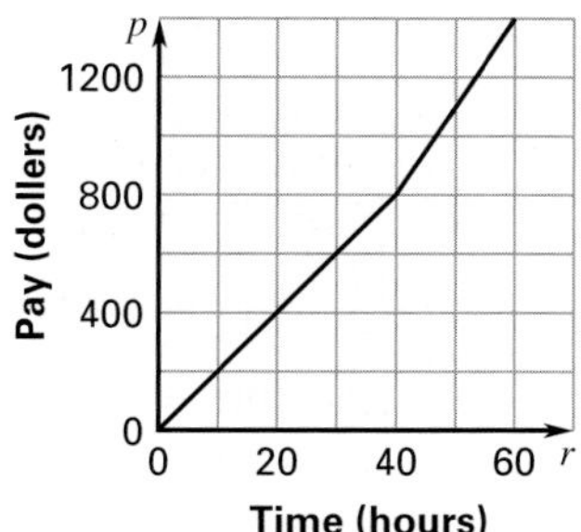

9.

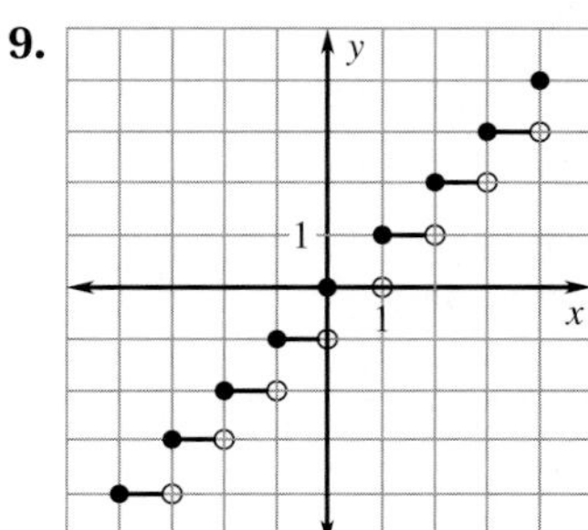

Yes; yes; the function is a piecewise function because, for every integer value of n, there is a unique equation that applies to the part of the domain defined by $n \le x < n + 1$. The function is a step function because it is defined by a constant value over each part of its domain.

6.6 Skill Practice **1.** solution **3.** not a solution **5.** not a solution **7.** A

9.

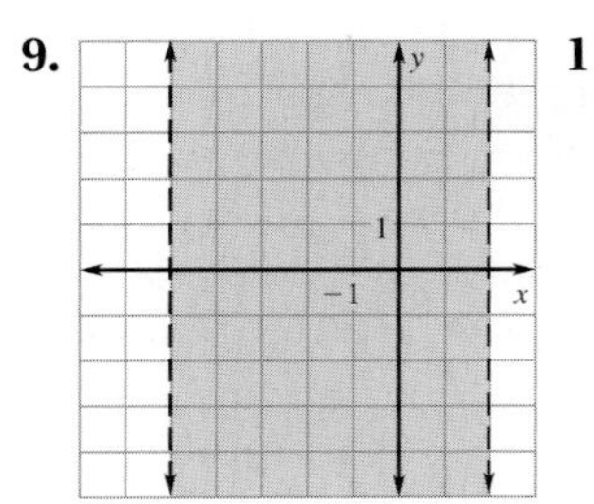

11.

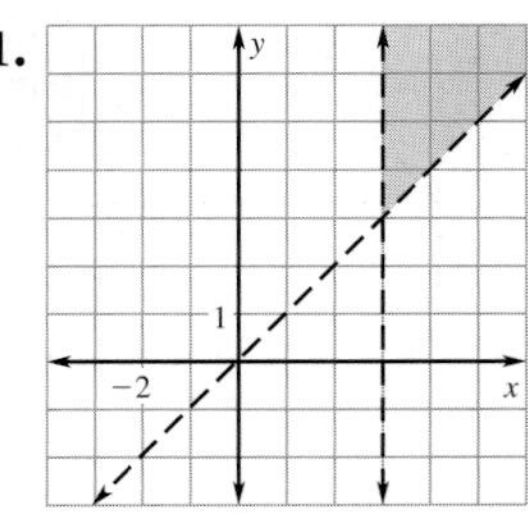

13.

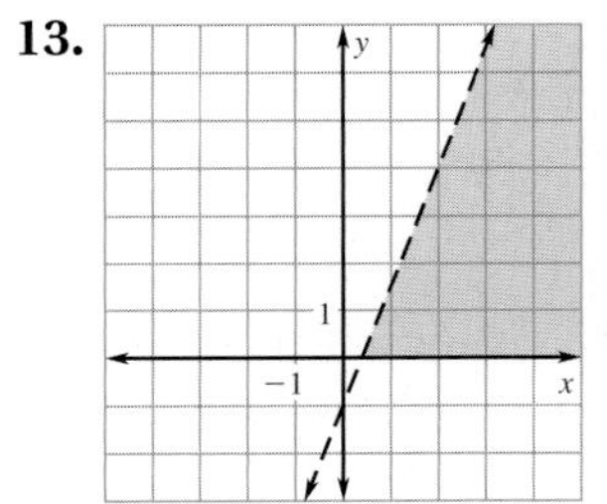

15.

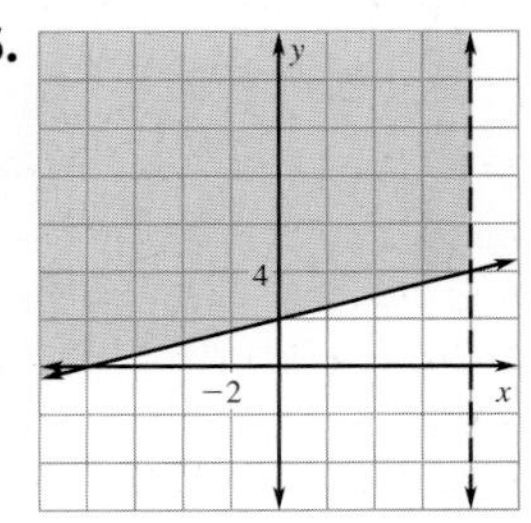

17. 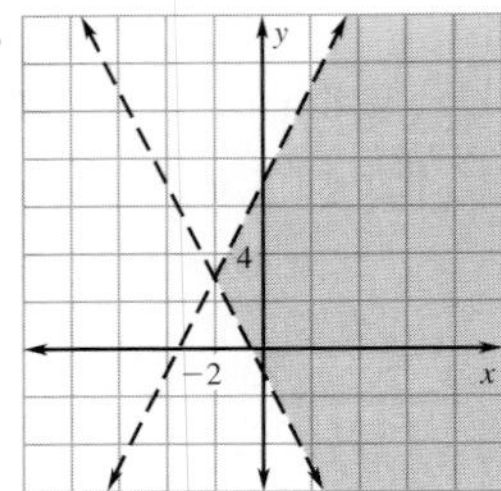

19. 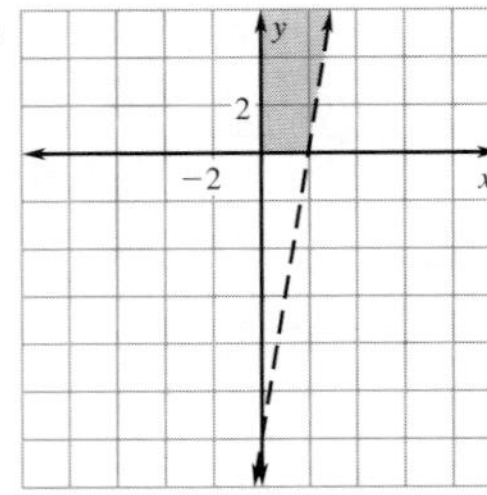

23. The graph is shaded to include $x + y > 3$, not $x + y < 3$.

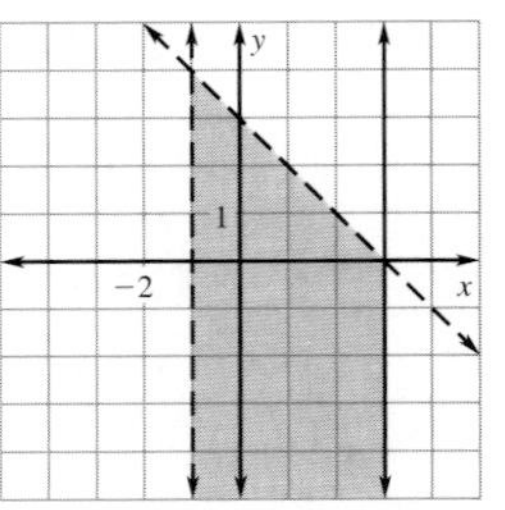

25. $y > -1, y < 4$ **27.** $y \leq 5x + 1, y > x - 2$ **29.** $y \leq x - 3, y > -2x - 1, y > -6$

31. 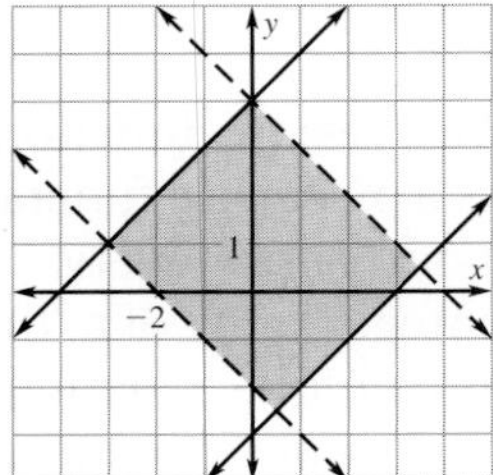

33. No; there are no possible values for x and y that satisfy both equations.

6.6 Problem Solving

37. $14x + 7y < 70$, $x + y < 8, x \geq 0, y \geq 0$

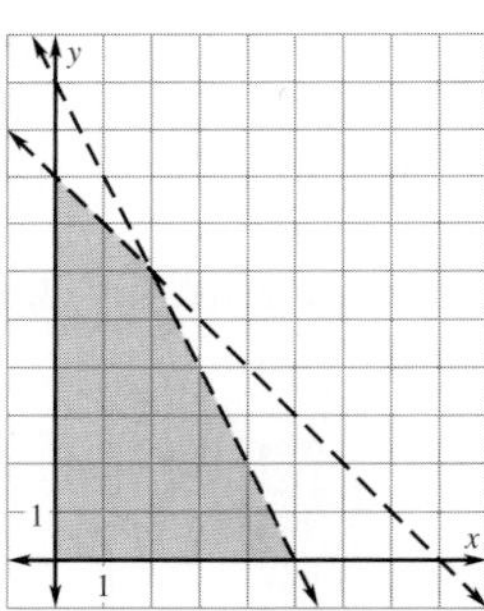

39. a. $20 \leq x \leq 65$, $154 - 0.7x \leq y \leq 187 - 0.85x$

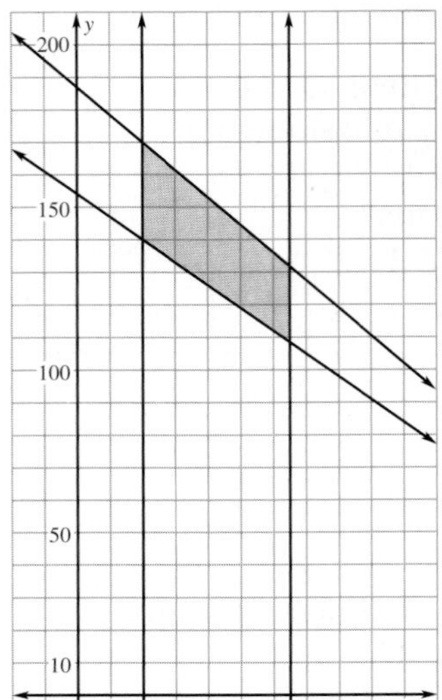

b. No. *Sample answer:* The heart rate is below 70% of the maximum heart rate.

Chapter Review **1.** system of linear inequalities **3.** *Sample answer:* Graph each inequality then shade the region that is the intersection of the solutions to each inequality. Then check the solution with a test point. **5.** $(2, -5)$ **7.** $(4, -1)$ **9.** $(5, 1)$ **11.** 4 tubes of paint, 8 brushes **13.** $(1, -2)$ **15.** $(6, 10)$ **17.** $(-7, 8)$ **19.** $(-2, 5)$ **21.** $(4, 5)$ **23.** $(1, 6)$ **25.** No solution. *Sample answer:* When the variables are eliminated, a false statement remains, which means there is no solution. **27.** One solution. *Sample answer:* The lines have different slopes, so there is only one solution.

29. 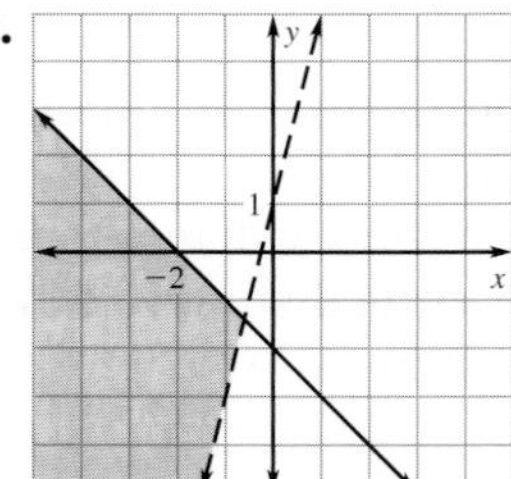

31. Let m represent the number of matinee movies and n represent the number of evening movies; $5m + 8n \leq 40, m \geq 0, n \geq 0$.

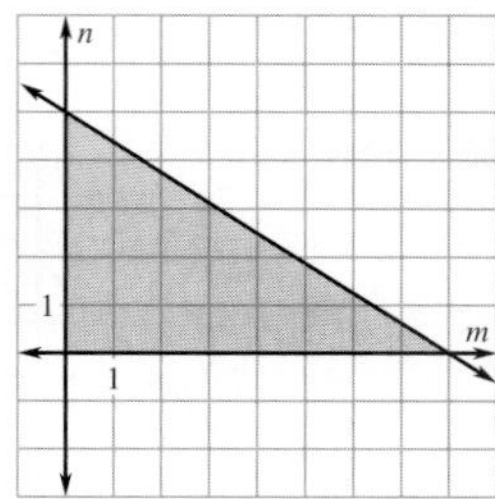

Chapter 6
Extra Practice

1. (3, 2) **3.** (1, −3) **5.** (−3, −2) **7.** (−3, 0) **9.** (9, 7) **11.** (3, −7) **13.** (−4, 3) **15.** (−9, −2) **17.** (−3, −5) **19.** (−6, 3) **21.** (11, 9) **23.** $\left(10, -\frac{3}{2}\right)$

25.
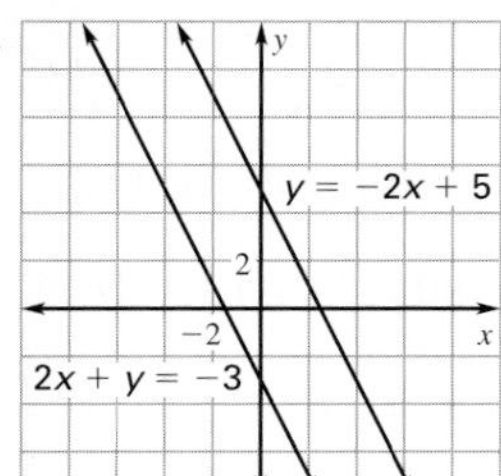

no solution

27.
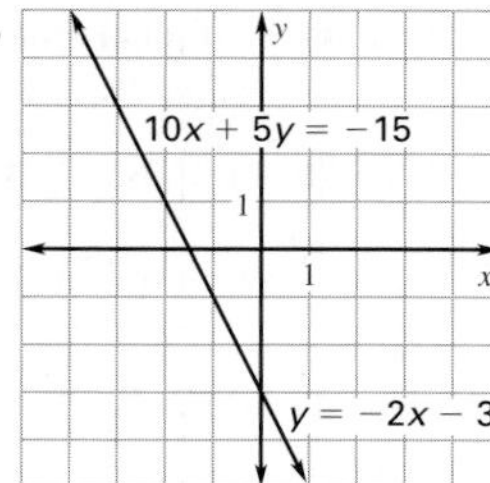

infinitely many solutions

29. (20, 48) **31.** no solution **33.** (−30, 0)

35.
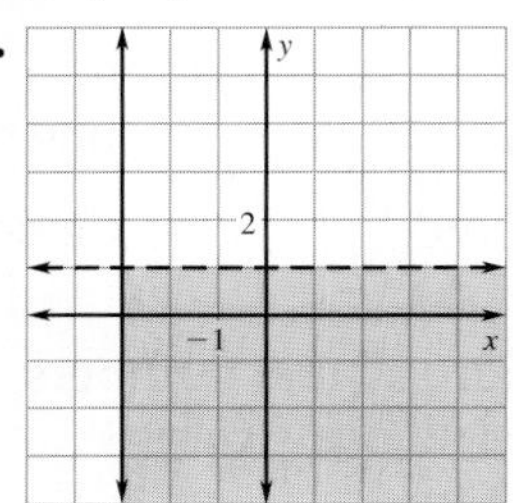

37.
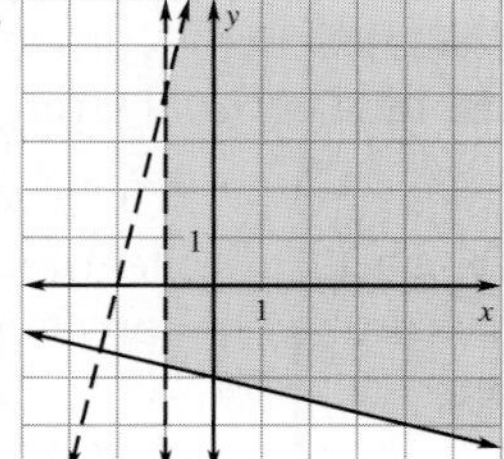

39.
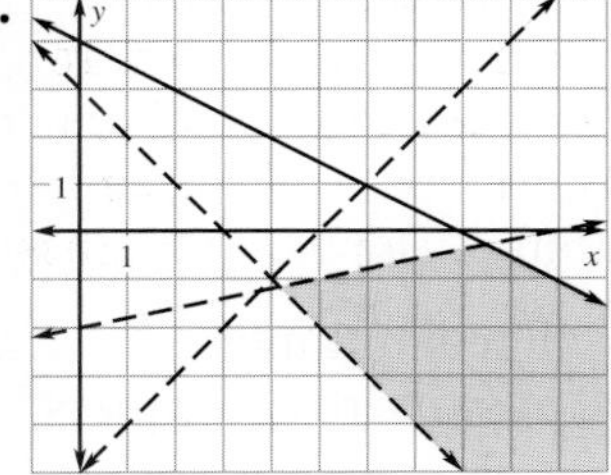

Chapter 7

7.1 Skill Practice **1.** order of magnitude **3.** 4^8 **5.** 3^4 **7.** $(-7)^9$ **9.** 2^{14} **11.** 3^{10} **13.** $(-5)^{12}$ **15.** $15^3 \cdot 29^3$ **17.** $132^6 \cdot 9^6$ **19.** x^6 **21.** z^6 **23.** x^{10} **25.** $(b-2)^{12}$ **27.** $25x^2$ **29.** $49x^2y^2$ **31.** $100x^{14}$ **33.** $96d^{22}$ **35.** $12p^{19}$ **37.** $108x^{29}$ **39.** *Sample answer:* The exponents should be added, not multiplied; $c^1 \cdot c^4 \cdot c^5 = c^{1+4+5} = c^{10}$. **43.** 2 **45.** 2 **47.** $-3267x^{12}y^{13}$ **49.** $1000r^{17}s^6t^{17}$

7.1 Problem Solving **53.** 10^{26} m

55. a.

Ounces of gold	10	100	1000	10,000	100,000
Number of atoms	10^{24}	10^{25}	10^{26}	10^{27}	10^{28}

b. $10^5 \cdot 10^{23}$; 10^{28} atoms **57.** 10^{27}

7.2 Skill Practice **1.** base, exponent **3.** 5^4 **5.** 3^4 **7.** $(-4)^3$ **9.** 10^6 **11.** $\frac{1}{3^5}$ **13.** $\frac{5^4}{4^4}$ **15.** 7^7 **17.** 3^8 **21.** y^7 **23.** $\frac{a^9}{y^9}$ **25.** $\frac{p^4}{q^4}$ **27.** $-\frac{64}{x^3}$ **29.** $\frac{64c^3}{d^6}$ **31.** $\frac{x^4}{9y^6}$ **33.** $\frac{9x^4}{4y^2}$ **35.** $\frac{3m^7}{8n^6}$ **39.** 8 **41.** 4 **43.** $54s^3t^3$ **45.** $\frac{27x^{11}y^5}{25}$ **47.** Identity property of multiplication; Multiply fractions; Quotient of powers property

7.2 Problem Solving

49. a.

Step	Number of new squares	Side length of new square
1	$4 = 4^1$	$\frac{1}{2} = \left(\frac{1}{2}\right)^1$
2	$16 = 4^2$	$\frac{1}{4} = \left(\frac{1}{2}\right)^2$
3	$64 = 4^3$	$\frac{1}{8} = \left(\frac{1}{2}\right)^3$
4	$256 = 4^4$	$\frac{1}{16} = \left(\frac{1}{2}\right)^4$

b. $\frac{4^4}{4^2}$; 16 times

51. about 31,710 yr **53.** 31^3 times greater

7.3 Skill Practice **1.** Product of powers property and definition of zero exponent; the expression simplifies using the product of powers property to 3^0, which by definition equals 1. **3.** $\frac{1}{64}$ **5.** $-\frac{1}{3}$ **7.** 1 **9.** 1 **11.** $\frac{49}{4}$ **13.** undefined **15.** $\frac{1}{32}$ **17.** $\frac{1}{32}$ **19.** 27 **21.** $\frac{1}{243}$ **23.** $\frac{8}{3}$ **25.** 16 **27.** 3^0 is not equivalent to 0, but to 1; $-6 \cdot 3^0 = -6 \cdot 1 = -6$. **29.** $\frac{2}{y^3}$ **31.** $\frac{1}{121h^2}$ **33.** $\frac{5}{m^3n^4}$ **35.** 1 **37.** $\frac{1}{x^5y^2}$ **39.** $\frac{y^8}{15x^{10}}$ **41.** $243d^3$ **43.** $\frac{3x^{12}y^5}{4}$

7.3 Problem Solving **51.** about 10^5 grains of rice **53.** about 10^{11} red blood cells

55. a.

Number of folds	0	1	2	3
Fraction of original area	1	$\frac{1}{2}$	$\frac{1}{4}$	$\frac{1}{8}$

b. $\left(\frac{1}{2}\right)^x$ where x is the number of folds **57. a.** 112.5 watts **b.** $I = 9d^{-2}$ **c.** The intensity is divided by 4.

Extension **1.** 1000 **3.** $\frac{1}{729}$ **5.** $\frac{1}{3}$ **7.** 81 **9.** $\frac{1}{216}$ **11.** $-\frac{1}{4}$ **13.** For $0 < x < 1$, $x^{1/2} < x^{-1/2}$; for $x = 1$, $x^{1/2} = x^{-1/2}$; for $x > 1$, $x^{1/2} > x^{-1/2}$.

7.4 Skill Practice **1.** growth factor **3.** The graph would be a vertical stretch. *Sample answer:* Since the y-values of $y = 2 \cdot 5^x$ are double those of $y = 5^x$. **5.** $y = 125 \cdot 5^x$ **7.** $y = \frac{1}{9} \cdot 3^x$

9.

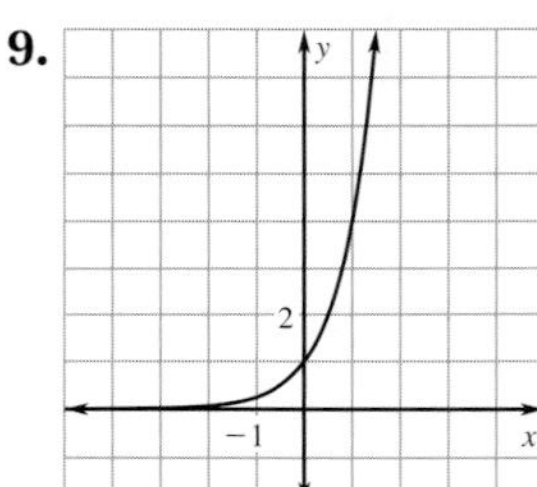

domain: all real numbers, range: all positive real numbers

11. domain: all real numbers, range: all positive real numbers

13.

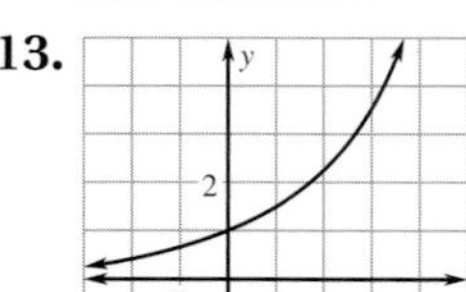

domain: all real numbers, range: all positive real numbers

15.

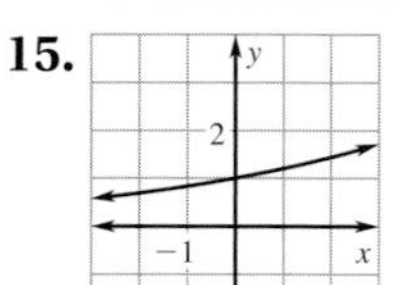

domain: all real numbers, range: all positive real numbers

17. 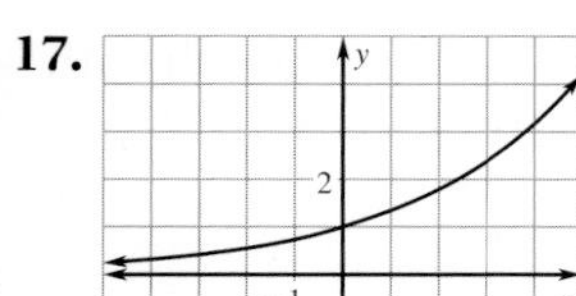

domain: all real numbers, range: all positive real numbers

19. 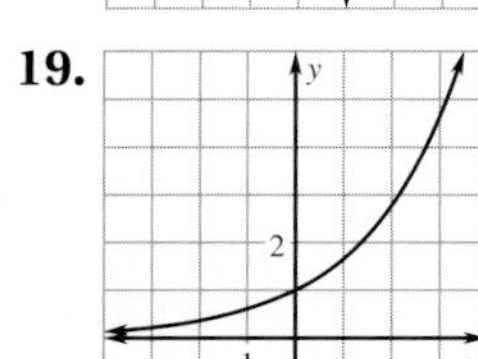
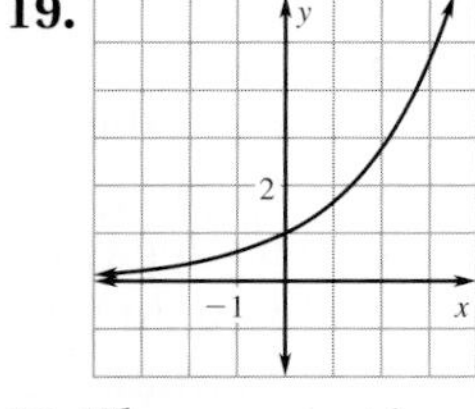

domain: all real numbers, range: all positive real numbers

21. The percent increase was not written as a decimal; $0.27(1 + 0.02)^3 = 0.27(1.02)^3 \approx \$.29$.

23. 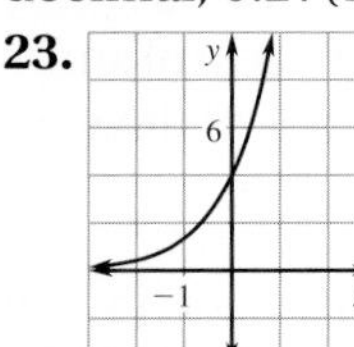

The graph is a vertical stretch.

25. 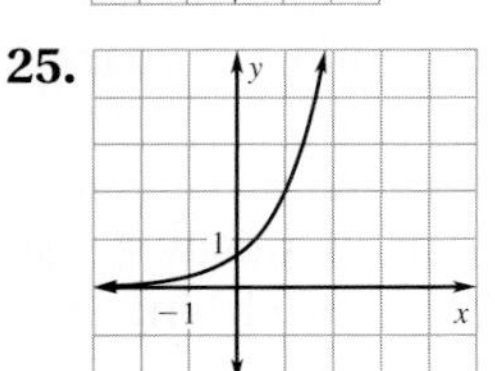

The graph is a vertical shrink.

27. 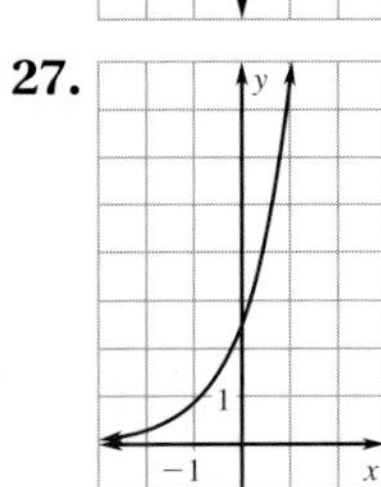

The graph is a vertical stretch.

29. 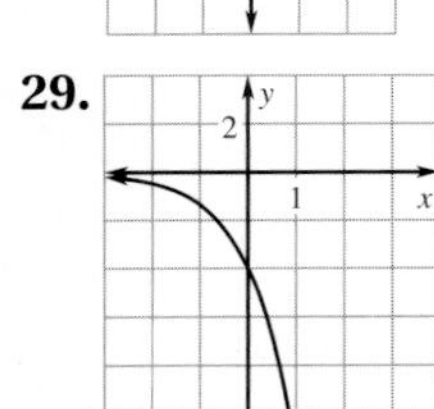

The graph is a vertical stretch with a reflection in the x-axis.

31. 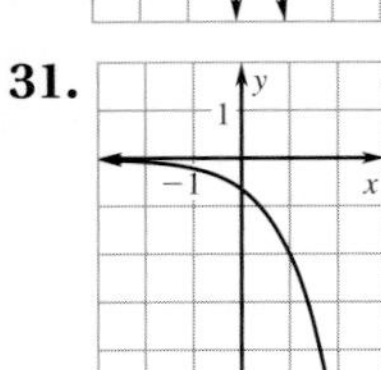

The graph is a vertical shrink with a reflection in the x-axis.

33. 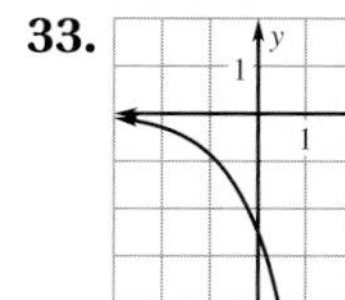

The graph is a vertical stretch with a reflection in the x-axis.

35. 200%. *Sample answer:* A growth rate of 200% would create a growth factor of $1 + 2 = 3$, which would represent the tripling of the population every year.

7.4 Problem Solving **39. a.** Let x represent the number of years since 2001 and $f(x)$ represent the number of computers (in hundreds of millions); $f(x) = 6 \cdot (1.1)^x$. **b.** about 1,286,153,286 computers **41. a.** tree 1: $A = 154 \cdot (1.06)^t$, tree 2: $A = 113 \cdot (1.1)^t$

b. 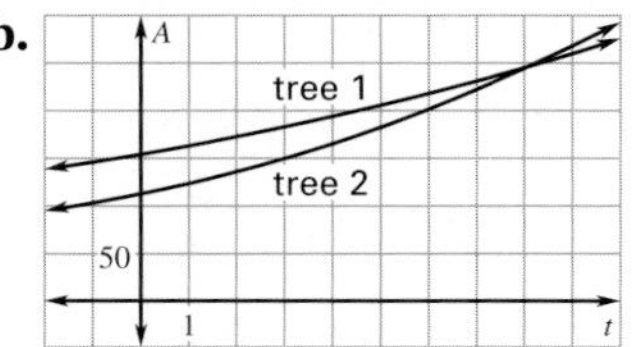

about 8.4 yr

45. $y = 25.96(1.059)^x$; about 145 Hz **47.** $1266.77 **49.** $1271.24

7.4 Problem Solving Workshop

1. a. Let t represent the number of years since 1997 and F represent the bus fare; $F = 20(1.12)^t$. **b.** $22.40 **c.** 2000. *Sample answer:* Make a table of values. **3. a.** $T = 7.5(1.039)^t$ **b.** about 37.4 million

7.5 Skill Practice **1.** $1 - r$ **3.** exponential function; $y = 8 \cdot 4^x$ **5.** exponential function; $y = 2\left(\frac{1}{3}\right)^x$

7. 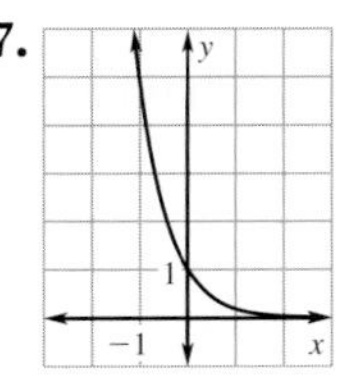

domain: all real numbers, range: all positive real numbers

9. 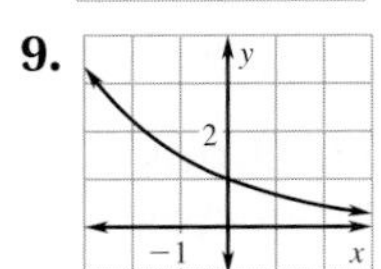

domain: all real numbers, range: all positive real numbers

11. 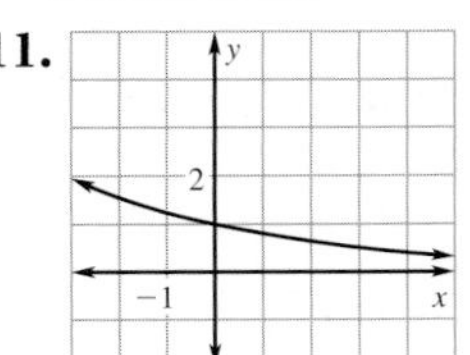

domain: all real numbers, range: all positive real numbers

13. 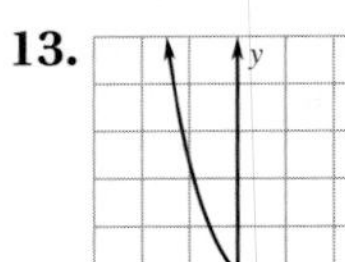 domain: all real numbers, range: all positive real numbers

15. 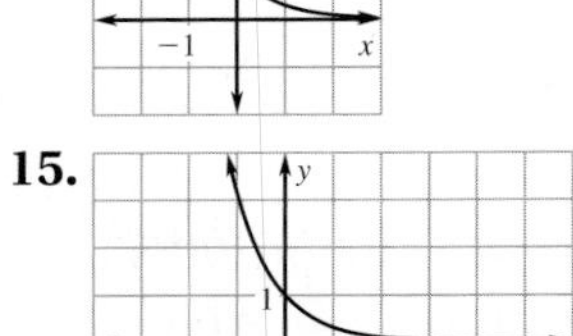 domain: all real numbers, range: all positive real numbers

17. 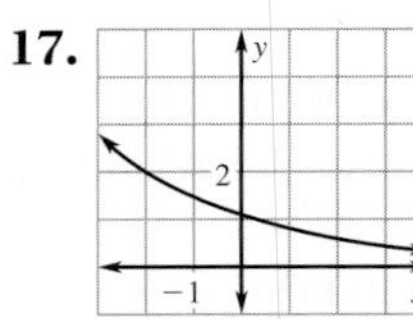 domain: all real numbers, range: all positive real numbers

21. 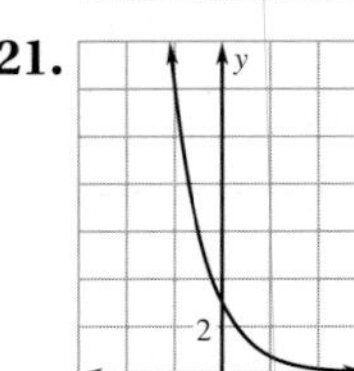 The graph is a vertical stretch.

23. 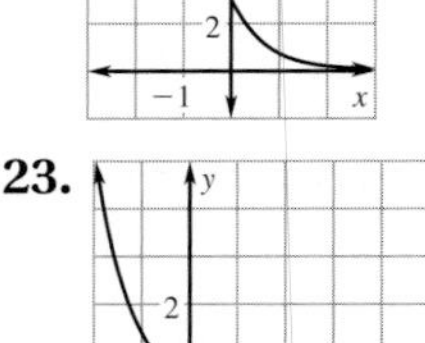 The graph is a vertical shrink.

25. 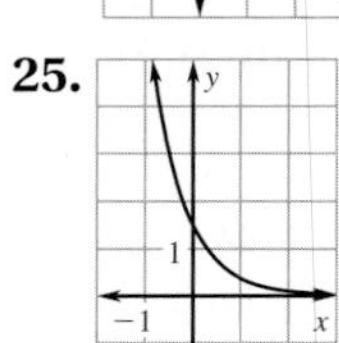 The graph is a vertical stretch.

27. 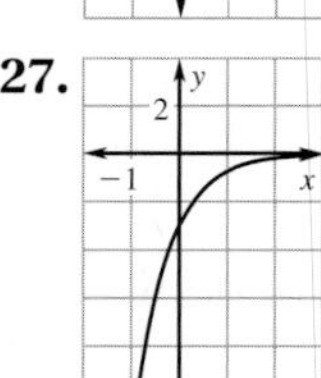 The graph is a vertical stretch with a reflection in the x-axis.

29. 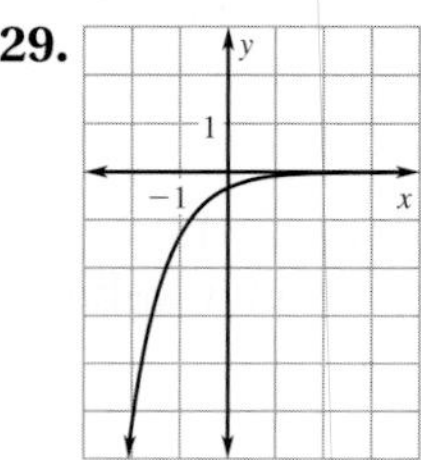 The graph is a vertical shrink with a reflection in the x-axis.

31. 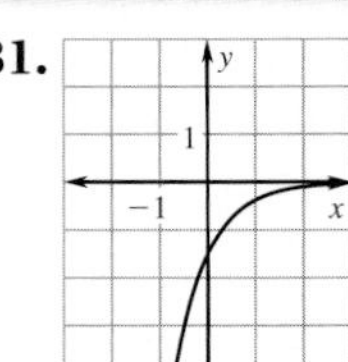 The graph is a vertical stretch with a reflection in the x-axis.

33. C **35.** initial amount: 90,000 people, decay factor: 0.975, decay rate: 2.5%; Let P represent the population and t represent the number of years; $P = 90{,}000(0.975)^t$. **37.** *Sample answer:* The decay rate, r, is 0.14. So the decay factor $(1 - r)$ should be 0.86, not 0.14; $y = 25{,}000(0.86)^t$. **39.** exponential decay; $y = 8 \cdot 0.6^x$ **41. a.** The graph is a vertical shrink. **b.** The graph is a vertical stretch with a reflection in the x-axis. **c.** The graph is a vertical shift up 1 unit. **45.** To find t, divide the number of days, 40, by the half-life, 10. Then $A = 100(0.5)^4 =$ 6.25 grams.

7.5 Problem Solving **47.** Let V represent the value of the cell phone and t represent the number of years since purchase, $V = 125(0.8)^t$; $64.
49. No. *Sample answer:* The boat's value is about $3217. **51. a.** decay factor: 0.9439, decay rate: 5.61% **b.** about 1.431 in. **c.** about 0.716 in.
53. a. $y = 4(0.995)^x$, $y = 3.5(0.995)^x$

b. 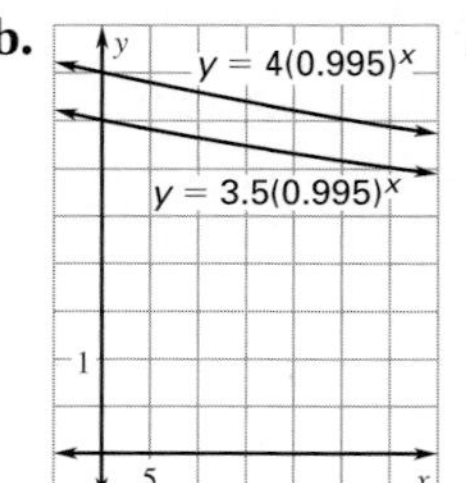

c. about 52 yr

Extension

1. geometric

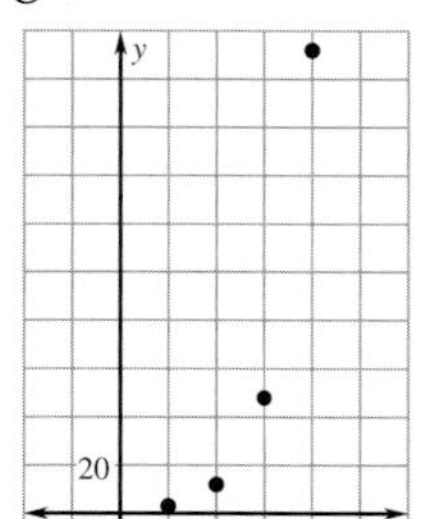

3. arithmetic

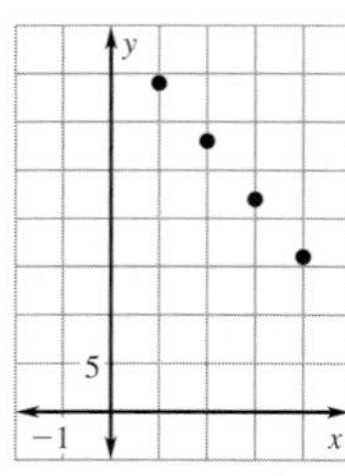

5. geometric

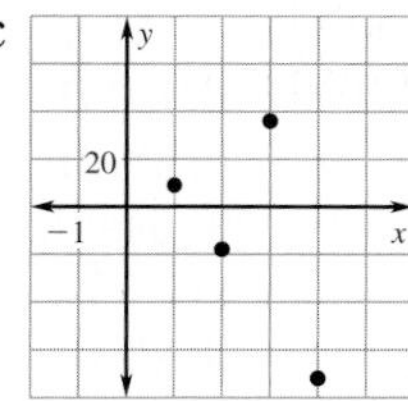

7. $a_n = (-5)^{n-1}$; 15,625 **9.** $a_n = 432\left(\frac{1}{6}\right)^{n-1}$; $\frac{1}{108}$

Extension

11. $a_1 = 256$, $a_n = 0.25a_{n-1}$
13. $a_1 = 3$, $a_n = a_{n-1} + 4$
15. $a_1 = -5$, $a_n = a_{n-1} + 2$
17. $a_1 = -2$, $a_n = -2a_{n-1}$
19. $a_1 = 1$, $a_2 = 3$, $a_n = a_{n-2} + a_{n-1}$; 18, 29
21. $a_1 = 1$, $a_2 = 1$, $a_3 = 1$, $a_n = a_{n-3} + a_{n-2} + a_{n-1}$; 17, 31
23. $a_1 = 64$, $a_2 = 16$, $a_n =$; 4, 0.25
25.a. 3, 5, 7, 9, 11, 13, 15, 17, 19, 21 **b.** 3, 12, 48, 192, 768, 3072, 12,288, 49,152, 196,608, 786, 432
27.a. This is the explicit rule with $n - 1$ substituted for n. **b.** Explicit rule for arithmetic seq.; ident. prop. of add.; inv. prop. of add.; assoc. prop. of add.; dist. prop.; subst. prop. (from part (a))

Chapter Review **1.** decay, decay factor **3.** Exponential decay; $b = 0.85$ which is between 0 and 1, therefore it's exponential decay. **5.** Exponential growth; $b = 2.1$ which is greater than 1, therefore it's exponential growth. **7.** $(-3)^8$ **9.** y^{20} **11.** $(b + 2)^{24}$ **13.** $-64x^2y^2$ **15.** 10^{21} **17.** 5^3 **19.** 17^4 **21.** $\frac{49x^{10}}{y^4}$ **23.** $\frac{6r^{15}}{7s^5}$ **25.** 1 **27.** $\frac{27}{8}$ **29.** 10^6

31.

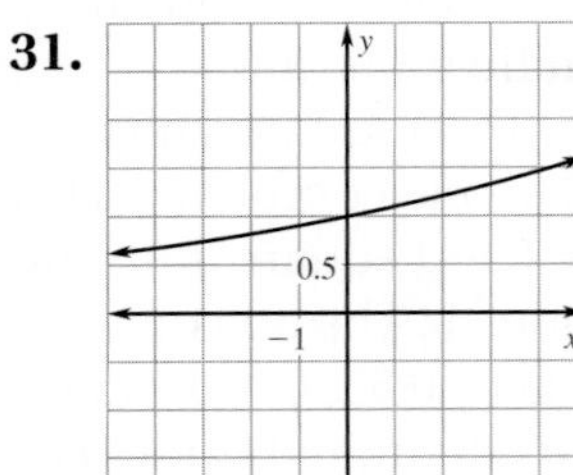

domain: all real numbers, range: all positive real numbers

33. domain: all real numbers, range: all positive real numbers

Chapter 7 Extra Practice

1. 5^7 **3.** $(-2)^9$ **5.** $(-4)^6$ **7.** m^7 **9.** y^{15} **11.** $54d^8$ **13.** 8^5 **15.** $-\frac{2^5}{3^5}$ **17.** 7^5 **19.** $\frac{p^7}{q^7}$ **21.** $\frac{64y^9}{27}$ **23.** $\frac{25x^2y^6}{4}$ **25.** $\frac{1}{81}$ **27.** 1 **29.** 8 **31.** 32 **33.** $\frac{1}{y^{10}}$ **35.** $\frac{10c^5}{b^3}$ **37.** $\frac{y^5}{x^4}$ **39.** $-96z^5$

41.

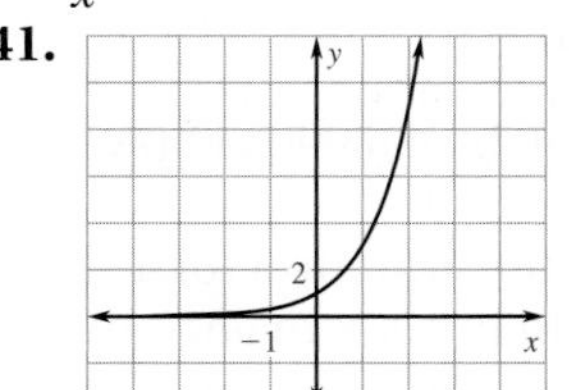

43.

45.

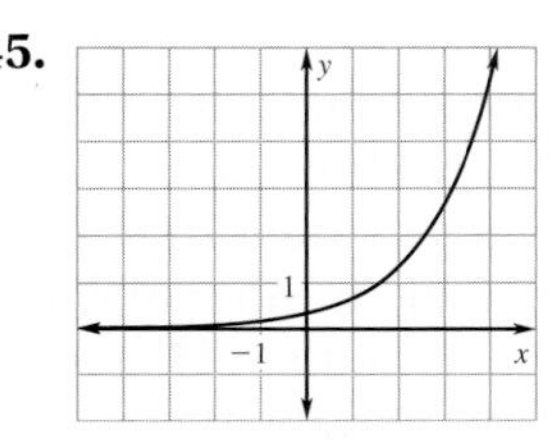

47.

49.

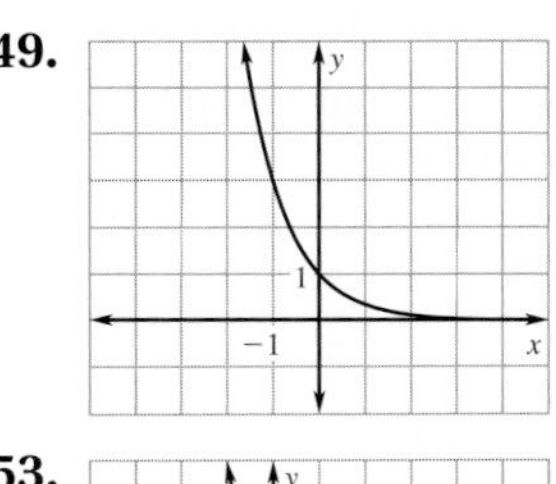

51.

53.

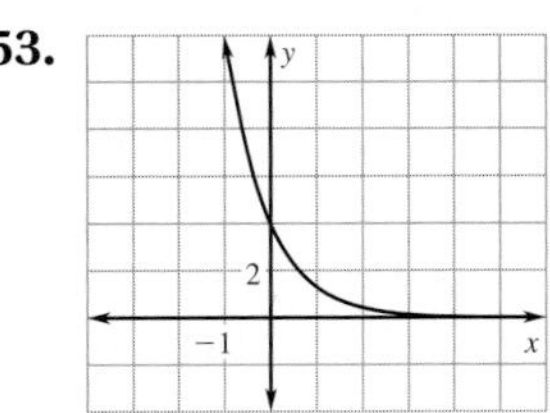

55.

57. exponential; $y = 5 \bullet 2x$ **59.** not exponential

Selected Answers

Chapter 8

8.1 Skill Practice **1.** monomial **3.** $9m^5$; 5, 9 **5.** $2x^2y^2 - 8xy$; 4, 2 **7.** $3z^4 + 2z^3 - z^2 + 5z$; 4, 3 **11.** not a polynomial; variable exponent **13.** polynomial; 1, binomial **15.** polynomial; 3, trinomial **17.** $13a^2 - 4$ **19.** $m^2 + 9m + 9$ **21.** $6c^2 + 14$ **23.** $-2n^3 + n - 12$ **25.** $-15d^3 + 3d^2 - 3d + 2$ **27.** Two unlike terms, $-4x^2$ and $8x$, were combined; $-2x^3 - 4x^2 + 8x + 1$. **29.** $3x^5$, $x + 2x^3 + x^2$, $1 - 3x + 5x^2$, $12x + 1$ **31.** $12x - 3$ **33.** $-x^2 + 10xy + y^2$ **35.** $6a^2b - 6a + 4b - 19$

8.1 Problem Solving **37.** about 39,800,000 people **39. a.** $T = 9.5t^3 - 73t^2 + 130t + 860$ **b.** 1998; substitute $t = 0$ into the equation for T to find the number of books sold in 1998 to get 860 million books. Substitute 4 into the equation for T to find the number of books sold in 2002 to get 820 million books. More books were sold in 1998. **41. a.** $D = -0.44t^2 + 49t + 19.7$ **b.** about 855 decisions **c.** about 61%; Cy Young's career lasted $1911 - 1890 = 21$ years. To find the number of wins in his career, find the value of W when $t = 21$; about 525 wins. From part (b), we know that the total number of decisions in his career is about 855, so to find the percent of the decisions that were wins, find $525 \div 855 \approx 0.614$, or about 61%.

8.1 Graphing Calculator Activity **1.** $7x^2 + 2x + 1$ **3.** correct

8.2 Skill Practice **1.** binomials **3.** $2x^3 - 3x^2 + 9x$ **5.** $4z^6 + z^5 - 11z^4 - 6z^2$ **7.** $9a^7 - 5a^6 - 13a^5$ **9.** $x^2 - x - 6$ **11.** $4b^2 - 31b + 21$ **13.** $12k^2 + 23k - 9$ **15.** The second term of the first binomial is -5, not 5, so the entries in the second row of the diagram should be $-15x$ and -5; $3x^2 - 14x - 5$. **17.** $y^2 + y - 30$ **19.** $77w^2 + 34w - 15$ **21.** $s^3 + 10s^2 + 19s - 20$ **23.** $-15x^3 + 14x^2 + 3x - 2$ **25.** $54z^3 - 21z^2 - 14z + 5$ **27.** $10r^2 + r - 3$ **29.** $8m^2 + 46m + 63$ **31.** $48x^2 - 88x + 35$ **33.** $3p^2 - 3p - 9$ **35.** $-3c^3 - 45c^2 + 23c - 10$ **37.** $2x^2 + x - 45$ **39.** $x^2 + 8x + 15$ **41.** $80 - 6x^2$ **43.** $2x^2 - 10x - 132$ **45.** $2x^4 - 11x^3 - 20x^2 - 7x$; graph $Y_1 = (x^2 - 7x)(2x^2 + 3x + 1)$ and $Y_2 = 2x^4 - 11x^3 - 20x^2 - 7x$ in the same viewing window. Because the graphs coincide, the expressions for Y_1 and Y_2 must be equivalent.

8.2 Problem Solving **49. a.** $4x^2 + 84x + 440$ **b.** 840 in.^{2} **51. a.** \$12,300 million, 0.171; for $t = 0$, the amount of money (in millions of dollars) people between 15 and 19 years old spent on sound recordings in the U.S. in 1997 **b.** $R \cdot P \approx -1.18t^4 + 14.4t^3 - 57.4t^2 - 10.4t + 2100$ **c.** about \$1680 million **53. a.** *Sample answer:* $T = t + 90$; use the data points from 1995–1999: (5, 95), (6, 96), (7, 97), (8, 98), (9, 99). All these points lie on a line with slope $m = 1$; use any one of the points to find the y-intercept $b = 90$. The other data points, (0, 92), (10, 101), and (11, 102), lie close to the line $T = t + 90$. **b.** $V = -0.0015t^3 - 0.103t^2 + 2.949t + 6.21$ **c.** about 24.2 million households, about 22.2 million households

8.3 Skill Practice **1.** *Sample answer:* $x - 5$, $x + 5$ **3.** $x^2 + 16x + 64$ **5.** $4y^2 + 20y + 25$ **7.** $n^2 - 22n + 121$ **9.** The middle term of the product, $2(s)(-3) = -6s$, was left out; $s^2 - 6s + 9$. **11.** $t^2 - 16$ **13.** $4x^2 - 1$ **15.** $49 - w^2$ **19.** Use the sum and difference pattern to find the product $(20 - 4)(20 + 4)$. **21.** Use the square of a binomial pattern to find the product $(20 - 3)^2$. **23.** $r^2 + 18rs + 81s^2$ **25.** $9m^2 - 121n^2$ **27.** $9m^2 - 42mn + 49n^2$ **29.** $9f^2 - 81$ **31.** $9x^2 + 48xy + 64y^2$ **33.** $4a^2 - 25b^2$ **35.** $9x^2 - 0.25$ **37.** $9x^2 - 3x + 0.25$

8.3 Problem Solving

41. a.

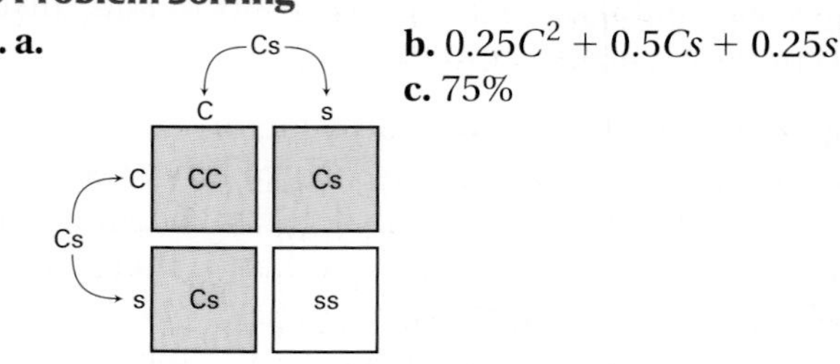

b. $0.25C^2 + 0.5Cs + 0.25s^2$ **c.** 75%

43. a. 88.1%; the areas of the four regions are: 2 complete passes: $0.655^2 \approx 0.429$ square units; 1 complete pass, 1 incomplete pass: $0.655(0.345) \approx 0.226$ square units; 1 incomplete pass, 1 complete pass: $0.345(0.655) \approx 0.226$ square units; and 2 incomplete passes: $0.345^2 \approx 0.119$ square units. The regions that involve at least one complete pass cover $0.429 + 0.226 + 0.226 = 0.881$ square units, or 88.1% of the whole square region. **b.** The outcome of each attempted pass is modeled by $0.655C + 0.345I$, so the possible outcomes of two attempted passes is modeled by $(0.655C + 0.345I)^2 = 0.429C^2 + 0.452CI + 0.119I^2$. Because any combination of outcomes with a C results in at least one completed pass, the coefficients of the first two terms show that 42.9% + 45.2% = 88.1% of the outcomes will have at least one completed pass, and the coefficient of the last term shows that 11.9% of the outcomes will have two incomplete passes.

8.4 Skill Practice **1.** The vertical motion model is the equation $h = -16t^2 + vt + s$, where h is the height (in feet) of a projectile after t seconds in the air, given an initial vertical velocity of v feet per second and an initial height of s feet. **3.** 5, -3 **5.** 13, 14 **7.** 7, $-\frac{4}{3}$ **9.** ± 3 **11.** $-\frac{11}{3}$, -1 **13.** $-\frac{5}{2}, \frac{5}{7}$ **17.** $2(x + y)$ **19.** $s(3s^3 + 16)$ **21.** $7w^2(w^3 - 5)$ **23.** $5n(3n^2 + 5)$ **25.** $\frac{1}{2}x^4(5x^2 - 1)$ **27.** 0, -6 **29.** 0, $\frac{7}{2}$ **31.** 0, $-\frac{1}{3}$ **33.** 0, 2 **35.** 0, $\frac{5}{2}$ **37.** 0, $-\frac{2}{7}$ **41.** $2ab(4a - 3b)$ **43.** $v(v^2 - 5v + 9)$ **45.** $3q^2(2q^3 - 7q^2 - 5)$ **47.** 0, $\frac{1}{2}$

8.4 Problem Solving **51.** about 0.69 sec **53.** 0, about 0.28; the zero $t = 0$ seconds means that the penguin begins at a height of 0 feet in the air as it leaves the water; the zero $t \approx 0.28$ second means that the penguin lands back in the water (at a height of 0 feet in the air) after about 0.28 second. **55. a.** $h = -4.9t^2 + 4.9t$ **b.** $0 \leq t \leq 1$; a reasonable domain for the function will cover the time from when the rabbit leaves the ground until the rabbit lands back on the ground; these times t are the zeros of the function, 0 seconds and 1 second. **57. a.** $w(w + 2) = w(10 - w)$ **b.** 4 ft **c.** 48 ft^2

8.5 Skill Practice **1.** factors **3.** $(x + 3)(x + 1)$ **5.** $(b - 9)(b - 8)$ **7.** $(z + 12)(z - 4)$ **9.** $(y - 9)(y + 2)$ **11.** $(x + 10)(x - 7)$ **13.** $(m - 15)(m + 8)$ **15.** $(p + 16)(p + 4)$ **17.** $(c + 11)(c + 4)$ **19.** In order to have a product of $+24$, p and q must have the same sign; $(m - 6)(m - 4)$. **21.** 10, -3 **23.** -10, 5 **25.** -5, -4 **27.** -22, -1 **31.** -3, -2 **33.** 9, 5 **35.** 17, -3 **37.** 14, 2 **39.** -9, 8 **41.** -17, -2 **43.** 20 in., 5 in. **45.** 26 yd, 6 yd **47.** $(x - 2y)^2$ **49.** $(c + 9d)(c + 4d)$ **51.** $(a + 5b)(a - 3b)$ **53.** $(m - 7n)(m + 6n)$ **55.** $(g + 10h)(g - 6h)$

8.5 Problem Solving **59.** 10 cm^2 **61.** 40 in.; the side lengths of the rectangular picture can be represented by $x - 5$ and $x - 6$; the area of the picture is 20 square inches, so to find the side length x of the original square picture, solve the equation $(x - 5)(x - 6) = 20$. The equation has two solutions, 10 and 1, but when $x = 1$ inch, both $x - 5$ and $x - 6$ are negative, which does not make sense in this situation. So, $x = 10$ inches, and the perimeter of the original picture was $4(10) = 40$ inches.

8.5 Problem Solving Workshop **1.** 2 ft **3.** 9 ft

8.6 Skill Practice **1.** roots **3.** To factor the polynomial that has a leading coefficient of 1, $x^2 - x - 2$, you only need to find factors of the constant term, -2, that add to the coefficient of the middle term, -1. To factor the polynomial that has a leading coefficient that is not 1, $6x^2 - x - 2$, you must also take into account how the factors of the leading coefficient, 6, affect the coefficient of the middle term. **5.** $-(y - 4)(y + 2)$ **7.** $(5w - 1)(w - 1)$ **9.** $(6s + 5)(s - 1)$ **11.** $(2c - 1)(c - 3)$ **13.** $-(2h + 1)(h - 3)$ **15.** $(2x + 3)(5x - 9)$ **17.** $(3z + 7)(z - 2)$ **19.** $(2n + 3)(2n + 5)$ **21.** $(3y - 4)(2y + 1)$ **23.** $-\frac{7}{2}$, 5 **25.** $\frac{1}{4}$, -3 **27.** $\frac{3}{4}, -\frac{1}{2}$ **29.** $-\frac{1}{4}, \frac{2}{5}$ **31.** $\frac{1}{3}$, -5 **33.** $\frac{2}{5}$, 1 **35.** $\frac{11}{2}$, -3 **37.** $-\frac{4}{3}, \frac{1}{2}$ **39.** The factorization of the polynomial should be $(3x + 2)(4x - 1)$ instead of $(3x - 1)(4x + 2)$; $-\frac{2}{3}, \frac{1}{4}$. **41.** $9\frac{1}{2}$ in.; to find the width, solve the equation $w(4w + 1) = 3$ to get $w = \frac{3}{4}$ or $w = -1$. The width cannot be negative, so the width is $\frac{3}{4}$ inch. Then the length is $4\left(\frac{3}{4}\right) + 1 = 4$ inches, and the perimeter is $2\left(\frac{3}{4}\right) + 2(4) = 9\frac{1}{2}$ inches. **43.** 5, 7 **45.** $-\frac{7}{3}$, 2 **47.** $\frac{7}{2}, -\frac{3}{2}$ **49.** $-\frac{1}{4}, \frac{5}{2}$ **53.** $2x^2 - 9x - 5 = 0$; any root $x = \frac{r}{s}$ of $ax^2 + bx + c = 0$ comes from setting the factor $sx - r$ equal to 0 after $ax^2 + bx + c$ is written in factored form; so, the roots $-\frac{1}{2}$ and 5 come from the factors $2x - (-1)$, or $2x + 1$, and $x - 5$. The product of these factors is $(2x + 1)(x - 5) = 2x^2 - 10x + x - 5 = 2x^2 - 9x - 5$.

8.6 Problem Solving **59. a.** $24x^2 + 48x + 24$ **b.** 4 cm, 2 cm **61.** 70 m, 31 m

8.7 Skill Practice **1.** perfect square **3.** $(x + 5)(x - 5)$ **5.** $(9c + 2)(9c - 2)$ **7.** $-3(m + 4n)(m - 4n)$ **9.** $(x - 2)^2$ **11.** $(7a + 1)^2$ **13.** $\left(m + \frac{1}{2}\right)^2$ **15.** $4(c + 10)(c - 10)$ **17.** $(2s + 3r)(2s - 3r)$ **19.** $8(3 + 2y)(3 - 2y)$ **21.** $(2x)^2 - 3^2$ is in the form $a^2 - b^2$, so it must be factored using the difference of two squares pattern, not the perfect square trinomial pattern; $9(2x + 3)(2x - 3)$. **25.** -4 **27.** ± 3 **29.** -2 **31.** ± 12 **33.** $\pm\frac{7}{2}$ **35.** $\frac{5}{6}$ **37.** $\pm\frac{4}{3}$ **39.** 0, 1

8.7 Problem Solving **47.** 2.5 sec **49.** Once; the ball's height (in feet) is modeled by the equation $h = -16t^2 + 56t + 5$, where t is the time (in seconds) since it was thrown. To find when the height is 54 feet, substitute 54 for h and solve the equation $54 = -16t^2 + 56t + 5$, or $16t^2 - 56t + 49 = 0$.

Because the left side of the equation factors as a perfect square trinomial, $(4t - 7)^2$, the equation has only one solution, 1.75; so, the ball reaches a height of 54 feet only once, after 1.75 seconds.
51. a. $4d^2 - 9$ **b.** 10 in.

8.8 Skill Practice **1.** The polynomial is written as a monomial or as a product of a monomial and one or more prime polynomials.
3. $(x - 8)(x + 1)$ **5.** $(z - 4)(6z - 7)$ **7.** $(b + 5)(b^2 - 3)$ **9.** $(x + 13)(x - 1)$ **11.** $(z - 1)(12 + 5z^2)$ **13.** $(x + 1)(x^2 + 2)$ **15.** $(z - 4)(z^2 + 3)$ **17.** $(a + 13)(a^2 - 5)$ **19.** $(5n - 4)(n^2 + 5)$ **21.** $(y + 1)(y + 5x)$ **23.** $x^2(x - 1)(x + 1)$ **25.** $3n^3(n - 4)(n + 4)$ **27.** $3c^7(5c - 1)(5c + 1)$ **29.** $8s^2(2s - 1)(2s + 1)$ **31.** cannot be factored **33.** $3w^2(w + 4)^2$ **35.** $(b - 5)(b - 2)(b + 2)$ **37.** $(9t - 1)(t^2 + 2)$ **39.** $7ab^3(a - 3)(a + 3)$ **43.** $-1, \pm 2$ **45.** $\frac{7}{4}, \pm 2$ **47.** $0, -5, -3$ **49.** $0, \pm 9$ **51.** $0, \pm 2$ **53.** $-\frac{1}{3}, \pm 1$
55. No; when the polynomial is factored completely, the equation becomes $(x + 2)(x^2 + 3) = 0$. When the factor $x^2 + 3$ is set equal to 0, the resulting equation, $x^2 + 3 = 0$, or $x^2 = -3$, has no real number solutions because x^2 cannot be negative. **57.** 12 yd, 4 yd, 2 yd **59.** $(2b - a)(2b - 3)(2b + 3)$ **61.** $(3x + 4)(2x - 1)$ **63.** $(4n - 3)(3n - 1)$ **65.** $(3w + 2)(7w - 2)$

8.8 Problem Solving **69. a.** $4w^2 + 16w$ **b.** 4 in. long by 4 in. wide by 8 in. high **71. a.** 1, about -0.2
b. The zero $t \approx -0.2$ has no meaning because t, which represents time in seconds, cannot be negative in this situation. The zero $t = 1$ means that the ball lands on the ground 1 second after you throw it.
73. a. $-h^3 + 5h^2 + 36h$ **b.** 4 in. long by 9 in. wide by 5 in. high, 3 in. long by 10 in. wide by 6 in. high
c. 4 in. long by 9 in. wide by 5 in. high; the 4-inch long box has a surface area of 202 square inches and the 3-inch long box has a surface area of 216 square inches.

Chapter Review **1.** degree of the polynomial
3. A factorable polynomial with integer coefficients is factored completely if it is written as a product of unfactorable polynomials with integer coefficients. *Sample answer:* $3x(x - 4)(2x + 1)$ **5.** A
7. $x^3 - 8x^2 + 15x$ **9.** $11y^5 + 4y^2 - y - 3$ **11.** $5s^3 - 7s + 13$ **13.** $x^3 - 5x^2 + 7x - 3$ **15.** $x^2 - 2x - 8$ **17.** $z^2 - 3z - 88$ **19.** $18n^2 + 27n + 7$ **21.** $3x^2 + 10x - 8$ **23.** $36y^2 + 12y + 1$ **25.** $16a^2 - 24a + 9$ **27.** $9s^2 - 25$ **29.** 0, 11 **31.** 0, 9 **33.** $0, \frac{1}{3}$ **35.** $(s + 11)(s - 1)$ **37.** $(a + 12)(a - 7)$ **39.** $(x + 8)(x - 4)$ **41.** $(c + 5)(c + 3)$ **43.** $\frac{1}{7}, 1$ **45.** $\frac{2}{3}, -2$ **47.** $-\frac{3}{2}, -3$ **49.** 3 sec

51. $(z - 15)(z + 15)$ **53.** $12(1 - 2n)(1 + 2n)$ **55.** $(4p - 1)^2$ **57.** 1 sec **59.** $(y + 3)(y + x)$ **61.** $5s^2(s - 5)(s + 5)$ **63.** $2z(z + 6)(z - 5)$ **65.** $(2b + 3)(b - 2)(b + 2)$

Chapter 8 Extra Practice

1. $7x^2 - 2$ **3.** $7m^2 - 5m - 3$ **5.** $6b^3 - 3b^2 - 8b + 8$ **7.** $10x^7 - 15x^6 + 25x^5 - 5x^4$ **9.** $8x^2 + 16x + 6$ **11.** $3x^2 + 8x - 35$ **13.** $x^2 + 20x + 100$ **15.** $16x^2 - 4$ **17.** $36 - 9t^2$ **19.** $-8, 2$ **21.** $\frac{3}{5}, 2$ **23.** $-\frac{1}{4}, 0$ **25.** $(y + 3)(y + 4)$ **27.** $(x - 4)(x + 9)$ **29.** $(m - 25)(m - 4)$ **31.** 2, 5 **33.** 4, 9 **35.** 2, 5 **37.** $-(x - 3)(x - 2)$ **39.** $(2k - 1)(2k - 5)$ **41.** $-(3s + 1)(s + 2)$ **43.** $\frac{2}{3}, 4$ **45.** $-2, \frac{1}{2}$ **47.** $-1, \frac{1}{16}$ **49.** $(y + 6)(y - 6)$ **51.** $3(2y - 3)(2y + 3)$ **53.** $(2x - 3)^2$ **55.** $(g + 5)^2$ **57.** $(2w + 7)^2$ **59.** $(3z - 1)(z - 5)$ **61.** $(3y^2 + 2)(y + 5)$ **63.** $2m(7m - 3)(7m + 3)$ **65.** $(h + 3)(h - 3)(2h - 3)$

Chapter 9

9.1 Skill Practice **1.** parabola **3.** C **5.** B

7. 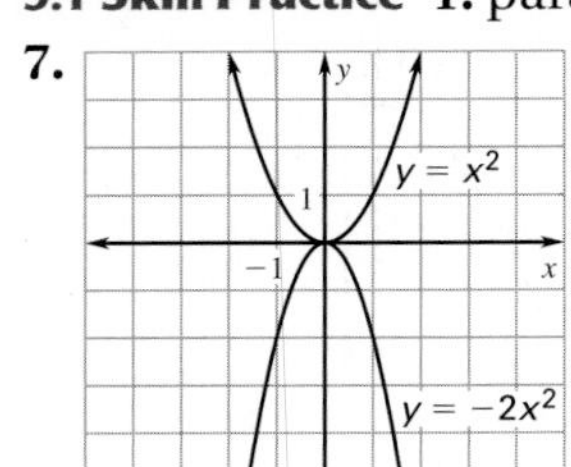

The graph is a vertical stretch (by a factor of 2) with a reflection in the x-axis of the graph of $y = x^2$.

9. 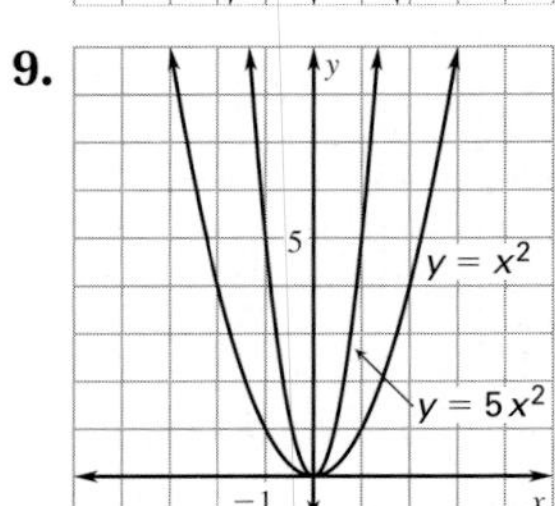

The graph is a vertical stretch (by a factor of 5) of the graph of $y = x^2$.

11. 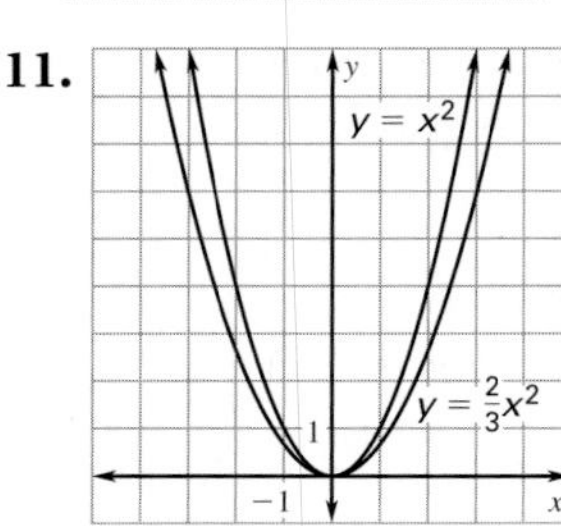

The graph is a vertical shrink $\left(\text{by a factor of } \frac{2}{3}\right)$ of the graph of $y = x^2$.

13. 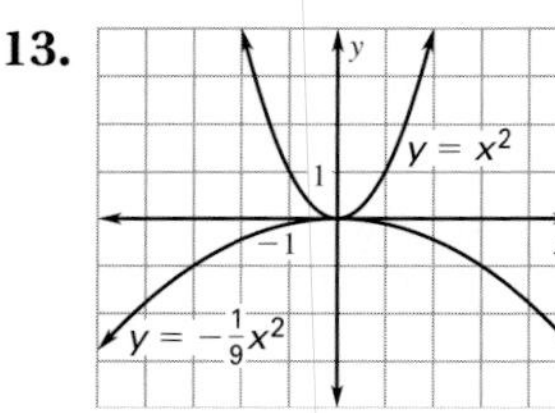

The graph is a vertical shrink $\left(\text{by a factor of } \frac{1}{9}\right)$ with a reflection in the x-axis of the graph of $y = x^2$.

15. 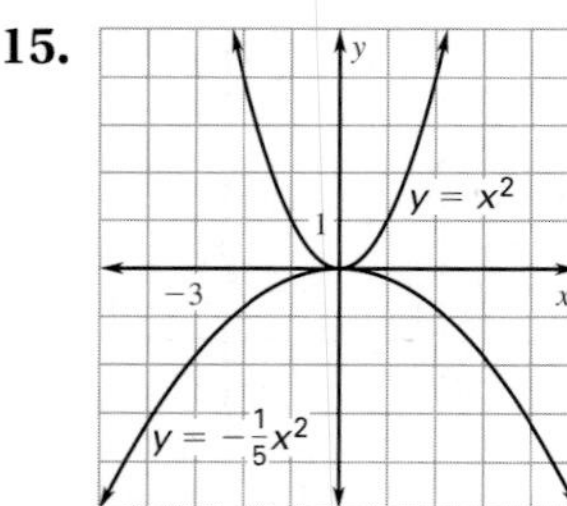

The graph is a vertical shrink $\left(\text{by a factor of } \frac{1}{5}\right)$ with a reflection in the x-axis of the graph of $y = x^2$.

17. 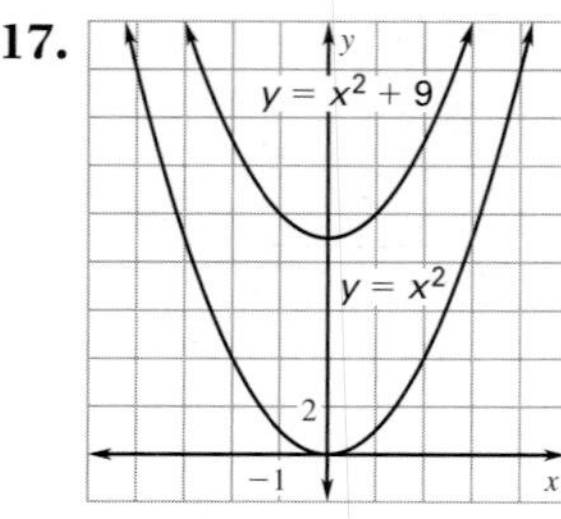

The graph is a vertical translation (of 9 units up) of the graph of $y = x^2$.

19. 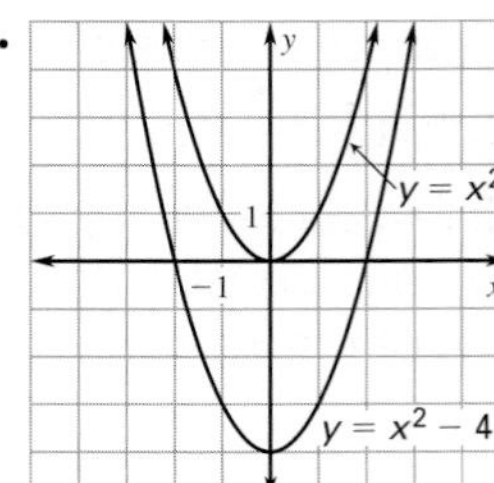

The graph is a vertical translation (of 4 units down) of the graph of $y = x^2$.

21. 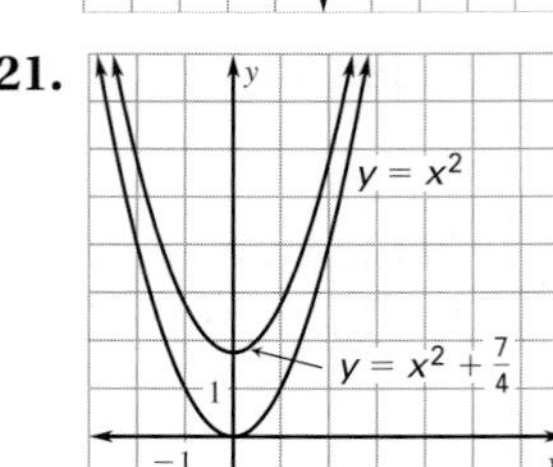

The graph is a vertical translation $\left(\text{of } \frac{7}{4} \text{ units up}\right)$ of the graph of $y = x^2$.

23. The graph of $y = x^2 - 2$ should be shifted 2 units down, not 2 units up. The vertex should be at $(0, -2)$.

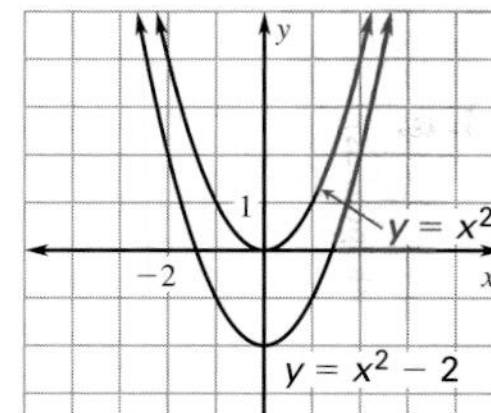

25. 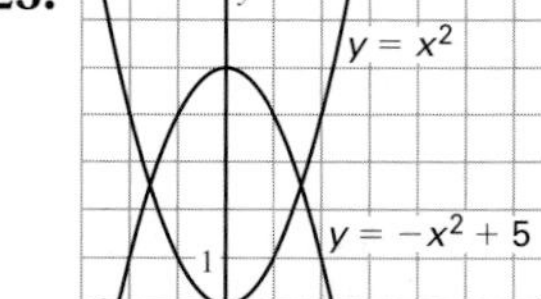

The graph is a reflection in the x-axis with a vertical translation (of 5 units up) of the graph of $y = x^2$.

27. 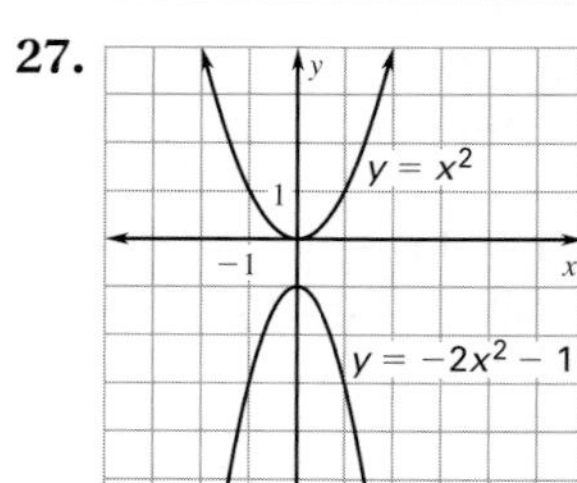

The graph is a vertical stretch (by a factor of 2) with a vertical translation (of 1 unit down) and a reflection in the x-axis of the graph of $y = x^2$.

29. 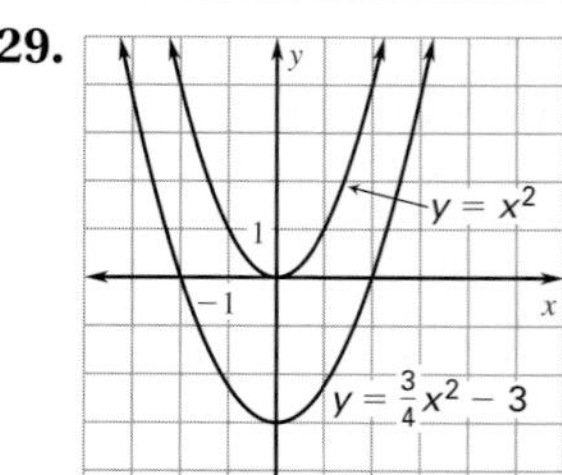

The graph is a vertical shrink $\left(\text{by a factor of } \frac{3}{4}\right)$ with a vertical translation (of 3 units down) of the graph of $y = x^2$.

31. 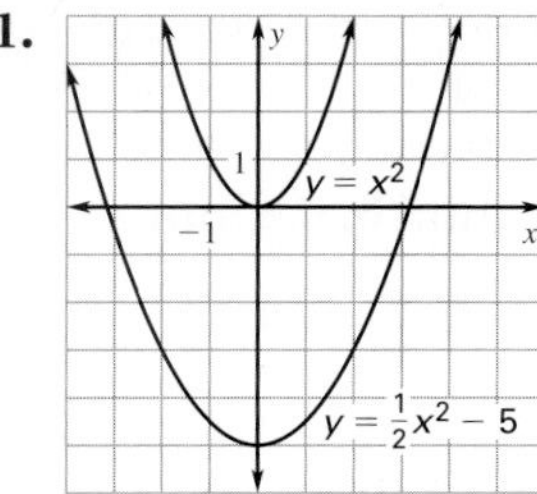

The graph is a vertical shrink $\left(\text{by a factor of } \frac{1}{2}\right)$ with a vertical translation (of 5 units down) of the graph of $y = x^2$.

35. Translate the graph of f 5 units down.

9.1 Problem Solving

41. a. 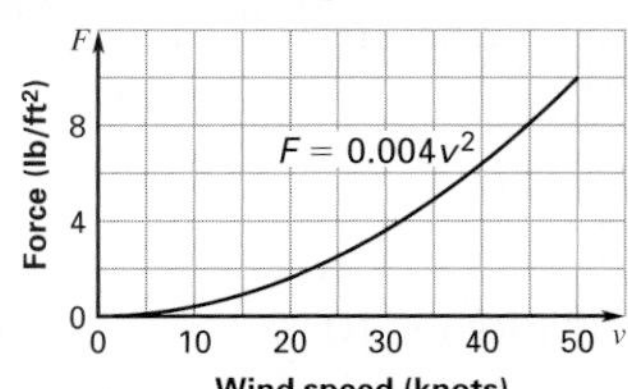

b. about 16 knots **c.** about 35 knots

43. a. 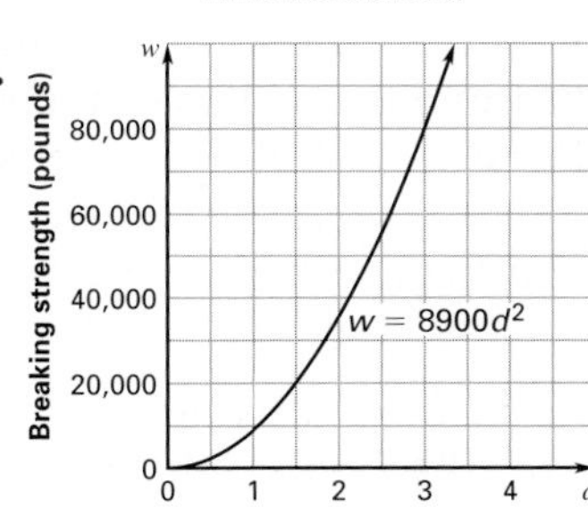

b. No. *Sample answer:* Let D be the diameter of a rope with 4 times the breaking strength of a rope with diameter d. Then $8900D^2 = 4(8900d^2)$; $D^2 = 4d^2$; $D = \sqrt{4d^2}$; $D = 2d$. Thus, the diameter of the rope with 4 times the breaking strength is only two times the diameter of the other rope.

9.2 Skill Practice **1.** When the function is in standard form, $y = ax^2 + bx + c$, it will have a minimum value if $a > 0$ and a maximum value if $a < 0$. **3.** $x = 2$, $(2, -2)$ **5.** $x = 4$, $(4, 26)$ **7.** $x = -\frac{1}{2}$, $\left(-\frac{1}{2}, -\frac{3}{2}\right)$

9. $x = 0$, $(0, -1)$ **11.** $x = 6$, $(6, 7)$

13. The equation of the axis of symmetry is $x = \frac{-b}{2a}$, not $x = \frac{b}{2a}$; $x = \frac{-b}{2a} = \frac{-16}{2(2)}$, $x = -4$.

15. 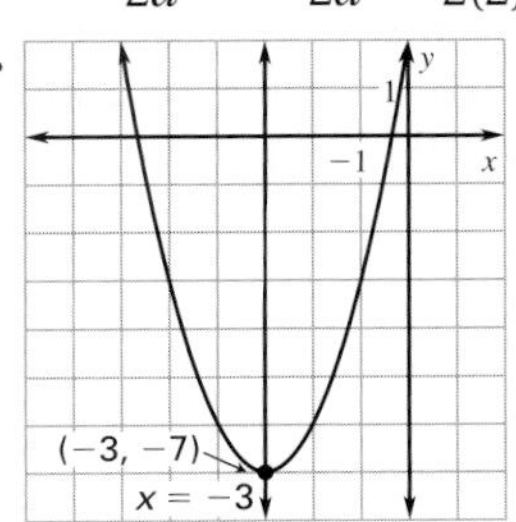

17. 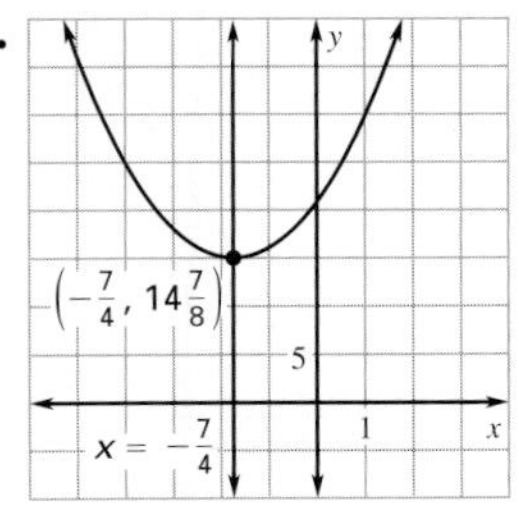

19. 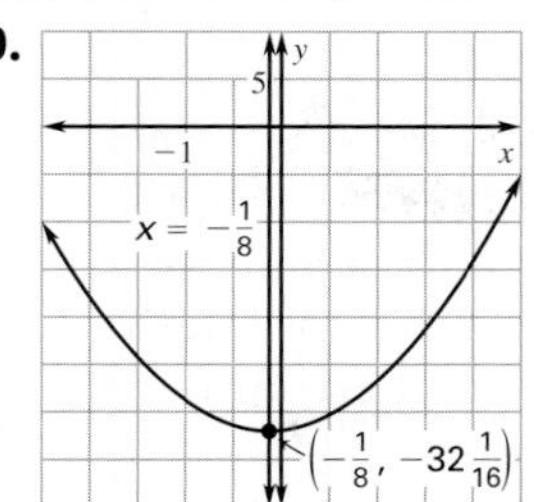

21. 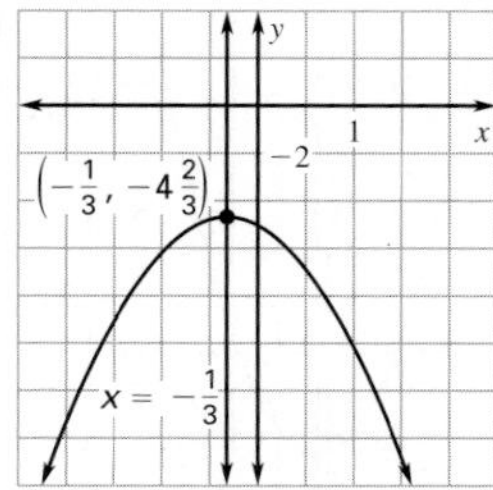

23. 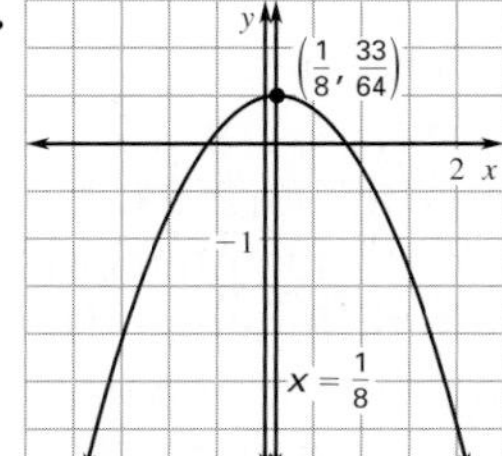

25. 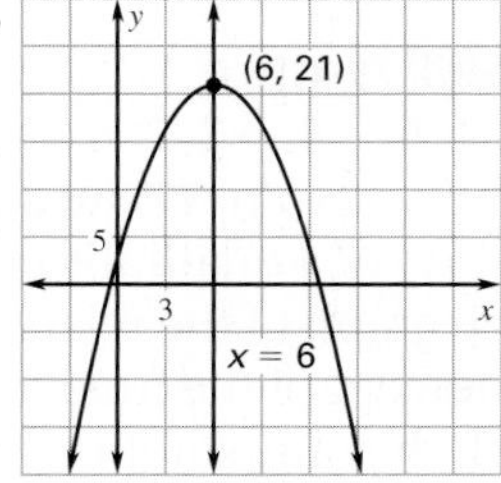

29. maximum value; 7 **31.** maximum value; −8 **33.** maximum value; $\frac{81}{8}$ **35.** maximum value; 54 **37.** The graph of $y = x^2 + 4x + 1$ is a horizontal translation (of 4 units left) of the graph of $y = x^2 - 4x + 1$.

9.2 Problem Solving **41.** about 66 ft

43. 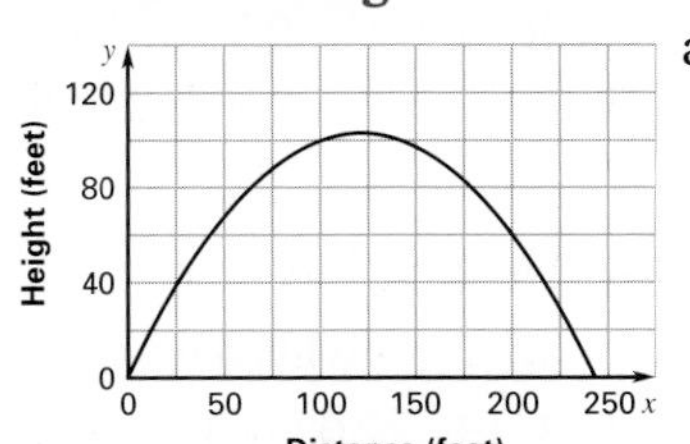

about 243 ft

Extension

1. 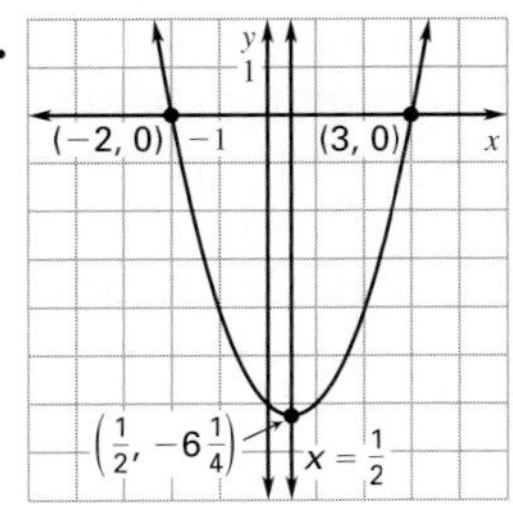

3. 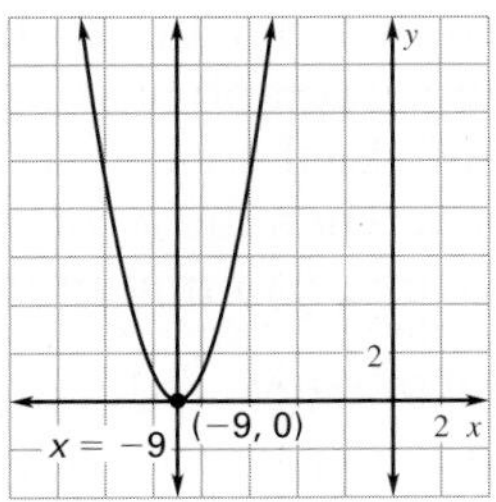

5. 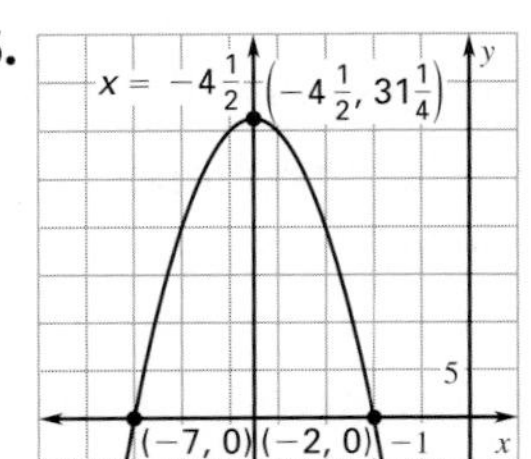

7. 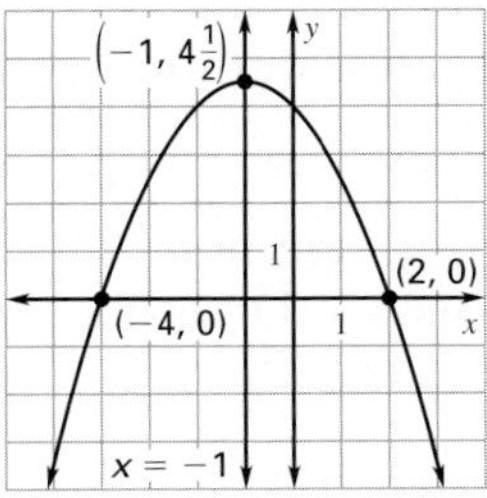

9. 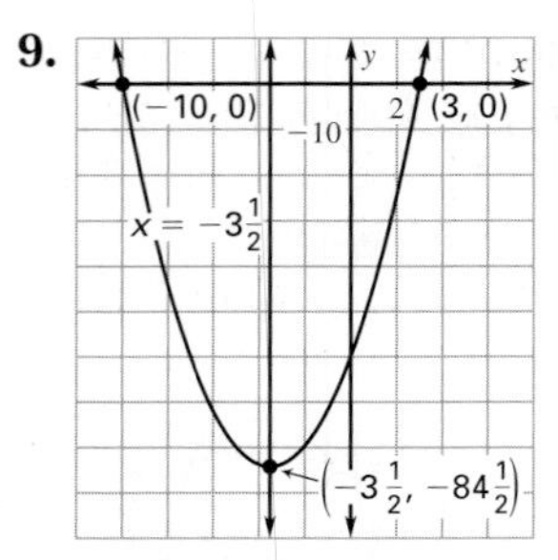

11. 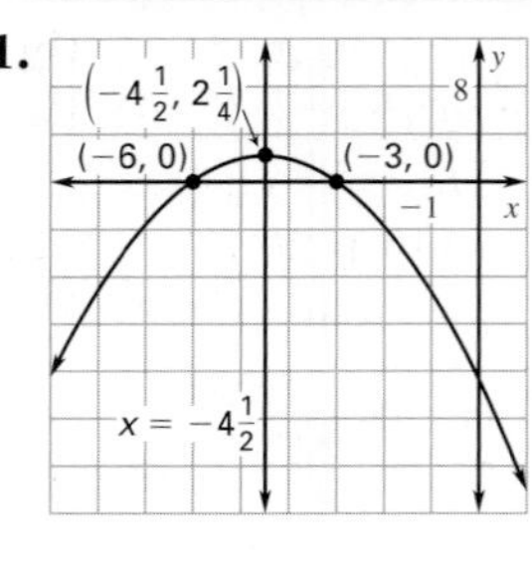

9.3 Skill Practice **1.** $2x^2 - 9x + 11 = 0$ **3.** 4, 1 **5.** −4, −2 **7.** 8, −2 **9.** 3 **11.** −5 **13.** −7 **15.** no solution **17.** no solution **19.** −6, 2 **21.** Any solution of a quadratic equation is an x-intercept of the graph of the related quadratic function. The x-intercept of the function shown in the graph is 2, not 4; the only solution of the equation is 2. **23.** −3, 4 **25.** −5, 2 **27.** −5, 4 **29.** 1, 11 **31.** $-1\frac{1}{2}$, 1 **33.** $\frac{1}{2}$ **35.** no solution **37.** −3.4, −0.6 **39.** −1.4, 3.4 **41.** 0.8, 6.2 **43.** −1.3, 0.8 **45.** −4.7, −1.3

9.3 Problem Solving **51.** 24.1 ft **53.** 16 ft; the distance from the nozzle to the circle is the distance between the x-intercepts of $y = -0.75x^2 + 6x$. Substitute 0 for y and solve for x: $0 = -0.75x^2 + 6x$ has solutions 0 and 8. The radius of the display circle is 8 feet, so the diameter is 16 feet.

9.3 Graphing Calculator Activity

1. $1\frac{2}{3}$ **3.** −3.75 **5.** about −3.5 **7.** −1.11, 3.61 **9.** −1.61, 5.61 **11.** 0.90, 2.18 **13.** −7.03, 2.15 **15.** 0; the maximum or minimum value of a quadratic function occurs at the vertex of the parabola that is the graph of the function. When a quadratic function has only one zero, its graph has only one x-intercept, which must also be the x-coordinate of the vertex of the parabola. Then the y-coordinate of the vertex is 0, so the maximum or minimum value of the function is 0.

9.4 Skill Practice **1.** square root **3.** ±1 **5.** ±10 **7.** 0 **9.** $\pm\frac{1}{2}$ **11.** $\pm\frac{7}{3}$ **13.** 0 **17.** ±2.65 **19.** no solution **21.** 0 **23.** ±2.24 **25.** ±3.78 **27.** ±1.32 **31.** Negative numbers do not have real number square roots, so $\pm\sqrt{-\frac{11}{7}}$ are not real numbers; there is no solution. **33.** 0.76, 5.24 **35.** −8.16, −1.84 **37.** −16.65, −11.35 **39.** −5.69, 3.69 **41.** ±4 **43.** ±1.41 **45.** 0.37, 13.63 **47.** 12 in. **49.** 11.66 ft **51.** $\pm\frac{6}{5}$, or ±1.2. *Sample answer:* Rewrite the decimal as a fraction and then take square roots of each side of the equation: $x^2 = \frac{144}{100}$, so $x = \pm\sqrt{\frac{144}{100}} = \pm\frac{12}{10} = \pm\frac{6}{5}$ or ±1.2.

9.4 Problem Solving **59. a.** 6.8 mm **b.** 5.9 mm **c.** 5.6 mm **61. a.** $D = 4 \pm \sqrt{\frac{16V}{L}}$ **b.** 11.1 in., 10.7 in., 10.3 in., 10.0 in.

9.4 Problem Solving Workshop **1.** about 1.5 sec **3. a.** $V = 25x^2$ **b.** length: about 9 in., width: 5 in., height: about 1.8 in.

c.

Height, x (inches)	1.7	1.8	1.9
Width (inches)	5	5	5
Length, $5x$ (inches)	8.5	9	9.5
Volume, V (cubic inches)	72.25	81	90.25

The volume in the table closest to 83 cubic inches is 81 cubic inches. To the nearest tenth of an inch, the height of the box is about 1.8 inches. The length of the box is $5x \approx 9$ inches, and the width is 5 inches. **5.** To rewrite the equation $6 = -16t^2 + 54$ so that one side is 0, you must subtract 6 from each side; $0 = -16t^2 + 48$, replace 48 with the closest perfect square, 49. $0 = -16t^2 + 49 = -(16t^2 - 49) = -(4t + 7)(4t - 7)$, so the approximate solutions of this equation are $\pm\frac{7}{4}$. Disregard the negative solution because time cannot be negative; so, it takes about $\frac{7}{4}$, or 1.75, seconds for the shoe to hit the net.

9.5 Skill Practice **1.** completing the square **3.** 9; $(x + 3)^2$ **5.** 4; $(x - 2)^2$ **7.** $\frac{9}{4}$; $\left(x - \frac{3}{2}\right)^2$ **9.** 1.44; $(x + 1.2)^2$ **11.** $\frac{4}{9}$; $\left(x - \frac{2}{3}\right)^2$ **13.** −12, 2 **15.** −6, 12 **17.** −7, 3 **19.** −10.5, −0.5 **21.** −0.80, 8.80 **23.** −2.5, −0.5 **27.** The perfect square trinomial $x^2 - 2x + 1$ factors as $(x - 1)^2$ not $(x + 1)^2$, $(x - 1)^2 = 5$, $x - 1 = \pm\sqrt{5}$, $x = 1 \pm \sqrt{5}$. **29.** −11.57, −0.43 **31.** −1.91, 0.91 **33.** −0.96, 6.96 **35.** 0.79, 2.21 **37.** −3.68, −0.32 **39.** −0.25, 0.75 **41.** 4.87

9.5 Problem Solving

45. 3 ft **47. a.** $1904 = 7x^2 - 4x + 392$, 2000

b. 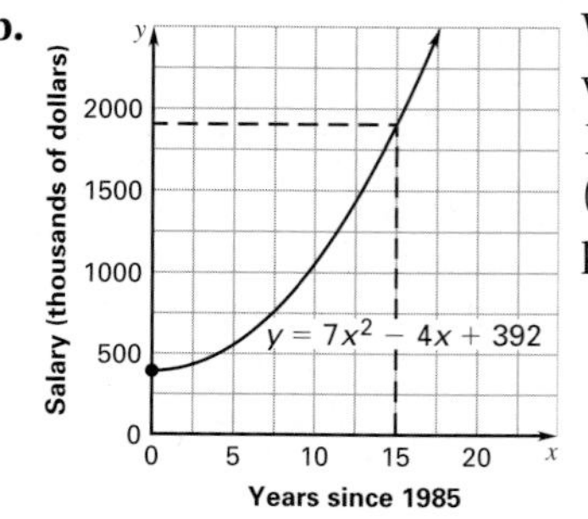

When $y \approx 1904$, the value of x is about 15. So the year 2000 (1985 + 15) found in part (a) is correct.

49. Yes; to find the number of days x after which the stock price was \$23.50 per share, substitute 23.5 for y and solve for x by completing the square to find that the solutions are 10 and 30. You could have sold the stock for \$23.50 per share 10 days after you purchased it.

Extension

1.

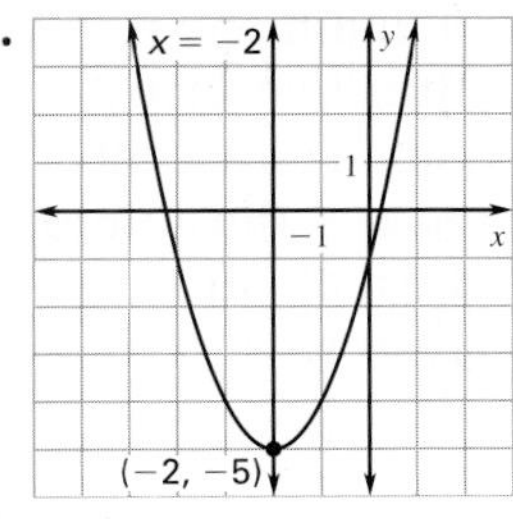

3.

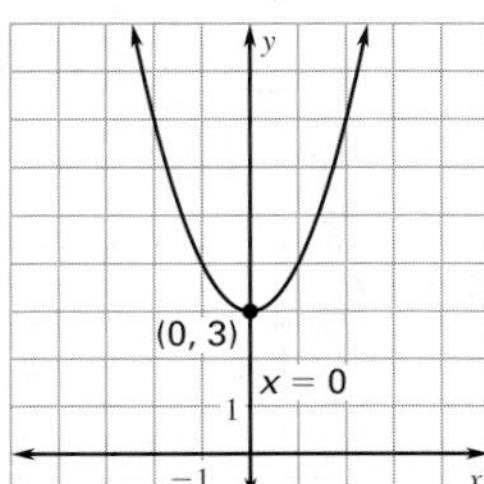

5.

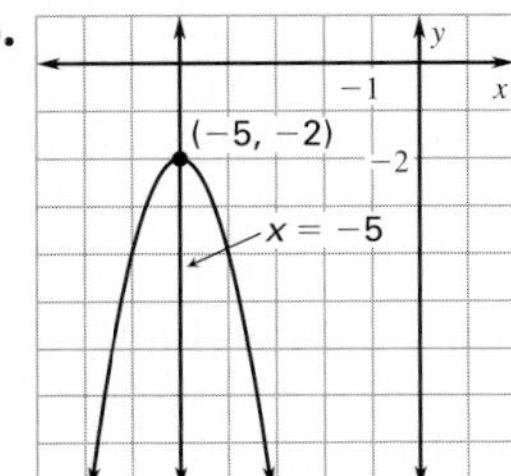

7. $y = (x - 6)^2$

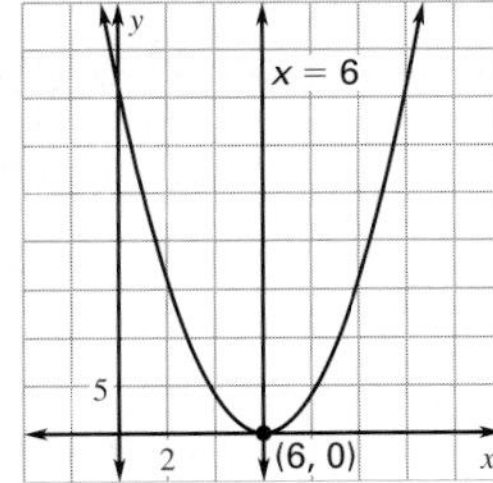

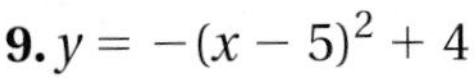
9. $y = -(x - 5)^2 + 4$

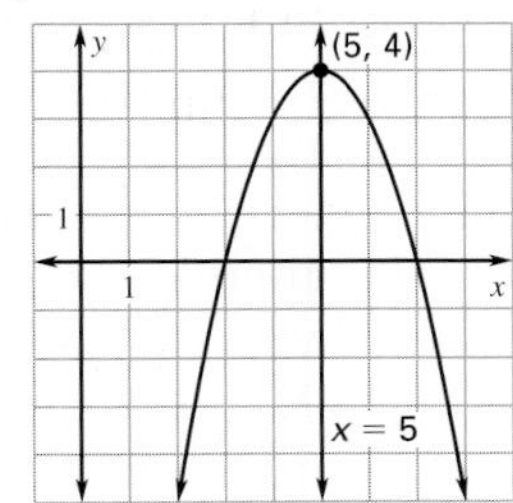

11. $y = -3(x + 1)^2 + 2$

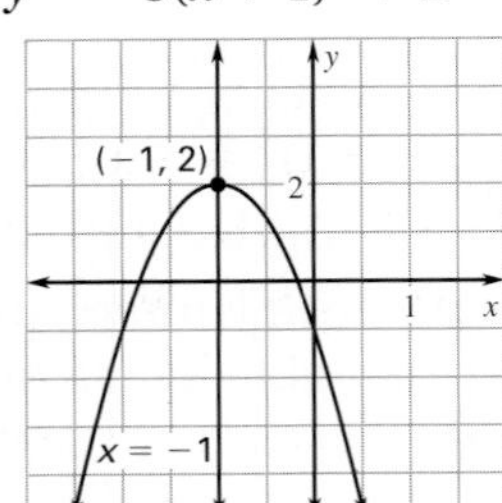

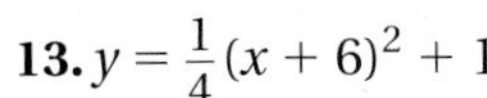
13. $y = \frac{1}{4}(x + 6)^2 + 1$

9.6 Skill Practice **1.** quadratic formula **3.** −13, 8 **5.** −2, 2.33 **7.** −3.27, 4.27 **9.** −2.5 **11.** −0.63, 2.13 **13.** −2, 7 **15.** −1, 1.29 **17.** 3.27, 6.73 **19.** −0.54, 2.29 **21.** −0.66, 1.09 **23.** −1.77, −0.57 **27.** Before identifying the values of a, b, and c, the equation must be written in standard form $ax^2 + bx + c = 0$; $-2x^2 + 3x - 1 = 0$, so $c = -1$, not 1; $x = \frac{-3 \pm \sqrt{3^2 - 4(-2)(-1)}}{2(-2)}$, $x = \frac{-3 \pm \sqrt{1}}{-4}$, $x = \frac{1}{2}$ and $x = 1$. **29–33.** Sample answers are given.

29. Using square roots, the equation can be written in the form $x^2 = d$. **31.** Factoring, the expression $m^2 + 5m + 6$ factors easily. **33.** Quadratic formula, the equation does not factor easily. **35.** 4 **37.** 6 **39.** −1.94, 2.19 **41.** −0.41, 2.41 **43.** 5; 13 m by 7 m

9.6 Problem Solving

47. 1993 **49. a.** 2001 **b.**

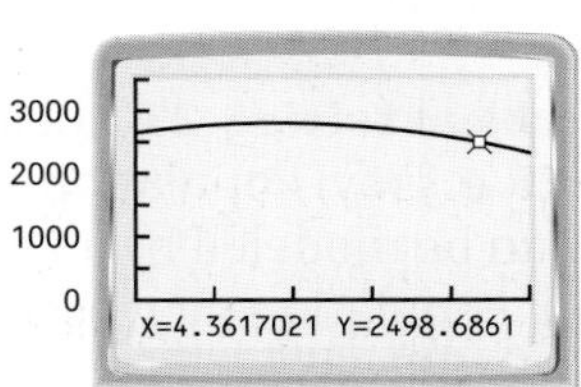

Extension **1.** $-2 - \sqrt{2}, -2 + \sqrt{2}$ **3.** $-4 - 2\sqrt{2}, -4 + 2\sqrt{2}$ **5.** $-1 - \frac{2\sqrt{3}}{3}, -1 + \frac{2\sqrt{3}}{3}$ **7.** $\frac{1}{5} - \frac{\sqrt{11}}{5}, \frac{1}{5} + \frac{\sqrt{11}}{5}$ **9.** $\frac{1}{2} - \frac{\sqrt{13}}{2}, \frac{1}{2} + \frac{\sqrt{13}}{2}$ **11.** $\frac{7}{2} - \frac{\sqrt{61}}{2}, \frac{7}{2} + \frac{\sqrt{61}}{2}$ **13.** $2 - \sqrt{2}, 2 + \sqrt{2}$ **15.** $-\frac{\sqrt{6}}{3}, \frac{\sqrt{6}}{3}$ **17.** $-\frac{1}{6} - \frac{\sqrt{73}}{6}, -\frac{1}{6} + \frac{\sqrt{73}}{6}$ **21.** Sum: $-\frac{b}{a}$, product: $\frac{c}{a}$. *Sample answer:* $y = 2x^2 - 4x + 1$

9.7 Skill Practice **1.** First solve one of the equations for a variable. Then substitute that expression for the variable in the other equation. Solve the resulting equation in one variable. Use that solution to substitute into one of the original equations to find the value of the other variable. **3.** (−1, 4) and (3, 8) **5.** (−2, 6) and $\left(\frac{1}{2}, -\frac{1}{4}\right)$ **7.** (−2, 6) and (1, −3) **9.** The student substituted incorrectly. Substitute 4 for y and then the solutions are (0, 4) and (2, 4). **11.** C **13.** (–1, 10) and (3, 14) **15.** (2, 0) and (6, 4) **17.** (–3, 14) and (1, 2) **19.** –1 **21.** 1 and –2 **23.** (0, –1) **25.** no solution **27.** (–1, 2.5), (0, 1) **29.** 1 and 2 **31.** 3 **33.** (1, –1)

9.7 Problem Solving **35.** No; *Sample answer:* The graphs of the equations that model the paths do not intersect, so the dogs' paths will not cross. **37.** The graphs intersect when the two girls have the same amount of money saved. Miranda has more money saved for the first 20 months, and then again after 104 months, because the graphs intersect near $x = 20$ and $x = 104$. **39. a.** (1, 4) and (2.5, 8.5) **b.** (1, 4) **c.** (0, 6) and (1, 4) **d.** yes; (1, 4)

9.8 Skill Practice **1.** exponential function **3.** B **5.** A **7.** linear function **9.** exponential function **11.** quadratic function **13.** quadratic function; $y = -x^2$ **15.** linear function; $y = 3x + 1$

17. exponential function; $y = 4\left(\frac{1}{4}\right)^x$ **19.** The x- and y-values were reversed when substituting the coordinates of the ordered pair (2, 10) into the equation $y = ax^2$. Substituting 2 for x and 10 for y gives $10 = a(2)^2$, $a = 2.5$; so, the equation is $y = 2.5x^2$. **21.** $A = \left(\frac{\sqrt{3}}{4}\right)s^2$; $25\sqrt{3}$ cm^2

9.8 Problem Solving **23.** linear function; $y = 0.34x + 24.6$ **25. a.** Troy: Population doubled every decade; data can be modeled by an exponential function. Union: Population increased by a fixed amount every decade; data can be modeled by a linear function.

b.

Decades since 1970	Troy's pop.
0	3000
1	6000
2	12,000
3	24,000
4	48,000

Decades since 1970	Union's pop.
0	3000
1	6000
2	9000
3	12,000
4	15,000

Troy: Ratios of successive y-values are equal. Union: First differences are constant. **c.** Let P = population and n = number of decades since 1970. Troy: $P = 3000 \cdot 2^n$, 192,000; Union: $P = 3000n + 3000$, 21,000 **27. a.** quadratic function; $\ell = 0.82t^2$ **b.** 0.205 ft **c.** The period decreases by about 71%. For example, consider $t = 4$ for $\ell = 13.12$. To find t for 50% of ℓ, solve $0.5(13.12) = 0.82t^2$; $t \approx 2.83$, and $\frac{2.83}{4} = 0.708$, so the period decreased by about 71%. Consider $t = 2$ for $\ell = 3.28$. To find t for 50% of ℓ, solve $0.5(3.28) = 0.82t^2$; $t \approx 1.41$, and $\frac{1.41}{2} = 0.705$, so the period decreased by about 71%. Consider $t = 1$ for $\ell = 0.82$. To find t for 50% of ℓ, solve $0.5(0.82) = 0.82t^2$; $t \approx 0.707$, and $\frac{0.707}{1} = 0.707$, so the period decreased by about 71%.

9.8 Graphing Calculator Activity

1. $y = 15{,}600(0.866)^x$; about \$5698
3. $y = 179(0.987)^x$, $y = 0.040x^2 - 4.13x + 197$

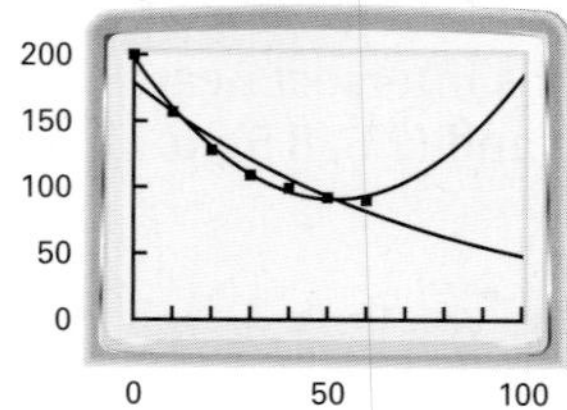

The exponential model; although the quadratic model appears to fit the given data points more closely than the exponential model does, the graph shows that after the last data point, (60, 90), the quadratic model implies increasing temperatures as time goes on, while the exponential model shows gradually decreasing temperatures as time goes on; the exponential model is a more accurate model of what will happen as the hot chocolate continues to cool.

9.9 Skill Practice **1.** verbal model

3.

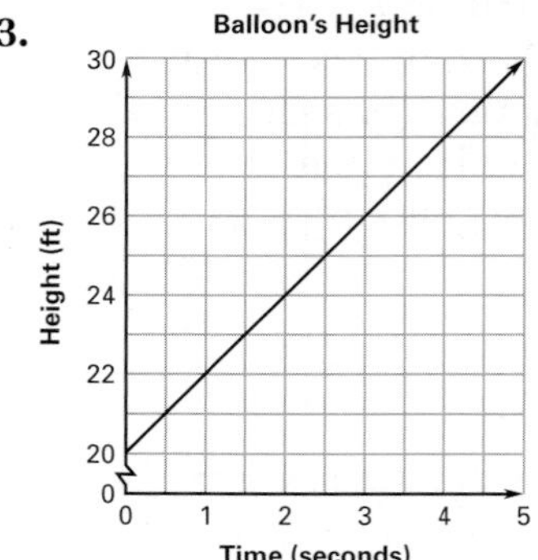

The function is increasing throughout its domain, $x \geq 0$. As the time since it resumed its ascent increases, the altitude of the balloon increases.

5.

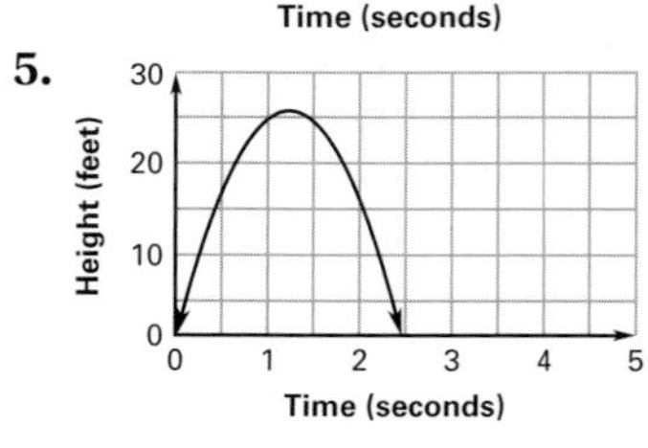

The function is increasing from $x = 0$ to about $x = 1.25$. This is the time during which the ball is traveling upward until it reaches its maximum height at about 1.25 seconds. The graph is decreasing from about $x = 1.25$ to $x = 2.5$. This is the time during which the ball is traveling downward until the juggler catches it at 2.5 seconds. **7.** A function that increases by a constant percent should be modeled by an exponential growth function. **9.** The slope of Linear Function 1 is –1 while the slope of Linear Function 2 is –2. So Linear Function 2 is decreasing more rapidly. **11.** C

9.9 Problem Solving **13.** Connie's playlist is growing faster. **15.** The number of spores in the Petri dish represents growth; the growth rate is 50%. There are no intercepts. If there were an x-intercept, there would be no area. If there were a y-intercept, the fountain would have no measurable length or width. **17.** The rowing crew's distances are decaying by a constant percent rate per unit interval of time. The decay rate is 20%. **19a.** the exponential function $y = 2^x$ **b.** the exponential function $y = 3^x + 1$ **c.** the exponential growth function

9.9 Graphing Calculator Activity

1. Depending on the interval, the average rate of change can be very large or very small, but it is always positive. **3.** For $y = 2x - 3$, the average rate of change is the constant 2. **5.** $y = x + 1$: 1, 1; $y = x^2 + 1$: 1100, 11,000; $y = 2^x$: very large, very large, extremely large; as x increases, the average rate of change of the exponential function increases much more rapidly than the average rate of change of the quadratic function. The linear function maintains a constant rate of change.

Chapter Review

1. axis of symmetry **3.** maximum

5. 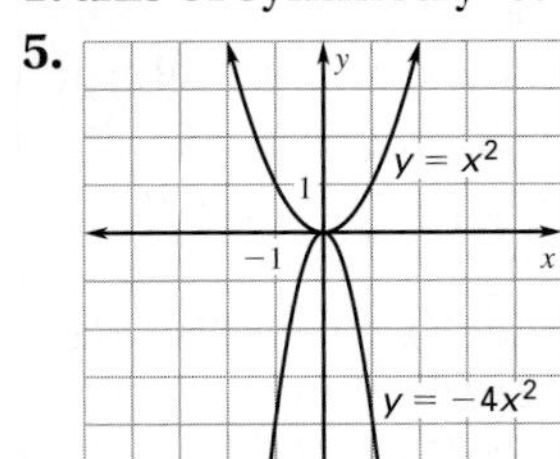

The graph is a vertical stretch (by a factor of 4) with a reflection in the x-axis of the graph of $y = x^2$.

7. 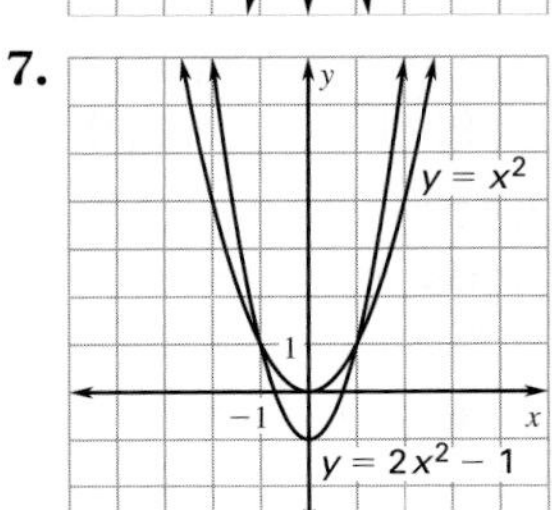

The graph is a vertical stretch (by a factor of 2) with a vertical translation (of 1 unit down) of the graph of $y = x^2$.

9. 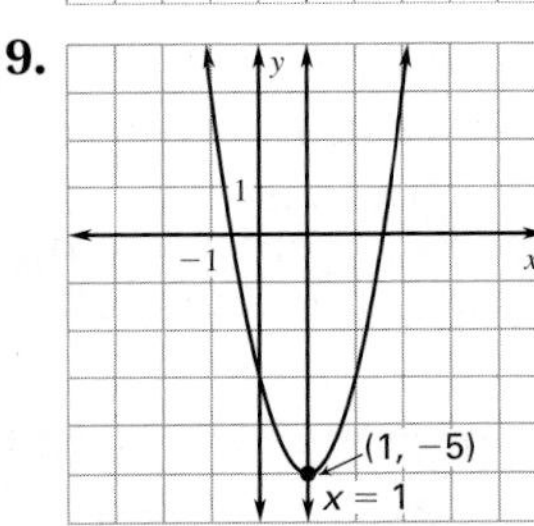

11. no solution **13.** −8, 1 **15.** no solution **17.** ±0.76 **19.** 2.71, 5.29 **21.** 0.32, −6.32 **23.** −0.62, 1.62 **25.** −3.89, 0.39 **27.** 0.16, 1.24 **29.** −1.22, 1 **31.** (−1, 1), (2, −2) **33.** (−0.5, 1), (1.5, 5) **35.** linear function **37.** exponential

Chapter 9 Extra Practice

1. 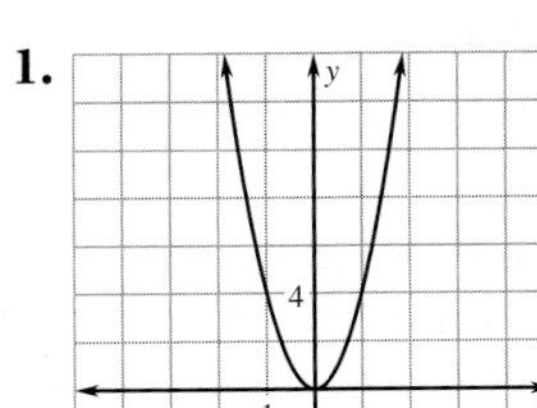

The graph is a vertical stretch by a factor of 4 of the graph of $y = x^2$.

3. 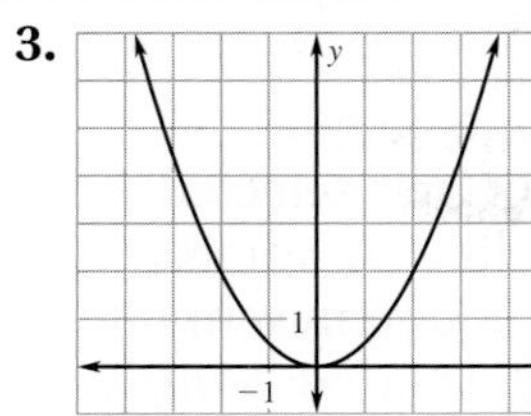

The graph is a vertical shrink by a factor of $\frac{1}{2}$ of the graph of $y = x^2$.

5. 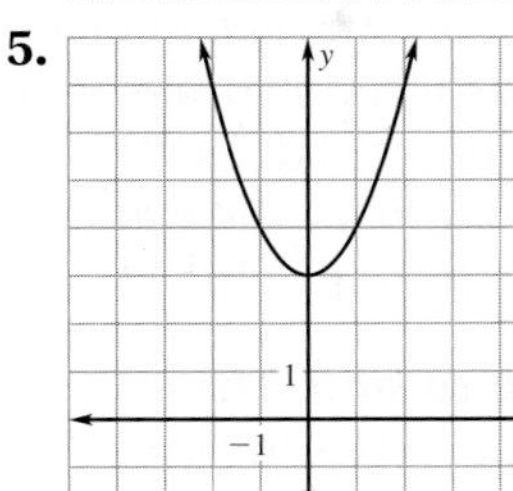

The graph is a vertical translation 3 units up of the graph of $y = x^2$.

7. 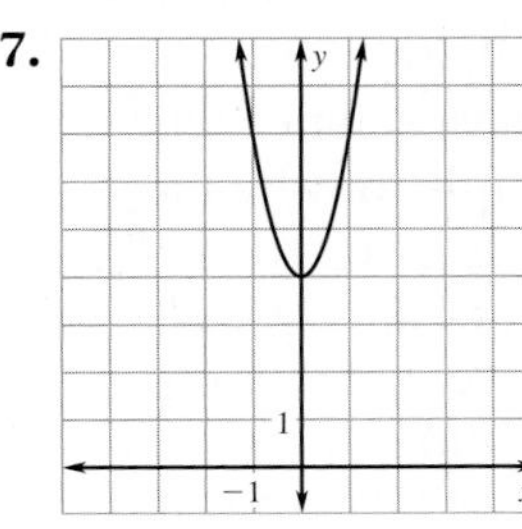

The graph is a vertical stretch by a factor of 3 with a vertical translation 4 units up of the graph of $y = x^2$.

9. 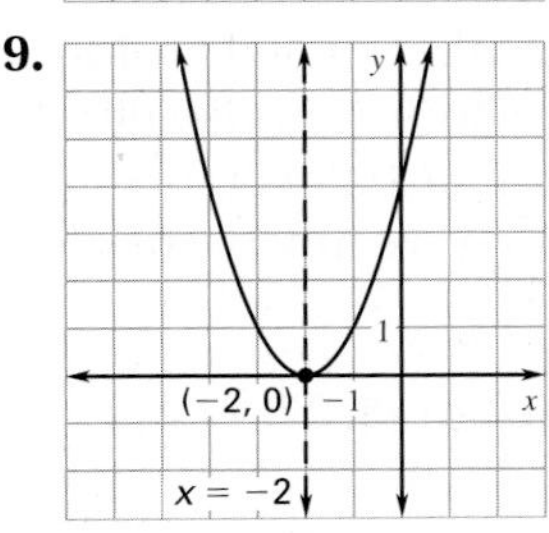

11.

$\left(\frac{3}{2}, \frac{1}{2}\right)$, $x = \frac{3}{2}$

13. 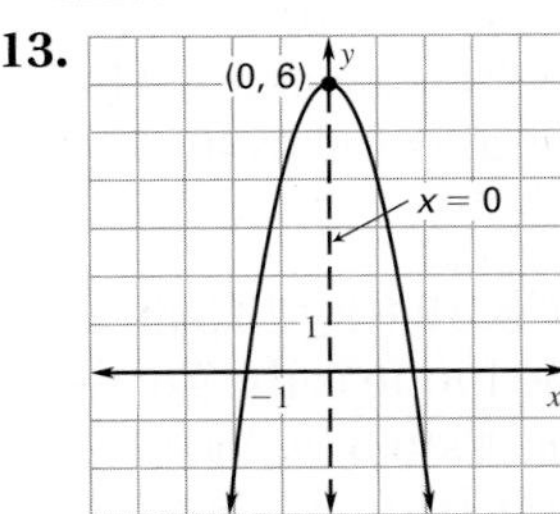

15. −5, 2 **17.** −3, 6 **19.** $-2, \frac{3}{2}$ **21.** ±7 **23.** ±0.75 **25.** ±1.73 **27.** −7, 3 **29.** −2.66, 0.66 **31.** 0.33, 2 **33.** 0.21, 4.79 **35.** −0.35, 1.15 **37.** (0, −1) and (3, −4)

39. quadratic function; $y = 3x^2$ **41.** exponential function; $y = 0.5 \cdot 2^x$ **43.** The slope of Linear Function 1 is $\frac{5}{2}$, while the slope of Linear Function 2 is $\frac{5}{3}$. So Linear Function 1 is increasing more rapidly.

Chapter 10

10.1 Skill Practice **1.** systematic **3.** people who have eaten at the restaurant, self-selected **5.** passengers of the airline, random **7.** Not likely. *Sample answer:* The sample should represent the neighborhood. **9.** Not potentially biased. *Sample answer:* This question simply presents the two choices. **11.** *Sample answer:* The new question presumes that the driving age should be changed, and does not present the option that it should remain the same; "What do you think about the current driving age?"

10.1 Problem Solving **13.** *Sample answer:* This question is phrased to prompt people into agreeing that the athletic field is more important than the science lab; "Which do you think the school needs more: a new athletic field or a new science lab?" **15.** No. *Sample answer:* The sample may be biased. It does not include fans who only listen to or watch games on radio or television. The sample is also self-selected. Fans in attendance have to choose to turn in their surveys in order to be counted. **17.** *Sample answer:* Obtain a list of everyone at the school and select names randomly using a random number generator. "How many hours per day do you study?"; This question is unbiased because it does not prompt respondents to give any particular answer.

10.2 Skill Practice **1.** mode **3.** 3, 3, 1 **5.** 22, 21, no mode **7.** 5.223, 5.48, no mode **11.** 65, 21.2 **13.** 70, 12.56 **15.** 0.85, 0.23 **17.** *Sample answer:* The range only considers the two extreme values, while the mean absolute deviation is affected by all of the values.

10.2 Problem Solving **19. a.** 19 **b.** 19.6 lb, 23.5 lb, 24 lb **c.** Median. *Sample answer:* The mode is the greatest data value and the mean is less than 8 of the 10 data values. **21. a.** The range for Team 2 is 56 and the range for Team 1 is 52, so the scores for Team 2 cover a slightly wider range. **b.** The mean absolute deviation for Team 1 is 15.75 and the mean absolute deviation for Team 2 is 22.5, so the scores for Team 2 are more dispersed.

Extension **1.** 6.3, 2.5 **3.** 76,656.6; 276.9 **5.** 29.1 **7. a.** 5.6 **b.** *Sample answer:* Since 136 is much greater than the mean, the standard deviation will increase. **c.** 17.7. *Sample answer:* The standard deviation more than tripled, so the prediction was correct.

10.3 Skill Practice **1.** joint frequency **3.** 5 **5.** 2
7.

	0 brothers	1 brother	2 brothers	Total
0 sisters	9	7	11	27
1 sister	10	15	8	33
2 sisters	12	6	4	22
Total	31	28	23	82

9. Junior 11. Katy

10.3 Problem Solving **13.** 56 **15.** ham because 97 is the greatest number of wheat bread sandwiches sold **17. a.** Soil fertilized every 2 weeks **b.** Fertilizer-fortified soil **c.** Fertilizer-fortified soil; no, this is the better choice for green peppers, but is not as good for tomatoes. **19. a.** $x = 249$, $y = 93$ **b.** 435 **c.** 209

10.4 Skill Practice **1.** frequency

3.

Stem	Leaves
1	7
2	0 0 4
3	0 1 3 5 8 8 9
4	2
5	5

Key: 1 | 7 = 17

5.

Stem	Leaves
10	5 9
11	1
12	1 4 7
13	3
14	2
15	6
16	
17	9
18	2

Key: 10 | 5 = 105

7. There is no key given for the stem-and-leaf plot; Key: 1 | 8 = 18.

11. **13.**

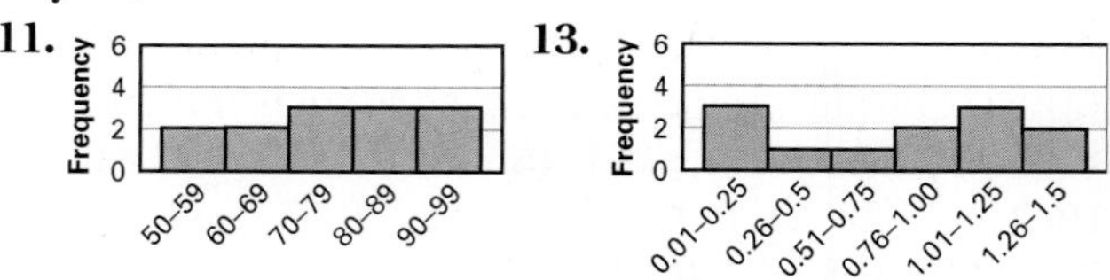

15. *Sample answer:* The given data range from 10 to 21, so a stem-and-leaf plot would place all the data into only two intervals, making it difficult to see the distribution of the data. The histogram could use more than two intervals.

10.4 Problem Solving

17. Heights

Stem	Leaves
6	8 9 9
7	0 2 4 4 6 8 8
8	0 1 1 1 1

Key: 6 | 8 = 68 in.

19. a.

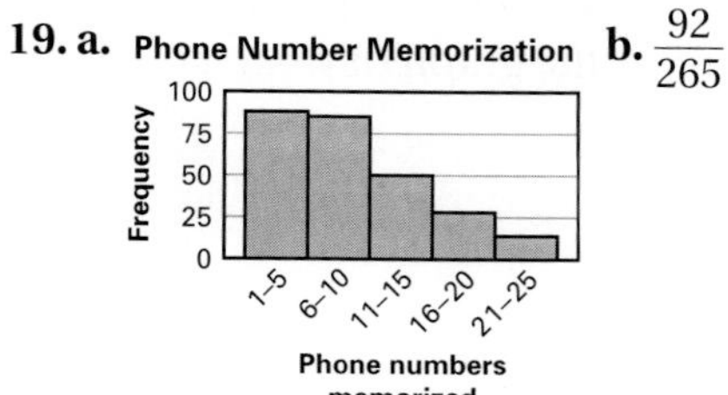

b. $\frac{92}{265}$

21. a.

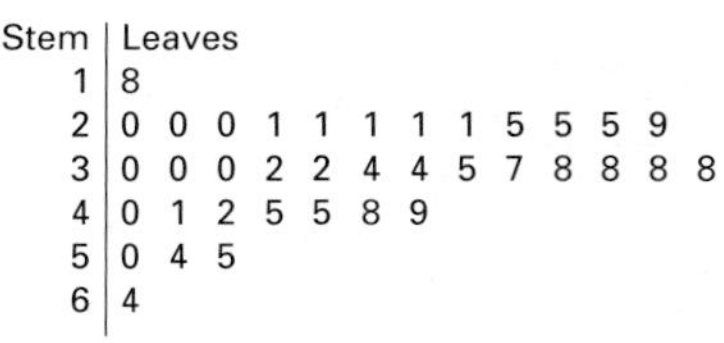

Ages of *Mayflower* Passengers

Stem	Leaves
1	8
2	0 0 0 1 1 1 1 1 5 5 5 9
3	0 0 0 2 2 4 4 5 7 8 8 8 8
4	0 1 2 5 5 8 9
5	0 4 5
6	4

Key: 1 | 8 = 18 years

b. median: 34 yr, range: 46 yr **c.** $\frac{1}{3}$. *Sample answer:* Since 13 of the 39 passengers or $\frac{1}{3}$ of them were ages 18–29, we can predict that another passenger about whom we have no information has a $\frac{1}{3}$ probability of being in that age group.

10.4 Graphing Calculator Activity **1.** *Sample answer:* The majority of the data are at the lower end of the scale, between 3000 and 12,000, with the highest frequency between 3000 and 6000.

10.5 Skill Practice **1.** the difference of the upper quartile and the lower quartile

3. **5.**

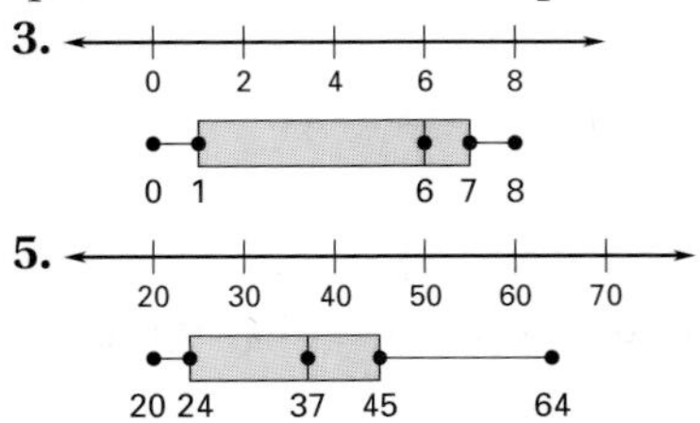

7. *Sample answer:* The upper quartile is incorrect. The upper quartile should be the median of 8 and 10, or 9.

11. There are no outliers.

13. There are no outliers.

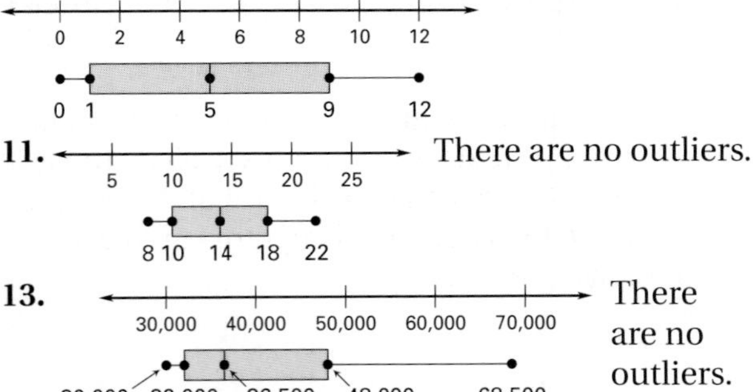

10.5 Problem Solving

15. **17. a.** **b.** none

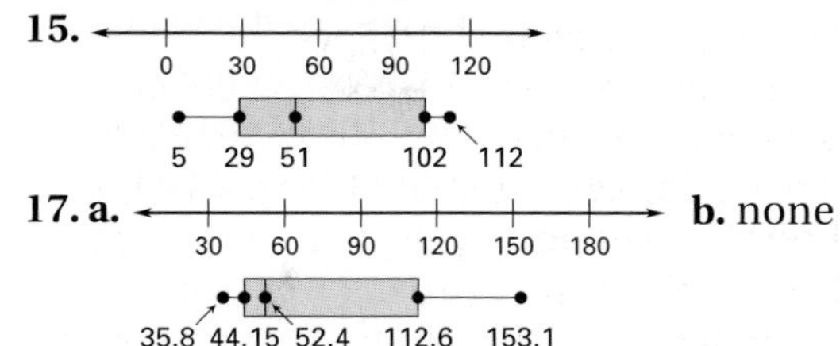

19. a. *Sample answer:* The craters on Ganymede are generally smaller than the craters on Callisto. The lower extreme, lower quartile, median, upper quartile, and upper extreme values are all lower for Ganymede than for Callisto. **b.** *Sample answer:* Chesapeake Bay is larger than between 50% and 75% of the craters on both Callisto and Ganymede. **c.** *Sample answer:* Vredefort is larger than at least 75% of the craters on both Callisto and Ganymede.

10.5 Problem Solving Workshop **1.** minimum: 4; first quartile: 18; median: 33.5; third quartile: 58.5; maximum: 350

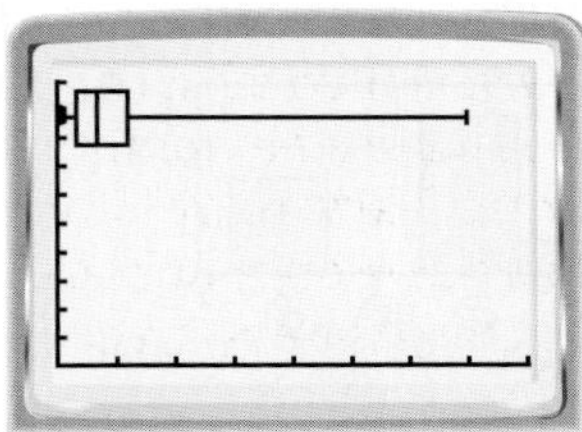

10.5 Extension **1.** Since the data are close together with no outliers, it is appropriate to use a histogram. The mean is 15.44 and the standard deviation is about 3.49. **3.** Since the data are close together with no outliers, it is appropriate to use a histogram. The mean is 9.51 minutes and the standard deviation is about 1.44 minutes. **5.** Since the data are close together with no outliers, it is appropriate to use a histogram. The mean is 25.7 cookies and the standard deviation is about 6.27 cookies.

Chapter Review **1.** systematic **3.** The box represents the middle half of the data, and the whiskers represent the first and last quarter of the data.

5. a. about 5.045, 4.5, 1 **b.** Median. *Sample answer:* The mode is much lower than many of the values, and the mean is affected by the two extreme values (17 and 19) that are much greater than the rest of the data. So, the median best represents the data.

7.

Stem	Leaves
0	0 0 0 0 0 5
1	0 0 5
2	0 0 0 0 5 5
3	0 0 5
4	0 5

Key: 1 | 0 = 10 minutes

Chapter 10
Extra Practice

1. Population: parents or guardians of high school students, sampling method: systematic sample
3. Potentially biased. *Sample answer*: The question encourages the listener to agree with the researcher.
5. fries; salad; fries

7.

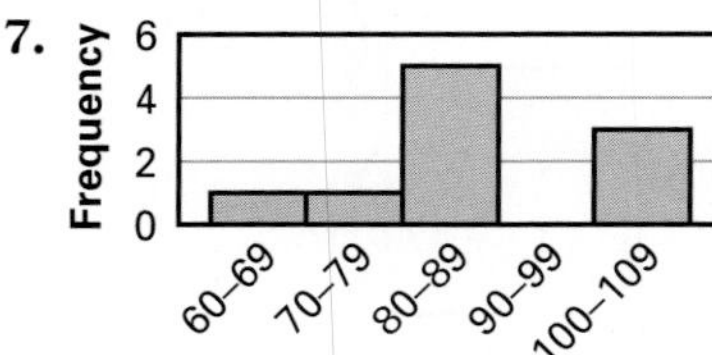

Stem	Leaves
6	9
7	8
8	0 8 8 8 8
9	
10	1 2 8

Key: 6 | 9 = 69

9. 13,500 ft

Chapter 11

11.1 Skill Practice **1.** probability **3.** 12 outcomes; R1, R2, R3, R4, W1, W2, W3, W4, B1, B2, B3, B4 **5.** 48; HHH1, HHH2, HHH3, HHH4, HHH5, HHH6, HHT1, HHT2, HHT3, HHT4, HHT5, HHT6, HTH1, HTH2, HTH3, HTH4, HTH5, HTH6, HTT1, HTT2, HTT3, HTT4, HTT5, HTT6, THH1, THH2, THH3, THH4, THH5, THH6, THT1, THT2, THT3, THT4, THT5, THT6, TTH1, TTH2, TTH3, TTH4, TTH5, TTH6, TTT1, TTT2, TTT3, TTT4, TTT5, TTT6 **7.** $\frac{9}{10}$ **9.** $\frac{1}{10}$ **11.** $\frac{3}{7}$ or 3 : 7 **13.** *Sample answer:* Odds in favor is the number of favorable outcomes divided by the number of unfavorable outcomes; odds in favor of a multiple of 3 $= \frac{\text{Number of favorable outcomes}}{\text{Number of unfavorable outcomes}} = \frac{9}{1}$ or 9 : 1. **15.** *Sample answer:* Rolling a standard number cube and getting a 0, flipping a coin and getting heads or tails. **17.** *Sample answer:* route A; The experimental probability that he will encounter heavy traffic on route A is 0.25, and the experimental probability that he will encounter heavy traffic on route B is 0.375.

11.1 Problem Solving **19.** $\frac{1}{7}$ **21.** $\frac{4}{9}; \frac{4}{5}$. *Sample answer:* The probability and odds of choosing a boy are related because both compare the number of boys to another number. The probability of choosing a boy compares the number of boys to the total number of outcomes, while the odds of choosing a boy compare the number of boys to the total number of outcomes minus the number of boys.

Extension **1.** Answers will vary. **3.** *Sample answer:* There are 3 prizes to win, but since the prizes do not have an equal likelihood of being won, generating a list of random integers from 1 to 3 would not represent the situation. The probability of winning a CD is $\frac{1}{6}$, so if there were only 3 possible outcomes in the simulation you could not represent winning a CD properly.

11.2 Skill Practice **1.** permutation **3. a.** 2 ways **b.** 2 ways **5. a.** 24 ways **b.** 12 ways **7. a.** 120 ways **b.** 20 ways **9. a.** 120 ways **b.** 20 ways **11.** *Sample answer:* 5 people are running in a race. How many different results can there be for first and second place? **13.** 6 **15.** 120 **17.** 3,628,800 **19.** 6,227,020,800 **21.** 210 **23.** 720 **25.** 1 **27.** 6,375,600 **29.** The denominator should be $(5 - 3)! = 2!$, not 3!; ${}_5P_3 = \frac{5!}{(5-3)!} = \frac{5!}{2!} = 60.$

11.2 Problem Solving **35. a.** $\frac{1}{2}$. *Sample answer:* Make a list of possible permutations, count the number in which you are first or second, and divide it by the total number of outcomes. **b.** $\frac{1}{2}$; the answers are the same. **37.** $\frac{1}{720}$

11.3 Skill Practice **1.** combination **3.** 20 combinations **5.** *Sample answer:* The answer given is for ${}_9P_4$, not ${}_9C_4$; ${}_9C_4 = \frac{9!}{(9-4)! \cdot 4!} = \frac{9!}{5! \cdot 4!} = 126.$ **7.** 56 **9.** 28 **11.** 330 **13.** 15,504 **17.** Permutations; since the roles are different, the order in which students are selected for the roles matters; 720 ways. **19.** Permutations; the arrangement of people in the car matters; 120 ways. **21.** ${}_nC_r = {}_nP_r \cdot \frac{1}{r!}$. *Sample answer:* To find the number of combinations, you find the number of permutations and then divide by the number of ways the items being chosen can be arranged, or $r!$.

11.3 Problem Solving **23.** 840 burritos **25. a.** 84 combinations **b.** $\frac{5}{21}$. *Sample answer:* There are 84 possible outcomes of the choice. Find the number of combinations that include you and your 2 friends. After you and your friends are chosen, 3 other contestants from a pool of 6 can be chosen in any combination, so the number of favorable combinations is ${}_6C_3 = 20$. The probability that you and your friends are chosen is $\frac{20}{84} = \frac{5}{21}$.

11.3 Graphing Calculator Activity **1.** 35 **3.** 120 **5.** 15,120 **7.** 6,652,800 **9. a.** 3276 groups **b.** 6 ways

11.4 Skill Practice **1.** compound event **3.** 0.4 **5.** 0.65 **7.** $\frac{7}{12}$ **9.** 0.65 **11.** 0.21 **13.** $\frac{5}{7}$ **17.** 1 **19.** $\frac{3}{8}$ **21.** $\frac{4}{13}$ **23.** $\frac{2}{13}$ **25.** $\frac{3}{4}$ **27.** The probability of a club and 9 must be subtracted instead of added; $P(\text{club}) + P(9) - P(\text{club and } 9) = \frac{13}{52} + \frac{4}{52} - \frac{1}{52} = \frac{4}{13}$. **29.** 0.67; not disjoint **31.** $\frac{1}{5}$; not disjoint **33.** 24%; not disjoint **35.** $\frac{5}{36}$ **37.** $\frac{5}{6}$

11.4 Problem Solving **43.** 0.7 **45.** about 0.8488 **47. a.** 58% **b.** 53% **c.** No; what percent of the tomatoes have been fed on by insects *and* are partially rotten *and* have bite marks. **49.** $\frac{17}{20}$

11.5 Skill Practice **1.** conditional probability **3.** dependent **5.** dependent **7.** 0.21 **9.** 0.325 **11.** $P(A|B) = 0.3$ and $P(B|A) = 0.2$; A and B are independent because $P(A) = P(A|B)$ and $P(B) = P(B|A)$. **13.** 0.8 **15.** $\frac{1}{10}$ **17.** $\frac{4}{11}$ **19. a.** $\frac{1}{16}$ **b.** $\frac{13}{204}$ **21. a.** $\frac{3}{169}$ **b.** $\frac{4}{221}$ **23. a.** $\frac{1}{2197}$ **b.** $\frac{8}{16,575}$ **25.** *Sample answer:* Independent; the result of the first spin has no effect on the result of the second spin. **27.** The probabilities should be multiplied instead of being added; $P(A \text{ and } B) = 0.4 \cdot 0.5 = 0.2$. **29. a.** $\frac{4}{12} = \frac{1}{3}$ **b.** $\frac{6}{10} = 0.6$ **c.** $\frac{6}{15} = \frac{2}{5} = 0.4$ **d.** *Sample answer:* In part (b), the sample space consists of all 6 ounce bottles of juice (apple or orange), but in part (c) the sample space consists of all bottles of orange juice (6 oz or 8 oz). **31.** The formula can be written as $P(B \text{ and } A) = P(B) \cdot P(A|B)$, so $P(A) \cdot P(B|A) = P(B) \cdot P(A|B)$. Solve for $P(A|B)$ to get Bayes's Theorem.

11.5 Problem Solving **33. a.** about 22.6% **b.** about 36.7% **c.** no; $P(\text{senior}) \neq P(\text{senior}|\text{bikes to school})$ **35.** 51% **37.a.** 0%; about 2%; about 98% **b.** about 29%; about 30%; about 50% **c.** Yes; go for 2 points after the first touchdown. If the 2 points are scored, go for 1 point after the second touchdown. If the 2 points are not scored, go for 2 points after the second touchdown; win: about 45%, lose: about 30%.

Extension **1.** Yes; Leon did 7 of the total of 53 completed puzzlers. He was assigned 7 of the 53 possible winning numbers. **3.a.** 0.09 **b.** 0.12 **c.** Remove the goalie.

Chapter Review **1.** compound event **3.** *Sample answer:* Theoretical probability is based on knowing the likelihood of all possible outcomes of an event. Experimental probability is based on the results of an experiment. **5.** $\frac{2}{9}$ **7.** 30 **9.** 1,037,836,800 **11.** 7 **13.** 56 **15.** 126 ways **17.** 0.68 **19.a.** $\frac{5}{32}$ **b.** $\frac{1}{6}$ **21.a.** $\frac{1}{4}$ **b.** $\frac{7}{30}$

Chapter 11 Extra Practice

1. 6 possible outcomes; heads, yellow; heads, red; heads, blue; tails, yellow; tails, red; tails, blue **3.** 5:3 **5.** 60 ways **7.** 336 **9.** 120 **11.** 200 **13.** 35 **15.** 15,504 **17.** 0.8 **19.** 0.6; not disjoint **21.** 0.17; not disjoint **23.** $\frac{1}{52}$ **25.** $\frac{4}{13}$ **27.** 0.125 **29.** 0.24 **31.** 0.2 **33.a.** $\frac{1}{16}$ **b.** $\frac{13}{204}$

Selected Answers

Skills Review Handbook

Comparing and Ordering Decimals **1.** > **3.** > **5.** > **7.** < **9.** > **11.** 7.01, 7.03, 7.13, 7.3 **13.** 0.15, 0.3, 0.47, 0.9 **15.** 10.9, 11, 11.9, 12.6 **17.** 0.3, 1.33, 3.1, 3.3

Factors and Multiples **1.** $2^2 \cdot 7$ **3.** prime **5.** 3^4 **7.** $2^2 \cdot 3 \cdot 5$ **9.** $2^2 \cdot 3^2 \cdot 5$ **11.** $3 \cdot 17$ **13.** 4 **15.** 6 **17.** 9 **19.** 4 **21.** 8 **23.** 4 **25.** 18 **27.** 45 **29.** 130 **31.** 90 **33.** 14 **35.** 49

Finding Equivalent Fractions and Simplifying Fractions **1–5.** Sample answers are given. **1.** $\frac{3}{4}$ and $\frac{18}{24}$ **3.** $\frac{2}{4}$ and $\frac{3}{6}$ **5.** $\frac{5}{7}$ and $\frac{20}{28}$ **7.** $\frac{1}{4}$ **9.** $\frac{1}{8}$ **11.** $\frac{1}{4}$ **13.** $\frac{7}{20}$ **15.** $\frac{4}{5}$ **17.** $\frac{3}{7}$ **19.** $\frac{4}{13}$

Mixed Numbers and Improper Fractions **1.** $\frac{5}{3}$ **3.** $\frac{103}{10}$ **5.** $\frac{9}{2}$ **7.** $\frac{23}{12}$ **9.** $\frac{53}{8}$ **11.** $\frac{65}{8}$ **13.** $\frac{65}{9}$ **15.** $\frac{38}{3}$ **17.** $2\frac{2}{5}$ **19.** $6\frac{1}{4}$ **21.** $1\frac{3}{4}$ **23.** $2\frac{9}{10}$ **25.** $10\frac{4}{5}$ **27.** $4\frac{2}{5}$ **29.** $4\frac{7}{9}$

Adding and Subtracting Fractions **1.** $\frac{1}{4}$ **3.** $\frac{1}{6}$ **5.** 1 **7.** $\frac{1}{2}$ **9.** $1\frac{1}{5}$ **11.** $\frac{3}{16}$ **13.** $\frac{25}{48}$ **15.** $1\frac{17}{24}$ **17.** $\frac{11}{20}$ **19.** $\frac{4}{5}$ **21.** $6\frac{3}{4}$ **23.** 5 **25.** $1\frac{1}{16}$

Multiplying and Dividing Fractions **1.** $\frac{1}{2}$ **3.** $\frac{1}{2}$ **5.** $1\frac{1}{8}$ **7.** $\frac{3}{64}$ **9.** $\frac{1}{8}$ **11.** $1\frac{1}{2}$ **13.** $\frac{1}{2}$ **15.** $\frac{2}{7}$ **17.** $\frac{1}{50}$ **19.** $\frac{3}{5}$ **21.** $3\frac{3}{32}$ **23.** $4\frac{3}{8}$ **25.** $1\frac{1}{3}$

Fractions, Decimals, and Percents **1.** 0.7, $\frac{7}{10}$ **3.** 0.03, $\frac{3}{100}$ **5.** 0.35, $\frac{7}{20}$ **7.** 1.1, $1\frac{1}{10}$ **9.** 0.003, $\frac{3}{1000}$ **11.** $\frac{7}{25}$, 28% **13.** $\frac{1}{20}$, 5% **15.** $\frac{13}{25}$, 52% **17.** $\frac{1}{40}$, 2.5% **19.** $\frac{3}{2}$, 150% **21.** 0.188, 18.8% **23.** 0.61, 61% **25.** 0.19, 19% **27.** 0.36, 36% **29.** 0.571, 57.1%

Mean, Median, and Mode **1.** 92.4; 93; 94 **3.** 41 yr; 41 yr; 52 yr **5.** \$7; \$7; \$6.75 **7.** 2.25; 2; 2

The Coordinate Plane **1.** (5, 4) **3.** (10, 8) **5.** (9, 2) **7.** (2, 6) **9.** (10, 0) **11.** (0, 5)

13–23.

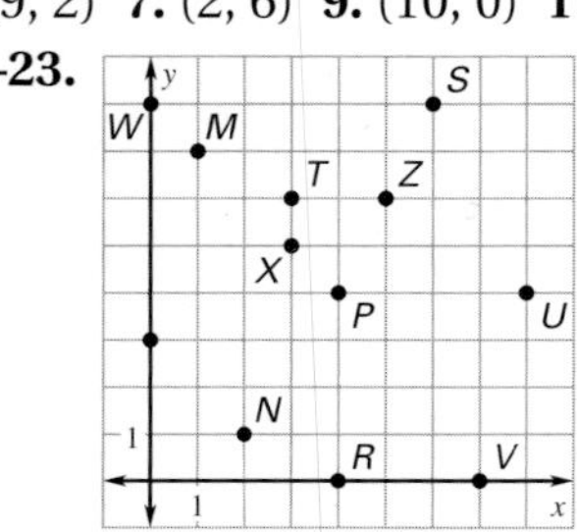

Transformations

1. **3.**

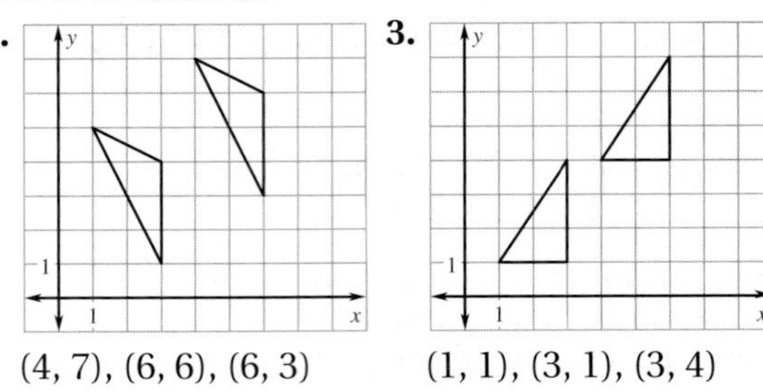

(4, 7), (6, 6), (6, 3) (1, 1), (3, 1), (3, 4)

5.

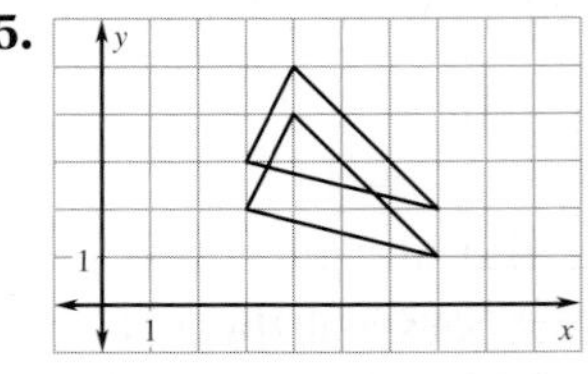

(4, 4), (7, 1), (3, 2)

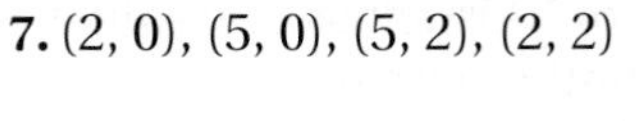

7. (2, 0), (5, 0), (5, 2), (2, 2)

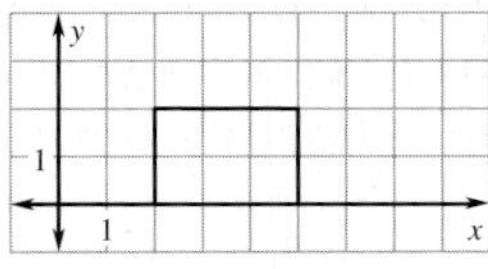

9.

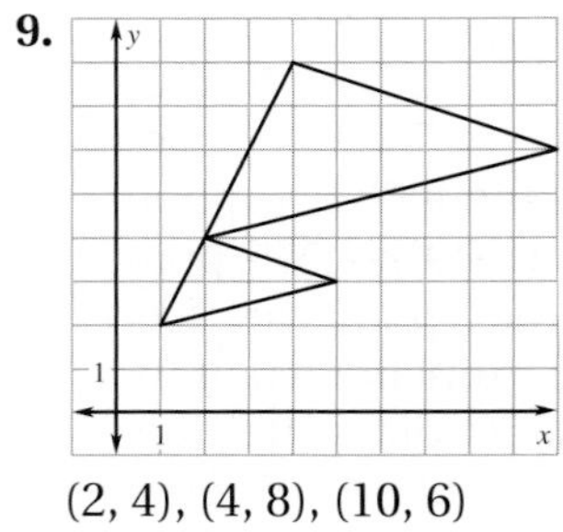

(2, 4), (4, 8), (10, 6)

11. (4, 12), (12, 12), (12, 4), (4, 4)

13.

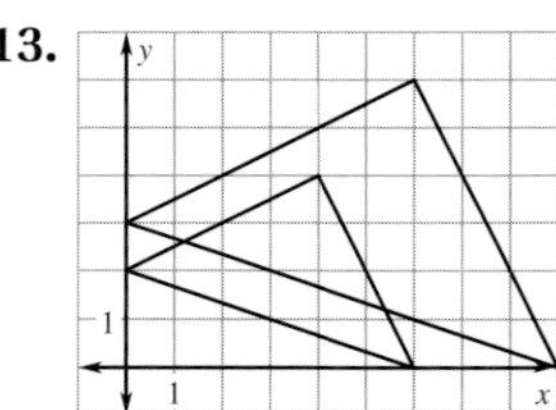

(0, 3), (6, 6), (9, 0)

Perimeter and Area **1.** 36 ft **3.** 20 ft **5.** 66 yd^2 **7.** 110 in.^{2} **9.** 21 ft^2 **11.** 70 yd^2

Circumference and Area of a Circle **1.** 12π in. or 37.7 in., 36π in.^{2} or 113.0 in.^{2} **3.** 16π in. or 50.2 in., 64π in.^{2} or 201.0 in.^{2} **5.** 4π ft or 12.6 ft, 4π ft^2 or 12.6 ft^2 **7.** 18π m or 56.5 m, 81π m^2 or 254.3 m^2

Surface Area and Volume **1.** 320 cm^2, 336 cm^3 **3.** 900π m^2 or 2826 m^2, 4500π m^3 or 14,130 m^3 **5.** 200π in.^{2} or 628 in.^{2}, 320π in.^{3} or 1004.8 in.^{3} **7.** 96 in.^{2}, 48 in.^{3} **9.** 1888π in.^{2} or 5928.3 in.^{2}, $11{,}008\pi$ in.^{3} or 34,565.1 in.^{3} **11.** 96π m^2 or 301.4 m^2, 96π m^3 or 301.4 m^3

Selected Answers

Converting Units of Measurement **1.** 5 **3.** 4 **5.** 6 **7.** 14 **9.** 300 **11.** 70,000 **13.** 3000 **15.** $14\frac{2}{3}$ yd or 44 ft

Converting Between Systems **1.** 845 **3.** 6 **5.** 22 **7.** 4 **9.** 32 **11.** 4 **13.** 2 **15.** 5

Venn Diagrams and Logical Reasoning

1.

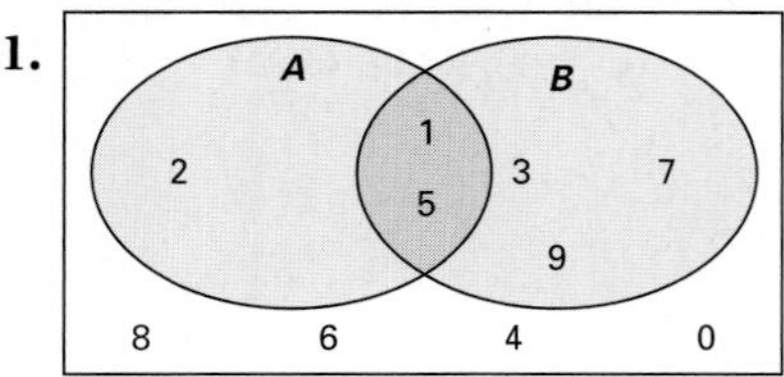

3. a. False; there are whole numbers less than 10 that are odd but are not factors of 10, such as 3, 7, and 9. **b.** False; there is a whole number less than 10 that is a factor of 10 but is not odd, 2.

Counting Methods **1.** 6 ways **3.** 17,576 3-letter monograms **5.** 1,679,616 computer passwords **7.** 72 dinners

Bar Graphs **1.** bronze **3.** 103 medals **5.** 25 medals **7.** Switzerland **9.** United States **11.** 96 medals

Line Graphs **1.** about 24 lb **3.** between ages 4 and 5 **5.** about 15 lb **7.** about 2 years old **9.** between ages 3 and 4 **11.** between ages 1 and 2 **13.** about 4 yr

Circle Graphs **1.** 9% **3.** 24.5% **5.** 37% **7.** woodwinds **9.** brass

Misleading Data Displays **1.** The angle at which the graph is displayed emphasizes the region at the front. Although regions A and D represent the same percent of the data, region D appears larger. **3.** The break in the vertical axis exaggerates the differences in the data.

Problem Solving Strategies **1.** Pam owes \$4 that she can pay to Bonnie who is owed a total of \$5. Holly should pay both Barb and Bonnie \$1. **3.** 25 years old **5.** 10 ways **7.** 1:45 P.M. **9.** 3 soccer games per week **11.** Quinn

Selected answers for the Extra Practice section are at the end of each chapter.